COLLEGE PLANNING/SEARCH BOOK

a guide to COLLEGE PLANNING

1991-92 edition

Library of Congress Catalog Card Number—75:28517

ISBN 1-56009-007-3

Contents

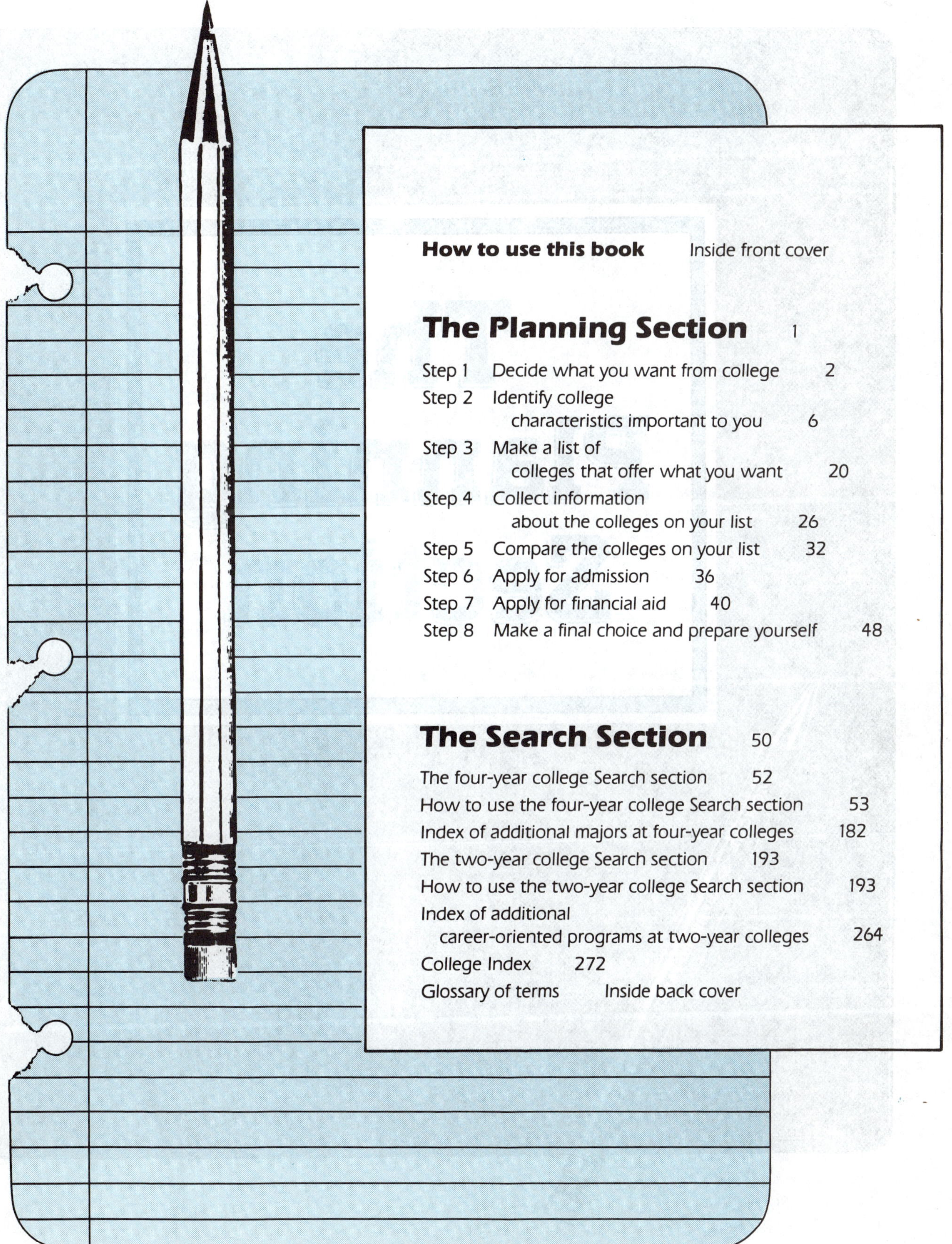

How to use this book Inside front cover

The Planning Section 1

Step 1 Decide what you want from college 2
Step 2 Identify college characteristics important to you 6
Step 3 Make a list of colleges that offer what you want 20
Step 4 Collect information about the colleges on your list 26
Step 5 Compare the colleges on your list 32
Step 6 Apply for admission 36
Step 7 Apply for financial aid 40
Step 8 Make a final choice and prepare yourself 48

The Search Section 50

The four-year college Search section 52
How to use the four-year college Search section 53
Index of additional majors at four-year colleges 182
The two-year college Search section 193
How to use the two-year college Search section 193
Index of additional career-oriented programs at two-year colleges 264
College Index 272
Glossary of terms Inside back cover

The Planning Section

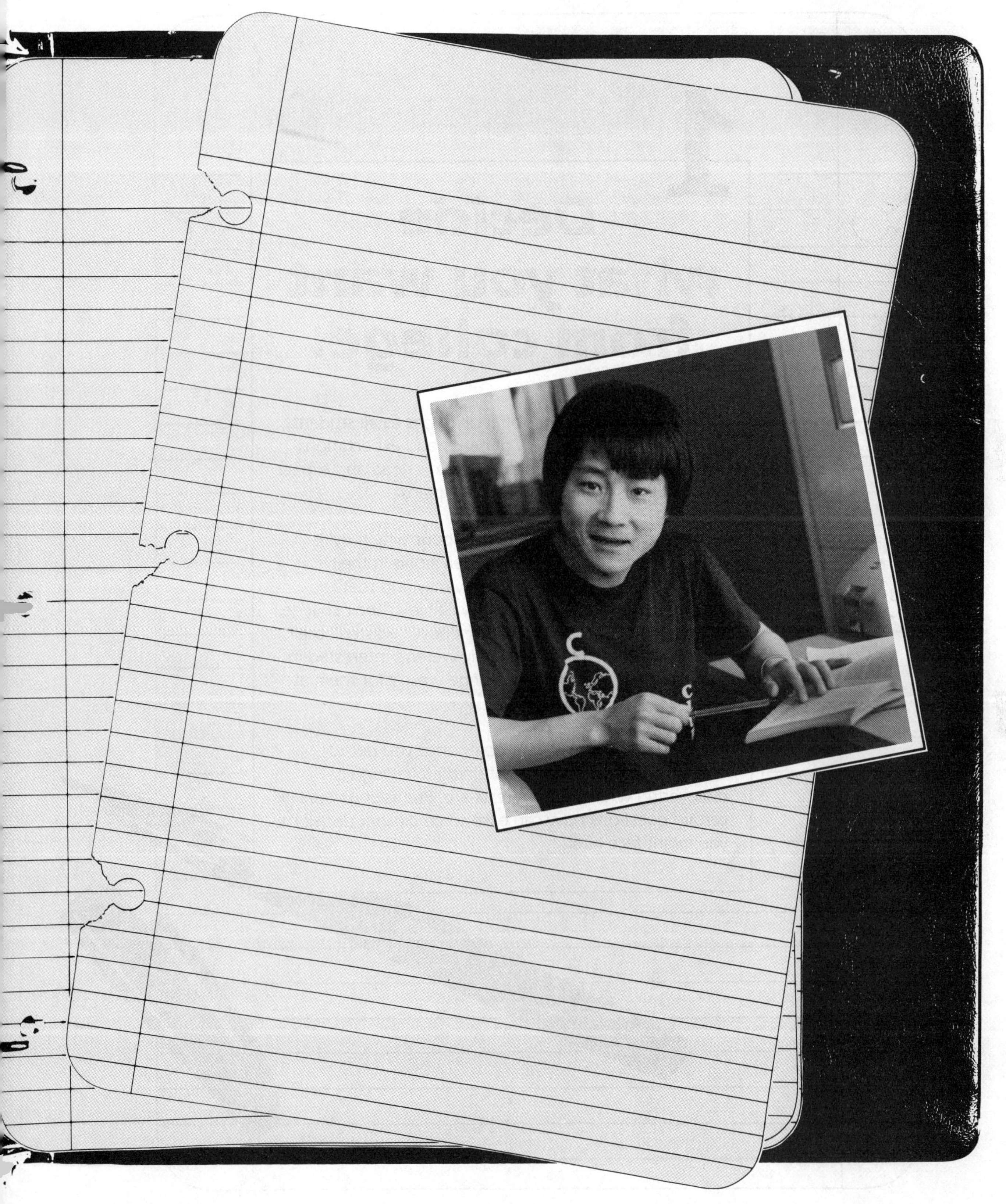

1 Decide what you want from college.

Although college cannot offer all things to all students, it can meet a great variety of needs and expectations. But it's important to identify what you need and expect from college as you begin to make plans.

Some students don't really think about why they're going to college until they are well along in their college careers. By that time, they may find that the program they really want is unavailable at their college, or they may feel that they've somehow "wasted" their time doing something they really weren't interested in. They may even decide that college wasn't for them at all.

It is natural to rethink your goals once you get to college. Part of the process of going to college is discovering what your interests are. But asking yourself certain questions now can ease some difficult decisions you might face later.

Why are you going to college?

How solid are your reasons? Have you examined them? You may want to consider each of your reasons in relation to the "picture" of yourself that you construct on pages 4 and 5. Considering your background and interests, will college help you develop your abilities and achieve your goals?

Ask yourself "Why am I going to college?" Think of as many reasons as you can, and write them here.

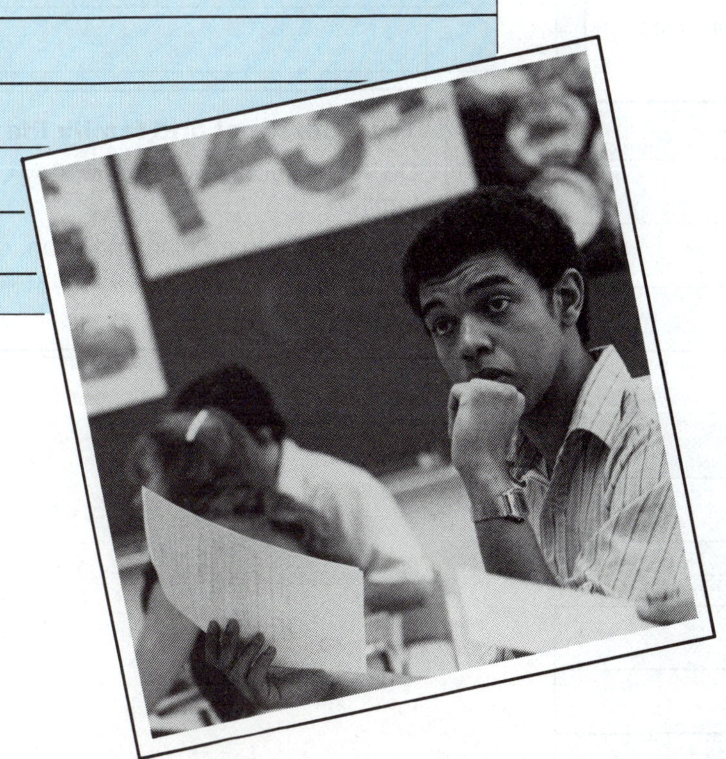

Take a look at yourself.

As you decide what you want from college, examine both the way you picture yourself now and the way you'd like to see yourself in the future. Your personality, interests, and experiences can and should guide the choices you make—as should your ambitions, goals, and dreams.

For example, suppose you're thinking about college in terms of preparing yourself for a career in the foreign service. In taking a close look at yourself, however, you realize that being near your family and friends has always been important to you, that any traveling you've done has been limited to weekend trips to the beach, and that you've never been much interested in politics.

This isn't to say that you should forget the foreign service and think about becoming an engineer. Perhaps you'll find that the way you'd like to see yourself in five years is very different from the way you are now. In that case, you'll probably want to look carefully at the types of colleges that offer the best means of effecting some of the changes you'd like to make.

On the other hand, the view you have of yourself in five years may closely resemble your present one. In that case, you'll probably want to keep your present values strongly in mind as you make your college plans.

On the next two pages, put together a picture of yourself by making notes in response to the questions.

What are you like now?

Your academic progress

What kinds of courses have you taken?

What courses have you particularly enjoyed?

What academic successes and difficulties have you had?

What skills have you developed?

How much academic challenge are you comfortable with?

Your spare-time activities

What work or volunteer work have you done?

What clubs, hobbies, and sports interest you?

What social activities are important to you?

Have you done much traveling?

Your style

Do you take the lead or prefer to join in?

Do you make the best of what comes or search for what you want?

Do you prefer to work alone or with others?

Your career

What do you want to accomplish during your working life?

What careers seem to fit your skills and interests, your likes and dislikes?

Your personal and family life

Do you go your own way or stay close to your family?

Do you anticipate marrying soon, or is marriage a distant possibility—or something you haven't considered much at all?

Where do you want to be five years from now?

Your academic progress

Your career

Your spare-time activities

Your style

Your personal and family life

Discuss your self-portrait with your parents, your friends, and your school counselor.

How complete do they think your portrait is?

How do they view your college plans?

Can they suggest colleges—or types of colleges—that will help you?

2
Identify college characteristics important to you.

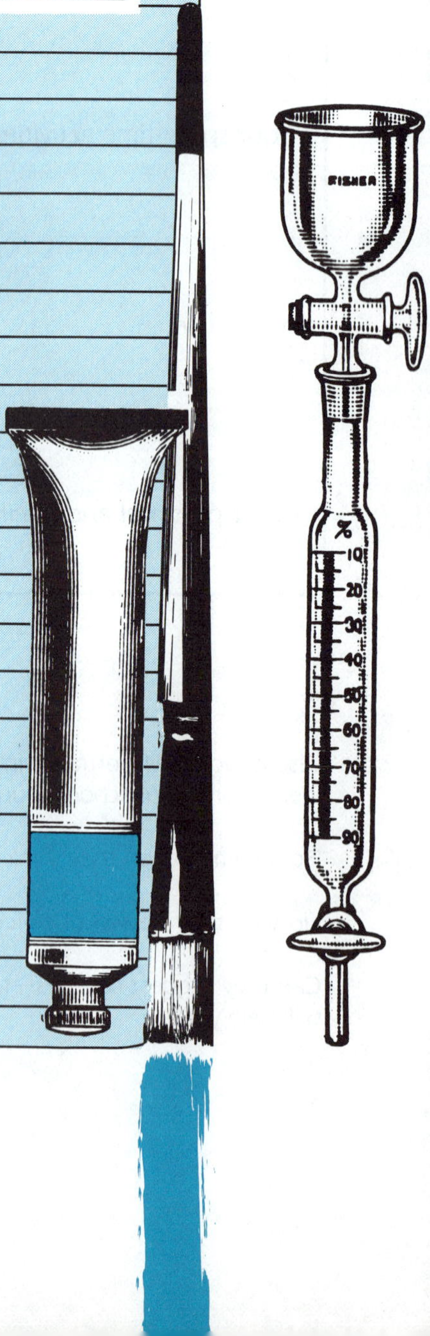

Your goals

You've just taken a good look at yourself—as you are now and as you'd like to be in five years. Focusing on your specific goals will help you in the college selection process. What do you want from college?

What abilities do you want to develop?

What career interests do you want to pursue?

What new experiences and new people do you want to encounter?

What personal goals have you set for yourself?

How to find colleges that can help you reach your goals

Your next step is to relate your goals to the characteristics of particular colleges. Pages 8 and 9 contain detailed information about the characteristics of different types of colleges. As you read them, think about the relationship between your goals and these characteristics. Then use the charts on pages 22 and 23 to summarize your own preferences.

The next few pages discuss:

- Kinds of colleges
- College location
- Admissions selectivity
- College size
- College costs
- Majors and study programs
- Accreditation and affiliation

Kinds of colleges

Four-year colleges

There are more than 1,700 colleges in the United States that offer programs leading to a bachelor of arts (BA) or a bachelor of science (BS) degree. Most have residence facilities on campus, although some enroll predominantly commuter students. Several major types of schools are included in the four-year college category.

Liberal arts colleges offer BA degree programs that combine a broad four-year education in the arts, humanities, social sciences, and sciences, with a major in a subject or area such as political science, literature, mathematics, or biology. A large proportion of these are private colleges with fewer than 5,000 students.

Specialized colleges or schools offer BS degree programs with less emphasis on broad liberal arts education and more focus on preparation for a specific career—such as education, music, art, engineering, business, agriculture, or home economics.

Universities usually include a liberal arts college and several other specialized colleges, such as business, engineering, education, agriculture, law, or medicine. Each of these individual colleges may have its own set of entrance requirements for freshmen. In addition to bachelor's degree programs for undergraduate students, universities may offer graduate programs leading to the master of arts (MA) or master of science (MS) degree, the doctor of philosophy degree (PhD), or to other professional degrees such as law (LLD) or medicine (MD).

Two-year colleges and vocational-technical schools

Two-year colleges

There are about 1,400 two-year colleges in the United States today; approximately three-fourths of them are public.[1] The three major types of two-year institutions are: (1) junior colleges, (2) community colleges, and (3) vocational-technical schools, colleges, or institutes.

Junior colleges, which are generally the oldest two-year colleges, were originally established as transfer institutions that provided courses to parallel the freshman and sophomore offerings at four-year colleges and universities. Now, most two-year institutions are called community colleges. These public community-based colleges, which are often part of statewide college systems, provide educational services to meet the diverse needs of a mixed student population. As a result, community colleges are constantly working to expand the educational opportunities they offer and to help students make better educational choices by emphasizing personalized career guidance.

Students who attend two-year colleges may enroll in various kinds of programs:

- associate degree programs (usually two years in length)
- associate degree and transfer programs for students who plan to continue study at a four-year college
- career-oriented programs (some awarding a certificate or associate degree) for students who are primarily concerned with finding employment after six months to two years of postsecondary education
- noncredit courses (often referred to as "lifelong learning" or "life enrichment") that are not part of a regular academic program

In many community colleges, liberal arts and vocational-technical programs exist side by side, with considerable interaction; in others, the programs operate independently. Programs with courses that must be taken in sequence usually require students to begin in the fall term, but other programs may have flexible entry policies.

[1] The "two-year" category includes schools that offer some programs that require more or less than two years to complete. "Two-year" refers basically to the time required for a full-time student to complete the coursework for an associate degree.

Many students who begin their college education at a two-year college do so because it is convenient, economical, or academically beneficial. Two-year college tuition is generally low (compared to four-year schools) and most students live at home. Students often find that a two-year college enables them to combine work with schooling. Approximately 60 percent of the students enrolled in two-year institutions last year were part-time; many colleges have programs that allow students to earn an associate degree or certificate while attending classes part-time. Students who have not done well academically in high school may enroll in a two-year college to "test the water," to sample the courses and determine the level or type of education that best suits their abilities and needs. Other students may choose the two-year college because they want concentrated training to prepare them for entry into technical and skilled occupations that do not require a four-year college education.

Because most of their students live at home and commute to school, many public two-year colleges do not have on-campus residence facilities. However, many private and church-related two-year colleges enroll students from all over the country and do have dormitories. The campus life and activities at these colleges may be similar to campus life at residential four-year colleges.

Transferring

Students who enroll at one college with the intention of transferring credits to another college should study the catalog and work with the admissions staff of the second college in order to understand clearly which courses meet its requirements for freshmen and sophomores. Four-year institutions may vary greatly, even within a given state, in the kind and amount of transfer credit they will accept from two-year or other four-year colleges. Difficulties may also arise, for example, in converting quarter-hours of credit into semester hours or in transferring courses with grades of C or lower. For the student who intends to continue at a four-year college, the importance of verifying the transferability of courses—if possible, before enrollment—cannot be overemphasized.

Vocational-technical schools

Vocational technical schools are similar to community colleges in that they offer career-oriented programs. As is the case with community colleges, not all the programs are two years in length. Programs may last a year, two semesters, one semester, three quarters, two quarters, or one quarter. Some are even shorter.

Vocational-technical schools differ from community colleges in a number of important ways. Unlike community colleges, vocational-technical schools do not offer transfer programs or programs parallel to those of four-year colleges. Virtually all vocational-technical programs are directly related to specific occupations. Because vocational-technical schools are concerned mainly with the preparation of students for immediate employment, they are less likely than community colleges to include nonvocational or general subject matter in their career-related offerings. This may be an advantage or disadvantage, depending upon your goals and point of view. Training offered by a vocational-technical school is usually more detailed and may be of shorter duration than that offered by a community college, because the concentration is on strictly technical training. On the other hand, a community college may offer a more reasonable balance between breadth and specialization by including some general education courses in its career-related offerings.

Unlike community colleges, which usually maintain "open-door" or "modified open-door" admissions policies, vocational-technical schools are sometimes relatively selective. One reason for this is that some vocational-technical schools offer programs that are highly specialized and not available at many other institutions. Thus, competition for places in some of these programs may be fairly intense. Be sure to apply early enough to be considered for programs that may have a limited number of openings.

College location

The college closest to your home may not be the best one for you. Even your home state may not offer all of the best educational and financial aid resources for you. On the other hand, a distant college may not be the best either.

Which areas of the country can you realistically consider? Should you consider climate, scenic beauty, recreational possibilities, or your own health as you look for a college?

You should consider the relation between location and costs. Private colleges usually charge the same tuition for all students no matter where they are from; publicly supported colleges usually have higher tuition rates for students from out of state. Travel costs and travel time go up the farther away from home you go. How frequently will you want to come home? Every weekend? Once a month? For major vacations only?

What are you looking for—and ready for—in terms of psychological distance or separation from your family? One hundred miles may be just right for some, but too close to home for others; 2,000 miles may be comfortable for some, but too far for others.

The map on the opposite page divides the country into seven regions. If you have interests or goals that are tied to a specific location or climate, use it to identify the states or regions of the country you would like to explore. Or, if a college's distance from your home is an important consideration for you, use the map to determine which states and regions you should concentrate on.

To help you focus your search for colleges, we've grouped the four-year colleges in the **Search** section of this book according to these regions. The two-year colleges are listed alphabetically by state.

List regions in order of preference here:

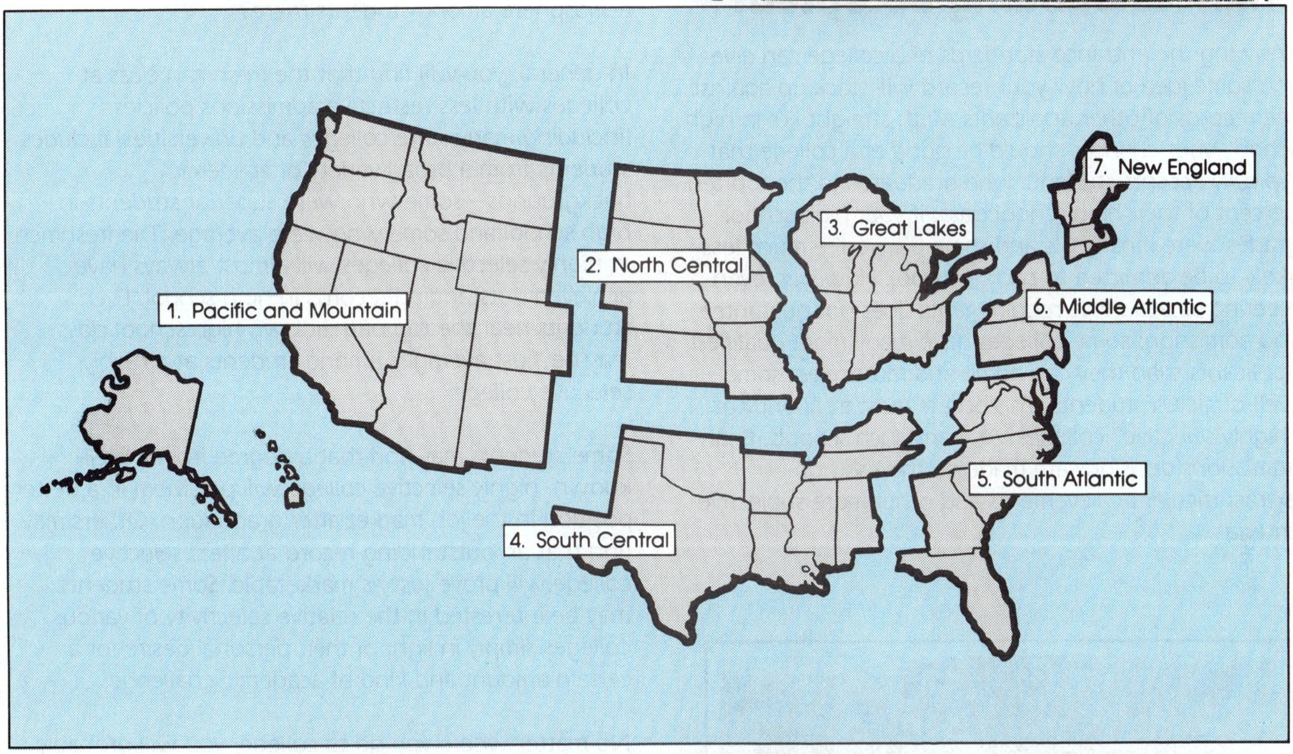

7. New England

3. Great Lakes

2. North Central

6. Middle Atlantic

1. Pacific and Mountain

5. South Atlantic

4. South Central

Admissions selectivity

Admissions selectivity refers to the level of academic qualifications a college looks for in applicants as part of its entrance requirements. Information about the admissions selectivity of a college—its standards for entrance—will help you answer some important questions.

Are you eligible for admission? What are your chances of being accepted?

Knowing the entrance standards of a college can give you some idea of how your record will stack up against the records of other applicants. With straight A's in high school, your chances should be good at a college that typically accepts students who graduated in the top ten percent of their high school class; if your high school grades were mostly C's and some B's, you're much less likely to be admitted to such a school. However, even meeting all academic requirements does not guarantee you admission; some colleges have many more qualified applicants than they can admit and must reject some well-qualified students. This occurs most frequently at "highly selective" colleges. At many such schools, final admissions decisions are made on the basis of extracurricular achievements and other more subjective criteria.

What academic demands can you expect to find at a specific college?

If your grades and other qualifications suggest you are eligible for acceptance at a particular school, you'll want to get a good idea of what your academic life would be like there. Compare your academic skills with those of the school's freshmen. What are the performance standards at the school? What are your own grade standards and goals? What is the competitive atmosphere among students there?

In general, you will find that the freshman class at colleges with less restrictive admissions policies (including many state colleges and universities) includes students from a broad variety of academic backgrounds—some who were superior students in high school and some who were average. The freshmen at highly selective colleges will almost always have achieved outstanding records in high school. Even students near the top of their own high school class may be "just average" among students at a highly selective college.

Some students may find that a degree from a well-known, highly selective college will put them in a better position in the job market after graduation. Others may find that an outstanding record at a less selective college will prove just as marketable. Some students may be interested in the relative selectivity of various colleges simply in light of their personal desire for a certain amount and kind of academic challenge.

No matter where you go to college, you will probably find the competition more demanding than it was in high school. While the right amount of academic competition from other students can be a good thing, jumping in where the competition is too tough may discourage you. On the other hand, coasting along where the competition isn't tough enough might not stimulate you to do your best work.

We've asked colleges to describe their admissions policies using the categories listed on the chart below. These are general descriptions; some schools may accept students with special talents or needs who do not quite meet the standards listed. Also, average entrance test scores differ among colleges in the same admissions category.

We've tried to give you an idea of the kinds of students attending colleges in each admission category. The table shows average ACT and SAT scores for the middle two-thirds of colleges in each category. For example, about two-thirds of the highly selective colleges have average ACT Composite scores between 27 and 31 (see lower right). Of course, many students score above or below the averages for their colleges. Admissions tests are discussed in detail on page 25.

To review your opportunities thoroughly as you conduct your search, consider colleges in more than one of these admissions selectivity categories. For example, if you are in the top ten percent of your class, you may meet the eligibility requirements for almost every college and thus can seriously consider colleges in all of the admissions categories. If you are just above the middle of your high school class, your chances for admission may be best at colleges in the Open, Liberal, and Traditional categories.

Note. An Open admissions policy does not guarantee a degree for students who have not done well in high school. Colleges with less stringent entrance requirements may also have a higher freshman dropout rate. Students who underestimate the academic standards at such schools may find that the "open door" is also a "revolving door."

Admissions Policy

Admissions Category	Typical Test Score Averages Reported by Colleges	
	SAT Total (V + M)	**ACT** Composite
OPEN All high school graduates accepted, to limit of capacity	680-810	17-20
LIBERAL Some freshmen from lower half of high school graduating class	720-860	18-21
TRADITIONAL Majority of accepted freshmen in top 50 percent of high school graduating class	810-950	20-23
SELECTIVE Majority of accepted freshmen in top 25 percent of high school graduating class	920-1090	22-27
HIGHLY SELECTIVE Majority of accepted freshmen in top 10 percent of high school graduating class	1120-1290	27-31

College size

Colleges vary greatly in size. Some enroll fewer than 100 students; others, such as large universities, may have as many as 40,000 students on a campus. The size of a college may mean more to you than just the number of students. Listed below are some of the characteristics that frequently come to mind when people think about differences between colleges of different sizes.

Not all of these statements are true for all colleges in a particular size category. Not all of these characteristics may be equally important to you. For example, a small library with a collection of basic books in your major may be sufficient to support your study as an undergraduate. At a large college, the residence hall you live in may provide your primary social group, and thus the overall size of the college may not concern you. Before you eliminate colleges on the basis of size, you should decide how important the differences between large and small colleges are to you.

Large colleges MAY offer

- more areas of specialized study
- more courses in each area
- more privacy and anonymity
- greater freedom to find your own way
- greater range of extracurricular activities and organizations
- opportunities to meet students and faculty from a greater variety of backgrounds
- larger, more specialized libraries
- more laboratory facilities
- more famous professors, more research-oriented faculty
- graduate departments, advanced degree programs

Small colleges MAY offer

- a less cold, more personal atmosphere
- small classes, more discussion, and fewer lectures
- less distance between students and faculty
- greater chance for individual participation and experience in athletics, clubs, leadership positions
- less chance for an individual to get lost in the shuffle
- more teachers interested in students and teaching
- more flexible programs, more opportunity for students to experiment

College costs

For most students, costs are an important factor in selecting a college. Here are four steps that will help you decide whether you can afford to go to a particular school.

- Determine the cost of attending the college.
- See how far your resources will go toward the cost.
- Look into financial aid from the school and other sources.
- Develop a realistic perspective on costs of education.

Determine the cost.

For each college you're considering, add up the direct and indirect costs of attendance. **Direct costs** include tuition and fees, and books and supplies. **Indirect costs** include room and board, transportation to and from home, and miscellaneous personal expenses like clothing, laundry, entertainment, and recreation. Tuition and room and board costs will account for a major share of your bill for a year at college. You can find these figures in the **Search** section of the book or in the current edition of the school's catalog.

Tuition expenses vary considerably according to the type of college. Tuition and fees are quite often higher for students at private colleges than for in-state students at tax-supported public colleges. Two-year public colleges frequently charge lower tuition and fees than do four-year colleges and universities. Out-of-state students frequently pay higher tuition at public colleges than do in-state residents.

Room and board in a college dormitory will probably cost you more than room and board at home. The cost of books and supplies can vary greatly according to the nature of your program. On the average, however, undergraduate students spend $400-$500 per year on books and supplies. The cost of transportation varies, too. Your miscellaneous expenses will depend largely on your personal spending habits. A good rule of thumb is to allow at least $1,200-$1,500 per year for miscellaneous expenses.

See how far your resources will go.

Estimate the amount of money you and your family can provide for a year of your college education. Although federal, state, and local taxes support part of the costs of postsecondary education, you and your family have the primary responsibility for financing your college education. You should expect to draw on your summer earnings and on any other resources you may have, such as savings, stocks, bonds, or trust funds. Your parents will be expected to continue at least the same level of support they provided while you were in high school and will also be expected to draw on some of their assets.

Estimated Funds Available

Your Resources	**Estimated Amount**
Savings and other assets (35% per year)	$ ______
Summer earnings	$ ______
Part-time work during school year	$ ______
Miscellaneous	$ ______
Your Total Resources	**$** ______
Parents' Resources	**Available to You**
From their current income	$ ______
From college savings (total amount divided by years of education planned)	$ ______
Miscellaneous (insurance, annuities, stocks, trusts)	$ ______
Parents' Total Resources	**$** ______
Total Estimated Resources Available	**$** ______

If you had to stop right here, your "total resources available" figure would tell you clearly what price range you could afford in college. But, like many students, you may find the bill for colleges that interest you is greater than your "total resources available" figure. Your next step should be:

Look into financial aid.

Many students whose resources fall short of their college costs receive financial aid in the form of a scholarship or grant, a loan, a work-study job, or some combination of the three. You owe it to yourself to explore all these possibilities. About one-third of the full-time freshmen at universities and two-year colleges receive some kind of financial aid to help them meet college expenses. Nearly half the freshmen at four-year colleges (including many private schools) receive this kind of assistance.

Eligibility for need-based financial aid is not determined solely by family income level. Your chances of getting financial aid depend on several factors:

- Your family's **total** financial picture (income, assets, debts, retirement needs, family size, number of students in college)
- Total costs at the specific college
- Amount of aid funds available from all possible sources
- Needs of other applicants (Colleges often award aid to neediest students first and may not have sufficient funds to help every student with need.)
- Specific program of study (Individual programs, such as nursing or various health professions, may have special federal funds available.)

For example, if you are an only child in a family with average income and debts, you probably would be ineligible for need-based aid at a local college with low annual tuition. However, if your family has four children and two of you attend private colleges where annual costs are high, the picture changes significantly. Living in a state that offers aid to students attending higher-priced private colleges or studying a major for which federal funds are available also increases your possibilities for aid. At a college with strong endowment funding for financial aid, your chances of getting aid may be further increased.

Develop a realistic perspective on costs.

Because most schools make financial aid awards during the spring of the applicant's senior year in high school, you'll begin looking for the "right" college a long time before you can have an exact idea of the amount of financial aid for which you might be eligible.

So first estimate how much money you and your family can spend for your first year of college. Then, instead of searching only for those colleges where your expenses will be equal to or less than your own resources, identify colleges that "look good" on most of your other key preferences, and investigate each school's financial aid program. Don't rule out a school that's ideal for you in all other respects simply because it appears to be too expensive. With careful checking and planning, you may be able to match all your other needs and preferences with a school that offers the financial aid you need.

You'll find more information about financial aid, including lists of aid sources, when you get to Step 7. In the meantime, you may want to consult or order copies of the following:

- **Applying for Financial Aid** from ACT Financial Aid Services, P.O. Box 168, Iowa City, Iowa 52243 (free).
- **The College Cost Book, 1992** (12th ed.) from College Board Publications, Box 886, New York, New York 10101 ($14.95).
- **Financial Aids for Higher Education: A Catalog for Undergraduates** from Wm. C. Brown Publishers, Dubuque, Iowa 52001 ($45.00; paperback).
- **The Student Guide to Financial Aid, 1991-92,** from U.S. Department of Education, Office of Grants, Loans, and Work Study, Washington, D.C. 20202 (free).
- **Meeting College Costs** from College Board Scholarship Service, 45 Columbus Ave., New York, New York 10023 (free).
- **Need a Lift?** from The American Legion, National Emblem Sales, P.O. Box 1050, Indianapolis, Indiana 46206 ($2.00 prepaid). This annually revised booklet devotes over 100 pages to scholarship and aid program descriptions.

Your high school library or local public library may have a copy of **Scholarships, Fellowships, and Loans,** Vol. 8 (Arlington, Massachusetts: Bellman Publishing, 1987, $80.00). This comprehensive resource lists more than ten billion dollars in student aid available annually. It describes the number of awards, required qualifications, funds for special fields of interest, and how and when to apply for the various kinds of financial aid.

Majors and study programs

Choosing a major

If you have a clear idea of your life direction, you may also know which programs and majors you want. For example, if you are seriously planning to teach science at the high school level, you'll want to identify schools that offer majors in secondary education, particularly those with strong, quality programs in several science areas. If you're thinking of a social work career in the inner city, you may wish to look for social work majors at schools that also offer a language you'd find useful in that career. If you decide on engineering, you may want to identify colleges which have business administration programs as well, because many engineers find training in business useful.

On the other hand, if your long-range goals are uncertain, you may want to investigate schools that offer exposure to several areas. A school with a narrow range of programs (for example, one that prepares only engineers) may not provide you with sufficient flexibility and diversity of choice.

As you examine college programs, you may also find that there is some flexibility about the time when you must choose a major area of study. Though the general practice is to declare a major during the sophomore year, some schools allow you to make preliminary choices about majors as early as the freshman year. Some schools encourage you to design your own major in consultation with an adviser; others provide quite specific guidelines about what to study in each area.

If you have a specific career in mind, it is advisable to find out as much as possible about the study programs that are considered best for that particular line of work. A strong background in specific career-related courses can provide a good preparation for some jobs, but employers in other fields might prefer graduates with liberal arts majors.

Career information

The Bureau of Labor Statistics of the U.S. Department of Labor publishes several reference works containing detailed career information. The most comprehensive resource book is the **Occupational Outlook Handbook** (published every two years), which provides recent employment statistics and makes projections, based on current trends, about probable employment opportunities in the coming five to ten years. This employment guide contains "occupational statements," which furnish information on the nature of the work; places of employment; education, skills, and abilities required for job entry; employment outlook; earnings; and working conditions. Your local public library can help you find a copy of this publication.

Another Bureau publication, the **Occupational Outlook Quarterly,** features articles about the latest developments in specific job areas, as well as periodic job outlook projections based on recent studies. The Winter 1990-91 issue contains an article entitled "Entry Level Jobs: Defining Them and Counting Them," which describes occupations traditionally available to workers who are just getting their start in the labor force.

Beginning in the late '60s, and continuing through the '70s, the number of bachelor's degrees awarded significantly exceeded the number of job openings for college graduates; as a result, many graduates found the professional and technical job fields closed and had to enter jobs in, for example, sales, clerical, craft, or service areas. Since projections indicate that, in certain areas, qualified graduates will continue to outnumber job openings, career outlook information might be an important factor as you think about college majors and programs of study.

Exploring program areas

Twelve general areas of study are listed at the right, and several specific four-year college majors are shown in each area. In the four-year college **(blue)** section of this book, you can find which of these specific majors (and about 30 others) are available at each college. You can consult the **Index of Additional Majors at Four-year Colleges** on page 182 to locate colleges with 63 additional majors not listed in the **Search** sections.

In the two-year **(purple)** section, 15 subject areas indicate which general groups of transfer courses are available at each college. The **Search** pages also show 39 additional career-oriented programs. For more specialized, hard-to-find programs, consult the **Index of Additional Career-oriented Programs at Two-year Colleges** on page 264.

Check the study areas that are important to you as you search for colleges. Add those of interest to you that are not shown on this list.

- ☐ **Agriculture**
  Agronomy, Animal Husbandry, Fish, Wildlife Management, Forestry
- ☐ **Business**
  Accounting, Business Management/Administration, Marketing/Purchasing, Secretarial Studies
- ☐ **Communications**
  Journalism, Radio/TV Broadcasting, Advertising
- ☐ **Education**
  Art Education, Elementary Education, Secondary Education, Special Education
- ☐ **Engineering**
  Chemical Engineering, Civil Engineering, Electrical Engineering, Mechanical Engineering
- ☐ **Fine/Applied Arts**
  Architecture, Art, Dance, Dramatic Arts, Music
- ☐ **Foreign Language**
  French, German, Spanish, Russian
- ☐ **Health Professions**
  Predentistry, Premedicine, Medical Technology, Nursing, Occupational Therapy, Physical Therapy
- ☐ **Home Economics**
  Clothing and Textiles, Family Relations, Child Development, Foods and Nutrition
- ☐ **Humanities**
  Creative Writing, History, Literature, Philosophy, Religion, Speech
- ☐ **Math and Physical Science**
  Mathematics, Computer Sciences, Biology, Chemistry, Physics
- ☐ **Social Sciences**
  Law Enforcement, Correction, Social Work, Geography, Prelaw, Psychology, Sociology

Accreditation and affiliation

Accreditation

Accreditation indicates that a college or educational program has met certain minimum standards for its program of study, staff, and facilities. Accreditation is somewhat like a "pass-fail" grading system. In such a system, "pass" may be assigned to a student who meets minimum requirements as well as to one who has done outstanding work. Similarly, among schools that have been accredited there are many different levels of quality.

Although credits and degrees earned at accredited colleges are more likely to be eligible for transfer recognition by other colleges or by graduate schools, accreditation does not guarantee such transfer. Decisions about which credits or degrees are transferable are made by individual institutions.

Institutional accreditation applies to the total institution and indicates that the school as a whole has been judged to be meeting its objectives and operating at an acceptable standard. However, it does not necessarily mean that all of its parts or departments are equal in quality. For example, an accredited college may have an outstanding program in one area but be about average in another.

The **Search** pages of this book note whether or not a college is accredited. Accreditation denoted by footnote 5 means the college has reported that it is accredited or is a recognized candidate for accreditation by one of the following six regional associations of schools and colleges: the Middle States Association, the New England Association, the North Central Association, the Northwest Association, the Southern Association, or the Western Association.

Colleges may also be accredited by one of many national accrediting bodies. Institutions that have indicated accreditation by a nationally recognized accrediting organization (**other** than one of the six regional associations) are indicated by the symbol †. The "Accreditation Information" section of the College Index (pages 304-305) lists those colleges that are accredited by the American Association of Bible Colleges or the Association of Independent Colleges and Schools. Other national accrediting agencies for specific areas include the National Association of Trade and Technical Schools and the National Home Study Council. Some accrediting organizations, such as the National Association of Schools of Music and the National Association of Schools of Art, evaluate institutions devoted to particular professions or occupations, but they are primarily involved with accreditation of individual programs within institutions.

Specialized accreditation of individual programs is granted by national professional organizations. Specialized accreditation is independent of institutional accreditation and is intended to ensure that specific programs meet the needs of society and the profession. Particularly in health professions, states may require that students graduate from an accredited program. Specialized program accreditation is not reported in this book.

For more information on accreditation, consult the latest edition of **Accredited Institutions of Postsecondary Education.** This book, which may be available through your counselor or library, contains information on both institutional and specialized accreditation.

Affiliation

Knowing that a college is public, private-independent, or private-church-related does not automatically provide information about the quality or nature of the institution. At some colleges, however, affiliation does have an effect on the religious life of students on the campus.

You can expect public colleges and universities and private-independent colleges to have no requirements that affect the religious activity of their students. Among church-related colleges, the influence of denominations on campus life varies. At some, this influence may be less apparent; at others, attendance at chapel or other worship services and study in religious courses is actively encouraged or required.

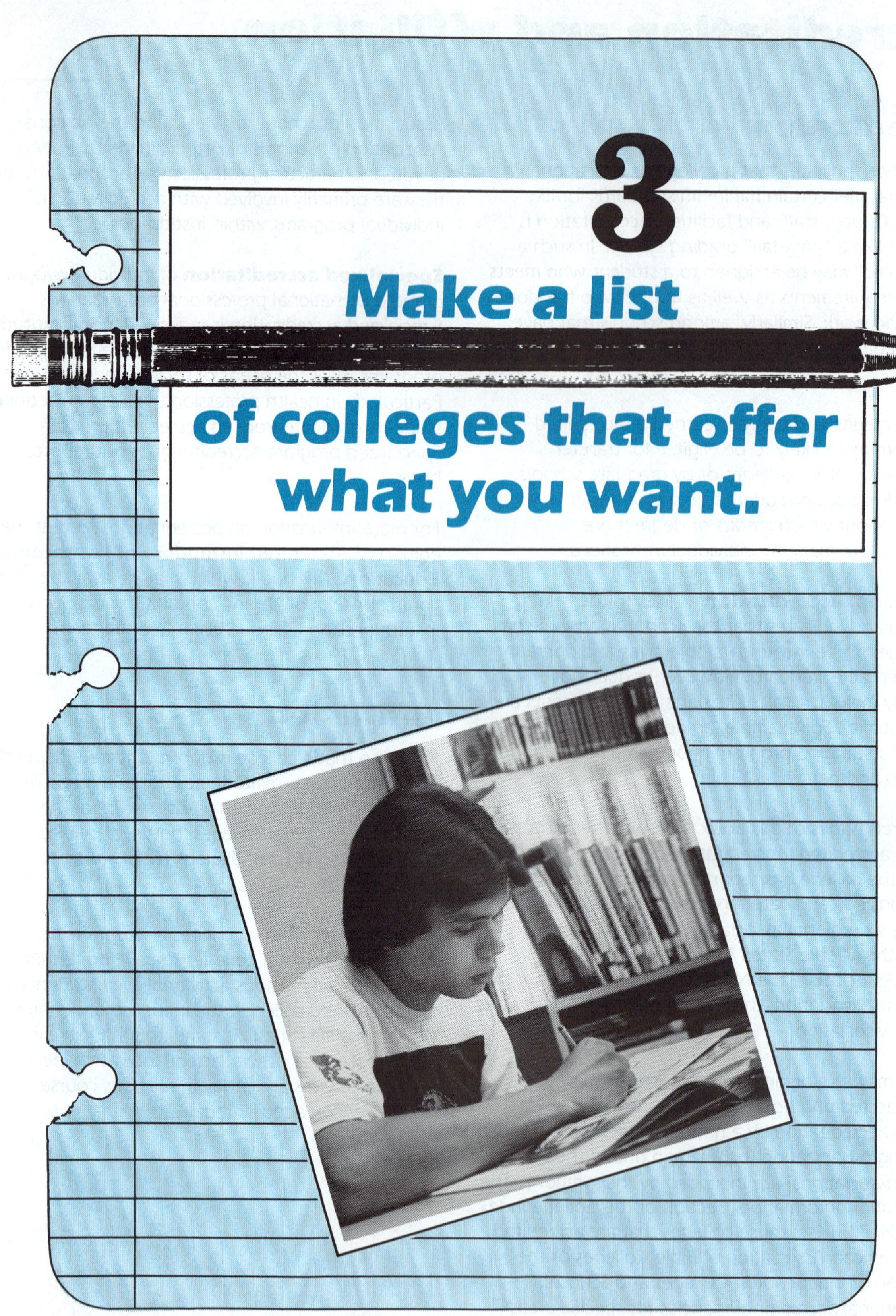

3

Make a list of colleges that offer what you want.

Sum up characteristics that are important to you.

So far you've been considering tangible factors that can guide your preliminary search for colleges. Now, use the worksheets in Step 3 to help you summarize your thinking. Then use the **Search** section to locate colleges that seem to fit your preferences.

After your search, investigate the colleges carefully to form a close-up picture of each. Evaluate how well each college fits your needs and preferences in some of the more intangible areas. Step 4, "Collect information about the colleges on your list," and Step 5, "Compare the colleges on your list," will help you with these tasks.

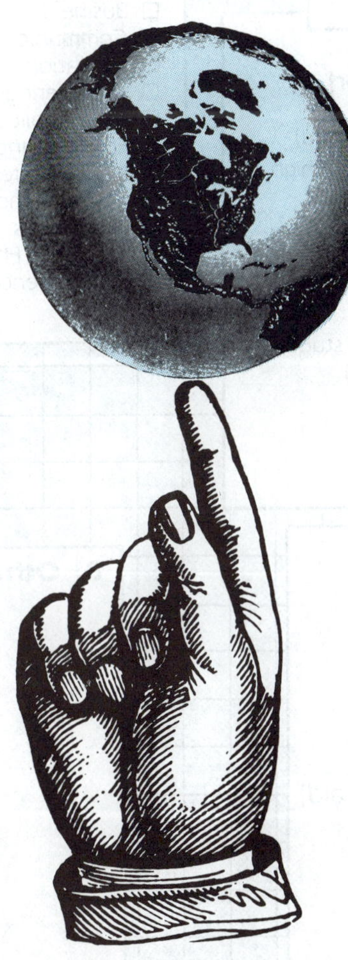

Summarize your four-year college preferences.

1. Region (check those you prefer)

- ☐ Pacific and Mountain States
  Alaska, Arizona, California, Colorado, Hawaii, Idaho, Montana, Nevada, New Mexico, Oregon, Utah, Washington, Wyoming
- ☐ North Central States
  Iowa, Kansas, Minnesota, Missouri, Nebraska, North Dakota, South Dakota
- ☐ Great Lakes States
  Illinois, Indiana, Michigan, Ohio, Wisconsin
- ☐ South Central States
  Alabama, Arkansas, Kentucky, Louisiana, Mississippi, Oklahoma, Tennessee, Texas
- ☐ South Atlantic States
  Delaware, District of Columbia, Florida, Georgia, Maryland, North Carolina, South Carolina, Virginia, West Virginia
- ☐ Middle Atlantic States
  New Jersey, New York, Pennsylvania
- ☐ New England States
  Connecticut, Maine, Massachusetts, New Hampshire, Rhode Island, Vermont

2. Admissions Selectivity (check those you are eligible for)

- ☐ Open (all high school graduates accepted)
- ☐ Liberal (some freshmen from lower half of high school class)
- ☐ Traditional (majority of accepted freshmen in upper half of high school class)
- ☐ Selective (majority of accepted students in top 25 percent of high school class)
- ☐ Highly selective (majority of accepted students in top 10 percent of high school class)

3. Size (check those you prefer)

- ☐ Up to 1,000 students
- ☐ 1,000 to 5,000 students
- ☐ 5,000 to 15,000 students
- ☐ More than 15,000 students

4. Cost (check the resources you and your parents have available each year, without aid)

- ☐ Up to $500
- ☐ Up to $1,000
- ☐ Up to $1,500
- ☐ Up to $2,000
- ☐ Up to $2,500
- ☐ Up to $3,000
- ☐ More than $3,000

5. Affiliation (check those you prefer)

- ☐ Public
- ☐ Private, no special religious emphasis
- ☐ Private, some emphasis on religious observance or study
  - _____ Baptist
  - _____ Jewish
  - _____ Latter Day Saints
  - _____ Lutheran
  - _____ Methodist
  - _____ Presbyterian
  - _____ Roman Catholic
  - _____ United Church of Christ
  - _____ Other

6. Majors Available (check areas you prefer)

- ☐ Agriculture
- ☐ Business
- ☐ Communications
- ☐ Education
- ☐ Engineering
- ☐ Fine/Applied Arts
- ☐ Foreign Languages
- ☐ Health Professions
- ☐ Home Economics
- ☐ Humanities
- ☐ Math and Physical Sciences
- ☐ Social Sciences

7. Student Body

- ☐ Coed
- ☐ All women
- ☐ All men

8. Other Factors:

Summarize your two-year college preferences.

1. States (list states you prefer)

2. Admissions Selectivity

Most two-year colleges accept all high school graduates. Schools that do not use this admissions policy are indicated by footnote 8.

3. Size (check those you prefer)

- ☐ Up to 1,000 students
- ☐ 1,000 to 5,000 students
- ☐ 5,000 to 15,000 students
- ☐ More than 15,000 students

4. Cost (check the resources you and your parents have available each year, without aid)

- ☐ Up to $500
- ☐ Up to $1,000
- ☐ Up to $1,500
- ☐ Up to $2,000
- ☐ Up to $3,000
- ☐ More than $3,000

5. Affiliation (check those you prefer)

- ☐ Public
- ☐ Private, no special religious emphasis
- ☐ Private, some emphasis on religious observance or study
  - _____ Baptist
  - _____ Jewish
  - _____ Latter Day Saints
  - _____ Lutheran
  - _____ Methodist
  - _____ Presbyterian
  - _____ Roman Catholic
  - _____ United Church of Christ
  - _____ Other

6. Career-oriented Programs Available (check areas you prefer)

- ☐ Agriculture
- ☐ Business
- ☐ Education
- ☐ Liberal Arts
- ☐ Health
- ☐ Home Economics
- ☐ Math and Physical Sciences
- ☐ Social Sciences
- ☐ Technical/Skilled Trades (including Engineering)

7. College Transfer Courses Available (check those you prefer)

- ☐ Agriculture
- ☐ Business
- ☐ Communications
- ☐ Education
- ☐ Engineering
- ☐ Fine/Applied Arts
- ☐ Foreign Languages
- ☐ Health Professions
- ☐ Home Economics
- ☐ Humanities
- ☐ Math and Physical Sciences
- ☐ Social Sciences

8. Other Factors:

Make a list.

After you've thought carefully about the college characteristics you prefer, use the four-year and two-year **Search** sections and the **College Index** to make a list of colleges that offer what you want. The **Search** sections in the book contain descriptive information for about 97 percent of all American four- and two-year colleges. Except as noted, all of them admit students directly after high school.

If you're interested in four-year colleges

Turn to the four-year (blue) **Search** section, which begins on page 52. Here you'll find a description of how colleges are arranged within this section. You'll also find directions for using the four-year **Search** section and a detailed guide to reading the entries there. Carefully read through all the directions on these pages and work through the sample entry. Then begin your search. After you've finished, return to this page and list the colleges you wish to investigate further.

If you're interested in two-year colleges

Turn to the two-year (purple) **Search** section, which begins on page 193. Here you'll find a description of how colleges are arranged within this section. You'll also find directions for using the two-year **Search** section and a detailed guide to reading the entries there. Carefully read through all the directions on these pages and work through the sample entry. Then begin your search. After you've finished, return to this page and list the colleges you wish to investigate further.

If you want to look up information about specific colleges

Turn to the **College Index,** which begins on page 272. Find the college or colleges you're interested in. Each college has a sequence number; use this number to locate the college in the **Search** pages.

If a college that interests you is in the four-year (blue) **Search** section, consult page 54 for a detailed guide to reading the four-year college entries.

If a college that interests you is in the two-year (purple) **Search** section, consult page 194 for a detailed guide to reading the two-year college entries.

After you've finished your search, return to this page and list the colleges you wish to investigate further.

College admission tests[1]

Many colleges require or recommend that students submit results from one of two national tests (ACT or SAT) as part of their application for admission. Reports of these results are also provided to the student to help in educational and career planning. As soon as you've begun to develop a list of colleges that interest you, you should register to take the appropriate college admission test.

The ACT Assessment (American College Testing, Iowa City, Iowa 52243) includes four tests—**English, Mathematics, Reading,** and **Science Reasoning**—designed to measure current level of educational development and ability to perform tasks frequently required in college coursework. The ACT Assessment also includes an **Interest Inventory** to help you compare your interests with those of students who have completed various college majors and identify groups of jobs (job families) you may want to explore. The **Student Profile Section** lets you describe to colleges some of your accomplishments, plans, and needs.

The Admissions Testing Program (The College Entrance Examination Board, Princeton, New Jersey 08540) consists of the Scholastic Aptitude Test (SAT) and Achievement Tests in 14 subject areas. Individual colleges may require only the SAT, or the SAT in combination with one or more specific achievement tests. The SAT is designed to measure your **Verbal Reasoning** (reported in reading comprehension and vocabulary subscores) and **Mathematical Reasoning** abilities, and includes an experimental test of **Written English.** The SAT also includes a **Student Descriptive Questionnaire** that allows you to describe to colleges some of your plans and experiences.

The basic steps to follow are similar for both testing programs.

1. Find out which test is preferred or required by each of the colleges you are considering. (This is shown for each college on the **Search** pages of this book.) Check with your counselor about which test(s) to take and when (late in junior year, during the following summer, or early in senior year).
2. Register by mail for the desired test about six weeks before one of the national test dates on which it is given. Registration forms, fees, and listings of dates and deadlines for each test are available in your school guidance office.
3. After registering, you will be sent an admission blank, which you must take with you to your test center on the day of the test.
4. The tests, which last about three to four hours, are given on Saturday mornings at specified test centers selected to be accessible to as many students as possible. Non-Saturday testing is available for students whose religious faith prohibits them from taking the test on a Saturday.
5. About five to six weeks after the test, copies of your results will be sent to you or your high school and to colleges and scholarship agencies you listed. For an additional fee, you may request that your results be sent to other colleges or scholarship agencies by using a special form available from your counselor.

[1]**Important note for students who plan to take college admission tests in New York State:** Legislation has resulted in the reduced availability of certain testing services in that state. See your counselor or contact the appropriate testing service for up-to-date information.

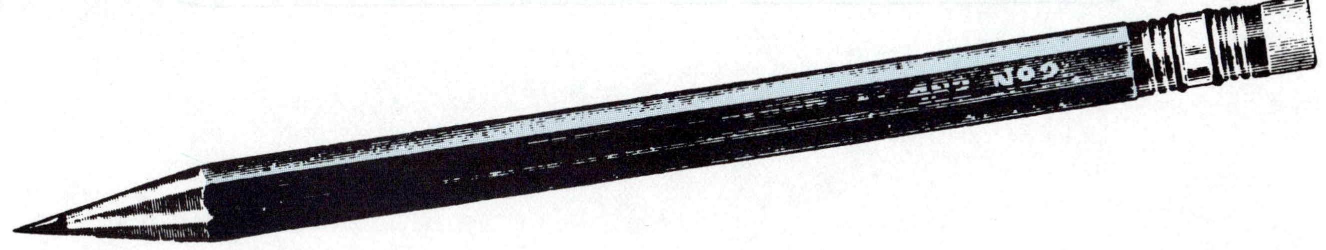

4

Collect information about the colleges on your list.

After you have developed a list of colleges to consider, try to construct a detailed and complete picture of each college. Be sure to balance your investigations; gather information from several different sources. Careful reading at home and in your school guidance office, combined with campus visits and discussions with students, will give you an accurate sense of your own feelings about a college. Talking with your parents, counselors, teachers, and friends about the information you gather will help you put together a clearer picture of each college.

This section describes sources of information about what to look for as you investigate colleges. Consult these sources before you begin. Then study the colleges on your list, making notes to keep track of what you find. Use the College Comparison Outline on pages 34 and 35 as a model for organizing your notes.

Keep your own preferences in mind. You may want to review the first part of this book to rethink your goals. Knowing your own priorities can help you put the advantages and disadvantages of individual colleges into perspective as you compare one college with another.

1. Alpha College

Admissions Office
Alpha College
Beta CA 92345

Please send me a catalog giving information about

Sources of information about colleges

The school counselor

Your high school counselor can be a very helpful source of information about colleges, and can often help you weigh critically the pros and cons of individual colleges.

- Your counselor may have access to school-related information about you that can help in your college planning. Discussions of your high school experiences, career plans, abilities, and preferences can help you choose and rank your own college search factors.
- Your counselor probably helps students answer college planning questions every day. He or she will be able to answer your questions about application forms and financial aid opportunities, and can refer you quickly to information resources such as college directories and catalogs.
- Your counselor can help you get in touch with graduates of your high school who are attending a particular college, can let you know when college representatives will be visiting your high school, and can help you arrange visits to specific colleges.
- As your plans develop, your counselor can act as a sounding board for your ideas, and can help you to clarify and organize your evaluation of each particular college.

Although you should take full advantage of your counselor's advice and help, remember that you (and not your counselor) will have to make the final decisions and live with them. That's why it's so important for you to gather as much information as you can and to evaluate that information carefully.

College directories

A college directory brings capsule descriptions of colleges across the country together in a single book. The **College Planning/Search Book** is one type of college directory, with its own way of presenting information about colleges. Although each kind of directory presents many of the same basic facts about a college, each has a slightly different format and emphasis. For these reasons, it may be useful to read descriptions of colleges in more than one directory.

Keep in mind that college directories are intended to provide a very general introduction to each campus. Be sure to use the most recent editions. For a more specific and complete description of each college and its policies, read the college's catalog.

Selected college directories

The college directories below provide capsule descriptions of two-year and four-year colleges. Copies are likely to be available in your counselor's office or in your school or public library. Be sure to consult the latest edition available.

The College Handbook, 1992 (29th ed.). New York: The College Board, 1991, $18.95 (paperback).

Who's Who in Community, Technical and Junior Colleges. Fairfax, VA.: American Association of Community and Junior Colleges, 1991. $37.50 (paperback).

Index of Majors, 1992 (14th ed.). New York: The College Board, 1991. $15.95 (paperback).

Lovejoy's College Guide (19th ed.). New York: Simon & Schuster, Inc., 1989. $18.95 (paperback).

Profiles of American Colleges (18th ed.). Hauppauge, N.Y.: Barron's Educational Series, Inc., 1991. $17.95 (paperback).

College catalogs

As you begin to consider a college seriously, study of its catalog becomes a must. The college catalog is a complete and authoritative source of information about college policies, rules, and regulations; it provides detailed information about programs and courses of study. Catalogs for many colleges may be on file in your guidance office or on the shelves in the reference section of your public library. You can get your own copy of a college's catalog by writing directly to its admissions office. Some schools will respond to your inquiry by sending a short informational brochure and a catalog request card or form. To receive a catalog, you should fill out and return the request form. Some colleges provide catalogs at no cost upon request; others charge a fee (usually $1-$3) to cover printing costs.

The college catalog will tell you many of the facts you need to know about the college:

- Steps necessary to apply for admission, housing, and financial aid
- Costs
- Course requirements for various degree programs
- Courses available in specific areas of study
- Academic credentials of instructors
- Student body composition
- Student activities and services available
- Social, cultural, religious opportunities and requirements
- Library and other educational facilities available
- Nature of the surrounding community
- Calendar for the school year

In addition to their catalogs, many schools publish supplementary brochures or pamphlets for particular subjects and programs of study. These often give more detailed information than the college catalog, and describe new courses that might not be included in the catalog. Some community colleges, for example, publish a comprehensive catalog only once every two years; students should look for the current course information releases, which are often published in newspapers or newsletters, to find out which courses are available in a given year, semester, or quarter.

Many four-year liberal arts colleges publish a **viewbook,** a short pamphlet that conveys, through photographs and words, a more personalized view of the school and its philosophy and approach to higher education. Viewbooks characteristically include statements from faculty and students, profiles of individual students, and short articles on experimental or innovative programs. At its best, the viewbook combines specific information with glimpses into the less tangible aspects of college life.

Recruitment and college representatives

Recent studies show that enrollment in colleges leveled off during the second half of the 1970s. Because of a decline in the national birth rate after 1964, the number of traditional-age students entering college has also declined during the 1980s. At the same time, overall college dropout rates generally range between 40 and 60 percent. Consequently, colleges place great emphasis on the **recruitment** and **retention** of students.

Recruitment refers to the various means by which colleges make their programs and services known to prospective students. Most schools still rely on direct mail to make and maintain contacts. Once you have expressed interest in attending a college, you will probably receive follow-up letters as well as detailed information about programs of interest to you. Both four-year and two-year colleges have increased their efforts to attract applicants from nontraditional segments of the population: minorities, women, and older persons. Colleges frequently send representatives to high schools; or they may arrange for you to meet with an alumnus living in your area. From college representatives and alumni you can often gain information and insights that are not available in college catalogs or brochures.

Retention describes the efforts colleges make to keep students once they have enrolled. Because significant numbers of students drop out without completing a program or degree, many colleges are trying to lower the rate at which students withdraw by expanding and redefining programs of study and by offering more services and activities.

Faced with declining enrollment and a tightening job market, colleges are attempting to provide programs that meet student needs and relate learning to employment. They are stressing the expansion of internships (on-the-job training), business offerings, health science offerings, and career planning centers. As you weigh the advantages of one college against another, the college's commitment to career-oriented activities might be an influential factor.

You might also want to ask how the college's advising system works. Many colleges have developed individualized guidance systems that help students make sensible, step-by-step plans and decisions. Some colleges have large guidance centers, while at others the advising job is assigned largely to faculty members.

College students and alumni

Current students and alumni of a college you are considering can be very useful sources of information. Your counselor may be able to help you locate them. Be sure you accurately interpret what they tell you, however. For example, if a student says the study load at a college is "just right," you may ask, "Just right for whom?—the student who received mostly A's in high school?—the student who loves to study 40 hours a week and has little interest in other campus or social activities?" What does a student mean when she says, "The college is great—tough—exciting"? Colleges change, and a person who graduated three years ago may be describing a college campus quite different from the campus you will encounter. As you talk to students and alumni, be sure that you understand their points of reference. Try to convert the information they give you into a personally useful form: "How will **I** like it? Will it be good for **me**?"

Ask about the amount and kind of studying necessary, and what campus life is like in terms of such things as dating, student freedom, and student activities. Find out what surprises other students found and what students might have done differently. Ask about the reasons behind their reactions to your questions.

College visits

A visit to a college campus is probably the best way to learn about many of its qualities and to get a feel for what it would be like to study there.

Your counselor can probably help you arrange to visit a campus. Write to the admissions office ahead of time to make arrangements for a place to stay and, if appropriate, schedule interviews with admissions personnel. Before you go, study the college catalog and copies of the school newspaper if you can obtain them. Develop a list of questions and things to look for when you get to the campus. The College Comparison Outline on pages 34 and 35 can help you prepare for your visit.

Plan to visit when classes are in session and the admissions office is open. Visit classes and stay overnight in the living facilities you are considering. Talk to students about the college environment and its academic, extracurricular, and social life.

Specialized services for students with disabilities

Section 504 of the Rehabilitation Act of 1973 states that "no otherwise qualified individual . . . shall, solely by reason of . . . handicap be excluded from participation in, be denied the benefits of, or be subjected to discrimination under any program or activity receiving federal financial assistance."

Section 504 requires that all postsecondary institutions receiving federal financial assistance must provide equal opportunity to all qualified students and must make all programs and courses readily accessible to them; it prohibits discrimination against students with disabilities in recruitment, admission, and treatment after admission; it requires that colleges and universities (a) make reasonable adjustments (smaller course loads, more test time) to permit students with disabilities to fulfill academic requirements, and (b) ensure that the students are not excluded from programs because of the absence of auxiliary facilities or services.

As a result of federal legislation, federal funding, and efforts by many colleges to create barrier-free campuses, educational opportunities and services for students with disabilities have increased markedly since the mid-1970s. Many institutions have set up specialized services committees—with members typically drawn from planners, counselors, faculty, and representative students—to evaluate existing facilities and programs, and to make recommendations aimed at ensuring that the institution's environment does not handicap students or their performance in college. Pre-admission interviews, specialized orientation programs, flexible, individualized study plans, and expanded intramural/social activities are some of the features for students with disabilities that are now common on many campuses.

Information about specialized services and accessibility of facilities is routinely included in most general college catalogs, and many institutions provide booklets, brochures, or guides specifically to answer questions that students might have. For information about nationwide opportunities in higher education for students with disabilities, check to see if your library has a copy of the **Directory of College Facilities and Services for the Disabled, 3rd Edition** (Oryx Press, 1991, $115.00).

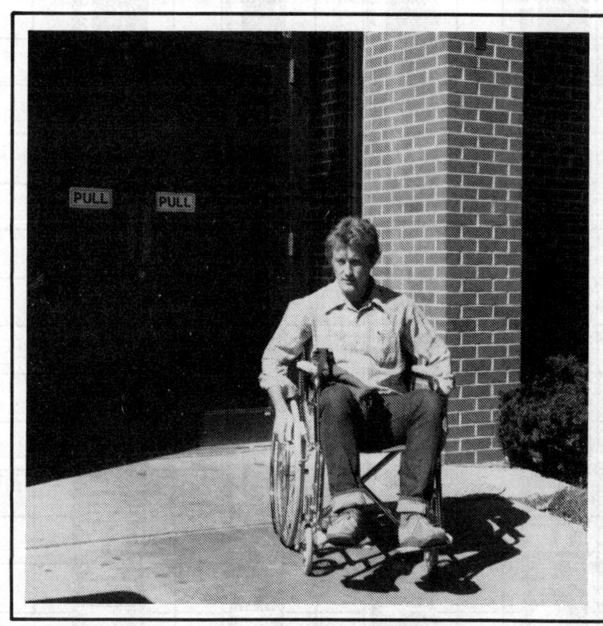

5 Compare the colleges on your list.

Organizing your information about colleges

By now you have gathered information about a number of colleges. Your next step is to organize that information in a way that will allow you to compare those colleges easily. The next two pages outline several significant factors to consider. Not all of the ideas there will be equally important to you; you may have others that we haven't listed. Use the space provided under each heading to list additional factors that will help you organize your information and impressions.

Next, using a separate sheet of paper for each college you wish to consider, systematically copy the phrases from the "master outline" that are important to you. Leave space under each heading to jot down your notes. Then record information about each college on the outlines you've constructed.

Using your outlines to compare colleges

After you've completed outlines for all the colleges that interest you, place them on a table in front of you. Carefully compare each college with the others for which you've recorded information. This comparison is not likely to be simple. You will have to decide whether the advantages of a certain college outweigh its disadvantages. And you may have to decide between different kinds of advantages available at different schools. College A may be in a better location than College B, but College B may offer a greater variety of programs of study. Then again, College C might offer the same programs as College B, but cost less.

Examine the advantages and disadvantages of each college thoughtfully. Though you will probably not find a "perfect" college, you can determine which colleges have most of the characteristics you want. Weigh the strengths and weaknesses of each to find the one that is most likely to meet your needs.

Once you have narrowed the number of colleges to three or four, you should begin the process of applying for admission and financial aid. Steps 6 and 7 describe general procedures for doing this. They also provide sample charts that you can use to keep track of your admissions and financial aid applications.

College comparison outline

To compare colleges, follow these steps:

1. Review the factors listed on these two pages. Choose the ones that you think are important in comparing colleges.
2. Add any other factors that are important to you.
3. Make an outline for each of the colleges on your list.
4. On each outline, fill in the information that you have for that college.
5. Then compare the colleges, point by point.

Academic environment

Admissions selectivity

- ☐ Academic standing required for admission
- ☐ Other admission factors
- ☐ My chances for admission

Admission steps

- ☐ Tests required or recommended
- ☐ Admissions application deadline
- ☐ Other special applications requirements

Academic orientation of students

- ☐ Emphasis of students and faculty on academic life
- ☐ High school grade point average of accepted students
- ☐ Percent of freshman students who return as sophomores
- ☐ Percent of graduates who continue their education

Educational opportunities available

- ☐ Institutional accreditation
- ☐ Specialized program accreditation
- ☐ Availability of my preferred major
- ☐ Availability of related majors
- ☐ Reputation of the department
- ☐ Requirements for a degree
- ☐ Qualifications of faculty
- ☐ Learning opportunities available outside the classroom
- ☐ Advising system
- ☐ Special opportunities: credit by exam, honors programs, summer school

Student and campus life

Student characteristics

- ☐ Size and diversity of student body
- ☐ Percent women, minority, from out of state, full time, undergraduate, live in dorms, leave on weekends, major in various areas
- ☐ Social and economic backgrounds

Student lifestyle and activities

- ☐ Orientation of students: academic, scientific, social service, arts, mixed
- ☐ Social life: informal or fraternity/sorority oriented
- ☐ Religious or political activities
- ☐ Campus rules that affect student lifestyle
- ☐ Campus atmosphere
- ☐ Active clubs and interest groups

Campus characteristics

- ☐ Location of campus
- ☐ Physical characteristics: number, layout, condition of buildings
- ☐ Special facilities available in your area of interest
- ☐ Housing options

Community characteristics

- ☐ Community size and location
- ☐ Cultural and social facilities
- ☐ Transportation

Financial considerations

Costs

- ☐ Tuition and fees
- ☐ Room and board
- ☐ Books and supplies
- ☐ Transportation costs (distance, frequency of visits)
- ☐ Miscellaneous
- ☐ Total costs

Your available resources

- ☐ Scholarship
- ☐ Grant
- ☐ Loan
- ☐ Work
- ☐ Family contribution
- ☐ Your contribution

Additional notes

How you will feel about your attendance there

How the reactions of others—parents, friends, relatives—to your decision will affect you

Benefits you expect from the school

Challenges or difficulties you expect at the school

6

Apply for admission.

Alpha College

State University

Decide where to apply.

The number of colleges you should apply to depends on several factors: the educational opportunities for you at individual colleges, your chances for admission there, and in some cases, your possibilities for financial aid. For example, if **after careful study of colleges** you find that your first-choice college fits within your financial resources and there is no doubt about your admission there, you may need to apply only to that school. On the other hand, you may find that your first-choice college cannot accept all qualified applicants, or that your attendance there may depend heavily on a financial aid offer. In this case, you will want to apply to one or more second-choice colleges as well. If possible, include at least one that's a "sure thing" for you in terms of admissions standards and costs.

Don't rule out applying to a college that seems to be out of your price range if you qualify for admission and the college looks good in other respects. Financial aid programs are set up to help many students in this situation. However, you must apply, be accepted for admission, and complete the financial aid application procedures at a college before you will know your exact chances for aid there. Because you won't receive a definite decision on financial aid at the college until the spring of your senior year, it's important to include among your applications for admission at least one college that's within your financial resources.

Obtain application materials.

Write to the admissions offices of the colleges you've chosen and request the materials and forms you need in order to apply there. Be sure to consult the most recent catalog of each college for information about its procedures and deadlines for admissions and financial aid applications. Many colleges encourage students to submit admissions applications in the fall of their senior year in high school. Some schools prefer earlier applications; for others, it may be possible to apply later in your senior year without jeopardizing your chances for admission. However, it may be risky to wait until the stated admissions deadline to submit your application, because some colleges fill their classes before this date.

As you complete your applications for admission, follow instructions carefully. The application form is often the admissions committee's first contact with you, so prepare a neat and legible form. Be certain to have your high school send an official transcript and, if necessary, have your ACT or SAT results sent to the college. Some colleges ask that you identify people who would serve as references. Select people who know you and can support their recommendations well—and always obtain their permission to list their names as references. Other colleges may require a personal interview or examples of your work in special areas such as art or music.

Keep track of your applications.

Develop a file for each college so your catalogs, letters, and records will be organized and accessible. Also put together a log of the necessary application steps for each college to help you keep track of your progress on each application. (One model for this appears on the next page.) Enter information about the requirements of each college, such as the application deadline or the required test, and record the date you complete each step. Be sure to determine whether the school has any additional requirements.

Some colleges will respond to your admission application two to three weeks after they receive all the required information. Others will wait until spring to let you know your admission status. The response you receive from a college may range from unqualified admittance to rejection of your application. In between, there are several kinds of "qualified admittance" such as admission contingent on attendance at summer school, or admission on probation. If you receive an acceptance notice from a school, note carefully whether there are required additional steps, such as sending a deposit, completing a health form, or making arrangements for housing. Be sure to complete the follow-through steps before their deadlines.

National Association of College Admission Counselors (NACAC)

Statement of Students' Rights and Responsibilities

in the College Admissions Process

As a student making application to colleges and universities, you have both rights and responsibilities.

Your rights include:

- Receiving full information from colleges and universities about their admissions, financial aid and scholarship policies
- Not responding to an offer of admission and/or financial aid until you have heard from all colleges and universities to which you have applied or by May 1, whichever comes earlier.

If you think your rights have been denied, you should contact the college or university immediately to request additional information or the extension of a reply date. In addition, you should ask your counselor to notify the President of your State or Regional Association of College Admission Counselors.

If you need further assistance, send a copy of any correspondence you have had with the college or university and a copy of your letter of admission to: Executive Director, NACAC, 1800 Diagonal Road, Suite 430, Alexandria, Virginia 22314.

Your responsibilities include:

- Making sure you understand the admissions, financial aid and scholarship policies of the colleges and universities where you plan to apply. This includes being aware of deadlines, restrictions, etc.

Before you apply, you should understand each college or university's policies and procedures regarding application fees, financial aid and scholarships, and housing. You should also be sure you understand each college or university's policies about deposits you may be required to make before you enroll, and the policy about when refunds of those deposits are available.

- Completing and submitting all materials which are required for application and meeting all deadlines.
- Following the application procedures of your high school.
- Notifying each college or university which admits you whether you are accepting or rejecting their offer. You should make these notifications as soon as you have heard from all the colleges where you applied or by May 1, whichever is earlier.
- Confirming your intention to enroll and submitting a deposit to only one college or university by its required notification date, usually May 1.

If you are put on a waiting list by a college and are later admitted by that college, you may accept the offer and send a deposit to that college. However, you must immediately notify any other college where you indicated your intention to enroll of your change in plans.

This statement is part of the Code of Ethics of the National Association of College Admission Counselors and is endorsed by the National Association of Secondary School Principals.

Sample College Admission Log

College ______________________ **Sequence No.** __________

City ______________________ **State** __________

Application deadline and fees

Date __________ $ __________

Application form

Requested from college ☐ Yes Date __________

Submitted to college ☐ Yes Date __________

Other steps required

Tests required or recommended __________

Test registration completed ☐ Yes Date __________

Test taken ☐ Yes Date __________

Results forwarded to college ☐ Yes Date __________

Necessary high school courses completed ☐ Yes

High school transcript submitted ☐ Yes Date __________

References submitted ☐ Yes Date __________

Interview completed ☐ Yes Date __________

College reply

Expected by Date __________

College decision __________

Follow-through steps required

(List steps and completion dates.)

1. __________ Date __________
2. __________ Date __________
3. __________ Date __________
4. __________ Date __________
5. __________ Date __________

____

____

College admissions office notified of your decision

☐ Yes Date __________

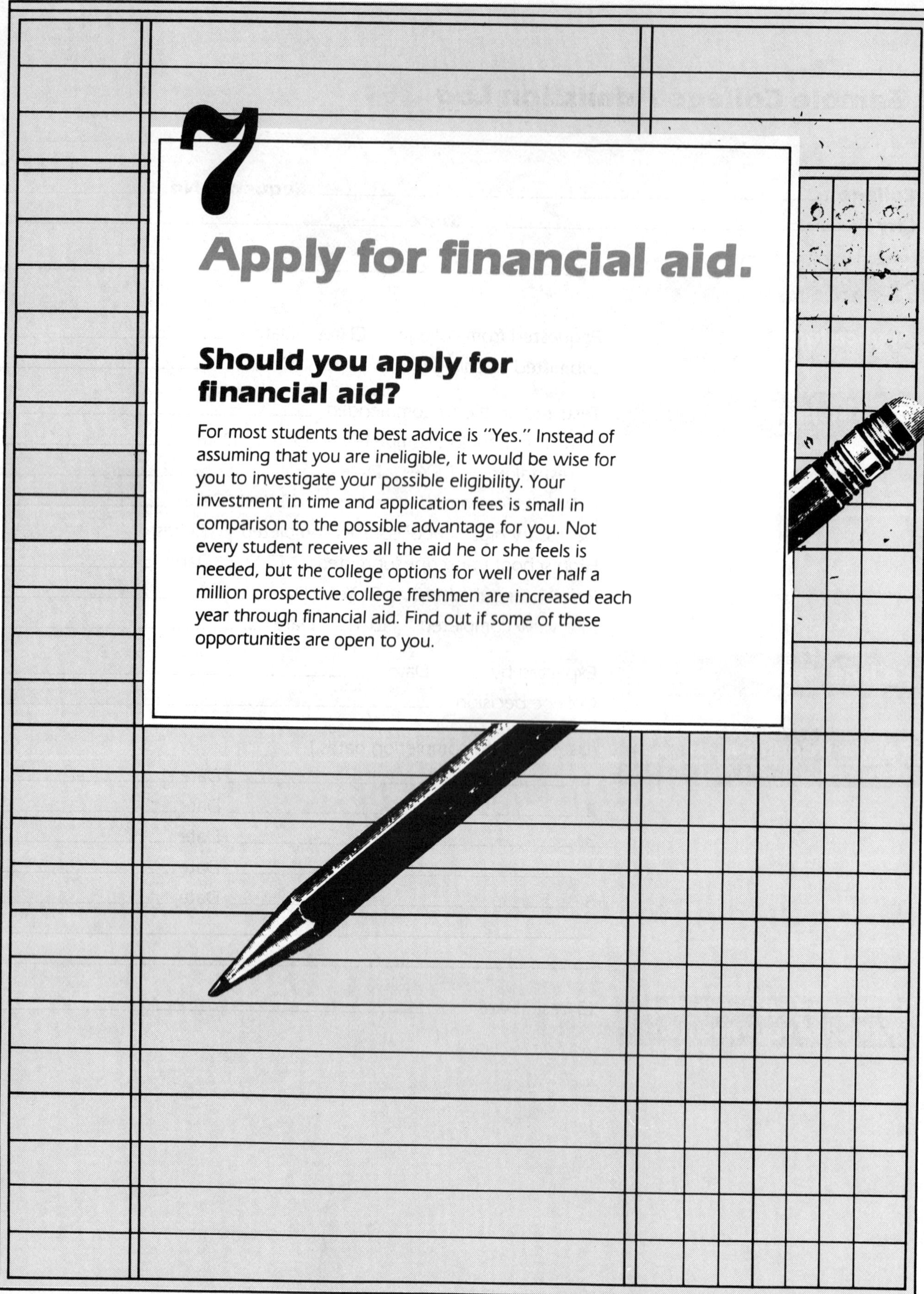

7 Apply for financial aid.

Should you apply for financial aid?

For most students the best advice is "Yes." Instead of assuming that you are ineligible, it would be wise for you to investigate your possible eligibility. Your investment in time and application fees is small in comparison to the possible advantage for you. Not every student receives all the aid he or she feels is needed, but the college options for well over half a million prospective college freshmen are increased each year through financial aid. Find out if some of these opportunities are open to you.

What kinds of aid are available?

The chart on page 42 outlines the major forms of financial aid that are based on need. This aid is frequently awarded in a "package" that consists of a combination of scholarships or grants, loans, and employment. One type of aid, the Pell Grant, is offered directly to the student to be used at any eligible college the student chooses; however, most aid money is offered or coordinated through the financial aid office of the individual college for use at that school only. Schools vary greatly in the kind and amount of financial aid they have available; thus their ability to offer aid to individual students also varies.

Be sure to investigate sources of aid not offered directly by colleges, such as state grants and loans. (See page 16 for a list of financial aid resources.) Deadlines and application requirements vary. Aside from state and federal programs, there are many local financial aid awards sponsored by civic, business, or church groups. Check with your high school counselor to learn whether you are eligible for any such awards in your area.

To help you keep track of the progress of your financial aid applications, the basic steps in applying for aid are listed in the Sample Financial Aid Log on page 43. Enter information about the requirements at each college, such as the type of application form required and the application deadline, and record the date you complete each step. Be sure to find out if the school has any additional requirements for financial aid applicants.

Colleges usually do not make decisions about financial aid until after students have been accepted for admission. However, many schools may suggest that you complete the college's aid application form and a specific need analysis form in the early winter of your senior year. (Review pages 15 and 16 for more information about college costs.)

Filing a need analysis form

To help distribute limited funds fairly, all college financial aid offices and state scholarship and grant programs require aid applicants to submit a need analysis form. On this form, you and your parents will supply detailed information about income, assets, and expenses. The information you supply will be analyzed to determine the amount that can be fairly expected as a total family contribution toward the expenses for your postsecondary education. A report of this amount will be sent to schools or agencies you specify. The **Search** sections of this book indicate which of the two major need analysis forms—American College Testing's Family Financial Statement (FFS) or the College Scholarship Service's Financial Aid Form (FAF)—each college accepts or requires. If the school accepts or requires a need analysis form other than the FAF or the FFS (for example, the United Student Aid Fund's form [Single File], CSX Commercial Services' Application for Federal and State Student Aid, or the U.S. Department of Education's Application for Federal Student Aid), the **Search** sections will list the abbreviation "oth" for other. Contact the school directly for specific information on which form to file. Any of these forms may also be used to apply for the Pell Grant.

With few exceptions, your expected total family contribution will be the same for all colleges. Because your "amount of need" is calculated by subtracting your "expected family contribution" from the cost at a particular school, your "amount of need" will change from one college to another. If it is possible, the financial aid office of each college will develop a package of scholarships, loans, and employment assistance to meet your need at that school.

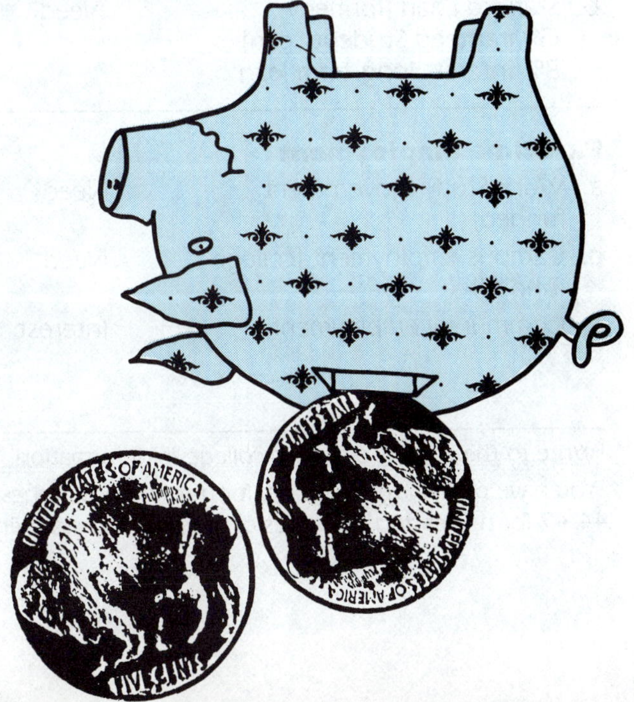

Major Sources of Financial Aid

TYPE OF AID	AWARD BASIS	WHERE AVAILABLE
Scholarship (no repayment required)	Ability, but need is usually taken into account	■ College-administered scholarships[1] ■ State scholarship programs[2] ■ Community organizations, unions, employers[2] ■ Private foundations, scholarship programs such as National Merit Scholarship, etc.[2]
Grant (no repayment required)		
a. State grant	Need	a. Grant program office in your state[2]
b. Pell Grant	Need	b. Eligibility determined by federal government; apply using the ACT FFS, CSS FAF, USAF SingleFile, CSX AFSSA, or the Application for Federal Student Aid
c. Supplemental Educational Opportunity Grant (SEOG)	Need	c. Aid offices of participating colleges[1]
Loan (repayment required)		
a. Perkins Loan (formerly National Direct Student Loan) 5% interest long-term loan	Need	a. Aid offices of participating colleges[1]
b. Stafford Loan (formerly Guaranteed Student Loan) 8% interest long-term loan	Need	b. Through participating banks, credit unions, savings and loan associations[2]
Part-time employment		
a. Work-Study (government funded)	Need	a. Aid offices of participating colleges[1]
b. Campus employment (college funded)	Need	b. Aid offices of participating colleges[1]
c. Community employment	Interest	c. Campus or community employment office; newspapers; employment bulletin boards[2]

[1]Write to the aid office at each college for information.

[2]You have primary responsibility for tracking down these opportunities. Start in your counselor's office. See pages 44-47 for names and addresses of national and state financial aid programs.

Sample Financial Aid Log

College ______________________ **Sequence No.** ____________

City ______________________ **State** ____________

Application deadline
Date ____________

Application form
Requested from college ☐ Yes Date ____________
Submitted to college ☐ Yes Date ____________

Need analysis forms
Which one(s) ____________
Forms completed ☐ Yes Date ____________
Results forwarded to college ☐ Yes Date ____________

College reply
Expected by Date ____________
College decision ____________

Follow-through steps required
(List steps and completion dates.)
1. ____________ Date ____________
2. ____________ Date ____________
3. ____________ Date ____________
4. ____________ Date ____________
5. ____________ Date ____________

____

____

College admissions office notified of your decision
☐ Yes Date ____________

Some specific sources of financial aid

National financial aid programs

There are many national financial aid programs available to qualified students. These programs vary widely in terms of eligibility requirements and the types and amount of aid they provide. Consult either your school counselor or a good financial aid guide (page 16 lists some examples) for help in determining programs for which you may be eligible and for information on how to apply.

Some of the national programs are:

Federal Student Aid Programs provide grants, loans, and subsidized work opportunities for students. Use the ACT FFS, CSS FAF, USAF SingleFile, CSX AFSSA, or Application for Federal Student Aid to apply. For more information, read the **1991-92 Federal Student Guide.** To get a free copy, write to: U.S. Department of Education, Office of Student Financial Assistance, Washington, D.C. 20202-5464.

Vocational Rehabilitation programs provide benefits to people with physical or mental disabilities that are handicaps to employment; contact State Vocational Rehabilitation Offices.

Veterans' educational benefits for qualified servicemen and women; provided through nearest Veterans Administration Office.

The Department of the Interior
Bureau of Indian Affairs Higher Education Program
123 4th Street
P.O. Box 1788
Albuquerque, New Mexico 87103

The National Achievement Scholarship Program for Outstanding Negro Students
National Merit Scholarship Corporation
One American Plaza
Evanston, Illinois 60201

The National Merit Scholarship Program
One American Plaza
Evanston, Illinois 60201

State financial aid programs

Listed on the next three pages are the names and addresses of the scholarship, grant, and loan agencies of the individual states. In many states, special awards are made directly through the state office, in addition to aid that may be available at individual colleges.

Programs in different states vary greatly in their eligibility requirements and in the kinds and amount of aid available, as well as in limits on where the aid may be used.

For many programs, students may need to file only a single application form (the ACT Family Financial Statement, the CSS Financial Aid Form, USAF SingleFile form, or CSX Application for Federal and State Student Aid) to simultaneously apply for the state aid program, campus-based funds, and the federal Pell Grant program. In other state programs, a separate state application form may be required in addition to the form used to apply for campus-based aid and Pell Grants.

Information and application forms for each program may be obtained from your high school guidance office or directly from the offices listed on pages 45-47.

Remember—almost all colleges have significant financial aid resources of their own. You should investigate aid programs available in your state and at the colleges you're considering.

Alabama
Alabama Commission on Higher Education
One Court Square, Suite 221
Montgomery, Alabama 36197-0001
(205) 269-2700

Alaska
Alaska Commission on Postsecondary Education
Box F.P.
Juneau, Alaska 99811
(907) 465-2854

Arizona
Arizona Commission for Postsecondary Education
3030 North Central Avenue, Suite 1407
Phoenix, Arizona 85012
(602) 255-3109

Arkansas
Department of Higher Education
State Scholarship Program
1220 West 3rd St.
Little Rock, Arkansas 72201
(501) 371-1441

California
California Student Aid Commission
1515 S Street, Suite 500, North Bldg.
Sacramento, California 94245-0001
(916) 322-1904

Colorado
Colorado Commission on Higher Education
Colorado Heritage Center
1300 Broadway, 2nd Floor
Denver, Colorado 80203
(303) 866-2723

Connecticut
Connecticut Department of Higher Education
61 Woodland Street
Hartford, Connecticut 06105
(203) 566-2618

Delaware
Delaware Postsecondary Education Commission
Carvel State Office Building
820 North French Street, Fourth Floor
Wilmington, Delaware 19801
(302) 571-3240

District of Columbia
Office of Postsecondary Education, Research and Assistance
1331 H Street, N.W., Suite 600
Washington, D.C. 20005
(202) 727-3685

Florida
Florida Department of Education
Office of Student Financial Assistance
Knott Building
Tallahassee, Florida 32399
(904) 488-4095

Georgia
Georgia Student Finance Commission
2082 East Exchange Place, Suite 200
Tucker, Georgia 30084
(404) 493-5402

Hawaii
State Postsecondary Education Commission
2444 Dole Street
Honolulu, Hawaii 96822
(808) 956-8213

Idaho
Office of State Board of Education
Len B. Jordan Bldg., Room 307
650 W. State Street
Boise, Idaho 83720
(208) 334-2270

Illinois
Illinois Student Assistance Commission
106 Wilmot Road
Deerfield, Illinois 60015
(708) 948-8550

Indiana
State Student Assistance Commission of Indiana
964 Pennsylvania Street
Indianapolis, Indiana 46204
(317) 232-2350

Iowa
Iowa College Student Aid Commission
201 Jewett Building
9th & Grand Avenue
Des Moines, Iowa 50309
(515) 281-3501

Kansas
Kansas Board of Regents
Suite 609, Capitol Tower
400 W. 8th Street
Topeka, Kansas 66603
(913) 296-3421

Kentucky
Higher Education Assistance Authority
1050 U.S. 127 South
Frankfort, Kentucky 40601
(502) 564-7992

Louisiana
Governor's Special Commission on Education Services
P.O. Box 91202
Baton Rouge, Louisiana 70821-9202
1-800-433-9578

Maine
Finance Authority of Maine
Maine Education Assistance Division
State House, Station #119-One Weston Court
Augusta, Maine 04333
(207) 289-2183

Maryland
Maryland Higher Education Commission
16 Francis Street, 2nd Floor
Annapolis, Maryland 21401
(301) 974-5370

Massachusetts
State Scholarship Office
330 Stuart Street
Boston, Massachusetts 02116
(617) 727-9420

Michigan
Michigan Higher Education Assistance Authority
Box 30008
Lansing, Michigan 48909
(517) 373-3399

Minnesota
Minnesota Higher Education Coordinating Board
550 Cedar Street, Suite 400
Capitol Square Building
St. Paul, Minnesota 55101
(612) 296-5715

Mississippi
Mississippi Postsecondary Education Financial Assistance Board
3825 Ridgewood Road
Jackson, Mississippi 39211-6453
(601) 982-6661

Missouri
Coordinating Board for Higher Education
101 Adams Street
Jefferson City, Missouri 65101
(314) 751-2361

Montana
Montana Guaranteed Student Loan Program
33 South Last Chance Gulch
Helena, Montana 59620-3104
(406) 444-6594

Nebraska
Nebraska Coordinating Commission for Postsecondary Education
6th Floor State Capitol
P.O. Box 95005
Lincoln, Nebraska 68509-5005
(402) 471-2847

Nevada
Department of Education
400 West King Street
Capitol Complex
Carson City, Nevada 89710
(702) 687-5914

New Hampshire
New Hampshire Postsecondary Education Commission
Two Industrial Park Drive
Concord, New Hampshire 03301-8512
(603) 271-2555

New Jersey
New Jersey Department of Higher Education
CN 540
Trenton, New Jersey 08625
(609) 588-3225

New Mexico
Commission on Higher Education
1068 Cerrillos Road
Santa Fe, New Mexico 87501-4295
(505) 827-8300

New York
New York State Higher Education Services Corporation
99 Washington Avenue
Albany, New York 12255
(518) 474-5592

North Carolina
North Carolina State Education Assistance Authority
P.O. Box 2688
Chapel Hill, North Carolina 27515-2688
(919) 549-8614

North Dakota
Student Financial Assistance Program
State Board of Higher Education
State Capitol, 10th Floor
Bismarck, North Dakota 58505-0154
(701) 224-4114

Ohio
Ohio Board of Regents
30 East Broad Street
Columbus, Ohio 43266-0417
(614) 466-7420

Oklahoma
Oklahoma State Regents for Higher Education
Oklahoma Tuition Aid Grant Program
P.O. Box 54009
Oklahoma City, Oklahoma 73754-2054
(405) 840-8356

Oregon
Oregon State Scholarship Commission
1445 Willamette Street
Eugene, Oregon 97401
(503) 346-4166

Pennsylvania
Pennsylvania Higher Education Assistance Agency
660 Boas Street
Harrisburg, Pennsylvania 17102
(717) 257-2500

Rhode Island
Rhode Island Higher Education Assistance Authority
560 Jefferson Boulevard
Warwick, Rhode Island 02886
(401) 277-2050

South Carolina
South Carolina Higher Education Tuition Grants Agency
411 Keenan Building, P.O. Box 12159
1310 Lady Street
Columbia, South Carolina 29211
(803) 734-1200

South Dakota
Department of Education and Cultural Affairs
700 Governors Drive
Pierre, South Dakota 57501-2291
(605) 773-3134

Tennessee
Tennessee Student Assistance Corporation
404 James Robertson Parkway, Suite 1950, Parkway Towers
Nashville, Tennessee 37243-0820
(615) 741-1346

Texas
Higher Education Coordinating Board
P.O. Box 12788, Capitol Station
Austin, Texas 78711
(512) 462-6325

Utah
Utah State Board of Regents
355 West North Temple
#3 Triad, Suite 550
Salt Lake City, Utah 84180-1205
(801) 538-5457

Vermont
Vermont Student Assistance Corporation
P.O. Box 2000
Champlain Mill
Winooski, Vermont 05404
(802) 655-9602

Virginia
State Council of Higher Education
101 North Fourteenth Street
Richmond, Virginia 23219
(804) 225-2137

Washington
Higher Education Coordinating Board
917 Lakeridge Way, M/S GV-11
Olympia, Washington 98504
(206) 586-6404

West Virginia
Higher Education Grant Programs
P.O. Box 4007
Charleston, West Virginia 25364
(304) 347-1211

Wisconsin
Higher Educational Aids Board
131 West Wilson Street, Suite 902
P.O. Box 7885
Madison, Wisconsin 53707-7885
(608) 267-2208

Wyoming
Wyoming Community College Commission
2301 Central Avenue
Barrett Building, 3rd Floor
Cheyenne, Wyoming 82002
(307) 777-7763

American Samoa
Department of Education
Pago Pago, American Samoa 96799
(684) 633-5237

Commonwealth of the Northern Mariana Islands
Northern Marianas College
P.O. Box NMCC
Saipan, Mariana Islands 96950
(overseas) Saipan 7312

Guam
Student Financial Assistance Office
University of Guam
P.O. Box EK
Agana, Guam 96910
(overseas) 734-9256

Puerto Rico
Council on Higher Education
Box 23305, U.P.R. Station
San Juan, Puerto Rico 00931
(809) 758-3350

Trust Territories of the Pacific Islands
Headquarters Department of Education
Trust Territory of the Pacific Islands
Saipan, Mariana Islands 96950
(overseas) Saipan 9870

Virgin Islands
Virgin Islands of Education
Commandant Gade O.V. #11
P.O. Box 9128
St. Thomas, Virgin Islands 00801
(809) 774-4546

8
Make a final choice and prepare yourself.

As you move into the spring of your senior year, you will have to make a final college choice. Keep in mind that your careful study and preparation to this point have focused your attention on one or more colleges that offer the best mix of opportunities, given your preferences and needs. Your information may point clearly to one school or may require that you choose among several schools, all of which offer a high possibility of meeting your major needs. Your decision may require weighing the importance of your preferences for the opportunities offered by a higher cost school against the greater financial burden you would have to carry there. Keep rethinking your goals and plans, and evaluate your options at each college. Talk them over with your counselors and your parents.

If you have done your homework to this point, you will have maximized your chances for selecting a college which meets your needs and preferences. Notify all the colleges you applied to of your final decision and turn your attention to the task of preparing yourself for the college you've chosen. Learning as much as you can beforehand about life at the college will help you get off to a good start when you reach the campus. Determine what you'll have to do to take advantage of the many opportunities that college offers you.

Now that you're nearing the end of the college planning process, you can look forward to a new phase in your life. In many ways, you may be on your own for the first time. And new freedoms will bring new responsibilities—among them the responsibility for ensuring the quality of your own education.

A good education will not just be given to you. You must work at it. Although college offers a rich assortment of educational resources, you'll have to prepare yourself in order to take advantage of them. If you are aware of the unique educational opportunities your college offers, you can begin to benefit from them as soon as you arrive on campus.

The pursuit of knowledge is an active process. It's up to you to determine the kind and quality of education you receive. Your own curiosity, hard work, and perseverance will make the difference.

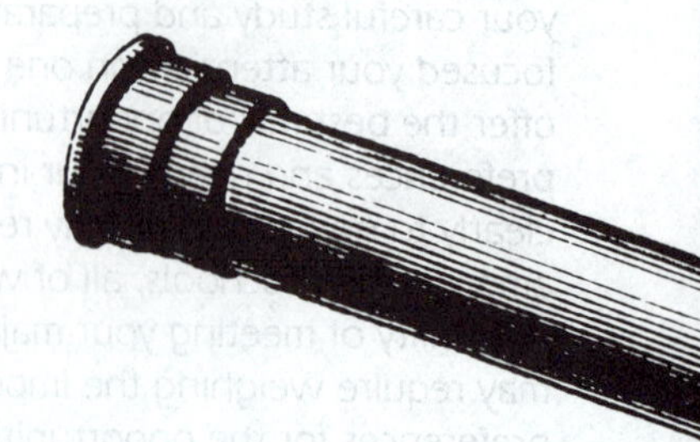

The Search Section

20 1 18 4 13 6 10 15 2 17 3 19 7 16 8 11 14 9 12 5

The four-year college Search section

This section will help you search for four-year colleges that meet your needs and preferences. To use the section most effectively, read through the directions on these two pages and the sample entry on pages 54 and 55 **before** you turn to the college listings. (You may also find it helpful to review the list of abbreviations on page 271.)

For example, you will find that all four-year colleges in the Pacific and Mountain states are listed together. Among schools in that region, you can quickly identify those that have open admissions, enroll up to 1,000 students, and cost under $2,500. You can search for colleges using any combinations of these factors you prefer.

The reading guide card

To make it easy for you to use the **Search** section, we've attached a reading guide card inside the front cover of this book. Tear out the card and use it to read the college entries. If the reading guide card is missing, use the sample guide card on pages 54 and 55 to make your own. Or, use a ruler as you read.

How is the four-year college Search section organized?

The four-year colleges are displayed on blue pages and ordered according to four key factors:

1. **Region:** Colleges from neighboring states are grouped together to form a REGION. (See map on page 11.)
2. **Admissions selectivity:** Within each region, colleges with similar ADMISSIONS requirements are grouped together.
3. **Size:** Colleges within each admissions category in a region are grouped according to their SIZE (based on full-time student enrollment).
4. **Cost:** Within each size category, colleges are ordered according to their total COST for resident tuition and fees plus room and board, from least expensive to most. (Please note that all cost figures are rounded to the nearest $100.)

Additional majors

The four-year college **Search** pages show which of 92 majors are offered by each college. If you're interested in a particular major that doesn't appear on these pages, turn to page 183 to see if it is listed as one of the 63 additional majors at four-year colleges.

How to use the four-year college Search section (purple pages)

1. If you want to look up specific colleges, turn to the **College Index** on page 272. Use the Index to find the sequence number for each college. Use the sequence number to locate each college in the **Search** section. Then follow steps 5, 6, 9, and 10 below.

2. If you have no specific colleges in mind, or if you want to add others to your list, use the **Search** section to identify colleges that fit your needs. Review the preferences you've summarized on page 22. Then consult the list below and find the page number of the region you're interested in. Turn to that page in the **Search** section.

3. Locate the admissions selectivity category you want to consider first.

4. Find the size category you're interested in. Then look for colleges that are within the cost range you've decided on. (In each category, colleges are listed in order of increasing costs for resident tuition plus room and board. For colleges with no on-campus facilities, the cost figure represents resident tuition only.) Keep in mind that financial aid might be available to allow you to attend a college that has everything you're looking for but seems too expensive.

5. Use your reading guide card to help you read information about each college.

6. As you read about a college, circle favorable characteristics; cross out entries that are unfavorable (such as wrong state or affiliation, lack of preferred majors).

7. After reviewing a group of colleges, circle the sequence numbers of those you want to consider further. Review once again the colleges you have not circled, before dropping them from consideration.

8. Repeat these steps for other combinations of characteristics that you prefer. You will probably want to look at colleges in different regions or admissions selectivity or size categories.

9. After you've investigated various combinations of characteristics, return to page 24 and list those colleges (and their sequence numbers) that seem promising on the basis of these tangible factors. Add to your list the names and numbers of additional colleges you may want to investigate or reconsider in the light of other, less tangible factors.

10. Now, focus your attention on the colleges on your list. Read the section about college admission tests on page 25; register to take the tests, if you haven't already taken them. Then turn to Steps 4 and 5 for ideas about investigating and comparing colleges. Use the suggestions there as you work toward making your college choice.

Region	Page in **Search** section
Pacific and Mountain States	56
North Central States	72
Great Lakes States	86
South Central States	108
South Atlantic States	128
Middle Atlantic States	148
New England States	168

How to read the entries in the four-year college Search section

(using a hypothetical example)

Left-hand page

The College: Sequence number 0000; Alpha College located in Beta, California; accepts all high school graduates (Open Admissions) and enrolls up to 1,000 full-time students.

Costs: $2,600 tuition, room and board (9-month academic year), includes $1,200 for room and board; no additional tuition/fees charged to out-of-state students. (Important note on cost figures: **Figures for tuition, room and board, and combined costs are rounded to the nearest $100.** As a result: (1) figures shown for room and board alone are within $50 of the actual fee at an institution; (2) combined figures shown for room and board plus tuition/fees are within $100 of the actual combined fees; and (3) any reported figures less than $50 have been rounded to zero.)

General Information: A Catholic school with religious study encouraged or required; located in a suburban area of a large city (population 100,000 to 500,000). Bachelor's degree is highest offered.

Admission: Admissions application deadline is July 31 for fall term; ACT Assessment preferred for admission, SAT also accepted. Semester system; early admission and deferred admission available.

Financial Aid: Aid application deadline is April 1 for fall term. The FFS and FAF need analysis forms are

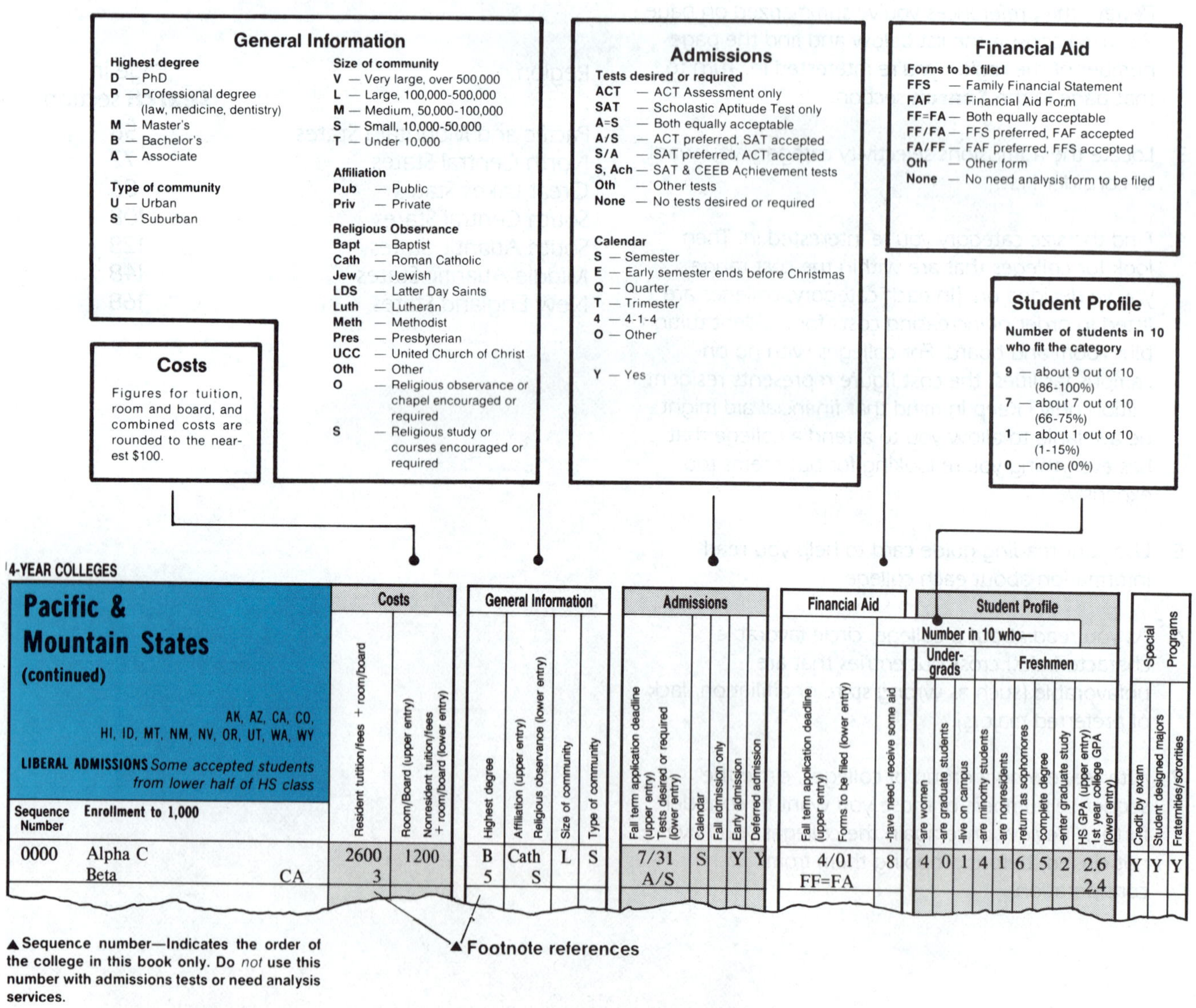

equally acceptable. **In a recent freshman class:** about 8 out of 10 with financial need were offered some aid.

Student Profile: About 4 out of 10 undergraduates are women and there are no graduate students at the school. Of the freshmen, 1 out of 10 lives on campus, 4 out of 10 are minority students, 1 out of 10 is not a resident of the state, 6 out of 10 return as sophomores, and 5 out of 10 complete the bachelor's degree.

About 2 out of 10 graduates attend graduate school. A recent freshman class had a high school grade point average of 2.6 and a first-year college grade point average of 2.4.

Special Programs: Credit by exam, student-designed majors, and fraternities or sororities are available.

Footnotes:
[3]Most freshmen required to live on campus
[5]Accredited by a regional accrediting association or a recognized candidate for accreditation

Right-hand page

What Students Study: 40 percent of the students study in the area of business, 15 percent in education, 20 percent in the health area, and 20 percent in social sciences.

Majors Available: General business and business management majors are available; no engineering majors are available, and so on.

Footnotes:
[1]Additional majors are available in the communications, education, health, and social sciences areas; see the "Index of Additional Majors at Four-year Colleges" section beginning on page 182.

■ Major available

% = Refers to the percentage of undergraduates studying in a family or group of related majors or programs

[1] = Additional majors available in this area

MAJORS AVAILABLE AND PERCENT OF STUDENTS STUDYING IN EACH AREA

	Agri.					Business							Comm.			
Sequence Number	Agriculture, general	Agronomy (crops & mgmt)	Animal Science (husbandry)	Fish, Wildlife Mgmt	Forestry	Business/Commerce, general	Accounting	Banking/Finance	Business Economics	Business Mgmt/Admin	Marketing/Purchasing	Secretarial Studies	Communications, general	Journalism	Radio/TV (broadcasting)	Advertising
					■	40% ■				■			■		1	■

	Education												
Sequence Number	Art Education	Distributive Education	Elementary Education	English Education	Mathematics Education	Music Education	Physical Education	Science Education	Secondary Education	Social Science Education	Special Education	Speech Education
	■	■	■	■	15% ■	■	■	■	■	■	1 ■	

	Engineering						Fine/App. Arts								Lang.					
Sequence Number	Engineering, general	Chemical	Civil	Electrical/Electronics/Comm	Industrial/Management	Mechanical	Architecture	Fine/Applied Arts, general	Art (Paint, draw, sculpt)	Art History/Appreciation	Dance	Dramatic Arts (theater arts)	Music (liberal arts)	Music (perform, compos, theory)	French	German	Italian	Latin	Spanish	Russian

	Health									Home Ec.					
Sequence Number	Predentistry	Premedicine	Medical/Lab Technology	Nursing (registered nurse)	Occupational Therapy	Preoptometry	Prepharmacy	Physical Therapy	Preveterinary Medicine	Home Economics, general	Clothing and Textiles	Consumer Ec/Home Mgmt	Family Relations/Child Devel	Food and Nutrition/Dietetics	Institution Mgmt
		■	20% ■				1								

	Humanities							Math-Sciences								
Sequence Number	Humanities, general	Creative Writing	English, general	Literature, English	Philosophy	Religion	Speech/Forensic Science	Mathematics, general	Computer/Info Sciences	Biological Sciences, general	Biology	Botany	Zoology	Physical Sciences, general	Chemistry	Physics
																■

	Social Sciences												GS	ROTC		
Sequence Number	Crim Just/Law Enforce	Social Work	Social Sciences, general	Anthropology	Area Studies (Amer., African, etc.)	Economics	Geography	History	Prelaw	Political Science	Psychology	Sociology	General Studies	Air Force	Army	Navy
	■	■		20% ■	■	■	■		■	■	1 ■					

Pacific & Mountain States

AK, AZ, CA, CO, HI, ID, MT, NM, NV, OR, UT, WA, WY

OPEN ADMISSIONS *All HS graduates accepted, to limit of capacity*

Sequence Number	School name (upper entry) / City (lower entry)	State	Costs: Resident tuition/fees + room/board	Costs: Room/Board (upper entry) / Nonresident tuition/fees + room/board (lower entry)	General Information: Highest degree	General Information: Affiliation (upper entry) / Religious observance (lower entry)	General Information: Size of community	General Information: Type of community	Admissions: Fall term application deadline (upper entry) / Tests desired or required (lower entry)	Admissions: Calendar	Admissions: Fall admission only	Admissions: Early admission	Admissions: Deferred admission	Financial Aid: Fall term application deadline (upper entry) / Forms to be filed (lower entry)	Student Profile (Number in 10 who—): -have need, receive some aid	Undergrads: -are women	Undergrads: -are graduate students	Freshmen: -live on campus	Freshmen: -are minority students	Freshmen: -are nonresidents	Freshmen: -return as sophomores	Freshmen: -complete degree	Freshmen: -enter graduate study	HS GPA (upper entry) / 1st year college GPA (lower entry)	Special Programs: Credit by exam	Special Programs: Student designed majors	Special Programs: Fraternities/sororities
Enrollment to 1,000																											
0001	Alas Juneau,U of Juneau	AK	2900 [2]	1700 5400	M [5]	Pub	S		A=S	E		Y	Y	6/01 FAF	4	6	1-		2						Y		
0002	Morrison C/Reno B C Reno	NV	4600	[1]	B †	Priv	M	U	None	O				FF=FA	8	6	0	0	2	1	9			2.3 3.0	Y		
0003	Rocky Mtn C Art Dsn Denver	CO	4600	[1]	B †	Priv	V	U	A/S	T		Y	Y	FF=FA	7	5	0		1	4	7				Y		
0004	Heritage C Toppenish	WA	4700	[1]	M [5]	Priv	T		A=S	S		Y		4/15 FA/FF	7	8	4	0	5	0	6				Y		
0005	Great Falls,C of Great Falls	MT	4800 [2]	1000	M [5]	Cath OS	M		9/01 A=S	E		Y		FAF	7	5	1	1	1	1	6	3	1		Y		
0006	Ariz C of Bible Phoenix	AZ	5800 [2]	1400	B †	Oth OS	V	S	A=S	E		Y	Y	3/31 FF/FA	1	3	0	1	1	2	6	4	1	3.0 3.0	Y		
0007	Pacific States U Los Angeles	CA	5800	[1]	D	Priv	V	U	10/01 A/S	T				None		2	8	0	9	9	6	4	5	2.7 2.9	Y		
0008	West Coast Chrstn C Fresno	CA	6000	2900	B [5]	Oth OS	L	S	8/15 ACT	E		Y		10/15 FA/FF	9	4	0	2	4	8	2	2	2				
0009	Marylhurst C Marylhurst	OR	6800	[1]	M [5]	Cath	S		None	Q			Y	5/15 FAF	9	7	2	0	1	1	9	9	2		Y	Y	
0010	Humphreys C Stockton	CA	7800 [2]	4100	P [5]	Priv	L	S	9/05 None	Q		Y	Y	FF=FA	6	9	2	1	3	1	5	6			Y		Y
0011	Northwest Christian Eugene	OR	9100	3300	M [5]	Oth O	M	U	S/A	Q		Y		FA/FF		5	1	8	1	4		3	2	2.0	Y	Y	
0012	Sheldon Jackson C Sitka	AK	9500 [3]	4100	B [5]	Pres S	T		A/S	4		Y		FF=FA	9	5	0	8	4	5	4				Y		
Enrollment 1,000 to 5,000																											
0013	Western NM U Silver City	NM	3000 [3]	2000 6300	M [5]	Pub	S		9/02 A/S	E		Y	Y	4/01 FF=FA	9	6	1	1	4	2	5	2	5	2.2 2.8	Y		
0014	Lewis-Clark St C Lewiston	ID	3800	2700 5700	B [5]	Pub	S		A/S	S		Y		3/15 FA/FF	7	6	0	1	1	1	4	2	2	2.7 2.6	Y	Y	
0015	Southern Utah U Cedar City	UT	3800	2300 6100	M [5]	Pub	S		9/15 A/S	Q		Y		3/01 FFS	4	5	0	6	1	1	6	3	1	3.2 2.7	Y		Y
0016	Eastern Montana C Billings	MT	4100	2700 5800	M [5]	Pub	M	U	10/03 A/S	Q		Y		FF=FA	7	7	1	1	1	1	4	3	1	2.7 2.7	Y		
0017	Mesa St C Grand Junction	CO	4300 [3]	2900 6600	B [5]	Pub	S		8/15 A/S	E		Y		FFS	5	6	0	4	2	1	3	3		2.6 2.7	Y	Y	
0018	City U Bellevue	WA	5600	[1]	M [5]	Priv	V	U	None	O				FAF		4	5	0	4			7	3		Y		
0019	West Coast U Los Angeles	CA	8300	[1]	M [5]	Priv	V	U	Oth	O				FAF	1	2	4	0	5		8	2	2	 2.4	Y		
Enrollment 5,000 to 15,000																											
0020	Alas Anchorage,U Anchorage	AK	3300 [2]	2000 5900	M [5]	Pub	M	U	A=S	S		Y	Y	FA/FF	3	6	1		2					2.9	Y	Y	Y
0021	Idaho St U Pocatello	ID	3700	2500 5700	D [5]	Pub	M		A/S	E		Y	Y	2/15 FAF	7	5	1	1	1	1	5	4	2	3.0 2.4	Y	Y	Y
0022	Weber St U Ogden	UT	4000	2600 6400	M [5]	Pub	M		9/15 A/S	Q		Y	Y		3	5	0	1	2	1	6	6	2	3.1 2.5	Y	Y	Y
LIBERAL ADMISSIONS *Some accepted students from lower half of HS class*																											
Enrollment to 1,000																											
0023	Antioch U Los Ang Marina Del Rey	CA		[1]	M [5]	Priv	V	U	7/23 None	Q				7/23 FAF	5	8	7		1						Y	Y	
0024	Antioch U Seattle Seattle	WA		[1]	M [5]	Priv	V	U	7/23 None	Q			Y	7/23 FAF	5	8	8		1			5			Y	Y	
0025	Valley C Comm/Tech Kent	WA	1800	[1]	B [5]	Priv	L	S	A/S	O		Y	Y	Oth			0								Y		
0026	Yellowstone Bapt C Billings	MT	3500	1800	B	Oth OS	M	S	A/S	E		Y		FF/FA	5	5	0	2	1	4	9	4	8	2.3 2.4	Y		
0027	Lincoln U San Francisco	CA	3600	[1]	P †	Priv	V	U	Oth	E				Oth		3	4	0	9	8	9	2	8	2.5 3.0			

▲ **Sequence number—indicates the order of the college in this book only. Do *not* use this number with admissions tests or need analysis services.**

[1] No campus room and board facilities
[2] Room only or board only
[3] Most freshmen required to live on campus
[4] City or district residence requirements
[5] Accredited by a regional accrediting association or a recognized candidate for accreditation
[6] All female freshman class
[7] All male freshman class

MAJORS AVAILABLE AND PERCENT OF STUDENTS STUDYING IN EACH AREA

Sequence Number	Agri.: Agriculture, general	Agronomy (crops & mgmt)	Animal Science (husbandry)	Fish, Wildlife Mgmt	Forestry	Business: Business/Commerce, general	Accounting	Banking/Finance	Business Economics	Business Mgmt/Admin	Marketing/Purchasing	Secretarial Studies	Comm.: Communications, general	Journalism	Radio/TV (broadcasting)	Advertising
0001						■	0 ■	3	4	% ■					1	%
0002							0	5	5	% ■						
0003																
0004						■	0	1	3	%						
0005							0 ■	2	2	% ■			■		2 ■	%
0006																
0007						■	0 ■	7	5	% ■	■					
0008							0	2	0	%						
0009						■	0	2	5	%			0 ■	1	7	%
0010							0 ■	1	4	%						
0011																
0012	0	3	7	% ■	[1]		0	1	7	% ■						
0013						■	0 ■	2	2 ■	% ■	■	[1]	■			
0014						■	0	2	5	% ■						
0015			1	%			0 ■	2	0	% ■			■		3	%
0016						■	0 ■	3 ■	2 ■	% ■	■		■		4	%
0017						■	0 ■	2	7 ■	% ■	■		■			
0018						■	0 ■	9	0	% ■					5	%
0019						■	0 ■	3	0	% ■		[1]				
0020						■	0 ■	1 ■	4 ■	% ■	■		■	■	3 ■	%
0021			1	% ■		■	0 ■	1 ■	8	% ■	■		■	■	1	%
0022					■		0 ■	1 ■	4 ■	% ■	■	[1] ■	■	■	1 ■	%
0023																
0024																
0025							■									
0026																
0027							0 ■	6	0 ■	% ■		[1]	■		1	%

Sequence Number	Education: Art Education	Distributive Education	Elementary Education	English Education	Mathematics Education	Music Education	Physical Education	Science Education	Secondary Education	Social Science Education	Special Education	Speech Education
0001		■	■		0 ■	1	1	% ■	■			[1]
0002												
0003												
0004			■	■	0	4	9	% ■	■	■		[1]
0005			■	■	0 ■	1	5 ■	% ■	■	■		
0006			■		0	2	1	%				
0007												
0008					0	2	0	%				
0009												
0010							3	%				
0011												
0012			■		0	2	5	%				[1]
0013	■	■	■	■	0 ■	2 ■	4 ■	% ■	■	■	■	[1]
0014			■	■	0 ■	2	3 ■	% ■	■	■	■	[1]
0015	■	■	■	■	0 ■	2 ■	3 ■	% ■	■	■		[1] ■
0016	■	■	■	■	0 ■	2 ■	1 ■	% ■	■	■	■	[1]
0017												
0018												
0019												
0020	■		■	■	0 ■	1 ■	2 ■	% ■	■	■		[1]
0021	■	■	■	■	0 ■	2 ■	1 ■	% ■	■	■	■	[1] ■
0022	■	■	■	■	■	■	9 ■	% ■	■	■		[1]
0023												
0024												
0025												
0026												
0027												

Sequence Number	Engineering: Engineering, general	Chemical	Civil	Electrical/Electronics/Comm	Industrial/Management	Mechanical	Fine/App. Arts: Architecture	Fine/Applied Arts, general	Art (Paint, draw, sculpt)	Art History/Appreciation	Dance	Dramatic Arts (theater arts)	Music (liberal arts)	Music (perform, compos, theory)
0001											1	%	■	
0002														
0003								■	1 ■	0	0	%		[1]
0004														
0005														
0006														
0007		0	1	9 ■	%									
0008														
0009								■	0 ■	1	3	%	■	[1] ■
0010														
0011														
0012											1	%		
0013								■	■		3	% ■	■	■
0014				1	%						1	% ■		
0015				2	%				■		2 ■	% ■	■	■
0016				1	%			■	■		3	% ■	■	
0017				2	%			■						
0018														
0019	■	0	4	5 ■	% ■	[1] ■								
0020			■	4	%			■	■		3	% ■	■	■
0021	■			5	%			■	■		1	% ■	■	■
0022	■			1 ■	% ■	■		■	■		1	% ■	■	[1]
0023														
0024														
0025	■													
0026														
0027														

Sequence Number	Lang.: French	German	Italian	Latin	Spanish	Russian	Health: Predentistry	Premedicine	Medical/Lab Technology	Nursing (registered nurse)	Occupational Therapy	Preoptometry	Prepharmacy	Physical Therapy	Preveterinary Medicine
0001				1	%										
0002															
0003															
0004											3	%			
0005											1	%			[1]
0006															
0007															
0008															
0009															
0010															
0011															
0012															
0013															
0014				1	%				0	1 ■	0	%			
0015		■		1	% ■		■	■		■	3	%	■		■
0016		■		1	% ■						2	%			[1]
0017									0	1 ■	0	%			
0018										■	5	%			[1]
0019															
0020										■	7	%			
0021	■	■		1	% ■		■	■	0 ■	1 ■	4	% ■	■	■	[1] ■
0022	■	■		1	% ■		■	■	0 ■	1 ■	4	%	■		[1] ■
0023															
0024															
0025															
0026															
0027															

Sequence Number	Home Ec.: Home Economics, general	Clothing and Textiles	Consumer Ec/Home Mgmt	Family Relations/Child Devel	Food and Nutrition/Dietetics	Institution Mgmt	Humanities: Humanities, general	Creative Writing	English, general	Literature, English	Philosophy	Religion	Speech/Forensic Science
0001				1 ■	%					8	%		
0002													
0003													
0004							■		■	1	%		
0005									■	3	%		
0006								0	7	9	%	■	
0007													
0008								0	6	0	%	■	
0009							■			4	%		
0010													
0011								1	0	0	%	■	
0012							■			5	%		
0013									■	3	%		
0014							■		■	1	%		■
0015	■			3 ■	%				■	2 ■	%		■
0016									■	■			■
0017							■	0	1 ■	1	%		
0018													
0019													
0020									■	2	%		
0021	■		■	1	%		■		■	2 ■	% ■		■
0022	■		■	2	%				■	4 ■	% ■		■
0023													
0024													
0025													
0026								0	9 ■	9	%	■	
0027													

Sequence Number	Math-Sciences: Mathematics, general	Computer/Info Sciences	Biological Sciences, general	Biology	Botany	Zoology	Physical Sciences, general	Chemistry	Physics
0001		■	0 ■	1 ■	1	%			
0002			0	2	5	%			
0003									
0004		■	0	1	1	%			
0005	■	■	0	1 ■	9	%		■	[1]
0006									
0007		■			6	%			[1]
0008									
0009	■				1	%			
0010		■			3	%			
0011									
0012									
0013	■	■	0 ■	1 ■	1 ■	% ■	■	■	[1]
0014	■		■	■	2	%	■	■	[1]
0015	■	■	■		3 ■	% ■	■	■	
0016	■	■	0 ■	1 ■	3	%	■	■	[1]
0017	■	■	0 ■	1 ■	3	%	■		[1] ■
0018									[1]
0019		■	0	2	5	%			[1]
0020	■	■	■	■	6	%	■	■	
0021	■	■	0 ■	1 ■	0 ■	% ■	■	■	[1] ■
0022	■	■	0 ■	1 ■	3 ■	% ■	■	■	[1] ■
0023									
0024									
0025									
0026									
0027		■							[1]

Sequence Number	Social Sciences: Crim Just/Law Enforce	Social Work	Social Sciences, general	Anthropology	Area Studies (Amer., African, etc.)	Economics	Geography	History	Prelaw	Political Science	Psychology	Sociology	GS: General Studies	ROTC: Air Force	Army	Navy
0001							2	%		■		[1]	■			
0002																
0003																
0004			■		0	1	9	% ■	■				■			
0005	■	■	■		0	2	3	% ■		■		■	■			
0006																
0007																
0008																
0009			■		0	2	5	%								
0010																
0011																
0012			■				5	%					■			
0013	■	■	■		0	1 ■	2 ■	% ■		■	■	[1] ■	■			
0014	■		■				2	% ■					■	Y	Y	
0015			■				2	% ■	■	■	■	■			Y	
0016			■			■	7	% ■			■	[1] ■			Y	
0017			■		0	1 ■	2	% ■		■	■	[1] ■	■			
0018																
0019																
0020	■	■	■	■		■	8	% ■		■	■	■				
0021		■	■	■	0	1 ■	1	% ■	■	■	■	[1] ■	■		Y	
0022	■	■	■			■	4 ■	% ■	■	■	■	■	■	Y	Y	Y
0023													■			
0024													■			
0025																
0026							1	%			■					
0027					0	3 ■	9	%	■							

1 Additional majors available in this area
2 ROTC available

†Accredited by a nationally recognized accrediting body other than one of the regional accrediting associations

Pacific & Mountain States (continued)

AK, AZ, CA, CO, HI, ID, MT, NM, NV, OR, UT, WA, WY

LIBERAL ADMISSIONS *Some accepted students from lower half of HS class*

Sequence Number	School name (upper entry) City (lower entry)	State	Costs: Resident tuition/fees + room/board	Costs: Room/Board (upper entry) Nonresident tuition/fees + room/board (lower entry)	General Information: Highest degree	Affiliation (upper entry) Religious observance (lower entry)	Size of community	Type of community	Admissions: Fall term application deadline (upper entry) Tests desired or required (lower entry)	Calendar	Fall admission only	Early admission	Deferred admission	Financial Aid: Fall term application deadline (upper entry) Forms to be filed (lower entry)	Number in 10 who— -have need, receive some aid	Under-grads: -are women	-are graduate students	Freshmen: -live on campus	-are minority students	-are nonresidents	-return as sophomores	-complete degree	-enter graduate study	HS GPA (upper entry) 1st year college GPA (lower entry)	Special Programs: Credit by exam	Student designed majors	Fraternities/sororities
Enrollment to 1,000																											
0028	Western Montana C Dillon	MT	4200 [3]	2800 5800	M [5]	Pub	T		 A/S	E		Y		 FA/FF	6		0	9	1	1				2.6	Y	Y	
0029	Cal Maritime Acad Vallejo	CA	5000 [3]	3600 7900	B [5]	Pub	M	S	7/01 A=S	O				3/01 FF=FA	6	1	0	9	2	2	8	7	1	3.0 2.8	Y		
0030	Alas Bible C Glennallen	AK	5400 [3]	3200	B †	Oth OS	T		7/31 A=S	S		Y		9/30 FF=FA	9	5	0	9	2	1	5	4		3.1 2.6	Y		
0031	New C of Cal San Francisco	CA	5500	[1]	P [5]	Priv	V	U	 None	T		Y	Y	5/30 FAF	8	6	2	0	1	4	6	8	6	2.0	Y	Y	
0032	International Bapt C Tempe	AZ	5700 [3]	2700	M	Bapt OS	V	U	8/15 A/S	4		Y				4	3	5	1	5	9	2	1				Y
0033	Colo Tech C Colorado Sprgs	CO	6000	[1]	M [5]	Priv	L	S	10/08 Oth	Q		Y		 FF=FA	6	2	1	0	3	1	8	8	1		Y		
0034	Southwestern C Phoenix	AZ	6300	2000	B †	Bapt	V	S	8/10 A/S	O		Y	Y	4/15 FF/FA	5	5	0	6	1	3	5	3	6	2.9 3.0	Y		
0035	John F Kennedy U Orinda	CA	6400	[1]	P [5]	Priv	S		 None	Q				 FAF	3	8	9		3			1	6		Y	Y	
0036	Life Bible C Los Angeles	CA	6700	2800	B †	Oth OS	V	U	7/15 A=S	E			Y	7/01 Oth	4	3	0	7	2		7			2.8 2.9	Y		
0037	Pacific NW C of Art Portland	OR	6800	[1]	B [5]	Priv	L	U		E			Y	 FAF	7	6	0	0	1	3	7						
0038	Puget Sound Chrstn C Edmonds	WA	7200 [3]	3000	B †	Oth OS	S		9/15 A=S	Q		Y		5/01 FAF	7	4	0	7	1	4	5	2	2	2.9 2.8			
0039	San Jose Christian C San Jose	CA	7200	2600	B †	Oth OS	V	U	8/01 A=S	Q		Y		8/01 FA/FF	9	3	0	3	5	1	6	3	4		Y		
0040	Cornish C Seattle	WA	7400	[1]	B [5]	Priv	V	U	8/15 Oth	E		Y	Y	3/31 FAF	7	6	0	0	1	2	7	2	1	2.5 2.5	Y		
0041	Northwest C Kirkland	WA	8200	2900	B [5]	Oth OS	S		 A/S	E			Y	3/31 FA/FF	5	5	0	6	1	5	4			2.8 2.6	Y	Y	
0042	Cal Baptist C Riverside	CA	8600	3000	M [5]	Oth OS	L	S	 A/S	4		Y		3/02 FA/FF	9	5	1	7	4	2	5	5	6	3.0 2.8	Y		
0043	San Fran Consv Music San Francisco	CA	8600	[1]	M [5]	Priv	V	U	7/01 Oth	E		Y	Y	 FAF	6	6	4	0	5	4	8	5	6	 3.2	Y		
0044	Northwest Nazarene C Nampa	ID	9000 [3]	2500	M [5]	Oth OS	S		 ACT	Q		Y		2/15 FA/FF	5	5	0	8	1	7	7	3	1	3.1 2.4	Y	Y	
0045	Bethany Bible C Santa Cruz	CA	9100	3000	B [5]	Oth OS	T		8/01 ACT	E			Y	5/01 FAF	9	5	0	7	1	3	7		3	2.9	Y		
0046	Sierra Nevada C Incline Village	NV	9100 [2]	2200	B [5]	Priv	T		 A=S	E		Y	Y	5/30 FF=FA	5	4	0	2	1	9	7	4	3	2.5 2.5	Y	Y	
0047	Pacific Christian C Fullerton	CA	9400 [3]	4000	M [5]	Oth OS	M	U	9/01 S/A	4		Y		4/15 FA/FF	7	5	1	8	1	3	5	3	5	2.8 2.5	Y	Y	
0048	Bassist C Portland	OR	10000 [2]	2400	B [5]	Priv	L	U	9/04 A=S	O		Y	Y	 FA/FF	7	9	0	2	1	1	7	1	1	3.0 3.0			
0049	Concordia C Portland	OR	10000	2600	B [5]	Oth OS	L	U	9/20 S/A	Q			Y	5/01 FA/FF	9	6	0	8	2	7	6	5		3.0 2.8	Y		
0050	Warner Pacific C Portland	OR	10600 [3]	3200	M [5]	Oth OS	L	U	 Oth	E				5/01 FF=FA	8	5	0	4	2	3	4	3	1		Y		
0051	Western Baptist C Salem	OR	10600	3400	B [5]	Bapt OS	M	U	9/01 A=S	S				 FA/FF	8	5	0	8	1	5	6	3		3.0 2.8	Y		
0052	Santa Fe,C of Santa Fe	NM	11200 [3]	2800	M [5]	Cath S	M		 A=S	E		Y	Y	 FAF	8	5	1	1	4	2	5	4	4	2.7 2.8	Y	Y	Y
0053	Cal C of Arts Oakland	CA	11900 [2]	2100	M [5]	Priv	L	U	 None	E			Y	 FAF	4	6	1	8	3	3	8	2	1	2.8 2.9	Y	Y	
0054	Saint Martin's C Lacey	WA	13200 [3]	3700	P [5]	Cath S	S		 A=S	E		Y	Y	3/01 FA/FF	5	5	3	6	1	3	7	5	2	3.0 2.9	Y		Y
0055	Menlo C Atherton	CA	18400 [3]	6000	B [5]	Priv	S		 S/A	4		Y	Y	3/02 FA/FF	2	3	0	9	2	4	7	7	2	2.5 2.5			Y
Enrollment 1,000 to 5,000																											
0056	Eastern NM U Portales	NM	3400	2200 6500	M [5]	Pub	S		7/15 A/S	E		Y		3/01 FA/FF	9	6	1	7	3	3	6	3	1	2.8 2.6	Y	Y	Y
0057	NM Highlands U Las Vegas	NM	3400	2200 6300	M [5]	Pub	S		7/15 A/S	E		Y	Y	3/01 FA/FF	9	5	1	1	8	1	1	3	4		Y		Y

▲ Sequence number—indicates the order of the college in this book only. Do *not* use this number with admissions tests or need analysis services.

[1] No campus room and board facilities
[2] Room only or board only
[3] Most freshmen required to live on campus
[4] City or district residence requirements
[5] Accredited by a regional accrediting association or a recognized candidate for accreditation
[6] All female freshman class
[7] All male freshman class

MAJORS AVAILABLE AND PERCENT OF STUDENTS STUDYING IN EACH AREA

Sequence Number	Agri.	Business	Comm.	Education	Engineering	Fine/App. Arts	Lang.	Health	Home Ec.	Humanities	Math-Sciences	Social Sciences	GS	ROTC
0028		014%	1%	074% [1]		1%				2%	3%	2%		
0029					050%									Y
0030										100%				
0031			1%	1% [1]		1%	1%	1%		089%	3%	2%		
0032		2%		047%						051%				
0033		023%			052%						025%			Y
0034				028%						063%				
0035		028%												
0036										100%				
0037						100% [1]								
0038										100%				
0039				1% [1]			1%			096%		1%		
0040						100% [1]								
0041		2%	1%	011%		1%	1%	1%		054%	2%	012%		
0042		026%		023% [1]		6%	1%			015%	4%	016% [1]		
0043						100%								
0044		024% [1]	1%	013% [1]	1%	6%	1%	1%	2%	014%	013% [1]	011% [1]		Y
0045		7%	5%	6%		8%				042%		015%		
0046	[1]	030% [1]		010% [1]		9% [1]				025%	020% [1]	5%		Y
0047		6%	2%	6%		6%			1%	031%		015%		
0048		045%	1%			048%			1%	1%	1%	1%		
0049		040%		030% [1]				8% [1]		[1]				
0050		040%		031%		2%				013%	4%	6%		
0051		015%		035%				3%		020%		016%		
0052		013%	019%	8% [1]		040% [1]				6%	9% [1]	5% [1]		
0053						100% [1]								
0054		023%	1%	021% [1]	020%	1%		4%		5%	012% [1]	013% [1]		YY
0055		042%	016%							8%	012% [1]	9%		Y
0056	1% [1]	022% [1]	4%	016% [1]	1%	1%	1%	1% [1]	1%	2%	3% [1]	2%		Y
0057		014% [1]	1%	017% [1]	2%	1%		5% [1]		1%	7% [1]	014% [1]		Y

[1] Additional majors available in this area
[2] ROTC available

†Accredited by a nationally recognized accrediting body other than one of the regional accrediting associations

Pacific & Mountain States
(continued)

AK, AZ, CA, CO, HI, ID, MT, NM, NV, OR, UT, WA, WY

LIBERAL ADMISSIONS *Some accepted students from lower half of HS class*

Sequence Number	School name (upper entry) City (lower entry)	State	Costs: Resident tuition/fees + room/board	Costs: Room/Board (upper entry) Nonresident tuition/fees + room/board (lower entry)	General Information: Highest degree	General Information: Affiliation (upper entry) Religious observance (lower entry)	General Information: Size of community	General Information: Type of community	Admissions: Fall term application deadline (upper entry) Tests desired or required (lower entry)	Admissions: Calendar	Admissions: Fall admission only	Admissions: Early admission	Admissions: Deferred admission	Financial Aid: Fall term application deadline (upper entry) Forms to be filed (lower entry)	Student Profile (Number in 10 who—): Undergrads -have need, receive some aid	Freshmen -are women	-are graduate students	-live on campus	-are minority students	-are nonresidents	-return as sophomores	-complete degree	-enter graduate study	HS GPA (upper entry) 1st year college GPA (lower entry)	Special Programs: Credit by exam	Student designed majors	Fraternities/sororities
Enrollment 1,000 to 5,000																											
0058	Brigham Young Hawaii Laie	HI	4200 [3]	2600	B [5]	LDS OS	T		8/15 ACT	T		Y		8/07 Oth	2	6	0	9	6	7	4	2			Y		
0059	Fort Lewis C Durango	CO	4300	2800 8200	B [5]	Pub	S		8/01 A/S	T		Y	Y	3/01 FF/FA	6	4	0	3	2	2	6		2	2.5 2.6	Y	Y	
0060	Oregon Inst of Techn Klamath Falls	OR	4800	3100 7900	B [5]	Pub	S		9/15 A=S	Q		Y		3/01 FA/FF	7	3	0	3	1	1	8	7	1	2.9 2.9	Y		Y
0061	Southern Oregon St C Ashland	OR	4800 [3]	3000 8000	M [5]	Pub	S		A=S	Q		Y		3/01 FAF	6	5	1	8	1	1	6	3	2	3.0 2.6	Y	Y	
0062	DeVry Inst of Techn Phoenix	AZ	5000	[1]	B [5]	Priv	V	S	A=S	T			Y	FA/FF	8	2	0	0	3	6	5	3			Y		Y
0063	DeVry Inst Techn City Industry	CA	5000	[1]	B [5]	Priv	V		A=S	T			Y	FA/FF	7	2	0	0	7	1	5	3			Y		Y
0064	Westminster C Salt Lake City	UT	10400	3400	M [5]	Priv	V	U	A=S	O		Y	Y	FF/FA	9	6	2	1	2	1	6	5	1	3.2 3.1	Y	Y	
0065	Walla Walla C College Place	WA	11000 [3]	2500	M [5]	Oth OS	T		ACT	Q		Y		4/01 FA/FF	7	4	1	8	1			2		2.9	Y		
0066	Pacific Union C Angwin	CA	12200	3400	M [5]	Oth OS	T		ACT	Q		Y		3/02 Oth	6	5	1	9	4	2				2.7	Y	Y	
0067	Loma Linda U Riverside	CA	12600	3200	D [5]	Oth S	M	S	A/S	Q		Y		5/01 FA/FF	8	5	1	7	5	3	6	5	3	3.0 2.6	Y		
Enrollment 5,000 to 15,000																											
0068	Metropolitan St C Denver	CO	1600	[1] 4700	B [5]	Pub	V	U	8/23 A/S	E		Y	Y		5	5	0	0	2	1		1		2.7 2.6	Y	Y	
0069	Idaho,U of Moscow	ID	3800	2600 6100	D [5]	Pub	S		8/01 A=S	E		Y	Y	3/01 FA/FF	4	4	1	9	1	4	7	3	2	3.2 2.5	Y	Y	Y
0070	Boise St U Boise	ID	4100	2800 6100	M [5]	Pub	M	U	7/31 A/S	E		Y		3/01 FAF	3	6	1	1	1	1	5	3		3.1 2.2	Y		Y
0071	Utah St U Logan	UT	4400	2700 7100	D [5]	Pub	S		9/01 A/S	Q		Y	Y	3/15 FAF	9	5	1	7	1	2	5	1	2	3.2 2.5	Y		Y
0072	Nevada Reno,U of Reno	NV	4500	3100 6400	D [5]	Pub	L	U	7/01 A/S	E		Y	Y	2/15 FF/FA	6	5	1	2	1	2	7	3	3	3.2 2.6	Y		Y
0073	National U San Diego	CA	5400	[1]	P [5]	Priv	V	U	Oth	O			Y	FAF	6	5	5	0	3			5	4	3.0	Y		
Enrollment over 15,000																											
0074	NM,U of Albuquerque	NM	4600	3100 8300	D [5]	Pub	L	U	7/26 A/S	E		Y		3/01 FA/FF	5	5	2		3	2	7	2		2.9 2.6	Y	Y	Y
TRADITIONAL ADMISSIONS *Majority of accepted students in top 50% of HS class*																											
Enrollment to 1,000																											
0075	Saint John's Sem C Camarillo	CA	4000	1200	B [5]	Cath S	M		8/01 SAT	S			[7]	5/01 Oth	9	0	0	9	5	1	7	6	7	2.7	Y		
0076	Southwest,C of the Hobbs	NM	4000 [2]	1400	B [5]	Priv S	S		A/S	E		Y	Y	4/01 FF=FA	5	6	0	5	2	5	5	2	4	2.9 2.5	Y	Y	
0077	Beth-El C of Nsg Colorado Sprgs	CO	4100	[1]	B [5]	Pub	L	U	A/S	S				6/01 FFS	4	8	0	0	1	0	8	8	1	2.9 3.1	Y		
0078	Armstrong C Berkeley	CA	5400	[1]	P [5]	Priv	M	U	None	Q		Y		10/05 FAF	6	3	5	0	6	7	8	7		2.3 2.6	Y	Y	
0079	Mount Angel Seminary St Benedict	OR	6100 [3]	3100	M [5]	Cath OS	T		8/01 SAT	S			[7]	FAF	9	0	7	9	2	6	8	7	5	2.8			
0080	Cogswell C Cupertino	CA	6200	[1]	B [5]	Priv	V	U	8/21 A=S	T		Y		8/26 FA/FF	3	1	0	0	6	1	8	7	1	2.7 2.8	Y		
0081	Brooks Inst Photog Santa Barbara	CA	6400	[1]	M †	Priv	M	S	None	O			Y	4/15 FF=FA	3	3	1	0	3	4			1		Y		
0082	Patten C Oakland	CA	7200	3700	B [5]	Oth OS	L	U	8/10 A=S	E		Y		8/01 FA/FF	8	4	0	4	7	1	7	4	7	3.2 2.9	Y		
0083	Colo Christian U Lakewood	CO	8300	3200	M [5]	Oth OS	V	S	8/15 A/S	E		Y	Y	4/01 FF/FA	7	6	1	7	1	3	4	1		3.0 2.9	Y	Y	
0084	Multnomah Sch Bible Portland	OR	8300	3200	M †	Oth OS	L	U	7/15 S/A	E			Y	5/01 FA/FF	7	4	3	6.	1	7	7			3.3	Y		
Sequence Number	School name (upper entry) City (lower entry)	State	Costs		General Information				Admissions					Financial Aid	Student Profile										Programs		

▲ Sequence number—indicates the order of the college in this book only. Do *not* use this number with admissions tests or need analysis services.

[1] No campus room and board facilities
[2] Room only or board only
[3] Most freshmen required to live on campus
[4] City or district residence requirements
[5] Accredited by a regional accrediting association or a recognized candidate for accreditation
[6] All female freshman class
[7] All male freshman class

MAJORS AVAILABLE AND PERCENT OF STUDENTS STUDYING IN EACH AREA

Sequence Number	Agri. (Agriculture, general; Agronomy (crops & mgmt); Animal Science (husbandry); Fish, Wildlife Mgmt; Forestry)	Business (Business/Commerce, general; Accounting; Banking/Finance; Business Economics; Business Mgmt/Admin; Marketing/Purchasing; Secretarial Studies)	Comm. (Communications, general; Journalism; Radio/TV (broadcasting); Advertising)	Education (Art Education; Distributive Education; Elementary Education; English Education; Mathematics Education; Music Education; Physical Education; Science Education; Secondary Education; Social Science Education; Special Education; Speech Education)	Engineering (Engineering, general; Chemical; Civil; Electrical/Electronics/Comm; Industrial/Management; Mechanical; Architecture)	Fine/App. Arts (Fine/Applied Arts, general; Art (Paint, draw, scuplt); Art History/Appreciation; Dance; Dramatic Arts (theater arts); Music (liberal arts); Music (perform, compos, theory))	Lang. (French; German; Italian; Latin; Spanish; Russian)	Health (Predentistry; Premedicine; Medical/Lab Technology; Nursing (registered nurse); Occupational Therapy; Preoptometry; Prepharmacy; Physical Therapy; Preveterinary Medicine)	Home Ec. (Home Economics, general; Clothing and Textiles; Consumer Ec/Home Mgmt; Family Relations/Child Devel; Food and Nutrition/Dietetics; Institution Mgmt)	Humanities (Humanities, general; Creative Writing; English, general; Literature, English; Philosophy; Religion; Speech/Forensic Science)	Math-Sciences (Mathematics, general; Computer/Info Sciences; Biological Sciences, general; Biology; Botany; Zoology; Physical Sciences, general; Chemistry; Physics)	Social Sciences (Crim Just/Law Enforce; Social Work; Social Sciences, general; Anthropology; Area Studies (Amer., African, etc.); Economics; Geography; History; Prelaw; Political Science; Psychology; Sociology)	GS (General Studies)	ROTC (Air Force; Army; Navy)
0058		036%	2%	7%		1%	1%	2%	2%	6%	012%	9%		YY
0059	1%	030%	2%	022%	9%	1%	1%	1%		4%	013%	013%		
0060		5%	1%	1%	035%		1%	010%		1%	012%	2%		
0061		022%	5%	018%	1%	3%	1%	5%		3%	010%	011%		Y
0062		025%			058%						017%			
0063		018%	018%		048%						016%			
0064		038%	3%	6%		1%	1%	9%		2%	7%	2%		YYY
0065		014%	3%	8%	014%	3%	1%	012%	3%	3%	6%	4%		
0066		021%	3%	5%	3%	3%	1%	025%	1%	5%	013%	3%		
0067		016%	2%	011%	2%	1%	1%	021%		2%	010%	2%		
0068		014%	2%	5%	4%	3%	1%	2%		2%	8%	013%		YY
0069	4%	9%	8%	015%	014%	9%	2%	1%	4%	3%	9%	012%		YYY
0070	1%	034%	3%	015%	3%	2%	1%	010%	1%	2%	3%	2%		Y
0071	5%	015%	1%	014%	010%	6%	1%	5%	2%	3%	7%	8%		YY
0072	5%	015%	4%	9%	9%	3%	2%	012%	3%	6%	013%	015%		Y
0073		040%		022%	1%			3%			017%	013%		YY
0074		013%	1%	011%	011%	8%	1%	010%		3%	9%	016%		YYY
0075														
0076		027%		043%										
0077								100%						Y
0078		099%									1%			
0079			1%			5%	1%			076%	2%	015%		
0080		1%			084%					1%	010%	1%		
0081			010%			090%								
0082				9%						090%				
0083		015%	9%	015%		011%		2%		022%	013%	013%		Y
0084										100%				
Sequence Number	Agri.	Business	Comm.	Education	Engineering	Fine/App. Arts	Lang.	Health	Home Ec.	Humanities	Math-Sciences	Social Sciences	GS	ROTC

[1] Additional majors available in this area
[2] ROTC available

†Accredited by a nationally recognized accrediting body other than one of the regional accrediting associations

Pacific & Mountain States

(continued)

AK, AZ, CA, CO, HI, ID, MT, NM, NV, OR, UT, WA, WY

TRADITIONAL ADMISSIONS *Majority of accepted students in top 50% of HS class*

Sequence Number	School name (upper entry) City (lower entry)	State	Costs: Resident tuition/fees + room/board	Costs: Room/Board (upper entry) Nonresident tuition/fees + room/board (lower entry)	General Information: Highest degree	General Information: Affiliation (upper entry) Religious observance (lower entry)	General Information: Size of community	General Information: Type of community	Admissions: Fall term application deadline (upper entry) Tests desired or required (lower entry)	Admissions: Calendar	Admissions: Fall admission only	Admissions: Early admission	Admissions: Deferred admission	Financial Aid: Fall term application deadline (upper entry) Forms to be filed (lower entry)	Number in 10 who—: -have need, receive some aid	Under-grads: -are women	Under-grads: -are graduate students	Freshmen: -live on campus	Freshmen: -are minority students	Freshmen: -are nonresidents	Freshmen: -return as sophomores	Freshmen: -complete degree	Freshmen: -enter graduate study	Freshmen: HS GPA (upper entry) 1st year college GPA (lower entry)	Special Programs: Credit by exam	Special Programs: Student designed majors	Special Programs: Fraternities/sororities
	Enrollment to 1,000																										
0085	Simpson C Redding	CA	8300[3]	3000	M[5]	Oth OS	M		8/15 A=S	E			Y	FA/FF	8	5	1	8	1	3	6	4		3.1 2.6	Y	Y	
0086	Columbia Christian C Portland	OR	8700	2700	B[5]	Oth OS	L	S	A=S	E		Y		FAF	8	6	0	8	1	7	5	1		2.9 2.4	Y		Y
0087	Carroll C Montana Helena	MT	9800[3]	3200	B[5]	Cath S	S		7/31 A=S	E		Y	Y	FA/FF	6	6	0	9	1	4	7	4	5	3.0 3.0	Y	Y	
0088	Alas Pacific U Anchorage	AK	10100	3900	D[5]	Meth	M	S	8/15 A=S	E		Y	Y	4/01 FA/FF	7	7	2	5	3	1	6	1		2.9	Y		
0089	Christian Heritage C El Cajon	CA	10200	3400	B[5]	Bapt O	V	S	8/01 S/A	S			Y	6/01 FA/FF	9	5	0	6	1	3	7	4	3	3.2	Y		
0090	Southern Cal C Costa Mesa	CA	10200[3]	3300	M[5]	Oth OS	M	S	7/31 A=S	4			Y	3/01 Oth	8	5	0	7	2	3	7	4		2.9 2.8	Y		
0091	Rocky Mountain C Billings	MT	10400[3]	3300	B[5]	Oth S	M	S	8/15 A/S	E		Y	Y	FA/FF	8	5	0	4	1	3	7		2	2.9 2.6	Y	Y	
0092	Master's C, The Newhall	CA	10700[3]	3700	B[5]	Oth OS	M		8/15 A=S	E				6/15 FAF	7	5	1	9	1	3	6	4	1	3.2	Y		
0093	Christ C Irvine Irvine	CA	11100[2]	2300	M[5]	Oth OS	M	S	6/30 S/A	Q		Y	Y	4/15 FA/FF	4	6	1	6	3	3	8	3	3	3.3	Y		
0094	Idaho,C of Caldwell	ID	11400[3]	2500	M[5]	Pres S	S		A/S	4		Y	Y	FA/FF	8	5	1	9	3	3	8		5	3.3	Y	Y	Y
0095	Fresno Pacific C Fresno	CA	11600	3400	M[5]	Oth S	L	S	7/31 A/S	E		Y		3/02 FAF	8	6	1	8	2	1	7				Y	Y	
0096	George Fox C Newberg	OR	12400	3400	D[5]	Oth O	S		8/01 S/A	E			Y	FA/FF	9	5	0	8	1	5	7	4		3.2 2.9	Y	Y	
0097	Hawaii Loa C Kaneohe Oahu	HI	12800	4400	B[5]	Oth	M	S	8/01 S/A	S		Y	Y	FA/FF	8	6	0	4	6	5	6			2.3	Y	Y	
0098	Notre Dame,C of Belmont	CA	13500	4300	M[5]	Cath S	S		S/A	E			Y	FA/FF	8	7	3	7	5	4	7	3	3	3.0 2.7	Y	Y	
0099	Northrop U Los Angeles	CA	13600[2]	3000	P[5]	Priv	V	U	A=S	Q		Y	Y	5/01 FA/FF	3	1	4	3	6	6	6	5	3	2.8 2.8	Y		Y
0100	World C West Petaluma	CA	13800[3]	4300	B[5]	Priv	S		A=S	E		Y	Y	FA/FF	9	6	0	9	3	4	8	5	5	3.1	Y	Y	
0101	Samuel Merritt C Oakland	CA	14500	4400	M[5]	Priv S	V	U	7/15 A=S	4		Y	Y	3/01 FF=FA	8	9	1	5	3	1	9	7	3	2.9 2.9	Y		
0102	Dominican C San Raf San Rafael	CA	15200	5000	M[5]	Cath S	S		S/A	E		Y	Y	3/02 FAF	6	8	3		3		6	3	2		Y	Y	
0103	Woodbury U Burbank	CA	15600	5200	M[5]	Priv	M	U	A=S	Q			Y	FA/FF	8	6	1	5	5	1	7	4	1	3.1	Y		Y
	Enrollment 1,000 to 5,000																										
0104	Colo-Colo Spgs,U of Colorado Sprgs	CO	1700	[1] 5100	D[5]	Pub	L	S	7/01 A=S	E			Y	4/01 FFS	8	6	2	0	1	1				2.7	Y		
0105	Golden Gate U San Francisco	CA	3900	[1]	D[5]	Priv	V	U	A=S	T		Y	Y	FF=FA	1	5	7	0	3		8	5	4	3.1 2.8	Y		
0106	Adams St C Alamosa	CO	4000[3]	2600 6400	M[5]	Pub	S		8/01 A/S	E		Y	Y	3/01 FF/FA	6	6	1	6	3	2	6	4	2	3.1 2.5	Y	Y	Y
0107	Alas Fairbanks,U of Fairbanks	AK	4200	2500 6600	D[5]	Pub	S		8/01 A/S	E				5/15 FAF	6	6	1	7	3	1	6	4	2	2.4	Y	Y	
0108	Northern Montana C Havre	MT	4200[3]	2900 5900	M[5]	Pub	S		9/25 A/S	Q		Y		FA/FF	5	5	1	7	1	1	7	3	1	2.6 2.5	Y	Y	
0109	Montana C Minrl Sci Butte	MT	4300[3]	3000 6400	M[5]	Pub	S		A/S	E		Y	Y	4/01 FA/FF	7	4	1	1	1	1	5	3	2	3.2 2.5	Y		
0110	Western St C Gunnison	CO	4500[3]	3000 7600	B[5]	Pub	T		A/S	E		Y	Y	4/15 FFS	4	4	0	9	1	3	6	4	2	2.7 2.4	Y		Y
0111	Western Oregon St U Monmouth	OR	4700[3]	2900 7900	M[5]	Pub	T		6/01 S/A	Q		Y	Y	3/01 FA/FF	6	6	0	7	1	1	7	4	5	3.1 2.5	Y	Y	
0112	Evergreen St C Olympia	WA	5000	3400 9000	M[5]	Pub	S		3/01 S/A	Q			Y	4/15 FAF		6	1	8	1	3	7	5	5	3.1	Y	Y	
0113	Southern Colo,U of Pueblo	CO	5000[3]	3400 8900	M[5]	Pub	M	U	7/21 A=S	E		Y	Y	FA/FF	6	5	0	3	3	1	6	2	1	2.7 2.4	Y		Y
0114	Eastern Oregon St C La Grande	OR	5400	2900	M[5]	Pub	S		A=S	Q		Y	Y	FA/FF	7	5	1	4	2	3	6	3	2		Y	Y	

▲ Sequence number—indicates the order of the college in this book only. Do *not* use this number with admissions tests or need analysis services.

[1] No campus room and board facilities
[2] Room only or board only
[3] Most freshmen required to live on campus
[4] City or district residence requirements
[5] Accredited by a regional accrediting association or a recognized candidate for accreditation
[6] All female freshman class
[7] All male freshman class

MAJORS AVAILABLE AND PERCENT OF STUDENTS STUDYING IN EACH AREA

Sequence Number	Agri.	Business	Comm.	Education	Engineering	Fine/App. Arts	Lang.	Health	Home Ec.	Humanities	Math-Sciences	Social Sciences	GS	ROTC
0085		9%		021%						036%				
0086		014%	1%	042%		2%				6%	012%			
0087		022%	2%	010%	4%	1%	1%	024%		4%	017%	014%		
0088		038%	025%	013%	1%	1%	1%			2%	2%	1%		
0089		015%		025%					5%	027%	3%	025%		Y Y Y
0090		018%	010%	012%		2%				024%	7%	019%		
0091		020%	1%	7%	2%	6%	1%	2%		010%	014%	012%		Y (Army)
0092		012%	7%	017%				2%	4%	024%	7%	015%		
0093		017%	1%	028%		3%				016%	9%	018%		
0094		022%		013%	6%	3%		011%		4%	011%	015%		
0095		012%	1%	040%		1%	1%			013%	011%	6%		
0096		013%	013%	020%	1%	2%		2%	4%	9%	9%	015%		
0097		016%			1%		010%	048%		6%	7%	7%		Y Y (Air Force, Army)
0098		034%	4%			9%	1%			6%	010%	023%		Y (Air Force)
0099		021%			022%						1%			Y Y Y
0100		015%		1%		8%	3%			7%	2%	046%		
0101								100%						
0102		011%		4%		8%		019%		020%	010%	020%		Y (Air Force)
0103		050%				041%			7%		2%			
0104		017%	7%	5%	012%	2%	1%	3%		3%	016%	017%		Y (Army)
0105		079%	2%					2%			8%	5%		
0106		032%	1%	035%	1%	2%	1%	6%		1%	3%	1%		
0107	2%	9%	2%	9%	6%	2%	1%	1%		3%	010%	6%		Y (Army)
0108	2%	023%		020%		4%		014%			4%			
0109		014%	3%	1%	045%			1%		2%	018%	2%		
0110	1%	026%	7%	012%		1%	1%	6%		3%	013%	9%		
0111		014%		050%		1%		2%		1%	8%	2%		Y (Army)
0112	1%	014%	7%	010%	3%	2%	4%	7%	1%	016%	018%	016%		
0113		026%	7%		019%		1%	5%		6%	010%	015%		
0114	6%	020%	1%	023%	1%	1%	1%	4%		2%	017%	3%		Y (Army)

[1] Additional majors available in this area
[2] ROTC available

†Accredited by a nationally recognized accrediting body other than one of the regional accrediting associations

Pacific & Mountain States

(continued)

AK, AZ, CA, CO, HI, ID, MT, NM, NV, OR, UT, WA, WY

TRADITIONAL ADMISSIONS *Majority of accepted students in top 50% of HS class*

Sequence Number	School name (upper entry) City (lower entry)	State	Costs: Resident tuition/fees + room/board	Costs: Room/Board (upper entry) Nonresident tuition/fees + room/board (lower entry)	General Information: Highest degree	General Information: Affiliation (upper entry) Religious observance (lower entry)	General Information: Size of community	General Information: Type of community	Admissions: Fall term application deadline (upper entry) Tests desired or required (lower entry)	Admissions: Calendar	Admissions: Fall admission only	Admissions: Early admission	Admissions: Deferred admission	Financial Aid: Fall term application deadline (upper entry) Forms to be filed (lower entry)	Student Profile (Number in 10 who—): -have need, receive some aid	Under-grads: -are women	Under-grads: -are graduate students	Freshmen: -live on campus	Freshmen: -are minority students	Freshmen: -are nonresidents	Freshmen: -return as sophomores	Freshmen: -complete degree	Freshmen: -enter graduate study	Freshmen: HS GPA (upper entry) 1st year college GPA (lower entry)	Special Programs: Credit by exam	Special Programs: Student designed majors	Special Programs: Fraternities/sororities
Enrollment 1,000 to 5,000																											
0115	Hawaii Pacific U Honolulu	HI	8700 [2]	3600	M [5]	Priv	V	U	A=S	4		Y	Y	FF=FA	4	4	1	1	6	2	8	5	5	3.0 2.8	Y	Y	
0116	Grand Canyon U Phoenix	AZ	9200 [3]	2800	M [5]	Oth OS	V	U	A/S	S		Y		FF/FA	8	6	1	3	2	2	8	6	7	2.9 2.4	Y		
0117	Embry-Riddle Aero U Prescott	AZ	9500	3200	B [5]	Priv	S		A=S	O			Y	4/15 FFS	4	1	0		1	9	6	3		3.2 2.9	Y		Y
0118	Chaminade U Honolulu Honolulu	HI	9800	3600	M [5]	Cath S	V	S	8/01 A=S	E		Y	Y	3/31 FA/FF	4	5	3	3	5	3				2.5 2.7	Y	Y	
0119	Point Loma Nazarene San Diego	CA	10600	3400	M [5]	Oth OS	V	U	S/A	Q		Y	Y	3/02 FA/FF	6	6	1	9	2	2	6	3	6	2.7	Y		Y
0120	Azusa Pacific U Azusa	CA	12500	3900	M [5]	Oth OS	S		A=S	O				3/02 FF=FA	8	6	1	9	2	5	8	4	4	3.1 3.2	Y	Y	
0121	Cal Lutheran U Thousand Oaks	CA	13500 [3]	4200	M [5]	Luth OS	M	S	8/01 A=S	4		Y	Y	3/01 FA/FF	7	5	1	8	1	1	8	6	2	3.2	Y	Y	
0122	La Verne,U of La Verne	CA	14100	4000	D [5]	Oth	S		S/A	4		Y	Y	FA/FF	8	5	5	7	5	1	7	5	5	3.1	Y	Y	Y
0123	Seattle Pacific U Seattle	WA	14600 [3]	4000	M [5]	Oth OS	V	U	9/01 A=S	Q		Y		3/01 FAF	6	6	1	8	1	4	5	4		3.3	Y	Y	
0124	Chapman C Orange	CA	16500	4600	M [5]	Oth	M	S	A=S	4		Y		3/01 FAF	4	6	1	6	2	2	8	4	2	3.0 3.0	Y	Y	
0125	Loyola Marymount U Los Angeles	CA	17000	5600	P [5]	Cath S	V	S	2/01 A=S	E		Y	Y	2/15 Oth	5	6	1	9	4	3	9	7		3.4	Y	Y	Y
Enrollment 5,000 to 15,000																											
0126	Cal St U Los Ang Los Angeles	CA	3700 [2]	2800 9900	M [5]	Pub	V	U	8/07 A=S	O		Y		3/01 FF=FA	5	6	1	2	8	1	8				Y	Y	Y
0127	Northern Ariz U Flagstaff	AZ	3800	2400 7400	D [5]	Pub	S		A/S	O		Y		FF=FA	6	5	1	9	2	2	4	4	2	2.9	Y		Y
0128	NM St U Main Cam Las Cruces	NM	4100	2600 7800	D [5]	Pub	M		8/01 A/S	E		Y	Y	3/01 FF=FA		5	1	5	4	1	7				Y	Y	Y
0129	Oregon St U Corvallis	OR	4500 [3]	2700 8200	D [5]	Pub	S		5/01 A=S	Q		Y		FA/FF	6	4	1	9	2	2	8	4		3.2 2.6	Y		Y
0130	Wyoming,U of Laramie	WY	4500	3200 7200	D [5]	Pub	S		A/S	E		Y	Y	FA/FF	5	5	1	8	1	2	7	4	3	3.2 2.4	Y		Y
0131	Eastern Washington U Cheney	WA	4600	3000 8600	M [5]	Pub	S		9/01 A=S	Q		Y	Y	2/15 FAF	4	5	1	6	2	1	7			3.1	Y	Y	Y
0132	Montana,U of Missoula	MT	4600 [3]	3100 6600	D [5]	Pub	M		A/S	Q		Y	Y	3/01 FA/FF	5	5	1	7	1	2	6		2	3.1	Y		Y
0133	Central Washington U Ellensburg	WA	4700	3100 8800	M [5]	Pub	S		7/01 A=S	Q		Y	Y			5	1	9	1	1	8	3		3.1 2.8	Y	Y	
0134	Montana St U Bozeman	MT	4800 [3]	3100 6900	D [5]	Pub	S		9/01 A=S	Q		Y	Y	FF/FA	5	4	1	9	1	2	7	4	1	3.0 2.7	Y		Y
0135	Northern Colo,U of Greeley	CO	5000 [3]	3200 8400	D [5]	Pub	M		8/15 A=S	S		Y		3/31 FF/FA	5	6	1	9	1	1	6			3.0 2.5	Y	Y	Y
0136	Portland St U Portland	OR	5600	3700 9400	D [5]	Pub	V	U	7/01 A=S	Q		Y	Y	3/01 FF=FA	5	5	1		3	1				3.0 2.5	Y	Y	Y
Enrollment over 15,000																											
0137	Nevada Las Vegas,U Las Vegas	NV	5000	4000 7300	D [5]	Pub	V	U	8/17 A=S	4		Y	Y	2/15 FF/FA	5	5	1	1	1	2	6			2.8 2.5	Y	Y	Y
0138	Utah,U of Salt Lake City	UT	5100	3200 8500	D [5]	Pub	L	U	7/01 A/S	Q		Y		4/01 Oth	9	4	2	1	1	1	6	3	2	3.1 2.6	Y	Y	Y
0139	San Diego St U San Diego	CA	5300	4400 10900	D [5]	Pub	V	S	11/30 A=S	E		Y		3/02 FF=FA	2	5	1		3			2		3.0 2.2	Y	Y	Y
0140	Washington St U Pullman	WA	5300 [3]	3300 8700	D [5]	Pub	S		A=S	E				FAF	4	5	1	9	1	1	9	5	1	3.3 2.7	Y		Y
SELECTIVE ADMISSIONS *Majority of accepted students in top 25% of HS class*																											
Enrollment to 1,000																											
0141	San Fran Art Inst San Francisco	CA	10100 [2]	0	M [5]	Priv	V	U	A=S	E			Y	FAF	7	5	2	0	2	5	8	7					
Sequence Number	School name (upper entry) City (lower entry)	State	Costs		General Information				Admissions					Financial Aid	Student Profile										Programs		

▲ Sequence number—indicates the order of the college in this book only. Do *not* use this number with admissions tests or need analysis services.

[1] No campus room and board facilities
[2] Room only or board only
[3] Most freshmen required to live on campus
[4] City or district residence requirements
[5] Accredited by a regional accrediting association or a recognized candidate for accreditation
[6] All female freshman class
[7] All male freshman class

MAJORS AVAILABLE AND PERCENT OF STUDENTS STUDYING IN EACH AREA

Sequence Number	Agri.	Business	Comm.	Education	Engineering	Fine/App. Arts	Lang.	Health	Home Ec.	Humanities	Math-Sciences	Social Sciences	GS	ROTC: Air Force	ROTC: Army	ROTC: Navy
0115		065% [1]	1%	5% [1]		1%	1%			1% [1]	3% [1]	2% [1]		Y	Y	
0116		022%	2%	020%		4% [1]	1%	7%		6%	8% [1]	010%		Y	Y	
0117					030% [1]									Y	Y	
0118		047%	2%	4% [1]		7% [1]		[1]		2%	010% [1]	014% [1]		Y	Y	
0119		018% [1]	4%	3%	1%	6%		010% [1]	3%	8%	010% [1]	012%		Y	Y	Y
0120		018%	7%	4% [1]	1%	9%		7%		7%	8% [1]	017% [1]				
0121		032%	9%	010% [1]		4%	1%	3%		010%	019% [1]	4%		Y	Y	
0122		034%	015%	010% [1]	8%	1%	2%	5% [1]		6%	016% [1]	2% [1]				
0123		010%	3%	8% [1]	3%	2%		5% [1]	3%	5% [1]	9%	8%		Y	Y	Y
0124		030%	020%	5%		010%	1%	1%		5%	012% [1]	016%		Y		
0125		028%	011%		6%	7% [1]	1%			017% [1]	8%	019% [1]		Y		
0126		028% [1]	2%	2% [1]	7%	4%	1%	7% [1]	7%	2%	011% [1]	015% [1]		Y	Y	Y
0127	1% [1]	021% [1]	5%	013% [1]	5%	3% [1]		5% [1]	2%	2%	7% [1]	010% [1]		Y	Y	
0128	7% [1]	021% [1]	3%	010% [1]	017% [1]	2% [1]	1%	3% [1]	1%	3%	7% [1]	8% [1]		Y	Y	
0129	6% [1]	019% [1]	3%	5% [1]	016% [1]	2%		8% [1]	5%	4%	9% [1]	9% [1]		Y	Y	Y
0130	6% [1]	016%	4%	015% [1]	011% [1]	2% [1]	1%	013% [1]	1%	2% [1]	010% [1]	8% [1]		Y	Y	
0131		024% [1]	4%	017% [1]		1% [1]	1%	3% [1]		026% [1]	022% [1]	1% [1]			Y	
0132	8% [1]	023%	7%	014% [1]		5% [1]	2%	5% [1]		5% [1]	8% [1]	016% [1]			Y	
0133	1% [1]	031% [1]	2%	027% [1]	1%	1%	1%	2% [1]	2%	2%	3% [1]	2% [1]		Y	Y	
0134	6% [1]	016%	4%	9% [1]	021% [1]	6% [1]	1%	6% [1]	2%	3%	010% [1]	5% [1]		Y	Y	
0135		014%	3%	011% [1]		6%	1%	8% [1]	1%	4%	8% [1]	017% [1]		Y	Y	
0136		025%		7%	7%	5% [1]	2%	4%		7% [1]	8% [1]	019% [1]		Y	Y	
0137		036% [1]	3%	8% [1]	4%	2% [1]	1%	7% [1]		2% [1]	3% [1]	2% [1]			Y	
0138		014%	4%	4% [1]	011% [1]	8% [1]	1%	012% [1]	2%	8% [1]	9% [1]	011% [1]		Y	Y	Y
0139		022%	1%	1%	7% [1]	2% [1]	1%	3% [1]	1%	4% [1]	013% [1]	7% [1]		Y	Y	Y
0140	6% [1]	018% [1]	5%	010% [1]	012% [1]	4% [1]	1%	010% [1]	4%	7% [1]	7% [1]	016% [1]		Y	Y	Y
0141						100% [1]										

[1] Additional majors available in this area
[2] ROTC available

†Accredited by a nationally recognized accrediting body other than one of the regional accrediting associations

Pacific & Mountain States

(continued)

AK, AZ, CA, CO, HI, ID, MT, NM, NV, OR, UT, WA, WY

SELECTIVE ADMISSIONS *Majority of accepted students in top 25% of HS class*

Sequence Number	School name (upper entry) City (lower entry)	State	Costs: Resident tuition/fees + room/board	Costs: Room/Board (upper entry) Nonresident tuition/fees + room/board (lower entry)	General Information: Highest degree	General Information: Affiliation (upper entry) Religious observance (lower entry)	General Information: Size of community	General Information: Type of community	Admissions: Fall term application deadline (upper entry) Tests desired or required (lower entry)	Admissions: Calendar	Admissions: Fall admission only	Admissions: Early admission	Admissions: Deferred admission	Financial Aid: Fall term application deadline (upper entry) Forms to be filed (lower entry)	Financial Aid: Number in 10 who— -have need, receive some aid	Student Profile: Number in 10 who— Undergrads -are women	Undergrads -are graduate students	Freshmen -live on campus	Freshmen -are minority students	Freshmen -are nonresidents	Freshmen -return as sophomores	Freshmen -complete degree	Freshmen -enter graduate study	HS GPA (upper entry) 1st year college GPA (lower entry)	Special Programs: Credit by exam	Special Programs: Student designed majors	Special Programs: Fraternities/sororities
	Enrollment to 1,000																										
0142	Linfield Sch Nsg Portland	OR	11800[2,3]	1500	B[5]	Bapt	L	U	 A=S	4		Y	Y	 FAF	9	9	0	9	1	2	8			3.2 2.9	Y		
0143	Holy Names C Oakland	CA	12700	4200	M[5]	Cath OS	L	U	8/01 S/A	E			Y	 FA/FF	7	6	3	3	6	1	8				Y	Y	
0144	Judaism,U of/Lee C Los Angeles	CA	13300[3]	5300	M[5]	Jew	V	U	1/31 A=S	S		Y	Y	 FAF	7	7	5	6	1	5	9	7	8	3.4 3.0	Y	Y	
0145	Otis Art Inst Los Angeles	CA	13300[2]	2600	M[5]	Priv	V	U	 S/A	E		Y	Y	3/01 Oth	6	6	1	2	4	4	9						
0146	Thomas Aquinas C Santa Paula	CA	14800[3]	4400	B[5]	Cath O	S		 S/A	S		Y	Y	 FF=FA	7	4	0	9	2	6	8	7	5	 3.0			
0147	Mount Saint Mary's C Los Angeles	CA	15000	4700	M[5]	Cath S	V	S	3/01 S/A	E		Y	Y	3/01 FA/FF	7	9	1	7	6	1	8	6	4	3.4	Y	Y	Y
0148	Saint John's C Santa Fe	NM	19000	4700	M[5]	Priv	M	S	 A=S	E		Y	Y	 FAF	6	6	1	8	1	9	8	6	8				
0149	Scripps C Claremont	CA	19800[3]	6000	B[5]	Priv	S		2/01 A=S	E		Y	Y[6]	2/01 FAF	5	9	0	9	2	5	9	7	7	3.5		Y	
0150	Pitzer C Claremont	CA	21200[3]	5700	B[5]	Priv	S		2/01 S/A	E		Y	Y	2/01 FAF	5	5	0	9	3	6	9	7	7	3.4 3.0	Y	Y	
	Enrollment 1,000 to 5,000																										
0151	Colo Denver,U of Denver	CO	1700	[1] 6800	D[5]	Pub	V	U	7/22 A=S	E		Y	Y	3/30 FF/FA	2	5	2	0	2	1				3.1	Y	Y	
0152	Cal St U Dominguez Carson	CA	3000[2]	1800 7500	M[5]	Pub	M	U	6/01 A=S	E		Y		5/01 FAF	1	6	2	1	6	1	6			2.9	Y	Y	Y
0153	NM Inst Mining/Tech Socorro	NM	4200	2800 7600	D[5]	Pub	T		8/15 A/S	E		Y	Y	3/01 FA/FF	6	4	1	7	3	3	7		2	3.4 2.5	Y		
0154	Cal St U Bakersfield Bakersfield	CA	4400	3500 10600	M[5]	Pub	M	S	 A=S	Q		Y	Y	3/02 Oth	6	6	1	3	4	1	7	3	3	3.2 2.8	Y	Y	Y
0155	Cal St U Stanislaus Turlock	CA	5000	4100 9100	M[5]	Pub	S		 A=S	4		Y	Y	3/01	2	6	1	2	3	1	7	5		3.3 2.5	Y	Y	Y
0156	Art Center C Design Pasadena	CA	11000	[1]	M[5]	Priv	L	S	 A=S	O			Y	3/02 FA/FF	6	3	1	0	4	4	8	6	1	 3.0			
0157	Portland,U of Portland	OR	11500	3300	M[5]	Cath S	L	U	8/30 A=S	E			Y	3/15 FA/FF	7	5	1	7	2	5	7	4	2	3.3 2.9	Y	Y	Y
0158	US International U San Diego	CA	13500[3]	4400	D[5]	Priv	V	S	 S/A	Q		Y	Y	 FA/FF	8	5	5	8	6	7	6	3	4	3.0 3.2	Y		
0159	Pacific U Forest Grove	OR	13600[3]	3200	D[5]	UCC	S		8/01 S/A	4			Y	6/01 FA/FF	8	5	3	9	2	5	8	5		3.3	Y		Y
0160	Seattle U Seattle	WA	13600[3]	3600	D[5]	Cath S	V	U	9/01 A=S	Q		Y	Y	6/01 FF=FA	7	5	3	9	3	4	8	6	3	3.3	Y	Y	Y
0161	Biola U La Mirada	CA	14000	4100	D[5]	Oth OS	S		 S/A	4			Y	3/02	8	6	1	6	2	3	7	6	3	2.3	Y		
0162	Gonzaga U Spokane	WA	14000[3]	3700	D[5]	Cath S	M	U	8/15 A=S	E			Y	3/15 FAF	8	5	3	9	1	5	8	5	3	3.2 3.0	Y	Y	
0163	Regis C Denver	CO	14000[3]	4600	M[5]	Cath OS	V	S	8/15 A=S	E			Y	3/15 FF=FA	9	5	2	5	2	4	7	5	3	2.9	Y	Y	
0164	Whitworth C Spokane	WA	14300[3]	3900	M[5]	Pres OS	L	S	 A=S	4		Y	Y	 FA/FF	9	6	3	9	1	4	7	4		3.2	Y	Y	
0165	Linfield C McMinnville	OR	14400[3]	3500	M[5]	Bapt	S		9/01 A=S	4			Y	8/15 FA/FF	9	5	1	9	1	4	8	6	4	3.3 2.8	Y	Y	Y
0166	Pacific Lutheran U Tacoma	WA	15000[3]	3900	M[5]	Luth O	M	S	5/01 A=S	4		Y	Y	 FAF	8	6	1	9	1	4	8	7	3	3.5 2.6	Y	Y	
0167	Puget Sound,U of Tacoma	WA	15100	3800	P[5]	Meth	M	S	3/01 A=S	E		Y	Y	 FAF	6	6	1	9	1	6	8	6	5	3.5 3.0			Y
0168	Whitman C Walla Walla	WA	16000[3]	4100	B[5]	Priv	S		3/01 S/A	E		Y	Y	2/15 FA/FF	7	5	0	9	1	5	9	8	7	3.6 3.0		Y	Y
0169	San Diego,U of San Diego	CA	16100[3]	5600	D[5]	Cath	V	U	5/01 S/A	4			Y	3/01 FA/FF	9	6	2	9	2	4	9	6	4	3.4 2.9	Y		Y
0170	San Fran,U of San Francisco	CA	16100[3]	5100	D[5]	Cath	V	U	 S/A	E		Y	Y	3/02 FA/FF	4	6	2	6	4	5	8	6	4	3.0 2.6	Y	Y	Y
0171	Cal Inst of the Arts Valencia	CA	16300	4100	M[5]	Priv	M		 None	S		Y	Y	3/01 FAF	8	4	3	5	3	5	7		1			Y	

▲ **Sequence number—indicates the order of the college in this book only. Do *not* use this number with admissions tests or need analysis services.**

[1] No campus room and board facilities
[2] Room only or board only
[3] Most freshmen required to live on campus
[4] City or district residence requirements
[5] Accredited by a regional accrediting association or a recognized candidate for accreditation
[6] All female freshman class
[7] All male freshman class

MAJORS AVAILABLE AND PERCENT OF STUDENTS STUDYING IN EACH AREA

Sequence Number	Agri.	Business	Comm.	Education	Engineering	Fine/App. Arts	Lang.	Health	Home Ec.	Humanities	Math-Sciences	Social Sciences	ROTC: Air Force	ROTC: Army	ROTC: Navy
0142								100%					Y		
0143		019%			5%	4%	5%	010%		021%	015% [1]	011% [1]	Y	Y	
0144		010%								010%		030% [1]			
0145						100% [1]									
0146						1%	8%			045%	039%	7%			
0147		014%		8% [1]		3%	2%	040% [1]		7%	5% [1]	6% [1]	Y	Y	Y
0148															
0149		4%				018%	6%			026% [1]	4% [1]	042% [1]	Y	Y	
0150		010%	2%	1% [1]		1%	3%	6%		016% [1]	012%	049% [1]		Y	
0151		016% [1]	3%		013%	1%	1%	3%		3%	011% [1]	013%	Y	Y	
0152		033% [1]	4%	010% [1]		2%	1%	4% [1]		5%	013% [1]	014% [1]	Y	Y	
0153			3%	1%	030% [1]	1%	1%	1%			031% [1]	2%			
0154		022% [1]	3%	019% [1]		3%	1%	8% [1]		8%	010% [1]	2% [1]			
0155		014%	5%	010% [1]		1%	1%	8%		2%	3% [1]	2% [1]			
0156			030%			070% [1]									
0157		023%	7%	010%	013%	1%	1%	011% [1]		2%	9%	011%	Y	Y	
0158		042% [1]		[1]	4%	021%				2%		020% [1]		Y	
0159		019%	2%	012% [1]	5%	1%	3%	025% [1]		2%	018%	011% [1]		Y	
0160		021%	1%		014% [1]	1%	1%	7% [1]		6%	6%	8% [1]	Y	Y	Y
0161		015%	010%	9% [1]	1%	6%	1%	010%		014%	014% [1]	020% [1]	Y	Y	Y
0162		026%	010%	2%	014%	2%	1%	2%		4% [1]	9%	018% [1]		Y	
0163		030%	5%	8%	1%	2%	1%	1%		5%	7% [1]	2%	Y	Y	
0164		018%	5%	022% [1]		6%	1%	3% [1]	1%	011%	012%	017% [1]		Y	
0165		039%	2%	9% [1]	2%	2%	2%	018%	1%	010%	7% [1]	8%	Y		
0166		027% [1]	3%	013% [1]	2%	1% [1]	1%	015%		6% [1]	014% [1]	017% [1]		Y	
0167		023%	5%	8%		3%	1%	4% [1]		011%	019% [1]	024% [1]		Y	
0168				1%	1%	013%	3%	1%		018%	026% [1]	036%			
0169		045%	2%	3% [1]	1%	3%	1%	3%		010%	012% [1]	019% [1]	Y	Y	Y
0170	[1]	024% [1]	6%	2% [1]	1%	4% [1]	1%	8%		5%	018% [1]	016% [1]	Y	Y	
0171						100% [1]									

[1] Additional majors available in this area
[2] ROTC available

†Accredited by a nationally recognized accrediting body other than one of the regional accrediting associations

Pacific & Mountain States
(continued)

AK, AZ, CA, CO, HI, ID, MT, NM, NV, OR, UT, WA, WY

SELECTIVE ADMISSIONS *Majority of accepted students in top 25% of HS class*

Sequence Number	School name (upper entry) City (lower entry)	State	Costs		General Information				Admissions					Financial Aid		Student Profile: Number in 10 who—									Special Programs		
			Resident tuition/fees + room/board	Room/Board (upper entry) Nonresident tuition/fees + room/board (lower entry)	Highest degree	Affiliation (upper entry) Religious observance (lower entry)	Size of community	Type of community	Fall term application deadline (upper entry) Tests desired or required (lower entry)	Calendar	Fall admission only	Early admission	Deferred admission	Fall term application deadline (upper entry) Forms to be filed (lower entry)	-have need, receive some aid	Undergrads: -are women	Undergrads: -are graduate students	Freshmen: -live on campus	Freshmen: -are minority students	Freshmen: -are nonresidents	Freshmen: -return as sophomores	Freshmen: -complete degree	Freshmen: -enter graduate study	HS GPA (upper entry) 1st year college GPA (lower entry)	Credit by exam	Student designed majors	Fraternities/sororities
	Enrollment 1,000 to 5,000																										
0172	Saint Marys C of Ca Moraga	CA	16400	5400	M[5]	Cath OS	S		6/01 A=S	4		Y	Y	3/15 FA/FF	6	5	1	6	2	3	9	8	4	3.3 2.9	Y	Y	
0173	Westmont C Santa Barbara	CA	16800	4700	B[5]	Oth OS	M	S	 A=S	E			Y	 FA/FF	8	6	0	8	1	2	8	5	7	3.3 3.2	Y	Y	
0174	Lewis and Clark C Portland	OR	17300[3]	4400	P[5]	Pres	V	S	2/01 A=S	Q		Y	Y	2/15 FA/FF	5	5	3	9	2	7	8	6	4	3.3 3.0	Y	Y	Y
0175	Whittier C Whittier	CA	17700[3]	4500	P[5]	Priv	M	S	 A=S	4		Y	Y	2/15 FA/FF	7	5	3	7	3	5	8	6	5	3.0		Y	Y
0176	Mills C Oakland	CA	18100[3]	5400	M[5]	Priv	V	S	8/01 A=S	E			Y[6]	2/15 FAF	7	9	3	9	3	5	9	6	6	3.3	Y	Y	
0177	Redlands,U of Redlands	CA	18100	5100	M[5]	Priv	M		3/01 A=S	4		Y	Y	 FAF	8	5	2	9	2	4	9	5	6	3.4 2.8		Y	Y
0178	Pacific,U of the Stockton	CA	19300[3]	5100	D[5]	Meth	M	S	 S/A	E		Y	Y	3/01 FA/FF	6	5	1	9	3	2	8	6	5	3.1	Y	Y	Y
0179	Reed C Portland	OR	21300	4600	M[5]	Priv	V	S	2/01 A=S	E		Y	Y	3/01 FAF	4	4	0	9	2	9	7	6	6	3.7		Y	
	Enrollment 5,000 to 15,000																										
0180	Cal St U Hayward Hayward	CA	3400[2]	2500 8200	M[5]	Pub	M	U	7/05 A=S	Q		Y		 Oth	2	6	1	1	5	1				3.0	Y	Y	Y
0181	Cal St U Fullerton Fullerton	CA	3500[2]	2500 9600	M[5]	Pub	M	S	 A=S	E		Y		3/01 Oth	3	5	1	1	4	1	7	2		 2.2	Y	Y	Y
0182	Hawaii Manoa,U of Honolulu	HI	4500	3100 7000	D[5]	Pub	V	U	6/15 S/A	E		Y		 FAF		5	2		8						Y	Y	Y
0183	Cal St U San Bern San Bernardino	CA	4700	3700 9600	M[5]	Pub	L	S	8/25 A=S	Q		Y		3/01 FA/FF	2	5	1	2	2	1	7	2		3.1 2.6	Y	Y	Y
0184	Sonoma St U Rohnert Park	CA	4700	3800 10000	M[5]	Pub	S		 A=S	E		Y		 FAF	2	6	2	4	3	1				2.9 2.4	Y	Y	Y
0185	Cal St Poly U Pomona Pomona	CA	5000	4100 9900	M[5]	Pub	M	S	9/13 A=S	O		Y		 FA/FF	4	4	1	6	5	1	8	3		3.2 2.4	Y		Y
0186	Humboldt St U Arcata	CA	5000	4000 10200	M[5]	Pub	S		 A=S	S		Y		 FA/FF	5	5	1		1	1	7	2	2	2.9 2.6	Y	Y	Y
0187	Cal St U Chico Chico	CA	5100	4200 10400	M[5]	Pub	M		 A=S	E		Y	Y	3/01 Oth	3	5	1	6	2	1	8	4	3	2.9 2.5	Y	Y	Y
0188	Western Washington U Bellingham	WA	5400	3700 9400	M[5]	Pub	S		3/01	Q		Y		3/31 FA/FF	7	5	1	3	1	1	7	2	2	3.4 2.7	Y	Y	
0189	Santa Clara U Santa Clara	CA	15500	5000	D[5]	Cath S	M	S	2/01 S/A	Q				2/01 FAF	5	5	3	9	3	4	9	8	7	3.5 2.8	Y	Y	Y
0190	Denver,U of Denver	CO	17100[3]	4200	D[5]	Meth	V	S	8/01 A=S	Q		Y	Y	4/01 FF/FA	5	5	5	9	2	7	9	7	5	3.0 2.7	Y		Y
	Enrollment over 15,000																										
0191	San Fran St U San Francisco	CA	4600[3]	3800 9500	D[5]	Pub	V	U	 A=S	E		Y		3/01 FA/FF	8	6	1	1	6	1					Y		
0192	Cal St U Fresno Fresno	CA	4700	3800 9200	M[5]	Pub	V	U	 A=S	E				3/01 Oth	4	5	1	2	4	2	8	5		 2.5	Y	Y	Y
0193	Oregon,U of Eugene	OR	4800	2800 8500	D[5]	Pub	M	U	3/01 A=S	Q				3/01	9	5	2	6	2	3	8	5		3.4 2.7	Y		Y
0194	Brigham Young U Provo	UT	5000	3100	D[5]	LDS S	M	S	2/15 ACT	O		Y		4/30 FFS	4	5	1	8	1	7	8	2	2	3.5 2.3	Y	Y	
0195	Cal St U Long Beach Long Beach	CA	5100	4200 11200	M[5]	Pub	L	U	 A=S	E		Y		3/02 FF=FA	3	5	1		5	1	7	2		 2.4	Y	Y	Y
0196	Cal St U Sacramento Sacramento	CA	5100	4000 12700	M[5]	Pub	L	U	2/15 A=S	E		Y		3/01 FF=FA	2	5	1	2	3	1	7	2		3.2 2.4	Y	Y	Y
0197	Ariz,U of Tucson	AZ	5300	3700 10700	D[5]	Pub	V	U	4/01 S/A	E		Y	Y	3/01 FF=FA	3	5	1	6	2	4	8	6	3	3.2 2.4	Y		Y
0198	Ariz St U Tempe	AZ	5400	3900 10400	D[5]	Pub	M	S	 A=S	E				3/15 FA/FF	5	5	1	5	1	5	7	4		3.0	Y	Y	Y
0199	Colo Boulder,U of Boulder	CO	5600[3]	3300 12700	D[5]	Pub	M	S	 A=S	E			Y	 FF=FA	3	5	2	9	1	4	8	5	4	3.4	Y	Y	Y
0200	San Jose St U San Jose	CA	5700	4600 10900	M[5]	Pub	V	U	 A=S	E				3/01 FA/FF	2	5	1	3	5	1	8	2		3.1 2.5	Y	Y	Y
Sequence Number	School name (upper entry) City (lower entry)	State	Costs		General Information				Admissions					Financial Aid		Student Profile									Programs		

▲ Sequence number—indicates the order of the college in this book only. Do *not* use this number with admissions tests or need analysis services.

[1] No campus room and board facilities
[2] Room only or board only
[3] Most freshmen required to live on campus
[4] City or district residence requirements
[5] Accredited by a regional accrediting association or a recognized candidate for accreditation
[6] All female freshman class
[7] All male freshman class

MAJORS AVAILABLE AND PERCENT OF STUDENTS STUDYING IN EACH AREA

Sequence Number	Agri.	Business	Comm.	Education	Engineering	Fine/App. Arts	Lang.	Health	Home Ec.	Humanities	Math-Sciences	Social Sciences	GS	ROTC Air Force	ROTC Army	ROTC Navy
0172		020%	5%	3% [1]		5%	2%	7%		028% [1]	010%	013%		Y	Y	Y
0173		024%	016%	8%	2%	3%	1%	2%		019%	8%	016% [1]			Y	
0174		015%	7%	2%	1%	6%	4%	2%		9%	014%	015% [1]				
0175		016%		8%		8%	2%	9% [1]	1%	014%	018% [1]	024% [1]				
0176		2%	4%	3% [1]		6%	3%			6% [1]	6% [1]	015% [1]		Y	Y	Y
0177		020%		7% [1]	5%	010% [1]	2%	2% [1]		015%	016%	016% [1]				
0178		019%	9%	5% [1]	016%	7%	1%	4% [1]		3% [1]	011% [1]	9% [1]		Y		
0179	1%	3%		2%	2%	6%	3%	2%		020% [1]	034% [1]	020% [1]			Y	
0180		038%	3%	1%		2%		6% [1]		1%	9% [1]	017% [1]		Y	Y	Y
0181		032%	011%	2%	5%	6% [1]	1%	3% [1]	4%	3% [1]	9% [1]	014% [1]			Y	
0182	2% [1]	7% [1]	1%	9%	6%	5%	3%	2% [1]		7%	9% [1]	010% [1]		Y	Y	
0183		020%	2%	8% [1]		3%	1%	5% [1]	1%	3%	010%	018% [1]			Y	
0184		018%	2%	011%		5%	1%	4%		4%	011% [1]	020% [1]				
0185	4% [1]	022% [1]	2%	1%	026% [1]	9% [1]			1%	1%	015% [1]	6% [1]			Y	
0186	013% [1]	014% [1]	1%	1% [1]	5% [1]	7%	1%	8% [1]	1%	6%	017% [1]	010% [1]				
0187	2% [1]	020%	013%	4% [1]	9%	2%	1%	3% [1]	4%	4%	8% [1]	019% [1]			Y	
0188		014% [1]	5%	3% [1]	3%	6% [1]	1%	1% [1]	1%	6% [1]	012% [1]	011% [1]				
0189		027%	5%		015%	2%	1%			6% [1]	9%	017%		Y	Y	Y
0190		056% [1]	7%	1%	1%	4%	1%			6% [1]	8%	014% [1]		Y	Y	
0191		025%	4%	1% [1]	4%	1% [1]	1%	2% [1]	1%	2% [1]	3% [1]	2% [1]		Y		
0192	5% [1]	024% [1]	4%	022% [1]	7%	2%	1%	8% [1]	2%	4% [1]	7% [1]	014% [1]		Y	Y	
0193		020%	011%	7%	1%	011% [1]	2%	1%		5% [1]	010% [1]	017% [1]			Y	
0194	2% [1]	013% [1]	5%	8% [1]	010%	6% [1]	3%	6%	4%	6% [1]	012% [1]	013% [1]		Y	Y	
0195		021% [1]	4%	3% [1]	015% [1]	9% [1]		5% [1]	2%	4% [1]	8% [1]	012% [1]		Y	Y	
0196		030% [1]	7%	5% [1]	010%	4% [1]	1%	012% [1]	1%	2%	8% [1]	8% [1]		Y	Y	
0197	2% [1]	026% [1]	4%	7% [1]	011% [1]	6% [1]	2%	4% [1]	3%	5% [1]	6% [1]	010% [1]		Y	Y	Y
0198	1% [1]	024% [1]	7%	7% [1]	011% [1]	9% [1]	1%	3% [1]	1%	2%	6% [1]	014% [1]		Y	Y	
0199		016% [1]	012%		010% [1]	6% [1]	2%	[1]		8% [1]	013% [1]	031% [1]		Y	Y	Y
0200		024% [1]	6%	1% [1]	015% [1]	9% [1]	1%	010% [1]	1%	6% [1]	011% [1]	012% [1]		Y	Y	

[1] Additional majors available in this area
[2] ROTC available

†Accredited by a nationally recognized accrediting body other than one of the regional accrediting associations

Pacific & Mountain States
(continued)

AK, AZ, CA, CO, HI, ID, MT, NM, NV, OR, UT, WA, WY

SELECTIVE ADMISSIONS *Majority of accepted students in top 25% of HS class*

Sequence Number	School name (upper entry) / City (lower entry)	State	Costs: Resident tuition/fees + room/board	Costs: Room/Board (upper entry) / Nonresident tuition/fees + room/board (lower entry)	General Information: Highest degree	General Information: Affiliation (upper entry) / Religious observance (lower entry)	General Information: Size of community	General Information: Type of community	Admissions: Fall term application deadline (upper entry) / Tests desired or required (lower entry)	Admissions: Calendar	Admissions: Fall admission only	Admissions: Early admission	Admissions: Deferred admission	Financial Aid: Fall term application deadline (upper entry) / Forms to be filed (lower entry)	Financial Aid: -have need, receive some aid	Student Profile (Number in 10 who—) Undergrads: -are women	Undergrads: -are graduate students	Undergrads: -live on campus	Freshmen: -are minority students	Freshmen: -are nonresidents	Freshmen: -return as sophomores	Freshmen: -complete degree	Freshmen: -enter graduate study	Freshmen: HS GPA (upper entry) / 1st year college GPA (lower entry)	Special Programs: Credit by exam	Special Programs: Student designed majors	Special Programs: Fraternities/sororities
	Enrollment over 15,000																										
0201	Washington,U of / Seattle	WA	5700	3500 / 9600	D[5]	Pub	V	U	A=S	Q		Y		3/01 / FAF	3	5	2	5	3	1	9	5		3.5 / 3.0	Y	Y	Y
0202	Cal St U Northridge / Northridge	CA	6000	5100 / 10500	M[5]	Pub	V	S	10/30 / A=S	E				FA/FF	2	5	1	1	4	1	7	2		3.1 / 2.5	Y	Y	Y
0203	Colo St U / Fort Collins	CO	6100[3]	3900 / 10500	D[5]	Pub	M		A=S	E		Y		FF=FA	4	5	1	9	1	3	8	5		3.3 / 2.5	Y		Y
0204	Cal Poly-San Luis Ob / San Luis Obispo	CA	6700	5700 / 10600	M[5]	Pub	S		/00 / A=S	O				3/01 / FAF	1	4	1	8	3	1	8	5	1	3.3 / 2.5	Y		Y
0205	Southern Cal,U of / Los Angeles	CA	20100	5700	D[5]	Priv	V	U	A=S	E			Y	FF=FA	6	4	2	8	4	3	8	6		3.5 / 2.8	Y	Y	Y
	HIGHLY SELECTIVE *Majority of accepted students in top 10% of HS class*																										
	Enrollment to 1,000																										
0206	Claremont McKenna C / Claremont	CA	18700	4800	B[5]	Priv	S		2/01 / S/A	E		Y	Y	2/01 / FA/FF	7	4	0	9	3	5	9	9	8	3.8 / 3.1	Y	Y	
0207	Harvey Mudd C / Claremont	CA	20900	6000	M[5]	Priv	S		2/15 / Oth	E		Y	Y	2/15 / FAF	6	2	1	9	3	5	9	8	7	3.8	Y	Y	
	Enrollment 1,000 to 5,000																										
0208	US Air Force Acad / USAF Academy	CO	0[3]	0	B[5]	Pub	L	S	1/31 / A=S	E				None		1	0	9	2	9	8	7	7	2.8			
0209	Colo Sch of Mines / Golden	CO	7600	3700 / 13900	D[5]	Pub	S		8/15 / A=S	E				FF/FA	5	2	2	8	1	3	9	6	1	3.7 / 2.8	Y		Y
0210	Willamette U / Salem	OR	14500[3]	3800	P[5]	Meth	M		2/15 / A=S	E		Y	Y	3/01 / FA/FF	7	5	3	9	2	5	9	7	5	3.5 / 3.0	Y		Y
0211	Colo C / Colorado Sprgs	CO	16100[3]	3400	M[5]	Priv	L	S	2/01 / A=S	O		Y	Y	2/15 / FA/FF	5	5	1	9	1	7	9	8	5			Y	Y
0212	Cal Inst of Techn / Pasadena	CA	18700	5400	D[5]	Priv	M	S	1/01 / Oth	Q		Y	Y	2/01 / FAF	7	3	6	9	4	7	9	7	5	3.9	Y	Y	
0213	Pomona C / Claremont	CA	19100[3]	5200	B[5]	Priv	S		1/15 / A=S	E		Y	Y	2/01 / FAF	5	5	0	9	3	6	9	9	8	3.8 / 3.0		Y	Y
0214	Occidental C / Los Angeles	CA	19700	5200	M[5]	Priv	V	U	2/01 / S/A	O		Y	Y	2/01 / FA/FF	7	5	0	9	3	6	9	7	6	3.8 / 2.9		Y	Y
0215	Pepperdine U Malibu / Malibu	CA	21400[3]	6100	D[5]	Oth / OS	S		2/01 / A=S	E		Y		4/01 / FA/FF	9	6	1	9	3	5				3.3 / 2.9	Y		Y
	Enrollment 5,000 to 15,000																										
0216	Cal Riverside,U of / Riverside	CA	6800	4900 / 13300	D[5]	Pub	L	S	A=S	Q		Y		3/02 / Oth	5	5	2	4	4	1	9	5	5	3.4 / 2.9		Y	Y
0217	Cal Santa Cruz,U of / Santa Cruz	CA	7800	5300 / 13000	D[5]	Pub	S		11/30 / A=S	Q				FAF	5	5	1		2		9	4		3.4		Y	
0218	Stanford U / Stanford	CA	19200[3]	5600	D[5]	Priv	M	S	12/16 / S/A	Q			Y	2/01 / FAF	4	4	5	9	4	7	9	9				Y	Y
	Enrollment over 15,000																										
0219	Cal Davis,U of / Davis	CA	6500	4700 / 12900	D[5]	Pub	M		11/30 / A=S	Q			Y	2/10	7	5	2	9	4	1	7	6	4	3.7 / 2.9		Y	Y
0220	Cal Irvine,U of / Irvine	CA	6600	4700 / 13000	D[5]	Pub	M	S	11/30 / S/A	Q		Y		3/02 / Oth		5	1	7	6	1	8	5		2.9	Y		Y
0221	Cal Los Ang,U of / Los Angeles	CA	6600	4900 / 13000	D[5]	Pub	V	U	11/30 / A=S	Q				2/11 / FAF	5	5	3		5	1	9	6	6	3.8 / 3.0		Y	Y
0222	Cal Santa Barbara,U / Santa Barbara	CA	6600	5000 / 10800	D[5]	Pub	M	S	A=S	Q		Y		3/02 / FAF	6	5	1	5	3	1	9	5	3	3.5 / 2.7	Y	Y	Y
0223	Cal Berkeley,U of / Berkeley	CA	7600	5600 / 14200	D[5]	Pub	M	U	11/30 / A=S	S				3/02	5	5	3	5	6	2	9	7		3.7	Y	Y	Y
0224	Cal San Diego,U of / La Jolla	CA	8700	6200 / 16400	D[5]	Pub	S		11/30 / A=S	Q		Y	Y	3/02 / FF=FA	4	5	2	8	4	1	9	5	4	3.7 / 2.9		Y	Y

▲ Sequence number—indicates the order of the college in this book only. Do *not* use this number with admissions tests or need analysis services.

[1] No campus room and board facilities
[2] Room only or board only
[3] Most freshmen required to live on campus
[4] City or district residence requirements
[5] Accredited by a regional accrediting association or a recognized candidate for accreditation
[6] All female freshman class
[7] All male freshman class

MAJORS AVAILABLE AND PERCENT OF STUDENTS STUDYING IN EACH AREA

Sequence Number	Agri.	Business	Comm.	Education	Engineering	Fine/App. Arts	Lang.	Health	Home Ec.	Humanities	Math-Sciences	Social Sciences	GS	ROTC
0201	1% [1]	6%	1%	1%	6% [1]	5% [1]	1%	6% [1]		7% [1]	7% [1]	011%		YYY
0202		019% [1]	7%	4% [1]	6%	6% [1]	1%	7% [1]	1%	9% [1]	8% [1]	012% [1]		YY
0203	011% [1]	018% [1]	2%	1% [1]	7% [1]	9% [1]	1%	4% [1]	4%	1% [1]	011% [1]	3% [1]		YY
0204	021% [1]	010%	5%	2% [1]	024% [1]	011% [1]			3%	2%	013% [1]	7% [1]		Y
0205				[1]	[1]	[1]		[1]		[1]	[1]	[1]		YYY
0206					1%	1%	2%			012% [1]	013%	057% [1]		YY
0207					046%						050%			YY
0208		015%			031% [1]						019% [1]	023% [1]		
0209					083% [1]						017% [1]			YYY
0210		010%		3%		5%	3%	2% [1]		010%	021%	041% [1]		
0211						8%	2%			022% [1]	023% [1]	032% [1]		Y
0212					042% [1]						055% [1]	1% [1]		YYY
0213					1%	5%	3%			023% [1]	024% [1]	040% [1]		YY
0214				5% [1]	1%	1% [1]	5%			017% [1]	025% [1]	1% [1]		YYY
0215		026%	019%	1% [1]		4%	1%	4%	1%	4%	6% [1]	014% [1]		YYY
0216	1% [1]	019%			2% [1]	2%	2%	6%		010% [1]	021% [1]	022% [1]		YY
0217						[1]				[1]	[1]	[1]		
0218			2%		021% [1]	3%	2%			9% [1]	017% [1]	038% [1]		YYY
0219	028% [1]			[1]	012% [1]	4% [1]	1%			9% [1]	027% [1]	018% [1]		Y
0220				1%	7%	5%	2%			8% [1]	035%	025% [1]		Y Y
0221			1%		8% [1]	5% [1]	2%			9% [1]	017%	038% [1]		YYY
0222		013%	4%		7% [1]	5%	2%	[1]		014% [1]	013% [1]	022%		Y
0223	1% [1]	2%	1%	1%	012% [1]	4% [1]	1%	1%	1%	6% [1]	9% [1]	012% [1]		YYY
0224			5%	1%	020% [1]	4%	1%			6% [1]	029%	025% [1]		YYY

[1] Additional majors available in this area
[2] ROTC available

†Accredited by a nationally recognized accrediting body other than one of the regional accrediting associations

Pacific & Mountain States

(continued)

AK, AZ, CA, CO, HI, ID, MT, NM, NV, OR, UT, WA, WY

ADVANCED STANDING *Freshmen not accepted; college junior standing often required*

Enrollment to 1,000

Sequence Number	School name (upper entry) City (lower entry)	State	Costs: Resident tuition/fees + room/board	Costs: Room/Board (upper entry) Nonresident tuition/fees + room/board (lower entry)	General Information: Highest degree	Affiliation (upper entry) Religious observance (lower entry)	Size of community	Type of community	Admissions: Fall term application deadline (upper entry) Tests desired or required (lower entry)	Calendar	Fall admission only	Early admission	Deferred admission	Financial Aid: Fall term application deadline (upper entry) Forms to be filed (lower entry)	-have need, receive some aid	Under-grads: -are women	-are graduate students	Freshmen: -live on campus	-are minority students	-are nonresidents	-return as sophomores	-complete degree	-enter graduate study	HS GPA (upper entry) 1st year college GPA (lower entry)	Special Programs: Credit by exam	Student designed majors	Fraternities/sororities
0225	Antioch U Santa Barb Santa Barbara	CA		[1]	M [5]	Priv	M	U	8/23 None	Q				8/26 FAF	5	7	7		1						Y	Y	
0226	West Los Ang,U of Los Angeles	CA	3600	[1]	P [5]	Priv	V	U	None	T			Y	Oth		7	6	0	4			4	2		Y		
0227	Pacific Oaks C Pasadena	CA	9000	[1]	M [5]	Priv	L	S	None	E				4/14 FAF		9	5	0	3						Y		
0228	Monterey Inst Intern Monterey	CA	11300	[1]	M [5]	Priv	M		Oth	E			Y	Oth		7	9	0	4						Y		

North Central States

IA, KS, MN, MO, ND, NE, SD

OPEN ADMISSIONS *All HS graduates accepted, to limit of capacity*

Sequence Number	School name (upper entry) City (lower entry)	State	Costs: Resident tuition/fees + room/board	Costs: Room/Board (upper entry) Nonresident tuition/fees + room/board (lower entry)	General Information: Highest degree	Affiliation (upper entry) Religious observance (lower entry)	Size of community	Type of community	Admissions: Fall term application deadline (upper entry) Tests desired or required (lower entry)	Calendar	Fall admission only	Early admission	Deferred admission	Financial Aid: Fall term application deadline (upper entry) Forms to be filed (lower entry)	-have need, receive some aid	Under-grads: -are women	-are graduate students	Freshmen: -live on campus	-are minority students	-are nonresidents	-return as sophomores	-complete degree	-enter graduate study	HS GPA (upper entry) 1st year college GPA (lower entry)	Special Programs: Credit by exam	Student designed majors	Fraternities/sororities
	Enrollment to 1,000																										
0229	Sinte Gleska C Rosebud	SD	1800	[1]	B [5]	Pub	T		9/01 Oth	E		Y		FF=FA	7	6	0	0	8	1	8			1.8 2.0			
0230	Platte Valley Bible Scottsbluff	NE	2000 [2]	600	B †	Oth OS	S		8/01 A=S	S		Y		8/01 Oth	4	4	0	6	0	5	7	1	1				
0231	Valley City St U Valley City	ND	3400 [3]	1800 6700	B [5]	Pub	T		ACT	Q		Y		FF/FA	8	6	0	4	1	1	6	3	1	2.8 2.8	Y	Y	Y
0232	Baptist Bible C Springfield	MO	3800 [3]	2200	M †	Bapt OS	M	U	A/S	E				Oth	6	4	1	6	1	9	4		1	2.8 2.5			
0233	Mayville St U Mayville	ND	3800 [3]	2100 6300	B [5]	Pub	T		A/S	Q		Y		FF/FA	7	5	0	8	1	2	7	4	1	2.9 2.7	Y		Y
0234	Nebraska Christian C Norfolk	NE	4800	2500	B †	Oth O	S		A/S	E		Y		FA/FF	9	5	0	9	1	6	4		3	2.6			
0235	Ozark Christian C Joplin	MO	5000	2300	B †	Oth OS	S		8/15 A/S	S				7/15 FF=FA		5	0	9	1	9	8	2	1	2.9			
0236	Manhattan Christian Manhattan	KS	5700 [3]	2400	B †	Oth OS	S		A/S	E		Y	Y	4/01 FF/FA	6	5	0	9	1	4	7	2		2.6	Y		
0237	Pillsbury Bible C Owatonna	MN	5900 [3]	2500	B [5]	Bapt OS	S		ACT	E		Y		8/01 FFS	7	5	0	9	1		6						
0238	Trinity Bible C Ellendale	ND	7500 [3]	3100	B †	Oth OS	T		ACT	E				5/15 FF/FA	9	5	0	9	1	6	6	2	1		Y		
0239	National C Rapid City	SD	8700	3000	B [5]	Priv	M		ACT	Q				FF/FA	9	7	0	4	1	4	4	3	1	2.8 2.5	Y		Y
0240	Grand View C Des Moines	IA	10500	2900	B [5]	Luth S	L	U	A/S	E		Y		4/15 FA/FF	7	6	0	2	2	1	6	4	2	2.6 2.2	Y	Y	
	Enrollment 1,000 to 5,000																										
0241	Missouri Western St St Joseph	MO	3500	2100 4800	B [5]	Pub	M		ACT	E		Y		4/01 FF/FA	6	6	0	3	1	1	5	3	2	2.8 2.6	Y		Y
0242	Chadron St C Chadron	NE	3600	2200 4200	M [5]	Pub	T		ACT	S		Y	Y	FF=FA	9	6	1	8	1	2	6	4	1	3.0 2.8	Y	Y	
0243	Dickinson St U Dickinson	ND	3700	2000 6100	B [5]	Pub	S		A/S	E				FF/FA	7	6	0	5	1	2	6	3	1	2.7 2.4	Y	Y	Y
0244	Wayne St C Wayne	NE	3700 [3]	2300 4500	M [5]	Pub	T		A/S	E		Y	Y	FA/FF	7	6	1	9	1	3	6	4	1	2.5	Y		Y
0245	Emporia St U Emporia	KS	3800 [3]	2400 5900	M [5]	Pub	S		ACT	E		Y	Y	3/15 FF/FA	7	6	1	7	2	1	7	4	2	2.9 2.5	Y	Y	Y
0246	Pittsburg St U Pittsburg	KS	3900 [3]	2600 5800	M [5]	Pub	S		ACT	E				FFS	7	5	1	4	1	1	7	3	1	3.0	Y	Y	Y
0247	Peru St C Peru	NE	4000 [3]	2500 4800	M [5]	Pub	T		A/S	E		Y		4/01 FA/FF	7	5	0	9	1	1	7	4	1	2.6	Y		Y
0248	Fort Hays St U Hays	KS	4100 [3]	2600 6200	M [5]	Pub	S		A/S	E		Y	Y	3/15 FF/FA	7	5	1	4	1	1	4	3		2.3	Y		Y
0249	Lincoln U Jefferson City	MO	4200	2700 5500	M [5]	Pub	S		8/22 ACT	E		Y		3/01 FA/FF	5	6	1	1	4	1		5		2.5	Y	Y	Y

▲ Sequence number—indicates the order of the college in this book only. Do *not* use this number with admissions tests or need analysis services.

[1] No campus room and board facilities
[2] Room only or board only
[3] Most freshmen required to live on campus
[4] City or district residence requirements
[5] Accredited by a regional accrediting association or a recognized candidate for accreditation
[6] All female freshman class
[7] All male freshman class

MAJORS AVAILABLE AND PERCENT OF STUDENTS STUDYING IN EACH AREA

Sequence Number	Agri.	Business	Comm.	Education	Engineering	Fine/App. Arts	Lang.	Health	Home Ec.	Humanities	Math-Sciences	Social Sciences	GS	ROTC
0225														
0226												100%		
0227				1%								2%		
0228							030%					070%		
0229		020%		020%		3%		2%				024%		
0230				040%										
0231		025%		060%		1%	1%			1%	3%	2%		
0232		8%		011%						020%				
0233	1%	035%	1%	040%		1%		4%		1%	4%	2%		
0234										100%				
0235										100%				
0236	1%	5%	1%	030%		3%		1%	2%	049%	2%	6%		
0237		010%	1%	030%		9%	2%		2%	020%	013%	010%		
0238		9%		015%						050%	1%	010%		
0239	1%	063%	1%		4%		1%	013%		1%	011%	1%		Y
0240		028%	010%		1%	3%		020%		1%	5%	9%		YY
0241	1%	023%		012%	3%	3%	1%	010%		4%	9%	022%		Y
0242	3%	026%		031%		5%			3%	2%	011%	4%		
0243	1%	025%	1%	042%	1%	1%	1%	1%	1%	2%	3%	2%		
0244		025%	3%	032%		3%		1%	1%	1%	4%	013%		
0245		027%	2%	027%	1%	3%	1%		1%	2%	012%	7%		Y
0246		020%	2%	017%	8%	2%	2%	9%	2%	2%	014%	010%		Y
0247		033%		037%	9%	1%		3%		5%	9%	2%		Y
0248	4%	021%	6%	017%	1%	6%	1%	5%	1%	3%	011%	016%		
0249	6%	026%	2%	018%	4%	3%		011%	2%	1%	8%	9%		Y

1 Additional majors available in this area
2 ROTC available

†Accredited by a nationally recognized accrediting body other than one of the regional accrediting associations

North Central States

(continued)

IA, KS, MN, MO, ND, NE, SD

OPEN ADMISSIONS *All HS graduates accepted, to limit of capacity*

Sequence Number	School name (upper entry) City (lower entry)	State	Costs: Resident tuition/fees + room/board	Costs: Room/Board (upper entry) Nonresident tuition/fees + room/board (lower entry)	General Information: Highest degree	General Information: Affiliation (upper entry) Religious observance (lower entry)	General Information: Size of community	General Information: Type of community	Admissions: Fall term application deadline (upper entry) Tests desired or required (lower entry)	Admissions: Calendar	Admissions: Fall admission only	Admissions: Early admission	Admissions: Deferred admission	Financial Aid: Fall term application deadline (upper entry) Forms to be filed (lower entry)	Number in 10 who— Undergrads: -have need, receive some aid	Undergrads: -are women	Undergrads: -are graduate students	Freshmen: -live on campus	Freshmen: -are minority students	Freshmen: -are nonresidents	Freshmen: -return as sophomores	Freshmen: -complete degree	Freshmen: -enter graduate study	Freshmen: HS GPA (upper entry) 1st year college GPA (lower entry)	Special Programs: Credit by exam	Special Programs: Student designed majors	Special Programs: Fraternities/sororities
	Enrollment 1,000 to 5,000																										
0250	Washburn U Topeka	KS	5000	2700 6300	P [5]	Pub	M	U	8/01 A/S	E		Y		3/15 FF/FA	7	6	1	1	2	1	6	4	2	3.0 2.3	Y	Y	Y
0251	Minot St U Minot	ND	5200	3600 7000	M [5]	Pub	S		A/S	Q		Y		FF/FA	7	6	1	5	1	1	6	4	1	3.0 2.3	Y	Y	
0252	Missouri Baptist C St Louis	MO	8100	2500	B [5]	Oth OS	V	S	A=S	E		Y	Y	7/01 FF/FA	9	6	0	3	2	1	4	7	3	3.0 2.5	Y	Y	
0253	Southwest Baptist U Bolivar	MO	8200 [3]	2300	M [5]	Oth OS	T		9/10 A/S	4		Y	Y	4/30 FF/FA	9	6	0	7	1	5	7	4	4	2.9 2.9	Y	Y	
0254	Mid-Amer Nazarene C Olathe	KS	8800	3200	M [5]	Oth OS	M	S	9/01 A/S	E		Y		8/01 FF/FA	9	5	0	7	1	6	6	4	2	3.0 3.1	Y		
	Enrollment 5,000 to 15,000																										
0255	ND Main Cam,U of Grand Forks	ND	4300	2300 7400	D [5]	Pub	M		7/01 A/S	E		Y		3/15 FF/FA	8	5	1	5	1	4	8	5		3.1 2.6	Y	Y	Y
0256	ND St U Main Cam Fargo	ND	4300 [3]	2200 7400	D [5]	Pub	M		A/S	Q		Y	Y	4/15 FF/FA	4	4	1	6	1	4	7	4	1	3.1 2.3	Y	Y	Y
0257	Wichita St U Wichita	KS	4400	2800 7500	D [5]	Pub	L	U		O		Y		3/15 FF/FA	2	5	1	2	2	1	7	3	5	2.9 2.3	Y		Y
	Enrollment over 15,000																										
0258	Kansas,U of Lawrence	KS	4100	2500 7200	D [5]	Pub	M		ACT	E			Y	FFS	2	5	2		1	4	8	5		2.6	Y	Y	Y
0259	Kansas St U Manhattan	KS	4200	2600 7300	D [5]	Pub	S		A/S	S		Y	Y	FF/FA	6	4	1	8	1	1	9	4	3	3.1 2.4	Y		Y
	LIBERAL ADMISSIONS *Some accepted students from lower half of HS class*																										
	Enrollment to 1,000																										
0260	Bellevue C Bellevue	NE	2700	[1]	B [5]	Priv	S		ACT	O		Y		FAF	5	5	0	0	1		5		1		Y		
0261	Gateway C Evangelism Florissant	MO	3800	2300	B	Oth OS	V	S	A=S	S				6/01 Oth	2	5	0	7	1	5	5	1	1				
0262	Minn Bible C Rochester	MN	4200 [23]	1100	B †	Oth OS	M		8/01 A/S	Q		Y	Y	8/30 FFS	5	5	0	9	1	2	7	2	1	2.6	Y		
0263	Martin Luther C New Ulm	MN	5100 [3]	1800	B [5]	Oth OS	S		7/20 ACT	E				FF/FA	7	7	0	9	1	9	8	6	2	3.0 2.8	Y		
0264	Saint Louis Christn Florissant	MO	5300	2100	B †	Oth OS	M	S	8/01 A/S	E		Y		8/01 FF=FA	5	4	0	9	1	6	7	5	2	2.4	Y		
0265	Oak Hills Bible C Bemidji	MN	5600 [3]	2300	B †	Priv OS	S		9/01 ACT	Q		Y		7/31 FFS	6	6	0	9	1	2	6	3	2	2.9 2.7	Y		
0266	Kansas City C Bible Overland Park	KS	5800 [3]	3200	B †	Oth OS	V	S	7/29 A=S	S		Y		Oth		5	0		1						Y	Y	
0267	Calvary Bible C Kansas City	MO	6000 [3]	2600	P †	Oth OS	V	S	A/S	E		Y		7/01 Oth	5	5	0	8	1	8	7	4			Y		
0268	Vennard C University Park	IA	6000 [3]	2100	B †	Oth OS	S		9/07 A/S	O		Y		8/25 FA/FF	9	3	0	8	1	6	7		3	3.0			
0269	Divine Word C Epworth	IA	6100 [3]	1200	B [5]	Cath OS	T		8/01 S/A	E		Y	[7]	8/01 FF/FA	9	0	0	9	9	7	3	3	6	2.9 3.0	Y		
0270	Hannibal-La Grange C Hannibal	MO	6600	2000	B [5]	Oth OS	S		8/25 A/S	E		Y		6/01 FFS	9	6	0	3	1	1		5			Y		
0271	North Central Bible Minneapolis	MN	7600	2900	B [5]	Oth OS	V	U	ACT	E			Y	8/15 FFS	8	5	0	8	1	7					Y		
0272	Barclay C Haviland	KS	7900 [3]	2500	B †	Oth OS	T		8/25 A/S	E		Y		FF/FA	9	5	0	9	1	6	8	4	1	2.8 3.1	Y		
0273	Presentation C Aberdeen	SD	7900	2400	B [5]	Cath OS	S		ACT	E				3/01 FF/FA	9	8	0	6	2	1	6			2.9 2.8	Y		
0274	Mount Marty C Yankton	SD	8800	2600	M [5]	Cath S	S		8/15 A=S	4		Y		3/01 FF=FA	9	6	1	8	1	6	8	6	2	3.2 3.0	Y	Y	
0275	Saint Mary of Plains Dodge City	KS	8800 [3]	3000	B [5]	Cath OS	S		A/S	E		Y		FF/FA	9	7	0	7	2	5	6	3	1	2.4 2.2	Y		
0276	Central C McPherson	KS	9000 [3]	2900	B [5]	Oth OS	S		A/S	4			Y	FF/FA	9	5	0	9	1	8	6			2.8	Y		

▲ Sequence number—indicates the order of the college in this book only. Do *not* use this number with admissions tests or need analysis services.

[1] No campus room and board facilities
[2] Room only or board only
[3] Most freshmen required to live on campus
[4] City or district residence requirements
[5] Accredited by a regional accrediting association or a recognized candidate for accreditation
[6] All female freshman class
[7] All male freshman class

MAJORS AVAILABLE AND PERCENT OF STUDENTS STUDYING IN EACH AREA

Sequence Number	Agri.	Business	Comm.	Education	Engineering	Fine/App. Arts	Lang.	Health	Home Ec.	Humanities	Math-Sciences	Social Sciences	GS	ROTC Air Force	ROTC Army	ROTC Navy
0250		021%	5%	010% [1]	1%	3%	1%	012%	1%	3%	9% [1]	023% [1]		Y	Y	
0251	1%	028% [1]	2%	022% [1]	3%	1%	1%	017% [1]	1%	2%	3% [1]	2%				
0252		030%	5%	020% [1]		1%	1%	012%		2%	012%	011%			Y	
0253		030% [1]	5%	019% [1]	1%	8%	1%	3%	2%	019%	4%	7%			Y	
0254	4% [1]	023%	2%	020%				011%		5%	4%					
0255		019% [1]	3%	8% [1]	7% [1]	2%	1%	013% [1]	1%	1%	6% [1]	010% [1]			Y	
0256	8% [1]	013% [1]	2%	2% [1]	024% [1]	7% [1]	1%	9% [1]	7%	2%	010% [1]	7% [1]		Y	Y	
0257		020% [1]	3%	9% [1]	9% [1]	4% [1]	1%	8% [1]		1%	7% [1]	010% [1]			Y	
0258		016%	016%	9% [1]	9% [1]	011% [1]	2%	6% [1]		3% [1]	010% [1]	017% [1]		Y	Y	Y
0259	010% [1]	015% [1]	3%	7% [1]	013% [1]	8% [1]	1%	010% [1]	6%	3% [1]	8% [1]	5% [1]		Y	Y	
0260		069%		2%		6%	1%			2%	3%	017%		Y	Y	
0261						8%				027%						
0262			1%	1%		1%	1%			095%		1%				
0263				100%												
0264		1%								099%						
0265										099%						
0266				020% [1]			1%			050%		1%				
0267			4%	036%		2%	1%			040%						
0268		1% [1]		1% [1]		1%	1%	1%		093%		1%				
0269										022%	010%	024%				
0270		022%	3%	023% [1]	1%	1%	1%	8%		8%	010% [1]	2%				
0271			3%	010% [1]		5%				076%		6%				
0272		020%		020%						060%						
0273		023%		014%				058%			1%	4%				
0274		021%	1%	020% [1]		1%	1%	030% [1]	8%	2%	4%	2%			Y	
0275		015%	1%	022% [1]		2%	1%	031% [1]		3%	5% [1]	8%				
0276	3%	025%	1%	3%	1%	2%		5%	5%	026%	3%	2%				

[1] Additional majors available in this area
[2] ROTC available

†Accredited by a nationally recognized accrediting body other than one of the regional accrediting associations

North Central States (continued)

IA, KS, MN, MO, ND, NE, SD

LIBERAL ADMISSIONS *Some accepted students from lower half of HS class*

Sequence Number	School name (upper entry) City (lower entry)	State	Costs: Resident tuition/fees + room/board	Costs: Room/Board (upper entry) Nonresident tuition/fees + room/board (lower entry)	General Information: Highest degree	General Information: Affiliation (upper entry) Religious observance (lower entry)	General Information: Size of community	General Information: Type of community	Admissions: Fall term application deadline (upper entry) Tests desired or required (lower entry)	Admissions: Calendar	Admissions: Fall admission only	Admissions: Early admission	Admissions: Deferred admission	Financial Aid: Fall term application deadline (upper entry) Forms to be filed (lower entry)	Financial Aid: Number in 10 who— -have need, receive some aid	Student Profile: Under-grads -are women	Student Profile: Under-grads -are graduate students	Student Profile: Freshmen -live on campus	Student Profile: Freshmen -are minority students	Student Profile: Freshmen -are nonresidents	Student Profile: Freshmen -return as sophomores	Student Profile: Freshmen -complete degree	Student Profile: Freshmen -enter graduate study	Student Profile: HS GPA (upper entry) 1st year college GPA (lower entry)	Special Programs: Credit by exam	Special Programs: Student designed majors	Special Programs: Fraternities/sororities
	Enrollment to 1,000																										
0277	Huron U Huron	SD	9000	2800	B[5]	Priv	S		9/01 A/S	E		Y		FA/FF	9	6	0	7	2	5	4	2	1	2.6	Y		
0278	Mount St Clare C Clinton	IA	9500	2900	B[5]	Cath S	S		8/15 A/S	E		Y		8/01 FA/FF	8	6	0	5	1	4	7			2.7 2.4	Y		
0279	Saint Paul Bible C St Bonifacius	MN	9700[3]	3300	B[5]	Oth OS	T		A/S	E		Y	Y	FF/FA	9	5	0	9	1	4	8	3	3	2.6	Y		
0280	Sterling C Sterling	KS	9700	3000	B[5]	Pres OS	T		8/15 A/S	4		Y	Y		9	5	0	9	2	6	7	4	2	2.8 2.3	Y	Y	
0281	Graceland C Lamoni	IA	9900[3]	2500	B[5]	Oth O	T		8/15 A=S	4		Y	Y	4/15 FA/FF	6	5	0	7	1	7	7	4	3	3.0 2.8	Y	Y	
0282	Union C Lincoln	NE	10200	2500	B[5]	Oth OS	M	S	ACT	E		Y		6/15 FF=FA		5	0	9	1	8	6	3	2		Y	Y	
0283	Avila C Kansas City	MO	10600[3]	3200	M[5]	Cath S	V	S	A/S	E				7/01 FF/FA	9	9	1	5	1	1	8	6		3.1 2.9	Y		
0284	Iowa Wesleyan C Mount Pleasant	IA	10800[3]	3000	B[5]	Meth OS	T		8/15 A=S	4		Y	Y	8/15 FF=FA	9	6	0	8	1	4	8	4	1		Y	Y	Y
0285	Kansas City Art Inst Kansas City	MO	14400	4200	B[5]	Priv	V	U	A=S	E		Y	Y	FAF	6	5	0	8	1	7	8		5	2.6 2.8	Y		
	Enrollment 1,000 to 5,000																										
0286	Missouri Southern St Joplin	MO	3500[3]	2300 4700	B[5]	Pub	M	S	A/S	E		Y	Y	4/30 FFS	8	6	0	1	1	1	6	6	1	3.0 2.2	Y		Y
0287	Black Hills St U Spearfish	SD	3800[3]	2100 5000	M[5]	Pub	S		A/S	E		Y	Y	9/01 FF/FA	8	6	0	5	2	1	6			2.7 2.3	Y		Y
0288	Southwest St U Marshall	MN	4600	2500 5800	B[5]	Pub	S		A=S	Q		Y	Y	FFS	8	5	0	5	1	2	8			2.9	Y	Y	
0289	DeVry Inst Techn Kansas City	MO	5000	[1]	B[5]	Priv	V	S	A=S	T			Y	FA/FF	7	2	0	0	2	5	5	3			Y		Y
0290	Evangel C Springfield	MO	9100	2900	B[5]	Oth OS	M		8/12 A/S	S		Y		FA/FF	8	5	0	8	1	7	5	6		3.2 2.6	Y		
0291	Friends U Wichita	KS	9300	2500	M[5]	Oth S	L	U	A/S	E		Y		FF/FA	6	5	4	2	2	1	7	3	3	3.1 2.8	Y	Y	Y
0292	Northwestern C St Paul	MN	10900[3]	2600	B[5]	Oth OS	V	S	A/S	Q		Y	Y	FF/FA	8	6	0		1			3	2	3.1	Y		
	Enrollment 5,000 to 15,000																										
0293	Nebraska Omaha,U of Omaha	NE	1500	[1] 3800	M[5]	Pub	L	U	8/01 A/S	E				4/01 FA/FF	4	5	1	0	1	1	5	1	2	2.9 2.6	Y	Y	Y
0294	Nebraska-Kearney,U Kearney	NE	3500[3]	2100 4300	M[5]	Pub	S		8/01 A/S	E		Y		4/01 FF/FA	8	5	1	6	1	1	6			3.1	Y		Y
0295	Central Missouri St Warrensburg	MO	4300[3]	2600 5700	M[5]	Pub	S		ACT	E		Y	Y	FF/FA	6	5	1	9	1	1	6	4	1	3.0 2.5	Y	Y	Y
0296	SE Missouri St U Cape Girardeau	MO	4500[3]	2800 6000	M[5]	Pub	S		ACT	E		Y	Y	3/31 FF/FA	9	6	0	5	1	1	6	5	1	3.0 2.2	Y	Y	Y
	TRADITIONAL ADMISSIONS *Majority of accepted students in top 50% of HS class*																										
	Enrollment to 1,000																										
0297	Bethany C of Mission Bloomington	MN	500[3]	0	B†	Oth OS	M	S	Oth	4				None	0	6	0	9	3	9	8			2.8 2.9	Y		
0298	Harris-Stowe St C St Louis	MO	1500	[1] 2900	B[5]	Pub	V	U	A=S	E		Y	Y	FAF	9	6	0	0	6	1	6		5				
0299	Emmaus Bible C Dubuque	IA	3000[3]	3000	B†	Oth OS	M		A=S	E		Y		8/01 FA/FF	6	5	0	9	1	9		1	4	2.8 2.5	Y		
0300	Dakota St U Madison	SD	3800[3]	2000	B[5]	Pub	T		A/S	E		Y	Y	FF=FA	8	6	0	8	1	1	7	6	1	2.8 2.4	Y		
0301	Clarkson C Nursing Omaha	NE	5600[2]	1500	M[5]	Oth	V	U	A/S	O		Y	Y	5/30 FA/FF	9	9	0	1	1	2	9	7	1	2.8 2.5	Y		
0302	Central Bible C Springfield	MO	5700	2600	B†	Oth OS	L	U	8/15 ACT	S				5/01 FA/FF	6	4	0	8	1	7	7	6	2	2.5 2.4	Y		
0303	Grace C of Bible Omaha	NE	6100[3]	2400	B†	Oth OS	L	U	ACT	E				7/15 FF=FA	7	4	0	6	1	0	8	4			Y		

▲ Sequence number—indicates the order of the college in this book only. Do *not* use this number with admissions tests or need analysis services.

[1] No campus room and board facilities
[2] Room only or board only
[3] Most freshmen required to live on campus
[4] City or district residence requirements
[5] Accredited by a regional accrediting association or a recognized candidate for accreditation
[6] All female freshman class
[7] All male freshman class

MAJORS AVAILABLE AND PERCENT OF STUDENTS STUDYING IN EACH AREA

Columns: **Agri.** — Agriculture, general; Agronomy (crops & mgmt); Animal Science (husbandry); Fish, Wildlife Mgmt; Forestry. **Business** — Business/Commerce, general; Accounting; Banking/Finance; Business Economics; Business Mgmt/Admin; Marketing/Purchasing; Secretarial Studies. **Comm.** — Communications, general; Journalism; Radio/TV (broadcasting); Advertising. **Education** — Art Education; Distributive Education; Elementary Education; English Education; Mathematics Education; Music Education; Physical Education; Science Education; Secondary Education; Social Science Education; Special Education; Speech Education. **Engineering** — Engineering, general; Chemical; Civil; Electrical/Electronics/Comm; Industrial/Management; Mechanical; Architecture. **Fine/App. Arts** — Fine/Applied Arts, general; Art (Paint, draw, sculpt); Art History/Appreciation; Dance; Dramatic Arts (theater arts); Music (liberal arts); Music (perform, compos, theory). **Lang.** — French; German; Italian; Latin; Spanish; Russian. **Health** — Predentistry; Premedicine; Medical/Lab Technology; Nursing (registered nurse); Occupational Therapy; Preoptometry; Pharmacy; Physical Therapy; Preveterinary Medicine. **Home Ec.** — Home Economics, general; Clothing and Textiles; Consumer Ec/Home Mgmt; Family Relations/Child Devel; Food and Nutrition/Dietetics; Institution Mgmt. **Humanities** — Humanities, general; Creative Writing; English, general; Literature, English; Philosophy; Religion; Speech/Forensic Science. **Math-Sciences** — Mathematics, general; Computer/Info Sciences; Biological Sciences, general; Biology; Botany; Zoology; Physical Sciences, general; Chemistry; Physics. **Social Sciences** — Crim Just/Law Enforce; Social Work; Social Sciences, general; Anthropology; Area Studies (Amer., African, etc.); Economics; Geography; History; Prelaw; Political Science; Psychology; Sociology. **GS** — General Studies. **ROTC** — Air Force; Army; Navy.

Sequence Number	Agri.	Business	Comm.	Education	Engineering	Fine/App. Arts	Lang.	Health	Home Ec.	Humanities	Math-Sciences	Social Sciences	GS	ROTC
0277		33%[1]	3%	19%[1]				14%			2%	21%[1]		
0278		56%[1]		15%		1%	1%	5%		2%	3%	1%		
0279		10%	1%	36%[1]		1%			3%	31%	1%	4%		
0280		20%	1%	22%[1]		4%	1%	1%	3%	7%	13%[1]	9%		
0281		19%		11%[1]	2%	9%	1%	11%[1]		5%	14%[1]	9%[1]		
0282		24%[1]	6%	15%[1]	2%	3%	1%	20%		6%	11%[1]	9%		
0283		28%	1%	11%		6%		26%[1]		5%	13%[1]	10%[1]		Y
0284		35%	5%	21%[1]		3%		4%		2%	13%	7%		
0285						100%[1]								
0286		25%	2%	15%[1]	1%	1%[1]	1%	4%[1]		1%	11%[1]	9%		Y
0287	1%	34%[1]	3%	17%[1]	1%	4%	1%	1%		4%	8%[1]	14%[1]		Y
0288	1%[1]	22%[1]	3%	14%[1]	4%	1%	1%	2%		1%	4%[1]	7%		
0289		13%	21%		44%						22%[1]			
0290		23%[1]	8%	16%[1]		1%[1]	1%	5%		2%	3%	2%[1]		Y
0291		45%	2%	18%[1]		6%		3%[1]		3%	8%	7%[1]		
0292		20%[1]	11%	30%[1]		9%				12%	4%[1]	14%		Y
0293		28%[1]	3%	10%[1]	7%[1]	2%[1]	1%	1%[1]	2%	2%	8%[1]	7%[1]		YY
0294	1%[1]	30%[1]	2%	27%[1]		3%[1]	1%	7%[1]	3%	1%	5%[1]	5%[1]		Y
0295	1%[1]	17%[1]	4%	15%[1]	10%	2%[1]		3%[1]	1%	1%	3%[1]	11%[1]		Y
0296	1%[1]	35%[1]	6%	20%[1]	1%	2%[1]	1%	8%[1]	4%	2%[1]	3%[1]	2%[1]		YY
0297										100%				
0298		1%		92%[1]		1%	1%			1%	3%	1%		YY
0299							1%			99%				
0300		22%		12%[1]		1%		8%[1]		3%	12%[1]			Y
0301								100%						Y
0302										100%				
0303			4%	12%		1%				83%				

[1] Additional majors available in this area
[2] ROTC available

†Accredited by a nationally recognized accrediting body other than one of the regional accrediting associations

North Central States
(continued)

IA, KS, MN, MO, ND, NE, SD

TRADITIONAL ADMISSIONS *Majority of accepted students in top 50% of HS class*

Sequence Number	Enrollment to 1,000 School name (upper entry) City (lower entry)	State	Costs: Resident tuition/fees + room/board	Costs: Room/Board (upper entry) Nonresident tuition/fees + room/board (lower entry)	General Information: Highest degree	General Information: Affiliation (upper entry) Religious observance (lower entry)	General Information: Size of community	General Information: Type of community	Admissions: Fall term application deadline (upper entry) Tests desired or required (lower entry)	Admissions: Calendar	Admissions: Fall admission only	Admissions: Early admission	Admissions: Deferred admission	Financial Aid: Fall term application deadline (upper entry) Forms to be filed (lower entry)	Financial Aid: Number in 10 who— -have need, receive some aid	Student Profile: Number in 10 who— Under-grads: -are women	Under-grads: -are graduate students	Freshmen: -live on campus	Freshmen: -are minority students	Freshmen: -are nonresidents	Freshmen: -return as sophomores	Freshmen: -complete degree	Freshmen: -enter graduate study	HS GPA (upper entry) 1st year college GPA (lower entry)	Special Programs: Credit by exam	Special Programs: Student designed majors	Special Programs: Fraternities/sororities
0304	Assoc Arts,C of St Paul	MN	6700	[1]	B †	Priv	V	U	7/31 A=S	E			Y	FF/FA	8	5	0		1		7	5	1	2.8 2.8	Y		
0305	Faith Baptist Bible Ankeny	IA	6800	2800	P †	Bapt OS	S		8/01 A/S	E			Y	3/01 FF/FA	6	6	1	9	1	6	7	4	1		Y		
0306	Conception Seminary Conception	MO	7000[3]	2700	B [5]	Cath OS	T		ACT	E			Y[7]	3/01 FFS	9	0	0	9	1	7	7	4	7	3.2 3.0	Y		
0307	Deaconess C Nursing St Louis	MO	7100	2100	B [5]	UCC	V	U	8/01 A/S	E				6/01 FF/FA	8	9	0	3	2	2	7	5	2	3.0 2.9	Y		
0308	Southwestern C Winfield	KS	7300[3]	2700	M [5]	Meth O	S		A/S	4		Y	Y	FF/FA	8	5	0	9	1	3	6	6	2	3.1 3.1	Y	Y	Y
0309	Barnes C of Nsg St Louis	MO	7700	1600	B †	Priv	V	U	A/S	S		Y		8/15 FF/FA	6	9	0	7	1	2	9	7		3.0	Y		
0310	Tarkio C Tarkio	MO	8000	2800	B [5]	Pres OS	T		9/01 A=S	S				FF=FA	7	4	0	9	3	6	7	4	2	2.9 2.5	Y		Y
0311	Concordia C Seward	NE	8600[3]	2600	M [5]	Oth OS	T		8/01 A/S	S		Y		FA/FF	7	6	1	9	1	6	7		1	3.1	Y	Y	
0312	Culver-Stockton C Canton	MO	8600[3]	2300	B [5]	Oth OS	T		A=S	S		Y		4/01 FA/FF	7	6	0	9	1	5	7	4	1	3.2 2.4	Y		Y
0313	Dakota Wesleyan U Mitchell	SD	8800[3]	2500	M [5]	Meth OS	S		8/01 A/S	S		Y		4/01 FF/FA	9	6	0	5	1	1	7	5		2.8 2.7	Y	Y	
0314	Kansas Wesleyan U Salina	KS	9100[3]	2900	B [5]	Meth OS	S		8/01 A/S	4		Y		4/15 FF/FA	9	6	0	7	2	4	4	6	1	2.8 2.5	Y	Y	Y
0315	Park C Parkville	MO	9200	3000	M [5]	Oth	T		8/25 A/S	E		Y	Y	4/01 FF/FA	8	5	1	7	3	5	5	6	3	2.4 2.4	Y	Y	
0316	Tabor C Hillsboro	KS	9300[3]	2800	B [5]	Oth OS	T		8/01 A/S	4		Y		6/30 FF/FA	7	5	0	9	1	5	6	4	1	3.1 2.4	Y	Y	
0317	Bethel C North Newton	KS	9600	2800	B [5]	Oth OS	S		8/15 A/S	4		Y	Y	5/01 FF/FA	6	5	0	9	1	4	6	4	3	3.4 2.9	Y	Y	
0318	Dana C Blair	NE	9600	2600	B [5]	Luth O	T		A/S	4		Y	Y	FA/FF	9	5	0	9	1	4	6	5	3	3.0 2.8	Y		
0319	Saint Louis C Pharm St Louis	MO	9600	3700	P [5]	Priv	V	U	8/01 A/S	E		Y		5/30 FAF	4	6	0	6	1	6	8	6	1	3.4 2.4	Y		Y
0320	Jamestown C Jamestown	ND	9700[3]	3000	B [5]	Pres OS	S		A/S	S		Y	Y	FF/FA	8	5	0	9	1	6	6	5	3	3.2	Y	Y	
0321	Kansas Newman C Wichita	KS	9700[3]	3200	B [5]	Cath S	L	U	A/S	S		Y	Y	FF/FA	9	6	0	1	1	2	6	4	3	3.0 2.8	Y		
0322	Maharishi Intern U Fairfield	IA	9700[3]	2500	D [5]	Priv	T			S				3/15	9	5	4	9	6	7	7	6	1		Y		
0323	Bethany C Lindsborg	KS	9800	3300	B [5]	Luth S	T		A/S	4		Y	Y	FF/FA	7	5	0	9	1	5	6	5	1		Y	Y	Y
0324	Ottawa U Ottawa	KS	9800	3300	B [5]	Bapt S	S		A=S	E		Y	Y	FF/FA	9	5	0	9	2	4	6	4	4	2.8 2.4	Y	Y	
0325	Saint Mary C Leavenworth	KS	9800[3]	3300	B [5]	Cath OS	S		A/S	E		Y	Y	8/01 FF/FA	8	5	0	6	4	4	9	4	1	3.2 2.8	Y	Y	
0326	Columbia C Columbia	MO	9900[3]	3100	B [5]	Oth	M		A/S	E		Y	Y	FF/FA	7	5	0	8	1	4	6	2		2.7	Y	Y	
0327	Central Methodist C Fayette	MO	10000[3]	3300	B [5]	Meth OS	T		A/S	4		Y	Y	4/01 FF/FA	8	5	0	9	1	1	6	4	3	3.0 2.5	Y	Y	Y
0328	Saint Mary,C of Omaha	NE	10300[3]	3000	B [5]	Cath OS	L	S	A/S	E		Y	Y	FA/FF	9	9	0	5	1	4	7	4	1	 2.8	Y		
0329	McPherson C McPherson	KS	10500[3]	3300	B [5]	Oth	S		8/15 A/S	4		Y		8/15 FF/FA	9	4	0	9	1	6	7			3.1 2.7	Y	Y	
0330	Sioux Falls C Sioux Falls	SD	10500[3]	3000	M [5]	Bapt OS	M	S	A/S	4				FF/FA	9	6	0	9	1	3	5	4	1	2.9 2.6	Y	Y	
0331	Fontbonne C St Louis	MO	10600	3500	M [5]	Cath	V	S	8/01 A/S	S		Y	Y	4/01 FA/FF	8	6	1	2	3	2	7	5	3		Y	Y	
0332	Midland Lutheran C Fremont	NE	10700[3]	2600	B [5]	Luth OS	S		9/01 ACT	4		Y		5/01 FF=FA	9	5	0	6	1	3	9	5	2	3.1 2.9	Y	Y	Y
0333	Teikyo Marycrest U Davenport	IA	10700	2900	M [5]	Priv	L	U	A/S	E		Y	Y	4/15 FF/FA	9	7	1	8	1	4	7	5	1	2.9 2.8	Y	Y	
0334	Doane C Crete	NE	10900[3]	2600	B [5]	UCC	T		A=S	4		Y	Y	FA/FF	9	5	0	9	1	2	7	5	2		Y	Y	Y

▲ Sequence number—indicates the order of the college in this book only. Do *not* use this number with admissions tests or need analysis services.

[1] No campus room and board facilities
[2] Room only or board only
[3] Most freshmen required to live on campus
[4] City or district residence requirements
[5] Accredited by a regional accrediting association or a recognized candidate for accreditation
[6] All female freshman class
[7] All male freshman class

MAJORS AVAILABLE AND PERCENT OF STUDENTS STUDYING IN EACH AREA

Agri.: Agriculture, general; Agronomy (crops & mgmt); Animal Science (husbandry); Fish, Wildlife Mgmt; Forestry
Business: Business/Commerce, general; Accounting; Banking/Finance; Business Economics; Business Mgmt/Admin; Marketing/Purchasing; Secretarial Studies
Comm.: Communications, general; Journalism; Radio/TV (broadcasting); Advertising
Education: Art Education; Distributive Education; Elementary Education; English Education; Mathematics Education; Music Education; Physical Education; Science Education; Secondary Education; Social Science Education; Special Education; Speech Education
Engineering: Engineering, general; Chemical; Civil; Electrical/Electronics/Comm; Industrial/Management; Mechanical
Fine/App. Arts: Architecture; Fine/Applied Arts, general; Art (Paint, draw, sculpt); Art History/Appreciation; Dance; Dramatic Arts (theater arts); Music (liberal arts); Music (perform, compos, theory)
Lang.: French; German; Italian; Latin; Spanish; Russian
Health: Predentistry; Premedicine; Medical/Lab Technology; Nursing (registered nurse); Occupational Therapy; Preoptometry; Prepharmacy; Physical Therapy; Preveterinary Medicine
Home Ec.: Home Economics, general; Clothing and Textiles; Consumer Ec/Home Mgmt; Family Relations/Child Devel; Food and Nutrition/Dietetics; Institution Mgmt
Humanities: Humanities, general; Creative Writing; English, general; Literature, English; Philosophy; Religion; Speech/Forensic Science
Math-Sciences: Mathematics, general; Computer/Info Sciences; Biological Sciences, general; Biology; Botany; Zoology; Physical Sciences, general; Chemistry; Physics
Social Sciences: Crim Just/Law Enforce; Social Work; Social Sciences, general; Anthropology; Area Studies (Amer., African, etc.); Economics; Geography; History; Prelaw; Political Science; Psychology; Sociology
GS: General Studies
ROTC: Air Force; Army; Navy

Sequence Number	Agri.	Business	Comm.	Education	Engineering	Fine/App. Arts	Lang.	Health	Home Ec.	Humanities	Math-Sciences	Social Sciences	GS	ROTC
0304						100% [1]								
0305		8%		022%		5%				056%				
0306										074%		026%		
0307			1%	1%				092%		2%	2%	1%		
0308	1%	016%	2%	019% [1]	1%	2%	1%	013%		2%	3% [1]	2%		
0309								100%						
0310		040%	3%		1%	015%		3%		9%	015%	6%		
0311		012%	2%	075% [1]		1% [1]		1% [1]		2%	3%	4%		YYY
0312		031%	1%	026% [1]		5%		014%		5%	3%	4%		
0313	1%	030%	3%	014% [1]	1%	1%	1%	029% [1]		2%	3%	2% [1]		
0314		019%	3%	011% [1]	1%	2%	1%	018% [1]		2%	010%	015%		
0315		035%	010%	7%	1%	2%	1%	2% [1]		6%	019% [1]	013% [1]		Y
0316	1%	012%	1%	8% [1]	1%	2%		010% [1]		7%	6% [1]	012% [1]		
0317		018%	2%	012% [1]		5%	2%	019%	2%	3%	013% [1]	018%		
0318		024%	015%	022% [1]		5% [1]	5%	4% [1]		6%	9% [1]	5%		Y
0319								100%						YY
0320		015%		7%	2%	3%		018%		5%	014% [1]	014%		
0321		055%	2%	013% [1]				012% [1]		7%	7% [1]	1%		
0322		023%		1%	4%	010%	1%	1%		010%	015% [1]	8%		
0323		013%		021%		3%				2%	7% [1]	9% [1]		
0324		029%	5%	018% [1]	2%	3%		5%		3%	018% [1]	012%		
0325		029%		015%		010%	1%	2%		015%	017%	011% [1]		
0326		037% [1]	1%	6% [1]		1%	1%		9%	2%	3%	2% [1]		YYY
0327		019%	4%	018% [1]	1%	6%	1%	024%		8% [1]	6% [1]	8%		Y
0328		011%	1%	011% [1]		5%		033% [1]		2%	015% [1]	018% [1]		YY
0329	2%	022%	2%	012% [1]		5% [1]	1%	3%	1%	5%	9%	9%		
0330		035% [1]	2%	025%		2%	1%	1% [1]		8%	7% [1]	016%		
0331		026%	7%	015% [1]		1%	2%	2% [1]	017%	2%	3% [1]	2% [1]		Y
0332	1%	025%	4%	020% [1]	1%	1%	1%	024% [1]		2%	012% [1]	3%		Y
0333		015%	4%	6% [1]		6%		010%	1%	4%	8% [1]	5% [1]		
0334		034%	4%	9% [1]		4%				2%	019%	027% [1]		YY

[1] Additional majors available in this area
[2] ROTC available

†Accredited by a nationally recognized accrediting body other than one of the regional accrediting associations

North Central States
(continued)

IA, KS, MN, MO, ND, NE, SD

TRADITIONAL ADMISSIONS *Majority of accepted students in top 50% of HS class*

Sequence Number	School name (upper entry) City (lower entry)	State	Costs		General Information				Admissions					Financial Aid		Student Profile: Number in 10 who—									Special Programs		
			Resident tuition/fees + room/board	Room/Board (upper entry) Nonresident tuition/fees + room/board (lower entry)	Highest degree	Affiliation (upper entry) Religious observance (lower entry)	Size of community	Type of community	Fall term application deadline (upper entry) Tests desired or required (lower entry)	Calendar	Fall admission only	Early admission	Deferred admission	Fall term application deadline (upper entry) Forms to be filed (lower entry)	-have need, receive some aid	Under-grads: -are women	Under-grads: -are graduate students	Freshmen: -live on campus	Freshmen: -are minority students	Freshmen: -are nonresidents	Freshmen: -return as sophomores	Freshmen: -complete degree	Freshmen: -enter graduate study	HS GPA (upper entry) 1st year college GPA (lower entry)	Credit by exam	Student designed majors	Fraternities/sororities
	Enrollment to 1,000																										
0335	Mount Mercy C Cedar Rapids	IA	10900 [3]	3100	B [5]	Cath OS	M	U	A=S	4		Y	Y	8/15 FF=FA	8	7	0	7	1	1	7	5	1	3.1 2.7	Y	Y	
0336	William Penn C Oskaloosa	IA	10900 [3]	2500	B [5]	Oth OS	S		8/20 A=S	E		Y	Y	8/20 FA/FF	9	5	0	8	1	2	7	4	2	2.7 2.3	Y		Y
0337	Hastings C Hastings	NE	11100 [3]	3000	M [5]	Pres	S		7/15 A=S	4		Y	Y	5/01 FF=FA	9	5	0	8	1	2	8	6	3	3.2 2.8	Y	Y	Y
0338	Benedictine C Atchison	KS	11200 [3]	3400	B [5]	Cath S	S		8/01 A/S	E		Y	Y	8/15 FF/FA	8	5	0	9	1	6	7	5	2	2.9 2.6	Y	Y	
0339	Upper Iowa U Fayette	IA	11400 [3]	2900	B [5]	Priv	T		A=S	O		Y	Y	3/01 FF/FA	9	4	0	9	1	4	7	6	1	2.8 2.7	Y		Y
0340	Mpls C Art & Design Minneapolis	MN	11600 [2]	1900	B [5]	Priv	V	U	A=S	S			Y	FF/FA	9	5	0	5	1	4	8	5	1		Y	Y	
0341	William Woods C Fulton	MO	11700 [3]	3600	B [5]	Oth	S		A=S	S		Y	Y [6]	FA/FF	5	9	0	9	1	5	8		1	3.1 2.6	Y		Y
0342	Clarke C Dubuque	IA	12000 [3]	3000	M [5]	Cath OS	M		A=S	E		Y	Y	8/01 FF=FA	7	7	0	7	1	7	9	6	1	3.0 3.0	Y	Y	
0343	Research C Nursing Kansas City	MO	12000	3600	B †	Cath S	V	U	6/30 A=S	S		Y	Y	FA/FF	9	9	0	6	1	2	8	6		3.2 2.5	Y		Y
0344	Teikyo Westmar U Lemars	IA	12000	3300	B [5]	Meth OS	T		A/S	4		Y	Y	FF=FA	9	4	0	8	1	2	5	4	1	2.6 2.4	Y	Y	
0345	Dubuque,U of Dubuque	IA	12200	3100	M [5]	Pres	M	S	8/01 A/S	E		Y	Y	8/01 Oth	8	5	2	8	3	6	6	5	2		Y	Y	Y
0346	Morningside C Sioux City	IA	12200 [3]	3000	M [5]	Meth S	M	S	A=S	E		Y	Y	FF/FA	9	6	0	7	1	2	7	6	2		Y	Y	Y
	Enrollment 1,000 to 5,000																										
0347	Northern St U Aberdeen	SD	3500 [3]	1900 4800	M [5]	Pub	S		8/15 A/S	E		Y	Y	3/01 FF=FA	7	6	1	7	1	1	6	3	3	2.9 2.2	Y		
0348	Bemidji St U Bemidji	MN	4200	2400 5500	M [5]	Pub	S		8/15 ACT	Q		Y	Y	4/20 FFS	7	5	0	8	1	1	7	4	1	2.5	Y		Y
0349	Mary,U of Bismarck	ND	7600 [3]	2400	M [5]	Cath O	S		A=S	E		Y	Y	7/01 FF/FA	8	6	0	7	1	3	7	3	1	3.3	Y	Y	
0350	Dordt C Sioux Center	IA	9200 [3]	2100	B [5]	Oth O	T		8/30 ACT	E				4/15 FA/FF	8	5	0	9	1	6	8	6	1	3.0 3.0	Y		
0351	Webster U St Louis	MO	10200 [3]	3400	D [5]	Priv	V	S	8/01 A=S	E		Y	Y	4/01 FA/FF	7	7	1	5	1	3	8	4	2		Y	Y	
0352	Baker U Baldwin City	KS	10500 [3]	3400	M [5]	Meth O	T		A=S	4		Y	Y	3/01 FF/FA	9	5	2	9	1	4	7	4	3	2.9 2.7	Y		Y
0353	Northwestern C Orange City	IA	10800	2800	M [5]	Oth OS	T		8/15 A/S	E				7/15 FF/FA	9	6	1	9	1	3	7	5	2	3.1 2.7	Y	Y	
0354	Briar Cliff C Sioux City	IA	11000 [3]	3000	B [5]	Cath S	M	S	A/S	O		Y	Y	FF/FA	9	7	0	8	1	3	7	4	1	3.0 2.8	Y	Y	
0355	Concordia C St Paul St Paul	MN	11200	2900	M [5]	Oth OS	V	U	8/15 A/S	Q				6/01 FF=FA	9	6	0	8	1	3	6	5	3	3.0 2.7	Y	Y	
0356	Saint Mary's C Winona	MN	11600 [3]	3000	M [5]	Cath OS	S		A/S	E		Y	Y	FF/FA	7	5	1	9	1	6	9	6	5	2.7 2.6	Y	Y	Y
0357	Saint Ambrose U Davenport	IA	11900 [3]	3400	M [5]	Cath S	L	U	A/S	E		Y	Y	6/01 FFS	8	8	1	8	1	3	7	7	2	3.0 2.8	Y	Y	
0358	Loras C Dubuque	IA	12300 [3]	3200	M [5]	Cath O	M	S	8/15 A/S	E		Y	Y	4/15 FF/FA	7	5	1	8	1	4	9	6	4	2.7 2.4	Y	Y	Y
0359	Lindenwood C St Charles	MO	12600	4400	D [5]	Pres	M	S	9/01 A=S	E			Y	9/01 FF/FA	9	7	1	5	2	3	8	6	3	3.0 2.9	Y	Y	Y
0360	Bethel C St Paul	MN	12700 [3]	3400	B [5]	Bapt OS	V	S	A/S	4			Y	FF/FA	9	5	0	9	1						Y	Y	
0361	Saint Catherine,C of St Paul	MN	12700	3400	M [5]	Cath S	L	U	8/15 A=S	4			Y [6]	4/01 FF/FA	7	9	1	8	1	2	8	5	3		Y	Y	
0362	Buena Vista C Storm Lake	IA	12900 [3]	2900	B [5]	Pres	S		A/S	4		Y	Y	FF/FA	9	5	0	9	1	2	7	5	2	3.3 2.9	Y	Y	Y
0363	Missouri Valley C Marshall	MO	12900	4700	B [5]	Pres	S		A=S	4		Y	Y	FA/FF	9	4	0	9	3	4	8	6	2	2.9	Y	Y	Y
0364	Saint Scholastica,C Duluth	MN	13200	3300	M [5]	Cath	M	S	A/S	Q		Y	Y	FF/FA	9	7	1	6	1	1	8	6	1	3.2 3.2	Y	Y	
Sequence Number	School name (upper entry) City (lower entry)	State	Costs		General Information				Admissions					Financial Aid		Student Profile									Programs		

▲ Sequence number—indicates the order of the college in this book only. Do *not* use this number with admissions tests or need analysis services.

[1] No campus room and board facilities
[2] Room only or board only
[3] Most freshmen required to live on campus
[4] City or district residence requirements
[5] Accredited by a regional accrediting association or a recognized candidate for accreditation
[6] All female freshman class
[7] All male freshman class

MAJORS AVAILABLE AND PERCENT OF STUDENTS STUDYING IN EACH AREA

Majors by area:

- **Agri.**: Agriculture, general; Agronomy (crops & mgmt); Animal Science (husbandry); Fish, Wildlife Mgmt; Forestry
- **Business**: Business/Commerce, general; Accounting; Banking/Finance; Business Economics; Business Mgmt/Admin; Marketing/Purchasing; Secretarial Studies
- **Comm.**: Communications, general; Journalism; Radio/TV (broadcasting); Advertising
- **Education**: Art Education; Distributive Education; Elementary Education; English Education; Mathematics Education; Music Education; Physical Education; Science Education; Secondary Education; Social Science Education; Special Education; Speech Education
- **Engineering**: Engineering, general; Chemical; Civil; Electrical/Electronics/Comm; Industrial/Management; Mechanical; Architecture
- **Fine/App. Arts**: Fine/Applied Arts, general; Art (Paint, draw, sculpt); Art History/Appreciation; Dance; Dramatic Arts (theater arts); Music (liberal arts); Music (perform, compos, theory)
- **Lang.**: French; German; Italian; Latin; Spanish; Russian
- **Health**: Predentistry; Premedicine; Medical/Lab Technology; Nursing (registered nurse); Occupational Therapy; Preoptometry; Pharmacy; Prepharmacy; Physical Therapy; Preveterinary Medicine
- **Home Ec.**: Home Economics, general; Clothing and Textiles; Consumer Ec/Home Mgmt; Family Relations/Child Devel; Food and Nutrition/Dietetics; Institution Mgmt
- **Humanities**: Humanities, general; Creative Writing; English, general; Literature, English; Philosophy; Religion; Speech/Forensic Science
- **Math-Sciences**: Mathematics, general; Computer/Info Sciences; Biological Sciences, general; Biology; Botany; Zoology; Physical Sciences, general; Chemistry; Physics
- **Social Sciences**: Crim Just/Law Enforce; Social Work; Social Sciences, general; Anthropology; Area Studies (Amer., African, etc.); Economics; Geography; History; Prelaw; Political Science; Psychology; Sociology
- **GS**: General Studies
- **ROTC**: Air Force; Army; Navy

Sequence Number	Agri.	Business	Comm.	Education	Engineering	Fine/App. Arts	Lang.	Health	Home Ec.	Humanities	Math-Sciences	Social Sciences	GS	ROTC
0335		41%	4%	15%		3%		10%			14%	13%		
0336		20%	1%	19% [1]	5%	2% [1]	1%	1% [1]	2%	2%	10% [1]	3%		
0337		20%	10%	20% [1]	3%	8%	1%	9%		2%	3%	6%		
0338		19% [1]	2%	18% [1]	2%	2%	4%	8%	2%	2% [1]	3% [1]	2%		Y
0339	1%	25%		20% [1]	1%	4%	1%	6%		3%	31%	7% [1]		
0340						100% [1]								
0341	15% [1]	24%	6%	9% [1]		15% [1]	2%		4%	2%	4% [1]	10% [1]		Y
0342		17%	6%	14% [1]		12%	2%	4% [1]		3%	26% [1]	16%		
0343								100%						Y
0344		35%	1%	19% [1]		5%	1%	[1]		2%	12%	24% [1]		
0345		21%	1%	13% [1]		2%		15%		5%	13% [1]	15% [1]		
0346	[1]	21% [1]	6%	24% [1]	1%	8% [1]		4% [1]		2%	10%	19% [1]		
0347		40% [1]	1%	30% [1]	1%	2% [1]	1%	3%		2%	3%	2%		Y
0348		25% [1]	4%	20% [1]	2%	2% [1]	1%	1% [1]	1%	5%	17% [1]	12% [1]		
0349		29%	4%	20% [1]		1%	1%	20% [1]		3%	12%	8%		
0350	10% [1]	27%	4%	19% [1]	2% [1]	3%	1%	2%		5% [1]	11% [1]	5%		
0351		34% [1]	13%	5% [1]		14% [1]	1%	1% [1]		4% [1]	7% [1]	10%		
0352		24%	5%	8% [1]	1%	5%	1%	5%	2%	6%	10%	7%		
0353	1%	26%	3%	23%	1%	3%	1%	7%		5%	10%	12% [1]		
0354		25%	6%	10% [1]	1%	5%		14% [1]		5%	10%	21% [1]		
0355		25%	4%	36% [1]	1%	2%	4%	4%		15%	6%	3%		Y
0356		11%	3%	4%		5%	3%	1% [1]		7%	22% [1]	14%		
0357	[1]	33%	22%	6% [1]	1%	4%	1%	2% [1]		7%	5% [1]	8%		
0358		30%	7%	5% [1]	5%	2%	1%	10% [1]		2% [1]	3% [1]	2%		
0359		37%	11%	10% [1]	1%	1%	1%	5%		6%	17% [1]	5%		
0360		18%	5%	12% [1]	1%	7%	1%	8%	1%	10%	15%	19% [1]		YYY
0361		14%	4%	13% [1]		4%	3%	22% [1]	4%	9%	6% [1]	16% [1]		Y
0362		39%	11%	14% [1]	1%	1%	1%	4% [1]		2%	10% [1]	2%		
0363	2% [1]	29%	5%	31%		1%	1%	1%		2%	3%	2% [1]		
0364		6%	2%	4% [1]		1%	1%	62%	2%	2%	3%	2%		

[1] Additional majors available in this area
[2] ROTC available

†Accredited by a nationally recognized accrediting body other than one of the regional accrediting associations

4-YEAR COLLEGES

North Central States
(continued)

IA, KS, MN, MO, ND, NE, SD

TRADITIONAL ADMISSIONS *Majority of accepted students in top 50% of HS class*

Sequence Number	School name (upper entry) City (lower entry)	State	Costs: Resident tuition/fees + room/board	Costs: Room/Board (upper entry) Nonresident tuition/fees + room/board (lower entry)	General Information: Highest degree	General Information: Affiliation (upper entry) Religious observance (lower entry)	General Information: Size of community	General Information: Type of community	Admissions: Fall term application deadline (upper entry) Tests desired or required (lower entry)	Admissions: Calendar	Admissions: Fall admission only	Admissions: Early admission	Admissions: Deferred admission	Financial Aid: Fall term application deadline (upper entry) Forms to be filed (lower entry)	Financial Aid: Number in 10 who -have need, receive some aid	Student Profile: Undergrads -are women	Undergrads -are graduate students	Freshmen -live on campus	Freshmen -are minority students	Freshmen -are nonresidents	Freshmen -return as sophomores	Freshmen -complete degree	Freshmen -enter graduate study	HS GPA (upper entry) 1st year college GPA (lower entry)	Special Programs: Credit by exam	Special Programs: Student designed majors	Special Programs: Fraternities/sororities
	Enrollment 1,000 to 5,000																										
0365	Stephens C Columbia	MO	16000 [3]	4500	B [5]	Priv	M		8/15 A=S	E			Y	FA/FF	4	9	0	9	1	8	8	4	2	3.0 2.9	Y	Y	Y
	Enrollment 5,000 to 15,000																										
0366	SD St U Brookings	SD	3600 [3]	1700 5200	D [5]	Pub	S		8/01 ACT	E		Y		5/01 FF=FA	8	4	1	9	1	2	7	5	2	3.1 2.6	Y	Y	Y
0367	Northwest Missouri U Maryville	MO	3900 [3]	2400 5100	M [5]	Pub	S		ACT	E		Y		4/01 FF/FA	8	6	1	9	1	5	6	5	3	2.9 2.8	Y		Y
0368	SD,U of Vermillion	SD	4000 [3]	2100 5500	D [5]	Pub	S		A/S	E		Y		2/15 FF/FA	8	5	2	7	1	2	7	5		3.1	Y	Y	Y
0369	Northern Iowa,U of Cedar Falls	IA	4200	2300 7100	D [5]	Pub	S		A/S	E		Y	Y	3/01 FF=FA	7	6	1	7	1	1	8	5	1	2.6	Y	Y	Y
0370	Mankato St U Mankato	MN	4400	2400 5600	M [5]	Pub	S		A/S	Q		Y		FFS	6	5	1	5	1	1	7	4	1	2.9 2.6	Y	Y	Y
0371	Moorhead St U Moorhead	MN	4400	2400 5600	M [5]	Pub	M		8/15 A=S	Q		Y	Y	FFS	8	6	1	6	1	4	7	4		2.2	Y	Y	Y
0372	Saint Cloud St U St Cloud	MN	4400	2400 5600	M [5]	Pub	M		8/15	Q		Y	Y	5/15 FFS	9	5	1	6	1	1	7	3	1	2.6	Y	Y	Y
0373	SW Missouri St U Springfield	MO	4600 [3]	2800 6400	M [5]	Pub	M	S	8/01 ACT	E		Y		3/31 FF/FA	5	5	1	7	1	1	7			2.4	Y	Y	Y
0374	Winona St U Winona	MN	4700	2600 6100	M [5]	Pub	S		A/S	Q		Y	Y	FFS	7	6	1	8	1	3	7	5	2	2.9 2.7	Y	Y	Y
0375	Minn Duluth,U of Duluth	MN	5500	3000 8600	M [5]	Pub	M	S	ACT	O			Y	FFS	8	5	1	7	1	1	8	3	2		Y	Y	Y
	Enrollment over 15,000																										
0376	Nebraska Lincoln,U Lincoln	NE	4500 [3]	2600 7300	D [5]	Pub	M	U	A/S	E				FF/FA	5	4	1	6	1	1	7	4		3.2 2.7	Y	Y	Y
0377	Iowa,U of Iowa City	IA	4900	2900 9400	D [5]	Pub	M		5/15 A=S	E		Y	Y	FF/FA	5	5	2	9	1	3	8	5		3.2	Y	Y	Y
0378	Minn Twin Cities,U Minneapolis	MN	5800	3200 9200	D [5]	Pub	V	U	ACT	Q		Y	Y	FFS	6	5	2	6	2	3	8	3		2.7	Y	Y	Y
	SELECTIVE ADMISSIONS *Majority of accepted students in top 25% of HS class*																										
	Enrollment to 1,000																										
0379	Nebraska Meth C Nsg Omaha	NE	6600	2100	B [5]	Meth	V	U	8/01 ACT	S			Y	5/01 FFS	6	9	0	5	1	0	8	9	1	2.9 2.8	Y		
0380	Maryville C St Louis St Louis	MO	10900	3500	M [5]	Priv	V	S	A/S	E		Y	Y	3/01 FA/FF	5	7	0	2	1	1	8	5		3.3 3.0	Y		
0381	Westminster C Fulton	MO	11500 [3]	3300	B [5]	Pres	S		A/S	O			Y	FA/FF	4	4	0	9	1	5	9	7	4	3.6 2.6	Y	Y	Y
0382	Coe C Cedar Rapids	IA	14300 [3]	3900	B [5]	Pres	M	U	A=S	4		Y	Y	3/01 FA/FF	8	5	0	9	1	4	8	6	4	3.3 2.9	Y	Y	Y
	Enrollment 1,000 to 5,000																										
0383	Ozarks,C of the Point Lookout	MO	1700	1600	B [5]	Pres OS	T		A/S	E		Y		FF/FA	9	5	0	3	1	1	8	7	1	3.1 2.5	Y	Y	
0384	SD Sch Mines & Techn Rapid City	SD	4600 [3]	2200 6400	D [5]	Pub	M		A/S	E				5/01 FF=FA	5	3	1	3	2	2	7	4	2	3.3 2.4	Y		Y
0385	Missouri Rolla,U of Rolla	MO	5500 [3]	3100 9000	D [5]	Pub	S		7/01 A/S	E		Y	Y	4/01 FFS	6	2	1	9	1	2	7	5	3	2.5	Y		Y
0386	Nebraska Wesleyan U Lincoln	NE	10500 [3]	2800	B [5]	Meth	M	S	8/22 A=S	E		Y	Y	8/15 FA/FF	9	6	0	8	1	1	8	5		2.9	Y		Y
0387	Drury C Springfield	MO	10700	3200	M [5]	Oth	L	U	8/01 A=S	E		Y		6/15 FF/FA	5	6	1	5	1	1	8	5	2	3.4 2.7	Y	Y	Y
0388	William Jewell C Liberty	MO	11000	2700	B [5]	Bapt OS	V	S	A=S	4		Y		3/15 FF/FA	6	5	0	8	1	3		6	3	3.3 2.9	Y	Y	Y
0389	Concordia C Moorhead Moorhead	MN	11400 [3]	2700	B [5]	Luth OS	M	S	A=S	E		Y	Y	7/01 FF/FA	7	6	0	9	1	4	8	7	4		Y	Y	
0390	Wartburg C Waverly	IA	11600	2900	B [5]	Luth S	T		A=S	O		Y	Y	FA/FF	7	5	0	9	1	3	7	6	2	3.3 2.8	Y	Y	

▲ Sequence number—indicates the order of the college in this book only. Do *not* use this number with admissions tests or need analysis services.

[1] No campus room and board facilities
[2] Room only or board only
[3] Most freshmen required to live on campus
[4] City or district residence requirements
[5] Accredited by a regional accrediting association or a recognized candidate for accreditation
[6] All female freshman class
[7] All male freshman class

MAJORS AVAILABLE AND PERCENT OF STUDENTS STUDYING IN EACH AREA

Sequence Number	Agri.	Business	Comm.	Education	Engineering	Fine/App. Arts	Lang.	Health	Home Ec.	Humanities	Math-Sciences	Social Sciences	GS	ROTC: Air Force	ROTC: Army	ROTC: Navy
0365	5%	016%	011%	6% [1]	1%	019% [1]	1%	9%	013%	3%	5%	3%		Y	Y	Y
0366	014% [1]	2% [1]	4%	7% [1]	016% [1]	2% [1]		020% [1]	6%	3%	7% [1]	017% [1]		Y	Y	
0367	010% [1]	033% [1]	3%	027% [1]	1%	3% [1]	1%	2%	3%	2%	9% [1]	4% [1]			Y	
0368		019%	6%	016% [1]		1% [1]	1%	6% [1]		3% [1]	011% [1]	8% [1]			Y	
0369		028%	5%	021% [1]	3%	5% [1]	1%	1% [1]	1%	1%	6% [1]	013% [1]			Y	
0370		028% [1]	2%	015% [1]	6%	4% [1]	1%	7% [1]	2%	2%	7% [1]	016% [1]			Y	
0371		026% [1]	6%	017% [1]	2%	5% [1]	1%	3% [1]	1%	4%	7% [1]	014%		Y	Y	
0372	1%	034% [1]	5%	013% [1]	7%	1% [1]	1%	5% [1]	1%	2%	3% [1]	2% [1]			Y	
0373	3% [1]	023% [1]	5%	014% [1]	3%	4% [1]		1% [1]	4%	1%	5% [1]	010% [1]			Y	
0374		024% [1]	3%	014% [1]	3% [1]	1% [1]	1%	010% [1]		014%	016% [1]	013% [1]				
0375	1%	019%	5%	011% [1]	9%	5%	1%	6%	1%	2%	8% [1]	012% [1]		Y	Y	
0376	5% [1]	015% [1]	6%	9% [1]	010% [1]	4%	1%	5% [1]	5%	2% [1]	6% [1]	8% [1]		Y	Y	Y
0377		019% [1]	012%	7%	6% [1]	3% [1]	2%	9% [1]		6% [1]	4% [1]	015% [1]		Y	Y	
0378	[1]			[1]	[1]	[1]		[1]		[1]	[1]	[1]		Y	Y	Y
0379								100% [1]								
0380		032%	5%	4% [1]		2% [1]	1%	045% [1]		2%	3% [1]	2%			Y	
0381		028%		3% [1]	1%	1%	1%	026%		2%	5%	3% [1]				
0382		035%	1%	6% [1]	1%	7%	2%	011%		6% [1]	012% [1]	011% [1]			Y	
0383	5% [1]	020%	4%	016% [1]	1%	9% [1]	1%	2%	2%	3%	011%	018%				
0384					061% [1]						013% [1]				Y	
0385					083% [1]					2%	011% [1]	4%		Y	Y	
0386		019%	5%	013% [1]		6%	1%	9%		6%	022% [1]	018%		Y	Y	Y
0387		027%	9%	7% [1]	1%	8%	1%	8%		3%	3% [1]	4%			Y	
0388		016%	6%	8%		6%	1%	4% [1]		6%	012% [1]	015% [1]				
0389		021% [1]	8%	9% [1]		6%	7%	6% [1]	2%	8% [1]	015% [1]	017% [1]		Y	Y	
0390		028%	4%	012% [1]	2%	5%	3%	5% [1]		3%	021% [1]	013% [1]				

[1] Additional majors available in this area
[2] ROTC available

†Accredited by a nationally recognized accrediting body other than one of the regional accrediting associations

North Central States
(continued)

IA, KS, MN, MO, ND, NE, SD

Sequence Number	School name (upper entry) City (lower entry)	State	Costs: Resident tuition/fees + room/board	Costs: Room/Board (upper entry) Nonresident tuition/fees + room/board (lower entry)	General Information: Highest degree	General Information: Affiliation (upper entry) Religious observance (lower entry)	General Information: Size of community	General Information: Type of community	Admissions: Fall term application deadline (upper entry) Tests desired or required (lower entry)	Admissions: Calendar	Admissions: Fall admission only	Admissions: Early admission	Admissions: Deferred admission	Financial Aid: Fall term application deadline (upper entry) Forms to be filed (lower entry)	Student Profile: Number in 10 who— Undergrads -have need, receive some aid	Undergrads -are women	Undergrads -are graduate students	Freshmen -live on campus	Freshmen -are minority students	Freshmen -are nonresidents	Freshmen -return as sophomores	Freshmen -complete degree	Freshmen -enter graduate study	HS GPA (upper entry) 1st year college GPA (lower entry)	Special Programs: Credit by exam	Special Programs: Student designed majors	Special Programs: Fraternities/sororities
	SELECTIVE ADMISSIONS *Majority of accepted students in top 25% of HS class*																										
	Enrollment 1,000 to 5,000																										
0391	Rockhurst C Kansas City	MO	12100 [3]	3600	M [5]	Cath S	V	U	6/30 A/S	E		Y	Y	 FA/FF	9	6	0	5	1	5	7	5	1	3.2 2.8	Y		Y
0392	Saint Thomas,U of St Paul	MN	12100	3100	D [5]	Cath S	V	U	 A=S	4			Y	3/01 FF=FA	7	5	1	5	1	1	9			 2.8	Y	Y	Y
0393	Augustana C Sioux Falls	SD	12200	2900	M [5]	Luth OS	M	S	7/15 A/S	4		Y	Y	 FF/FA	8	6	0	7	1	5	8	6	2	3.4 2.8	Y	Y	
0394	Central C Pella	IA	12700 [3]	3400	B [5]	Oth	T		8/01 A/S	Q			Y	 FF=FA	9	6	0	9	1	2	8	7	2	3.5 2.9	Y	Y	Y
0395	Saint Benedict,C of St Joseph	MN	12900	3400	B [5]	Cath S	T		 A=S	4		Y	Y	 FF/FA	7	9	0	9	1	2	8	6	4	3.3 2.8	Y	Y	Y
0396	Simpson C Indianola	IA	12900 [3]	3400	B [5]	Meth	S		8/01 A=S	O		Y	Y	8/01 FF=FA	9	6	0	9	1	1	7	6	2	 2.7	Y	Y	Y
0397	Saint John's U Collegeville	MN	13000	3500	M [5]	Cath	T		 A=S	4		Y	Y	 FF/FA	6	1	1	9	1	2	9	7	4	3.1 2.8	Y	Y	
0398	Augsburg C Minneapolis	MN	13100	3600	M [5]	Luth OS	V	U	8/15 A=S	4		Y	Y	7/01 FF/FA	8	6	1	8	2	2	8	6	5	 2.8	Y	Y	
0399	Gustavus Adolphus C St Peter	MN	13800 [3]	2900	B [5]	Luth O	T		 A=S	4		Y	Y	 FF=FA	6	5	0	9	1	3	9	7	3	3.4 2.8		Y	Y
0400	Luther C Decorah	IA	13900 [3]	3300	B [5]	Luth OS	T		6/01 A/S	4		Y	Y	3/01 FF/FA	7	6	0	9	1	6	9	8	5	3.3 2.9	Y	Y	Y
0401	Drake U Des Moines	IA	14100 [3]	3800	D [5]	Priv	L	U	 A=S	E		Y	Y	3/01 FF=FA	5	5	1	9	1	7	8	7	2	3.1 2.9	Y	Y	Y
0402	Hamline U St Paul	MN	15300	3600	P [5]	Meth	V	U	 A=S	4		Y	Y	 FF/FA	8	6	4	9	1	3	8		3	 3.2	Y	Y	Y
0403	Saint Olaf C Northfield	MN	15400 [3]	3300	B [5]	Luth OS	S		 A=S	4		Y	Y	3/01 FF=FA	6	5	0	9	1	5	9	7	7	3.5 2.9	Y	Y	
0404	Cornell C Mount Vernon	IA	16300 [3]	4000	B [5]	Meth	T		4/01 A=S	O		Y	Y	3/01 FF=FA	8	5	0	9	1	7	8	9	7	3.4 3.0	Y	Y	Y
	Enrollment 5,000 to 15,000																										
0405	Missouri St Louis,U St Louis	MO	2300	[1] 6100	D [5]	Pub	V	U	 A=S	E		Y		3/01 FF/FA	5	6	1	0	1	1	6	3			Y		Y
0406	Northeast Missouri U Kirksville	MO	4400 [3]	2600 6100	M [5]	Pub	S		4/01 A/S	E		Y		3/01 FF/FA	6	6	1	9	1	3	8	6	3	 2.6	Y		Y
0407	Missouri KC,U of Kansas City	MO	5300	3100 9100	D [5]	Pub	V	U	 ACT	E		Y	Y	 FFS	4	6	3	2	2	1	6	2	1		Y		Y
0408	Creighton U Omaha	NE	11800 [3]	3500	D [5]	Cath OS	V	U	8/01 A/S	E			Y	 FA/FF	7	5	4	9	1	5	8	6	3	3.2 2.8	Y		Y
0409	Saint Louis U St Louis	MO	13300	4200	D [5]	Cath OS	V	U	 A=S	E		Y	Y	 FF=FA	8	5	2	4	2	4	8	7	6	3.3 2.8	Y	Y	Y
	Enrollment over 15,000																										
0410	Iowa St U Ames	IA	4900	2900 9300	D [5]	Pub	M		8/24 A/S	E			Y	 FF=FA	7	4	1	8	1	2	8	6	1	3.2 2.5	Y	Y	Y
0411	Missouri Columbia,U Columbia	MO	4900	2900 8400	D [5]	Pub	M		5/15 ACT	E		Y	Y	 FF/FA	3	5	1	7	1	1	8	5		 2.5	Y	Y	Y
	HIGHLY SELECTIVE *Majority of accepted students in top 10% of HS class*																										
	Enrollment 1,000 to 5,000																										
0412	Minn Morris,U of Morris	MN	5300	2800 8700	B [5]	Pub	T		3/15 ACT	Q		Y	Y	5/01 FFS	9	5	0	9	1	2	9	4	3	3.3 2.9	Y	Y	Y
0413	Macalester C St Paul	MN	16200	3700	B [5]	Pres	V	U	2/01 A=S	4		Y	Y	3/01 FA/FF	6	5	0	9	2	8	9	7				Y	
0414	Grinnell C Grinnell	IA	17600 [3]	3900	B [5]	Priv	T		2/01 A=S	E		Y	Y	3/01 FAF	6	5	0	9	2	8	9	8				Y	
0415	Carleton C Northfield	MN	18300 [3]	3100	B [5]	Priv	S		2/01 A=S	O		Y	Y	3/01 Oth	5	5	0	9	1	7	9	8	7	 3.1	Y	Y	
	Enrollment 5,000 to 15,000																										
0416	Washington U St Louis	MO	21300 [3]	5200	D [5]	Priv	V	S	2/01 A=S	S		Y	Y	2/15 FAF	4	5	1	6	2	9	9	8	8		Y	Y	Y

▲ Sequence number—indicates the order of the college in this book only. Do *not* use this number with admissions tests or need analysis services.

[1] No campus room and board facilities
[2] Room only or board only
[3] Most freshmen required to live on campus
[4] City or district residence requirements
[5] Accredited by a regional accrediting association or a recognized candidate for accreditation
[6] All female freshman class
[7] All male freshman class

MAJORS AVAILABLE AND PERCENT OF STUDENTS STUDYING IN EACH AREA

Agri.: Agriculture, general; Agronomy (crops & mgmt); Animal Science (husbandry); Fish, Wildlife Mgmt; Forestry
Business: Business/Commerce, general; Accounting; Banking/Finance; Business Economics; Business Mgmt/Admin; Marketing/Purchasing; Secretarial Studies
Comm.: Communications, general; Journalism; Radio/TV (broadcasting); Advertising
Education: Art Education; Distributive Education; Elementary Education; English Education; Mathematics Education; Music Education; Physical Education; Science Education; Secondary Education; Social Science Education; Special Education; Speech Education
Engineering: Engineering, general; Chemical; Civil; Electrical/Electronics/Comm; Industrial/Management; Mechanical
Fine/App. Arts: Architecture; Fine/Applied Arts, general; Art (Paint, draw, sculpt); Art History/Appreciation; Dance; Dramatic Arts (theater arts); Music (liberal arts); Music (perform, compos, theory)
Lang.: French; German; Italian; Latin; Spanish[1]; Russian
Health: Predentistry; Premedicine; Medical/Lab Technology; Nursing (registered nurse); Occupational Therapy; Preoptometry; Prepharmacy; Physical Therapy; Preveterinary Medicine
Home Ec.: Home Economics, general; Clothing and Textiles; Consumer Ec/Home Mgmt; Family Relations/Child Devel; Food and Nutrition/Dietetics; Institution Mgmt
Humanities: Humanities, general; Creative Writing; English, general; Literature, English; Philosophy; Religion; Speech/Forensic Science
Math-Sciences: Mathematics, general; Computer/Info Sciences; Biological Sciences, general; Biology; Botany; Zoology; Physical Sciences, general; Chemistry; Physics
Social Sciences: Crim Just/Law Enforce; Social Work; Social Sciences, general; Anthropology; Area Studies (Amer., African, etc.); Economics; Geography; History; Prelaw; Political Science; Psychology; Sociology
GS: General Studies
ROTC: Air Force; Army; Navy

Sequence Number	Agri.	Business	Comm.	Education	Engineering	Fine/App. Arts	Lang.	Health	Home Ec.	Humanities	Math-Sciences	Social Sciences	ROTC
0391		045% [1]	1%	2% [1]			2%	014% [1]		010%	5% [1]	4% [1]	Y
0392		050%	8%	2%			4%	1%		6%	010% [1]	015%	Y
0393		013%	4%	019% [1]	1%	1%	1%	020% [1]		2% [1]	3% [1]	2% [1]	
0394		025%	6%	019%		3%	8%	1% [1]		5% [1]	016% [1]	6% [1]	
0395		015%		016%		6%	4%	012% [1]		9% [1]	010%	014%	Y
0396		024%	6%	020% [1]		7%	3%	[1]		4%	018%	015% [1]	
0397		031%		1%	2%	2%	2%	4% [1]		011% [1]	023%	023%	Y
0398		027%	6%	9% [1]	1%	010%	3%	2% [1]		016%	011% [1]	012% [1]	YYY
0399		022%	5%	012% [1]	1%	2%	5%	2%		6% [1]	022% [1]	023%	Y
0400		018%	5%	8%		8%	2%	8%		8% [1]	018% [1]	023% [1]	
0401		027% [1]	010%	8% [1]		4% [1]	1%	012%		3%	012% [1]	010% [1]	YY
0402		013%	3%	3%		3%	5%	1% [1]		014%	015%	035% [1]	Y
0403		9%	1%	3% [1]	1%	013%	8%	5% [1]	1%	016% [1]	030% [1]	9% [1]	
0404		013%		010%		9%	6%			017%	017% [1]	020% [1]	
0405		037%	3%	016% [1]		1%	1%	3%		3%	9% [1]	8% [1]	YY
0406	3% [1]	021%	7%	7% [1]	1%	5%	4%	7% [1]	3%	6%	019% [1]	016%	Y
0407		012% [1]	1%	7% [1]	9%	4%	1%	014% [1]		2%	4% [1]	3% [1]	Y
0408		027%	5%	4% [1]		1%	1%	027% [1]		5% [1]	015% [1]	015%	YY
0409		014% [1]	5%	5% [1]	6% [1]	2% [1]	1%	023% [1]		8% [1]	022% [1]	013%	YY
0410	8% [1]	021% [1]	3%	010% [1]	021% [1]	9% [1]		3%	3%	2% [1]	7% [1]	7% [1]	YYY
0411	6% [1]	7% [1]	3%	7% [1]	8% [1]	2% [1]	1%	2% [1]	4%	5% [1]	6% [1]	010% [1]	YYY
0412		011%	3%	011% [1]	5%	4%	4%	4%		8%	021% [1]	025% [1]	
0413						010%	8%			019% [1]	015% [1]	043% [1]	Y Y
0414		8%			2%	5%	7%	1% [1]		014% [1]	026% [1]	033% [1]	
0415						6%	5%			021% [1]	019% [1]	044% [1]	
0416		7% [1]		1%	018%	010% [1]	3%	[1]		9% [1]	016% [1]	016% [1]	YY

[1] Additional majors available in this area
[2] ROTC available

†Accredited by a nationally recognized accrediting body other than one of the regional accrediting associations

North Central States
(continued)

IA, KS, MN, MO, ND, NE, SD

ADVANCED STANDING *Freshmen not accepted; college junior standing often required*

Sequence Number	School name (upper entry) / City (lower entry)	State	Costs: Resident tuition/fees + room/board	Costs: Room/Board (upper entry) / Nonresident tuition/fees + room/board (lower entry)	General Information: Highest degree	General Information: Affiliation (upper entry) / Religious observance (lower entry)	General Information: Size of community	General Information: Type of community	Admissions: Fall term application deadline (upper entry) / Tests desired or required (lower entry)	Admissions: Calendar	Admissions: Fall admission only	Admissions: Early admission	Admissions: Deferred admission	Financial Aid: Fall term application deadline (upper entry) / Forms to be filed (lower entry)	Number in 10 who— -have need, receive some aid	Under-grads: -are women	Under-grads: -are graduate students	Freshmen: -live on campus	Freshmen: -are minority students	Freshmen: -are nonresidents	Freshmen: -return as sophomores	Freshmen: -complete degree	Freshmen: -enter graduate study	HS GPA (upper entry) / 1st year college GPA (lower entry)	Special Programs: Credit by exam	Special Programs: Student designed majors	Special Programs: Fraternities/sororities
	Enrollment to 1,000																										
0417	Metropolitan St U St Paul	MN	1800	[1] 3000	M [5]	Pub	V	U	 None	Q				 FF/FA		6	1	0	1				2		Y	Y	
0418	Medcenter One Sc Nsg Bismarck	ND	2800 [2]	700	B †	Priv	M		 A/S	E				 FFS	7	9	0		1			5	1		Y		
0419	St Mary Plains C Nsg Topeka	KS	4900	[1]	B [5]	Cath	M	U		S						9	0		1								
	Enrollment 1,000 to 5,000																										
0420	Nebraska Med Ctr,U Omaha	NE	1500	[1] 4000	D [5]	Pub	L	U	 A/S	E				 FA/FF		9	7		1						Y		
0421	Palmer C Chiropractc Davenport	IA	9500	2600	P [5]	Priv	L	U	 A=S	T		Y	Y	 Oth	9		9	0	2	8	9			 3.1	Y		Y

Great Lakes States

IL, IN, MI, OH, WI

OPEN ADMISSIONS *All HS graduates accepted, to limit of capacity*

Sequence Number	School name (upper entry) / City (lower entry)	State	Costs: Resident tuition/fees + room/board	Costs: Room/Board (upper entry) / Nonresident tuition/fees + room/board (lower entry)	General Information: Highest degree	General Information: Affiliation (upper entry) / Religious observance (lower entry)	General Information: Size of community	General Information: Type of community	Admissions: Fall term application deadline (upper entry) / Tests desired or required (lower entry)	Admissions: Calendar	Admissions: Fall admission only	Admissions: Early admission	Admissions: Deferred admission	Financial Aid: Fall term application deadline (upper entry) / Forms to be filed (lower entry)	Number in 10 who— -have need, receive some aid	Under-grads: -are women	Under-grads: -are graduate students	Freshmen: -live on campus	Freshmen: -are minority students	Freshmen: -are nonresidents	Freshmen: -return as sophomores	Freshmen: -complete degree	Freshmen: -enter graduate study	HS GPA (upper entry) / 1st year college GPA (lower entry)	Special Programs: Credit by exam	Special Programs: Student designed majors	Special Programs: Fraternities/sororities
	Enrollment to 1,000																										
0422	Marietta Bible C Marietta	OH	1700 [3]	1400		Oth OS	S		 A/S	S						5	0	6	1	7	9	2	1				
0423	Ohio U Chillicothe Chillicothe	OH	2200	[1] 5300	A [5]	Pub	S		9/01 A/S	Q		Y	Y	4/01 FAF	3	6	0	0	1	1	5			3.0 2.6	Y	Y	
0424	Ohio St Lima Lima	OH	2300	[1] 6900	B [5]	Pub	M		7/01 A/S	Q		Y		4/01 FA/FF	7	6	0	0	1	1	5				Y	Y	
0425	Ohio St Mansfield Mansfield	OH	2300	[1] 6900	B [5]	Pub	M		7/01 A/S	Q		Y		4/01 FA/FF	7	6	1	0	1	1	5				Y		
0426	Ohio St Marion Marion	OH	2300	[1] 6900	B [5]	Pub	S		7/01 A/S	Q		Y		4/01 FA/FF	7	6	0	0	1	1	6				Y	Y	
0427	Ohio St Newark Newark	OH	2300	[1] 6900	B [5]	Pub	M		7/01 A/S	Q		Y		4/01 FA/FF	7	6	0	0	1	1	5				Y	Y	
0428	Temple Baptist C Cincinnati	OH	2300	[1]	B †	Bapt OS	V	U	 A/S	Q		Y		 FF=FA	3	1	0	0	3	0	8	1	6	2.9 2.9	Y		
0429	Baker C-Mt Clemens Mount Clemens	MI	4000	[1]	B [5]	Priv	L	S	 A=S	Q		Y	Y	9/01 FA/FF	7	7	0		2						Y		
0430	Oregon Bible C Oregon	IL	4000	2000		Oth OS	T		 A=S	O		Y		7/15 None	6	4	0	9	0	8	5	3	2	2.9 2.9			
0431	Lockyear C Evansville	IN	4500 [2]	1000	B †	Priv	L	U	 None	Q		Y	Y	 Oth	8	6	0	1	2	4	7						Y
0432	Cleary C Ypsilanti	MI	5000	[1]	B †	Priv	S		9/23 None	Q		Y	Y	5/01 FA/FF	4	7	0	0	1	1	5	2	1		Y	Y	
0433	Detroit C Business Warren	MI	5300	[1]	B [5]	Priv	S		 None	Q			Y	3/15 FAF	6	8	0		4		7						
0434	East-West U Chicago	IL	5400	[1]	B [5]	Priv	V	U	 ACT	Q				 FFS		7	0	0	9	0	4						
0435	Baker C-Owosso Owosso	MI	6000 [2]	1500	B [5]	Priv	S		 None	Q				 FA/FF		8	0		1	0					Y	Y	
0436	Maranatha Bapt Bible Watertown	WI	6000 [3]	2600	M [5]	Bapt OS	S		 A/S	S		Y	Y	 FF/FA	3	5	1	8	1	7	7	5		3.1 2.9	Y		
0437	Cinci Bible C Cincinnati	OH	6200 [3]	2800	M †	Oth OS	L	U	8/01 ACT	E			Y	6/01 FF/FA	9	4	3	9	1	5	7	4	3	2.9 2.9	Y		
0438	Davenport C-Kalamazoo Kalamazoo	MI	6900	[1]	B [5]	Priv	M	S	 None	Q		Y		3/15 FA/FF	8	8	0	0	2	1	7			2.2 3.0	Y		
0439	Mich Christian C Rochester Hills	MI	7200	3000	B [5]	Oth OS	M	S	 ACT	E		Y	Y	8/01 FF/FA		5	0	7	2	3				2.5	Y		
0440	Reformed Bible C Grand Rapids	MI	7600	2800	M †	Oth OS	L	S	 A=S	S		Y	Y	4/30 FAF	8	5	0	5	4	5	7	2	2	3.0 2.5	Y		
0441	Oakland City C Oakland City	IN	9000 [3]	2700	M [5]	Bapt S	T		9/01 A=S	E		Y	Y	5/01 FAF	9	5	1	7	1	2	8	6	3	2.7 2.4	Y		

▲ Sequence number—indicates the order of the college in this book only. Do *not* use this number with admissions tests or need analysis services.

[1] No campus room and board facilities
[2] Room only or board only
[3] Most freshmen required to live on campus
[4] City or district residence requirements
[5] Accredited by a regional accrediting association or a recognized candidate for accreditation
[6] All female freshman class
[7] All male freshman class

MAJORS AVAILABLE AND PERCENT OF STUDENTS STUDYING IN EACH AREA

Majors listed under each area:

- **Agri.**: Agriculture, general; Agronomy (crops & mgmt); Animal Science (husbandry); Fish, Wildlife Mgmt; Forestry
- **Business**: Business/Commerce, general; Accounting; Banking/Finance; Business Economics; Business Mgmt/Admin; Marketing/Purchasing; Secretarial Studies
- **Comm.**: Communications, general; Journalism; Radio/TV (broadcasting); Advertising
- **Education**: Art Education; Distributive Education; Elementary Education; English Education; Mathematics Education; Music Education; Physical Education; Science Education; Secondary Education; Social Science Education; Special Education; Speech Education
- **Engineering**: Engineering, general; Chemical; Civil; Electrical/Electronics/Comm; Industrial/Management; Mechanical
- **Fine/App. Arts**: Architecture; Fine/Applied Arts, general; Art (Paint, draw, sculpt); Art History/Appreciation; Dance; Dramatic Arts (theater arts); Music (liberal arts); Music (perform, compos, theory)
- **Lang.**: French; German; Italian; Latin; Spanish; Russian
- **Health**: Predentistry; Premedicine; Medical/Lab Technology; Nursing (registered nurse); Occupational Therapy; Preoptometry; Prepharmacy; Physical Therapy; Preveterinary Medicine
- **Home Ec.**: Home Economics, general; Clothing and Textiles; Consumer Ec/Home Mgmt; Family Relations/Child Devel; Food and Nutrition/Dietetics; Institution Mgmt
- **Humanities**: Humanities, general; Creative Writing; English, general; Literature, English; Philosophy; Religion; Speech/Forensic Science
- **Math-Sciences**: Mathematics, general; Computer/Info Sciences; Biological Sciences, general; Biology; Botany; Zoology; Physical Sciences, general; Chemistry; Physics
- **Social Sciences**: Crim Just/Law Enforce; Social Work; Social Sciences, general; Anthropology; Area Studies (Amer., African, etc.); Economics; Geography; History; Prelaw; Political Science; Psychology; Sociology
- **GS**: General Studies
- **ROTC**: Air Force; Army; Navy

Sequence Number	Agri.	Business	Comm.	Education	Engineering	Fine/App. Arts	Lang.	Health	Home Ec.	Humanities	Math-Sciences	Social Sciences	GS	ROTC
0417		025% ■ Accounting	010% ■ Communications, general			5%	5%	5% ■ Nursing		010%	010%	010%	■	
0418								100%						
0419								100% ■ Nursing						
0420								100% ■ Medical/Lab Technology ■ Nursing ■ Physical Therapy [1]						
0421								100% [1]						
0422				050% [1]						050% ■ Religion				
0423	1%	6%	3%	019%	3%	2%	1%	6%	1%	1%	012%	6%		Y (Air Force) Y (Army)
0424	2%	016%	1%	038% ■ Elementary Education	5%	2%		7%	1%	1%	3%	3%		
0425	1%	020%	1%	037% ■ Elementary Education	5%	3%		7%	1%	1%	3%	5%		
0426	1%	016%	2%	034% ■ Elementary Education	3%	3%	1%	4%	1%	1%	3%	9%		
0427	1%	026%	2%	028% ■ Elementary Education	7%	2%		6%	1%	1%	3%	7%		
0428		015% ■ Business/Commerce, general		025% ■ Elementary Education [1]		■ Music (liberal arts) ■ Music (perform, compos, theory)				060% ■ Religion				
0429		075% ■ Business Mgmt/Admin						010%			015%			
0430										100%				
0431		070% ■ Accounting ■ Business Mgmt/Admin [1]						5%			011% [1]	■ Social Sciences, general		
0432		086% ■ Business/Commerce, general ■ Accounting ■ Business Mgmt/Admin ■ Marketing/Purchasing ■ Secretarial Studies		1%				8%		1%	2% [1]	1%		
0433		100% ■ Accounting ■ Business Mgmt/Admin [1]												
0434		036% ■ Business/Commerce, general			027%					■ English, general	034% ■ Mathematics, general ■ Computer/Info Sciences	3% ■ Social Sciences, general		
0435		075% ■ Business/Commerce, general ■ Accounting ■ Business Mgmt/Admin [1]			3%	1%		011%	2%		8% [1]			
0436		014% ■ Business Mgmt/Admin ■ Secretarial Studies		039% ■ Distributive Education ■ Elementary Education ■ English Education ■ Mathematics Education ■ Music Education ■ Physical Education ■ Secondary Education ■ Social Science Education [1]		3% ■ Music (liberal arts) ■ Music (perform, compos, theory)	1% ■ Latin	3%		034% ■ Religion	4%	2%		
0437		3%	1% ■ Journalism							096% ■ Religion				
0438		065%						8%			1%	1%		
0439		022%	1%	010%	3%	3%	1%	8%	5%	011% ■ Religion	6%	5% ■ Psychology		
0440										100% ■ Religion				
0441		024% ■ Business/Commerce, general ■ Accounting ■ Business Mgmt/Admin		020% ■ Art Education ■ Distributive Education ■ Elementary Education ■ English Education ■ Mathematics Education ■ Music Education ■ Physical Education ■ Science Education ■ Secondary Education		1% ■ Fine/Applied Arts, general ■ Art (Paint, draw, sculpt) ■ Music (liberal arts)				2% ■ Humanities, general ■ English, general ■ Religion	3% ■ Computer/Info Sciences ■ Biology ■ Chemistry [1]	1%	■	

[1] Additional majors available in this area
[2] ROTC available

†Accredited by a nationally recognized accrediting body other than one of the regional accrediting associations

Great Lakes States (continued)

IL, IN, MI, OH, WI

OPEN ADMISSIONS *All HS graduates accepted, to limit of capacity*

Sequence Number	School name (upper entry) City (lower entry)	State	Costs: Resident tuition/fees + room/board	Costs: Room/Board (upper entry) Nonresident tuition/fees + room/board (lower entry)	General Information: Highest degree	General Information: Affiliation (upper entry) Religious observance (lower entry)	General Information: Size of community	General Information: Type of community	Admissions: Fall term application deadline (upper entry) Tests desired or required (lower entry)	Admissions: Calendar	Admissions: Fall admission only	Admissions: Early admission	Admissions: Deferred admission	Financial Aid: Fall term application deadline (upper entry) Forms to be filed (lower entry)	Number in 10 who— -have need, receive some aid	Under-grads: -are women	Under-grads: -are graduate students	Freshmen: -live on campus	Freshmen: -are minority students	Freshmen: -are nonresidents	Freshmen: -return as sophomores	Freshmen: -complete degree	Freshmen: -enter graduate study	HS GPA (upper entry) 1st year college GPA (lower entry)	Special Programs: Credit by exam	Special Programs: Student designed majors	Special Programs: Fraternities/sororities
	Enrollment to 1,000																										
0442	Davenport C Lansing Lansing	MI	9200	[1]	B [5]	Priv	M	U	9/23 None	Q		Y		8/15 FA/FF	8	7	0	0	2	0	4				Y		
	Enrollment 1,000 to 5,000																										
0443	Shawnee St U Portsmouth	OH	1600	[1] 2000	B [5]	Pub	S		9/18 A/S	Q		Y		9/15 FAF	9	7	0	1	1	1	5			2.7 2.8	Y	Y	Y
0444	Ohio U Ironton Ironton	OH	2000	[1] 2100	M [5]	Pub	S		A/S	Q		Y	Y	6/13 FAF	7	5	1	0	1	1	7	5	2			Y	
0445	Southern Ind,U of Evansville	IN	3000 [2]	1300 5400	M [5]	Pub	M	S	8/15 A=S	E		Y	Y	3/01 FAF	6	6	0	2	1	1	8				Y		Y
0446	Franklin U Columbus	OH	3600	[1]	B [5]	Priv	V	U		T		Y	Y	9/06	5	5	0	0	2	1		1	1	2.4 2.4	Y		
0447	Jordan C Cedar Springs	MI	4300	[1]	B [5]	Priv	T		Oth	S		Y	Y	3/31 FA/FF	9	8	0	0	7	1	4				Y		
0448	Hyles-Anderson C Crown Point	IN	4400	2100	M	Bapt OS	T		9/14 ACT	S				None		4	1	5		7		6	1				
0449	Rio Grande,U of Rio Grande	OH	4800 [3]	2900 7700	B [5]	Priv	T		8/23 ACT	Q		Y	Y	4/15 FAF	9	5	0	5	1	1	5	3	2	2.5 2.3	Y	Y	Y
0450	Columbia C Chicago	IL	5100	[1]	M [5]	Priv	V	U		S			Y	FF=FA	4	5	1	0	4	1		5	2		Y	Y	Y
0451	Detroit C of Bus Dearborn	MI	5300	[1]	B [5]	Priv	M	S	None	Q			Y	2/15	6	8	0	0	6	0	7				Y		Y
0452	Central St U Wilberforce	OH	6000 [3]	3800 8600	M [5]	Pub	T		A/S	Q		Y	Y	4/15 FA/FF	9	5	0	5	9	2		4	1	2.5 2.3	Y		Y
0453	Baker C Flint	MI	6100 [2]	1500	B [5]	Priv	M	U	None	Q		Y	Y	FA/FF	7	7	0	1	2	0	7				Y		
0454	Union Inst Cincinnati	OH	6300	[1]	D [5]	Priv	V	U	None	Q		Y		FA/FF	9	4	7		3			8	4		Y	Y	
0455	Baker C-Muskegon Muskegon	MI	7100	2600	B [5]	Priv	S		None	Q		Y		9/01 FF=FA	8	7	0	1	1	1	8				Y		Y
0456	Davenport C Gr Rpds Grand Rapids	MI	9100 [2]	1900	B [5]	Priv	L	U	None	Q		Y	Y	3/15 FA/FF	7	7	0	2	1	1	8	2	1	2.9 3.0	Y		
0457	Andrews U Berrien Springs	MI	12100	3600	D [5]	Oth OS	T		8/15 Oth	Q			Y	6/01 FA/FF	9	5	3	8	5	6	6	5	3	2.9 2.7	Y	Y	
	Enrollment 5,000 to 15,000																										
0458	Wright St U Dayton	OH	5600	3100 8000	D [5]	Pub	L	S	A/S	Q			Y	4/19 FA/FF	9	5	1	3	1	1	7	3	2	2.8	Y	Y	Y
0459	Youngstown St U Youngstown	OH	5600	3400 6800	M [5]	Pub	V	U	8/15 A=S	Q		Y	Y	4/01 FA/FF	6	5	1	1	1	1	8	3			Y	Y	Y
0460	Cleveland St U Cleveland	OH	5700	3200 8300	D [5]	Pub	V	U	9/15 A=S	Q		Y		FA/FF	3	5	1	1	2	1	5			2.2	Y	Y	Y
	Enrollment over 15,000																										
0461	Akron,U of Akron	OH	5600	3200 9200	D [5]	Pub	L	U	8/16 A=S	E		Y		3/15 FAF	5	5	1	1	1	1	7			2.7	Y	Y	Y
	LIBERAL ADMISSIONS *Some accepted students from lower half of HS class*																										
	Enrollment to 1,000																										
0462	Allegheny Wesleyan C Salem	OH	3400	1700	B	Oth	S		8/15 A=S	E		Y	Y	None		5	0	5	0	6	4	4	0	3.0			
0463	Heritage Baptist U Indianapolis	IN	3800	1900	D	Bapt OS	V	S	8/01 ACT	S		Y	Y	6/01 None	1	2	1	1	1	2	5	2	1	2.7 3.0	Y		
0464	Jordan Energy Inst Cedar Springs	MI	4300	[1]	B [5]	Priv	T		Oth	S		Y	Y	3/31 FA/FF	9	7	0	0	1		3				Y		
0465	Dyke C Cleveland	OH	4500	[1]	B [5]	Priv	V	U	A=S	S		Y		8/01	8	6	0	0	6	1		6	2		Y		Y
0466	God's Bible Sch & C Cincinnati	OH	4600 [3]	2100	B †	Priv OS	L	U	A=S	E				7/15 FF=FA	7	5	0	9	1	7	5	3	2	3.0 2.6	Y		
0467	Lourdes C Sylvania	OH	4700	[1]	B [5]	Cath	S		A/S	E		Y		9/01 FA/FF	9	8	0	0	1	1	5	1	1		Y	Y	Y

▲ Sequence number—indicates the order of the college in this book only. Do *not* use this number with admissions tests or need analysis services.

[1] No campus room and board facilities
[2] Room only or board only
[3] Most freshmen required to live on campus
[4] City or district residence requirements
[5] Accredited by a regional accrediting association or a recognized candidate for accreditation
[6] All female freshman class
[7] All male freshman class

MAJORS AVAILABLE AND PERCENT OF STUDENTS STUDYING IN EACH AREA

Sequence Number	Agri.	Business	Comm.	Education	Engineering	Fine/App. Arts	Lang.	Health	Home Ec.	Humanities	Math-Sciences	Social Sciences	GS	ROTC
0442		100%												
0443		026%	2%	8%	015%	1%	1%	020% [1]		5%	8%	8%		Y
0444		049%	4%	034% [1]	5%	1%	1%		1%	1%	3%	1%		
0445		032% [1]	2%	9% [1]	4%	1%	1%	3% [1]		9%	7% [1]	011%		
0446		051% [1]	2%		8%	1%		4%		2%	6%	2% [1]		Y
0447	1% [1]	046%			2%			1%	8%		010%	016%		
0448		5%		035% [1]					3%	045%	7%	4%		
0449		025% [1]	5%	030% [1]	1%	1%		6%		1%	3% [1]	2% [1]		Y
0450		5%	038%			038% [1]			1%	5%				
0451		082% [1]						[1]			018% [1]			
0452		026% [1]	3%	3% [1]	5%	1% [1]	1%	5%		2%	3% [1]	2% [1]		YY
0453		067% [1]			1%	1% [1]		5%			1% [1]			
0454	2% [1]	035% [1]	5%	6% [1]		5% [1]	1%	010% [1]	2%	025% [1]	3% [1]	5% [1]		
0455		074% [1]			1%			1%			1% [1]			
0456		080% [1]	5%					010%			5%			
0457	1%	012% [1]	4%	6% [1]	5%	9% [1]	1%	015% [1]	2%	5%	012% [1]	2%		
0458		025%	4%	014%	014% [1]	5% [1]	1%	6%		2% [1]	010% [1]	5% [1]		YY
0459		017% [1]	2%	012% [1]	010% [1]	4%		6% [1]	2%	3%	7% [1]	010% [1]		Y
0460		030%	9%	8% [1]	014%	2%	1%	6% [1]		3% [1]	8% [1]	019%		Y
0461		031%	2%	6% [1]	8%	[1]	1%	010%	1%	[1]	022% [1]	5%		YY
0462				050% [1]						050%				
0463		7%	1%	021% [1]		1%	1%		1%	064%	3%	1%		
0464	2% [1]	050%			031%						3%			
0465		097% [1]										3% [1]		
0466				4% [1]		1%	1%		4%	044%	1%	5%		
0467		025%		1%		1%	1%	030%	2%	7%	2%	7%		

[1] Additional majors available in this area
[2] ROTC available

†Accredited by a nationally recognized accrediting body other than one of the regional accrediting associations

Great Lakes States (continued)

IL, IN, MI, OH, WI

LIBERAL ADMISSIONS *Some accepted students from lower half of HS class*

Enrollment to 1,000

Sequence Number	School name (upper entry) City (lower entry)	State	Costs: Resident tuition/fees + room/board	Costs: Room/Board (upper entry) Nonresident tuition/fees + room/board (lower entry)	General Information: Highest degree	General Information: Affiliation (upper entry) Religious observance (lower entry)	General Information: Size of community	General Information: Type of community	Admissions: Fall term application deadline (upper entry) Tests desired or required (lower entry)	Admissions: Calendar	Admissions: Fall admission only	Admissions: Early admission	Admissions: Deferred admission	Financial Aid: Fall term application deadline (upper entry) Forms to be filed (lower entry)	Financial Aid: Number in 10 who—have need, receive some aid	Student Profile (Number in 10 who—), Undergrads: -are women	Undergrads: -are graduate students	Freshmen: -live on campus	Freshmen: -are minority students	Freshmen: -are nonresidents	Freshmen: -return as sophomores	Freshmen: -complete degree	Freshmen: -enter graduate study	HS GPA (upper entry) 1st year college GPA (lower entry)	Special Programs: Credit by exam	Special Programs: Student designed majors	Special Programs: Fraternities/sororities
0468	Amer Islamic C Chicago	IL	4800 [2]	1800	B †	Oth S	V	U	 A=S	S		Y	Y	7/15 FF=FA	7	2	0	6	6	0		1		3.2 2.5	Y		
0469	Christian Union C Greenfield	OH	5000	2700		Oth OS	T		9/07 A/S	E		Y		8/01 Oth	9	2	0	9	0		9	1	1	 3.0			
0470	Sacred Heart Sem Detroit	MI	5300	2400	P [5]	Cath OS	V	U	8/01 Oth	E		Y	Y	4/01 FF=FA	9		0		3						Y		
0471	Circleville Bible C Circleville	OH	6100	2600	B †	Oth OS	S		8/01 A/S	E				5/01 Oth	9	4	0	5	1	1	6	3		2.8 2.8			
0472	Lincoln Christian C Lincoln	IL	6100 [3]	2500	B [5]	Oth OS	S		 ACT	E			Y	 FF/FA	9	5	0	9	1	2	8	4	4	3.0 2.6			
0473	Great Lakes Bible C Lansing	MI	6300 [3]	2800	B †	Oth OS	M	S	7/30 ACT	S			Y	8/01 FFS	8	5	0	9	1	2	6	2	1				
0474	Saint Mary's C Orchard Lake	MI	6700	2900	B [5]	Cath OS	T		9/01 Oth	S		Y		4/30	4	6	0		2	1	8	5	7	3.0 2.9	Y		Y
0475	Amer Consv of Music Chicago	IL	6800	[1]	D †	Priv	V	U	8/01 Oth	E		Y	Y	6/01	3	3	1	0	5	1	6	4					
0476	ITT Tech Inst Fort Wayne	IN	6800	[1]	B †	Priv	L	S	9/07 Oth	Q					9	1	0	0	1	4	7			2.8 2.7			
0477	Pontifical C Joseph Columbus	OH	7000 [3]	2800	P [5]	Cath OS	L	S	7/15 A/S	S		Y	[7]	7/15 FAF	3	0	6	9	2	8	6		9	2.5 2.7	Y		
0478	Ray C of Design Chicago	IL	7300	[1]	B †	Priv	V	U	 A=S	S				8/01	8	6	0			2	8						
0479	Kendall C Art/Design Grand Rapids	MI	7600	[1]	B [5]	Priv	M	U	 A=S	S		Y	Y	2/15 FA/FF	8	6	0	0	1	1	6	6	1	2.8 2.5	Y		
0480	William Tyndale C Farmington Hill	MI	7700	3200	B [5]	Oth OS	M	S	7/27 A/S	E		Y	Y	8/29 FAF	6	4	0	1	4	1	6	2	7	2.6	Y		
0481	Graceland U New Albany	IN	8300	2500	B [5]	Oth OS	M	U	 A=S	E							0	7	1	1					Y		
0482	Mount Vernon Nazaren Mount Vernon	OH	8300 [3]	2800	B [5]	Oth OS	S		8/15 ACT	4		Y		5/30 FA/FF	9	6	0	7	1	2	6	4	3	2.9 2.8	Y		
0483	Hebrew Theol C Skokie	IL	8400	3600	D †	Jew OS	M	S	4/20 Oth	S		Y		4/20 FAF	4	5	4	5	1	4	8		6	2.9			
0484	Mount Senario C Ladysmith	WI	9000 [3]	2600	B [5]	Priv	T		 A/S	E			Y	 FA/FF	9	5	0	6	3	1	5		1	 2.2	Y	Y	
0485	Saint Meinrad C St Meinrad	IN	9500 [3]	4100	B [5]	Cath OS	T		4/01 A/S	E			[7]	 FAF	9	0	0	9	1	8	7	4	7		Y		
0486	Tiffin U Tiffin	OH	9500 [3]	3400	M [5]	Priv	S		8/11 A/S	E		Y	Y	4/30 FA/FF	8	4	1	9	1	1	5	5	1	2.5 2.5	Y		Y
0487	Edgewood C Madison	WI	9700	3200	M [5]	Cath OS	M	U	 A/S	4		Y	Y	 FAF	6	7	1	7	4	2	7	4	2	2.9 2.8	Y	Y	
0488	Ohio Dominican C Columbus	OH	9800	3500	B [5]	Cath S	V	S	 A=S	E			Y		8	7	0	5	3	1	7	4	3	2.8 2.7	Y	Y	
0489	Ind Inst of Techn Fort Wayne	IN	9900 [3]	3100	B [5]	Priv	L	U	 A=S	S		Y		3/01 FAF	9	3	0	9	4	5	6	6	2	2.9 2.5	Y		Y
0490	Shimer C Waukegan	IL	9900 [2]	1500	B [5]	Priv	M	S	 A=S	4		Y	Y		9	4	0	7	2	3	6	5	7	2.8 2.8	Y	Y	
0491	Silver Lake C Manitowoc	WI	10400	2900	M [5]	Cath S	S		8/01 A=S	E		Y		8/01 FAF	9	7	0		1		6	4	1	2.8	Y	Y	
0492	Kendall C Evanston	IL	10600	4100	B [5]	Meth	M	S	9/01 A/S	Q				 FA/FF	7	5	0	4	3	1	6			2.5 2.3			
0493	Defiance C Defiance	OH	10900 [3]	3000	B [5]	UCC O	S		8/15 A/S	4			Y	8/27 FA/FF	8	6	0	3	1	1	7	5	2	2.8 2.5	Y	Y	Y
0494	Niles C of Loyola Chicago	IL	11200 [3]	2700	B [5]	Cath OS	V	U	 A/S	E			[7]	6/30 FAF	9	0	0	9	5			5	5	2.8 2.7	Y		
0495	Urbana U Urbana	OH	11400 [3]	3900	B [5]	Oth	S		 A=S	E		Y	Y	 FA/FF	9	4	0	7	3	1	7	6		2.6	Y	Y	
0496	Northland C Ashland	WI	11800 [3]	3500	B [5]	UCC	T		8/15 A=S	O		Y	Y	7/15 FA/FF	8	5	0	8	1	6	7	4	2		Y	Y	Y
0497	Vandercook C Music Chicago	IL	12200	4200	M [5]	Priv	V	U	8/01 A=S	S				8/01 FF=FA	7	3	5	8	3	2	9	8		 2.6			Y

▲ **Sequence number—indicates the order of the college in this book only. Do *not* use this number with admissions tests or need analysis services.**

[1] No campus room and board facilities
[2] Room only or board only
[3] Most freshmen required to live on campus
[4] City or district residence requirements
[5] Accredited by a regional accrediting association or a recognized candidate for accreditation
[6] All female freshman class
[7] All male freshman class

MAJORS AVAILABLE AND PERCENT OF STUDENTS STUDYING IN EACH AREA

Column headings by area:

- **Agri.**: Agriculture, general; Agronomy (crops & mgmt); Animal Science (husbandry); Fish, Wildlife Mgmt; Forestry
- **Business**: Business/Commerce, general; Accounting; Banking/Finance; Business Economics; Business Mgmt/Admin; Marketing/Purchasing; Secretarial Studies
- **Comm.**: Communications, general; Journalism; Radio/TV (broadcasting); Advertising
- **Education**: Art Education; Distributive Education; Elementary Education; English Education; Mathematics Education; Music Education; Physical Education; Science Education; Secondary Education; Social Science Education; Special Education; Speech Education
- **Engineering**: Engineering, general; Chemical; Civil; Electrical/Electronics/Comm; Industrial/Management; Mechanical
- **Fine/App. Arts**: Architecture; Fine/Applied Arts, general; Art (Paint, draw, sculpt); Art History/Appreciation; Dance; Dramatic Arts (theater arts); Music (liberal arts); Music (perform, compos, theory)
- **Lang.**: French; German; Italian; Latin; Spanish; Russian
- **Health**: Predentistry; Premedicine; Medical/Lab Technology; Nursing (registered nurse); Occupational Therapy; Preoptometry; Prepharmacy; Physical Therapy; Preveterinary Medicine
- **Home Ec.**: Home Economics, general; Clothing and Textiles; Consumer Ec/Home Mgmt; Family Relations/Child Devel; Food and Nutrition/Dietetics; Institution Mgmt
- **Humanities**: Humanities, general; Creative Writing; English, general; Literature, English; Philosophy; Religion; Speech/Forensic Science
- **Math-Sciences**: Mathematics, general; Computer/Info Sciences; Biological Sciences, general; Biology; Botany; Zoology; Physical Sciences, general; Chemistry; Physics
- **Social Sciences**: Crim Just/Law Enforce; Social Work; Social Sciences, general; Anthropology; Area Studies (Amer., African, etc.); Economics; Geography; History; Prelaw; Political Science; Psychology; Sociology
- **GS**: General Studies
- **ROTC**: Air Force; Army; Navy

Sequence Number	Agri.	Business	Comm.	Education	Engineering	Fine/App. Arts	Lang.	Health	Home Ec.	Humanities	Math-Sciences	Social Sciences	GS	ROTC
0468							029%			061% ■ Religion	4%			
0469										100%				
0470										■ Humanities, general; English, general; Literature, English; Philosophy		■ History	■	
0471										100% ■ Religion				
0472		010% ■ Business Mgmt/Admin; Secretarial Studies		016% [1] ■ Elementary Education; Secondary Education		4% ■ Music (perform, compos, theory)				053% ■ Religion				
0473		012%		7% [1]			1%			078% ■ Religion		2%		
0474		020% ■ Business Mgmt/Admin	015% ■ Communications, general				5%	020% [1]		015% ■ English, general; Philosophy; Religion	010% [1] ■ Computer/Info Sciences; Biology; Chemistry	010% [1] ■ Social Sciences, general; Area Studies; Psychology	■	
0475				1%		099% ■ Music (perform, compos, theory)								
0476		8%			079%									
0477										075% ■ English, general; Literature, English; Philosophy; Religion		025% ■ History; Psychology		
0478		1% ■ Marketing/Purchasing	1% ■ Communications, general; Advertising			097% [1] ■ Fine/Applied Arts, general			1% ■ Home Economics, general; Clothing and Textiles					
0479			8% ■ Radio/TV (broadcasting); Advertising			092% [1] ■ Fine/Applied Arts, general; Art (Paint, draw, sculpt)								
0480			■ Communications, general	010% [1]		7% ■ Music (liberal arts); Music (perform, compos, theory)				023% ■ Religion		033% ■ Social Sciences, general; Psychology	■	
0481		040% [1] ■ Business/Commerce, general; Business Mgmt/Admin; Marketing/Purchasing	040% ■ Communications, general	[1]		■ Fine/Applied Arts, general				020% ■ Religion	■ Mathematics, general; Computer/Info Sciences	[1] ■ Social Sciences, general	■	
0482		022% [1] ■ Business/Commerce, general; Accounting; Business Mgmt/Admin; Secretarial Studies	5% ■ Communications, general; Radio/TV (broadcasting)	015% [1] ■ Art; Distributive; Elementary; English; Mathematics; Music; Physical; Science; Secondary; Social Science; Special Education		6% ■ Art (Paint, draw, sculpt); Music (liberal arts); Music (perform, compos, theory)	1% ■ Spanish	8% ■ Predentistry; Premedicine; Medical/Lab Technology; Preoptometry; Prepharmacy; Preveterinary Medicine	2% ■ Home Economics, general	014% ■ Humanities, general; English, general; Philosophy; Religion; Speech/Forensic Science	012% [1] ■ Mathematics, general; Computer/Info Sciences; Biological Sciences, general; Biology; Physical Sciences, general; Chemistry	012% ■ Crim Just/Law Enforce; Social Work; Social Sciences, general; History; Prelaw; Psychology; Sociology		
0483		010%		020% ■ Special Education	5%	1%	1%	5%		020% ■ Philosophy; Religion	010%	015% ■ Social Work; History		
0484		011% ■ Accounting; Business Economics; Business Mgmt/Admin	8%	016% [1] ■ Art; Elementary; English; Mathematics; Music; Physical; Science; Secondary; Social Science Education	1% ■ Engineering, general	8% [1] ■ Art (Paint, draw, sculpt); Music (liberal arts); Music (perform, compos, theory)	1%	1% ■ Nursing (registered nurse)		2% ■ English, general	6% ■ Mathematics, general; Biological Sciences, general; Biology	010% ■ Crim Just/Law Enforce; Social Work; Social Sciences, general; History; Psychology; Sociology		
0485			1%	1%		1%	9% ■ Latin; Spanish			052% ■ English, general; Philosophy	7%	029% ■ History; Psychology		
0486		086% [1] ■ Business/Commerce, general; Accounting; Business Mgmt/Admin									2% ■ Computer/Info Sciences	011% ■ Crim Just/Law Enforce		
0487		037% ■ Business/Commerce, general; Accounting; Business Mgmt/Admin	1%	015% [1] ■ Art; Distributive; Elementary; English; Mathematics; Science; Social Science; Special Education		2% ■ Fine/Applied Arts, general; Art (Paint, draw, sculpt); Dramatic Arts (theater arts)	1% ■ French; Spanish	012% ■ Predentistry; Premedicine; Medical/Lab Technology; Nursing (registered nurse); Prepharmacy; Preveterinary Medicine		5% ■ Humanities, general; English, general; Literature, English; Religion	7% [1] ■ Mathematics, general; Computer/Info Sciences; Biological Sciences, general; Biology	010% [1] ■ Crim Just/Law Enforce; Social Sciences, general; Economics; History; Prelaw; Political Science; Psychology; Sociology	■	
0488		030% ■ Business/Commerce, general; Accounting; Business Mgmt/Admin	6% ■ Communications, general	011% [1] ■ Art; Elementary; English; Mathematics; Physical; Science; Secondary; Social Science; Special Education		2% ■ Art (Paint, draw, sculpt)	1%	1% ■ Predentistry; Premedicine; Medical/Lab Technology; Prepharmacy; Preveterinary Medicine	1%	2% ■ English, general; Philosophy; Religion	012% ■ Mathematics, general; Computer/Info Sciences; Biology; Chemistry	014% [1] ■ Crim Just/Law Enforce; Social Work; Social Sciences, general; Economics; History; Prelaw; Political Science; Psychology; Sociology		Y
0489		040% ■ Business/Commerce, general; Accounting; Business Mgmt/Admin; Marketing/Purchasing	1% ■ Communications, general		035% ■ Engineering, general; Civil; Electrical/Electronics/Comm; Mechanical			[1]			020% [1] ■ Computer/Info Sciences	4% [1] ■ Social Work		
0490										020% ■ Humanities, general	010%	030% ■ Social Sciences, general	■	
0491		045% ■ Accounting; Business Mgmt/Admin		030% ■ Art; Elementary; Music; Special Education		5% ■ Fine/Applied Arts, general; Music (liberal arts)		5% ■ Nursing (registered nurse)	1%	3% ■ English, general; Religion	8% ■ Mathematics, general; Computer/Info Sciences; Biology	2% ■ Social Sciences, general; History		
0492		035% [1] ■ Business/Commerce, general	1%	010% [1]				010%	015% ■ Food and Nutrition/Dietetics	1%		2% [1]		
0493		016% ■ Business/Commerce, general; Accounting; Banking/Finance; Business Mgmt/Admin; Marketing/Purchasing	4% ■ Communications, general	026% [1] ■ Art; Distributive; Elementary; English; Mathematics; Music; Physical; Science; Secondary; Social Science; Special Education		1% ■ Fine/Applied Arts, general; Art (Paint, draw, sculpt); Music (liberal arts)	1%	1% ■ Predentistry; Premedicine; Medical/Lab Technology; Preveterinary Medicine		2% ■ English, general; Philosophy; Religion; Speech/Forensic Science	6% [1] ■ Mathematics, general; Computer/Info Sciences; Biological Sciences, general; Biology; Physical Sciences, general; Chemistry	3% ■ Crim Just/Law Enforce; Social Work; Social Sciences, general; History; Prelaw; Psychology	■	
0494			010% ■ Communications, general	3%		3% ■ Fine/Applied Arts, general; Dramatic Arts (theater arts)	3% ■ French; German; Italian; Latin; Spanish			030% [1] ■ Humanities, general; English, general; Literature, English; Philosophy; Religion	6% ■ Mathematics, general; Computer/Info Sciences; Biological Sciences, general; Biology; Physical Sciences, general; Chemistry; Physics	045% ■ Social Work; Social Sciences, general; Anthropology; Economics; History; Political Science; Psychology; Sociology		
0495		042% ■ Business/Commerce, general; Accounting; Banking/Finance; Business Economics; Business Mgmt/Admin; Marketing/Purchasing	■ Communications, general	029% [1] ■ Distributive; Elementary; English; Mathematics; Physical; Science; Secondary; Social Science; Special Education				1% ■ Predentistry; Premedicine; Preveterinary Medicine		2% ■ Humanities, general; English, general; Philosophy; Religion	010% ■ Biological Sciences, general; Biology; Physical Sciences, general; Chemistry	011% ■ Crim Just/Law Enforce; Social Work; Social Sciences, general; Prelaw; Psychology; Sociology		Y
0496	8% [1] ■ Fish, Wildlife Mgmt; Forestry	016% ■ Business/Commerce, general; Accounting; Business Economics; Business Mgmt/Admin	1%	010% [1] ■ Elementary; English; Mathematics; Music; Science; Secondary; Social Science Education	1%	3% ■ Music (liberal arts); Music (perform, compos, theory)	1%	2% [1] ■ Predentistry; Premedicine; Occupational Therapy; Preoptometry; Prepharmacy; Preveterinary Medicine		4% ■ English, general; Literature, English; Religion	023% [1] ■ Mathematics, general; Computer/Info Sciences; Biological Sciences, general; Biology; Physical Sciences, general; Chemistry	7% [1] ■ Social Sciences, general; Anthropology; Economics; History; Prelaw; Psychology; Sociology		
0497				099% ■ Music Education		1%								

[1] Additional majors available in this area
[2] ROTC available

†Accredited by a nationally recognized accrediting body other than one of the regional accrediting associations

Great Lakes States
(continued)

IL, IN, MI, OH, WI

LIBERAL ADMISSIONS *Some accepted students from lower half of HS class*

Sequence Number	School name (upper entry) / City (lower entry)	State	Costs: Resident tuition/fees + room/board	Costs: Room/Board (upper entry) / Nonresident tuition/fees + room/board (lower entry)	General Information: Highest degree	Affiliation (upper entry) / Religious observance (lower entry)	Size of community	Type of community	Admissions: Fall term application deadline (upper entry) / Tests desired or required (lower entry)	Calendar	Fall admission only	Early admission	Deferred admission	Financial Aid: Fall term application deadline (upper entry) / Forms to be filed (lower entry)	Number in 10 who— -have need, receive some aid	Under-grads: -are women	-are graduate students	Freshmen: -live on campus	-are minority students	-are nonresidents	-return as sophomores	-complete degree	-enter graduate study	HS GPA (upper entry) / 1st year college GPA (lower entry)	Special Programs: Credit by exam	Student designed majors	Fraternities/sororities
	Enrollment 1,000 to 5,000																										
0498	Chicago St U Chicago	IL	1800	[1] 4900	M[5]	Pub	V	U	A=S	S				7/01 FF=FA	8	7	1	0	9	1	5	2	2	2.6 2.7	Y	Y	Y
0499	Purdue North Central Westville	IN	1800	[1] 4500	M[5]	Pub	S		S/A	E		Y		2/15 FA/FF	5	6	0	0	1	0	6	1		3.0 2.4	Y		
0500	Northeastern Ill U Chicago	IL	1900	[1] 5100	M[5]	Pub	V	U	8/15 ACT	S				4/01	4	6	1	0	4	1	7	2		2.8	Y	Y	Y
0501	DeVry Inst of Techn Chicago	IL	5000	[1]	M[5]	Priv	V	U	A=S	T			Y	FA/FF	8	3	0	0	7	1	5	5			Y		Y
0502	DeVry Inst of Techn Lombard	IL	5000	[1]	M[5]	Priv	M	S	A=S	T			Y	FA/FF	7	2	0	0	2	2	5	4			Y		Y
0503	DeVry Inst of Techn Columbus	OH	5000	[1]	B[5]	Priv	V	S	A=S	T			Y	FA/FF	8	2	0	0	2	4	4	4			Y		Y
0504	Olivet Nazarene U Kankakee	IL	10000	3500	M[5]	Oth OS	M		ACT	E		Y		8/01 FAF	7	5	1	9	1	6	7	4	2	3.0	Y	Y	
0505	Marian C Fond Du Lac Fond Du Lac	WI	10300[3]	2900	M[5]	Cath OS	S		A/S	E		Y	Y	FA/FF	8	7	1	6	1	2	8	6	1	2.7 2.7	Y	Y	Y
0506	Concordia U Mequon	WI	10500	3100	M[5]	Oth O	S		A/S	4		Y	Y	4/15 FAF	8	5	0	5	1	1	8	4		2.9 2.9	Y	Y	
0507	Northwood Inst Midland	MI	11100[3]	3600	B[5]	Priv	S		9/01 A/S	Q		Y	Y	3/01 FA/FF	5	4	0	9	2	3	8	3	1	2.1	Y		Y
0508	Aurora U Aurora	IL	11600	3500	M[5]	Priv	M	S	A/S	Q		Y	Y	8/15 FA/FF	9	5	2	7	2	1	7		1		Y	Y	Y
	Enrollment 5,000 to 15,000																										
0509	Wis Stout,U of Menomonie	WI	4400[3]	2500 8000	M[5]	Pub	S		A/S	E		Y	Y	2/15 FFS	6	5	1	8	1	3	9	5	1	2.8 2.6	Y		Y
0510	Northern Mich U Marquette	MI	5300[3]	3300 6600	M[5]	Pub	S		A/S	E		Y	Y	FA/FF	6		1	4	1	1	7	4	2	2.8	Y	Y	Y
0511	Ferris St U Big Rapids	MI	5400[3]	3000 7900	P[5]	Pub	S		8/01 ACT	Q			Y	8/01 FA/FF	6	4	0	7	1	1		8	1	2.6 2.6	Y		Y
	TRADITIONAL ADMISSIONS *Majority of accepted students in top 50% of HS class*																										
	Enrollment to 1,000																										
0512	Ind U East Richmond	IN	1800	[1] 4500	B[5]	Pub	S		A=S	E		Y	Y	3/01 FAF		7	0	0	1	1	5				Y		
0513	Ctr for Robotic Tech Chicago	IL	3100	[1]	B	Priv	V	U	9/28 Oth	O				9/28 Oth		1	0	0	4	1				2.5 2.8	Y		
0514	Immanuel Lutheran C Eau Claire	WI	3100[3]	1700	B	Luth OS	M	S	A/S	E		Y		6/15 None	3	4	0	2	1	7	8			3.1 3.1	Y		
0515	Calumet C St Joseph Whiting	IN	4000	[1]	B[5]	Cath S	M	U	A=S	E		Y	Y		6	7	0	0	4	2	6	4		2.5 2.4	Y	Y	Y
0516	Lakeview C Nsg Danville	IL	4500	[1]	B[5]	Priv	S		A/S	S					9	9	0	0	1	1	9				Y		
0517	Northwestern C Wis Watertown	WI	5000	1800	B[5]	Luth OS	S		ACT	S		Y	[7]	5/01 FA/FF	6	0	0	9	0		8	6	9	3.2 2.7			
0518	Northland Baptist C Dunbar	WI	5300	2700	M †	Bapt OS	T		8/20 A=S	E			Y	None	9	6	0	9	1	8	8	7	1	3.1 2.8	Y		
0519	Lutheran C Hlth Prof Fort Wayne	IN	5700[2]	1600	B[5]	Luth	M	U	7/01 A=S	E				6/15 FA/FF	5	9	0	4	1	2	8				Y		
0520	Aero-Space Inst Chicago	IL	6000	[1]	B	Priv	V	U	A/S	E				10/01 FF=FA	8	1	0	0	8	1	9	7	1	2.5 2.2	Y		Y
0521	ETI Tech C-Cleveland Cleveland	OH	6000	2200	B †	Priv	V	U	Oth	Q		Y	Y	Oth	8	1	0	2	2	2	8	7	1	2.5 2.7	Y		
0522	Grace Bible C Grand Rapids	MI	6400	2800	B[5]	Oth OS	L	S	7/15 ACT	E		Y	Y	6/01 FA/FF	7	5	0	8	1	4	8		1	2.6 2.3	Y		
0523	Milwaukee Inst Art Milwaukee	WI	6400	[1]	B[5]	Priv	V	U	A=S	S			Y	FAF	7	5	0	0	1	1	8	6		2.4			
0524	D'Etre U Grosse Pointe	MI	7400[3]	2500 10500	M	Priv	V	U	9/01 A=S	S		Y	Y	3/01 FF=FA	6	7	1	5	7	5			6		Y		
0525	Summit Christian C Fort Wayne	IN	8700	2700	B[5]	Oth OS	L	U	8/15 S/A	E		Y	Y	7/30 FA/FF	9	5	0		1	1	7				Y		

▲ Sequence number—indicates the order of the college in this book only. Do *not* use this number with admissions tests or need analysis services.

[1] No campus room and board facilities
[2] Room only or board only
[3] Most freshmen required to live on campus
[4] City or district residence requirements
[5] Accredited by a regional accrediting association or a recognized candidate for accreditation
[6] All female freshman class
[7] All male freshman class

MAJORS AVAILABLE AND PERCENT OF STUDENTS STUDYING IN EACH AREA

Sequence Number	Agri.	Business	Comm.	Education	Engineering	Fine/App. Arts	Lang.	Health	Home Ec.	Humanities	Math-Sciences	Social Sciences	GS	ROTC
0498		026% [1]	1%	010% [1]		1%	1%	011% [1]	1%	1%	014% [1]	6%		YYY
0499	1%	024% [1]	1%	4%	2%	1%	1%	017%	1%	2%	3%	2%		
0500		027%		017% [1]		2%	1%			5% [1]	012% [1]	014%		YY
0501		019%			054%						027% [1]			
0502		012%	014%		051%						023% [1]			Y
0503		022%			057%						021% [1]			YY
0504	[1]	020%	4%	024% [1]	3%	3%	1%	7%	3%	8%	011% [1]	015%		Y
0505		020%		018% [1]		4%		042% [1]		2%	2%	2%		Y
0506	1%	030%	1%	032% [1]	2%	3% [1]	2%	014%		4%	5%	4%		
0507		093% [1]	2%								4%			Y
0508		026%		9% [1]	1%			015% [1]		2%	3% [1]	2% [1]		
0509		036% [1]		011% [1]	018%	010%			6%		4% [1]	4%		
0510	[1]	017% [1]	011%	017% [1]	1%	4% [1]	1%	012% [1]	1%	5%	5% [1]	012% [1]		Y
0511	1%	024% [1]	1%	5% [1]	3%	1%	1%	023% [1]		1%	7% [1]	2%		
0512		020%		011%				020%		1%	3%	7%		
0513		1%			1%					2%	2%	1%		
0514				034%						024%				
0515		063% [1]	3%	2%						2%	9% [1]	019%		
0516								100%						
0517							1%			099%				
0518		9%		023% [1]		3%			8%	033%	6%	3%		
0519								100%						
0520		052% [1]			048% [1]									
0521					067%	018%						015%		
0522		013%		[1]						070%		9%		
0523						100% [1]								
0524		050%	2%		6%		020%			2% [1]	010% [1]	010% [1]		
0525		6%		018% [1]						029%				
Sequence Number	Agri.	Business	Comm.	Education	Engineering	Fine/App. Arts	Lang.	Health	Home Ec.	Humanities	Math-Sciences	Social Sciences	GS	ROTC

1 Additional majors available in this area
2 ROTC available

†Accredited by a nationally recognized accrediting body other than one of the regional accrediting associations

Great Lakes States
(continued)

IL, IN, MI, OH, WI

TRADITIONAL ADMISSIONS *Majority of accepted students in top 50% of HS class*

Enrollment to 1,000

Sequence Number	School name (upper entry) City (lower entry)	State	Costs: Resident tuition/fees + room/board (upper entry) Nonresident tuition/fees + room/board (lower entry)	Costs: Room/Board	General Information: Highest degree	General Information: Affiliation (upper entry) Religious observance (lower entry)	General Information: Size of community	General Information: Type of community	Admissions: Fall term application deadline (upper entry) Tests desired or required (lower entry)	Admissions: Calendar	Admissions: Fall admission only	Admissions: Early admission	Admissions: Deferred admission	Financial Aid: Fall term application deadline (upper entry) Forms to be filed (lower entry)	Financial Aid: -have need, receive some aid	Undergrads: -are women	Undergrads: -are graduate students	Freshmen: -live on campus	Freshmen: -are minority students	Freshmen: -are nonresidents	Freshmen: -return as sophomores	Freshmen: -complete degree	Freshmen: -enter graduate study	HS GPA (upper entry) 1st year college GPA (lower entry)	Special Programs: Credit by exam	Special Programs: Student designed majors	Special Programs: Fraternities/sororities
0526	Walsh C Canton	OH	8700	3100	M[5]	Cath OS	L	S	8/15 A=S	E		Y	Y	7/15 FF=FA	9	6	0	4	1	1	9	7	1	3.0 2.9	Y	Y	
0527	Grand Rapids Bapt C Grand Rapids	MI	8900	3500	P[5]	Bapt OS	V	S	8/15 ACT	E		Y	Y	3/01 FA/FF	7	5	1		1	2	6	4		3.1	Y		
0528	Wilberforce U Wilberforce	OH	9100	3200	B[5]	Oth	T		6/01	T		Y	Y	6/01 FA/FF	9	6	0	8	9	7	7	5	2	2.4	Y		Y
0529	Bethel C Mishawaka	IN	9300	2500	M[5]	Oth OS	L	U	A=S	E		Y	Y	3/01 FA/FF	8	5	1	5	9	2	7	6		2.8 2.9	Y		
0530	Blessing C of Nsg Quincy	IL	9300	2600	B[5]	Priv	S		7/01 A/S	S				5/01	9	9	0	5	1	4	7	7	1	3.3	Y		
0531	McKendree C Lebanon	IL	9300 [3]	3000	B[5]	Meth O	T		A/S	S			Y	8/31 FA/FF	8	5	0	5	2	1	8	6	1	3.3 2.5	Y	Y	Y
0532	Mount Mary C Milwaukee	WI	9400	2400	M[5]	Cath OS	V	S	8/15 A=S	S		Y	[6]	FA/FF	6	9	1	4	1	1	8	5	1	2.9 2.8	Y	Y	
0533	Notre Dame C-Ohio Cleveland	OH	9500 [3]	3200	B[5]	Cath S	V	S	8/01 A=S	S			Y[6]	3/01 FAF	9	9	0	7	3	1	7	7	1	3.0	Y		
0534	Art Acad Cincinnati Cincinnati	OH	9800 [2]	2600	B[5]	Priv	L	U	8/15 A=S	S			Y	6/15 Oth	9	5	0	1	1	2	7	7	4	2.7	Y		
0535	Grace C Winona Lake	IN	9800	3200	B[5]	Oth OS	T		9/01 A=S	E		Y		4/01 FAF	9	6	0	9	1	6	7	5	2	3.1 2.8	Y		
0536	Ill C Jacksonville	IL	9900	3300	B[5]	Pres OS	S		8/15 A=S	E				8/01 FA/FF	8	5	0	7	1	1	7	5	2	2.5	Y	Y	
0537	Wis Lutheran C Milwaukee	WI	9900	3100	B[5]	Luth OS	V	S	8/15 A/S	E		Y	Y	4/01 FA/FF	9	6	0	8	1	2	7	5	4	2.9	Y		
0538	Siena Heights C Adrian	MI	10000	3400	M[5]	Cath	S		8/15 A/S	E		Y	Y	FA/FF	9	6	1	6	1	1	7	4	2	2.8	Y	Y	Y
0539	Spring Arbor C Spring Arbor	MI	10000 [3]	2800	B[5]	Oth OS	T		8/01 A/S	4		Y		2/15 FA/FF	9	6	0	8	1	1	7	4	1	3.0 2.8	Y	Y	
0540	Olivet C Olivet	MI	10100 [3]	2700	B[5]	UCC	T		8/15 ACT	E		Y	Y	1/31 FF=FA	9	4	0	9	1	1	8	5	2	2.7 2.6	Y	Y	Y
0541	Concordia C Ann Arbor	MI	10600	3500	B[5]	Oth OS	M	S	A=S	E		Y	Y	7/01 FA/FF	9	6	0	9	1	2	8	5	8		Y		
0542	Wilmington C Wilmington	OH	10600 [3]	3100	B[5]	Oth	S		A=S	E		Y	Y	3/31 FAF	9	5	0	8	1	1	8	5	3	2.7	Y	Y	Y
0543	Marian C Indianapolis	IN	10700 [3]	3100	B[5]	Cath S	V	S	8/15 A=S	E			Y	3/01 FAF	8	6	0	5	1	1	8	4	2	2.7 2.6	Y		
0544	Saint Francis C Fort Wayne	IN	10700 [3]	3500	M[5]	Cath S	M	S	A=S	E		Y		7/01 FA/FF	8	7	1	6	1	2	7	3	1		Y		Y
0545	Trinity Christian C Palos Heights	IL	10800	3100	B[5]	Oth O	S		8/15 A/S	4		Y		8/15 FA/FF	8	5	0	6	2	4	7	4	2	2.8	Y		
0546	Concordia U of Ill River Forest	IL	10900	3600	M[5]	Oth OS	S		ACT	Q			Y	7/15 FAF	7	7	1	7	1	4	8	6	2	3.1 2.8	Y		
0547	MacMurray C Jacksonville	IL	10900	3200	B[5]	Meth	S		A=S	4		Y		FA/FF	9	5	0	9	1	1	8	6	1	2.9 2.7	Y		Y
0548	West Suburban C Nsg Oak Park	IL	10900	3600	B[5]	Priv	M	S	8/31 ACT	Q				4/01 FAF	9	9	0	6	2	1	7	7	2	2.9	Y		
0549	Goshen C Goshen	IN	11000	3300	B[5]	Oth OS	S		A=S	T		Y	Y	FA/FF	9	5	0	8	1	6	8	6	2	3.3 3.0	Y	Y	
0550	Huntington C Huntington	IN	11000	3100	M[5]	Oth OS	S		A=S	4		Y	Y	FA/FF	6	5	1	9	1	4	7	6	2	2.9 2.9	Y		Y
0551	Ind Wesleyan U Marion	IN	11000	3400	M[5]	Oth OS	S		9/01 S/A	4		Y		4/15 FA/FF	9	6	1	7	1	2	8	5	4	3.0 3.3	Y		
0552	Barat C Lake Forest	IL	11100	3200	B[5]	Cath S	S		A=S	4		Y	Y	FF/FA	7	7	0	6	2	2	6	5	4	2.5 2.5	Y	Y	
0553	Ursuline C Pepper Pike	OH	11100	3700	M[5]	Cath S	S		A=S	E		Y	Y	FAF	4	9	1	2	2	1	9	7	1	2.8 3.3	Y	Y	
0554	Lakeland C Sheboygan	WI	11400	3300	M[5]	UCC S	S		A/S	4			Y	FA/FF	9	5	0	8	1	3	6	5	1	2.8 2.5	Y		Y
0555	Greenville C Greenville	IL	11500 [3]	3600	B[5]	Oth OS	T		A=S	4				FA/FF	9	5	0	8	1	5	6	4	2	2.8 2.6	Y	Y	
0556	Mundelein C Chicago	IL	11500	3400	M[5]	Cath S	V	U	9/16 A=S	O				4/01 FAF	9	9	1	6	4	2	8			3.1	Y	Y	

▲ **Sequence number—indicates the order of the college in this book only. Do *not* use this number with admissions tests or need analysis services.**

[1] No campus room and board facilities
[2] Room only or board only
[3] Most freshmen required to live on campus
[4] City or district residence requirements
[5] Accredited by a regional accrediting association or a recognized candidate for accreditation
[6] All female freshman class
[7] All male freshman class

MAJORS AVAILABLE AND PERCENT OF STUDENTS STUDYING IN EACH AREA

Sequence Number	Agri.	Business	Comm.	Education	Engineering	Fine/App. Arts	Lang.	Health	Home Ec.	Humanities	Math-Sciences	Social Sciences	GS	ROTC
0526		043%	4%	014% [1]		1%	1%	013%		4%	010%	3% [1]		
0527		020%	1%	010% [1]		6%				026%	5%	011%		Y (Army)
0528		030%	010%			2%		9% [1]		1%	021% [1]	026%		YY (Air Force, Army)
0529		018%		031% [1]	2% [1]	7% [1]		016%		6%	5% [1]	9% [1]		YYY
0530								100%						
0531		037%	2%	018% [1]		3%		9%		4%	8%	018% [1]		Y (Air Force)
0532		025% [1]	4%	013% [1]		016% [1]	1%	018% [1]	012%	2%	3%	6%		
0533		050%	2%	012% [1]		1%	1%		2%	5%	7% [1]	7%		Y (Army)
0534						067% [1]								YYY
0535		024%	5%	027%		5%	4%	1%		8%	7%	016%		
0536		041%	5%	010%	5%	1%	2%	2% [1]		3%	7% [1]	7% [1]		
0537		020%	020%	020% [1]		2%				015%	7%	016%		
0538		028% [1]		010%		010% [1]	1%		1%	8%	013% [1]	016% [1]		
0539		017%	7%	030%	1%	8%		3%		9%	013% [1]	010%		
0540		031% [1]	9%	9%	1%	1%	1%	1%		2%	3% [1]	2% [1]		
0541		050%		025% [1]		5%		1%		012%		5%		YY
0542	7% [1]	028%	6%	020% [1]	1%	2%	3%	2% [1]		3% [1]	7% [1]	018% [1]		
0543		021%	2%	022% [1]		2%	2%	010% [1]	4%	2%	6%	4%		YY
0544		026%	013%	019% [1]		5% [1]		010% [1]		2%	4% [1]	015%		
0545		026%		015% [1]		4%	3%	016%		010% [1]	9% [1]	8%		
0546		011%	4%	051% [1]			1%	012%		6%	8% [1]	7%		
0547		013%	1%	029%	1%	2%	1%	8% [1]		2%	6% [1]	019%		
0548								100%						
0549		015%	5%	013% [1]		8%	1%	010%	1%	6%	013% [1]	014%		
0550		022% [1]	3%	027% [1]		5%		2%		012%	012% [1]	9% [1]		
0551		018%	1%	011%		6%	1%	026%		5%	3% [1]	014%		Y (Army)
0552		037%	3%	8% [1]		8% [1]		4% [1]		010%	2% [1]	9%		
0553		013%	2%	6% [1]	1%	6% [1]	1%	051% [1]	1%	3%	3% [1]	8% [1]		
0554		072%		015% [1]		1%	1%	1%		3%	5% [1]	1% [1]		
0555		017%	2%	019% [1]		1%	1%	011%		2%	3% [1]	2%		
0556		033%	1%	1% [1]		7% [1]	1%	1%	1%	8%	3%	5%		

[1] Additional majors available in this area
[2] ROTC available

†Accredited by a nationally recognized accrediting body other than one of the regional accrediting associations

Great Lakes States

(continued)

IL, IN, MI, OH, WI

TRADITIONAL ADMISSIONS *Majority of accepted students in top 50% of HS class*

Sequence Number	School name (upper entry) City (lower entry)	State	Costs: Resident tuition/fees + room/board	Costs: Room/Board (upper entry) Nonresident tuition/fees + room/board (lower entry)	General Information: Highest degree	General Information: Affiliation (upper entry) Religious observance (lower entry)	General Information: Size of community	General Information: Type of community	Admissions: Fall term application deadline (upper entry) Tests desired or required (lower entry)	Admissions: Calendar	Admissions: Fall admission only	Admissions: Early admission	Admissions: Deferred admission	Financial Aid: Fall term application deadline (upper entry) Forms to be filed (lower entry)	Financial Aid: -have need, receive some aid	Student Profile (Number in 10 who—), Undergrads: -are women	Undergrads: -are graduate students	Freshmen: -live on campus	Freshmen: -are minority students	Freshmen: -are nonresidents	Freshmen: -return as sophomores	Freshmen: -complete degree	Freshmen: -enter graduate study	Freshmen: HS GPA (upper entry) 1st year college GPA (lower entry)	Special Programs: Credit by exam	Special Programs: Student designed majors	Special Programs: Fraternities/sororities
	Enrollment to 1,000																										
0557	Trinity C of Ill Deerfield	IL	11600	3600	B[5]	Oth OS	T		 A/S	E				 FA/FF	8	5	0	8	2	4	7	5	4	3.0 2.6	Y		
0558	Eureka C Eureka	IL	11700	3000	B[5]	Oth	T		 A/S	O			Y	 FA/FF	9	5	0	9	1	1	8	6	3	 2.8	Y	Y	Y
0559	Lake Erie C Painesville	OH	11700	3900	M[5]	Priv	S		 A/S	S		Y	Y	4/01 FF=FA	9	8	2	7	1	6	7	6	2	2.8 3.0	Y	Y	
0560	Center Creative Stud Detroit	MI	11800[2]	2900	B[5]	Priv	V	U	/00 A=S	E				3/01 FF=FA	4	4	0	2	1	2	8	4	1	2.8 2.8	Y	Y	
0561	Judson C Elgin	IL	12200[3]	4100	B[5]	Bapt OS	M		8/15 A=S	O		Y	Y	5/01 FA/FF	9	5	0	7	1	3				2.9			
0562	Rosary C River Forest	IL	12200	3800	M[5]	Cath S	S		 A=S	E		Y	Y	 FAF	6	7	1	6	2		8			3.0 3.0	Y	Y	
0563	Franklin C Franklin	IN	12400[3]	3400	B[5]	Bapt O	S		8/15 A=S	4		Y	Y	 FF=FA	9	5	0	9	1	1		5	2	 2.7	Y		Y
0564	Saint Mary-of-Woods St Mary-Woods	IN	12700[3]	3600	M[5]	Cath S	M		 A=S	E		Y	Y[6]	 FA/FF	8	9	0	9	1	3	8	7	2	3.0 3.0	Y	Y	
0565	Rockford C Rockford	IL	12800	3400	M[5]	Priv	M	S	 A/S	E		Y	Y	 FA/FF	8	6	1	7	1	3	9	5	2	3.0 2.4	Y	Y	
0566	Clevelnd Inst of Art Cleveland	OH	14000[3]	4200	B[5]	Priv	V	U	8/01 A=S	E		Y	Y	4/01 FA/FF	7	5	0	5	1	3	8	4	2	2.7 2.4	Y	Y	
0567	North Park C Chicago	IL	14700	4000	M[5]	Oth OS	V	U	9/04 A=S	Q		Y		7/01 FA/FF	8	5	0	5	3	3	7	4	3	2.9 2.4	Y		
0568	Principia C Elsah	IL	14700[3]	4200	B[5]	Oth O	T		 S/A	Q				 FAF	7	6	0	9	1	9	9	6	3	3.3 2.9	Y	Y	
0569	Antioch C Yellow Springs	OH	16500	3500	B[5]	Priv	T		3/01 A=S	Q		Y	Y	5/01 FA/FF	6	6	0	9	1	8	8	5			Y	Y	
	Enrollment 1,000 to 5,000																										
0570	Ind U at Kokomo Kokomo	IN	1800	[1] 4500	M[5]	Pub	M		8/05 A=S	E		Y	Y	3/01	4	7	1	0	1	1	5			 2.3	Y		
0571	Ind U South Bend South Bend	IN	1800	[1] 4500	M[5]	Pub	L	U	 A=S	E		Y		3/01 FAF	2	6	1	0	1	1	5			 2.5	Y		Y
0572	Ind U Northwest Gary	IN	1800	[1] 4500	M[5]	Pub	L	U	7/15 A=S	E		Y	Y	2/15 FAF	6	6	1	0	3	1	6				Y		
0573	Ind U Southeast New Albany	IN	1800	[1] 4500	M[5]	Pub	S		7/15 A=S	E		Y	Y	3/01 FAF	6	6	0	0	1	1	6			2.5 2.5	Y		Y
0574	Purdue U Calumet Hammond	IN	1800	[1] 4500	M[5]	Pub	L	S	 S/A	E		Y		3/01 FA/FF	4	5	1	0	2		6	2			Y		Y
0575	Ind U-Purdue F W Fort Wayne	IN	2200	[1]	M[5]	Pub	M	S	8/01 A=S	E		Y	Y	3/01 FAF	8	5	0	0	1	1						Y	Y
0576	Wis River Falls,U River Falls	WI	4000[3]	2200 7300	M[5]	Pub	S		 ACT	E		Y	Y	 FAF	7	5	1	8	1	4	7	7	1	 2.3	Y	Y	Y
0577	Wis Superior,U of Superior	WI	4000[3]	2200 7200	M[5]	Pub	S		8/01 ACT	E		Y		 FA/FF	8	5	1	5	1	3	6	4	2	2.9 2.4	Y	Y	
0578	Wis Green Bay,U of Green Bay	WI	4100	2300 7700	M[5]	Pub	M		6/15 ACT	4		Y		4/01 FA/FF	7	6	0	6	1	1	6	3	2	 2.5	Y	Y	Y
0579	Moody Bible Inst Chicago	IL	4700[3]	3800	M[5]	Oth OS	V	U	5/01 ACT	E			Y	 None	9	4	1	9	1	8		6		3.0	Y		
0580	Wis Parkside,U of Kenosha	WI	4900	3100 8500	M[5]	Pub	M	S	 A/S	E		Y	Y	3/15 FF/FA	4	5	0		1	1	7				Y		
0581	Lake Superior St C Sault Ste Marie	MI	5400[3]	3200 7400	M[5]	Pub	S		8/01 ACT	Q				4/01 FA/FF	6	5	1	4	3	1	6			2.9 2.8	Y	Y	Y
0582	Saginaw Valley St U University Ctr	MI	5500	3200 7900	M[5]	Pub	T		 A/S	E		Y		4/01 FA/FF	5	6	0	1	1	1	6	3	3	2.9 2.7	Y	Y	Y
0583	Madonna C Livonia	MI	7300	3200	M[5]	Cath OS	M	S	 ACT	E		Y		2/15 FA/FF	2	8	1	1	2	1	7	3	4	3.0 2.8	Y		
0584	Lawrence Tech U Southfield	MI	8000	3400	P[5]	Priv	M	S	8/14 ACT	Q		Y	Y	6/01 FF/FA	4	2	0	1	1	1	8			2.9	Y	Y	Y
0585	Cedarville C Cedarville	OH	8300[3]	3300	B[5]	Bapt OS	T		 A/S	Q		Y	Y	4/01 FAF	7	6	0	9	1	6	7	4	2	3.3	Y		
0586	Alverno C Milwaukee	WI	9300	2900	B[5]	Cath O	V	S	8/01 Oth	E		Y	Y[6]	 FA/FF	7	9	0	4	2	1	9	6	3	3.0	Y		

▲ **Sequence number—indicates the order of the college in this book only. Do *not* use this number with admissions tests or need analysis services.**

[1] No campus room and board facilities
[2] Room only or board only
[3] Most freshmen required to live on campus
[4] City or district residence requirements
[5] Accredited by a regional accrediting association or a recognized candidate for accreditation
[6] All female freshman class
[7] All male freshman class

MAJORS AVAILABLE AND PERCENT OF STUDENTS STUDYING IN EACH AREA

Sequence Number	Agri.	Business	Comm.	Education	Engineering	Fine/App. Arts	Lang.	Health	Home Ec.	Humanities	Math-Sciences	Social Sciences	GS	ROTC
0557		8%	2%	26%		1%		2%		26%	6%	28%		
0558		22%	4%	18%	2%	1%	1%	10%		2%	6%	2%		
0559		19%		10%		3%	6%			15%	7%	7%		
0560						100%								
0561		6%	3%	12%	1%	5%		1%		5%	8%	11%		Y
0562		40%	7%			2%	2%		9%	9%	12%	16%		
0563		17%	17%	12%		3%	4%			8%	15%	22%		Y
0564		17%	13%	17%		8%	1%	1%	1%	2%	11%	11%		Y
0565		39%		23%		2%	2%	6%		3%	9%	14%		Y
0566				2%										
0567		11%	4%	4%	1%	4%	6%	14%		7%	13%	10%		Y Y
0568		9%	4%	6%		10%	4%			14%	10%	7%		
0569		1%	3%	1%		4%	1%			3%	3%	6%		
0570		19%		11%				27%		1%	4%	8%		
0571		17%	1%	14%		2%	1%	9%		2%	7%	10%		YYY
0572		23%	2%	9%		2%	1%	24%		3%	5%	12%		Y
0573		10%	2%	13%		1%		9%		2%	4%	7%		YY
0574		15%	2%	3%	23%		1%	11%	1%	1%	14%	3%		
0575	1%	12%	2%	7%	12%	1%	1%	6%	2%	2%	7%	6%		
0576	20%	18%	2%	16%	1%	4%	1%	4%		4%	11%	11%		
0577	1%	19%	4%	14%		2%		4%		18%	15%	14%		Y
0578		17%	5%	19%	1%	4%	3%	1%		2%	31%	17%		
0579			11%							77%				
0580		25%	7%	10%	3%	3%	2%	5%		4%	9%	12%		Y
0581	8%	18%		1%	12%			9%		3%	7%	29%		
0582		20%	2%	18%	5%	1%		2%		2%	7%	13%		
0583		28%	2%	10%		1%		18%	5%	2%	3%	15%		
0584		20%			51%	15%					8%			YY
0585		17%	7%	19%	1%	3%	1%	9%		10%	17%	5%		YY
0586		42%	10%	6%	1%	2%		29%		2%	2%	3%		Y

1 Additional majors available in this area
2 ROTC available

†Accredited by a nationally recognized accrediting body other than one of the regional accrediting associations

Great Lakes States

(continued)

IL, IN, MI, OH, WI

TRADITIONAL ADMISSIONS *Majority of accepted students in top 50% of HS class*

Enrollment 1,000 to 5,000

Sequence Number	School name (upper entry) City (lower entry)	State	Costs: Resident tuition/fees + room/board	Costs: Room/Board (upper entry) Nonresident tuition/fees + room/board (lower entry)	General Information: Highest degree	General Information: Affiliation (upper entry) Religious observance (lower entry)	General Information: Size of community	General Information: Type of community	Admissions: Fall term application deadline (upper entry) Tests desired or required (lower entry)	Admissions: Calendar	Admissions: Fall admission only	Admissions: Early admission	Admissions: Deferred admission	Financial Aid: Fall term application deadline (upper entry) Forms to be filed (lower entry)	Financial Aid: Number in 10 who— -have need, receive some aid	Student Profile: Number in 10 who— Undergrads -are women	Undergrads -are graduate students	Freshmen -live on campus	Freshmen -are minority students	Freshmen -are nonresidents	Freshmen -return as sophomores	Freshmen -complete degree	Freshmen -enter graduate study	HS GPA (upper entry) 1st year college GPA (lower entry)	Special Programs: Credit by exam	Special Programs: Student designed majors	Special Programs: Fraternities/sororities
0587	Marygrove C Detroit	MI	9300	3300	M [5]	Cath	V	U	8/15 A=S	E		Y		3/15 FA/FF	9	9	1	1	8	1			1	2.7 2.6	Y	Y	
0588	Cardinal Stritch C Milwaukee	WI	9600	3100	M [5]	Cath S	V	S	8/15 A/S	E		Y	Y	3/01 FA/FF	9	6	2	6	1	1	8	5	2	2.9 2.6	Y		
0589	Viterbo C La Crosse	WI	10200 [3]	3000	M [5]	Cath	M		8/31 A/S	E		Y		 FF/FA	9	6	0	7	1	1	8	6	1	3.2	Y		
0590	Calvin C Grand Rapids	MI	10500 [3]	3100	M [5]	Oth OS	L	S	 A/S	4		Y	Y	2/15 FA/FF	6	5	1	7	1	5	8	5	2	3.2 2.6	Y	Y	
0591	Adrian C Adrian	MI	10600 [3]	2500	B [5]	Meth OS	S		8/15 A=S	E			Y	 FA/FF	8	6	0	9	1	3	8	6	2	3.0 2.7	Y	Y	Y
0592	Art Inst of Chicago Chicago	IL	10600	[1]	M [5]	Priv	V	U	 A=S	S			Y	 FA/FF	6	6	2	0	2	7	9	7			Y		
0593	Parks C-St Louis U Cahokia	IL	10700	3700	B [5]	Cath	S		 A=S	E		Y	Y	8/01 FF=FA	8	1	0	6	2	4	8	6	1	2.9 2.2	Y		Y
0594	Franciscan U Steubenville	OH	10900	3900	M [5]	Cath OS	S		7/31 A=S	E		Y	Y	5/01 FA/FF	9	6	1	9	1	7	7	5		3.1 2.6	Y		Y
0595	Tri-State U Angola	IN	10900 [3]	3300	B [5]	Priv	T		 S/A	Q		Y	Y	3/01 FF=FA	6	3	0	9	2	4	7	3		 2.4	Y		Y
0596	Anderson U Anderson	IN	11000 [3]	2900	M [5]	Oth O	M	S	9/01 A=S	E		Y	Y	3/01 FA/FF	8	6	1	9	1	5	8	5			Y	Y	
0597	Elmhurst C Elmhurst	IL	11000	3200	B [5]	UCC OS	S		8/15 A=S	4		Y	Y	 FA/FF	6	6	0	6	1	1	7	5	2	2.8 2.5	Y		Y
0598	Manchester C N Manchester	IN	11200 [3]	3200	M [5]	Oth O	T		9/01 S/A	4		Y		3/01 FAF	9	5	0	9	1	2	9	5	2	 2.5	Y	Y	
0599	National-Louis U Evanston	IL	11200	4100	D [5]	Priv	M	S	 A=S	Q			Y	7/15 FF/FA	9	7	3	5	4	1	6	5	3	2.5	Y	Y	Y
0600	Mount St Joseph,C of Mount St Joseph	OH	11300	3700	M [5]	Cath OS	L	S	 A=S	E		Y	Y	 FA/FF	6	7	1	4	2	1	8	7	1	2.9 2.8	Y	Y	
0601	Findlay,U of Findlay	OH	11500 [3]	3500	M [5]	Oth O	S		8/15 A/S	E		Y	Y	 FA/FF	8	5	0	8	2	2	7	4		2.8 2.7	Y	Y	Y
0602	Columbus C of Art Columbus	OH	11600 [3]	4200	B [5]	Priv	V	U	 A=S	E			Y	5/01 FAF	7	5	0	6	1	2	8	4	1	2.7 2.5			
0603	Indianapolis,U of Indianapolis	IN	11600	3300	M [5]	Meth S	V	S	8/15 A=S	O		Y	Y	3/01 FAF	8	7	1	6	1	1	8	7	2		Y		
0604	Aquinas C Grand Rapids	MI	12000 [3]	3700	M [5]	Cath	V	S	8/15 A/S	S		Y	Y	3/15 FA/FF	9	6	0	5	1	1	8	5	2	3.0 2.6	Y	Y	
0605	Roosevelt U Chicago	IL	12000	4500	D [5]	Priv	V	U	8/01 A=S	E		Y	Y	 FF/FA	7	5	1	1	4	1	7	3			Y	Y	Y
0606	Saint Xavier C Chicago	IL	12000	3500	M [5]	Cath S	V	U	8/15 A=S	4		Y	Y	8/20 FA/FF	8	8	1	2	2	1	8	7	5	2.8 2.9	Y	Y	
0607	Taylor U Upland	IN	12200 [3]	3400	B [5]	Oth OS	T		 A=S	4		Y	Y	3/01 FA/FF	7	5	0	9	1	6	9	7	1	3.4	Y	Y	
0608	Lewis U Romeoville	IL	12300	4000	M [5]	Cath	S		9/01 A/S	E		Y	Y	4/01 FAF	8	4	0	4	2	1	7	4	2	2.8 2.4	Y	Y	Y
0609	Ill Benedictine C Lisle	IL	12600	3600	M [5]	Cath S	S		 A/S	E			Y	 FA/FF	9	5	3	3	1	1	8	5	3		Y		
0610	North Central C Naperville	IL	12700	3500	M [5]	Meth	M	S	 A=S	O		Y	Y	8/01 FF/FA	9	5	1	8	1	8	8	6	2	3.0	Y	Y	
0611	Ashland C Ashland	OH	13000 [3]	3800	M [5]	Oth	S		 A/S	E			Y	8/15 FA/FF	9	6	2	9	3	1	7	6	1	2.8 2.8	Y		Y
0612	Carthage C Kenosha	WI	13000 [3]	3200	M [5]	Luth O	M	S	 A=S	4		Y	Y	3/01 FA/FF	7	5	1	9	1	5	7	7	2	2.8 2.5	Y	Y	Y
0613	Saint Joseph's C Rensselaer	IN	13000	3600	M [5]	Cath	T		 A=S	E		Y	Y	5/01 FA/FF	9	5	0	9	1	4	7	6	3	2.7 2.5	Y	Y	
0614	Otterbein C Westerville	OH	14700 [3]	3900	M [5]	Meth S	S		 A=S	Q		Y	Y	5/01 FA/FF	9	6	0	9	1	1	8	6	7	3.2 2.8	Y	Y	Y
0615	Capital U Columbus	OH	14800 [3]	3700	P [5]	Luth OS	V	S	7/01 A=S	E		Y	Y	6/01 FA/FF	8	6	3	8	1	1	8	6	3	3.3 2.9	Y	Y	Y
0616	Muskingum C New Concord	OH	15300 [3]	3500	M [5]	Pres OS	T		8/01 A=S	E		Y	Y	3/01 FAF	8	5	0	8	1	1	8	6	3	3.1 2.7	Y	Y	Y

▲ Sequence number—indicates the order of the college in this book only. Do *not* use this number with admissions tests or need analysis services.

1 No campus room and board facilities
2 Room only or board only
3 Most freshmen required to live on campus
4 City or district residence requirements
5 Accredited by a regional accrediting association or a recognized candidate for accreditation
6 All female freshman class
7 All male freshman class

MAJORS AVAILABLE AND PERCENT OF STUDENTS STUDYING IN EACH AREA

Sequence Number	Agri.	Business	Comm.	Education	Engineering	Fine/App. Arts	Lang.	Health	Home Ec.	Humanities	Math-Sciences	Social Sciences	GS	ROTC Air Force	ROTC Army	ROTC Navy
0587		022%	1%	8% [1]		8% [1]	1%	013% [1]	6%	1%	021% [1]	018%				
0588		030%	4%	018% [1]		010%	1%	010%		8%	013%	5%			Y	
0589		025%		010% [1]		4% [1]		022% [1]		016%	011%	011%			Y	
0590	[1]	017%	1%	015% [1]	7%	1%	4%	5%		3% [1]	4% [1]	6%				
0591		024%	3%	011% [1]	1%	3% [1]	2%	4%	3%	9%	012% [1]	013% [1]			Y	
0592				2%		083% [1]				2%	2%	1%				
0593		024% [1]			052% [1]						2% [1]			Y	Y	Y
0594		014%	4%	015% [1]	3%			7%		014%	011% [1]	010%				
0595		018% [1]	1%	010% [1]	053% [1]	1%				1%	6% [1]	1%				
0596		032%	4%	011% [1]		010%	1%	6% [1]		011%	011%	8% [1]				
0597		043% [1]	5%	015% [1]		4%	1%	8% [1]		3%	010% [1]	010%		Y	Y	
0598		024% [1]	5%	026% [1]	1%	3%	1%	9% [1]		2% [1]	4% [1]	023%				
0599		017%		030% [1]		1%		012% [1]			5%	030%				
0600		028%	3%	011% [1]		013% [1]		012% [1]		7%	8%	9%		Y	Y	
0601	3% [1]	042%	3%	010% [1]	1%	1%	1%	3% [1]		3%	022% [1]	3% [1]		Y	Y	
0602			1%			096% [1]				1%	1%	1%				
0603		031% [1]	4%	018% [1]	1%	4%	1%	015% [1]		2%	010% [1]	9%			Y	
0604		050%	4%	9% [1]		2% [1]	1%	3%		2%	011% [1]	2% [1]				
0605		033% [1]	2%	8% [1]	3%	5% [1]		1% [1]		2% [1]	027%	8% [1]				
0606		025%	1%	037% [1]	1%	1% [1]	1%	012% [1]		2%	3% [1]	2% [1]		Y		
0607		016%	6%	012%	1%	3%	1%	1%		7%	017%	014% [1]				
0608		024%	3%	2% [1]		2%		011%		1%	5% [1]	019% [1]		Y	Y	
0609		033%	3%	8%	1% [1]		1%	9% [1]		011%	024% [1]	010%			Y	
0610		035%	8%	4% [1]	2%	3%	3%	4% [1]		3% [1]	028%	9% [1]		Y	Y	Y
0611		036% [1]	010%	020% [1]		2%	1%	2%	4%	3%	014% [1]	3% [1]		Y		
0612		039%	1%	018% [1]		4% [1]	1%	[1]		3% [1]	2%	021% [1]				
0613		039%	8%	010% [1]	1%	1%		011%		2%	011% [1]	011% [1]				
0614		026%	012%	9% [1]		8%	1%	9%	2%	4%	013%	012% [1]		Y	Y	Y
0615		019%	6%	017% [1]		011%	1%	010% [1]		3%	9%	016% [1]			Y	
0616		024%	4%	026%	1%	6%	2%	2%		9%	016% [1]	8% [1]			Y	

[1] Additional majors available in this area
[2] ROTC available

†Accredited by a nationally recognized accrediting body other than one of the regional accrediting associations

Great Lakes States
(continued)

IL, IN, MI, OH, WI

Sequence Number	School name (upper entry) City (lower entry)	State	Costs: Resident tuition/fees + room/board	Costs: Room/Board (upper entry) Nonresident tuition/fees + room/board (lower entry)	General Information: Highest degree	Affiliation (upper entry) Religious observance (lower entry)	Size of community	Type of community	Admissions: Fall term application deadline (upper entry) Tests desired or required (lower entry)	Calendar	Fall admission only	Early admission	Deferred admission	Financial Aid: Fall term application deadline (upper entry) Forms to be filed (lower entry)	Number in 10 who— -have need, receive some aid	Under-grads: -are women	-are graduate students	Freshmen: -live on campus	-are minority students	-are nonresidents	-return as sophomores	-complete degree	-enter graduate study	HS GPA (upper entry) 1st year college GPA (lower entry)	Special Programs: Credit by exam	Student designed majors	Fraternities/sororities
	TRADITIONAL ADMISSIONS *Majority of accepted students in top 50% of HS class*																										
	Enrollment 5,000 to 15,000																										
0617	Ind U-Purdue Indpls Indianapolis	IN	3400 [2]	1300 7600	D [5]	Pub	V	U	6/15 A=S	E		Y	Y	3/01 FAF	3	6	2	1	1	1	6				Y		Y
0618	Wis Oshkosh,U of Oshkosh	WI	3900 [3]	2100 7500	M [5]	Pub	M		 A/S	S		Y		 FAF	6	6	1	7	1	1	7	4	1	2.9 2.4	Y	Y	Y
0619	Wis Eau Claire,U of Eau Claire	WI	4200	2400 7900	M [5]	Pub	M		 A/S	E		Y		 FF=FA	5	6	1	8	1	2	8	4	1	 2.6	Y		Y
0620	Wis Platteville,U of Platteville	WI	4200 [3]	2300 7800	M [5]	Pub	S		 ACT	E				 FF/FA	9	3	1	8	1	1	7	5	1	3.1 2.3	Y	Y	Y
0621	Wis Whitewater,U of Whitewater	WI	4200 [3]	2200 8000	M [5]	Pub	S		 A/S	E		Y		 FF/FA	5	5	1	9	1	1	8	5		2.8 2.5	Y	Y	Y
0622	Wis Stevens Pt,U of Stevens Point	WI	4500 [3]	2600 8100	M [5]	Pub	S		 ACT	E				 FFS	6	5	1	9	1	1	7	3	1	 2.5	Y	Y	Y
0623	Eastern Ill U Charleston	IL	4600 [3]	2500 7700	M [5]	Pub	S		 A/S	E		Y	Y	 FF=FA	6	6	1	8	1	1	8	5		2.9 2.5	Y		Y
0624	Western Ill U Macomb	IL	4800 [3]	2700 8000	M [5]	Pub	S		8/15 A=S	E		Y		 FF/FA	5	5	1	9	2	1	7	4	4	 2.4	Y	Y	Y
0625	Southern Ill U Edwardsville	IL	4900	3100 7800	D [5]	Pub	S		9/06 A/S	Q		Y		4/01 Oth	8	6	1		2	1	7			 2.3	Y		Y
0626	Ind St U Terre Haute	IN	5200 [3]	3000 8100	D [5]	Pub	M	U	8/15 S/A	E		Y		3/01 FAF	5	5	1	7	1	1	6	5		2.8 2.5	Y		Y
0627	Wis Milwaukee,U of Milwaukee	WI	5200	3000 9900	D [5]	Pub	V	U	 A/S	E		Y	Y	 FF/FA	4	5	1	2	1	1	7				Y	Y	Y
0628	Grand Valley St U Allendale	MI	5400	3300 8200	M [5]	Pub	L	S	7/19 A/S	E		Y	Y	2/15 FA/FF	5	6	1	4	1	1	8		3	3.3 2.6	Y		Y
0629	Eastern Mich U Ypsilanti	MI	5500 [3]	3400 8400	D [5]	Pub	S		 A=S	E		Y	Y	4/01 FF=FA	6	6	1	7	2	1	7	7	3	3.0 2.7	Y	Y	Y
0630	Cinci,U of Cincinnati	OH	7200	4200 11400	D [5]	Pub	L	U	 A=S	Q				3/01 FA/FF		5	2		1		8				Y	Y	Y
0631	Dayton,U of Dayton	OH	13200 [3]	3800	D [5]	Cath OS	M	S	 A=S	T		Y	Y	 FA/FF	5	5	1	9	1	4	9	7			Y	Y	Y
	Enrollment over 15,000																										
0632	Ball St U Muncie	IN	4900 [3]	2800 7700	D [5]	Pub	M	S	 S/A	E			Y	3/01 FA/FF	6	6	1	9	1	1	7	5	2	2.9 2.3	Y	Y	Y
0633	Ill St U Normal	IL	4900 [3]	2600 8300	D [5]	Pub	M		 A/S	E		Y		 FF=FA	4	6	1	9	1	1	8	5		 2.4	Y	Y	Y
0634	Southern Ill U Carbondale	IL	5100	2800 8300	D [5]	Pub	S		 A/S	E		Y		 FF=FA	8	4	1	4	2	1	7	5		2.7 2.4	Y	Y	Y
0635	Northern Ill U De Kalb	IL	5200 [3]	2700 8700	D [5]	Pub	S		8/01 A=S	E		Y		3/01 FAF	6	5	1	9	2	1	8	5		 2.0	Y	Y	Y
0636	Toledo,U of Toledo	OH	5300	2800 8600	D [5]	Pub	L	S	 A/S	Q		Y	Y	 FA/FF	5	5	1	5	2	1	7			2.9 2.5	Y	Y	Y
0637	Ind U Bloomington Bloomington	IN	5600	3200 10100	D [5]	Pub	M		2/15 A=S	E			Y	3/01 FAF	3	5	2	9	1	3	8	6		 2.8	Y	Y	Y
0638	Kent St U Main Cam Kent	OH	6000 [3]	3000 9000	D [5]	Pub	M		3/15 A/S	E		Y		4/01 FAF	7	6	1	8	1	1	8	3		2.9 2.5	Y	Y	Y
	SELECTIVE ADMISSIONS *Majority of accepted students in top 25% of HS class*																										
	Enrollment to 1,000																										
0639	Bellin C Nsg Green Bay	WI	6000	[1] 9600	B [5]	Priv	M	U	 ACT	4			Y	 FAF		9	0	0	1	1	9			 3.1	Y		
0640	Blackburn C Carlinville	IL	8800	1400	B [5]	Pres	T		 A=S	E		Y	Y	 FF=FA	9	5	0	9	2	3	7	4	1	2.8 2.4	Y	Y	
0641	Mt Carmel C of Nsg Columbus	OH	9000 [2]	1800	B †	Cath S	V	U	 ACT	E				6/30 FA/FF	6	9	0	5	1	0	8			3.1 2.7	Y		
0642	Saint Francis,C of Joliet	IL	10700	3400	M [5]	Cath S	M	S	8/15 A/S	E		Y	Y	8/01 FF/FA	8	5	1	5	1	1	8	6	2	3.0 2.5	Y		
0643	Bluffton C Bluffton	OH	10800 [3]	3100	B [5]	Oth OS	T		8/15 A=S	Q		Y	Y	8/15 FA/FF	9	5	0	9	1	1	7	6	1	3.2 2.8	Y	Y	
0644	Wabash C Crawfordsville	IN	14500 [3]	3700	B [5]	Priv	S		7/15 S/A	E			[7]	7/15 FAF	8	0	0	9	1	2	9	7	8	3.4 2.8	Y		Y

▲ Sequence number—indicates the order of the college in this book only. Do *not* use this number with admissions tests or need analysis services.

[1] No campus room and board facilities
[2] Room only or board only
[3] Most freshmen required to live on campus
[4] City or district residence requirements
[5] Accredited by a regional accrediting association or a recognized candidate for accreditation
[6] All female freshman class
[7] All male freshman class

MAJORS AVAILABLE AND PERCENT OF STUDENTS STUDYING IN EACH AREA

Sequence Number	Agri.	Business	Comm.	Education	Engineering	Fine/App. Arts	Lang.	Health	Home Ec.	Humanities	Math-Sciences	Social Sciences	GS	ROTC
0617		18% [1]	1%	7% [1]	9%	2% [1]	1%	15% [1]		4%	4% [1]	8% [1]		YY
0618		25%	7%	17% [1]		6% [1]	1%	6%		2%	6% [1]	18% [1]		Y
0619		24% [1]	4%	22% [1]	1%	3% [1]	1%	9% [1]		5%	6% [1]	12% [1]		
0620	8% [1]	14%	6%	8% [1]	28%	2%	1%	1%		2%	8% [1]	4%		
0621		46% [1]	5%	22% [1]	1%	4%	1%	1% [1]	1%	2%	5% [1]	9% [1]		Y
0622	17% [1]	14%	7%	7% [1]	3%	2% [1]	1%	2% [1]	7%	2%	3%	2% [1]		Y
0623		7% [1]	2%	19% [1]	2%	4%	1%	2% [1]	6%	7%	8% [1]	14% [1]		Y
0624	2%	16% [1]	7%	12% [1]	2%	4%	1%	2% [1]	3%	3%	8% [1]	21% [1]		Y
0625		15%	4%	7% [1]	6%	3% [1]		1% [1]		2%	5% [1]	4% [1]		YY
0626		17% [1]	4%	13% [1]	7%	4% [1]	1%	4% [1]	1%	1%	5% [1]	10% [1]		YY
0627		15% [1]	6%	8% [1]	8% [1]	12% [1]	1%	9% [1]		4% [1]	17% [1]	18% [1]		
0628	1% [1]	17% [1]	2%	5% [1]	1%	2% [1]	1%	9% [1]		2%	3% [1]	2% [1]		
0629		20% [1]	5%	16% [1]	5%	5% [1]	2%	14% [1]	2%	6% [1]	15% [1]	10% [1]		YYY
0630		17% [1]	3%	10% [1]	15% [1]	14% [1]	1%	6% [1]	2%	2% [1]	7% [1]	14% [1]		YY
0631		20%	9%	9% [1]	20%	2% [1]	1%	3% [1]	1%	5%	7% [1]	12% [1]		YY
0632	1% [1]	22% [1]	8%	16% [1]	2%	8% [1]	1%	5% [1]	2%	2%	5% [1]	12% [1]		Y
0633	1% [1]	19% [1]	4%	13% [1]	3%	4% [1]	1%	2% [1]	3%	3%	9% [1]	16% [1]		Y
0634	2% [1]	8% [1]	4%	9% [1]	11% [1]	5% [1]	1%	3% [1]	2%	3% [1]	7% [1]	8% [1]		YY
0635		26% [1]	1%	11% [1]	5%	8% [1]	1%	8% [1]	3%	4%	9% [1]	12% [1]		Y
0636		[1]		[1]		[1]		[1]		[1]	[1]			YY
0637		21% [1]	7%	9% [1]		4% [1]	2%	4% [1]	2%	5% [1]	9% [1]	20% [1]		YY
0638	[1]	23% [1]	5%	16% [1]	3%	9% [1]	1%	8% [1]	5%	4% [1]	6% [1]	5% [1]		YY
0639								100%						Y
0640		30%	3%	14%		2%	1%	1%		2%	19%	19% [1]		
0641								100%						
0642		36%	9%	13%				4% [1]		4%	17%	17% [1]		
0643		28% [1]	5%	23% [1]		6%	1%	6%	4%	1%	11%	10% [1]		
0644		1%	1%	1%	1%	5%	7%	1%		16% [1]	27%	40%		

[1] Additional majors available in this area
[2] ROTC available

†Accredited by a nationally recognized accrediting body other than one of the regional accrediting associations

Great Lakes States (continued)

IL, IN, MI, OH, WI

SELECTIVE ADMISSIONS *Majority of accepted students in top 25% of HS class*

Sequence Number	School name (upper entry) / City (lower entry)	State	Costs: Resident tuition/fees + room/board	Costs: Room/Board (upper entry) / Nonresident tuition/fees + room/board (lower entry)	General Information: Highest degree	General Information: Affiliation (upper entry) / Religious observance (lower entry)	General Information: Size of community	General Information: Type of community	Admissions: Fall term application deadline (upper entry) / Tests desired or required (lower entry)	Admissions: Calendar	Admissions: Fall admission only	Admissions: Early admission	Admissions: Deferred admission	Financial Aid: Fall term application deadline (upper entry) / Forms to be filed (lower entry)	Number in 10 who— -have need, receive some aid	Under-grads: -are women	Under-grads: -are graduate students	Freshmen: -live on campus	Freshmen: -are minority students	Freshmen: -are nonresidents	Freshmen: -return as sophomores	Freshmen: -complete degree	Freshmen: -enter graduate study	HS GPA (upper entry) / 1st year college GPA (lower entry)	Special Programs: Credit by exam	Special Programs: Student designed majors	Special Programs: Fraternities/sororities
Enrollment to 1,000																											
0645	Columbia C Nsg / Waukesha	WI	14700 [3]	3600	B [5]	Priv / S	V	S	A=S	4		Y		FA/FF	9	9	0	8	1	1	9	9			Y		Y
0646	Monmouth C / Monmouth	IL	14700 [3]	3200	B [5]	Pres	S		5/01 / A/S	E		Y	Y	5/01 / FA/FF	9	5	0	9	2	2	9	7	3	3.2	Y		Y
0647	Hiram C / Hiram	OH	15600	3800	B [5]	Oth	T		4/15 / A=S	Q		Y	Y	8/01 / FA/FF	7	5	0	9	1	2		7	3	3.4 / 2.9	Y	Y	
0648	Ripon C / Ripon	WI	15900 [3]	3200	B [5]	Priv	T		A=S	E		Y	Y	FAF	8	5	0	9	1	4	9	7	5	3.3 / 2.9	Y	Y	Y
0649	Cleveland Inst Music / Cleveland	OH	16100	4600	D [5]	Priv	V	U	2/01 / Oth	E		Y		4/01 / FAF	7	5	4	9	2	8	9	4	9	3.1	Y		Y
0650	Knox C / Galesburg	IL	16500 [3]	3700	B [5]	Priv	S		A=S	O		Y	Y	FA/FF	6	5	0	9	2	4	9	7	6	2.7	Y	Y	Y
Enrollment 1,000 to 5,000																											
0651	Mich Flint,U of / Flint	MI	2200	[1] / 7400	M [5]	Pub	M	U	A=S	E		Y	Y	4/15 / FF/FA	4	6	1	0	1	1	5	4	2	3.1	Y	Y	Y
0652	Hanover C / Hanover	IN	8900 [3]	2700	B [5]	Pres	T		3/15 / S/A	O		Y	Y	4/15 / FA/FF	6	5	0	9	1	4	9	6	4	3.0 / 2.7			Y
0653	Malone C / Canton	OH	10900 [3]	3000	M [5]	Oth / OS	M	S	A/S	E		Y	Y	4/15 / FAF	8	6	1	8	1	1	7	4	1	3.3	Y	Y	
0654	Quincy C / Quincy	IL	11100 [3]	3100	M [5]	Cath / OS	S		A/S	E			Y	FA/FF	8	5	0	7	1	3	9	6	2	3.3 / 2.8	Y	Y	
0655	Valparaiso U / Valparaiso	IN	11800 [3]	2700	P [5]	Luth / OS	S		A=S	E		Y	Y	FA/FF	7	5	2	9	1	7	9	7	4	3.2 / 2.6	Y	Y	Y
0656	Milwaukee Sch Engr / Milwaukee	WI	12400 [3]	3200	M [5]	Priv	V	U	A/S	Q			Y	FA/FF	8	1	1	6	1	2	7	7	2	3.2 / 2.9	Y		Y
0657	Baldwin-Wallace C / Berea	OH	12900 [3]	3700	M [5]	Meth	S		A=S	Q			Y	9/01 / FA/FF	7	6	0	8	1	1	8	7	5	3.1 / 2.7	Y	Y	Y
0658	Hope C / Holland	MI	13000 [3]	3600	B [5]	Oth / OS	S		A/S	E		Y	Y	2/15 / FA/FF	6	6	0	9	1	2	8	6	4		Y	Y	Y
0659	Detroit,U Mercy MC / Detroit	MI	13100	3500	D [5]	Cath	V	U	A/S	E		Y		4/01 / FF/FA	7	6	3	4	4	1	8	5	2	2.9 / 2.6	Y		Y
0660	Evansville,U of / Evansville	IN	13200 [3]	3500	M [5]	Meth	M	S	8/25 / A=S	E		Y	Y	3/01 / FA/FF	9	6	0	9	2	5	8	5	2	2.6	Y		Y
0661	Hillsdale C / Hillsdale	MI	13200 [3]	3800	B [5]	Priv	T		A=S	E		Y		4/15 / FA/FF	7	5	0	9		5	9	7	2	3.2 / 2.8	Y		Y
0662	Wheaton C / Wheaton	IL	13300	3800	M [5]	Oth / OS	S		2/15 / A=S	E		Y		3/15 / FA/FF	8	5	1	9	1	8	9	8		3.6 / 3.0	Y	Y	
0663	Alma C / Alma	MI	13500 [3]	3600	B [5]	Pres	S		8/30 / A/S	O		Y	Y	3/15 / FA/FF	7	5	0	9	1	1	9	7	6	3.3 / 2.9	Y	Y	Y
0664	Carroll C / Waukesha	WI	13600 [3]	3300	M [5]	Pres	M	S	A=S	4		Y	Y	FA/FF	9	6	0	9	1	1	8	6	2	2.6	Y	Y	Y
0665	Saint Mary's C / Notre Dame	IN	13600	4200	B [5]	Cath / S	M	S	A=S	E		Y	Y [6]	3/01 / FAF	4	9	0	9	1	8	9	8	2	3.4 / 2.9	Y		
0666	Xavier U / Cincinnati	OH	13800 [3]	4100	M [5]	Cath / S	L	S	A=S	E		Y	Y	4/15 / FA/FF	8	5	1	6	1	4	9	6	5	3.0 / 2.8	Y	Y	Y
0667	Millikin U / Decatur	IL	13900 [3]	3800	B [5]	Pres	M		A=S	E			Y	FAF	8	6	0	9	1	1	8	6	1	3.2 / 2.9		Y	Y
0668	Albion C / Albion	MI	14000 [3]	3900	B [5]	Meth	S		A=S	E		Y	Y	3/01 / FA/FF	5	5	0	9	1	1	9	7	3	3.4 / 2.8	Y	Y	Y
0669	Saint Norbert C / De Pere	WI	14100 [3]	3900	M [5]	Cath / S	S		A=S	E			Y	FA/FF	8	6	0	9	1	3	8	7	2	3.2 / 2.9	Y	Y	Y
0670	Butler U / Indianapolis	IN	14300 [3]	3800	M [5]	Priv	V	S	S/A	E		Y	Y	3/01 / FAF	8	6	1	6	1	3	9	6		2.6	Y		Y
0671	Heidelberg C / Tiffin	OH	14400 [3]	3500	M [5]	UCC	S		7/30 / A=S	E		Y	Y	6/01 / FA/FF	6	5	1	9	1	3	8	6	4	3.0 / 2.8	Y	Y	Y
0672	Mount Union C / Alliance	OH	14600 [3]	3300	B [5]	Meth / S	S		A=S	E			Y	FAF	9	4	0	9	1	2	9	6	4	2.7	Y	Y	Y
0673	John Carroll U / University Hts	OH	14700	5100	M [5]	Cath / S	S		8/01 / A=S	E		Y	Y	3/01 / FAF	5	5	1	8	1	4	9	7	4	3.2	Y	Y	Y
0674	Augustana C of ILL / Rock Island	IL	14800 [3]	3700	B [5]	Luth / S	L	U	A=S	Q		Y	Y	FA/FF	9	5	0	9	1	2	8	6	3	3.2 / 2.9	Y	Y	Y

▲ Sequence number—indicates the order of the college in this book only. Do *not* use this number with admissions tests or need analysis services.

[1] No campus room and board facilities
[2] Room only or board only
[3] Most freshmen required to live on campus
[4] City or district residence requirements
[5] Accredited by a regional accrediting association or a recognized candidate for accreditation
[6] All female freshman class
[7] All male freshman class

MAJORS AVAILABLE AND PERCENT OF STUDENTS STUDYING IN EACH AREA

Majors by area: **Agri.** — Agriculture, general; Agronomy (crops & mgmt); Animal Science (husbandry); Fish, Wildlife Mgmt; Forestry. **Business** — Business/Commerce, general; Accounting; Banking/Finance; Business Economics; Business Mgmt/Admin; Marketing/Purchasing; Secretarial Studies. **Comm.** — Communications, general; Journalism; Radio/TV (broadcasting); Advertising. **Education** — Art Education; Distributive Education; Elementary Education; English Education; Mathematics Education; Music Education; Physical Education; Science Education; Secondary Education; Social Science Education; Special Education; Speech Education. **Engineering** — Engineering, general; Chemical; Civil; Electrical/Electronics/Comm; Industrial/Management; Mechanical. **Fine/App. Arts** — Architecture; Fine/Applied Arts, general; Art (paint, draw, sculpt); Art History/Appreciation; Dance; Dramatic Arts (theater arts); Music (liberal arts); Music (perform, compos, theory). **Lang.** — French; German; Italian; Latin; Spanish; Russian. **Health** — Predentistry; Premedicine; Medical/Lab Technology; Nursing (registered nurse); Occupational Therapy; Preoptometry; Pharmacy; Physical Therapy; Preveterinary Medicine. **Home Ec.** — Home Economics, general; Clothing and Textiles; Consumer Ec/Home Mgmt; Family Relations/Child Devel; Food and Nutrition/Dietetics; Institution Mgmt. **Humanities** — Humanities, general; Creative Writing; English, general; Literature, English; Philosophy; Religion; Speech/Forensic Science. **Math-Sciences** — Mathematics, general; Computer/Info Sciences; Biological Sciences, general; Biology; Botany; Zoology; Physical Sciences, general; Chemistry; Physics. **Social Sciences** — Crim Just/Law Enforce; Social Work; Social Sciences, general; Anthropology; Area Studies (Amer., African, etc.); Economics; Geography; History; Prelaw; Political Science; Psychology; Sociology. **GS** — General Studies. **ROTC** — Air Force; Army; Navy.

Sequence Number	Agri.	Business	Comm.	Education	Engineering	Fine/App. Arts	Lang.	Health	Home Ec.	Humanities	Math-Sciences	Social Sciences	GS	Air Force	Army	Navy
0645								100%								
0646		26%	5%	15%	2%	5%	4%	2%		7%	21%	8%			Y	
0647		25%	7%	8%		6%	4%			14%	15%	20%				
0648		16%		1%	1%	3%	8%	7%		12%	24%	28%			Y	
0649						100%										
0650				3%		2%	3%			12%	15%	41%				
0651		23%	3%	13%	4%	1%	1%	10%		3%	14%	14%				
0652		30%	15%	13%	1%	1%	10%	1%		2%	3%	11%				
0653		31%	4%	23%		1%		9%		6%	8%	10%				
0654		30%	6%	12%		6%		5%		5%	17%	12%				
0655		18%	6%	6%	12%	1%	1%	9%	2%	5%	11%	14%				
0656		5%	4%		75%						15%			Y	Y	
0657		40%	5%	9%	1%	7%	1%	1%	1%	2%	10%	12%		Y	Y	
0658		18%	4%	17%	1%	6%	3%	2%		10%	17%	21%				
0659		21%	4%	5%	13%	7%		20%		2%	4%	11%				
0660		17%	6%	11%	15%	10%	1%	8%		4%	12%	11%				
0661		36%	2%	10%		3%	5%			16%	9%	19%				
0662		8%	9%	6%	1%	7%	3%	1%		24%	13%	20%			Y	
0663		29%		5%		4%	3%	5%		7%	12%	31%			Y	
0664		20%	9%	8%		5%	1%	14%		6%	15%	19%				
0665		21%	8%	8%		4%	3%	4%		12%	11%	20%		Y	Y	Y
0666		25%	7%	6%		2%	1%	5%		4%	10%	12%		Y	Y	
0667		28%	6%	15%	2%	17%		7%		5%	13%	7%				
0668		15%	3%			4%	3%			10%	11%	9%				
0669		25%	9%	8%	1%	4%	1%	1%		8%	14%	10%			Y	
0670		22%	14%	13%		2%	1%	15%	6%	2%	11%	2%		Y	Y	
0671		29%	6%	15%	2%	5%	2%	7%		2%	23%	8%				
0672		23%	5%	13%		2%	1%	3%		7%	27%	11%		Y	Y	
0673		32%	11%	6%	1%	1%	2%			17%	13%	17%			Y	
0674		17%	3%	6%	1%	12%	4%	7%		11%	19%	20%				

1 Additional majors available in this area
2 ROTC available

†Accredited by a nationally recognized accrediting body other than one of the regional accrediting associations

Great Lakes States (continued)

IL, IN, MI, OH, WI

SELECTIVE ADMISSIONS *Majority of accepted students in top 25% of HS class*

Sequence Number	School name (upper entry) / City (lower entry)	State	Costs: Resident tuition/fees + room/board	Costs: Room/Board (upper entry) / Nonresident tuition/fees + room/board (lower entry)	General Information: Highest degree	General Information: Affiliation (upper entry) / Religious observance (lower entry)	General Information: Size of community	General Information: Type of community	Admissions: Fall term application deadline (upper entry) / Tests desired or required (lower entry)	Admissions: Calendar	Admissions: Fall admission only	Admissions: Early admission	Admissions: Deferred admission	Financial Aid: Fall term application deadline (upper entry) / Forms to be filed (lower entry)	Financial Aid: Number in 10 who -have need, receive some aid	Student Profile: Under-grads -are women	Student Profile: Under-grads -are graduate students	Student Profile: Freshmen -live on campus	Student Profile: Freshmen -are minority students	Student Profile: Freshmen -are nonresidents	Student Profile: Freshmen -return as sophomores	Student Profile: Freshmen -complete degree	Student Profile: Freshmen -enter graduate study	Student Profile: Freshmen HS GPA (upper entry) / 1st year college GPA (lower entry)	Special Programs: Credit by exam	Special Programs: Student designed majors	Special Programs: Fraternities/sororities
Enrollment 1,000 to 5,000																											
0675	Beloit C Beloit	WI	15200 [3]	3200	M [5]	UCC	S		3/15 A=S	E		Y	Y	4/01 FA/FF	6	6	1	9	1	8	9	6	7	3.3 2.6	Y	Y	Y
0676	Ohio Northern U Ada	OH	15200 [3]	3200	P [5]	Meth	T		8/15 A/S	Q		Y		FA/FF	7	5	2	9	1	1	8	6	2	3.3 2.5	Y		Y
0677	Kalamazoo C Kalamazoo	MI	15300	3800	B [5]	Priv	M	S	5/01 A=S	Q		Y	Y	FA/FF	6	5	0	9	1	2	9	7	8	3.5 2.9	Y		
0678	Marietta C Marietta	OH	15300	3500	M [5]	Priv	S		7/01 A=S	E			Y	5/01 FA/FF	6	4	1	9	1	5	8	7	3	3.0 2.6	Y	Y	Y
0679	De Pauw U Greencastle	IN	15700 [3]	4200	B [5]	Meth	T		2/15 A=S	4		Y	Y	2/15	3	6	0	9	1	6	9	8	5	2.8	Y	Y	Y
0680	Ill Inst of Techn Chicago	IL	15900 [3]	4100	D [5]	Priv	V	U	5/01 A=S	E		Y	Y		9	2	3	8	5	4	8	7	4	3.3 2.6	Y		Y
0681	Earlham C Richmond	IN	16100 [3]	3600	B [5]	Oth	S		2/15 S/A	O		Y	Y	FA/FF	6	6	0	9	1	8	9	7	6	3.3	Y	Y	
0682	Ohio Wesleyan U Delaware	OH	16800 [3]	4500	B [5]	Meth	S		3/01 A=S	E		Y	Y	3/15 FAF	5	5	0	9	2	6	9	7	5	3.4 2.8		Y	
0683	Lake Forest C Lake Forest	IL	17000 [3]	3100	B [5]	Pres	S		2/15 A=S	E		Y	Y	3/01 FF=FA	6	5	0	9	1	7	9	7	3			Y	Y
0684	Wittenberg U Springfield	OH	17200 [3]	4400	B [5]	Luth O	M	S	3/15 A=S	O		Y	Y	3/15 FA/FF	5	5	0	9	1	5	9	7	7	3.4 2.9	Y	Y	Y
0685	Wooster,C of Wooster	OH	17700 [3]	4200	B [5]	Pres S	S		2/15 A=S	E		Y	Y	2/15 FA/FF	6	5	0	9	1	6	9	7	4	3.0 2.9		Y	
0686	Kenyon C Gambier	OH	18200 [3]	3300	B [5]	Oth	T		2/15 A=S	E		Y	Y	2/15 FA/FF	3	5	0	9	1	8	9	8	8	3.3 3.0		Y	Y
0687	Denison U Granville	OH	18700 [3]	4000	B [5]	Priv	T		2/01 A=S	E		Y	Y	3/15 FAF	4	5	0	9	1	7	9	8	5	3.3 2.7	Y	Y	Y
Enrollment 5,000 to 15,000																											
0688	Wis La Crosse,U of La Crosse	WI	4200	2200 6000	M [5]	Pub	M		ACT	S				FA/FF	4	6	1	8	1	1	7	3		3.0 2.5	Y		Y
0689	Central Mich U Mt Pleasant	MI	5500 [3]	3400 8400	D [5]	Pub	S		A/S	E			Y	3/01 FA/FF	7	6	1	9	1	1	8	5		3.1 2.5	Y	Y	Y
0690	Oakland U Rochester	MI	5500	3100 9100	D [5]	Pub	S		7/15 ACT	E		Y	Y	FA/FF	3	6	1	2	1	1	7	6	2	3.2 2.9	Y	Y	Y
0691	Mich Techn U Houghton	MI	5600 [3]	3200 9100	D [5]	Pub	T		8/01 A=S	Q		Y		3/01 FA/FF	7	2	1	8	1	2	8	6	2	2.8	Y	Y	Y
0692	Miami U Oxford	OH	6800 [3]	3400 10600	D [5]	Pub	S		1/31 A=S	E		Y		FA/FF	6	5	1	9	1	3	9	7	4	3.4 2.9	Y	Y	Y
0693	Loyola U of Chicago Chicago	IL	12700	4300	D [5]	Cath OS	V	U	7/14 A=S	E				FAF	7	6	3	3	2	2	8	6		2.7	Y		Y
0694	Marquette U Milwaukee	WI	13000 [3]	4000	D [5]	Cath OS	V	U	A=S	E				FA/FF	8	5	3	8	1	5	9	7	2	2.9	Y	Y	Y
0695	Bradley U Peoria	IL	13100 [3]	4000	M [5]	Priv	L	S	A=S	E			Y	FA/FF	9	4	1	9	2	3	9	6	2	3.1 2.7	Y	Y	Y
0696	De Paul U Chicago	IL	13600	4300	D [5]	Cath O	V	U	8/15 A=S	Q		Y	Y	FAF	7	6	2	3	3	2	8		2	3.3	Y		Y
Enrollment over 15,000																											
0697	Bowling Green St U Bowling Green	OH	5300 [3]	2500 8700	D [5]	Pub	S		A/S	E				4/01	5	6	1	9	1	1	8	5		3.2 2.5	Y	Y	Y
0698	Wis Madison,U of Madison	WI	5500	3400 10200	D [5]	Pub	M	U	2/01 A=S	E		Y		2/15 FA/FF	4	5	3	8	1	3		6	4	3.2 2.7	Y	Y	Y
0699	Purdue U West Lafayette	IN	5600	3400 10100	D [5]	Pub	M		A=S	E		Y		FA/FF	5	4	1	9	1	3	9	7		2.6	Y	Y	Y
0700	Western Mich U Kalamazoo	MI	5700	3400 8800	D [5]	Pub	M	S	ACT	E				3/01 FF/FA	6	5	1	7	1	1	8	4	1	3.2 2.7	Y	Y	Y
0701	Mich St U East Lansing	MI	6100 [3]	3200 11000	D [5]	Pub	M	S	8/15 A=S	Q			Y	FF/FA	5	5	2	9	1	1	9	6	2	3.3 2.7	Y		Y
0702	Ohio St U Columbus Columbus	OH	6100 [3]	3800 10700	D [5]	Pub	V	U	2/15 A/S	Q		Y		3/01 FA/FF	7	5	1	5	1	1	8	5			Y	Y	Y
0703	Ohio U Athens Athens	OH	6200 [3]	3500 9300	D [5]	Pub	S		3/15 A/S	Q		Y	Y	3/15 FAF	6	5	1	9	2	2	9	8	4	3.1 2.8	Y	Y	Y

▲ **Sequence number—indicates the order of the college in this book only. Do *not* use this number with admissions tests or need analysis services.**

[1] No campus room and board facilities
[2] Room only or board only
[3] Most freshmen required to live on campus
[4] City or district residence requirements
[5] Accredited by a regional accrediting association or a recognized candidate for accreditation
[6] All female freshman class
[7] All male freshman class

MAJORS AVAILABLE AND PERCENT OF STUDENTS STUDYING IN EACH AREA

Agri.: Agriculture, general; Agronomy (crops & mgmt); Animal Science (husbandry); Fish, Wildlife Mgmt; Forestry
Business: Business/Commerce, general; Accounting; Banking/Finance; Business Economics; Business Mgmt/Admin; Marketing/Purchasing; Secretarial Studies
Comm.: Communications, general; Journalism; Radio/TV (broadcasting); Advertising
Education: Art Education; Distributive Education; Elementary Education; English Education; Mathematics Education; Music Education; Physical Education; Science Education; Secondary Education; Social Science Education; Special Education; Speech Education
Engineering: Engineering, general; Chemical; Civil; Electrical/Electronics/Comm; Industrial/Management; Mechanical
Fine/App. Arts: Architecture; Fine/Applied Arts, general; Art (Paint, draw, sculpt); Art History/Appreciation; Dance; Dramatic Arts (theater arts); Music (liberal arts); Music (perform, compos, theory)
Lang.: French; German; Italian; Latin; Spanish; Russian
Health: Predentistry; Premedicine; Medical/Lab Technology; Nursing (registered nurse); Occupational Therapy; Preoptometry; Prepharmacy; Physical Therapy; Preveterinary Medicine
Home Ec.: Home Economics, general; Clothing and Textiles; Consumer Ec/Home Mgmt; Family Relations/Child Devel; Food and Nutrition/Dietetics; Institution Mgmt
Humanities: Humanities, general; Creative Writing; English, general; Literature, English; Philosophy; Religion; Speech/Forensic Science
Math-Sciences: Mathematics, general; Computer/Info Sciences; Biological Sciences, general; Biology; Botany; Zoology; Physical Sciences, general; Chemistry; Physics
Social Sciences: Crim. Just/Law Enforce; Social Work; Social Sciences, general; Anthropology; Area Studies (Amer., African, etc.); Economics; Geography; History; Prelaw; Political Science; Psychology; Sociology
GS: General Studies
ROTC: Air Force; Army; Navy

Sequence Number	Agri.	Business	Comm.	Education	Engineering	Fine/App. Arts	Lang.	Health	Home Ec.	Humanities	Math-Sciences	Social Sciences	ROTC
0675		6%		5%	1%	011%	7%	1%		016% [1]	021%	026% [1]	
0676		015%	2%	3% [1]	020%	2%	1%	031%		2%	010% [1]	010% [1]	YY
0677		020%	3%	4%	1%	8%	5%	5% [1]		6%	023%	025% [1]	
0678	[1]	032%	010%	011% [1]	011% [1]	4%	1%	010%		3%	011% [1]	2% [1]	Y
0679			011%	4%		7%	5%	3% [1]		017%	012% [1]	041% [1]	YY
0680		6% [1]			061% [1]	026%		1% [1]		2%	3% [1]	1% [1]	YYY
0681		2%		3% [1]		4%	5%			014%	023% [1]	033% [1]	
0682		016%	5%	6% [1]	3%	8%	4%	6%		8% [1]	023% [1]	021% [1]	Y
0683		013%		2% [1]	1%	2%	4%	2% [1]		2% [1]	3% [1]	2% [1]	
0684	1%	022%	1%	8%	1%	7% [1]	3%	3% [1]		012% [1]	021% [1]	016% [1]	YY
0685		6%	1%	2%	1%	8%	2%	1%		020% [1]	013% [1]	035%	
0686						9%	4%			027% [1]	027% [1]	033% [1]	
0687		1%	4%	1% [1]	1%	5%	3%	5%		023% [1]	019% [1]	031% [1]	
0688		020%	4%	023% [1]		1%	1%	011% [1]		2%	7% [1]	017% [1]	Y
0689	1%	037% [1]	7%	014% [1]	2%	3% [1]	1%	5% [1]	6%	6% [1]	7% [1]	8% [1]	Y
0690		023%	8%	8% [1]	014%	1%	1%	014%		4% [1]	010% [1]	013% [1]	
0691	2%	6%	2%		069% [1]	[1]	1%	1%		2%	012% [1]	1% [1]	YY
0692		025%	8%	6% [1]	4%	6% [1]	2%	6% [1]	1%	3% [1]	015% [1]	013% [1]	Y Y
0693		027%	010%	3% [1]		2%	1%	8% [1]		7% [1]	019% [1]	023%	Y
0694		023%	014%	1% [1]	020%	1%	3%	012% [1]		4%	9% [1]	013% [1]	YYY
0695		018%	012%	4% [1]	020%	1% [1]	1%	7%	2%	3%	011% [1]	6% [1]	Y
0696		054% [1]	6%	3% [1]	1%	5% [1]	1%	2%		3%	010% [1]	8% [1]	Y
0697		026% [1]	012%	021% [1]	3%	4% [1]	1%	7% [1]	3%	1% [1]	6% [1]	012% [1]	YY
0698	4% [1]	010% [1]	9%	6% [1]	011% [1]	4% [1]	2%	7% [1]	2%	6% [1]	010% [1]	027% [1]	YYY
0699	4% [1]	013% [1]	5%	8% [1]	034% [1]	3% [1]		7% [1]	2%	4% [1]	010% [1]	5% [1]	YYY
0700	[1]	028% [1]	4%	017% [1]	010% [1]	5% [1]		5% [1]		1% [1]	4% [1]	010% [1]	Y
0701	010% [1]	020% [1]	015%	5% [1]	8% [1]	3% [1]	1%	4% [1]	4%	8% [1]	7% [1]	015% [1]	YY
0702	3% [1]	016% [1]	4%	012% [1]	010% [1]	5% [1]	1%	010% [1]	4%	3% [1]	5% [1]	9% [1]	YYY
0703		017% [1]	019%	010% [1]	012% [1]	5% [1]	1%	7% [1]	3%	8% [1]	9% [1]	7% [1]	YY

1 Additional majors available in this area
2 ROTC available

†Accredited by a nationally recognized accrediting body other than one of the regional accrediting associations

Great Lakes States
(continued)

IL, IN, MI, OH, WI

Sequence Number	School name (upper entry) City (lower entry)	State	Costs: Resident tuition/fees + room/board	Costs: Room/Board (upper entry) Nonresident tuition/fees + room/board (lower entry)	General Information: Highest degree	Affiliation (upper entry) Religious observance (lower entry)	Size of community	Type of community	Admissions: Fall term application deadline (upper entry) Tests desired or required (lower entry)	Calendar	Fall admission only	Early admission	Deferred admission	Financial Aid: Fall term application deadline (upper entry) Forms to be filed (lower entry)	Number in 10 who— -have need, receive some aid	Undergrads -are women	-are graduate students	-live on campus	Freshmen -are minority students	-are nonresidents	-return as sophomores	-complete degree	-enter graduate study	HS GPA (upper entry) 1st year college GPA (lower entry)	Special Programs: Credit by exam	Student designed majors	Fraternities/sororities
	SELECTIVE ADMISSIONS *Majority of accepted students in top 25% of HS class*																										
	Enrollment over 15,000																										
0704	Ill Chicago,U of Chicago	IL	7000	4300 10600	D 5	Pub	V	U	8/01 A/S	Q		Y	Y	5/01 FF=FA	7	5	2		4	1	7	2		3.0 2.6	Y	Y	Y
0705	Wayne St U Detroit	MI	7900 2	4900 11500	D 5	Pub	V	U	8/01 A/S	E				5/01 FF=FA	5	6	3		3		7	4		3.1	Y		Y
	HIGHLY SELECTIVE *Majority of accepted students in top 10% of HS class*																										
	Enrollment 1,000 to 5,000																										
0706	Mich Dearborn,U of Dearborn	MI	2400	1 7900	M 5	Pub	M	S	A/S	T		Y	Y	FF/FA	5	5	1	0	1	1	7		2	3.2 2.8		Y	Y
0707	General Motors Inst Flint	MI	9900 3	2400	M 5	Priv	M	S	A=S	S			Y	FA/FF	5	2	0	9	2	5	9	7	5	3.6 3.1			Y
0708	Rose-Hulman Inst Terre Haute	IN	13200 3	3300	M 5	Priv	M	S	A=S	Q			Y 7	3/15 FA/FF	8	0	1	9	1	4	9	7	5	3.7 2.9	Y		Y
0709	Ill Wesleyan U Bloomington	IL	14700	3700	B 5	Meth S	M	S	A=S	4		Y		3/01 FA/FF	7	5	0	9	1	2	9	8	3	3.3 2.7	Y	Y	Y
0710	Lawrence U Appleton	WI	19400 3	3400	B 5	Priv	M		2/15 A=S	O		Y	Y	3/01 FA/FF	6	5	0	9	1	6	9	7	6	3.6 2.7	Y	Y	Y
0711	Oberlin C Oberlin	OH	22200 3	5200	M 5	Priv	T		1/15 A=S	4		Y	Y	2/01 FAF	4	5	0	9	2	9	9	8	7		Y	Y	
	Enrollment 5,000 to 15,000																										
0712	Notre Dame,U of Notre Dame	IN	17800 3	5400	D 5	Cath OS	L	S	1/10 SAT	E		Y	Y	2/28 FAF	7	4	2	9	1	9	9	9	2	3.9 3.0	Y	Y	
0713	Northwestern U Evanston	IL	18300	4600	D 5	Priv	M	S	1/01 A=S	Q		Y	Y	2/15 FAF	6	5	4	9	2	7	9	8	7	 3.7		Y	Y
0714	Case Western Reserve Cleveland	OH	18500	4900	D 5	Priv	V	U	3/01 A=S	E		Y	Y	FA/FF	7	4	5	8	3	4	9	7	7		Y	Y	Y
0715	Chicago,U of Chicago	IL	20100 3	5300	D 5	Priv	V	U	1/15 A=S	Q		Y	Y	2/01 FAF	7	4	6	9	2	8	9	8	8	 2.9	Y	Y	Y
	Enrollment over 15,000																										
0716	Ill-Urbana Chpgn,U Champaign	IL	6500 3	3700 10000	D 5	Pub	M		1/01 A=S	E		Y	Y	3/15 FF/FA	8	4	2	7	2	1	9	7	3	3.4 3.0	Y	Y	Y
0717	Mich Ann Arbor,U of Ann Arbor	MI	7400	3900 15900	D 5	Pub	M	U	2/01 A=S	T			Y	2/15 FA/FF	8	5	4	9	2	3	9	7	8	3.7 3.2	Y	Y	Y
	ADVANCED STANDING *Freshmen not accepted; college junior standing often required*																										
	Enrollment to 1,000																										
0718	Antioch Sch Adult Lr Yellow Springs	OH		1	M 5	Priv	T		7/23 None	Q				7/23 FAF	5	7	1		1						Y		
0719	Governors St U University Park	IL	1600	1 4800	M 5	Pub	S			T				FAF		6	1		2						Y	Y	
0720	Cinci C Mort Sci Cincinnati	OH	4600	1	B 5	Priv	V	U	A=S	O				FF=FA	7	2	0		1	5		2					
0721	Saint Joseph C Nsg Joliet	IL	6000	1	B 5	Cath O	M		A/S	E			Y	FFS	6	9	0	0	1	0		4	2	2.4 2.9	Y		
0722	Saint Francis C Nsg Peoria	IL	6200 2	1000	B 5	Cath	M	U	A/S	E				FF/FA	9	9	0		1					3.0 2.9	Y		
0723	St Anthony C Nsg Rockford	IL	7200 2	1000	B †	Cath OS	L	U	A/S	S		Y	Y	6/01 FF=FA	0	9	0	0	1	0	0				Y		
0724	St John's Sch Nsg Springfield	IL	7300 2	1600	B †	Cath	M	U	A/S	E		Y	7	5/30 FF/FA	0	0	0	0		0	0						
0725	Mennonite C of Nsg Bloomington	IL	9000	2100	B 5	Oth	M		A=S	Q				4/01 FFS	6	9	0	4	1	0					Y		
0726	Natl C Chiropractic Lombard	IL	9200 2	1900	P 5	Priv	M	S	None	T				FF/FA		3	0		1								Y
0727	Rush U Chicago	IL	9200 2	1800	D 5	Priv	V	U	A=S	Q				FA/FF	7	8	8		3								

Sequence Number | School name (upper entry) City (lower entry) | State | Costs | General Information | Admissions | Financial Aid | Student Profile | Programs

▲ Sequence number—indicates the order of the college in this book only. Do *not* use this number with admissions tests or need analysis services.

1 No campus room and board facilities
2 Room only or board only
3 Most freshmen required to live on campus
4 City or district residence requirements
5 Accredited by a regional accrediting association or a recognized candidate for accreditation
6 All female freshman class
7 All male freshman class

MAJORS AVAILABLE AND PERCENT OF STUDENTS STUDYING IN EACH AREA

Sequence Number	Agri.	Business	Comm.	Education	Engineering	Fine/App. Arts	Lang.	Health	Home Ec.	Humanities	Math-Sciences	Social Sciences	ROTC
0704		021%	5%	4%	015%	6%	1%	014%		1%	6%	012%	YYY
0705		017%	6%	010%	012%	6%	1%	012%	1%	8%	7%	015%	YY
0706		018%		6%	018%	1%		2%		4%	011%	014%	YYY
0707		9%			091%								
0708					080%						020%		YY
0709		025%	1%	5%	2%	011%	2%	9%		3%	021%	011%	Y
0710				4%		015%	7%			024%	021%	028%	
0711													
0712		013%			010%	4%	1%	7%		6%	6%	012%	YYY
0713			017%	1%	013%	013%	1%	3%		7%	8%	033%	YYY
0714		011%	1%	1%	041%	3%	1%	1%	1%	5%	015%	017%	YY
0715						1%	2%			022%	037%	032%	YYY
0716	3%	015%	3%	3%	020%	6%	1%		2%	7%	014%	014%	YYY
0717	5%	010%	5%	5%	011%	5%	5%	011%		7%	024%	011%	YYY
0718		058%								1%		030%	
0719		026%	2%	012%		2%		8%		1%	6%	6%	YY
0720												100%	
0721								100%					
0722								100%					
0723								100%					
0724								100%					
0725								100%					
0726								100%					
0727								100%					

1 Additional majors available in this area
2 ROTC available

†Accredited by a nationally recognized accrediting body other than one of the regional accrediting associations

Great Lakes States
(continued)

IL, IN, MI, OH, WI

ADVANCED STANDING *Freshmen not accepted; college junior standing often required*

Enrollment 1,000 to 5,000

Sequence Number	School name (upper entry) City (lower entry)	State	Costs: Resident tuition/fees + room/board	Costs: Room/Board (upper entry) Nonresident tuition/fees + room/board (lower entry)	General Information: Highest degree	Affiliation (upper entry) Religious observance (lower entry)	Size of community	Type of community	Admissions: Fall term application deadline (upper entry) Tests desired or required (lower entry)	Calendar	Fall admission only	Early admission	Deferred admission	Financial Aid: Fall term application deadline (upper entry) Forms to be filed (lower entry)	-have need, receive some aid	Under-grads: -are women	-are graduate students	Freshmen: -live on campus	-are minority students	-are nonresidents	-return as sophomores	-complete degree	-enter graduate study	HS GPA (upper entry) 1st year college GPA (lower entry)	Credit by exam	Student designed majors	Fraternities/sororities
0728	Sangamon St U Springfield	IL	2600[2]	800 5800	M[5]	Pub	M	S		E				FF/FA		6	2		1						Y	Y	

South Central States

AL, AR, KY, LA, MS, OK, TN, TX

OPEN ADMISSIONS *All HS graduates accepted, to limit of capacity*

Enrollment to 1,000

Sequence Number	School name (upper entry) City (lower entry)	State	Costs: Resident tuition/fees + room/board	Costs: Room/Board (upper entry) Nonresident tuition/fees + room/board (lower entry)	General Information: Highest degree	Affiliation (upper entry) Religious observance (lower entry)	Size of community	Type of community	Admissions: Fall term application deadline (upper entry) Tests desired or required (lower entry)	Calendar	Fall admission only	Early admission	Deferred admission	Financial Aid: Fall term application deadline (upper entry) Forms to be filed (lower entry)	-have need, receive some aid	Under-grads: -are women	-are graduate students	Freshmen: -live on campus	-are minority students	-are nonresidents	-return as sophomores	-complete degree	-enter graduate study	HS GPA (upper entry) 1st year college GPA (lower entry)	Credit by exam	Student designed majors	Fraternities/sororities
0729	Okla Msnry Bapt C Marlow	OK	1000	[1]	P †	Bapt OS	T		A/S	E		Y				2	0	0	1	0	6	4	1	2.5 2.5			
0730	Troy St U Montgomery Montgomery	AL	1300	[1] 1900	M[5]	Pub	L	U	9/01 A/S	Q		Y		9/01 FAF		6	3	0	3	0	6				Y	Y	
0731	Clarksville Bapt C Clarksville	TN	1600	800	B	Bapt OS	M	S	A=S	E				None	0		0					2			Y		
0732	Faith Baptist Inst-C Oliver Springs	TN	2100	[1]	D	Priv	T		A=S	S		Y	Y			8	6	9		8	9			2.5 3.2			
0733	Bay Ridge Chr C Kendleton	TX	2600	900	B †	Oth OS	T			S				10/23	7	1	0		9	6		6	3				
0734	Magnolia Bible C Kosciusko	MS	2900[3]	1100	B †	Oth OS	S		A/S	S				8/01 FF/FA	6	3	0	2	4	2	6	1	7	2.4	Y		
0735	Midcontinent Bible C Mayfield	KY	2900[2]	1300	B[5]	Bapt OS	S		A/S	E		Y		Oth	7	2	0	1	1	1	4		2				
0736	Selma U Selma	AL	3300	1600	B †	Bapt	S		A/S	E				FF/FA	9	5	1	6	9	1	3			2.5 2.0			
0737	Texas Baptist C Longview	TX	3800[3]	1800	B[5]	Bapt OS	M		8/15 A/S	S			Y			5	0	6	1	5	7	4	1				
0738	Arkansas Baptist C Little Rock	AR	3900	2200	B[5]	Bapt OS	L	U	7/01 A/S	E				4/01 FFS	8	2	0	1	9	1	5	5	3	3.8 2.8		Y	
0739	Southeastern Bapt C Laurel	MS	3900	1700	B †	Bapt OS	S		A=S	S		Y		8/20	8	4	0	4	1	1	2	3	4	2.8			
0740	Amer Baptist C Nashville	TN	4000	2000	B †	Bapt OS	V	S	7/01 Oth	S				7/01 FA/FF	9	1	0	5	9	5	7	5	7				
0741	Okla Baptist C-Inst Oklahoma City	OK	5100	2700	B	Bapt OS	V	U	9/01 A/S	S				9/01		4	0	3	1	5	4	5	1		Y		
0742	Jimmy Swaggart Bible Baton Rouge	LA	5200	2600	M[5]	Oth OS	L	S	ACT	E		Y		8/01 FAF	5	4	1		2	7					Y		
0743	Hillsdale FW Bapt C Moore	OK	5300[3]	2600	B †	Oth OS	M	S	8/16 A/S	S		Y		FFS	7	4	0	8	1	5	7	1	1	3.1 3.0	Y		
0744	Paul Quinn C Waco	TX	5600	2800	B[5]	Oth O	M	U	A/S	E				8/01 FA/FF	9	5	0	8	9	2					Y		Y
0745	Miles C Birmingham	AL	5800	2100	P[5]	Meth OS	S		5/01 ACT	E		Y		4/15 FA/FF	9	6	0	5	9	2	6	6	3	2.5 2.5		Y	Y
0746	Free Will Baptist C Nashville	TN	6000[3]	2900	B †	Oth OS	V	U	7/15 ACT	E		Y		6/01	4	4	0	9	1	7	7	2	1	2.8	Y		
0747	Tomlinson C Cleveland	TN	6000	2600	B[5]	Oth OS	S		8/26 A/S	S		Y	Y	5/01 FF/FA	9	5	0	9	2	8	6			2.9	Y		Y
0748	Pikeville C Pikeville	KY	6100	2300	B[5]	Pres OS	T		9/04 ACT	S		Y			8	7	0	2	1	1	6	8	2	3.2	Y		
0749	Texas C Tyler	TX	6100[3]	2500	B[5]	Oth OS	M		8/01 A/S	E		Y	Y	5/15 FF/FA	9	5	0	8	9	5	6	9	1	2.5 2.0			Y
0750	Wayland Baptist U Plainview	TX	6200[3]	2500	M[5]	Oth OS	S		8/30 A/S	4		Y		5/01 FF/FA	8	6	0	9	2	2	7				Y		
0751	Southwest Assem God Waxahachie	TX	6300	2800	B[5]	Oth OS	S		8/01 ACT	E		Y		6/01 FFS	7	4	0	8	1	3	8	2		2.7 2.5	Y		
0752	Wiley C Marshall	TX	6300	2500	B[5]	Meth OS	S		A=S	S		Y	Y	6/01 FA/FF	9	6	0	8	9	3	5	7	1	2.5 2.0	Y		Y
0753	Lane C Jackson	TN	6900	2500	B[5]	Meth OS	M		A/S	E				4/15 FF=FA	9	5	0		9	2	6	5	2	2.3 2.1	Y		Y

Sequence Number | School name (upper entry) City (lower entry) | State | Costs | General Information | Admissions | Financial Aid | Student Profile | Programs

▲ Sequence number—indicates the order of the college in this book only. Do *not* use this number with admissions tests or need analysis services.

[1] No campus room and board facilities
[2] Room only or board only
[3] Most freshmen required to live on campus
[4] City or district residence requirements
[5] Accredited by a regional accrediting association or a recognized candidate for accreditation
[6] All female freshman class
[7] All male freshman class

MAJORS AVAILABLE AND PERCENT OF STUDENTS STUDYING IN EACH AREA

Sequence Number	Agri. (Agriculture, general; Agronomy (crops & mgmt); Animal Science (husbandry); Fish, Wildlife Mgmt; Forestry)	Business (Business/Commerce, general; Accounting; Banking/Finance; Business Economics; Business Mgmt/Admin; Marketing/Purchasing; Secretarial Studies)	Comm. (Communications, general; Journalism; Radio/TV (broadcasting); Advertising)	Education (Art Education; Distributive Education; Elementary Education; English Education; Mathematics Education; Music Education; Physical Education; Science Education; Secondary Education; Social Science Education; Special Education; Speech Education)	Engineering (Engineering, general; Chemical; Civil; Electrical/Electronics/Comm; Industrial/Management; Mechanical)	Fine/App. Arts (Architecture; Fine/Applied Arts, general; Art (Paint, draw, sculpt); Art History/Appreciation; Dance; Dramatic Arts (theater arts); Music (liberal arts); Music (perform, compos, theory))	Lang. (French; German; Italian; Latin; Spanish; Russian)	Health (Predentistry; Premedicine; Medical/Lab Technology; Nursing (registered nurse); Occupational Therapy; Preoptometry; Prepharmacy; Physical Therapy; Preveterinary Medicine)	Home Ec. (Home Economics, general; Clothing and Textiles; Consumer Ec/Home Mgmt; Family Relations/Child Devel; Food and Nutrition/Dietetics; Institution Mgmt)	Humanities (Humanities, general; Creative Writing; English, general; Literature, English; Philosophy; Religion; Speech/Forensic Science)	Math-Sciences (Mathematics, general; Computer/Info Sciences; Biological Sciences, general; Biology; Botany; Zoology; Physical Sciences, general; Chemistry; Physics)	Social Sciences (Crim Just/Law Enforce; Social Work; Social Sciences, general; Anthropology; Area Studies (Amer., African, etc.); Economics; Geography; History; Prelaw; Political Science; Psychology; Sociology)	GS (General Studies)	ROTC (Air Force; Army; Navy)
0728		■ ■ 038% ■ ¹	■ 6%			■ 1%		■ ■ 7% ¹		■ 2%	■ ■ ■ 6% ■	■ ■ ■ 026% ■ ■ ■ ■ ■ ¹		
0729		7%				6%	3%			057% ■	9%	012%		
0730		■ ■ 053% ■								■	■ ■ 022%	■ ■ 012% ■ ■ ■ ■	■	YY
0731										100% ■				
0732				■ ■ 100% ■ ■ ■ ¹						■				
0733		2%								098% ■				
0734										100% ■				
0735										100% ■				
0736		015%		080%						■	5%			
0737		■ 3% ¹ ■		■ ■ ■ 033% ■			1%		2%	059% ■ ■ ■ ■ ■ ■	1%	1%		
0738		■ 039%		■ 019% ■ ■ ¹						1% ■		■ 039%	■	
0739		011%		026%		013% ■				043% ■	6%	1%		
0740										■ 075% ■		025% ■ ■		
0741		010%		■ ■ ■ ■ ■ 020% ■ ■ ■ ■ ■ ¹		1% ■	1%		■ 1%	■ 064% ■	■ 2%	1% ■		
0742		1%	8% ■	■ 015% ¹		1% ■ ■	1%			040% ■	021%	■ ¹		
0743		013%		012%		6%		4%		046% ■	2%	2%		
0744		■ 040% ■ ■ ¹		■ 020% ■ ■		1% ■		■ 6%		■ 2% ■	■ ■ ■ ■ 6%	■ ■ 020% ■ ¹ ■		Y
0745		■ 032% ■	■ 5%	■ 012% ■ ■ ¹	■ ■ 1% ■ ■	1%	1%	■ 2%		■ 2% ■	■ ■ ■ 3% ■ ■	■ 2% ■		YY
0746		2%		■ ■ 027% ■ ■		2%				038% ■ ■				Y
0747		018%		014%		4%				033%	8%			
0748		■ ■ 015% ■ ¹ ■		■ ■ ■ ■ ■ 040% ■ ■ ■ ■ ■ ¹		■ 1%		015% ■		■ 3% ■	■ ■ ■ 014% ■ ¹	3% ■ ■		
0749		023% ■ ¹		■ ■ ■ ■ ■ ■ ■ ■ 018% ■ ¹		■ 5% ■				■ ■ 1%	■ ■ ■ ■ 014% ■ ■	■ ■ 015% ■ ■ ■		
0750		■ ■ 015% ■ ■ ■ ¹	■ 3%	■ ■ ■ ■ ■ ■ ■ ■ 014% ¹		■ 8% ■ ■	1%	5%		■ 011% ■ ■	■ ■ ■ ■ 6% ■ ■ ¹	■ 8% ■ ■ ■		
0751		■ 016% ■ ¹	1%	■ ■ 017% ■		2% ■	1%			057% ■		1%		
0752		■ 042% ¹ ■	■ 010%	■ 018% ■ ■ ¹			1%	5% ¹		■ 2% ■	■ ■ ■ 012% ■ ■	■ 2% ■ ■		
0753		■ ■ 036% ■	■ 3%	■ ■ 020% ■	■ ■ ■ 1%	1% ■	1%	1%		■ ■ 1% ■	■ ■ ■ ■ 016% ■ ■ ¹	011% ■ ■		
Sequence Number	Agri.	Business	Comm.	Education	Engineering	Fine/App. Arts	Lang.	Health	Home Ec.	Humanities	Math-Sciences	Social Sciences	GS	ROTC

[1] Additional majors available in this area
[2] ROTC available

†Accredited by a nationally recognized accrediting body other than one of the regional accrediting associations

South Central States

(continued)

AL, AR, KY, LA, MS, OK, TN, TX

OPEN ADMISSIONS *All HS graduates accepted, to limit of capacity*

Sequence Number	School name (upper entry) City (lower entry)	State	Costs: Resident tuition/fees + room/board	Costs: Room/Board (upper entry) Nonresident tuition/fees + room/board (lower entry)	General Information: Highest degree	General Information: Affiliation (upper entry) Religious observance (lower entry)	General Information: Size of community	General Information: Type of community	Admissions: Fall term application deadline (upper entry) Tests, desired or required (lower entry)	Admissions: Calendar	Admissions: Fall admission only	Admissions: Early admission	Admissions: Deferred admission	Financial Aid: Fall term application deadline (upper entry) Forms to be filed (lower entry)	Number in 10 who— -have need, receive some aid	Under-grads: -are women	Under-grads: -are graduate students	Freshmen: -live on campus	Freshmen: -are minority students	Freshmen: -are nonresidents	Freshmen: -return as sophomores	Freshmen: -complete degree	Freshmen: -enter graduate study	HS GPA (upper entry) 1st year college GPA (lower entry)	Special Programs: Credit by exam	Special Programs: Student designed majors	Special Programs: Fraternities/sororities
	Enrollment to 1,000																										
0754	Huston-Tillotson C Austin	TX	7700 [3]	3300	B [5]	Meth OS	V	U	A=S	S				5/01 FF/FA	9	5	0	6	9	1	8	6	5	2.5 2.8			Y
0755	Southwestern Advent Keene	TX	9700 [3]	3200	M [5]	Oth OS	T		S/A	E		Y		7/15	9	6	0	4	3	5	6	3		2.7	Y	Y	
	Enrollment 1,000 to 5,000																										
0756	Ark Med Sci,U of Little Rock	AR	1500 [2]	1500	D [5]	Pub	L	U		S				5/01 Oth		7	5			0					Y		
0757	La St U Shreveport Shreveport	LA	1500	[1] 3800	M [5]	Pub	L	S	7/15 A/S	E		Y		FFS	9	5	1	0	1	1	5	5	2	2.6 1.8	Y	Y	Y
0758	Southern U New Orls New Orleans	LA	1500	[1] 3000	M [5]	Pub	V	U	7/01 ACT	E				7/01 Oth		7	1	0	9	1	4	3	1				Y
0759	Okla Panhandle St U Goodwell	OK	3100 [3]	1800 4800	B [5]	Pub	T		ACT	O		Y		FF/FA	3	5	0	6	1	4	6	4	2	2.8 2.6	Y		
0760	Arkansas Montic,U of Monticello	AR	3200	1800 4900	B [5]	Pub	S		8/12 ACT	E		Y	Y	6/01 FFS	8	6	0	4	2	1	5	4	2	2.7 2.4	Y		Y
0761	Arkansas P Bluff,U Pine Bluff	AR	3200	1900 5000	B [5]	Pub	M		A/S	S		Y		7/01 FF/FA	8	6	0	4	8	2	6	7	3	2.7 2.6	Y		Y
0762	Henderson St U Arkadelphia	AR	3200 [3]	2000 4400	M [5]	Pub	S		A/S	E		Y		4/01 Oth	5	5	0	5	2	1	6	6	1	2.2	Y		Y
0763	Alabama St U Montgomery	AL	3300	2000 4400	M [5]	Pub	L	U	A/S	O		Y	Y	6/01 FF/FA	6	6	1		9	4	6	6	3	2.4 2.3			Y
0764	Tenn St U Nashville	TN	3600	2300 6500	D [5]	Pub	V	U	A/S	E		Y		FA/FF	7	6	1	7	8	3	7	7	3	2.6	Y		Y
0765	Langston U Langston	OK	3700 [3]	2400 5000	M [5]	Pub	T		A/S	S		Y		5/01 FA/FF	7	5	1	9		3	4	8	2				
0766	Houston Downtown,U Houston	TX	3900	3000 6400	B [5]	Pub	V	U	8/15 A=S	S				FF/FA	4	5	0	1	6	1	4	1			Y		Y
0767	Northwest St U of La Natchitoches	LA	3900 [3]	2100 5700	M [5]	Pub	S		8/30 A/S	E		Y		5/01 FF/FA	7	6	1	5	3	1	5	4		2.8	Y	Y	Y
0768	Howard Payne U Brownwood	TX	6500 [3]	2500	B [5]	Oth OS	S		A/S	E		Y		8/15 FF/FA	7	5	0	7	1	1	6	4	3	2.9	Y		
0769	Trevecca Nazarene C Nashville	TN	7700	2500	M [5]	Oth	V	U	A/S	Q		Y	Y	FFS	8	5	4	9	1	6	7	3	3		Y		
0770	Lindsey Wilson C Columbia	KY	8500	3300	B [5]	Meth OS	T		A/S	E		Y		9/01 FA/FF	9	6	0	6	1	1	5	3	1	2.7 2.4	Y		
	Enrollment 5,000 to 15,000																										
0771	Arkansas Little Rk,U Little Rock	AR	1600	[1] 3900	D [5]	Pub	M	U	A/S	E		Y	Y	Oth		6	1	0	2	1	9				Y	Y	Y
0772	Northern Kentucky U Highland Height	KY	2700 [2]	1300 5300	P [5]	Pub	M	S	ACT	E		Y		4/01 FAF	2	5	1	1	1	3	6	2	1	2.4	Y	Y	Y
0773	Arkansas St U St University	AR	3400	2000 4700	M [5]	Pub	S		ACT	E		Y		4/01 FFS	6	6	1	3	1	1	6	4		2.9 2.2	Y		Y
0774	Jacksonville St U Jacksonville	AL	3400 [3]	2100 4100	M [5]	Pub	T		A/S	E		Y	Y	4/01 FAF	2	5	1	5	2	2	6	4	2		Y		Y
0775	McNeese St U Lake Charles	LA	3600	2000 5000	M [5]	Pub	M	S	7/01 A/S	E		Y		5/01 FFS	4	6	1	2	2	1	6	3	2	2.7 2.7	Y		Y
0776	Nicholls St U Thibodaux	LA	3600 [3]	2000 5400	M [5]	Pub	S		ACT	E		Y		6/01 Oth	4	6	1	4	1	1	6	3		2.5 2.2	Y		Y
0777	Northeast La U Monroe	LA	3600	2000 5200	D [5]	Pub	M	U	ACT	E		Y		FF=FA	5	6	1	4	2	1	3	2		2.6	Y		Y
0778	Southwestern La,U of Lafayette	LA	3700 [3]	2200 5500	D [5]	Pub	M	U	A/S	E		Y		3/01	4	5	1		2	1	5	4	1		Y	Y	Y
0779	La Tech U Ruston	LA	3900	2100 5100	D [5]	Pub	S		8/15 A/S	Q		Y			5	4	1	7	2	1	6	3	3	2.7 2.0	Y		Y
0780	Southeastern La U Hammond	LA	4000 [3]	2300 6200	M [5]	Pub	S		7/23 ACT	E		Y		5/01 Oth	6	5	1		1	1		3	2	2.6 2.0	Y		Y
0781	Southern U Baton Rouge	LA	4000	2500 5500	D [5]	Pub	L	U	7/01 A=S	S		Y		4/14 FF=FA	8	5	1	5	9	2	6			2.8 2.5	Y		Y
0782	Pan American U Edinburg	TX	4200	3200 7900	M [5]	Pub	S		8/01 A/S	E		Y		4/16 FFS	8	6	1		8	1	5	3	3	2.8 2.0	Y		Y

▲ Sequence number—indicates the order of the college in this book only. Do *not* use this number with admissions tests or need analysis services.

[1] No campus room and board facilities
[2] Room only or board only
[3] Most freshmen required to live on campus
[4] City or district residence requirements
[5] Accredited by a regional accrediting association or a recognized candidate for accreditation
[6] All female freshman class
[7] All male freshman class

MAJORS AVAILABLE AND PERCENT OF STUDENTS STUDYING IN EACH AREA

Sequence Number	Agri.	Business	Comm.	Education	Engineering	Fine/App. Arts	Lang.	Health	Home Ec.	Humanities	Math-Sciences	Social Sciences	GS	ROTC
0754		060%		7%				6%			018%	9%		Y
0755		021%	6%	022%			1%	1%		8%	014%	5%		
0756								100%						Y
0757	1%	021%	6%	9%	5%	1%	1%	019%		2%	7%	011%		Y
0758		022%	1%	011%	1%	2%	1%	1%		3%	5%	3%		YYY
0759	018%	023%	5%	020%	1%	1%	1%	1%	2%	2%	3%	2%		
0760	5%	027%		019%		2%		9%		1%	3%	2%		
0761	3%	019%		015%	2%	1%		7%	3%	3%	012%	012%		Y
0762		025%	4%	030%	1%	2%	1%	8%	2%	2%	5%	3%		
0763		026%	9%	015%	1%	4%		1%		1%	021%	022%		YY
0764		027%	5%	5%	015%	5%		013%			8%	013%		Y
0765	2%	018%	9%	026%		1%		010%	1%	1%	3%	2%		Y
0766		029%	1%	5%	010%	1%	1%	6%	1%	2%	017%	021%		YY
0767	1%	023%	3%	7%	2%	2%	1%	018%	1%	2%	5%	6%		Y
0768		013%	3%	015%		1%	1%			6%	4%	6%		Y
0769		028%	4%	015%		6%		8%		012%	8%	012%		YYY
0770	1%	041%		019%		1%					7%	010%		
0771		010%	3%	2%	3%	1%		3%		1%	4%	6%		Y
0772		025%	6%	010%	5%	4%		7%		4%	016%	019%		YY
0773	3%	020%	7%	020%	4%	2%	1%	8%		1%	011%	3%		Y
0774		023%	2%	017%	1%	1%	1%	4%	1%	2%	3%	8%		Y
0775	4%	013%	3%	024%	7%	2%	1%	8%	2%	2%	9%	011%		Y
0776	1%	024%	3%	020%	6%			015%	4%		9%	010%		
0777	1%	016%	4%	014%	1%	1%		031%	1%	1%	3%	010%		Y
0778	1%	019%	4%	014%	9%	6%		012%	3%	1%	3%	010%		
0779	5%	020%	1%	014%	013%	6%	1%	5%	3%	1%	4%	5%		Y
0780	2%	030%	1%	017%	4%	1%	1%	9%	1%	1%	8%	7%		Y
0781	1%	010%	1%	013%	012%	2%	1%	1%	1%	2%	3%	2%		YY
0782		034%	2%	023%		1%	1%	9%		1%	3%	2%		Y

[1] Additional majors available in this area
[2] ROTC available

†Accredited by a nationally recognized accrediting body other than one of the regional accrediting associations

South Central States
(continued)

AL, AR, KY, LA, MS, OK, TN, TX

OPEN ADMISSIONS *All HS graduates accepted, to limit of capacity*

Sequence Number	School name (upper entry) City (lower entry)	State	Costs: Resident tuition/fees + room/board	Costs: Room/Board (upper entry) Nonresident tuition/fees + room/board (lower entry)	General Information: Highest degree	General Information: Affiliation (upper entry) Religious observance (lower entry)	General Information: Size of community	General Information: Type of community	Admissions: Fall term application deadline (upper entry) Tests desired or required (lower entry)	Admissions: Calendar	Admissions: Fall admission only	Admissions: Early admission	Admissions: Deferred admission	Financial Aid: Fall term application deadline (upper entry) Forms to be filed (lower entry)	Financial Aid: -have need, receive some aid	Student Profile (Number in 10 who—), Undergrads: -are women	Undergrads: -are graduate students	Freshmen: -live on campus	Freshmen: -are minority students	Freshmen: -are nonresidents	Freshmen: -return as sophomores	Freshmen: -complete degree	Freshmen: -enter graduate study	Freshmen: HS GPA (upper entry) 1st year college GPA (lower entry)	Special Programs: Credit by exam	Special Programs: Student designed majors	Special Programs: Fraternities/sororities
	Enrollment 5,000 to 15,000																										
0783	Grambling St U Grambling	LA	4400[3]	2600 5900	D[5]	Pub	T		8/01 Oth	E		Y		6/01 FF=FA	8	6	1	8	9	5	8	6	3	2.8	Y		Y
0784	Texas Southern U Houston	TX	4400	3300 7700	D[5]	Pub	V	U	8/09 A/S	E				3/01 FAF	7	4	2	3	9	1	6	6	6	2.7 2.5			Y
0785	Eastern Kentucky U Richmond	KY	5800	3000 6800	D[5]	Pub	S		ACT	E				FAF	7	5	1	9	1	1	6	3	5	2.7 2.1	Y		Y
	LIBERAL ADMISSIONS *Some accepted students from lower half of HS class*																										
	Enrollment to 1,000																										
0786	Texas Hlth Sci Ctr,U San Antonio	TX	800	[1] 4000	D[5]	Pub	V	S	2/01 Oth	E		Y		FA/FF	7	8	3	0	3		9	9		2.5 2.8	Y		
0787	Lexington Baptist C Lexington	KY	900	[1]	B†	Bapt OS	M	U	A/S	E		Y	Y		0	1	0	0	2	2	9	6	2	2.5	Y		
0788	Troy St U Dothan Dothan	AL	1500	[1] 1800	M[5]	Pub	M	S	9/05 A=S	Q		Y	Y	4/15 FF=FA	6	6	2	0	1	1		7	2		Y		
0789	Alice Lloyd C Pippa Passes	KY	2600	2600 5600	B[5]	Priv	T		A/S	S		Y	Y	2/15 FA/FF	8	6	0	7	1	1	4	4		3.1 3.0	Y		
0790	Mid-South Christian Memphis	TN	2700[2]	900	M†	Oth OS	V	U	8/01 A/S	E		Y		8/01 FF=FA	5	4	2	5	4	6	5		2	2.8 3.0	Y		
0791	International Bible Florence	AL	2900[2]	800	B†	Oth OS	M		7/15 None	E				7/01 FFS	8	1	0	2	3	8							
0792	Wesley C Florence	MS	3700	2000	B†	Oth OS	T		A=S	E		Y		7/01 FA/FF	7	5	0	8	1	8	5	5	3	2.2 2.3	Y		
0793	Philander Smith C Little Rock	AR	4000	2300	B[5]	Meth	L	U	A/S	S				FFS	8	5	0		9			2		2.2 1.7			
0794	Dallas Christian C Dallas	TX	4700[3]	2600	B†	Oth OS	V	S	8/25 ACT	S		Y	Y	6/01 FFS	6	4	0	9	1	4	8	2	2	2.5 2.5			
0795	Crichton C Memphis	TN	4800[2]	1400	B[5]	Priv OS	V	S	8/10 A/S	4		Y		7/15 FFS	4	5	0	1	2	2	7	3	8		Y	Y	
0796	Williams Baptist C Walnut Ridge	AR	4800[3]	1900	B[5]	Bapt OS	T		8/15 A/S	S		Y	Y	FFS	9	6	0	6	1	1	5			2.9	Y		
0797	Rust C Holly Springs	MS	5000	2000	B[5]	Meth OS	S		7/15 A/S	E		Y		7/01	9	6	0	9	9	4	6	5	4	2.5			Y
0798	Blue Mountain C Blue Mountain	MS	5200[3]	2000	B[5]	Oth OS	T		8/01 A/S	E		Y	Y[6]	4/30 Oth	9	9	0	7	1	3	6	5	5	3.0 2.8	Y		
0799	Tougaloo C Tougaloo	MS	5900	1700	B[5]	UCC	L	S	A=S	S		Y		4/15 FF=FA	9	7	0	7	9	1	9	7	4	3.0	Y		Y
0800	Stillman C Tuscaloosa	AL	6000	2400	B[5]	Pres OS	M	U	A=S	S		Y		6/15 FA/FF	9	7	0	9	9	3	7	4	1	2.0 2.0	Y		Y
0801	Kentucky Christian C Grayson	KY	6300[3]	3000	B[5]	Oth OS	T		8/01 A/S	E				FA/FF	8	5	0	9	1	6	5	3			Y		
0802	Jarvis Christian C Hawkins	TX	6500[3]	2800	B[5]	Oth OS	T		8/15 A=S	E				4/15 FF/FA	9	5	0	9	9	6	4	5	1	2.5 2.0	Y	Y	Y
0803	Johnson Bible C Knoxville	TN	6600[3]	3200	M[5]	Oth OS	L	S	ACT	E			Y	FF/FA		4	1	9	1	8	7	3			Y		
0804	Mid-America Bible C Oklahoma City	OK	6800	2600	B[5]	Oth OS	L	U	8/15 A/S	S		Y		8/15 FAF	7	4	0	9	1	7	8	4	1	2.8	Y		
0805	Tenn Temple U Chattanooga	TN	6800	3200	D†	Bapt OS	L	U	8/01 A=S	E		Y		6/01 FF/FA	4	6	1	7	1	6	7	8	3		Y		
0806	Cumberland U Lebanon	TN	7100	2700	M[5]	Priv	S		A/S	E		Y		8/01 FF/FA	7	5	0	3	1	1	6			3.0	Y		Y
0807	Faulkner U Montgomery	AL	7600	2900	P[5]	Oth OS	M	S	9/19 A/S	S		Y	Y	FF/FA	9	5	3	6	3	3	4			2.4	Y		
0808	Campbellsville C Campbellsville	KY	7700[3]	3200	B[5]	Oth OS	S		8/23 A/S	E		Y	Y	4/01 FAF	9	5	0	5	1	1	7	3	8	2.9 2.7	Y		
0809	Bartlesvl Wesleyan C Bartlesville	OK	7900	2800	B[5]	Oth OS	S		A=S	E		Y		5/01 FF/FA	7	6	0	8	1	6	6	1	1	2.8 2.8	Y		Y
0810	Tenn Wesleyan C Athens	TN	8000[3]	3000	B[5]	Meth OS	S		A/S	E		Y		6/01 FAF	5	5	0	4	2	1		7		2.8 2.5	Y		Y
0811	Lubbock Christian U Lubbock	TX	8100[3]	2500	M[5]	Oth OS	M	U	A/S	E		Y		8/15 FF/FA	9	5	0	6	1	2	6	2	1	 2.4	Y		

▲ Sequence number—indicates the order of the college in this book only. Do *not* use this number with admissions tests or need analysis services.

[1] No campus room and board facilities
[2] Room only or board only
[3] Most freshmen required to live on campus
[4] City or district residence requirements
[5] Accredited by a regional accrediting association or a recognized candidate for accreditation
[6] All female freshman class
[7] All male freshman class

MAJORS AVAILABLE AND PERCENT OF STUDENTS STUDYING IN EACH AREA

Sequence Number	Agri.	Business	Comm.	Education	Engineering	Fine/App. Arts	Lang.	Health	Home Ec.	Humanities	Math-Sciences	Social Sciences	GS	ROTC (Air Force, Army, Navy)
0783		024% [1]	6%	8% [1]	5%	4% [1]		010% [1]	1%	1%	013% [1]	014% [1]		Y Y
0784		017% [1]	5%	025% [1]			1%	5% [1]	1%	1%	1% [1]	2% [1]		
0785	3% [1]	019% [1]	6%	010% [1]		2% [1]	1%	014% [1]	5%	2%	023% [1]	8% [1]		Y
0786								100% [1]						
0787										100%				
0788		042%		025% [1]						1%	010% [1]	010% [1]		
0789		025%		032%	3%	1%		010%		2%	3%	2%		
0790		1%	1%				1%			096%		1%		
0791										100%				
0792				040%						049%				
0793		033%		011% [1]	1%	1%	1%	1%	3%	2%	3%	2%		Y
0794		010%		2%		5%				082%				
0795		011%		020%				6%		040%	1%	015%		
0796		022%		026% [1]						015%	6%	5%		
0797		030% [1]	8%	012% [1]	3%	4%	1%	1%		3%	9% [1]	019%		Y
0798		013% [1]		030%		9%	1%	1%	2%	024%	4%	3%		
0799		019%	3%	5% [1]	1%	4%	1%	1%		4%	044% [1]	017%		Y
0800		025%	9%	012%						3%	025%	012% [1]		Y Y
0801		015%	1%	036% [1]		1%				023%		015%		
0802		030% [1]		016% [1]		4%		011% [1]		2%	3%	028%		
0803				014% [1]		1%				085%				
0804				026%		1%	1%	3%		046%	2%	014%		
0805		012% [1]	3%	015% [1]		8%		1%	1%	022%	010% [1]	1%		Y
0806		040%		025% [1]		1%		1% [1]		6%	7%	015%		
0807		023%		016%				4%		7%	8%	9%		
0808		030% [1]		030% [1]	1%	1%		1%		2%	8% [1]	2%		
0809		033%		022%						014%	8%	012%		
0810		038%	3%	019% [1]		1%		2%		5%	012% [1]	012%		
0811	3% [1]	015%	3%	025% [1]		2% [1]			2%	8%	016%	010%		Y Y

[1] Additional majors available in this area
[2] ROTC available

†Accredited by a nationally recognized accrediting body other than one of the regional accrediting associations

South Central States
(continued)

AL, AR, KY, LA, MS, OK, TN, TX

LIBERAL ADMISSIONS *Some accepted students from lower half of HS class*

Sequence Number	School name (upper entry) City (lower entry)	State	Costs: Resident tuition/fees + room/board	Costs: Room/Board (upper entry) Nonresident tuition/fees + room/board (lower entry)	General Information: Highest degree	Affiliation (upper entry) Religious observance (lower entry)	Size of community	Type of community	Admissions: Fall term application deadline (upper entry) Tests desired or required (lower entry)	Calendar	Fall admission only	Early admission	Deferred admission	Financial Aid: Fall term application deadline (upper entry) Forms to be filed (lower entry)	-have need, receive some aid	Undergrads -are women	-are graduate students	Freshmen -live on campus	-are minority students	-are nonresidents	-return as sophomores	-complete degree	-enter graduate study	HS GPA (upper entry) 1st year college GPA (lower entry)	Credit by exam	Student designed majors	Fraternities/sororities
	Enrollment to 1,000																										
0812	Sullivan C Louisville	KY	8700[2]	2500	B[5]	Priv	L	S	9/20 Oth	Q		Y		9/30 FAF	9	7	0	1	2	1	3			3.0 2.8	Y		
0813	Midway C Midway	KY	8900	3400	B[5]	Oth OS	T		8/15 A=S	E		Y	[6]	4/30 FA/FF	8	9	0	6	1	1	8			2.7 3.0	Y	Y	
0814	Saint Joseph Sem-C St Benedict	LA	9100[3]	3500	B[5]	Cath OS	S		ACT	E				FAF	7	4	0	9	2	4	9	7	6	3.1 3.3	Y		
0815	Concordia Lutheran C Austin	TX	9300	3200	B[5]	Oth OS	V	U	8/15 A=S	E		Y		6/01 FFS	8	6	0	6	2	1	7	3	2	3.1 2.4	Y		
0816	Memphis C of Art Memphis	TN	11900	3800	M[5]	Priv	V	U	A=S	E		Y	Y	FF/FA	8	5	1	1	2	4	7	6	2	2.9 2.3	Y	Y	
	Enrollment 1,000 to 5,000																										
0817	East Central U Ada	OK	2600	1800 4100	M[5]	Pub	S		8/15 A/S	E				7/01 FFS	6	5	1	4	1	1	6	5	2	3.0 2.4	Y		Y
0818	Southwest Okla St U Weatherford	OK	2700	1500 4700	P[5]	Pub	S		8/30 A/S	E				6/01 FF/FA	4	6	1	6	1	1	7	6	3	3.2 2.8	Y		Y
0819	Auburn U Montgomery Montgomery	AL	2800[2]	1400 5700	M[5]	Pub	L	S	9/07 A=S	Q		Y		3/15 FFS	3	5	1	1	2	1	7	7	6	2.9	Y	Y	Y
0820	Northwest Okla St U Alva	OK	2900	1700 4900	M[5]	Pub	T		A/S	E		Y		5/01 FF=FA	1	6	1	3	1	1	5	2	2	2.8 2.5	Y		Y
0821	Southeast Okla St U Durant	OK	2900[3]	1900 4500	M[5]	Pub	S		A/S	E		Y	Y	4/01 FFS	6	5	1	4	4	1	6	3	4	3.0 2.5	Y		Y
0822	Southern Arkansas U Magnolia	AR	3200[3]	2100 3800	M[5]	Pub	S		A/S	E		Y	Y	Oth	6	6	0	4	2	1	8	4	3	2.9 2.3	Y		Y
0823	Arkansas Tech U Russellville	AR	3400	2100 4600	M[5]	Pub	S		9/05 A/S	E		Y	Y	5/01 Oth	6	5	0		1	1	4			2.9	Y		Y
0824	Delta St U Cleveland	MS	3400	1700 4600	D[5]	Pub	S		8/07 ACT	E		Y		4/01 FF/FA	6	6	1	6	2	1	6	4	2	2.5	Y		Y
0825	Livingston U Livingston	AL	3600[3]	2100	M[5]	Pub	T		A/S	Q		Y	Y	4/20 FFS	8	5	1	8	3	3	6	3	1	2.5 2.3	Y		Y
0826	Alcorn St U Lorman	MS	3700	1900 4800	M[5]	Pub	T		7/27 ACT	E		Y		4/15 FAF	8	6	1	9	9	1	6	5		2.5 2.2	Y		Y
0827	LeMoyne-Owen C Memphis	TN	3700	[1]	B[5]	UCC O	V	U	7/15 A/S	E				4/15 FF=FA	8	7	0	0	9		7	8		2.5	Y	Y	Y
0828	Midwestern St U Wichita Falls	TX	3700	2700 6200	M[5]	Pub	M	S	8/07 A=S	E		Y		5/01 FF/FA	2	5	1	2	1	1	8		2	2.8 2.5	Y		Y
0829	West Texas St U Canyon	TX	3700[3]	2700 6800	M[5]	Pub	S		8/15 A=S	E		Y		FF/FA	6	5	1	6	1		6	3		3.1 2.2	Y		Y
0830	Kentucky St U Frankfort	KY	3800[3]	2500 6200	M[5]	Pub	S		A/S	E		Y		FAF	8	6	1	7	7	3	6	2	1	2.4 2.3	Y	Y	Y
0831	Sul Ross St U Alpine	TX	3900[3]	2900 7200	M[5]	Pub	T		A=S	E		Y		FF/FA	7	6	1	9	4	1	4	6	3	2.8	Y		
0832	Miss Valley St U Itta Bena	MS	4000	1800 5200	M[5]	Pub	T		A/S	E		Y	Y	8/01 FF/FA	9	5	0	8	9	1	8	5		2.8			Y
0833	DeVry Inst of Techn Irving	TX	5000	[1]	B[5]	Priv	M	S	A=S	T			Y	FA/FF	8	2	0	0	5	1	5	3			Y		Y
0834	Miss U for Women Columbus	MS	5900	2000 7100	M[5]	Pub	S		8/30 A/S	E		Y	Y	FF/FA	6	8	1	3	2	1	6	4		3.0 2.3	Y		Y
0835	Lee C Cleveland	TN	6500[3]	2800	B[5]	Oth OS	S		A/S	S		Y		FA/FF	9	5	0	9	1	8	8	6	2	2.8 2.4	Y		Y
0836	Okla Christian U Oklahoma City	OK	7200	2700	M[5]	Oth OS	V	S	A/S	T		Y		4/15 FFS	6	5	0	9	1			3	3	3.1	Y		
0837	Mobile C Mobile	AL	7700	3000	M[5]	Bapt OS	L	S	A/S	E		Y	Y	3/31 FF/FA	6	5	1	3	2	2	7	8	4		Y		
0838	David Lipscomb U Nashville	TN	8100[3]	3200	M[5]	Oth OS	V	S	ACT	E		Y		6/01 FA/FF	7	5	1	7	1	5	6	6	5		Y		
0839	Xavier U of La New Orleans	LA	8500	3000	P[5]	Cath OS	V	U	7/15 A=S	S			Y	FA/FF	9	7	1	4	9	5	7	4	5	2.7 2.5	Y		Y
0840	Abilene Christian U Abilene	TX	8700[3]	2600	D[5]	Oth OS	M	U	A/S	E		Y	Y	5/01 FF/FA	6	5	1	9	1	3	7	4	4	3.1 2.6	Y		Y
0841	Knoxville C Knoxville	TN	8700[3]	3500	B[5]	Pres	L	U	A=S	Q				FA/FF	9	5	0	9	9	7	5	5	2	2.5 2.4			Y

▲ Sequence number—indicates the order of the college in this book only. Do *not* use this number with admissions tests or need analysis services.

[1] No campus room and board facilities
[2] Room only or board only
[3] Most freshmen required to live on campus
[4] City or district residence requirements
[5] Accredited by a regional accrediting association or a recognized candidate for accreditation
[6] All female freshman class
[7] All male freshman class

MAJORS AVAILABLE AND PERCENT OF STUDENTS STUDYING IN EACH AREA

Majors by area:

- **Agri.:** Agriculture, general; Agronomy (crops & mgmt); Animal Science (husbandry); Fish, Wildlife Mgmt; Forestry
- **Business:** Business/Commerce, general; Accounting; Banking/Finance; Business Economics; Business Mgmt/Admin; Marketing/Purchasing; Secretarial Studies
- **Comm.:** Communications, general; Journalism; Radio/TV (broadcasting); Advertising
- **Education:** Art Education; Distributive Education; Elementary Education; English Education; Mathematics Education; Music Education; Physical Education; Science Education; Secondary Education; Social Science Education; Special Education; Speech Education
- **Engineering:** Engineering, general; Chemical; Civil; Electrical/Electronics/Comm; Industrial/Management; Mechanical
- **Fine/App. Arts:** Architecture; Fine/Applied Arts, general; Art (Paint, draw, sculpt); Art History/Appreciation; Dance; Dramatic Arts (theater arts); Music (liberal arts); Music (perform, compos, theory)
- **Lang.:** French; German; Italian; Latin; Spanish; Russian
- **Health:** Predentistry; Premedicine; Medical/Lab Technology; Nursing (registered nurse); Occupational Therapy; Preoptometry; Prepharmacy; Physical Therapy; Preveterinary Medicine
- **Home Ec.:** Home Economics, general; Clothing and Textiles; Consumer Ec/Home Mgmt; Family Relations/Child Devel; Food and Nutrition/Dietetics; Institution Mgmt
- **Humanities:** Humanities, general; Creative Writing; English, general; Literature, English; Philosophy; Religion; Speech/Forensic Science
- **Math-Sciences:** Mathematics, general; Computer/Info Sciences; Biological Sciences, general; Biology; Botany; Zoology; Physical Sciences, general; Chemistry; Physics
- **Social Sciences:** Crim Just/Law Enforce; Social Work; Social Sciences, general; Anthropology; Area Studies (Amer., African, etc.); Economics; Geography; History; Prelaw; Political Science; Psychology; Sociology
- **GS:** General Studies
- **ROTC:** Air Force; Army; Navy

Sequence Number	Agri.	Business	Comm.	Education	Engineering	Fine/App. Arts	Lang.	Health	Home Ec.	Humanities	Math-Sciences	Social Sciences	GS	ROTC
0812		85%									1%	7%		
0813	13%	20%		10%				38%	2%	5%	3%	8%		YY
0814										100%				
0815		31%	14%	22%		1%	1%				2%	8%		YY
0816						100%								
0817		22%	2%	15%	1%	1%		12%	2%	1%	8%	1%		Y
0818		16%	1%	27%		1%	1%	18%	3%	2%	3%	2%		
0819		29%	1%	20%	1%	1%	1%	1%		2%	13%	2%		YY
0820	4%	18%	3%	10%	1%	2%		19%	1%		12%	11%		
0821	2%	13%	2%	27%	4%	1%			1%	1%	11%	10%		Y
0822	8%	23%	2%	19%	1%	2%	2%	10%		1%	3%	2%		
0823	6%	25%	1%	20%	5%	3%	1%	4%		2%	11%	7%		
0824		33%		31%		1%		11%	3%	1%	3%	2%		YY
0825		27%		24%		4%	1%	8%		3%	29%	4%		
0826	4%	33%	1%	35%	1%		1%	10%	2%	1%	3%	2%		Y
0827		31%		6%	1%	1%		4%		2%	2%	1%		YYY
0828		25%	2%	10%	2%	2%	1%	10%		2%	8%	5%		Y
0829	7%	21%	2%	22%	1%	1%	1%	8%		2%	3%	2%		
0830		19%		9%	3%	1%		5%	2%	2%	13%	11%		YY
0831	15%	13%	2%	23%		2%		2%		2%	7%	13%		
0832		21%		14%				1%						YY
0833		19%			57%						24%			
0834		27%	5%	10%		1%		16%	1%	2%	12%	1%		Y
0835		22%	2%	12%		1%	1%	8%		2%	3%	1%		
0836		22%	9%	17%	9%	2%		1%	2%	9%	13%	9%		YY
0837		17%	3%	20%	1%	4%		20%		7%	9%	8%		Y
0838		20%	1%	33%	1%	1%	1%	5%	4%	2%	3%	2%		
0839		20%	3%	5%	5%	1%	1%	39%		2%	7%	1%		YYY
0840	3%	23%	5%	22%	1%	2%	1%	7%	3%	8%	10%	8%		Y
0841		47%		20%	2%			8%						YY

[1] Additional majors available in this area
[2] ROTC available

†Accredited by a nationally recognized accrediting body other than one of the regional accrediting associations

South Central States
(continued)

AL, AR, KY, LA, MS, OK, TN, TX

LIBERAL ADMISSIONS *Some accepted students from lower half of HS class*

Sequence Number	School name (upper entry) City (lower entry)	State	Costs: Resident tuition/fees + room/board	Costs: Room/Board (upper entry) Nonresident tuition/fees + room/board (lower entry)	General Information: Highest degree	General Information: Affiliation (upper entry) Religious observance (lower entry)	General Information: Size of community	General Information: Type of community	Admissions: Fall term application deadline (upper entry) Tests desired or required (lower entry)	Admissions: Calendar	Admissions: Fall admission only	Admissions: Early admission	Admissions: Deferred admission	Financial Aid: Fall term application deadline (upper entry) Forms to be filed (lower entry)	Number in 10 who—: -have need, receive some aid	Under-grads: -are women	Under-grads: -are graduate students	Freshmen: -live on campus	Freshmen: -are minority students	Freshmen: -are nonresidents	Freshmen: -return as sophomores	Freshmen: -complete degree	Freshmen: -enter graduate study	HS GPA (upper entry) 1st year college GPA (lower entry)	Special Programs: Credit by exam	Special Programs: Student designed majors	Special Programs: Fraternities/sororities
	Enrollment 1,000 to 5,000																										
0842	Oakwood C Huntsville	AL	8900	3300	B [5]	Oth OS	M	U	A=S	Q				FAF	7	6	0	7	9	9				2.5	Y		
0843	Southern C Collegedale	TN	10100	3000	B [5]	Oth OS	T		ACT	E		Y		7/15 FF/FA	8	6	0	7	2	7	6	5	4	2.9 2.7	Y		
	Enrollment 5,000 to 15,000																										
0844	Alabama A&M U Normal	AL	3200	2000 4200	D [5]	Pub	M	S	A=S	E		Y	Y	4/01 FF/FA	8	6	1	8	9	2	7	7	3	2.8 2.5	Y		Y
0845	Central Okla,U of Edmond	OK	3200	2000 4900	M [5]	Pub	M	S	8/23 A=S	E		Y		6/01 FF/FA	3	6	1	1	2	1	6	1		2.9 2.3	Y		Y
0846	Middle Tenn St U Murfreesboro	TN	3300	1900 6500	D [5]	Pub	S		A/S	S		Y	Y	5/15 FF/FA	8	5	1	4	1	1	5	3	1	2.9 2.2	Y		Y
0847	Lamar U Beaumont	TX	3400	2600 5900	D [5]	Pub	M	S	8/08 A=S	S		Y		4/01 FA/FF	3	3	1	2	2	1	6	5	1	2.9 2.2	Y		Y
0848	Central Arkansas,U Conway	AR	3500 [3]	2200 4800	M [5]	Pub	S		8/15 A/S	E		Y	Y	FFS	7	6	1		1	1	6		2	3.0	Y		Y
0849	Texas El Paso,U of El Paso	TX	3500	2600 6600	D [5]	Pub	V	U	A=S	E		Y	Y	4/01 FF/FA	5	5	1		7	1	6	2			Y		Y
0850	Tarleton St U Stephenville	TX	3600 [3]	2500 6700	M [5]	Pub	S		8/15 A=S	E		Y	Y	6/01 FAF	4	5	1	6	1	1	6	2	1		Y		Y
0851	Morehead St U Morehead	KY	3800	2500 6100	M [5]	Pub	T		8/01 A/S	E		Y	Y	4/01 FAF	7	6	1	8	1	2	7	3		2.9	Y	Y	Y
0852	Austin Peay St U Clarksville	TN	4300 [3]	2500 6900	M [5]	Pub	M		8/15 A/S	S		Y		8/01 FF/FA	7	6	1	3	2	1	7	3	2	3.0 2.3	Y		Y
0853	Jackson St U Jackson	MS	4300	2500 5500	D [5]	Pub	V	U	8/01 A/S	S		Y	Y	4/01 FA/FF	8	6	1	4	9	4	7		3	2.5	Y		Y
0854	Western Kentucky U Bowling Green	KY	4300 [3]	2900 6900	M [5]	Pub	M		8/01 ACT	E		Y	Y	4/01 FA/FF	3	6	1	8	1	2	7	3		2.9 2.4	Y	Y	Y
0855	Miss St U Miss State	MS	4800	2800 6000	D [5]	Pub	S		8/04 A/S	E		Y		4/01 FF/FA	7	4	1		2	3	8	4		2.5	Y		Y
	TRADITIONAL ADMISSIONS *Majority of accepted students in top 50% of HS class*																										
	Enrollment to 1,000																										
0856	Christ C of Okla Tulsa	OK	1100	[1]	B †	Oth OS	L	S	9/12 A/S	S						3	0		1	5	7			3.0			
0857	Sci & Arts Okla,U of Chickasha	OK	3100	1800 5100	B [5]	Pub	S		A/S	T		Y		7/15 FFS	7	7	0	2	1	1	6	4	3	2.9 2.7	Y		
0858	Texas Tech U Sch Nsg Lubbock	TX	3500 [3]	2600 5600	M †	Pub	L	U	5/15 A=S	E		Y		FF/FA	2	9	1	3	2	1	9	6			Y		Y
0859	Central Baptist C Conway	AR	3700	1700	B †	Bapt OS	S		8/15 ACT	E		Y		8/15	6	5	0	8	1	1	7	1	5	3.0 2.8	Y		
0860	Texas A&M Galveston Galveston	TX	4300 [3]	3100 7600	B [5]	Pub	M	S	9/01 A=S	E		Y	Y	6/01 FAF	3	4	0	9	1	3		1	2		Y		
0861	Southwest C Chr Min Bethany	OK	4600	2100	B [5]	Oth O	V	S	8/15 A/S	E		Y	Y	7/01 FFS	8	4	0	8	1	4	7	6	1	2.7 2.8	Y		
0862	Ozarks,U of the Clarksville	AR	5200	2200	B [5]	Pres OS	T		A/S	S		Y	Y	7/01 FFS	8	5	0	7	2	1	7		3	2.9 2.6	Y		Y
0863	Baptist Christian Shreveport	LA	5700	2400	B	Bapt OS	M	U	9/01 A/S	S				9/01	5	4	0	1	2	1	7	7	9	2.0 2.5	Y	Y	
0864	Southeastern Bible C Birmingham	AL	5700	2500	M †	Priv OS	V	S	8/15 A/S	E				7/15 FA/FF	7	3	1	5	1	5	6	5	2	3.0 2.8	Y		
0865	Bethel C McKenzie	TN	6500	2400	M [5]	Oth S	T		8/01 A/S	S		Y		7/01 FF/FA	9	6	1	5	1	2	6	5	2	2.5	Y	Y	Y
0866	Talladega C Talladega	AL	6500	2000	B [5]	Priv O	T		A=S	E		Y		FA/FF	9	6	0	3	9	5	6	5	4	2.8 2.5	Y		Y
0867	La C Pineville	LA	7000	2800	B [5]	Oth OS	M	S	A/S	E		Y	Y	5/01 FF/FA	8	5	0	5	1	1	5	3		3.2 2.6	Y	Y	Y
0868	San Antonio Art Inst San Antonio	TX	7000	[1]	B [5]	Priv	V	U	A=S	E				3/01 FA/FF	8	4	0	0	4	1	8			2.8 2.8	Y		
0869	William Carey C Hattiesburg	MS	7000	2800	M [5]	Oth OS	M		8/15 A=S	E		Y		4/15 FA/FF	7	7	1	5	4	3	5		5	3.0	Y		Y

Sequence Number | School name (upper entry) City (lower entry) | State | Costs | General Information | Admissions | Financial Aid | Student Profile | Programs

▲ Sequence number—indicates the order of the college in this book only. Do *not* use this number with admissions tests or need analysis services.

[1] No campus room and board facilities
[2] Room only or board only
[3] Most freshmen required to live on campus
[4] City or district residence requirements
[5] Accredited by a regional accrediting association or a recognized candidate for accreditation
[6] All female freshman class
[7] All male freshman class

MAJORS AVAILABLE AND PERCENT OF STUDENTS STUDYING IN EACH AREA

Agri.: Agriculture, general; Agronomy (crops & mgmt); Animal Science (husbandry); Fish, Wildlife Mgmt; Forestry
Business: Business/Commerce, general; Accounting; Banking/Finance; Business Economics; Business Mgmt/Admin; Marketing/Purchasing; Secretarial Studies
Comm.: Communications, general; Journalism; Radio/TV (broadcasting); Advertising
Education: Art Education; Distributive Education; Elementary Education; English Education; Mathematics Education; Music Education; Physical Education; Science Education; Secondary Education; Social Science Education; Special Education; Speech Education
Engineering: Engineering, general; Chemical; Civil; Electrical/Electronics/Comm; Industrial/Management; Mechanical
Fine/App. Arts: Architecture; Fine/Applied Arts, general; Art (Paint, draw, sculpt); Art History/Appreciation; Dance; Dramatic Arts (theater arts); Music (liberal arts); Music (perform, compos, theory)
Lang.: French; German; Italian; Latin; Spanish; Russian
Health: Predentistry; Premedicine; Medical/Lab Technology; Nursing (registered nurse); Occupational Therapy; Preoptometry; Prepharmacy; Physical Therapy; Preveterinary Medicine
Home Ec.: Home Economics, general; Clothing and Textiles; Consumer Ec/Home Mgmt; Family Relations/Child Devel; Food and Nutrition/Dietetics; Institution Mgmt
Humanities: Humanities, general; Creative Writing; English, general; Literature, English; Philosophy; Religion; Speech/Forensic Science
Math-Sciences: Mathematics, general; Computer/Info Sciences; Biological Sciences, general; Biology; Botany; Zoology; Physical Sciences, general; Chemistry; Physics
Social Sciences: Crim Just/Law Enforce; Social Work; Social Sciences, general; Anthropology; Area Studies (Amer., African, etc.); Economics; Geography; History; Prelaw; Political Science; Psychology; Sociology
GS: General Studies
ROTC: Air Force; Army; Navy

Sequence Number	Agri.	Business	Comm.	Education	Engineering	Fine/App. Arts	Lang.	Health	Home Ec.	Humanities	Math-Sciences	Social Sciences	GS	ROTC
0842		17%	4%	6%	2%	3%		10%	5%	17%	9%	7%		
0843		17%	3%	15%	1%	1%	1%	32%	2%	2%	3%	2%		
0844	7%	30%	5%	13%	9%	2%	1%	4%	1%	2%	18%	6%		Y
0845		23%	5%	15%		3%	1%	4%	1%	1%	8%	6%		Y
0846	3%	25%	13%	9%	5%	3%	1%	6%	2%	2%	11%	12%		Y
0847		21%	6%	17%	12%	2%	1%	9%	2%	2%	3%	2%		Y
0848		28%	3%	22%	1%	2%	1%	17%	2%	2%	3%	2%		Y
0849		8%	3%	6%	7%	2%	1%	1%		3%	7%	13%		YY
0850	18%	19%		3%	2%	4%		7%	2%	2%	9%	10%		Y
0851	1%	13%	5%	17%	4%	2%		4%	2%	2%	10%	12%		Y
0852	2%	22%	5%	19%	2%	5%	1%	10%		3%	9%	11%		Y
0853		28%	5%	12%	4%	1%	1%	1%		3%	25%	6%		Y
0854	3%	16%	11%	15%	6%	1%	1%	11%	2%	4%	6%	14%		YY
0855	11%	25%	3%	15%	19%	5%	1%	1%	2%	1%	10%	6%		YY
0856										100%				
0857		25%	7%	30%		10%		3%	2%		14%	9%		
0858								100%						YYY
0859	1%	12%	2%	20%	1%	1%	1%	7%		38%	4%	5%		
0860	3%	19%			13%						59%			Y
0861				10%						90%				
0862		39%	1%	21%		1%	1%	2%		2%	3%	2%		Y
0863		25%		50%										
0864				25%						75%				
0865		25%		30%		1%		2%		2%	3%	1%		
0866		28%	1%	5%	1%	1%	1%	1%		3%	29%	12%		
0867		25%	3%	10%		2%	1%	15%		15%	8%	17%		
0868						100%								
0869		21%	1%	17%	1%	14%	1%	18%		20%	3%	2%		

[1] Additional majors available in this area
[2] ROTC available

†Accredited by a nationally recognized accrediting body other than one of the regional accrediting associations

South Central States

(continued)

AL, AR, KY, LA, MS, OK, TN, TX

TRADITIONAL ADMISSIONS *Majority of accepted students in top 50% of HS class*

Sequence Number	School name (upper entry) City (lower entry)	State	Costs: Resident tuition/fees + room/board	Costs: Room/Board (upper entry) Nonresident tuition/fees + room/board (lower entry)	General Information: Highest degree	General Information: Affiliation (upper entry) Religious observance (lower entry)	General Information: Size of community	General Information: Type of community	Admissions: Fall term application deadline (upper entry) Tests desired or required (lower entry)	Admissions: Calendar	Admissions: Fall admission only	Admissions: Early admission	Admissions: Deferred admission	Financial Aid: Fall term application deadline (upper entry) Forms to be filed (lower entry)	Financial Aid: Number in 10 who -have need, receive some aid	Student Profile: Number in 10 who — Undergrads -are women	Undergrads -are graduate students	Freshmen -live on campus	Freshmen -are minority students	Freshmen -are nonresidents	Freshmen -return as sophomores	Freshmen -complete degree	Freshmen -enter graduate study	HS GPA (upper entry) 1st year college GPA (lower entry)	Special Programs: Credit by exam	Special Programs: Student designed majors	Special Programs: Fraternities/sororities
	Enrollment to 1,000																										
0870	East Texas Baptist U Marshall	TX	7100	2800	B[5]	Oth OS	S		9/01 A/S	4		Y		 FA/FF	9	5	0	7	1	1	7	3	3	3.1 3.0	Y		
0871	Lambuth C Jackson	TN	7100	2900	B[5]	Meth OS	M		 A/S	E		Y		 FF/FA	7	5	0	7	2	3	7	4	3	3.3 2.6	Y	Y	Y
0872	Texas Sch All H S,U Houston	TX	7500	6600 12300	B[5]	Pub	V	U	5/15 Oth	O				4/15 FAF	7	5	2		2	1	9			2.4 2.8	Y		
0873	Union C Barbourville	KY	7700[3]	2300	M[5]	Meth OS	T		8/30 A=S	E		Y	Y	7/15 FA/FF	9	5	1	5	1	2	6	4	3	2.8 2.7	Y	Y	
0874	Belhaven C Jackson	MS	8000	2100	B[5]	Pres OS	L	U	 A/S	E		Y	Y	4/15 FA/FF	5	5	0	8	1	4	9		1		Y		
0875	Dallas Baptist U Dallas	TX	8000	2900	M[5]	Oth OS	V	U	 A=S	4		Y		5/01 FA/FF		5	1	5	3	2	6				Y		
0876	Brescia C Owensboro	KY	8200	2600	B[5]	Cath OS	M		 A/S	E				3/30 FAF	7	5	0	1	1	1	7	6		3.1 3.0	Y		
0877	John Brown U Siloam Springs	AR	8500	3100	B[5]	Priv OS	T		 A/S	E		Y		4/01 FFS	7	5	0	9	1	8	7	4	3	3.0 2.7	Y		
0878	Milligan C Milligan	TN	8900[3]	2700	M[5]	Oth OS	S		8/01 A/S	E		Y	Y	4/01 FF/FA	7	5	1	8	1	7	6	4	1	 2.4	Y		
0879	Tusculum C Greeneville	TN	9000[3]	3100	M[5]	Pres	S		 A=S	S		Y	Y	5/01 FF/FA	9	6	2	8	1	4	6		2	2.8 2.8	Y	Y	
0880	Spalding U Louisville	KY	9400	2800	D[5]	Cath S	V	U	8/15 A=S	E		Y	Y	3/15 FAF	8	8	1	2	1	2	7	7	2	3.1	Y	Y	
0881	Bryan C Dayton	TN	9900	3500	B[5]	Priv OS	T		7/31 A/S	E		Y		5/01 FF/FA	8	6	0	9	1	8	7	4	2	3.2	Y	Y	
0882	Thomas More C Crestview Hills	KY	10900	3400	B[5]	Cath S	M	S	9/01 A=S	E		Y		 FA/FF	7	6	0	5	3	4	8	5	3	3.0 3.1	Y	Y	Y
0883	Le Tourneau U Longview	TX	11000[3]	3600	B[5]	Oth OS	M		8/15 A=S	E				 FA/FF	8	2	0	8	1	7	8	5		3.2 2.6	Y		
0884	Northwood of Texas Cedar Hill	TX	11300[3]	3700	B[5]	Priv	S		9/02 A/S	Q			Y	8/31 FA/FF	7	4	0	6	1	3	8	6	1	2.8	Y		Y
0885	Phillips U Enid	OK	11300[3]	2800	M[5]	Oth OS	S		 A=S	E		Y	Y	 FA/FF	8	6	2	4	1	2	8	8		3.1	Y	Y	Y
0886	Schreiner C Kerrville	TX	12000[3]	4700	B[5]	Pres OS	S		8/15 A=S	4		Y	Y	6/15 FA/FF	7	5	0	7	3	1	5	2	4	2.9 2.3	Y	Y	Y
	Enrollment 1,000 to 5,000																										
0887	Texas A&I U Kingsville	TX	3500[3]	2600 6600	D[5]	Pub	S		 A/S	S				5/17 FA/FF	6	5	1		7			2		2.7 2.3	Y		Y
0888	Cameron U Lawton	OK	3600	2200 5500	M[5]	Pub	M		 A/S	E		Y		8/01 FFS	5	5	1	1	2	1	5	4	2	3.0 2.5	Y		Y
0889	North Alabama,U of Florence	AL	3700	2400 4200	M[5]	Pub	S		 A=S	E		Y	Y	4/01	3	6	1	3	1	1	7	3		2.9 2.0	Y		Y
0890	Troy St U-Troy Troy	AL	3700[3]	2300 4400	M[5]	Pub	S		 A=S	Q			Y	5/01	7	5	1	5	2	3	7	7	1	3.2 3.0	Y	Y	Y
0891	Tenn Martin,U of Martin	TN	4000[3]	2500 7300	M[5]	Pub	S		 A/S	S		Y		3/01 FF/FA	6	5	0	6	2	1	7	4		2.9	Y	Y	Y
0892	Texas Woman's U Denton	TX	4000[3]	2900 7100	D[5]	Pub	M	S	 Oth	E		Y	Y	4/01 FF/FA		9	2		3	1	6				Y		Y
0893	Montevallo,U of Montevallo	AL	4600[3]	2800 6200	M[5]	Pub	T		8/01 A/S	E		Y	Y	6/01 FA/FF	6	7	1	7	1	1	7	5	2	3.1 2.6	Y		Y
0894	Prairie View A&M U Prairie View	TX	4600	3200 7200	M[5]	Pub	T		 A=S	S		Y	Y	4/01 FF=FA	7	5	1	7	9	1	6	7	2	2.6 2.4	Y		Y
0895	East Texas St U Commerce	TX	5100[3]	4100 8200	D[5]	Pub	T		8/01 A=S	E		Y		5/01 FF/FA	3	5	1	6	2	1	7			 2.3	Y		Y
0896	Lincoln Memorial U Harrogate	TN	6700[3]	2400	M[5]	Priv	T		 A/S	E		Y	Y	 FF/FA	9	7	0	3	1	5	7	5	2	3.2 2.5	Y	Y	Y
0897	Okla Baptist U Shawnee	OK	6700	2600	B[5]	Oth OS	S		8/01 A/S	E				4/15 FFS	9	5	0	7	1	3	7	7	4	3.2 2.8	Y	Y	Y
0898	Ouachita Baptist U Arkadelphia	AR	6900[3]	2100	B[5]	Bapt OS	S		8/15 A/S	E		Y		 FF/FA	7	5	0	9	1	2	7	5	4	3.2 2.6	Y		Y
0899	Hardin-Simmons U Abilene	TX	7400[3]	2600	M[5]	Bapt OS	M		 A=S	E		Y	Y	3/15 FF/FA	9	5	1	6	1	1	6	3	2	3.0	Y		Y

▲ Sequence number—indicates the order of the college in this book only. Do *not* use this number with admissions tests or need analysis services.

[1] No campus room and board facilities
[2] Room only or board only
[3] Most freshmen required to live on campus
[4] City or district residence requirements
[5] Accredited by a regional accrediting association or a recognized candidate for accreditation
[6] All female freshman class
[7] All male freshman class

MAJORS AVAILABLE AND PERCENT OF STUDENTS STUDYING IN EACH AREA

Sequence Number	Agri.	Business	Comm.	Education	Engineering	Fine/App. Arts	Lang.	Health	Home Ec.	Humanities	Math-Sciences	Social Sciences	GS	ROTC
0870		016%	3%	024%		4%	1%	2%		013%	6% [1]	9%		
0871		018%	3%	7% [1]		7% [1]	1%	[1]	1%	4%	016% [1]	7% [1]		
0872								100% [1]						
0873		021% [1]	3%	022% [1]	3%	2%	2%	4%		5%	022%	012%		Army
0874		039%	1%	9%		6%	1%	1%		9% [1]	010%	7%		Army
0875		047% [1]	1%	8% [1]		2%		6% [1]		6%	8% [1]	010% [1]		Air Force, Army
0876		032%		025%	2%	1%	1%	8%		2%	3% [1]	2%		
0877		030%	8%	015% [1]	013%	1%				3%	2%	1%		Army
0878		022% [1]	015%	011%		3%		4% [1]		4%	015%	016% [1]		Army
0879		072%	2%	010% [1]		1%				1%	4%	4%		
0880		012%	8%	010% [1]		1%	1%	030%	2%	3%	3%	3% [1]		Air Force, Army
0881		018%	2%	018%		4%		1%		020%	010%	018%		
0882		035%		5% [1]	3% [1]	1%	1%	017%		3%	025% [1]	9%		Air Force, Army, Navy
0883		013%		1%	063% [1]			1%		2%	013%	1% [1]		
0884		100%												
0885		021% [1]	6%	014% [1]	3%	8%	1%	5% [1]		5%	6% [1]	011% [1]		
0886		049% [1]	1%	9% [1]	4%	9%	1%	011%		2%	7%	2%		
0887	5% [1]	022% [1]	2%	024% [1]	014% [1]	3%	1%	3%	2%	1%	7% [1]	7% [1]		Army
0888	3%	021%	010%	012% [1]	4%			5%	3%	3%	015% [1]	6%		Army
0889		034% [1]	5%	023% [1]	2%	4% [1]	1%	6%	1%	2%	010%	012%		Army
0890		039% [1]	7%	013% [1]				8%			[1]			Air Force
0891	6% [1]	026% [1]	3%	5% [1]	6%	4% [1]	2%	015% [1]	2%	6%	015% [1]	9% [1]		Army
0892		8% [1]	2%	014% [1]		4% [1]	1%	045% [1]	3%	1%	4%	010% [1]		Air Force, Army
0893		019%	4%	020% [1]		010% [1]		7% [1]	4%	5%	5%	012%		Air Force, Army
0894	2% [1]	025% [1]	2%	7% [1]	020% [1]	2%		015%	1%	1%	022% [1]	2%		Army, Navy
0895	5% [1]	026% [1]	012%	030% [1]	1%	2% [1]	1%	1%		2% [1]	7% [1]	2% [1]		
0896	1%	038% [1]	2%	020% [1]		1% [1]		012%		2%	8%	2%		Army
0897		011% [1]	5%	019% [1]		4%	1%	7% [1]		024%	6% [1]	011% [1]		
0898		020% [1]	4%	017% [1]	1%	7%	1%	5% [1]	1%	021%	011% [1]	012%		
0899		015% [1]	2%	020% [1]		6%		8%		8%	8% [1]	017% [1]		Army

[1] Additional majors available in this area
[2] ROTC available

†Accredited by a nationally recognized accrediting body other than one of the regional accrediting associations

South Central States (continued)

AL, AR, KY, LA, MS, OK, TN, TX

TRADITIONAL ADMISSIONS *Majority of accepted students in top 50% of HS class*

Sequence Number	School name (upper entry) City (lower entry)	State	Costs: Resident tuition/fees + room/board	Costs: Room/Board (upper entry) Nonresident tuition/fees + room/board (lower entry)	General Information: Highest degree	General Information: Affiliation (upper entry) Religious observance (lower entry)	General Information: Size of community	General Information: Type of community	Admissions: Fall term application deadline (upper entry) Tests desired or required (lower entry)	Admissions: Calendar	Admissions: Fall admission only	Admissions: Early admission	Admissions: Deferred admission	Financial Aid: Fall term application deadline (upper entry) Forms to be filed (lower entry)	Financial Aid: Number in 10 who— -have need, receive some aid	Student Profile: Undergrads -are women	Undergrads -are graduate students	Freshmen -live on campus	Freshmen -are minority students	Freshmen -are nonresidents	Freshmen -return as sophomores	Freshmen -complete degree	Freshmen -enter graduate study	HS GPA (upper entry) 1st year college GPA (lower entry)	Special Programs: Credit by exam	Special Programs: Student designed majors	Special Programs: Fraternities/sororities
	Enrollment 1,000 to 5,000																										
0900	Mary Hardin Baylor,U Belton	TX	7500 [3]	3000	M [5]	Oth OS	S		A/S	E		Y		FFS	8	7	1	8	2	1	7	6	2	3.0	Y		Y
0901	Cumberland C Williamsburg	KY	7600	2700	M [5]	Oth OS	T		A=S	E		Y	Y	3/15 FF=FA	8	5	1	7	1	4	6	2		3.0 2.5	Y		
0902	Miss C Clinton	MS	7600	2600	P [5]	Bapt O	S		8/15 A/S	E		Y		4/01 FA/FF	7	6	2	5	2	2	9	6	4	2.7	Y		
0903	Freed-Hardeman U Henderson	TN	7800	2800	M [5]	Oth OS	T		9/01 A/S	E		Y	Y	9/01 FF/FA	7	6	0	9	1	4	7	4	2	3.0 2.6	Y	Y	
0904	McMurry U Abilene	TX	8000 [3]	2700	B [5]	Meth OS	M	S	A=S	E		Y		FF/FA	6	5	0	8	2	1	6	3	3	3.2 2.5	Y		Y
0905	Southern Nazarene U Bethany	OK	8000 [3]	3000	M [5]	Oth OS	V	S	8/01 A/S	E		Y	Y	6/01 FF/FA	8	6	1	8	1	6	7	5	5	3.0 2.7	Y		
0906	Okla City U Oklahoma City	OK	8200 [3]	3400	P [5]	Meth S	V	U	A=S	E		Y	Y	3/01 FA/FF	8	5	5	7	3	1	7			3.2	Y		Y
0907	Texas Wesleyan U Fort Worth	TX	8500	3200	M [5]	Meth S	L	U	A=S	S		Y		4/15 FA/FF	8	5	2	4	1	1	7	3	4	3.4 2.6	Y		Y
0908	Asbury C Wilmore	KY	8600	2200	B [5]	Oth OS	T		8/15 A/S	E		Y		3/15 FA/FF	8	5	0	9	1	7	8	7	5	3.0 2.8	Y		
0909	Tuskegee U Tuskegee	AL	8600 [3]	2800	P [5]	Priv	S		6/15 A=S	E		Y		3/31 FF=FA	9	5	0	9	9	8	6	4	2		Y		Y
0910	Dillard U New Orleans	LA	8700	3200	B [5]	Oth O	V	U	7/01 A=S	E		Y		6/01 FF/FA	9	7	0	5	9	4	6	7	4	3.0 3.0	Y		Y
0911	Georgetown C Georgetown	KY	9000 [3]	3300 9100	M [5]	Oth OS	S		8/01 A/S	E				FA/FF	6	5	0	9	1	2	7	5	4	3.2 2.6	Y	Y	Y
0912	Oral Roberts U Tulsa	OK	9000 [3]	3400	D [5]	Oth OS	L	S	A=S	E		Y	Y	6/01 FAF	8	5	1	9	3	7	5			3.3 2.8	Y	Y	
0913	Belmont C Nashville	TN	9100 [3]	3200	M [5]	Bapt O	V	U	8/04 A/S	E		Y	Y	3/15 FAF	8	6	1	7	1	3	6	3	3		Y		
0914	Carson-Newman C Jefferson City	TN	9400 [3]	2900	M [5]	Bapt OS	T		A/S	E		Y		4/01 FA/FF	9	6	1	8		3	7	5	3	3.1 2.5	Y	Y	Y
0915	Our Lady of the Lake San Antonio	TX	9900	3300	D [5]	Cath S	V	U	A=S	E		Y		FF/FA	8	7	2	4	6	1	6	4	2	3.0 2.5	Y		
0916	Saint Thomas,U of Houston	TX	10000	3200	D [5]	Cath	V	U	A=S	S		Y	Y	5/31 FAF	4	6	1	2	3	1	7		3		Y		
0917	Incarnate Word C San Antonio	TX	10700	3500	M [5]	Cath S	V	U	A=S	E		Y	Y	FA/FF	6		1	4	5	1	9	7	2	3.2 3.0	Y		Y
	Enrollment 5,000 to 15,000																										
0918	Sam Houston St U Huntsville	TX	3400 [3]	2300 6500	D [5]	Pub	S		A=S	E		Y		7/15 FFS	5	5	1	7	1	1	6			2.0	Y		Y
0919	East Tenn St U Johnson City	TN	3700	2300 6900	D [5]	Pub	S		A/S	E		Y		4/15 FF/FA	4	5	1	3	1	1	7	3		2.8 2.5	Y		Y
0920	Northeast Okla St U Tahlequah	OK	3700 [3]	2400 5700	P [5]	Pub	S		8/01 ACT	E			Y	4/01 FF=FA	8	5	1	2	2	1	6	3	1	2.8 2.3	Y		
0921	Murray St U Murray	KY	3800 [3]	2400 6400	M [5]	Pub	S		A/S	E		Y	Y	4/01 FAF	9	5	1	5	1	2	7	7	1	3.0	Y		Y
0922	Stephen Austin U Nacogdoches	TX	3900 [3]	3000 7000	D [5]	Pub	S		A=S	E		Y	Y	4/01	3	5	1	8	1	1	6	4	1	3.2 2.0	Y		Y
0923	Memphis St U Memphis	TN	4100	2500 7300	D [5]	Pub	V	S	8/01 A/S	E		Y	Y	4/01 FF/FA	3	5	1		2	1	7	3		2.9 2.0	Y	Y	Y
0924	Tenn Tech U Cookeville	TN	4100 [3]	2700 7300	D [5]	Pub	S		8/01 ACT	E		Y		5/01 FF/FA	6	4	1	7	1	1	6	4	1	2.8 2.2	Y		Y
0925	Alabama Birmingham,U Birmingham	AL	4300 [2]	2400 5900	D [5]	Pub	V	U	9/06 A/S	Q		Y	Y	8/01 FA/FF	3	5	3		2	1				2.3 2.2	Y	Y	Y
0926	New Orls,U of New Orleans	LA	4300	2400 7000	D [5]	Pub	V	U	8/15 A/S	E		Y		5/01	4	5	1	1	2	1	6	2				Y	Y
0927	Arkansas Main Cam,U Fayetteville	AR	4400 [3]	2900 6800	D [5]	Pub	S		9/01 A=S	E				FF/FA	7	5	2	8	1	1	6	3		3.1 2.4	Y		Y
0928	South Alabama,U of Mobile	AL	4400	2500 5000	D [5]	Pub	L	S	9/10 A/S	Q		Y		4/01 FFS	3	6	1	3	2	2	6	3	1	2.8 2.2	Y	Y	Y
0929	Okla,U of Norman	OK	4800	3200 7700	D [5]	Pub	M	S	A/S	E		Y		6/01 FF/FA	4	4	1	5	2	2	7	3		3.2 2.3	Y	Y	Y

▲ Sequence number—indicates the order of the college in this book only. Do *not* use this number with admissions tests or need analysis services.

[1] No campus room and board facilities
[2] Room only or board only
[3] Most freshmen required to live on campus
[4] City or district residence requirements
[5] Accredited by a regional accrediting association or a recognized candidate for accreditation
[6] All female freshman class
[7] All male freshman class

MAJORS AVAILABLE AND PERCENT OF STUDENTS STUDYING IN EACH AREA

Sequence Number	Agri.	Business	Comm.	Education	Engineering	Fine/App. Arts	Lang.	Health	Home Ec.	Humanities	Math-Sciences	Social Sciences	GS	ROTC: Air Force	ROTC: Army	ROTC: Navy
0900		22%	1%	28%		1%	1%	12%	1%	4%	7%	9%		Y		
0901		27%		22%	1%	6%	1%	11%		5%	21%	3%			Y	
0902		23%	4%	14%		1%	1%	12%	2%	2%	7%	2%			Y	
0903	1%	20%	6%	18%	4%	2%		7%	4%	8%	5%	7%				
0904		28%	2%	27%		3%		5%		5%	14%	16%			Y	
0905		18%	3%	14%	1%	5%	1%	5%	2%	16%	11%	3%			Y	
0906		23%	9%	2%		22%		12%		10%	13%	9%		Y		
0907		34%	10%	14%	2%	8%	1%	2%		5%	20%	3%			Y	
0908		8%	6%	16%		4%	2%			15%	10%	16%				
0909	6%	20%	1%	7%	22%	6%		14%	1%	1%	15%	7%		Y	Y	
0910		22%	4%	5%	3%	1%	2%	24%		2%	17%	2%		Y	Y	Y
0911		22%	5%	11%	2%	5%	1%	1%	1%	9%	25%	11%		Y	Y	
0912		20%	9%	6%	2%	8%	1%	2%	1%	12%	22%	7%			Y	
0913		44%	4%	7%		10%	1%	2%		13%	8%	7%		Y	Y	Y
0914		17%	9%	15%	1%	2%	1%	10%	4%	3%	20%	12%			Y	
0915		45%	1%	9%		1%	1%	6%		2%	3%	2%			Y	
0916		28%	5%	6%	2%	3%	1%	3%		5%	8%	20%			Y	Y
0917		36%	6%	11%		8%		13%	3%	3%	4%	9%			Y	
0918	4%	22%	4%	17%	1%	6%	1%	2%	1%	2%	7%	18%			Y	
0919		20%	3%	16%	1%	6%	1%	13%	2%	5%	10%	6%			Y	
0920	1%	25%	7%	25%	1%	2%	2%	2%	2%	2%	5%	3%			Y	
0921	3%	20%	3%	25%	2%	2%	1%	3%	1%	2%	3%	2%			Y	
0922	3%	26%	6%	17%		5%		6%	1%	2%	7%	12%			Y	
0923		25%	3%	8%	10%	5%		4%	1%	1%	5%	8%		Y	Y	Y
0924	3%	22%	2%	16%	26%			4%	2%	3%	6%	5%			Y	
0925		20%	3%	10%	7%	2%	1%	11%		1%	13%	12%		Y	Y	
0926		30%	5%	9%	8%	3%	1%	10%		3%	7%	11%		Y	Y	
0927	4%	24%	7%	15%	18%	6%	1%	1%	3%	3%	8%	9%		Y	Y	
0928		22%	6%	18%	8%	3%		19%		2%	5%	8%		Y	Y	
0929		21%	9%	7%	12%	8%	1%	1%	1%	4%	9%	10%		Y	Y	Y

[1] Additional majors available in this area
[2] ROTC available

†Accredited by a nationally recognized accrediting body other than one of the regional accrediting associations

South Central States

(continued)

AL, AR, KY, LA, MS, OK, TN, TX

TRADITIONAL ADMISSIONS *Majority of accepted students in top 50% of HS class*

Sequence Number	School name (upper entry) City (lower entry)	State	Costs: Resident tuition/fees + room/board	Costs: Room/Board (upper entry) Nonresident tuition/fees + room/board (lower entry)	General Information: Highest degree	Affiliation (upper entry) Religious observance (lower entry)	Size of community	Type of community	Admissions: Fall term application deadline (upper entry) Tests desired or required (lower entry)	Calendar	Fall admission only	Early admission	Deferred admission	Financial Aid: Fall term application deadline (upper entry) Forms to be filed (lower entry)	Student Profile: Number in 10 who— -have need, receive some aid	Undergrads: -are women	-are graduate students	Freshmen: -live on campus	-are minority students	-are nonresidents	-return as sophomores	-complete degree	-enter graduate study	HS GPA (upper entry) 1st year college GPA (lower entry)	Special Programs: Credit by exam	Student designed majors	Fraternities/sororities
Enrollment 5,000 to 15,000																											
0930	Miss,U of University	MS	4900[3]	2800 6000	D[5]	Pub	S		A/S	E		Y		FA/FF	3	5	1	9	1	4	8	5	3	3.0 2.5	Y		Y
0931	Texas Arlington,U of Arlington	TX	4900	3900 8000	D[5]	Pub	L	S	8/01 A=S	S		Y	Y	6/01 FA/FF	4	4	1	1	3	1	6	2	3	3.2 2.2	Y		Y
0932	Tenn Chattanooga,U Chattanooga	TN	5000	3500 8200	M[5]	Pub	L	U	A/S	E		Y		2/01 FF/FA	6	5	1	1	1	1	7	3		3.0 2.3	Y		Y
0933	Texas San Antonio,U San Antonio	TX	5000	4000 8100	D[5]	Pub	V	S	7/01 A=S	E		Y	Y	3/31 FAF	4	5	1		4	1					Y		Y
Enrollment over 15,000																											
0934	North Texas,U of Denton	TX	4300	3300 7500	D[5]	Pub	M	S	6/15 A=S	E		Y		6/01 FAF	3	5	1	3	2					2.5	Y		Y
0935	Texas Tech U Lubbock	TX	4400[3]	3200 7500	D[5]	Pub	M	U	8/15 A=S	E				4/15 FF/FA	3	5	1	5	1	1	7	3		2.1	Y		Y
0936	Okla St U Stillwater	OK	4500[3]	2900 7400	D[5]	Pub	S		A/S	E		Y		3/01 FFS	3	5	1	5	1	1	7	4		3.3 2.3	Y	Y	Y
0937	Louisville,U of Louisville	KY	4600	3000 7600	D[5]	Pub	V	U	8/26 ACT	S		Y	Y	4/15 FA/FF	3	5	2	1	1	1		3	1	2.8	Y	Y	Y
0938	La St U A&M Batn Rge Baton Rouge	LA	4700	2700 7900	D[5]	Pub	L	U	7/01 A/S	E		Y		FFS	2	5	1	5	1	1	7	3		2.9 2.4	Y		Y
0939	Tenn Knoxville,U of Knoxville	TN	4700[3]	3000 7900	D[5]	Pub	L	U	7/01 A=S	E		Y	Y	4/01 FF=FA	3	5	2	7	1	1	8	5		3.1 2.6	Y	Y	Y
0940	Southwest Texas St U San Marcos	TX	4800[3]	3700 7900	M[5]	Pub	S		8/01 A=S	O				4/01 FF/FA	6	5	1	5	3	1	6	4	1	2.9 2.3	Y		Y
SELECTIVE ADMISSIONS *Majority of accepted students in top 25% of HS class*																											
Enrollment to 1,000																											
0941	La St U Sch Dentstry New Orleans	LA	3500	[1] 8100	P †	Pub	V	U	2/15 ACT	O				8/25 Oth	6	4	0	0	2	0				2.9			Y
0942	Amber U Garland	TX	3800	[1]	M[5]	Oth S	V	S	None	O					0	5	7	0	3	0				2.7	Y	Y	
0943	Judson C Marion	AL	6900	2700	B[5]	Bapt OS	T		8/15 A/S	O		Y	Y[6]	8/01 FFS	6	9	0	9	1	2	7	6	3	3.0	Y		
0944	Texas Lutheran C Seguin	TX	7900[3]	2600	B[5]	Luth O	S		A=S	E			Y	FA/FF	5	5	0	7	2	1	7	3	1	3.2 2.7	Y		Y
0945	Fisk U Nashville	TN	8100[3]	3100	M[5]	UCC	L	U	6/15 S/A	E		Y		4/01 FAF	7	7	1	9	9	9	7	7	6	3.0	Y	Y	
0946	Arkansas C Batesville	AR	9200[3]	2800	B[5]	Pres OS	T		8/15 A=S	4		Y	Y	FF=FA	9	6	0	7	1	2	6	3	1	3.3 2.5	Y	Y	Y
0947	Kentucky Wesleyan C Owensboro	KY	9500[3]	3400	B[5]	Meth	M		9/01 A=S	E		Y	Y	8/01 FAF	8	5	0	6	1	2	7	5	3	3.1 2.6	Y	Y	Y
0948	Huntingdon C Montgomery	AL	9600[3]	3200	B[5]	Meth O	M	S	A/S	O		Y		6/01 FA/FF	9	6	0	8	1	2	7	5	2	3.0 2.8	Y	Y	Y
0949	King C Bristol	TN	9700[3]	3400	B[5]	Pres OS	M	S	A=S	O		Y		FAF	8	5	0	8	1	5	7	5	4	2.8 2.4	Y		
0950	Centenary C of La Shreveport	LA	10100	3100	M[5]	Meth	L	S	8/01 A=S	4		Y	Y	3/15 FA/FF	6	5	0	6	1	4	8	7	6	3.2 3.0	Y		Y
0951	Maryville C Maryville	TN	11200	3600	B[5]	Pres O	S		A=S	4		Y	Y	FA/FF	6	6	0	8	1	4	6	3	4	3.0 2.5	Y	Y	
0952	Spring Hill C Mobile	AL	12700[3]	4000	M[5]	Cath S	L	S	A=S	E		Y	Y	3/01 FA/FF	7	5	1	7	1	7	8	6	5	3.0 2.8	Y	Y	Y
0953	Transylvania U Lexington	KY	13600[3]	4000	B[5]	Oth	M	U	6/01 A=S	O		Y	Y	3/15 FA/FF	7	5	0	9	1	2	8	6	4	3.3	Y	Y	Y
Enrollment 1,000 to 5,000																											
0954	Texas at Dallas,U Richardson	TX	1000	[1] 4100	D[5]	Pub	V	S	S/A	E			Y	11/01 FA/FF		5	3	0	2	1					Y	Y	
0955	Berea C Berea	KY	2500[3]	2300	B[5]	Priv OS	T		A=S	4		Y		8/01 FF=FA	9	6	0		1	5	7	5	6	3.2	Y	Y	
0956	Angelo St U San Angelo	TX	4300	3300 7400	M[5]	Pub	M		8/19 A=S	E		Y		7/15 FF/FA		6	0	3	2	1	6				Y		Y

▲ Sequence number—indicates the order of the college in this book only. Do *not* use this number with admissions tests or need analysis services.

[1] No campus room and board facilities
[2] Room only or board only
[3] Most freshmen required to live on campus
[4] City or district residence requirements
[5] Accredited by a regional accrediting association or a recognized candidate for accreditation
[6] All female freshman class
[7] All male freshman class

MAJORS AVAILABLE AND PERCENT OF STUDENTS STUDYING IN EACH AREA

Sequence Number	Agri.	Business	Comm.	Education	Engineering	Fine/App. Arts	Lang.	Health	Home Ec.	Humanities	Math-Sciences	Social Sciences	ROTC Air Force	ROTC Army	ROTC Navy
0930		037% [1]	3%	010% [1]	7% [1]	4% [1]	1%	012% [1]	2%	6% [1]	9% [1]	8% [1]	Y	Y	Y
0931		028% [1]	5%	1%	017% [1]	6% [1]	2%	7%		3%	9% [1]	011%	Y	Y	
0932		028%	6%	013% [1]	010%	6%	1%	5%	3%	3%	010% [1]	9% [1]		Y	
0933		024%		9% [1]	7%	2% [1]	1%	2% [1]		1%	012% [1]	9%	Y	Y	
0934		030% [1]	6%	012% [1]		012% [1]		1% [1]	3%	2%	7% [1]	010% [1]	Y		
0935	5% [1]	017% [1]	5%	9% [1]	9% [1]	5% [1]		[1]	9%	2% [1]	4% [1]	010% [1]	Y	Y	Y
0936	5% [1]	023% [1]	3%	012% [1]	014% [1]	3% [1]	1%	5% [1]	4%	1%	5% [1]	7% [1]	Y	Y	
0937		014% [1]	3%	7% [1]	012% [1]	2% [1]	1%	2% [1]		2% [1]	3% [1]	2% [1]	Y	Y	
0938	1% [1]	014% [1]	4%	7% [1]	011% [1]	6% [1]	1%	6% [1]	2%	4%	6% [1]	013% [1]	Y	Y	Y
0939	4% [1]	029% [1]	5%	010% [1]	014% [1]	6% [1]	1%	2% [1]	4%	3% [1]	4% [1]	011% [1]	Y	Y	
0940	2% [1]	020%	6%	012% [1]		4% [1]		6% [1]	4%	1%	9% [1]	018% [1]	Y	Y	
0941								100% [1]							
0942		073%	1%								1%				
0943		011%	2%	013% [1]		011% [1]	2%	4%	4%	010%	023% [1]	018%		Y	
0944		022%	6%	025%		2%	1%			3%	018% [1]	018%			
0945		025%	1%	3%		1%	1%	4%		2%	3%	2%	Y	Y	Y
0946		027%	4%	029%		4%				7%	017% [1]	012%			
0947		015%	015%	9% [1]	2%	1%	1%	019%		2%	010% [1]	2%			
0948		020%		010% [1]	1%	5%	1%	015%		3%	020% [1]	3% [1]	Y	Y	
0949		022%		8%	1%	1%	3%	018%		2%	3% [1]	1%		Y	
0950		025%	2%	9% [1]	5%	5%	1%	9% [1]		012%	017% [1]	011%		Y	
0951		010%		3%	5%	1%	1%	1%		2%	3%	1%			
0952		028%	020%	8% [1]				[1]		8%	016% [1]	020% [1]		Y	
0953		030%		8% [1]		3%				5%	024%	030%	Y	Y	
0954		038%			4%	1%		1% [1]		4% [1]	012% [1]	021% [1]	Y	Y	
0955	5%	018% [1]		018% [1]		3%	2%	9%	5%	012%	014%	6%			
0956	2% [1]	025% [1]	1%	010% [1]	1%	3%	1%	011%		3%	010%	011% [1]	Y		

[1] Additional majors available in this area
[2] ROTC available

†Accredited by a nationally recognized accrediting body other than one of the regional accrediting associations

South Central States

(continued)

AL, AR, KY, LA, MS, OK, TN, TX

SELECTIVE ADMISSIONS *Majority of accepted students in top 25% of HS class*

Sequence Number	School name (upper entry) City (lower entry)	State	Costs: Resident tuition/fees + room/board	Costs: Room/Board (upper entry) Nonresident tuition/fees + room/board (lower entry)	General Information: Highest degree	General Information: Affiliation (upper entry) Religious observance (lower entry)	General Information: Size of community	General Information: Type of community	Admissions: Fall term application deadline (upper entry) Tests desired or required (lower entry)	Admissions: Calendar	Admissions: Fall admission only	Admissions: Early admission	Admissions: Deferred admission	Financial Aid: Fall term application deadline (upper entry) Forms to be filed (lower entry)	Student Profile (Number in 10 who—): -have need, receive some aid	Under-grads: -are women	Under-grads: -are graduate students	Freshmen: -live on campus	Freshmen: -are minority students	Freshmen: -are nonresidents	Freshmen: -return as sophomores	Freshmen: -complete degree	Freshmen: -enter graduate study	Freshmen: HS GPA (upper entry) 1st year college GPA (lower entry)	Special Programs: Credit by exam	Special Programs: Student designed majors	Special Programs: Fraternities/sororities
	Enrollment 1,000 to 5,000																										
0957	Alabama Huntsville,U Huntsville	AL	4800	2800 6800	D[5]	Pub	M	S	8/13 A/S	O		Y	Y	4/01 FF/FA	3	5	1	1	1	1			2	3.2 2.3	Y		Y
0958	Union U Jackson	TN	6900	2300	M[5]	Oth OS	M		9/01 A/S	4		Y		5/15 FFS	8	6	0		1	2	8			3.0	Y	Y	Y
0959	Houston Baptist U Houston	TX	7200	2600	M[5]	Oth OS	V	U	8/15 S/A	Q		Y	Y	7/01 FA/FF	7	6	3	1	3	1	7		4	 2.7	Y		Y
0960	Harding U Searcy	AR	7400[3]	3000	M[5]	Oth OS	S		 A/S	E		Y	Y	5/01 FF=FA	7	5	1	9	1	7	7	5	3	3.0 3.0	Y		
0961	Bellarmine C Louisville	KY	8400	2400	M[5]	Cath	V	S	8/15 A/S	E		Y		5/01 FA/FF	9	6	1	4	1	1	9	7	3	3.1 2.8	Y		
0962	Hendrix C Conway	AR	9200	2600	B[5]	Meth	S		 A=S	O			Y	 Oth	7	5	0	9	1	2	8	7	5	3.4	Y	Y	
0963	Samford U Birmingham	AL	9200[3]	3200	P[5]	Oth OS	L	S	8/20 A=S	4		Y		 FA/FF	4	6	2	6	1	5	8	7	4	3.1 2.7	Y		Y
0964	Saint Mary's U San Antonio	TX	9600[3]	3200	D[5]	Cath OS	V	S	8/15 A=S	E			Y	 FA/FF	7	5	3	6	6	1	9	6	4	3.2 2.8	Y		Y
0965	Christian Brothers C Memphis	TN	10300	3600	M[5]	Cath OS	V	U	 A/S	E		Y	Y	 FF=FA	5	5	1	4	2	3	8	4	1	3.0 2.5	Y		Y
0966	Saint Edward's U Austin	TX	11000[3]	3400	M[5]	Cath	L	S	8/01 A=S	E		Y	Y	4/01	6	5	1	7	3	1	7	4	2	3.0 2.6	Y		
0967	Dallas,U of Irving	TX	11500	3600	D[5]	Cath	M	S	 A=S	E		Y	Y	2/15 FA/FF	6	5	3	8	3	4	8	6	6	 2.8	Y	Y	
0968	Tulsa,U of Tulsa	OK	12000[3]	3300	D[5]	Pres	V	U	 A=S	E		Y	Y	3/01 FA/FF	7	5	2	5	2	3	7	6	3	3.4 2.9	Y	Y	Y
0969	Birmingham-Sthn C Birmingham	AL	12100[3]	3100	M[5]	Meth O	V	U	 A=S	4		Y	Y	 FA/FF	5	5	1	9	1	4	9	7	4	3.2 2.8	Y	Y	Y
0970	Austin C Sherman	TX	13200[3]	3700	M[5]	Pres	S		 A=S	4		Y	Y	5/15 FA/FF	8	5	0	9	1	1	8	5	6	3.5 2.9	Y	Y	Y
0971	Loyola U New Orleans New Orleans	LA	13300[3]	4800	P[5]	Cath S	V	U	8/01 A=S	S		Y	Y	5/01 FAF	5	6	2	7	3	5	8			3.2	Y	Y	Y
0972	Millsaps C Jackson	MS	13300[3]	3600	M[5]	Meth	L	U	 A=S	E		Y	Y	3/01 FAF	6	5	0	7	1	5	8	6	4	3.1 2.6	Y		Y
0973	South,U of the Sewanee	TN	16000[3]	3300	D[5]	Oth O	T		2/01 A=S	E		Y	Y	3/01 FA/FF	5	5	1	9	1	8	9	8	7	3.3 2.6	Y		Y
	Enrollment 5,000 to 15,000																										
0974	Southern Miss,U of Hattiesburg	MS	4100	2200 5300	D[5]	Pub	M		8/19 ACT	S		Y	Y	3/15 FF/FA	6	6	1	5	2	2	7	5	4	2.8 2.3	Y		Y
0975	Baylor U Waco	TX	9800	3700	D[5]	Bapt OS	M	S	 S/A	E		Y	Y	 FAF	4	5	1	9	1	2	8	7		 2.9	Y		Y
0976	Texas Christian U Fort Worth	TX	10900	2700	D[5]	Oth S	V	S	2/01 S/A	E		Y	Y	3/01	7	6	1	9	1	3	8	6	3	3.1 2.7	Y	Y	Y
0977	Southern Methodist U Dallas	TX	15500[3]	4700	D[5]	Meth	V	S	4/01 A=S	S			Y	 FAF	6	5	2	9	1	5	9	7		3.2	Y		Y
0978	Tulane U New Orleans	LA	22500[3]	5500	D[5]	Priv	V	U	1/15 A=S	S		Y	Y	 FAF	9	5	4	9	2	8	9	7	9	 2.6	Y	Y	Y
	Enrollment over 15,000																										
0979	Kentucky,U of Lexington	KY	4400	2700 7400	D[5]	Pub	M	U	6/01 A/S	E			Y	4/01 FAF	5	6	1	8	1	2	7	5	4	3.2	Y	Y	Y
0980	Houston Main Cam,U Houston	TX	4800	3800 7900	D[5]	Pub	V	U	6/29 A=S	E		Y		4/02 FF/FA	3	3	2		3	1					Y		Y
0981	Alabama,U of Tuscaloosa	AL	4900	3100 7600	D[5]	Pub	M	S	8/01 A=S	E		Y		3/15 FF/FA	3	5	1	7	2	4	8	5		3.1 2.3	Y	Y	Y
0982	Auburn U Auburn	AL	4900	3300 8100	D[5]	Pub	S		9/01 A=S	Q		Y	Y	 FFS	4	4	1	3	1	4	8	5	2	3.2 2.5	Y		Y
0983	Texas A&M U Main Cam College Station	TX	5100	3800 8100	D[5]	Pub	M		 A=S	E		Y	Y	 FF=FA	3	4	2	5	2	1	8	6	3	 2.5	Y		Y

▲ Sequence number—indicates the order of the college in this book only. Do *not* use this number with admissions tests or need analysis services.

[1] No campus room and board facilities
[2] Room only or board only
[3] Most freshmen required to live on campus
[4] City or district residence requirements
[5] Accredited by a regional accrediting association or a recognized candidate for accreditation
[6] All female freshman class
[7] All male freshman class

MAJORS AVAILABLE AND PERCENT OF STUDENTS STUDYING IN EACH AREA

Sequence Number	Agri.	Business	Comm.	Education	Engineering	Fine/App. Arts	Lang.	Health	Home Ec.	Humanities	Math-Sciences	Social Sciences	GS	ROTC
0957		016%	1%	2% [1]	026%	2% [1]	1%	4%		3%	012%	3% [1]		YY
0958		021% [1]	6%	015% [1]		6%	1%	030%		5%	7% [1]	9%		
0959		013%	1%	011% [1]		8%	6%	023% [1]		021%	4% [1]	010%		YY
0960		022% [1]	2%	013% [1]		1%	1%	8%	1%	013%	016% [1]	8%	[1]	
0961		042%	1%	5% [1]	1%	1%	1%	025% [1]		2%	3% [1]	1%		YY
0962		018%		6% [1]	2%	2%	2%			013%	028%	027%		
0963		023% [1]	1%	010% [1]	1%	5% [1]	1%	028%	4%	010%	7% [1]	010%	[1]	YY
0964		038% [1]	010%	5% [1]	3%		1%	1%		2%	018% [1]	013%	[1]	Y
0965		045%	2%	1%	019%			2% [1]		4%	015% [1]	7%		YYY
0966		029%	4%	6%		6% [1]	2%			8%	018%	022%	[1]	
0967				3%		8% [1]	4%	025%		012% [1]	013% [1]	032%		Y
0968		031% [1]	3%	1% [1]	018% [1]	1%	1%	8% [1]		2% [1]	8% [1]	3%	[1]	Y
0969		031%		4% [1]		3%	1%			011%	029%	018%	[1]	YY
0970		021%	6%	5%		3%	3%			013% [1]	016%	030%	[1]	
0971		033%	018%	5% [1]	1%	5%	1%	5% [1]		4%	4% [1]	014%		YYY
0972		023%		4%	1%	2%	3%	1%		018% [1]	027% [1]	020%		
0973	4% [1]			1%		6%	4%	1%		021% [1]	015% [1]	041%	[1]	
0974	1% [1]	023% [1]	4%	013% [1]	5%	6% [1]	2%	4% [1]	3%	4% [1]	024% [1]	3%	[1]	YY
0975		031% [1]	4%	013% [1]	2%	3% [1]		3% [1]	1%	4% [1]	010% [1]	010%	[1]	Y
0976		020%	015%	4% [1]		9% [1]	1%	010% [1]		4% [1]	013% [1]	013%	[1]	YY
0977		021% [1]	016%		6%	9% [1]	2%			013% [1]	010% [1]	023%	[1]	YY
0978		014%	5%	1%	010%	8%	2%			8% [1]	9%	039%	[1]	YYY
0979	5% [1]	017% [1]	5%	6% [1]	9% [1]	2% [1]	1%	6% [1]	3%	2% [1]	7% [1]	5%	[1]	YY
0980		018% [1]	6%	7% [1]	016%	3% [1]	1%	6%	2%	3% [1]	6% [1]	4%		YY
0981		027% [1]	010%	011% [1]	011% [1]	1% [1]	1%	5% [1]	4%	2% [1]	5% [1]	8%	[1]	YY
0982	4% [1]	021% [1]	3%	8% [1]	020% [1]	8% [1]	1%	9% [1]	3%	2% [1]	5% [1]	8%	[1]	YYY
0983	010% [1]	018%	4%	7% [1]	022% [1]	4% [1]	1%	3%		3%	9% [1]	011%	[1]	YYY

[1] Additional majors available in this area
[2] ROTC available

†Accredited by a nationally recognized accrediting body other than one of the regional accrediting associations

South Central States
(continued)

AL, AR, KY, LA, MS, OK, TN, TX

HIGHLY SELECTIVE *Majority of accepted students in top 10% of HS class*

Sequence Number	School name (upper entry) City (lower entry)	State	Costs: Resident tuition/fees + room/board	Costs: Room/Board (upper entry) Nonresident tuition/fees + room/board (lower entry)	General Information: Highest degree	General Information: Affiliation (upper entry) Religious observance (lower entry)	General Information: Size of community	General Information: Type of community	Admissions: Fall term application deadline (upper entry) Tests desired or required (lower entry)	Admissions: Calendar	Admissions: Fall admission only	Admissions: Early admission	Admissions: Deferred admission	Financial Aid: Fall term application deadline (upper entry) Forms to be filed (lower entry)	Financial Aid: Number in 10 who— -have need, receive some aid	Student Profile: Under-grads -are women	Student Profile: Under-grads -are graduate students	Student Profile: Freshmen -live on campus	Student Profile: Freshmen -are minority students	Student Profile: Freshmen -are nonresidents	Student Profile: Freshmen -return as sophomores	Student Profile: Freshmen -complete degree	Student Profile: Freshmen -enter graduate study	HS GPA (upper entry) 1st year college GPA (lower entry)	Special Programs: Credit by exam	Special Programs: Student designed majors	Special Programs: Fraternities/sororities
	Enrollment to 1,000																										
0984	International Inst Lewisville	TX	4800	2800	D	Oth OS	S			E						5	0	9	1	7	5	6	1				
0985	Centre C Danville	KY	12900[3]	3600	B[5]	Pres	S		3/01 A=S	O		Y	Y	3/15 FAF	5	5	0	9	1	3	9	7	5	3.5 2.5	Y	Y	Y
	Enrollment 1,000 to 5,000																										
0986	Rice U Houston	TX	12900	4900	D[5]	Priv	V	U	1/02 Oth	E		Y	Y	FAF	8	4	3	7	2	5	9	9	7		Y	Y	
0987	Southwestern U Georgetown	TX	13500[3]	4100	B[5]	Meth OS	S		A=S	E		Y	Y	3/15 FA/FF	6	5	0	9	2	1	9	7	7	3.4 2.9	Y	Y	Y
0988	Trinity U San Antonio	TX	15000[3]	4800	M[5]	Pres	V	U	2/01 S/A	E		Y	Y	2/01 FAF	5	5	1	9	2	6	9	8	7	3.6 2.8			Y
0989	Rhodes C Memphis	TN	17500	4500	B[5]	Pres S	V	S	2/01 A=S	E		Y	Y	3/01 FA/FF	5	5	0	9	1	7	9	7	4	3.5 2.8		Y	Y
	Enrollment 5,000 to 15,000																										
0990	Vanderbilt U Nashville	TN	19600[3]	5100	D[5]	Priv	V	U	Oth	E		Y	Y	2/15 FAF	3	5	4	9	1	9	9	8	7		Y	Y	Y
	Enrollment over 15,000																										
0991	Texas Austin,U of Austin	TX	5100	4100 8200	D[5]	Pub	L	U	3/01 A=S	O			Y	FF=FA	3	5	2	3	3	1	8	5		2.5	Y	Y	Y
	ADVANCED STANDING *Freshmen not accepted; college junior standing often required*																										
	Enrollment to 1,000																										
0992	Baylor C Dentistry Dallas	TX		[1]	P[5]	Priv	V	U	Oth	Q			[6]	FAF		9	9		2								Y
0993	Texas Hlth Sci,U of Dallas	TX	1000	[1] 4700	D[5]	Pub	V	U		O				FAF		7	6	0	2			9	1				
0994	Tex Permian Basin,U Odessa	TX	2100[2]	1200 5200	M[5]	Pub	M		None	E				4/01 FFS		6	1		2	0	0	5	2				
0995	La St U Sch All Hlth Shreveport	LA	2200	[1] 3000	M[5]	Pub	L	U	ACT	T				12/15	9	7	2	0	1			9	1	3.0			
0996	Central Texas,U of Killeen	TX	8000	3500	M[5]	Priv	M	S	None	E				FFS		4	3		3				3		Y		
0997	Tenn Memphis,U of Memphis	TN	8200	6500 11200	D[5]	Pub	V	U	A=S	E			Y	FA/FF	7	9	1		2	1					Y		Y
	Enrollment 1,000 to 5,000																										
0998	Houston Clear Lake,U Houston	TX	900	[1] 4000	M[5]	Pub	V	S	None	E				FAF		6	3	0	2						Y		
0999	Texas at Tyler,U of Tyler	TX	900	[1] 4000	M[5]	Pub	M		None	E				7/01 FF/FA		6	2		1							Y	
1000	Athens St C Athens	AL	1900[2]	700 3000	B[5]	Pub	S		None	Q				FAF		6	0		1						Y		Y
1001	Okla Hlth Sci Ctr,U Oklahoma City	OK	1900	[1] 6000	D[5]	Pub	L	U		E				FAF		7	2		2			3			Y		
1002	Corpus Christi St U Corpus Christi	TX	2400[2]	1400 5500	M[5]	Pub	L	U		S		Y		4/01 FF=FA		6	3		3			8	2				
1003	Miss Med Ctr,U of Jackson	MS	2600[2]	1000 3800	D[5]	Pub	L	U	2/15 Oth	S				4/15 FF/FA	8	8	6		2			9	5	3.4	Y		
1004	Tex Medl Br Galv,U Galveston	TX	6600[2]	5700 15400	D[5]	Pub	M		Oth	O				FA/FF		8	6		3			9			Y		Y

Sequence Number | School name (upper entry) City (lower entry) | State | Costs | General Information | Admissions | Financial Aid | Student Profile | Programs

▲ Sequence number—indicates the order of the college in this book only. Do *not* use this number with admissions tests or need analysis services.

[1] No campus room and board facilities
[2] Room only or board only
[3] Most freshmen required to live on campus
[4] City or district residence requirements
[5] Accredited by a regional accrediting association or a recognized candidate for accreditation
[6] All female freshman class
[7] All male freshman class

MAJORS AVAILABLE AND PERCENT OF STUDENTS STUDYING IN EACH AREA

Sequence Number	Agri.	Business	Comm.	Education	Engineering	Fine/App. Arts	Lang.	Health	Home Ec.	Humanities	Math-Sciences	Social Sciences	GS	ROTC Air Force	ROTC Army	ROTC Navy
0984			1%	010% [1]			1%			087%		1%				
0985		016%	1%	2%	1%	1%	5%	014%		2%	3% [1]	2%		Y	Y	
0986		2%	2%		030% [1]	019%	3%			012% [1]	026% [1]	6%			Y	Y
0987		022%	5%	012%		010%	2%			013%	015%	021% [1]				
0988		023%	7%	5% [1]	1%	6%	5%	1% [1]		015% [1]	011% [1]	026% [1]		Y	Y	
0989		011%		1%		010%	011%			023% [1]	018% [1]	026% [1]		Y	Y	
0990			2%	5% [1]	015%	3%	1%			010% [1]	014% [1]	045% [1]		Y	Y	Y
0991		021% [1]	9%	4% [1]	013% [1]	6% [1]	1%	3% [1]	2%	3% [1]	014% [1]	014% [1]		Y	Y	Y
0992								100% [1]			[1]					
0993								099% [1]			1% [1]					
0994		033%	3%	6%	3%	2%	1%			5%	022% [1]	013%				
0995								100% [1]								
0996		025%		1%							012%	033%			Y	
0997								100% [1]								
0998		035% [1]	1%	012% [1]	1%	1% [1]		2% [1]		8%	023% [1]	011% [1]				
0999		019%	2%	021% [1]		2%		8% [1]		4% [1]	011%	011%				
1000		035%		038% [1]						2%	018%	7% [1]				
1001								100% [1]								
1002		033%	3%	014%		4%	1%	9%		1%	013% [1]	013%			Y	
1003								100% [1]								
1004								094% [1]			1% [1]					

Majors listed under each area: Agri.: Agriculture, general; Agronomy (crops & mgmt); Animal Science (husbandry); Fish, Wildlife Mgmt; Forestry. Business: Business/Commerce, general; Accounting; Banking/Finance; Business Economics; Business Mgmt/Admin; Marketing/Purchasing; Secretarial Studies. Comm.: Communications, general; Journalism; Radio/TV (broadcasting); Advertising. Education: Art Education; Distributive Education; Elementary Education; English Education; Mathematics Education; Music Education; Physical Education; Science Education; Secondary Education; Social Science Education; Special Education; Speech Education. Engineering: Engineering, general; Chemical; Civil; Electrical/Electronics/Comm; Industrial/Management; Mechanical. Fine/App. Arts: Architecture; Fine/Applied Arts, general; Art (Paint, draw, sculpt); Art History/Appreciation; Dance; Dramatic Arts (theater arts); Music (liberal arts); Music (perform, compos, theory). Lang.: French; German; Italian; Latin; Spanish; Russian. Health: Predentistry; Premedicine; Medical/Lab Technology; Nursing (registered nurse); Occupational Therapy; Preoptometry; Prepharmacy; Physical Therapy; Preveterinary Medicine. Home Ec.: Home Economics, general; Clothing and Textiles; Consumer Ec/Home Mgmt; Family Relations/Child Devel; Food and Nutrition/Dietetics; Institution Mgmt. Humanities: Humanities, general; Creative Writing; English, general; Literature, English; Philosophy; Religion; Speech/Forensic Science. Math-Sciences: Mathematics, general; Computer/Info Sciences; Biological Sciences, general; Biology; Botany; Zoology; Physical Sciences, general; Chemistry; Physics. Social Sciences: Crim Just/Law Enforce; Social Work; Social Sciences, general; Anthropology; Area Studies (Amer., African, etc.); Economics; Geography; History; Prelaw; Political Science; Psychology; Sociology. GS: General Studies. ROTC: Air Force; Army; Navy.

[1] Additional majors available in this area
[2] ROTC available

†Accredited by a nationally recognized accrediting body other than one of the regional accrediting associations

South Atlantic States

DC, DE, FL, GA, MD, NC, SC, VA, WV

OPEN ADMISSIONS *All HS graduates accepted, to limit of capacity*

Sequence Number	School name (upper entry) City (lower entry)	State	Costs: Resident tuition/fees + room/board	Costs: Room/Board (upper entry) Nonresident tuition/fees + room/board (lower entry)	General Information: Highest degree	General Information: Affiliation (upper entry) Religious observance (lower entry)	General Information: Size of community	General Information: Type of community	Admissions: Fall term application deadline (upper entry) Tests desired or required (lower entry)	Admissions: Calendar	Admissions: Fall admission only	Admissions: Early admission	Admissions: Deferred admission	Financial Aid: Fall term application deadline (upper entry) Forms to be filed (lower entry)	Financial Aid: Number in 10 who— -have need, receive some aid	Student Profile: Undergrads -are women	Undergrads -are graduate students	Freshmen -live on campus	Freshmen -are minority students	Freshmen -are nonresidents	Freshmen -return as sophomores	Freshmen -complete degree	Freshmen -enter graduate study	HS GPA (upper entry) 1st year college GPA (lower entry)	Special Programs: Credit by exam	Special Programs: Student designed majors	Special Programs: Fraternities/sororities
	Enrollment to 1,000																										
1005	Florida Baptist C Brandon	FL	1700 [2]	1000	B	Bapt OS	M		8/01 A=S	E		Y			0	2	0	5	1	2	6	2	1				
1006	Winston-Salem Bible Winston-Salem	NC	1700 [2]	400	B †	Oth OS	M	S	Oth	E		Y		8/26 None	3	3	0	2	8	1	8	1	2	2.3	Y	Y	
1007	Antietam Bible C Hagerstown	MD	2400	1200	D	Oth OS	S		8/15 A/S	S		Y	Y	8/15 FF/FA	1	5	2		2	5	9	3	7	3.0 3.0	Y		
1008	Fla Bapt Theol C Graceville	FL	2500 [2]	1100	B [5]	Oth OS	T		None	O		Y		5/15 FF/FA	7	3	0	4	1	6	8	5	3		Y		
1009	Thomas C Thomasville	GA	2800	[1]	B [5]	Priv	S		S/A	Q		Y	Y	FAF	3	7	0	0	2	1	3			2.8	Y		
1010	Beulah Hghts Bible C Atlanta	GA	3100	1500	B †	Oth OS	V	U	A/S	E		Y	Y	Oth	1	2	0	2	7	2	7	6	5	2.5	Y		
1011	Md Baptist Bible C Elkton	MD	3200 [3]	1600	M	Bapt OS	S		A/S	S				None		5	0	8	1	6	9	6			Y		
1012	Liberty Christian C Pensacola	FL	4300	2300	M †	Oth OS	M	S	8/01 A/S	S		Y	Y	8/01 FF/FA	5	4	0	3	1	3	6	8	1	2.0 3.0	Y		
1013	Eastern Christian C Bel Air	MD	4600	2300	B	Oth OS	S		8/30 A/S	S				8/30 FF=FA	8	5	0	9	1	6	6	6	4	2.0 2.5	Y		
1014	Atlantic Bapt Bible Chester	VA	4700	2400	B	Bapt OS	M	S	A/S	S						4	0	4	1	2	5	2					
1015	Heritage C Orlando	FL	4800	2000	M †	Bapt	V	U	8/31 A/S	E		Y		FFS		4	1		3		7	5		2.0 2.0			
1016	East Coast Bible C Charlotte	NC	5000	2000	B [5]	Oth OS	L	U	ACT	E			Y	5/01 FFS	7	3	0	6	1	4	5	2	1	2.7	Y		Y
1017	Spurgeon Baptist C Mulberry	FL	5100 [3]	2000	B †	Bapt OS	T		A=S	Q				8/01 FAF	3	4	0	7	1	6	8	5	3		Y		
1018	Trinity C of Fla Holiday	FL	5200	2400	M †	Oth OS	M	S	8/15 A=S	E		Y		8/01	3	4	1	4	1	1	5	3	3	2.5 2.2	Y		
1019	Voorhees C Denmark	SC	5800	2500	B [5]	Oth	T		8/21 A=S	E				3/01 FAF	9	7	0	9	9	2	5	5		2.0 1.9	Y		
1020	Fort Lauderdale C Ft Lauderdale	FL	6000 [2]	2600	M †	Priv	L	U	A=S	Q		Y		FF/FA	6	5	1	3	6	4	7	5	1	2.7 2.7	Y		
1021	Intl Acad Merch Tampa	FL	6200	[1]	B †	Priv	V	U	None	Q		Y	Y	Oth	4	9	0		2	1	7			2.8 2.6	Y	Y	
1022	Allen U Columbia	SC	6300	2800	B	Oth OS	M			S				4/15		6	0										
1023	Morris C Sumter	SC	6300	2400	B [5]	Bapt	M			S				5/01 FF=FA	8	6	0		9								Y
1024	Clearwater Christian Clearwater	FL	7800	3000	B [5]	Oth OS	M	S	8/01 A/S	E		Y		8/01 FF=FA	7	6	0		1						Y		
	Enrollment 1,000 to 5,000																										
1025	Md U C,U of College Park	MD		[1]	M [5]	Pub	S		None	E		Y		FAF		5	1	0	3						Y		
1026	Bluefield St C Bluefield	WV	1300	[1] 3200	B [5]	Pub	S		9/01 A/S	E		Y		3/01 FAF	7	6	0	0	1	1	7	5	1	2.8 2.4	Y	Y	Y
1027	Orlando C Orlando	FL	3600	[1]	M †	Priv	V	U	None	Q		Y	Y		9	7	1	0		0	8		1	2.4 2.6	Y		
1028	Glenville St C Glenville	WV	3900 [3]	2600 5800	B [5]	Pub	T		A/S	E		Y		4/01 FAF	9	6	0	6	1	1	7	5		2.8 2.3	Y		Y
1029	Fairmont St C Fairmont	WV	4100	2700 6100	B [5]	Pub	S		6/15 A/S	E		Y		3/01 FAF	6	5	0	1	1	1	6	3		2.0 2.6	Y	Y	Y
1030	Tampa C Tampa	FL	4500	[1]	M †	Priv	V	U	10/09 None	Q				FF/FA	8	6	1	0	4	1	8	6	1		Y		
1031	Brewton-Parker C Mt Vernon	GA	5800 [3]	2200	B [5]	Oth OS	T		9/01 A=S	Q		Y		6/01 FAF	9	5	0	7	2	1	7			3.0			
1032	National Ed Ctr Fort Lauderdale	FL	6800 [2]	2000	B †	Priv	L	U	Oth	Q				Oth		5	0		3	3							Y
1033	Benedict C Columbia	SC	6900	2300	B [5]	Bapt O	L	U	A=S	O		Y		3/15 FA/FF	9	7	0	8	9		6	5	1	2.0	Y		Y
1034	Florida Memorial C Miami	FL	7000	2800	B [5]	Bapt	V	U	8/15 A/S	S				4/01 FA/FF	8	5	0	7	9	2	7	7	3				

▲ Sequence number—indicates the order of the college in this book only. Do *not* use this number with admissions tests or need analysis services.

[1] No campus room and board facilities
[2] Room only or board only
[3] Most freshmen required to live on campus
[4] City or district residence requirements
[5] Accredited by a regional accrediting association or a recognized candidate for accreditation
[6] All female freshman class
[7] All male freshman class

MAJORS AVAILABLE AND PERCENT OF STUDENTS STUDYING IN EACH AREA

Sequence Number	Agri.	Agriculture, general	Agronomy (crops & mgmt)	Animal Science (husbandry)	Fish, Wildlife Mgmt	Forestry	Business	Business/Commerce, general	Accounting	Banking/Finance	Business Economics	Business Mgmt/Admin	Marketing/Purchasing	Secretarial Studies	Comm.	Communications, general	Journalism	Radio/TV (broadcasting)	Advertising
1005																			
1006																			
1007																			
1008																			
1009							039%					■							
1010																			
1011																			
1012							1%												
1013																			
1014							017%	■											
1015																			
1016																			
1017																			
1018												■							
1019							030%		■			■		[1] ■					
1020							094%	■	■	■		■	■	[1]					
1021							030%						■						
1022									■		■	■							
1023							030%					■			5%				
1024							012%					■		[1]					
1025							034%								2%				
1026							030%	■				■							
1027							070%	■	■			■	■						
1028	8%						035%	■	■	■		■	■	[1] ■					
1029							030%	■	■	■			■	[1] ■	2%				
1030							054%	■	■			■	■		1%				
1031							020%	■	■			■							
1032							1%								012%				
1033							021%		■	■		■	■	[1]	3%		■	■	
1034							030%		■			■							

Sequence Number	Education	Art Education	Distributive Education	Elementary Education	English Education	Mathematics Education	Music Education	Physical Education	Science Education	Secondary Education	Social Science Education	Special Education	Speech Education	Engineering	Engineering, general	Chemical	Civil	Electrical/Electronics/Comm	Industrial/Management	Mechanical
1005	015%												[1]							
1006													[1]							
1007	040%		■	■	■	■	■	■	■	■	■		[1] ■							
1008																				
1009	011%																			
1010																				
1011																				
1012																				
1013																				
1014	028%			■																
1015	040%			■	■	■			■	■	■		[1]							
1016	020%			■																
1017																				
1018	7%			■																
1019	011%		■	■	■	■			■	■	■			1%	■					
1020																				
1021																				
1022			■	■				■					[1]							
1023	010%			■																
1024	044%		■	■	■	■	■	■	■		■		[1]							
1025																				
1026	019%	■		■	■	■		■	■	■	■	■		1%						
1027																				
1028	035%	■	■	■	■	■	■	■	■	■	■	■	[1] ■	1%						
1029	015%	■	■	■	■	■	■	■	■		■	■	[1] ■	1%						
1030																				
1031	020%			■			■	■					[1]	1%						
1032																				
1033	8%	■	■	■	■	■	■	■	■		■		[1]	2%	■					
1034	030%	■		■	■	■	■	■	■	■			[1]							

Sequence Number	Fine/App. Arts	Architecture	Fine/Applied Arts, general	Art (Paint, draw, sculpt)	Art History/Appreciation	Dance	Dramatic Arts (theater arts)	Music (liberal arts)	Music (perform, compos, theory)	Lang.	French	German	Italian	Latin	Spanish	Russian
1005																
1006																
1007								■		2%						
1008	014%															
1009	2%															
1010																
1011																
1012	1%															
1013																
1014																
1015	1%							■								
1016																
1017																
1018																
1019																
1020																
1021	040%								[1]							
1022								■								
1023	5%															
1024	1%							■		1%						
1025																
1026	1%									1%						
1027																
1028	1%															
1029	2%								[1]	3%	■					
1030																
1031	1%							■		1%						
1032	1%								[1]							
1033	1%			■				■								
1034	2%							■		1%						

Sequence Number	Health	Predentistry	Premedicine	Medical/Lab Technology	Nursing (registered nurse)	Occupational Therapy	Preoptometry	Prepharmacy	Physical Therapy	Preveterinary Medicine	Home Ec.	Home Economics, general	Clothing and Textiles	Consumer Ec/Home Mgmt	Family Relations/Child Devel	Food and Nutrition/Dietetics	Institution Mgmt
1005																	
1006																	
1007					■							■					
1008																	
1009	018%																
1010																	
1011																	
1012																	
1013																	
1014																	
1015																	
1016																	
1017																	
1018																	
1019	1%		■														
1020																	
1021												■					
1022																	
1023																	
1024																	
1025	1%																
1026	015%																
1027	013%																
1028	2%	■	■		■		■	■		■							
1029	5%				■						5%	■					
1030	015%																
1031	3%										2%						
1032											020%						
1033																	
1034																	

Sequence Number	Humanities	Humanities, general	Creative Writing	English, general	Literature, English	Philosophy	Religion	Speech/Forensic Science	Math-Sciences	Mathematics, general	Computer/Info Sciences	Biological Sciences, general	Biology	Botany	Zoology	Physical Sciences, general	Chemistry	Physics
1005	085%						■											
1006	100%						■											
1007	050%			■	■		■	■	2%	■								
1008	086%						■											
1009	018%								8%									
1010	100%						■											
1011	100%						■											
1012	080%						■											
1013	100%						■											
1014	055%						■											
1015	056%						■		2%									
1016	071%						■											
1017	100%						■											
1018	093%						■											
1019									3%	■	■		■					
1020									5%		■							[1]
1021																		
1022				■						■						■	■	
1023	8%			■					025%	■			■					
1024	2%			■			■		2%	■			■					
1025	2%								018%									
1026	1%			■					3%	■		■	■					
1027									014%									[1]
1028	1%			■				■	3%	■	■	■	■			■	■	
1029	2%			■					3%	■	■		■				■	
1030									6%		■							[1]
1031	015%						■		016%									
1032																		
1033	2%			■		■	■		010%	■	■		■				■	
1034	2%			■			■		4%	■		■	■			■	■	

Sequence Number	Social Sciences	Crim Just/Law Enforce	Social Work	Social Sciences, general	Anthropology	Area Studies (Amer., African, etc.)	Economics	Geography	History	Prelaw	Political Science	Psychology	Sociology	GS: General Studies	ROTC: Air Force	Army	Navy
1005																	
1006				■													
1007	2%			■		■			■			■	[1] ■	■			
1008																	
1009	1%																
1010																	
1011																	
1012	018%											■					
1013																	
1014																	
1015	1%			■					■								
1016																	
1017																	
1018																	
1019	2%	■	■						■		■		■			Y	
1020	1%																
1021																	
1022													■				
1023	017%			■					■		■					Y	
1024	1%											■			Y		
1025	013%													■			
1026	2%	■		■					■								
1027	1%																
1028	1%								■								
1029	2%	■					■		■		■	■	■			Y	
1030	1%			■													
1031	010%													■			
1032																	
1033	019%	■	■				■		■		■		[1] ■		Y	Y	
1034	030%			■											Y		

[1] Additional majors available in this area
[2] ROTC available

†Accredited by a nationally recognized accrediting body other than one of the regional accrediting associations

South Atlantic States (continued)

DC, DE, FL, GA, MD, NC, SC, VA, WV

Sequence Number	School name (upper entry) / City (lower entry)	State	Costs: Resident tuition/fees + room/board	Costs: Room/Board (upper entry) / Nonresident tuition/fees + room/board (lower entry)	General Information: Highest degree	General Information: Affiliation (upper entry) / Religious observance (lower entry)	General Information: Size of community	General Information: Type of community	Admissions: Fall term application deadline (upper entry) / Tests desired or required (lower entry)	Admissions: Calendar	Admissions: Fall admission only	Admissions: Early admission	Admissions: Deferred admission	Financial Aid: Fall term application deadline (upper entry) / Forms to be filed (lower entry)	Financial Aid: Number in 10 who -have need, receive some aid	Student Profile: Under-grads -are women	Under-grads -are graduate students	Freshmen -live on campus	Freshmen -are minority students	Freshmen -are nonresidents	Freshmen -return as sophomores	Freshmen -complete degree	Freshmen -enter graduate study	HS GPA (upper entry) / 1st year college GPA (lower entry)	Special Programs: Credit by exam	Special Programs: Student designed majors	Special Programs: Fraternities/sororities
OPEN ADMISSIONS *All HS graduates accepted, to limit of capacity*																											
	Enrollment 1,000 to 5,000																										
1035	Art Inst Ft Lauderda Fort Lauderdale	FL	10200[2]	3000	B †	Priv	T		Oth	Q			Y	9/26 FA/FF	7	5	0	3	2	5	8			2.5 2.8			
	Enrollment 5,000 to 15,000																										
1036	DC, U of Washington	DC	700	[1] 2500	M[5]	Pub	V	U	8/02 None	E			Y	4/15 FF/FA	2	6	1	0	9	1	3	3	1	2.0 2.0			Y
1037	Norfolk St U Norfolk	VA	5400	3200 7800	M[5]	Pub	L	U	S/A	E		Y	Y	5/01 FA/FF	8	6	1		9	1	7	4	2	2.5 2.2	Y		Y
1038	Liberty U Lynchburg	VA	9900	4000	M[5]	Bapt	M	S	8/01 A=S	E		Y		4/15 FAF	9	4	1	9	1	7	6	3	2	3.2 2.6	Y	Y	
LIBERAL ADMISSIONS *Some accepted students from lower half of HS class*																											
	Enrollment to 1,000																										
1039	Holmes C of Bible Greenville	SC	0	0	B	Oth OS	L	U	9/05 ACT	S		Y				4	0	9	1	5	7		1	2.4	Y		
1040	Manna Christian C Fayetteville	NC	900	600	B	Oth	L	S	A=S	Q				None	0	1	0	5	1	0	8	9		2.6 3.2			
1041	Jones C Jacksonville	FL	3600	[1]	B †	Priv	V	S	A=S	T		Y			9	6	0	0	4	1	7	6	1	2.3 2.5	Y		Y
1042	Ambassador Baptist C Shelby	NC	3800	2400	B	Bapt OS	S		8/22	E		Y		8/15		2	0	7	1	7	8						
1043	John Wesley C High Point	NC	4200[2]	1200	B †	Priv OS	M		Oth	E		Y	Y	6/01 FAF	6	3	0	4	1	3	5	5	2	2.4 2.4	Y		
1044	Florida Christian C Kissimmee	FL	4300[23]	1200	B †	Oth O	M	S	7/15 ACT	Q		Y	Y	5/01 FFS	9	6	0	9	1	2	7	6	5	2.8 2.6	Y	Y	
1045	Life Bible C East Christiansburg	VA	4500[3]	2300	B	Oth OS	S		A=S	S						4	0	9	1	9	8			2.7			
1046	NC Sch of the Arts Winston-Salem	NC	4600	3000 9600	M[5]	Pub	M	U	S/A	O				4/01 FF=FA	6	5	1	8	1	5	5	4		2.9 2.2	Y		
1047	Wilmington C New Castle	DE	4700	[1]	M[5]	Priv	S		A=S	T		Y	Y	7/11 FF/FA	2	6	1	0	2	2	8	6	1	2.5 2.7	Y		Y
1048	Southeast FW Bapt C Wendell	NC	4900	2400	B †	Bapt OS	S		A=S	O						5	0		1								
1049	Florida Bible C Kissimmee	FL	5000	1800	B †	Priv OS	S		8/01 A/S	E				5/01		5	0	9	1	5	8	4	2	2.9 2.6	Y		
1050	Piedmont Bible C Winston-Salem	NC	5500	2500	B †	Bapt OS	L	U	8/26 ACT	E		Y		1/01 FF=FA	5	3	0	7	1	4	7	4		2.8	Y		
1051	Atlanta Christian C East Point	GA	5600	2200	B †	Oth OS	S		8/01 S/A	E		Y	Y	6/01 FAF	9	4	0	7	2	2	6	4	3		Y		Y
1052	Southeastern U Washington	DC	5700	[1]	M[5]	Priv	V	U	Oth	O		Y	Y	FA/FF	9	3	3	0	8	5	7	5	2	2.0	Y		
1053	Claflin C Orangeburg	SC	6000	2000	B[5]	Meth	S		8/01 A=S	E		Y		6/01 FF=FA	9	7	0	9	9	1	9	9	1	2.0	Y		Y
1054	Appalachian Bible C Bradley	WV	6100[3]	2700	B †	Bapt OS	T		8/20 ACT	E				FAF	8	5	0	8	1	3			3		Y		
1055	Barber-Scotia C Concord	NC	6500	2500	B[5]	Pres	S		8/01 A=S	E				FF=FA	9	6	0	5	9	5	6	4	1		Y		Y
1056	Piedmont C Demorest	GA	6700[3]	3100	B[5]	Oth OS	T		8/01 S/A	E		Y	Y	7/15 FF=FA	8	5	0	4	1	1					Y		
1057	Ohio Valley C Parkersburg	WV	7000	2800	B[5]	Oth OS	M	S	ACT	E		Y	Y	FA/FF	9	5	0	8	1	6	6			2.7 2.3	Y		
1058	Paine C Augusta	GA	7400	2500	B[5]	Meth OS	L	U	8/01 S/A	S		Y	Y	3/15 FF=FA	9	7	0		9	3	7	2	1	2.6 2.3	Y		Y
1059	Saint Paul's C Lawrenceville	VA	7600[3]	3000	B[5]	Oth OS	T		SAT	E				8/01 FAF	9	6	0	8	9	3	5	3	1		Y		Y
1060	Montreat-Anderson C Montreat	NC	7700	2900	B[5]	Pres O	T		S/A	E		Y		FA/FF	5	5	0	9	1	5	7	4		2.5 2.3	Y		
1061	Chowan C Murfreesboro	NC	7800	2600	B[5]	Oth S	T		8/30 A=S	E		Y	Y	FA/FF	8	3	0	9	3	5	4			2.4 2.2	Y	Y	
1062	Washington Bible C Lanham	MD	7800	3100	M †	Priv OS	S		8/25 A=S	E		Y		5/30 FAF	5	4	3	3	4	3	7		3		Y		

▲ Sequence number—indicates the order of the college in this book only. Do *not* use this number with admissions tests or need analysis services.

[1] No campus room and board facilities
[2] Room only or board only
[3] Most freshmen required to live on campus
[4] City or district residence requirements
[5] Accredited by a regional accrediting association or a recognized candidate for accreditation
[6] All female freshman class
[7] All male freshman class

MAJORS AVAILABLE AND PERCENT OF STUDENTS STUDYING IN EACH AREA

Sequence Number	Agri. (Agriculture, general; Agronomy (crops & mgmt); Animal Science (husbandry); Fish, Wildlife Mgmt; Forestry)	Business (Business/Commerce, general; Accounting; Banking/Finance; Business Economics; Business Mgmt/Admin; Marketing/Purchasing; Secretarial Studies)	Comm. (Communications, general; Journalism; Radio/TV (broadcasting); Advertising)	Education (Art Education; Distributive Education; Elementary Education; English Education; Mathematics Education; Music Education; Physical Education; Science Education; Secondary Education; Social Science Education; Special Education; Speech Education)	Engineering (Engineering, general; Chemical; Civil; Electrical/Electronics/Comm; Industrial/Management; Mechanical)	Fine/App. Arts (Architecture; Fine/Applied Arts, general; Art (Paint, draw, sculpt); Art History/Appreciation; Dance; Dramatic Arts (theater arts); Music (liberal arts); Music (perform, compos, theory))	Lang. (French; German; Italian; Latin; Spanish; Russian)	Health (Predentistry; Premedicine; Medical/Lab Technology; Nursing (registered nurse); Occupational Therapy; Preoptometry; Prepharmacy; Physical Therapy; Preveterinary Medicine)	Home Ec. (Home Economics, general; Clothing and Textiles; Consumer Ec/Home Mgmt; Family Relations/Child Devel; Food and Nutrition/Dietetics; Institution Mgmt)	Humanities (Humanities, general; Creative Writing; English, general; Literature, English; Philosophy; Religion; Speech/Forensic Science)	Math-Sciences (Mathematics, general; Computer/Info Sciences; Biological Sciences, general; Biology; Botany; Zoology; Physical Sciences, general; Chemistry; Physics)	Social Sciences (Crim Just/Law Enforce; Social Work; Social Sciences, general; Anthropology; Area Studies (Amer., African, etc.); Economics; Geography; History; Prelaw; Political Science; Psychology; Sociology)	GS (General Studies)	ROTC (Air Force; Army; Navy)
1035		025% ■■ [1]	030% ■■■			040% ■■ [1]			5% ■					
1036	1% [1]	022% ■■■ [1]	1% ■	015% ■■■■■■■■■ [1]	1% ■■■■	4% ■■■ [1]	2% ■■■	3% ■ [1]	1% ■■■	013% ■■	022% ■■■■■■ [1]	3% ■■■■■■■■■■		YYY
1037	[1]	026% ■■■■■ [1]	6% ■■■	010% ■■■■■■■■■■■■ [1]	1% ■	■■■■ [1]		4% ■■■ [1]	1% ■■■	3% ■■	8% ■■■■■■■	9% ■■■■■■■■ [1]	■	YY
1038		022% ■■■ [1]	7% ■■■■	020% ■■■■■■■■ [1]		1% ■■	1%	1% ■■■■	1% ■■	8% ■■■	3% ■■■■ [1]	6% ■■■■■■ [1]		Y
1039										100% ■				
1040				1%						098% ■		1%		
1041		087% ■■■■ [1]						013%			[1]			
1042										100% ■				
1043				1% ■						083% ■		016% ■		
1044				010%						080% ■		010%		
1045										100% ■				
1046						100% ■■■■ [1]								
1047		050% ■■■■	3% ■■■	015% ■ [1]				010% ■				016% ■■		YY
1048		5%		050% [1]						041% ■	2%	1%		
1049				022% ■■						074% ■	3%	1%		
1050				029% ■ [1]	015% [1]					056% ■				
1051		9%		1%		1% ■	1%			086% ■		1%		
1052		092% ■■■■■■				1%				2%	3% [1]	2% ■ [1]		
1053		7% ■■■■		025% ■■■■■■■■		1% ■■		■■		2% ■■■	3% ■■■■■ [1]	2% ■■■■		Y
1054										100% ■				
1055		033% ■■■ [1]		018% ■■■				3% ■■■			014% ■■■	014% ■		Y
1056	1%	030% ■■■	1%	020% ■■■■■■ [1]		1% ■■■	4% ■	1%		2% ■	3% ■■■■■■	2% ■■■■■		
1057	1%	042%	5%	010%		1%	1%	6%	1%	5% ■	3%	2%		Y
1058		024% ■	4% ■	010% ■■ [1]		2%				3% ■	020% ■■■	019% ■■■		Y
1059		035% ■■■ [1]		020% ■■■■■■■ [1]						5% ■	7% ■■■	020% ■■■■	■	Y
1060		9% ■				1%	4%			2% ■■■	3%	2% ■	■	
1061	2%	032% ■	■	014% ■■■ [1]	4%	3%	1%	8%		5% ■	014%	8% [1]	■	
1062				010% ■		■■				090% ■				
Sequence Number	Agri.	Business	Comm.	Education	Engineering	Fine/App. Arts	Lang.	Health	Home Ec.	Humanities	Math-Sciences	Social Sciences	GS	ROTC

[1] Additional majors available in this area
[2] ROTC available

†Accredited by a nationally recognized accrediting body other than one of the regional accrediting associations

South Atlantic States
(continued)

DC, DE, FL, GA, MD, NC, SC, VA, WV

LIBERAL ADMISSIONS *Some accepted students from lower half of HS class*

Sequence Number	School name (upper entry) City (lower entry)	State	Costs: Resident tuition/fees + room/board	Costs: Room/Board (upper entry) Nonresident tuition/fees + room/board (lower entry)	General Information: Highest degree	General Information: Affiliation (upper entry) Religious observance (lower entry)	General Information: Size of community	General Information: Type of community	Admissions: Fall term application deadline (upper entry) Tests desired or required (lower entry)	Admissions: Calendar	Admissions: Fall admission only	Admissions: Early admission	Admissions: Deferred admission	Financial Aid: Fall term application deadline (upper entry) Forms to be filed (lower entry)	Financial Aid: Number in 10 who -have need, receive some aid	Student Profile: Undergrads -are women	Student Profile: Undergrads -are graduate students	Student Profile: Freshmen -live on campus	Student Profile: Freshmen -are minority students	Student Profile: Freshmen -are nonresidents	Student Profile: Freshmen -return as sophomores	Student Profile: Freshmen -complete degree	Student Profile: Freshmen -enter graduate study	Student Profile: HS GPA (upper entry) 1st year college GPA (lower entry)	Special Programs: Credit by exam	Special Programs: Student designed majors	Special Programs: Fraternities/sororities
Enrollment to 1,000																											
1063	Goldey Beacom C Wilmington	DE	7900 [2]	2600	B [5]	Priv	M	S	Oth	4		Y	Y	4/01 FAF	4	7	0	3	1	4	6	7		2.6 2.3	Y		Y
1064	Warner Southern C Lake Wales	FL	8100	2900	B [5]	Oth OS	T		8/15 A=S	E		Y	Y	4/01 FF/FA	8	6	0	8	1	5	5	5	2	2.7 2.7	Y		
1065	Anderson C Anderson	SC	8200 [3]	3000	B [5]	Bapt O	S		8/22 A=S	E		Y	Y	5/01 FA/FF	9	5	0	5	1	2	6			2.1 2.3	Y		
1066	Lees-McRae C Banner Elk	NC	8300 [3]	2800	B [5]	Priv S	T		A=S	S		Y		4/01 FAF	5	4	0	9	1	4	6			2.0 2.0	Y	Y	
1067	Bluefield C Bluefield	VA	9000	3600	B [5]	Oth OS	S		8/15 A=S	S		Y	Y	5/01 FAF	9	6	0	5	1	1	6	5	4	2.8 2.5	Y		
1068	Capitol C Laurel	MD	9000 [2]	2500	B [5]	Priv	S		S/A	E		Y		3/01 FAF	5	1	0	4	3	2	6	3	1	2.6	Y		
1069	Mount Olive C Mount Olive	NC	9200	2600	B [5]	Oth OS	T		A=S	E		Y		FF=FA	9	5	0	7	2	1	7	3	7	2.5 2.6	Y		
1070	Salem Teikyo U Salem	WV	9800 [3]	3600	M [5]	Priv	T		7/15 A/S	T		Y		4/15 FF=FA	3	5	0	9	1	7	8	5	2	2.0 2.2	Y		Y
1071	Central Wesleyan C Central	SC	10100 [3]	3000	B [5]	Oth OS	T		A=S	E		Y	Y	FA/FF	9	5	0	6	1	4	7	4	1	2.0	Y		
1072	Virginia Intermont C Bristol	VA	10500	3900	B [5]	Bapt S	S		A=S	E		Y	Y	4/15 FF/FA	7	7	0	7	1	4	6	4		2.7 2.5	Y	Y	
1073	Davis & Elkins C Elkins	WV	10800	3700	B [5]	Pres OS	T		9/01 A=S	S		Y	Y	5/01 FA/FF	6	5	0	7	1	6	6			2.5	Y	Y	Y
1074	Wesley C Dover	DE	11900	3800	B [5]	Meth	T		A=S	S		Y	Y	4/15 FF=FA	7	5	0	8	1	6	7			2.6 2.7	Y		Y
1075	Northwood Inst West Palm Beach	FL	12300 [3]	4700	B [5]	Priv	M	S	A=S	Q				FA/FF	6	4	0	8	2	7	9	7	1	2.5 2.4	Y		
1076	Schiller Intl U Dunedin	FL	13300	3600	B †	Priv	M	S	A=S	S		Y	Y			5	0		8								
1077	Ringling Sch Art/Des Sarasota	FL	13600	4700	B [5]	Priv	M	S	A=S	S					7	5	0	5	1	5	8	7			Y		Y
Enrollment 1,000 to 5,000																											
1078	Clayton St C Morrow	GA	1200	[1] 3500	B [5]	Pub	M	S	9/01 A=S	Q		Y	Y	9/01 FAF	3	6	0	0	1	1	6			2.7 1.8	Y		
1079	Kennesaw C Marietta	GA	1300	[1] 8800	M [5]	Pub	M	S	8/31 S/A	Q		Y	Y	FA/FF	2	6	1	0	1	1	7	3	1	2.8 2.4	Y		Y
1080	Coppin St C Baltimore	MD	2100	[1] 3800	M [5]	Pub	V	U	7/15 SAT	E		Y	Y	5/01 FA/FF	9	7	1	0	9	1			3	2.7 2.5	Y		Y
1081	Georgia C Milledgeville	GA	3300	2100 6000	M [5]	Pub	S		8/31 A=S	Q		Y		4/15 FAF	6	5	1	5	2	1	8	6	2	2.9 2.3	Y	Y	Y
1082	Western Carolina U Cullowhee	NC	3400 [3]	2200 7900	M [5]	Pub	T		8/01 SAT	E		Y	Y	4/01 FAF	9	5	1	9	1	1	7	4	2	2.5 2.3	Y	Y	Y
1083	Columbus C Columbus	GA	3500	2100 6000	M [5]	Pub	M	S	9/11 S/A	Q		Y	Y	FAF	4	6	1		2	1	8	6	1	2.6 2.5	Y		Y
1084	Elizabeth City St U Elizabeth City	NC	3500	2400 7500	B [5]	Pub	S		SAT	S				FF=FA	9	6	0	7	8	1	8	4	3	2.7 2.4			Y
1085	Georgia Southwest C Americus	GA	3700 [3]	2200 6200	M [5]	Pub	S		9/01 S/A	Q				8/15 FAF	3	6	1	4	2	1	6	3	2	2.8 2.2	Y		Y
1086	Savannah St C Savannah	GA	3700 [3]	2100 6100	M [5]	Pub	M	U	8/25 A=S	Q		Y		FAF	6	6	1	5	9	1	7			2.3 2.0	Y		Y
1087	Winston-Salem St U Winston-Salem	NC	3700	2600 7600	B [5]	Pub	M	U	A=S	S				5/01 FF=FA	6	6	0	7	8	1	7	5	1		Y		Y
1088	W Va St C Institute	WV	3800 [3]	2600 5600	B [5]	Pub	S		A/S	E		Y		3/15 FAF	4	6	0	1	1	1		5	2	2.6 2.3	Y		Y
1089	Fort Valley St C Fort Valley	GA	3900	2300 6300	M [5]	Pub	T		A=S	Q		Y		8/22		5	1										
1090	West Liberty St C West Liberty	WV	3900 [3]	2600 5800	B [5]	Pub	T		8/01 A/S	E		Y		3/01 FAF	5	5	0	9	1	3	7	5	1	2.8 2.3	Y	Y	Y
1091	Albany St C Albany	GA	4000	2400	M [5]	Pub	M		9/01 A=S	Q		Y	Y	8/01 FA/FF	8	6	0		8	1			1	2.0 2.2	Y		Y
1092	Concord C Athens	WV	4100 [3]	2700 6100	B [5]	Pub	T		A/S	S		Y		FA/FF	5	6	0	6	1	1	6	5	2	3.0 2.1	Y		Y

▲ Sequence number—indicates the order of the college in this book only. Do *not* use this number with admissions tests or need analysis services.

[1] No campus room and board facilities
[2] Room only or board only
[3] Most freshmen required to live on campus
[4] City or district residence requirements
[5] Accredited by a regional accrediting association or a recognized candidate for accreditation
[6] All female freshman class
[7] All male freshman class

MAJORS AVAILABLE AND PERCENT OF STUDENTS STUDYING IN EACH AREA

Agri.: Agriculture, general; Agronomy (crops & mgmt); Animal Science (husbandry); Fish, Wildlife Mgmt; Forestry
Business: Business/Commerce, general; Accounting; Banking/Finance; Business Economics; Business Mgmt/Admin; Marketing/Purchasing; Secretarial Studies
Comm.: Communications, general; Journalism; Radio/TV (broadcasting); Advertising
Education: Art Education; Distributive Education; Elementary Education; English Education; Mathematics Education; Music Education; Physical Education; Science Education; Secondary Education; Social Science Education; Special Education; Speech Education
Engineering: Engineering, general; Chemical; Civil; Electrical/Electronics/Comm; Industrial/Management; Mechanical
Fine/App. Arts: Architecture; Fine/Applied Arts, general; Art (paint, draw, sculpt); Art History/Appreciation; Dance; Dramatic Arts (theater arts); Music (liberal arts); Music (perform, compos, theory)
Lang.: French; German; Italian; Latin; Spanish; Russian
Health: Predentistry; Premedicine; Medical/Lab Technology; Nursing (registered nurse); Occupational Therapy; Preoptometry; Prepharmacy; Physical Therapy; Preveterinary Medicine
Home Ec.: Home Economics, general; Clothing and Textiles; Consumer Ec/Home Mgmt; Family Relations/Child Devel; Food and Nutrition/Dietetics; Institution Mgmt
Humanities: Humanities, general; Creative Writing; English, general; Literature, English; Philosophy; Religion; Speech/Forensic Science
Math-Sciences: Mathematics, general; Computer/Info Sciences; Biological Sciences, general; Biology; Botany; Zoology; Physical Sciences, general; Chemistry; Physics
Social Sciences: Crim Just/Law Enforce; Social Work; Social Sciences, general; Anthropology; Area Studies (Amer., African, etc.); Economics; Geography; History; Prelaw; Political Science; Psychology; Sociology
GS: General Studies
ROTC: Air Force; Army; Navy

Sequence Number	Agri.	Business	Comm.	Education	Engineering	Fine/App. Arts	Lang.	Health	Home Ec.	Humanities	Math-Sciences	Social Sciences	GS	ROTC
1063		97%									3%			
1064		13%	2%	41%						13%		4%		
1065	1%	22%	3%	10%	4%	5%	1%	6%	8%	4%	5%	8%		YY
1066		30%	1%	20%		3%	1%	2%		2%	3%	2%		
1067		24%		18%	3%	5%		2%		5%	10%	16%		
1068			5%		95%									
1069	3%	40%	2%	10%	2%	7%		6%		2%	4%	6%		
1070		20%	3%	28%	1%	1%		15%		2%	3%	2%		
1071		22%	1%	27%		1%				17%	9%	14%		YY
1072		17%		6%		11%		3%		2%	2%	20%		
1073		29%	3%	7%	1%	2%	1%	15%		5%	8%	12%		
1074		48%	3%	8%	1%	1%	1%	16%		2%	3%	2%		
1075		95%									5%			
1076														
1077						100%								
1078		48%	1%	5%	2%	1%		12%		1%	6%	3%		
1079		33%	1%	16%		1%	1%	7%		1%	18%	5%		Y
1080		30%	5%	15%	5%	1%	1%	20%		1%	8%	6%		Y
1081		45%	1%	25%	1%	1%	1%	4%	1%	2%	11%	3%		Y
1082	1%	19%		15%	3%	5%	1%	8%	4%	2%	10%	14%		Y
1083	1%	35%		10%	1%	1%	1%	17%		2%	3%	2%		Y
1084		11%		10%		2%				1%	7%	8%		Y
1085		22%		41%		1%		6%		2%	15%	13%		Y
1086		47%	5%		17%	1%				1%	12%	12%		YY
1087		30%	2%	16%		1%	1%	10%		3%	24%	3%		Y
1088		29%	3%	13%	1%	1%	1%	1%	1%	2%	14%	9%		Y
1089														
1090		24%	3%	26%		2%		15%		1%	7%	12%		
1091		35%	1%	10%		1%	1%	10%		3%	11%	6%		Y
1092		18%	2%	20%		4%	1%	2%		1%	4%	12%		

[1] Additional majors available in this area
[2] ROTC available

†Accredited by a nationally recognized accrediting body other than one of the regional accrediting associations

South Atlantic States (continued)

DC, DE, FL, GA, MD, NC, SC, VA, WV

LIBERAL ADMISSIONS *Some accepted students from lower half of HS class*

Sequence Number	School name (upper entry) City (lower entry)	State	Costs: Resident tuition/fees + room/board	Costs: Room/Board (upper entry) Nonresident tuition/fees + room/board (lower entry)	General Information: Highest degree	General Information: Affiliation (upper entry) Religious observance (lower entry)	General Information: Size of community	General Information: Type of community	Admissions: Fall term application deadline (upper entry) Tests desired or required (lower entry)	Admissions: Calendar	Admissions: Fall admission only	Admissions: Early admission	Admissions: Deferred admission	Financial Aid: Fall term application deadline (upper entry) Forms to be filed (lower entry)	Financial Aid: Number in 10 who -have need, receive some aid	Student Profile: Undergrads -are women	Undergrads -are graduate students	Freshmen -live on campus	Freshmen -are minority students	Freshmen -are nonresidents	Freshmen -return as sophomores	Freshmen -complete degree	Freshmen -enter graduate study	HS GPA (upper entry) 1st year college GPA (lower entry)	Special Programs: Credit by exam	Special Programs: Student designed majors	Special Programs: Fraternities/sororities
	Enrollment 1,000 to 5,000																										
1093	West Georgia C Carrollton	GA	4200 [3]	2300 6500	M [5]	Pub	S		9/01 A=S	Q		Y		3/01 FAF	6	6	1	5	2	1	5	2		2.8	Y		Y
1094	Armstrong St C Savannah	GA	4400	2900 6800	M [5]	Pub	L	S	9/01 A=S	Q		Y		7/01 FAF	3	6	1	1	2	1	6	3	1	2.6 2.1	Y		Y
1095	Strayer C Arlington	VA	4500	[1]	M [5]	Priv	V	U	Oth	Q		Y	Y	5/15 FA/FF	6	5	2	0	7	5	5	4	2	2.5 2.5	Y		
1096	Francis Marion C Florence	SC	4700	2900 6500	M [5]	Pub	S		S/A	E		Y		3/01 FA/FF		5	0	4	1	1	7	3	1		Y		Y
1097	DeVry Inst Techn Decatur	GA	5000	[1]	B [5]	Priv	S		A=S	T			Y	FA/FF	8	3	0	0	7	6	4	3			Y		Y
1098	SE C Assembly God Lakeland	FL	5200 [3]	2400	B [5]	Oth OS	M		A/S	E		Y		FAF	7	4	0	8	1	5	7	5	2		Y		
1099	Pensacola Christ C Pensacola	FL	5300 [3]	2800	D †	Oth OS	M	S	9/04 A=S	E		Y	Y	9/04		6	0	9		9					Y		
1100	Md Eastern Cam,U of Princess Anne	MD	5600	3500 9300	D [5]	Pub	T		SAT	S				4/01 FF/FA	9	5	1	8	8	3	7	4	1	2.4 2.5	Y	Y	Y
1101	Virginia St U Petersburg	VA	6700	4000 9900	M [5]	Pub	M		5/01 S/A	O			Y	3/31 FA/FF	8	6	1	9	9	5	6	3		2.4 2.4	Y		Y
1102	Bethune-Cookman C Daytona Beach	FL	7100	2600	B [5]	Meth OS	M	U	7/30 A=S	E				3/01 FF/FA	8	6	0	8	9	2	7	4	1	2.7 2.3	Y		Y
1103	Bob Jones U Greenville	SC	7300 [3]	3400	D	Priv OS	M	U	ACT	E				Oth	5	5	1	9		9	8	5	3		Y		
1104	Johnson C Smith U Charlotte	NC	7400	2300	B [5]	Priv	L	U	8/01 S/A	S		Y	Y	FF=FA	9	6	0	9	9	7	6	3	2	2.3 2.2			Y
1105	Shaw U Raleigh	NC	7500 [3]	3200	B [5]	Bapt	L	U	8/11 S/A	S		Y		6/01 FF/FA	4	5	0	9	9	5	6	4	1	2.0 2.0			
1106	Palm Beach-Atlantic West Palm Beach	FL	8000 [3]	2600	M [5]	Oth OS	M	U	A=S	4		Y	Y	5/01 FF/FA	9	6	0	6	1	2	5	4	5		Y		
1107	Saint Augustine's C Raleigh	NC	8200	4000	B [5]	Priv	M	U	8/01	S				3/30 FFS	8	6	0	9	9	5	7	5	3				
1108	Virginia Union U Richmond	VA	8800	3000	P [5]	Bapt OS	V	U	S/A	E		Y	Y	5/15 FA/FF	9	6	1	8	9	5	6				Y		Y
1109	Clark Atlanta U Atlanta	GA	8900	2700	B [5]	Meth	V	U	S/A	S		Y		4/15 FA/FF	9	7	0	5	9	5	7	4		2.5 2.0	Y		Y
1110	Belmont Abbey C Belmont	NC	9900 [3]	3700 11000	B [5]	Cath S	T		8/01 A=S	S		Y	Y	4/15 FA/FF	7	5	0	8	1	6	6	5	2	2.4 2.0	Y		Y
1111	Boca Raton,C of Boca Raton	FL	16900 [3]	4700	M [5]	Priv	M	S	A=S	S		Y	Y	2/15 FF/FA	4	5	1	7	2	7	7	6		2.5 2.5	Y	Y	
	Enrollment 5,000 to 15,000																										
1112	Augusta C Augusta	GA	3000 [2]	1600 5500	M [5]	Pub	L	S	8/15 S/A	Q		Y	Y	6/01 FAF	9	6	1	1	2	0	8			2.4	Y		Y
1113	NC Agrl & Tech St U Greensboro	NC	3400	2300 7900	M [5]	Pub	L	U	6/01 S/A	S		Y		5/15 FA/FF		4	1	8	9	2	9	3		2.8 2.5	Y		Y
1114	Florida A&M U Tallahassee	FL	3900 [3]	2500 7200	D [5]	Pub	M	U	7/01 A=S	E		Y	Y	4/01 FF/FA	7	6	1	8	9	4	7	7	2	2.9 2.3	Y		Y
1115	Georgia Southern U Statesboro	GA	4300	2700 6800	M [5]	Pub	S		9/01 A=S	Q		Y	Y	4/15 FA/FF	7	5	1	5	1	1	8	4		2.4 2.1	Y		Y
	TRADITIONAL ADMISSIONS *Majority of accepted students in top 50% of HS class*																										
	Enrollment to 1,000																										
1116	Georgia Baptist C College Park	GA	1600	[1]	M	Bapt S	M	S	9/01 A=S	S				None		1	2	1	5	2	2	0	0	3.5 3.0			
1117	Georgia Bapt Sch Nsg Atlanta	GA	3100 [2]	800 6700	B †	Bapt O	V	U	7/10 A=S	O		Y	[6]	FA/FF	8	9	0		1	1					Y		
1118	Landmark Baptist C Haines City	FL	4700 [2]	800	D	Bapt OS	S		A/S	S		Y		None		2	1	6	3	2	9	8		2.5 3.2	Y		
1119	Villa Julie C Stevenson	MD	5700	[1]	B [5]	Priv	V	S	S/A	E		Y	Y	FA/FF	6	8	0	0	2	1	7	6	2		Y	Y	
1120	Livingstone C Salisbury	NC	5900	2300	M [5]	Oth OS	S		S/A	S			Y	7/31 FA/FF	7	4	1	9	9	6	6	6	1	2.2 2.0	Y		Y

▲ Sequence number—indicates the order of the college in this book only. Do *not* use this number with admissions tests or need analysis services.

[1] No campus room and board facilities
[2] Room only or board only
[3] Most freshmen required to live on campus
[4] City or district residence requirements
[5] Accredited by a regional accrediting association or a recognized candidate for accreditation
[6] All female freshman class
[7] All male freshman class

MAJORS AVAILABLE AND PERCENT OF STUDENTS STUDYING IN EACH AREA

Sequence Number	Agri.	Business	Comm.	Education	Engineering	Fine/App. Arts	Lang.	Health	Home Ec.	Humanities	Math-Sciences	Social Sciences	GS	ROTC
1093		030%	1%	013%		2%		3%		1%	5%	9%		Y
1094				8%		1%	1%	015%		2%	3%	2%		YY
1095		034%	1%							2%	2%	1%		
1096	1%	023%	1%	013%	3%	2%	1%	3%		4%	016%	016%		Y
1097		027%			047%						026%			
1098		1%		035%		1%	1%			2%	2%	7%		Y
1099		020%	1%	026%	2%	4%	1%	012%	3%	016%	6%	5%		
1100	2%	023%		5%	8%	1%		010%	2%	5%	7%	8%		Y
1101	1%	036%		016%	7%	1%			4%	3%	5%	6%		Y
1102		029%	5%	019%	2%	1%		5%		2%	8%	021%		
1103	1%	020%	2%	021%	2%	8%	1%	6%	4%	017%	5%	7%		
1104		028%	014%	9%	1%					5%	026%	015%		YY
1105		022%	7%	023%	4%	2%		2%		1%	3%	2%		YY
1106		022%	4%	011%		1%				6%	010%	011%		
1107		017%	1%	017%	4%	1%	2%	1%		1%	3%	2%		Y
1108		034%	2%	8%	3%	4%	1%			1%	011%	021%		Y
1109		027%	018%	4%	1%	1%	1%	8%	1%	2%	8%	2%		YYY
1110		047%		011%	2%			3%		4%	011%	021%		YY
1111		050%	5%	5%		5%		2%		010%		015%		
1112	1%	023%	3%	013%	1%	1%	1%	7%		2%	3%	2%		Y
1113	2%	021%	4%	012%	018%	2%	1%	3%	1%	1%	9%	5%		YY
1114	1%	014%	4%	6%	7%	3%		011%		1%	9%	013%		YYY
1115	1%	026%	8%	012%	1%	4%	1%	3%	2%	2%	012%	5%		Y
1116		1%								098%		1%		
1117								100%						
1118		5%	1%	033%		1%	1%			040%	010%	1%		
1119		021%	4%	7%		3%		2%			026%	024%		Y
1120		046%		017%		1%				6%	7%	011%		Y

[1] Additional majors available in this area
[2] ROTC available

†Accredited by a nationally recognized accrediting body other than one of the regional accrediting associations

South Atlantic States (continued)

DC, DE, FL, GA, MD, NC, SC, VA, WV

TRADITIONAL ADMISSIONS *Majority of accepted students in top 50% of HS class*

Enrollment to 1,000

Sequence Number	School name (upper entry) City (lower entry)	State	Costs: Resident tuition/fees + room/board	Costs: Room/Board (upper entry) Nonresident tuition/fees + room/board (lower entry)	General Information: Highest degree	General Information: Affiliation (upper entry) Religious observance (lower entry)	General Information: Size of community	General Information: Type of community	Admissions: Fall term application deadline (upper entry) Tests desired or required (lower entry)	Admissions: Calendar	Admissions: Fall admission only	Admissions: Early admission	Admissions: Deferred admission	Financial Aid: Fall term application deadline (upper entry) Forms to be filed (lower entry)	Number in 10 who—have need, receive some aid	Student Profile (Undergrads): -are women	-are graduate students	Student Profile (Freshmen): -live on campus	-are minority students	-are nonresidents	-return as sophomores	-complete degree	-enter graduate study	HS GPA (upper entry) 1st year college GPA (lower entry)	Special Programs: Credit by exam	Student designed majors	Fraternities/sororities
1121	Bennett C Greensboro	NC	7500	2300	B[5]	Meth OS	M	U	8/10 A=S	S		Y	Y[6]	4/15 FA/FF	7	9	0	9	9	6	7		3	2.5 2.0			Y
1122	Toccoa Falls C Toccoa Falls	GA	7800	3100	B[5]	Oth OS	S		 A=S	4		Y	Y	 FA/FF	7	5	0	9	1	8	8	4	7	3.0	Y		
1123	Columbia Bible C Columbia	SC	7900	2900	D[5]	Priv OS	L	S	 S/A	Q			Y	3/15 FF/FA	3	5	1		1		7	4			Y		
1124	Miami Christian C Miami	FL	8100	2900	M†	Priv OS	V	U	8/15 A/S	O		Y	Y	 FF/FA	8	5	0	6	4	2	7	3	5	2.9 2.9	Y		
1125	Webber C Babson Park	FL	8100[3]	2700	B[5]	Priv	T		9/01 A=S	E		Y	Y	9/01 FF/FA	6	5	0	9	4	4	8	6	2	2.5 2.3	Y		Y
1126	Saint John Vianney C Miami	FL	8500[3]	3000	B[5]	Cath OS	V	U	7/01 A=S	S		Y	[7]		5	0	0	9	5	2	8	8	9		Y		
1127	LaGrange C LaGrange	GA	8700	3100	M[5]	Meth	S		7/31 A=S	Q		Y		6/01 FAF	6	5	0	8	1	3	8	6	3	3.2 2.3	Y		Y
1128	Greensboro C Greensboro	NC	9200[3]	3000	B[5]	Meth OS	M	U	 A=S	E		Y	Y	 FA/FF	6	7	0	9	1	6	7	4	1	2.7 2.3	Y	Y	
1129	Warren Wilson C Swannanoa	NC	9200	800	M[5]	Pres	M		 A=S	S		Y	Y	4/15 FF/FA	9	5	1	9	2	6	7	8	3	2.4 2.5	Y	Y	
1130	Shorter C of Georgia Rome	GA	9300	3500	B[5]	Oth OS	M		 A=S	E		Y	Y	7/01 FAF	5	6	0	5	1		9	4	6	3.1 2.6	Y	Y	Y
1131	Limestone C Gaffney	SC	9500	3000	B[5]	Priv O	S		8/20 Oth	E		Y		6/01 FAF	9	5	0	6	2	1	7	7	2	2.5 2.5	Y	Y	Y
1132	Pfeiffer C Misenheimer	NC	9600	3000	M[5]	Meth O	T		 S/A	E		Y	Y	5/01 FA/FF	8	5	0	9	1	4	7	4	2	2.6 2.4	Y		
1133	Eastern Mennonite C Harrisonburg	VA	10000	3100	B[5]	Oth OS	S		8/01 A=S	E		Y	Y	8/01 FA/FF	9	6	0	9	1	6	8	6	1	3.1	Y		
1134	Newberry C Newberry	SC	10100[3]	3000	B[5]	Luth	S		 A=S	S		Y		4/01 FA/FF	8	4	0	8	2	2	7	4	1	2.6	Y		Y
1135	Atlanta C of Art Atlanta	GA	10200[2]	2700	B[5]	Priv	V	U	 S/A	E		Y	Y	 FA/FF	8	5	0	5	2	6	7	5	4	2.5 3.0	Y	Y	
1136	Gardner-Webb C Boiling Springs	NC	10200	3500	M[5]	Oth O	T		8/01 A=S	E		Y		6/01 FF/FA	9	5	1	7	2	4	7	6	2	2.5 2.0	Y		
1137	Alderson-Broaddus C Philippi	WV	10500	2700	B[5]	Bapt O	T		 A/S	S		Y	Y	 FA/FF	9	6	0	9	1	4	8	5	2	3.2 2.7	Y	Y	Y
1138	NC Wesleyan C Rocky Mount	NC	10700[3]	3500	B[5]	Meth S	M		 A=S	S		Y	Y	 FA/FF	7	4	0	6	2	6	7	4		2.5 2.3	Y		Y
1139	Catawba C Salisbury	NC	10800[3]	3500	M[5]	UCC O	S		 S/A	E		Y	Y	 FA/FF	4	5	1	8	1	5	8	5	6	2.8	Y	Y	
1140	Charleston,U of Charleston	WV	10900[3]	3500	M[5]	Priv	M		 A=S	E			Y	3/01 FA/FF	7	6	0	3	1	2	8			2.8 2.7	Y	Y	Y
1141	Coker C Hartsville	SC	10900	3200	B[5]	Priv	S		 S/A	E			Y	7/01 FA/FF	8	6	0	7	3	3	7			2.8	Y	Y	
1142	Christendom C Front Royal	VA	11100	3400	B[5]	Cath O	S		4/01 S/A	E				4/01 FA/FF	6	5	0	9	1	7	8	4	1	3.3 2.5			
1143	Emory & Henry C Emory	VA	11300[3]	4000	B[5]	Meth OS	T		 A=S	E		Y	Y	 FAF	8	5	0	9	1	2	8	6	3			Y	Y
1144	Saint Leo C Saint Leo	FL	11500[3]	3400	B[5]	Cath S	T		 A=S	E		Y	Y	 FA/FF	7	5	0	9	1	5	7	4		2.5 2.7	Y		Y
1145	Covenant C Lookout Mt	GA	11600[3]	3500	B[5]	Oth OS	T		6/01 A=S	E		Y	Y	3/31 FA/FF	9	5	0	9	1	8	7	4		3.1	Y		
1146	Wheeling Jesuit C Wheeling	WV	11700[3]	3700	M[5]	Cath S	M	S	6/01 A=S	E		Y	Y	5/01 FA/FF	8	5	0	7	1	6	8	6	3	3.1 2.8	Y	Y	
1147	Columbia Union C Takoma Park	MD	11900	3800	B[5]	Oth OS	S		8/01 A/S	E		Y	Y	3/31 FF=FA	6	6	0	4	5	6	6	6	2	3.2 2.9	Y	Y	
1148	Erskine C Due West	SC	11900	3100	B[5]	Oth OS	T		 S/A	4			Y	 FA/FF	7	5	0	9	1	3	9	7	4	3.4 2.3	Y		Y
1149	Saint Andrew's Presb Laurinburg	NC	11900	3700	B[5]	Pres	S		8/15 S/A	4		Y	Y	 FA/FF	9	5	0	9	1	6		6	4	2.9 2.8	Y	Y	
1150	Brenau Women's C Gainesville	GA	12000[3]	5400	M[5]	Priv	M		9/01 A=S	Q		Y	Y[6]	8/01 FA/FF	6	9	0	8	1	4	7	5	3		Y	Y	Y
1151	Shenandoah C Winchester	VA	12000	3900	M[5]	Meth S	S		3/15 A=S	E		Y	Y	3/15 FAF	8	6	1	6	1	4	6	6	3	2.5	Y		

▲ **Sequence number—indicates the order of the college in this book only. Do *not* use this number with admissions tests or need analysis services.**

[1] No campus room and board facilities
[2] Room only or board only
[3] Most freshmen required to live on campus
[4] City or district residence requirements
[5] Accredited by a regional accrediting association or a recognized candidate for accreditation
[6] All female freshman class
[7] All male freshman class

MAJORS AVAILABLE AND PERCENT OF STUDENTS STUDYING IN EACH AREA

Agri.: Agriculture, general; Agronomy (crops & mgmt); Animal Science (husbandry); Fish, Wildlife Mgmt; Forestry
Business: Business/Commerce, general; Accounting; Banking/Finance; Business Economics; Business Mgmt/Admin; Marketing/Purchasing; Secretarial Studies
Comm.: Communications, general; Journalism; Radio/TV (broadcasting); Advertising
Education: Art Education; Distributive Education; Elementary Education; English Education; Mathematics Education; Music Education; Physical Education; Science Education; Secondary Education; Social Science Education; Special Education; Speech Education
Engineering: Engineering, general; Chemical; Civil; Electrical/Electronics/Comm; Industrial/Management; Mechanical
Fine/App. Arts: Architecture; Fine/Applied Arts, general; Art (Paint, draw, sculpt); Art History/Appreciation; Dance; Dramatic Arts (theater arts); Music (liberal arts); Music (perform, compos, theory)
Lang.: French; German; Italian; Latin; Spanish; Russian
Health: Predentistry; Premedicine; Medical/Lab Technology; Nursing (registered nurse); Occupational Therapy; Preoptometry; Prepharmacy; Physical Therapy; Preveterinary Medicine
Home Ec.: Home Economics, general; Clothing and Textiles; Consumer Ec/Home Mgmt; Family Relations/Child Devel; Food and Nutrition/Dietetics; Institution Mgmt
Humanities: Humanities, general; Creative Writing; English, general; Literature, English; Philosophy; Religion
Math-Sciences: Speech/Forensic Science; Mathematics, general; Computer/Info Sciences; Biological Sciences, general; Biology; Botany; Zoology; Physical Sciences, general; Chemistry; Physics
Social Sciences: Crim Just/Law Enforce; Social Work; Social Sciences, general; Anthropology; Area Studies (Amer., African, etc.); Economics; Geography; History; Prelaw; Political Science; Psychology; Sociology
GS: General Studies
ROTC: Air Force; Army; Navy

Sequence Number	Agri.	Business	Comm.	Education	Engineering	Fine/App. Arts	Lang.	Health	Home Ec.	Humanities	Math-Sciences	Social Sciences	GS	ROTC
1121		19%		14%	1%	1%			2%	3%	24%	18%		
1122			5%	14%		1%	1%			23%	10%	4%		
1123										100%				
1124		2%	9%	17%		8%	5%			25%		15%		
1125		90%									10%			
1126										100%				
1127		25%		20%		5%	1%	10%	1%	9%	8%	20%		
1128		38%		16%		1%				8%	14%	19%		Y Y
1129		13%		9%		3%				9%	22%	19%		
1130		25%	6%	19%		15%	1%			6%	11%	15%		Y
1131		70%		10%		1%	1%	1%		1%	3%	2%		
1132		40%		12%	1%	1%		5%		6%	8%	8%		Y
1133	1%	17%		23%		1%	1%	6%		13%	10%	19%		
1134		30%		20%	2%	3%	1%	2%		5%	14%	13%		Y
1135						100%								
1136		43%	1%	12%		1%	1%	8%		5%	16%	12%		
1137		11%	3%	13%				48%		3%	4%	2%		
1138														Y
1139		28%	9%	18%		5%	1%	4%		3%	12%	9%		Y
1140		17%	2%	9%		2%		42%		2%	7%	9%		Y
1141		30%	4%	13%		18%		1%		2%	5%	26%		
1142							5%			45%		50%		
1143		25%	4%	17%	2%	1%	3%	3%		8%	19%	18%		
1144		31%		14%		4%				5%	5%	20%		
1145		17%		24%	5%	2%		1%		14%	11%	19%		Y
1146		24%			3%		1%	23%		6%	13%	21%		Y
1147		34%	6%	4%	1%	1%	3%	17%		7%	9%	8%		
1148		20%		15%		2%	1%			11%	29%	17%		
1149		22%	1%	7%		4%	1%	1%		19%	24%	20%		
1150		29%	6%	19%		9%		18%			3%	12%		Y
1151		15%		14%		1%		21%		2%	3%	1%		

[1] Additional majors available in this area
[2] ROTC available

†Accredited by a nationally recognized accrediting body other than one of the regional accrediting associations

South Atlantic States (continued)

DC, DE, FL, GA, MD, NC, SC, VA, WV

TRADITIONAL ADMISSIONS *Majority of accepted students in top 50% of HS class*

Sequence Number	School name (upper entry) City (lower entry)	State	Costs: Resident tuition/fees + room/board	Costs: Room/Board (upper entry) Nonresident tuition/fees + room/board (lower entry)	General Information: Highest degree	General Information: Affiliation (upper entry) Religious observance (lower entry)	General Information: Size of community	General Information: Type of community	Admissions: Fall term application deadline (upper entry) Tests desired or required (lower entry)	Admissions: Calendar	Admissions: Fall admission only	Admissions: Early admission	Admissions: Deferred admission	Financial Aid: Fall term application deadline (upper entry) Forms to be filed (lower entry)	Financial Aid: Number in 10 who- -have need, receive some aid	Student Profile: Number in 10 who- Under-grads -are women	Student Profile: Under-grads -are graduate students	Student Profile: Freshmen -live on campus	Student Profile: Freshmen -are minority students	Student Profile: Freshmen -are nonresidents	Student Profile: Freshmen -return as sophomores	Student Profile: Freshmen -complete degree	Student Profile: Freshmen -enter graduate study	Student Profile: HS GPA (upper entry) 1st year college GPA (lower entry)	Special Programs: Credit by exam	Special Programs: Student designed majors	Special Programs: Fraternities/sororities
	Enrollment to 1,000																										
1152	Corcoran Sch of Art Washington	DC	13400[2]	3900	B[5]	Priv	V	U	A=S	S		Y	Y	3/15 FA/FF	5	6	0	3	3	4	7	7	2	2.8 2.9	Y		
1153	Mary Baldwin C Staunton	VA	14600	6100	B[5]	Pres	S		3/15 A=S	O		Y	Y[6]	3/15 FAF	4	9	0	9	1	5	8	7	4	2.9 2.4		Y	
1154	Md Inst C Art Baltimore	MD	14800	4100	M[5]	Priv	V	U	A=S	E		Y	Y	3/01 FA/FF	6	5	1		1	6	8	5	2				
1155	Trinity C of DC Washington	DC	16000[3]	6000	M[5]	Cath OS	V	U	2/01 A=S	E		Y	Y[6]	3/01 FF=FA	8	9	0	9	2	8		9	7	3.0 2.8	Y	Y	
1156	Washington C Chestertown	MD	16100[3]	4700	M[5]	Priv	T		3/01 A=S	E		Y	Y	2/15 FA/FF	5	5	0	9	1	5	9	6	3	3.0 2.5	Y	Y	Y
1157	Mount Vernon C Washington	DC	18600[3]	6100	B[5]	Priv	V	U	A=S	S		Y	Y[6]	2/01 FAF	3	9	0	8	3	9	7	5	1	2.8	Y	Y	
	Enrollment 1,000 to 5,000																										
1158	Christopher Newport Newport News	VA	2000	[1] 4400	M[5]	Pub	M	S	8/01 S/A	E		Y	Y	4/01 FAF	3	6	0	0	2	1	7	3	3	2.8 2.2	Y	Y	Y
1159	Pembroke St U Pembroke	NC	2800	2000 6800	M[5]	Pub	T		7/15 A=S	E		Y		3/15 FA/FF	6	6	0	4	4	1	7	3		2.7 2.0	Y		Y
1160	Medical C of Georgia Augusta	GA	2900[2]	1000 6200	D[5]	Pub	L	U	A=S	Q		Y		FAF	8	8	6		1					2.9	Y		
1161	Fayetteville St U Fayetteville	NC	3300	2200 7900	M[5]	Pub	L	U	8/15 SAT	S		Y	Y	5/01 FF/FA		6	1		8	1		4	1	2.5	Y		Y
1162	North Georgia C Dahlonega	GA	3700[3]	2200 6200	M[5]	Pub	T		9/01 A=S	Q		Y	Y	9/01 FA/FF	4	6	1	7	1	1	8	6	2	3.1 2.5	Y		Y
1163	NC Asheville,U of Asheville	NC	3900	2800 7900	M[5]	Pub	M		7/01 S/A	E		Y	Y	3/01 FF=FA	3	6	0	6	1	1	7	3	3	3.1 2.6	Y	Y	Y
1164	NC Central U Durham	NC	3900	2800 8400	P[5]	Pub	L	U	7/01 A=S	E				5/01 FF/FA	9	6	1	7	9	2	7	2		2.3 2.0	Y		Y
1165	Del St C Dover	DE	4000	2700 5900	M[5]	Pub	S		6/01 A=S	E		Y		3/15 FF/FA	7	6	1	7	7	5	5		1	2.4 2.1	Y		Y
1166	SC at Aiken,U of Aiken	SC	4200	2400 6900	M[5]	Pub	S		8/01 S/A	S		Y	Y	3/15 FA/FF	4	6	2	1	2	2	4	2		2.5 2.2	Y	Y	Y
1167	SC Spartanburg,U of Spartanburg	SC	4200	2300 7100	B[5]	Pub	M		8/15 S/A	E			Y	FF/FA	4	6	0	1	1	1	7				Y	Y	Y
1168	Lander C Greenwood	SC	4500	2400 5400	M[5]	Pub	M		A=S	E		Y	Y	4/15 FA/FF	5	7	0	5	2	1	7	4	1	2.5	Y	Y	Y
1169	Southern C Tech Inst Marietta	GA	4600	3200 7100	M[5]	Pub	S		8/28 A=S	Q		Y	Y	3/15 FA/FF	3	2	1	1	2	1	6	1	1	2.7 2.0	Y		Y
1170	W Va Inst of Techn Montgomery	WV	4700[3]	3300 6800	M[5]	Pub	T		8/15 A=S	E		Y		4/01 FAF	6	3	0	3	2	2	7			2.8 2.5	Y		Y
1171	SC Coastal Cam,U of Conway	SC	4800	2900 7700	B[5]	Pub	S		8/15 A=S	E				4/01 FF/FA	5	6	0	2	1	2	7	3	4	2.9 2.5	Y	Y	Y
1172	Virginia Clinch,U of Wise	VA	5000	2900 6600	B[5]	Pub	T		8/15 S/A	E		Y		4/01 FAF	6	5	0	3	1	1	6	2	1	2.8 2.5		Y	Y
1173	Citadel of SC,The Charleston	SC	5200[3]	2300 8400	M[5]	Pub	L	U	3/01 A=S	E				3/15 FAF	3	1	1	9	1	5	7	7		3.0 2.2	Y		
1174	Winthrop C Rock Hill	SC	5300	2700 7300	M[5]	Pub	S		5/01 A=S	E		Y		FAF	4	7	1	8	2	2	7	4			Y		Y
1175	Bowie St U Bowie	MD	5700	3600 7400	M[5]	Pub	S		7/01 SAT	E		Y	Y	7/01	5	6	1	6	8	2	7	2	2	2.5	Y		Y
1176	Frostburg St U Frostburg	MD	5800	3700 7400	M[5]	Pub	T		SAT	E				4/01 FAF	6	5	1	8	1	1	7	4	2	2.7 2.5	Y		Y
1177	Salisbury St C Salisbury	MD	6100	3800 7800	M[5]	Pub	M		S/A	E		Y		3/01 FAF	6	5	1	8	1	2	8	6	2	2.8 2.5	Y	Y	Y
1178	SC St C Orangeburg	SC	6100	4100 8000	D[5]	Pub	S		7/31 S/A	S				6/01 FA/FF	8	6	1	9	9	1	9	4	2	2.5	Y		Y
1179	Longwood C Farmville	VA	6300[3]	3400 9000	M[5]	Pub	T		6/15 S/A	E		Y	Y	4/01 FAF	5	7	0	9	1	1	8	5	1	3.0 2.3	Y		Y
1180	Morgan St U Baltimore	MD	6500	4400 8400	D[5]	Pub	V	U	5/01 A=S	E		Y		4/01 FAF	8	5	1	4	9	4	7		5	2.5	Y		Y
1181	Hampton U Hampton	VA	7000	2500	M[5]	Priv	L	U	6/30 A=S	S		Y	Y	6/30 FA/FF		6	1	9	9	7	7	6	2	3.2 2.5	Y		Y

▲ Sequence number—indicates the order of the college in this book only. Do *not* use this number with admissions tests or need analysis services.

[1] No campus room and board facilities
[2] Room only or board only
[3] Most freshmen required to live on campus
[4] City or district residence requirements
[5] Accredited by a regional accrediting association or a recognized candidate for accreditation
[6] All female freshman class
[7] All male freshman class

MAJORS AVAILABLE AND PERCENT OF STUDENTS STUDYING IN EACH AREA

Sequence Number	Agri.: Agriculture, general	Agri.: Agronomy (crops & mgmt)	Agri.: Animal Science (husbandry)	Agri.: Fish, Wildlife Mgmt	Agri.: Forestry	Business: Business/Commerce, general	Business: Accounting	Business: Banking/Finance	Business: Business Economics	Business: Business Mgmt/Admin	Business: Marketing/Purchasing	Business: Secretarial Studies	Comm.: Communications, general	Comm.: Journalism	Comm.: Radio/TV (broadcasting)	Comm.: Advertising
1152																
1153						■	0	1	5 ■	% ■	■		0 ■	1	0	%
1154																
1155							0	2	3 ■	% ■			■		5	% ■
1156							0	1	9	% ■						
1157						■	0	1 ■	9	% ■	■		0 ■	1	8	%
1158					[1] ■	■	0 ■	4 ■	7 ■	% ■	■	[1]		■	1	%
1159						■	0 ■	2	3	% ■		[1]	■	■	7 ■	%
1160																
1161							0 ■	3 ■	3	% ■	■	[1]				
1162						■	0 ■	2 ■	4 ■	% ■	■					
1163							■		9	% ■			■		2	%
1164			1	%		■	0 ■	3 ■	5 ■	% ■	■				5	%
1165	■		5	% ■	[1] ■	■	0 ■	3	0 ■	% ■	■	[1]	■	■	1	%
1166						■	0 ■	4 ■	6 ■	% ■	■					
1167						■	0 ■	2 ■	6 ■	% ■	■			■	3	%
1168						■	0	2	3	%						
1169									3	%						
1170							0 ■	2	3	% ■		[1] ■			1	%
1171							0 ■	2 ■	5	% ■	■	[1]				
1172						■	0 ■	5	4 ■	% ■	■	[1]				
1173						■	0	3	2	%						
1174							0	2	7	% ■			■		6	%
1175						■	0	3	1	% ■			■	■	8	%
1176			1	% ■	[1]		0 ■	3	3	% ■			■		1	%
1177						■	0 ■	1	9	% ■			■		7 ■	%
1178			1	%	[1]	■	0 ■	2	5 ■	% ■	■	[1]			1	%
1179							0	2	9	% ■						
1180							0 ■	2 ■	5 ■	% ■		■	■		1 ■	%
1181						■	0 ■	2 ■	1 ■	% ■	■	■	0 ■	1 ■	0 ■	% ■

Sequence Number	Education: Art Education	Education: Distributive Education	Education: Elementary Education	Education: English Education	Education: Mathematics Education	Education: Music Education	Education: Physical Education	Education: Science Education	Education: Secondary Education	Education: Social Science Education	Education: Special Education	Education: Speech Education	Engineering: Engineering, general	Engineering: Chemical	Engineering: Civil	Engineering: Electrical/Electronics/Comm	Engineering: Industrial/Management	Engineering: Mechanical
1152																		
1153					0	1	0	%										
1154	■						4	%										
1155			■			■	8	%	■		■	[1]						
1156																		
1157			■				6	%										
1158			■				9 ■	%	■			[1]				2	%	
1159	■	■	■	■	0 ■	2 ■	6 ■	% ■	■	■	■	[1]						
1160																		
1161	■	■	■	■	0 ■	1 ■	6 ■	% ■		■								
1162	■	■	■	■	0 ■	2 ■	0 ■	% ■		■	■	[1]				1	%	
1163							1	%										
1164	■	■	■	■	0 ■	1 ■	2 ■	%	■	■		[1] ■				1	%	
1165	■	■	■	■	0 ■	2 ■	0 ■	% ■	■	■	■	[1]		■	■	1 ■	%	[1] ■
1166		■	■	■	0 ■	2 ■	7 ■	% ■	■	■		[1]						
1167			■	■	0 ■	1	6 ■	% ■	■	■		[1]				1	%	
1168	■	■	■	■	0 ■	1 ■	7 ■	%		■		[1] ■						
1169														0	8	2	%	
1170		■		■	0 ■	1 ■	6 ■	% ■		■		[1]		0 ■	2 ■	7 ■	%	[1] ■
1171	■		■	■	0 ■	2 ■	0 ■	% ■	■	■		[1]						
1172			■		0	2	4	%										
1173							4 ■	%	■					0	1 ■	8 ■	%	
1174		■	■		0	1 ■	7 ■	%	■		■	[1]						
1175	■		■	■	0 ■	1 ■	0 ■	% ■	■	■	■	[1]						
1176	■	■	■		0	1 ■	3 ■	%				[1]						
1177	■		■	■	0 ■	1 ■	0 ■	% ■	■	■		[1] ■				2	%	
1178	■	■	■	■	0 ■	1 ■	8 ■	%		■	■	[1]		0	1	2	%	
1179	■		■	■	0 ■	2 ■	5 ■	% ■	■	■	■	[1]				2	%	
1180	■	■	■	■	■	■	8 ■	% ■	■	■		[1]	■	0	1 ■	0 ■	% ■	
1181	■	■	■	■	0 ■	1 ■	2 ■	% ■	■	■	■	[1] ■	■	■	■	3 ■	%	■

Sequence Number	Fine/App. Arts: Architecture	Fine/App. Arts: Fine/Applied Arts, general	Fine/App. Arts: Art (Paint, draw, sculpt)	Fine/App. Arts: Art History/Appreciation	Fine/App. Arts: Dance	Fine/App. Arts: Dramatic Arts (theater arts)	Fine/App. Arts: Music (liberal arts)	Fine/App. Arts: Music (perform, compos, theory)	Lang.: French	Lang.: German	Lang.: Italian	Lang.: Latin	Lang.: Spanish	Lang.: Russian
1152		■	1 ■	0	0	%		[1]						
1153		■	0 ■	1 ■	2	% ■			■			4	% ■	
1154		■	0 ■	9	6	%		[1]						
1155		■	■	■	1	%	■		■			3	% ■	
1156			■		3	% ■	■		■	■		2	% ■	
1157					2	%		[1]						
1158		■	■		3	% ■	■	[1] ■	■	■		2	% ■	
1159			■		2	% ■	■	■						
1160														
1161		■			2	%								
1162			■						■			1	%	
1163		■	■		5	% ■	■	■	■	■		1	% ■	
1164		■	■		2	% ■	■		■			1	% ■	
1165		■			2	% ■	■		■			1	% ■	
1166														
1167														
1168			■		5	% ■	■		■					
1169	■				4	%		[1]						
1170														
1171			■		1	% ■								
1172		■			1	%								
1173									■	■		1	% ■	
1174		■	0 ■	1	1	% ■	■	■				1	%	
1175		■			1	% ■								
1176		■	■		4	% ■	■		■			1	% ■	
1177		■	■	■	1	% ■	■		■			1	% ■	
1178					1	% ■			■			1	% ■	
1179		■	■		6	% ■	■	■	■	■		2	% ■	
1180			■		2	% ■	■	[1]	■			1	% ■	
1181	■		■	■	2	% ■	■					1	%	

Sequence Number	Health: Predentistry	Health: Premedicine	Health: Medical/Lab Technology	Health: Nursing (registered nurse)	Health: Occupational Therapy	Health: Preoptometry	Health: Prepharmacy	Health: Physical Therapy	Health: Preveterinary Medicine	Home Ec.: Home Economics, general	Home Ec.: Clothing and Textiles	Home Ec.: Consumer Ec/Home Mgmt	Home Ec.: Family Relations/Child Devel	Home Ec.: Food and Nutrition/Dietetics	Home Ec.: Institution Mgmt
1152															
1153			■		1	%									
1154															
1155		■													
1156															
1157					1	%			[1]						
1158	■	■		■	2	%									
1159			■		1	%									
1160			1 ■	0 ■	0 ■	%		■	[1]						
1161			■		2	%									
1162			0	1 ■	4	%									
1163															
1164	■		0	2 ■	0	%				■	■		3	% ■	
1165		■		■	6	%			[1] ■	■	■		3 ■	% ■	
1166	■	■		■											
1167	■	■	0	1 ■	5	%									
1168			0 ■	1 ■	1	%				■			1	%	
1169															
1170			0	1	0	%									
1171	■	■			4	% ■	■		■						
1172			■		1	%									
1173															
1174			■							■			1	% ■	
1175				■	3	%									
1176															
1177	■	■	■	■	9	% ■	■		[1] ■						
1178				■	7	%			[1]	■			6 ■	% ■	
1179	■	■	■		1	%	■		[1] ■						
1180		■	■		7	%	■			■			1	% ■	
1181	■	■	0	2 ■	0	%			■	■	■		5	% ■	

Sequence Number	Humanities: Humanities, general	Humanities: Creative Writing	Humanities: English, general	Humanities: Literature, English	Humanities: Philosophy	Humanities: Religion	Humanities: Speech/Forensic Science	Math-Sciences: Mathematics, general	Math-Sciences: Computer/Info Sciences	Math-Sciences: Biological Sciences, general	Math-Sciences: Biology	Math-Sciences: Botany	Math-Sciences: Zoology	Math-Sciences: Physical Sciences, general	Math-Sciences: Chemistry	Math-Sciences: Physics
1152																
1153			■	4 ■	%			■	■	0 ■	1 ■	4	%	■	■	[1]
1154																
1155		0	1 ■	1 ■	% ■	■		■		■	■	8	%	■	■	[1]
1156	■	0	1 ■	7 ■	% ■			■	■	0	1 ■	3	%		■	■
1157	■	0	1	0	%							4	%			[1]
1158	■		■	3 ■	% ■			■	■	0 ■	1 ■	7	%	■	■	■
1159		■	■	2	% ■	■		■	■	0 ■	1 ■	8	%	■	■	■
1160																
1161			■	1 ■	%		■	■	■		■	8	%		■	
1162			■	1	%			■	■	■	■	8	%	■	■	■
1163			■	3 ■	% ■		[1]	■		0 ■	1 ■	0	%	■	■	[1] ■
1164			■	2	% ■			■	■	■	■	3	%	■	■	■
1165			■	2	%			■	■	■	■	3	%	■	■	■
1166	■		■	3	%			■	■		■	4	%		■	
1167			■	2	%			■	■	■	■	8	%	■	■	[1]
1168			■	3	%			■	■	■	■	9	%	■	■	
1169				2	%			■				9	%			[1] ■
1170				1	%			■	■	■	■	3	%	■	■	■
1171			■	3	%				■	0	1 ■	3	%			[1]
1172			■	1 ■	%			■	■	■	■	4	%	■	■	[1]
1173			■	1	%			■	■		■	3	%		■	■
1174			■	2	% ■	■	■	■	■		■	7	%		■	
1175			■	1	%		[1] ■	■	■	0 ■	1 ■	3	%			[1]
1176			■	6	% ■		■	■	■	0 ■	2 ■	2	%	■	■	■
1177			■	3	% ■		■	■		0 ■	1 ■	7	%	■	■	[1] ■
1178			■	3	%			■	■	0 ■	1 ■	0	%	■	■	■
1179			■	4	%			■		0 ■	1 ■	0	%	■	■	■
1180	■		■	2	% ■	■	■	■	■	■	■	3	%	■	■	■
1181			■	2	%		■	■	■	■	■	3	%	■	■	[1] ■

Sequence Number	Social Sciences: Crim Just/Law Enforce	Social Sciences: Social Work	Social Sciences: Social Sciences, general	Social Sciences: Anthropology	Social Sciences: Area Studies (Amer., African, etc.)	Social Sciences: Economics	Social Sciences: Geography	Social Sciences: History	Social Sciences: Prelaw	Social Sciences: Political Science	Social Sciences: Psychology	Social Sciences: Sociology	GS: General Studies	ROTC: Air Force	ROTC: Army	ROTC: Navy
1152																
1153		■			0	1 ■	6	% ■		■	■	■			Y	
1154																
1155					0	4 ■	0	% ■	■	■	■	[1] ■		Y	Y	Y
1156					0	4 ■	6	% ■		■	■	[1] ■				
1157			■				6	%		■		[1]				
1158	■	■	■		0	1 ■	0	% ■	■	■	■	[1] ■	■		Y	
1159	■	■			0 ■	1 ■	9	% ■	■	■	■	[1] ■	■	Y	Y	
1160																
1161	■		■		0	1 ■	7 ■	% ■		■	■	■		Y		
1162	■		■		0	1	7	% ■		■	■	[1] ■			Y	
1163			■		0	1 ■	3	% ■		■	■	■				
1164	■		■				2 ■	% ■	■	■	■	[1] ■		Y	Y	Y
1165		■	■			■	2	% ■	■	■	■	[1] ■		Y	Y	
1166	■	■			0	1	1	% ■	■	■	■	[1] ■	■		Y	
1167	■						8	% ■	■	■	■	[1] ■			Y	
1168					0	1	4	% ■		■	■	■	■		Y	
1169														Y	Y	Y
1170							2	% ■				[1]			Y	
1171					0	1	2	% ■	■	■	■	■	■			
1172			■		0	1 ■	0	% ■		■	■	[1]	■			
1173							1	% ■		■	■			Y	Y	Y
1174		■			0	1	5	% ■		■	■	[1] ■				
1175		■			0	1	4	% ■		■	■	[1] ■			Y	
1176	■	■	■		0	1 ■	8 ■	% ■		■	■	[1] ■			Y	
1177		■	■			■	6 ■	% ■	■	■	■	■	■		Y	
1178	■	■	■			■	6	% ■		■	■	[1] ■		Y	Y	
1179		■	■	■	0	2	1	% ■	■	■	■	■			Y	
1180	■	■	■		■	■	2 ■	% ■	■	■	■	[1] ■			Y	
1181	■	■				■	2	% ■	■	■	■	■			Y	Y

[1] Additional majors available in this area
[2] ROTC available

†Accredited by a nationally recognized accrediting body other than one of the regional accrediting associations

South Atlantic States
(continued)

DC, DE, FL, GA, MD, NC, SC, VA, WV

TRADITIONAL ADMISSIONS *Majority of accepted students in top 50% of HS class*

Sequence Number	School name (upper entry) City (lower entry)	State	Costs: Resident tuition/fees + room/board	Costs: Room/Board (upper entry) Nonresident tuition/fees + room/board (lower entry)	General Information: Highest degree	General Information: Affiliation (upper entry) Religious observance (lower entry)	General Information: Size of community	General Information: Type of community	Admissions: Fall term application deadline (upper entry) Tests desired or required (lower entry)	Admissions: Calendar	Admissions: Fall admission only	Admissions: Early admission	Admissions: Deferred admission	Financial Aid: Fall term application deadline (upper entry) Forms to be filed (lower entry)	Financial Aid: Number in 10 who -have need, receive some aid	Student Profile (Number in 10 who—), Undergrads: -are women	Undergrads: -are graduate students	Freshmen: -live on campus	Freshmen: -are minority students	Freshmen: -are nonresidents	Freshmen: -return as sophomores	Freshmen: -complete degree	Freshmen: -enter graduate study	Freshmen: HS GPA (upper entry) 1st year college GPA (lower entry)	Special Programs: Credit by exam	Special Programs: Student designed majors	Special Programs: Fraternities/sororities
	Enrollment 1,000 to 5,000																										
1182	Flagler C St Augustine	FL	7400[3]	2800	B[5]	Priv	S		3/01 A=S	E		Y	Y	4/01 FA/FF	5	6	0	9	1	5	8	5	3	2.8 2.5	Y	Y	
1183	Barton C Wilson	NC	8200	2600	B[5]	Oth	S		S/A	E		Y	Y	5/01 FF/FA	8	6	0	6	2	2	8	6	2	2.8 2.8	Y		Y
1184	Gallaudet U Washington	DC	8200	4200	D[5]	Priv	V	U	1/01 Oth	S		Y	Y	4/01 FAF		5	1	9	2	9	6	7	2	2.9	Y		Y
1185	Wingate C Wingate	NC	8500[3]	2800	M[5]	Oth S	T		8/01 A=S	E		Y	Y	3/15	7	5	0	8	1	3	8	7	2	2.5 2.3	Y		
1186	Mars Hill C Mars Hill	NC	8800[3]	2900	B[5]	Oth OS	T		8/15 A=S	S		Y		4/01 FA/FF	7	5	0	9	1	4	7	4	3	2.8	Y		Y
1187	Charleston Southrn U Charleston	SC	9000	2900	M[5]	Bapt OS	V	S	S/A	4		Y	Y	5/01 FAF	9	5	1	5	3	1	5	7			Y		
1188	Embry Riddle Aero U Daytona Beach	FL	9500	3200	M[5]	Priv	M	S	A=S	O			Y	4/15 FFS	3	1	1	5	2	8	6	4		3.1 2.7	Y		Y
1189	Ferrum C Ferrum	VA	9500	3000	B[5]	Meth OS	T		S/A	E			Y	6/01 FA/FF	9	4	0	9	1	1	6			2.5 2.3	Y	Y	
1190	Morris Brown C Atlanta	GA	9800	3800	B[5]	Meth	L	U	S/A	E		Y		FF=FA		6	0	6	9	3	6			2.0 2.0			
1191	High Point C High Point	NC	9900[3]	3200	B[5]	Meth OS	M		A=S	S		Y	Y	3/01 FA/FF	4	5	0	7	1	6	8	4	1	2.5 2.3	Y	Y	Y
1192	Elon C Elon College	NC	10100	3300	M[5]	UCC S	T		S/A	4			Y	5/01 FAF	4	5	0	9	1	6	8	5	2	2.7 2.3	Y		Y
1193	Nova U Ft Lauderdale	FL	10100[2]	2700	D[5]	Priv	M	S	A=S	T		Y	Y	FAF	9	6	5	4	3	5	7	8	5	2.8 2.6	Y		
1194	Methodist C Fayetteville	NC	10200	3000	B[5]	Meth OS	M	S	A=S	E		Y	Y	FF=FA	9	5	0	4	2	4	6	5	2	2.8 2.4	Y		Y
1195	Florida Southern C Lakeland	FL	10800[3]	4200	M[5]	Meth	M		8/01 A=S	E		Y	Y	4/01 FA/FF		5	0	8	1	3	8		4	3.0 2.8	Y		Y
1196	Saint Thomas U Miami	FL	11200	3800	P[5]	Cath S	V	S	A=S	E		Y	Y	5/01 FA/FF	8	5	3	5	5	4	7	6		2.5 2.9	Y		Y
1197	Jacksonville U Jacksonville	FL	12200	3800	M[5]	Priv	V	S	A=S	E		Y	Y	3/15 FA/FF	8	5	1	6	2	5	7	5	4	3.1 2.9	Y	Y	Y
1198	Queens C Charlotte	NC	12700[3]	4200	M[5]	Pres OS	L	S	A=S	4		Y		FA/FF	7	7	1	8	2	6	8	6	2	3.4 2.8	Y		Y
1199	Averett C Danville	VA	13000[3]	4200	M[5]	Oth S	M	S	8/01 S/A	E		Y	Y	FA/FF	7	6	3	7	2	4	7	6	3	2.8 2.6	Y	Y	Y
1200	Virginia Wesleyan C Norfolk	VA	13100	4400	B[5]	Meth	V	S	3/01 S/A	4		Y	Y	FAF	6	6	0	7	1	4	8	7	3	3.0 2.8	Y	Y	Y
1201	Mercer U Macon Macon	GA	13400[3]	4000	P[5]	Bapt	L	S	A=S	Q		Y		FA/FF	6	5	1	8	2	4	7	4	4	3.2	Y	Y	Y
1202	Bridgewater C Bridgewater	VA	13500[3]	4300	B[5]	Oth	T		8/15 S/A	O		Y		3/15 FA/FF	9	5	0	9	1	2	8	6	2		Y		
1203	Roanoke C Salem	VA	14000[3]	3800	B[5]	Luth	S		5/01 S/A	E		Y	Y	3/01 FA/FF	4	6	0	9	1	5	7	6		2.7 2.3	Y		Y
1204	Barry U Miami	FL	14300	5000	D[5]	Cath	S		8/01 A=S	E		Y	Y	4/01 FAF	7	6	2	4	5	4	7	5		3.0	Y		Y
1205	Marymount U of Va Arlington	VA	14400	4700	M[5]	Cath	M	S	A=S	E			Y	FA/FF	5	8	2	7	3	5	7	4	1	2.7 2.8	Y		
1206	Mount St Mary's C Emmitsburg	MD	14400	5300	M[5]	Cath S	T		3/01 S/A	E		Y	Y	3/15 FAF	7	5	1	9	1	6	9	7	4	 2.6	Y	Y	
1207	W Va Wesleyan C Buckhannon	WV	15000[3]	3200	M[5]	Meth O	T		A=S	4		Y	Y	7/31 FAF	7	5	1	9	1	6	8	5	4	2.9 2.7	Y	Y	Y
1208	Lynchburg C Lynchburg	VA	15400[3]	5100	M[5]	Oth S	M	S	A=S	E		Y	Y	4/01 FAF	3	6	1	9	1	7	8	5	3	2.9 2.4	Y		
	Enrollment 5,000 to 15,000																										
1209	Appalachian St U Boone	NC	3500[3]	2200 8000	M[5]	Pub	S		S/A	E				3/15 FF=FA	6	5	1	9	1	1	9	5		3.1 2.3	Y	Y	Y
1210	NC Charlotte,U of Charlotte	NC	3600	2600 8200	M[5]	Pub	L	U	7/01 A=S	E		Y	Y	4/15 FA/FF	5	5	1	5	2	1	8	4			Y		Y
1211	East Carolina U Greenville	NC	3800	2700 8300	D[5]	Pub	S		S/A	E		Y		4/15 Oth		5	1	9	1	2	8	4	2	 2.1	Y		Y

▲ Sequence number—indicates the order of the college in this book only. Do *not* use this number with admissions tests or need analysis services.

[1] No campus room and board facilities
[2] Room only or board only
[3] Most freshmen required to live on campus
[4] City or district residence requirements
[5] Accredited by a regional accrediting association or a recognized candidate for accreditation
[6] All female freshman class
[7] All male freshman class

MAJORS AVAILABLE AND PERCENT OF STUDENTS STUDYING IN EACH AREA

Sequence Number	Agri.	Business	Comm.	Education	Engineering	Fine/App. Arts	Lang.	Health	Home Ec.	Humanities	Math-Sciences	Social Sciences	GS	ROTC
1182		032%	010%	022%		3%	1%			8%	3%	016%		
1183		027%	3%	019%		3%	1%	020%		2%	7%	5%		
1184		015%	1%	1%		1%	1%		010%	2%	3%	2%		
1185		028%	012%	015%	1%	1%	1%	1%		3%	011%	018%		YY
1186		024%	1%	019%		7%	1%	4%	3%	6%	8%	018%		
1187														Y
1188		014%			024%						3%			YY
1189	8%	027%				1%	2%	1%		3%	015%	018%		
1190		031%	3%	015%	2%	2%	1%	013%	3%	2%	3%	020%		YYY
1191		058%	6%	5%		4%	1%	1%		4%	012%	9%		
1192		034%	9%	010%		1%	1%	3%		6%	9%	019%		Y
1193		045%		015%	1%						020%	015%		
1194		034%	1%	012%		3%	1%	1%		7%	3%	017%		YY
1195	4%	041%	6%	011%		1%	1%	6%		2%	3%	2%		YY
1196		042%	3%	8%			4%	1%		2%	3%	2%		YY
1197		035%	5%	6%	5%	2%	1%	4%		2%	018%	2%		YY
1198		026%	017%	7%		7%	2%	5%		013%	011%	6%		YY
1199		023%	5%	013%		2%		1%		9%	014%	017%		
1200		024%	011%	012%		5%	1%			6%	9%	010%		
1201		033%		6%	014%	1%				044%	2%			Y
1202	1%	029%	1%	016%	1%	1%	2%	1%	3%	2%	3%	2%		
1203		015%		2%		2%	1%	1%		3%	6%	013%		
1204		030%	2%	8%	1%	2%	1%	014%		4%	5%	2%		YY
1205		030%	5%	7%		011%		9%	1%	9%	4%	6%		Y
1206		040%	1%	6%	1%	1%	1%	2%		2%	6%	2%		Y
1207		029%	2%	017%	2%	2%	1%	8%	1%	8%	6%	013%		
1208	1%	036%	4%	011%	1%	1%	1%	010%		2%	5%	2%		Y
1209	1%	024%	010%	017%	1%	5%	1%	2%	3%	4%	015%	8%		Y
1210	1%	020%	1%	8%	011%	6%	1%	4%		5%	8%	017%		YY
1211		6%	1%	9%	2%	9%		5%	3%	2%	3%	7%		YY

1 Additional majors available in this area
2 ROTC available

†Accredited by a nationally recognized accrediting body other than one of the regional accrediting associations

South Atlantic States
(continued)

DC, DE, FL, GA, MD, NC, SC, VA, WV

TRADITIONAL ADMISSIONS *Majority of accepted students in top 50% of HS class*

Sequence Number	School name (upper entry) City (lower entry)	State	Costs: Resident tuition/fees + room/board	Costs: Room/Board (upper entry) Nonresident tuition/fees + room/board (lower entry)	General Information: Highest degree	Affiliation (upper entry) Religious observance (lower entry)	Size of community	Type of community	Admissions: Fall term application deadline (upper entry) Tests desired or required (lower entry)	Calendar	Fall admission only	Early admission	Deferred admission	Financial Aid: Fall term application deadline (upper entry) Forms to be filed (lower entry)	Student Profile: Number in 10 who—have need, receive some aid	Undergrads -are women	-are graduate students	Freshmen -live on campus	-are minority students	-are nonresidents	-return as sophomores	-complete degree	-enter graduate study	HS GPA (upper entry) 1st year college GPA (lower entry)	Special Programs: Credit by exam	Student designed majors	Fraternities/sororities
	Enrollment 5,000 to 15,000																										
1212	Valdosta St C Valdosta	GA	4000[3]	2400 6400	D[5]	Pub	M		9/01 S/A	Q		Y		4/15 FF=FA	4	6	1	8	2	1	6		1	2.8 2.7	Y		Y
1213	NC Wilmington,U of Wilmington	NC	4200	3000 8700	M[5]	Pub	M	S	5/01 S/A	E				FA/FF	4	6	1	8	1	2	8	4	2	2.9 2.1	Y		Y
1214	Marshall U Huntington	WV	4900[3]	3400 7200	D[5]	Pub	M		8/15 A/S	E		Y	Y	3/01 FA/FF	5	5	1	5	1	1	7			2.9 2.2	Y		Y
1215	Charleston,C of Charleston	SC	5200	2900 7500	M[5]	Pub	M	U	7/01 SAT	S				FF/FA		6	1		1	3	8			2.3	Y		Y
1216	Virginia Commonwlth Richmond	VA	5600	3100 8600	D[5]	Pub	L	U	2/01 A=S	E		Y	Y	2/15 FA/FF	6	6	2	6	2	1	8	5	4	2.9 2.5	Y	Y	Y
1217	Radford U Radford	VA	5800[3]	3600 8300	M[5]	Pub	S		4/01 S/A	S		Y		3/15 FAF	4	6	1	9	1	1	7	8	1	2.9 2.3	Y	Y	
1218	George Mason U Fairfax	VA	7000	4500 10500	D[5]	Pub	V	S	2/01 A=S	E		Y		3/01 FA/FF	4	6	1	4	2	2	8	3	2	3.1	Y	Y	Y
1219	James Madison U Harrisonburg	VA	7000[3]	3900 10000	M[5]	Pub	S		2/01 SAT	E				3/17 FAF	4	6	1	9	1	2	8	8	2	2.7	Y		Y
1220	Campbell U Buies Creek	NC	9300	2500	D[5]	Oth O	T		8/01 S/A	E		Y		3/15 FF/FA	9	5	2	7	3	3	8	7	4	2.8 2.6	Y	Y	
1221	Howard U Washington	DC	9300	3400	D[5]	Priv	V	U	4/01 A=S	E		Y		4/01 FA/FF	8	6	2	8	9	7	8		7	3.0	Y	Y	Y
	Enrollment over 15,000																										
1222	Georgia St U Atlanta	GA	1800	[1] 5800	D[5]	Pub	V	U	8/11 S/A	Q		Y		4/01 FA/FF	5	6	3	0	3	1				2.6	Y	Y	Y
1223	South Florida,U of Tampa	FL	4300	2900 7600	D[5]	Pub	L	S	6/01 A=S	E		Y		FF/FA		5	1	6	2	3	7	5		3.0	Y		Y
1224	W Va U Morgantown	WV	5400[3]	3600 8200	D[5]	Pub	S		A=S	E		Y	Y	3/01 FAF	3	5	1	8	1	5	8	5		3.0 2.4	Y	Y	Y
1225	Old Dominion U Norfolk	VA	6700	4100 10000	D[5]	Pub	L	S	5/01 S/A	E		Y	Y	FAF	8	5	3	6	1	2	8			2.8 2.2	Y	Y	Y
	SELECTIVE ADMISSIONS *Majority of accepted students in top 25% of HS class*																										
	Enrollment to 1,000																										
1226	Baltimore Hebrew C Baltimore	MD	3400	[1]	D[5]	Priv	V	S	4/15 SAT	4		Y	Y	FAF	0	7	7	0	0		7			3.3	Y		
1227	Edward Waters C Jacksonville	FL	6500	3400	B[5]	Oth	V	U	7/01 Oth	S				5/01		6	0	5		1	8						Y
1228	Columbia C Columbia	SC	11000	3000	M[5]	Meth OS	L	U	8/01 S/A	E		Y	Y[6]	4/01 FA/FF	8	9	0	7	2	1	7	5	3	2.8	Y	Y	
1229	Wesleyan C Macon	GA	12600[3]	3900	B[5]	Meth OS	M	S	S/A	E		Y	Y[6]	4/01 FA/FF	9	9	0	9	2	4	7	5	5	3.2 2.8	Y		
1230	Converse C Spartanburg	SC	13600[3]	3200	M[5]	Priv	M	U	S/A	O		Y	[6]	3/15 FAF	6	9	1	9	1	5	8	6	2	3.2 2.8	Y		
1231	Hampden-Sydney C Hampden-Sydney	VA	14200[3]	3400	B[5]	Pres	T		3/01 A=S	E		Y	[7]	3/01 FF=FA	4	0	0	9	1	5	9	7	7	3.0 2.5			Y
1232	Notre Dame of Md Baltimore	MD	14300	4800	M[5]	Cath S	V	S	2/15 S/A	4		Y	Y[6]	2/15 FAF	9	9	0	8	3	2	8	8	4	3.2		Y	
1233	Oglethorpe U Atlanta	GA	14300	4000	M[5]	Priv	V	S	8/01 A=S	E		Y	Y	4/01 FF=FA	9	7	0	9	2	3	8	6	2	3.3	Y	Y	Y
1234	Bethany C Bethany	WV	14400[3]	3700	B[5]	Oth S	T		5/01 A=S	4		Y	Y	4/01 FA/FF	7	5	0	9	1	8	8	5	3	3.0 2.7	Y	Y	Y
1235	Agnes Scott C Decatur	GA	14500[3]	4200	B[5]	Pres	V	S	S/A	E		Y	Y[6]	FAF	5	9	0	9	2	5	8	6	5		Y	Y	
1236	Salem C Winston-Salem	NC	14600[3]	5600	M[5]	Oth	M	U	A=S	4		Y	Y	FF=FA	7	9	1	9	1	6	7	6	3	3.0 2.5	Y	Y	
1237	Hollins C Roanoke	VA	15100[3]	4400	M[5]	Priv	M	S	A=S	4		Y	Y[6]	3/31 FAF	4	9	1	9	1	7	8	7	3	2.9 2.8		Y	
1238	Randolph-Macon Wom C Lynchburg	VA	15700[3]	4800	B[5]	Meth	M	S	A=S	E		Y	Y[6]	3/01 FA/FF	4	9	0	9	1	6	8	6	5	3.0	Y	Y	
1239	Sweet Briar C Sweet Briar	VA	16000[3]	4300	B[5]	Priv	T		2/15 Oth	4		Y	Y[6]	3/01 FAF	4	9	0	9	1	8	8	6	4	2.9 2.7	Y	Y	

▲ **Sequence number—indicates the order of the college in this book only. Do *not* use this number with admissions tests or need analysis services.**

[1] No campus room and board facilities
[2] Room only or board only
[3] Most freshmen required to live on campus
[4] City or district residence requirements
[5] Accredited by a regional accrediting association or a recognized candidate for accreditation
[6] All female freshman class
[7] All male freshman class

MAJORS AVAILABLE AND PERCENT OF STUDENTS STUDYING IN EACH AREA

Agri.: Agriculture, general; Agronomy (crops & mgmt); Animal Science (husbandry); Fish, Wildlife Mgmt; Forestry
Business: Business/Commerce, general; Accounting; Banking/Finance; Business Economics; Business Mgmt/Admin; Marketing/Purchasing; Secretarial Studies
Comm.: Communications, general; Journalism; Radio/TV (broadcasting); Advertising
Education: Art Education; Distributive Education; Elementary Education; English Education; Mathematics Education; Music Education; Physical Education; Science Education; Secondary Education; Social Science Education; Special Education; Speech Education
Engineering: Engineering, general; Chemical; Civil; Electrical/Electronics/Comm; Industrial/Management; Mechanical
Fine/App. Arts: Architecture; Fine/Applied Arts, general; Art (Paint, draw, sculpt); Art History/Appreciation; Dance; Dramatic Arts (theater arts); Music (liberal arts); Music (perform, compos, theory)
Lang.: French; German; Italian; Latin; Spanish; Russian
Health: Predentistry; Premedicine; Medical/Lab Technology; Nursing (registered nurse); Occupational Therapy; Preoptometry; Prepharmacy; Physical Therapy; Preveterinary Medicine
Home Ec.: Home Economics, general; Clothing and Textiles; Consumer Ec/Home Mgmt; Family Relations/Child Devel; Food and Nutrition/Dietetics; Institution Mgmt
Humanities: Humanities, general; Creative Writing; English, general; Literature, English; Philosophy; Religion; Speech/Forensic Science
Math-Sciences: Mathematics, general; Computer/Info Sciences; Biological Sciences, general; Biology; Botany; Zoology; Physical Sciences, general; Chemistry; Physics
Social Sciences: Crim. Just/Law Enforce; Social Work; Social Sciences, general; Anthropology; Area Studies (Amer., African, etc.); Economics; Geography; History; Prelaw; Political Science; Psychology; Sociology
GS: General Studies
ROTC: Air Force; Army; Navy

Sequence Number	Agri.	Business	Comm.	Education	Engineering	Fine/App. Arts	Lang.	Health	Home Ec.	Humanities	Math-Sciences	Social Sciences	GS	ROTC
1212		020%	3%	029% [1]	1%	1%	1%	7% [1]		2%	3% [1]	2%		Y (Air Force)
1213		019%		011% [1]		2%	1%	5%		8%	010% [1]	016% [1]		
1214		022% [1]	3%	016% [1]	2%	2% [1]		011% [1]	1%	3% [1]	6% [1]	017% [1]		Y (Army)
1215		029%		014% [1]	1%	5%	1%			8% [1]	020% [1]	016%		Y (Air Force)
1216		019% [1]	5%	7% [1]	1%	013% [1]	1%	011% [1]	2%	3% [1]	6% [1]	011% [1]		Y (Army)
1217		024% [1]	6%	018% [1]		5% [1]	1%	9% [1]		2%	8% [1]	011% [1]		Y (Army)
1218		019%	4%	2% [1]	6%	3%	1%	4%		4% [1]	011% [1]	026% [1]		Y Y (Air Force, Army)
1219		032% [1]	9%	010% [1]		5%	1%	4%	2%	4%	013% [1]	018% [1]		Y (Army)
1220		029%	010%	010% [1]		2% [1]	1%	5% [1]	2%	015%	021% [1]	3% [1]		Y (Army)
1221		016% [1]	010%	1% [1]	012%	7% [1]	1%	8% [1]	5%	2% [1]	016% [1]	013% [1]		Y Y (Air Force, Army)
1222		036% [1]	5%	8% [1]		7% [1]	1%	7% [1]		010% [1]	017% [1]	8% [1]		Y (Army)
1223		027%	5%	010% [1]	016% [1]	3%	1%	1%		2% [1]	013% [1]	014% [1]		Y Y (Air Force, Army)
1224	3% [1]	018%	6%	9% [1]	010% [1]	4% [1]	1%	010% [1]	2%	1% [1]	7% [1]	011% [1]		Y Y (Air Force, Army)
1225		017% [1]	2%	6% [1]	015%	1%	1%	5% [1]		2%	016% [1]	8% [1]		Y Y (Army, Navy)
1226				010% [1]			020%			040% [1]		030% [1]		
1227		063%	1%	5% [1]						2% [1]	4% [1]	025% [1]		
1228		020%		027% [1]		9%	2%	[1]		5%	6%	020% [1]		Y Y (Air Force, Army)
1229		013%	012%	017% [1]	3%	7% [1]	1%			017%	011%	018% [1]		
1230		018%	1%	014% [1]		021% [1]	1%	1%		4%	7%	012%		
1231		030%					2%			7% [1]	017% [1]	044%		Y (Army)
1232		027%	012%	6%	[1]	3%	1%	011%		4%	9% [1]	011% [1]		Y (Army)
1233		028%	5%	7% [1]	4%	1%	2%	010% [1]		6%	8%	8% [1]		Y Y Y (Air Force, Army, Navy)
1234		015%	016%	014% [1]	1%	1%	5%	1%		8%	010% [1]	011%		
1235						014%	7%			025% [1]	015% [1]	030% [1]		Y Y (Air Force, Navy)
1236		018%	015%			014% [1]	3%			9% [1]	8%	027% [1]		Y (Army)
1237			4%	017%		014%	5%			014% [1]	8%	035% [1]		
1238			011%	3%		011%	6%			014% [1]	013%	041% [1]		Y (Army)
1239						014%	9%	[1]		017% [1]	9% [1]	041% [1]		Y (Army)

[1] Additional majors available in this area
[2] ROTC available

†Accredited by a nationally recognized accrediting body other than one of the regional accrediting associations

South Atlantic States (continued)

DC, DE, FL, GA, MD, NC, SC, VA, WV

SELECTIVE ADMISSIONS *Majority of accepted students in top 25% of HS class*

Sequence Number	School name (upper entry) City (lower entry)	State	Costs: Resident tuition/fees + room/board	Costs: Room/Board (upper entry) Nonresident tuition/fees + room/board (lower entry)	General Information: Highest degree	Affiliation (upper entry) Religious observance (lower entry)	Size of community	Type of community	Admissions: Fall term application deadline (upper entry) Tests desired or required (lower entry)	Calendar	Fall admission only	Early admission	Deferred admission	Financial Aid: Fall term application deadline (upper entry) Forms to be filed (lower entry)	Number in 10 who— -have need, receive some aid	Under-grads: -are women	-are graduate students	Freshmen: -live on campus	-are minority students	-are nonresidents	-return as sophomores	-complete degree	-enter graduate study	HS GPA (upper entry) 1st year college GPA (lower entry)	Special Programs: Credit by exam	Student designed majors	Fraternities/sororities
Enrollment to 1,000																											
1240	Hood C Frederick	MD	17100	5600	M [5]	UCC	S		3/31 S/A	E		Y	Y	3/31 FA/FF	8	9	1	9	2	5	8	6	7	3.0 2.5	Y	Y	
1241	Peabody Inst Baltimore	MD	17100	5100	D [5]	Priv	V	U	5/01 S/A	S		Y		1/15 FAF	4	5	4	9	2	7	8			3.4			
1242	Saint John's C Annapolis	MD	17400 [3]	4400	M [5]	Priv	S		 A=S	S		Y	Y	 FAF	5	4	1	9	1	8	8	6	6				
1243	Goucher C Towson	MD	18400	5700	M [5]	Priv	M	S	 S/A	E		Y	Y	2/15 FAF	5	8	1	9	1	8	8	6	8	3.2 2.6	Y	Y	
Enrollment 1,000 to 5,000																											
1244	US Naval Acad Annapolis	MD	0 [3]	0	B [5]	Pub	M		2/28 A=S	E		Y		 None		1	0	9	2	9		7	5	3.2 2.5	Y		
1245	North Florida,U of Jacksonville	FL	4300	3000 7600	D [5]	Pub	V	S	7/01 A=S	E		Y		4/01 FF=FA	6	6	1		2	1				3.4	Y		Y
1246	West Florida,U of Pensacola	FL	4500	3200 7700	M [5]	Pub	M	S	7/15 A=S	S		Y	Y	4/01 FA/FF	4	6	1	5	1	1	8			3.2	Y		Y
1247	Shepherd C Shepherdstown	WV	4800 [3]	3300 6900	B [5]	Pub	T		2/01 A/S	E		Y	Y	3/01 FAF	5	6	0	3	1	3	8	6	5	3.4 2.2	Y	Y	Y
1248	Mary Washington C Fredericksburg	VA	6200	3900 8900	M [5]	Pub	S		2/01 SAT	E		Y	Y	3/01 FAF	5	7	0	9	1	3	9	6	3	3.4 2.4	Y	Y	
1249	Saint Mary's C of Md St Mary's City	MD	6500	3900 8100	B [5]	Pub	T		 SAT	E		Y	Y	3/15	2	6	0	7	1	2	9	6	2	3.2 2.8	Y	Y	
1250	Virginia Mil Inst Lexington	VA	6800 [3]	3200 11800	B [5]	Pub	T		3/01 A=S	E		Y	[7]	3/01 FA/FF	7	0	0	9	1	4	8	7	3	2.9 2.2			
1251	Meredith C Raleigh	NC	7900 [3]	2600	M [5]	Bapt OS	L	S	 S/A	E		Y	Y [6]	2/15 FAF	3	9	0	9	1	2	9	7	2	3.0 2.6	Y	Y	
1252	Berry C Rome	GA	10400	3400	M [5]	Priv OS	S		8/01 A=S	E		Y	Y	 FF/FA	9	6	0	9	1	2	7	4	2	3.4	Y	Y	
1253	Morehouse C Atlanta	GA	10700	4500	B [5]	Priv S	V	U	2/15 S/A	E		Y	Y [7]	4/01 FAF	5	0	0	8	9	8	7	5	6	2.9 2.4	Y		Y
1254	Spelman C Atlanta	GA	11600	4700	B [5]	Priv	V	U	2/01 A=S	E		Y	[6]	4/01 FA/FF	8	9	0	9	9	8	8	8	5	3.4	Y		Y
1255	Lenoir-Rhyne C Hickory	NC	11900 [3]	3300	M [5]	Luth	S		 S/A	S		Y	Y	 FA/FF	6	6	1	8	1	5	9	6	1	 2.4	Y	Y	Y
1256	Savannah C Art Des Savannah	GA	12100	4500	M [5]	Priv	M	U	 A=S	Q		Y		6/01 FF=FA	5	5	1	8	1	7	6	6	1	3.0 2.9			
1257	Presbyterian C Clinton	SC	13000 [3]	3100	B [5]	Pres OS	S		 S/A	E		Y	Y	5/10 FA/FF	7	5	0	9	1	5	9	7		3.2 2.4	Y		Y
1258	Wofford C Spartanburg	SC	13000	4000	B [5]	Meth S	M	U	2/01 A=S	4		Y	Y	3/01 FA/FF	7	4	0	9	1	3	9	7	5	 2.4	Y	Y	Y
1259	Florida Inst Techn Melbourne	FL	13300 [3]	3300	D [5]	Priv	M		5/01 S/A	Q		Y	Y	3/15 FAF	6	3	1	9	2	6	7	5	3	3.0 2.9	Y		Y
1260	Tampa,U of Tampa	FL	13800	3700	M [5]	Priv	L	U	 A=S	E		Y	Y	3/15 FA/FF	7	5	1	8	2	7	6	4			Y		Y
1261	Stetson U De Land	FL	14100	4100	P [5]	Bapt OS	S		3/01 A=S	4		Y		 FF=FA	6	5	2	9	1	3	8	6	4	3.3 2.5	Y	Y	Y
1262	Randolph-Macon C Ashland	VA	14200	4300	B [5]	Meth	T		3/01 S/A	4		Y	Y	3/01 FA/FF	3	5	0	9	1	5	9	7	6		Y		Y
1263	Richmond,U of Richmond	VA	14600	2900	P [5]	Bapt	V	S	2/01 Oth	E		Y	Y	2/25	2	5	1	9	1	8	9	8	3	3.0 3.0	Y	Y	Y
1264	Guilford C Greensboro	NC	14700	4200	B [5]	Oth	L	S	3/01 A=S	E		Y	Y	3/01 FA/FF	4	5	0	9	1	6	8	6	3	3.0 2.4	Y	Y	
1265	Loyola C Baltimore	MD	15700	5400	M [5]	Cath	V	S	3/01 S/A	S		Y	Y	3/01 FAF	7	5	1	7	1	5	9	7	2	3.2 2.5	Y		
1266	Western Md C Westminster	MD	16000	4400	M [5]	Priv	S		3/15 S/A	4		Y	Y	3/01 FA/FF	7	5	1	9	1	5	8	6	6	3.1 2.5	Y	Y	Y
1267	Catholic U of Amer Washington	DC	16200	5300	D [5]	Cath S	V	S	2/15 A=S	E		Y	Y	 FAF	6	5	3	8	1	9	9	7	6	3.3		Y	Y
1268	Eckerd C St Petersburg	FL	16200 [3]	3200	B [5]	Pres	L	S	 A=S	4		Y	Y	3/01 FA/FF	5	5	0	9	2	8	8	7	5	3.1 2.5	Y	Y	
1269	Rollins C Winter Park	FL	16900	4000	M [5]	Priv	S		2/15 A=S	4		Y	Y	2/15 FAF	5	5	2	8	2	7	9	7	3	3.0 2.7	Y	Y	Y

▲ **Sequence number—indicates the order of the college in this book only. Do *not* use this number with admissions tests or need analysis services.**

[1] No campus room and board facilities
[2] Room only or board only
[3] Most freshmen required to live on campus
[4] City or district residence requirements
[5] Accredited by a regional accrediting association or a recognized candidate for accreditation
[6] All female freshman class
[7] All male freshman class

MAJORS AVAILABLE AND PERCENT OF STUDENTS STUDYING IN EACH AREA

Sequence Number	Agri.	Business	Comm.	Education	Engineering	Fine/App. Arts	Lang.	Health	Home Ec.	Humanities	Math-Sciences	Social Sciences	GS	ROTC: Air Force	ROTC: Army	ROTC: Navy
1240		026%	8%	011% [1]		2% [1]	2%	1%	7%	4%	017% [1]	021% [1]			Y	
1241																
1242																
1243		010%	6%	5% [1]		9%	5%			015%	012%	035% [1]			Y	
1244					035% [1]					5%	040% [1]	020%				
1245		035% [1]	3%	018% [1]	1%	1%		4% [1]		2%	3% [1]	2%			Y	
1246		024% [1]	6%	020% [1]	1%	4%	1%	2%	1%	2%	026% [1]	012% [1]			Y	
1247		023% [1]	2%	010% [1]	1%	5% [1]	1%	4% [1]	1%	3% [1]	5% [1]	012% [1]		Y	Y	
1248		018%				7%	5%	1%		016% [1]	029% [1]	021% [1]				
1249				8%		8%	8%	1%		7%	018%	050%				
1250		022%			040%		1%			5%	011% [1]	021% [1]		Y	Y	Y
1251		030%		1%		6% [1]	3%	[1]	025%	7%	6% [1]	017% [1]		Y	Y	
1252	3% [1]	013%	1%	012% [1]	1%	3%	1%	1%	3%	4%	6%	3%			Y	
1253		026% [1]	4%	1% [1]	016%	1%	1%			5%	028%	012%		Y	Y	Y
1254				4% [1]	7% [1]	2%	2%			014%	028% [1]	040%		Y	Y	Y
1255		028%	5%	019%	2%	3%	3%	9%		2% [1]	7% [1]	010% [1]				
1256						100% [1]										
1257	1%	028%		8%	1%	2%	3%	1%		010%	020% [1]	026%			Y	
1258		021%					6%			013%	024%	035%			Y	
1259		028%		2%	038% [1]					1%	018% [1]	3%			Y	
1260		036%	6%	010% [1]	1%	1%	1%	3%		4%	016% [1]	015%		Y	Y	
1261		039%		9% [1]		4%	2%			6%	010% [1]	017% [1]			Y	
1262		029%				2%	4%			012% [1]	019%	034% [1]			Y	
1263		025%	1%	2% [1]		1%	6%	1%		012% [1]	9% [1]	035% [1]			Y	
1264		018%		3% [1]	1%	3%	4%	010%		5%	018% [1]	014% [1]				
1265		030%	1%	2% [1]	1%	2% [1]	1%	2%		2% [1]	033% [1]	026% [1]			Y	
1266		019%	011%	011%		6%	2%			7% [1]	3%	024%			Y	
1267		6%	1%	5% [1]	9% [1]	7% [1]	3%	015%		2% [1]	6% [1]	5% [1]		Y	Y	Y
1268		027%		1% [1]		5%	2%			011% [1]	015% [1]	020% [1]			Y	
1269		1%		1% [1]	1%	5%	3%	2%		011% [1]	6%	030% [1]				

Majors listed under each area — Agri.: Agriculture, general; Agronomy (crops & mgmt); Animal Science (husbandry); Fish, Wildlife Mgmt; Forestry. Business: Business/Commerce, general; Accounting; Banking/Finance; Business Economics; Business Mgmt/Admin; Marketing/Purchasing; Secretarial Studies. Comm.: Communications, general; Journalism; Radio/TV (broadcasting); Advertising. Education: Art Education; Distributive Education; Elementary Education; English Education; Mathematics Education; Music Education; Physical Education; Science Education; Secondary Education; Social Science Education; Special Education; Speech Education. Engineering: Engineering, general; Chemical; Civil; Electrical/Electronics/Comm; Industrial/Management; Mechanical. Fine/App. Arts: Architecture; Fine/Applied Arts, general; Art (Paint, draw, sculpt); Art History/Appreciation; Dance; Dramatic Arts (theater arts); Music (liberal arts); Music (perform, compos, theory). Lang.: French; German; Italian; Latin; Spanish; Russian. Health: Predentistry; Premedicine; Medical/Lab Technology; Nursing (registered nurse); Occupational Therapy; Preoptometry; Prepharmacy; Physical Therapy; Preveterinary Medicine. Home Ec.: Home Economics, general; Clothing and Textiles; Consumer Ec/Home Mgmt; Family Relations/Child Devel; Food and Nutrition/Dietetics; Institution Mgmt. Humanities: Humanities, general; Creative Writing; English, general; Literature, English; Philosophy; Religion; Speech/Forensic Science. Math-Sciences: Mathematics, general; Computer/Info Sciences; Biological Sciences, general; Biology; Botany; Zoology; Physical Sciences, general; Chemistry; Physics. Social Sciences: Crim Just/Law Enforce; Social Work; Social Sciences, general; Anthropology; Area Studies (Amer., African, etc.); Economics; Geography; History; Prelaw; Political Science; Psychology; Sociology. GS: General Studies. ROTC: Air Force; Army; Navy.

[1] Additional majors available in this area
[2] ROTC available

†Accredited by a nationally recognized accrediting body other than one of the regional accrediting associations

South Atlantic States
(continued)

DC, DE, FL, GA, MD, NC, SC, VA, WV

SELECTIVE ADMISSIONS *Majority of accepted students in top 25% of HS class*

Sequence Number	School name (upper entry) City (lower entry)	State	Costs: Resident tuition/fees + room/board	Costs: Room/Board (upper entry) Nonresident tuition/fees + room/board (lower entry)	General Information: Highest degree	General Information: Affiliation (upper entry) Religious observance (lower entry)	General Information: Size of community	General Information: Type of community	Admissions: Fall term application deadline (upper entry) Tests desired or required (lower entry)	Admissions: Calendar	Admissions: Fall admission only	Admissions: Early admission	Admissions: Deferred admission	Financial Aid: Fall term application deadline (upper entry) Forms to be filed (lower entry)	Financial Aid: Number in 10 who -have need, receive some aid	Student Profile: Under-grads -are women	Under-grads -are graduate students	Freshmen -live on campus	Freshmen -are minority students	Freshmen -are nonresidents	Freshmen -return as sophomores	Freshmen -complete degree	Freshmen -enter graduate study	HS GPA (upper entry) 1st year college GPA (lower entry)	Special Programs: Credit by exam	Special Programs: Student designed majors	Special Programs: Fraternities/sororities
	Enrollment 5,000 to 15,000																										
1270	Florida Internatl U Miami	FL	4700	3400 9400	D[5]	Pub	V	U	7/01 A=S	E		Y	Y	4/15 FAF	3	6	1	3	6	1	9	6	4	3.4	Y		Y
1271	NC Greensboro,U of Greensboro	NC	4700	3300 9400	D[5]	Pub	L	U	8/01 S/A	E		Y	Y	 FAF	4	7	1	7	1	2	8	5		3.0 2.4	Y	Y	Y
1272	Florida Atlantic U Boca Raton	FL	4900	3500 8200	D[5]	Pub	M	S	5/31 A=S	E		Y	Y	4/01 FA/FF	5	5	2	3	1	1	8	6	2	3.4 2.5	Y	Y	Y
1273	Central Florida,U of Orlando	FL	5000	3700 8400	D[5]	Pub	V	S	3/15 A=S	S		Y	Y	3/15 FF=FA	2	5	1		2	1	7	6		3.3 2.7	Y	Y	Y
1274	Clemson U Clemson	SC	5800	3200 10200	D[5]	Pub	S		 SAT	E		Y		4/01 FAF	6	4	1	8	1	3	9	7		3.4 2.5	Y		Y
1275	Md Baltimore Co,U of Baltimore	MD	6500	4000 11100	D[5]	Pub	M	S	7/31 SAT	4		Y	Y	3/01 FAF	4	5	1	4	3	1	8	3	3	2.9 2.7	Y	Y	Y
1276	Towson St U Towson	MD	6500	4300 8300	M[5]	Pub	V	S	3/01 S/A	4		Y		3/15 FAF	2	6	1	7	1	2	8	5		2.9 2.5	Y	Y	Y
1277	Del,U of Newark	DE	6600	3300 11400	D[5]	Priv	S		3/01 S/A	4		Y	Y	5/01 FA/FF	5	6	1	9	1	7	9	7	2	3.1 2.6		Y	Y
1278	Amer U Washington	DC	19500	6000	D[5]	Meth	V	S	2/01 S/A	E		Y	Y	3/01 FAF	7	6	3	9	2	9	9	6		3.2	Y	Y	Y
1279	George Washington U Washington	DC	19600	6000	D[5]	Priv	V	U	2/01 Oth	E		Y	Y	2/01 FAF	4	5	4	9	3	9	8	6		3.0 2.7	Y	Y	Y
1280	Miami,U of Coral Gables	FL	19700[3]	5600	D[5]	Priv	M	S	 A=S	E		Y	Y	3/01 FAF	7	5	4	8	4	6					Y	Y	Y
	Enrollment over 15,000																										
1281	NC St U Raleigh	NC	4000	2900 8500	D[5]	Pub	L	U	2/01 S/A	E				3/01 FA/FF	4	4	1	9	1	2	9	6	3	3.5 2.6	Y	Y	Y
1282	Florida,U of Gainesville	FL	4600	3300 7300	D[5]	Pub	M	S	2/01 A=S	E		Y		3/01 FF=FA	6	5	2	8	2	1	9	6	3	3.6	Y	Y	Y
1283	Georgia,U of Athens	GA	5200	3100 8600	D[5]	Pub	M		 S/A	Q		Y	Y	3/01 FF/FA	3	5	2	8	1	1	8	6	2	3.7 2.5	Y	Y	Y
1284	SC Main Cam,U of Columbia	SC	5500[3]	2900 9300	D[5]	Pub	L	U	 S/A	E				4/15 FFS	2	5	2	8	2	2	8	6		 2.5	Y	Y	Y
1285	Virginia Tech Blacksburg	VA	5700[3]	2700 9300	D[5]	Pub	S		2/01 SAT	E		Y		2/15 FAF	4	4	2	9	1	2	9	7	1	 2.4		Y	Y
1286	Md-C Park Cam,U of College Park	MD	7100	4700 12000	D[5]	Pub	S		4/30 A=S	S		Y		2/15 FAF	5	5	2	5	3	3		5		3.0 2.6	Y	Y	Y
	HIGHLY SELECTIVE *Majority of accepted students in top 10% of HS class*																										
	Enrollment to 1,000																										
1287	New C-U of S Florida Sarasota	FL	4900[3]	3400 8900	B[5]	Pub	M	S	7/01 A=S	4		Y	Y	 FF/FA	5	5	0	9	1	5	9	4	7	3.5		Y	
	Enrollment 1,000 to 5,000																										
1288	Furman U Greenville	SC	13400[3]	3600	M[5]	Bapt S	L	S	2/01 SAT	O		Y		2/01 FA/FF	6	5	1	9	1	6	9	8	4	3.5 2.7	Y	Y	Y
1289	Washington and Lee U Lexington	VA	14800[3]	3900	P[5]	Priv	T		2/01 A=S	O			Y	 FA/FF	2	3	2	9	1	8	9	8	4	 2.8	Y	Y	Y
1290	Davidson C Davidson	NC	17900[3]	4200	B[5]	Pres S	T		2/01 A=S	E		Y	Y	2/01 FAF	3	4	0	9	1	7	9	9	7	3.5 2.8		Y	Y
1291	Johns Hopkins U Baltimore	MD	21000[3]	5600	D[5]	Priv	V	U	1/01 S/A	4		Y	Y	1/01 FAF	6	3	3	9	2	8	9	8	7	 3.0		Y	Y
	Enrollment 5,000 to 15,000																										
1292	Georgia Inst Techn Atlanta	GA	5700	3700 9500	D[5]	Pub	V	U	2/01 S/A	Q		Y	Y	3/01 Oth	3	2	2	8	2	4	8	6	2	3.6 2.4			Y
1293	Wm & Mary,C of Williamsburg	VA	7100[3]	3700 12900	D[5]	Pub	S		1/15 SAT	E		Y	Y	2/15 FAF	3	5	3	9	1	3	9	8	3	 2.6	Y	Y	Y
1294	Wake Forest U Winston-Salem	NC	14500[3]	3700	D[5]	Priv S	M	S	1/15 SAT	S		Y	Y	3/01 FAF	3	4	3	9	1	7	9	8	5		Y		Y
1295	Emory U Atlanta	GA	19800[3]	4500	D[5]	Meth	V	S	2/01 A=S	S		Y	Y	2/15 FAF	5	5	5	9	2	8	9	8	6	3.5 3.0		Y	Y

▲ Sequence number—indicates the order of the college in this book only. Do *not* use this number with admissions tests or need analysis services.

[1] No campus room and board facilities
[2] Room only or board only
[3] Most freshmen required to live on campus
[4] City or district residence requirements
[5] Accredited by a regional accrediting association or a recognized candidate for accreditation
[6] All female freshman class
[7] All male freshman class

MAJORS AVAILABLE AND PERCENT OF STUDENTS STUDYING IN EACH AREA

Columns by area — Agri.: Agriculture, general; Agronomy (crops & mgmt); Animal Science (husbandry); Fish, Wildlife Mgmt; Forestry. Business: Business/Commerce, general; Accounting; Banking/Finance; Business Economics; Business Mgmt/Admin; Marketing/Purchasing; Secretarial Studies. Comm.: Communications, general; Journalism; Radio/TV (broadcasting); Advertising. Education: Art Education; Distributive Education; Elementary Education; English Education; Mathematics Education; Music Education; Physical Education; Science Education; Secondary Education; Social Science Education; Special Education; Speech Education. Engineering: Engineering, general; Chemical; Civil; Electrical/Electronics/Comm; Industrial/Management; Mechanical. Fine/App. Arts: Architecture; Fine/Applied Arts, general; Art (Paint, draw, sculpt); Art History/Appreciation; Dance; Dramatic Arts (theater arts); Music (liberal arts); Music (perform, compos, theory). Lang.: French; German; Italian; Latin; Spanish; Russian. Health: Predentistry; Premedicine; Medical Lab Technology; Nursing (registered nurse); Occupational Therapy; Preoptometry; Prepharmacy; Physical Therapy; Preveterinary Medicine. Home Ec.: Home Economics, general; Clothing and Textiles; Consumer Ec/Home Mgmt; Family Relations/Child Devel; Food and Nutrition/Dietetics; Institution Mgmt. Humanities: Humanities, general; Creative Writing; English, general; Literature, English; Philosophy; Religion; Speech/Forensic Science. Math-Sciences: Mathematics, general; Computer/Info Sciences; Biological Sciences, general; Biology; Botany; Zoology; Physical Sciences, general; Chemistry; Physics. Social Sciences: Crim Just/Law Enforce; Social Work; Social Sciences, general; Anthropology; Area Studies (Amer., African, etc.); Economics; Geography; History; Political Science; Prelaw; Psychology; Sociology. GS: General Studies. ROTC: Air Force; Army; Navy.

Sequence Number	Agri.	Business	Comm.	Education	Engineering	Fine/App. Arts	Lang.	Health	Home Ec.	Humanities	Math-Sciences	Social Sciences	GS	ROTC
1270		024% ¹	3%	010% ¹	7% ¹	2% ¹	1%	4% ¹	1%	1% ¹	013% ¹	012% ¹		YY
1271		023% ¹		016% ¹		8% ¹	1%	8% ¹	9%	013% ¹	5% ¹	016% ¹		YY
1272		020% ¹	3%	012% ¹	020% ¹	1% ¹	1%	5% ¹		2% ¹	017% ¹	019% ¹		Y
1273		028% ¹	8%	014% ¹	015% ¹	2% ¹	1%	4% ¹		2%	8% ¹	011% ¹		YY
1274	3% ¹	028% ¹		011% ¹	021% ¹	7% ¹	2%	3%		3%	9% ¹	9% ¹		YY
1275					7%	6% ¹	1%	011% ¹		4% ¹	026% ¹	025% ¹		Y
1276		027%	9%	014% ¹		4%	1%	7% ¹		3%	010% ¹	012% ¹		YY
1277	4% ¹	012% ¹	3%	8% ¹	8% ¹	1% ¹	4%	2%	6%	3% ¹	010%	019% ¹		YY
1278		029% ¹	015%	2%		2% ¹	1%	1%		2%	9% ¹	030% ¹		YYY
1279		023%	4%	2% ¹	9%	3%	2%	7% ¹		8% ¹	3% ¹	026% ¹		Y
1280		023% ¹	8%	1%	010% ¹	013% ¹	1%	3% ¹		3%	015% ¹	011% ¹		YY
1281	010% ¹	011%	2%	2% ¹	037% ¹	1% ¹	1%			3%	3% ¹	2% ¹		YYY
1282	3% ¹	011% ¹	8% ¹	3% ¹	012% ¹	5% ¹	1%	9% ¹		3% ¹	7% ¹	011% ¹		YYY
1283	5% ¹	025% ¹	8%	014% ¹	1% ¹	5% ¹	1%	4% ¹	2%	7% ¹	5% ¹	012% ¹		YY
1284		025% ¹	6%	1%	8%	4% ¹	1%	6%		5% ¹	9% ¹	019% ¹		YYY
1285	7% ¹	018% ¹	3%	4% ¹	025% ¹	6% ¹	1%	1%	7%	2%	014% ¹	8% ¹		YYY
1286	2% ¹	8% ¹	3%	5% ¹	011% ¹	2% ¹	1%	1% ¹	2%	011% ¹	010% ¹	014% ¹		Y
1287						2%	3%			032% ¹	023% ¹	040% ¹		YY
1288		015%		5%	5%	5%	5%	010%		010%	015% ¹	020%		Y
1289		010%	9%		1%	3%	010%			8% ¹	012% ¹	043% ¹		
1290		1%		1%	1%	3%	5%	1%		015% ¹	026% ¹	042%		YY
1291					022% ¹		2%	6%		9% ¹	031% ¹	020% ¹		YY
1292		020%			064% ¹	4%					011% ¹	1%		YYY
1293										¹	¹	¹		Y
1294		018%	8%	5% ¹		3%	2%	2% ¹		011% ¹	015% ¹	036%		Y
1295		010%		1% ¹		3% ¹	4%	6%		014% ¹	014% ¹	032% ¹		

[1] Additional majors available in this area
[2] ROTC available

†Accredited by a nationally recognized accrediting body other than one of the regional accrediting associations

Sequence Number	School name (upper entry) City (lower entry)	State	Costs: Resident tuition/fees + room/board	Costs: Room/Board (upper entry) Nonresident tuition/fees + room/board (lower entry)	General Information: Highest degree	General Information: Affiliation (upper entry) Religious observance (lower entry)	General Information: Size of community	General Information: Type of community	Admissions: Fall term application deadline (upper entry) Tests desired or required (lower entry)	Admissions: Calendar	Admissions: Fall admission only	Admissions: Early admission	Admissions: Deferred admission	Financial Aid: Fall term application deadline (upper entry) Forms to be filed (lower entry)	Number in 10 who—: -have need, receive some aid	Under-grads: -are women	Under-grads: -are graduate students	Freshmen: -live on campus	Freshmen: -are minority students	Freshmen: -are nonresidents	Freshmen: -return as sophomores	Freshmen: -complete degree	Freshmen: -enter graduate study	HS GPA (upper entry) 1st year college GPA (lower entry)	Special Programs: Credit by exam	Special Programs: Student designed majors	Special Programs: Fraternities/sororities
	South Atlantic States (continued) DC, DE, FL, GA, MD, NC, SC, VA, WV **HIGHLY SELECTIVE** *Majority of accepted students in top 10% of HS class*																										
	Enrollment 5,000 to 15,000																										
1296	Duke U Durham	NC	20100	5000	D[5]	Meth	M	S	1/01 A=S	E		Y	Y	 FAF	4	4	4	9	2	9	9	9	5	3.6 3.0		Y	Y
1297	Georgetown U Washington	DC	22100 [3]	6300	D[5]	Cath	V	U	1/10 A=S	E		Y	Y	1/15 FAF	6	5	4	8	2	9	9	9	9			Y	
	Enrollment over 15,000																										
1298	NC Chapel Hill,U of Chapel Hill	NC	4600	3500 9300	D[5]	Pub	M		1/15 SAT	E		Y		 FA/FF	3	6	2	9	2	2	9	7	4	 2.7	Y	Y	Y
1299	Florida St U Tallahassee	FL	5000	3600 8500	D[5]	Pub	M	S	3/02 A=S	S		Y		4/01 FF/FA	4	5	1	5	1	2	8	5		3.5	Y		Y
1300	Virginia,U of Charlottesville	VA	6100 [3]	3200 11400	D[5]	Pub	M	S	1/02 SAT	E				3/01 FAF	3	5	3	9	2	3	9	9	7	 2.9		Y	Y
	ADVANCED STANDING *Freshmen not accepted; college junior standing often required*																										
	Enrollment 1,000 to 5,000																										
1301	Baltimore,U of Baltimore	MD	1800	[1] 3200	P[5]	Pub	V	U	 None	S				5/01 FA/FF		5	1		2			6	2		Y		
	Middle Atlantic States NJ, NY, PA **OPEN ADMISSIONS** *All HS graduates accepted, to limit of capacity*																										
	Enrollment to 1,000																										
1302	Rutgers-UC,New Bruns New Brunswick	NJ		[1]	B[5]	Pub	S		6/29 A=S	E			Y	 FAF		5	0	0	2	1					Y	Y	
1303	Manna Bible Inst Philadelphia	PA	2200	[1]	†	Oth OS	V	U	8/29 A=S	4		Y		8/29 None	7	4	0	0	9	1	7	1	6	 2.8			
1304	Acad the New Church Bryn Athyn	PA	6100	2900	P[5]	Oth OS	T		3/01 S/A	O			Y	4/15 Oth	9	5	0	7		5	7	8	1		Y		
1305	Rabbinical C of Amer Morristown	NJ	10000	4500	B †	Jew OS	S		 Oth	S			[7]	9/30		0	0	9	0								
	Enrollment 1,000 to 5,000																										
1306	CUNY Medgar Evers C Brooklyn	NY	1300	[1] 2100	B[5]	Pub	V	U	 None	E			Y	9/30 Oth		7	0	0	9	1	6	3			Y		
1307	SUNY Empire St C Saratoga Sprgs	NY	1700	[1] 5000	M[5]	Pub	S		 None	O		Y		 FA/FF	6	4	0	0	2	1					Y		
1308	Boricua C New York	NY	5300	[1]	B[5]	Priv	V	U	 Oth	O			Y	5/01 FAF	2	8	0	0	9	0	6	2			Y		
	Enrollment 5,000 to 15,000																										
1309	Edison St Ext Deg C Trenton	NJ	400	[1] 600	B[5]	Pub	M	U	 None	O				7/01 FAF	1	4	0	0	2				5		Y	Y	
1310	USNY Reg C Degree Albany	NY	400	[1]	B[5]	Pub	M		 None	O				5/01 FFS		5	0						5		Y		
1311	CUNY NY City Tech C Brooklyn	NY	1500	[1] 4100	B[5]	Pub	V	U	7/01 None	E				6/30 Oth	6	5	0	0	9	1	6			 2.5	Y		
1312	CUNY C Staten Island Staten Island	NY	1600	[1] 4200	M[5]	Pub	L	S	9/01 None	S				5/31 Oth	2	6	0	0	2	1	6	2	2	 2.0	Y	Y	
1313	Mercy C-NY Dobbs Ferry	NY	6600	[1]	M[5]	Priv	T		 S/A	4		Y	Y	2/01 FAF	7	6	0	0	4	1		6	3	2.8 2.5	Y	Y	
	Enrollment over 15,000																										
1314	CUNY NY City New York	NY	1500	[1] 4100	D[5]	Pub	V	U	1/15 None	S		Y	Y	10/15 Oth	8	6	9		7	1	7				Y	Y	

▲ Sequence number—indicates the order of the college in this book only. Do *not* use this number with admissions tests or need analysis services.

[1] No campus room and board facilities
[2] Room only or board only
[3] Most freshmen required to live on campus
[4] City or district residence requirements
[5] Accredited by a regional accrediting association or a recognized candidate for accreditation
[6] All female freshman class
[7] All male freshman class

MAJORS AVAILABLE AND PERCENT OF STUDENTS STUDYING IN EACH AREA

Percent of students studying in each area ([1] = additional majors available in this area) and ROTC:

Sequence Number	Agri.	Business	Comm.	Education	Engineering	Fine/App. Arts	Lang.	Health	Home Ec.	Humanities	Math-Sciences	Social Sciences	GS	ROTC Air Force	ROTC Army	ROTC Navy
1296					011%	3%	2%	2%		011% [1]	015% [1]	052% [1]		Y	Y	Y
1297		019%		[1]		1%	013%	4%		9% [1]	8%	046% [1]		Y	Y	Y
1298		017% [1]	010%	5% [1]		2%	1%	011% [1]		011% [1]	010% [1]	028% [1]		Y		Y
1299		027% [1]	7%	013% [1]	2%	6% [1]	1%	3% [1]	4%	5% [1]	5% [1]	027% [1]		Y	Y	Y
1300		6%		1%	012% [1]	4% [1]	1%	3% [1]		7% [1]	5% [1]	016% [1]		Y	Y	Y
1301		071% [1]								4%	1% [1]	9% [1]			Y	
1302	[1]	020% [1]	6%	[1]		3%	1%		1%	010% [1]	017% [1]	037% [1]		Y	Y	
1303				015%		2%		2%		060%	5%	015%				
1304				020%						060%						
1305										100%						
1306		044%		010%				020%			014%	010% [1]				
1307		051% [1]		5% [1]		2%				[1]	[1]	018% [1]				
1308		5%		010%						2%		012% [1]				
1309	[1]	032% [1]	1%		022%	1% [1]	1%	6% [1]		012%	4% [1]	020% [1]				
1310		010%			8%			042%			[1]					
1311		038% [1]	1%		1%	2%		016%		1%	3%	2%				
1312		029%		[1]	4%	3% [1]	1%	011%		7% [1]	7% [1]	031% [1]				
1313		057%				2%	4%	[1]		9%	014% [1]	014%		Y		
1314	[1]	033% [1]	1%	2% [1]	2%	2% [1]	1%	011% [1]	1%	2% [1]	010% [1]	013% [1]			Y	

Majors available (■) — Agri., Business, Comm., Education, Engineering:

Sequence Number	Agriculture, general	Agronomy (crops & mgmt)	Animal Science (husbandry)	Fish, Wildlife Mgmt	Forestry	Business/Commerce, general	Accounting	Banking/Finance	Business Economics	Business Mgmt/Admin	Marketing/Purchasing	Secretarial Studies	Communications, general	Journalism	Radio/TV (broadcasting)	Advertising	Art Education	Distributive Education	Elementary Education	English Education	Mathematics Education	Music Education	Physical Education	Science Education	Secondary Education	Social Science Education	Special Education	Speech Education	Engineering, general	Chemical	Civil	Electrical/Electronics/Comm	Industrial/Management	Mechanical
1296																													■		■	■		■
1297						■	■	■		■	■																		■					
1298						■	■							■	■		■		■	■	■	■	■	■	■	■	■	■						
1299						■	■	■		■	■		■		■	■	■		■	■	■	■	■	■	■	■	■			■	■	■	■	■
1300						■													■				■		■		■		■	■	■	■		■
1301						■	■	■	■	■	■		■			■																		
1302							■	■		■	■		■	■																				
1303																																		
1304																			■															
1305																																		
1306						■	■												■															
1307						■				■																								
1308						■													■															
1309					■	■	■	■		■	■		■	■																				
1310						■	■	■		■	■																							
1311													■																					
1312						■	■	■		■			■																■					
1313						■	■	■		■				■																				
1314						■	■	■	■	■	■	■	■	■	■	■	■	■	■	■	■	■	■	■	■	■	■	■	■	■	■	■		■

Majors available (■) — Fine/App. Arts, Lang., Health, Home Ec.:

Sequence Number	Architecture	Fine/Applied Arts, general	Art (Paint, draw, sculpt)	Art History/Appreciation	Dance	Dramatic Arts (theater arts)	Music (liberal arts)	Music (perform, compos, theory)	French	German	Italian	Latin	Spanish	Russian	Predentistry	Premedicine	Medical/Lab Technology	Nursing (registered nurse)	Occupational Therapy	Preoptometry	Prepharmacy	Physical Therapy	Preveterinary Medicine	Home Economics, general	Clothing and Textiles	Consumer Ec/Home Mgmt	Family Relations/Child Devel	Food and Nutrition/Dietetics	Institution Mgmt
1296		■		■		■	■		■	■	■	■	■	■															
1297		■							■	■	■		■	■				■											
1298			■	■		■	■	■	■	■	■	■	■	■	■	■	■	■			■	■							
1299		■	■	■	■	■	■	■	■	■	■	■	■	■	■	■	■	■		■	■		■	■	■		■	■	
1300	■		■			■	■		■	■	■		■					■											
1301																													
1302		■	■	■	■	■	■		■	■	■	■	■	■														■	
1303																													
1304																													
1305																													
1306																■		■											
1307		■																											
1308																													
1309			■		■		■		■	■	■		■	■			■	■									■		
1310							■		■	■			■					■											
1311																													
1312			■	■		■	■						■				■	■											
1313		■						■	■		■		■				■						■						
1314	■	■	■	■	■	■	■	■	■	■	■	■	■	■			■	■	■			■		■		■		■	

Majors available (■) — Humanities, Math-Sciences, Social Sciences, General Studies:

Sequence Number	Humanities, general	Creative Writing	English, general	Literature, English	Philosophy	Religion	Speech/Forensic Science	Mathematics, general	Computer/Info Sciences	Biological Sciences, general	Biology	Botany	Zoology	Physical Sciences, general	Chemistry	Physics	Crim Just/Law Enforce	Social Work	Social Sciences, general	Anthropology	Area Studies (Amer., African, etc.)	Economics	Geography	History	Prelaw	Political Science	Psychology	Sociology	General Studies
1296			■		■	■		■	■		■				■	■				■	■	■		■		■	■	■	
1297			■		■	■		■	■	■	■			■	■	■						■		■		■	■	■	■
1298			■	■	■	■	■	■	■	■	■			■	■	■	■		■	■	■	■	■	■		■	■	■	■
1299	■	■	■	■	■	■		■	■	■	■			■	■	■	■	■	■	■	■	■	■	■		■	■	■	
1300			■		■	■	■	■	■		■				■	■				■	■	■		■		■	■	■	
1301		■	■	■					■								■					■		■	■	■	■	■	■
1302			■		■	■		■	■	■	■			■	■	■	■		■	■	■	■	■	■	■	■	■	■	
1303						■			■																				
1304	■					■																							■
1305						■																							
1306											■																		
1307	■	■	■	■	■	■	■	■	■	■	■			■	■	■	■	■	■	■		■	■	■		■	■	■	
1308																													■
1309	■		■	■	■	■		■	■		■				■	■	■	■	■	■		■	■	■		■	■	■	■
1310				■	■			■	■		■				■	■						■	■	■		■	■	■	■
1311																													
1312	■		■	■	■			■	■	■	■			■	■	■					■	■		■		■	■	■	■
1313				■				■	■	■	■						■	■	■					■		■	■	■	■
1314	■	■	■	■	■		■	■	■	■	■	■	■	■	■	■	■	■		■	■	■	■	■	■	■	■	■	■

[1] Additional majors available in this area
[2] ROTC available

†Accredited by a nationally recognized accrediting body other than one of the regional accrediting associations

Middle Atlantic States
(continued)

NJ, NY, PA

LIBERAL ADMISSIONS *Some accepted students from lower half of HS class*

Sequence Number	School name (upper entry) City (lower entry)	State	Costs: Resident tuition/fees + room/board	Costs: Room/Board (upper entry) Nonresident tuition/fees + room/board (lower entry)	General Information: Highest degree	Affiliation (upper entry) Religious observance (lower entry)	Size of community	Type of community	Admissions: Fall term application deadline (upper entry) Tests desired or required (lower entry)	Calendar	Fall admission only	Early admission	Deferred admission	Financial Aid: Fall term application deadline (upper entry) Forms to be filed (lower entry)	Number in 10 who— -have need, receive some aid	Under-grads: -are women	-are graduate students	Freshmen: -live on campus	-are minority students	-are nonresidents	-return as sophomores	-complete degree	-enter graduate study	HS GPA (upper entry) 1st year college GPA (lower entry)	Special Programs: Credit by exam	Student designed majors	Fraternities/sororities
	Enrollment to 1,000																										
1315	Rutgers-UC,Newark Newark	NJ		[1]	B [5]	Pub	L	U	8/01 A=S	E		Y	Y	FAF		6	0	0	6	1					Y	Y	
1316	Gratz C Melrose Park	PA	3300	[1]	M [5]	Jew	V	S		S		Y	Y	Oth	7	7	1	0		4	5	1	6				
1317	Baptist Bible C Pa Clarks Summit	PA	7700 [3]	2800	P [5]	Bapt OS	T		8/15 A=S	E		Y	Y	7/01 None	7	6	1	9	1	6	7	5		2.8 2.7	Y		
1318	Lancaster Bible C Lancaster	PA	8400 [3]	2700	B [5]	Oth OS	M	S	A/S	E		Y	Y	7/01 FFS	8	5	0	6	1	2	7	5	5	2.8 2.3	Y		
1319	Human Services,C of New York	NY	9500	[1]	M [5]	Priv	V	U	Oth	T			Y	Oth	8	6	1		8	1	7	3	6		Y		
1320	Dominican C Orangeburg	NY	10800	4800	B [5]	Cath	T		A=S	S		Y	Y	FAF	5	7	0	1	1	3	6	6	3	2.7 2.5	Y		
1321	Bloomfield C Bloomfield	NJ	11000	3700	B [5]	Pres	M	S	S/A	S		Y	Y	FA/FF	9	6	0	4	7	1	8	8	1	2.7 2.5	Y	Y	Y
1322	Centenary C Hackettstown	NJ	14200	4700	B [5]	Meth	S		A=S	E			Y	4/30 FAF	8	8	0	7	3	4	9	5	1	2.4 2.6	Y	Y	Y
	Enrollment 1,000 to 5,000																										
1323	CUNY York C Jamaica	NY	1500	[1] 4500	B [5]	Pub	V	U	None	S		Y		5/15 Oth	8	6	0	0	9	0	6			2.0	Y		
1324	Lincoln U Lincoln Univ	PA	5200 [3]	2700 6400	M [5]	Pub OS	T		S/A	T		Y	Y	3/15 FF=FA	9	6	1	9	9	5	7	3	4	2.5			Y
1325	SUNY at Old Westbury Old Westbury	NY	5400	3600 8500	B [5]	Pub	T		8/15 A=S	E			Y	5/01 FF=FA	5	6	0	2	4	1	6	3	4	 2.0	Y		Y
1326	Acad of Aeronautics Flushing	NY	5500	3000	B [5]	Priv	V	U	A=S	E		Y		6/30 FAF	7	1	0	0	7	1	6	7		2.5 2.5	Y		
1327	Cheyney U Cheyney	PA	5500	3000 7500	M [5]	Pub	T		6/30 S/A	E				4/01 FF=FA	9	5	1	7	9	5	2	3	1		Y		Y
1328	Medaille C Buffalo	NY	6600	[1]	B [5]	Priv	M	U	8/01 Oth	E		Y	Y	3/15 FAF	9	5	0	0	3	1	5	3	2		Y	Y	
1329	Pittsbg Greensburg,U Greensburg	PA	7300	3000 11600	B [5]	Priv	S		8/01 A=S	T		Y	Y	5/01 FAF	6	5	0	2	1	1	7	6	2	2.6 2.4	Y	Y	Y
1330	Robert Morris C Cora Coraopolis	PA	8900	3500	M [5]	Priv	S		A=S	E		Y	Y	5/01 Oth	7	5	2	5	1	1	8	6	2		Y		Y
1331	Dowling C Oakdale Long Is	NY	9100 [2]	2500	M [5]	Priv	T		A=S	S		Y	Y	4/01 FA/FF	7	6	0	1	1	1	6	3	4	2.7 2.5	Y		
1332	Cazenovia C Cazenovia	NY	11800	4100	B [5]	Priv	T		9/01 A=S	O		Y	Y	9/01 FA/FF	9	6	0	9	1	2	7			2.3 2.3	Y		
	Enrollment 5,000 to 15,000																										
1333	Kean College of NJ Union	NJ	5100	3000 5800	M [5]	Pub	L	S	6/01 S/A	4		Y	Y	4/01 FF=FA	5	6	1	2	3	1	8	7	1		Y		Y
1334	NY Inst Techn Old Westbury	NY	12100	4900	P [5]	Priv	T		A=S	S		Y	Y	FAF	6	3	1	1	3	1	6	5	2	2.6 2.4	Y		Y
	TRADITIONAL ADMISSIONS *Majority of accepted students in top 50% of HS class*																										
	Enrollment to 1,000																										
1335	Rutgers-UC,Camden Camden	NJ		[1]	B [5]	Pub	M		7/15 A=S	E		Y	Y	FAF		5	0	0	2	1					Y	Y	
1336	Valley Forge Chr C Phoenixville	PA	6000 [3]	2500	B †	Oth OS	S		8/15 A=S	E		Y		Oth	7	4	0		1			4	1	2.5 2.3	Y		
1337	SUNY Health Syracuse Syracuse	NY	6200 [2]	4500 10000	D [5]	Pub	L	U	A=S	E		Y	Y	FFS	7	4	8		1		9	9	2		Y		
1338	Wadhams Hall Sem-C Ogdensburg	NY	6600	3200	B [5]	Cath O	S		8/01 Oth	E				8/01 FA/FF	8	1	0	9	3	3	6	5	9		Y		
1339	Felician C Lodi	NJ	7000	[1]	B [5]	Cath S	S		S/A	S			Y	FAF	5	8	0	0	2	1	8	5	1	 2.5	Y	Y	Y
1340	Rutgers-M Gross Art New Brunswick	NJ	7200	3800 10200	D [5]	Pub	S		1/15 A=S	E		Y	Y	FAF	4	6	3	9	2	2	8	5			Y		Y
1341	NY Sch Interior Des New York	NY	7300	[1]	B †	Priv	V	U	S/A	4			Y	7/01 FAF	5	9	0	0	3	1	8	9		 2.6	Y		

▲ Sequence number—indicates the order of the college in this book only. Do *not* use this number with admissions tests or need analysis services.

[1] No campus room and board facilities
[2] Room only or board only
[3] Most freshmen required to live on campus
[4] City or district residence requirements
[5] Accredited by a regional accrediting association or a recognized candidate for accreditation
[6] All female freshman class
[7] All male freshman class

MAJORS AVAILABLE AND PERCENT OF STUDENTS STUDYING IN EACH AREA

Sequence Number	Agri.	Business	Comm.	Education	Engineering	Fine/App. Arts	Lang.	Health	Home Ec.	Humanities	Math-Sciences	Social Sciences	GS	ROTC
	Agriculture, general; Agronomy (crops & mgmt); Animal Science (husbandry); Fish, Wildlife Mgmt; Forestry	Business/Commerce, general; Accounting; Banking/Finance; Business Economics; Business Mgmt/Admin; Marketing/Purchasing; Secretarial Studies	Communications, general; Journalism; Radio/TV (broadcasting); Advertising	Art Education; Distributive Education; Elementary Education; English Education; Mathematics Education; Music Education; Physical Education; Science Education; Secondary Education; Social Science Education; Special Education; Speech Education	Engineering, general; Chemical; Civil; Electrical/Electronics/Comm; Industrial/Management; Mechanical; Architecture	Fine/Applied Arts, general; Art (Paint, draw, sculpt); Art History/Appreciation; Dance; Dramatic Arts (theater arts); Music (liberal arts); Music (perform, compos, theory)	French; German; Italian; Latin; Spanish; Russian	Predentistry; Premedicine; Medical/Lab Technology; Nursing (registered nurse); Occupational Therapy; Preoptometry; Prepharmacy; Physical Therapy; Preveterinary Medicine	Home Economics, general; Clothing and Textiles; Consumer Ec/Home Mgmt; Family Relations/Child Devel; Food and Nutrition/Dietetics; Institution Mgmt	Humanities, general; Creative Writing; English, general; Literature, English; Philosophy; Religion; Speech/Forensic Science	Mathematics, general; Computer/Info Sciences; Biological Sciences, general; Biology; Botany; Zoology; Physical Sciences, general; Chemistry; Physics	Crim Just/Law Enforce; Social Work; Social Sciences, general; Anthropology; Area Studies (Amer., African, etc.); Economics; Geography; History; Prelaw; Political Science; Psychology; Sociology	General Studies	Air Force; Army; Navy
1315		057% [1]					1%			4%	5% [1]	030%		YY
1316				015% [1]			015%					[1]		
1317		6%		033%		3%				031%				
1318										100%				
1319		018%												
1320		036%		3% [1]				018% [1]		8%	9% [1]	023%		Y
1321		056%	4%			1%	1%	015%		2%	3% [1]	2%		YYY
1322	017%	031%	4%	018% [1]		7% [1]			4%	1%	8% [1]			
1323		030%		013% [1]		1%	1%	014% [1]		1%	015% [1]	025%		
1324		024%	4%	012% [1]	1%		1%	2%		7% [1]	015% [1]	011% [1]		Y
1325		030% [1]	1%	014% [1]	1%	3%	1%			1% [1]	013%	9% [1]		YY
1326					100% [1]									Y
1327		027% [1]	5%	013% [1]	5%	2%		1%	3%	1%	010%	016% [1]		Y
1328	4%	020%	7%	7% [1]				1%	1%	1%	6% [1]	014% [1]		Y
1329		035%	2%	1%	014%	1%	1%	010%	1%	2%	5% [1]	013%		
1330		089% [1]	2%	2% [1]				2%		1%	2% [1]	1%		YY
1331		043% [1]		9% [1]	9%	3%	1%	1%		4%	011% [1]	012%		YY
1332	8%	020%	1%	8%		038%			2%			2%		
1333		027%	3%	016% [1]	3%	6% [1]		9%		2%	011% [1]	016% [1]		YY
1334		017%	[1] 010%		020%	019% [1]		[1]		013%	8% [1]	3%		Y
1335										022%	052%	026% [1]		YYY
1336				025%						075%				
1337								100% [1]						
1338										100%				
1339		012%		010%		2%		037%		7%	010% [1]	011%		
1340						100%								YY
1341						100% [1]								
Sequence Number	Agri.	Business	Comm.	Education	Engineering	Fine/App. Arts	Lang.	Health	Home Ec.	Humanities	Math-Sciences	Social Sciences	GS	ROTC

[1] Additional majors available in this area
[2] ROTC available

†Accredited by a nationally recognized accrediting body other than one of the regional accrediting associations

Middle Atlantic States
(continued)

NJ, NY, PA

TRADITIONAL ADMISSIONS *Majority of accepted students in top 50% of HS class*

Sequence Number — Enrollment to 1,000

Sequence Number	School name (upper entry) City (lower entry)	State	Costs: Resident tuition/fees + room/board	Costs: Room/Board (upper entry) Nonresident tuition/fees + room/board (lower entry)	General Information: Highest degree	General Information: Affiliation (upper entry) Religious observance (lower entry)	General Information: Size of community	General Information: Type of community	Admissions: Fall term application deadline (upper entry) Tests desired or required (lower entry)	Admissions: Calendar	Admissions: Fall admission only	Admissions: Early admission	Admissions: Deferred admission	Financial Aid: Fall term application deadline (upper entry) Forms to be filed (lower entry)	Number in 10 who— -have need, receive some aid	Under-grads: -are women	Under-grads: -are graduate students	Freshmen: -live on campus	Freshmen: -are minority students	Freshmen: -are nonresidents	Freshmen: -return as sophomores	Freshmen: -complete degree	Freshmen: -enter graduate study	Freshmen: HS GPA (upper entry) 1st year college GPA (lower entry)	Special Programs: Credit by exam	Special Programs: Student designed majors	Special Programs: Fraternities/sororities
1342	Neumann C Aston	PA	7500	[1]	M [5]	Cath	S		S/A	E		Y	Y	4/01 FAF	6	8	0	0	1	2	8		1	2.9 3.0	Y	Y	Y
1343	Pittsbg Bradford,U Bradford	PA	7800 [3]	3500 12400	B [5]	Pub	S		7/01 A=S	E		Y	Y	3/01 FF=FA	7	5	0	6	1	1	9	7	2	3.0	Y	Y	Y
1344	Lab Inst of Merchand New York	NY	8300	[1]	B [5]	Priv	V	U	A=S	4			Y	4/01 FF=FA	8	9	0	0	2	5	9	9	1	2.5 2.5	Y		
1345	Phila C of the Bible Langhorne	PA	9300	3400	B [5]	Oth OS	T		S/A	E		Y	Y	5/01 FA/FF	9	5	0	7	2	4	6	4	5	2.9	Y		
1346	La Roche C Pittsburgh	PA	10100	3600	M [5]	Cath	L	S	S/A	E		Y	Y	Oth	8	7	3	6	1	1	6	6		2.6	Y		Y
1347	Nyack C Nyack	NY	10300 [3]	3300	M [5]	Oth OS	S		S/A	E			Y	FAF	9	5	2	8	2	5	6	5	6	2.7	Y		
1348	Georgian Court C Lakewood	NJ	10400	3700	M [5]	Cath OS	S		8/01 SAT	E		Y		10/01 FAF	8	9	0	4	1	1	8	6	2		Y		
1349	Mount Saint Mary C Newburgh	NY	10600	4000	M [5]	Cath	S		8/15 A=S	4		Y	Y	FA/FF	9	7	1	7	1	2	7	7	4	2.9 2.7	Y	Y	
1350	Allentown C Center Valley	PA	11000	3800	M [5]	Cath OS	T		S/A	E		Y	Y	Oth	8	5	0	8	1	3	8	6	2	3.0 2.4	Y		Y
1351	Caldwell C Caldwell	NJ	11000	3800	B [5]	Cath S	S		A=S	S		Y	Y	8/15 FA/FF	7	7	0	5	3	1	7	4	1		Y		Y
1352	Misericordia,C Dallas	PA	11500	4000	M [5]	Cath S	T		A=S	E		Y		4/01 Oth	9	7	1	5	1	2	9	8	1	3.2 2.9	Y	Y	Y
1353	Seton Hill C Greensburg	PA	11500	3400	B [5]	Cath S	S		8/15 A=S	E		Y	Y	8/01 FF=FA	8	9	0	9	1	3	8	5	3	2.9	Y	Y	
1354	King's C Briarcliff	NY	11800	3800	B [5]	Priv OS	T		A=S	E		Y		FA/FF	8	6	0	9	2	7	8	4		2.5	Y		
1355	Gwynedd-Mercy C Gwynedd Valley	PA	11900	4000	M [5]	Cath S	T		8/01 A=S	E		Y	Y	3/01 Oth	5	8	1	3	2	1	8	8			Y		
1356	Immaculata C Immaculata	PA	12200	4000	M [5]	Priv OS	T		6/01 A=S	E		Y	Y	3/15 Oth	6	9	1	9	3	4	9	7	2	3.2 2.8	Y	Y	
1357	Carlow C Pittsburgh	PA	12300	4000	M [5]	Cath	L	U	S/A	S		Y	Y	3/15 FF=FA	8	9	1	7	2	1	7	5	1		Y	Y	
1358	Rosemont C Rosemont	PA	12400	4800	B [5]	Cath	T		SAT	E			Y [6]	FAF	4	9	0	8	1	6	9	7	2	3.0 3.0	Y	Y	
1359	Spring Garden C Philadelphia	PA	12400 [3]	4000	B [5]	Priv	V	S	7/01 S/A	4		Y	Y	5/01 FAF	7	3	0	5	2	1	8	5	1	2.8 2.6	Y		Y
1360	Concordia C Bronxville	NY	12600	4200	B [5]	Oth OS	T		8/30 S/A	E		Y	Y	4/15 FA/FF	8	6	0	7	2	2	7	5		2.7 2.4	Y		
1361	Pace U White Plains White Plains	NY	12700	4200	P [5]	Priv	M	S	8/15 A=S	O		Y	Y	3/15 FF=FA	6	6	2	3	2	3	8	5		3.1	Y		
1362	Marymount Manhattan New York	NY	12800 [2]	4200	B [5]	Priv	V	U	A=S	4		Y	Y	4/01 FA/FF	5	9	0	1	4		6	3	3	2.9	Y		
1363	Mount St Vincent,C Riverdale	NY	13500	4600	M [5]	Priv	V	S	8/15 S/A	E		Y	Y	3/15 FAF	7	9	0	6	3	2	8	6	3	3.0 2.7	Y	Y	
1364	New Rochelle,C of New Rochelle	NY	13600	4300	M [5]	Priv	M	S	S/A	E		Y	Y	FAF	7	9	1	6	4	1	8	6	1		Y	Y	
1365	Thiel C Greenville	PA	13700	4300	B [5]	Luth OS	S		A=S	S		Y		5/01 FF=FA	9	5	0	9	1		9	5	2	3.0 2.3	Y		Y
1366	Friends World C Huntington	NY	14500 [3]	5500	B [5]	Priv	M	S	A=S	S		Y	Y	FA/FF	7	6	0	9	2	4	8	4	4	2.8	Y	Y	
1367	Wilson C Chambersburg	PA	14600 [3]	4500	B [5]	Pres	S		A=S	4		Y	Y	5/01 FF=FA	7	8	0	9	1	5	7	7	5	2.8 2.7	Y	Y	
1368	Marymount C Tarrytown	NY	14700	5300	B [5]	Cath	S		S/A	S		Y	Y	5/01 FA/FF	6	9	0	9	2	4	8	6	2		Y	Y	
1369	Lebanon Valley C Annville	PA	14900	4200	M [5]	Meth	T		5/01 A=S	E		Y	Y	3/01 Oth	8	5	1	9	1	2	8	7	6	2.4	Y	Y	Y
1370	Upsala C E Orange East Orange	NJ	15000	4600	M [5]	Luth	M	S	S/A	S		Y	Y	8/15 FAF	8	4	0	5	4	1	7	6	1	2.0 2.0	Y	Y	Y
1371	Moore C of Art Philadelphia	PA	15500	4600	B [5]	Priv	V	U	A=S	E		Y	Y [6]	4/01 FA/FF	7	9	0	7	1	5		8	1	3.0 2.8	Y	Y	
1372	Westminster Choir C Princeton	NJ	15900	4800	M [5]	Priv	S		8/01 Oth	S		Y	Y	5/01 FAF	8	6	2	9	2	6	8	6	1	3.0	Y		

▲ **Sequence number—indicates the order of the college in this book only. Do *not* use this number with admissions tests or need analysis services.**

[1] No campus room and board facilities
[2] Room only or board only
[3] Most freshmen required to live on campus
[4] City or district residence requirements
[5] Accredited by a regional accrediting association or a recognized candidate for accreditation
[6] All female freshman class
[7] All male freshman class

MAJORS AVAILABLE AND PERCENT OF STUDENTS STUDYING IN EACH AREA

Sequence Number	Agri.	Business	Comm.	Education	Engineering	Fine/App. Arts	Lang.	Health	Home Ec.	Humanities	Math-Sciences	Social Sciences	GS	ROTC Air Force	ROTC Army	ROTC Navy
1342		022%	6%	013% (1)				038%		3%	8%	010%				
1343		018%	010%	3% (1)	010% (1)		1%	015% (1)		2%	019% (1)	017% (1)			Y	
1344		100%														
1345		5%	5%	025% (1)						057%		8%		Y	Y	Y
1346		020%	3%			016% (1)		034% (1)		2%	7%	8%		Y	Y	
1347		1%	1%	023%		1%	1%	1%		031%		026%				
1348		032%		022%		4%	1%			013%	8% (1)	020%				
1349		021%	5%	025%		1%	1%	026%		3%	6%	9%			Y	
1350		027%	5%	1%		013%	2%	022%		2%	020% (1)	6%		Y	Y	
1351		041%		8%		4%	1%	1%		9%	7%	020%			Y	
1352		015%		015%				045% (1)		010%	9% (1)	6%		Y	Y	
1353		012%	7%	4%		020% (1)	1%	4%	8%	7%	010% (1)	020%			Y	
1354		018%		028%		2%	2%	2%		012%	012%	016%				
1355		016%		011% (1)				060% (1)		4%	7%	2%			Y	
1356		015%	1%	9% (1)			3%	1%	012%	015%	027% (1)	016% (1)				
1357		016%	5%	011% (1)		1%		026% (1)		3%	9% (1)	7%		Y	Y	Y
1358		9%		1%		1%	4%	1%		2%	3%	1%				
1359		020%			019%	031% (1)		3%			021% (1)	1%				
1360		024%	1%	030%		3%	1%	1%		011%	014% (1)	012%				
1361		061%	2%	6%			1%	1%		5%	021% (1)	3%		Y		
1362		031%	5%	1%		8%	1%			6%	5%	020% (1)				
1363		018%	012%	010%			2%	030%		5%	010% (1)	011%		Y		
1364		7%	7%	5%		3%	1%	046%		5% (1)	3%	4% (1)				
1365	4%	029%	4%	3%	2%	4%	1%	012% (1)		3%	012% (1)	9%				
1366	5% (1)	3%	010%	015% (1)		5% (1)	5%	5% (1)	2%	010% (1)	2% (1)	037%				
1367	020%	020%	4%	3%		1%		022% (1)		6%	019%	5% (1)				
1368		047%		6% (1)		8% (1)			7%	010% (1)	4% (1)	018% (1)				
1369		024% (1)		018% (1)	1%	3%	1%	5% (1)		4%	027% (1)	4% (1)			Y	
1370		043% (1)	1%	3% (1)		1%	5%	1%		2% (1)	3% (1)	2% (1)		Y	Y	
1371			1%	3%		096% (1)										
1372				048%		052%										

Majors listed by area: Agri.: Agriculture, general; Agronomy (crops & mgmt); Animal Science (husbandry); Fish, Wildlife Mgmt; Forestry. Business: Business/Commerce, general; Accounting; Banking/Finance; Business Economics; Business Mgmt/Admin; Marketing/Purchasing; Secretarial Studies. Comm.: Communications, general; Journalism; Radio/TV (broadcasting); Advertising. Education: Art Education; Distributive Education; Elementary Education; English Education; Mathematics Education; Music Education; Physical Education; Science Education; Secondary Education; Social Science Education; Special Education; Speech Education. Engineering: Engineering, general; Chemical; Civil; Electrical/Electronics/Comm; Industrial/Management; Mechanical. Fine/App. Arts: Architecture; Fine/Applied Arts, general; Art (Paint, draw, sculpt); Art History/Appreciation; Dance; Dramatic Arts (theater arts); Music (liberal arts); Music (perform, compos, theory). Lang.: French; German; Italian; Latin; Spanish; Russian. Health: Predentistry; Premedicine; Medical/Lab Technology; Nursing (registered nurse); Occupational Therapy; Preoptometry; Prepharmacy; Physical Therapy; Preveterinary Medicine. Home Ec.: Home Economics, general; Clothing and Textiles; Consumer Ec/Home Mgmt; Family Relations/Child Devel; Food and Nutrition/Dietetics; Institution Mgmt. Humanities: Humanities, general; Creative Writing; English, general; Literature, English; Philosophy; Religion; Speech/Forensic Science. Math-Sciences: Mathematics, general; Computer/Info Sciences; Biological Sciences, general; Biology; Botany; Zoology; Physical Sciences, general; Chemistry; Physics. Social Sciences: Crim Just/Law Enforce; Social Work; Social Sciences, general; Anthropology; Area Studies (Amer., African, etc.); Economics; Geography; History; Prelaw; Political Science; Psychology; Sociology. GS: General Studies. ROTC: Air Force; Army; Navy.

[1] Additional majors available in this area
[2] ROTC available

†Accredited by a nationally recognized accrediting body other than one of the regional accrediting associations

Middle Atlantic States (continued)

NJ, NY, PA

TRADITIONAL ADMISSIONS *Majority of accepted students in top 50% of HS class*

Sequence Number	School name (upper entry) City (lower entry)	State	Costs: Resident tuition/fees + room/board	Costs: Room/Board (upper entry) Nonresident tuition/fees + room/board (lower entry)	General Information: Highest degree	General Information: Affiliation (upper entry) Religious observance (lower entry)	General Information: Size of community	General Information: Type of community	Admissions: Fall term application deadline (upper entry) Tests desired or required (lower entry)	Admissions: Calendar	Admissions: Fall admission only	Admissions: Early admission	Admissions: Deferred admission	Financial Aid: Fall term application deadline (upper entry) Forms to be filed (lower entry)	Number in 10 who—: Undergrads -have need, receive some aid	Undergrads -are women	Undergrads -are graduate students	Freshmen -live on campus	Freshmen -are minority students	Freshmen -are nonresidents	Freshmen -return as sophomores	Freshmen -complete degree	Freshmen -enter graduate study	HS GPA (upper entry) 1st year college GPA (lower entry)	Special Programs: Credit by exam	Special Programs: Student designed majors	Special Programs: Fraternities/sororities
	Enrollment to 1,000																										
1373	Cedar Crest C Allentown	PA	17100 [3]	4900	B [5]	UCC	M	S	8/01 A=S	E		Y	Y	3/01 FAF	7	9	0	8	1	1	8	5	2	3.0 2.5	Y	Y	
	Enrollment 1,000 to 5,000																										
1374	CUNY-John J Crim Jus New York	NY	1600	[1] 4200	D [5]	Pub	V	U	 None	E		Y		 Oth	9	5	1	0	7	1	8		5		Y		
1375	East Stroudsburg U E Stroudsburg	PA	5000 [3]	2700 7000	M [5]	Pub	S		3/01 A=S	E				3/31 Oth	7	6	1	8	1	3	8	5	2	2.8 2.5	Y		Y
1376	Lock Haven U Lock Haven	PA	5300 [3]	2700 7300	B [5]	Pub	T		6/01 S/A	E		Y	Y	4/15 FAF	9	5	0	9	1	2	7	5		 2.2	Y	Y	
1377	Saint Francis C Brooklyn	NY	5300	[1]	B [5]	Cath S	V	U	 S/A	E			Y	2/15 FAF	8	5	0	0	4	0	8	3	5		Y		Y
1378	SUNY at Fredonia Fredonia	NY	5400 [3]	3600 8800	M [5]	Pub	S		5/01 A=S	E		Y	Y	 FAF	7	6	1	9	1	1	8	5	2	3.1 2.5	Y	Y	Y
1379	Fashion Inst Techn New York	NY	6200	4600 8500	M [5]	Pub	V	U	1/15 A=S	4				3/01 FAF	5	8	1	2	5	4	8			2.7	Y		
1380	Saint Joseph's C Brooklyn	NY	6300	[1]	B [5]	Priv	V	U	8/15 S/A	E		Y	Y	3/15 FAF	8	8	0	0	4	1	9	7	4	3.0 2.7	Y		Y
1381	St Joseph's/Suffolk Patchogue	NY	6400	[1]	B [5]	Priv	S		8/15 S/A	E			Y		7	8	0		1		7	5	5		Y		
1382	Holy Family C Philadelphia	PA	6500	[1]	M [5]	Cath OS	V	S	 A=S	S		Y	Y	7/01 FA/FF	9	7	1	0	2	1	8	6	4	3.5 2.8	Y		
1383	Ramapo C of NJ Mahwah	NJ	6600	4000 7200	B [5]	Pub	T		3/15 A=S	E		Y	Y	5/01 FAF	5	5	0		2	1	7	2	2	2.9 2.4	Y	Y	Y
1384	Jersey City St C Jersey City	NJ	6700	4500 7400	M [5]	Pub	L	U	7/01 S/A	S		Y	Y	 FAF	6	6	0	1	6	1	8	7	2	2.5	Y		Y
1385	York C of Pa York	PA	7000	2800	M [5]	Priv	M	S	 A=S	E		Y	Y	4/15 FA/FF	6	6	0	7	1	4	8	6		3.0 2.4	Y		Y
1386	Mansfield U Mansfield	PA	7500 [3]	2300 9400	M [5]	Pub	T		7/15 A=S	S		Y	Y	4/15 Oth	9	6	1	8	1	2	8	7		2.8 2.5	Y	Y	Y
1387	Pa St U Erie Behrend Erie	PA	7500	3500 11900	M [5]	Pub	L	S	 S/A	E				 FA/FF	6	3	0	3	1	1	8	6		3.0 2.6	Y		
1388	Molloy C Rockville Centr	NY	8200	[1]	M [5]	Cath S	S		8/15 A=S	4		Y	Y	3/01 FA/FF	9	8	0	0	2	1	9	7	2	3.3 2.9	Y	Y	
1389	Saint Thomas Aquinas Sparkill	NY	9800 [2]	3200	M [5]	Priv	S		 S/A	4		Y	Y	3/01 FAF	7	5	0	1	1	2	8	7	5	2.6	Y		
1390	Waynesburg C Waynesburg	PA	9900 [3]	2900	M [5]	Pres	T		 A=S	S		Y		 FF=FA	9	6	0	5	1	1	7	5			Y		Y
1391	Alvernia C Reading	PA	10400	3600	B [5]	Cath OS	M	S	4/01 A=S	E		Y	Y	4/01 Oth	8	6	0	4	1	1	8	8	2	2.6 2.7	Y	Y	
1392	Geneva C Beaver Falls	PA	10700 [3]	3500	M [5]	Oth OS	S		 A=S	E		Y	Y	4/15 FA/FF	7	5	0	8	1	3	7	5	1		Y	Y	
1393	D'Youville C Buffalo	NY	11000	3600	M [5]	Priv	V	U	8/15 A=S	S				 FAF	9	8	2	3	4	1	8	6	2	3.2 2.9	Y		
1394	Hahnemann U Philadelphia	PA	11300 [2]	3800	D [5]	Priv	V	U	 A=S	S			Y	5/01 Oth	8	9	6		2	4	9	8			Y		
1395	Daemen C Amherst	NY	11600	4000	B [5]	Priv	M	S	 S/A	S		Y	Y	 FAF	9	6	0	5	1	1	6		2	3.0 2.5	Y	Y	Y
1396	Saint Peter's C Jersey City	NJ	11800	4500	M [5]	Cath S	L	U	 S/A	E		Y	Y	3/01 FA/FF	7	6	1	1	4	1	8	5	3	 2.8	Y	Y	Y
1397	Mercyhurst C Erie	PA	11900 [3]	3200	M [5]	Cath S	M	S	 A=S	O		Y	Y	 Oth	9	5	1	7	2	3	8	7	1	3.0 2.5	Y	Y	
1398	Saint Rose,C of Albany	NY	11900	4100	M [5]	Priv	M	U	8/15 A=S	E			Y	3/01 FA/FF	8	7	1	7	1	1	8	6	1	3.0 2.7	Y	Y	
1399	Marywood C Scranton	PA	12000	3800	M [5]	Cath OS	M	S	7/01 A=S	S		Y	Y	2/15 FAF	8	8	1	5	1	2	9	7	4	3.0 2.9	Y	Y	
1400	Wilkes C Wilkes-Barre	PA	12000 [3]	3800	M [5]	Priv	M		 S/A	S		Y	Y	3/01 FF=FA	8	4	1	5	1	3	8	5	2	3.0 2.5	Y	Y	
1401	Cabrini C Radnor	PA	12100	4800	M [5]	Cath S	S		 S/A	E		Y	Y	2/15 FAF	8	7	0	7	1	3	8	6	3		Y	Y	
1402	Delaware Valley C Doylestown	PA	12100	3900	B [5]	Priv	S		 S/A	E			Y	5/01 Oth	7	3	0	7	1	3	9	6	1	 2.5	Y		

▲ Sequence number—indicates the order of the college in this book only. Do *not* use this number with admissions tests or need analysis services.

[1] No campus room and board facilities
[2] Room only or board only
[3] Most freshmen required to live on campus
[4] City or district residence requirements
[5] Accredited by a regional accrediting association or a recognized candidate for accreditation
[6] All female freshman class
[7] All male freshman class

MAJORS AVAILABLE AND PERCENT OF STUDENTS STUDYING IN EACH AREA

Sequence Number	Agri.	Business	Comm.	Education	Engineering	Fine/App. Arts	Lang.	Health	Home Ec.	Humanities	Math-Sciences	Social Sciences	GS	ROTC
1373		19%	4%	8%		4%	2%	24%		4%	9%	19%		YY
1374														Y
1375		7%	6%	29%		1%	1%	8%		2%	3%	2%		YY
1376		10%	6%	39%	2%	1%	1%	5%		2%	3%	2%		Y
1377		49%	5%	7%				13%		3%	3%	8%		YY
1378		26%	9%	21%	3%	7%	1%	6%		4%	8%	14%		Y
1379		50%				50%								
1380		20%		55%		1%	1%	15%		1%	3%	1%		
1381														YY
1382		16%		18%		1%	1%	37%		7%	8%	8%		
1383		50%	7%	1%		2%	1%			2%	3%	2%		
1384		23%	4%	16%		4%	1%	20%		3%	11%	15%		YY
1385		28%	4%	17%	1%	1%	1%	13%		2%	4%	14%		
1386		10%	5%	18%	3%	9%	1%	10%	8%	2%	11%	13%		Y
1387	1%	22%	4%	2%	21%					1%	3%	5%		Y
1388		13%	2%	6%		1%	2%	46%		2%	3%	2%		YY
1389		40%	2%	10%		7%	2%	2%		2%	8%	7%		Y
1390		28%	4%	12%	2%			21%		8%	13%	10%		
1391		46%	4%	5%		1%		10%		2%	3%	2%		
1392		28%	4%	9%	14%	2%		2%		8%	18%	6%		
1393		15%		20%				50%		2%	4%	2%		Y
1394								100%						
1395		17%	1%	12%		1%	1%	28%		2%	3%	4%		Y
1396		53%		5%			1%			6%	21%	13%		YY
1397		23%	2%	12%		4%		7%	6%	2%	3%	2%		Y
1398		28%	12%	26%		7%		1%		3%	11%	8%		YYY
1399		19%	5%	23%		12%	1%	12%	3%	1%	8%	13%		Y
1400		22%	3%	1%	19%	1%	1%	12%		3%	13%	9%		Y
1401		27%	15%	28%		1%	1%	2%		3%	7%	16%		Y
1402	54%	34%						1%			2%			

[1] Additional majors available in this area
[2] ROTC available

†Accredited by a nationally recognized accrediting body other than one of the regional accrediting associations

Middle Atlantic States
(continued)

NJ, NY, PA

TRADITIONAL ADMISSIONS *Majority of accepted students in top 50% of HS class*

Enrollment 1,000 to 5,000

Sequence Number	School name (upper entry) City (lower entry)	State	Costs: Resident tuition/fees + room/board	Costs: Room/Board (upper entry) Nonresident tuition/fees + room/board (lower entry)	General Information: Highest degree	General Information: Affiliation (upper entry) Religious observance (lower entry)	General Information: Size of community	General Information: Type of community	Admissions: Fall term application deadline (upper entry) Tests desired or required (lower entry)	Admissions: Calendar	Admissions: Fall admission only	Admissions: Early admission	Admissions: Deferred admission	Financial Aid: Fall term application deadline (upper entry) Forms to be filed (lower entry)	Financial Aid: Number in 10 who— -have need, receive some aid	Student Profile: Number in 10 who— Undergrads -are women	Undergrads -are graduate students	Freshmen -live on campus	Freshmen -are minority students	Freshmen -are nonresidents	Freshmen -return as sophomores	Freshmen -complete degree	Freshmen -enter graduate study	HS GPA (upper entry) 1st year college GPA (lower entry)	Special Programs: Credit by exam	Special Programs: Student designed majors	Special Programs: Fraternities/sororities
1403	Niagara U Niagara	NY	12100 [3]	3900	M [5]	Priv S	M		8/15 A=S	E		Y	Y	 FA/FF	9	6	1	7	1	1	8	6		3.0 2.5	Y		
1404	Eastern C St Davids	PA	12200	3500	M [5]	Oth OS	S		8/15 S/A	E		Y	Y	 FA/FF	9	5	2	8	2	4	7	5	2	 2.5	Y	Y	
1405	Saint John Fisher C Rochester	NY	12200	3700	M [5]	Cath S	L	S	 A=S	E		Y	Y	3/01 FA/FF	9	5	0	8	2	1	8	6	3	3.0 2.5	Y	Y	
1406	Point Park C Pittsburgh	PA	12400	4400	M [5]	Priv	L	U	 A=S	E		Y	Y	 Oth	8	5	1	6	1	3	6	5	1	2.8 2.8	Y	Y	Y
1407	King's C Wilkes-Barre	PA	12500 [3]	4000	B [5]	Cath S	M		8/15 S/A	E		Y	Y	4/15 Oth	8	5	0	7	1	3	8	7	1		Y	Y	
1408	Long Is U Brklyn Cam Brooklyn	NY	12500	4000	D [5]	Priv	V	U	 A=S	S		Y		5/15 FF=FA	8	6	1	2	5	1	7	6	7	2.0 2.3	Y		
1409	Amer U of Paris New York	NY	12700	[1]	B [5]	Priv	V	U	5/01 S/A	S		Y	Y	7/01	1	6	0	0			6			3.2	Y		
1410	Pace U NY City New York	NY	12700	4200	D [5]	Priv	V	U	8/15 A=S	E		Y	Y	3/15 FF=FA	6	6	1	1	5	1	8	5		3.1	Y		Y
1411	Pace U Pleasantville Pleasantville	NY	12700	4200	M [5]	Priv	S		8/15 A=S	O		Y	Y	3/15 FF=FA	6	6	1	5	1	2	8	7		3.1	Y		Y
1412	Saint Bonaventure U St Bonaventure	NY	12800 [3]	4300	M [5]	Cath S	S		 A=S	E		Y	Y	3/01 FAF	5	5	1	9	1	3	9	6	3	3.0 2.6	Y		
1413	Saint Elizabeth,C of Convent Station	NJ	12800	4000	B [5]	Cath OS	S		8/15 S/A	E		Y	Y	4/01 FA/FF	7	9	0	8	4	1	8	6	2	2.9 2.8	Y		
1414	Monmouth C W Long Branch	NJ	12900	3900	M [5]	Priv	S		8/01 S/A	E			Y	3/01 FAF	7	5	3	5	2	1	8	6	2	2.8 2.4	Y		Y
1415	Messiah C Grantham	PA	13000 [3]	4400	B [5]	Oth OS	T		4/01 A=S	E		Y	Y	4/01 FF=FA	8	6	0	9	1	5	9	7	3	3.2 2.5	Y	Y	
1416	Saint Francis C Loretto	PA	13000 [3]	4100	M [5]	Cath S	T		 A=S	E		Y	Y	5/01 FF=FA	8	5	1	6	1	4	8	6	2	3.0 2.7	Y	Y	Y
1417	Phila C Textiles-Sci Philadelphia	PA	13100	4200	M [5]	Priv	V	S	 A=S	E			Y	4/15 FF=FA	7	7	1	7	1	4	7	7	2	2.9	Y		Y
1418	Canisius C Buffalo	NY	13400	4700	M [5]	Cath S	L	U	 A=S	S		Y		2/01 FA/FF	8	4	1	3	1	1	9	6	3	3.1 2.2	Y		Y
1419	Marist C Poughkeepsie	NY	13400 [3]	4900	M [5]	Cath	M		 A=S	S		Y	Y	3/01 FA/FF	6	5	1	9	1	5	9	7	2	2.9 2.7	Y		Y
1420	Nazareth C Rochester	NY	13400	4400	M [5]	Priv	L	S	 A=S	E		Y	Y	3/30 FAF	8	7	1	5	1	1	8	6	2	3.3 2.8	Y		
1421	Visual Arts,Sch of New York	NY	13700 [2]	3500	M [5]	Priv	V	U	 A=S	S			Y	3/01 FAF	7	5	1		1	3	9	6	1	3.0	Y		
1422	Farlgh Dcksn U Madsn Madison	NJ	13900	5100	M [5]	Priv	S		 S/A	E		Y	Y	 FAF	9	6	1	7	1	2	8	5		2.8	Y		Y
1423	Farlgh Dcksn U Rthfd Rutherford	NJ	13900	5100	M [5]	Priv	S		 S/A	E		Y	Y	 FAF	9	5	2	5	3	2	8	5		2.8	Y		Y
1424	Farlgh Dcksn U Tneck Teaneck	NJ	13900	5100	D [5]	Priv	M	S	 S/A	E		Y	Y	 FAF	9	5	1	5	3	2	8	5		2.8	Y		Y
1425	Iona C New Rochelle	NY	13900	5600	M [5]	Cath	M	S	 S/A	4		Y	Y	4/15 FA/FF	9	5	1	2	2	1	8	6	3	2.7	Y		Y
1426	Long Is U Sthampton Southampton	NY	13900 [3]	4700	M [5]	Priv	S		 A=S	4		Y	Y	6/15 FA/FF	8	5	0	9	1	4	9	5	5	2.8 2.7	Y		
1427	Russell Sage C Troy	NY	14000 [3]	4200	M [5]	Priv	M		8/15 A=S	4		Y	Y [6]	 FAF	8	9	1	8	1	3	9	7	4	3.2 2.8	Y	Y	
1428	Rider C Lawrenceville	NJ	14300	4300	M [5]	Priv	S		 A=S	4			Y	3/01 FAF	6	5	0	7	2	2	8	7	3	2.9 2.2	Y		Y
1429	Wagner C Staten Island	NY	14700	4800	M [5]	Luth	L	S	7/15 S/A	E		Y	Y	 FA/FF	7	5	1	6	2	4	8	6	4	2.7 2.7	Y		Y
1430	Lycoming C Williamsport	PA	15000 [3]	4000	B [5]	Meth	S		4/01 A=S	O		Y	Y	4/01 FAF	8	5	0	8	1	4	8	7	2	2.8 2.4	Y		Y
1431	Widener U Chester	PA	15100 [3]	4600	D [5]	Priv	M	S	 A=S	E		Y	Y	3/01 FA/FF	9	4	2	6	1	4	8	6	1	2.8 2.4	Y	Y	
1432	Beaver C Glenside	PA	15500	4800	M [5]	Pres	S		7/01 A=S	S		Y	Y	3/01 FAF	5	7	3	8	1	3	9	6	5	3.0 3.0	Y	Y	
1433	Seton Hall U South Orange	NJ	16600	5500	D [5]	Cath OS	S		3/01 S/A	E			Y	4/15 FAF	7	5	1	6	2	2	9	5		2.6	Y	Y	Y

▲ Sequence number—indicates the order of the college in this book only. Do *not* use this number with admissions tests or need analysis services.

[1] No campus room and board facilities
[2] Room only or board only
[3] Most freshmen required to live on campus
[4] City or district residence requirements
[5] Accredited by a regional accrediting association or a recognized candidate for accreditation
[6] All female freshman class
[7] All male freshman class

MAJORS AVAILABLE AND PERCENT OF STUDENTS STUDYING IN EACH AREA

Sequence Number	Agri.	Business	Comm.	Education	Engineering	Fine/App. Arts	Lang.	Health	Home Ec.	Humanities	Math-Sciences	Social Sciences	ROTC: Air Force	ROTC: Army	ROTC: Navy
1403		037%	3%	6%	1%	2%	1%	8%		2%	7%	016%		Y	
1404		9%	1%	010%		1%	1%	013%		5%	3%	012%	Y	Y	
1405		039%	9%	2%	1%		1%	2%		4%	010%	025%	Y	Y	Y
1406		020%	010%	3%	024%	015%		3%		1%	016%	2%	Y	Y	
1407		033%	8%	6%		1%	1%	5%		6%	015%	019%	Y	Y	
1408		020%	5%	5%		1%	1%	039%		2%	3%	2%		Y	
1409		048%				013%	5%			010%	3%	021%			
1410		072%		2%		1%	1%	2%		2%	015%	4%	Y		
1411		046%	1%	2%	1%	1%	1%	029%		1%	3%	2%	Y		
1412		036%	011%	011%	1%	1%	1%	1%		2%	4%	2%		Y	
1413		042%	1%	011%		1%	1%	7%	3%	010%	014%	9%			
1414		035%	2%	3%	7%	1%	1%	3%		2%	3%	2%			
1415		018%	3%	8%	7%	2%	2%	4%	1%	2%	020%	3%			
1416		029%	4%	012%	2%		1%	012%		011%	013%	012%		Y	
1417		060%			3%	020%		2%	7%		8%				
1418		040%	6%	8%	1%	1%	1%	1%		7%	010%	019%		Y	
1419		030%	020%	5%		1%	2%	3%		2%	6%	021%		Y	
1420		021%		030%		7%	5%	6%		012%	7%	012%	Y	Y	Y
1421			047%	1%		048%				1%	2%	1%			
1422		054%	1%			1%	1%	3%		012%	016%	012%	Y	Y	
1423		056%	1%			1%	1%	019%		1%	3%	2%	Y	Y	
1424		028%	4%	1%	032%	1%	1%	2%		8%	013%	010%	Y	Y	
1425		040%	8%	3%			1%	2%		4%	015%	014%	Y	Y	
1426		016%	5%	9%		6%				5%	037%	4%			
1427		012%		013%	1%	3%	1%	038%	1%	4%	010%	016%	Y	Y	Y
1428		050%	010%	010%		2%	1%			2%	9%	013%	Y	Y	
1429		023%	1%	010%	1%	9%	2%	020%		011%	012%	011%	Y	Y	
1430	1%	026%	010%		1%	5%	2%	011%		4%	012%	028%		Y	
1431		034%	1%	2%	026%	1%	1%	021%		1%	3%	2%	Y	Y	
1432		012%	1%	010%		015%		3%		6%	027%	019%			
1433		023%	8%	5%	1%	1%	1%	5%		4%	9%	019%	Y	Y	

[1] Additional majors available in this area
[2] ROTC available

†Accredited by a nationally recognized accrediting body other than one of the regional accrediting associations

Middle Atlantic States (continued)

NJ, NY, PA

Sequence Number	School name (upper entry) City (lower entry)	State	Costs: Resident tuition/fees + room/board	Costs: Room/Board (upper entry) Nonresident tuition/fees + room/board (lower entry)	General Information: Highest degree	General Information: Affiliation (upper entry) Religious observance (lower entry)	General Information: Size of community	General Information: Type of community	Admissions: Fall term application deadline (upper entry) Tests desired or required (lower entry)	Admissions: Calendar	Admissions: Fall admission only	Admissions: Early admission	Admissions: Deferred admission	Financial Aid: Fall term application deadline (upper entry) Forms to be filed (lower entry)	Financial Aid: -have need, receive some aid	Student Profile (Number in 10 who—) Under-grads: -are women	Under-grads: -are graduate students	Freshmen: -live on campus	Freshmen: -are minority students	Freshmen: -are nonresidents	Freshmen: -return as sophomores	Freshmen: -complete degree	Freshmen: -enter graduate study	HS GPA (upper entry) 1st year college GPA (lower entry)	Special Programs: Credit by exam	Special Programs: Student designed majors	Special Programs: Fraternities/sororities
TRADITIONAL ADMISSIONS *Majority of accepted students in top 50% of HS class*																											
Enrollment 1,000 to 5,000																											
1434	Pratt Inst Brooklyn	NY	17000	5600	M [5]	Priv	V	U	3/01 S/A	4		Y	Y	3/01 FA/FF	7	4	2	7	4	6	8	6	5	2.8 2.7	Y	Y	Y
1435	Gannon U Erie	PA	17400 [3]	4000	M [5]	Cath OS	L	U	A=S	E		Y		3/01 Oth	8	5	1	6	1	1	7	6	3	2.9 2.7	Y		Y
1436	Hartwick C Oneonta	NY	17900 [3]	4400	B [5]	Priv	S		3/01 A=S	4		Y	Y	4/01 FAF	6	6	0	9	1	4	8	7	2	2.7	Y	Y	Y
Enrollment 5,000 to 15,000																											
1437	CUNY Brooklyn C Brooklyn	NY	1400	[1] 4200	M [5]	Pub	V	U	5/15 S/A	S		Y	Y	6/15 Oth	9	6	1	0	5	1		3	5	2.5	Y		Y
1438	CUNY Bernard Baruch New York	NY	1500	[1] 4200	D [5]	Pub	V	U	1/15 None	E		Y		Oth	5	6	1	0	8	1		5			Y	Y	
1439	CUNY-City College New York	NY	1500	[1] 4100	M [5]	Pub	V	U	Oth	E				5/01 Oth	7	4	1	0	9	1	8	5	5	2.5 2.4			
1440	Kutztown U Kutztown	PA	5100	2500 7100	M [5]	Pub	T		3/01 S/A	S		Y	Y	2/15 Oth	8	6	1	5	1	2	8	5	1		Y	Y	Y
1441	SUNY at Cortland Cortland	NY	5100	3400	M [5]	Pub	S		3/01 S/A	E		Y	Y	5/01 FA/FF	9	6	1	9	1	1	6	6	2	2.8 2.3	Y	Y	Y
1442	Clarion U Clarion	PA	5200	2500 6900	M [5]	Pub	T		5/01 A=S	E		Y	Y	3/30 Oth	7	5	1	7	1	1	8	7	2	3.0 2.5	Y		Y
1443	Shippensburg U Shippensburg	PA	5300	2600 7300	M [5]	Pub	S		S/A	E		Y	Y	5/01 Oth	6	5	1	8	1	1	8	6	1	2.5	Y		Y
1444	Edinboro U Edinboro	PA	5500 [3]	2900 7500	M [5]	Pub	S		A=S	E		Y	Y	5/01 Oth	8	6	1	8	1	2	7	4			Y	Y	Y
1445	Slippery Rock U Slippery Rock	PA	5500 [3]	2800 7500	M [5]	Pub	T		5/01 A=S	E		Y	Y	5/01 Oth	7	6	1	7	1	1	7	4		2.7 2.5	Y		Y
1446	SUNY at Buffalo Buffalo	NY	5500	3700 8800	M [5]	Pub	L	U	None	E		Y	Y	FA/FF	8	6	1	4	2	1	7	4		2.4	Y		Y
1447	SUNY at New Paltz New Paltz	NY	5500 [3]	3700 8900	M [5]	Pub	T		6/01 A=S	S		Y	Y	2/15 FAF	6	6	1	5	2	1	7		3	2.7 2.3	Y	Y	Y
1448	Cal U of Pa California	PA	5600	2900 7600	M [5]	Pub	T		8/01 S/A	E		Y	Y	5/01 Oth	5	5	1	5	1	1	8	5	3	2.6 2.5	Y		Y
1449	SUNY at Brockport Brockport	NY	5600 [3]	3800 9000	M [5]	Pub	T		7/15 A=S	S		Y	Y	5/01 FA/FF	8	5	1	8	1	1	8	4	3	3.4	Y	Y	Y
1450	West Chester U West Chester	PA	5700	3200 7800	M [5]	Pub	S		7/01 A=S	S		Y	Y	5/01 Oth	7	6	1	9	1	3	9	6	2	3.0	Y	Y	Y
1451	William Paterson C Wayne	NJ	5900	3600 6600	M [5]	Pub	M	S	6/30 S/A	E		Y	Y	FF=FA	4	6	1	2	1	1	7	3	1	2.5	Y		Y
1452	Glassboro St C Glassboro	NJ	6400 [3]	4100 7300	M [5]	Pub	S		3/15 A=S	E		Y	Y	4/15 FA/FF	5	5	0	7	2	1	8	6	3	3.2 2.8	Y		Y
1453	Saint John's U Jamaica	NY	7600	[1]	D [5]	Cath	V	U	S/A	E		Y	Y	4/01 FAF	9	5	1	0	3	1	9	7		3.0 3.0	Y		Y
1454	Touro C New York	NY	9800 [2]	3600	P [5]	Priv	V	U	4/15 S/A	S		Y	Y	4/15 FAF	8	7	1	2	7	4	8	8	8	3.4 2.9	Y	Y	
1455	Long Is U C W Post Brookville	NY	13600	4600	M [5]	Priv	S		S/A	E		Y	Y	FAF	9	5	2	2	2	1	8	5	3		Y	Y	Y
1456	Ithaca C Ithaca	NY	17200	5100	M [5]	Priv	S		3/01 A=S	S		Y	Y	3/01 FAF	5		1	8	1	5	8	6	3				Y
Enrollment over 15,000																											
1457	Temple U Philadelphia	PA	8600	4400 12200	D [5]	Pub	V	U	6/15 A=S	E		Y		5/01 FF=FA	7	5	2	3	3	2	8				Y	Y	Y
SELECTIVE ADMISSIONS *Majority of accepted students in top 25% of HS class*																											
Enrollment to 1,000																											
1458	US Merchant Mar Acad Kings Point	NY	2900 [3]	0	B [5]	Pub	S		3/01 A=S	O		Y		1/30 FF=FA		1	0	9	1	9	8	7	8	2.7	Y		
1459	Rabbinical Sem Amer New York	NY	6000	3000	P	Jew	V	S	Oth	S		Y	[7]	FA/FF	9	0	3	9	1	1	9	9	9	3.2 3.4			
1460	SUNY Maritime C Ft Schylr Bronx	NY	7000 [3]	3900 9900	M [5]	Pub	V	S	A=S	S		Y	Y	5/01 FAF	7	1	1	9	2	2	8	8	2	3.0 2.6	Y		

▲ Sequence number—indicates the order of the college in this book only. Do *not* use this number with admissions tests or need analysis services.

[1] No campus room and board facilities
[2] Room only or board only
[3] Most freshmen required to live on campus
[4] City or district residence requirements
[5] Accredited by a regional accrediting association or a recognized candidate for accreditation
[6] All female freshman class
[7] All male freshman class

MAJORS AVAILABLE AND PERCENT OF STUDENTS STUDYING IN EACH AREA

Sequence Number	Agri.	Business	Comm.	Education	Engineering	Fine/App. Arts	Lang.	Health	Home Ec.	Humanities	Math-Sciences	Social Sciences	GS	ROTC
1434				1%	025%	074% [1]								Y
1435		020% [1]	3%	1% [1]	9%	2%	1%	040% [1]		015%	3% [1]	4%		Y
1436		016%				5%	2%	6% [1]		8%	014% [1]	028%		
1437		011%	2%	4% [1]		9%	3%	3% [1]		015% [1]	032% [1]	015% [1]		
1438		088% [1]	1%	3% [1]			1%			1%	3% [1]	2% [1]		
1439		1%	3%	5% [1]	030%	9% [1]	1%	014%		[1]	8% [1]	7% [1]		
1440		017%	5%	026% [1]		011% [1]		[1]		3%	5% [1]	013% [1]		YY
1441		7%	5%	033% [1]	1%	1%	2%	3% [1]		2%	5% [1]	8%		YYY
1442		036% [1]	023%	021% [1]		1%	1%	2%		2%	3% [1]	1% [1]		Y
1443		022% [1]	5%	013%		1%	1%			5%	013% [1]	023% [1]		Y
1444		010%	5%	022% [1]	1%	5% [1]	1%	4% [1]	1%	3%	7% [1]	014%		Y
1445		014%	4%	025% [1]		2%	1%	016% [1]		1%	7% [1]	011% [1]		Y
1446		7%	4%	029% [1]	8%	011% [1]	1%		4%	3%	010% [1]	022% [1]		
1447		014%	9%	023% [1]	4%	8% [1]	1%	4% [1]		4% [1]	8% [1]	013% [1]		Y
1448	1% [1]	020%	2%	020% [1]	6% [1]	2% [1]	2%	010% [1]		3%	010% [1]	7% [1]		Y
1449		020%	7%	9%		3%	1%	7% [1]		5%	012% [1]	032% [1]		Y
1450		010%	3%	015% [1]		1%	1%	010% [1]		3% [1]	7% [1]	7%		YY
1451		022%	016%	018% [1]		6% [1]	1%	6% [1]		2%	6% [1]	010% [1]		
1452		022%	010%	036% [1]		1% [1]	1%		1%	2%	3% [1]	2% [1]		Y
1453		037%	4%	8% [1]	1%	1% [1]	1%	013% [1]		010%	010% [1]	9% [1]		Y
1454		038%	2%	1%		1%	4%	7%		4%	7%	6% [1]		
1455		036%	9%	013% [1]	1%	1% [1]	1%	3% [1]		1%	9% [1]	021% [1]		YY
1456		020% [1]	8%	5%		1% [1]	2%	012%		2%	3% [1]	2% [1]		YYY
1457	1% [1]	029% [1]	013%	9% [1]	6%	9% [1]	1%	2% [1]		3% [1]	7% [1]	015% [1]		YYY
1458					050%						4%	031%		
1459										100%				
1460		048%			046%						6% [1]			Y Y

[1] Additional majors available in this area
[2] ROTC available

†Accredited by a nationally recognized accrediting body other than one of the regional accrediting associations

Middle Atlantic States
(continued)

NJ, NY, PA

SELECTIVE ADMISSIONS *Majority of accepted students in top 25% of HS class*

Sequence Number	School name (upper entry) City (lower entry)	State	Costs: Resident tuition/fees + room/board	Costs: Room/Board (upper entry) Nonresident tuition/fees + room/board (lower entry)	General Information: Highest degree	General Information: Affiliation (upper entry) Religious observance (lower entry)	General Information: Size of community	General Information: Type of community	Admissions: Fall term application deadline (upper entry) Tests desired or required (lower entry)	Admissions: Calendar	Admissions: Fall admission only	Admissions: Early admission	Admissions: Deferred admission	Financial Aid: Fall term application deadline (upper entry) Forms to be filed (lower entry)	Number in 10 who— -have need, receive some aid	Undergrads: -are women	Undergrads: -are graduate students	Freshmen: -live on campus	Freshmen: -are minority students	Freshmen: -are nonresidents	Freshmen: -return as sophomores	Freshmen: -complete degree	Freshmen: -enter graduate study	HS GPA (upper entry) 1st year college GPA (lower entry)	Special Programs: Credit by exam	Special Programs: Student designed majors	Special Programs: Fraternities/sororities
	Enrollment to 1,000																										
1461	Rutgers-C of Nursing Newark	NJ	7100	3800 10000	D [5]	Pub	L	U	5/01 A=S	E		Y	Y	 FAF	5	9	1	6	5	1	9	6			Y		Y
1462	Albany C of Pharmacy Albany	NY	9200 [3]	2800	B [5]	Priv	M	U	 S/A	E				2/01 FFS	8	6	0	9	1	1	9	8	1	 2.7	Y		Y
1463	Jewish Theol Sem New York	NY	10000	3100	D [5]	Jew	V	U	 S/A	S		Y	Y	2/15 FAF	5	6	7	9	0	6	9	9	8	3.6 3.0		Y	Y
1464	Keuka C Keuka Park	NY	11300	3600	B [5]	Bapt	T		 A=S	4		Y	Y	 FA/FF	9	8	0	9	1	1	8	6	1	 2.3	Y	Y	
1465	Roberts Wesleyan C Rochester	NY	11500	3000	B [5]	Oth OS	V	S	8/01 A=S	S		Y	Y	7/15 FA/FF	7	6	0	8	2	2	7	5	2	3.1	Y		
1466	Chestnut Hill C Philadelphia	PA	12400	4100	M [5]	Cath OS	V	S	 S/A	E		Y	Y	 Oth	7	9	4	7	1	3	9	8	3	3.0 2.9	Y	Y	
1467	Mannes C of Music New York	NY	14600 [2]	4600	M [5]	Priv	V	U	7/15 Oth	S				7/15 FAF	8	6	5	1	5	7	8	5	4		Y		
1468	Chatham C Pittsburgh	PA	14700	4500	B [5]	Priv	L	U	 A=S	4		Y	Y [6]	5/01 Oth	8	9	0	8	2	3	7	7	7	3.0	Y	Y	
1469	Insurance,C of New York	NY	14900	6300	M [5]	Priv	V	U	8/01 A=S	T		Y	Y	6/01 FA/FF	9	5	6	3	3	5	8	8	3	3.4 3.0	Y		
1470	Wells C Aurora	NY	16000 [3]	4300	B [5]	Priv	T		8/01 A=S	4		Y	Y [6]	2/15 FA/FF	7	9	0	9	1	6	9	8	5	3.0 2.8	Y	Y	
1471	Eugene Lang C New York	NY	17800	6800	B [5]	Priv	V	U	2/01 A=S	E		Y	Y	3/01 FAF	8	6	0	8	2	6	7	7	8	3.0 3.0		Y	
1472	Eastman Sch Music Rochester	NY	18400 [3]	5100	D †	Priv	V	U	 Oth	E		Y		2/01 FA/FF	9	5	3	9	2	8	9	8	6	 3.4	Y		
1473	William Smith C Geneva	NY	21000	5000	B [5]	Priv	S		2/15 A=S	O		Y	Y [6]	2/15 FA/FF	5	9	0	9	1	5	9	8	6	3.4 2.9	Y	Y	
	Enrollment 1,000 to 5,000																										
1474	US Military Acad West Point	NY	0 [3]	0	B [5]	Pub	T		3/21 A=S	E		Y	Y	 None		1	0	9	1	9	9	7	9	3.6 2.6			
1475	CUNY-Lehman C Bronx	NY	1500	[1] 4600	M [5]	Pub	V	U	8/25 None	E		Y	Y	 Oth	8	7	1	0	7	1	7	1	2	2.8 2.3	Y	Y	
1476	SUNY at Potsdam Potsdam	NY	4500 [3]	2800 7800	M [5]	Pub	S		 A=S	E		Y	Y	3/01 FAF	8	6	1	9	1	1	8	6	4		Y	Y	Y
1477	SUNY at Purchase Purchase	NY	5600	3800 9000	M [5]	Pub	T		 A=S	S		Y	Y	3/15 FA/FF	7	6	1	6	2	2	7	4	3	3.4 2.6	Y	Y	
1478	Stockton St C Pomona	NJ	6000	3800 6700	B [5]	Pub	T		5/01 S/A	S		Y		3/01 FAF	9	5	0	9	1	1	8		3		Y	Y	Y
1479	Grove City C Grove City	PA	6800 [3]	2400	B [5]	Pres OS	T		 A=S	E		Y	Y	5/01 FA/FF	4	5	0	9	1	4	9	8	1	 2.9	Y	Y	Y
1480	Rutgers-Camden C A&S Camden	NJ	7100	3800 10000	B [5]	Pub	M		5/01 A=S	E		Y	Y	 FAF	4	5	0	4	2	1	8	5			Y	Y	
1481	Rutgers-Newark C A&S Newark	NJ	7100	3800 10000	B [5]	Pub	L	U	5/01 A=S	E		Y	Y	 FAF	5	5	0	2	5	1	8	5			Y	Y	Y
1482	Rutgers-Douglass C New Brunswick	NJ	7200 [3]	3800 10200	B [5]	Pub	S		1/15 A=S	E		Y	Y [6]	 FAF	4	9	0	9	3	1	9	8			Y	Y	Y
1483	Rutgers-Livingston C New Brunswick	NJ	7200	3800 10200	B [5]	Pub	S		1/15 A=S	E		Y	Y	 FAF	4	4	0	8	3	1	9	5			Y	Y	Y
1484	Pittsbg Johnstown,U Johnstown	PA	7500	3200 12000	B [5]	Pub	M	S	 A=S	O			Y	4/01 Oth	8	5	0	6	1	1			2	3.0	Y	Y	Y
1485	Rutgers-Cook C New Brunswick	NJ	7600	3800 10900	B [5]	Pub	S		1/15 A=S	E		Y	Y	 FAF	4	5	0	9	2	1	9	7			Y	Y	Y
1486	SUNY Envi Sci-Forest Syracuse	NY	8000 [3]	5600 11400	D [5]	Pub	V	U	7/01 A=S	E			Y	3/15 FF/FA	8	3	2	9	1	1	9	8	2	3.5 2.7	Y	Y	Y
1487	NJ Inst Techn Newark	NJ	8600	4600 12100	D [5]	Pub	L	U	4/01 S/A	E		Y		3/15 FAF	7	1	2	3	5	1	8	4	2	 2.7	Y	Y	Y
1488	Houghton C Houghton	NY	11100 [3]	3000	B [5]	Oth OS	T		6/30 A=S	E		Y	Y	3/15 FAF	9	6	0	9	1	6	9	6	3	3.1 2.7	Y		
1489	Saint Vincent C Latrobe	PA	11600 [3]	3300	B [5]	Cath OS	S		5/01 A=S	S		Y	Y	3/31 FF=FA	8	5	0	9	1	1	9	6	3	 2.8	Y	Y	
1490	Phila C Pharm Sci Philadelphia	PA	12600 [3]	4100	D [5]	Priv	V	U	 SAT	E			Y	3/15 Oth	7	6	1	4	2	3	8	8	2		Y		Y

▲ Sequence number—indicates the order of the college in this book only. Do *not* use this number with admissions tests or need analysis services.

[1] No campus room and board facilities
[2] Room only or board only
[3] Most freshmen required to live on campus
[4] City or district residence requirements
[5] Accredited by a regional accrediting association or a recognized candidate for accreditation
[6] All female freshman class
[7] All male freshman class

MAJORS AVAILABLE AND PERCENT OF STUDENTS STUDYING IN EACH AREA

Sequence Number	Agri.	Business	Comm.	Education	Engineering	Fine/App. Arts	Lang.	Health	Home Ec.	Humanities	Math-Sciences	Social Sciences	GS	ROTC Air Force	ROTC Army	ROTC Navy
1461								100%						Y	Y	
1462								100%								
1463				010% [1]						2% [1]		2%				
1464		015% [1]		024% [1]				030% [1]		3%	5% [1]	018% [1]			Y	
1465		024%	3%	020%	2%	5%		010%		5%	6%	015%		Y	Y	Y
1466		017%		021% [1]		4%	2%			010% [1]	014% [1]	022%			Y	
1467						100%										
1468		018%	015%	8%		2%	4%	8% [1]		011%	013% [1]	016%		Y	Y	Y
1469		079% [1]									021% [1]					
1470		1%	1%	1%	5%	1%	016%	2%		4%	012%	7% [1]		Y	Y	
1471			3%	4%		010%	2%			030% [1]	1%	020%				
1472				013%		087%										Y
1473						6%	4%			028% [1]	022% [1]	027% [1]				
1474		5%			036%		5%			2%	019%	033%			Y	
1475		022% [1]	5%	5%		2%	2%	015% [1]		010% [1]	021% [1]	018% [1]			Y	
1476		[1]		041% [1]		014% [1]	2%			010%	013% [1]	020%		Y	Y	
1477						038%	2%			022%	011%	021%				
1478		039%				3%	1%	6% [1]		2% [1]	025% [1]	022%			Y	
1479		036%	6%	015%	011%	1%	1%			2%	019% [1]	7%				
1480		039%				5%		010%		6%	015%	025% [1]		Y	Y	Y
1481		044%				3%	2%			7% [1]	017% [1]	025% [1]		Y	Y	
1482		8% [1]	014%	1%		4%	3%	3% [1]	2%	013% [1]	7% [1]	043% [1]		Y	Y	
1483		8% [1]	013%	1%		3%	1%	5% [1]		6% [1]	6% [1]	053% [1]		Y	Y	
1484		021%	4%	016% [1]	011%	1%		010% [1]		2%	013% [1]	011%				
1485	016% [1]		5%	8% [1]	[1]	025% [1]		5%	4%		018% [1]	018%		Y	Y	
1486	014% [1]				010% [1]	018% [1]					030% [1]	022%		Y	Y	
1487		4%			071% [1]	012%					010% [1]			Y		
1488		011%	4%	029% [1]	1%	5%	2%	2% [1]		025%	014%	6%			Y	
1489		036%	5%	1% [1]		2% [1]	1%	[1]		6%	021% [1]	018%		Y	Y	
1490								093%			7% [1]				Y	

[1] Additional majors available in this area
[2] ROTC available

†Accredited by a nationally recognized accrediting body other than one of the regional accrediting associations

Middle Atlantic States

(continued)

NJ, NY, PA

SELECTIVE ADMISSIONS *Majority of accepted students in top 25% of HS class*

Enrollment 1,000 to 5,000

Sequence Number	School name (upper entry) City (lower entry)	State	Costs: Resident tuition/fees + room/board Nonresident tuition/fees + room/board (lower entry)	Costs: Room/Board (upper entry)	General Information: Highest degree	Affiliation (upper entry) Religious observance (lower entry)	Size of community	Type of community	Admissions: Fall term application deadline (upper entry) Tests desired or required (lower entry)	Calendar	Fall admission only	Early admission	Deferred admission	Financial Aid: Fall term application deadline (upper entry) Forms to be filed (lower entry)	Student Profile: Number in 10 who— -have need, receive some aid	Undergrads: -are women	-are graduate students	Freshmen: -live on campus	-are minority students	-are nonresidents	-return as sophomores	-complete degree	-enter graduate study	HS GPA (upper entry) 1st year college GPA (lower entry)	Special Programs: Credit by exam	Student designed majors	Fraternities/sororities
1491	Scranton,U of Scranton	PA	12600[3]	4000	M[5]	Cath OS	M	U	3/01 A=S	4		Y	Y		8	5	1	7	1	5	9	8	5	 3.0	Y	Y	
1492	Siena C Loudonville	NY	12600[3]	4300	B[5]	Cath S	S		3/01 A=S	S		Y	Y	2/01 FF=FA	8	5	0	7	1	2	9	8	3	 2.6	Y		
1493	Arts,U of the Philadelphia	PA	13000[23]	3400	M[5]	Priv	V	U	 S/A	E		Y	Y	 FAF	7	6	1	8	2	6	8	4	2	 3.0	Y		
1494	La Salle U Philadelphia	PA	13300	4200	M[5]	Cath S	V	U	8/15 A=S	E		Y	Y	2/15 Oth	8	5	1	6	2	2	9	8	5	3.0 2.6	Y	Y	Y
1495	Le Moyne C Syracuse	NY	13300[3]	4000	B[5]	Cath S	M	S	3/15 A=S	E		Y	Y	2/15 FAF	7	5	0	9	1	1	9	7	4	3.0 2.6	Y		
1496	Westminster C New Wilmington	PA	13700[3]	3100	M[5]	Pres OS	T		 A=S	4			Y		7	5	1	9	1	2	9	7	4	3.0 2.6	Y	Y	Y
1497	Utica C Utica	NY	13900	4200	B[5]	Priv	M	S	 A=S	E		Y	Y	 FF=FA	9	6	0	8	2	3	9	6	1	3.0 2.8	Y		Y
1498	Adelphi U Garden City	NY	14400	4900	D[5]	Priv	S		 A=S	4		Y	Y	5/01 FAF	7	7	2	5	2	2	8	7		3.3	Y		Y
1499	Elmira C Elmira	NY	15300[3]	3900	B[5]	Priv	S		6/30 A=S	O		Y	Y	7/15 FA/FF	7		0	9	2	3	9	7	3	2.9 2.8	Y	Y	
1500	Saint Joseph's U Philadelphia	PA	15300	5000	M[5]	Cath S	V	S	3/01 A=S	S		Y	Y	2/15 FAF	7	5	0	6	1	4	9	7	4			Y	Y
1501	Yeshiva U New York	NY	15400	5100	D[5]	Priv	V	U	4/15 SAT	S		Y	Y	4/15 FAF	7	4	6	9		4	8	4	8	3.4 3.0	Y	Y	
1502	Juniata C Huntingdon	PA	16200	3700	B[5]	Oth	T		3/01 S/A	E		Y	Y	3/01 Oth	7	5	0	9	1	2	9	7	6	 2.6	Y	Y	
1503	Washington & Jeff C Washington	PA	16200[3]	3300	B[5]	Priv	S		3/01 A=S	4		Y	Y	3/15 FAF	7	4	0	8	1	3	9	8	6	3.4 2.7	Y	Y	Y
1504	Moravian C Bethlehem	PA	16700	4000	B[5]	Oth S	M	S	3/01 S/A	4		Y	Y	 FA/FF	7	5	1	8	1	5	9	6	3	3.2 2.5	Y	Y	Y
1505	Manhattanville C Purchase	NY	16800	5300	M[5]	Priv	T		3/01 A=S	E		Y	Y	3/01 FA/FF	6	6	1	9	3	5	9	7	7	3.1 2.7	Y	Y	
1506	Manhattan C Riverdale	NY	16900	5800	M[5]	Priv S	V	S	3/01 S/A	4		Y	Y	2/01 FA/FF	9	4	1	5	2	3	9	7	4		Y		Y
1507	Ursinus C Collegeville	PA	16900	4500	B[5]	UCC	T		2/15 S/A	E		Y	Y	2/15 FA/FF	7	5	0	9	1	4	9	7	6	3.5 2.7	Y	Y	Y
1508	Albright C Reading	PA	17400[3]	4000	B[5]	Meth S	M	S	3/15 A=S	4		Y	Y	4/01 FAF	6	5	0	9	2	6	9	8	7	3.2 2.8	Y	Y	Y
1509	Susquehanna U Selinsgrove	PA	17900[3]	4000	B[5]	Luth	T		3/15 A=S	S		Y	Y	5/01 FA/FF	6	5	0	9	1	5	8	7	3	 2.6		Y	Y
1510	Parsons Sch Design New York	NY	18200	6000	M[5]	Priv	V	U	 A=S	E		Y		3/01 FAF	8	6	1	7	2	7	9	7	1	3.2 2.8			
1511	Alfred U Alfred	NY	18600[3]	4500	D[5]	Priv	T		 A=S	E		Y	Y	 FAF	7	5	1	9	1	3	9	7	3	3.5	Y	Y	Y
1512	Allegheny C Meadville	PA	19000[3]	4100	M[5]	Meth	S		2/15 A=S	S		Y	Y	2/15 FA/FF	9	5	0	7	1	5	9	7	7	3.2 2.5	Y	Y	Y
1513	Muhlenberg C Allentown	PA	19300[3]	4300	B[5]	Luth S	M	S	2/15 S/A	E		Y	Y	2/15 FAF	6	5	0	9	1	6	9	8	3	 2.6	Y	Y	Y
1514	Saint Lawrence U Canton	NY	19300[3]	4700	M[5]	Priv	T		2/01 A=S	E		Y	Y	2/01 FAF	5	5	0	9	1	5	9	8	6	 2.7	Y	Y	Y
1515	Skidmore C Saratoga Sprgs	NY	19600[3]	4900	B[5]	Priv	S		2/01 A=S	E		Y	Y	2/01 FA/FF	3	5	0	9	1	7	9	8	6	 2.8	Y	Y	
1516	Stevens Inst Techn Hoboken	NJ	19700	4800	D[5]	Priv	S		4/01 S/A	S		Y	Y	3/01 FAF	7	2	2	8	4	4	8	7		 2.6			Y
1517	Gettysburg C Gettysburg	PA	20000[3]	3500	B[5]	Luth	T		2/15 A=S	E		Y	Y	2/01 FF=FA	6	5	0	9	1	7	9	7	4	 2.7		Y	Y
1518	Bard C Annandale Hudsn	NY	20500[3]	5200	M[5]	Priv	T		2/15 A=S	4		Y	Y	2/15 FAF	6	5	1	9	2	6	8	7	5	3.0 2.8		Y	
1519	Franklin-Marshall C Lancaster	PA	21000[3]	0	B[5]	Priv	M	S	2/10 S/A	S		Y	Y	3/01 FAF	4	5	0	7	1	7	9	8	6	 2.7	Y	Y	
1520	Hobart C Geneva	NY	21000	5000	B[5]	Oth	S		2/15 A=S	O		Y	Y[7]	2/15 FA/FF	5	0	0	9	1	6	9	8	7	 2.8	Y	Y	Y
1521	Sarah Lawrence C Bronxville	NY	21500	6000	M[5]	Priv	S		2/01 A=S	E		Y	Y	2/01 FAF	5	7	1	9	3	7	9	8	7	3.0		Y	

▲ Sequence number—indicates the order of the college in this book only. Do *not* use this number with admissions tests or need analysis services.

[1] No campus room and board facilities
[2] Room only or board only
[3] Most freshmen required to live on campus
[4] City or district residence requirements
[5] Accredited by a regional accrediting association or a recognized candidate for accreditation
[6] All female freshman class
[7] All male freshman class

MAJORS AVAILABLE AND PERCENT OF STUDENTS STUDYING IN EACH AREA

Sequence Number	Agri.	Business	Comm.	Education	Engineering	Fine/App. Arts	Lang.	Health	Home Ec.	Humanities	Math-Sciences	Social Sciences	GS	ROTC: Air Force	ROTC: Army	ROTC: Navy
1491		28%	6%	6%	2%		2%	11%		7%	16%	20%		Y	Y	
1492	1%	54%		1%	1%	1%	1%	7%		7%	10%	15%		Y	Y	Y
1493				2%		98%										
1494		37%	3%	7%		1%	1%	16%		2%	3%	2%		Y	Y	Y
1495		33%		4%			1%			14%	12%	18%		Y	Y	
1496		23%	7%	13%	2%	4%	1%			9%	19%	15%				
1497		28%	11%	1%	1%	1%	1%	19%		4%	10%	11%		Y	Y	
1498		29%		8%				11%				8%				
1499		26%		15%		4%	2%	6%		3%	9%	24%				
1500		51%		1%	1%	1%	1%			21%	3%	1%		Y		
1501		21%	7%	3%	2%			6%		9%	15%	32%				
1502		17%	3%	13%	1%	1%	1%	14%		4%	20%	17%				
1503		36%					4%	30%		2%	24%	4%				
1504		23%	3%	8%		4%	2%	1%		9%	24%	26%		Y	Y	
1505		10%	1%	2%	1%	10%	5%	1%		22%	24%	21%				
1506		32%	2%	5%	34%		1%	2%		1%	18%	5%		Y		
1507		12%	5%	9%			6%	4%		12%	30%	21%				
1508		26%	1%	1%	1%		2%	22%	3%	6%	22%	13%			Y	
1509		30%	10%	7%		2%	3%	1%		6%	13%	17%			Y	
1510		5%				95%										
1511		17%	1%	5%	24%	12%	1%	15%		2%	9%	10%			Y	
1512	1%	17%	4%	3%	1%	2%	3%	17%		2%	3%	2%			Y	
1513		29%	9%	5%		3%	4%			10%	20%	11%		Y	Y	
1514		1%	1%	2%		2%	3%	8%		6%	15%	51%			Y	
1515		15%		2%		14%	6%	5%		19%	16%	18%				
1516		5%			80%			1%		2%	11%	1%		Y	Y	
1517		22%	1%	3%	2%	3%	5%	3%		12%	15%	34%			Y	
1518																
1519		14%				2%	6%			17%	18%	39%				
1520						2%				21%	11%	55%				
1521																

[1] Additional majors available in this area
[2] ROTC available

†Accredited by a nationally recognized accrediting body other than one of the regional accrediting associations

Middle Atlantic States (continued)

NJ, NY, PA

SELECTIVE ADMISSIONS *Majority of accepted students in top 25% of HS class*

Sequence Number	School name (upper entry) City (lower entry)	State	Costs: Resident tuition/fees + room/board	Costs: Room/Board (upper entry) Nonresident tuition/fees + room/board (lower entry)	General Information: Highest degree	General Information: Affiliation (upper entry) Religious observance (lower entry)	General Information: Size of community	General Information: Type of community	Admissions: Fall term application deadline (upper entry) Tests desired or required (lower entry)	Admissions: Calendar	Admissions: Fall admission only	Admissions: Early admission	Admissions: Deferred admission	Financial Aid: Fall term application deadline (upper entry) Forms to be filed (lower entry)	Financial Aid: Number in 10 who— -have need, receive some aid	Student Profile: Under-grads -are women	Student Profile: Under-grads -are graduate students	Freshmen -live on campus	Freshmen -are minority students	Freshmen -are nonresidents	Freshmen -return as sophomores	Freshmen -complete degree	Freshmen -enter graduate study	HS GPA (upper entry) 1st year college GPA (lower entry)	Special Programs: Credit by exam	Special Programs: Student designed majors	Special Programs: Fraternities/sororities
Enrollment 5,000 to 15,000																											
1522	CUNY Queens C Flushing	NY	1600	[1] 4200	P [5]	Pub	V	U	8/01 A=S	E		Y	Y	7/31 Oth	5	6	1	0	4	1	7	3		3.3 2.5	Y	Y	Y
1523	CUNY Hunter C New York	NY	3100 [2]	1600 5700	M [5]	Pub	V	U	1/15	E				5/13	7	7	1		6	1		2			Y	Y	Y
1524	Bloomsburg U Bloomsburg	PA	5000 [3]	2400 6900	M [5]	Pub	S		 SAT	E		Y	Y	3/15 Oth	8	6	1	9	1	1	9	7	2	3.3 2.7	Y		Y
1525	SUNY at Albany Albany	NY	5000	3300 8300	D [5]	Pub	M	S	4/01 S/A	E		Y	Y	3/01 FAF	8	5	2	9	3	1	9	7	4	3.5 2.8	Y	Y	Y
1526	SUNY at Oswego Oswego	NY	5000 [3]	3200 8400	M [5]	Pub	S		4/15 A=S	E		Y	Y	3/01	6	5	1	9	1	1	9	5	1	3.2 2.4	Y	Y	Y
1527	Indiana U of Pa Indiana	PA	5100	2500 7100	D [5]	Pub	S		 S/A	E		Y	Y	5/01 Oth	8	6	1	7	1	1	8	7			Y		Y
1528	Millersville U Millersville	PA	5400 [3]	2800 7500	M [5]	Pub	T		 A=S	4		Y	Y	5/01 Oth	7	6	1	9	1	1	8	6		 2.5	Y		Y
1529	SUNY at Stony Brook Stony Brook	NY	5700	3900 9100	D [5]	Pub	S		 A=S	S		Y	Y	2/19 FAF		5	2	7	5	1	8	5	4	3.3	Y		Y
1530	SUNY at Oneonta Oneonta	NY	5800	3900 9300	M [5]	Pub	S		4/01 A=S	E		Y	Y	4/15 FA/FF	6	6	1	9	1	1	8	6	4	3.0 2.5	Y		Y
1531	SUNY at Plattsburgh Plattsburgh	NY	6200 [3]	3600 9000	M [5]	Pub	S		7/15 A=S	E			Y	4/15 FAF	5	6	1	9	1	1	8	5	3	3.4 2.4	Y	Y	Y
1532	Montclair St C Upper Montclair	NJ	6400	4100 7300	M [5]	Pub	S		3/01 SAT	E				3/01 FAF	5	6	1	5	3	1	8	5			Y		Y
1533	Duquesne U Pittsburgh	PA	13200 [3]	4300	D [5]	Cath	L	U	7/01 S/A	S		Y	Y	5/01 FA/FF	8	6	2	7	1	2	9	7	3	3.4 2.6	Y		Y
1534	Hofstra U Hempstead	NY	14100	5000	D [5]	Priv	S		 A=S	4		Y	Y	2/15 FF=FA	8	5	1	6	2	2	9	6	6	 2.8	Y	Y	Y
1535	Villanova U Villanova	PA	15800	5200	D [5]	Cath OS	S		1/15 A=S	E		Y	Y	3/15 FA/FF	4	5	3	8	1	7	9	8	3	3.4 2.8	Y		Y
1536	Rochester Inst Techn Rochester	NY	15900 [3]	4700	D [5]	Priv	V	S	 A=S	Q		Y	Y	 FA/FF	7	3	1	9	2	3	8	5	4	3.2 2.7	Y	Y	Y
1537	Drexel U Philadelphia	PA	16200 [3]	5400	D [5]	Priv	V	U	3/01 S/A	O		Y	Y	3/01 Oth	8	3	1	7	1	4	8	8	3	3.0 2.4			Y
1538	Fordham U Bronx	NY	16200	6000	D [5]	Priv	V	U	 A=S	E		Y	Y	2/15 FF=FA	7	5	3	5	3	1	8	8	7	 3.0	Y	Y	
1539	Lehigh U Bethlehem	PA	20600 [3]	4900	D [5]	Priv	M		2/15 Oth	S		Y	Y	2/06 Oth	4	4	3	9	1	8	9	8	5	3.3 2.6	Y	Y	Y
Enrollment over 15,000																											
1540	SUNY at Buffalo Buffalo	NY	5600	4100 9000	D [5]	Pub	L	S	1/05 A=S	E		Y		 FA/FF	7	4	2	6	2	1	8	5			Y	Y	Y
1541	Pa St U-U Park University Park	PA	7500 [3]	3500 11900	D [5]	Pub	S		 S/A	E				 FA/FF	6	4	1	9	1	3	8	6		3.0 2.6	Y	Y	Y
1542	Pittsbg,U of Pittsburgh	PA	7800	3500 12400	D [5]	Pub	L	U	 A=S	O		Y	Y	3/01 FAF	7	5	3	7	1	1	8		4		Y	Y	Y
1543	Syracuse U Syracuse	NY	18900 [3]	5900	D [5]	Priv	L	U	2/01 S/A	S		Y	Y	2/01 FAF	6	5	2	8	2	6	9	8	5		Y	Y	Y
1544	NY U New York	NY	21400	6900	D [5]	Priv	V	U	2/01 S/A	S		Y	Y	2/15 FF/FA	8	6	3	6	5	5	9	8	6	3.3	Y	Y	Y
HIGHLY SELECTIVE *Majority of accepted students in top 10% of HS class*																											
Enrollment to 1,000																											
1545	Webb Inst Naval Arch Glen Cove	NY	4200 [3]	4200	B [5]	Priv	S		2/15 S/A	E				7/05 FF=FA	1	2	0	9	1	6	9	8	9	3.6 3.4			
1546	Rutgers-C of Pharmcy New Brunswick	NJ	7600	3800 10800	D [5]	Pub	S		1/15 A=S	E		Y	Y	 FAF	3	7	1	9	4	2	9	6			Y		Y
1547	Manhattan Sch of Mus New York	NY	13700 [2]	4000	D [5]	Priv	V	U	7/01 A=S	E		Y	Y	7/01 FAF	7	5	4	2	5	5	8	7	8		Y		
1548	Juilliard Sch,The New York	NY	16100	5800	D [5]	Priv	V	U	3/15 Oth	E		Y		 FAF	9	5	4	0	4	8	9		5			Y	
1549	Columbia U Sch Gen S New York	NY	24400	9500	M [5]	Priv	V	U	7/15 Oth	S			Y	 FAF		5	0			1			7		Y	Y	

▲ Sequence number—indicates the order of the college in this book only. Do *not* use this number with admissions tests or need analysis services.

[1] No campus room and board facilities
[2] Room only or board only
[3] Most freshmen required to live on campus
[4] City or district residence requirements
[5] Accredited by a regional accrediting association or a recognized candidate for accreditation
[6] All female freshman class
[7] All male freshman class

MAJORS AVAILABLE AND PERCENT OF STUDENTS STUDYING IN EACH AREA

Majors listed under each area:
- **Agri.:** Agriculture, general; Agronomy (crops & mgmt); Animal Science (husbandry); Fish, Wildlife Mgmt; Forestry
- **Business:** Business/Commerce, general; Accounting; Banking/Finance; Business Economics; Business Mgmt/Admin; Marketing/Purchasing; Secretarial Studies
- **Comm.:** Communications, general; Journalism; Radio/TV (broadcasting); Advertising
- **Education:** Art Education; Distributive Education; Elementary Education; English Education; Mathematics Education; Music Education; Physical Education; Science Education; Secondary Education; Social Science Education; Special Education; Speech Education
- **Engineering:** Engineering, general; Chemical; Civil; Electrical/Electronics/Comm; Industrial/Management; Mechanical; Architecture
- **Fine/App. Arts:** Fine/Applied Arts, general; Art (Paint, draw, sculpt); Art History/Appreciation; Dance; Dramatic Arts (theater arts); Music (liberal arts); Music (perform, compos, theory)
- **Lang.:** French; German; Italian; Latin; Spanish; Russian
- **Health:** Predentistry; Premedicine; Medical/Lab Technology; Nursing (registered nurse); Occupational Therapy; Preoptometry; Prepharmacy; Physical Therapy; Preveterinary Medicine
- **Home Ec.:** Home Economics, general; Clothing and Textiles; Consumer Ec/Home Mgmt; Family Relations/Child Devel; Food and Nutrition/Dietetics; Institution Mgmt
- **Humanities:** Humanities, general; Creative Writing; English, general; Literature, English; Philosophy; Religion; Speech/Forensic Science
- **Math-Sciences:** Mathematics, general; Computer/Info Sciences; Biological Sciences, general; Biology; Botany; Zoology; Physical Sciences, general; Chemistry; Physics
- **Social Sciences:** Crim Just/Law Enforce; Social Work; Social Sciences, general; Anthropology; Area Studies (Amer., African, etc.); Economics; Geography; History; Prelaw; Political Science; Psychology; Sociology
- **GS:** General Studies
- **ROTC:** Air Force; Army; Navy

Sequence Number	Agri.	Business	Comm.	Education	Engineering	Fine/App. Arts	Lang.	Health	Home Ec.	Humanities	Math-Sciences	Social Sciences	GS	ROTC Air Force	ROTC Army	ROTC Navy
1522		013% [1]	6%	012% [1]		4%	1%	1% [1]	2%	5% [1]	020% [1]	9% [1]				
1523								7% [1]		029% [1]	8% [1]	041% [1]				
1524		028% [1]	3%	024% [1]		1%		8% [1]		1%	010% [1]	012%		Y	Y	
1525		017%	5%	1% [1]		2% [1]	5%	1%		013% [1]	021% [1]	034% [1]		Y	Y	Y
1526		019%	7%	021% [1]		3%	2%			3% [1]	011% [1]	013%			Y	
1527	1% [1]	023% [1]	2%	022% [1]	1%	2% [1]	1%	010% [1]	5%	2%	3% [1]	2% [1]			Y	
1528		011%	3%	019% [1]	2%	3%	2%	2%		4%	017% [1]	012%			Y	
1529		1%			7%	1%	1%	5% [1]		5% [1]	013% [1]	019% [1]				
1530		025%	1%	025% [1]	2%	1%	1%	1%	8%	2%	3% [1]	1%				
1531		[1]		[1]				[1]			[1]	[1]				
1532		015%		6% [1]		7%	2%	2% [1]	5%	6% [1]	7% [1]	017% [1]		Y	Y	
1533		023% [1]	8%	011% [1]	1%	3%	1%	025% [1]		8% [1]	7% [1]	8% [1]		Y	Y	
1534		043%	7%	3% [1]	3%	3%	1%	1% [1]		4% [1]	7% [1]	014% [1]			Y	
1535		031%	2%	1%	013%		1%	6% [1]		4% [1]	9% [1]	8%		Y	Y	Y
1536	[1]	020% [1]	2%		025%	013% [1]		1% [1]			014% [1]	5%		Y	Y	Y
1537	1% [1]	038% [1]	1%	1%	040% [1]	2% [1]	1%	1%	1%	1%	010% [1]	2% [1]		Y	Y	Y
1538		016%	011%	1% [1]		2%	4%	3%		4% [1]	5% [1]	3% [1]			Y	Y
1539		020%	1%	1%	040% [1]	2%	1%	014%		2% [1]	6% [1]	6% [1]		Y	Y	
1540		018%	3%	1%	021% [1]	8% [1]	1%	013% [1]		4% [1]	010% [1]	020% [1]			Y	
1541	5% [1]	018% [1]	4%	9% [1]	016% [1]	4% [1]	1%	3% [1]	1%	2% [1]	6% [1]	9% [1]		Y	Y	Y
1542		4%	1%	2% [1]	9% [1]	1% [1]	1%	7% [1]	1%	4% [1]	6% [1]	010% [1]		Y	Y	Y
1543		019% [1]	013%	3% [1]	8% [1]	016% [1]	1%	2%	4%	8% [1]	4% [1]	022% [1]		Y	Y	
1544		015% [1]	1%	8% [1]		016% [1]	1%	2% [1]	1%	4% [1]	9% [1]	011% [1]		Y	Y	
1545					100% [1]											
1546								100%						Y	Y	
1547						100%										
1548						100%										
1549						1%	6%			024% [1]	014% [1]	041%				

[1] Additional majors available in this area
[2] ROTC available

†Accredited by a nationally recognized accrediting body other than one of the regional accrediting associations

Middle Atlantic States
(continued)

NJ, NY, PA

HIGHLY SELECTIVE *Majority of accepted students in top 10% of HS class*

Sequence Number	School name (upper entry) City (lower entry)	State	Costs: Resident tuition/fees + room/board	Costs: Room/Board (upper entry) Nonresident tuition/fees + room/board (lower entry)	General Information: Highest degree	General Information: Affiliation (upper entry) Religious observance (lower entry)	General Information: Size of community	General Information: Type of community	Admissions: Fall term application deadline (upper entry) Tests desired or required (lower entry)	Admissions: Calendar	Admissions: Fall admission only	Admissions: Early admission	Admissions: Deferred admission	Financial Aid: Fall term application deadline (upper entry) Forms to be filed (lower entry)	Number in 10 who— Under-grads: -have need, receive some aid	Under-grads: -are women	Under-grads: -are graduate students	Freshmen: -live on campus	Freshmen: -are minority students	Freshmen: -are nonresidents	Freshmen: -return as sophomores	Freshmen: -complete degree	Freshmen: -enter graduate study	HS GPA (upper entry) 1st year college GPA (lower entry)	Special Programs: Credit by exam	Special Programs: Student designed majors	Special Programs: Fraternities/sororities
Enrollment 1,000 to 5,000																											
1550	Cooper Union New York	NY	4600	4300	M [5]	Priv	V	U	2/01 S/A	E		Y	Y	2/15 FAF	4	3	1	0	5	4	9	7	5	4.0 2.9	Y		Y
1551	Rutgers-C of Engr New Brunswick	NJ	7600	3800 10800	D [5]	Pub	S		1/15 A=S	E		Y	Y	 FAF	4	2	2	9	4	1	9	7			Y		Y
1552	Elizabethtown C Elizabethtown	PA	14500 [3]	3800	B [5]	Oth	T		 S/A	E		Y	Y	4/01 Oth	7	6	0	9	1	5	8	6		3.3 2.7	Y		
1553	Polytechnic U Brooklyn	NY	17000	4200	D [5]	Priv	V	U	5/01 S/A	E		Y	Y	2/15 FA/FF	8	1	2	1	4	1	7	5	6	3.0			Y
1554	Clarkson U Potsdam	NY	18000	4700	D [5]	Priv	S		 A=S	S		Y	Y	2/15 FA/FF	7	2	1	9	1	2	9	8	2	 2.6		Y	Y
1555	Lafayette C Easton	PA	18600 [3]	4600	B [5]	Pres	S		2/01 S/A	E		Y	Y	2/15 FAF	5	5	0	9	1	8	9	9	2	3.5 2.8		Y	Y
1556	Drew U Madison	NJ	19000	4400	D [5]	Meth	S		2/15 Oth	S		Y	Y	3/01 FA/FF	5	6	1	9	1	5	9	8	3	 2.9	Y	Y	
1557	Bucknell U Lewisburg	PA	19500 [3]	3800	M [5]	Priv	T		1/01 S/A	4		Y	Y	1/15 FAF	6	5	1	9	1	7	9	9	3	3.3 2.9	Y	Y	Y
1558	Colgate U Hamilton	NY	19800 [3]	4800	M [5]	Priv	T		1/15 A=S	S		Y	Y	2/01 FAF	5	5	0	9	2	6	9	9	7	3.6 2.8	Y	Y	Y
1559	Dickinson C Carlisle	PA	20000	4500	B [5]	Meth	S		3/01 S/A	E		Y	Y	2/15 FA/FF	6	6	0	9	1	6	9	8	5	 2.7		Y	Y
1560	Haverford C Haverford	PA	20000 [3]	5100	B [5]	Priv	S		1/15 Oth	E		Y	Y	1/31 FAF	4	5	0	9	2	9	9	9	7			Y	
1561	Columbia Engr-Ap Sci New York	NY	20300	5700	D [5]	Priv	V	U	2/01 SAT	E		Y	Y	2/01 FAF	9	2	5	9	3	4	9	9	7				
1562	Hamilton C Clinton	NY	20300	4400	B [5]	Priv	T		1/15 A=S	E		Y	Y	2/01 FA/FF	6	5	0	9	1	6	9	9	5	 2.8		Y	Y
1563	Union C Schenectady	NY	21000 [3]	5400	D [5]	Priv	M		2/01	O		Y	Y	2/01 FAF	4	4	1	9	1	5	9	8	5			Y	Y
1564	Barnard C-Columbia U New York	NY	21400	6500	B [5]	Priv	V	U	2/01 Oth	E		Y	Y [6]	2/01 FAF	6	9	0	9	4	6	9	9	7	3.6		Y	Y
1565	Bryn Mawr C Bryn Mawr	PA	21500 [3]	5900	D [5]	Priv	S		1/15 Oth	E		Y	Y [6]	1/15 FAF		9	2	9	4	9	9	9	8			Y	
1566	Vassar C Poughkeepsie	NY	21600	5300	M [5]	Priv	M		1/15 A=S	E		Y	Y	1/15 FA/FF	6	6	0	9	2	7	9	8	8	 3.0	Y	Y	
1567	Swarthmore C Swarthmore	PA	22000	5500	B [5]	Priv	T		2/01 Oth	E			Y	2/08 FAF	5	5	0	9	2	8	9	9	7		Y	Y	Y
1568	Columbia U Columbia New York	NY	23900	8700	B [5]	Priv	V	U	1/15 Oth	E		Y	Y	2/01 FAF	6	5	0	9	3	8	9	9	9			Y	Y
Enrollment 5,000 to 15,000																											
1569	SUNY at Geneseo Geneseo	NY	5200 [3]	3300 8500	M [5]	Pub	T		 A=S	E		Y	Y	3/01 FAF	9	7	1	9	1	1	9	7	4	3.8 2.7	Y		Y
1570	SUNY at Binghamton Binghamton	NY	6200 [3]	4500 9800	D [5]	Pub	L	S	2/15 A=S	E		Y	Y	4/01 FF=FA	7	5	1	9	2	1	9	7	4	3.5	Y	Y	Y
1571	Rutgers-Rutgers C New Brunswick	NJ	7200	3800 10200	B [5]	Pub	S		1/15 A=S	E		Y	Y	 FAF	4	5	0	9	3	1	9	8			Y	Y	Y
1572	Trenton St C Trenton	NJ	7700	4500 8900	M [5]	Pub	S		2/15 A=S	E		Y	Y	4/01	5	6	0	8	1	1	9	6	3	3.4	Y		Y
1573	Rochester,U of Rochester	NY	20100 [3]	5500	D [5]	Priv	V	S	 A=S	E		Y	Y	 FA/FF	6	5	3	9	2	5	9	7	8		Y	Y	Y
1574	Carnegie-Mellon U Pittsburgh	PA	20400 [3]	5100	D [5]	Priv	L	U	2/01 A=S	E		Y	Y	2/15 FA/FF	6	4	3	8	4	7	9	7	3	3.6 2.7	Y	Y	Y
1575	Princeton U Princeton	NJ	20500 [3]	5100	D [5]	Priv	S		1/01 S/A	S		Y	Y	2/01 FAF	9	4	3	9	2	9	9	8	5		Y	Y	
1576	Rensselaer Polytech Troy	NY	20800 [3]	5200	D [5]	Priv	M		 S/A	E		Y	Y	 FAF	7	2	3	9	2	6	8	7	6	 2.8			Y
Enrollment over 15,000																											
1577	Cornell U Ithaca	NY	20200	5000	D [5]	Priv	S		1/01 A=S	E		Y	Y	2/15 FAF	5	4	3	9	2	5	9	8			Y	Y	Y
1578	Pa,U of Philadelphia	PA	20300	5700	D [5]	Priv	V	U	1/01 Oth	E		Y	Y	 FAF	5	5	5	9	3	8	9	8	6		Y	Y	Y
Sequence Number	School name (upper entry) City (lower entry)	State	Costs		General Information				Admissions					Financial Aid		Student Profile									Programs		

▲ Sequence number—indicates the order of the college in this book only. Do *not* use this number with admissions tests or need analysis services.

[1] No campus room and board facilities
[2] Room only or board only
[3] Most freshmen required to live on campus
[4] City or district residence requirements
[5] Accredited by a regional accrediting association or a recognized candidate for accreditation
[6] All female freshman class
[7] All male freshman class

MAJORS AVAILABLE AND PERCENT OF STUDENTS STUDYING IN EACH AREA

Sequence Number	Agri.	Business	Comm.	Education	Engineering	Fine/App. Arts	Lang.	Health	Home Ec.	Humanities	Math-Sciences	Social Sciences	GS	ROTC
1550					53%	47%								
1551					100%[1]									YY
1552		33%	7%	7%[1]		1%	1%	13%[1]		2%	3%[1]	2%		
1553			1%		75%[1]						2%[1]	1%		YY
1554		14%	1%		74%[1]	1%		1%			7%[1]	1%		YY
1555		9%			27%	1%	1%	4%		7%	18%[1]	33%[1]		YY
1556						7%	6%			22%[1]	14%[1]	43%		
1557		13%		3%[1]	18%	2%	5%			15%[1]	22%[1]	18%[1]		Y
1558				3%[1]		3%	8%			24%[1]	15%[1]	47%[1]		
1559						4%	14%			14%	10%[1]	43%[1]		Y
1560							1%			31%[1]	28%[1]	40%[1]		
1561					98%[1]						2%[1]			
1562						6%	4%			23%[1]	16%[1]	47%[1]		Y
1563					20%	1%	2%			9%[1]	30%[1]	27%[1]		YYY
1564						7%	3%			24%[1]	16%[1]	42%[1]		
1565						8%[1]	10%			15%[1]	27%[1]	30%		Y Y
1566						13%	6%			19%	11%[1]	40%[1]		
1567					5%	2%	8%			26%[1]	27%[1]	27%		
1568					2%	4%	4%			23%[1]	27%[1]	22%[1]		YY
1569		15%	6%	15%[1]		2%	1%	3%[1]		8%[1]	18%[1]	20%[1]		YYY
1570		15%	1%		7%	4%[1]	2%	5%		9%[1]	34%[1]	22%[1]		
1571		10%[1]	6%	1%	1%	2%	3%	1%[1]		13%[1]	15%[1]	47%[1]		YY
1572		17%[1]	4%	16%[1]	9%	9%[1]	1%	8%		3%[1]	11%[1]	14%[1]		YY
1573					14%[1]	14%[1]	1%	6%		5%[1]	17%[1]	40%[1]		YYY
1574		4%	1%	1%	24%[1]	21%[1]	1%	2%		2%[1]	36%[1]	7%[1]		YYY
1575					19%[1]	6%	3%			16%[1]	16%[1]	39%[1]		YY
1576		6%	1%		55%[1]	6%	1%	5%		2%	23%	1%		YYY
1577	16%[1]	10%[1]	3%	[1]	18%[1]	5%[1]	1%		9%	4%[1]	14%[1]	16%[1]		YYY
1578		15%[1]	5%	1%	15%[1]	3%[1]	4%	8%		2%[1]	28%[1]	18%[1]		YYY

[1] Additional majors available in this area
[2] ROTC available

†Accredited by a nationally recognized accrediting body other than one of the regional accrediting associations

Middle Atlantic States (continued)

NJ, NY, PA

ADVANCED STANDING *Freshmen not accepted; college junior standing often required*

Sequence Number	School name (upper entry) City (lower entry)	State	Costs: Resident tuition/fees + room/board	Costs: Room/Board (upper entry) Nonresident tuition/fees + room/board (lower entry)	General Information: Highest degree	General Information: Affiliation (upper entry) Religious observance (lower entry)	General Information: Size of community	General Information: Type of community	Admissions: Fall term application deadline (upper entry) Tests desired or required (lower entry)	Admissions: Calendar	Admissions: Fall admission only	Admissions: Early admission	Admissions: Deferred admission	Financial Aid: Fall term application deadline (upper entry) Forms to be filed (lower entry)	Number in 10 who— Financial Aid: -have need, receive some aid	Number in 10 who— Undergrads: -are women	Undergrads: -are graduate students	Undergrads: -live on campus	Undergrads: -are minority students	Undergrads: -are nonresidents	Freshmen: -return as sophomores	Freshmen: -complete degree	Freshmen: -enter graduate study	Freshmen: HS GPA (upper entry) 1st year college GPA (lower entry)	Special Programs: Credit by exam	Special Programs: Student designed majors	Special Programs: Fraternities/sororities
	Enrollment to 1,000																										
1579	SUNY Ag Tech Cbleskl Cobleskill	NY	5200	3500 8600	B[5]	Pub	T		A=S	S			Y	4/01 FA/FF		3	0		1			8			Y		
1580	SUNY C Tech Frmgdale Farmingdale	NY	5900	3900 9200	B[5]	Pub	T		A=S	S			[7]	FAF		0	0		3						Y		
1581	Thomas Jefferson U Philadelphia	PA	15600	5000	D[5]	Priv	V	U	S/A	S				5/01 FAF	7	9	0		1			9	1	3.1	Y		
1582	Columbia U,Sch Nsg New York	NY	20100	7100	M[5]	Priv	V	U	S/A	E				FA/FF	9	9	7		3				4				
	Enrollment 1,000 to 5,000																										
1583	SUNY Inst Tech-Utica Utica	NY	6100	4300 9500	M[5]	Pub	M	S	None	E				FA/FF		5	1	0	1			8	2		Y		Y
1584	Pa St U Harrisburg Middletown	PA	7500	3500 11900	D[5]	Pub	S			E				FA/FF		4	1		1			6			Y		
1585	SUNY Health Brooklyn Brooklyn	NY	9500	7100 14600	D[5]	Pub	V	U	S/A	Q		Y	Y	Oth		8	6		5			9			Y		

New England States

CT, MA, ME, NH, RI, VT

OPEN ADMISSIONS *All HS graduates accepted, to limit of capacity*

Sequence Number	School name (upper entry) City (lower entry)	State	Costs: Resident tuition/fees + room/board	Costs: Room/Board (upper entry) Nonresident tuition/fees + room/board (lower entry)	General Information: Highest degree	General Information: Affiliation (upper entry) Religious observance (lower entry)	General Information: Size of community	General Information: Type of community	Admissions: Fall term application deadline (upper entry) Tests desired or required (lower entry)	Admissions: Calendar	Admissions: Fall admission only	Admissions: Early admission	Admissions: Deferred admission	Financial Aid: Fall term application deadline (upper entry) Forms to be filed (lower entry)	Number in 10 who— Financial Aid: -have need, receive some aid	Number in 10 who— Undergrads: -are women	Undergrads: -are graduate students	Undergrads: -live on campus	Undergrads: -are minority students	Undergrads: -are nonresidents	Freshmen: -return as sophomores	Freshmen: -complete degree	Freshmen: -enter graduate study	Freshmen: HS GPA (upper entry) 1st year college GPA (lower entry)	Special Programs: Credit by exam	Special Programs: Student designed majors	Special Programs: Fraternities/sororities
	Enrollment to 1,000																										
1586	Maine Augusta,U of Augusta	ME	2000	[1] 4700	B[5]	Pub	S			S		Y	Y	FAF	3	7	1	0	1	1	7				Y	Y	Y
1587	Hebrew C Brookline	MA	3900	[1]	M[5]	Jew	V	U	9/01 None	S			Y	8/01 Oth		6	6	0	1	1	9	8	6				
1588	Baptist Bible C East Boston	MA	4100	2100	†	Bapt OS	V	S	8/15 ACT	E				Oth	2	4	0	7	1	6	7						
1589	Bridgeport Engr Inst Fairfield	CT	5100	[1]	B[5]	Priv	M	S	9/04 None	O		Y		10/09	1	1	0	0	1		9	2	2	2.3 2.3	Y		
1590	Burlington C Burlington	VT	6400	[1]	B[5]	Priv	M		A=S	E		Y		9/09 FF/FA	8	7	0	0	1	1	5	7	5		Y	Y	
1591	Holy Apostles C Cromwell	CT	7700	4300	M[5]	Cath O	T		8/30 Oth	S		Y		8/01	9	2	4	8	1	8	9	8	7	2.5	Y		
	Enrollment 1,000 to 5,000																										
1592	Husson C Bangor	ME	11100	3800	M[5]	Priv	M		A=S	S		Y	Y	FAF	9	6	1	5	2	1	7		1	2.5	Y		Y
1593	Mount Ida C Newton	MA	14200	5900	B[5]	Priv	M	S	A=S	S		Y	Y	FF=FA	5	5	0	6	2	5	7	5	1		Y		
1594	Clark U Worcester	MA	18900[3]	4500	D[5]	Priv	M	U	2/15 Oth	E		Y	Y	2/01 FA/FF	5	6	1	9	3	7	9	7	7	3.2		Y	

LIBERAL ADMISSIONS *Some accepted students from lower half of HS class*

Sequence Number	School name (upper entry) City (lower entry)	State	Costs: Resident tuition/fees + room/board	Costs: Room/Board (upper entry) Nonresident tuition/fees + room/board (lower entry)	General Information: Highest degree	General Information: Affiliation (upper entry) Religious observance (lower entry)	General Information: Size of community	General Information: Type of community	Admissions: Fall term application deadline (upper entry) Tests desired or required (lower entry)	Admissions: Calendar	Admissions: Fall admission only	Admissions: Early admission	Admissions: Deferred admission	Financial Aid: Fall term application deadline (upper entry) Forms to be filed (lower entry)	Number in 10 who— Financial Aid: -have need, receive some aid	Number in 10 who— Undergrads: -are women	Undergrads: -are graduate students	Undergrads: -live on campus	Undergrads: -are minority students	Undergrads: -are nonresidents	Freshmen: -return as sophomores	Freshmen: -complete degree	Freshmen: -enter graduate study	Freshmen: HS GPA (upper entry) 1st year college GPA (lower entry)	Special Programs: Credit by exam	Special Programs: Student designed majors	Special Programs: Fraternities/sororities
	Enrollment to 1,000																										
1595	Maine Ft Kent,U of Fort Kent	ME	5300	3400 8100	B[5]	Pub	T		8/15 S/A	E		Y	Y	FAF	9	6	0	5	1	2	6				Y		Y
1596	Montserrat C of Art Beverly	MA	7600	[1]	B[5]	Priv	S		A=S	S		Y	Y	FF=FA	7	5	0	0	1	4	9					Y	
1597	Art Inst Boston Boston	MA	7700	6300	B †	Priv	V	U	Oth	E		Y	Y	FAF	6	5	0	1	1	3	9	4			Y		
1598	Magdalen C Bedford	NH	8000[3]	3000	B[5]	Cath OS	T		A=S	E		Y		7/15	5	6	0	9	1	9	9	8	3	3.0 3.0			
1599	Thomas More Inst Merrimack	NH	9200[3]	3900	B	Cath OS	M	S	A=S	E			Y	7/15 FF=FA	6	5	0	9	1	9	8	7		2.9 3.2			
1600	Saint Joseph,C of Rutland	VT	9600[3]	3600	M[5]	Cath S	S		A=S	E		Y	Y	3/01 FF/FA	9	6	1	5	1	5	7	7	1			Y	

▲ Sequence number—indicates the order of the college in this book only. Do *not* use this number with admissions tests or need analysis services.

[1] No campus room and board facilities
[2] Room only or board only
[3] Most freshmen required to live on campus
[4] City or district residence requirements
[5] Accredited by a regional accrediting association or a recognized candidate for accreditation
[6] All female freshman class
[7] All male freshman class

MAJORS AVAILABLE AND PERCENT OF STUDENTS STUDYING IN EACH AREA

Sequence Number	Agri. %	Agriculture, general	Agronomy (crops & mgmt)	Animal Science (husbandry)	Fish, Wildlife Mgmt	Forestry	Business %	Business/Commerce, general	Accounting	Banking/Finance	Business Economics	Business Mgmt/Admin	Marketing/Purchasing	Secretarial Studies	Comm. %	Communications, general	Journalism	Radio/TV (broadcasting)	Advertising
1579	100%	■		■		[1]													
1580																			
1581																			
1582																			
1583							037%	■	■	■						■			
1584							022%	■	■	■		■	■		3%	■			
1585																			
1586							042%	■	■						1%				
1587																			
1588																			
1589																			
1590	5%	■					5%	■							5%	■	■		
1591																			
1592							072%	■	■	■		■	■	■ [1]	1%				
1593								■				■	■			■			
1594						[1]	8%	■				■							
1595	2%					[1]	6%					■			1%				
1596																■			
1597																■			
1598																			
1599																			
1600							041%		■			■							

Sequence Number	Education %	Art Education	Distributive Education	Elementary Education	English Education	Mathematics Education	Music Education	Physical Education	Science Education	Secondary Education	Social Science Education	Special Education	Speech Education
1579													
1580													
1581													
1582													
1583													
1584	6%			■	■								
1585													
1586													
1587	050%												
1588	025%												
1589													
1590	010%											■	[1]
1591													
1592	4%		■							■			
1593													
1594													
1595	8%			■									[1]
1596													
1597													
1598	010%												
1599													
1600	039%			■								■	[1]

Sequence Number	Engineering %	Engineering, general	Chemical	Civil	Electrical/Electronics/Comm	Industrial/Management	Mechanical	Fine/App. Arts %	Architecture	Fine/Applied Arts, general	Art (Paint, draw, sculpt)	Art History/Appreciation	Dance	Dramatic Arts (theater arts)	Music (liberal arts)	Music (perform, compos, theory)
1579																
1580	100%															
1581																
1582																
1583	023%															
1584	025%															
1585																
1586								8%								■
1587																
1588																
1589	100%				■		■									
1590								1%		■						
1591																
1592																
1593										■						[1]
1594								8%		■	■	■		■	■	■ [1]
1595								1%								
1596								100%		■	■					
1597								100%		■	■					[1]
1598								010%								
1599								5%								
1600																

Sequence Number	Lang. %	French	German	Italian	Latin	Spanish	Russian	Health %	Predentistry	Premedicine	Medical/Lab Technology	Nursing (registered nurse)	Occupational Therapy	Preoptometry	Prepharmacy	Physical Therapy	Preveterinary Medicine
1579																	
1580																	
1581								100%			■	■	■			■	[1]
1582								100%				■					
1583								020%				■					[1]
1584								2%									[1]
1585								100%		■		■	■			■	[1]
1586								025%									
1587	1%																
1588																	
1589																	
1590								5%									[1]
1591																	
1592								012%				■					[1]
1593																	
1594	3%	■	■			■											
1595	1%	■						8%				■					
1596																	
1597																	
1598	5%																
1599																	
1600																	

Sequence Number	Home Ec. %	Home Economics, general	Clothing and Textiles	Consumer Ec/Home Mgmt	Family Relations/Child Devel	Food and Nutrition/Dietetics	Institution Mgmt	Humanities %	Humanities, general	Creative Writing	English, general	Literature, English	Philosophy	Religion	Speech/Forensic Science
1579															
1580															
1581															
1582															
1583															
1584												■			
1585															
1586								1%			■				
1587								2%							
1588								067%							
1589															
1590	010%	■				■		2%	■						
1591								070%			■		■	■	
1592								2%							
1593		■							■						
1594								8%			■	■	■		[1]
1595	1%							6%			■				
1596															
1597															
1598								020%							
1599								045%				■	■		
1600															

Sequence Number	Math-Sciences %	Mathematics, general	Computer/Info Sciences	Biological Sciences, general	Biology	Botany	Zoology	Physical Sciences, general	Chemistry	Physics
1579										
1580										
1581										
1582										
1583	013%		■							[1]
1584	3%		■							[1]
1585									■	[1]
1586	5%	■								
1587										
1588										
1589										
1590	1%									[1]
1591										
1592	7%		■							[1]
1593										
1594	010%	■	■	■	■			■	■	■ [1]
1595	014%	■		■	■					
1596										
1597										
1598	020%									
1599	040%									
1600	1%		■							

Sequence Number	Social Sciences %	Crim Just/Law Enforce	Social Work	Social Sciences, general	Anthropology	Area Studies (Amer., African, etc.)	Economics	Geography	History	Prelaw	Political Science	Psychology	Sociology	General Studies (GS)	ROTC: Air Force	ROTC: Army	ROTC: Navy
1579																	
1580																	
1581															Y		
1582																	
1583	6%			■								■	■	■	Y	Y	Y
1584	013%	■		■			■						[1]				
1585																	
1586	4%			■							■		[1]				
1587																	
1588																	
1589																	
1590	2%											■	[1]	■			
1591	030%			■													
1592	1%														Y	Y	
1593				■										■			
1594	062%					■	■	■	■		■	■	■ [1]	■	Y	Y	Y
1595	9%			■					■					■			
1596																	
1597																	
1598	010%													■			
1599	010%										■		[1]				
1600	017%									■		■		■			

[1] Additional majors available in this area
[2] ROTC available

†Accredited by a nationally recognized accrediting body other than one of the regional accrediting associations

New England States (continued)

CT, MA, ME, NH, RI, VT

LIBERAL ADMISSIONS *Some accepted students from lower half of HS class*

Sequence Number	School name (upper entry) / City (lower entry)	State	Costs: Resident tuition/fees + room/board	Costs: Room/Board (upper entry) / Nonresident tuition/fees + room/board (lower entry)	General Information: Highest degree	General Information: Affiliation (upper entry) / Religious observance (lower entry)	General Information: Size of community	General Information: Type of community	Admissions: Fall term application deadline (upper entry) / Tests desired or required (lower entry)	Admissions: Calendar	Admissions: Fall admission only	Admissions: Early admission	Admissions: Deferred admission	Financial Aid: Fall term application deadline (upper entry) / Forms to be filed (lower entry)	Financial Aid: Number in 10 who -have need, receive some aid	Student Profile: Number in 10 who — Undergrads -are women	Undergrads -are graduate students	Freshmen -live on campus	Freshmen -are minority students	Freshmen -are nonresidents	Freshmen -return as sophomores	Freshmen -complete degree	Freshmen -enter graduate study	HS GPA (upper entry) / 1st year college GPA (lower entry)	Special Programs: Credit by exam	Special Programs: Student designed majors	Fraternities/sororities
	Enrollment to 1,000																										
1601	Eastern Nazarene C / Quincy	MA	10100	3100	M [5]	Oth / OS	M	S	8/15 / S/A	4		Y	Y	/ FA/FF	8	6	1	8	1						Y		
1602	Museum Fine Arts,Sch / Boston	MA	10200	[1]	M †	Priv	V	U	/ S/A	S		Y	Y	3/15 / FF=FA	5	7	1	0	1	6	7	2	2			Y	
1603	Unity C / Unity	ME	10200 [3]	4100 / 11500	B [5]	Priv	T		/ A=S	E		Y	Y	6/01 / FA/FF	9	4	0	9	1	8	7	5	1		Y	Y	
1604	Southern Vermont C / Bennington	VT	11200	3800	B [5]	Priv	S		/ A=S	S		Y	Y	/ FF=FA	9	6	0	8	1	7	6	4		2.5 / 2.5	Y	Y	
1605	Thomas C / Waterville	ME	11200	3900	M [5]	Priv	S		8/31 / A=S	E		Y	Y	/ FA/FF	8	5	3	8	1	1	8	7	1	2.9 / 2.5	Y		Y
1606	Teikyo Post U / Waterbury	CT	12700	3900	B [5]	Priv	M	S	/ S/A	S		Y	Y	4/15 / FAF	6	6	0	3	1	1	7	6	5		Y	Y	
1607	Nichols C / Dudley	MA	12800 [3]	4500	M [5]	Priv	T		/ S/A	S		Y	Y	/ FAF	6	3	0	7	1	3	8	6	1	2.4 / 2.6	Y		
1608	Endicott C / Beverly	MA	14200	5100	B [5]	Priv	S		/ A=S	4		Y	Y [6]	/ FAF	6	9	0	9	2	7	8				Y	Y	
1609	Goddard C / Plainfield	VT	15300	3900	M [5]	Priv	T		/ A=S	E		Y	Y	/ FF=FA	9	5	3	9	1	9	8	6	6		Y	Y	
1610	Wheelock C / Boston	MA	15400	4900	M [5]	Priv	V	U	2/15 / A=S	E		Y	Y	3/01 /	7	9	1	9	1	5	8	7		2.5 / 3.0	Y		
1611	Lasell C / Newton	MA	15500	5600	B [5]	Priv	S			E			Y [6]	/ FAF	6	9	0	8	1	5	8			2.3 / 2.6	Y	Y	
1612	New Eng C / Henniker	NH	16500 [3]	4800	M [5]	Priv	T		/ A=S	S			Y	3/01 / FA/FF	5	4	0	9	1	9	7	6	2	2.3 / 2.3	Y	Y	Y
1613	Pine Manor C / Chestnut Hill	MA	18300 [3]	5700	B [5]	Priv	V	S	/ A=S	E			Y [6]	3/15 / FA/FF	3	9	0	9	3	8	7	6	1	2.4 / 2.5	Y	Y	
	Enrollment 1,000 to 5,000																										
1614	Maine Presque Isle,U / Presque Isle	ME	5400	3300 / 8100	M [5]	Pub	S		/ S/A	E		Y	Y	5/15 / FAF	8	6	1	5	1	1	5	2	2	2.7 / 2.5	Y	Y	Y
1615	Champlain C / Burlington	VT	11900	4900	B [5]	Priv	M		/ A=S	E		Y	Y	5/01 / FA/FF	7	6	0	5	1	3	7			2.5 / 2.8	Y		
1616	Atlantic Union C / South Lancaster	MA	12700	3300	B [5]	Oth / OS	T		9/15 / A/S	E		Y		6/01 / FAF	7	6	0	6	5	8	7				Y		
1617	Wentworth Inst Techn / Boston	MA	13400	5200	P [5]	Priv	V	U	8/01 / A=S	S				3/01 / FAF	7	1	0	2	2	2	6	3	1	2.5	Y		
1618	Franklin Pierce C / Rindge	NH	14500 [3]	4000	B [5]	Priv	T		8/15 / A=S	E		Y	Y	/ FA/FF	5	5	0	9	1	9	7	4	3	2.3 / 2.3	Y	Y	
1619	Berklee C of Music / Boston	MA	15200	6200	B [5]	Priv	V	U	/ A=S	E			Y	3/31 / FF=FA	6	2	0	6		7					Y	Y	
	Enrollment 5,000 to 15,000																										
1620	Johnson & Wales U / Providence	RI	11600 [3]	3700	M †	Priv	M	U	/ A=S	Q		Y	Y	/ FF=FA	9	5	1	8	1	8	7	4	1		Y		Y
	TRADITIONAL ADMISSIONS *Majority of accepted students in top 50% of HS class*																										
	Enrollment to 1,000																										
1621	Maine Machias,U of / Machias	ME	5000	3100 / 7700	B [5]	Pub	T		/ A=S	E		Y	Y	5/01 / FA/FF	8	6	0	5	1	2	7	4	1	2.5	Y		Y
1622	Mass Maritime Acad / Buzzards Bay	MA	6000 [3]	3800 / 9800	B [5]	Pub	S		5/01 / S/A	O		Y	Y	5/01 / FAF	7	1	0	9	1	2	7	7	1	2.5 / 2.0	Y		
1623	Saint Johns Seminary / Brighton	MA	6500 [3]	3500	B [5]	Cath / OS	V	U	7/15 / Oth	E			[7]	8/15 / Oth	6	0	0	9	1	1	9	8	8	/ 2.5		Y	
1624	St Hyacinth C & Sem / Granby	MA	7600	4000	B [5]	Cath / OS	T		6/01 / S/A	E			[7]	/ FA/FF	5	0	0	9	1	8	8	8	9	2.0 / 2.0	Y		
1625	Maine Maritime Acad / Castine	ME	7900 [3]	4000 / 10300	M [5]	Pub	T		7/01 / S/A	T			Y	4/15 / FAF	7	1	1	9	1	3	7	7	1	/ 2.5	Y		Y
1626	Saint Basil's C / Stamford	CT	8000 [3]	3000	B †	Cath / OS	L	S	8/01 / A=S	E			[7]	8/01 / None	9	0	0	9	3	9	9	9	9	3.5 / 3.0	Y		
1627	Hellenic-Holy Cross / Brookline	MA	9700 [3]	3800	M [5]	Oth / OS	L	S	/ S/A	S			Y	4/01 / FA/FF	9	1	7	9	1	9	9	4	6		Y		

▲ Sequence number—indicates the order of the college in this book only. Do *not* use this number with admissions tests or need analysis services.

[1] No campus room and board facilities
[2] Room only or board only
[3] Most freshmen required to live on campus
[4] City or district residence requirements
[5] Accredited by a regional accrediting association or a recognized candidate for accreditation
[6] All female freshman class
[7] All male freshman class

MAJORS AVAILABLE AND PERCENT OF STUDENTS STUDYING IN EACH AREA

Sequence Number	Agri.	Business	Comm.	Education	Engineering	Fine/App. Arts	Lang.	Health	Home Ec.	Humanities	Math-Sciences	Social Sciences	GS	ROTC
1601		013%	4%	017% [1]	4% [1]	3%		3%		012%	014% [1]	016%		
1602				3%		097% [1]								
1603	060% [1]					1%					015% [1]	1% [1]		Y
1604		040% [1]	4%					5%	3%	3%		025%		
1605		083% [1]		5%				1%			010% [1]			Y
1606		075%	1%	1%		2% [1]	1%	1%		2%	3%	2%		Y
1607		090% [1]									[1]	010% [1]		Y
1608		038% [1]	013%	1%		031% [1]		3%	1%	1%	3%	4%		
1609	1%	010%	3%	015% [1]		3% [1]		2%		2%	3% [1]	2%		
1610				085% [1]								015%		
1611		041% [1]		025% [1]				4%						
1612		025%	017%	5% [1]	5%	011%	1%			3%	5% [1]	028% [1]		
1613		027%	020%	010% [1]		8%	1%					[1]		
1614		012%	2%	030% [1]		3%		5%			3% [1]	9% [1]		
1615		055%	1%	1%	1%			1%	6%	2%	1%	2%		YY
1616		015%		9%		7% [1]	1%	9% [1]		012%	012% [1]	015%		
1617					088% [1]	5% [1]		1%			1%			YY
1618		016% [1]	014%	9% [1]		020% [1]				7%	7% [1]	022% [1]		
1619				9%		091%								
1620	1%	072% [1]	1%	1% [1]				1%	022%		1%	1%		Y
1621		055% [1]	1%	025% [1]						2%	015% [1]	2% [1]		
1622		034% [1]			066%									
1623							013%			060% [1]		010%		
1624										100%				
1625		1% [1]			070%					1%	3%	2%		Y
1626										100%				
1627										100%				

[1] Additional majors available in this area
[2] ROTC available

†Accredited by a nationally recognized accrediting body other than one of the regional accrediting associations

New England States
(continued)

CT, MA, ME, NH, RI, VT

TRADITIONAL ADMISSIONS *Majority of accepted students in top 50% of HS class*

Sequence Number	School name (upper entry) City (lower entry)	State	Resident tuition/fees + room/board	Room/Board (upper entry) Nonresident tuition/fees + room/board (lower entry)	Highest degree	Affiliation (upper entry) Religious observance (lower entry)	Size of community	Type of community	Fall term application deadline (upper entry) Tests desired or required (lower entry)	Calendar	Fall admission only	Early admission	Deferred admission	Fall term application deadline (upper entry) Forms to be filed (lower entry)	-have need, receive some aid	-are women	-are graduate students	-live on campus	-are minority students	-are nonresidents	-return as sophomores	-complete degree	-enter graduate study	HS GPA (upper entry) 1st year college GPA (lower entry)	Credit by exam	Student designed majors	Fraternities/sororities
			Costs		**General Information**				**Admissions**					**Financial Aid**		**Student Profile** (Number in 10 who— Undergrads)		**Freshmen**							**Special Programs**		
	Enrollment to 1,000																										
1628	Notre Dame C of NH Manchester	NH	11900	4300	M[5]	Cath	M	S	8/05 A=S	E			Y	3/15 FA/FF	9	8	3	6	1	4	8	5	3	2.8	Y		
1629	Rivier C Nashua	NH	12100	4100	M[5]	Cath S	M		S/A	E		Y	Y	FF=FA	8	9	1	3	3	3	7	7	1	3.4 3.7	Y	Y	
1630	Green Mountain C Poultney	VT	12200[3]	4700	B[5]	Priv	T		8/15	S		Y	Y	FA/FF	3	5	0	9	1	9	8	6	4	2.7 2.3	Y	Y	
1631	Portland Sch of Art Portland	ME	12400	4100	B[5]	Priv	M	U	A=S	S			Y	3/01 FAF	7	6	0	5	1		9	6	2	2.6			
1632	Anna Maria C Paxton	MA	12600	4200	M[5]	Cath S	T		6/01 S/A	4		Y	Y	3/01 FAF	7	7	1	8	1	2	9	7	2	2.8	Y		
1633	Saint Joseph's C Windham	ME	12800	4300	M[5]	Cath	S		6/01 S/A	S		Y	Y	3/15 FAF	8	6	0	9	1	6	8	7	4	2.9 2.6	Y		
1634	Trinity C Vermont Burlington	VT	13100[3]	4500	M[5]	Cath S	S		A=S	E		Y	Y	3/01 FF=FA	6	8	0		1	4	7	6	3	3.0 2.8	Y	Y	
1635	Boston Consv Music Boston	MA	13200	5000	M[5]	Priv	V	U	S/A	S		Y	Y	3/15 FA/FF	8	7	1	4	2	5	8	8	2	3.0 2.6	Y		Y
1636	Elms C Chicopee	MA	13300	4400	M[5]	Cath S	M	S	S/A	E		Y	Y	FAF	8	9	1	7	2	4	8	8	8	2.9 2.8	Y	Y	
1637	Westbrook C Portland	ME	13600	4400	B[5]	Priv	M	S	SAT	E		Y	Y	FA/FF	8	9	0	7	1	4	7	7		2.6 2.8	Y		
1638	Daniel Webster C Nashua	NH	13800[3]	4100	B[5]	Priv	M	S	S/A	S			Y	3/01 FAF	6	2	0	9	1	8	7		1		Y		
1639	Albertus Magnus C New Haven	CT	14300	4900	B[5]	Cath S	L	U	S/A	E		Y	Y	2/15 FA/FF	7	7	0	8	1	3	7	7	5	3.0 2.5	Y	Y	
1640	Regis C Weston	MA	14400	4900	B[5]	Cath	S		S/A	S		Y	Y[6]	3/01 FA/FF	7	9	0	8	2	3	8	7	1	3.0 2.6		Y	
1641	Emmanuel C Boston	MA	14500	5100	M[5]	Cath S	V	U	S/A	S		Y	Y	FAF	7	9	1	6	3	2	9	7		2.6 2.7	Y		
1642	Atlantic,C of the Bar Harbor	ME	14800	3300	M[5]	Priv	T		A=S	O		Y	Y	3/01 FAF	6	6	0	9	1	8	7	5	3	2.9	Y	Y	
1643	Colby-Sawyer C New London	NH	15900	4500	B[5]	Priv	T		A=S	S			Y	2/15 FAF	5	9	0	9	1	7	9	6	3	2.4	Y	Y	
1644	Bradford C Bradford	MA	17500	5900	B[5]	Priv	S		3/01 S/A	E		Y	Y	3/15 FAF	5	5	0	9	1	6	7	6	5	2.5	Y	Y	
1645	Forsyth Sch Dent Hyg Boston	MA	18100	6700	B[5]	Priv	V	U	Oth	Q		Y	Y	3/01 FAF	9	9	0	2	1	2	8			2.8 3.8	Y		
	Enrollment 1,000 to 5,000																										
1646	Worcester St C Worcester	MA	4300	2900 7600	M[5]	Pub	M	U	8/25 SAT	E			Y	3/15 FF=FA	7	5	0	1	1	1	6	3	2	2.8 2.4	Y		
1647	Western Conn St U Danbury	CT	4500	2800 6500	M[5]	Pub	M	U	4/01 S/A	E			Y	5/01 FAF	2	6	1	4	1	1	8	6	1	3.1	Y		Y
1648	Westfield St C Westfield	MA	4700	3200 7200	M[5]	Pub	S		4/01 SAT	E				3/01 FAF	5	5	0	7	1	1	9	6	2	2.9 2.5	Y		
1649	Framingham St C Framingham	MA	4800	2800 7600	M[5]	Pub	M	S	S/A	S		Y	Y	4/15 FAF	4	6	1	5	1	1	6	6	2	2.7 1.8	Y	Y	
1650	Eastern Conn St U Willimantic	CT	5200	3300 8000	M[5]	Pub	S		5/01 SAT	E		Y	Y	4/15 FAF	4	5	0	8	1	1	8	5	2		Y	Y	
1651	Maine Farmington,U Farmington	ME	5400	3300 7900	B[5]	Pub	T		S/A	E		Y		3/15 FAF	9	6	0	9	1	2	8	5	1	2.4	Y	Y	
1652	Fitchburg St C Fitchburg	MA	5600	3100 8700	M[5]	Pub	S		3/01 S/A	S			Y	3/30 FAF	7	6	0	4	1	1	7	5	3	2.8 2.7	Y		Y
1653	Keene St C Keene	NH	5900	3400 9800	M[5]	Pub	S		4/01 SAT	S		Y	Y	3/01 FA/FF	7	6	1	7	1	4	8		4	2.5	Y	Y	Y
1654	North Adams St C North Adams	MA	6000	3500 8900	M[5]	Pub	S		6/01 A=S	S			Y	5/01 FAF	6	5	0	9	1	1	8	5	1	2.8 2.5	Y	Y	Y
1655	Plymouth St C Plymouth	NH	6000[3]	3400 9800	M[5]	Pub	T		4/01 S/A	E		Y		3/01 FAF	5	5	1	9	1	4	8	7	1		Y	Y	Y
1656	Southern Maine,U of Portland	ME	6000	3800 9700	P[5]	Pub	M		7/15 S/A	S		Y	Y	FAF	7	6	1	5	1	1		5		2.4	Y	Y	Y
1657	Castleton St C Castleton	VT	7200[3]	4100 10500	M[5]	Pub	T		5/01 S/A	S		Y	Y	3/15 FA/FF	6	6	1	7	1	5	7			2.6	Y	Y	
Sequence Number	School name (upper entry) City (lower entry)	State	**Costs**		**General Information**				**Admissions**					**Financial Aid**		**Student Profile**									**Programs**		

▲ Sequence number—indicates the order of the college in this book only. Do *not* use this number with admissions tests or need analysis services.

[1] No campus room and board facilities
[2] Room only or board only
[3] Most freshmen required to live on campus
[4] City or district residence requirements
[5] Accredited by a regional accrediting association or a recognized candidate for accreditation
[6] All female freshman class
[7] All male freshman class

MAJORS AVAILABLE AND PERCENT OF STUDENTS STUDYING IN EACH AREA

Sequence Number	Agri.					Business							Comm.				Education												Engineering						Fine/App. Arts								Lang.						Health									Home Ec.						Humanities							Math-Sciences									Social Sciences												GS	ROTC		
	Agriculture, general	Agronomy (crops & mgmt)	Animal Science (husbandry)	Fish, Wildlife Mgmt	Forestry	Business/Commerce, general	Accounting	Banking/Finance	Business Economics	Business Mgmt/Admin	Marketing/Purchasing	Secretarial Studies	Communications, general	Journalism	Radio/TV (broadcasting)	Advertising	Art Education	Distributive Education	Elementary Education	English Education	Mathematics Education	Music Education	Physical Education	Science Education	Secondary Education	Social Science Education	Special Education	Speech Education	Engineering, general	Chemical	Civil	Electrical/Electronics/Comm	Industrial/Management	Mechanical	Architecture	Fine/Applied Arts, general	Art (Paint, draw, sculpt)	Art History/Appreciation	Dance	Dramatic Arts (theater arts)	Music (liberal arts)	Music (perform, compos, theory)	French	German	Italian	Latin	Spanish	Russian	Predentistry	Premedicine	Medical/Lab Technology	Nursing (registered nurse)	Occupational Therapy	Preoptometry	Prepharmacy	Physical Therapy	Preveterinary Medicine	Home Economics, general	Clothing and Textiles	Consumer Ec/Home Mgmt	Family Relations/Child Devel	Food and Nutrition/Dietetics	Institution Mgmt	Humanities, general	Creative Writing	English, general	Literature, English	Philosophy	Religion	Speech/Forensic Science	Mathematics, general	Computer/Info Sciences	Biological Sciences, general	Biology	Botany	Zoology	Physical Sciences, general	Chemistry	Physics	Crim Just/Law Enforce	Social Work	Social Sciences, general	Anthropology	Area Studies (Amer., African, etc.)	Economics	Geography	History	Prelaw	Political Science	Psychology	Sociology	General Studies	Air Force	Army	Navy
1628						■	016%						010% ■				■	■	■	■	030%	■		■		■	■	[1]								■	014% ■					[1]				1%							5%		■											■	7% ■		■				■	■	4%							■		013%			■			■					
1629						■	032% ■			■	■	[1] ■	■	■	6%		■	■	■	■	026% ■			■	■	■	■	[1]								■	■		7%				■				■		■	■		■	1%				■									■	3% ■				■	■	011% ■	■			■	■				■				5%		■		■	■	■	Y		
1630						■	023% ■			■	■								■		014%						■									■	■		6%														3%				[1]								016%	■																■				7%					[1]	■			
1631													■																							■	100% ■					[1]																																																							
1632						■	010% ■	■		■	■		■		1%		■		■		020% ■	■						[1]	■			1%				■	■		6%		■	■	■			1%	■		■	■	■	■	4%				[1]									■	4%					■	■	■	8%				[1]	■	■	■				9%	■	■	■	■	■	■	Y	Y	Y
1633						■	026% ■			■	■		012% ■		■				■	■	014% ■		■	■	■	■																							■	■	019%	■			■		[1] ■									■	3%		■		■		013% ■	■			■		[1]		■			013%			■	■			■			Y	
1634							039% ■			■			■		1%			■	■		023%				■		■	[1]											1%				■			1%	■				■		8%												012%	■	■	■			■			■	2%			■			■			012%	■		■			■		■	Y		
1635																						■	1%														099%		■			■																																																								
1636						■	014% ■			■	■		■				■		■	■	025% ■			■	■	■		[1]								■	■		1%		■		■			4%	■		■	■	018% ■	■		■	■		[1] ■				■			■	■	■	4% ■		■		■	■	■	■	5%		■	■			■	■		011% ■			■	■		■	[1] ■	■	Y	Y	
1637						■	043% ■			■	■				1%				■				6%					[1]											1%							1%					042% ■	■					[1]									■	1%								2%											1%									
1638						■			6%	■																						2%																																			1%					■			4%				[1]														Y		
1639							030%		■				015% ■										5%													■	■		1%				■	010%	■	■	■						1%											■		■	2%	■	■	[1]	■	■			3%							■			■	2%	■		■	■	■	■			
1640						■			7%				■		6%								3%													■	■	■	9%		■		■	■		7%	■																		017%	■				[1]	■		016% ■	■			■	■			■			027%	■		■		■	■	■				
1641						■	010% ■						■		6%		■		■		010%	■			■						■		■	■		■	■	■	7%		■		■			1%	■		■	■	012% ■	■														■	9%		■		■			■	6%			■	[1] ■					014%	■		■	■	■	■	■			Y	
1642															5%				■		012%			■	■	■		[1]							■		010% ■					[1]																						■			5%						028% ■	■		■			[1]			■		010%				■	■		[1]	■			
1643							015%			■							■		■		024%			■	■	■		[1]								■	■		5%	■						1%					021%	■										1%					1%						■	■	3%											1%				■			Y	Y	
1644							037%			■					1%						010%															■	■		1% ■	■	■					1%			■	■														■			2%		■		■				3%							■				1%	■		■	■	[1] ■				
1645																																																			100%						[1]																																									
1646									9%	■			■		5% ■				■		012%																		1%				■			1%	■					■	6% ■				[1]									■	6%				■	■		■	9%			■	■			■		016%	■	■	■			■	■		Y		Y
1647						■	031% ■						■		9%				■	■	■	■	8%	■	■	■						1%				■			8%	■	■	■				1%	■				■	■	7%				[1]									■	6%				■	■		■	8%			■	[1]	■	■	■	■	015%	■		■		■	■	■				
1648						■	023%						■		4% ■				■		015%		■	■			■	[1]								■			2%		■		■			1%	■																			■	3%				■	■	■	■	5%				[1]	■		■			■	3%	■			■	■	■		Y	
1649			1%		[1]		010%			■	■		■		3%				■				6%					[1]									■	■	4%				■			1%	■				■	■	8%					■	■	■	7%	■				■	5% ■	■			■	■	010% ■	■			■	■	[1]					015%	■	■	■		■	■	■	■			
1650							024%			■			011% ■						■	■	012% ■		■	■	■	■		[1]									■		1%		■					2%	■						3%													■	4%				■	■	018% ■	■			■		[1]		■	■		024%	■		■		■	■	■	■	Y	Y	
1651						■			8% ■										■	■	028% ■			■	■	■	■	[1] ■								■			1%			[1]							■	■			8%				[1]	■			4%					■	5% ■				■	■	■	■	9%		■	■	[1]		■	■		018%		■	■	■		■		■			
1652						■	013%						011% ■						■	■	022% ■			■	■	■	■	[1]				5%				■															011% ■	■													■	■	3%				■	■	■	■	7%		■	■	[1]					014%	■	■	■			■	[1] ■			Y	
1653							025%			■				■	3%				■	■	025% ■	■	■	■	■	■	■	[1]				2%				■	■	■	3%	■	■	[1]	■			1%	■											■			5% ■	■				■	4% ■				■	■	010% ■	■			■	■	[1] ■			■				8% ■	■		■	■	■	■	Y	Y	
1654						■	030% ■	■	■	■	■		015% ■						■		015%							[1]																							■		5%													■	3% ■	■			■	■	■	■	6%		■	■	[1] ■				■	010%	■		■		■	■	■	■			
1655						■	035% ■		■	■	■						■		■	■	035% ■	■	■	■	■	■		[1]								■	■	■	1%	■	■		■			2%	■																		■	■	2% ■	■		[1]	■	■	■	■	3%		■	■	[1]		■	■	■		■	2% ■	■	■	■	■	[1] ■	■	Y	Y	
1656							022% ■		■	■			■		8%						017%	■						[1]				1% ■				■	■		3%	■	■	■	■	■		1% ■	■	■	■	■		■	7%				[1] ■									■	5%	■		[1]	■	■		■	5%			■	[1] ■	■	■	■	■	011%	■	■	■		■	■	■	■	Y	Y	
1657							022% ■	■		■	■		010% ■				■	■	■	■	021% ■	■	■	■	■	■	■	[1]									■		5%	■	■		■			1%	■						4%													■	4% ■				■	■	■	■	7%		■		[1]	■	■	■		011%			■			■	■	■			
Sequence Number	Agri.					Business							Comm.				Education												Engineering						Fine/App. Arts								Lang.						Health									Home Ec.						Humanities							Math-Sciences									Social Sciences												GS	ROTC		

[1] Additional majors available in this area
[2] ROTC available

†Accredited by a nationally recognized accrediting body other than one of the regional accrediting associations

New England States
(continued)

CT, MA, ME, NH, RI, VT

TRADITIONAL ADMISSIONS *Majority of accepted students in top 50% of HS class*

Sequence Number	School name (upper entry) / City (lower entry)	State	Costs: Resident tuition/fees + room/board	Costs: Room/Board (upper entry) / Nonresident tuition/fees + room/board (lower entry)	General Information: Highest degree	Affiliation (upper entry) / Religious observance (lower entry)	Size of community	Type of community	Admissions: Fall term application deadline (upper entry) / Tests desired or required (lower entry)	Calendar	Fall admission only	Early admission	Deferred admission	Financial Aid: Fall term application deadline (upper entry) / Forms to be filed (lower entry)	Number in 10 who— -have need, receive some aid	Undergrads -are women	-are graduate students	Freshmen -live on campus	-are minority students	-are nonresidents	-return as sophomores	-complete degree	-enter graduate study	HS GPA (upper entry) / 1st year college GPA (lower entry)	Special Programs: Credit by exam	Student designed majors	Fraternities/sororities
	Enrollment 1,000 to 5,000																										
1658	Johnson St C / Johnson	VT	7200[3]	4100 / 10500	M[5]	Pub	T		4/01 / A=S	S		Y	Y	3/01 / FF=FA	7	5	0	8	1	4	8	4	1	2.5 / 2.5	Y		
1659	Lyndon St C / Lyndonville	VT	7300[3]	4100 / 10600	M[5]	Pub	T		S/A	E		Y	Y	3/01 / FA/FF	6	5	1	7	1	4	7	5	2	2.8	Y	Y	Y
1660	Suffolk U / Boston	MA	8500	[1]	P[5]	Priv	V	U	6/01 / SAT	E		Y	Y	3/01 / FAF	6	5	3	1	1	1	7	6	1	2.7 / 2.4	Y		
1661	Amer International C / Springfield	MA	11700[3]	3900	D[5]	Priv	M	U	S/A	S		Y	Y	FA/FF	7	4	2	6	2	5	8	6	3	2.5	Y	Y	Y
1662	Western New Eng C / Springfield	MA	12100	4500	P[5]	Priv	M	S	A=S	E			Y	FA/FF	5	4	2	8	1	4	8	5		2.5	Y	Y	Y
1663	Sacred Heart U / Fairfield	CT	12800	5000	M[5]	Cath / S	M	S	4/15 / S/A	S		Y	Y	3/01 / FA/FF	8	6	0	0	2	0	8	7	1	2.0 / 2.5	Y		Y
1664	New Haven,U of / West Haven	CT	13600	4500	D[5]	Priv	M		8/15 / S/A	S			Y		6	3	2	4	3	3	7	2	3		Y		Y
1665	Quinnipiac C / Hamden	CT	13700	4600	M[5]	Priv	M	S	A=S	S			Y	3/01 / FF=FA	6	6	1	8	1	5	8	6	5	3.0	Y	Y	Y
1666	New Eng,U of / Biddeford	ME	13800[3]	4200	P[5]	Priv	S		S/A	4		Y	Y	4/01 / FF=FA	9	8	4	8	1	5	9	6	2	3.2 / 2.6	Y	Y	
1667	Springfield C / Springfield	MA	13800[3]	4400	D[5]	Priv	L	S	4/01 / S/A	S		Y	Y	4/01 / FAF	5	5	1	8	1	7	8	8	1		Y		
1668	Assumption C / Worcester	MA	13900	4700	M[5]	Cath / S	M	S	3/01 / S/A	S		Y	Y	2/01 / FA/FF	6	5	1	9	1	4	9	8	6	3.0 / 2.8	Y	Y	
1669	NH C / Manchester	NH	14000[3]	4500	M[5]	Priv	L	S	SAT	S			Y	FAF	8	5	2	8	1	8	8		1	2.8 / 2.7	Y		Y
1670	Saint Anselm C / Manchester	NH	14200[3]	4800	B[5]	Cath / OS	M	S	4/01 / S/A	E		Y	Y	4/15 / FA/FF	6	5	0	9	1	8	9	7	3	3.0 / 2.5	Y		
1671	Roger Williams C / Bristol	RI	14600	4800	B[5]	Priv	S		A=S	4		Y	Y	3/01 / FAF	4	4	0	8	1	9	8	5	3	2.8 / 2.7	Y	Y	
1672	Bridgeport,U of / Bridgeport	CT	15000[3]	4800	D[5]	Priv	M	U	S/A	S		Y	Y	FA/FF	6	5	3	6	3	6	6	5	2		Y	Y	Y
1673	Gordon C / Wenham	MA	15000[3]	3600	B[5]	Oth	T		S/A	Q		Y	Y	3/15 / FAF	8	6	0	9	1	7	8	8	5	2.8	Y	Y	
1674	Merrimack C / North Andover	MA	15000	5300	B[5]	Cath / S	S		3/01 / S/A	S		Y	Y	3/15 / FAF	6	5	0	7	1	3	8	7	1	/ 2.4	Y	Y	Y
1675	Mass C Pharm/Health / Boston	MA	15200	6000	D[5]	Priv	V	U	6/01 / Oth	Q		Y	Y	4/01 / FA/FF	8	6	1	6	4	4	8	7	1	2.9 / 2.9	Y		Y
1676	Lesley C / Cambridge	MA	15500	4800	D[5]	Priv	L	U	A=S	E		Y	Y[6]	3/01 / FAF	6	9	4	9	1	4	7		1	2.6 / 2.3	Y		
1677	Salve Regina-Newport / Newport	RI	15700	5200	D[5]	Cath / S	S		A=S	E		Y	Y	3/01 / FA/FF	5	7	1	9	1	8	9	8			Y		
1678	Norwich U / Northfield	VT	16300[3]	4500	M[5]	Priv	T		A=S	E		Y	Y	FA/FF	7	4	2	9	1	8	7	6	2	/ 2.2	Y	Y	
1679	Curry C / Milton	MA	17500	5600	M[5]	Priv	S		4/01 / S/A	E		Y	Y	4/15 / FA/FF	4	5	1	7	1	5	7	4		2.5 / 2.3	Y	Y	
1680	Hartford,U of / West Hartford	CT	17600	5100	D[5]	Priv	M	S	A=S	E		Y	Y	3/01 / FA/FF	4	5	1	9	2	7	7	4		/ 2.6	Y	Y	Y
1681	Emerson C / Boston	MA	19800[3]	7100	D[5]	Priv	V	U	S/A	E		Y	Y	FA/FF	7	6	1	9	1	6	8	5		2.9 / 3.0	Y	Y	Y
	Enrollment 5,000 to 15,000																										
1682	Bridgewater St C / Bridgewater	MA	5000	3200 / 7800	M[5]	Pub	S		3/01 / SAT	S			Y	FAF	5	6	1	5	1	1	6	3	1	3.0 / 2.0	Y	Y	Y
1683	Central Conn St U / New Britain	CT	5400	3500 / 8200	M[5]	Pub	M	S	7/01 / SAT	S				3/25 / FAF	3	5	1	3	1	1	7	4	2		Y	Y	Y
1684	Southern Conn St U / New Haven	CT	5700	4000 / 8500	M[5]	Pub	M	U	S/A	S			Y	3/15 / FA/FF	3	6	1	4	1	1	7	6	3	2.7 / 2.4	Y		Y
1685	Salem St C / Salem	MA	5800	3400 / 8800	M[5]	Pub	S		3/01 / S/A	E		Y		4/01 / FAF	6	6	0	2	1	1	7	7		2.8	Y	Y	
1686	Rhode Island C / Providence	RI	6100	4300 / 8900	M[5]	Pub	L	S	5/01 / S/A	S		Y		3/01 / FAF	9	6	2	2	1	1	7	5	7	3.2 / 2.7	Y	Y	
1687	Lowell,U of / Lowell	MA	6600	3900 / 10600	D[5]	Pub	M	U	S/A	S			Y	5/01 / FAF	4	4	1	2	2	1					Y		Y

▲ Sequence number—indicates the order of the college in this book only. Do *not* use this number with admissions tests or need analysis services.

[1] No campus room and board facilities
[2] Room only or board only
[3] Most freshmen required to live on campus
[4] City or district residence requirements
[5] Accredited by a regional accrediting association or a recognized candidate for accreditation
[6] All female freshman class
[7] All male freshman class

MAJORS AVAILABLE AND PERCENT OF STUDENTS STUDYING IN EACH AREA

Sequence Number	Agri.	Business	Comm.	Education	Engineering	Fine/App. Arts	Lang.	Health	Home Ec.	Humanities	Math-Sciences	Social Sciences	GS	ROTC
1658														
1659		016%	019%	016%		1%				6%	015%	022%		Y
1660		057%	3%	2%	1%	1%	1%	1%		6%	017%	6%		
1661		040%	1%	021%		1%	1%	7%		2%	6%	017%		YY
1662		051%			014%					2%	7%	8%		YY
1663		036%	3%	7%		3%	1%	2%		5%	010%	013%		Y
1664		021%	5%		019%	9%				2%	5%	022%		Y
1665		033%	5%			1%	1%	038%		2%	8%	6%		Y
1666		4%		2%				049%		3%	020%	012%		Y
1667		014%	2%	021%		2%	1%	027%		2%	7%	5%		YY
1668		030%		3%			3%	1%		2%	014%	016%		YYY
1669		090%	7%	1%							2%			YY
1670		021%		3%	3%		4%	8%		021%	016%	017%		YY
1671		025%	5%	2%	010%	024%				010%	012%	012%		Y
1672		015%	3%		011%	013%		012%	3%		7%	4%		Y
1673		012%	1%	015%		1%	2%	1%		2%	3%	2%		YYY
1674		054%		9%	9%					6%	7%	015%		
1675		020%						070%			010%			Y
1676		5%		065%				030%						
1677		017%		025%		4%	1%	9%		6%	6%	029%		Y
1678		015%	5%	4%	025%	4%		010%			012%	025%		YYY
1679		013%	010%	7%		1%		010%		1%	1%	6%		Y
1680		025%	9%	6%	016%	010%		4%		1%	4%	8%		YY
1681			074%			011%		2%		013%				
1682	1%	019%	5%	031%		3%	1%	1%		4%	6%	015%		YY
1683		034%	5%	018%	7%	2%	1%	1%		3%	7%	015%		YY
1684		024%	012%	018%		5%	1%	9%		2%	8%	011%		YY
1685		030%	2%	016%		1%	1%	010%		2%	3%	015%		
1686		012%	7%	014%		1%	1%	019%		2%	3%	2%		Y
1687		023%		1%	027%	5%		7%		2%	8%	012%		YY

[1] Additional majors available in this area
[2] ROTC available

†Accredited by a nationally recognized accrediting body other than one of the regional accrediting associations

New England States
(continued)

CT, MA, ME, NH, RI, VT

TRADITIONAL ADMISSIONS *Majority of accepted students in top 50% of HS class*

Sequence Number	School name (upper entry) / City (lower entry)	State	Costs: Resident tuition/fees + room/board	Costs: Room/Board (upper entry) / Nonresident tuition/fees + room/board (lower entry)	General Information: Highest degree	General Information: Affiliation (upper entry) / Religious observance (lower entry)	General Information: Size of community	General Information: Type of community	Admissions: Fall term application deadline (upper entry) / Tests desired or required (lower entry)	Admissions: Calendar	Admissions: Fall admission only	Admissions: Early admission	Admissions: Deferred admission	Financial Aid: Fall term application deadline (upper entry) / Forms to be filed (lower entry)	Number in 10 who— -have need, receive some aid	Under-grads: -are women	Under-grads: -are graduate students	Freshmen: -live on campus	Freshmen: -are minority students	Freshmen: -are nonresidents	Freshmen: -return as sophomores	Freshmen: -complete degree	Freshmen: -enter graduate study	HS GPA (upper entry) / 1st year college GPA (lower entry)	Special Programs: Credit by exam	Special Programs: Student designed majors	Special Programs: Fraternities/sororities
	Enrollment 5,000 to 15,000																										
1688	Maine Orono,U of Orono	ME	6900	3900 10100	D[5]	Pub	S		 S/A	E		Y	Y	3/01 FAF	5	5	1	9	1	2	8	5	2		Y	Y	Y
	Enrollment over 15,000																										
1689	Northeastern U Boston	MA	16400	6400	D[5]	Priv	V	U	 S/A	Q		Y	Y	3/01 FAF	8	4	1	6	4	4	7	5		2.7	Y	Y	Y
	SELECTIVE ADMISSIONS *Majority of accepted students in top 25% of HS class*																										
	Enrollment to 1,000																										
1690	Saint Joseph C West Hartford	CT	14500	4100	M[5]	Cath S	M	S	5/01 S/A	E		Y	Y[6]	2/01 FAF	7	9	1	7	1	1	8	7	4	 2.9	Y	Y	
1691	Simon's Rock of Bard Gr Barrington	MA	17700[3]	4400	B[5]	Priv	T		 A=S	S		Y	Y	 FA/FF	7	6	0	9	2	8	8		5				
1692	World Studies Prgm Marlboro	VT	18800	4800	B[5]	Priv	S		 A=S	S		Y	Y	3/15 FAF	8	6	0	9	1	9			6	3.0		Y	
1693	New Eng Consv Music Boston	MA	19600[3]	6200	M[5]	Priv	V	U	1/15 SAT	E			Y	3/01 FAF	7	5	5	9	2	8	9	8	6		Y		Y
1694	Marlboro C Marlboro	VT	21300[3]	5200	M[5]	Priv	T		 A=S	S		Y	Y	4/15 FA/FF	6	5	0	9	1	8	7	5	6		Y	Y	
1695	Bennington C Bennington	VT	23200	3800	M[5]	Priv	S		3/01 A=S	O		Y	Y	3/01 FAF	5	6	1	9	1	9		6	4			Y	
	Enrollment 1,000 to 5,000																										
1696	Bryant C Smithfield	RI	15700	5800	M[5]	Priv	S		 A=S	E		Y	Y	3/01 FAF	7	4	1	8	1	8	9	9	5	3.1 2.8	Y		Y
1697	Stonehill C North Easton	MA	15700	5400	B[5]	Cath S	S		2/15 S/A	E		Y	Y	 FAF	5	5	0	8	1	3	9	7		 2.9	Y	Y	
1698	Providence C Providence	RI	15900	5000	D[5]	Cath OS	M	S	2/01 A=S	S		Y	Y	2/15 FAF	5	5	1	9	1	8	9	9	2	 2.8	Y	Y	
1699	Bentley C Waltham	MA	16200	4800	M[5]	Priv	M	S	3/10 A=S	E		Y	Y	2/01 FA/FF	5	5	1	9	2	5	9	7	7	 2.7	Y	Y	Y
1700	Saint Michael's C Colchester	VT	16400[3]	5100	M[5]	Cath OS	S		2/15 S/A	E		Y	Y	3/15 FA/FF	6	5	1	9	1	8	9	7	5	3.3 2.3	Y	Y	
1701	Fairfield U Fairfield	CT	16900[3]	5100	M[5]	Cath S	M	S	3/01 S/A	E		Y	Y	2/01 FAF	6	5	1	9	1	7	9	8	1	3.0 2.8			
1702	Rhode Island Sch Des Providence	RI	18800[3]	5600	P[5]	Priv	M	U	2/15 S/A	4		Y	Y	2/15 FA/FF	6	6	1	9	2	9	9	8	2	3.1			
1703	Babson C Wellesley	MA	19700	5800	M[5]	Priv	S		2/01 Oth	4			Y	2/01 FAF	4	4	1	8	2	4	9	8	1	 2.0	Y	Y	Y
1704	Conn C New London	CT	20000	4800	M[5]	Priv	S		1/15 Oth	E		Y	Y	2/15 FAF	4	5	1	9	1	8	9	8	5	3.4		Y	
1705	Simmons C Boston	MA	20100	6000	D[5]	Priv	V	U	2/01 A=S	E		Y	Y[6]	2/01 FAF	5	9	2	9	1	6	8	7	2		Y	Y	
1706	Hampshire C Amherst	MA	20700	4200	B[5]	Priv	S		2/01 None	4		Y	Y	2/15 FAF	5	6	0	9	1	9	8	6	4			Y	
1707	Wheaton C Norton	MA	21300	5500	B[5]	Priv	S		2/01 S/A	E		Y	Y	2/15 FA/FF	5	8	0	9	1	7	9	7	3	3.0 3.0		Y	
	Enrollment 5,000 to 15,000																										
1708	Southeastern Mass U North Dartmouth	MA	6500	4100 10400	M[5]	Pub	S		 SAT	S		Y		 FAF	4	5	1	5	1	1	9	5	1	 2.5	Y	Y	Y
1709	Rhode Island,U of Kingston	RI	6800	4200 11300	D[5]	Pub	S		3/01 A=S	E		Y		3/01 FAF	7	5	1	9	2	6	8	5	2	3.0 2.5	Y		Y
1710	NH,U of Durham	NH	7100	3500 13100	D[5]	Pub	S		2/01 S/A	E		Y	Y	2/15 FAF	5	5	1	9	1	4	8	6		 2.5	Y	Y	Y
1711	Conn,U of Storrs	CT	7300	4300 12100	D[5]	Pub	S		4/01 SAT	E			Y	2/15 FAF	1	5	1	9	1	2	8	6				Y	Y
1712	Vermont,U of Burlington	VT	8200[3]	4000 16800	D[5]	Pub	S		2/01 S/A	E		Y	Y	3/01 FA/FF	4	5	1	9	1	5	9	7		 2.6	Y	Y	Y

Sequence Number | School name (upper entry) City (lower entry) | State | Costs | General Information | Admissions | Financial Aid | Student Profile | Programs

▲ **Sequence number—indicates the order of the college in this book only. Do *not* use this number with admissions tests or need analysis services.**

[1] No campus room and board facilities
[2] Room only or board only
[3] Most freshmen required to live on campus
[4] City or district residence requirements
[5] Accredited by a regional accrediting association or a recognized candidate for accreditation
[6] All female freshman class
[7] All male freshman class

MAJORS AVAILABLE AND PERCENT OF STUDENTS STUDYING IN EACH AREA

Sequence Number	Agri.					Business							Comm.				Education												Engineering						Fine/App. Arts								Lang.						Health									Home Ec.						Humanities							Math-Sciences									Social Sciences												GS	ROTC		
	Agriculture, general	Agronomy (crops & mgmt)	Animal Science (husbandry)	Fish, Wildlife Mgmt	Forestry	Business/Commerce, general	Accounting	Banking/Finance	Business Economics	Business Mgmt/Admin	Marketing/Purchasing	Secretarial Studies	Communications, general	Journalism	Radio/TV (broadcasting)	Advertising	Art Education	Distributive Education	Elementary Education	English Education	Mathematics Education	Music Education	Physical Education	Science Education	Secondary Education	Social Science Education	Special Education	Speech Education	Engineering, general	Chemical	Civil	Electrical/Electronics/Comm	Industrial/Management	Mechanical	Architecture	Fine/Applied Arts, general	Art (Paint, draw, sculpt)	Art History/Appreciation	Dance	Dramatic Arts (theater arts)	Music (liberal arts)	Music (perform, compos, theory)	French	German	Italian	Latin	Spanish	Russian	Predentistry	Premedicine	Medical/Lab Technology	Nursing (registered nurse)	Occupational Therapy	Preoptometry	Prepharmacy	Physical Therapy	Preveterinary Medicine	Home Economics, general	Clothing and Textiles	Consumer Ec/Home Mgmt	Family Relations/Child Devel	Food and Nutrition/Dietetics	Institution Mgmt	Humanities, general	Creative Writing	English, general	Literature, English	Philosophy	Religion	Speech/Forensic Science	Mathematics, general	Computer/Info Sciences	Biological Sciences, general	Biology	Botany	Zoology	Physical Sciences, general	Chemistry	Physics	Crim Just/Law Enforce	Social Work	Social Sciences, general	Anthropology	Area Studies (Amer., African, etc.)	Economics	Geography	History	Prelaw	Political Science	Psychology	Sociology	General Studies	Air Force	Army	Navy
1688	0 ■	1 ■	0 ■	% ■	[1] ■	■	0 ■	1 ■	6 ■	% ■	■		■	■	2 ■	%	■		■	■	■	■	8 ■	% ■	■	■	■	[1] ■	■	0 ■	1 ■	6 ■	%	[1] ■			■	■	5	% ■	■	[1]	■	■		1 ■	% ■		■	■	■	■	6	%			■	■	■	■	5 ■	% ■				■	4 ■	% ■		■	■	■	0 ■	1 ■	5 ■	% ■	■	■	[1] ■		■	■	■	0	1 ■	1	% ■	■	■	■	[1] ■		Y	Y	Y
1689						■	0 ■	2 ■	6	% ■	■	[1]	■	■	7	%			■				4 ■	%				[1]	■	0 ■	1 ■	8 ■	% ■	■		■			3 ■	% ■	■		■	■	■	1	% ■	■			0 ■	1 ■	0	%	■	■	[1]									■	2	% ■		[1]	■	■		■	5	%		■	[1] ■	■			■	0 ■	2 ■	2	% ■		■	■	[1] ■		Y	Y	Y
1690							■		9 ■	% ■							■		■	■	0 ■	2 ■	4	% ■	■	■	■	[1]										■	2	%			■			2	% ■			■	0 ■	2 ■	0	%				■		■	5	% ■		■		■	5	% ■	■		■	■	■	■	7	%	■	■			■	■		0	2 ■	0	% ■	■	■	■	■			Y	
1691															1	%																2	%			■			1	%				0	1	0	%			■			2	%			[1]								0	2	1 ■	%		[1]	■				6	%						■		0	2	0	%					■			
1692			1	%					1	%					1	%							1	%								1	%						1	%						3	%																				5	%							2	%								0	8	3	%				[1]				
1693																						■	1	%													0	9	9	%		■																																																						
1694					■																															■	0 ■	1 ■	1	% ■	■	[1] ■	■	■	■	■	■																	■	0 ■	3 ■	0 ■	% ■	■	[1]	■	■	0 ■	2 ■	4 ■	%	■	■	[1] ■			■	■	0	1 ■	5	% ■		■	■	[1] ■				
1695																												[1]							■	■	■		■	■	■	■	■	■			■																		■	■	■	■		[1]	■		■	■			■	■	[1] ■			■	■		■		■		■	■					
1696						■	0 ■	9 ■	7 ■	% ■	■		■		1	% ■																																																							■	■			2	%			[1]															Y	
1697							0 ■	2 ■	0	% ■	■		■		8	%			■	■	0 ■	1	0	% ■		■		[1]	■	■	■	1 ■	%	[1] ■												1	%		■	■	■		4	%			[1]									■	6	% ■	■		■	■	0	1 ■	0	%		■		■				0 ■	2 ■	6	% ■	■	■	■	[1] ■			Y	
1698						■	0 ■	3 ■	4 ■	% ■	■								■	■	■		1	% ■		■	■					1	%				■	■	1	% ■	■		■		■	1	% ■						5	%			[1]									■	8	% ■	■		■	■		■	9	%		■			■	■		0 ■	3 ■	8	% ■		■	■	[1] ■	■		Y	
1699							0 ■	8 ■	7 ■	% ■	■		■		3	%																																																		■		■							3	%			[1]								■					■	Y	Y	
1700							0 ■	2	8	% ■				■	4	%	■		■			■	8	%					■			1	%				■		2	% ■	■		■			1 ■	% ■																		0	1 ■	3 ■	% ■	■	[1]	■	■	0	1 ■	0	%		■	[1] ■					0 ■	1 ■	9	% ■		■	■	[1] ■		Y	Y	
1701							0 ■	2 ■	9	% ■	■		■		4	%													■	■	■	1 ■	%	■		■			1	%			■	■		1	% ■					■	4	%											0	1 ■	0 ■	% ■	■	[1]	■	■	0	1 ■	9	%		■	[1] ■					0 ■	1 ■	5	% ■		■	■	[1] ■				
1702																																			■	■	1 ■	0	0	%		[1]																■																																							
1703						■	0 ■	8 ■	2 ■	% ■	■		0 ■	1	1	%																																																											5	%			[1]						■	2	%								
1704																							3	%												■	0 ■	1 ■	3 ■	% ■	■		■	■	■	7 ■	% ■	■													■				0	1 ■	2 ■	% ■	■	[1]	■		■	■	8 ■	% ■	■	■	[1] ■			■	■	0 ■	5 ■	3	% ■		■	■	[1] ■				
1705						■	0 ■	2 ■	3 ■	% ■	■		0 ■	1 ■	0	% ■			■	■	■	■	7	% ■	■	■	■	[1]	■					[1]		■	■	■	3	%	■		■			1	% ■				0	1 ■	9	%	■	■						■				■	8 ■	% ■		[1]	■	■	■	■	7	%	■	■	[1] ■					0 ■	1 ■	6	% ■		■	■	[1] ■			Y	
1706	■		1 ■	%	[1]							[1]	■	■	2	%							2	%				[1]								■	0 ■	2 ■	7 ■	% ■	■	[1] ■							■	■			3	%			[1] ■				■			■	0 ■	1 ■	7 ■	% ■	■	[1]	■	■	■	■	9 ■	%	■	■	[1] ■			■	■	0 ■	2 ■	3	% ■	■	■	■	[1] ■	■			
1707																																					■	■	4	%	■		■	■	■	3	% ■	■					1	%											0	1 ■	3 ■	% ■	■	[1]	■		0	1 ■	0	%		■	[1] ■				■	0	5 ■	7	% ■		■	■	■				
1708							0 ■	2 ■	0	% ■	■	[1]			1	%	■						1	%					■	0	1 ■	0 ■	%	■		■	■	■	2	%	■	[1]	■	■		2	% ■				0 ■	1 ■	0	%												■	5	% ■			■	■		■	4	%		■	■	■	■				■	2	% ■		■	■	■			Y	
1709			2 ■	% ■	[1]	■	0 ■	1 ■	8	% ■	■	[1]	■	■	8	%	■		■	■	0 ■	1 ■	0 ■	% ■	■	■		[1] ■	■	■	■	8 ■	% ■	[1] ■		■	■	■	2	% ■	■	[1] ■	■	■	■	1 ■	% ■	■			■	■	9	%	■	■	[1]	■	0 ■	1 ■	3 ■	% ■				■	5 ■	% ■		[1] ■	■	■	■	■	5 ■	% ■	■	■	[1] ■			■	■	0 ■	1 ■	8 ■	% ■		■	■	[1] ■	■		Y	
1710		■	6 ■	% ■	[1] ■	■	0	1	2	% ■		[1]	■	■	4	%	■		■	■	■	■	2 ■	% ■			■	[1] ■	■	■	■	9 ■	%	[1] ■		■	■	■	4	% ■	■	[1] ■	■	■		2 ■	% ■	■			■	■	7 ■	%			[1] ■			■	2	%		■		■	7	% ■		[1]	■	■	0 ■	1 ■	0 ■	% ■	■	■	[1] ■		■		■	0	1 ■	7 ■	% ■		■	■	[1] ■		Y	Y	
1711	■	■	2 ■	%	[1]	■	■	■	8	% ■	■	[1]	■	■	5	%		■	■			■	3 ■	%	■		■	[1]	■	■	■	9 ■	%	■		■	■	■	5	% ■	■	[1] ■	■	■	■	1	% ■	■			■	■	7	%	■	■	[1]			■	4 ■	% ■				■	6 ■	% ■		[1]	■			■	9	%		■	[1] ■			■	■	0 ■	2 ■	2 ■	% ■		■	■	[1] ■	■	Y	Y	
1712	■		6 ■	% ■	[1] ■	■	0 ■	1 ■	1	% ■	■						■		■	■	■	■	6 ■	% ■	■	■	■	[1]			■	7 ■	% ■	■			■	■	3	% ■	■	■	■	■		2 ■	% ■	■		■	0 ■	1 ■	0	%		■	[1]	■	■		5 ■	% ■		■	■	■	9 ■	% ■	■	[1]	■	■	0 ■	1 ■	1 ■	% ■	■	■	[1] ■		■	■	■	0 ■	2 ■	2 ■	% ■		■	■	[1] ■	■	Y	Y	
Sequence Number	Agri.					Business							Comm.				Education												Engineering						Fine/App. Arts								Lang.						Health									Home Ec.						Humanities							Math-Sciences									Social Sciences												GS	ROTC		

[1] Additional majors available in this area
[2] ROTC available

†Accredited by a nationally recognized accrediting body other than one of the regional accrediting associations

New England States
(continued)

CT, MA, ME, NH, RI, VT

SELECTIVE ADMISSIONS *Majority of accepted students in top 25% of HS class*

Sequence Number	School name (upper entry) City (lower entry)	State	Costs: Resident tuition/fees + room/board	Costs: Room/Board (upper entry) Nonresident tuition/fees + room/board (lower entry)	General Information: Highest degree	Affiliation (upper entry) Religious observance (lower entry)	Size of community	Type of community	Admissions: Fall term application deadline (upper entry) Tests desired or required (lower entry)	Calendar	Fall admission only	Early admission	Deferred admission	Financial Aid: Fall term application deadline (upper entry) Forms to be filed (lower entry)	Number in 10 who— -have need, receive some aid	Under-grads: -are women	-are graduate students	Freshmen: -live on campus	-are minority students	-are nonresidents	-return as sophomores	-complete degree	-enter graduate study	HS GPA (upper entry) 1st year college GPA (lower entry)	Special Programs: Credit by exam	Student designed majors	Fraternities/sororities
	Enrollment over 15,000																										
1713	Mass Amherst,U of Amherst	MA	7100 [3]	3600 12200	D [5]	Pub	S		2/15 A=S	S				3/01 FAF	6	5	3	8	2	2	8	6	3	 2.6	Y	Y	Y
	HIGHLY SELECTIVE *Majority of accepted students in top 10% of HS class*																										
	Enrollment to 1,000																										
1714	U S Coast Guard Acad New London	CT	0 [3]	0	B [5]	Pub	S		12/15 A=S	S				 None	0	1	0	9	1	9	8	5	8	3.7	Y		
	Enrollment 1,000 to 5,000																										
1715	Mass C of Art Boston	MA	8400	5100 12200	M [5]	Pub	V	U	4/01 SAT	E			Y	 FF=FA	5	6	1	1	3	1	8	7	2		Y	Y	
1716	Worcester Poly Inst Worcester	MA	18600	4600	D [5]	Priv	L	U	2/15 A=S	O		Y	Y	3/01 FAF	8	2	1	9	1	6	9	8	6	3.5		Y	Y
1717	Wesleyan U Middletown	CT	19300	4700	D [5]	Priv	S		1/15 S/A	E		Y	Y	2/01 FF=FA	5	5	1	9	2	9	9	9	7		Y	Y	Y
1718	Mount Holyoke C South Hadley	MA	19600	4600	B [5]	Priv	S		2/01 Oth	4		Y	Y [6]	2/01 FA/FF	6	9	0	9	2	8	9	8	7	 3.1	Y	Y	
1719	Trinity C Hartford	CT	19600	4500	M [5]	Priv	L	U	1/15 Oth	E		Y	Y	2/01 FAF	4	5	0	9	2	8	9	8	7	3.4 2.9		Y	Y
1720	Wellesley C Wellesley	MA	20100	5300	B [5]	Priv	S		2/01 Oth	4		Y	Y [6]	2/01 FAF	4	9	0	9	3	8	9	8	6		Y	Y	
1721	Middlebury C Middlebury	VT	20300	0	D [5]	Priv	T		1/15 A=S	4			Y	2/01 FAF		5	0	9	1	9	9	8	4			Y	
1722	Smith C Northampton	MA	20300 [3]	5700	D [5]	Priv	S		1/15 A=S	4		Y	Y [6]	1/15 FAF	5	9	1	9	2	8	9	9	7	3.5		Y	
1723	Amherst C Amherst	MA	20400 [3]	4400	B [5]	Priv	S		1/01 A=S	4		Y	Y	1/15 FA/FF	5	5	0	9	2	9	9	9	8			Y	
1724	Bowdoin C Brunswick	ME	20400 [3]	5200	B [5]	Priv	S		1/15 None	E		Y	Y	3/01 FAF	6	5	0	9	1	8	9	9	7	3.5		Y	Y
1725	Colby C Waterville	ME	20400 [3]	5100	B [5]	Priv	S		1/15 Oth	4		Y	Y	2/01 FAF	7	5	0	9	1	9	9	9	6	 2.9	Y	Y	
1726	Dartmouth C Hanover	NH	20500 [3]	5100	D [5]	Priv	T		1/01 S/A	O			Y	1/15 FA/FF	4	4	2	9	4		9	9	8	 3.1		Y	Y
1727	Williams C Williamstown	MA	20800	5000	M [5]	Priv	T		1/01 A=S	4		Y	Y	1/01 FF=FA	4	4	1	9	2	9	9	9		 2.9	Y	Y	
1728	Holy Cross,C of the Worcester	MA	21200	5700	B [5]	Cath OS	M	S	2/01 S/A	S		Y	Y	2/01 FF=FA	6	5	0	8	1	5	9	9	8	 2.9		Y	
1729	Brandeis U Waltham	MA	21300	6000	D [5]	Priv	M	S	2/01 A=S	E		Y	Y	2/15 FAF	5	5	2	9	1	8	9	8	8			Y	
1730	Bates C Lewiston	ME	21400	0	B [5]	Priv	M		2/01 A=S	O		Y	Y	2/15 FAF	4	5	0	9	1	9	9	9	6	3.5 2.7		Y	
	Enrollment 5,000 to 15,000																										
1731	Harvard-Radcliffe U Cambridge	MA	19600	5100	D [5]	Priv	M		1/01 Oth	S		Y	Y	2/15 FAF	7	4	3	9	3	8	9	9		4.0 3.5	Y	Y	
1732	Boston C Chestnut Hill	MA	20300	6200	D [5]	Oth S	M		1/25 A=S	E		Y	Y	2/01 FA/FF	6	5	2	9	2	7	9	8	5	3.5 2.9	Y	Y	
1733	Mass Inst of Techn Cambridge	MA	20700 [3]	5100	D [5]	Priv	M	U	11/01 A=S	4		Y	Y	2/01	6	3	5	9	5	9	9	9	7		Y	Y	Y
1734	Yale U New Haven	CT	20800 [3]	5600	D [5]	Priv	M	U	12/31 A=S	S		Y	Y	1/15 FAF	4	4	5	9	3	9	9	9	7		Y	Y	
1735	Brown U Providence	RI	20900 [3]	5000	D [5]	Priv	L	U	1/01 S/A	E		Y	Y	1/15 FAF	9	5	2	9	2	9	9	9	6			Y	Y

▲ Sequence number—indicates the order of the college in this book only. Do *not* use this number with admissions tests or need analysis services.

[1] No campus room and board facilities
[2] Room only or board only
[3] Most freshmen required to live on campus
[4] City or district residence requirements
[5] Accredited by a regional accrediting association or a recognized candidate for accreditation
[6] All female freshman class
[7] All male freshman class

MAJORS AVAILABLE AND PERCENT OF STUDENTS STUDYING IN EACH AREA

Sequence Number	Agri.	Business	Comm.	Education	Engineering	Fine/App. Arts	Lang.	Health	Home Ec.	Humanities	Math-Sciences	Social Sciences	GS	ROTC Air Force	ROTC Army	ROTC Navy
1713	6% [1]	019% [1]	7%	4% [1]	010%	5% [1]	2%	2% [1]	4%	4% [1]	4% [1]	015% [1]		Y	Y	
1714		015%			037%						030% [1]	018%				
1715				6%		094% [1]										
1716		8%			069% [1]			1%		1%	018% [1]	2% [1]		Y	Y	Y
1717				1%	1%	6% [1]	2%			020% [1]	014% [1]	030% [1]				
1718										[1]	[1]	[1]		Y	Y	
1719					2%	5%	2%			021% [1]	024% [1]	042% [1]				
1720						9%	015%			014% [1]	021% [1]	032% [1]		Y	Y	Y
1721							8%			[1]	[1]	[1]				
1722				2% [1]		013%	6%			014% [1]	024% [1]	032% [1]		Y	Y	
1723						6%	5%			023% [1]	015% [1]	039% [1]				
1724						5%	6%			010% [1]	012% [1]	034% [1]				
1725		5%				6%	6%			017% [1]	016% [1]	040% [1]		Y	Y	
1726				1%	6%	6% [1]	6%			022% [1]	021% [1]	038% [1]			Y	
1727					1%	010%	4%	1%		023% [1]	010% [1]	044% [1]				
1728		5%				2%	5%			019% [1]	022% [1]	041% [1]		Y		Y
1729				1%	1%	6%	3%	1%		016% [1]	017% [1]	052% [1]				
1730						8%	6%			018%	015% [1]	049% [1]				
1731						[1]				[1]	[1]	[1]		Y	Y	Y
1732		022%	7%	8% [1]		1%	2%	012%		015% [1]	010% [1]	023% [1]		Y	Y	Y
1733		[1] 4%	[1]		053% [1]	4% [1]		1%		1% [1]	032% [1]	4% [1]		Y	Y	Y
1734					2%	010% [1]	1%			019% [1]	013% [1]	038% [1]		Y	Y	
1735				1%	010% [1]	2%	7%	012%		5% [1]	013% [1]	5% [1]				

1 Additional majors available in this area
2 ROTC available

†Accredited by a nationally recognized accrediting body other than one of the regional accrediting associations

New England States
(continued)

CT, MA, ME, NH, RI, VT

SELECTIVE ADMISSIONS *Majority of accepted students in top 25% of HS class*

Sequence Number	School name (upper entry) City (lower entry)	State	Costs: Resident tuition/fees + room/board	Costs: Room/Board (upper entry) Nonresident tuition/fees + room/board (lower entry)	General Information: Highest degree	General Information: Affiliation (upper entry) Religious observance (lower entry)	General Information: Size of community	General Information: Type of community	Admissions: Fall term application deadline (upper entry) Tests desired or required (lower entry)	Admissions: Calendar	Admissions: Fall admission only	Admissions: Early admission	Admissions: Deferred admission	Financial Aid: Fall term application deadline (upper entry) Forms to be filed (lower entry)	Financial Aid: Number in 10 who— -have need, receive some aid	Student Profile: Undergrads -are women	Undergrads -are graduate students	Freshmen -live on campus	Freshmen -are minority students	Freshmen -are nonresidents	Freshmen -return as sophomores	Freshmen -complete degree	Freshmen -enter graduate study	HS GPA (upper entry) 1st year college GPA (lower entry)	Special Programs: Credit by exam	Special Programs: Student designed majors	Special Programs: Fraternities/sororities
	Enrollment 5,000 to 15,000																										
1736	Tufts U Medford	MA	22100 3	5300	D 5	Priv	M	S	1/01 Oth	E		Y	Y	2/01 FAF	4	5	4	9	2	7	9	9	4			Y	Y
	Enrollment over 15,000																										
1737	Boston U Boston	MA	22300 3	6300	D 5	Priv	V	U	S/A	S		Y	Y	3/01 FAF	5	5	3	9	3	8	8	6		3.4 2.9	Y	Y	Y

▲ Sequence number—indicates the order of the college in this book only. Do *not* use this number with admissions tests or need analysis services.

[1] No campus room and board facilities
[2] Room only or board only
[3] Most freshmen required to live on campus
[4] City or district residence requirements
[5] Accredited by a regional accrediting association or a recognized candidate for accreditation
[6] All female freshman class
[7] All male freshman class

MAJORS AVAILABLE AND PERCENT OF STUDENTS STUDYING IN EACH AREA

Agri.

Sequence Number	Agriculture, general	Agronomy (crops & mgmt)	Animal Science (husbandry)	Fish, Wildlife Mgmt	Forestry	%
1736						
1737						

Business

Sequence Number	Business/Commerce, general	Accounting	Banking/Finance	Business Economics	Business Mgmt/Admin	Marketing/Purchasing	Secretarial Studies	%
1736								
1737	■	■			■	■		020% [1]

Comm.

Sequence Number	Communications, general	Journalism	Radio/TV (broadcasting)	Advertising	%
1736					
1737	■	■	■		016%

Education

Sequence Number	Art Education	Distributive Education	Elementary Education	English Education	Mathematics Education	Music Education	Physical Education	Science Education	Secondary Education	Social Science Education	Special Education	Speech Education	%
1736	■												1% [1]
1737	■	■	■	■	■	■	■	■	■	■	■	■	3% [1]

Engineering

Sequence Number	Engineering, general	Chemical	Civil	Electrical/Electronics/Comm	Industrial/Management	Mechanical	%
1736	■	■	■	■		■	018% [1]
1737	■			■	■	■	012% [1]

Fine/App. Arts

Sequence Number	Architecture	Fine/Applied Arts, general	Art (Paint, draw, sculpt)	Art History/Appreciation	Dance	Dramatic Arts (theater arts)	Music (liberal arts)	Music (perform, compos, theory)	%
1736		■		■		■	■		
1737		■	■	■		■	■	■	5% [1]

Lang.

Sequence Number	French	German	Italian	Latin	Spanish	Russian	%
1736	■	■	■	■	■	■	3%
1737	■	■	■	■	■	■	1%

Health

Sequence Number	Predentistry	Premedicine	Medical/Lab Technology	Nursing (registered nurse)	Occupational Therapy	Preoptometry	Prepharmacy	Physical Therapy	Preveterinary Medicine	%
1736										4%
1737	■	■	■		■			■		9% [1]

Home Ec.

Sequence Number	Home Economics, general	Clothing and Textiles	Consumer Ec/Home Mgmt	Family Relations/Child Devel	Food and Nutrition/Dietetics	Institution Mgmt	%
1736							
1737							

Humanities

Sequence Number	Humanities, general	Creative Writing	English, general	Literature, English	Philosophy	Religion	Speech/Forensic Science	%
1736			■		■	■		[1]
1737	■		■	■	■	■		5% [1]

Math-Sciences

Sequence Number	Mathematics, general	Computer/Info Sciences	Biological Sciences, general	Biology	Botany	Zoology	Physical Sciences, general	Chemistry	Physics	%
1736	■	■	■	■			■	■	■	†
1737	■	■	■	■			■	■	■	8% †

Social Sciences

Sequence Number	Crim Just/Law Enforce	Social Work	Social Sciences, general	Anthropology	Area Studies (Amer., African, etc.)	Economics	Geography	History	Prelaw	Political Science	Psychology	Sociology	%
1736				■	■	■		■		■	■	■	[1]
1737			■	■	■	■	■	■	■	■	■	■	020% [1]

GS / ROTC

Sequence Number	General Studies	Air Force	Army	Navy
1736		Y	Y	Y
1737	■	Y	Y	Y

[1] Additional majors available in this area
[2] ROTC available

†Accredited by a nationally recognized accrediting body other than one of the regional accrediting associations

Index of additional majors at four-year colleges

On the four-year college **Search** pages, indicators (■) show which of 92 majors are offered by each college. On the following pages, sequence numbers are provided to identify four-year schools offering the 63 **additional majors** shown in the outline on the next page.

These majors represent concentrated study in a subject area as part of the four-year bachelor's degree or a coordinated sequence of upper division courses in a preprofessional program such as predentistry or premedicine.

Suggestions for using this index

Which colleges in a region offer a specific major?

To identify colleges in a region that offer one of the majors listed on the next page, follow these steps:

1. Use the chart below to note the sequence number range for colleges in that region.

Region	Sequence No. Range
1. Pacific and Mountain States	0001-0228
2. North Central States	0229-0421
3. Great Lakes States	0422-0728
4. South Central States	0729-1004
5. South Atlantic States	1005-1301
6. Middle Atlantic States	1302-1585
7. New England States	1586-1737

2. Turn to the listings beginning on page 184 and find the major you are considering. Scan the numbers listed under that major to see if any are in the sequence number range for the region that interests you.

For example, assume you would like to find out which schools in the Pacific and Mountain States Region offer agricultural business majors. First, note that the sequence number range for colleges in that region is 0001-0228. Then, turn to the listing for **1. Agricultural Business** on page 184. You will see that there are 18 colleges with sequence numbers between 0001 and 0228 (0056, 0069, and so on). All of these colleges are located in the Pacific and Mountain States region, and all of them offer agricultural business majors. Jot down these sequence numbers and turn back to the **Search** pages to identify the colleges and check other information about them.

Is a specific major available at the college you're considering?

Identify the sequence number for the college you're interested in by checking the **College Index** or the **Search** pages. Then, look for the sequence number among those listed for the specific major.

Additional majors at four-year colleges

Agriculture*

1. Agricultural Business
2. Agricultural Economics
3. Agricultural and Farm Management
4. Agriculture, Forestry, Wildlife Technologies
5. Food Science and Technology
6. Horticulture/Ornamental Horticulture
7. Natural Resources Management

Business*

8. Hotel and Restaurant Management
9. Labor and Industrial Relations
10. Office Management
11. Real Estate and Insurance
12. Recreation and Tourism
13. Transportation

Communications (All majors in this area are shown on the four-year college **Search** pages.)

Education*

14. Education, general
15. Agricultural Education
16. Home Economics Education
17. Industrial Arts, Vocational/Technical Education

Engineering*

18. Aerospace, Aeronautical, and Astronautical Engineering
19. Agricultural Engineering
20. Architectural Engineering
21. Environmental and Ecological Engineering
22. Geological Engineering
23. Metallurgical and Materials Engineering
24. Mining and Mineral Engineering
25. Nuclear Engineering
26. Ocean Engineering
27. Petroleum Engineering

Fine/Applied Arts*

28. Architecture Technology
29. City, Community, and Regional Planning
30. Environmental Design, Landscape Architecture
31. Interior Design
32. Applied Design
33. Photography/Cinematography

Foreign Languages (All majors in this area are shown on the four-year college **Search** pages.)

General Studies (Majors in this area are shown only on the four-year college **Search** pages.)

Health Professions*

34. Health Professions, general
35. Dental Assistant
36. Dental Hygiene
37. Dental Lab Technology
38. Medical Assistant or Medical Office Assistant
39. Radiology
40. Radiologic Technology
41. Surgical Technology

Home Economics (All majors in this area are shown on the four-year college **Search** pages.)

Humanities*

42. Classics
43. Comparative Literature
44. Linguistics

Math/Physical Sciences*

45. Applied Mathematics
46. Statistics
47. Computer Programming
48. Information Systems and Sciences
49. Data Processing Technology
50. Computer Operating
51. Biochemistry
52. Ecology
53. Microbiology
54. Astronomy
55. Earth Sciences
56. Geology
57. Oceanography

Social Sciences*

58. Community Service, general
59. Parks and Recreation Management
60. Public Administration
61. Military
62. Ethnic Studies
63. International Relations

---

*Other majors in this area are shown on the right-hand pages of the four-year college **Search** section, which begins on page 56.

1. Agricultural Business

0056 0069 0071 0072 0114 0128 0129 0130 0134 0140
0185 0187 0192 0194 0198 0203 0204 0219 0241 0242
0244 0248 0249 0254 0259 0288 0294 0295 0296 0346
0350 0357 0363 0366 0367 0373 0376 0378 0383 0410
0542 0576 0620 0633 0634 0698 0699 0700 0701 0702
0716 0759 0760 0773 0775 0776 0777 0778 0779 0785
0811 0820 0822 0823 0829 0831 0840 0844 0846 0850
0852 0855 0891 0895 0903 0921 0922 0927 0935 0938
0939 0940 0956 0979 1085 1103 1113 1114 1115 1165
1178 1224 1252 1274 1277 1281 1286 1402 1541 1577
1579 1595 1688 1710

2. Agricultural Economics

0069 0071 0072 0128 0129 0134 0140 0182 0194 0197
0203 0219 0256 0259 0295 0366 0367 0376 0406 0411
0454 0542 0576 0620 0634 0698 0699 0701 0702 0716
0761 0765 0773 0781 0826 0829 0844 0850 0855 0887
0894 0895 0909 0921 0927 0935 0936 0938 0939 0979
0982 0983 1089 1113 1224 1274 1277 1281 1282 1283
1285 1286 1485 1541 1577 1688 1709 1711 1712 1713

3. Agricultural and Farm Management

0069 0114 0128 0130 0134 0194 0197 0203 0204 0219
0259 0295 0367 0410 0542 0576 0601 0698 0699 0716
0785 0831 0840 0844 0850 0887 0891 0935 0938 0940
0979 0983 1089 1165 1199 1485 1577 1688

4. Agricultural, Forestry, Wildlife Technologies

0069 0071 0128 0129 0140 0197 0236 0496 0542 0633
0634 0698 0699 0701 0702 0716 0785 0850 0855 0938
0939 0979 0983 1165 1282 1283 1286 1541 1577 1688
1712 1713

5. Food Science and Technology

0071 0128 0129 0130 0140 0182 0194 0197 0201 0203
0204 0219 0223 0256 0259 0341 0366 0376 0378 0410
0411 0504 0510 0576 0622 0634 0698 0699 0701 0702
0705 0716 0778 0779 0785 0844 0851 0855 0891 0909
0921 0927 0935 0936 0938 0939 0974 0979 0982 0983
1036 1037 1099 1113 1224 1274 1281 1282 1283 1285
1286 1302 1314 1386 1402 1485 1527 1536 1537 1541
1577 1649 1688 1706 1709 1712 1713 1733

6. Horticulture/Ornamental Horticulture

0069 0128 0129 0133 0134 0140 0182 0185 0194 0197
0203 0204 0219 0256 0259 0295 0296 0366 0367 0373
0376 0410 0411 0576 0633 0634 0698 0699 0701 0702
0716 0761 0773 0778 0779 0785 0844 0850 0855 0887
0921 0922 0927 0935 0936 0938 0939 0940 0979 0982
0983 1036 1089 1114 1158 1165 1195 1224 1252 1274
1281 1282 1283 1285 1286 1309 1402 1457 1541 1577
1579 1688 1710 1711 1712

7. Natural Resources Management

0012 0046 0069 0071 0072 0088 0107 0114 0127 0128
0129 0130 0132 0134 0170 0185 0186 0194 0197 0203
0204 0216 0219 0223 0249 0259 0295 0366 0376 0378
0410 0447 0464 0496 0542 0576 0578 0590 0622 0628
0632 0638 0678 0698 0699 0701 0702 0705 0706 0716
0717 0821 0844 0891 0920 0922 0927 0935 0939 0973
0983 1036 1074 1082 1165 1176 1189 1224 1281 1283
1286 1366 1448 1485 1486 1504 1541 1577 1594 1603
1682 1688 1706 1709 1710 1711 1712 1713

8. Hotel and Restaurant Management

0027 0046 0058 0068 0088 0105 0115 0127 0128 0129
0137 0140 0158 0170 0182 0185 0190 0256 0259 0277
0287 0288 0295 0338 0366 0371 0373 0410 0411 0456
0486 0492 0498 0507 0509 0510 0511 0532 0538 0574
0583 0603 0605 0611 0626 0628 0629 0634 0638 0659

8. Hotel and Restaurant Management (continued)

0689 0697 0699 0701 0702 0716 0752 0754 0764 0778
0783 0823 0841 0845 0854 0913 0917 0926 0934 0935
0936 0939 0955 0974 0979 0980 0981 0982 1020 1037
1055 1076 1092 1100 1101 1102 1109 1111 1125 1138
1144 1165 1190 1196 1204 1209 1219 1221 1222 1247
1270 1271 1273 1277 1283 1284 1285 1299 1301 1309
1311 1314 1327 1334 1369 1375 1397 1399 1403 1423
1431 1464 1527 1531 1536 1537 1541 1544 1577 1604
1608 1611 1620 1658 1664 1669 1678 1710 1713 1737

9. Labor and Industrial Relations

0071 0073 0088 0126 0133 0152 0166 0170 0192 0195
0200 0202 0259 0351 0374 0377 0391 0407 0409 0416
0459 0499 0511 0515 0563 0570 0571 0572 0574 0575
0580 0605 0617 0627 0628 0629 0630 0636 0638 0666
0680 0697 0699 0702 0703 0705 0717 0728 0772 0934
0979 0981 1037 1170 1221 1245 1278 1283 1286 1298
1301 1302 1307 1309 1315 1325 1334 1370 1410 1428
1433 1438 1442 1443 1456 1457 1476 1482 1483 1494
1495 1496 1500 1522 1527 1537 1541 1543 1571 1577
1578 1661 1672 1706 1708 1709 1733

10. Office Management

0013 0022 0044 0056 0057 0060 0065 0066 0067 0069
0070 0071 0072 0105 0106 0119 0126 0131 0133 0154
0186 0188 0194 0195 0202 0231 0242 0243 0244 0245
0248 0251 0253 0255 0268 0278 0282 0287 0288 0290
0292 0294 0295 0296 0330 0346 0347 0348 0367 0370
0371 0372 0373 0374 0376 0389 0431 0433 0435 0445
0449 0451 0452 0453 0454 0455 0457 0465 0481 0482
0486 0498 0510 0511 0577 0581 0595 0598 0603 0619
0621 0623 0624 0626 0629 0630 0632 0633 0635 0689
0697 0700 0719 0737 0744 0748 0749 0750 0751 0752
0755 0758 0760 0763 0764 0766 0768 0769 0772 0773
0776 0777 0778 0779 0780 0781 0782 0783 0785 0798
0802 0805 0808 0817 0818 0820 0821 0822 0823 0824
0826 0829 0834 0835 0836 0838 0840 0842 0843 0844
0845 0846 0847 0848 0850 0851 0852 0853 0857 0869
0873 0878 0885 0887 0889 0890 0891 0892 0894 0895
0896 0897 0898 0899 0902 0903 0905 0913 0918 0919
0920 0921 0922 0923 0927 0935 0937 0958 0960 0974
0980 0998 1019 1024 1028 1029 1033 1036 1037 1038
1041 1059 1063 1072 1081 1082 1083 1085 1087 1090
1091 1093 1099 1103 1109 1113 1121 1136 1139 1147
1159 1161 1165 1172 1178 1185 1187 1189 1190 1199
1205 1209 1216 1217 1219 1222 1246 1247 1271 1284
1309 1314 1330 1385 1393 1399 1411 1425 1428 1438
1442 1443 1475 1524 1527 1537 1572 1592 1605 1618
1629 1661 1683 1685 1709

11. Real Estate and Insurance

0073 0126 0128 0133 0137 0140 0152 0182 0185 0190
0192 0196 0197 0198 0199 0202 0203 0257 0293 0351
0372 0373 0401 0411 0446 0465 0511 0540 0617 0629
0630 0637 0638 0698 0700 0702 0709 0766 0771 0777
0785 0797 0824 0845 0851 0855 0875 0886 0887 0923
0927 0929 0930 0931 0934 0938 0956 0963 0964 0968
0974 0975 0977 0981 0991 1115 1158 1171 1209 1211
1221 1222 1245 1253 1271 1272 1278 1280 1282 1283
1284 1299 1309 1410 1442 1443 1457 1469 1494 1533
1541 1607 1680 1689 1709 1711 1733

12. Recreation and Tourism

0046 0058 0074 0088 0105 0107 0115 0127 0128 0129
0137 0158 0182 0194 0199 0202 0239 0277 0287 0294
0326 0372 0373 0409 0550 0581 0593 0603 0605 0628
0629 0634 0643 0696 0699 0700 0701 0783 0818 0840
0913 0920 0939 1035 1073 1088 1090 1092 1111 1125
1196 1200 1216 1222 1225 1247 1270 1271 1274 1284
1375 1380 1386 1395 1403 1435 1536 1608 1611 1620
1621 1658 1664 1667 1685 1710 1713

13. Transportation

0019 0105 0126 0151 0182 0192 0198 0199 0239 0255
0409 0410 0459 0520 0593 0597 0624 0630 0636 0637
0673 0698 0701 0702 0758 0784 0785 0855 0923 0927
0939 0981 0982 1036 1113 1115 1214 1245 1309 1330
1331 1395 1403 1443 1541 1543 1622 1625 1664 1682
1689 1733

14. Education, general

0001 0004 0012 0013 0014 0015 0016 0020 0021 0022
0028 0031 0039 0042 0044 0046 0049 0052 0054 0056
0057 0058 0061 0064 0066 0068 0069 0070 0071 0073
0074 0082 0085 0086 0087 0088 0090 0091 0093 0096
0098 0106 0107 0108 0111 0114 0115 0118 0120 0121
0122 0123 0128 0129 0130 0131 0132 0133 0134 0135
0137 0138 0140 0147 0150 0152 0154 0155 0158 0159
0161 0164 0165 0166 0169 0170 0172 0176 0177 0178
0186 0187 0188 0191 0194 0196 0197 0198 0200 0202
0205 0214 0215 0219 0235 0236 0237 0240 0242 0243
0244 0245 0246 0247 0248 0249 0250 0251 0252 0253
0255 0256 0257 0258 0259 0266 0268 0270 0271 0274
0275 0277 0279 0281 0282 0284 0286 0287 0288 0290
0291 0292 0293 0294 0295 0296 0298 0300 0308 0311
0312 0313 0314 0316 0317 0318 0321 0324 0326 0327
0328 0329 0331 0332 0333 0334 0336 0337 0338 0339
0341 0342 0344 0345 0346 0348 0349 0350 0351 0352
0354 0355 0356 0357 0358 0359 0360 0361 0362 0363
0364 0365 0366 0367 0368 0369 0370 0371 0372 0373
0374 0375 0376 0378 0380 0381 0382 0383 0386 0387
0389 0390 0391 0393 0396 0398 0399 0401 0405 0407
0408 0409 0410 0411 0412 0416 0422 0428 0436 0444
0445 0448 0449 0452 0454 0459 0460 0461 0462 0463
0466 0472 0473 0480 0481 0482 0484 0487 0488 0492
0493 0495 0496 0498 0500 0504 0505 0506 0508 0509
0510 0518 0522 0525 0526 0527 0529 0531 0532 0533
0537 0541 0542 0543 0544 0545 0546 0549 0550 0552
0553 0554 0555 0556 0559 0563 0564 0565 0567 0568
0569 0571 0574 0576 0577 0578 0582 0583 0585 0586
0587 0588 0589 0590 0591 0594 0595 0596 0597 0598
0599 0600 0601 0603 0604 0605 0606 0607 0608 0610
0611 0612 0613 0614 0615 0617 0618 0619 0620 0621
0622 0623 0625 0626 0627 0628 0629 0630 0632 0633
0634 0635 0636 0637 0638 0643 0646 0650 0651 0652
0653 0655 0657 0658 0660 0661 0663 0664 0666 0667
0669 0670 0671 0672 0673 0674 0678 0681 0682 0683
0684 0687 0688 0689 0690 0692 0693 0694 0695 0696
0697 0698 0699 0700 0701 0702 0703 0704 0705 0706
0713 0714 0716 0717 0732 0738 0741 0742 0745 0748
0749 0750 0752 0754 0755 0757 0758 0760 0761 0762
0763 0764 0767 0768 0769 0770 0772 0773 0774 0775
0777 0778 0779 0781 0782 0783 0784 0785 0788 0796
0797 0799 0801 0802 0803 0805 0806 0808 0810 0811
0817 0818 0819 0820 0821 0822 0825 0828 0829 0830
0831 0834 0835 0836 0837 0838 0839 0840 0841 0842
0844 0845 0846 0847 0848 0851 0852 0853 0854 0855
0857 0863 0871 0873 0875 0877 0879 0880 0882 0885
0886 0887 0889 0890 0891 0892 0893 0895 0896 0897
0898 0899 0900 0901 0902 0905 0906 0907 0908 0909
0910 0912 0913 0914 0915 0916 0917 0918 0919 0921
0922 0923 0924 0925 0926 0928 0929 0932 0933 0934
0935 0936 0937 0940 0943 0947 0948 0950 0952 0953
0956 0957 0958 0959 0960 0961 0962 0963 0964 0968
0969 0971 0974 0975 0976 0979 0980 0981 0982 0984
0988 0990 0991 0998 0999 1000 1005 1006 1007 1015
1022 1024 1028 1029 1031 1033 1034 1036 1037 1038
1047 1048 1050 1056 1058 1059 1061 1066 1067 1072
1073 1074 1079 1080 1081 1082 1083 1084 1085 1087
1088 1089 1091 1092 1093 1094 1096 1098 1099 1100
1103 1104 1106 1108 1109 1111 1113 1114 1115 1118
1120 1121 1122 1127 1128 1129 1130 1131 1133 1136
1137 1138 1139 1140 1141 1143 1144 1145 1147 1148
1149 1150 1155 1158 1159 1162 1164 1165 1166 1167
1168 1171 1174 1175 1176 1177 1178 1179 1180 1181
1183 1184 1185 1187 1189 1190 1191 1192 1193 1194

14. Education, general (continued)

1195 1197 1198 1199 1200 1201 1203 1204 1205 1207
1208 1209 1210 1211 1212 1213 1214 1215 1216 1217
1218 1219 1220 1221 1222 1223 1224 1225 1226 1227
1228 1229 1230 1233 1234 1240 1243 1245 1246 1247
1252 1253 1254 1255 1260 1261 1263 1264 1265 1267
1268 1269 1270 1271 1272 1273 1276 1277 1279 1281
1282 1283 1285 1286 1294 1295 1297 1298 1299 1307
1312 1314 1316 1320 1322 1323 1324 1325 1327 1328
1330 1331 1342 1343 1345 1355 1356 1357 1366 1368
1369 1370 1373 1375 1377 1378 1380 1381 1382 1384
1385 1386 1388 1389 1392 1393 1395 1396 1397 1399
1401 1403 1404 1406 1408 1410 1412 1413 1414 1415
1418 1425 1428 1429 1432 1433 1435 1437 1438 1439
1440 1441 1442 1444 1445 1446 1447 1448 1450 1451
1452 1453 1455 1457 1463 1464 1466 1476 1484 1488
1489 1491 1494 1499 1501 1502 1504 1506 1511 1512
1524 1525 1526 1527 1530 1531 1533 1534 1538 1541
1543 1544 1552 1557 1558 1569 1572 1577 1590 1595
1600 1601 1609 1610 1611 1612 1613 1614 1618 1620
1621 1628 1629 1632 1634 1636 1637 1642 1643 1648
1649 1650 1651 1652 1653 1654 1655 1657 1658 1659
1660 1661 1663 1667 1672 1673 1674 1676 1677 1678
1680 1682 1683 1684 1685 1688 1689 1690 1695 1697
1705 1706 1710 1712 1713 1722 1732 1736 1737

15. Agricultural Education

0069 0071 0128 0130 0134 0140 0192 0197 0203 0204
0219 0236 0249 0256 0259 0295 0296 0308 0366 0367
0373 0376 0378 0410 0411 0457 0542 0576 0620 0624
0633 0634 0698 0699 0700 0701 0702 0716 0759 0761
0765 0773 0778 0779 0780 0781 0785 0822 0826 0844
0846 0850 0851 0852 0854 0855 0887 0888 0891 0894
0895 0909 0918 0921 0924 0927 0935 0936 0938 0939
0940 0979 0982 0983 1089 1100 1101 1113 1165 1189
1224 1274 1277 1281 1282 1283 1285 1286 1541 1577
1710 1711 1712

16. Home Economics Education

0013 0015 0021 0022 0044 0056 0058 0065 0066 0069
0071 0089 0096 0123 0127 0128 0130 0131 0133 0134
0138 0140 0165 0186 0188 0191 0194 0196 0197 0198
0203 0215 0236 0242 0244 0245 0246 0248 0249 0255
0256 0259 0280 0293 0294 0295 0296 0317 0331 0336
0361 0364 0366 0367 0369 0370 0373 0375 0376 0378
0383 0389 0403 0410 0411 0454 0457 0459 0461 0466
0482 0504 0509 0510 0518 0532 0533 0543 0545 0583
0591 0598 0611 0622 0623 0624 0626 0629 0632 0633
0634 0635 0638 0643 0657 0689 0692 0695 0697 0698
0699 0700 0701 0702 0703 0705 0716 0741 0755 0759
0761 0762 0765 0767 0774 0775 0776 0777 0778 0779
0780 0781 0783 0784 0785 0793 0811 0817 0818 0820
0821 0824 0826 0834 0838 0840 0844 0845 0846 0847
0848 0850 0851 0854 0857 0871 0887 0888 0889 0891
0892 0893 0894 0898 0900 0902 0905 0909 0914 0918
0919 0920 0921 0924 0927 0930 0935 0936 0938 0939
0940 0955 0960 0963 0974 0975 0979 0981 0982 0991
1007 1029 1036 1037 1081 1082 1089 1100 1103 1109
1113 1115 1121 1164 1165 1168 1174 1178 1180 1181
1202 1207 1209 1211 1214 1220 1221 1224 1246 1247
1252 1270 1271 1277 1283 1285 1286 1299 1314 1327
1356 1368 1386 1397 1399 1413 1415 1437 1457 1489
1508 1522 1530 1531 1541 1577 1651 1653 1688 1690
1709 1710 1711 1712 1713

17. Industrial Arts, Vocational/Technical Education

0015 0021 0028 0056 0058 0065 0066 0068 0069 0071
0073 0074 0106 0108 0110 0113 0126 0127 0128 0129
0130 0131 0133 0134 0137 0140 0183 0186 0187 0188
0192 0194 0195 0198 0200 0203 0231 0242 0244 0245
0246 0247 0248 0249 0255 0257 0286 0287 0293 0294
0295 0296 0300 0311 0329 0336 0347 0348 0367 0369
0370 0371 0372 0373 0375 0376 0378 0383 0406 0410

17. Industrial Arts, Vocational/Technical Education (continued)

0411 0452 0454 0457 0461 0498 0509 0510 0511 0545 0574 0583 0620 0623 0624 0626 0629 0632 0633 0634 0635 0636 0638 0676 0689 0697 0699 0700 0702 0703 0705 0716 0759 0761 0765 0767 0773 0778 0780 0781 0783 0784 0785 0817 0818 0820 0821 0822 0825 0826 0829 0831 0840 0844 0845 0846 0848 0850 0851 0853 0854 0855 0887 0894 0895 0906 0909 0918 0919 0920 0921 0923 0924 0927 0936 0937 0938 0939 0940 0955 0974 0979 0980 0982 0983 0999 1000 1029 1036 1037 1070 1080 1082 1084 1100 1101 1109 1113 1114 1115 1165 1170 1178 1209 1211 1212 1214 1218 1219 1222 1223 1225 1245 1246 1252 1270 1273 1274 1281 1283 1285 1286 1302 1314 1327 1333 1439 1446 1448 1452 1457 1485 1526 1527 1528 1532 1541 1542 1572 1652 1653 1656 1683 1686 1710 1712

18. Aerospace, Aeronautical, and Astronautical Engineering

0019 0099 0112 0117 0139 0185 0195 0197 0198 0199 0200 0201 0204 0205 0208 0212 0219 0221 0224 0257 0258 0259 0378 0385 0409 0410 0411 0520 0593 0595 0609 0630 0680 0699 0700 0702 0712 0716 0717 0821 0846 0855 0882 0909 0929 0931 0936 0939 0981 0982 0983 0991 1050 1107 1165 1188 1207 1224 1232 1244 1254 1259 1273 1281 1282 1285 1286 1292 1300 1326 1376 1390 1416 1540 1541 1543 1553 1554 1575 1576 1601 1617 1697 1705 1716 1733 1737

19. Agricultural Engineering

0069 0071 0128 0130 0134 0140 0185 0197 0198 0203 0204 0219 0256 0259 0350 0366 0376 0378 0410 0411 0698 0699 0701 0702 0716 0773 0778 0855 0894 0927 0935 0936 0938 0939 0979 0982 0983 1113 1274 1277 1281 1282 1283 1285 1286 1376 1390 1416 1485 1486 1541 1551 1577 1688

20. Architectural Engineering

0130 0199 0204 0205 0258 0259 0293 0410 0630 0656 0764 0781 0882 0894 0929 0935 0936 0991 1113 1267 1280 1286 1537 1541 1617 1733

21. Environmental and Ecological Engineering

0071 0109 0129 0153 0160 0186 0205 0216 0222 0259 0293 0377 0634 0691 0698 0699 0700 0713 0717 0781 0832 0846 0847 0882 0929 0936 0937 0986 1223 1259 1270 1273 1282 1291 1376 1400 1415 1416 1448 1487 1516 1541 1543 1554 1574 1576 1577 1697 1733 1735 1736

22. Geological Engineering

0069 0072 0107 0109 0128 0138 0140 0153 0197 0198 0209 0221 0255 0378 0384 0385 0691 0698 0699 0882 0929 0930 0968 0982 1561 1573 1710 1733 1735

23. Metallurgical and Materials Engineering

0069 0072 0109 0138 0140 0153 0185 0195 0197 0198 0200 0201 0204 0205 0209 0219 0221 0222 0223 0374 0378 0384 0385 0410 0458 0459 0627 0630 0680 0691 0698 0699 0701 0702 0704 0705 0713 0714 0716 0717 0849 0882 0883 0925 0939 0979 0981 0982 1232 1281 1282 1285 1292 1343 1390 1400 1416 1487 1504 1516 1537 1539 1541 1542 1553 1574 1576 1577 1578 1664 1697 1709 1716 1733

24. Mining and Mineral Engineering

0069 0072 0107 0109 0138 0153 0197 0209 0223 0384 0385 0634 0691 0702 0979 0981 0983 1170 1224 1285 1343 1376 1416 1541 1542 1561 1733

25. Nuclear Engineering

0074 0129 0197 0198 0212 0221 0222 0223 0236 0259 0385 0410 0529 0630 0698 0699 0716 0717 0855 0882 0938 0939 0983 0986 1232 1281 1282 1286 1292 1300 1376 1390 1416 1541 1561 1576 1687 1716 1733 1735

26. Ocean Engineering

0195 0717 0847 0983 1244 1259 1272 1282 1285 1545 1709 1733 1735

27. Petroleum Engineering

0107 0109 0130 0153 0205 0209 0218 0223 0256 0258 0385 0678 0680 0778 0779 0855 0882 0887 0929 0935 0938 0968 0981 0983 0986 0991 1224 1343 1376 1416 1541

28. Architecture Technology

0108 0137 0198 0246 0373 0574 0617 0626 0629 0697 0777 0783 0923 0929 0938 0940 0974 1029 1037 1169 1270 1309 1333 1359 1417 1536 1617

29. City, Community, and Regional Planning

0068 0071 0074 0128 0131 0139 0185 0188 0193 0194 0197 0198 0202 0204 0205 0223 0259 0348 0373 0374 0409 0410 0416 0454 0510 0578 0618 0626 0627 0628 0629 0630 0632 0636 0655 0664 0692 0696 0699 0701 0702 0705 0713 0716 0717 0762 0778 0785 0844 0846 0855 0919 0921 0940 0974 0981 1036 1105 1158 1180 1209 1211 1216 1221 1222 1224 1267 1274 1282 1286 1300 1314 1366 1386 1446 1448 1525 1527 1543 1544 1565 1577 1578 1594 1651 1667 1685 1706 1710 1733

30. Environmental Design, Landscape architecture

0069 0071 0137 0140 0145 0156 0185 0193 0198 0199 0201 0203 0204 0219 0223 0256 0259 0366 0378 0410 0411 0510 0578 0632 0634 0691 0692 0697 0698 0699 0701 0702 0716 0717 0855 0927 0929 0931 0935 0936 0938 0979 0982 0983 1113 1169 1217 1224 1274 1281 1282 1283 1285 1366 1439 1448 1457 1485 1486 1510 1536 1540 1541 1543 1577 1594 1642 1688 1702 1706 1709 1711 1713 1731 1733

31. Interior Design

0003 0009 0040 0053 0066 0069 0072 0098 0103 0118 0134 0137 0140 0170 0188 0193 0194 0195 0196 0197 0198 0200 0203 0219 0236 0242 0244 0246 0256 0258 0259 0293 0295 0296 0329 0336 0341 0366 0367 0373 0378 0380 0401 0410 0411 0450 0453 0454 0478 0479 0506 0510 0523 0532 0553 0556 0560 0566 0584 0591 0592 0600 0602 0604 0605 0622 0626 0629 0630 0631 0632 0634 0635 0638 0655 0689 0692 0697 0698 0699 0700 0701 0702 0705 0717 0778 0779 0785 0811 0824 0834 0836 0840 0844 0845 0846 0847 0854 0871 0889 0891 0892 0902 0914 0917 0918 0922 0927 0929 0930 0931 0933 0934 0935 0937 0938 0939 0940 0943 0957 0963 0975 0976 0979 0981 0982 0991 1021 1032 1035 1065 1077 1111 1115 1135 1140 1150 1154 1157 1205 1209 1211 1216 1217 1220 1221 1224 1230 1236 1240 1251 1256 1270 1271 1277 1282 1283 1285 1286 1299 1322 1333 1334 1341 1346 1353 1359 1368 1371 1379 1397 1399 1406 1417 1421 1432 1434 1489 1493 1510 1527 1536 1537 1543 1572 1577 1593 1606 1608 1616 1617 1664 1672 1702 1713

32. Applied Design

0022 0037 0046 0053 0070 0125 0127 0130 0131 0132 0136 0145 0156 0166 0170 0177 0181 0188 0191 0193 0194 0195 0197 0198 0200 0201 0203 0204 0221 0240 0257 0258 0259 0285 0286 0290 0294 0311 0318 0347 0348 0351 0365 0367 0368 0369 0370 0371 0372 0373 0374 0377 0378 0383 0401 0410 0416 0452 0454 0461

32. Applied Design (continued)

0479 0484 0510 0529 0534 0538 0544 0552 0560 0566
0577 0587 0589 0592 0602 0604 0606 0612 0617 0618
0619 0625 0627 0628 0629 0631 0632 0634 0635 0637
0638 0660 0684 0689 0695 0696 0697 0699 0700 0702
0703 0705 0709 0712 0716 0717 0771 0777 0778 0782
0785 0816 0818 0819 0824 0829 0834 0845 0846 0847
0849 0852 0868 0892 0895 0896 0904 0906 0924 0929
0934 0938 0940 0967 0968 0975 0976 0980 0998 1046
1077 1085 1088 1135 1141 1152 1154 1183 1197 1211
1214 1216 1221 1224 1247 1256 1271 1277 1278 1280
1283 1286 1299 1334 1353 1366 1371 1379 1384 1386
1395 1399 1426 1432 1434 1440 1444 1446 1447 1448
1451 1452 1455 1457 1493 1510 1511 1536 1543 1572
1574 1597 1602 1609 1618 1628 1631 1653 1671 1672
1680 1694 1702 1708 1711 1713 1715

33. Photography/Cinematography

0009 0037 0052 0053 0067 0069 0081 0090 0096 0116
0125 0131 0134 0138 0141 0145 0156 0170 0171 0181
0194 0195 0198 0199 0200 0201 0205 0214 0217 0221
0223 0285 0304 0340 0346 0351 0368 0370 0377 0383
0450 0457 0458 0461 0478 0510 0523 0534 0552 0560
0578 0592 0602 0617 0618 0627 0628 0631 0632 0634
0697 0699 0702 0703 0704 0705 0712 0713 0716 0717
0719 0771 0779 0889 0892 0893 0895 0914 0918 0922
0929 0934 0935 0966 0976 0977 0980 1035 1072 1103
1119 1122 1135 1141 1152 1154 1183 1197 1204 1221
1222 1229 1247 1256 1265 1275 1278 1280 1295 1299
1309 1312 1353 1366 1371 1384 1399 1406 1421 1432
1434 1439 1444 1446 1447 1453 1455 1456 1457 1476
1489 1493 1510 1511 1518 1521 1536 1540 1541 1542
1543 1544 1570 1573 1594 1597 1602 1609 1631 1672
1680 1681 1685 1702 1706 1711 1715 1717 1726 1733
1734 1737

34. Health Professions, general

0005 0016 0018 0021 0022 0049 0056 0057 0065 0068
0070 0071 0072 0073 0074 0087 0097 0105 0109 0118
0119 0122 0123 0126 0127 0128 0129 0130 0131 0132
0133 0134 0135 0137 0138 0139 0140 0147 0152 0154
0157 0159 0160 0164 0167 0175 0177 0178 0180 0181
0182 0183 0186 0187 0188 0191 0192 0195 0196 0197
0198 0199 0200 0201 0202 0203 0205 0210 0222 0236
0244 0246 0255 0256 0257 0258 0259 0274 0281 0293
0294 0295 0296 0300 0311 0313 0314 0315 0316 0318
0321 0328 0331 0332 0336 0342 0344 0346 0348 0349
0351 0356 0357 0358 0361 0362 0366 0368 0369 0370
0371 0372 0374 0376 0377 0378 0379 0380 0388 0389
0390 0391 0393 0394 0395 0396 0397 0398 0402 0406
0408 0409 0411 0414 0416 0420 0421 0443 0445 0451
0454 0457 0459 0460 0474 0489 0496 0498 0508 0510
0511 0528 0532 0536 0542 0543 0547 0552 0553 0559
0563 0567 0572 0575 0576 0583 0586 0587 0589 0596
0597 0598 0599 0600 0601 0603 0605 0606 0609 0610
0612 0615 0617 0619 0621 0622 0623 0624 0625 0626
0627 0628 0629 0631 0632 0633 0634 0635 0636 0637
0638 0642 0648 0651 0653 0655 0657 0659 0660 0661
0663 0664 0666 0670 0671 0674 0677 0679 0680 0683
0684 0688 0689 0692 0694 0697 0698 0699 0700 0701
0702 0703 0704 0705 0706 0713 0714 0716 0719 0720
0726 0728 0752 0754 0756 0762 0764 0769 0771 0772
0773 0775 0777 0778 0779 0781 0782 0783 0784 0785
0786 0802 0806 0817 0818 0819 0822 0826 0827 0828
0835 0841 0842 0844 0845 0848 0849 0852 0854 0857
0862 0869 0871 0872 0875 0878 0885 0891 0892 0893
0897 0898 0901 0902 0908 0909 0910 0914 0917 0919
0921 0922 0925 0926 0927 0928 0929 0930 0933 0934
0935 0936 0937 0938 0939 0940 0950 0952 0954 0959
0961 0965 0968 0971 0974 0975 0976 0979 0981 0982
0988 0991 0993 0995 0997 0998 0999 1001 1003 1004
1036 1037 1073 1082 1083 1087 1094 1095 1100 1109
1111 1114 1119 1121 1128 1137 1139 1140 1143 1146
1147 1149 1151 1157 1160 1165 1177 1178 1179 1185

34. Health Professions, general (continued)

1190 1198 1204 1205 1208 1211 1212 1214 1216 1217
1220 1221 1222 1224 1228 1233 1239 1245 1247 1251
1270 1271 1272 1273 1275 1276 1279 1280 1282 1283
1294 1299 1300 1309 1313 1314 1320 1323 1337 1343
1346 1352 1355 1357 1365 1366 1367 1369 1373 1377
1378 1381 1384 1385 1388 1392 1393 1394 1395 1396
1397 1399 1400 1404 1406 1407 1408 1410 1416 1420
1427 1429 1435 1437 1439 1440 1441 1444 1445 1447
1448 1449 1450 1451 1453 1455 1457 1464 1468 1475
1478 1482 1483 1484 1488 1489 1491 1494 1497 1498
1499 1502 1503 1504 1506 1511 1512 1522 1523 1527
1529 1531 1532 1533 1534 1540 1541 1542 1544 1552
1569 1571 1581 1583 1584 1585 1590 1616 1630 1632
1636 1646 1647 1651 1656 1663 1665 1666 1667 1672
1674 1675 1676 1680 1681 1682 1685 1686 1689 1691
1697 1698 1706 1709 1710 1711 1712 1713 1737

35. Dental Assistant

0785 0842

36. Dental Hygiene

0021 0060 0074 0127 0130 0131 0201 0205 0286 0293
0368 0376 0377 0378 0407 0420 0575 0617 0659 0693
0694 0702 0717 0756 0764 0777 0785 0828 0840 0842
0854 0892 0919 0925 0926 0930 0937 0941 0975 0992
0997 1001 1003 1090 1094 1160 1216 1221 1224 1225
1286 1298 1309 1369 1444 1502 1524 1535 1581 1637
1645 1672 1709 1712

37. Dental Lab Technology

0785 0926 0930 0941 1221

38. Medical Assistant or Medical Office Assistant

0152 0457 0704 0756 0785 0823 0841 0842 0872 0925
0993 1109 1136 1221 1314 1380 1592

39. Radiology

0021 0060 0070 0074 0137 0200 0248 0251 0258 0274
0275 0283 0286 0291 0293 0294 0330 0349 0354 0373
0411 0420 0457 0474 0498 0505 0543 0544 0583 0599
0605 0617 0653 0702 0705 0756 0767 0772 0775 0777
0822 0828 0846 0848 0852 0862 0869 0902 0920 0925
0971 0979 0993 1001 1070 1128 1137 1140 1160 1199
1204 1216 1221 1273 1279 1286 1298 1309 1334 1337
1346 1352 1369 1422 1448 1455 1502 1506 1524 1535
1536 1581 1585 1633 1665 1675 1680 1686 1712

40. Radiologic Technology

0021 0060 0070 0074 0137 0200 0248 0251 0258 0274
0275 0283 0286 0291 0293 0294 0330 0349 0354 0373
0411 0420 0457 0474 0498 0505 0543 0544 0583 0599
0605 0617 0653 0702 0705 0756 0767 0772 0775 0777
0822 0828 0846 0848 0852 0862 0869 0902 0920 0925
0971 0979 0993 1001 1070 1128 1137 1140 1160 1199
1204 1216 1221 1273 1279 1286 1298 1309 1334 1337
1346 1352 1369 1422 1448 1455 1502 1506 1524 1535
1536 1581 1585 1633 1665 1675 1680 1686 1712

41. Surgical Technology

0152 0457 0704 0756 0785 0823 0841 0842 0872 0925
0993 1109 1136 1221 1314 1380 1592

42. Classics

0049 0074 0087 0093 0123 0125 0132 0139 0149 0150
0162 0166 0172 0178 0179 0188 0189 0190 0191 0193
0194 0197 0199 0201 0202 0205 0206 0211 0213 0216
0217 0218 0219 0220 0221 0222 0223 0224 0258 0259
0296 0338 0350 0358 0368 0376 0377 0378 0389 0393
0395 0397 0399 0400 0403 0408 0409 0411 0413 0414

42. Classics (continued)

0415 0416 0454 0458 0461 0494 0524 0565 0590 0610
0627 0630 0634 0636 0638 0644 0646 0647 0650 0652
0655 0658 0659 0661 0666 0670 0673 0674 0675 0682
0685 0686 0687 0692 0693 0697 0698 0701 0702 0704
0705 0710 0711 0712 0713 0714 0715 0716 0717 0874
0895 0927 0929 0930 0939 0967 0968 0970 0972 0973
0974 0976 0978 0979 0980 0981 0986 0988 0989 0990
0991 1143 1163 1214 1215 1218 1221 1222 1223 1224
1231 1235 1236 1237 1238 1239 1248 1255 1262 1263
1265 1267 1269 1271 1275 1277 1279 1282 1283 1284
1286 1287 1289 1290 1291 1293 1294 1295 1296 1297
1298 1299 1300 1302 1314 1364 1370 1396 1412 1433
1437 1439 1457 1463 1466 1471 1473 1475 1481 1482
1483 1491 1494 1499 1504 1505 1506 1507 1509 1513
1515 1517 1518 1519 1520 1521 1522 1523 1525 1532
1533 1534 1535 1538 1539 1540 1541 1542 1543 1544
1549 1556 1557 1558 1560 1562 1563 1564 1565 1567
1568 1570 1571 1573 1575 1577 1578 1623 1639 1640
1656 1668 1694 1700 1704 1707 1709 1710 1711 1712
1713 1717 1718 1719 1720 1721 1722 1723 1724 1725
1726 1727 1728 1729 1731 1732 1734 1735 1736 1737

43. Comparative Literature

0074 0088 0131 0137 0139 0140 0149 0162 0176 0179
0181 0190 0191 0193 0194 0195 0201 0205 0206 0211
0213 0214 0216 0217 0218 0219 0220 0221 0222 0223
0258 0259 0327 0351 0377 0382 0393 0403 0408 0409
0416 0454 0542 0545 0590 0598 0605 0612 0627 0630
0636 0637 0655 0660 0675 0682 0683 0684 0685 0690
0698 0699 0701 0702 0705 0711 0713 0714 0715 0716
0717 0895 0954 0973 0974 0977 0979 0981 0999 1143
1216 1224 1226 1227 1247 1266 1267 1268 1272 1277
1283 1286 1287 1293 1298 1299 1300 1302 1307 1312
1314 1325 1366 1368 1373 1382 1409 1430 1437 1447
1450 1473 1475 1478 1482 1483 1512 1518 1520 1521
1522 1523 1529 1538 1541 1543 1544 1549 1557 1562
1568 1569 1570 1571 1573 1574 1575 1577 1578 1594
1655 1671 1677 1684 1685 1691 1694 1695 1701 1705
1706 1709 1713 1717 1719 1721 1722 1726 1729 1731
1734 1735 1737

44. Linguistics

0074 0107 0115 0123 0130 0136 0138 0139 0149 0150
0178 0181 0192 0193 0194 0197 0199 0200 0201 0202
0203 0205 0213 0216 0217 0218 0219 0220 0221 0222
0223 0224 0258 0259 0377 0378 0394 0410 0411 0413
0416 0460 0500 0590 0627 0629 0630 0634 0636 0637
0689 0690 0698 0700 0701 0702 0703 0705 0713 0715
0716 0717 0849 0853 0895 0929 0930 0935 0937 0974
0978 0979 0986 0991 1175 1184 1195 1224 1270 1271
1272 1275 1283 1286 1293 1297 1298 1299 1302 1307
1314 1324 1366 1439 1457 1463 1475 1482 1483 1522
1525 1526 1529 1532 1540 1541 1542 1543 1544 1557
1564 1568 1570 1571 1573 1574 1577 1578 1673 1680
1685 1689 1706 1709 1710 1711 1713 1729 1731 1732
1733 1734 1735 1737

45. Applied Mathematics

0016 0022 0052 0057 0066 0069 0071 0074 0086 0087
0096 0104 0109 0111 0118 0124 0126 0127 0129 0130
0131 0132 0134 0137 0143 0151 0153 0165 0166 0175
0178 0181 0194 0195 0196 0198 0199 0202 0208 0209
0212 0218 0219 0221 0222 0223 0224 0240 0251 0259
0275 0280 0330 0331 0332 0348 0351 0358 0361 0362
0366 0367 0368 0370 0374 0377 0384 0385 0391 0392
0405 0408 0409 0414 0416 0441 0454 0458 0461 0487
0493 0509 0511 0533 0542 0561 0563 0571 0594 0595
0605 0618 0620 0623 0627 0629 0633 0634 0635 0636
0638 0651 0659 0660 0663 0675 0678 0680 0684 0686
0692 0695 0698 0699 0700 0701 0703 0707 0713 0714
0715 0717 0766 0778 0783 0785 0797 0810 0824 0826
0829 0830 0840 0841 0845 0865 0870 0871 0876 0885

45. Applied Mathematics (continued)

0895 0898 0900 0904 0908 0910 0916 0919 0921 0932
0935 0937 0944 0946 0949 0954 0957 0961 0968 0973
0977 0980 0981 0982 0983 0986 1036 1081 1084 1088
1094 1100 1137 1143 1171 1177 1181 1197 1212 1216
1222 1227 1240 1247 1255 1257 1259 1260 1265 1267
1270 1275 1277 1278 1279 1280 1281 1283 1286 1287
1291 1292 1298 1299 1300 1307 1314 1320 1322 1329
1331 1343 1353 1389 1392 1397 1402 1447 1451 1452
1466 1469 1479 1481 1484 1487 1492 1494 1502 1506
1507 1516 1522 1526 1527 1529 1533 1536 1539 1542
1544 1549 1553 1554 1557 1561 1562 1570 1572 1573
1574 1578 1584 1618 1654 1655 1656 1664 1667 1677
1685 1687 1694 1705 1706 1709 1711 1712 1714 1718
1731 1733 1734 1735 1736 1737

46. Statistics

0059 0069 0071 0074 0107 0127 0128 0130 0134 0135
0137 0139 0180 0181 0191 0193 0194 0195 0200 0201
0202 0203 0204 0216 0218 0219 0222 0223 0256 0259
0294 0321 0356 0367 0368 0374 0377 0378 0391 0406
0408 0409 0410 0411 0416 0461 0474 0574 0635 0659
0689 0692 0693 0694 0697 0698 0699 0700 0701 0702
0704 0713 0714 0715 0716 0717 0766 0775 0778 0783
0785 0818 0839 0846 0849 0855 0894 0913 0927 0928
0933 0935 0936 0938 0939 0954 0974 0976 0980 0981
0986 1177 1190 1209 1216 1217 1224 1245 1246 1247
1270 1271 1273 1277 1278 1279 1281 1282 1283 1284
1285 1286 1298 1299 1301 1302 1307 1314 1438 1453
1457 1482 1483 1487 1516 1523 1529 1530 1536 1539
1540 1542 1543 1544 1549 1553 1554 1557 1562 1564
1568 1571 1572 1573 1574 1578 1687 1706 1709 1711
1712 1713 1718 1731 1733 1735 1737

47. Computer Programming

0007 0013 0021 0022 0027 0052 0054 0056 0058 0060
0064 0065 0073 0078 0098 0107 0109 0113 0114 0115
0120 0132 0153 0163 0166 0193 0213 0215 0233 0239
0242 0247 0250 0251 0259 0270 0282 0288 0300 0308
0316 0321 0324 0327 0331 0332 0333 0336 0345 0357
0358 0359 0362 0367 0368 0374 0382 0391 0393 0405
0406 0416 0432 0435 0441 0451 0452 0453 0482 0489
0496 0498 0508 0510 0511 0515 0529 0539 0545 0550
0554 0555 0564 0567 0573 0574 0575 0576 0587 0595
0597 0606 0607 0617 0619 0626 0628 0629 0634 0635
0655 0660 0663 0664 0670 0671 0693 0694 0695 0697
0699 0701 0705 0753 0757 0761 0762 0778 0780 0783
0784 0799 0819 0825 0827 0829 0842 0843 0844 0846
0848 0871 0882 0885 0887 0891 0895 0897 0899 0902
0905 0907 0910 0919 0935 0947 0957 0958 0961 0971
0975 0981 0986 1020 1027 1030 1041 1053 1074 1079
1119 1163 1188 1190 1193 1197 1199 1200 1201 1208
1212 1216 1220 1227 1232 1240 1247 1255 1260 1301
1313 1320 1324 1333 1356 1359 1392 1399 1407 1414
1415 1429 1438 1442 1452 1494 1506 1507 1527 1536
1537 1538 1552 1616 1618 1638 1648 1651 1653 1654
1655 1657 1659 1665 1669 1671 1673 1677 1685 1688
1706 1733 1735

48. Information Systems and Sciences

0005 0016 0018 0019 0044 0046 0052 0054 0055 0062
0063 0066 0068 0071 0073 0074 0078 0083 0098 0099
0103 0104 0105 0109 0115 0119 0120 0121 0124 0126
0127 0128 0130 0131 0132 0133 0139 0151 0152 0155
0163 0165 0166 0167 0169 0170 0192 0193 0194 0196
0198 0199 0203 0217 0224 0241 0245 0246 0249 0250
0256 0259 0281 0283 0286 0288 0289 0291 0292 0295
0300 0315 0320 0323 0331 0333 0336 0341 0342 0350
0356 0357 0361 0362 0369 0370 0371 0372 0373 0374
0380 0386 0390 0391 0392 0393 0394 0398 0400 0401
0408 0416 0431 0449 0451 0453 0454 0457 0460 0461
0487 0489 0496 0498 0501 0502 0503 0508 0510 0528
0536 0538 0546 0547 0549 0551 0552 0555 0557 0563

48. Information Systems and Sciences (continued)

0564 0570 0572 0575 0576 0577 0578 0580 0581 0582
0583 0593 0594 0595 0599 0603 0605 0606 0607 0608
0610 0619 0621 0625 0627 0629 0630 0631 0633 0636
0638 0655 0659 0660 0663 0664 0666 0667 0672 0678
0680 0689 0690 0692 0694 0695 0696 0697 0698 0699
0700 0701 0702 0703 0705 0706 0707 0712 0713 0717
0755 0769 0772 0773 0777 0782 0783 0788 0805 0808
0819 0821 0824 0829 0833 0840 0846 0854 0870 0871
0875 0895 0897 0900 0904 0907 0910 0911 0912 0913
0919 0921 0922 0927 0931 0933 0934 0935 0940 0943
0948 0952 0957 0958 0963 0964 0965 0968 0971 0975
0977 0980 0991 0998 1027 1036 1038 1074 1078 1079
1081 1082 1092 1094 1097 1101 1102 1119 1132 1137
1143 1147 1151 1153 1157 1167 1169 1172 1175 1180
1185 1187 1192 1193 1196 1201 1203 1204 1207 1208
1209 1214 1216 1217 1218 1219 1220 1221 1222 1223
1227 1232 1240 1245 1247 1259 1260 1270 1272 1275
1278 1279 1280 1283 1286 1292 1299 1301 1314 1315
1320 1321 1328 1329 1330 1331 1350 1352 1357 1361
1368 1369 1382 1384 1386 1392 1397 1399 1401 1407
1408 1410 1411 1417 1418 1419 1426 1427 1428 1438
1439 1445 1448 1457 1468 1478 1481 1487 1491 1494
1500 1502 1504 1506 1513 1522 1526 1527 1529 1533
1536 1537 1538 1542 1543 1544 1569 1570 1572 1574
1577 1578 1583 1592 1601 1605 1607 1632 1638 1657
1658 1660 1661 1662 1663 1665 1667 1669 1671 1674
1677 1687 1696 1699 1701 1703 1706 1709 1733 1735

49. Data Processing Technology

0007 0022 0066 0069 0163 0166 0193 0239 0244 0333
0367 0373 0374 0388 0416 0482 0489 0498 0510 0511
0570 0572 0581 0605 0626 0699 0748 0750 0760 0761
0781 0783 0784 0785 0840 0844 0851 0857 0871 0887
0888 0927 0937 0961 0974 1041 1079 1125 1181 1220
1227 1245 1301 1309 1333 1339 1359 1399 1538 1592
1655 1669 1671

50. Computer Operating

0066 0071 0103 0106 0131 0154 0195 0233 0236 0239
0244 0287 0295 0372 0432 0435 0451 0455 0489 0524
0564 0603 0697 0699 0700 0748 0762 0766 0769 0771
0797 0805 0820 0846 0850 0851 0855 0857 0887 0914
0921 1041 1052 1099 1125 1271 1282 1309 1334 1339
1425 1443 1618 1621

51. Biochemistry

0021 0066 0067 0069 0071 0072 0074 0098 0119 0120
0122 0126 0128 0129 0130 0132 0135 0138 0140 0147
0149 0153 0154 0161 0168 0170 0175 0176 0178 0179
0181 0188 0191 0192 0193 0194 0195 0197 0200 0201
0202 0203 0204 0214 0216 0217 0219 0221 0222 0223
0224 0251 0257 0258 0259 0322 0331 0370 0376 0377
0378 0387 0407 0410 0411 0416 0445 0457 0510 0540
0562 0576 0582 0583 0590 0597 0598 0609 0611 0613
0627 0629 0630 0631 0634 0635 0637 0659 0663 0675
0676 0678 0682 0684 0690 0694 0695 0698 0699 0701
0702 0704 0705 0706 0711 0712 0713 0714 0716 0717
0821 0827 0836 0838 0839 0840 0842 0854 0855 0882
0895 0906 0908 0921 0931 0934 0935 0936 0938 0960
0964 0967 0978 0980 0981 0982 0983 0985 0986 0988
0989 0991 0992 0993 1004 1080 1120 1147 1149 1155
1198 1199 1206 1208 1211 1215 1221 1225 1231 1239
1240 1254 1259 1260 1267 1275 1277 1280 1281 1283
1285 1286 1293 1299 1302 1312 1314 1321 1348 1353
1356 1363 1369 1370 1373 1375 1376 1382 1391 1396
1400 1403 1411 1417 1418 1420 1424 1425 1427 1428
1436 1444 1447 1450 1456 1457 1464 1466 1475 1476
1479 1482 1483 1485 1486 1489 1490 1491 1498 1499
1502 1505 1506 1508 1509 1515 1516 1527 1529 1531
1532 1533 1534 1536 1537 1539 1540 1541 1542 1544
1549 1552 1555 1556 1557 1558 1562 1564 1566 1567
1568 1569 1570 1571 1573 1574 1576 1578 1585 1594

51. Biochemistry (continued)

1641 1660 1661 1663 1665 1684 1688 1694 1700 1704
1705 1706 1707 1710 1711 1712 1713 1716 1717 1718
1719 1720 1721 1722 1724 1725 1726 1729 1731 1732
1733 1734 1735

52. Ecology

0046 0071 0108 0112 0140 0163 0176 0181 0188 0192
0193 0197 0199 0200 0219 0222 0223 0224 0317 0318
0356 0367 0410 0416 0454 0496 0504 0510 0544 0569
0578 0581 0598 0601 0613 0620 0623 0626 0646 0651
0671 0684 0696 0699 0701 0703 0713 0716 0775 0824
0827 0851 0853 0895 0907 0911 0918 0936 0976 1073
1074 1086 1100 1180 1189 1240 1268 1270 1273 1279
1287 1307 1314 1360 1366 1399 1414 1425 1451 1453
1484 1485 1486 1499 1502 1511 1518 1537 1573 1577
1590 1594 1603 1609 1618 1621 1642 1653 1694 1695
1704 1706 1717 1721

53. Microbiology

0021 0022 0069 0126 0127 0128 0129 0130 0132 0133
0134 0139 0140 0182 0185 0187 0192 0193 0194 0195
0197 0198 0199 0200 0201 0202 0203 0204 0218 0219
0221 0222 0223 0224 0256 0258 0259 0366 0377 0378
0407 0410 0411 0416 0510 0574 0618 0627 0629 0633
0634 0637 0688 0692 0697 0698 0699 0701 0702 0703
0705 0706 0713 0716 0717 0766 0767 0775 0778 0779
0780 0785 0821 0827 0834 0839 0849 0852 0855 0895
0919 0927 0929 0931 0935 0936 0938 0939 0940 0974
0979 0981 0982 0983 0985 0991 0992 0993 1004 1137
1221 1223 1234 1259 1273 1274 1280 1281 1282 1283
1286 1294 1314 1429 1486 1490 1496 1502 1541 1542
1573 1577 1578 1585 1594 1664 1665 1684 1688 1694
1706 1709 1710 1711 1712 1713 1733 1734

54. Astronomy

0127 0130 0139 0188 0197 0201 0205 0212 0213 0217
0221 0223 0258 0338 0370 0377 0378 0401 0454 0637
0672 0681 0682 0698 0702 0705 0711 0713 0714 0716
0717 0785 0929 0976 0990 0991 1212 1221 1222 1235
1282 1283 1286 1291 1298 1300 1366 1404 1430 1529
1535 1541 1549 1558 1560 1565 1566 1567 1568 1570
1573 1575 1577 1578 1694 1713 1717 1718 1720 1722
1723 1726 1727 1731 1733 1734 1736 1737

55. Earth Sciences

0014 0021 0022 0067 0069 0070 0072 0074 0106 0107
0116 0126 0127 0128 0131 0133 0134 0135 0137 0152
0154 0166 0185 0188 0194 0195 0197 0200 0201 0202
0203 0212 0216 0217 0218 0219 0221 0223 0242 0243
0244 0245 0251 0255 0256 0259 0295 0296 0345 0348
0368 0369 0370 0371 0372 0373 0374 0375 0399 0401
0404 0407 0409 0410 0416 0452 0454 0459 0496 0500
0510 0542 0546 0575 0576 0578 0591 0603 0604 0611
0613 0616 0618 0620 0625 0628 0629 0638 0655 0669
0674 0679 0684 0687 0688 0689 0692 0695 0697 0698
0699 0700 0701 0703 0705 0712 0714 0715 0750 0777
0780 0785 0831 0846 0851 0854 0890 0891 0895 0899
0900 0918 0921 0927 0964 0968 0975 0978 0982 0983
0988 0994 1085 1093 1107 1139 1177 1201 1209 1210
1217 1220 1222 1225 1246 1247 1248 1268 1281 1291
1300 1307 1314 1333 1343 1365 1366 1375 1376 1386
1397 1399 1400 1435 1439 1440 1442 1443 1444 1445
1448 1449 1450 1457 1473 1476 1485 1494 1498 1502
1520 1524 1525 1526 1527 1528 1530 1532 1534 1539
1541 1569 1570 1612 1633 1647 1649 1650 1652 1653
1682 1683 1684 1685 1706 1710 1717 1726 1733 1737

56. Geology

0013 0014 0017 0021 0022 0056 0059 0061 0067 0069
0070 0071 0072 0074 0091 0106 0107 0109 0110 0121
0126 0127 0128 0129 0130 0131 0132 0133 0134 0135

56. Geology (continued)

0136 0137 0138 0139 0140 0149 0151 0153 0154 0155
0166 0167 0168 0175 0178 0180 0181 0182 0184 0185
0186 0187 0188 0191 0192 0193 0194 0195 0196 0197
0198 0199 0200 0201 0202 0203 0205 0211 0212 0213
0214 0216 0218 0219 0221 0222 0223 0248 0251 0255
0257 0258 0259 0293 0295 0296 0348 0367 0369 0373
0374 0375 0376 0377 0378 0384 0385 0392 0399 0404
0407 0409 0410 0411 0412 0413 0415 0416 0452 0454
0458 0459 0460 0461 0496 0504 0572 0575 0576 0578
0580 0581 0590 0611 0616 0617 0618 0619 0620 0623
0624 0626 0627 0628 0629 0630 0631 0632 0633 0634
0635 0636 0637 0638 0646 0652 0655 0657 0658 0662
0668 0672 0674 0675 0678 0679 0681 0682 0684 0685
0687 0689 0691 0692 0695 0697 0698 0699 0700 0701
0702 0703 0704 0705 0710 0711 0713 0714 0715 0716
0717 0760 0767 0772 0775 0776 0777 0778 0779 0785
0823 0828 0829 0831 0846 0847 0849 0850 0851 0852
0854 0855 0885 0887 0899 0904 0918 0919 0921 0922
0923 0924 0925 0926 0927 0928 0929 0930 0931 0932
0933 0935 0936 0937 0938 0939 0950 0954 0968 0972
0974 0975 0976 0977 0978 0979 0980 0981 0982 0983
0986 0988 0990 0991 0994 1002 1036 1082 1083 1084
1085 1093 1101 1115 1209 1211 1213 1214 1215 1217
1218 1219 1221 1222 1223 1224 1225 1248 1261 1264
1270 1272 1274 1277 1279 1280 1281 1282 1283 1284
1285 1286 1288 1289 1293 1296 1298 1299 1302 1307
1310 1314 1323 1343 1365 1378 1384 1386 1397 1426
1428 1435 1436 1437 1439 1440 1441 1444 1445 1446
1447 1448 1449 1455 1457 1473 1475 1476 1478 1481
1482 1483 1484 1485 1494 1497 1502 1504 1509 1511
1512 1514 1515 1519 1520 1522 1523 1524 1525 1526
1527 1528 1529 1530 1531 1534 1539 1540 1541 1542
1543 1549 1555 1557 1558 1559 1560 1562 1563 1565
1566 1568 1569 1570 1571 1573 1575 1576 1577 1578
1614 1651 1656 1657 1678 1682 1684 1685 1687 1688
1689 1706 1709 1710 1711 1712 1713 1717 1718 1720
1721 1722 1723 1724 1725 1726 1727 1730 1731 1732
1733 1734 1735 1736 1737

57. Oceanography

0097 0107 0169 0186 0201 0454 0717 0847 1086 1115
1171 1181 1193 1197 1204 1244 1259 1260 1268 1280
1284 1314 1333 1366 1422 1424 1426 1439 1440 1448
1460 1478 1528 1666 1671 1706 1733

58. Community Service, general

0016 0021 0054 0108 0111 0114 0126 0152 0188 0193
0194 0196 0227 0231 0240 0255 0259 0277 0287 0291
0293 0295 0328 0347 0348 0367 0369 0374 0410 0412
0454 0481 0488 0489 0492 0510 0581 0583 0601 0617
0627 0628 0630 0634 0636 0690 0697 0700 0702 0717
0728 0770 0784 0785 0818 0819 0820 0848 0854 0878
0880 0885 0891 0892 0895 0897 0908 0914 0919 0921
0929 0934 0936 0938 0939 0979 1165 1170 1185 1191
1192 1216 1222 1225 1247 1286 1307 1308 1309 1314
1327 1328 1366 1384 1390 1401 1427 1440 1442 1443
1448 1455 1491 1499 1543 1544 1577 1590 1618 1652
1655 1658 1659 1664 1666 1667 1684 1705 1706 1716

59. Parks and Recreation Management

0017 0021 0066 0069 0071 0072 0110 0120 0127 0128
0129 0130 0131 0132 0133 0134 0135 0138 0139 0140
0152 0180 0182 0185 0186 0187 0188 0192 0194 0195
0196 0198 0199 0200 0202 0203 0204 0241 0242 0245
0255 0256 0258 0259 0281 0294 0295 0296 0313 0323
0339 0344 0346 0347 0353 0366 0367 0368 0369 0370
0372 0373 0374 0376 0377 0378 0390 0394 0410 0411
0454 0489 0496 0508 0510 0529 0540 0542 0550 0576
0581 0607 0612 0623 0624 0625 0626 0627 0628 0629
0633 0634 0636 0637 0638 0643 0688 0689 0697 0698
0699 0700 0701 0702 0703 0705 0716 0717 0744 0761
0762 0763 0779 0781 0783 0785 0800 0821 0823 0824

59. Parks and Recreation Management (continued)

0829 0836 0840 0851 0854 0891 0892 0899 0908 0911
0921 0923 0929 0930 0935 0937 0940 0948 0974 0982
0983 1033 1037 1061 1069 1073 1082 1083 1086 1088
1093 1108 1110 1111 1113 1115 1128 1130 1137 1139
1158 1159 1162 1165 1176 1180 1182 1185 1186 1189
1196 1199 1200 1205 1208 1209 1211 1213 1214 1216
1217 1218 1221 1222 1224 1225 1247 1270 1271 1274
1277 1281 1282 1283 1286 1298 1299 1309 1314 1327
1333 1366 1375 1381 1385 1415 1445 1448 1449 1456
1457 1532 1541 1544 1603 1614 1618 1621 1630 1659
1667 1684 1688 1689 1710 1711 1712 1713

60. Public Administration

0001 0013 0042 0052 0057 0070 0073 0074 0087 0098
0112 0115 0126 0127 0128 0130 0131 0134 0137 0139
0140 0152 0154 0155 0160 0167 0170 0178 0181 0183
0184 0187 0188 0190 0192 0193 0194 0196 0197 0202
0205 0222 0244 0249 0250 0255 0257 0259 0283 0290
0293 0295 0315 0325 0331 0334 0356 0357 0363 0367
0368 0369 0370 0372 0373 0374 0401 0404 0405 0410
0416 0446 0449 0452 0454 0459 0465 0487 0489 0496
0510 0524 0531 0538 0542 0554 0571 0572 0575 0578
0582 0583 0585 0596 0605 0608 0610 0612 0615 0617
0621 0622 0628 0629 0636 0637 0640 0642 0651 0671
0674 0678 0683 0688 0689 0690 0692 0697 0700 0701
0703 0705 0706 0717 0719 0728 0757 0762 0772 0781
0783 0784 0785 0819 0829 0830 0831 0847 0848 0852
0853 0855 0862 0866 0867 0875 0883 0887 0891 0895
0902 0906 0910 0915 0921 0923 0925 0927 0929 0930
0935 0938 0939 0940 0954 0956 0957 0960 0963 0975
0981 0982 0998 1033 1052 1079 1081 1083 1086 1091
1101 1105 1115 1139 1144 1150 1157 1158 1159 1164
1167 1172 1174 1175 1178 1192 1196 1197 1199 1207
1218 1219 1220 1221 1222 1227 1228 1246 1270 1272
1273 1283 1285 1286 1289 1296 1298 1301 1306 1307
1309 1314 1324 1328 1333 1343 1366 1370 1373 1374
1385 1390 1397 1399 1406 1416 1427 1438 1440 1443
1445 1451 1453 1455 1464 1491 1494 1499 1500 1502
1511 1525 1538 1541 1542 1544 1572 1574 1577 1584
1586 1607 1612 1642 1655 1660 1661 1664 1667 1671
1680 1686 1688 1689 1697 1737

61. Military

0058 0131 0133 0160 0326 0410 0761 0774 0780 0783
0785 0891 0929 0936 1105 1140 1166 1205 1217 1220
1660 1678

62. Ethnic Studies

0057 0068 0069 0071 0074 0088 0097 0098 0106 0107
0125 0126 0128 0129 0130 0131 0135 0140 0144 0147
0149 0152 0162 0167 0169 0173 0176 0179 0180 0181
0184 0187 0190 0193 0194 0195 0196 0197 0199 0201
0202 0205 0206 0210 0213 0216 0217 0219 0221 0223
0224 0255 0257 0258 0259 0281 0293 0313 0345 0348
0360 0369 0370 0372 0373 0376 0377 0378 0381 0382
0394 0398 0400 0401 0402 0403 0404 0407 0411 0412
0413 0415 0416 0459 0474 0524 0553 0562 0563 0569
0572 0585 0605 0619 0622 0623 0626 0627 0628 0629
0630 0632 0636 0637 0638 0648 0651 0655 0674 0679
0681 0683 0684 0685 0687 0690 0692 0694 0696 0697
0698 0699 0700 0702 0703 0704 0705 0711 0712 0714
0716 0717 0742 0783 0815 0849 0857 0897 0903 0906
0911 0923 0929 0930 0932 0938 0940 0954 0957 0964
0970 0973 0975 0976 0977 0978 0979 0981 0982 0988
0989 0990 0991 1007 1065 1149 1159 1180 1182 1198
1201 1210 1218 1221 1223 1224 1226 1233 1235 1237
1239 1240 1243 1246 1261 1263 1264 1268 1269 1270
1271 1275 1276 1278 1279 1280 1282 1284 1289 1291
1293 1295 1296 1298 1299 1300 1302 1312 1314 1316
1325 1335 1366 1369 1383 1404 1419 1425 1437 1439
1446 1449 1451 1453 1454 1455 1457 1470 1473 1475
1480 1481 1482 1483 1498 1500 1505 1506 1507 1518

62. Ethnic Studies (continued)

1519 1520 1521 1522 1523 1525 1529 1531 1534 1538
1539 1540 1541 1542 1543 1544 1558 1559 1560 1562
1563 1564 1566 1568 1569 1570 1571 1574 1577 1578
1594 1613 1636 1677 1681 1687 1689 1697 1698 1700
1701 1704 1705 1706 1709 1711 1712 1713 1717 1718
1719 1720 1722 1723 1724 1725 1727 1729 1730 1731
1733 1734 1735 1736 1737

63. International Relations

0044 0061 0069 0072 0087 0096 0097 0100 0102 0118
0120 0122 0126 0128 0130 0131 0135 0136 0140 0143
0149 0150 0158 0159 0161 0164 0166 0167 0169 0174
0175 0176 0177 0178 0179 0187 0190 0191 0193 0194
0199 0201 0205 0206 0208 0210 0213 0214 0215 0218
0219 0228 0281 0316 0333 0334 0341 0351 0360 0361
0370 0372 0374 0375 0376 0378 0381 0388 0389 0391
0393 0394 0396 0398 0401 0402 0404 0410 0413 0416
0454 0458 0487 0526 0531 0536 0567 0580 0591 0596
0604 0606 0611 0613 0614 0615 0616 0618 0621 0627
0628 0630 0631 0635 0636 0638 0650 0652 0655 0657
0664 0666 0669 0670 0671 0675 0676 0677 0681 0682
0683 0685 0686 0687 0690 0692 0694 0695 0696 0698
0701 0702 0703 0705 0712 0713 0717 0755 0772 0788
0800 0819 0827 0846 0871 0907 0913 0916 0923 0940
0952 0963 0964 0966 0968 0969 0970 0973 0975 0978
0981 0987 0989 1000 1038 1076 1079 1101 1105 1129
1134 1139 1140 1144 1146 1149 1155 1156 1157 1158
1175 1176 1180 1189 1196 1197 1200 1202 1203 1204
1208 1214 1218 1221 1223 1224 1226 1229 1232 1233
1235 1236 1238 1239 1243 1246 1248 1250 1251 1255
1262 1263 1267 1268 1269 1270 1276 1277 1278 1279
1284 1285 1287 1291 1293 1295 1297 1299 1300 1307
1312 1314 1356 1362 1364 1366 1367 1368 1370 1376
1385 1386 1388 1400 1403 1405 1409 1411 1418 1423
1424 1425 1427 1430 1431 1439 1447 1448 1491 1496
1497 1499 1500 1502 1505 1507 1508 1512 1513 1521
1523 1527 1533 1537 1539 1541 1543 1544 1555 1557
1558 1559 1562 1566 1575 1578 1594 1599 1636 1644
1668 1678 1688 1692 1694 1697 1704 1705 1706 1710
1717 1718 1720 1721 1725 1733 1735 1736 1737

The two-year college Search section

This section will help you search for two-year colleges that meet your needs and preferences. To use the section most effectively, read through the directions on this page and the sample entry on page 194. (You may also find it helpful to review the list of abbreviations on page 271.)

The reading guide card

To make it easy for you to use the **Search** section, we've attached a reading guide card inside the front cover of this book. Tear out the card and use it to read the college entries. If the reading guide card is missing, use the sample guide card on page 194 to make your own. Or, use a ruler as you read.

How is the two-year college Search section organized?

Two-year colleges are displayed on purple pages and are ordered alphabetically within each state. The states are also listed in alphabetical order.

For example, you will find that all two-year colleges in Alabama are listed together in alphabetical order. Among schools in Alabama, you can quickly review the entries to identify those that have both college transfer and career-oriented programs in the business area, have residence hall facilities on campus, and cost under $2,500. You can search for two-year colleges using any combinations of factors you prefer.

Additional career-oriented programs

The two-year **Search** pages show which of 15 college transfer course areas and 35 career-oriented programs are offered by each college. If you're interested in a particular program that isn't included on these pages, turn to page 265 to see if it appears in the index there of 39 additional career-oriented programs at two-year colleges.

How to use the two-year college Search section (purple pages)

1. If you want to look up specific colleges, turn to the **College Index** on page 272. Find the colleges you're interested in. Each college has a sequence number; use this number to locate the college in the **Search** pages. Then follow steps 3, 4, 7, and 8.

2. If you have no specific colleges in mind, or if you want to add others to your list, review the preferences you summarized on page 23. Then, turn to the pages in the **Search** section for a state you want to search. Colleges in that state are listed in alphabetical order. You'll be able to see the total full-time enrollment and the costs for each college.

3. Use your reading guide card to help you read information about a college.

4. For each college, circle favorable characteristics; cross out entries that are unfavorable (such as wrong state or affiliation, lack of preferred majors). Keep in mind that financial aid might be available to allow you to attend a college that has everything you're looking for but seems too expensive.

5. After reviewing the colleges in a state, circle the sequence numbers for those you want to consider further. Also review once more the colleges you have not circled before you drop them from consideration.

6. Repeat these steps for other states you want to consider.

7. Return to page 24 and list the colleges (and their sequence numbers) that seem promising on the basis of these tangible factors. Add the names and sequence numbers of other colleges you want to consider in the light of other, less tangible, factors.

8. Now focus your attention on the colleges on your list. If any of them require admission tests, read the section about admission tests on page 25; register to take the tests, if you haven't already done so. Then turn to Steps 4 and 5 for ideas about investigating and comparing the colleges on your list. Use the suggestions there as you work toward making your college choice.

How to read the entries in the two-year college Search section (using a hypothetical example)

Alpha Community College, sequence number 2000, is located in Beta, California and has 15,266 students. Tuition and fees are $100 for residents and $1,300 for out-of-state students. No campus room-and-board facilities are available (footnote 1) and in-state students who do not live in the city or district pay higher costs than residents (footnote 4). The college is publicly supported, has no religious requirements, and is located in an urban area of a city with a population between 100,000 and 500,000. Alpha lists no fall term application deadline, requires no tests for admission, is on an early semester system, and is either accredited or a candidate for accreditation by a regional accrediting association (footnote 5). No deadline is given for financial aid application. The FFS need analysis form and the FAF are equally acceptable. **In a recent freshman class:** about 4 of 10 with financial need were offered some aid. About 3 of 10 students are women. Of the freshmen, 3 of 10 are minority students, 4 of 10 return as sophomores, and 2 of 10 transfer to a four-year college. Transfer courses and career-oriented programs available are indicated by the symbol ■.

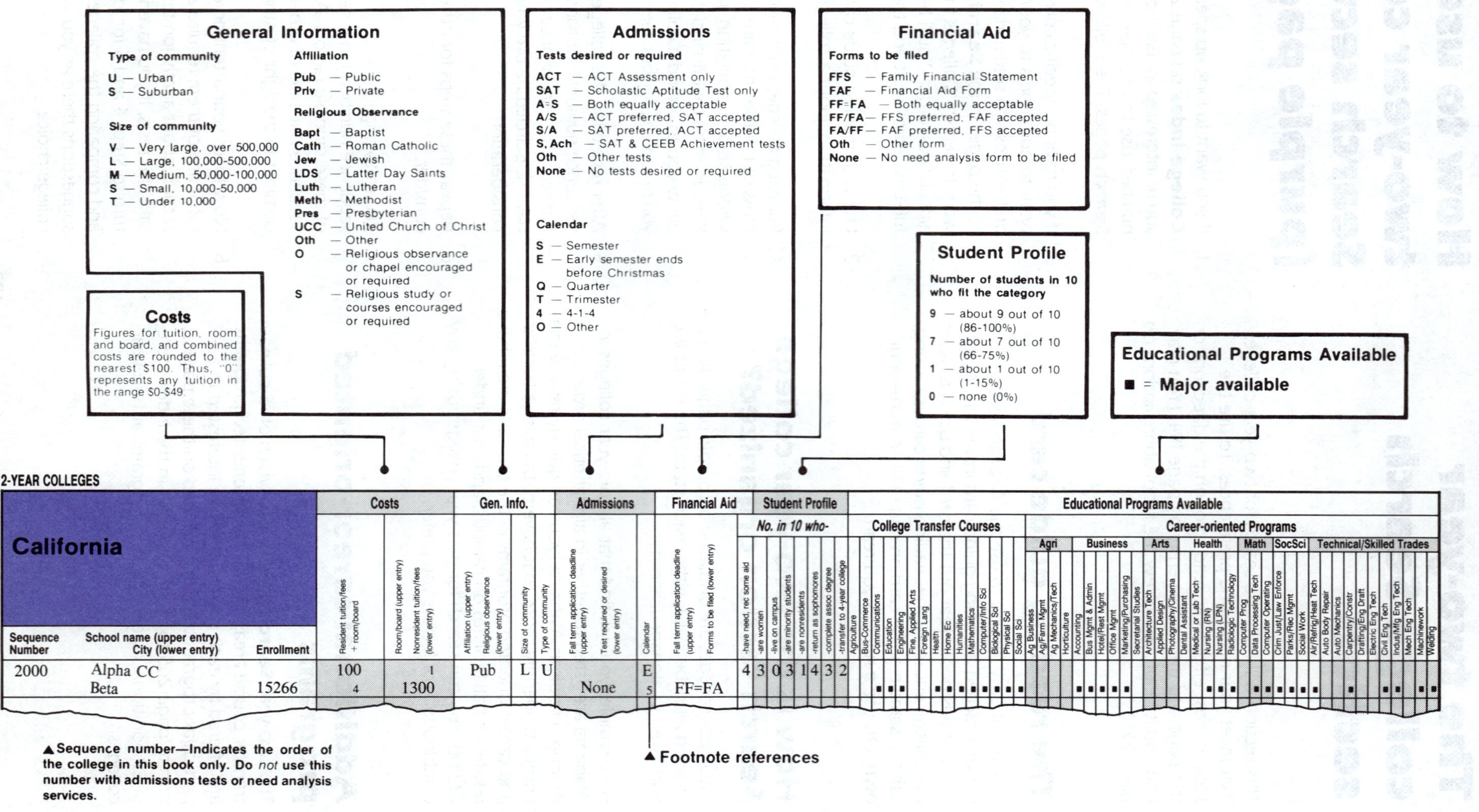

Alabama

Sequence Number	School name (upper entry) City (lower entry)	Enrollment	Costs: Resident tuition/fees + room/board	Costs: Room/board (upper entry) Nonresident tuition/fees (lower entry)	Gen. Info.: Affiliation (upper entry) Religious observance (lower entry)	Gen. Info.: Size of community	Gen. Info.: Type of community	Admissions: Fall term application deadline (upper entry) Test required or desired (lower entry)	Admissions: Calendar	Financial Aid: Fall term application deadline (upper entry) Forms to be filed (lower entry)	Student Profile (No. in 10 who-): -have need, rec some aid	-are women	-live on campus	-are minority students	-are nonresidents	-return as sophomores	-complete assoc degree	-transfer to 4-year college
2001	Alabama Aviat & Tech Ozark	386	4800	2900 5500	Pub	S			Q[5]		9	1	1	2	2			
2002	Alabama Bible C Guin	12	2800[3]	1400	Bapt OS	T[8]		Oth	S			6	0	0	0	9		
2003	Alexander City CC Alexander City	1233	800	[1] 1400	Pub	S		None	Q[5]		6	5	0	1	1	6	4	3
2004	Ayers Tech C Anniston	532	1000	[1] 1800	Pub	S		None	Q[5]	FFS	6	4	0	2			7	
2005	Bessemer St Tech Bessemer	879	900	[1] 1500	Pub	S		Oth	Q[5]	Oth	7	4	0	3	0	5	5	1
2006	Brewer St JC Fayette	488	800	[1] 1400	Pub	T			Q[5]	8/01 FA/FF	8	5	0	1	1	6		8
2007	Carver St Tech Inst Mobile	468	800	[1] 1600	Pub	L	U	Oth	O[5]	FFS	8	6	0	8	0	7	9	1
2008	Central Ala CC-Child Childersburg	532	600	[1] 1100	Pub	T		9/02 Oth	O[5]		8	4	0	4	0		1	1
2009	Chattahoochee Vly CC Phenix City	1196	600	[1] 1100	Pub	M	S	9/20 Oth	Q[5]	9/01 FFS	4	6	0	3	2	4	4	6
2010	Concordia C-Alabama Selma	380	6900	4000	Luth S	S		8/15 A/S	E[5]	9/01 FFS	8	7	7	9	1	9	9	6
2011	Coosa Valley Sch Nsg Sylacauga	47	1900	[1]	Pub	S[8]		8/07 Oth	Q†	7/01	5	9	0	1	0			
2012	Drake St Tech Huntsville	432	1200	[1] 2100	Pub	L	U	9/07 Oth	Q[5]	FFS	3	4	0	4	1	5	2	1
2013	Enterprise St JC Enterprise	2113	600	[1] 1100	Pub	S		A=S	Q[5]	FF/FA	6	6	0	2	0	3	3	4
2014	Faulkner St JC Bay Minette	3109	2900	1900 3900	Pub	T		9/25 None	Q[5]	9/01 FF/FA	3	6	1	1	1	5	5	
2015	Faulkner U Birminghm Birmingham	183	4700	[1]	Oth S	V[8]	U	9/12 A/S	Q[5]	FF/FA	9	7	0	8	0	4	2	2
2016	Faulkner U Florence Florence	86	4700	[1]	Oth S	M[8]		8/31 None	Q[5]	Oth	8	7	0	1	0	4	1	2
2017	Faulkner U Huntsvle Huntsville	45	4700	[1]	Oth S	M[8]	S	8/15 A/S	O[5]	FF/FA	9	5	0	4	0			
2018	Faulkner U Mobile Mobile	92	3900	[1]	Oth S	L[8]	U	8/15 A/S	4[5]	FF/FA	9	7	0	3	0	0		
2019	Fredd St Tech C Tuscaloosa	316	1400	[1]	Pub	M			Q[5]	FF=FA	9	6	0	9				
2020	Gadsden St CC Gadsden	5426	2600	1800 3200	Pub	M	S	Oth	Q[5]	FF/FA	3	5	1	2	1	5	6	4
2021	Herzing Inst Alabama Birmingham	450	4400	[1]	Priv	L[8]	U	Oth	Q†	9/15 FF=FA	9	6	0	5	1	0	7	
2022	Hobson St Tech Thomasville	455	900	[1] 1400	Pub	T		Oth	O[5]	Oth	7	5	0	5	0	4		1
2023	Holy Name Sch Nsg Gadsden	32	2900[2]	700	Cath O	S[8]	[6]	8/15 Oth	Q†	9/15 FF=FA	4	9	1	1	0	8		

Educational Programs Available — College Transfer Courses

Sequence Number	Agriculture	Bus-Commerce	Communications	Education	Engineering	Fine, Applied Arts	Foreign Lang	Health	Home Ec	Humanities	Mathematics	Computer/Info Sci	Biological Sci	Physical Sci	Social Sci
2001															
2002		■		■		■	■		■	■		■	■		■
2003	■	■	■	■	■	■	■	■	■	■	■	■	■	■	■
2004															
2005															
2006	■	■	■	■	■	■		■		■	■	■	■	■	■
2007				■							■	■			
2008		■						■							
2009	■	■	■	■	■	■	■	■		■	■	■	■	■	■
2010		■	■	■		■				■	■		■	■	■
2011								■							
2012															
2013	■	■	■	■	■	■	■	■	■	■	■	■			■
2014	■	■	■	■	■	■	■	■	■	■	■	■	■	■	■
2015		■	■	■		■				■	■	■	■	■	■
2016		■		■						■	■	■		■	■
2017		■	■	■				■		■	■	■			■
2018		■	■			■		■		■		■	■	■	■
2019															
2020	■	■	■	■	■	■		■	■	■	■	■	■	■	■
2021		■									■	■			
2022															
2023															

Educational Programs Available — Career-oriented Programs (Agri: Ag Business–Horticulture; Business: Accounting–Secretarial Studies; Arts: Architecture Tech–Photography/Cinema; Health: Dental Assistant–Radiologic Technology; Math: Computer Prog–Computer Operating; SocSci: Crim Just/Law Enforce–Social Work; Technical/Skilled Trades: Air/Refrig/Heat Tech–Welding)

Sequence Number	Ag Business	Ag/Farm Mgmt	Ag Mechanics/Tech	Horticulture	Accounting	Bus Mgmt & Admin	Hotel/Rest Mgmt	Office Mgmt	Marketing/Purchasing	Secretarial Studies	Architecture Tech	Applied Design	Photography/Cinema	Dental Assistant	Medical or Lab Tech	Nursing (RN)	Nursing (LPN)	Radiologic Technology	Computer Prog	Data Processing Tech	Computer Operating	Crim Just/Law Enforce	Parks/Rec Mgmt	Social Work	Air/Refrig/Heat Tech	Auto Body Repair	Auto Mechanics	Carpentry/Constr	Drafting/Eng Draft	Electric Eng Tech	Civil Eng Tech	Indus/Mfg Eng Tech	Mech Eng Tech	Machinework	Welding
2001																											■			■					
2002																																			
2003						■		■		■					■			■	■	■	■	■			■		■			■					■
2004					■					■							■		■						■	■	■		■	■				■	■
2005				■	■				■	■			■	■			■		■	■					■		■	■	■	■				■	■
2006						■				■										■															
2007					■	■		■		■											■				■	■									■
2008					■					■							■		■	■					■	■	■	■	■	■				■	■
2009					■	■		■	■	■						■	■	■	■	■	■	■													
2010																																			
2011																■																			
2012					■					■							■		■		■				■		■	■	■	■				■	■
2013		■			■	■		■	■	■									■			■	■												
2014						■	■	■	■	■				■	■			■				■													
2015															■			■																	
2016								■																											
2017															■			■																	
2018										■					■			■																	
2019										■																■		■		■					
2020	■								■	■					■	■	■	■		■		■		■	■	■	■	■	■	■	■	■		■	■
2021										■									■	■	■									■					
2022					■					■							■				■				■	■	■	■		■					■
2023																■																			

▲ Sequence Number—indicates the order of the college in this book only. Do *not* use this number with admissions tests or need analysis services.

[1] No campus room and board facilities
[2] Room only or board only
[3] Most freshmen required to live on campus
[4] City or district residency requirements
[5] Accredited by regional accrediting association or a recognized candidate for accreditation
[6] All female freshman class
[7] All male freshman class
[8] Some admission selectivity; not all hs graduates accepted
[9] Requirements more stringent for nonresidents
†Accredited by a nationally recognized accrediting body other than one of the regional accrediting associations

Alabama
(continued)

Sequence Number	School name (upper entry) / City (lower entry)	Enrollment	Costs: Resident tuition/fees + room/board	Costs: Room/board (upper entry) / Nonresident tuition/fees (lower entry)	Gen. Info.: Affiliation (upper entry) / Religious observance (lower entry)	Gen. Info.: Size of community	Gen. Info.: Type of community	Admissions: Fall term application deadline (upper entry) / Test required or desired (lower entry)	Calendar	Financial Aid: Fall term application deadline (upper entry) / Forms to be filed (lower entry)	No. in 10 who- -have need, rec some aid	-are women	-live on campus	-are minority students	-are nonresidents	-return as sophomores	-complete assoc degree	-transfer to 4-year college
2024	Jefferson Davis CC Brewton	716	800	[1] 1400	Pub	T		9/01 None	Q[5]	3/15 FF=FA	3	6	0	2	1	4	3	3
2025	Jefferson St CC Birmingham	3386	1100	[1] 1800	Pub	L	S	None	Q[5]	Oth	3	6	0	2			4	
2026	John C Calhoun St CC Decatur	3336	900	[1] 1500	Pub	M	S	None	Q[5]	3/15 FF/FA	5	5	0	1	1	4	2	4
2027	Lawson St CC Birmingham	1413	900	[1] 1600	Pub	L	U	None	Q[5]	9/15 FA/FF	8	6	0	9	0	5	7	3
2028	Lurleen Wallace JC Andalusia	871	900	[1] 1500	Pub	S		None	Q[5]	6/15 Oth	9	6	0	1	1			
2029	Marion Military Inst Marion	405	6700[3]	2500	Priv	T[8]		8/28 Oth	E[5]	8/30 FFS	9	1	9	1	5	7	7	9
2030	National Career C Decatur	161	4800	[1]	Priv	S[8]		ACT	Q†	None	8	7	0	1	1	2		
2031	National Career C Tuscaloosa	205	5000	[1]	Priv	M[8]	U	Oth	Q†	10/01 Oth	8	9	0	4	0	8	9	1
2032	National Ed Ctr Ala Birmingham	200	4900	[1]	Priv	V[8]	S	Oth	Q†	FF=FA	7	5	0	6	1	8	6	1
2033	Northeast Alabama JC Rainsville	994	900	[1] 1500	Pub	T		9/05 None	Q[5]	8/25 FFS	9	3	0	1	1	5	3	2
2034	Northwest CC Phil Campbell	1430	1500[2]	500 2200	Pub	T		9/10 A/S	Q[5]	9/15 FF=FA	7	6	0	1	1	4	4	4
2035	Opelika St Tech Opelika	606	800	[1] 1200	Pub	S		Oth	Q[5]	FFS	5	5	0	4	0	6	5	1
2036	Patrick Henry C Monroeville	587	1000	[1] 1600	Pub	T		A/S	Q[5]	7/15 FF=FA	5	6	0	2	1	4	3	2
2037	Patterson Tech C Montgomery	751	1300	[1] 2600	Pub	M	S	Oth	Q[5]	Oth		4	0	3	1		5	1
2038	Reid St Tech C Evergreen	393	900	[1] 1700	Pub	T		None	O[5]	FF/FA	8	8	0	4	1	7		
2039	S D Bishop CC Mobile	1857	1000	[1] 1800	Pub	L	U	9/13 None	Q[5]	FFS	6	7	0	7	1			
2040	Shelton St CC Tuscaloosa	1953	900	[1] 1700	Pub	M	U	A=S	Q[5]	8/01	5	5	0	3	1	4	2	7
2041	Shoals CC Muscle Shoals	2026	600	[1] 1100	Pub	M	S	Oth	Q[5]	8/01 FF=FA	4	4	0	2	1			
2042	Snead St JC Boaz	1691	2400	1600 2900	Pub	T		9/15 None	Q[5]	9/15 FFS	3	6	1	1	1	4		
2043	Southern JC Birmingham	800	3500	[1]	Priv	L	U	Oth	Q[5]		9	8	0	9			7	1
2044	Southern JC-Huntsvll Huntsville	426	4400	[1]	Priv	M[8]	U	8/27 Oth	Q[5]	8/27 Oth	9	7		3	1	7	6	1
2045	Southern Union JC Wadley	2896	2700	1800 3300	Pub	T		None	Q[5]	FF/FA	6	6	1	2	1		1	
2046	Southern Voc C Tuskegee	125	3000	[1]	Priv	S		None	Q[5]	7/30 FFS	9	9	0	9	1	8	8	1

Educational Programs Available — College Transfer Courses

Sequence Number	Agriculture	Bus-Commerce	Communications	Education	Engineering	Fine, Applied Arts	Foreign Lang	Health	Home Ec	Humanities	Mathematics	Computer/Info Sci	Biological Sci	Physical Sci	Social Sci
2024	■	■		■	■	■		■	■	■	■	■	■	■	■
2025	■	■	■	■	■	■	■	■		■	■	■	■	■	■
2026		■		■	■	■	■	■		■	■	■	■	■	■
2027		■	■	■		■		■		■	■	■	■	■	■
2028	■	■	■					■		■		■			■
2029	■	■	■	■	■	■	■	■		■	■	■	■	■	■
2030															
2031															
2032															
2033	■	■	■	■	■	■	■	■	■	■	■		■	■	
2034	■	■	■	■	■	■	■	■	■	■	■	■	■	■	■
2035															
2036	■	■	■	■	■	■	■	■		■	■	■	■	■	■
2037		■									■	■			
2038		■										■			
2039		■	■	■	■	■		■		■	■		■	■	■
2040	■	■		■	■	■	■	■	■		■	■	■	■	■
2041	■	■	■	■	■	■	■	■		■	■	■	■	■	■
2042	■	■		■	■	■		■			■	■	■	■	■
2043		■								■	■				
2044		■				■		■	■			■			■
2045	■	■	■	■	■	■		■	■	■	■	■	■	■	■
2046		■		■		■		■	■	■	■	■	■	■	■

Educational Programs Available — Career-oriented Programs (Agri, Business, Arts, Health)

Sequence Number	Agri: Ag Business	Ag/Farm Mgmt	Ag Mechanics/Tech	Horticulture	Business: Accounting	Bus Mgmt & Admin	Hotel/Rest Mgmt	Office Mgmt	Marketing/Purchasing	Secretarial Studies	Arts: Architecture Tech	Applied Design	Photography/Cinema	Health: Dental Assistant	Medical or Lab Tech	Nursing (RN)	Nursing (LPN)	Radiologic Technology
2024																		
2025					■		■		■	■	■				■	■		■
2026				■	■	■		■	■	■		■		■	■	■	■	■
2027										■				■	■	■		■
2028					■	■				■								
2029																		
2030					■	■		■	■	■								
2031					■			■	■	■								
2032																		
2033										■		■		■		■		■
2034					■	■		■		■					■	■	■	■
2035					■			■		■							■	
2036								■		■								
2037																		
2038								■		■							■	
2039					■	■		■	■	■					■	■		■
2040			■					■		■					■		■	
2041					■			■		■							■	
2042								■	■	■					■	■		■
2043								■										
2044						■		■	■	■								
2045								■		■						■		■
2046						■			■	■				■	■		■	

Educational Programs Available — Career-oriented Programs (Math, SocSci, Technical/Skilled Trades)

Sequence Number	Math: Computer Prog	Data Processing Tech	Computer Operating	SocSci: Crim Just/Law Enforce	Parks/Rec Mgmt	Social Work	Technical/Skilled Trades: Air/Refrig/Heat Tech	Auto Body Repair	Auto Mechanics	Carpentry/Constr	Drafting/Eng Draft	Electric Eng Tech	Civil Eng Tech	Indus/Mfg Eng Tech	Mech Eng Tech	Machinework	Welding
2024																	
2025		■	■	■	■						■		■		■		
2026			■	■			■	■	■		■	■				■	■
2027		■		■				■		■	■	■					
2028				■													
2029																	
2030		■	■														
2031		■	■														
2032																	
2033	■	■															
2034	■	■	■	■	■		■	■	■	■	■	■			■	■	■
2035	■	■					■	■	■	■	■	■				■	■
2036	■	■	■														
2037	■						■		■		■					■	■
2038								■		■		■					■
2039	■	■															
2040							■		■	■	■	■				■	■
2041	■		■	■			■	■	■	■	■	■				■	■
2042		■															
2043	■	■															
2044																	
2045																	
2046				■													

▲ Sequence Number—indicates the order of the college in this book only. Do *not* use this number with admissions tests or need analysis services.

[1] No campus room and board facilities
[2] Room only or board only
[3] Most freshmen required to live on campus
[4] City or district residency requirements
[5] Accredited by regional accrediting association or a recognized candidate for accreditation
[6] All female freshman class
[7] All male freshman class
[8] Some admission selectivity; not all hs graduates accepted
[9] Requirements more stringent for nonresidents
†Accredited by a nationally recognized accrediting body other than one of the regional accrediting associations

Alabama
(continued)

Sequence Number	School name (upper entry) City (lower entry)	Enrollment	Costs: Resident tuition/fees + room/board	Costs: Room/board (upper entry) Nonresident tuition/fees (lower entry)	Gen. Info.: Affiliation (upper entry) Religious observance (lower entry)	Gen. Info.: Size of community	Gen. Info.: Type of community	Admissions: Fall term application deadline (upper entry) Test required or desired (lower entry)	Admissions: Calendar	Financial Aid: Fall term application deadline (upper entry) Forms to be filed (lower entry)
2047	Southwest St Tech C Mobile	850	1400	[1] 2200	Pub	L	U	9/21 Oth	O [5]	FFS
2048	Sparks St Tech CC Eufaula	350	800	[1] 1600	Pub	S		None	Q [5]	Oth
2049	Trenholm St Tech Montgomery	500	900	[1] 1800	Pub	L	U	Oth	O [5]	8/01 Oth
2050	Twentieth Century C Mobile	100	4000	[1]	Priv	L [8]	U	Oth	O †	FFS
2051	Walker C Jasper	524	4000	2000	Priv	S		9/05 ACT	E [5]	7/15 Oth
2052	Walker St Tech Sumiton	1084	1000	[1] 1800	Pub	M		Oth	Q [5]	Oth
2053	Wallace St CC-Dothan Dothan	1829	700	[1] 1100	Pub	M		None	Q [5]	FFS
2054	Wallace St CC-Hancev Hanceville	2723	1200 [2]	600 1700	Pub	T		Oth	Q [5]	
2055	Wallace St CC-Selma Selma	1164	600	[1] 1100	Pub	S		9/01 None	Q [5]	8/16 FAF
Alaska										
2056	Kenai Peninsula C Soldotna	250	800	[1] 1800	Pub	T		Oth	E [5]	FAF
2057	Ketchikan Cam,U Alas Ketchikan	83	1200	[1] 3800	Pub	S		9/03 None	E [5]	5/15 FAF
2058	Kodiak C Kodiak	20	1000	[1] 3600	Pub	T		None	S [5]	
2059	Kuskokwim C Bethel	75	5800	4800 8200	Pub	T		5/15 A=S	E [5]	8/15 FAF
2060	Matanuska-Susitna C Palmer	235	1000	[1] 3600	Pub	S		None	E [5]	5/01 FA/FF
2061	Northwest C Nome	255	900	[1] 1700	Pub	T		Oth	S [5]	8/15 FAF
2062	Prince Wm Sound CC Valdez	57	2500 [2]	1400 5300	Pub	T		None	E	9/30 FAF
2063	Sitka Cam,U Alas Sitka	64	2800 [2]	1800	Pub	S		None	E [5]	5/15 FAF
Arizona										
2064	ABC Tech Trade Sch Tucson	252	6000	[1]	Priv	L	U	Oth	O †	Oth
2065	Ariz Western C Yuma	1239	3200	2500 7300	Pub	M		None	E [5]	FF/FA
2066	Central Ariz C Coolidge	1045	2800	2200 6700	Pub	S		8/15 None	E [5]	FFS
2067	Chandler Gilbert CC Chandler	3500	700	[1] 4500	Pub	M	S	None	E [5]	FA/FF

Student Profile — No. in 10 who-

Sequence Number	-have need, rec some aid	-are women	-live on campus	-are minority students	-are nonresidents	-return as sophomores	-complete assoc degree	-transfer to 4-year college
2047	4	4	0	4	0	5	2	1
2048	8	5	0	4	1	6		
2049	8	5	0	7	0	7		
2050		9	0	4				
2051	5	6	2	1	1	6	5	7
2052	4	5	0	1	0	5	6	1
2053	6	6	0	1	1		3	3
2054	5	5	1	1	1	6	3	4
2055	6	6	0	3	0	5	2	1
Alaska								
2056	8	5	0	2			7	1
2057	1	6		2		8	1	4
2058	1	5	0					2
2059	9	6	8	6	0	7	2	7
2060	3	7	0	1	0		4	4
2061	8	6	0	4	0			
2062	8	7	2	3			1	1
2063	5	6	0	3	1	3	1	1
Arizona								
2064	7	1			5	9		
2065	7	6	4	6	3	7		
2066		6		3				
2067	1	6	0	2	1			

Educational Programs Available — College Transfer Courses

Sequence Number	Agriculture	Bus-Commerce	Communications	Education	Engineering	Fine, Applied Arts	Foreign Lang	Health	Home Ec	Humanities	Mathematics	Computer/Info Sci	Biological Sci	Physical Sci	Social Sci
2047															
2048															
2049															
2050		■										■			
2051	■	■	■	■	■	■	■	■	■	■	■	■	■	■	■
2052		■		■				■		■	■	■		■	■
2053		■		■	■	■				■	■	■	■	■	■
2054	■	■				■		■		■	■		■	■	■
2055	■	■	■	■	■	■		■	■	■	■	■	■	■	■
Alaska															
2056		■		■	■	■		■			■	■			■
2057		■		■		■	■	■	■	■	■	■	■	■	■
2058		■				■	■			■	■	■			■
2059	■	■	■	■		■	■	■	■	■	■	■	■	■	■
2060	■	■	■	■		■	■	■	■	■	■	■	■	■	■
2061	■	■	■	■		■	■	■		■	■	■		■	■
2062		■	■	■		■			■	■	■	■			■
2063	■	■	■	■	■	■	■	■	■	■	■	■	■	■	■
Arizona															
2064															
2065	■	■	■	■	■	■	■	■	■	■	■	■	■	■	■
2066	■	■	■	■	■	■	■	■	■	■	■	■	■	■	■
2067		■	■		■	■	■		■	■	■	■	■	■	■

Educational Programs Available — Career-oriented Programs (Agri, Business, Arts, Health)

Sequence Number	Agri: Ag Business	Agri: Ag/Farm Mgmt	Agri: Ag Mechanics/Tech	Agri: Horticulture	Business: Accounting	Business: Bus Mgmt & Admin	Business: Hotel/Rest Mgmt	Business: Office Mgmt	Business: Marketing/Purchasing	Business: Secretarial Studies	Arts: Architecture Tech	Arts: Applied Design	Arts: Photography/Cinema	Health: Dental Assistant	Health: Medical or Lab Tech	Health: Nursing (RN)	Health: Nursing (LPN)	Health: Radiologic Technology
2047									■								■	
2048					■			■		■							■	
2049				■	■					■				■			■	
2050					■	■												
2051								■		■						■		■
2052					■	■		■		■						■	■	
2053					■			■		■					■	■	■	■
2054					■	■		■						■	■	■	■	■
2055										■						■	■	
Alaska																		
2056										■								
2057					■	■	■	■	■	■								
2058								■		■								
2059																		
2060					■	■				■								
2061					■	■		■		■							■	
2062										■								
2063																		
Arizona																		
2064																		
2065	■							■	■	■						■		
2066	■	■			■	■	■	■	■	■						■	■	
2067								■		■								

Educational Programs Available — Career-oriented Programs (Math, SocSci, Technical/Skilled Trades)

Sequence Number	Math: Computer Prog	Math: Data Processing Tech	Math: Computer Operating	SocSci: Crim Just/Law Enforce	SocSci: Parks/Rec Mgmt	SocSci: Social Work	Tech: Air/Refrig/Heat Tech	Tech: Auto Body Repair	Tech: Auto Mechanics	Tech: Carpentry/Constr	Tech: Drafting/Eng Draft	Tech: Electric Eng Tech	Tech: Civil Eng Tech	Tech: Indus/Mfg Eng Tech	Tech: Mech Eng Tech	Tech: Machinework	Tech: Welding
2047							■		■	■	■	■				■	
2048		■	■				■	■	■	■	■	■			■		■
2049								■		■		■					
2050		■															
2051																	
2052	■	■					■	■	■		■	■				■	■
2053		■		■			■	■	■	■	■	■			■	■	■
2054	■			■		■	■	■	■	■	■	■				■	■
2055				■			■	■	■	■	■	■				■	■
Alaska																	
2056	■	■									■						■
2057									■								■
2058																	
2059	■	■															
2060							■			■	■						■
2061										■							
2062																	
2063			■	■													■
Arizona																	
2064							■		■			■					■
2065	■	■	■	■		■	■		■		■	■		■		■	■
2066	■	■	■	■			■	■	■	■	■	■	■	■		■	
2067		■	■														

▲ **Sequence Number—indicates the order of the college in this book only. Do *not* use this number with admissions tests or need analysis services.**

[1] No campus room and board facilities
[2] Room only or board only
[3] Most freshmen required to live on campus
[4] City or district residency requirements
[5] Accredited by regional accrediting association or a recognized candidate for accreditation
[6] All female freshman class
[7] All male freshman class
[8] Some admission selectivity; not all hs graduates accepted
[9] Requirements more stringent for nonresidents
†Accredited by a nationally recognized accrediting body other than one of the regional accrediting associations

Arizona
(continued)

Sequence Number	School name (upper entry) / City (lower entry)	Enrollment	Costs: Resident tuition/fees + room/board	Costs: Room/board (upper entry) / Nonresident tuition/fees (lower entry)	Gen. Info.: Affiliation (upper entry) / Religious observance (lower entry)	Gen. Info.: Size of community	Gen. Info.: Type of community	Admissions: Fall term application deadline (upper entry) / Test required or desired (lower entry)	Admissions: Calendar	Financial Aid: Fall term application deadline (upper entry) / Forms to be filed (lower entry)	No. in 10 who- -have need, rec some aid	-are women	-live on campus	-are minority students	-are nonresidents	-return as sophomores	-complete assoc degree	-transfer to 4-year college
2068	Cochise C / Douglas	2252	3500	2800 / 7100	Pub	S		None	E[5]	FF/FA	4	5	1	6	1	2		
2069	Eastern Ariz C / Thatcher	903	3200	2600 / 6300	Pub	T		A/S	E[5]	4/15 / FA/FF	7	5	4	3	1	5	3	3
2070	Gateway CC / Phoenix	682	700	[1] / 4400	Pub	V	U	None	S[5]		2	6	0	3	1	1	1	1
2071	Glendale CC / Glendale	4552	700	[1] / 4400	Pub	M	S	8/23 / Oth	E[5]		2	6	0	2	1	4	4	
2072	Mesa CC / Mesa	4811	900	[1] / 5400	Pub	L	U	8/15 / None	E[5]	FF/FA	7	5	0	1	1			
2073	Mohave CC / Kingman	458	500	[1] / 3400	Pub	S			S[5]	FF/FA	5	6		1			1	1
2074	Navajo CC / Tsaile	698	2900	2500	Pub	T		8/02 / A=S	E[5]	6/30 / FFS	5	7	1	9	1	6	2	4
2075	Northland Pioneer C / Holbrook	699	1900[2]	1700 / 4600	Pub	T		None	S[5]	FF=FA	5	6	0	3	0	6		
2076	Paradise Valley CC / Phoenix	4613	700	[1] / 5100	Pub	L	U	Oth	E[5]	4/15 / FFS		6	0	1			1	
2077	Phoenix C / Phoenix	3146	700	[1] / 4500	Pub	V	U	8/30 / Oth	E[5]	FF/FA		6	0	2	1	3		
2078	Pima CC / Tucson	6868	500	[1] / 2800	Pub	V	U	9/01 / None	E[5]	FF/FA	2	6	0	3	1	4	1	3
2079	Rio Salado CC / Phoenix	467	700	[1] / 4500	Pub	V	U	None	O[5]	12/01 / FF=FA		6	0	2	1		1	
2080	Scottsdale CC / Scottsdale	2367	700	[1] / 4500	Pub	L	S		E[5]	4/15 / FFS	9	6	0	1	1	2		8
2081	South Mountain CC / Phoenix	2984	700	[1] / 4400	Pub	V	U	8/22 / None	S[5]	FF=FA	1	6	0	7	2	1	1	1
2082	Yavapai C / Prescott	1218	3100	2500 / 7100	Pub	S		None	4[5]	FA/FF	6	6	2	1	1	3	1	2
Arkansas																		
2083	Arkansas St U Beebe / Beebe	961	2600	1700 / 3100	Pub	T		8/25 / ACT	E[5]	FFS	9	6	1	1	1	8	5	7
2084	Bapt System Sch Nsg / Little Rock	643	5400	[1]	Bapt	M[8]	S	Oth	S†	8/01		9		1		8		
2085	Capital City Bus C / Little Rock	275	6000	[1]	Priv	M	U	Oth	O[5]	10/07		8						
2086	Crowley's Ridge C / Paragould	110	5400[3]	2200	Oth / OS	S			S†	FFS	7	5	5	1	1	6	2	5
2087	East Arkansas CC / Forrest City	830	600	[1] / 900	Pub	S		8/27 / A/S	E[5]	4/15	7	7	0	4	1	3	2	3
2088	Garland Co CC / Hot Springs	1100	800	[1] / 1700	Pub	S		A=S	E[5]	5/01 / FFS	2	6	0	1	1	3	1	3
2089	Jefferson Sch Nsg / Pine Bluff	140	1200	[1]	Priv	M[8]		7/01 / Oth	S†	11/01	2	9	0	2	0		6	

Educational Programs Available — College Transfer Courses

Sequence Number	Agriculture	Bus-Commerce	Communications	Education	Engineering	Fine, Applied Arts	Foreign Lang	Health	Home Ec	Humanities	Mathematics	Computer/Info Sci	Biological Sci	Physical Sci	Social Sci
2068	■	■	■	■	■	■	■	■		■		■	■	■	■
2069	■	■		■	■	■	■	■	■	■	■	■	■	■	■
2070		■	■			■	■	■	■	■	■	■	■	■	■
2071	■	■	■	■	■	■	■	■	■	■	■	■	■	■	■
2072	■	■	■	■	■	■	■	■	■	■	■	■	■	■	■
2073		■	■	■	■	■	■	■	■	■	■	■	■	■	■
2074	■	■	■	■	■	■	■	■	■	■	■	■	■	■	■
2075	■	■	■	■	■	■	■	■	■	■	■	■	■	■	■
2076	■	■	■	■	■	■	■	■	■	■	■	■	■	■	■
2077		■	■	■	■	■	■	■	■	■	■	■	■	■	■
2078	■	■	■	■	■	■	■	■	■	■	■		■	■	■
2079		■				■	■			■					■
2080	■	■	■	■	■	■	■	■	■	■	■	■	■	■	■
2081		■				■	■		■	■	■	■			■
2082	■	■	■	■	■	■	■	■	■	■	■	■	■	■	■
2083	■	■	■	■	■	■	■	■		■	■	■	■	■	■
2084															
2085															
2086		■		■	■	■		■		■	■		■	■	■
2087	■	■	■	■	■	■	■	■		■	■	■	■	■	■
2088		■	■	■	■	■	■	■		■	■	■	■	■	■
2089															

Educational Programs Available — Career-oriented Programs

Sequence Number	Agri: Ag Business	Ag/Farm Mgmt	Ag Mechanics/Tech	Horticulture	Business: Accounting	Bus Mgmt & Admin	Hotel/Rest Mgmt	Office Mgmt	Marketing/Purchasing	Secretarial Studies	Arts: Architecture Tech	Applied Design	Photography/Cinema	Health: Dental Assistant	Medical or Lab Tech	Nursing (RN)	Nursing (LPN)	Radiologic Technology	Math: Computer Prog	Data Processing Tech	Computer Operating	SocSci: Crim Just/Law Enforce	Parks/Rec Mgmt	Social Work	Technical/Skilled Trades: Air/Refrig/Heat Tech	Auto Body Repair	Auto Mechanics	Carpentry/Constr	Drafting/Eng Draft	Electric Eng Tech	Civil Eng Tech	Indus/Mfg Eng Tech	Mech Eng Tech	Machinework	Welding
2068	■	■			■	■		■		■						■	■		■			■		■					■			■		■	■
2069						■		■	■	■									■			■					■		■	■				■	■
2070					■	■		■		■						■	■	■	■	■	■				■		■		■	■					
2071	■			■	■				■	■						■						■		■			■		■						
2072	■	■						■		■						■	■			■		■					■		■	■					
2073					■	■		■		■							■					■			■		■								■
2074					■	■		■		■									■	■	■			■			■								■
2075								■		■												■		■			■	■							■
2076								■	■	■						■			■	■		■		■				■	■	■					
2077					■	■	■	■	■	■				■	■	■				■	■	■		■					■		■		■		
2078					■	■	■	■	■	■		■		■		■	■	■	■	■	■	■	■	■	■		■	■	■				■	■	■
2079							■			■											■			■				■	■	■		■			
2080					■	■	■	■	■	■						■	■		■	■	■	■						■	■	■					
2081						■				■																									
2082					■	■		■	■	■	■					■			■	■							■	■	■			■		■	■
2083										■																						■			
2084															■	■	■	■																	
2085					■	■		■		■									■	■	■														
2086																																			
2087	■									■						■				■		■							■						
2088					■	■				■		■			■	■		■		■	■	■													
2089																■		■																	

▲ **Sequence Number—indicates the order of the college in this book only. Do *not* use this number with admissions tests or need analysis services.**

[1] No campus room and board facilities
[2] Room only or board only
[3] Most freshmen required to live on campus
[4] City or district residency requirements
[5] Accredited by regional accrediting association or a recognized candidate for accreditation
[6] All female freshman class
[7] All male freshman class
[8] Some admission selectivity; not all hs graduates accepted
[9] Requirements more stringent for nonresidents
†Accredited by a nationally recognized accrediting body other than one of the regional accrediting associations

Arkansas
(continued)

Sequence Number	School name (upper entry) / City (lower entry)	Enrollment	Resident tuition/fees + room/board	Room/board (upper entry) / Nonresident tuition/fees (lower entry)	Affiliation (upper entry) / Religious observance (lower entry)	Size of community	Type of community	Fall term application deadline (upper entry) / Test required or desired (lower entry)	Calendar	Fall term application deadline (upper entry) / Forms to be filed (lower entry)	-have need, rec some aid	-are women	-live on campus	-are minority students	-are nonresidents	-return as sophomores	-complete assoc degree	-transfer to 4-year college
			Costs		**Gen. Info.**			**Admissions**		**Financial Aid**	**Student Profile — No. in 10 who-**							
2090	Miss Co CC Blytheville	684	600	[1] 1900	Pub	S		8/20	E[5]	4/15 FFS	8	7	0	2	2	5	1	2
2091	Natl Ed Ctr Ark Tech Little Rock	500	6700	[1]	Priv	L	U	Oth	O†	10/21 Oth	9	3	0	4	1	8	6	
2092	North Arkansas CC Harrison	663	500	[1] 1000	Pub	T			E[5]	5/01 FFS	6	6	0	1	1	5	1	5
2093	Oil Belt Voc-Tech El Dorado	300	500	[1]	Pub	S		Oth	E†	5/01 FFS		3		3				
2094	Petit Jean Voc Tech Morrilton	285	200	[1]	Pub	T[8]		Oth	E[5]	Oth	7	6		1	1		8	
2095	Phillips Co CC Helena	1467	700	[1] 1100	Pub	S		Oth	E[5]	FF=FA	9	7	0	5	1	5	4	2
2096	Rich Mountain CC Mena	308	600	[1] 1800	Pub	T		8/28 Oth	S[5]	8/01	7	7	0	1	1			
2097	Shorter C Arkansas N Little Rock	120	2800	1100	Oth OS	M[8]		Oth	E[5]		9	5	3	9	1	8	8	6
2098	Southern Ark U Tech Camden	401	2600	1900 3000	Pub	S		A/S	S[5]	8/01 FFS	7	5	2	2	1	4	5	1
2099	Southern Arkansas U El Dorado	360	800	[1] 1200	Pub	S		A/S	E[5]	FF=FA	5	7	0	2	1	3		
2100	Westark CC Fort Smith	5206	700	[1] 1600	Pub	M		8/21 A=S	E[5]	6/01 FFS	4	6	0	1	1	5	2	3
California																		
2101	Alameda,C of Alameda	1598	100	[1] 3000	Pub	M	U	9/17 None	Q[5]	8/15 FA/FF	7	5	0	7	1	4	2	1
2102	Amer River C Sacramento	21514	100	[1] 2900	Pub	L	S	9/18 A/S	S[5]	8/15 Oth	2	5	0	2	1	6	5	2
2103	Antelope Valley C Lancaster	1978	100	[1] 4000	Pub	M	S	Oth	S[5]	8/01 Oth	2	6	0	2		5		
2104	Bakersfield C Bakersfield	3435	3500	3400 6400	Pub	L	U	Oth	E[5]	FAF	1	5	1	3	1	6	3	2
2105	Barstow C Barstow	418	100	[1] 2700	Pub	S		9/13 Oth	S[5]	Oth	2	5	0	4	1	6	1	1
2106	Brooks C Long Beach	886	9300	3600	Priv	L[8]	S	None	Q[5]	6/01 FAF	8	9	8	3	7	7	6	1
2107	Butte C Oroville	3084	200	[1] 2300	Pub	M		Oth	E[5]	5/01 FA/FF		5	0	2	1			
2108	Cabrillo C Aptos	4130	200	[1] 3000	Pub	S		8/03 None	S[5]	FF=FA	3	6	0	2	1	3	1	3
2109	Canada C Redwood City	1000	100	[1] 2900	Pub	M	S	9/01 Oth	S[5]	6/30 FF=FA	4	6	0	2	1		1	
2110	Canyons,C of the Valencia	1848	100	[1] 2300	Pub	M	S	A=S	E[5]	6/15 Oth	1	6	0	2	1		1	2
2111	Cerritos C Norwalk	20440	100	[1] 2600	Pub	L	S	Oth	E[5]	FF=FA	1	5	0	7			1	

Educational Programs Available — College Transfer Courses

Sequence Number	Agriculture	Bus-Commerce	Communications	Education	Engineering	Fine, Applied Arts	Foreign Lang	Health	Home Ec	Humanities	Mathematics	Computer/Info Sci	Biological Sci	Physical Sci	Social Sci
2090	■	■	■	■		■		■		■	■	■	■	■	■
2091															
2092	■	■	■	■	■	■		■		■	■	■	■	■	■
2093															
2094															
2095	■	■	■	■	■	■		■		■	■	■	■	■	■
2096		■		■		■	■	■	■	■	■	■	■	■	■
2097															
2098		■	■	■				■		■	■	■			■
2099		■		■		■				■	■	■	■		■
2100	■	■	■	■	■	■	■	■	■	■	■	■	■	■	■
2101		■		■		■	■	■	■	■	■	■	■	■	■
2102	■	■	■		■	■	■	■	■	■	■	■	■	■	■
2103	■	■	■	■	■	■	■	■	■	■	■	■	■	■	■
2104	■	■	■	■	■	■	■	■	■	■	■	■	■	■	■
2105		■	■	■	■	■	■	■	■	■	■	■	■	■	■
2106						■									
2107	■	■	■	■	■	■	■	■	■	■	■	■	■	■	■
2108	■	■	■	■	■	■	■	■	■	■	■	■	■	■	■
2109		■	■	■	■	■	■	■	■	■	■	■	■	■	■
2110		■	■	■	■	■	■	■	■	■	■	■	■	■	■
2111	■	■	■	■	■	■	■	■	■	■	■	■	■	■	■

Educational Programs Available — Career-oriented Programs

Sequence Number	Agri: Ag Business	Agri: Ag/Farm Mgmt	Agri: Ag Mechanics/Tech	Agri: Horticulture	Business: Accounting	Business: Bus Mgmt & Admin	Business: Hotel/Rest Mgmt	Business: Office Mgmt	Business: Marketing/Purchasing	Business: Secretarial Studies	Arts: Architecture Tech	Arts: Applied Design	Arts: Photography/Cinema	Health: Dental Assistant	Health: Medical or Lab Tech	Health: Nursing (RN)	Health: Nursing (LPN)	Health: Radiologic Technology	Math: Computer Prog	Math: Data Processing Tech	Math: Computer Operating	SocSci: Crim Just/Law Enforce	SocSci: Parks/Rec Mgmt	SocSci: Social Work	Tech: Air/Refrig/Heat Tech	Tech: Auto Body Repair	Tech: Auto Mechanics	Tech: Carpentry/Constr	Tech: Drafting/Eng Draft	Tech: Electric Eng Tech	Tech: Civil Eng Tech	Tech: Indus/Mfg Eng Tech	Tech: Mech Eng Tech	Tech: Machinework	Tech: Welding
2090	■	■			■	■				■						■			■			■		■								■			
2091	■				■	■		■	■	■									■	■	■				■							■			
2092	■				■	■		■		■						■			■	■		■													
2093					■			■	■	■						■	■				■				■		■							■	■
2094				■					■	■							■								■		■	■	■					■	■
2095					■	■		■		■		■			■	■	■	■	■	■	■	■		■	■		■		■		■				■
2096						■				■							■		■	■							■	■						■	■
2097						■				■														■											
2098							■			■									■	■	■											■			
2099					■					■					■			■			■	■													
2100					■			■		■	■					■	■		■	■	■						■	■	■	■		■		■	■
2101					■				■																	■	■								
2102				■	■	■	■	■	■	■						■			■	■		■	■	■		■	■	■	■	■	■				■
2103										■					■	■	■	■	■			■				■	■			■					■
2104	■	■	■	■	■	■	■	■	■	■			■	■	■	■	■	■	■	■	■	■	■				■		■	■				■	■
2105					■	■		■	■	■							■		■			■		■	■		■		■	■					■
2106						■			■																										
2107	■		■	■	■		■	■	■	■			■			■	■		■	■	■	■	■	■			■		■	■	■				■
2108				■	■			■		■						■	■	■	■		■	■													
2109					■			■		■								■	■		■									■					
2110					■	■	■	■	■	■						■	■					■							■						■
2111					■			■	■	■				■		■	■			■		■				■	■		■	■					■

▲ Sequence Number—indicates the order of the college in this book only. Do *not* use this number with admissions tests or need analysis services.

[1] No campus room and board facilities
[2] Room only or board only
[3] Most freshmen required to live on campus
[4] City or district residency requirements
[5] Accredited by regional accrediting association or a recognized candidate for accreditation
[6] All female freshman class
[7] All male freshman class
[8] Some admission selectivity; not all hs graduates accepted
[9] Requirements more stringent for nonresidents
†Accredited by a nationally recognized accrediting body other than one of the regional accrediting associations

California
(continued)

Sequence Number	School name (upper entry) City (lower entry)	Enrollment	Costs: Resident tuition/fees + room/board	Costs: Room/board (upper entry) Nonresident tuition/fees (lower entry)	Gen. Info.: Affiliation (upper entry) Religious observance (lower entry)	Gen. Info.: Size of community	Gen. Info.: Type of community	Admissions: Fall term application deadline (upper entry) Test required or desired (lower entry)	Admissions: Calendar	Financial Aid: Fall term application deadline (upper entry) Forms to be filed (lower entry)	No. in 10 who- -have need, rec some aid	-are women	-live on campus	-are minority students	-are nonresidents	-return as sophomores	-complete assoc degree	-transfer to 4-year college
2112	Cerro Coso CC Ridgecrest	526	100	[1] 2800	Pub	S		 Oth	E[5]	5/01 FA/FF	1	6	0	2		1		
2113	Chabot C Hayward	4281	100	[1] 3300	Pub	M	S	 None	Q[5]	 FFS		5	0	1	1		1	1
2114	Chaffey C Rancho Cucamung	4167	100	[1] 3100	Pub	M	S	9/18 None	Q[5]	 FAF	4	6	0	3	1			2
2115	Citrus C Glendora	2702	100	[1] 2300	Pub	M	S	9/15 Oth	S[5]	8/01 FF=FA	1	5	0	4	1	5	7	4
2116	City C of San Fran San Francisco	7003	100	[1] 3400	Pub	V	U	7/07 None	E[5]	7/21 FAF		5	0	7			1	
2117	Coastline CC Fountain Valley	350	100	[1] 2900	Pub	V	U	9/19 None	S[5]	3/15 FAF	1	6	0	1	1		1	1
2118	Columbia C Columbia	477	1500[2]	1400 4200	Pub	T		8/01 None	E[5]	 Oth	5	6	1	1	1	5	4	3
2119	Compton CC Compton	1392	100	[1] 2400	Pub	M		 Oth	S[5]	 FA/FF	7	6	0	9	1	2		
2120	Contra Costa C San Pablo	2070	100	[1] 2900	Pub	M		9/02 Oth	E[5]	8/01 FAF	3	6	0	7	1	3	1	2
2121	Cosumnes River C Sacramento	1484	100	[1] 3600	Pub	L	S	8/24 None	E[5]	7/07 Oth		6	0	3	0			
2122	Crafton Hills C Yucaipa	2951	100	[1] 3000	Pub	S		 Oth	S[5]	7/01 FAF	4	6	0	3	1	3	3	2
2123	Cuesta C San Luis Obispo	3315	100	[1] 3000	Pub	M		 Oth	E[5]	5/03 Oth	5	6	0	2	1	3	2	2
2124	Cuyamaca C El Cajon	902	100	[1] 3200	Pub	M	S	8/29	E[5]	11/06 FA/FF	1	5	0	2				
2125	Cypress C Cypress	4027	100	[1] 3000	Pub	M	S	8/14 A=S	E[5]	3/02 Oth	2	6	0	3	1	5	3	2
2126	D-Q U Davis	94	6100	3100	Priv	S		 A=S	S[5]	9/30	9	6		9	1	8	9	
2127	De Anza C Cupertino	6542	100	[1] 2500	Pub	V	S	 A=S	Q[5]	 Oth		5	0	4	1	2		1
2128	Deep Springs C Via Dyer NV	25	0[3]		Priv	T[8]	[7]	1/15 S/A	O[5]	2/15 None	9	0	9	1	9	9		9
2129	Desert,C of the Palm Desert	1400	100	[1] 2900	Pub	M		 None	E[5]	5/01 FFS		5	0	1	1	5		
2130	Diablo Valley C Pleasant Hill	7184	100	[1] 3000	Pub	L	S	8/15 A=S	E[5]		1	5	0	2	0		3	3
2131	Don Bosco Tech Inst Rosemead	227	3700	[1]	Cath OS	S[8]	[7]	 Oth	S[5]	 FF=FA	1	0	0	8	0	7	6	8
2132	East Los Ang C Monterey Park	14000	100	[1] 3000	Pub	V	U	9/21 None	S[5]	3/31 Oth	2	5	0	9	1	7	1	3
2133	El Camino C Torrance	6380	100	[1] 2500	Pub	L	U	 Oth	S[5]	6/01 FA/FF		5	0	6				
2134	Evergreen Valley C San Jose	5683	100	[1]	Pub	V	S	 Oth	E[5]	7/13 FF=FA		5	0	6	1	2	1	1

Educational Programs Available — College Transfer Courses

Sequence Number	Agriculture	Bus-Commerce	Communications	Education	Engineering	Fine, Applied Arts	Foreign Lang	Health	Home Ec	Humanities	Mathematics	Computer/Info Sci	Biological Sci	Physical Sci	Social Sci
2112	■	■	■	■	■	■	■		■	■	■	■	■	■	■
2113	■	■	■	■	■	■	■	■	■	■	■	■	■	■	■
2114	■	■	■	■	■	■	■	■	■	■	■	■	■	■	■
2115	■	■	■	■	■	■	■	■		■	■	■	■	■	■
2116	■	■	■		■	■	■	■	■	■	■	■	■	■	■
2117	■	■	■	■		■	■		■	■	■	■	■	■	■
2118		■	■	■		■	■	■		■	■	■	■	■	■
2119	■	■	■	■	■	■	■	■	■	■	■	■	■	■	■
2120		■	■		■	■	■	■	■	■	■	■	■	■	■
2121	■	■	■	■	■	■	■	■	■	■	■	■	■	■	■
2122		■	■	■	■	■	■	■		■	■	■	■	■	■
2123		■	■		■	■	■	■	■	■	■	■	■	■	■
2124	■	■	■	■	■	■	■		■	■	■	■	■	■	■
2125		■	■	■	■	■	■	■	■	■	■	■	■	■	■
2126	■	■	■	■		■	■		■	■	■		■	■	■
2127		■	■		■	■	■	■	■	■	■	■	■	■	■
2128															
2129	■	■	■	■	■	■	■	■	■	■	■	■	■	■	■
2130	■	■	■		■	■	■	■	■	■	■	■	■	■	■
2131			■			■									
2132		■	■	■	■	■	■	■	■	■	■	■	■	■	■
2133	■	■	■	■	■	■	■	■	■	■	■	■	■	■	■
2134		■	■		■	■	■	■	■	■	■	■	■	■	■

Educational Programs Available — Career-oriented Programs (Agri, Business, Arts, Health)

Sequence Number	Agri: Ag Business	Ag/Farm Mgmt	Ag Mechanics/Tech	Horticulture	Business: Accounting	Bus Mgmt & Admin	Hotel/Rest Mgmt	Office Mgmt	Marketing/Purchasing	Secretarial Studies	Arts: Architecture Tech	Applied Design	Photography/Cinema	Health: Dental Assistant	Medical or Lab Tech	Nursing (RN)	Nursing (LPN)	Radiologic Technology
2112						■				■							■	
2113	■			■	■	■			■	■	■			■		■		
2114					■	■	■	■	■	■		■	■	■		■	■	■
2115										■				■			■	
2116				■	■	■	■		■	■		■		■	■	■	■	■
2117					■	■		■	■	■								
2118						■	■	■										
2119					■	■		■		■	■					■	■	■
2120					■	■	■	■		■			■	■		■		
2121	■		■	■	■	■	■	■	■	■								
2122					■	■		■	■	■					■			
2123										■						■		
2124				■	■	■		■										
2125					■	■	■	■	■	■		■	■	■	■	■	■	■
2126		■																
2127					■				■	■			■			■		
2128																		
2129	■		■	■	■	■	■	■	■	■		■		■		■		
2130				■	■	■	■	■	■	■				■				
2131																		
2132					■	■		■	■	■		■	■		■	■		
2133					■	■				■	■		■			■	■	
2134					■			■	■	■						■		

Educational Programs Available — Career-oriented Programs (Math, SocSci, Technical/Skilled Trades)

Sequence Number	Math: Computer Prog	Data Processing Tech	Computer Operating	SocSci: Crim Just/Law Enforce	Parks/Rec Mgmt	Social Work	Technical/Skilled Trades: Air/Refrig/Heat Tech	Auto Body Repair	Auto Mechanics	Carpentry/Constr	Drafting/Eng Draft	Electric Eng Tech	Civil Eng Tech	Indus/Mfg Eng Tech	Mech Eng Tech	Machinework	Welding
2112	■	■		■			■		■		■	■				■	■
2113	■	■	■	■	■	■			■		■	■	■		■	■	■
2114	■	■	■	■				■	■		■	■			■		■
2115	■			■			■	■	■		■	■			■	■	
2116	■	■		■		■	■				■	■	■		■		
2117										■		■					
2118	■								■								
2119								■		■		■		■	■		■
2120	■	■	■	■			■	■	■		■	■	■				■
2121	■	■	■	■					■	■	■	■					
2122				■													
2123				■				■	■	■	■						
2124									■		■						■
2125	■	■	■		■	■	■	■	■								
2126																	
2127	■	■	■	■					■		■				■	■	■
2128																	
2129	■	■		■	■		■	■	■	■	■	■	■		■	■	■
2130	■			■			■			■	■	■	■		■	■	■
2131							■									■	
2132				■					■		■	■	■		■		
2133	■	■	■	■		■	■	■	■	■	■	■				■	■
2134	■			■					■								

▲ Sequence Number—indicates the order of the college in this book only. Do *not* use this number with admissions tests or need analysis services.

1 No campus room and board facilities
2 Room only or board only
3 Most freshmen required to live on campus
4 City or district residency requirements
5 Accredited by regional accrediting association or a recognized candidate for accreditation
6 All female freshman class
7 All male freshman class
8 Some admission selectivity; not all hs graduates accepted
9 Requirements more stringent for nonresidents
†Accredited by a nationally recognized accrediting body other than one of the regional accrediting associations

California
(continued)

Sequence Number	School name (upper entry) / City (lower entry)	Enrollment	Resident tuition/fees + room/board	Room/board (upper entry)	Nonresident tuition/fees (lower entry)	Affiliation (upper entry) / Religious observance (lower entry)	Size of community	Type of community	Fall term application deadline (upper entry)	Test required or desired (lower entry)	Calendar	Fall term application deadline (upper entry)	Forms to be filed (lower entry)	-have need, rec some aid	-are women	-live on campus	-are minority students	-are nonresidents	-return as sophomores	-complete assoc degree	-transfer to 4-year college
			Costs			**Gen. Info.**			**Admissions**			**Financial Aid**		**Student Profile: No. in 10 who-**							
2135	Feather River C / Quincy	350	100	[1]	3000	Pub	T		9/07	Oth	E [5]	7/01	FF=FA	6	5	0	1	1	4	6	4
2136	Foothill C / Los Altos Hills	4083	1200	[1]	2100	Pub	M	S	9/01	Oth	Q [5]	6/11	FF/FA	6	6	0	2	1	3	1	1
2137	Fresno City C / Fresno	5713	100	[1]	2800	Pub	L	U	7/18	Oth	E [5]		FA/FF	3	5	0	4	0	7	1	1
2138	Fullerton C / Fullerton	6490	100	[1]	3300	Pub	V	U		Oth	S [5]		FFS		5	0	3	1		2	2
2139	Gavilan C / Gilroy	1751	1300	[1]	2200	Pub	S			Oth	S [5]	8/15	FA/FF	8	5	0	4	0		2	2
2140	Glendale CC / Glendale	4210	300	[1]	3200	Pub	M	U	9/10	Oth	S [5]		FAF	3	6	0	4		3	1	2
2141	Golden West C / Huntingtn Beach	2940	100	[1]	2900	Pub	L	S		None	S [5]	6/01	Oth	1	5	0	3	1		1	1
2142	Grossmont C / El Cajon	6113	100	[1]	3200	Pub	M	S	8/23	None	E [5]		FA/FF	1	6	0	2				
2143	Hartnell C / Salinas	2127	100	[1]	3100	Pub	M		8/15	Oth	S [5]	5/15	FAF	6	5	0	4	2		1	
2144	Heald Inst of Tech / San Francisco	500	6000	[1]		Priv	V [8]	U		Oth	Q [5]				1			1	7		
2145	Imperial Valley C / Imperial	2314	100	[1]	3200	Pub	T			Oth	S [5]		FAF	7	6	0	8	1			3
2146	Kings River CC / Reedley	3500	1400 [2]	1300	4100	Pub	S		7/01	Oth	E [5]	4/15	Oth	9	6	1	4	1	5	2	2
2147	Lake Tahoe CC / S Lake Tahoe	275	100	[1]	3400	Pub	S		9/20	None	Q [5]	9/15	FAF	1	6	0	1	1	1		
2148	Laney C / Oakland	2152	100	[1]	2500	Pub	L	U		None	S [5]	6/15	FF/FA	4	5	0	7	1	4	7	1
2149	Las Positas C / Livermore		100	[1]	2500	Pub	M	S		Oth	Q [5]	8/01								2	3
2150	Lassen C / Susanville	747	3400	3300	5800	Pub	T			Oth	E [5]	6/30	FAF	8	4	1	1	1	4	4	
2151	Long Beach City C / Long Beach	4850	100	[1]	3000	Pub	L	U		Oth	E [5]	5/15	FF=FA	9	6		5				
2152	Los Ang City C / Los Angeles	3213	100	[1]	3400	Pub	V	U	8/30	Oth	S [5]	3/02	FA/FF	2	5	0	8	1		1	2
2153	Los Ang Harbor C / Wilmington	2400	100	[1]	2900	Pub	V	U	9/20	Oth	S [5]	3/01	FFS	1	6	0	6	1	7	1	2
2154	Los Ang Mission / San Fernando	1326	100	[1]	2800	Pub	V	U		None	S [5]	8/01	FAF	9	7	0	6	0	0	1	
2155	Los Ang Pierce C / Woodland Hills	5616	100	[1]	2700	Pub	V	S	9/01	None	E [5]		FF=FA	1	5	0	3	1			
2156	Los Ang Southwest C / Los Angeles	1218	100	[1]	2800	Pub	V	U	9/06	Oth	S [5]	7/01	Oth	9	4	0	9	1	7	3	4
2157	Los Ang Trade-Tech C / Los Angeles	13701	100	[1]	2900	Pub	V	U		Oth	S [5]	5/31	FF/FA	5	4	0	8				

Educational Programs Available — College Transfer Courses

Sequence Number	Agriculture	Bus-Commerce	Communications	Education	Engineering	Fine, Applied Arts	Foreign Lang	Health	Home Ec	Humanities	Mathematics	Computer/Info Sci	Biological Sci	Physical Sci	Social Sci
2135	■	■		■	■	■	■	■	■	■	■	■	■	■	■
2136	■	■	■	■	■	■	■	■		■	■	■	■	■	■
2137	■	■	■	■	■	■	■	■	■	■	■	■	■	■	■
2138	■	■	■	■	■	■	■	■	■	■	■	■	■	■	■
2139		■	■	■	■	■	■	■		■	■	■	■		■
2140						■	■	■	■	■	■	■	■	■	■
2141		■	■	■	■	■	■	■		■	■	■	■	■	■
2142		■	■	■		■	■	■	■	■	■	■	■	■	■
2143	■	■	■	■	■	■	■	■	■	■	■	■	■	■	■
2144															
2145	■	■	■	■	■	■	■	■		■	■	■	■	■	■
2146	■	■	■	■	■	■	■	■	■	■	■	■	■	■	■
2147	■	■		■		■	■	■	■	■	■	■	■	■	■
2148	■	■	■	■	■	■	■	■	■	■	■	■	■	■	■
2149	■	■	■	■	■	■			■	■	■	■	■	■	■
2150	■	■	■	■	■	■		■	■	■	■	■	■	■	■
2151	■	■	■		■	■	■	■	■	■	■	■	■	■	■
2152	■	■	■	■	■	■	■	■	■	■	■	■	■	■	■
2153		■	■	■	■	■	■	■	■	■	■	■	■	■	■
2154		■	■	■	■	■	■	■	■	■	■	■	■	■	■
2155	■	■	■		■	■	■	■		■	■	■	■	■	■
2156		■	■	■		■	■	■	■	■	■	■	■	■	■
2157		■	■	■	■	■	■	■	■	■	■	■	■	■	■

Career-oriented Programs — Agri / Business / Arts / Health

Sequence Number	Ag Business	Ag/Farm Mgmt	Ag Mechanics/Tech	Horticulture	Accounting	Bus Mgmt & Admin	Hotel/Rest Mgmt	Office Mgmt	Marketing/Purchasing	Secretarial Studies	Architecture Tech	Applied Design	Photography/Cinema	Dental Assistant	Medical or Lab Tech	Nursing (RN)	Nursing (LPN)	Radiologic Technology
2135	■				■			■		■							■	
2136				■	■				■	■		■	■	■				■
2137	■				■	■		■	■							■	■	■
2138				■	■	■		■	■	■			■					
2139					■	■			■	■						■	■	
2140					■	■	■			■						■	■	
2141					■	■		■	■	■						■		
2142					■	■	■	■	■	■		■	■		■	■		
2143	■	■		■						■						■	■	
2144																		
2145	■		■			■			■	■						■	■	
2146	■	■	■	■	■	■		■	■	■				■				
2147					■	■	■	■	■	■								
2148					■			■	■	■	■		■					
2149				■				■		■								
2150	■		■		■	■		■		■			■				■	
2151				■	■	■	■	■	■	■	■			■		■	■	■
2152					■			■		■								■
2153				■	■					■		■				■	■	
2154					■	■		■		■								
2155				■	■	■		■	■	■	■					■		
2156					■	■			■	■						■		
2157					■	■	■	■	■			■				■	■	

Career-oriented Programs — Math / SocSci / Technical/Skilled Trades

Sequence Number	Computer Prog	Data Processing Tech	Computer Operating	Crim Just/Law Enforce	Parks/Rec Mgmt	Social Work	Air/Refrig/Heat Tech	Auto Body Repair	Auto Mechanics	Carpentry/Constr	Drafting/Eng Draft	Electric Eng Tech	Civil Eng Tech	Indus/Mfg Eng Tech	Mech Eng Tech	Machinework	Welding
2135			■	■	■												■
2136	■	■									■						
2137	■	■		■	■		■	■	■	■	■	■			■	■	■
2138	■	■	■	■	■	■			■		■	■	■			■	
2139	■			■				■	■	■	■						■
2140				■							■					■	
2141		■	■	■				■	■		■	■					
2142	■		■	■	■												
2143	■			■	■			■	■	■	■	■				■	■
2144	■											■					
2145		■		■		■			■				■				■
2146	■			■					■		■					■	■
2147	■			■													
2148	■		■				■			■	■	■	■		■	■	■
2149		■	■	■													
2150	■			■				■	■	■						■	■
2151	■					■	■	■	■	■	■	■				■	■
2152	■	■		■							■	■			■		
2153				■		■	■		■		■	■				■	
2154																	
2155	■	■	■						■	■	■	■		■		■	■
2156	■	■				■					■	■					
2157	■	■	■				■	■	■	■	■	■	■			■	■

▲ Sequence Number—indicates the order of the college in this book only. Do *not* use this number with admissions tests or need analysis services.

[1] No campus room and board facilities
[2] Room only or board only
[3] Most freshmen required to live on campus
[4] City or district residency requirements
[5] Accredited by regional accrediting association or a recognized candidate for accreditation
[6] All female freshman class
[7] All male freshman class
[8] Some admission selectivity; not all hs graduates accepted
[9] Requirements more stringent for nonresidents
†Accredited by a nationally recognized accrediting body other than one of the regional accrediting associations

California
(continued)

Sequence Number	School name (upper entry) / City (lower entry)	Enrollment	Resident tuition/fees + room/board	Room/board (upper entry) / Nonresident tuition/fees (lower entry)	Affiliation (upper entry) / Religious observance (lower entry)	Size of community	Type of community	Fall term application deadline (upper entry) / Test required or desired (lower entry)	Calendar	Fall term application deadline (upper entry) / Forms to be filed (lower entry)	-have need, rec some aid	-are women	-live on campus	-are minority students	-are nonresidents	-return as sophomores	-complete assoc degree	-transfer to 4-year college
2158	Los Ang Valley C Van Nuys	1313	100	[1] 3000	Pub	V	U	8/19 None	S[5]	3/15 FAF		6	0	4		5	6	4
2159	Los Medanos C Pittsburg	1444	100	[1] 3000	Pub	M		9/05 None	E[5]	6/15 FA/FF	2	6	0	3	1	5	1	1
2160	Marin,C of Kentfield	7980	100	[1] 3600	Pub	L	S	8/29 None	E[5]	3/30 FAF	4	6	0	2	1			
2161	Marymount C Rancho Palos Ve	749	13100[2]	3300	Cath	S[8]		None	4[5]	3/02 FF=FA	4	6	5	5	4	5	6	7
2162	Mendocino C Ukiah	655	100	[1] 3400	Pub	S		8/15 A=S	E[5]	11/15 Oth	7	7	0	2	0	4	3	1
2163	Merced C Merced	2850	100	[1] 3000	Pub	S		8/17 Oth	E[5]	FF=FA	8	6	0	3	1	8	4	2
2164	Merritt C Oakland	1340	100	[1] 2400	Pub	L	U	8/31 Oth	E[5]	FAF	4	6	0	6	1		3	
2165	Miracosta C Oceanside	1602	100	[1] 2700	Pub	M		None	S[5]	6/16 FA/FF	1	6	0	2	1			
2166	Mission C Santa Clara	1311	100	[1] 3100	Pub	M	S	None	S[5]	5/01 FF=FA	1	5	0	6			1	1
2167	Modesto JC Modesto	4884	100	[1] 3100	Pub	L	S	None	E[5]	FA/FF	2	6	0	3				1
2168	Monterey Peninsula C Monterey	1622	100	[1] 3200	Pub	M		None	E[5]	5/01 Oth	2	6	0	3	1		4	4
2169	Moorpark C Moorpark	7102	100	[1] 3200	Pub	S		9/07 None	S[5]	6/08 FAF	6	5	0	2	1		2	
2170	Mount San Antonio C Walnut	6000	200	[1] 3000	Pub	S		8/14 A=S	S[5]	1/06 FF=FA	1	5	0	5	1	5	1	3
2171	Mount San Jacinto C San Jacinto	938	100	[1] 2700	Pub	S		Oth	E[5]	6/01 FAF	8	6	0	2	1	5	2	3
2172	Napa Valley C Napa	1622	100	[1] 3000	Pub	M		Oth	S[5]	5/01 FAF	7	6	0	3	1	5	4	2
2173	Ohlone C Fremont	2395	100	[1] 2900	Pub	M	S	None	S[5]	6/30 FA/FF	1	6	0	4	1	2	1	2
2174	Orange Coast C Costa Mesa	8000	100	[1] 3000	Pub	M	S	None	E[5]	FAF	5	5	0	3	1	3	3	2
2175	Oxnard C Oxnard	1303	100	[1] 3000	Pub	M	S	9/10 None	E[5]	5/10 FF=FA	8	5	0	6	1	5		
2176	Palo Verde C Blythe	220	100	[1] 1200	Pub	S		None	E[5]	Oth	7	7	0	6	1	6	1	1
2177	Palomar C San Marcos	5443	100	[1] 3000	Pub	M	S	8/01 Oth	E[5]	5/01 FA/FF	6	6	0	3		5	1	1
2178	Pasadena City C Pasadena	7595	100	[1] 2900	Pub	L	U	9/09 None	S[5]	6/30 FAF	8	5	0	6	1			
2179	Porterville C Porterville	650	100	[1] 2700	Pub	S		None	E[5]	FF=FA	8	5	0	3	1	3	1	1
2180	Rancho Santiago CC Santa Ana	4401	100	[1] 3200	Pub	L	U	8/23 Oth	E[5]	10/31 Oth	9	5	0	4		3		

Costs | Gen. Info. | Admissions | Financial Aid | Student Profile (No. in 10 who-)

Educational Programs Available — College Transfer Courses

Sequence Number	Agriculture	Bus-Commerce	Communications	Education	Engineering	Fine, Applied Arts	Foreign Lang	Health	Home Ec	Humanities	Mathematics	Computer/Info Sci	Biological Sci	Physical Sci	Social Sci
2158		■	■	■	■	■	■	■	■	■	■	■	■	■	■
2159		■	■			■		■	■		■		■	■	■
2160	■	■	■	■	■	■	■	■	■	■	■	■	■	■	■
2161		■	■	■		■	■		■	■	■	■	■	■	■
2162	■	■		■		■	■	■		■	■	■	■	■	■
2163	■	■		■	■	■	■	■	■	■	■	■	■	■	■
2164		■	■	■	■	■	■	■	■	■	■	■	■	■	■
2165	■	■	■	■		■	■	■	■	■	■		■	■	■
2166		■	■		■	■	■	■	■	■	■	■	■	■	■
2167	■	■	■	■	■	■	■	■	■	■	■	■	■	■	■
2168	■	■		■	■	■	■	■	■	■	■	■	■	■	■
2169	■	■	■	■	■	■	■	■	■	■	■	■	■	■	■
2170	■	■	■	■	■	■	■	■	■	■	■	■	■	■	■
2171		■	■	■	■	■	■	■	■	■	■	■	■	■	■
2172	■	■		■	■	■	■	■	■	■	■	■	■	■	■
2173		■	■	■	■	■	■	■	■	■	■	■	■	■	■
2174	■	■	■	■	■	■	■		■	■	■	■	■	■	■
2175	■	■	■	■	■	■	■		■	■	■	■	■	■	■
2176	■	■					■			■	■	■		■	■
2177		■	■	■	■	■	■	■	■	■	■	■	■	■	■
2178	■	■	■	■	■	■	■	■	■	■	■	■	■	■	■
2179	■	■	■	■	■	■	■	■	■	■	■	■	■	■	■
2180	■	■	■	■	■	■	■	■	■	■	■	■	■	■	■

Educational Programs Available — Career-oriented Programs (Agri, Business, Arts)

Sequence Number	Ag Business	Ag/Farm Mgmt	Ag Mechanics/Tech	Horticulture	Accounting	Bus Mgmt & Admin	Hotel/Rest Mgmt	Office Mgmt	Marketing/Purchasing	Secretarial Studies	Architecture Tech	Applied Design	Photography/Cinema
2158					■	■	■	■	■	■			
2159					■	■				■			
2160				■	■	■			■	■		■	
2161													
2162				■	■	■				■			
2163	■	■	■	■	■	■		■	■	■			
2164					■	■		■		■			
2165				■	■	■	■	■		■			
2166					■		■		■	■			
2167	■	■	■	■	■	■		■	■	■		■	
2168							■	■	■	■			
2169	■			■	■	■		■	■				■
2170	■	■	■	■	■	■	■	■	■	■		■	■
2171					■	■		■		■		■	
2172				■	■	■		■	■	■			■
2173				■	■	■				■		■	
2174	■			■	■	■	■	■	■	■	■	■	■
2175	■	■	■	■	■	■	■	■	■	■			
2176					■	■		■	■				
2177					■		■		■	■		■	■
2178					■	■			■	■		■	
2179								■		■			
2180					■	■		■	■	■		■	■

Educational Programs Available — Career-oriented Programs (Health, Math, SocSci, Technical/Skilled Trades)

Sequence Number	Dental Assistant	Medical or Lab Tech	Nursing (RN)	Nursing (LPN)	Radiologic Technology	Computer Prog	Data Processing Tech	Computer Operating	Crim Just/Law Enforce	Parks/Rec Mgmt	Social Work	Air/Refrig/Heat Tech	Auto Body Repair	Auto Mechanics	Carpentry/Constr	Drafting/Eng Draft	Electric Eng Tech	Civil Eng Tech	Indus/Mfg Eng Tech	Mech Eng Tech	Machinework	Welding
2158			■			■			■								■	■		■	■	
2159				■		■			■			■		■		■	■					■
2160	■		■	■		■	■		■		■			■			■	■		■	■	
2161																						
2162						■	■							■								■
2163	■			■	■				■		■	■	■	■	■	■	■					■
2164			■		■	■	■	■	■	■					■		■					■
2165				■					■				■	■		■				■		
2166				■												■						
2167	■		■	■		■	■		■		■	■	■	■		■	■				■	■
2168	■		■	■			■	■	■					■		■						
2169			■				■		■													
2170			■	■	■	■	■	■	■	■		■				■	■	■			■	■
2171			■	■		■		■	■		■		■	■		■	■					
2172			■	■					■							■					■	■
2173			■			■			■							■						
2174	■	■			■	■	■					■			■	■		■				■
2175									■			■	■	■	■		■					■
2176									■					■								
2177	■		■						■	■		■	■	■	■	■	■					■
2178	■		■	■	■		■			■		■	■	■	■	■	■	■			■	■
2179				■					■					■	■	■						■
2180			■			■	■	■	■				■	■	■	■	■	■		■	■	■

▲ **Sequence Number—indicates the order of the college in this book only. Do *not* use this number with admissions tests or need analysis services.**

[1] No campus room and board facilities
[2] Room only or board only
[3] Most freshmen required to live on campus
[4] City or district residency requirements
[5] Accredited by regional accrediting association or a recognized candidate for accreditation
[6] All female freshman class
[7] All male freshman class
[8] Some admission selectivity; not all hs graduates accepted
[9] Requirements more stringent for nonresidents
†Accredited by a nationally recognized accrediting body other than one of the regional accrediting associations

California
(continued)

Sequence Number	School name (upper entry) City (lower entry)	Enrollment	Costs: Resident tuition/fees + room/board	Costs: Room/board (upper entry) Nonresident tuition/fees (lower entry)	Gen. Info.: Affiliation (upper entry) Religious observance (lower entry)	Gen. Info.: Size of community	Gen. Info.: Type of community	Admissions: Fall term application deadline (upper entry) Test required or desired (lower entry)	Admissions: Calendar	Financial Aid: Fall term application deadline (upper entry) Forms to be filed (lower entry)	No. in 10 who- -have need, rec some aid	-are women	-live on campus	-are minority students	-are nonresidents	-return as sophomores	-complete assoc degree	-transfer to 4-year college
2181	Redwoods,C of the Eureka	2128	3900	3800 7100	Pub	S		 Oth	S [5]	3/01 FF=FA	2	5	1	2				
2182	Rio Hondo C Whittier	6500	100	[1] 2800	Pub	L	S	 None	E [5]	7/01 Oth		4	0	7	0			1
2183	Riverside CC Riverside	4650	100	[1] 3100	Pub	L	U	 Oth	S [5]	 FAF	1	6	0	4	1		1	
2184	Sacramento City C Sacramento	4293	100	[1] 3100	Pub	L	U	 A=S	S [5]	 FA/FF	6	6	0	5	1	4	1	1
2185	Saddleback C Mission Viejo	3349	100	[1] 2700	Pub	M	S	 A/S	E [5]	 FAF	1	6	0	2	1	4	2	3
2186	San Bernardino Vly C San Bernardino	2522	100	[1] 2400	Pub	L	U	 Oth	S [5]	 Oth	6	6	0	4				
2187	San Diego City C San Diego	4094	100	[1] 2900	Pub	V	U	 None	S [5]	 FA/FF	3	5	0	5	1	6	3	2
2188	San Diego Mesa C San Diego	27445	100	[1] 2500	Pub	V	U	 Oth	S [5]	7/01 FAF		6	0					
2189	San Fran Mort Sci San Francisco	60	8100	[1]	Priv	V	U	9/30 None	T [5]	9/30 FF=FA	8	2	0	3	2	8		
2190	San Joaquin Delta C Stockton	5247	100	[1] 2800	Pub	L	U	8/20 A=S	S [5]	10/15 FAF	8	5	0	4	1		2	2
2191	San Jose City C San Jose	3000	100	[1] 2600	Pub	V	U	 Oth	E [5]	6/15 Oth	1	5	0	9	1	5	2	
2192	San Mateo,C of San Mateo	39740	100	[1] 3100	Pub	M	S	8/15 A=S	S [5]	 Oth	1	5	0	3			3	2
2193	Santa Barbara CC Santa Barbara	4070	100	[1] 3100	Pub	M	S	7/30 Oth	S [5]	5/15 FAF	2	5	0	3	1	5	4	4
2194	Santa Monica C Santa Monica	5604	100	[1] 3400	Pub	M	S	9/05 A=S	S [5]	10/05 FAF	6	6	0	4	1	5	1	
2195	Santa Rosa JC Santa Rosa	5725	5200	5100 7500	Pub	M	U	9/10 A=S	S [5]	 FF=FA	3	6	1	2	1			
2196	Sequoias,C of the Visalia	3771	100	[1] 2900	Pub	M		8/17 Oth	E [5]	5/01 Oth	3	6	0	4	1	5	2	3
2197	Shasta C Redding	3000	1900 [2]	1800 4400	Pub	M		 None	S [5]	4/15 FF=FA	6	5					1	2
2198	Sierra C Rocklin	3873	3700	3600 6600	Pub	S		8/10 A=S	S [5]	3/15 FA/FF	3	6	1	1	1	5		3
2199	Siskiyous,C of the Weed	863	3700	3600 6600	Pub	T		 A=S	E [5]	4/30 FA/FF	4	6	3	2	1	5	2	2
2200	Skyline C San Bruno	2090	100	[1] 3100	Pub	M	S	8/24 A=S	S [5]	7/04 FAF	1	6	0	5				
2201	Solano CC Suisun City	2418	100	[1] 3000	Pub	M		9/04 Oth	E [5]	6/01 FAF	7	5	0	4	0	4	6	1
2202	Southwestern C Chula Vista	4312	100	[1] 2900	Pub	L	S	8/29 Oth	S [5]	4/30 FAF	7	5	0	6		6		
2203	Taft C Taft	414	1700 [3]	1600 4800	Pub	S		9/04 Oth	E [5]	9/05 FF=FA	8	6	1	2	1	3	3	2

Educational Programs Available — College Transfer Courses

Sequence Number	Agriculture	Bus-Commerce	Communications	Education	Engineering	Fine, Applied Arts	Foreign Lang	Health	Home Ec	Humanities	Mathematics	Computer/Info Sci	Biological Sci	Physical Sci	Social Sci
2181	■	■		■	■	■	■	■	■	■	■	■	■	■	■
2182		■	■	■	■	■	■	■	■	■	■	■	■	■	■
2183	■	■	■	■	■	■	■	■	■	■	■	■	■	■	■
2184		■	■	■	■	■	■	■	■	■	■	■	■	■	■
2185	■	■	■	■	■	■	■	■	■	■	■	■	■	■	■
2186	■	■	■	■	■	■	■	■	■	■	■	■	■	■	■
2187		■	■	■	■	■	■	■	■	■	■	■	■	■	■
2188		■	■	■	■	■	■	■	■	■	■	■	■	■	■
2189															
2190	■	■	■		■	■	■	■	■	■	■	■	■	■	■
2191	■	■	■	■	■	■	■	■	■	■	■	■	■	■	■
2192	■	■	■	■	■	■	■	■	■	■	■	■	■	■	■
2193	■	■	■		■	■	■	■	■	■	■	■	■	■	■
2194		■	■	■	■	■	■	■	■	■	■	■	■	■	■
2195	■	■	■	■	■	■	■	■	■	■	■	■	■	■	■
2196	■	■	■	■	■	■	■	■	■	■	■	■	■	■	■
2197	■	■	■	■	■	■	■	■		■	■	■	■	■	■
2198	■	■	■	■	■	■	■	■	■	■	■	■	■	■	■
2199	■	■	■	■	■	■	■	■	■	■	■	■	■	■	■
2200		■	■			■	■		■	■	■	■	■	■	■
2201	■	■	■	■	■	■	■	■	■	■	■	■	■	■	■
2202	■	■	■	■	■	■	■	■		■	■	■	■	■	■
2203	■	■	■	■	■	■	■	■		■	■	■			■

Educational Programs Available — Career-oriented Programs (Agri, Business, Arts, Health)

Sequence Number	Agri: Ag Business	Ag/Farm Mgmt	Ag Mechanics/Tech	Horticulture	Business: Accounting	Bus Mgmt & Admin	Hotel/Rest Mgmt	Office Mgmt	Marketing/Purchasing	Secretarial Studies	Arts: Architecture Tech	Applied Design	Photography/Cinema	Health: Dental Assistant	Medical or Lab Tech	Nursing (RN)	Nursing (LPN)	Radiologic Technology
2181				■		■				■				■		■	■	
2182					■	■		■		■		■		■		■	■	
2183	■				■	■		■	■	■			■			■	■	
2184					■			■		■				■		■	■	
2185	■			■	■	■		■	■	■						■	■	
2186						■	■	■	■	■	■		■			■		
2187					■	■		■	■	■		■				■	■	
2188					■	■	■	■	■	■				■				■
2189																		
2190	■	■	■	■	■	■		■	■	■		■			■	■	■	■
2191					■	■		■	■	■				■				
2192				■	■	■		■	■	■			■	■		■		
2193				■		■	■	■	■	■				■		■	■	■
2194					■	■		■	■	■		■	■			■	■	
2195	■	■	■	■	■	■		■	■	■		■	■	■		■	■	■
2196	■			■	■	■			■							■	■	
2197	■		■	■	■	■		■	■	■		■				■	■	
2198	■			■	■	■			■	■			■			■	■	
2199					■	■		■		■							■	
2200					■	■	■	■	■	■								
2201				■	■	■			■	■						■		
2202				■	■	■	■	■	■	■						■	■	
2203					■	■		■		■								

Educational Programs Available — Career-oriented Programs (Math, SocSci, Technical/Skilled Trades)

Sequence Number	Math: Computer Prog	Data Processing Tech	Computer Operating	SocSci: Crim Just/Law Enforce	Parks/Rec Mgmt	Social Work	Technical/Skilled Trades: Air/Refrig/Heat Tech	Auto Body Repair	Auto Mechanics	Carpentry/Constr	Drafting/Eng Draft	Electric Eng Tech	Civil Eng Tech	Indus/Mfg Eng Tech	Mech Eng Tech	Machinework	Welding
2181	■			■					■	■	■					■	■
2182	■	■	■	■				■	■		■					■	■
2183		■	■	■			■	■	■		■			■			■
2184				■		■	■				■	■	■		■	■	
2185		■	■	■					■	■	■	■				■	■
2186	■	■	■	■	■	■	■	■	■	■	■		■		■	■	■
2187	■	■	■			■	■	■	■	■	■	■		■	■	■	■
2188			■			■											
2189																	
2190	■	■		■		■	■	■	■	■	■	■	■		■	■	■
2191				■			■			■	■	■	■				
2192	■		■	■							■					■	■
2193	■	■	■	■					■								
2194	■	■		■	■			■	■	■	■	■			■	■	■
2195		■	■	■	■			■	■			■	■		■	■	■
2196							■		■	■	■	■					■
2197	■		■	■				■	■	■	■		■		■		■
2198	■	■		■					■	■	■	■					■
2199	■	■	■	■					■								■
2200		■		■	■				■								
2201	■			■				■	■		■	■				■	■
2202	■	■		■	■	■	■	■	■	■	■	■	■		■		
2203		■	■	■					■		■						

▲ **Sequence Number—indicates the order of the college in this book only. Do *not* use this number with admissions tests or need analysis services.**

[1] No campus room and board facilities
[2] Room only or board only
[3] Most freshmen required to live on campus
[4] City or district residency requirements
[5] Accredited by regional accrediting association or a recognized candidate for accreditation
[6] All female freshman class
[7] All male freshman class
[8] Some admission selectivity; not all hs graduates accepted
[9] Requirements more stringent for nonresidents
†Accredited by a nationally recognized accrediting body other than one of the regional accrediting associations

California
(continued)

Sequence Number	School name (upper entry) / City (lower entry)	Enrollment	Resident tuition/fees + room/board	Room/board (upper entry) / Nonresident tuition/fees (lower entry)	Affiliation (upper entry) / Religious observance (lower entry)	Size of community	Type of community	Fall term application deadline (upper entry) / Test required or desired (lower entry)	Calendar	Fall term application deadline (upper entry) / Forms to be filed (lower entry)	-have need, rec some aid	-are women	-live on campus	-are minority students	-are nonresidents	-return as sophomores	-complete assoc degree	-transfer to 4-year college
			Costs		**Gen. Info.**			**Admissions**		**Financial Aid**	**Student Profile: No. in 10 who-**							
2204	Ventura C / Ventura	3200	100	[1] / 3000	Pub	M		Oth	E [5]	7/05 / FA/FF	1	6	0	3	1		2	3
2205	Victor Valley C / Victorville	1700	100	[1] / 2600	Pub	M		Oth	E [5]	FAF	1	1	0	2	1	6	1	1
2206	Vista C / Berkeley	1586	100	[1] / 2600	Pub	L	U	A=S	S [5]	FAF		6	0	6		2		
2207	West Hills C / Coalinga	759	3700	[1] / 6400	Pub	T		9/03 / A=S	E [5]	FF=FA	7	5	3	4	1	9	2	3
2208	West Los Ang C / Culver City	9471	100	[1] / 1300	Pub	M	U	None	S [5]	5/14 / FAF	6	6	0	7	1	6	1	1
2209	West Valley C / Saratoga	3841	100	[1] / 3000	Pub	S		7/20 / A=S	S [5]	FA/FF		6	0	3		5	1	
2210	Yuba C / Marysville	2100	3200	3100 / 6200	Pub	S		8/09 / A=S	S [5]	4/30 / FF/FA	4	6	1	2	1	4	2	1
	Colorado																	
2211	Aims CC / Greeley	2098	600	[1] / 3800	Pub	M		A=S	Q [5]	6/01 / FF/FA		6	0	3	1			
2212	Arapahoe CC / Littleton	1969	1100	[1] / 3900	Pub	M	S	A/S	E [5]	5/01 / FF/FA	2	6	0	2	1	3	2	2
2213	Aurora,CC of / Aurora	654	1100	[1] / 4300	Pub	M	S		S [5]	6/01 / FF/FA	1	7	0	3	1	4		
2214	Bel-Rea Animal Techn / Denver	220	4200	[1]	Priv	V [8]	S	6/01 / A=S	O †	9/01 / FF=FA	7	8	0	1	4	8	8	1
2215	Colo Mtn C Alpine / Steamboat Sprgs	350	4100	3200 / 8000	Pub	T		A=S	E [5]	FF/FA	8	5	5	1	4	5	6	3
2216	Colo Mtn C Spr Vly / Glenwood Sprgs	400	4100	3200 / 8000	Pub	T		A=S	E [5]	FF/FA	8	5	1	1	2	4	4	2
2217	Colo Mtn C Timberln / Leadville	190	4100	3200 / 8000	Pub	T		A=S	E [5]	FF/FA	6	4	6	2	4	7	6	3
2218	Colo Northwestern CC / Rangely	364	2800 [3]	2600 / 5100	Pub	T		8/15 / None	E [5]	5/01 / FFS	8	6	8	1	1	6	4	3
2219	Denver, CC of / Denver	5929	900	[1] / 3800	Pub	L	U	None	E [5]	6/01 / FFS	5	6	0	4			3	2
2220	Front Range CC / Westminster	3074	1000	[1] / 3800	Pub	L	S	Oth	E [5]	5/15 / FF/FA	3	6	0	2		3	1	2
2221	Lamar CC / Lamar	677	3700 [3]	2500 / 5600	Pub	T		8/15 / A/S	S [5]	5/15 / FFS	8	5	6	1	1	6	6	4
2222	Morgan CC / Fort Morgan	256	1000	[1] / 3800	Pub	S		None	E [5]	5/01 / FF/FA	9	7	0	1	1			
2223	Nazarene Bible C / Colorado Sprgs	225	2500	[1]	Oth / OS	L	U	9/06 / None	Q †		8	4	0	1	9	4		
2224	Northeastern JC / Sterling	902	4400 [3]	3800 / 5900	Pub	S		9/01 / A/S	Q [5]	4/01 / FF/FA	9	5	5	1	1	6	6	5
2225	Otero JC / La Junta	556	3900 [3]	2800 / 5800	Pub	T			S [5]	FFS	8	5	2	4	1	4	4	4

Educational Programs Available — College Transfer Courses (Agriculture … Social Sci); Career-oriented Programs: Agri (Ag Business … Horticulture), Business (Accounting … Secretarial Studies), Arts (Architecture Tech … Photography/Cinema), Health (Dental Assistant … Radiologic Technology), Math (Computer Prog … Computer Operating), SocSci (Crim Just/Law Enforce … Social Work), Technical/Skilled Trades (Air/Refrig/Heat Tech … Welding)

Sequence Number	Agriculture	Bus-Commerce	Communications	Education	Engineering	Fine, Applied Arts	Foreign Lang	Health	Home Ec	Humanities	Mathematics	Computer/Info Sci	Biological Sci	Physical Sci	Social Sci	Ag Business	Ag/Farm Mgmt	Ag Mechanics/Tech	Horticulture	Accounting	Bus Mgmt & Admin	Hotel/Rest Mgmt	Office Mgmt	Marketing/Purchasing	Secretarial Studies	Architecture Tech	Applied Design	Photography/Cinema	Dental Assistant	Medical or Lab Tech	Nursing (RN)	Nursing (LPN)	Radiologic Technology	Computer Prog	Data Processing Tech	Computer Operating	Crim Just/Law Enforce	Parks/Rec Mgmt	Social Work	Air/Refrig/Heat Tech	Auto Body Repair	Auto Mechanics	Carpentry/Constr	Drafting/Eng Draft	Electric Eng Tech	Civil Eng Tech	Indus/Mfg Eng Tech	Mech Eng Tech	Machinework	Welding
2204	■	■	■	■	■	■	■	■	■	■	■	■	■	■	■	■	■	■	■	■	■		■	■	■		■				■	■		■	■		■	■				■	■	■	■	■		■	■	■
2205	■	■			■	■	■	■	■	■	■	■	■	■	■				■	■	■		■	■	■						■			■	■		■					■			■					■
2206		■				■	■			■	■	■		■	■					■	■		■		■									■					■											
2207	■	■	■	■	■	■	■	■		■	■	■	■	■	■	■	■	■	■	■	■			■	■		■								■	■	■					■								■
2208		■	■	■	■	■	■	■	■	■	■	■	■	■	■					■	■		■	■	■						■			■	■		■													
2209	■	■	■	■	■	■	■	■	■	■	■	■	■	■	■					■	■		■	■	■		■							■	■	■	■	■						■						
2210	■	■	■	■	■	■	■	■	■	■	■	■	■	■	■	■	■	■	■	■	■	■	■	■	■		■	■			■	■	■	■		■	■		■		■	■		■	■	■	■	■	■	■
2211	■	■						■	■			■			■		■																				■				■	■	■	■						■
2212	■	■	■	■	■	■	■	■	■	■	■	■	■	■	■					■	■		■	■	■	■				■	■			■		■	■			■	■	■	■	■				■	■	
2213		■	■						■			■	■	■	■					■			■		■			■						■	■	■						■								■
2214								■																																										
2215		■	■	■		■	■	■		■	■	■	■	■	■					■	■	■		■																										
2216		■	■	■		■	■	■		■	■	■	■	■	■						■							■									■													
2217		■		■		■	■			■	■	■	■	■	■					■	■			■	■										■	■														
2218		■		■						■	■	■			■		■				■		■		■												■													
2219				■		■	■	■		■	■		■	■	■					■	■	■	■	■	■						■	■	■	■	■	■			■	■		■		■	■					■
2220		■	■			■	■	■		■	■	■	■	■	■				■	■	■		■	■	■				■		■	■		■	■						■	■		■					■	
2221	■	■	■	■	■	■	■	■		■	■	■	■	■	■										■																	■								■
2222		■	■			■				■	■	■	■	■	■		■			■	■				■						■										■	■								■
2223										■																																								
2224	■	■	■	■	■	■	■	■	■	■	■	■	■	■	■	■	■	■		■	■	■	■	■	■							■				■					■	■	■	■				■		■
2225		■	■	■	■	■	■	■		■	■	■			■		■			■	■				■						■	■												■					■	■

▲ **Sequence Number—indicates the order of the college in this book only. Do *not* use this number with admissions tests or need analysis services.**

[1] No campus room and board facilities
[2] Room only or board only
[3] Most freshmen required to live on campus
[4] City or district residency requirements
[5] Accredited by regional accrediting association or a recognized candidate for accreditation
[6] All female freshman class
[7] All male freshman class
[8] Some admission selectivity; not all hs graduates accepted
[9] Requirements more stringent for nonresidents
†Accredited by a nationally recognized accrediting body other than one of the regional accrediting associations

Colorado
(continued)

Sequence Number	School name (upper entry) City (lower entry)	Enrollment	Costs: Resident tuition/fees + room/board	Costs: Room/board (upper entry) Nonresident tuition/fees (lower entry)	Gen. Info.: Affiliation (upper entry) Religious observance (lower entry)	Gen. Info.: Size of community	Gen. Info.: Type of community	Admissions: Fall term application deadline (upper entry) Test required or desired (lower entry)	Admissions: Calendar	Financial Aid: Fall term application deadline (upper entry) Forms to be filed (lower entry)	Student Profile (No. in 10 who-): -have need, rec some aid	-are women	-live on campus	-are minority students	-are nonresidents	-return as sophomores	-complete assoc degree	-transfer to 4-year college
2226	Pickens Tech Ctr Aurora	521	1300	[1] 2500	Pub	M	S	8/24	S [5]	 FFS	7	5	0	2	0	0	7	
2227	Pikes Peak CC Colorado Sprgs	2397	1000	[1] 3900	Pub	L	S	9/01 A/S	S [5]	7/02 FF/FA	6	6	0	2	1		2	1
2228	Pueblo CC Pueblo	1960	1600	[1] 5100	Pub	M		8/15 Oth	E [5]	7/24 FF/FA	7	6	0	4	1	6	3	1
2229	Red Rocks CC Lakewood	1438	1000	[1] 3900	Pub	L	S		E [5]	6/01 FFS	3	6	0	2	1	5	2	3
2230	Trinidad St JC Trinidad	719	4400	3300 6200	Pub	S		8/10 A/S	E [5]	5/01	7	4	3	5	2	7	7	3
Connecticut																		
2231	Asnuntuck CC Enfield	215	900	[1] 2900	Pub	S		 Oth	S [5]	 Oth	2	7	0	2	1	4	1	3
2232	Greater Hartford CC Hartford	433	900	[1] 2700	Pub	V	U	 None	S [5]	 FF=FA	2	7	0	5	1		2	
2233	Hartfd Camerata Cons Hartford	28	5500	[1]	Priv	L [8]	U	 None	E [5]	 FAF	7	5	0					
2234	Hartford C for Women Hartford	120	13700	4700	Priv	L [8]	S [6]	 S/A	E [5]	 FA/FF	7	9	4	4	1	8	8	9
2235	Hartford St Tech C Hartford	322	1600	[1] 4200	Pub	M [8]	U	 Oth	S [5]	 FF=FA	3	1	0	2	1			2
2236	Housatonic CC Bridgeport	1297	900	[1] 2700	Pub	L	U	 None	S [5]	7/01 Oth		7		4	1	6		
2237	Katharine Gibbs Sch Norwalk	225	6700	[1]	Priv	M [8]	S	 A=S	Q †	9/01 FF=FA	6	9	1	1	1	9	9	1
2238	Manchester CC Manchester	1623	1000	[1] 2900	Pub	S		 None	E [5]	6/01 FAF	2	3	0	1	1	7		
2239	Mattatuck CC Waterbury	1473	900	[1] 2600	Pub	L	U	9/01 Oth	E [5]	6/30 FA/FF	6	7	0	1	0	7	1	3
2240	Middlesex CC Middletown	3230	900	[1] 2700	Pub	S		 None	S [5]	 FF=FA	2	7	0	1	1	6	4	6
2241	Mitchell C New London	614	13200	4100	Priv	S [8]		 A=S	E [5]	 FAF	4	4	9	2	7	7	7	9
2242	Mohegan CC Norwich	701	1000	[1] 2900	Pub	S		 None	E [5]	 FA/FF	3	7	0	1	1	6	4	4
2243	Northwestern Conn CC Winsted	472	1000	[1] 3000	Pub	S		9/01 None	E [5]	 FA/FF	3	6	0	1	1	6	5	3
2244	Norwalk CC Norwalk	669	900	[1] 2600	Pub	M	U	 None	E [5]	7/01 FF/FA	5	7	0	2	1	5	2	2
2245	Norwalk St Tech C Norwalk	310	1200	[1] 3800	Pub	M [8]	S	9/01 Oth	E [5]	10/01	3	2	0	4	0	5	4	7
2246	Quinebaug Valley CC Danielson	306	900	[1] 2200	Pub	T		9/01 None	S [5]	 FAF	3	8	0	1	1	3	1	3
2247	South Central CC New Haven	1214	1000	[1] 2900	Pub	M	U	 Oth	E [5]	9/01 FF=FA	3	7	0	3	1			1

Educational Programs Available — College Transfer Courses

Sequence Number	Agriculture	Bus-Commerce	Communications	Education	Engineering	Fine, Applied Arts	Foreign Lang	Health	Home Ec	Humanities	Mathematics	Computer/Info Sci	Biological Sci	Physical Sci	Social Sci
2226															
2227	■	■	■	■	■	■	■	■	■	■	■	■	■	■	■
2228															
2229	■	■	■	■	■	■	■	■		■	■	■	■	■	■
2230	■	■	■	■	■	■	■	■		■	■	■	■	■	■
2231		■	■			■						■			■
2232		■		■		■	■	■	■	■		■	■		■
2233															
2234						■	■			■	■	■	■	■	■
2235															
2236	■	■	■		■	■	■	■			■	■			■
2237															
2238		■	■	■		■	■	■		■	■	■	■	■	■
2239	■	■	■	■		■	■	■	■	■	■	■	■	■	■
2240		■	■		■	■	■			■	■	■		■	■
2241		■	■	■	■	■		■		■	■	■	■	■	■
2242		■	■	■		■	■	■		■	■	■	■	■	■
2243		■	■	■	■	■		■	■	■	■	■	■	■	■
2244		■	■	■			■	■		■	■		■	■	■
2245		■			■	■					■	■			
2246		■		■		■				■	■	■			■
2247		■	■	■		■	■	■	■	■	■	■			■

Educational Programs Available — Career-oriented Programs (Agri, Business, Arts, Health)

Sequence Number	Agri: Ag Business	Ag/Farm Mgmt	Ag Mechanics/Tech	Horticulture	Business: Accounting	Bus Mgmt & Admin	Hotel/Rest Mgmt	Office Mgmt	Marketing/Purchasing	Secretarial Studies	Arts: Architecture Tech	Applied Design	Photography/Cinema	Health: Dental Assistant	Medical or Lab Tech	Nursing (RN)	Nursing (LPN)	Radiologic Technology
2226				■	■		■	■	■	■			■	■	■		■	
2227					■	■	■	■	■	■	■	■		■		■	■	
2228		■			■	■		■		■						■	■	■
2229					■	■		■	■	■		■						
2230								■		■							■	
2231					■	■		■		■								
2232					■	■			■	■						■		
2233																		
2234																		
2235											■							
2236					■	■				■					■	■		
2237					■		■	■		■								
2238					■	■	■		■	■					■			■
2239				■	■	■	■		■	■						■		■
2240					■	■			■									■
2241					■	■		■		■								
2242					■	■	■		■	■						■		
2243					■	■			■	■			■					
2244					■		■		■	■						■		
2245											■							
2246					■			■		■								
2247					■		■			■								■

Educational Programs Available — Career-oriented Programs (Math, SocSci, Technical/Skilled Trades)

Sequence Number	Math: Computer Prog	Data Processing Tech	Computer Operating	SocSci: Crim Just/Law Enforce	Parks/Rec Mgmt	Social Work	Technical/Skilled Trades: Air/Refrig/Heat Tech	Auto Body Repair	Auto Mechanics	Carpentry/Constr	Drafting/Eng Draft	Electric Eng Tech	Civil Eng Tech	Indus/Mfg Eng Tech	Mech Eng Tech	Machinework	Welding
2226		■	■				■	■	■	■	■					■	■
2227		■	■	■		■	■	■	■	■	■				■	■	■
2228	■	■		■			■	■	■		■					■	■
2229	■	■	■	■					■	■	■	■					■
2230	■			■				■	■	■	■	■	■				■
2231																	
2232	■																
2233																	
2234																	
2235							■					■	■	■	■		
2236	■	■	■	■													
2237			■														
2238	■			■		■											
2239				■		■			■								
2240	■																
2241						■											
2242				■													
2243	■			■	■	■											
2244		■		■	■	■											
2245	■	■								■		■	■	■	■		
2246						■											
2247	■					■											

▲ **Sequence Number—indicates the order of the college in this book only. Do *not* use this number with admissions tests or need analysis services.**

[1] No campus room and board facilities
[2] Room only or board only
[3] Most freshmen required to live on campus
[4] City or district residency requirements
[5] Accredited by regional accrediting association or a recognized candidate for accreditation
[6] All female freshman class
[7] All male freshman class
[8] Some admission selectivity; not all hs graduates accepted
[9] Requirements more stringent for nonresidents
†Accredited by a nationally recognized accrediting body other than one of the regional accrediting associations

Connecticut (continued)

Sequence Number	School name (upper entry) / City (lower entry)	Enrollment	Costs: Resident tuition/fees + room/board	Costs: Room/board (upper entry) / Nonresident tuition/fees (lower entry)	Gen. Info.: Affiliation (upper entry) / Religious observance (lower entry)	Gen. Info.: Size of community	Gen. Info.: Type of community	Admissions: Fall term application deadline (upper entry) / Test required or desired (lower entry)	Admissions: Calendar	Financial Aid: Fall term application deadline (upper entry) / Forms to be filed (lower entry)	No. in 10 who- have need, rec some aid	-are women	-live on campus	-are minority students	-are nonresidents	-return as sophomores	-complete assoc degree	-transfer to 4-year college
2248	Thames Valley St C / Norwich	375	1200	1 / 3800	Pub	S		A=S	E 5	FAF	6	2	0	1	1	6	6	4
2249	Tunxis CC / Farmington	906	900	1 / 2700	Pub	S		None	S 5	FA/FF	2	7	0	1	1	5		5
Delaware																		
2250	Del Tech & CC-South / Georgetown	1361	900	1 / 2300	Pub	T		Oth	Q 5	FFS		6	0	2	1	5	2	1
2251	Del Tech CC Stanton / Newark	2088	900	1 / 2300	Pub	M		8/01 / Oth	Q 5	7/01 / FFS	9	6	0	2	1	5	2	1
2252	Del Tech CC Terry / Dover	588	900	1 / 2300	Pub	S		8/15 / Oth	Q 5	FF/FA		6	0	2	1	4	1	1
Florida																		
2253	Atlantic Voc-Tech / Coconut Creek	3500	200	1 / 400	Pub	S		Oth	O 5		1	5	0					
2254	Brevard CC / Cocoa	4690	800	1 / 1600	Pub	S		A=S	S 5	FA/FF	3	5	0	1	1	5	1	5
2255	Broward CC / Fort Lauderdale	8488	700	1 / 1500	Pub	V	U	None	T 5	FAF	9	6	0	3	1	7		6
2256	Central Florida CC / Ocala	1924	900	1 / 1800	Pub	M		8/10 / A/S	E 5	FF/FA	4	6	0	1	1	6	3	4
2257	Chipola JC / Marianna	1061	2300	1600 / 2900	Pub	T		A/S	E 5	4/01 / FF/FA	7	5	1	1	1	8	5	4
2258	Daytona Beach CC / Daytona Beach	4045	800	1 / 1600	Pub	M	S	A=S	E 5	FA/FF	3	6	0	1	2		7	6
2259	Edison CC / Fort Myers	2407	700	1 / 1500	Pub	M		8/17 / A/S	E 5	7/01 / FF/FA	3	6	0	1	1	6	3	2
2260	Florida C / Temple Terrace	367	6100	2400	Priv / OS	S 8		8/15 / ACT	E 5	FF/FA	8	5	9	1	8			
2261	Florida CC Jacksonvl / Jacksonville	5677	800	1 / 1600	Pub	V	U	A=S	O 5	FA/FF		6	0	2	1	5	3	2
2262	Florida Keys CC / Key West	294	700	1 / 1400	Pub	S		A=S	E 5	5/01 / FA/FF	5	5	0	1	1	3	5	4
2263	Gulf Coast CC / Panama City	3200	700	1 / 1200	Pub	M		Oth	E 5	FF/FA	2	5	0	1	1	7	4	5
2264	Haney Voc-Tech Ctr / Panama City	1100	500	1 / 900	Pub	M	S	Oth	O 5			3	0	1				
2265	Hillsborough CC / Tampa	5405	800	1 / 1600	Pub	L	U	Oth	E 5	FF/FA	3	6	0	2	1		5	5
2266	Indian River CC / Fort Pierce	2219	800	1 / 1500	Pub	M		A/S	O 5	6/01	2	5	0	1	1	2		
2267	Intern Fine Arts C / Miami	613	10300 2	2500	Priv	V	U	8/25 / Oth	S 5	4/01 / FAF	5	7	5	5	5	8	8	
2268	L Hopkins Tech Ctr / Miami	2600	300	1	Pub	V	U	None	T 5		2	6	0	8	1			

Educational Programs Available (College Transfer Courses: Agriculture – Social Sci; Career-oriented Programs: Agri: Ag Business – Horticulture; Business: Accounting – Secretarial Studies; Arts: Architecture Tech – Photography/Cinema; Health: Dental Assistant – Radiologic Technology; Math: Computer Prog – Computer Operating; SocSci: Crim Just/Law Enforce – Social Work; Technical/Skilled Trades: Air/Refrig/Heat Tech – Welding)

Seq.	Agriculture	Bus-Commerce	Communications	Education	Engineering	Fine, Applied Arts	Foreign Lang	Health	Home Ec	Humanities	Mathematics	Computer/Info Sci	Biological Sci	Physical Sci	Social Sci	Ag Business	Ag/Farm Mgmt	Ag Mechanics/Tech	Horticulture	Accounting	Bus Mgmt & Admin	Hotel/Rest Mgmt	Office Mgmt	Marketing/Purchasing	Secretarial Studies	Architecture Tech	Applied Design	Photography/Cinema	Dental Assistant	Medical or Lab Tech	Nursing (RN)	Nursing (LPN)	Radiologic Technology	Computer Prog	Data Processing Tech	Computer Operating	Crim Just/Law Enforce	Parks/Rec Mgmt	Social Work	Air/Refrig/Heat Tech	Auto Body Repair	Auto Mechanics	Carpentry/Constr	Drafting/Eng Draft	Electric Eng Tech	Civil Eng Tech	Indus/Mfg Eng Tech	Mech Eng Tech	Machinework	Welding
2248					■	■						■		■																					■									■		■		■		
2249		■	■			■	■	■	■	■	■	■	■	■	■					■	■			■	■		■		■						■		■													
2250	■	■	■		■	■		■				■			■	■				■	■	■		■	■					■	■	■			■		■		■	■		■		■	■	■		■		■
2251																				■	■				■				■		■				■		■			■				■	■	■		■		
2252		■		■	■					■	■	■			■					■	■		■	■	■							■		■	■		■		■					■	■	■				
2253																			■	■			■	■	■							■		■	■	■				■	■	■	■	■					■	■
2254		■	■	■	■	■	■	■	■	■	■	■	■	■	■				■		■	■	■	■	■			■	■	■	■	■	■				■			■		■	■	■	■				■	■
2255	■	■	■	■	■	■	■	■	■	■	■	■	■	■	■				■	■	■	■	■	■	■		■		■	■	■		■	■	■		■			■		■	■		■	■		■		
2256	■	■	■	■	■	■	■	■	■	■	■	■	■	■	■				■		■	■			■						■	■					■			■	■	■		■	■				■	■
2257	■	■	■	■	■	■	■	■	■	■	■	■	■	■	■										■										■		■			■		■			■					■
2258	■	■	■	■	■	■	■	■	■	■	■	■	■	■	■					■	■	■	■	■	■	■		■	■		■	■	■	■	■	■	■			■	■	■	■	■		■	■		■	
2259	■	■	■	■	■	■	■	■		■	■	■	■	■	■					■					■					■	■			■			■							■	■	■				
2260																																																		
2261		■	■	■		■	■	■	■	■	■	■	■	■	■					■	■	■	■	■	■	■				■	■		■	■	■	■	■			■						■				
2262		■		■		■	■			■	■	■	■	■	■					■	■	■			■						■			■	■		■								■					
2263	■	■	■	■	■	■	■	■	■	■	■	■	■	■	■					■	■	■		■	■				■		■				■		■							■	■	■		■		
2264																			■	■		■	■		■		■			■		■								■	■	■	■	■	■				■	■
2265	■	■	■	■	■	■	■	■	■	■	■	■	■	■	■				■	■		■	■	■	■	■					■	■	■	■		■	■			■		■								
2266	■	■	■	■	■	■	■	■	■	■	■	■	■	■	■					■	■		■	■	■	■			■	■	■	■	■	■	■	■	■			■				■						
2267		■	■			■			■																																									
2268																				■		■	■		■		■		■			■		■	■	■				■		■		■	■					

▲ Sequence Number—indicates the order of the college in this book only. Do *not* use this number with admissions tests or need analysis services.

[1] No campus room and board facilities
[2] Room only or board only
[3] Most freshmen required to live on campus
[4] City or district residency requirements
[5] Accredited by regional accrediting association or a recognized candidate for accreditation
[6] All female freshman class
[7] All male freshman class
[8] Some admission selectivity; not all hs graduates accepted
[9] Requirements more stringent for nonresidents
†Accredited by a nationally recognized accrediting body other than one of the regional accrediting associations

Florida

(continued)

Sequence Number	School name (upper entry) City (lower entry)	Enrollment	Costs: Resident tuition/fees + room/board	Costs: Room/board (upper entry) Nonresident tuition/fees (lower entry)	Gen. Info.: Affiliation (upper entry) Religious observance (lower entry)	Gen. Info.: Size of community	Gen. Info.: Type of community	Admissions: Fall term application deadline (upper entry) Test required or desired (lower entry)	Admissions: Calendar	Financial Aid: Fall term application deadline (upper entry) Forms to be filed (lower entry)	No. in 10 who- -have need, rec some aid	-are women	-live on campus	-are minority students	-are nonresidents	-return as sophomores	-complete assoc degree	-transfer to 4-year college
2269	Lake City CC Lake City	2358	3400	2600 4200	Pub	S		A/S	E [5]	6/01 FFS	3	5	1	2	1	5	5	3
2270	Lake Co Voc-Tech Ctr Eustis	550	300	[1] 600	Pub	M [8]	S	Oth	O [5]	Oth	2	5	0	2				
2271	Lake-Sumter CC Leesburg	749	700	[1] 1500	Pub	S		Oth	T [5]	3/15 FA/FF	3	6	0	1	0	4	4	6
2272	Lively Voc-Tech Ctr Tallahassee	2600	300	[1] 600	Pub	L	S	Oth	O [5]	FFS		5	0	3				
2273	Manatee CC Bradenton	3100	800	[1] 1400	Pub	L	S	8/25 Oth	E [5]	6/01 FFS	4	6	0	1	1	6	2	4
2274	McFatter Voc-Tech Davie	3000		[1]	Pub	V			[5]									
2275	Miami-Dade CC Miami	18753	800	[1] 2000	Pub	V	U	A=S	O [5]	4/01 FA/FF	8	6	0	8	1	6	2	2
2276	Mid-Florida Tech Orlando	3000	300	[1] 600	Pub	V	S	Oth	O [5]	Oth	1	4	0	3	1	9		
2277	North Florida JC Madison	466	700	[1] 1400	Pub	T		A/S	O [5]	FA/FF	3	6	0	2	1	6	8	6
2278	North Tech Educ Ctr Riviera Beach	800	300	[1] 700	Pub	L	S	Oth	O [5]	Oth		4	0	4				
2279	Okaloosa-Walton JC Niceville	1406	700	[1] 1300	Pub	S		A=S	T [5]	FF/FA	3	5	0	1	1			
2280	Orlando Voc Tech Orlando	1225	400	[1]	Pub	V		Oth	O [5]	Oth	2	7		6			6	1
2281	Palm Beach CC Lake Worth	3200	800	[1] 1500	Pub	S		7/27 A/S	O [5]	4/01 FF/FA	8	6	0	1	1	9	7	6
2282	Palm Beaches,C of West Palm Beach	200	5600	[1]	Priv	L	U	A/S	O †	Oth	8	9	0	7			7	1
2283	Pasco-Hernando CC Dade City	1673	900	[1] 1700	Pub	S		8/22 Oth	O [5]	6/01 FA/FF	4	6	0	1	1	6	4	3
2284	Pensacola JC Pensacola	3848	800	[1] 1600	Pub	L	S	Oth	E [5]	FA/FF	2	6	0	1	1	7	3	3
2285	Pinellas Voc-Tech Clearwater	2500	400	[1] 700	Pub	L	S	Oth	O [5]		5	3	0	1	0	7	3	0
2286	Polk CC Winter Haven	1492	600	[1] 1400	Pub	M		8/01 Oth	O [5]	5/01 FF/FA	9	5	0	2	1	6	3	2
2287	Prospect Hall C Hollywood	325	4800	[1]	Priv	L	S	0/04 Oth	Q †	9/30 FF=FA	7	7	0	5	1	8		2
2288	Saint Augustine Tech St Augustine	810	200	[1] 400	Pub	S		Oth	O [5]	3/15 Oth		3	0	2	1	7		
2289	Saint Johns River CC Palatka	1171	700	[1] 1400	Pub	S		A=S	T [5]	5/15 FF=FA	2	6	0	1	1	5	3	3
2290	Saint Petersburg JC St Petersburg	5782	800	[1] 1600	Pub	V	S		E [5]	4/15 FFS	9	6		1	1	4	8	4
2291	Saint Petersburg V-T St Petersburg	1183	500	[1] 1000	Pub	L	U	Oth	O [5]	Oth	5	5	0	4	1			

Educational Programs Available — College Transfer Courses

Sequence Number	Agriculture	Bus-Commerce	Communications	Education	Engineering	Fine, Applied Arts	Foreign Lang	Health	Home Ec	Humanities	Mathematics	Computer/Info Sci	Biological Sci	Physical Sci	Social Sci
2269	■	■	■	■	■	■	■	■	■	■	■	■	■	■	■
2270															
2271	■	■	■	■	■	■	■	■	■	■	■	■	■	■	■
2272															
2273	■	■	■	■	■	■	■	■	■	■	■	■	■	■	■
2274															
2275	■	■	■	■	■	■	■	■	■	■	■	■	■	■	■
2276															
2277		■	■	■		■	■		■	■	■	■	■	■	■
2278															
2279	■	■		■	■	■	■	■	■	■	■	■	■	■	■
2280															
2281	■	■	■	■	■	■	■	■	■	■	■	■	■	■	■
2282															
2283		■	■	■		■	■	■	■	■	■	■	■	■	■
2284	■	■	■	■	■	■	■	■	■	■	■	■	■	■	■
2285															
2286	■	■	■	■	■	■	■	■	■	■	■	■	■	■	■
2287		■										■			
2288															
2289	■	■	■	■	■	■	■	■		■	■	■	■	■	■
2290		■						■							
2291															

Educational Programs Available — Career-oriented Programs (Agri, Business, Arts, Health)

Sequence Number	Agri: Ag Business	Agri: Ag/Farm Mgmt	Agri: Ag Mechanics/Tech	Agri: Horticulture	Business: Accounting	Business: Bus Mgmt & Admin	Business: Hotel/Rest Mgmt	Business: Office Mgmt	Business: Marketing/Purchasing	Business: Secretarial Studies	Arts: Architecture Tech	Arts: Applied Design	Arts: Photography/Cinema	Health: Dental Assistant	Health: Medical or Lab Tech	Health: Nursing (RN)	Health: Nursing (LPN)	Health: Radiologic Technology
2269				■					■	■					■	■		
2270			■	■	■					■							■	
2271						■	■	■		■		■			■	■		
2272				■	■			■		■	■		■				■	
2273							■	■	■	■	■					■		■
2274																	■	
2275				■	■	■	■	■	■	■	■	■	■		■	■		■
2276					■	■	■	■	■	■	■		■					
2277					■	■		■		■	■						■	
2278				■	■	■		■		■							■	
2279						■	■	■		■								
2280					■			■		■				■			■	
2281					■		■	■	■			■		■	■	■		■
2282					■			■	■	■								
2283				■		■		■	■					■		■	■	
2284	■			■	■	■	■	■	■	■	■			■	■	■	■	■
2285				■	■			■		■	■						■	
2286					■	■		■		■						■		■
2287					■	■												
2288	■		■	■	■	■		■		■			■				■	
2289					■	■		■	■	■								
2290					■	■		■	■	■	■				■	■		■
2291				■	■		■	■	■	■		■	■	■			■	

Educational Programs Available — Career-oriented Programs (Math, SocSci, Technical/Skilled Trades)

Sequence Number	Math: Computer Prog	Math: Data Processing Tech	Math: Computer Operating	SocSci: Crim Just/Law Enforce	SocSci: Parks/Rec Mgmt	SocSci: Social Work	Tech: Air/Refrig/Heat Tech	Tech: Auto Body Repair	Tech: Auto Mechanics	Tech: Carpentry/Constr	Tech: Drafting/Eng Draft	Tech: Electric Eng Tech	Tech: Civil Eng Tech	Tech: Indus/Mfg Eng Tech	Tech: Mech Eng Tech	Tech: Machinework	Tech: Welding
2269	■	■		■	■					■							
2270	■	■	■	■			■	■	■	■	■						■
2271		■	■	■													
2272	■	■	■	■			■	■	■	■	■	■				■	■
2273	■			■								■	■	■			
2274				■					■		■					■	■
2275	■	■		■			■			■	■	■	■	■	■		
2276	■	■	■	■			■	■	■		■	■				■	■
2277	■	■	■	■							■						
2278							■	■	■	■	■	■				■	■
2279	■	■	■	■			■		■		■	■					■
2280	■	■	■				■				■						
2281	■	■		■							■	■	■				
2282		■	■														
2283	■	■	■	■						■							■
2284	■	■	■			■	■	■	■	■	■	■	■			■	■
2285		■	■				■	■	■	■	■					■	■
2286		■		■		■			■		■	■	■				
2287	■	■															
2288	■	■	■	■			■	■	■	■	■	■			■	■	■
2289		■	■									■					
2290	■	■	■	■						■							
2291	■	■	■				■	■	■	■	■	■				■	■

▲ **Sequence Number—indicates the order of the college in this book only. Do *not* use this number with admissions tests or need analysis services.**

[1] No campus room and board facilities
[2] Room only or board only
[3] Most freshmen required to live on campus
[4] City or district residency requirements
[5] Accredited by regional accrediting association or a recognized candidate for accreditation
[6] All female freshman class
[7] All male freshman class
[8] Some admission selectivity; not all hs graduates accepted
[9] Requirements more stringent for nonresidents
†Accredited by a nationally recognized accrediting body other than one of the regional accrediting associations

Florida
(continued)

Sequence Number	School name (upper entry) / City (lower entry)	Enrollment	Costs: Resident tuition/fees + room/board	Costs: Room/board (upper entry) / Nonresident tuition/fees (lower entry)	Gen. Info.: Affiliation (upper entry) / Religious observance (lower entry)	Size of community	Type of community	Admissions: Fall term application deadline (upper entry) / Test required or desired (lower entry)	Calendar	Financial Aid: Fall term application deadline (upper entry) / Forms to be filed (lower entry)	No. in 10 who- -have need, rec some aid	-are women	-live on campus	-are minority students	-are nonresidents	-return as sophomores	-complete assoc degree	-transfer to 4-year college
2292	Santa Fe CC / Gainesville	5493	800	[1] / 1500	Pub	L	S	A=S	E [5]	FF/FA	6	5	0	2	1	7		6
2293	Seminole CC / Sanford	2507	800	[1] / 1500	Pub	V	S	8/22 / A/S	E [5]	5/01 / FF/FA	3	6	0	1	1	6	5	3
2294	Sheridan Vo-Tech Ctr / Hollywood	1750		[1]	Pub	M	U		O [5]	FFS								
2295	South Florida CC / Avon Park	602	800	1600	Pub	S		A=S	T [5]	FA/FF		5		2			7	
2296	Suwannee-Hamilton VT / Live Oak	550	300	[1]	Pub	T		Oth	S [5]	None		7	0	2				
2297	Tallahassee CC / Tallahassee	4435	700	[1] / 1300	Pub	M	S	A=S	E [5]	6/01 / FF/FA	2	5	0	2	1			8
2298	Traviss Voc-Tech Ctr / Lakeland	3372	300	[1] / 500	Pub	M	S	Oth	S [5]	Oth	1	5	0	1				
2299	Valencia CC / Orlando	6044	800	[1] / 1800	Pub	V	U	8/23 / None	E [5]	4/01 / FA/FF	4	6	0	3	1	3		6
2300	Walker Voc-Tech / Naples	397	300	[1] / 700	Pub	L	U		O [5]	FAF	2	5	0	2	1	0	4	
2301	Washington-Holms V-T / Chipley	650	300	[1] / 700	Pub	T		Oth	S [5]	FAF	5	4	0	2	1	7		
2302	Westside Voc Tech / Winter Garden	870	300	[1] / 500	Pub	S		Oth	S [5]	FF=FA	2	6		6			7	1
Georgia																		
2303	Abraham Baldwin Ag C / Tifton	1802	3200	2000 / 4900	Pub	S		9/01 / A=S	Q [5]	5/01 / FA/FF	6	5	4	1	1		2	2
2304	Albany Tech Inst / Albany	776	600	[1] / 1200	Pub	M [8]	S	Oth	O [5]	Oth	6	6	0	5	0			
2305	Andrew C / Cuthbert	309	7500	3500	Meth	T [8]		A=S	Q [5]	FF=FA	9	5	8	3	5	8	8	9
2306	Athens Area Tech C / Athens	733	500	[1] / 800	Pub	M [8]		Oth	O [5]	FAF	4	6	0	3	1	5		
2307	Atlanta Area Tech Sc / Atlanta	1600	400	[1] / 700	Pub	V	U	8/30 / Oth	O [5]	8/01 / FF=FA	5	5	0	7	0	2		
2308	Atlanta Metro C / Atlanta	746	1000	[1] / 2700	Pub	V [8]	U	9/13 / A=S	Q [5]	9/10 / FAF	3	6	0	9	2	5	3	6
2309	Augusta Area Tech Sc / Augusta	1450	500	[1] / 700	Pub	L	U	9/15 / Oth	O [5]	9/15 / FA/FF	5	5	0	4	1	3		1
2310	Bainbridge C / Bainbridge	370	1000	[1] / 2800	Pub	S [8]		9/20 / A=S	Q [5]	8/30 / FAF	3	6	0	2	1	6	3	5
2311	Bauder Fashion C / Atlanta	500	8200 [2]	2200	Priv	V [8]	S	None	T [5]	FF=FA	4	9	9	3	7	6	9	1
2312	Ben Hill Irwin Tech / Fitzgerald	309	600	[1] / 2400	Pub	M		0/01 / Oth	Q [5]	9/01 / FF=FA	6	4	0	3	0	8		
2313	Brunswick JC / Brunswick	776	1100	[1] / 2900	Pub	S [8]		9/01 / A=S	Q [5]	6/01 / FAF	4	7	0	2	1	4	3	2

Educational Programs Available — College Transfer Courses

Sequence Number	Agriculture	Bus-Commerce	Communications	Education	Engineering	Fine, Applied Arts	Foreign Lang	Health	Home Ec	Humanities	Mathematics	Computer/Info Sci	Biological Sci	Physical Sci	Social Sci
2292	■	■	■	■	■	■	■	■	■	■	■	■	■	■	■
2293		■		■	■	■	■	■	■	■	■	■		■	■
2294															
2295	■	■	■	■	■	■	■	■		■	■	■	■	■	■
2296															
2297		■	■	■	■	■	■	■	■	■	■	■	■	■	■
2298															
2299		■	■	■	■	■	■	■		■	■	■	■	■	■
2300															
2301															
2302															
2303	■	■	■	■	■	■	■	■	■	■	■	■	■	■	■
2304															
2305	■	■	■	■	■	■	■	■	■	■	■	■	■	■	■
2306		■						■				■	■	■	■
2307															
2308	■	■	■	■	■	■	■	■	■	■	■	■		■	■
2309	■	■	■					■				■			■
2310	■	■	■	■		■	■	■	■	■	■		■	■	■
2311															
2312															
2313		■		■	■		■	■		■	■	■	■	■	■

Educational Programs Available — Career-oriented Programs

Sequence Number	Agri: Ag Business	Ag/Farm Mgmt	Ag Mechanics/Tech	Horticulture	Business: Accounting	Bus Mgmt & Admin	Hotel/Rest Mgmt	Office Mgmt	Marketing/Purchasing	Secretarial Studies	Arts: Architecture Tech	Applied Design	Photography/Cinema	Health: Dental Assistant	Medical or Lab Tech	Nursing (RN)	Nursing (LPN)	Radiologic Technology	Math: Computer Prog	Data Processing Tech	Computer Operating	SocSci: Crim Just/Law Enforce	Parks/Rec Mgmt	Social Work	Technical/Skilled Trades: Air/Refrig/Heat Tech	Auto Body Repair	Auto Mechanics	Carpentry/Constr	Drafting/Eng Draft	Electric Eng Tech	Civil Eng Tech	Indus/Mfg Eng Tech	Mech Eng Tech	Machinework	Welding
2292				■	■	■		■	■	■				■		■	■	■				■	■		■		■	■	■	■					■
2293						■		■	■	■	■					■	■		■	■	■	■			■		■		■						■
2294								■		■					■		■		■	■	■				■	■	■		■					■	■
2295	■				■	■	■	■	■	■		■				■	■		■	■	■	■		■	■	■	■	■	■						■
2296			■	■	■					■							■			■						■	■	■	■						■
2297						■				■						■			■	■		■													
2298				■	■			■	■	■	■						■		■	■	■				■	■	■	■	■	■			■	■	■
2299				■	■	■	■	■	■		■				■	■		■	■			■							■		■	■			
2300				■						■							■		■	■							■	■							
2301				■				■	■	■							■		■	■	■	■			■	■	■		■						■
2302				■	■			■	■	■										■	■				■			■							■
2303	■	■	■	■	■	■		■	■	■						■				■	■	■		■											
2304				■	■				■	■				■			■	■	■	■	■				■	■	■	■	■	■			■	■	■
2305																																			
2306					■				■	■							■		■						■	■	■		■					■	
2307					■				■	■				■	■		■		■		■				■	■	■	■	■					■	■
2308					■	■																			■	■	■		■	■					
2309				■	■	■			■	■				■	■		■		■	■					■	■	■	■	■	■	■	■	■	■	■
2310					■				■	■							■								■		■		■	■					■
2311									■																										
2312					■			■		■							■			■	■				■	■	■	■	■	■		■		■	
2313					■				■	■					■	■	■	■	■	■		■							■				■	■	■

▲ Sequence Number—indicates the order of the college in this book only. Do *not* use this number with admissions tests or need analysis services.

[1] No campus room and board facilities
[2] Room only or board only
[3] Most freshmen required to live on campus
[4] City or district residency requirements
[5] Accredited by regional accrediting association or a recognized candidate for accreditation
[6] All female freshman class
[7] All male freshman class
[8] Some admission selectivity; not all hs graduates accepted
[9] Requirements more stringent for nonresidents
†Accredited by a nationally recognized accrediting body other than one of the regional accrediting associations

Georgia
(continued)

Sequence Number	School name (upper entry) City (lower entry)	Enrollment	Costs: Resident tuition/fees + room/board	Costs: Room/board (upper entry) Nonresident tuition/fees (lower entry)	Gen. Info.: Affiliation (upper entry) Religious observance (lower entry)	Gen. Info.: Size of community	Gen. Info.: Type of community	Admissions: Fall term application deadline (upper entry) Test required or desired (lower entry)	Admissions: Calendar	Financial Aid: Fall term application deadline (upper entry) Forms to be filed (lower entry)	No. in 10 who- -have need, rec some aid	-are women	-live on campus	-are minority students	-are nonresidents	-return as sophomores	-complete assoc degree	-transfer to 4-year college
2314	Chattahoochee Tech Marietta	565	800	[1]	Pub	L	S	A=S	O [5]	FF=FA	1	5	0	2			3	2
2315	Columbus Tech Inst Columbus	934	500	[1]	Pub	L	S	Oth	O [5]		6	4	0	3	1		8	1
2316	Coosa Valley Voc-Tec Rome	645	500	[1] 800	Pub	M		Oth	O [5]	9/01 FA/FF	1	5	0	2	1			
2317	Dalton C Dalton	1100	1000	[1] 2700	Pub	S		9/01 S/A	Q [5]	8/01 FAF	9	6	0	1	1	7		
2318	Dalton Voc Sch Dalton	43	1500	[1] 1900	Pub	S [8]		Oth	O [5]	FF=FA	2	9	0	1	0	0		
2319	Darton C Albany	1046	1000	[1] 2800	Pub	M [8]	U	8/30 A=S	Q [5]	8/30 FA/FF	6	7	0	2	1	6	4	4
2320	DeKalb C Decatur	7367	1000	[1] 2500	Pub	V [8]	S	8/25 A=S	Q [5]	7/01 FA/FF	8	6	0	3	1	8	2	3
2321	East Georgia C Swainsboro	607	1000	[1]	Pub	T		S/A	Q [5]	FAF	3	6	0	1	0	7	4	5
2322	Emmanuel C Franklin Sprgs	372	6100	2600	Oth OS	T [8]		9/01 A=S	Q [5]	8/15 FF=FA	7	5	5	2	3	7	6	5
2323	Floyd C Rome	1685	900	[1] 2700	Pub	S [8]		A=S	Q [5]	FAF		6	0	1	1			
2324	Gainesville C Gainesville	1996	1000	[1] 2700	Pub	S		9/03 A=S	Q [5]	4/15 FAF	2	5	0	1	1	6	4	7
2325	Georgia Military C Milledgeville	1535	6000	3300	Pub	S [8]		Oth	Q [5]	8/01 FF=FA	5	4	1	4	3	7	9	9
2326	Gordon C Barnesville	967	3000	2000 4700	Pub	T [8]		S/A	Q [5]		3	6	2	2	0	5	3	5
2327	Griffin-Spaulding VT Griffin	540	600	[1] 2400	Pub	S		Oth	Q [5]	Oth		5						
2328	Lanier Tech Inst Oakwood	455	700	[1] 1400	Pub	M		Oth	Q [5]	FF=FA	2	5	0	1				
2329	Macon C Macon	1304	1000	[1] 3000	Pub	M [8]	S	A=S	Q [5]	Oth	2	7	0	2				
2330	Macon Technical Inst Macon	702	600	[1]	Pub	M [8]	U	0/01 Oth	Q [5]	9/20 FFS	4	6	0	4				
2331	Massey Business C Atlanta	480	7500	[1]	Priv	L [8]	U	Oth	Q †	None		6	0					
2332	Med Ctr-Sch Rad Tec Columbus	25	800	[1]	Pub	M [8]	U	5/01 A=S	O	5/01		8	0	1		9		
2333	Med/Dental,C of Atlanta	300	5000	[1]	Priv	V	U	Oth	O †	FF=FA	9	7	0	9	0	1	8	
2334	Middle Georgia C Cochran	936	3400 [3]	2200 5100	Pub	T [8]		9/01 A=S	Q [5]	7/01 FA/FF	2	5	1	2	1	5	7	7
2335	Middle Georgia Tech Warner Robins	393	600	[1]	Pub	M	S	Oth	O [5]		4	5	0	2				
2336	North Georgia Tech Clarkesville	550	1900	1500 2300	Pub	T		Oth	Q [5]	10/15 Oth	3	4	4	1	1			

Educational Programs Available — College Transfer Courses

Sequence Number	Agriculture	Bus-Commerce	Communications	Education	Engineering	Fine, Applied Arts	Foreign Lang	Health	Home Ec	Humanities	Mathematics	Computer/Info Sci	Biological Sci	Physical Sci	Social Sci
2314		■								■	■			■	■
2315		■			■							■			
2316															
2317	■	■	■	■	■	■	■	■	■	■	■		■	■	■
2318															
2319	■	■	■	■	■	■	■	■	■	■	■	■	■	■	■
2320	■	■	■	■	■	■	■	■		■	■	■	■	■	■
2321	■	■	■	■	■	■	■	■	■	■	■	■	■	■	■
2322		■		■		■		■		■					
2323	■	■	■	■	■	■	■	■		■	■	■	■	■	■
2324	■	■	■	■	■	■	■	■	■	■	■	■	■	■	■
2325		■	■	■	■	■	■			■	■		■	■	■
2326		■	■	■	■	■	■	■		■	■	■	■	■	■
2327															
2328															
2329	■	■	■	■	■	■	■	■		■	■	■	■	■	■
2330															
2331															
2332															
2333								■							
2334	■	■	■	■	■	■	■	■	■	■	■	■	■	■	■
2335															
2336															

Educational Programs Available — Career-oriented Programs

Sequence Number	Agri: Ag Business	Ag/Farm Mgmt	Ag Mechanics/Tech	Horticulture	Business: Accounting	Bus Mgmt & Admin	Hotel/Rest Mgmt	Office Mgmt	Marketing/Purchasing	Secretarial Studies	Arts: Architecture Tech	Applied Design	Photography/Cinema	Health: Dental Assistant	Medical or Lab Tech	Nursing (RN)	Nursing (LPN)	Radiologic Technology	Math: Computer Prog	Data Processing Tech	Computer Operating	SocSci: Crim Just/Law Enforce	Parks/Rec Mgmt	Social Work	Technical/Skilled Trades: Air/Refrig/Heat Tech	Auto Body Repair	Auto Mechanics	Carpentry/Constr	Drafting/Eng Draft	Electric Eng Tech	Civil Eng Tech	Indus/Mfg Eng Tech	Mech Eng Tech	Machinework	Welding
2314					■			■		■	■						■		■		■	■			■	■	■		■					■	■
2315					■			■	■	■							■		■	■	■				■	■	■	■	■	■		■	■	■	■
2316					■			■	■	■							■		■	■	■				■	■	■	■	■				■	■	■
2317					■			■	■	■					■	■			■	■		■			■	■	■		■	■					■
2318																	■																		
2319					■	■		■	■	■					■	■			■		■				■	■	■	■	■					■	■
2320				■	■				■	■		■			■		■		■	■		■	■		■		■		■	■			■	■	■
2321					■	■				■																									
2322																																			
2323				■	■					■					■	■				■		■	■	■						■			■		
2324					■	■	■		■	■				■					■	■	■	■			■	■	■	■		■			■		■
2325																						■													
2326					■	■		■		■									■	■		■													
2327					■				■	■			■				■	■	■	■	■				■	■	■	■	■	■		■		■	■
2328					■					■				■	■		■		■						■	■	■	■		■				■	■
2329					■			■		■					■	■			■	■	■	■													
2330					■				■	■					■		■		■	■	■	■			■	■	■	■	■	■				■	■
2331						■				■										■															
2332																		■																	
2333														■	■																				
2334								■	■							■					■	■							■		■				
2335					■				■	■							■								■		■		■						■
2336				■	■					■			■		■		■		■	■	■				■	■	■	■	■	■			■	■	■

▲ Sequence Number—indicates the order of the college in this book only. Do *not* use this number with admissions tests or need analysis services.

[1] No campus room and board facilities
[2] Room only or board only
[3] Most freshmen required to live on campus
[4] City or district residency requirements
[5] Accredited by regional accrediting association or a recognized candidate for accreditation
[6] All female freshman class
[7] All male freshman class
[8] Some admission selectivity; not all hs graduates accepted
[9] Requirements more stringent for nonresidents
†Accredited by a nationally recognized accrediting body other than one of the regional accrediting associations

Georgia
(continued)

Sequence Number	School name (upper entry) City (lower entry)	Enrollment	Resident tuition/fees + room/board	Room/board (upper entry) Nonresident tuition/fees (lower entry)	Affiliation (upper entry) Religious observance (lower entry)	Size of community	Type of community	Fall term application deadline (upper entry) Test required or desired (lower entry)	Calendar	Fall term application deadline (upper entry) Forms to be filed (lower entry)	-have need, rec some aid	-are women	-live on campus	-are minority students	-are nonresidents	-return as sophomores	-complete assoc degree	-transfer to 4-year college
			Costs		**Gen. Info.**			**Admissions**		**Financial Aid**	**Student Profile** No. in 10 who-							
2337	Oxford C of Emory U Oxford	512	14200[3]	3900	Meth	S[8]		8/15 S/A	E[5]	4/01 FA/FF	6	5	9	2	5	8	6	9
2338	Phillips C Atlanta	300	5000	[1]	Priv	V	U	 Oth	O[5]	 FF=FA	9	6	0	8	0	7	7	
2339	Pickens Tech Inst Jasper	275	600	[1] 1000	Pub	S		 A=S	Q[5]	 Oth	4	5	0	1	1		7	
2340	Reinhardt C Waleska	560	6200	3000	Meth	T[8]		 S/A	Q[5]	4/01 FA/FF	8	5	7	1	1	8	5	5
2341	Savannah Area Tech Savannah	751	600	[1] 1000	Pub	M	U	 Oth	Q[5]	7/01 FF=FA	4	6	0	5	0	0	2	
2342	South Georgia C Douglas	730	3200[3]	2200 4900	Pub	S[8]		 A=S	Q[5]	8/01 FAF	5	6	2	2	1	4	3	5
2343	South Georgia Tech Americus	480	3100	2300 3700	Pub	S[8]		 Oth	O[5]	 Oth	4	3	3	4	1	7		
2344	Swainsboro Tech Inst Swainsboro	300	400	[1] 1200	Pub	S[8]		9/10 Oth	O[5]	 Oth	4	4	0					
2345	Thomas Tech Inst Thomasville	440	500	[1] 800	Pub	T		 Oth	O[5]	8/15	6	5	0	5	1	8		
2346	Truett-McConnell C Cleveland	524	5900[3]	2400	Oth OS	T		 A=S	Q[5]	7/30 FA/FF	6	6	4	2	1	8	8	
2347	Upson Co Voc-Tech Thomaston	480	400	[1]	Pub	T		 Oth	O[5]	 FAF		3	0	4	0			
2348	Walker Tech Inst Rock Spring	470	600	[1]	Pub	T		 Oth	Q[5]	 Oth	6	5	0	1	1			
2349	Waycross C Waycross	474	1000	[1] 3000	Pub	S[8]		9/21 A=S	Q[5]		3	7	0	1	1	4	2	3
2350	Waycross Ware Tech Waycross	335	600	[1]	Pub	S		 Oth	Q[5]	 FF=FA	4	5	0	3		2		
2351	West Georgia Tech Lagrange	528	800	[1]	Pub	S[8]		9/01 Oth	O[5]	9/01 FF=FA	3	5	0	2	1			
2352	Young Harris C Young Harris	444	7200	3100	Meth O	T[8]		 S/A	Q[5]	 FAF	6	5	8	1	1	5	6	9
Hawaii																		
2353	Hawaii Hilo,U of Hilo	2578	3300	2800 5300	Pub	S		7/01 Oth	S[5]	3/01 FAF	5							
2354	Honolulu CC,U Hawaii Honolulu	1861	400	[1] 3500	Pub	L	U	7/01 None	S[5]	5/01 FAF	1	4	0	9	1	3		1
2355	Kapiolani CC,U Hwaii Honolulu	4000	400	[1] 2500	Pub	V	U	7/01 None	S[5]	5/01 FAF	1	6	0	7	1	3	3	2
2356	Kauai CC,U Hawaii Lihue	411	400	[1] 2600	Pub	T		8/15 Oth	E[5]	6/01 FAF		6	0	7	1			1
2357	Leeward CC,U Hawaii Pearl City	2428	400	[1] 2500	Pub	S		8/01 None	E[5]	5/01 FAF	9	6	0	8	1			
2358	Maui CC,U Hawaii Kahlului	2280	1800[2]	1400 4000	Pub	S		7/30 A=S	E[5]	5/01 FAF		4	1	7	1	3		

Educational Programs Available

Sequence Number	College Transfer Courses															Career-oriented Programs: Agri				Business						Arts			Health					Math			SocSci			Technical/Skilled Trades										
	Agriculture	Bus-Commerce	Communications	Education	Engineering	Fine, Applied Arts	Foreign Lang	Health	Home Ec	Humanities	Mathematics	Computer/Info Sci	Biological Sci	Physical Sci	Social Sci	Ag Business	Ag/Farm Mgmt	Ag Mechanics/Tech	Horticulture	Accounting	Bus Mgmt & Admin	Hotel/Rest Mgmt	Office Mgmt	Marketing/Purchasing	Secretarial Studies	Architecture Tech	Applied Design	Photography/Cinema	Dental Assistant	Medical or Lab Tech	Nursing (RN)	Nursing (LPN)	Radiologic Technology	Computer Prog	Data Processing Tech	Computer Operating	Crim Just/Law Enforce	Parks/Rec Mgmt	Social Work	Air/Refrig/Heat Tech	Auto Body Repair	Auto Mechanics	Carpentry/Constr	Drafting/Eng Draft	Electric Eng Tech	Civil Eng Tech	Indus/Mfg Eng Tech	Mech Eng Tech	Machinework	Welding
2337		■		■	■	■	■	■		■	■	■	■	■	■																																				
2338		■									■	■			■					■	■				■									■	■	■														
2339																				■			■		■							■		■	■	■				■	■	■	■	■	■			■	■	■
2340	■	■		■		■		■		■	■		■	■	■				■	■	■																													
2341					■														■	■				■	■				■			■		■	■	■	■			■	■	■	■	■	■				■	■
2342	■	■	■	■	■	■	■	■		■	■	■	■	■	■	■	■			■				■	■						■			■	■		■	■												
2343																		■		■					■			■				■		■						■	■	■	■	■			■		■	■
2344																				■				■	■							■			■					■		■		■	■				■	
2345																				■					■					■		■	■		■	■				■		■		■					■	■
2346	■	■	■	■	■	■	■	■		■	■	■	■	■	■					■			■		■			■		■																				
2347																				■			■		■							■			■	■				■		■	■	■	■			■		■
2348		■										■								■				■	■							■		■						■	■	■		■					■	■
2349	■	■	■	■	■	■	■	■		■	■	■	■	■	■					■	■			■	■					■				■		■														
2350																				■					■					■		■	■	■	■					■	■	■		■	■					■
2351																				■					■							■	■	■							■	■	■	■					■	■
2352	■	■	■	■	■	■	■	■	■	■	■	■	■	■	■																																			
Hawaii																																																		
2353						■			■						■				■	■				■	■						■	■			■	■					■	■	■	■	■				■	■
2354		■	■	■		■	■		■	■	■	■	■	■	■										■	■											■			■	■	■	■	■	■	■			■	■
2355																				■		■		■	■				■	■	■	■	■		■	■													
2356	■					■		■		■	■			■	■					■				■	■						■	■									■	■	■		■					■
2357	■	■	■	■	■	■	■	■		■	■	■	■	■	■					■	■		■	■	■													■				■		■						
2358	■	■						■							■				■	■		■	■	■	■						■	■					■				■	■	■	■						■

▲ **Sequence Number—indicates the order of the college in this book only. Do *not* use this number with admissions tests or need analysis services.**

[1] No campus room and board facilities
[2] Room only or board only
[3] Most freshmen required to live on campus
[4] City or district residency requirements
[5] Accredited by regional accrediting association or a recognized candidate for accreditation
[6] All female freshman class
[7] All male freshman class
[8] Some admission selectivity; not all hs graduates accepted
[9] Requirements more stringent for nonresidents
†Accredited by a nationally recognized accrediting body other than one of the regional accrediting associations

Hawaii
(continued)

Sequence Number	School name (upper entry) City (lower entry)	Enrollment	Resident tuition/fees + room/board	Room/board (upper entry) Nonresident tuition/fees (lower entry)	Affiliation (upper entry) Religious observance (lower entry)	Size of community	Type of community	Fall term application deadline (upper entry) Test required or desired (lower entry)	Calendar	Fall term application deadline (upper entry) Forms to be filed (lower entry)	-have need, rec some aid	-are women	-live on campus	-are minority students	-are nonresidents	-return as sophomores	-complete assoc degree	-transfer to 4-year college
2359	Windward CC,U Hawaii Kaneohe	538	400	[1] 2500	Pub	S		8/01 None	E[5]	7/01 FAF	1	6	0	6	1		6	5
Idaho																		
2360	East Idaho Tech C Idaho Falls	355	900	[1] 2100	Pub	S		Oth	O[5]	5/15 Oth	6	4	0	1	1	1	8	
2361	North Idaho C Coeur D'Alene	1664	3400	2600 4600	Pub	S		None	E[5]	4/15 FA/FF	4	6	1	1	2	5	2	3
2362	Ricks C Rexburg	7795	4200	2700	LDS OS	S		5/01 A/S	E[5]	3/15 None	9	6	2	1	6	5	3	5
2363	Southern Idaho,C of Twin Falls	2787	2900	2100 3900	Pub	S		Oth	E[5]	FA/FF	6	6		1				2
Illinois																		
2364	Amer Acad of Art Chicago	417	7100	[1]	Priv	V[8]	U	Oth	S†	7/31 FF=FA	5	5	0	1	2	7	7	
2365	Belleville Area C Belleville	3351	900	[1] 3600	Pub	M	S	Oth	E[5]	5/01 FF=FA	5	6	0	1	0			
2366	Bl-Nl Sch of Radiogr Normal	15	1000	[1]	Priv	M[8]		5/30 A/S	T†	8/31 FAF	2	8	0	0	0	9	9	
2367	Black Hawk C Moline	2048	1200	[1] 4800	Pub	M	S	8/15 None	E[5]	5/15 FF=FA	6	6	0	1	1			
2368	Black Hawk C East Kewanee	450	1200	[1] 4800	Pub	S		None	E[5]	Oth	5	6	0	1	0		6	3
2369	Carl Sandburg C Galesburg	1200	800	[1] 4900	Pub	S		ACT	S[5]	FFS	7	6	0	1	0		3	4
2370	Chicago C Commerce Chicago	280	5600	[1]	Priv	V	U	Oth	Q†	7/15 Oth	5	9	0	4	1	9	7	
2371	Chicago City-Wide C Chicago	252	800	[1] 3300	Pub	V	U	None	S[5]	FF=FA		5	0	7	0	1	1	
2372	Daley C Chicago	1905	800	[1] 3300	Pub	V	U	ACT	E[5]	Oth	2	6	0	5	0	5	2	
2373	Danville Area CC Danville	1178	900	[1] 4000	Pub	S		A=S	E[5]	9/30 Oth	7	6	0	1	1	4	3	3
2374	Dawson Tech Inst Chicago	1800	600	[1] 3800	Pub	V	U	None	O[5]	Oth		5	0	9			0	0
2375	DuPage,C of Glen Ellyn	8049	900	[1] 3800	Pub	S		A/S	Q[5]		1	6	0	1	0	6	1	2
2376	Elgin CC Elgin	4337	1000	[1] 4100	Pub	M	S	A=S	S[5]	FA/FF	3	5	0	2	1	6	3	2
2377	Frontier CC Fairfield	221	600	[1] 4600	Pub	T		Oth	S[5]	Oth	1	7	0	1		9	1	1
2378	Graham Hosp Sch Nsg Canton	37	4200[2]	500	Priv	S[8]		7/01 A/S	S†	FFS	9	9	1	1		9		
2379	Harold Washington C Chicago	1623	800	[1] 4100	Pub	V	U	A/S	E[5]	Oth	4	6	0	8	1	3		2

Educational Programs Available — College Transfer Courses

Sequence Number	Agriculture	Bus-Commerce	Communications	Education	Engineering	Fine, Applied Arts	Foreign Lang	Health	Home Ec	Humanities	Mathematics	Computer/Info Sci	Biological Sci	Physical Sci	Social Sci
2359	■	■	■			■	■			■	■	■	■	■	■
2360		■								■	■				■
2361	■	■	■	■	■	■	■	■	■	■	■	■	■	■	■
2362	■	■	■	■	■	■	■	■	■	■	■	■	■	■	■
2363	■	■	■	■	■	■	■	■	■	■	■	■	■	■	■
2364						■									
2365		■	■	■	■	■	■	■		■	■		■	■	■
2366															
2367		■	■	■	■	■	■	■		■	■	■	■	■	■
2368	■	■	■	■	■	■	■	■	■	■	■	■	■	■	■
2369	■	■	■	■	■	■	■	■	■	■	■	■	■	■	■
2370															
2371		■		■		■	■	■	■	■	■	■	■	■	■
2372		■	■	■	■	■	■			■	■	■	■	■	■
2373	■	■	■	■	■	■		■		■	■		■	■	■
2374															
2375		■	■	■	■	■	■	■		■	■	■	■	■	■
2376		■	■	■	■	■	■	■		■	■		■	■	■
2377	■	■	■	■	■	■	■	■	■	■	■		■	■	■
2378															
2379		■	■	■	■	■	■	■	■	■	■	■	■	■	■

Educational Programs Available — Career-oriented Programs

Sequence Number	Agri				Business						Arts			Health					Math			SocSci			Technical/Skilled Trades										
	Ag Business	Ag/Farm Mgmt	Ag Mechanics/Tech	Horticulture	Accounting	Bus Mgmt & Admin	Hotel/Rest Mgmt	Office Mgmt	Marketing/Purchasing	Secretarial Studies	Architecture Tech	Applied Design	Photography/Cinema	Dental Assistant	Medical or Lab Tech	Nursing (RN)	Nursing (LPN)	Radiologic Technology	Computer Prog	Data Processing Tech	Computer Operating	Crim Just/Law Enforce	Parks/Rec Mgmt	Social Work	Air/Refrig/Heat Tech	Auto Body Repair	Auto Mechanics	Carpentry/Constr	Drafting/Eng Draft	Electric Eng Tech	Civil Eng Tech	Indus/Mfg Eng Tech	Mech Eng Tech	Machinework	Welding
2359					■					■																	■								
2360			■		■	■		■	■	■				■			■										■					■			■
2361						■				■		■				■	■			■	■	■			■	■	■	■	■						■
2362		■	■	■	■	■	■	■	■	■						■					■						■	■	■			■			■
2363	■	■	■					■		■							■				■	■				■	■		■						■
2364																																			
2365	■			■	■	■			■	■		■			■	■		■		■	■	■			■	■	■	■	■	■					■
2366																		■																	
2367					■	■	■	■	■	■				■		■	■		■	■	■	■			■	■	■		■	■	■		■	■	■
2368	■		■		■	■		■	■	■						■			■							■	■								
2369	■	■			■	■			■	■						■	■	■		■	■	■			■	■	■		■					■	■
2370								■		■																									
2371					■	■	■	■	■	■	■						■	■		■	■	■	■	■	■	■	■		■	■	■			■	■
2372					■	■			■	■						■			■			■													
2373	■		■	■	■				■	■							■		■	■		■					■		■	■			■		■
2374								■		■							■				■								■					■	
2375				■	■	■	■	■	■	■	■		■			■		■	■	■	■	■	■		■		■		■	■		■	■	■	■
2376					■	■	■	■	■	■				■		■			■	■		■			■		■		■						
2377								■		■																									
2378																■																			
2379					■	■	■	■	■	■			■							■		■		■											

▲ Sequence Number—indicates the order of the college in this book only. Do *not* use this number with admissions tests or need analysis services.

[1] No campus room and board facilities
[2] Room only or board only
[3] Most freshmen required to live on campus
[4] City or district residency requirements
[5] Accredited by regional accrediting association or a recognized candidate for accreditation
[6] All female freshman class
[7] All male freshman class
[8] Some admission selectivity; not all hs graduates accepted
[9] Requirements more stringent for nonresidents
†Accredited by a nationally recognized accrediting body other than one of the regional accrediting associations

Illinois
(continued)

Sequence Number	School name (upper entry) City (lower entry)	Enrollment	Costs: Resident tuition/fees + room/board	Costs: Room/board (upper entry) Nonresident tuition/fees (lower entry)	Gen. Info.: Affiliation (upper entry) Religious observance (lower entry)	Gen. Info.: Size of community	Gen. Info.: Type of community	Admissions: Fall term application deadline (upper entry) Test required or desired (lower entry)	Admissions: Calendar	Financial Aid: Fall term application deadline (upper entry) Forms to be filed (lower entry)	No. in 10 who- -have need, rec some aid	-are women	-live on campus	-are minority students	-are nonresidents	-return as sophomores	-complete assoc degree	-transfer to 4-year college
2380	Highland CC Freeport	995	700	[1] 3300	Pub	S			E [5]	FF=FA	4	6	0	1	0		5	6
2381	Ill Central C East Peoria	3999	1000	[1] 3800	Pub	M	S	A/S	E [5]	FA/FF	2	6	0	2	1	8		5
2382	Ill Tech C Chicago	120	4500	[1]	Priv	V [8]	U	9/07 A=S	T [5]	9/02 Oth	9	2	0	8	1	8	3	
2383	Ill Valley CC Oglesby	1741	700	[1] 3600	Pub	T			E [5]		5	5	0	1	0	5	6	5
2384	John A Logan C Carterville	2367	600	[1] 4700	Pub	T		ACT	E [5]	Oth	3	6	0	1		4	2	3
2385	John Wood CC Quincy	780	1000	[1] 4600	Pub	S		A=S	O [5]	FF=FA	7	5	0	1	0	7		2
2386	Joliet JC Joliet	3004	900	[1] 3800	Pub	M		8/05 A/S	E [5]	FF/FA	2	6	0	1	0	6	2	3
2387	Kankakee CC Kankakee	1000	800	[1] 5600	Pub	S		Oth	E [5]	FF=FA	5	6	0	1	0			
2388	Kaskaskia C Centralia	1160	800	[1] 4300	Pub	S		A/S	E [5]		2	6	0	1	1	3	5	3
2389	Kennedy-King C Chicago	2138	800	[1] 2600	Pub	V	U	8/20 Oth	S [5]	10/10 FF=FA	8	6	0	9	1		1	2
2390	Kishwaukee C Malta	1164	900	[1] 3300	Pub	M		A/S	E [5]	FF=FA	5	6	0	1	1	6	6	4
2391	Lake County,C of Grayslake	2682	1000	[1] 5300	Pub	T		A=S	E [5]	FF/FA		6	0	1	1			
2392	Lake Land C Mattoon	1628	1000	[1] 4200	Pub	S		ACT	S [5]	FFS	6	6	0	1	0	7		
2393	Lewis & Clark CC Godfrey	1728	800	[1] 4700	Pub	S		None	E [5]	Oth	6	6	0	1	0	3	3	
2394	Lexington Inst Chicago	35	6500	2700	Cath S	V [8]	U [6]		E [5]	FF=FA	8	9	3	7	1	8	7	1
2395	Lincoln C Lincoln	595	10400 [3]	3400	Priv	S [8]		A/S	E [5]	8/15 Oth	8	4	9	2	1	8	7	8
2396	Lincoln Land CC Springfield	2076	900	[1] 4100	Pub	M	S	A/S	E [5]	FF/FA	1	6	0	1	0			
2397	Lincoln Trail C Robinson	480	600	[1] 4600	Pub	T		Oth	S [5]	Oth	6	6	0	1	1	8	8	3
2398	MacCormac JC Chicago	500	5900	[1]	Priv	V [8]	U	A/S	Q [5]	FF=FA	8	7	0	5	1	7	7	2
2399	Malcolm X C Chicago	1956	800	[1] 4100	Pub	V	U	Oth	E [5]	FF=FA	9	5	0	9			2	5
2400	McHenry Co C Crystal Lake	843	900	[1] 4500	Pub	S		A/S	E [5]	FF/FA	3	6	0	1	1	5	4	4
2401	Methodist Ctr Sc Nsg Peoria	226	5800 [2]	1200	Meth	M [8]	U	A=S	S †	6/01 FFS	9	9	4	1	1	6		
2402	Midstate C Peoria	417	5300 [2]	1300	Priv	L [8]	U	0/01 None	Q [5]	10/01 FF=FA	8	9	1	1	1	8	7	1

Educational Programs Available — College Transfer Courses

Sequence Number	Agriculture	Bus-Commerce	Communications	Education	Engineering	Fine, Applied Arts	Foreign Lang	Health	Home Ec	Humanities	Mathematics	Computer/Info Sci	Biological Sci	Physical Sci	Social Sci
2380	■	■		■	■	■	■	■	■	■	■	■	■	■	■
2381	■	■	■	■	■	■	■	■	■	■	■	■	■	■	■
2382		■													
2383	■	■	■	■	■	■	■	■	■	■	■	■	■	■	■
2384	■	■	■	■	■	■	■			■	■	■	■	■	■
2385	■	■	■	■	■	■	■	■		■	■	■	■	■	■
2386	■	■	■	■	■	■	■		■	■	■	■	■	■	■
2387	■			■	■	■		■		■	■				■
2388	■	■	■	■	■	■	■	■	■	■	■	■	■	■	■
2389			■	■	■	■	■	■	■	■	■				■
2390	■	■	■	■	■	■	■	■	■	■	■	■	■	■	■
2391	■	■	■		■	■	■	■	■	■	■	■	■	■	■
2392	■	■	■	■	■	■	■	■	■	■	■	■	■	■	■
2393	■	■	■	■	■	■	■	■	■	■	■	■	■	■	■
2394		■	■			■			■	■					
2395	■	■	■	■		■	■	■		■	■	■	■	■	■
2396	■	■	■	■	■	■	■	■	■	■	■	■	■	■	■
2397	■	■	■	■	■	■	■	■	■	■	■	■	■	■	■
2398		■		■											■
2399		■	■	■	■	■	■	■	■	■	■	■	■	■	■
2400	■	■	■	■	■	■	■	■	■	■	■	■	■	■	■
2401															
2402		■						■	■			■			

Educational Programs Available — Career-oriented Programs

Sequence Number	Agri: Ag Business	Agri: Ag/Farm Mgmt	Agri: Ag Mechanics/Tech	Agri: Horticulture	Business: Accounting	Business: Bus Mgmt & Admin	Business: Hotel/Rest Mgmt	Business: Office Mgmt	Business: Marketing/Purchasing	Business: Secretarial Studies	Arts: Architecture Tech	Arts: Applied Design	Arts: Photography/Cinema	Health: Dental Assistant	Health: Medical or Lab Tech	Health: Nursing (RN)	Health: Nursing (LPN)	Health: Radiologic Technology	Math: Computer Prog	Math: Data Processing Tech	Math: Computer Operating	SocSci: Crim Just/Law Enforce	SocSci: Parks/Rec Mgmt	SocSci: Social Work	Technical/Skilled Trades: Air/Refrig/Heat Tech	Auto Body Repair	Auto Mechanics	Carpentry/Constr	Drafting/Eng Draft	Electric Eng Tech	Civil Eng Tech	Indus/Mfg Eng Tech	Mech Eng Tech	Machinework	Welding
2380	■				■	■			■	■						■	■		■	■				■	■	■	■		■				■	■	■
2381	■			■	■	■		■	■	■	■			■	■	■		■		■	■	■		■	■		■					■	■	■	■
2382					■					■																			■				■		
2383	■	■	■		■	■		■		■				■	■	■	■	■	■	■		■	■				■		■	■			■	■	■
2384					■			■	■	■				■		■	■			■	■	■			■	■	■	■	■					■	■
2385	■				■	■				■						■	■		■						■	■	■	■	■	■				■	■
2386	■	■		■	■	■	■		■	■						■	■		■	■	■	■				■	■	■	■	■			■	■	■
2387	■	■	■		■			■	■	■					■	■	■	■	■			■			■		■		■					■	■
2388	■	■			■	■			■	■				■		■	■	■	■	■	■	■			■	■	■		■				■		■
2389					■	■			■	■										■		■		■	■		■								
2390	■	■	■	■	■	■			■	■						■	■	■	■	■	■	■				■	■		■	■		■	■	■	■
2391				■	■	■		■	■	■					■	■		■	■	■	■	■		■	■	■	■	■	■		■		■	■	■
2392	■	■	■		■	■		■	■	■				■		■	■		■	■		■					■		■	■	■		■		■
2393	■	■			■	■	■	■	■	■				■	■	■			■	■	■	■				■	■	■	■	■				■	■
2394							■																												
2395	■	■				■																													
2396	■	■	■	■	■				■	■				■		■		■	■	■	■	■		■	■		■			■	■				■
2397								■		■									■	■	■				■				■				■	■	
2398					■	■	■	■		■																									
2399					■	■		■	■	■					■	■		■	■	■		■		■											
2400	■			■	■	■			■												■	■					■		■				■		
2401																■																			
2402					■				■	■									■	■															

▲ Sequence Number—indicates the order of the college in this book only. Do *not* use this number with admissions tests or need analysis services.

[1] No campus room and board facilities
[2] Room only or board only
[3] Most freshmen required to live on campus
[4] City or district residency requirements
[5] Accredited by regional accrediting association or a recognized candidate for accreditation
[6] All female freshman class
[7] All male freshman class
[8] Some admission selectivity; not all hs graduates accepted
[9] Requirements more stringent for nonresidents
†Accredited by a nationally recognized accrediting body other than one of the regional accrediting associations

Illinois
(continued)

Sequence Number	School name (upper entry) / City (lower entry)	Enrollment	Resident tuition/fees + room/board	Room/board (upper entry) / Nonresident tuition/fees (lower entry)	Affiliation (upper entry) / Religious observance (lower entry)	Size of community	Type of community	Fall term application deadline (upper entry) / Test required or desired (lower entry)	Calendar	Fall term application deadline (upper entry) / Forms to be filed (lower entry)	-have need, rec some aid	-are women	-live on campus	-are minority students	-are nonresidents	-return as sophomores	-complete assoc degree	-transfer to 4-year college
2403	Montay C Chicago	120	5000	[1]	Cath	V[8]	U		E[5]	Oth	3	8	0	5	0	8	8	8
2404	Moraine Valley CC Palos Hills	4595	1200	[1] 4400	Pub	S			E[5]	FF=FA		6	0	1			5	7
2405	Morrison Inst Techn Morrison	233	5500[2,3]	800	Priv	T		A=S	T†	9/15 FF=FA	7	1	5	1	1	8	7	1
2406	Morton C Cicero	878	1100	[1] 4300	Pub	M		8/26 A/S	E[5]	5/01 Oth	2	6	0	3	0	2		4
2407	Mt Vernon Chrstn C Mount Vernon	0	3600	[1]	Bapt OS	S		9/01 A/S	S†			5	0	1				
2408	Northwestern Bus C Chicago	693	4500	[1]	Priv	V[8]	U	A/S	Q†	FF=FA	7	8	0	7	0	6	4	1
2409	NW Bus C-SW Cam Palos Hills	86	4200	[1]	Priv	S[8]		Oth	Q†	9/30	5	8	0	1	0	9		
2410	Oakton CC Des Plaines	2424	600	[1] 3000	Pub	L	S	A/S	E[5]	6/01 Oth	1	5	0	1	1	5	2	2
2411	Olive-Harvey C Chicago	3657	800	[1] 3400	Pub	V	U	Oth	E[5]	Oth	6	6	0	9	1	6	2	1
2412	Olney Central C Olney	820	600	[1] 4600	Pub	S		Oth	S[5]	Oth	6	7	0	1	1	8	6	5
2413	Parkland C Champaign	3283	1000	[1] 4800	Pub	M	S		E[5]	FF=FA	6	6	0	1	1	4	6	3
2414	Prairie St C Chicago Heights	3000	1100	[1] 3400	Pub	M	S	A/S	E[5]	7/01 FF/FA	2	5	0	1	1	3	2	4
2415	Ravenswood Sch Nsg Chicago	87	4000[2]		Priv	V[8]	U	Oth	S†	6/01 FAF	9	9	2	4	0	8	9	
2416	Rend Lake C Ina	1450	600	[1] 3700	Pub	T		Oth	E[5]	10/31 Oth	9	5	0	1	0	6		6
2417	Richland CC Decatur	975	900	[1] 5700	Pub	M		A/S	E[5]	FF=FA	2	6	0	1	0	1	1	2
2418	Robert Morris C Springfield	134	6900	[1]	Priv	M[8]		9/01 A=S	Q[5]	FAF	9	8		1	1	9	9	1
2419	Robert Morris C Chi Chicago	1627	7400	[1]	Priv	V[8]	U	9/01 A=S	Q[5]	FAF	9	7	0	7	1	9	9	4
2420	Rock Valley C Rockford	2181	3600	2800 7600	Pub	L	S	Oth	E[5]	FF=FA	1	5	0	1	1	4	2	2
2421	Saint Augustine C Chicago	1355	4000	[1]	Oth	V	U	8/15 A=S	E[5]	7/15 FAF	3	7	0	9	0	8	3	2
2422	Saint Francis Rad Peoria	18	2300[2]	1800	Cath	M[8]	U	2/01 ACT	Q†	None	0	5	0	0	0	9		
2423	Sauk Valley CC Dixon	1038	900	[1] 2700	Pub	S		None	E[5]	FF/FA	6	6	0	1	0	4	6	2
2424	Shawnee C Ullin	550	700	[1] 3000	Pub	T		A/S	E[5]	FF/FA	7	6	0	1	0	7	6	5
2425	South Chicago Rad Chicago	21	900	[1]	UCC	V[8]	U	Oth	E†	6/01 FF=FA	8	5	0	4	2	7		

Educational Programs Available

College Transfer Courses

Sequence Number	Agriculture	Bus-Commerce	Communications	Education	Engineering	Fine, Applied Arts	Foreign Lang	Health	Home Ec	Humanities	Mathematics	Computer/Info Sci	Biological Sci	Physical Sci	Social Sci
2403		■	■	■		■	■			■	■	■	■		■
2404		■	■	■	■	■	■	■	■	■	■	■	■	■	■
2405						■									
2406	■	■	■	■	■	■	■	■		■	■	■	■	■	■
2407										■					
2408		■	■					■				■			
2409		■	■								■	■			
2410		■	■	■	■	■	■	■	■	■	■	■	■	■	■
2411		■		■	■	■	■	■		■	■	■	■	■	■
2412		■	■	■	■	■	■	■		■	■	■	■	■	■
2413	■	■	■	■	■	■	■	■	■	■	■	■	■	■	■
2414	■	■	■	■	■	■	■	■		■	■	■	■	■	■
2415															
2416	■	■	■	■	■	■	■	■	■	■	■	■	■	■	■
2417	■	■	■	■	■	■	■	■	■	■	■	■	■	■	■
2418		■						■				■			
2419		■	■			■		■				■			
2420	■	■	■	■	■	■	■	■	■	■	■	■	■	■	■
2421		■										■			■
2422								■							
2423		■	■	■	■	■	■	■	■	■	■	■	■	■	■
2424		■	■	■	■	■	■	■	■	■	■		■	■	■
2425															

Career-oriented Programs

Sequence Number	Agri: Ag Business	Agri: Ag/Farm Mgmt	Agri: Ag Mechanics/Tech	Agri: Horticulture	Business: Accounting	Business: Bus Mgmt & Admin	Business: Hotel/Rest Mgmt	Business: Office Mgmt	Business: Marketing/Purchasing	Business: Secretarial Studies	Arts: Architecture Tech	Arts: Applied Design	Arts: Photography/Cinema	Health: Dental Assistant	Health: Medical or Lab Tech	Health: Nursing (RN)	Health: Nursing (LPN)	Health: Radiologic Technology
2403																		
2404						■	■	■	■	■					■	■		■
2405											■							
2406					■			■	■	■				■		■		
2407										■								
2408					■	■	■	■	■	■								
2409					■	■		■	■	■								
2410					■	■	■	■	■	■					■	■	■	
2411					■	■			■	■						■		
2412					■			■		■						■	■	■
2413	■	■	■		■	■	■	■	■	■	■			■		■	■	■
2414						■		■		■	■					■		
2415																■		
2416	■	■	■			■				■		■				■	■	
2417	■			■	■	■		■	■	■								
2418					■	■				■								
2419					■	■				■								
2420			■		■	■		■	■	■				■		■		
2421										■								
2422																		
2423					■	■		■	■	■					■	■	■	■
2424	■	■		■	■	■	■			■						■	■	■
2425																		■

Sequence Number	Math: Computer Prog	Math: Data Processing Tech	Math: Computer Operating	SocSci: Crim Just/Law Enforce	SocSci: Parks/Rec Mgmt	SocSci: Social Work	Technical/Skilled Trades: Air/Refrig/Heat Tech	Auto Body Repair	Auto Mechanics	Carpentry/Constr	Drafting/Eng Draft	Electric Eng Tech	Civil Eng Tech	Indus/Mfg Eng Tech	Mech Eng Tech	Machinework	Welding
2403																	
2404	■		■	■	■		■		■	■	■	■			■	■	■
2405													■	■	■		
2406		■					■		■		■						■
2407																	
2408	■	■	■														
2409	■																
2410	■	■		■		■	■		■		■	■		■	■	■	■
2411		■											■				
2412				■				■	■	■							■
2413	■	■	■	■					■	■	■	■	■		■	■	
2414	■	■		■			■		■		■				■	■	■
2415																	
2416				■					■	■		■			■		■
2417		■	■	■							■	■		■		■	■
2418																	
2419		■									■						
2420	■	■	■	■	■				■	■	■	■		■	■		■
2421																	
2422																	
2423	■	■	■	■		■	■	■	■		■	■			■	■	
2424		■	■	■	■	■	■										■
2425																	

▲ **Sequence Number—indicates the order of the college in this book only. Do *not* use this number with admissions tests or need analysis services.**

[1] No campus room and board facilities
[2] Room only or board only
[3] Most freshmen required to live on campus
[4] City or district residency requirements
[5] Accredited by regional accrediting association or a recognized candidate for accreditation
[6] All female freshman class
[7] All male freshman class
[8] Some admission selectivity; not all hs graduates accepted
[9] Requirements more stringent for nonresidents
†Accredited by a nationally recognized accrediting body other than one of the regional accrediting associations

Illinois
(continued)

Sequence Number	School name (upper entry) City (lower entry)	Enrollment	Resident tuition/fees + room/board	Room/board (upper entry) Nonresident tuition/fees (lower entry)	Affiliation (upper entry) Religious observance (lower entry)	Size of community	Type of community	Fall term application deadline (upper entry) Test required or desired (lower entry)	Calendar	Fall term application deadline (upper entry) Forms to be filed (lower entry)	-have need, rec some aid	-are women	-live on campus	-are minority students	-are nonresidents	-return as sophomores	-complete assoc degree	-transfer to 4-year college
			Costs		Gen. Info.			Admissions		Financial Aid	Student Profile: No. in 10 who-							
2426	South Suburban C South Holland	2043	1200	[1] 4400	Pub	S		A=S	E[5]	Oth	6	6	0	4	1	4	4	
2427	Southeastern Ill C Harrisburg	1133	700	[1] 2500	Pub	S		8/20 Oth	E[5]		6	5	0	1	1	6	7	5
2428	Spoon River C Canton	900	1100	[1] 5900	Pub	S		Oth	E[5]	FF=FA	7	5	0	1	1	3	4	3
2429	Springfield C Ill Springfield	179	4800	[1]	Cath	M[8]		A/S	4[5]	FF/FA	9	7	0	1		8	8	9
2430	St Francis Sch Nsg Evanston	90	7000[2]	1000	Cath	M[8]	S	Oth	O†	FAF	7	9	2	3	1	9		
2431	St Johns Sch Resp Th Springfield	6	4000	[1]	Cath	M[8]	U[6]	Oth	T†	FA/FF	7	9	0	0	0	0		
2432	State CC East St Louis	759	900	[1] 5500	Pub	M	U		4[5]	FAF	8	7	0	9		5		
2433	Swedish-Amer Sch Rad Rockford	18	900[2]	100 1100	Priv	L[8]	U	3/01 Oth	O†		0	9	5	0		9	9	
2434	Triton C River Grove	4274	1100	[1] 5000	Pub	S		A=S	S[5]	FF=FA	4	5	0	4	0	5	2	5
2435	Truman C Chicago	3000	800	[1] 4100	Pub	V	U	ACT	E[5]	7/01 Oth	4	6	0	7	1	2	1	
2436	United Med Ctr Nsg Moline	61	6000	3000	Luth	L[8]	U	A/S	O†	5/01 FF/FA	7	9	4	1	1	7	9	
2437	United Samaritan RT Danville	17	1200	[1]	Cath	S[8]		4/01 A/S	T†	Oth	3	9	0	0	1	9		
2438	Wabash Valley C Mt Carmel	720	600	[1] 4600	Pub	T		Oth	S[5]	FFS	6	2	0	1	1	8	6	3
2439	Waubonsee CC Sugar Grove	1356	1000	[1] 4400	Pub	M	S		E[5]	FF=FA		6	0	2	0	6	1	
2440	William R Harper C Palatine	4485	900	[1] 4400	Pub	S		Oth	E[5]	FA/FF	1	6	0	2	0	5	2	5
2441	Worsham C Mort Sci Des Plaines	150	5600	[1]	Priv	L[8]	S	A=S	O†	FF=FA	3	1	0	4	5			
2442	Wright C Chicago	1646	800	[1] 4100	Pub	V	U	8/30 ACT	E[5]	10/01 FF/FA	4	5	0	5	1		3	2
Indiana																		
2443	Ancilla C Donaldson	175	1900	[1]	Cath	T[8]		Oth	S[5]	5/01 FA/FF	5	7	0	1	0	7	5	7
2444	Holy Cross C Notre Dame	387	4100	[1]	Cath	L[8]	S	7/01 S/A	E[5]	3/01 FAF	3	4	0	1	3	5	1	8
2445	Ind Voc Tech-Lafayet Lafayette	437	1500	[1] 2700	Pub	M		Oth	E[5]	FA/FF	5	6	0	1	0		2	
2446	Ind Voc Tech-S Bend South Bend	499	1500	[1] 2700	Pub	L	U	Oth	E[5]	FA/FF	4	5		1			2	
2447	Ind Voc Tech-Wabash Terre Haute	932	1500	[1] 2700	Pub	M	S	Oth	E[5]	FA/FF	6	6	0	1	1		3	1

Educational Programs Available — College Transfer Courses

Sequence Number	Agriculture	Bus-Commerce	Communications	Education	Engineering	Fine, Applied Arts	Foreign Lang	Health	Home Ec	Humanities	Mathematics	Computer/Info Sci	Biological Sci	Physical Sci	Social Sci
2426		■	■	■	■	■	■	■	■	■	■		■	■	■
2427	■	■	■	■	■	■	■	■	■	■	■	■	■	■	■
2428	■	■	■	■	■	■		■		■	■	■	■	■	■
2429		■		■	■	■	■	■	■	■	■		■	■	■
2430								■							
2431															
2432		■	■	■	■	■	■	■		■	■	■	■	■	■
2433															
2434	■	■	■	■	■	■	■	■	■	■	■	■	■	■	■
2435		■	■	■	■	■	■			■	■	■	■	■	
2436															
2437															
2438	■	■	■	■		■	■	■	■	■	■	■	■	■	■
2439		■	■	■	■	■	■		■	■	■	■	■	■	■
2440	■	■	■	■	■	■	■	■	■	■	■	■	■	■	■
2441															
2442	■	■	■	■	■	■	■	■		■	■	■	■	■	■
2443		■	■	■	■	■		■		■	■	■	■	■	■
2444		■					■			■	■	■			■
2445															
2446															
2447															

Educational Programs Available — Career-oriented Programs (Agri, Business, Arts, Health)

Sequence Number	Ag Business	Ag/Farm Mgmt	Ag Mechanics/Tech	Horticulture	Accounting	Bus Mgmt & Admin	Hotel/Rest Mgmt	Office Mgmt	Marketing/Purchasing	Secretarial Studies	Architecture Tech	Applied Design	Photography/Cinema	Dental Assistant	Medical or Lab Tech	Nursing (RN)	Nursing (LPN)	Radiologic Technology
2426					■	■		■	■	■						■	■	■
2427			■	■	■	■				■						■	■	
2428		■						■		■							■	
2429																		
2430																■		
2431																		
2432				■				■		■								
2433																		■
2434				■	■	■	■	■	■	■				■	■	■		■
2435					■	■			■	■						■		
2436																■		
2437																		■
2438	■							■	■	■								
2439					■	■		■	■	■						■		
2440				■	■	■		■	■	■	■					■	■	
2441																		
2442									■	■		■						■
2443					■	■		■		■		■						
2444																		
2445			■		■	■		■		■				■		■	■	
2446					■	■		■	■	■			■		■	■	■	
2447					■	■			■	■			■		■		■	■

Educational Programs Available — Career-oriented Programs (Math, SocSci, Technical/Skilled Trades)

Sequence Number	Computer Prog	Data Processing Tech	Computer Operating	Crim Just/Law Enforce	Parks/Rec Mgmt	Social Work	Air/Refrig/Heat Tech	Auto Body Repair	Auto Mechanics	Carpentry/Constr	Drafting/Eng Draft	Electric Eng Tech	Civil Eng Tech	Indus/Mfg Eng Tech	Mech Eng Tech	Machinework	Welding
2426	■	■		■		■				■	■	■			■		■
2427		■	■	■				■	■								■
2428	■	■		■					■		■	■					■
2429																	
2430																	
2431																	
2432	■	■	■	■			■	■	■	■	■						■
2433																	
2434		■	■	■	■		■		■	■	■	■		■	■	■	■
2435	■	■															
2436																	
2437																	
2438					■				■			■					
2439	■	■		■			■	■	■		■			■	■	■	■
2440		■	■	■	■		■				■				■		
2441																	
2442		■		■							■	■			■		
2443	■			■													
2444																	
2445	■						■	■	■		■					■	■
2446	■		■				■		■		■					■	■
2447	■	■						■	■		■						■

▲ **Sequence Number—indicates the order of the college in this book only. Do *not* use this number with admissions tests or need analysis services.**

1 No campus room and board facilities
2 Room only or board only
3 Most freshmen required to live on campus
4 City or district residency requirements
5 Accredited by regional accrediting association or a recognized candidate for accreditation
6 All female freshman class
7 All male freshman class
8 Some admission selectivity; not all hs graduates accepted
9 Requirements more stringent for nonresidents
†Accredited by a nationally recognized accrediting body other than one of the regional accrediting associations

Indiana
(continued)

Sequence Number	School name (upper entry) / City (lower entry)	Enrollment	Resident tuition/fees + room/board	Room/board (upper entry) / Nonresident tuition/fees (lower entry)	Affiliation (upper entry) / Religious observance (lower entry)	Size of community	Type of community	Fall term application deadline (upper entry) / Test required or desired (lower entry)	Calendar	Fall term application deadline (upper entry) / Forms to be filed (lower entry)	-have need, rec some aid	-are women	-live on campus	-are minority students	-are nonresidents	-return as sophomores	-complete assoc degree	-transfer to 4-year college
			Costs		**Gen. Info.**			**Admissions**		**Financial Aid**	**Student Profile: No. in 10 who-**							
2448	Ind Voc Tech-Whitewr / Richmond	341	1500	[1] / 2700	Pub	S		Oth	E [5]	FA/FF	8	6	0	1	1		3	
2449	Ind Voc-Tec C NE Ind / Fort Wayne	716	1500	[1] / 2700	Pub	L	U	Oth	E [5]	FA/FF	3	5	0	1	1		2	
2450	Ind Voc-Tech C / Columbus	605	1500	[1] / 2700	Pub	M		Oth	E [5]	FA/FF	6	6	0	1	0		2	
2451	Ind Voc-Tech C-East / Muncie	694	1500	[1] / 2700	Pub	S		Oth	E [5]	FA/FF	7	6	0	1	0		2	
2452	Ind Voc-Tech C-NW / Gary	887	1500	[1] / 2700	Pub	L	U	Oth	E [5]	FA/FF	9	5	0	4	0		1	
2453	Ind Voc-Tech C-SC / Sellersburg	556	1500	[1] / 2700	Pub	T		Oth	E [5]	FA/FF	7	5	0	1	1		2	
2454	Ind Voc-Tech C-SE / Madison	257	1500	[1] / 2700	Pub	T		Oth	E [5]	FA/FF	7	7	0	1	0		2	
2455	Ind Voc-Tech Cen Ind / Indianapolis	1533	1500	[1] / 2700	Pub	V	U	Oth	E [5]	FA/FF	5	5	0	2	0		1	
2456	Ind Voc-Tech Kokomo / Kokomo	276	1500	[1] / 2700	Pub	M	S	Oth	E [5]	FA/FF	8	5	0	1	0		1	0
2457	Ind Voc-Tech SW Ind / Evansville	583	1500	[1] / 2700	Pub	L	U	Oth	E [5]	FA/FF	5	5	0	1	1		2	
2458	International Bus C / Fort Wayne	504	9800 [2]	2800	Priv	L [8]	S	None	O †	Oth	4	8	2	1	1	7	9	2
2459	Mid Amer Funeral C / Jeffersonville	65	4900	[1]	Priv	S		None	O †	FF/FA	7	1	0	1	2	8	8	
2460	Saint Elizabeth Nsg / Lafayette	126	10400	4800	Cath / OS	S [8]		6/01 / A=S	E †	3/01 / FA/FF	9	9	4	1	1	8	7	
2461	Vincennes U / Vincennes	6300	4500	2900 / 7300	Pub	S		8/21 / A=S	S [5]	3/01 / FA/FF	6	4	5	1	1		6	5
Iowa																		
2462	Allen Hosp Sch Nsg / Waterloo	95	4600 [2]	1200	Priv	M [8]		8/01 / ACT	O †	FF/FA	6	9	3	1	0	8		
2463	Amer Inst Commerce / Davenport	666	4400	[1]	Priv	L [8]	S	9/11 / Oth	O †	FF/FA	8	8	0	1	3			1
2464	Amer Inst of Bus / Des Moines	788	5900 [23]	1400	Priv	L [8]	U	9/01 / Oth	Q [5]	4/01 / FF=FA	8	8	8	1	1	7	6	1
2465	Clinton CC / Clinton	624	1300	[1] / 1900	Pub	S		9/04 / A/S	S [5]	FF=FA	8	7	0	1	1	3	3	4
2466	Covenant Sch Rad / Waterloo	17	500	[1]	Cath	M [8]	S	ACT	E †	FF=FA	6	8	0	0	0			
2467	Des Moines Ar CC-Ank / Ankeny	4620	1300	[1] / 2400	Pub	S		Oth	E [5]	FF/FA	6	6	0	1	1		4	3
2468	Des Moines Ar CC-Bne / Boone	1000	1200	[1] / 1800	Pub	S		None	S [5]	FF/FA	6	6	0	1	1	4	4	2
2469	Des Moines Ar CC-Crl / Carroll	470	1200	[1] / 2400	Pub	S		A=S	S [5]	FF/FA	7	8		1		8	9	7

Educational Programs Available — College Transfer Courses

Sequence Number	Agriculture	Bus-Commerce	Communications	Education	Engineering	Fine, Applied Arts	Foreign Lang	Health	Home Ec	Humanities	Mathematics	Computer/Info Sci	Biological Sci	Physical Sci	Social Sci
2448															
2449															
2450															
2451															
2452															
2453															
2454															
2455															
2456															
2457															
2458															
2459								■							
2460															
2461	■	■	■	■	■	■	■	■	■	■	■	■	■	■	■
2462															
2463															
2464		■										■			
2465	■	■	■	■	■	■	■	■		■	■	■	■	■	■
2466															
2467	■	■	■	■	■	■	■	■	■	■	■	■	■	■	■
2468	■	■	■	■	■	■	■	■	■	■	■	■	■	■	■
2469		■	■	■		■	■	■		■	■	■	■	■	■

Educational Programs Available — Career-oriented Programs (Agri: cols 1–4; Business: 5–10; Arts: 11–13; Health: 14–18; Math: 19–21; SocSci: 22–24; Technical/Skilled Trades: 25–35)

Sequence Number	Ag Business	Ag/Farm Mgmt	Ag Mechanics/Tech	Horticulture	Accounting	Bus Mgmt & Admin	Hotel/Rest Mgmt	Office Mgmt	Marketing/Purchasing	Secretarial Studies	Architecture Tech	Applied Design	Photography/Cinema	Dental Assistant	Medical or Lab Tech	Nursing (RN)	Nursing (LPN)	Radiologic Technology	Computer Prog	Data Processing Tech	Computer Operating	Crim Just/Law Enforce	Parks/Rec Mgmt	Social Work	Air/Refrig/Heat Tech	Auto Body Repair	Auto Mechanics	Carpentry/Constr	Drafting/Eng Draft	Electric Eng Tech	Civil Eng Tech	Indus/Mfg Eng Tech	Mech Eng Tech	Machinework	Welding
2448					■	■		■		■						■	■		■						■		■	■						■	■
2449					■	■		■	■	■							■		■						■	■	■	■	■					■	■
2450					■	■		■		■			■				■		■	■					■		■	■	■						
2451					■	■		■	■	■							■		■	■					■	■	■	■	■					■	■
2452					■	■			■	■							■		■		■				■	■	■	■	■					■	■
2453					■	■		■		■			■			■	■		■						■	■	■	■	■						■
2454					■	■				■							■		■	■						■	■		■						■
2455					■	■	■	■	■	■							■	■	■	■					■	■	■	■	■					■	■
2456					■	■			■	■									■	■					■	■	■	■	■					■	■
2457					■	■		■	■	■			■			■	■		■	■					■		■		■						■
2458					■	■		■	■	■																									
2459																																			
2460																■																			
2461	■			■	■		■	■	■	■	■				■	■	■		■	■	■	■	■			■	■	■	■	■	■			■	■
Iowa																																			
2462																■																			
2463					■	■	■	■	■	■					■				■	■	■														
2464					■	■	■	■	■	■									■	■	■														
2465								■		■						■	■												■						
2466																		■																	
2467	■		■	■	■	■	■	■	■	■				■	■	■	■		■	■		■		■	■	■	■	■	■	■				■	■
2468					■	■		■		■						■	■		■	■	■		■												
2469						■				■							■																		

▲ **Sequence Number—indicates the order of the college in this book only. Do *not* use this number with admissions tests or need analysis services.**

[1] No campus room and board facilities
[2] Room only or board only
[3] Most freshmen required to live on campus
[4] City or district residency requirements
[5] Accredited by regional accrediting association or a recognized candidate for accreditation
[6] All female freshman class
[7] All male freshman class
[8] Some admission selectivity; not all hs graduates accepted
[9] Requirements more stringent for nonresidents
†Accredited by a nationally recognized accrediting body other than one of the regional accrediting associations

Iowa
(continued)

Sequence Number	School name (upper entry) City (lower entry)	Enrollment	Resident tuition/fees + room/board	Room/board (upper entry) Nonresident tuition/fees (lower entry)	Affiliation (upper entry) Religious observance (lower entry)	Size of community	Type of community	Fall term application deadline (upper entry) Test required or desired (lower entry)	Calendar	Fall term application deadline (upper entry) Forms to be filed (lower entry)	-have need, rec some aid	-are women	-live on campus	-are minority students	-are nonresidents	-return as sophomores	-complete assoc degree	-transfer to 4-year college
2470	Des Moines Ar CC-Urb Des Moines	1600	1000	[1] 2000	Pub	L	U	Oth	S [5]			6		3			6	2
2471	Ellsworth CC Iowa Falls	809	4000 [3]	2400 5400	Pub	T		ACT	E [5]	FF/FA	8	5	7	1	1	6	6	5
2472	Hawkeye Inst Techn Waterloo	1467	1400	[1] 2700	Pub	M [8]		Oth	Q [5]	FF/FA	8	5	0	1	1	6	6	1
2473	Indian Hills CC Centerville	502	1300	[1] 1800	Pub	T		A/S	Q [5]	FF=FA	6	6	0	1	1	7	7	6
2474	Indian Hills CC Ottumwa	2219	3000	1800 3600	Pub	S			Q [5]	FF=FA	6	6		1	1	3	8	6
2475	Iowa Central CC Eagle Grove	63	1000	[1] 1500	Pub	T		A=S	E [5]	FF=FA	6	7	0	1	0	4	4	2
2476	Iowa Central CC Fort Dodge	1540	3900	2500 4400	Pub	S		A/S	E [5]	FF=FA	6	5	3	1	1	3	6	7
2477	Iowa Central CC Webster City	160	1600	[1] 2300	Pub	S		A/S	E [5]	FF/FA		5	0	1	1	6	5	
2478	Iowa Lakes CC Emmetsburg	601	1800 [2]	500 2400	Pub	T		9/01 A/S	E [5]	FF=FA	9	4	0	1	1	4	7	
2479	Iowa Lakes CC Estherville	794	3400	2100 4000	Pub	T		A/S	E [5]	FF=FA	9	5	1	1	1	6	8	6
2480	Iowa Meth Sch Rad Des Moines	25	400	[1]	Meth	L [8]	U	ACT	O	FF=FA	3	7	0	0	0	9		
2481	Iowa Methodist Nsg Des Moines	189	5200	1600	Meth	L [8]	U	A/S	E †	7/01 FF=FA	9	9	6	1	1	8		
2482	Iowa Western CC Clarinda	191	2600 [2]	1100 3200	Pub	T		9/02 A/S	E [5]	FF=FA	6	6	0	1	0	4	3	7
2483	Iowa Western CC Council Bluffs	1639	4300	2800 5000	Pub	M	S	Oth	S [5]	5/30 FA/FF	8	5	2	1	1	5	5	4
2484	J E M H Sch Nsg Council Bluffs	82	4800	2600	Priv	M [8]		8/01 ACT	S †	6/01 FF=FA	9	9	3	0	1	9		
2485	J E M H Sch Rad Tech Council Bluffs	10	3000	2500	Priv	M [8]		3/31 ACT	O †		4	9	4	0	0	9	9	2
2486	Kirkwood CC Cedar Rapids	4699	1300	[1] 2600	Pub	M	S	Oth	E [5]	6/01 FF/FA	7	6	0	1	1			
2487	Marian Hlth Ctr Rad Sioux City	16	2000	[1]	Cath	M [8]		3/01 A/S	O †	4/15 FF/FA	8	1	0	0	4	0	7	2
2488	Marshalltown CC Marshalltown	835	1500	[1] 2900	Pub	S		A/S	E [5]	3/01 FA/FF	5	7	0	1	1	6	3	4
2489	Mercy Hosp Sch Nsg Des Moines	143	3100 [2]	1100	Cath	L [8]	U	ACT	S †	5/01 FF/FA	8	9	5	1	1	8	8	
2490	Mercy Hosp Sch Rad Des Moines	16	2100 [2]	1600	Cath	L [8]	U	5/01 ACT	S	10/31 FFS	4	8	4	0	0	9		
2491	Mercy-St Luke Rad T Cedar Rapids	33	2800 [2]	2200	Priv	M [8]	U	ACT	O †	5/01 FF=FA	8	9	5	0	1	9		1
2492	Muscatine CC Muscatine	1167	1300	[1] 1900	Pub	S		Oth	S [5]	8/15 FF=FA	5	6	0	1	1	6	4	6

Educational Programs Available — College Transfer Courses

Sequence Number	Agriculture	Bus-Commerce	Communications	Education	Engineering	Fine, Applied Arts	Foreign Lang	Health	Home Ec	Humanities	Mathematics	Computer/Info Sci	Biological Sci	Physical Sci	Social Sci
2470		■						■							■
2471	■	■	■	■	■	■	■	■	■	■	■	■	■	■	■
2472															
2473		■	■	■	■	■	■	■	■	■	■	■			■
2474		■	■	■	■	■	■			■	■				■
2475		■		■		■				■	■		■	■	■
2476	■	■	■	■	■	■	■	■	■	■	■	■	■	■	■
2477	■	■	■	■	■	■	■	■	■	■	■	■	■	■	■
2478	■	■		■	■		■	■		■	■	■	■	■	■
2479	■	■	■	■	■	■	■	■		■	■	■	■	■	■
2480															
2481								■							
2482	■	■	■	■	■	■		■	■	■	■	■	■	■	■
2483	■	■	■	■	■	■	■	■		■	■	■	■	■	■
2484								■							
2485															
2486	■	■	■	■	■	■	■	■	■	■	■	■	■	■	■
2487								■							
2488	■	■	■	■	■	■	■	■	■	■	■	■	■	■	■
2489															
2490															
2491															
2492	■	■	■	■	■	■	■	■		■	■	■	■	■	■

Educational Programs Available — Career-oriented Programs (Agri, Business, Arts, Health)

Sequence Number	Ag Business	Ag/Farm Mgmt	Ag Mechanics/Tech	Horticulture	Accounting	Bus Mgmt & Admin	Hotel/Rest Mgmt	Office Mgmt	Marketing/Purchasing	Secretarial Studies	Architecture Tech	Applied Design	Photography/Cinema	Dental Assistant	Medical or Lab Tech	Nursing (RN)	Nursing (LPN)	Radiologic Technology
2470					■			■		■								
2471	■	■			■	■		■	■	■						■	■	
2472	■	■	■	■	■			■	■	■	■		■	■	■	■	■	
2473										■							■	
2474			■	■						■						■	■	■
2475										■						■	■	
2476	■	■		■	■			■	■	■						■	■	
2477		■		■						■						■	■	
2478	■	■	■	■			■	■	■	■						■	■	
2479					■	■		■				■						
2480																		■
2481																■		
2482					■	■				■							■	
2483	■	■	■						■	■	■			■		■	■	
2484																■		
2485																		■
2486	■	■	■	■	■	■	■	■	■	■				■		■	■	
2487																		
2488					■	■				■				■		■	■	
2489																■		
2490																		■
2491															■			■
2492	■	■			■	■		■		■							■	

Educational Programs Available — Career-oriented Programs (Math, SocSci, Technical/Skilled Trades)

Sequence Number	Computer Prog	Data Processing Tech	Computer Operating	Crim Just/Law Enforce	Parks/Rec Mgmt	Social Work	Air/Refrig/Heat Tech	Auto Body Repair	Auto Mechanics	Carpentry/Constr	Drafting/Eng Draft	Electric Eng Tech	Civil Eng Tech	Indus/Mfg Eng Tech	Mech Eng Tech	Machinework	Welding
2470	■	■	■														
2471				■	■	■				■							
2472				■			■	■	■		■		■		■	■	■
2473										■	■						
2474	■			■			■	■	■	■	■					■	
2475																	
2476				■		■			■	■	■	■				■	■
2477	■	■		■	■	■											
2478								■	■	■							■
2479	■	■	■	■	■						■						
2480																	
2481																	
2482				■											■		
2483	■	■							■				■		■	■	■
2484																	
2485																	
2486	■	■	■		■	■	■	■	■	■	■	■		■	■	■	■
2487																	
2488	■										■	■			■	■	
2489																	
2490																	
2491																	
2492									■					■			■

▲ **Sequence Number—indicates the order of the college in this book only. Do *not* use this number with admissions tests or need analysis services.**

[1] No campus room and board facilities
[2] Room only or board only
[3] Most freshmen required to live on campus
[4] City or district residency requirements
[5] Accredited by regional accrediting association or a recognized candidate for accreditation
[6] All female freshman class
[7] All male freshman class
[8] Some admission selectivity; not all hs graduates accepted
[9] Requirements more stringent for nonresidents
†Accredited by a nationally recognized accrediting body other than one of the regional accrediting associations

Iowa
(continued)

Sequence Number	School name (upper entry) City (lower entry)	Enrollment	Costs: Resident tuition/fees + room/board	Costs: Room/board (upper entry) Nonresident tuition/fees (lower entry)	Gen. Info.: Affiliation (upper entry) Religious observance (lower entry)	Gen. Info.: Size of community	Gen. Info.: Type of community	Admissions: Fall term application deadline (upper entry) Test required or desired (lower entry)	Admissions: Calendar	Financial Aid: Fall term application deadline (upper entry) Forms to be filed (lower entry)	No. in 10 who- -have need, rec some aid	-are women	-live on campus	-are minority students	-are nonresidents	-return as sophomores	-complete assoc degree	-transfer to 4-year college
2493	National Ed Ctr Iowa West Des Moines	400	5100	[1]	Priv	L	S	None	Q †		9	2	0	1	1	8	6	1
2494	North Iowa Area CC Mason City	1867	3600	2200 4200	Pub	S		9/09	E [5]	9/01 FF/FA	6	5	2	1	1	4	5	5
2495	Northeast Iowa CC Calmar	564	2000	[1] 3900	Pub	T		Oth	Q [5]	FF=FA	8	5	0	1	1	3	2	
2496	Northeast Iowa CC Calmar	1224	1600	[1] 2900	Pub	M		Oth	Q [5]	4/01 FF/FA		7	0	1	1	2	4	
2497	Northwest Iowa Tech Sheldon	445	1200	[1] 1700	Pub	T		None	Q [5]	4/20 FF/FA	8	3	0	1			8	1
2498	Palmer Chiro Sch Tec Davenport	62	1300	[1]	Priv	L [8]	U	None	T [5]	9/15 Oth	9	9	0	1	4	9	9	1
2499	Scott CC Bettendorf	3300	1300	[1] 1900	Pub	L	S	9/01 A/S	E [5]	9/01 FF/FA	6	6	0	1	1	2	3	2
2500	Southeastern CC West Burlington	2018	3300	2200 4100	Pub	S		A/S	E [5]	4/15 FF=FA	6	6	1	1	1	6	3	5
2501	Southeastern CC S Ia Keokuk	603	1100	[1] 1700	Pub	S		Oth	E [5]	8/01 FF=FA	5	7	0	1	3			
2502	Southwestern CC Creston	1181	3600	2200 4000	Pub	T		A/S	S [5]	FF/FA	7	5	1	1	1	5	7	8
2503	Spencer Sch Business Spencer	169	8000 [2]	1800	Priv	S [8]		A=S	O †	7/01 FF/FA	9	9	8	1	1		9	1
2504	St Joseph Rad Tech Mason City	14	500	[1]	Cath	S [8]		A/S	S †			8	0	0	0	9	9	
2505	St Luke's Sch Nsg Sioux City	127	6300 [2]	1700	Oth	M [8]		8/15 A/S	O †	FF/FA	7	9	4	1	1	6		
2506	Waldorf C Forest City	517	10000 [3]	2900	Luth OS	T [8]		A/S	S [5]	9/01 FF/FA	7	4		1	3	7	8	8
2507	Western Iowa Tech CC Sioux City	1678	2800 [2]	1600 3900	Pub	M		ACT	O [5]	FF/FA	7	5		1	1	2	4	1

Kansas

Sequence Number	School name (upper entry) City (lower entry)	Enrollment	Costs: Resident tuition/fees + room/board	Costs: Room/board (upper entry) Nonresident tuition/fees (lower entry)	Gen. Info.: Affiliation (upper entry) Religious observance (lower entry)	Gen. Info.: Size of community	Gen. Info.: Type of community	Admissions: Fall term application deadline (upper entry) Test required or desired (lower entry)	Admissions: Calendar	Financial Aid: Fall term application deadline (upper entry) Forms to be filed (lower entry)	No. in 10 who- -have need, rec some aid	-are women	-live on campus	-are minority students	-are nonresidents	-return as sophomores	-complete assoc degree	-transfer to 4-year college
2508	Allen Co CC Iola	465	3100	2300 4300	Pub	T		9/06 A/S	E [5]		8	6	5	1	1	7	7	7
2509	Barton Co CC Great Bend	920	2700	2000 4100	Pub	S		A/S	E [5]	FF/FA	8	5	2	1	1	7		5
2510	Brown Mackie C Salina	430	6000	[1]	Priv	S [8]		Oth	O [5]		9	8	0	2	1	3		
2511	Butler Co CC El Dorado	1101	3000	2100 4800	Pub	S		8/20 A/S	E [5]	5/01 FFS		5	1	1	1	6	3	3
2512	Cloud Co CC Concordia	652	2700	1900 3600	Pub	T		A/S	E [5]	FF/FA	6	7	4	1	1	6	4	3
2513	Coffeyville CC Coffeyville	1037	3000	2200 4400	Pub	S		A/S	E [5]	FF/FA	6	4	2	2	1	7	4	5
2514	Colby CC Colby	643	3200	2400 4400	Pub	T		A/S	E [5]	FF/FA	8	5	3	1	1	8	6	5

Educational Programs Available — College Transfer Courses

Sequence Number	Agriculture	Bus-Commerce	Communications	Education	Engineering	Fine, Applied Arts	Foreign Lang	Health	Home Ec	Humanities	Mathematics	Computer/Info Sci	Biological Sci	Physical Sci	Social Sci
2493															
2494	■	■	■	■	■	■	■	■	■	■	■	■	■	■	■
2495	■	■	■			■		■	■			■			■
2496		■	■		■			■				■			■
2497		■													
2498								■							
2499		■	■	■	■	■	■	■		■	■	■	■	■	■
2500	■	■	■	■	■	■	■	■	■	■	■	■	■	■	■
2501		■	■	■	■	■	■	■	■	■	■	■	■	■	■
2502		■		■	■	■		■		■	■	■			■
2503		■						■							
2504															
2505															
2506	■	■	■	■	■	■	■	■	■	■	■	■	■	■	■
2507	■	■	■		■			■				■			■
2508	■	■	■	■	■	■	■	■	■	■	■	■	■	■	■
2509	■	■	■	■	■	■	■	■	■	■	■	■	■	■	■
2510															
2511	■	■	■	■	■	■	■	■	■	■	■	■	■	■	■
2512	■	■	■	■	■	■	■	■	■	■	■	■	■	■	■
2513	■	■	■	■	■	■	■	■	■	■	■	■	■	■	■
2514	■	■	■	■	■	■	■	■	■	■	■	■	■	■	■

Educational Programs Available — Career-oriented Programs (Agri, Business, Arts, Health)

Sequence Number	Agri: Ag Business	Ag/Farm Mgmt	Ag Mechanics/Tech	Horticulture	Business: Accounting	Bus Mgmt & Admin	Hotel/Rest Mgmt	Office Mgmt	Marketing/Purchasing	Secretarial Studies	Arts: Architecture Tech	Applied Design	Photography/Cinema	Health: Dental Assistant	Medical or Lab Tech	Nursing (RN)	Nursing (LPN)	Radiologic Technology
2493																		
2494	■	■			■	■		■	■	■						■	■	
2495	■		■		■				■	■				■		■	■	■
2496					■			■	■	■				■		■	■	■
2497	■				■				■	■							■	
2498																		
2499					■			■		■				■	■	■	■	■
2500	■				■			■							■	■	■	
2501								■		■						■	■	
2502			■		■				■	■						■	■	
2503					■	■	■	■	■	■								
2504																		■
2505																■		
2506					■	■				■								
2507			■		■	■			■	■				■		■	■	
2508	■	■			■			■	■	■								
2509	■	■			■			■	■	■					■	■	■	
2510					■	■	■	■	■	■								
2511	■	■			■	■		■	■	■						■	■	
2512	■	■			■	■	■	■		■						■	■	
2513	■	■			■	■				■						■	■	
2514	■	■				■		■		■		■				■	■	

Educational Programs Available — Career-oriented Programs (Math, SocSci, Technical/Skilled Trades)

Sequence Number	Math: Computer Prog	Data Processing Tech	Computer Operating	SocSci: Crim Just/Law Enforce	Parks/Rec Mgmt	Social Work	Technical/Skilled Trades: Air/Refrig/Heat Tech	Auto Body Repair	Auto Mechanics	Carpentry/Constr	Drafting/Eng Draft	Electric Eng Tech	Civil Eng Tech	Indus/Mfg Eng Tech	Mech Eng Tech	Machinework	Welding
2493																	
2494			■	■			■		■		■	■			■		■
2495								■	■	■						■	■
2496	■		■				■		■	■					■	■	■
2497	■						■	■	■	■	■	■			■	■	■
2498																	
2499	■	■		■			■	■	■		■	■				■	
2500	■	■		■			■	■	■		■			■	■	■	■
2501			■				■										
2502								■	■	■	■						■
2503																	
2504																	
2505																	
2506	■	■		■													
2507	■	■		■	■		■	■	■	■	■			■	■		■
2508	■			■			■			■	■	■		■		■	■
2509	■	■	■	■		■			■		■						
2510	■		■														
2511	■	■	■	■				■	■	■	■	■				■	■
2512		■															
2513	■							■	■	■	■					■	■
2514			■	■													

▲ **Sequence Number—indicates the order of the college in this book only. Do *not* use this number with admissions tests or need analysis services.**

[1] No campus room and board facilities
[2] Room only or board only
[3] Most freshmen required to live on campus
[4] City or district residency requirements
[5] Accredited by regional accrediting association or a recognized candidate for accreditation
[6] All female freshman class
[7] All male freshman class
[8] Some admission selectivity; not all hs graduates accepted
[9] Requirements more stringent for nonresidents
†Accredited by a nationally recognized accrediting body other than one of the regional accrediting associations

Kansas
(continued)

Sequence Number	School name (upper entry) City (lower entry)	Enrollment	Resident tuition/fees + room/board	Room/board (upper entry) Nonresident tuition/fees (lower entry)	Affiliation (upper entry) Religious observance (lower entry)	Size of community	Type of community	Fall term application deadline (upper entry) Test required or desired (lower entry)	Calendar	Fall term application deadline (upper entry) Forms to be filed (lower entry)	-have need, rec some aid	-are women	-live on campus	-are minority students	-are nonresidents	-return as sophomores	-complete assoc degree	-transfer to 4-year college
			Costs		**Gen. Info.**			**Admissions**		**Financial Aid**	**Student Profile — No. in 10 who-**							
2515	Cowley Co CC Arkansas City	910	3100	2300 4400	Pub	S		9/01 A/S	E[5]	4/01 FF=FA	7	5	1	1	1	5	1	1
2516	Dodge City CC Dodge City	870	3100	2400 4300	Pub	S		 Oth	E[5]	 FFS	9	6	4	1	1	7	7	7
2517	Donnelly C Kansas City	362	2300	[1]	Cath	M	U	 A=S	E[5]	 FFS	9	7	0	8	1	7	4	5
2518	Fort Scott CC Fort Scott	849	2900	2200 4300	Pub	S		 None	E[5]	 Oth	8	5	2	1	2	7	4	7
2519	Garden City CC Garden City	727	3200	2400 4300	Pub	S		9/05 Oth	S[5]	 FF/FA	7	6	1	2	1	6	4	6
2520	Haskell Indian JC Lawrence	831	0		Pub	M[8]	S	7/10	E[5]	5/01 FFS	3	5	8	9	9	5	3	1
2521	Hesston C Hesston	448	9200[3]	3300	Oth OS	T[8]		9/01 A/S	4[5]	8/31 FF/FA	8	5	8	2	7	7	7	5
2522	Highland CC Highland	562	3500[3]	2600 5300	Pub	T		8/10 A/S	E[5]	4/01 FFS	8	5	6	2	1	7	8	7
2523	Hutchinson CC Hutchinson	1468	2700	2000 4100	Pub	S		 A/S	E[5]	 FF/FA	7	6		1				
2524	Independence CC Independence	683	3100	2400 4400	Pub	S		 A/S	S[5]	 Oth		6	2	2	1	5	4	8
2525	Johnson Co CC Overland Park	4056	800	[1] 2800	Pub	M	S		E[5]	 FF/FA		6	0	1	1	2	1	4
2526	Kansas C of Tech Salina	311	3700[3]	2700 5900	Pub	S		9/10 A/S	E[5]	8/15 FFS	9	3	1	1	1	5		1
2527	Kansas City Kans CC Kansas City	1800	700	[1] 2000	Pub	M	S	8/13 None	S[5]	4/18 FF/FA	7	6	0	2	1			
2528	Labette CC Parsons	781	2700	2100 4600	Pub	S		8/20 A/S	E[5]	 FFS	8	7	1	1	1	5	4	3
2529	Neosho Co CC Chanute	1650	2800[3]	2200 3900	Pub	S		8/31 A/S	E[5]	5/01 FFS	9	5	2	1	1	8	7	6
2530	Newman Hosp Sch Nsg Emporia	65	2500[23]	1100	Pub	S[8]		7/15 ACT	E†	 Oth	7	7	2	1	0	9		
2531	North Central Vo-Tec Beloit	385	3400	2500 8300	Pub	T		 None	S[5]	 FF=FA	8	2	2	0	0	1		
2532	Pratt CC Pratt	750	3400	2500 4400	Pub	T		9/01 A/S	S[5]	 FF/FA	8	4	4	1	1	6	3	6
2533	Saint Francis Rad Wichita	18	1700	[1]	Cath	L[8]	U	6/01 ACT	O†		8	7	0	1	0	9	9	
2534	Saint Mary's C Saint Marys	35	6000	2000	Cath OS	T[8]		8/01 A=S	S	8/01 None	3	6	8	1	7	7	9	2
2535	Seward Co CC Liberal	442	3000	2300 4400	Pub	S		8/20	E[5]		9	6	3	1	2	6	7	3
2536	Topeka Tech C Topeka	175	5600	[1]	Priv	M	S	 Oth	Q†	 Oth	9	5	0	3		9	7	
2537	Wesley Ctr Rad Techn Wichita	14	1200	[1]	Priv	L[8]	U	4/30	S†	 Oth	5	7	0	0	0	9		

Educational Programs Available — College Transfer Courses; Career-oriented Programs: Agri, Business

Sequence Number	Agriculture	Bus-Commerce	Communications	Education	Engineering	Fine, Applied Arts	Foreign Lang	Health	Home Ec	Humanities	Mathematics	Computer/Info Sci	Biological Sci	Physical Sci	Social Sci	Ag Business	Ag/Farm Mgmt	Ag Mechanics/Tech	Horticulture	Accounting	Bus Mgmt & Admin	Hotel/Rest Mgmt	Office Mgmt	Marketing/Purchasing	Secretarial Studies
2515	■	■	■	■	■	■		■	■	■	■	■	■	■	■	■	■			■				■	■
2516	■	■	■	■	■	■	■	■	■	■	■	■	■	■	■	■	■	■		■	■		■	■	■
2517		■	■	■	■	■	■	■	■	■	■	■	■	■	■					■	■		■		■
2518	■	■	■	■	■	■	■	■	■	■	■	■	■	■	■										
2519	■	■	■	■	■	■	■	■	■	■	■	■	■	■	■	■	■	■		■	■		■	■	■
2520		■		■		■		■		■	■	■		■	■					■	■		■		■
2521		■		■	■	■		■				■	■	■	■						■	■	■		■
2522	■	■	■	■	■	■	■	■	■	■	■	■	■	■	■	■	■			■			■		■
2523	■	■	■	■	■	■	■	■	■	■	■	■	■	■	■	■	■	■		■	■	■		■	■
2524		■	■	■	■	■	■	■	■	■	■	■	■	■	■					■			■	■	■
2525	■	■	■	■	■	■	■	■	■	■	■	■	■	■	■	■				■	■	■		■	■
2526		■								■	■	■		■											
2527	■	■	■	■	■	■	■	■	■	■	■	■	■	■	■								■	■	■
2528	■	■	■	■	■	■	■	■	■	■	■	■	■	■	■					■			■	■	■
2529	■	■	■	■	■	■	■	■	■	■	■	■	■	■	■					■	■		■	■	■
2530								■																	
2531																■	■							■	■
2532	■	■	■	■	■	■	■	■	■	■	■	■	■	■	■	■	■	■					■	■	■
2533								■																	
2534							■			■	■			■	■										
2535	■	■	■	■	■	■	■	■	■	■	■	■		■	■		■			■			■	■	■
2536																				■	■	■	■	■	■
2537								■																	

Educational Programs Available — Career-oriented Programs: Arts, Health, Math, SocSci, Technical/Skilled Trades

Sequence Number	Architecture Tech	Applied Design	Photography/Cinema	Dental Assistant	Medical or Lab Tech	Nursing (RN)	Nursing (LPN)	Radiologic Technology	Computer Prog	Data Processing Tech	Computer Operating	Crim Just/Law Enforce	Parks/Rec Mgmt	Social Work	Air/Refrig/Heat Tech	Auto Body Repair	Auto Mechanics	Carpentry/Constr	Drafting/Eng Draft	Electric Eng Tech	Civil Eng Tech	Indus/Mfg Eng Tech	Mech Eng Tech	Machinework	Welding
2515										■	■	■					■	■	■					■	■
2516						■	■			■	■				■	■	■	■		■				■	■
2517											■			■											
2518						■	■																		
2519	■		■			■			■	■	■	■				■	■	■	■	■	■	■			■
2520		■		■						■															
2521						■				■	■						■								
2522										■	■	■													
2523				■		■		■	■	■	■	■		■	■		■	■	■	■		■		■	■
2524						■	■		■	■	■					■	■		■		■			■	■
2525					■	■		■		■		■			■		■		■	■	■	■			■
2526									■	■											■	■	■		
2527					■				■	■	■	■			■		■		■	■					
2528						■	■	■		■		■													
2529						■	■			■	■	■				■	■	■	■						■
2530						■																			
2531							■			■					■		■	■		■					■
2532						■	■										■	■		■			■		■
2533								■																	
2534																									
2535					■	■	■		■	■	■	■													
2536									■	■	■														
2537								■																	

▲ Sequence Number—indicates the order of the college in this book only. Do *not* use this number with admissions tests or need analysis services.

1 No campus room and board facilities
2 Room only or board only
3 Most freshmen required to live on campus
4 City or district residency requirements
5 Accredited by regional accrediting association or a recognized candidate for accreditation
6 All female freshman class
7 All male freshman class
8 Some admission selectivity; not all hs graduates accepted
9 Requirements more stringent for nonresidents
†Accredited by a nationally recognized accrediting body other than one of the regional accrediting associations

Kentucky

Sequence Number	School name (upper entry) City (lower entry)	Enrollment	Costs: Resident tuition/fees + room/board	Costs: Room/board (upper entry) Nonresident tuition/fees (lower entry)	Gen. Info.: Affiliation (upper entry) Religious observance (lower entry)	Gen. Info.: Size of community	Gen. Info.: Type of community	Admissions: Fall term application deadline (upper entry) Test required or desired (lower entry)	Admissions: Calendar	Financial Aid: Fall term application deadline (upper entry) Forms to be filed (lower entry)
2538	Ashland CC Ashland	3061	700	[1] 2000	Pub	S		8/28 ACT	E [5]	6/15 FAF
2539	Bowling Gr Voc-Tech Bowling Green	640	200	[1] 500	Pub	S		Oth	O [5]	None
2540	Central Kentucky V-T Lexington	443	400	[1] 800	Pub	L	U	8/19 Oth	Q [5]	5/01 Oth
2541	Elizabethtown CC Elizabethtown	1474	600	[1] 1900	Pub	S			S [5]	FAF
2542	Hazard CC Hazard	715	600	[1] 1900	Pub	T		8/15 ACT	E [5]	4/15 FAF
2543	Hazard St Voc-Tech Hazard	560	300	[1] 600	Pub	T		Oth	O [5]	Oth
2544	Henderson CC Henderson	612	600	[1] 1900	Pub	S		9/01 ACT	E [5]	4/01 FAF
2545	Hopkinsville CC Hopkinsville	740	700	[1] 2000	Pub	S		8/24 ACT	E [5]	4/01 FA/FF
2546	Jefferson CC Louisville	2265	600	[1] 1300	Pub	L	U	8/30 ACT	E [5]	6/15 FAF
2547	Jefferson St Vo-Tec Louisville	797	300	[1] 600	Pub	V	U	Oth	Q [5]	Oth
2548	Lees C Jackson	290	6500 [3]	2500	Pres O	T [8]		8/31 A/S	S [5]	8/31 FAF
2549	Lexington CC Lexington	2399	4600	2900 7600	Pub	M	U	8/22 ACT	E [5]	Oth
2550	Madisonville CC Madisonville	2136	600	[1] 1900	Pub	S		ACT	E [5]	4/01 FAF
2551	Maysville CC Maysville	412	600	[1] 1900	Pub	T			E [5]	FAF
2552	Natl Ed Ctr Ky Louisville	380	4900	[1]	Priv	L [8]	S	Oth	Q †	FF=FA
2553	North Kentucky St VT Covington	600	600	[1] 1100	Pub	M	S	8/01 Oth	O [5]	Oth
2554	Owensboro CC Owensboro	1004	600	[1] 1900	Pub	M		ACT	S [5]	4/01 FAF
2555	Owensboro JC of Bus Owensboro	295	3600	[1]	Priv	M [8]		Oth	Q †	FF/FA
2556	Paducah Area Voc Ctr Paducah	40	600	[1] 7100	Pub	S		Oth	O [5]	Oth
2557	Paducah CC Paducah	2812	600	[1] 1900	Pub	S		8/22 ACT	E [5]	4/01 FAF
2558	Prestonsburg CC Prestonsburg	1469	600	[1] 1900	Pub	T		ACT	S [5]	FAF
2559	S Ohio C-N KY Cam Fort Mitchell	308	5600	[1]	Priv	M [8]	S	Oth	Q [5]	Oth
2560	Saint Catharine C Saint Catharine	161	6300	2500	Cath OS	T		A=S	E [5]	3/01 FA/FF

Student Profile — No. in 10 who-

Sequence Number	-have need, rec some aid	-are women	-live on campus	-are minority students	-are nonresidents	-return as sophomores	-complete assoc degree	-transfer to 4-year college
2538	4	7	0	1	1	7	4	4
2539	3	4	0	1	1	8		
2540	6	4	0	1	0	7		
2541	6	7	0	1	1			
2542	9	7	0	1	0		4	
2543	7	3	0	1	0			
2544	4	7	0	1	1			
2545	4	7	0	1	1	3	6	3
2546	4	6	0	1	1	4	3	3
2547	4	4	0	4			7	1
2548	9	7	6	1	1	6	5	5
2549		6	1	1	1	4	6	2
2550	6	7	0	1	0	6	3	2
2551	6	7	0	1	1		5	5
2552	9	2	0	3	2	7	3	
2553	3	4	0	1	1		9	1
2554	4	7	0	1	0	5	1	6
2555	9	9	0	1		7		
2556	3	3	0	1		8		
2557	6	7	0	1	1		2	4
2558	6	7	0	1	1	6	3	6
2559	9	6	0	1		7	6	2
2560	9	6	2	2	1	5	5	4

Educational Programs Available — College Transfer Courses

Sequence Number	Agriculture	Bus-Commerce	Communications	Education	Engineering	Fine, Applied Arts	Foreign Lang	Health	Home Ec	Humanities	Mathematics	Computer/Info Sci	Biological Sci	Physical Sci	Social Sci
2538	■	■	■	■	■	■	■	■	■	■	■	■	■	■	■
2539															
2540															
2541	■	■	■	■	■	■	■	■	■	■	■	■	■	■	■
2542		■	■	■	■	■		■		■	■		■	■	■
2543															
2544	■	■	■	■	■	■	■	■	■	■	■		■	■	■
2545	■	■	■	■	■	■		■	■	■	■	■	■	■	■
2546	■	■	■	■	■	■	■	■	■	■	■	■	■	■	■
2547															
2548	■	■	■	■	■	■		■	■	■	■	■	■	■	■
2549		■										■			
2550	■	■	■	■	■	■	■	■	■	■	■	■	■	■	■
2551	■	■	■	■	■	■	■	■	■	■	■	■	■	■	■
2552															
2553															
2554		■	■	■		■	■	■	■	■	■	■	■	■	■
2555															
2556															
2557	■	■	■	■	■	■		■	■	■	■	■	■	■	■
2558	■	■	■	■	■	■		■	■	■	■	■	■	■	■
2559		■						■				■			
2560	■	■	■	■	■	■	■			■	■	■	■	■	■

Educational Programs Available — Career-oriented Programs (Agri, Business, Arts, Health)

Sequence Number	Agri: Ag Business	Agri: Ag/Farm Mgmt	Agri: Ag Mechanics/Tech	Agri: Horticulture	Business: Accounting	Business: Bus Mgmt & Admin	Business: Hotel/Rest Mgmt	Business: Office Mgmt	Business: Marketing/Purchasing	Business: Secretarial Studies	Arts: Architecture Tech	Arts: Applied Design	Arts: Photography/Cinema	Health: Dental Assistant	Health: Medical or Lab Tech	Health: Nursing (RN)	Health: Nursing (LPN)	Health: Radiologic Technology
2538					■	■		■	■	■						■		
2539									■	■				■			■	■
2540					■			■	■	■				■			■	
2541						■			■	■						■		
2542						■										■		
2543					■			■		■							■	
2544										■					■	■		
2545	■					■		■		■						■		
2546					■	■		■		■					■	■		
2547				■	■			■		■				■			■	■
2548					■	■		■		■								
2549					■	■			■	■	■					■		■
2550					■	■				■					■	■		■
2551	■					■		■	■	■						■		
2552					■	■		■		■								
2553								■		■								
2554					■	■												■
2555					■	■		■		■								
2556																		
2557					■	■		■	■	■						■		
2558								■	■							■		
2559										■								
2560	■	■		■		■		■		■								

Educational Programs Available — Career-oriented Programs (Math, SocSci, Technical/Skilled Trades)

Sequence Number	Math: Computer Prog	Math: Data Processing Tech	Math: Computer Operating	SocSci: Crim Just/Law Enforce	SocSci: Parks/Rec Mgmt	SocSci: Social Work	Air/Refrig/Heat Tech	Auto Body Repair	Auto Mechanics	Carpentry/Constr	Drafting/Eng Draft	Electric Eng Tech	Civil Eng Tech	Indus/Mfg Eng Tech	Mech Eng Tech	Machinework	Welding
2538	■		■									■					
2539							■	■	■	■	■	■		■		■	■
2540							■	■	■	■	■	■		■		■	■
2541		■															
2542		■	■														
2543							■	■	■	■	■	■	■			■	■
2544		■															
2545		■		■													
2546	■	■	■	■					■			■			■		
2547	■	■	■				■	■	■	■		■		■		■	■
2548						■						■	■				
2549												■			■		
2550		■										■			■		
2551		■															
2552		■	■						■								
2553		■	■				■	■	■	■	■	■				■	■
2554		■	■			■											
2555	■	■	■														
2556								■	■	■		■				■	■
2557		■	■														
2558																	
2559		■															
2560							■	■	■		■						■

▲ Sequence Number—indicates the order of the college in this book only. Do *not* use this number with admissions tests or need analysis services.

[1] No campus room and board facilities
[2] Room only or board only
[3] Most freshmen required to live on campus
[4] City or district residency requirements
[5] Accredited by regional accrediting association or a recognized candidate for accreditation
[6] All female freshman class
[7] All male freshman class
[8] Some admission selectivity; not all hs graduates accepted
[9] Requirements more stringent for nonresidents
†Accredited by a nationally recognized accrediting body other than one of the regional accrediting associations

Kentucky
(continued)

Sequence Number	School name (upper entry) City (lower entry)	Enrollment	Costs: Resident tuition/fees + room/board	Costs: Room/board (upper entry) Nonresident tuition/fees (lower entry)	Gen. Info.: Affiliation (upper entry) Religious observance (lower entry)	Gen. Info.: Size of community	Gen. Info.: Type of community	Admissions: Fall term application deadline (upper entry) Test required or desired (lower entry)	Admissions: Calendar	Financial Aid: Fall term application deadline (upper entry) Forms to be filed (lower entry)	No. in 10 who- -have need, rec some aid	-are women	-live on campus	-are minority students	-are nonresidents	-return as sophomores	-complete assoc degree	-transfer to 4-year college
2561	Somerset CC Somerset	1205	600	[1] 1900	Pub	S		 ACT	E [5]	4/01 FAF	7	7	0	1	1	7	5	5
2562	Southeast CC Cumberland	2065	600	[1] 1900	Pub	T		 ACT	E [5]	4/01 FAF	9	7	0	1		6	4	3
2563	Sue Bennett C London	359	5600	2200	Meth S	T		 A/S	E [5]	 FA/FF	7	6	1	1	1	6	1	6
2564	Watterson C Louisville	400	6700	[1]	Priv	L	S	 Oth	Q †	 Oth	8	7		2	1		5	
Louisiana																		
2565	Alexandria Voc-Tech Alexandria	400	300	[1] 600	Pub	M	S	 Oth	O [5]	 Oth	3	5	0	4	1		3	1
2566	Baton Rouge Rad Tech Baton Rouge	21	1500	[1]	Priv	L [8]	U	3/15 ACT	S †			5	0				7	0
2567	Baton Rouge Sch Nsg Baton Rouge	49	2300	[1]	Priv	L [8]	U	9/01 ACT	O †	 FFS	5	9	0	1	0	6		
2568	Baton Rouge Voc-Tech Baton Rouge	625	300	[1] 500	Pub	L	U	 Oth	O [5]	10/01 Oth		3	0	4	1			
2569	Bossier Parish CC Bossier City	1242	500	[1] 1000	Pub	L	S	8/11 ACT	E [5]	 FFS		7	0	1		6		6
2570	Charity Hosp Sch Nsg New Orleans	346	800 [2]	800	Pub	V [8]	U	5/01 Oth	S †	6/01 FFS	6	9	9	3	0			
2571	Charity Surg Tech New Orleans	46	1500	[1]	Pub	V	U	6/01 A/S	T †	 None		9	0	5	1			
2572	Collier Voc-Tech New Orleans	428	100	[1] 200	Pub	V	U	 Oth	O [5]	 Oth		6	0	9				
2573	Delgado CC New Orleans	5110	1000	[1] 2200	Pub	V	U	 A/S	E [5]	6/30 FFS	6	4	0	4	1	3	1	2
2574	Evangeline Voc-Tech St Martinville	300	300	[1] 600	Pub	T		 Oth	O [5]	 Oth	7	5	0	5				
2575	Gulf Area Voc-Tech Abbeville	330	300	[1] 500	Pub	S		 Oth	O [5]	 Oth	4	5	0	1			4	
2576	Hammond Area Tech Hammond	200	300	[1] 600	Pub	S		 Oth	O [5]	 Oth	2	6	0	4				
2577	Harris Voc-Tech Opelousas	651	300	[1] 600	Pub	S		 Oth	O [5]	 Oth	4	4	0	4	0	0		
2578	Huey Long Voc Sch Winnfield	165	200	[1] 1200	Pub	T		 None	O [5]		3	6		4				
2579	Jefferson Parish Voc Metairie	350	200	[1] 1200	Pub	V	U	 Oth	O [5]	 None	1	6	0	2				
2580	Jefferson Westbnk VT Harvey	300	300	[1] 600	Pub	M		 Oth	O [5]	 Oth	6	4	0	6				
2581	Jumonville Voc-Tech Port Allen	125	200	[1] 500	Pub	L	S	 Oth	O [5]	 Oth		1	0	5				
2582	La St U Alexandria Alexandria	1212	900	[1] 2300	Pub	M	S	 ACT	E [5]	 Oth	3	7	0	1	1		1	4

Educational Programs Available (■ = program offered)

Sequence Number	College Transfer Courses	Career-oriented: Agri	Business	Arts	Health	Math	SocSci	Technical/Skilled Trades
2561	Bus-Commerce, Communications, Education, Engineering, Fine, Applied Arts, Foreign Lang, Health, Humanities, Mathematics, Computer/Info Sci, Biological Sci, Physical Sci, Social Sci		Accounting, Bus Mgmt & Admin, Secretarial Studies		Medical or Lab Tech, Nursing (RN)	Data Processing Tech	Crim Just/Law Enforce	
2562	Bus-Commerce, Communications, Education, Engineering, Fine, Applied Arts, Foreign Lang, Health, Home Ec, Humanities, Mathematics, Computer/Info Sci, Biological Sci, Physical Sci, Social Sci		Marketing/Purchasing, Secretarial Studies		Nursing (RN)			
2563	Agriculture, Bus-Commerce, Communications, Education, Engineering, Fine, Applied Arts, Foreign Lang, Health, Home Ec, Humanities, Mathematics, Computer/Info Sci, Biological Sci, Physical Sci, Social Sci		Office Mgmt, Secretarial Studies			Computer Prog	Social Work	
2564			Accounting, Bus Mgmt & Admin, Hotel/Rest Mgmt, Secretarial Studies			Computer Prog, Data Processing Tech		
2565			Accounting, Office Mgmt, Secretarial Studies		Nursing (LPN)	Data Processing Tech, Computer Operating		Air/Refrig/Heat Tech, Auto Body Repair, Auto Mechanics, Carpentry/Constr, Drafting/Eng Draft, Electric Eng Tech, Machinework, Welding
2566					Radiologic Technology			
2567					Nursing (RN)			
2568			Accounting, Hotel/Rest Mgmt, Marketing/Purchasing, Secretarial Studies		Medical or Lab Tech, Nursing (LPN)	Computer Prog, Data Processing Tech		Air/Refrig/Heat Tech, Auto Body Repair, Auto Mechanics, Carpentry/Constr, Drafting/Eng Draft, Electric Eng Tech, Machinework, Welding
2569	Bus-Commerce, Communications, Education, Engineering, Fine, Applied Arts, Foreign Lang, Health, Home Ec, Humanities, Mathematics, Computer/Info Sci, Biological Sci, Physical Sci, Social Sci		Accounting, Bus Mgmt & Admin, Hotel/Rest Mgmt, Office Mgmt, Marketing/Purchasing, Secretarial Studies		Nursing (RN)	Data Processing Tech	Crim Just/Law Enforce	Air/Refrig/Heat Tech, Auto Mechanics, Drafting/Eng Draft, Electric Eng Tech, Welding
2570					Nursing (RN)			
2571					Dental Assistant, Nursing (RN), Nursing (LPN)			Drafting/Eng Draft, Mech Eng Tech
2572			Accounting, Office Mgmt, Secretarial Studies		Nursing (LPN)			Air/Refrig/Heat Tech, Auto Body Repair, Auto Mechanics, Carpentry/Constr, Drafting/Eng Draft
2573	Agriculture, Bus-Commerce, Communications, Education, Engineering, Fine, Applied Arts, Foreign Lang, Health, Home Ec, Humanities, Mathematics, Computer/Info Sci, Biological Sci, Physical Sci, Social Sci	Horticulture	Bus Mgmt & Admin, Secretarial Studies	Applied Design	Radiologic Technology	Data Processing Tech	Crim Just/Law Enforce	Air/Refrig/Heat Tech, Auto Body Repair, Auto Mechanics, Carpentry/Constr, Drafting/Eng Draft, Electric Eng Tech, Civil Eng Tech, Mech Eng Tech, Machinework, Welding
2574	Health		Accounting, Office Mgmt, Secretarial Studies			Computer Operating		Air/Refrig/Heat Tech, Auto Body Repair, Auto Mechanics, Electric Eng Tech, Machinework, Welding
2575			Accounting, Bus Mgmt & Admin, Office Mgmt, Secretarial Studies		Nursing (LPN)	Data Processing Tech, Computer Operating		Air/Refrig/Heat Tech, Auto Body Repair, Auto Mechanics, Drafting/Eng Draft, Welding
2576			Accounting, Bus Mgmt & Admin, Secretarial Studies		Nursing (LPN)			Auto Mechanics, Welding
2577			Accounting, Bus Mgmt & Admin, Secretarial Studies		Nursing (LPN)	Computer Prog, Data Processing Tech		Air/Refrig/Heat Tech, Auto Body Repair, Auto Mechanics, Carpentry/Constr, Drafting/Eng Draft, Electric Eng Tech, Civil Eng Tech, Machinework, Welding
2578			Office Mgmt, Secretarial Studies		Nursing (LPN)	Computer Operating		Air/Refrig/Heat Tech, Auto Mechanics, Carpentry/Constr, Welding
2579			Accounting, Secretarial Studies		Nursing (LPN)			Air/Refrig/Heat Tech, Auto Body Repair, Auto Mechanics, Carpentry/Constr, Drafting/Eng Draft, Electric Eng Tech, Welding
2580			Accounting, Secretarial Studies		Nursing (LPN)			Air/Refrig/Heat Tech, Auto Body Repair, Auto Mechanics, Carpentry/Constr, Drafting/Eng Draft, Electric Eng Tech, Welding
2581			Accounting, Bus Mgmt & Admin, Secretarial Studies			Computer Prog		Welding
2582	Agriculture, Bus-Commerce, Communications, Education, Engineering, Fine, Applied Arts, Foreign Lang, Health, Home Ec, Humanities, Mathematics, Computer/Info Sci, Biological Sci, Physical Sci, Social Sci		Bus Mgmt & Admin, Secretarial Studies	Photography/Cinema	Nursing (RN)	Computer Prog		

▲ Sequence Number—indicates the order of the college in this book only. Do *not* use this number with admissions tests or need analysis services.

1 No campus room and board facilities
2 Room only or board only
3 Most freshmen required to live on campus
4 City or district residency requirements
5 Accredited by regional accrediting association or a recognized candidate for accreditation
6 All female freshman class
7 All male freshman class
8 Some admission selectivity; not all hs graduates accepted
9 Requirements more stringent for nonresidents
†Accredited by a nationally recognized accrediting body other than one of the regional accrediting associations

Louisiana
(continued)

Sequence Number	School name (upper entry) / City (lower entry)	Enrollment	Costs: Resident tuition/fees + room/board	Costs: Room/board (upper entry) / Nonresident tuition/fees (lower entry)	Gen. Info.: Affiliation (upper entry) / Religious observance (lower entry)	Gen. Info.: Size of community	Gen. Info.: Type of community	Admissions: Fall term application deadline (upper entry) / Test required or desired (lower entry)	Admissions: Calendar	Financial Aid: Fall term application deadline (upper entry) / Forms to be filed (lower entry)	No. in 10 who- -have need, rec some aid	-are women	-live on campus	-are minority students	-are nonresidents	-return as sophomores	-complete assoc degree	-transfer to 4-year college
2583	La St U Eunice / Eunice	949	900	[1] / 1900	Pub	S		8/19 / ACT	S [5]	8/19 / FFS	4	6	0	1				
2584	Natchitoches Central / Natchitoches	250	300	[1] / 600	Pub	S		Oth	O [5]	Oth	5	7	0	6	1	6	4	
2585	North Central V-T / Farmerville	116	300	[1] / 600	Pub	T		None	O [5]	None	4	5	0	3	0		2	1
2586	Northeast La Voc Sch / Winnsboro	220	300	[1] / 600	Pub	T		Oth	O [5]	Oth	5	5	0	3	0			
2587	Northwest La Voc-Tec / Minden	275	300	[1] / 600	Pub	S		Oth	O [5]	Oth	1	6	0	3	0	6	7	
2588	Our Lady of Lake Nsg / Baton Rouge	132	5300	[1]	Cath / O	V [8]	U	5/15 / ACT	O †	10/15 / FFS	1	9	0	1	1	9	9	
2589	Our Lady Surgical / Baton Rouge		1200		Cath	L [8]	U	ACT	O †			9		2				
2590	Rapides Hosp Sch Rad / Alexandria	17	4500	[1]	Pub	M [8]		5/01 / ACT	O †	None		6	0	0	0	9	9	1
2591	Sabine Vly Voc-Tech / Many	109	300	[1] / 600	Pub	T		Oth	O [5]	Oth	2	4	0	3	1	7		
2592	Saint Bern Parish CC / Chalmette	248	300	[1]	Pub	S		8/31 / A/S	S [5]	8/15 / FFS	1	7	0	1	0	4	1	2
2593	Slidell Voc-Tec Sch / Slidell	300	300	[1] / 600	Pub	S		Oth	O [5]	None		4	0					
2594	South La Voc-Tech / Houma	230	300	[1] / 600	Pub	M		Oth	O [5]		5	5	0	2				
2595	Southern U Shreveprt / Shreveport	656	800	[1] / 1900	Pub	L	U	7/31 / ACT	E [5]	7/20 / FFS	7	7	0	9	0	9	4	6
2596	Sullivan Voc-Tech / Bogalusa	450	300	[1] / 600	Pub	S		8/20 / Oth	O [5]	9/01 / Oth	7	5	0	3	0	7	0	
2597	Teche Voc-Tech Sch / New Iberia	305	300	[1] / 600	Pub	S		Oth	O [5]	FF=FA	1	5	0	1			3	
Maine																		
2598	Beal C / Bangor	402	5000 [2]	1600	Priv	S [8]		9/08 / None	O †	5/01 / FAF	7	9	1	1	1	8	8	1
2599	Central Maine Sc Nsg / Lewiston	73	3500 [2]	1100	Priv	M [8]		6/30 / SAT	E [5]	FAF	7	9	2	1	0	7	7	
2600	Central Maine Tech C / Auburn	433	3700	2400 / 4900	Pub	M [8]	S		S [5]	FAF	4	2	2	1	1	8	8	1
2601	East Maine Tech C / Bangor	598	4200	2800 / 5400	Pub	S [8]		A=S	E [5]	4/01	5	4	3	1	1	6	7	1
2602	Kennebec Vly Voc-Tec / Fairfield	309	1300	[1] / 2400	Pub	S [8]		Oth	S [5]	Oth	6	6	0	0	0	3	7	1
2603	Maine U C,U of / Orono	1412	6900	3900 / 10100	Pub	S [8]		S/A	E [5]	3/01 / FAF	7	5	9	1	3	7	2	3
2604	North Maine Voc-Tech / Presque	670	3800	2400 / 5000	Pub	S [8]		None	S [5]	5/01 / FAF	7	4	4	1	1	7	7	1

Educational Programs Available — College Transfer Courses; Career-oriented Programs (Agri, Business)

Sequence Number	Agriculture	Bus-Commerce	Communications	Education	Engineering	Fine, Applied Arts	Foreign Lang	Health	Home Ec	Humanities	Mathematics	Computer/Info Sci	Biological Sci	Physical Sci	Social Sci	Agri: Ag Business	Ag/Farm Mgmt	Ag Mechanics/Tech	Horticulture	Business: Accounting	Bus Mgmt & Admin	Hotel/Rest Mgmt	Office Mgmt	Marketing/Purchasing	Secretarial Studies
2583	■	■	■	■	■	■	■	■	■	■	■	■	■	■	■	■	■		■	■	■	■	■	■	■
2584																				■					■
2585																									■
2586																		■		■					■
2587																				■					■
2588																									
2589																									
2590								■																	
2591																				■					■
2592		■	■	■		■	■			■	■	■	■	■	■										
2593																			■	■					■
2594																				■					■
2595		■	■	■	■	■	■	■		■	■	■	■	■	■					■	■	■	■	■	■
2596																			■	■			■	■	■
2597																				■					
2598		■						■				■			■					■	■	■	■		■
2599																									
2600		■	■			■		■															■		
2601								■		■	■				■						■				
2602		■						■				■												■	
2603		■				■		■		■	■	■	■	■	■						■				
2604		■								■	■	■		■	■			■		■	■				

Educational Programs Available — Career-oriented Programs (Arts, Health, Math, SocSci, Technical/Skilled Trades)

Sequence Number	Arts: Architecture Tech	Applied Design	Photography/Cinema	Health: Dental Assistant	Medical or Lab Tech	Nursing (RN)	Nursing (LPN)	Radiologic Technology	Math: Computer Prog	Data Processing Tech	Computer Operating	SocSci: Crim Just/Law Enforce	Parks/Rec Mgmt	Social Work	Technical/Skilled Trades: Air/Refrig/Heat Tech	Auto Body Repair	Auto Mechanics	Carpentry/Constr	Drafting/Eng Draft	Electric Eng Tech	Civil Eng Tech	Indus/Mfg Eng Tech	Mech Eng Tech	Machinework	Welding
2583				■		■						■							■				■		
2584							■								■		■	■		■					■
2585											■						■								■
2586							■			■							■		■						■
2587							■				■						■			■				■	■
2588						■																			
2589																									
2590							■	■																	
2591							■								■		■		■						
2592							■																		
2593							■		■	■					■		■	■	■	■					
2594							■								■		■		■					■	■
2595					■																				
2596							■		■	■	■				■		■	■	■					■	■
2597							■								■		■	■	■	■				■	■
2598									■	■															
2599						■																			
2600						■	■										■	■	■	■	■		■	■	■
2601					■	■	■	■							■		■	■		■				■	■
2602				■		■	■											■		■					
2603				■								■													
2604						■	■		■						■	■	■	■	■	■					

▲ Sequence Number—indicates the order of the college in this book only. Do *not* use this number with admissions tests or need analysis services.

[1] No campus room and board facilities
[2] Room only or board only
[3] Most freshmen required to live on campus
[4] City or district residency requirements
[5] Accredited by regional accrediting association or a recognized candidate for accreditation
[6] All female freshman class
[7] All male freshman class
[8] Some admission selectivity; not all hs graduates accepted
[9] Requirements more stringent for nonresidents
†Accredited by a nationally recognized accrediting body other than one of the regional accrediting associations

Maine (continued)

Sequence Number	School name (upper entry) / City (lower entry)	Enrollment	Resident tuition/fees + room/board	Room/board (upper entry) / Nonresident tuition/fees (lower entry)	Affiliation (upper entry) / Religious observance (lower entry)	Size of community	Type of community	Fall term application deadline (upper entry) / Test required or desired (lower entry)	Calendar	Fall term application deadline (upper entry) / Forms to be filed (lower entry)	-have need, rec some aid	-are women	-live on campus	-are minority students	-are nonresidents	-return as sophomores	-complete assoc degree	-transfer to 4-year college
			Costs		**Gen. Info.**			**Admissions**		**Financial Aid**	**Student Profile: No. in 10 who-**							
2605	South Maine Voc-Tech / South Portland	1182	3900	2500 / 5100	Pub	S [8]		S/A	S [5]	4/15 / FAF	7	4	2	1	1	7	6	1
2606	Washington Co Vo-Tec / Calais	181	2200 [2]	1000 / 3400	Pub	T		8/15 / None	S [5]	7/01 / FF=FA	7	1	6	1	1			
	Maryland																	
2607	Allegany CC / Cumberland	1488	1700	[1] / 3100	Pub	S		Oth	E [5]	3/15 / FA/FF	6	6	0	1	1	5	3	2
2608	Anne Arundel CC / Arnold	3404	1300	[1] / 5000	Pub	S		A=S	E [5]	5/01 / FA/FF	5	6	0	1	0		3	5
2609	Baltimore,CC of / Baltimore	1400	1100	[1] / 3200	Pub	V	U	8/31 / Oth	E [5]	6/01 / FF/FA	8	7	0	8	1	7		1
2610	Catonsville CC / Catonsville	2119	900	[1] / 2900	Pub	M	S	9/05 / A=S	4 [5]	9/01 / FAF	2	5	0	3	1	5	4	4
2611	Cecil CC / North East	332	1100	[1] / 3000	Pub	T		8/31 / Oth	S [5]	8/31 / FAF	5	6	0	1	1	2	1	1
2612	Charles Co CC / La Plata	1200	1300	[1] / 3700	Pub	T		ACT	E [5]	4/01 / FA/FF		6	0	1	1	3	2	3
2613	Chesapeake C / Wye Mills	462	1100	[1] / 4800	Pub	T		None	S [5]	6/01 / FA/FF	7	7	0	1		4	2	4
2614	Dundalk CC / Baltimore	506	1100	[1] / 3400	Pub	M	S	A=S	E [5]	FA/FF	3	6	0	1	1	5	2	3
2615	Essex CC / Baltimore Co	3154	1100	[1] / 3400	Pub	V	S	A=S	4 [5]	FA/FF	9	6	0	1	1			
2616	Frederick CC / Frederick	1209	1400	[1] / 5200	Pub	M		None	S [5]	7/01 / FAF	1	6	0	1	1			
2617	Garrett CC / McHenry	286	900	[1] / 3000	Pub	T		9/01 / None	S [5]	6/01 / FA/FF	7	6	0	1	1	4	5	4
2618	Hagerstown JC / Hagerstown	1151	1300	[1] / 3000	Pub	M	S	9/01 / A=S	E [5]	7/01 / FAF	5	5	0	1	2	6	5	6
2619	Harford CC / Bel Air	3897	1200	[1] / 3500	Pub	T			E [5]	FF=FA	5	6	0	1		3		
2620	Howard CC / Columbia	921	1400	[1] / 4900	Pub	M	S	None	4 [5]	9/01 / Oth	2	6	0	2	1	8		5
2621	MGW Sch Nsg / Easton	85	4200 [2]	1600	Priv	T [8]		A=S	E †	4/01 / FF=FA	7	9	2	1	1	8	8	5
2622	Montgomery C Rockvl / Rockville	4749	1500	[1] / 3900	Pub	M	S	None	S [5]	6/01 / FA/FF	1	5	0	3	1			
2623	Montgomery C Takoma / Takoma Park	1052	1500	[1] / 3900	Pub	S		None	S [5]	6/01 / FA/FF	1	6	0	6	1			
2624	Montgomery C-Germntn / Germantown	657	1500	[1] / 3900	Pub	S		None	S [5]	6/01 / FA/FF	1	6	0	1	1			
2625	Prince George's CC / Largo	3381	1600	[1] / 5900	Pub	S		Oth	E [5]	6/15 / FA/FF	3	6	0	5	1	4	1	3
2626	Union Memorial Nsg / Baltimore	100	3800	1800	Priv	V [8]	U	Oth	4 †	2/15 / FAF	3	9	5	1	1	9		

Educational Programs Available (continued for the same rows)

Sequence Number	Agriculture	Bus-Commerce	Communications	Education	Engineering	Fine, Applied Arts	Foreign Lang	Health	Home Ec	Humanities	Mathematics	Computer/Info Sci	Biological Sci	Physical Sci	Social Sci	Ag Business	Ag/Farm Mgmt	Ag Mechanics/Tech	Horticulture	Accounting	Bus Mgmt & Admin	Hotel/Rest Mgmt	Office Mgmt	Marketing/Purchasing	Secretarial Studies
	College Transfer Courses															**Career-oriented Programs: Agri**				**Business**					
2605	■	■			■	■		■	■			■		■	■				■			■	■		
2606																									■
2607	■	■	■	■	■	■	■	■		■	■	■	■	■	■					■			■		■
2608	■	■	■	■	■	■	■	■	■	■	■	■	■	■	■					■	■			■	■
2609		■	■	■	■	■	■	■	■	■	■	■	■	■	■					■	■	■			■
2610		■	■	■	■	■	■	■	■	■	■	■	■	■	■					■			■		■
2611		■		■		■	■			■	■		■	■	■					■	■		■		■
2612		■	■	■	■	■	■	■	■	■	■	■	■	■	■					■	■		■		■
2613	■	■		■	■	■		■		■	■	■	■	■	■					■	■				■
2614	■	■	■	■		■	■	■		■	■	■	■	■	■				■	■	■		■		■
2615	■	■	■	■	■	■	■	■		■	■	■	■	■	■					■	■	■		■	■
2616	■	■	■	■	■	■	■	■		■	■	■	■	■	■					■	■				■
2617	■	■	■	■	■	■		■		■	■	■	■	■	■						■	■		■	■
2618		■	■	■	■	■	■	■		■	■	■	■	■	■					■	■			■	■
2619		■	■	■	■	■		■		■	■	■	■	■	■					■		■		■	■
2620		■	■	■	■	■	■	■		■	■	■	■	■	■				■	■	■		■	■	■
2621								■																	
2622		■		■	■	■				■	■		■		■					■	■			■	■
2623		■		■	■			■		■	■				■					■					■
2624		■		■	■	■		■		■	■				■					■	■			■	■
2625		■	■	■	■	■	■		■	■	■	■	■	■	■				■	■	■	■	■	■	■
2626								■																	

Sequence Number	Architecture Tech	Applied Design	Photography/Cinema	Dental Assistant	Medical or Lab Tech	Nursing (RN)	Nursing (LPN)	Radiologic Technology	Computer Prog	Data Processing Tech	Computer Operating	Crim Just/Law Enforce	Parks/Rec Mgmt	Social Work	Air/Refrig/Heat Tech	Auto Body Repair	Auto Mechanics	Carpentry/Constr	Drafting/Eng Draft	Electric Eng Tech	Civil Eng Tech	Indus/Mfg Eng Tech	Mech Eng Tech	Machinework	Welding
	Arts			**Health**					**Math**			**SocSci**			**Technical/Skilled Trades**										
2605	■						■	■			■	■			■		■	■	■	■				■	
2606															■		■	■		■					■
2607				■	■	■	■	■	■	■		■									■		■		
2608						■			■	■		■		■						■			■		
2609		■		■		■				■		■		■	■		■	■	■	■	■		■		
2610	■					■			■	■	■	■	■				■		■		■	■		■	
2611						■				■		■			■			■		■					■
2612						■	■		■	■									■						
2613								■	■	■		■			■										
2614			■						■		■				■					■					
2615				■	■	■			■	■		■							■						
2616					■	■	■			■		■	■												
2617																		■							
2618						■		■		■		■								■			■		
2619					■	■	■		■	■		■					■		■						
2620						■			■	■	■							■		■					
2621						■																			
2622		■							■	■		■	■							■	■		■		
2623				■	■	■		■																	
2624										■							■		■	■					
2625						■		■	■			■													
2626						■																			

▲ **Sequence Number—indicates the order of the college in this book only. Do *not* use this number with admissions tests or need analysis services.**

[1] No campus room and board facilities
[2] Room only or board only
[3] Most freshmen required to live on campus
[4] City or district residency requirements
[5] Accredited by regional accrediting association or a recognized candidate for accreditation
[6] All female freshman class
[7] All male freshman class
[8] Some admission selectivity; not all hs graduates accepted
[9] Requirements more stringent for nonresidents
†Accredited by a nationally recognized accrediting body other than one of the regional accrediting associations

Maryland
(continued)

Sequence Number	School name (upper entry)	City (lower entry)	Enrollment	Resident tuition/fees + room/board	Room/board (upper entry)	Nonresident tuition/fees (lower entry)	Affiliation (upper entry)	Religious observance (lower entry)	Size of community	Type of community	Fall term application deadline (upper entry)	Test required or desired (lower entry)	Calendar	Fall term application deadline (upper entry)	Forms to be filed (lower entry)	-have need, rec some aid	-are women	-live on campus	-are minority students	-are nonresidents	-return as sophomores	-complete assoc degree	-transfer to 4-year college
				Costs			Gen. Info.				Admissions			Financial Aid		Student Profile: No. in 10 who-							
2627	Wor Wic Tech CC	Salisbury	244	1100	[1]	4400	Pub		S		9/01	None	E [5]	9/01	Oth	4	7	0	2	0	5	2	1

Massachusetts

Sequence Number	School name (upper entry)	City (lower entry)	Enrollment	Resident tuition/fees + room/board	Room/board (upper entry)	Nonresident tuition/fees (lower entry)	Affiliation (upper entry)	Religious observance (lower entry)	Size of community	Type of community	Fall term application deadline (upper entry)	Test required or desired (lower entry)	Calendar	Fall term application deadline (upper entry)	Forms to be filed (lower entry)	-have need, rec some aid	-are women	-live on campus	-are minority students	-are nonresidents	-return as sophomores	-complete assoc degree	-transfer to 4-year college
2628	Aquinas JC Milton	Milton	204	6900	[1]		Cath	OS	S [8]	[6]		Oth	O [5]		FAF	7	9	0	1	0	8	9	1
2629	Aquinas JC Newton	Newton	200	6800	[1]		Cath	O	M [8]	S [6]		None	4 [5]	9/01	FAF	7	9	0	1	0	9	8	5
2630	Bay Path C	Longmeadow	575	12400	4700		Priv		S [8]	[6]		None	S [5]		FA/FF	8	9	7	1	6	7	6	3
2631	Bay St C	Boston	760	11800	5400		Priv		V [8]	U		None	S [5]	3/01		8	8	4	2	2	7	9	3
2632	Becker C Worcester	Worcester	600	10700	3900		Priv		L [8]	U	9/01	None	S [5]	4/01	FA/FF	9	9	7	1	5	7	8	2
2633	Becker JC Leicester	Leicester	416	10700	3900		Priv		T [8]		9/01	None	S [5]	4/01	FA/FF	9	8	8	1	5	8	7	4
2634	Berkshire CC	Pittsfield	1088	2000	[1]	5000	Pub		M			A=S	S [5]	5/01	FA/FF	6	6	0	1	1			
2635	Bristol CC	Fall River	2809	1800	[1]	4900	Pub		M	U	8/01	S/A	E [5]		FAF	5	6	0	1	1	8		2
2636	Bunker Hill CC	Boston	3100	1200	[1]	4000	Pub		V	U		None	E [5]		FA/FF	5	5	0	4	1	5	5	3
2637	Burdett Sch	Boston	300	12200	5200		Priv		V [8]	U		None	O †	9/07		7	9	2	3	2		9	1
2638	Cape Cod CC	West Barnstable	2090	2100	[1]	6100	Pub		T		8/15	None	S [5]	5/01	FA/FF	6	6	0	1	1	6	4	6
2639	Dean JC	Franklin	1100	14400	5700		Priv		S [8]		9/01	A=S	E [5]	3/15	FA/FF	6	5	8	1	6	7	7	7
2640	Essex Agri Tech Inst	Hathorne	450	1700	[1]		Pub		T [8]			S/A	S [5]	5/01	FAF	2	6	0	1	0	7	9	2
2641	Fisher C	Boston	450	14200	5800		Priv		V [8]	U [6]		None	S [5]		FA/FF	7	9	7	3	5	6	6	4
2642	Franklin Inst Boston	Boston	315	12400	5500		Priv		V [8]	U	9/01	A=S	S [5]	3/01	FAF	5	1	0	3	1	8	6	4
2643	Greenfield CC	Greenfield	1108	1800	[1]	4600	Pub		S			None	E [5]		FA/FF	6	6	0	1	1		3	5
2644	Holyoke CC	Holyoke	2233	2600	[1]	9000	Pub		S			None	E [5]			3	6	0	1	1	5		4
2645	Katharine Gibbs Sch	Boston	420	13200	6200		Priv		L [8]	U			O †			6	9	5	2	4	7	8	1
2646	Laboure C	Boston	145	10600 [2]	2200		Cath	S	V [8]	U		None	O [5]	5/01	FA/FF	6	9	2	1	1	7	8	1
2647	Mass Bay CC	Wellesley Hills	2483	1400	[1]	3000	Pub		S			None	E [5]		FAF		6	0	2	1	6		4
2648	Massasoit CC	Brockton	3275	1500	[1]	4600	Pub		M	U		None	E [5]		FAF	4	5	0	1	0	5	2	4

Educational Programs Available — College Transfer Courses

Sequence Number	Agriculture	Bus-Commerce	Communications	Education	Engineering	Fine, Applied Arts	Foreign Lang	Health	Home Ec	Humanities	Mathematics	Computer/Info Sci	Biological Sci	Physical Sci	Social Sci
2627															
2628															
2629		■	■	■		■		■		■	■	■			■
2630				■		■	■		■	■	■		■	■	■
2631		■		■					■	■	■				
2632		■	■	■		■	■	■	■	■	■	■	■		■
2633	■	■	■	■		■	■	■	■	■	■	■	■	■	■
2634		■		■	■	■	■	■		■	■	■	■		■
2635		■	■	■	■	■	■	■		■	■	■	■	■	■
2636		■	■		■	■	■	■		■	■	■	■	■	■
2637															
2638		■	■	■	■	■	■	■	■	■	■	■	■	■	■
2639		■	■	■		■	■		■	■	■	■	■	■	■
2640	■	■		■					■		■		■	■	■
2641		■		■		■	■		■	■	■	■	■		■
2642					■	■		■				■			
2643	■	■	■	■	■	■		■				■			■
2644	■	■	■	■	■	■	■	■	■	■	■	■	■	■	■
2645		■													
2646								■	■						
2647		■	■		■	■	■	■	■	■	■	■	■	■	■
2648		■	■	■	■	■		■	■	■	■	■			■

Educational Programs Available — Career-oriented Programs

Sequence Number	Agri: Ag Business	Agri: Ag/Farm Mgmt	Agri: Ag Mechanics/Tech	Agri: Horticulture	Business: Accounting	Business: Bus Mgmt & Admin	Business: Hotel/Rest Mgmt	Business: Office Mgmt	Business: Marketing/Purchasing	Business: Secretarial Studies	Arts: Architecture Tech	Arts: Applied Design	Arts: Photography/Cinema	Health: Dental Assistant	Health: Medical or Lab Tech	Health: Nursing (RN)	Health: Nursing (LPN)	Health: Radiologic Technology	Math: Computer Prog	Math: Data Processing Tech	Math: Computer Operating	SocSci: Crim Just/Law Enforce	SocSci: Parks/Rec Mgmt	SocSci: Social Work	Technical/Skilled Trades: Air/Refrig/Heat Tech	Auto Body Repair	Auto Mechanics	Carpentry/Constr	Drafting/Eng Draft	Electric Eng Tech	Civil Eng Tech	Indus/Mfg Eng Tech	Mech Eng Tech	Machinework	Welding
2627					■	■	■			■						■	■	■	■			■													
2628					■	■		■	■	■											■														
2629					■	■		■		■					■						■														
2630					■	■	■	■	■	■											■														
2631					■	■	■	■	■	■																									
2632					■	■	■		■	■						■			■			■													
2633				■	■	■	■		■													■	■												
2634					■		■	■	■	■							■			■		■		■						■					
2635					■	■		■	■	■		■			■	■			■			■													
2636					■	■	■		■	■				■		■		■	■			■													
2637					■			■	■	■											■														
2638					■	■	■	■	■	■						■				■		■													
2639					■				■	■												■	■	■					■						
2640				■			■		■								■						■												
2641					■	■	■	■	■	■																									
2642															■												■		■	■	■		■		
2643					■	■		■	■	■						■						■	■												
2644					■	■	■		■	■						■		■				■													
2645					■		■	■		■																									
2646																																			
2647					■	■	■	■	■	■						■	■	■	■			■		■			■			■					
2648					■	■		■			■			■	■	■		■	■			■		■	■		■		■	■	■		■		

▲ Sequence Number—indicates the order of the college in this book only. Do *not* use this number with admissions tests or need analysis services.

[1] No campus room and board facilities
[2] Room only or board only
[3] Most freshmen required to live on campus
[4] City or district residency requirements
[5] Accredited by regional accrediting association or a recognized candidate for accreditation
[6] All female freshman class
[7] All male freshman class
[8] Some admission selectivity; not all hs graduates accepted
[9] Requirements more stringent for nonresidents
†Accredited by a nationally recognized accrediting body other than one of the regional accrediting associations

Massachusetts
(continued)

Sequence Number	School name (upper entry) City (lower entry)	Enrollment	Resident tuition/fees + room/board	Room/board (upper entry) Nonresident tuition/fees (lower entry)	Affiliation (upper entry) Religious observance (lower entry)	Size of community	Type of community	Fall term application deadline (upper entry) Test required or desired (lower entry)	Calendar	Fall term application deadline (upper entry) Forms to be filed (lower entry)	-have need, rec some aid	-are women	-live on campus	-are minority students	-are nonresidents	-return as sophomores	-complete assoc degree	-transfer to 4-year college
			Costs		**Gen. Info.**			**Admissions**		**Financial Aid**	**Student Profile** (No. in 10 who-)							
2649	Middlesex CC Bedford	3524	2200	[1] 4900	Pub	M	U	None	E [5]	FAF		6	0	1	1	5	9	4
2650	Mount Wachusett CC Gardner	1700	2000	[1] 5000	Pub	S		None	4 [5]	9/07 FA/FF	6	6	0	1	1	5	6	3
2651	Newbury C Brookline	907	13800	5300	Priv	L [8]	S	S/A	E [5]	FAF	5	6	4	4	3	8	6	4
2652	North Shore CC Beverly	3236	1900	[1] 4800	Pub	S		8/15 None	S [5]	6/01 FAF	3	5	0	1	1	5	8	4
2653	Northern Essex CC Haverhill	2694	1500	[1] 4500	Pub	M [8]	S		S [5]	4/01	5	6	0	1	1		7	7
2654	Quincy C Quincy	1437	1900	[1]	Pub	M	S	Oth	S [5]	5/01 FAF	6	7	0	2	0	7	5	3
2655	Quinsigamond CC Worcester	1856	1800	[1] 4700	Pub	L [8]	U	1/15 None	S [5]	FAF	7	6	0	2		6	4	4
2656	Roxbury CC Roxbury Crossng	485	1400	[1] 4500	Pub	V	U	9/01 None	E [5]	8/15 FAF	9	6	0	9	1	6		5
2657	Springfield Tech CC Springfield	2337	1400	[1] 4400	Pub	M	U	1/31 Oth	E [5]	4/30 FAF	7	6	0	3	1	7	6	2
2658	Worcester Tech Inst Worcester	404	1100	[1] 4800	Pub	L [8]	U	SAT	S [5]	9/01 FAF	3	3	0	1	0	8	9	2
Michigan																		
2659	Alpena CC Alpena	990	1200	[1] 2400	Pub	S		None	E [5]	FF=FA	9	6	0	1	1	0	4	3
2660	Baker C-Pontiac Pontiac	185	3400	[1]	Priv			A=S	Q [5]	9/01 FA/FF								
2661	Baker C-Port Huron Port Huron	271	3400	[1]	Priv			A=S	Q [5]	9/01 FA/FF								
2662	Bay De Noc CC Escanaba	1333	4500	3300 5800	Pub	S			S [5]	4/01 FAF	7	6	1	1	1	5	5	2
2663	Bronson Hosp Sch Nsg Kalamazoo	140	5700	2300	Priv	L [8]	U	8/01 A=S	S †	6/01 FFS	6	9	5	1	0	8	8	
2664	Bronson Hosp Sch Rad Kalamazoo	15	4000	2500	Meth	M [8]	U	2/15 A/S	Q †	FF=FA	5	8	0	1	0	9	9	1
2665	Delta C University Ctr	3763	4500	3100 5900	Pub	M	S	8/29 Oth	E [5]	Oth	3	6	1	1	1	4	3	3
2666	Glen Oaks CC Centreville	1374	1100	[1] 1500	Pub	T		None	T [5]	FA/FF	2	5	0	1	1			
2667	Gogebic CC Ironwood	643	1700 [2]	1000 2100	Pub	T		A/S	E [5]	4/01 FA/FF	8	6	1	3	1	7	8	6
2668	Grand Rapids Bible C Grand Rapids	118	5100	2700	Oth OS	V	U	A=S	E †	7/15 FAF	6	4	9	1	3	5	5	2
2669	Grand Rapids JC Grand Rapids	4442	1200	[1] 2300	Pub	V	U	8/20 Oth	4 [5]	FA/FF	6	5	0	1	1	6	5	5
2670	Henry Ford CC Dearborn	4585	1100	[1] 1500	Pub	M	S	None	S [5]	5/01 FF=FA	2	5	0	2	1		4	6

Educational Programs Available — College Transfer Courses

Sequence Number	Agriculture	Bus-Commerce	Communications	Education	Engineering	Fine, Applied Arts	Foreign Lang	Health	Home Ec	Humanities	Mathematics	Computer/Info Sci	Biological Sci	Physical Sci	Social Sci
2649		■	■	■	■			■				■			■
2650		■	■	■	■	■	■	■	■	■	■	■	■	■	■
2651	■	■	■	■		■		■	■	■	■	■	■	■	■
2652		■	■	■	■		■	■	■	■	■	■		■	■
2653		■	■		■	■	■	■		■	■		■	■	■
2654		■	■			■		■				■	■	■	■
2655		■		■	■	■	■	■		■	■	■	■	■	■
2656		■	■	■		■	■			■	■	■	■	■	■
2657		■		■	■	■		■		■	■	■	■	■	■
2658		■			■	■		■		■		■			■
2659		■	■	■	■	■		■		■	■	■	■	■	■
2660		■	■							■	■	■			■
2661		■	■							■	■	■			■
2662		■		■	■	■		■		■	■	■	■	■	■
2663								■							
2664															
2665	■	■	■	■	■	■	■	■	■	■	■	■	■	■	■
2666		■	■	■	■	■	■	■		■	■	■	■	■	■
2667	■	■	■	■	■	■	■	■	■	■	■	■	■	■	■
2668						■				■					
2669	■	■	■	■	■	■	■	■	■	■	■	■	■	■	■
2670	■	■	■	■	■	■	■	■	■	■	■	■	■	■	■

Educational Programs Available — Career-oriented Programs (Agri, Business, Arts, Health)

Sequence Number	Ag Business	Ag/Farm Mgmt	Ag Mechanics/Tech	Horticulture	Accounting	Bus Mgmt & Admin	Hotel/Rest Mgmt	Office Mgmt	Marketing/Purchasing	Secretarial Studies	Architecture Tech	Applied Design	Photography/Cinema	Dental Assistant	Medical or Lab Tech	Nursing (RN)	Nursing (LPN)	Radiologic Technology
2649					■	■	■		■	■				■	■	■		■
2650					■	■		■	■	■					■	■		
2651					■	■	■		■									
2652					■	■				■						■		■
2653					■	■	■	■		■				■		■	■	■
2654					■	■	■	■								■	■	
2655					■	■	■		■	■						■		■
2656					■	■				■								
2657				■	■	■			■	■				■	■	■		■
2658					■						■			■			■	
2659					■	■		■	■	■						■	■	
2660					■	■	■	■		■								
2661					■	■	■	■		■								
2662					■	■		■	■	■							■	
2663																■		
2664																		■
2665	■				■	■		■	■	■	■			■		■	■	■
2666					■	■		■	■	■						■	■	
2667					■	■	■	■	■	■						■	■	
2668																		
2669					■	■	■	■	■	■				■		■	■	■
2670					■	■	■	■	■	■	■	■	■		■	■		

Educational Programs Available — Career-oriented Programs (Math, SocSci, Technical/Skilled Trades)

Sequence Number	Computer Prog	Data Processing Tech	Computer Operating	Crim Just/Law Enforce	Parks/Rec Mgmt	Social Work	Air/Refrig/Heat Tech	Auto Body Repair	Auto Mechanics	Carpentry/Constr	Drafting/Eng Draft	Electric Eng Tech	Civil Eng Tech	Indus/Mfg Eng Tech	Mech Eng Tech	Machinework	Welding
2649	■			■				■			■	■					
2650	■	■	■	■					■								
2651																	
2652		■	■	■								■			■		
2653	■	■		■		■							■				
2654	■		■	■													
2655		■	■	■					■								
2656	■										■	■			■		■
2657	■	■		■			■		■		■	■	■		■	■	
2658	■	■					■				■	■	■		■	■	■
2659		■	■	■				■	■		■	■				■	
2660	■	■	■														
2661	■	■	■														
2662	■	■		■			■	■	■		■	■			■	■	■
2663																	
2664																	
2665	■	■	■	■					■	■	■			■	■	■	■
2666	■	■	■	■					■		■	■				■	■
2667	■	■	■					■	■	■	■				■		
2668																	
2669	■	■		■				■	■		■	■		■		■	■
2670	■	■	■	■			■		■		■	■	■	■	■	■	■

▲ Sequence Number—indicates the order of the college in this book only. Do *not* use this number with admissions tests or need analysis services.

[1] No campus room and board facilities
[2] Room only or board only
[3] Most freshmen required to live on campus
[4] City or district residency requirements
[5] Accredited by regional accrediting association or a recognized candidate for accreditation
[6] All female freshman class
[7] All male freshman class
[8] Some admission selectivity; not all hs graduates accepted
[9] Requirements more stringent for nonresidents
†Accredited by a nationally recognized accrediting body other than one of the regional accrediting associations

Michigan
(continued)

Sequence Number	School name (upper entry) City (lower entry)	Enrollment	Costs: Resident tuition/fees + room/board	Costs: Room/board (upper entry) Nonresident tuition/fees (lower entry)	Gen. Info.: Affiliation (upper entry) Religious observance (lower entry)	Gen. Info.: Size of community	Gen. Info.: Type of community	Admissions: Fall term application deadline (upper entry) Test required or desired (lower entry)	Admissions: Calendar	Financial Aid: Fall term application deadline (upper entry) Forms to be filed (lower entry)	No. in 10 who- -have need, rec some aid	-are women	-live on campus	-are minority students	-are nonresidents	-return as sophomores	-complete assoc degree	-transfer to 4-year college
2671	Highland Park CC Highland Park	1520	1200	[1] 1800	Pub	V	U	8/01 None	E [5]	 FA/FF	7	7	0	9	1	5	5	4
2672	Hurley Sch Nsg Flint	119	3900 [2]	1400	Pub	M [8]	U	 ACT	E †	8/01 FFS	6	9	3	1	0	9	9	
2673	Jackson Business Jackson	300	4600	[1]	Priv	S		9/25 A=S	Q †	9/25 Oth	9	8	0	1	0	8	7	1
2674	Jackson CC Jackson	2000	1200	[1] 1700	Pub	M		8/30 A=S	E [5]	4/01 FA/FF	3	5	0	1	0	6		6
2675	Kalamazoo Valley CC Kalamazoo	2717	800	[1] 2000	Pub	M	S	 A/S	E [5]	6/15 FF/FA	2	6	0	1	1			4
2676	Kellogg CC Battle Creek	1660	800	[1] 2100	Pub	M	S	8/28 A/S	E [5]	6/01 FA/FF	4	8	0	1	1	3		4
2677	Kirtland CC Roscommon	510	1300	[1] 2500	Pub	T		 None	E [5]	5/01 FA/FF	7	6	0	1	0			
2678	Lake Mich C Benton Harbor	820	1000	[1] 1600	Pub	S		 None	E [5]	 FA/FF	3	6	0	2	1	5		
2679	Lansing CC Lansing	7160	1100	[1] 2100	Pub	L	U	 None	Q [5]	 FF=FA	3	5	0	1	1	5	4	
2680	Lewis C of Business Detroit	180	4500	[1]	Priv	V	U	8/31 A/S	E [5]	 FA/FF	9	8	0	9	0	4	6	3
2681	Macomb CC Warren	6271	1300	[1] 2400	Pub	V	S	 None	E [5]	5/01 Oth	1	5	0	1	1	4	3	5
2682	Marquette Sch Rad Marquette	12	1000	[1] 1700	Priv	S [8]		4/24 Oth	O †	 FF=FA	7	9	0	0	0	9		
2683	Mid Mich CC Harrison	819	1100	[1] 1900	Pub	T		 None	E [5]	8/01 FF/FA	4	6	0	1	0	3	3	2
2684	Monroe Co CC Monroe	928	900	[1] 1000	Pub	S		 Oth	O [5]		7	6	0	1	1	6		4
2685	Montcalm CC Sidney	560	1000	[1] 1800	Pub	T		 None	S [5]	7/30 FAF	8	6	0	1	0	4	1	
2686	Mott CC Flint	2830	1300	[1] 2400	Pub	L	U	8/27 ACT	E [5]	 Oth	6	6	0	2	0	4	1	2
2687	Muskegon CC Muskegon	1319	1100	[1] 1500	Pub	M	U		E [5]	6/01 FA/FF	9	5	0	1	0	6	2	5
2688	North Central Mich C Petoskey	556	4100	3000 4700	Pub	T		 A/S	S [5]	4/15 FF=FA	2	6	1	1	1	6	4	3
2689	Northeastern Sch Com Bay City	169	2300	[1]	Priv	M [8]		9/09 None	Q †	8/01	6	8	0	1	0	7	6	1
2690	Northwestern Mich C Traverse City	2234	4500	3000 5600	Pub	S		9/18	Q [5]	5/01 FF=FA	6	6	1	1	1	6	3	5
2691	Oakland CC Bloomfield Hill	5941	1200	[1] 2700	Pub	V	S	9/01 None	E [5]	8/01 Oth	2	6	0	1	0	2	1	3
2692	Saint Clair Co CC Port Huron	1424	1300	[1] 2600	Pub	S		8/27 None	E [5]	6/01 FF/FA	6	7	0	1	1	4	7	4
2693	Saint John Sch Rad Detroit	19	800	[1]	Cath	V [8]	U	3/31 ACT	O †		0	7	0	0	0		9	

Educational Programs Available — College Transfer Courses

Sequence Number	Agriculture	Bus-Commerce	Communications	Education	Engineering	Fine, Applied Arts	Foreign Lang	Health	Home Ec	Humanities	Mathematics	Computer/Info Sci	Biological Sci	Physical Sci	Social Sci
2671		■	■	■	■	■	■	■		■	■				■
2672															
2673		■										■			
2674		■	■	■	■	■	■	■		■	■	■	■	■	■
2675	■	■	■	■	■	■	■	■		■	■	■	■	■	■
2676	■	■	■	■	■	■	■	■	■	■	■	■	■	■	■
2677		■	■	■	■	■	■	■		■	■	■	■	■	■
2678	■	■	■	■	■	■	■	■	■	■	■	■	■	■	■
2679	■	■	■	■	■	■	■	■	■	■	■	■	■	■	■
2680		■										■			
2681		■	■	■	■	■	■	■		■	■	■	■	■	■
2682															
2683		■	■	■		■				■	■	■	■	■	■
2684	■	■	■	■	■	■	■	■	■	■	■	■	■	■	■
2685		■	■	■		■		■	■	■	■	■		■	■
2686	■	■	■	■	■	■		■	■	■	■	■	■	■	■
2687	■	■	■	■	■	■	■	■		■	■	■	■	■	■
2688	■	■	■	■	■	■		■	■	■	■	■	■	■	■
2689		■						■				■			
2690	■	■	■	■	■	■	■	■	■	■	■	■	■	■	■
2691	■	■	■	■	■	■	■	■	■	■	■	■	■	■	■
2692	■	■	■	■	■	■	■	■	■	■	■	■	■	■	■
2693															

Educational Programs Available — Career-oriented Programs (Agri, Business, Arts)

Sequence Number	Agri: Ag Business	Ag/Farm Mgmt	Ag Mechanics/Tech	Horticulture	Business: Accounting	Bus Mgmt & Admin	Hotel/Rest Mgmt	Office Mgmt	Marketing/Purchasing	Secretarial Studies	Arts: Architecture Tech	Applied Design	Photography/Cinema
2671					■					■			
2672													
2673					■	■		■	■	■			
2674					■	■	■	■	■	■			
2675					■	■		■	■	■			
2676					■	■		■		■		■	
2677					■	■			■	■	■		
2678					■	■	■	■	■	■		■	
2679					■	■	■	■	■	■	■		■
2680					■	■		■		■			
2681					■	■		■	■	■	■		
2682													
2683					■	■			■	■			
2684		■	■		■	■		■	■	■			
2685					■	■			■	■			
2686					■	■		■	■	■			
2687					■	■	■	■		■			
2688								■	■	■			
2689					■	■		■		■			
2690					■	■	■	■		■			
2691				■	■	■	■	■	■	■	■	■	
2692	■			■	■	■			■	■		■	
2693													

Educational Programs Available — Career-oriented Programs (Health, Math, SocSci)

Sequence Number	Health: Dental Assistant	Medical or Lab Tech	Nursing (RN)	Nursing (LPN)	Radiologic Technology	Math: Computer Prog	Data Processing Tech	Computer Operating	SocSci: Crim Just/Law Enforce	Parks/Rec Mgmt	Social Work
2671		■	■	■		■	■				
2672			■								
2673								■			
2674			■	■	■		■		■		
2675		■	■			■	■	■	■		
2676		■	■	■	■	■	■		■		
2677			■	■			■		■		
2678	■		■	■	■		■		■		
2679	■		■	■	■	■	■	■	■		■
2680						■	■				
2681	■		■				■	■	■		
2682					■						
2683			■	■	■		■	■	■		
2684			■		■	■	■	■	■		
2685			■	■			■	■	■		
2686	■		■	■			■		■		■
2687			■	■		■	■	■	■		
2688			■			■	■		■		
2689											
2690	■	■	■	■		■	■	■	■		
2691		■	■	■	■	■	■		■		■
2692			■	■		■	■		■		■
2693					■						

Educational Programs Available — Career-oriented Programs (Technical/Skilled Trades)

Sequence Number	Air/Refrig/Heat Tech	Auto Body Repair	Auto Mechanics	Carpentry/Constr	Drafting/Eng Draft	Electric Eng Tech	Civil Eng Tech	Indus/Mfg Eng Tech	Mech Eng Tech	Machinework	Welding
2671			■		■	■					■
2672											
2673											
2674	■		■		■	■			■	■	■
2675	■		■		■	■		■	■	■	■
2676			■		■	■				■	■
2677			■		■			■		■	■
2678					■			■	■	■	
2679	■	■	■	■	■	■	■	■		■	■
2680											
2681	■	■	■	■	■	■	■	■	■	■	■
2682											
2683	■		■	■	■					■	■
2684			■		■	■		■	■	■	■
2685			■		■					■	■
2686	■		■	■	■	■	■		■	■	■
2687					■	■				■	■
2688				■						■	■
2689											
2690			■		■	■					
2691	■	■	■	■	■	■		■	■	■	■
2692					■			■		■	■
2693											

▲ **Sequence Number—indicates the order of the college in this book only. Do *not* use this number with admissions tests or need analysis services.**

[1] No campus room and board facilities
[2] Room only or board only
[3] Most freshmen required to live on campus
[4] City or district residency requirements
[5] Accredited by regional accrediting association or a recognized candidate for accreditation
[6] All female freshman class
[7] All male freshman class
[8] Some admission selectivity; not all hs graduates accepted
[9] Requirements more stringent for nonresidents
†Accredited by a nationally recognized accrediting body other than one of the regional accrediting associations

Michigan
(continued)

Sequence Number	School name (upper entry) / City (lower entry)	Enrollment	Costs: Resident tuition/fees + room/board	Costs: Room/board (upper entry) / Nonresident tuition/fees (lower entry)	Gen. Info.: Affiliation (upper entry) / Religious observance (lower entry)	Gen. Info.: Size of community	Gen. Info.: Type of community	Admissions: Fall term application deadline (upper entry) / Test required or desired (lower entry)	Admissions: Calendar	Financial Aid: Fall term application deadline (upper entry) / Forms to be filed (lower entry)	-have need, rec some aid	-are women	-live on campus	-are minority students	-are nonresidents	-return as sophomores	-complete assoc degree	-transfer to 4-year college
2694	Schoolcraft C Livonia	2184	1100	[1] 2300	Pub	L	S	 A=S	E[5]	3/30 Oth	2	5	0	1		7	4	4
2695	Southwestern Mich C Dowagiac	1148	4100	3000 4700	Pub	T		9/01 A/S	E[5]	 FF/FA	5	6	0	1	1	4	3	2
2696	Suomi C Hancock	575	10200	2800	Luth O	S[8]		 Oth	E[5]	 FAF	8	7	7	3	3	6	5	5
2697	Washtenaw CC Ann Arbor	2202	900	[1] 1900	Pub	M	S	9/05 None	S[5]	7/01 FA/FF	1	6	0	2	1		1	1
2698	Wayne Co CC Detroit	2121	1000	[1] 2000	Pub	V	U	 Oth	E[5]	8/31 FF=FA	2	7	0	7	1	6	3	2
2699	West Shore CC Scottville	510	1000	[1] 2000	Pub	T		 None	E[5]	 FF/FA	3	6	0	1	1	8	3	4
Minnesota																		
2700	Abbott NW Sch Rad T Minneapolis	19	600	[1]	Priv	V[8]	U	6/01 Oth	O	 FF=FA	5	7	0	0	1	9		
2701	Acad of Accountancy Minneapolis	180	6100	[1]	Priv	V	S	 Oth	Q†	 FFS	3	4	0	1		7		3
2702	Albert Lea Tech C Albert Lea	423	1600	[1] 3300	Pub	S		 None	Q[5]	 FFS	8	4	0	1	1	7		
2703	Alexandria Tech C Alexandria	1441	1600	[1] 3200	Pub	S[8]		 Oth	Q[5]	 FF/FA	9	5	0	1	1	6	8	
2704	Anoka Tech C Anoka	1600	1700	[1] 3400	Pub	M	S	 None	Q†	 FFS	3	5	0	1	1			
2705	Anoka-Ramsey CC Cambridge	325	1600	[1] 2400	Pub	T		 None	Q[5]	7/15 FFS	7	6	0	0	0	3	1	2
2706	Anoka-Ramsey CC Coon Rapids	2202	1600	[1] 2300	Pub	S		9/17 None	Q[5]	 FF/FA	3	6		1	1	4		
2707	Austin CC of Minn Austin	1250	1600	[1] 2400	Pub	S		 A=S	Q[5]	 FF/FA	7	7	0	1	1	6		
2708	Bemidji Tech C Bemidji	500	4100	2300 5800	Pub	S		 None	Q[5]	 FFS	8	4	1	1	1	9	6	1
2709	Bethany Lutheran C Mankato	285	7500[3]	2400	Luth OS	S[8]		8/15 A/S	E[5]	4/01 FF/FA	8	5	9	1	3	9	7	7
2710	Brainerd CC Brainerd	1837	1500	[1] 2200	Pub	S		9/09 A/S	Q[5]	 FF/FA	8	6	0	1	1	3	4	3
2711	Brainerd Tech C Brainerd	610	1600	[1] 3200	Pub	S		 None	Q[5]	8/01	7	6	0	1	1	3	9	1
2712	Dakota Co Tech C Rosemount	1939	1600	[1] 3200	Pub	T		 Oth	Q[5]	 FF/FA	7	5	0	1	1	7		
2713	Detroit Lakes Tech C Detroit Lakes	700	1500	[1] 3000	Pub	T		 None	Q[5]	 FFS	8	4	0	3	1		7	
2714	Duluth Tech C Duluth	1250	1400	[1] 2800	Pub	M		 Oth	Q[5]	 FF/FA	8	5	0	1			8	
2715	Dunwoody Inst Minneapolis	872	2800	[1]	Priv	L[8]	U	 Oth	Q†	 FF/FA	5	1		1				

Student Profile: No. in 10 who-

Educational Programs Available — College Transfer Courses

Sequence Number	Agriculture	Bus-Commerce	Communications	Education	Engineering	Fine, Applied Arts	Foreign Lang	Health	Home Ec	Humanities	Mathematics	Computer/Info Sci	Biological Sci	Physical Sci	Social Sci
2694	■	■	■	■	■	■	■	■	■	■	■	■	■	■	■
2695	■	■	■	■	■	■	■	■	■	■	■	■	■	■	■
2696		■	■	■	■	■	■	■		■		■	■	■	■
2697					■	■	■			■	■	■	■	■	■
2698	■	■			■	■	■	■	■	■	■	■	■	■	■
2699		■	■	■	■	■		■		■	■	■	■	■	■
Minnesota															
2700															
2701															
2702	■	■	■		■				■			■			
2703	■														■
2704															
2705		■	■	■		■	■	■		■	■		■	■	■
2706	■	■	■	■	■	■	■	■	■	■	■	■	■	■	■
2707		■	■	■	■	■	■	■	■	■	■	■	■	■	■
2708		■										■			
2709	■	■	■	■	■	■	■	■	■	■	■	■	■	■	■
2710	■	■	■	■	■	■	■	■	■	■	■	■	■	■	■
2711															
2712															
2713															
2714		■						■							■
2715			■		■	■						■			

Educational Programs Available — Career-oriented Programs (Agri, Business, Arts, Health)

Sequence Number	Agri: Ag Business	Agri: Ag/Farm Mgmt	Agri: Ag Mechanics/Tech	Agri: Horticulture	Business: Accounting	Business: Bus Mgmt & Admin	Business: Hotel/Rest Mgmt	Business: Office Mgmt	Business: Marketing/Purchasing	Business: Secretarial Studies	Arts: Architecture Tech	Arts: Applied Design	Arts: Photography/Cinema	Health: Dental Assistant	Health: Medical or Lab Tech	Health: Nursing (RN)	Health: Nursing (LPN)	Health: Radiologic Technology
2694					■			■	■	■					■	■	■	
2695	■				■	■		■	■	■						■	■	
2696					■	■	■	■		■						■	■	
2697					■		■	■	■	■			■	■		■	■	■
2698					■	■	■			■				■	■	■		
2699					■	■	■			■						■	■	
Minnesota																		
2700																		■
2701					■													
2702		■			■	■		■	■	■								
2703			■		■		■	■	■	■					■		■	
2704				■		■		■	■	■	■						■	
2705					■	■		■	■	■								
2706					■			■	■	■						■		
2707																■		
2708					■				■					■			■	
2709										■								
2710					■	■										■		
2711				■	■	■		■	■	■				■			■	
2712			■	■	■	■		■	■	■	■		■				■	
2713					■			■	■	■	■						■	
2714				■	■				■	■					■		■	
2715																		

Educational Programs Available — Career-oriented Programs (Math, SocSci, Technical/Skilled Trades)

Sequence Number	Math: Computer Prog	Math: Data Processing Tech	Math: Computer Operating	SocSci: Crim Just/Law Enforce	SocSci: Parks/Rec Mgmt	SocSci: Social Work	Air/Refrig/Heat Tech	Auto Body Repair	Auto Mechanics	Carpentry/Constr	Drafting/Eng Draft	Electric Eng Tech	Civil Eng Tech	Indus/Mfg Eng Tech	Mech Eng Tech	Machinework	Welding
2694	■	■		■					■		■			■	■	■	■
2695	■	■	■						■		■	■			■	■	■
2696	■		■	■	■	■											
2697	■	■		■				■	■	■	■	■			■	■	■
2698	■	■	■	■			■	■	■			■					■
2699	■	■	■	■					■			■				■	■
Minnesota																	
2700																	
2701																	
2702	■	■	■				■		■	■	■				■	■	■
2703	■			■					■	■				■		■	■
2704					■		■	■	■		■	■			■	■	■
2705	■	■															
2706																	
2707				■													
2708								■	■	■							
2709																	
2710				■													
2711		■	■					■	■								■
2712	■	■	■					■	■			■				■	■
2713		■	■				■	■	■	■	■	■					■
2714	■	■	■					■	■	■	■	■				■	
2715																	

▲ **Sequence Number—indicates the order of the college in this book only. Do *not* use this number with admissions tests or need analysis services.**

[1] No campus room and board facilities
[2] Room only or board only
[3] Most freshmen required to live on campus
[4] City or district residency requirements
[5] Accredited by regional accrediting association or a recognized candidate for accreditation
[6] All female freshman class
[7] All male freshman class
[8] Some admission selectivity; not all hs graduates accepted
[9] Requirements more stringent for nonresidents
†Accredited by a nationally recognized accrediting body other than one of the regional accrediting associations

Minnesota
(continued)

Sequence Number	School name (upper entry) / City (lower entry)	Enrollment	Resident tuition/fees + room/board	Room/board (upper entry) / Nonresident tuition/fees (lower entry)	Affiliation (upper entry) / Religious observance (lower entry)	Size of community	Type of community	Fall term application deadline (upper entry) / Test required or desired (lower entry)	Calendar	Fall term application deadline (upper entry) / Forms to be filed (lower entry)	-have need, rec some aid	-are women	-live on campus	-are minority students	-are nonresidents	-return as sophomores	-complete assoc degree	-transfer to 4-year college
			Costs		**Gen. Info.**			**Admissions**		**Financial Aid**	**Student Profile: No. in 10 who-**							
2716	East Grand Fork Tech / East Grand Fork	900	1700	[1]	Pub	M		8/30 / Oth	Q †	8/30 / FF/FA		5	0	1	4		8	
2717	Eveleth Tech C / Eveleth	410	1600	[1] / 3200	Pub	T [8]		Oth	Q †	FFS	9	5	0	1	1	9	8	1
2718	Faribault Tech C / Faribault	550	1600	[1] / 3300	Pub	S		None	Q †	FFS	8	5	0	1	1	3	9	1
2719	Fergus Falls CC / Fergus Falls	679	1500	[1] / 2200	Pub	S			Q [5]	FF=FA	7	6		1	1	6	6	7
2720	Granite Falls Vo-Tec / Granite Falls	350	1700	[1] / 3500	Pub	T		None	Q [5]	6/01 / FF/FA	8	4	0	1	1	5	8	
2721	Hennepin TC-Brk Park / Minneapolis		1600	[1] / 3100	Pub	S		Oth	Q [5]	FF/FA	7	4		1				
2722	Hennepin TC-Eden Pra / Minneapolis		1600	[1] / 3100	Pub	S		Oth	Q [5]	FF/FA	7	6		1			9	
2723	Hibbing CC / Hibbing	425	1500	[1] / 2200	Pub	S			Q [5]	FF/FA	6	6	0	1	1	5	5	2
2724	Hibbing Tech C / Hibbing	648	1700	[1] / 3400	Pub	S		None	Q [5]	FFS	8	2	0	1	1		8	
2725	Hutchinson Tech C / Hutchinson	710	1900	[1] / 3700	Pub	S		None	Q [5]	FFS	6	4	0	1	1			
2726	Inver Hills CC / Inver Grove Hts	1691	1900	[2] / 2600	Pub	S		9/01 / None	Q [5]	6/01 / FF/FA	5	6	0	1	1	6	4	
2727	Itasca CC / Grand Rapids	905	1600	[1] / 2400	Pub	S		None	Q [5]	FF/FA	6	6	0	1	1	6	4	6
2728	Jackson Tech C / Jackson	400	1800	[1] / 3400	Pub	T		None	Q [5]	FF/FA	8	3	0	1	1	3	9	1
2729	Lakewood CC / White Bear Lake	2286	1500	[1] / 2200	Pub	M	S	None	Q [5]	FF/FA	4	6	0	1	1			
2730	Lowthian C / Minneapolis	153	8200	2700	Priv	L [8]	U [6]	Oth	Q †	FFS	8	9	3	1	3	6	7	1
2731	Mankato Tech C / North Mankato	1450	1700	[1] / 3400	Pub	S [8]		None	Q [5]	5/01 / FFS	8	5	0	1		8	7	
2732	Medical Inst of Minn / Minneapolis	550	5000	[1]	Priv	V [8]	U	Oth	Q †	9/15 / FFS	8	8	0	1	2			
2733	Mesabi CC / Virginia	638	1600	[1] / 2400	Pub	T		9/16 / None	Q [5]	9/01 / FF/FA	8	6	0	1	1	5	4	5
2734	Minn Rivlnd Tech C / Austin	685	2000	[1] / 3600	Pub	S		None	Q †	FF/FA	8	4	0	1	1	2		
2735	Minn Tech Inst,U of / Crookston	834	5500	3100 / 8900	Pub	T		9/01 / A/S	Q [5]	4/30 / FF/FA	8	6	5	1	1	6	5	2
2736	Minn Waseca,U of / Waseca	774	4900	2500 / 8300	Pub	T		Oth	O [5]	FFS	8	6	5	1			6	2
2737	Minneapolis CC / Minneapolis	1682	1500	[1] / 2200	Pub	L	U	9/15 / None	Q [5]	FF/FA	7	6	0	3				
2738	Minneapolis Tech C / Minneapolis	1700	1600	[1] / 3200	Pub	L	U	Oth	Q †	FFS	8	4	0	4	1	4		

Educational Programs Available

Sequence Number	Agriculture	Bus-Commerce	Communications	Education	Engineering	Fine, Applied Arts	Foreign Lang	Health	Home Ec	Humanities	Mathematics	Computer/Info Sci	Biological Sci	Physical Sci	Social Sci	Ag Business	Ag/Farm Mgmt	Ag Mechanics/Tech	Horticulture	Accounting	Bus Mgmt & Admin	Hotel/Rest Mgmt	Office Mgmt	Marketing/Purchasing	Secretarial Studies	Architecture Tech	Applied Design	Photography/Cinema	Dental Assistant	Medical or Lab Tech	Nursing (RN)	Nursing (LPN)	Radiologic Technology	Computer Prog	Data Processing Tech	Computer Operating	Crim Just/Law Enforce	Parks/Rec Mgmt	Social Work	Air/Refrig/Heat Tech	Auto Body Repair	Auto Mechanics	Carpentry/Constr	Drafting/Eng Draft	Electric Eng Tech	Civil Eng Tech	Indus/Mfg Eng Tech	Mech Eng Tech	Machinework	Welding
	College Transfer Courses															**Career-oriented Programs: Agri**				**Business**						**Arts**			**Health**					**Math**			**SocSci**			**Technical/Skilled Trades**										
2716		■						■				■					■	■		■			■		■					■		■	■		■	■						■	■							■
2717								■												■			■		■							■			■							■	■				■			■
2718		■			■			■				■								■				■	■					■		■			■	■							■	■	■		■	■	■	■
2719	■	■	■	■	■	■	■	■	■	■	■	■	■	■	■								■	■	■					■	■	■					■													
2720		■																		■			■	■	■										■						■			■	■				■	
2721																				■			■	■	■	■		■	■			■		■	■	■				■	■	■		■			■	■	■	■
2722																				■			■	■	■	■		■						■	■	■				■	■	■	■	■	■		■		■	■
2723	■	■	■	■	■	■	■	■	■	■	■	■	■	■	■										■					■	■		■											■						
2724																								■					■	■							■			■		■			■					■
2725																		■			■		■	■	■							■										■		■				■	■	■
2726	■	■	■	■	■	■	■	■	■	■	■	■	■	■	■					■	■		■	■	■						■			■			■		■		■	■								
2727	■	■		■	■	■	■	■	■		■	■			■					■				■	■							■																		
2728																				■			■	■	■															■	■	■	■	■	■			■		
2729	■	■	■	■	■	■	■	■	■	■	■	■	■	■	■					■				■	■						■		■		■		■		■											
2730																								■																									
2731																■	■	■		■			■	■	■	■			■			■		■	■	■				■	■	■		■		■		■	■	■
2732																														■																			
2733	■	■	■	■	■	■	■	■	■	■	■	■	■	■	■									■	■												■													
2734	■	■	■					■				■			■	■	■	■			■		■	■	■							■	■		■						■		■				■		■	■
2735	■	■	■	■	■	■			■	■	■	■	■	■	■	■	■	■	■	■	■	■	■	■	■										■			■												
2736	■	■		■	■			■	■	■	■	■			■	■	■	■	■		■		■	■	■													■												
2737		■				■	■	■		■	■	■	■	■	■					■	■			■				■			■			■			■													
2738		■	■																	■			■	■	■							■		■	■	■				■		■			■				■	■

▲ Sequence Number—indicates the order of the college in this book only. Do *not* use this number with admissions tests or need analysis services.

[1] No campus room and board facilities
[2] Room only or board only
[3] Most freshmen required to live on campus
[4] City or district residency requirements
[5] Accredited by regional accrediting association or a recognized candidate for accreditation
[6] All female freshman class
[7] All male freshman class
[8] Some admission selectivity; not all hs graduates accepted
[9] Requirements more stringent for nonresidents
†Accredited by a nationally recognized accrediting body other than one of the regional accrediting associations

Minnesota
(continued)

Sequence Number	School name (upper entry) / City (lower entry)	Enrollment	Costs: Resident tuition/fees + room/board	Costs: Room/board (upper entry) / Nonresident tuition/fees (lower entry)	Gen. Info.: Affiliation (upper entry) / Religious observance (lower entry)	Gen. Info.: Size of community	Gen. Info.: Type of community	Admissions: Fall term application deadline (upper entry) / Test required or desired (lower entry)	Admissions: Calendar	Financial Aid: Fall term application deadline (upper entry) / Forms to be filed (lower entry)	-have need, rec some aid	-are women	-live on campus	-are minority students	-are nonresidents	-return as sophomores	-complete assoc degree	-transfer to 4-year college
2739	Moorhead Tech C / Moorhead	1089	1600	[1] / 3200	Pub	M [8]		9/05 / None	Q [5]	FF/FA	8	5	0	1	4	3	8	1
2740	Normandale CC / Bloomington	4177	1500	[1] / 2200	Pub	M	S	9/01 / None	Q [5]	FF/FA	3	6	0	1	1	5	4	2
2741	North Hennepin CC / Brooklyn Park	3000	2000	[1] / 2800	Pub	V	S	9/20 / None	Q [5]	FF/FA	7	6	0	1	1	6	1	2
2742	Northeast Metro Tech / White Bear Lake	2000	1500	[1] / 3100	Pub	S		None	Q [5]	FF/FA	7	5	0	1	1	6	6	1
2743	Northland CC / Thief Rvr Falls	456	1600	[1] / 2300	Pub	T		9/16 / None	Q [5]	9/01 / FF/FA	6	6	0	1	1	6	6	6
2744	Northwest Tech Inst / Eden Prairie	171	6500	[1]	Priv	V [8]	S	0/15 / Oth	S †	8/01 / FFS	8	1	0	1	1	8	8	1
2745	Pine Tech C / Pine City	300	1500	[1] / 3000	Pub	T		Oth	Q [5]	FF/FA	8	3	0	1	1	4		
2746	Rainy River CC / Internatl Falls	460	3100 [2]	1600 / 3700	Pub	T		A/S	Q [5]	FF/FA	9	5	0	2	1	5	4	4
2747	Red Wing Tech C / Red Wing	425	1700	[1] / 3300	Pub	S		None	Q [5]	8/01 / FF/FA	9	4	0	1	3		9	1
2748	Rochester CC / Rochester	2141	1500	[1] / 2200	Pub	M		9/11 / Oth	Q [5]	FF/FA	6	6	0	1	1	6		
2749	Rochester Tech C / Rochester	802	1500	[1] / 3100	Pub	M		9/06 / Oth	Q [5]	FFS	8	5	0	1	1	2	7	1
2750	Saint Cloud Hos Xray / St Cloud	15	400	[1]	Cath	S [8]		2/31 / A/S	O †	FFS	5	9	0	0	0	9	9	
2751	Saint Paul Tech C / St Paul	2000	1400	[1] / 2800	Pub	L	U	Oth	Q [5]	FF=FA	8	4	0	3		8	2	
2752	Southwest Tech C / Canby	200	1900	[1] / 3400	Pub	T		9/20 / None	Q [5]	FFS	8	3	0	1	2	5	9	1
2753	Southwestern Tech C / Pipestone	300	1600	[1] / 3200	Pub	T		None	Q [5]	FF/FA	8	4	0	1	2		9	
2754	St Cloud Tech C / St Cloud	2200	1600	[1] / 3200	Pub	M		None	Q [5]	FF/FA	7	4	0	1		4	8	
2755	St Marys of St Cath / Minneapolis	287	8300 [2]	800	Cath	V [8]	U		4 [5]	FF/FA	8	9	2	1	1	8	8	1
2756	Staples Tech C / Staples	720	1600	[1] / 3200	Pub	T		A=S	Q	FF/FA	9	2	0	2	1	9	9	1
2757	Thief Rvr Falls Tech / Thief Rvr Falls	850	1600	[1] / 3200	Pub	T		None	Q	FF/FA	8	5	0	1	1	7	1	1
2758	Vermilion CC / Ely	550	4500 [3]	2800 / 5300	Pub	T		None	Q [5]	9/01 / FF/FA	9	4	4	1	1	7	7	6
2759	Wadena Tech C / Wadena	600	1900	[1] / 3800	Pub	T		None	O [5]	FFS	8	5	0	1	1	3	9	
2760	Willmar CC / Willmar	908	1600	[1] / 2400	Pub	S		9/01	Q [5]	6/01 / FF/FA	8	6	0	1	1	7	6	6
2761	Willmar Tech C / Willmar	1150	2900 [2]	1200 / 4600	Pub	S		None	Q [5]	FF/FA	7	5	0	1	1	3	8	1

Student Profile: No. in 10 who-

Educational Programs Available — College Transfer Courses

Sequence Number	Agriculture	Bus-Commerce	Communications	Education	Engineering	Fine, Applied Arts	Foreign Lang	Health	Home Ec	Humanities	Mathematics	Computer/Info Sci	Biological Sci	Physical Sci	Social Sci
2739		■	■												
2740	■	■	■	■	■	■	■	■	■	■	■	■	■	■	■
2741	■	■	■	■	■	■	■	■		■	■	■	■	■	■
2742	■	■	■			■		■	■			■			■
2743	■	■	■	■	■	■	■	■	■	■	■	■	■	■	■
2744															
2745		■										■			
2746	■	■	■	■	■	■	■	■	■	■	■	■	■	■	■
2747															
2748	■	■	■	■	■	■	■	■	■	■	■	■	■	■	■
2749															
2750															
2751															
2752										■	■				■
2753															
2754															
2755				■				■	■						■
2756															
2757		■													
2758	■	■	■	■	■	■	■	■	■	■	■	■	■	■	■
2759															
2760	■	■	■	■	■	■	■	■	■	■	■	■	■	■	■
2761	■	■	■			■									

Educational Programs Available — Career-oriented Programs (Agri; Business; Arts; Health; Math; SocSci; Technical/Skilled Trades)

Sequence Number	Ag Business	Ag/Farm Mgmt	Ag Mechanics/Tech	Horticulture	Accounting	Bus Mgmt & Admin	Hotel/Rest Mgmt	Office Mgmt	Marketing/Purchasing	Secretarial Studies	Architecture Tech	Applied Design	Photography/Cinema	Dental Assistant	Medical or Lab Tech	Nursing (RN)	Nursing (LPN)	Radiologic Technology	Computer Prog	Data Processing Tech	Computer Operating	Crim Just/Law Enforce	Parks/Rec Mgmt	Social Work	Air/Refrig/Heat Tech	Auto Body Repair	Auto Mechanics	Carpentry/Constr	Drafting/Eng Draft	Electric Eng Tech	Civil Eng Tech	Indus/Mfg Eng Tech	Mech Eng Tech	Machinework	Welding
2739					■				■	■				■					■		■				■		■	■	■						■
2740					■		■	■						■		■		■	■		■	■							■				■		
2741					■	■		■	■	■		■				■		■				■	■				■								
2742				■	■	■		■	■	■			■	■	■				■	■	■				■	■	■						■	■	
2743						■		■		■						■						■													
2744											■																		■				■		
2745					■	■		■	■	■											■						■							■	■
2746					■			■		■							■																		
2747		■	■		■			■		■		■					■		■		■		■		■		■	■						■	■
2748						■			■	■					■	■		■				■								■	■		■		
2749		■			■			■		■				■			■				■				■		■	■	■				■	■	
2750																		■																	
2751					■		■			■	■				■		■		■	■	■				■	■	■	■	■		■		■	■	■
2752	■	■	■		■					■				■													■								■
2753	■	■			■			■	■	■							■			■	■						■	■							
2754		■			■	■			■	■	■			■			■		■	■	■				■	■	■	■	■	■	■		■	■	■
2755																■																			
2756										■																	■		■				■	■	
2757					■					■							■				■					■	■		■						■
2758					■					■													■												
2759					■					■										■	■					■	■								
2760	■				■	■		■		■										■	■	■		■					■						
2761	■	■	■		■	■		■	■	■			■				■									■	■	■	■					■	■

▲ Sequence Number—indicates the order of the college in this book only. Do *not* use this number with admissions tests or need analysis services.

[1] No campus room and board facilities
[2] Room only or board only
[3] Most freshmen required to live on campus
[4] City or district residency requirements
[5] Accredited by regional accrediting association or a recognized candidate for accreditation
[6] All female freshman class
[7] All male freshman class
[8] Some admission selectivity; not all hs graduates accepted
[9] Requirements more stringent for nonresidents
†Accredited by a nationally recognized accrediting body other than one of the regional accrediting associations

Minnesota
(continued)

Sequence Number	School name (upper entry) City (lower entry)	Enrollment	Costs: Resident tuition/fees + room/board	Costs: Room/board (upper entry) Nonresident tuition/fees (lower entry)	Gen. Info.: Affiliation (upper entry) Religious observance (lower entry)	Gen. Info.: Size of community	Gen. Info.: Type of community	Admissions: Fall term application deadline (upper entry) Test required or desired (lower entry)	Calendar	Financial Aid: Fall term application deadline (upper entry) Forms to be filed (lower entry)	No. in 10 who- have need, rec some aid	-are women	-live on campus	-are minority students	-are nonresidents	-return as sophomores	-complete assoc degree	-transfer to 4-year college
2762	Winona Tech C Winona	531	1800	[1] 3800	Pub	S		None	Q[5]	FF/FA	8	4	0	1	4	3	4	
2763	Worthington CC Worthington	472	1600	[1] 2400	Pub	S		A=S	Q[5]	FF/FA	8	6	0	1	2	5	7	5
Mississippi																		
2764	Clarke C Newton	116	5600	2300	Oth OS	T		9/14 A/S	E[5]	4/01 FA/FF	9	4	6	2	2	4	2	7
2765	Coahoma CC Clarksdale	1478	2800	2100 4200	Pub	S		ACT	S[5]	7/15 FA/FF	9	5	3	9	1	5	7	7
2766	Copiah-Lincoln CC Natchez	195	700	[1] 1700	Pub	M		ACT	O[5]	FFS	3	6	0	3	1	8	2	5
2767	Copiah-Lincoln CC Wesson	1246	2900	2200 3200	Pub	T		ACT	S[5]	6/01 FFS	3	5	6	3	1	8	6	8
2768	East Central JC Decatur	818	2400	1600 3300	Pub	T		ACT	E[5]	FFS	6	6	4	3	1	6		
2769	East Miss CC Mayhew	450	900	[1] 1900	Pub	S		9/15 A=S	S[5]	12/15	6	4	0	2	0	3	8	1
2770	East Miss CC Scooba	717	2700	1800 3700	Pub	T		9/10 A/S	S[5]	FFS	7	5	4	5	1	6	6	4
2771	Hinds CC-Jackson Jackson	766	700	[1] 3700	Pub	L	U	ACT	O[5]	Oth	7	7	0	7				
2772	Hinds CC-Rankin Pearl	955	700	[1] 3700	Pub	S		ACT	E[5]	FA/FF	1	5	0	1	0	0		
2773	Hinds CC-Raymond Raymond	3858	2200	1500 5200	Pub	T		8/11 ACT	E[5]	Oth	6	4	2	3	1		4	5
2774	Hinds CC-Utica Cam Utica	591	2200	1500 5200	Pub	T		8/20 ACT	E[5]	FA/FF	9	6		9	1		4	5
2775	Hinds CC-Vicksburg Vicksburg	111	700	[1] 3700	Pub	S		ACT	E[5]	FFS	1	6	0	3	1	6	4	2
2776	Holmes CC Goodman	667	1900	1200 2900	Pub	T[8]		8/29 ACT	E[5]	6/01 FF/FA	6	5	5	4	1	9	4	
2777	Itawamba CC Fulton	3358	2400	1600 3100	Pub	T		A/S	S[5]	FFS	7	5	3	2	1	5	4	
2778	Jones Co JC Ellisville	3100	2300	1700	Pub	T		A/S	E[5]	FF/FA	8	6		2	1	4	4	
2779	Mary Holmes C West Point	742	7800	3800	Pres S	S		None	E[5]	FAF	9	6	9	9	1	5	6	6
2780	Meridian CC Meridian	1525	2800	2100 3700	Pub	S		Oth	S[5]	Oth	4	7	0	3	1		2	
2781	Miss Bapt Rad Techn Jackson	28	600	[1]	Bapt	L[8]	U	5/01 ACT	O†	6/01 Oth	1	6	0	1		9		
2782	Miss Delta CC Moorhead	1583	2000	1300 3000	Pub	T		ACT	E[5]		7	6	3	4	1	8	8	3
2783	Miss Gulf CC Jackson Gautier	1996	800	[1] 1700	Pub	S		A/S	E[5]	FF=FA	5	6	0	2	1	6	3	4

Educational Programs Available — College Transfer Courses

Sequence Number	Agriculture	Bus-Commerce	Communications	Education	Engineering	Fine, Applied Arts	Foreign Lang	Health	Home Ec	Humanities	Mathematics	Computer/Info Sci	Biological Sci	Physical Sci	Social Sci
2762															
2763	■	■	■	■	■	■	■	■	■	■	■	■	■	■	■
2764		■		■		■	■	■		■	■	■	■	■	■
2765	■	■	■	■		■	■	■	■	■	■	■	■	■	■
2766	■	■	■	■	■	■	■	■	■	■	■	■	■	■	■
2767	■	■	■	■	■	■		■	■	■	■	■	■	■	■
2768	■	■	■	■	■	■	■	■		■	■	■	■	■	■
2769		■										■			
2770	■	■	■	■	■	■	■	■	■	■	■	■	■	■	■
2771		■	■	■	■	■		■	■	■	■	■			■
2772		■	■	■	■	■		■	■	■	■	■			■
2773	■	■	■	■	■	■	■	■	■	■	■	■	■	■	■
2774	■	■	■	■		■		■		■	■	■	■	■	■
2775	■	■	■	■	■	■	■	■		■	■	■			■
2776	■	■	■	■	■	■	■	■		■	■	■	■	■	■
2777	■	■	■	■	■	■	■	■	■	■	■	■	■	■	■
2778	■	■	■	■	■	■	■	■	■	■	■	■	■	■	■
2779		■	■	■	■	■		■		■	■	■	■	■	■
2780	■	■	■	■	■	■	■	■	■	■	■	■	■	■	■
2781															
2782	■	■	■	■	■	■	■	■	■	■	■	■			■
2783		■	■	■	■	■	■	■		■	■	■	■	■	■

Educational Programs Available — Career-oriented Programs

Sequence Number	Agri: Ag Business	Ag/Farm Mgmt	Ag Mechanics/Tech	Horticulture	Business: Accounting	Bus Mgmt & Admin	Hotel/Rest Mgmt	Office Mgmt	Marketing/Purchasing	Secretarial Studies	Arts: Architecture Tech	Applied Design	Photography/Cinema	Health: Dental Assistant	Medical or Lab Tech	Nursing (RN)	Nursing (LPN)	Radiologic Technology	Math: Computer Prog	Data Processing Tech	Computer Operating	SocSci: Crim Just/Law Enforce	Parks/Rec Mgmt	Social Work	Technical/Skilled Trades: Air/Refrig/Heat Tech	Auto Body Repair	Auto Mechanics	Carpentry/Constr	Drafting/Eng Draft	Electric Eng Tech	Civil Eng Tech	Indus/Mfg Eng Tech	Mech Eng Tech	Machinework	Welding
2762		■			■	■		■	■	■							■			■	■					■	■		■				■	■	
2763	■	■				■				■							■		■																
2764																																			
2765																										■	■	■	■	■					■
2766					■	■	■	■	■	■																		■							
2767																																			
2768																				■					■	■	■	■	■	■					
2769						■			■								■			■					■		■		■				■	■	■
2770								■	■	■							■				■				■		■		■	■				■	■
2771							■			■				■	■	■	■										■		■					■	■
2772			■																						■	■		■	■					■	■
2773	■	■	■					■	■	■		■								■	■	■			■	■	■	■	■	■				■	■
2774										■											■					■	■	■	■	■				■	■
2775			■				■	■		■							■		■	■		■			■		■	■	■		■		■	■	■
2776									■	■	■					■	■			■	■				■	■	■	■	■	■				■	■
2777			■						■	■						■	■	■	■						■	■	■	■	■	■	■				■
2778				■		■		■		■						■	■	■		■	■				■		■		■					■	■
2779					■	■				■					■				■	■															
2780				■			■		■	■					■	■	■			■					■				■	■				■	■
2781																		■																	
2782		■	■							■	■				■	■	■	■	■	■	■				■		■	■	■					■	■
2783						■			■	■					■	■	■	■			■			■			■							■	

▲ **Sequence Number—indicates the order of the college in this book only. Do *not* use this number with admissions tests or need analysis services.**

1 No campus room and board facilities
2 Room only or board only
3 Most freshmen required to live on campus
4 City or district residency requirements
5 Accredited by regional accrediting association or a recognized candidate for accreditation
6 All female freshman class
7 All male freshman class
8 Some admission selectivity; not all hs graduates accepted
9 Requirements more stringent for nonresidents
†Accredited by a nationally recognized accrediting body other than one of the regional accrediting associations

Mississippi (continued)

Sequence Number	School name (upper entry) / City (lower entry)	Enrollment	Resident tuition/fees + room/board	Room/board (upper entry) / Nonresident tuition/fees (lower entry)	Affiliation (upper entry) / Religious observance (lower entry)	Size of community	Type of community	Fall term application deadline (upper entry) / Test required or desired (lower entry)	Calendar	Fall term application deadline (upper entry) / Forms to be filed (lower entry)	-have need, rec some aid	-are women	-live on campus	-are minority students	-are nonresidents	-return as sophomores	-complete assoc degree	-transfer to 4-year college
			Costs		Gen. Info.			Admissions		Financial Aid	Student Profile: No. in 10 who-							
2784	Miss Gulf CC Jeff D / Gulfport	2258	800	[1] / 1700	Pub	M	S	8/29 / A/S	E[5]	8/29 / Oth	6	6	0	2	1	5	3	4
2785	Miss Gulf CC Prknstn / Perkinston	926	2000	1300 / 2900	Pub	T[8]		8/31 / A/S	S[5]	Oth	7	5	7	1	1	5	4	7
2786	Natchez C / Natchez	70	2400	800	Bapt / OS	S		None	S	Oth	9	6	6	9	4	5	6	8
2787	Northeast Miss CC / Booneville	2700	2200	1500 / 3000	Pub	T		9/05 / A=S	E[5]	FF/FA	4	5	2	1	1	8	8	6
2788	Northwest Miss CC / Senatobia	2790	2400	1600 / 3200	Pub	T		8/20 / A/S	S[5]	3/15 / FAF	8	5	4	3	1	4	3	2
2789	Pearl River CC / Poplarville	1945	2400	1700 / 3300	Pub	T		ACT	E[5]	7/01	8	6	3	2	1	2	2	2
2790	Southwest Miss CC / Summit	1160	2200	1500 / 3200	Pub	T		A/S	E[5]	8/01 / FFS	8	6		2	1		3	4
2791	Wood JC / Mathiston	348	4700	2500	Meth / O	T[8]		A/S	E[5]	FFS	9	6	1	1	1	5	2	7
Missouri																		
2792	Burge Sch of Nursing / Springfield	180	4400[2]	900	Priv	L[8]	U	A/S	O†	FFS	5	9	2	1	0	9	9	
2793	Clinton Area Voc Tec / Clinton		3200	[1]	Pub	T			S				0		0			
2794	Cottey C / Nevada	343	7200[3]	2600	Priv	T[8]	[6]	A=S	S[5]	FF/FA	5	9	9	1	9	6	6	9
2795	Crowder C / Neosho	773	2500	1900 / 3300	Pub	T		8/23 / A/S	E[5]	3/15	7	5	1	1	1	4	5	5
2796	East Central C / Union	1179	700	[1] / 1400	Pub	T		Oth	E[5]	FF/FA	6	6	0	1	0	8	5	3
2797	Jefferson C / Hillsboro	1785	700	[1] / 1400	Pub	T		Oth	S[5]	5/01	9	6	0	1	0	4	2	3
2798	Jewish Hosp Sch Nsg / St Louis	218	4600[2]	800	Priv	V[8]	U	A=S	E†	FFS	9	9	7	1	3	9		
2799	Kemper Military C / Boonville	179	11600[3]	2200	Priv	T		A=S	S[5]	8/01 / FF=FA	9	2	9	4	7	8	9	9
2800	Le Cox Sch Radiology / Springfield	35	2300[2]	1800	Priv	L[8]	S	3/31 / ACT	O†	FFS	6	4	3	1	1	9		
2801	Linn Tech C / Linn	725	2500	[1]	Pub	T		ACT	E[5]	FFS	8	2	0	1	1	8	8	1
2802	Longview CC / Lee's Summit	3005	1100	[1] / 2500	Pub	M	S	None	E[5]	FF/FA	1	6	0	1	1			
2803	Lutheran Med Sch Nsg / St Louis	126	6800	900	Priv	V[8]	U	6/01 / A/S	S†	6/01 / FFS	9	9	5	1	2	7		
2804	Maple Woods CC / Kansas City	1055	900	[1] / 2300	Pub	L	S	8/24 / Oth	E[5]	8/28 / FF=FA	1	6	0	1	1	4	3	5
2805	Metro Business Cape / Cape Girardeau	135	5900	[1]	Priv	S[8]		Oth	O†	FF=FA	8	9	0	1	1	0	8	1

Educational Programs Available — College Transfer Courses

Sequence Number	Agriculture	Bus-Commerce	Communications	Education	Engineering	Fine, Applied Arts	Foreign Lang	Health	Home Ec	Humanities	Mathematics	Computer/Info Sci	Biological Sci	Physical Sci	Social Sci
2784		■	■	■	■	■	■	■		■	■	■	■	■	■
2785	■	■	■	■	■	■	■	■		■	■	■	■	■	■
2786				■						■					
2787	■	■	■	■	■	■	■	■	■	■	■	■	■	■	■
2788	■	■	■	■	■	■	■	■		■	■	■	■	■	■
2789	■	■	■	■	■	■		■	■	■	■	■	■	■	■
2790	■	■	■	■	■	■		■				■	■		■
2791	■	■	■	■	■	■	■	■		■	■	■	■	■	■
2792															
2793															
2794	■	■	■	■	■	■	■	■	■	■	■	■	■	■	■
2795	■	■	■	■	■	■	■	■		■	■	■	■	■	■
2796	■	■	■	■	■	■	■	■	■	■	■	■	■	■	■
2797	■	■	■	■	■	■	■	■	■	■	■	■	■	■	■
2798															
2799		■	■	■		■	■			■	■	■	■	■	■
2800															
2801															
2802		■	■	■	■	■	■	■	■	■	■	■	■	■	■
2803															
2804	■	■	■	■	■	■	■	■	■	■	■	■	■	■	■
2805															

Educational Programs Available — Career-oriented Programs

Sequence Number	Agri: Ag Business	Ag/Farm Mgmt	Ag Mechanics/Tech	Horticulture	Business: Accounting	Bus Mgmt & Admin	Hotel/Rest Mgmt	Office Mgmt	Marketing/Purchasing	Secretarial Studies	Arts: Architecture Tech	Applied Design	Photography/Cinema	Health: Dental Assistant	Medical or Lab Tech	Nursing (RN)	Nursing (LPN)	Radiologic Technology	Math: Computer Prog	Data Processing Tech	Computer Operating	SocSci: Crim Just/Law Enforce	Parks/Rec Mgmt	Social Work	Technical/Skilled Trades: Air/Refrig/Heat Tech	Auto Body Repair	Auto Mechanics	Carpentry/Constr	Drafting/Eng Draft	Electric Eng Tech	Civil Eng Tech	Indus/Mfg Eng Tech	Mech Eng Tech	Machinework	Welding
2784					■		■	■	■	■						■	■			■	■	■			■	■	■	■	■					■	■
2785				■	■			■		■																	■		■						■
2786										■																									
2787			■												■	■	■			■					■	■	■	■	■	■	■			■	■
2788		■	■		■					■					■		■			■					■	■	■	■	■	■	■	■	■	■	■
2789								■	■	■				■		■	■	■	■	■	■				■	■	■	■	■	■				■	■
2790									■	■						■	■			■	■				■		■	■	■					■	■
2791										■																									
2792																■																			
2793	■		■	■	■	■		■	■	■											■				■		■	■	■					■	■
2794																																			
2795	■	■	■		■	■	■		■	■							■									■	■	■	■	■					
2796				■	■	■			■	■				■		■				■		■			■			■	■						■
2797					■	■	■			■	■					■	■		■		■	■			■		■		■				■	■	■
2798																■																			
2799																																			
2800																		■																	
2801					■			■		■									■						■	■	■		■	■				■	
2802					■	■		■	■	■									■	■	■	■					■		■	■			■	■	
2803																■																			
2804					■			■	■	■									■	■	■	■													■
2805					■			■		■					■				■	■	■														

▲ **Sequence Number—indicates the order of the college in this book only. Do *not* use this number with admissions tests or need analysis services.**

1 No campus room and board facilities
2 Room only or board only
3 Most freshmen required to live on campus
4 City or district residency requirements
5 Accredited by regional accrediting association or a recognized candidate for accreditation
6 All female freshman class
7 All male freshman class
8 Some admission selectivity; not all hs graduates accepted
9 Requirements more stringent for nonresidents
†Accredited by a nationally recognized accrediting body other than one of the regional accrediting associations

Missouri
(continued)

Sequence Number	School name (upper entry) City (lower entry)	Enrollment	Costs: Resident tuition/fees + room/board	Costs: Room/board (upper entry) Nonresident tuition/fees (lower entry)	Gen. Info.: Affiliation (upper entry) Religious observance (lower entry)	Gen. Info.: Size of community	Gen. Info.: Type of community	Admissions: Fall term application deadline (upper entry) Test required or desired (lower entry)	Calendar	Financial Aid: Fall term application deadline (upper entry) Forms to be filed (lower entry)	No. in 10 who- -have need, rec some aid	-are women	-live on campus	-are minority students	-are nonresidents	-return as sophomores	-complete assoc degree	-transfer to 4-year college
2806	Metro Business J Cty Jefferson City	77	7400	[1]	Priv	S[8]		Oth	O†	FF=FA	9	8	0	1	0	0	7	1
2807	Metro Business Rolla Rolla	102	7400	[1]	Priv	S[8]		Oth	O†	FF=FA	8	9	0	1	0	0	9	1
2808	Mineral Area C Flat River	1237	800	[1] 1400	Pub	T		ACT	E[5]	11/01 FF=FA	5	6	0	1	0	4	3	3
2809	Missouri Bap Med Ct St Louis	108	5900[2]	1400	Bapt	V[8]	S	6/01 ACT	O†	6/01 FFS	6	9	3	1	1	8		6
2810	Moberly Area CC Moberly	906	700	[1] 2600	Pub	S		9/09 ACT	E[5]	8/20 FFS	5	6	0	1	1	6	8	6
2811	N Central Missouri C Trenton	436	1700[2]	900 2700	Pub	T		9/03 ACT	E[5]	7/01 FFS	6	7	1	1	1	4	2	2
2812	Northwest MO AVT Sch Maryville	70	2800	[1]	Pub	T[8]		Oth	E[5]	10/01	9	8	0	1	1	0		
2813	Penn Valley CC Kansas City	1612	1100	[1] 2500	Pub	V	U	None	E[5]	FF=FA	6	6	0	5	1	5	1	6
2814	Platt CC St Joseph	250	2500	[1]	Priv	M[8]		Oth	Q[5]		7	7	0	1	1	7	7	
2815	Ranken Tech C St Louis	710	3800	[1]	Priv	V[8]	U	Oth	O[5]	FF=FA	8	1	0	1	6	8	7	
2816	Rutledge-Phillips C Springfield	500	4500	[1]	Priv	L	U	Oth	Q†	FF/FA	7	8	0	1	0		8	
2817	Saint Charles CC St Charles	936	900	[1] 2100	Pub	M	S	A=S	E[5]		2	7	0	1	0			
2818	Saint John's Rad Tec Springfield	30	800	[1]	Cath	M[8]	U	2/01 ACT	O†	FFS	5	6	0	0	0	9		
2819	Saint Lukes Sch Rad Kansas City	14	500	[1]	Oth	V[8]	U	6/01 A/S	O†	8/01	1	9	1	0	0	9	9	
2820	Snt Louis CC Flo Vly St Louis	2628	1000	[1] 1700	Pub	V	S	8/21 A=S	E[5]	FFS	2	6	0	2	1	5	2	4
2821	Snt Louis CC Frst Pk St Louis	1576	1000	[1] 1600	Pub	V	U	Oth	E[5]	FFS	8	6	0	4	1	5	1	4
2822	Snt Louis CC Meramec St Louis	4429	1000	[1] 1700	Pub	V	S	Oth	E[5]	Oth	2	5	0	1	1	5		5
2823	St John's Sch Nsg Springfield	251	4600	[1]	Cath	L[8]	U	None	E†	4/01 FFS	9	9	0	1		9	9	
2824	St Luke,C of Kansas City	100	5500[2]	1000	Oth	V	U[7]		S†	FA/FF		0	0	0	0	0		
2825	State Fair CC Sedalia	1014	800	[1] 2300	Pub	S		A/S	E[5]		5	6	0	1	1	6	6	4
2826	Three Rivers CC Poplar Bluff	1108	800	[1] 1800	Pub	S		8/15	S[5]	FF/FA	9	6	0	1	1	4	4	3
2827	Wentworth Mil Acad Lexington	93	11600	3400	Priv	T[8]	[7]	9/01 A/S	S[5]	9/01 FFS	6	0	9	2	8	6	8	9

Educational Programs Available

Sequence Number	College Transfer Courses: Agriculture	Bus-Commerce	Communications	Education	Engineering	Fine, Applied Arts	Foreign Lang	Health	Home Ec	Humanities	Mathematics	Computer/Info Sci	Biological Sci	Physical Sci	Social Sci	Career-oriented Programs – Agri: Ag Business	Ag/Farm Mgmt	Ag Mechanics/Tech	Horticulture	Business: Accounting	Bus Mgmt & Admin	Hotel/Rest Mgmt	Office Mgmt	Marketing/Purchasing	Secretarial Studies	Arts: Architecture Tech	Applied Design	Photography/Cinema	Health: Dental Assistant	Medical or Lab Tech	Nursing (RN)	Nursing (LPN)	Radiologic Technology	Math: Computer Prog	Data Processing Tech	Computer Operating	SocSci: Crim Just/Law Enforce	Parks/Rec Mgmt	Social Work	Technical/Skilled Trades: Air/Refrig/Heat Tech	Auto Body Repair	Auto Mechanics	Carpentry/Constr	Drafting/Eng Draft	Electric Eng Tech	Civil Eng Tech	Indus/Mfg Eng Tech	Mech Eng Tech	Machinework	Welding
2806																				■			■		■					■				■	■	■														
2807																				■			■		■					■				■	■	■														
2808		■	■	■	■	■	■	■	■	■	■	■	■	■	■						■		■	■	■				■		■	■				■	■								■	■	■			
2809																															■																			
2810	■	■	■	■	■	■	■	■	■	■	■	■	■	■	■					■	■		■	■	■						■	■		■		■														■
2811	■	■				■	■	■		■	■	■	■	■	■	■	■	■		■	■		■	■	■						■	■			■	■				■	■	■	■	■	■					■
2812																							■	■	■							■				■					■	■	■						■	■
2813		■	■	■	■	■	■	■	■	■	■	■	■	■	■					■		■	■		■				■		■		■	■	■		■			■				■	■					
2814		■	■	■	■	■		■		■	■	■	■	■	■					■	■		■	■	■						■	■		■	■	■	■							■						
2815																																								■	■	■	■	■					■	
2816		■						■				■			■					■	■		■		■										■															
2817		■	■	■	■	■	■			■	■	■	■	■	■					■	■		■	■	■						■	■				■	■													
2818																																	■																	
2819								■																									■																	
2820		■	■	■	■	■	■	■	■	■	■	■	■	■	■					■	■			■	■		■				■			■	■	■	■		■					■	■	■		■		
2821		■	■	■	■	■		■		■	■	■			■					■		■					■		■	■	■		■		■		■		■			■		■	■		■	■		
2822		■	■	■	■	■	■	■		■	■	■	■	■	■				■	■	■			■	■	■					■			■	■	■	■		■											
2823								■																							■																			
2824								■																																										
2825	■	■	■	■	■	■		■		■	■	■	■	■	■	■	■			■	■		■	■	■						■	■										■		■	■				■	■
2826		■		■	■	■	■	■		■	■			■	■	■	■	■		■	■			■	■				■	■	■				■		■							■		■		■		
2827		■	■	■	■	■	■			■	■	■	■	■	■																																			

▲ Sequence Number—indicates the order of the college in this book only. Do *not* use this number with admissions tests or need analysis services.

[1] No campus room and board facilities
[2] Room only or board only
[3] Most freshmen required to live on campus
[4] City or district residency requirements
[5] Accredited by regional accrediting association or a recognized candidate for accreditation
[6] All female freshman class
[7] All male freshman class
[8] Some admission selectivity; not all hs graduates accepted
[9] Requirements more stringent for nonresidents
†Accredited by a nationally recognized accrediting body other than one of the regional accrediting associations

Montana

Sequence Number	School name (upper entry) City (lower entry)	Enrollment	Costs: Resident tuition/fees + room/board	Costs: Room/board (upper entry) Nonresident tuition/fees (lower entry)	Gen. Info.: Affiliation (upper entry) Religious observance (lower entry)	Gen. Info.: Size of community	Gen. Info.: Type of community	Admissions: Fall term application deadline (upper entry) Test required or desired (lower entry)	Admissions: Calendar	Financial Aid: Fall term application deadline (upper entry) Forms to be filed (lower entry)	No. in 10 who- -have need, rec some aid	-are women	-live on campus	-are minority students	-are nonresidents	-return as sophomores	-complete assoc degree	-transfer to 4-year college
2828	Billings Voc-Tech Billings	298	1000	[1] 2000	Pub	M	S	None	E [5]	3/01 FFS	7	5	0	1	1	8	7	
2829	Butte Voc-Tech Ctr Butte	456	1000	[1] 1900	Pub	S		Oth	Q [5]	FF/FA	5	5	0	1	1			
2830	Dawson CC Glendive	342	1900 [2]	1100 2700	Pub	T		A/S	E [5]	7/01 FA/FF	6	6	2	1	1	3	4	2
2831	Dull Knife C Lame Deer	59	2900	2300	Pub	T		Oth	Q †	Oth	6	7	1	8	1	4	4	3
2832	Flathead Valley CC Kalispell	752	900	[1] 1600	Pub	S		None	Q [5]	5/01 FA/FF	7	7	0	1	1	3	1	5
2833	Fort Peck CC Poplar	161	1000	[1]	Pub	T		A=S	Q [5]	FFS	9	6	0	8			1	1
2834	Great Falls Voc-Tech Great Falls	540	900	[1] 1900	Pub	M		Oth	S [5]	FFS	6	7	0	1		6	7	1
2835	Helena Voc-Tech Ctr Helena	510	900	[1] 1800	Pub	S		9/01 None	S [5]	7/01 FF/FA	6	5	0	1	1	4		
2836	Miles CC Miles City	376	3600	2700 4300	Pub	S		A/S	E [5]	FA/FF	9	7	1	1	1	8	4	6
2837	Missoula Vo-Tech Ctr Missoula	554	900	[1] 1800	Pub	M		Oth	E [5]	FF/FA	5	5	0	1	1		5	
2838	St Patrick Rad Tech Missoula	10	200	[1]	Pub	S		2/01 A=S	O †	6/30 FFS	6	4		0				
Nebraska																		
2839	Bergan Mercy Sch RT Omaha	7	2000	[1]	Cath	M [8]	U [6]	2/15 A/S	O †	FF=FA	8	9	0	0	4	9		
2840	Bryan Mem Sch Nsg Lincoln	94	5000 [2]	1600	Priv	M [8]	U	A=S	O †	3/15 FAF		9		1			9	
2841	Central CC Platte Columbus	393	2500	1500 2900	Pub	S		A/S	E [5]	FF/FA	6	5	2	1	1	5	5	3
2842	Central CC-Hastings Hastings	707	2500	1600 3000	Pub	S		Oth	S [5]	8/01 FF=FA	8	5	2	1	1	5	2	1
2843	Lincoln Sch Commerce Lincoln	549	6600 [2]	1400	Priv	M [8]	U	Oth	Q †	7/15 FF=FA	9	8	2	1	1	4	6	1
2844	McCook CC McCook	441	2500	1800 2700	Pub	T		A=S	S [5]	FA/FF	6	7	4	1	1	5	7	7
2845	Metropolitan CC Omaha	1926	900	[1] 1800	Pub	V	U	None	Q [5]	FAF	9	6	0	2	1		1	
2846	Mid-Plains CC North Platte	690	1600 [2]	800 1700	Pub	S		8/20 Oth	E [5]	8/20 FF=FA	7	5		1	1	6	7	4
2847	Ne C of Tech Agri Curtis		3500	2300 4700	Pub	T		8/26 ACT	O [5]	FA/FF	7	4	5	1	1	8	8	1
2848	Nebraska C of Bus Omaha	550	5200	[1]	Priv	L	U	Oth	O †	FF=FA	9	6	0	3	1	7	6	2
2849	Northeastern CC Norfolk	1129	2000 [2]	1100 2100	Pub	S		A/S	E [5]	FA/FF	5	4	1	1	1	8	8	3

Educational Programs Available

Sequence Number	Agriculture	Bus-Commerce	Communications	Education	Engineering	Fine, Applied Arts	Foreign Lang	Health	Home Ec	Humanities	Mathematics	Computer/Info Sci	Biological Sci	Physical Sci	Social Sci	Ag Business	Ag/Farm Mgmt	Ag Mechanics/Tech	Horticulture	Accounting	Bus Mgmt & Admin	Hotel/Rest Mgmt	Office Mgmt	Marketing/Purchasing	Secretarial Studies	Architecture Tech	Applied Design	Photography/Cinema	Dental Assistant	Medical or Lab Tech	Nursing (RN)	Nursing (LPN)	Radiologic Technology	Computer Prog	Data Processing Tech	Computer Operating	Crim Just/Law Enforce	Parks/Rec Mgmt	Social Work	Air/Refrig/Heat Tech	Auto Body Repair	Auto Mechanics	Carpentry/Constr	Drafting/Eng Draft	Electric Eng Tech	Civil Eng Tech	Indus/Mfg Eng Tech	Mech Eng Tech	Machinework	Welding
	College Transfer Courses															Career-oriented Programs: Agri				Business						Arts			Health					Math			SocSci			Technical/Skilled Trades										
2828																									■							■								■	■	■		■						■
2829																				■					■							■			■							■		■	■	■			■	■
2830	■	■	■	■	■	■	■	■		■	■	■	■	■	■	■	■	■			■		■		■												■		■			■								
2831		■		■		■	■		■	■	■	■	■		■								■														■													
2832	■	■	■	■	■	■	■	■	■	■	■	■	■	■	■						■				■														■											
2833		■		■		■		■	■	■	■	■	■	■	■			■																			■					■	■							
2834		■	■					■	■			■								■	■		■		■				■			■			■	■					■									
2835																		■		■					■							■		■	■	■						■	■						■	■
2836	■	■	■	■	■	■	■	■	■	■	■	■	■	■	■		■				■				■			■			■			■	■	■						■								
2837		■	■		■				■			■								■												■		■	■	■						■								■
2838																																	■																	
2839																																	■																	
2840																															■																			
2841	■	■	■	■	■	■		■	■	■	■	■	■	■	■	■	■			■	■		■		■							■		■	■	■						■		■	■		■		■	■
2842	■	■	■	■				■	■	■	■	■	■	■	■	■	■	■	■	■	■	■	■	■	■				■			■		■	■	■			■	■	■	■	■	■	■				■	■
2843		■							■	■	■	■			■					■	■		■	■	■									■		■														
2844	■	■	■	■	■	■	■	■	■	■	■	■	■	■	■	■	■			■	■				■							■					■													
2845	■	■	■			■	■	■	■	■	■	■	■	■	■	■			■	■	■	■	■	■	■		■	■	■			■		■	■		■			■	■	■	■	■	■	■				■
2846	■	■	■	■	■	■	■	■		■	■	■	■	■	■					■	■		■		■				■	■		■		■	■		■			■	■	■	■	■	■				■	■
2847																■	■	■	■																															
2848		■	■									■			■					■	■	■	■	■	■										■	■														
2849	■	■	■	■	■	■	■	■	■	■	■	■	■	■	■	■	■	■	■	■	■			■	■						■	■		■	■	■	■			■	■	■	■	■	■				■	■

Sequence Number | School name (upper entry) City (lower entry) | Enrollment | Costs | Gen. Info. | Admissions | Financial Aid | Student Profile | Educational Programs Available

▲ Sequence Number—indicates the order of the college in this book only. Do *not* use this number with admissions tests or need analysis services.

[1] No campus room and board facilities
[2] Room only or board only
[3] Most freshmen required to live on campus
[4] City or district residency requirements
[5] Accredited by regional accrediting association or a recognized candidate for accreditation
[6] All female freshman class
[7] All male freshman class
[8] Some admission selectivity; not all hs graduates accepted
[9] Requirements more stringent for nonresidents
†Accredited by a nationally recognized accrediting body other than one of the regional accrediting associations

Nebraska
(continued)

Sequence Number	School name (upper entry) City (lower entry)	Enrollment	Resident tuition/fees + room/board	Room/board (upper entry) Nonresident tuition/fees (lower entry)	Affiliation (upper entry) Religious observance (lower entry)	Size of community	Type of community	Fall term application deadline (upper entry) Test required or desired (lower entry)	Calendar	Fall term application deadline (upper entry) Forms to be filed (lower entry)	-have need, rec some aid	-are women	-live on campus	-are minority students	-are nonresidents	-return as sophomores	-complete assoc degree	-transfer to 4-year college
			Costs		**Gen. Info.**			**Admissions**		**Financial Aid**	**Student Profile** No. in 10 who-							
2850	Omaha C of Health Omaha	250	5000 [2]	800	Priv	L [8]	U	8/30 Oth	O †	Oth	7	9	1	1		9		
2851	Southeast CC Beatrice	484	1900 [2]	1000 2200	Pub	S		Oth	S [5]	FA/FF	5	6	7	1	1	9	9	8
2852	Southeast CC Milford Milford	918	2500	1600 2800	Pub	T		None	O [5]	Oth	5	1	3	1	1	9	8	
2853	Southeast CC-Lincoln Lincoln	1515	900	[1] 1200	Pub	M	S	0/01 Oth	Q [5]	5/01 FA/FF	5	6	0	1	1	2	5	1
2854	Western Nebraska CC Scottsbluff	610	3200	2200	Pub	S		8/20 Oth	E [5]	3/01 FF=FA	7	6	1	1	1	4	3	5
2855	Western Nebraska CC Sidney	205	2200 [2]	1300 2300	Pub	T		None	E [5]	FF=FA	9	4	7	1	1	5		1
2856	York C York	303	6000 [3]	2600	Oth OS	T		ACT	E [5]	FF/FA	8	5	9	1	7	5	5	6
Nevada																		
2857	Northern Nevada CC Elko	150	700	[1] 3000	Pub	S		Oth	S [5]	7/01 FF=FA	5	5	1	2		5		1
2858	Southern Nevada,CC North Las Vegas	1615	1000	[1] 3500	Pub	V	U	None	E [5]	6/01 FFS	5	6	0	3	1	3	1	
2859	Truckee Meadows CC Reno	750	700	[1] 2200	Pub	L	U	None	E [5]	5/01 FAF	5	6	0	2	1	5	1	2
2860	Western Nevada CC Carson City	368	600	[1] 3600	Pub	S		None	E [5]	FF=FA	3	7	0	2		4	1	1
New Hampshire																		
2861	Hesser C Manchester	1925	9300	3400	Priv	M [8]		9/01 A=S	E [5]	6/30 FF=FA	9	7	6	1	6	7	8	1
2862	McIntosh C Dover	335	3600	[1]	Priv	S		8/30 Oth	O †	FAF	2	7	0	1	2	8	6	2
2863	NH Tech C Berlin Berlin	191	2000	[1] 4700	Pub	S [8]		9/01 Oth	S [5]	5/01 FA/FF	8	4	0	0	2	7	6	1
2864	NH Tech C-Claremnt Claremont	247	1900	[1] 4400	Pub	S [8]		Oth	S [5]	5/01 FF=FA	8	8	0	1	3	6	7	1
2865	NH Tech C-Laconia Laconia	280	1900	[1] 4600	Pub	S [8]		Oth	S [5]	4/01 FF=FA	7	3	0	1	2	7	5	1
2866	NH Tech C-Manchester Manchester	575	2300	[1] 5300	Pub	M [8]	S	8/15 Oth	S [5]	6/01 FAF	5	4	0	1	1	7	7	1
2867	NH Tech C-Nashua Nashua	471	2000	[1] 4500	Pub	M [8]	S	Oth	S [5]	5/01 FA/FF	6	3	0	1	1	6	6	2
2868	NH Tech C-Stratham Stratham	389	1700	[1] 4200	Pub	T [8]		Oth	E [5]	6/01 FA/FF	6	5	0	1	1	7	7	1
2869	NH Tech Inst Concord	1257	5000	2900 7700	Pub	S [8]		SAT	S [5]	5/01 FAF	4	5	2		1	6	6	2
2870	White Pines C Chester	75	9300	3600	Priv	T [8]		A=S	E [5]	FA/FF	4	6	7	2	7	8	6	4

Educational Programs Available — College Transfer Courses

Sequence Number	Agriculture	Bus-Commerce	Communications	Education	Engineering	Fine, Applied Arts	Foreign Lang	Health	Home Ec	Humanities	Mathematics	Computer/Info Sci	Biological Sci	Physical Sci	Social Sci
2850															
2851	■	■	■	■	■	■	■	■	■	■	■	■	■	■	■
2852															
2853		■						■	■		■	■	■	■	
2854	■	■	■	■	■	■	■	■	■	■	■	■	■	■	■
2855															
2856	■	■	■	■	■	■	■	■	■	■	■	■	■	■	■
2857	■	■		■	■	■		■	■	■		■		■	■
2858		■	■	■	■	■	■	■	■	■	■	■	■	■	■
2859	■	■	■	■	■	■	■			■	■	■	■	■	■
2860	■	■	■	■		■		■		■	■	■	■	■	■
2861		■	■	■								■			■
2862		■										■			■
2863	■	■			■			■	■						
2864															
2865		■	■			■									■
2866															■
2867		■										■			■
2868								■							
2869		■		■	■			■	■			■			■
2870		■	■			■				■					■

Educational Programs Available — Career-oriented Programs

Sequence Number	Agri: Ag Business	Agri: Ag/Farm Mgmt	Agri: Ag Mechanics/Tech	Agri: Horticulture	Business: Accounting	Business: Bus Mgmt & Admin	Business: Hotel/Rest Mgmt	Business: Office Mgmt	Business: Marketing/Purchasing	Business: Secretarial Studies	Arts: Architecture Tech	Arts: Applied Design	Arts: Photography/Cinema	Health: Dental Assistant	Health: Medical or Lab Tech	Health: Nursing (RN)	Health: Nursing (LPN)	Health: Radiologic Technology	Math: Computer Prog	Math: Data Processing Tech	Math: Computer Operating	SocSci: Crim Just/Law Enforce	SocSci: Parks/Rec Mgmt	SocSci: Social Work	Technical/Skilled Trades: Air/Refrig/Heat Tech	Auto Body Repair	Auto Mechanics	Carpentry/Constr	Drafting/Eng Draft	Electric Eng Tech	Civil Eng Tech	Indus/Mfg Eng Tech	Mech Eng Tech	Machinework	Welding
2850														■																					
2851	■	■	■		■			■	■	■							■		■	■	■														
2852											■								■						■	■	■	■	■	■	■		■	■	■
2853					■	■	■		■	■				■	■	■	■	■	■	■				■			■		■			■		■	■
2854	■	■	■		■	■	■			■							■		■	■				■			■								■
2855					■	■				■																■	■								■
2856					■			■																											
2857		■	■		■	■		■		■						■						■					■		■			■			■
2858				■	■	■	■	■	■	■					■	■	■			■	■	■	■	■			■		■	■					■
2859					■	■	■							■		■	■	■	■	■		■					■		■	■					■
2860						■		■		■						■	■		■			■					■							■	■
2861					■	■	■	■	■	■									■			■													
2862					■					■									■																
2863					■	■				■						■	■										■		■					■	
2864						■									■	■	■			■									■						
2865					■			■		■																	■			■					
2866								■		■						■	■								■		■	■		■					■
2867										■																									
2868					■	■		■		■						■	■		■		■						■	■	■	■				■	■
2869																																			
2870					■	■							■											■											

▲ Sequence Number—indicates the order of the college in this book only. Do *not* use this number with admissions tests or need analysis services.

[1] No campus room and board facilities
[2] Room only or board only
[3] Most freshmen required to live on campus
[4] City or district residency requirements
[5] Accredited by regional accrediting association or a recognized candidate for accreditation
[6] All female freshman class
[7] All male freshman class
[8] Some admission selectivity; not all hs graduates accepted
[9] Requirements more stringent for nonresidents
†Accredited by a nationally recognized accrediting body other than one of the regional accrediting associations

New Jersey

Sequence Number	School name (upper entry) / City (lower entry)	Enrollment	Costs: Resident tuition/fees + room/board	Costs: Room/board (upper entry) / Nonresident tuition/fees (lower entry)	Gen. Info.: Affiliation (upper entry) / Religious observance (lower entry)	Gen. Info.: Size of community	Gen. Info.: Type of community	Admissions: Fall term application deadline (upper entry) / Test required or desired (lower entry)	Admissions: Calendar	Financial Aid: Fall term application deadline (upper entry) / Forms to be filed (lower entry)	No. in 10 who- -have need, rec some aid	-are women	-live on campus	-are minority students	-are nonresidents	-return as sophomores	-complete assoc degree	-transfer to 4-year college
2871	Atlantic CC / Mays Landing	1564	1300	[1] / 3800	Pub	T		8/05 / Oth	S [5]	5/01 / FAF	6	6	0	2	1	4	3	
2872	Bergen CC / Paramus	4085	1200	[1] / 4400	Pub	S		7/31 / None	E [5]	FAF	2	6	0	3		5		4
2873	Berkeley C Business / Waldwick	188	8100	[1]	Priv	S [8]		None	Q †	FAF	7	9	0	1	1	9	9	
2874	Berkeley C Business / West Paterson	585	12200 [2]	4100	Priv	M [8]	S	None	Q [5]	FAF	7	9		4	1	8	9	
2875	Berkeley C Business / Woodbridge	141	8100	[1]	Priv	M [8]	S	None	Q [5]	FAF	7	9	0	4	1	9	9	
2876	Brookdale CC / Lincroft	3843	1400	[1] / 4900	Pub	S		None	O [5]	FAF	2	6	0	1	1		1	5
2877	Burlington Co C / Pemberton	1999	1100	[1] / 3300	Pub	S		8/31 / Oth	E [5]	8/31 / FAF	4	6	0	2	0	4	4	5
2878	Camden Co C / Blackwood	3610	1200	[1] / 1400	Pub	S		A=S	E [5]	7/01 / FA/FF	9	6	0	2	1	5	5	6
2879	Cumberland Co C / Vineland	994	1300	[1] / 5200	Pub	M	S	Oth	S [5]	8/20 / FAF	3	7	0	3	0	6	6	4
2880	DeVry Tech Inst / Woodbridge	1282	5000	[1]	Priv	M [8]	S	A=S	T [5]	FA/FF	6	1	0	4	2	5	4	
2881	Essex Co C / Newark	3281	1200	[1] / 3600	Pub	L	U	9/01 / Oth	E [5]	8/01 / FA/FF	6	5	0	8	0	3	1	5
2882	Farlgh Dckson U Ed W / Hackensack	1015	12600	4400	Priv	M [8]	S	A=S	E [5]	FAF	7	5	4	5	1	9	7	8
2883	Gloucester Co C / Sewell	4373	1400	[1] / 5000	Pub	S		A=S	E [5]	6/01 / FA/FF	7	6	0	1	0	5	3	4
2884	Helene Fuld Sch Nsg / Camden	230	3200 [2]	1000	Priv	M [8]		5/15 / Oth	E †	5/01 / Oth	2	9	3	2		9	8	1
2885	Hudson Co CC / Jersey City	1684	1200	[1] / 2400	Pub	L	U	Oth	S [5]	FAF	5	6	0	8				
2886	Katharine Gibbs Sch / Montclair	300	9300 [2]	2600	Priv	S		Oth	Q †		4	9	2	2	0	8		
2887	Mercer Co CC / Trenton	2769	1300	[1] / 4200	Pub	M	S	Oth	S [5]	5/01 / FF=FA	2	5	0	3	1	6	2	3
2888	Middlesex Co C / Edison	4232	1100	[1] / 2200	Pub	V	S	None	S [5]	FAF	4	5	0	3	1	7	3	3
2889	Morris,Co C of / Randolph	4403	1300	[1] / 3400	Pub	S		Oth	S [5]	7/15 / FAF	6	5	0	1	0	5	4	6
2890	Ocean Co C / Toms River	2707	1100	[1] / 2100	Pub	M	S	None	E [5]	FAF	4	6	0	1	0	6	4	6
2891	Passaic Co CC / Paterson	799	1700	[1] / 3400	Pub	L	U	None	S [5]	10/01 / FAF	5	6	0	9				4
2892	Raritan Valley CC / Somerville	1708	1400	[1] / 5600	Pub	T		None	S [5]	FAF	1	6	0	2	0	6	5	4
2893	Salem CC / Penns Grove	439	1300	[1] / 1900	Pub	M [8]		Oth	E [5]	FF=FA	9	6	0	2	1	4		

Educational Programs Available — College Transfer Courses

Sequence Number	Agriculture	Bus-Commerce	Communications	Education	Engineering	Fine, Applied Arts	Foreign Lang	Health	Home Ec	Humanities	Mathematics	Computer/Info Sci	Biological Sci	Physical Sci	Social Sci
2871		■	■	■		■	■	■	■	■	■	■	■	■	■
2872		■	■	■	■	■	■	■		■	■	■	■	■	■
2873															
2874															
2875															
2876	■	■	■	■	■	■	■	■		■	■	■	■	■	■
2877		■	■	■	■	■	■	■	■	■	■	■	■	■	■
2878	■	■	■	■	■	■		■		■	■	■	■	■	■
2879	■	■		■	■	■	■	■		■	■	■			■
2880															
2881		■	■	■	■	■	■	■		■		■	■	■	■
2882															
2883		■	■	■	■	■	■	■		■	■	■	■	■	■
2884								■							
2885		■	■	■	■			■	■	■	■	■		■	■
2886															
2887	■	■	■	■	■	■	■	■		■	■	■	■	■	■
2888		■	■	■	■	■	■			■	■	■	■	■	■
2889	■	■	■		■	■	■			■	■	■	■	■	■
2890		■	■	■	■	■	■	■		■	■	■			■
2891		■			■		■				■				
2892		■	■	■	■	■	■	■			■	■	■	■	■
2893		■	■		■	■	■	■		■	■	■	■	■	■

Educational Programs Available — Career-oriented Programs

Sequence Number	Agri: Ag Business	Ag/Farm Mgmt	Ag Mechanics/Tech	Horticulture	Business: Accounting	Bus Mgmt & Admin	Hotel/Rest Mgmt	Office Mgmt	Marketing/Purchasing	Secretarial Studies	Arts: Architecture Tech	Applied Design	Photography/Cinema	Health: Dental Assistant	Medical or Lab Tech	Nursing (RN)	Nursing (LPN)	Radiologic Technology	Math: Computer Prog	Data Processing Tech	Computer Operating	SocSci: Crim Just/Law Enforce	Parks/Rec Mgmt	Social Work	Technical/Skilled Trades: Air/Refrig/Heat Tech	Auto Body Repair	Auto Mechanics	Carpentry/Constr	Drafting/Eng Draft	Electric Eng Tech	Civil Eng Tech	Indus/Mfg Eng Tech	Mech Eng Tech	Machinework	Welding
2871					■	■	■		■	■					■	■						■		■											
2872				■	■	■	■		■	■					■	■		■	■	■	■	■					■		■	■					
2873						■			■	■																									
2874						■			■	■																									
2875					■	■			■	■										■															
2876				■	■	■		■	■	■	■				■	■			■			■					■		■						
2877					■	■	■	■	■	■	■		■				■	■	■	■	■	■									■		■		
2878										■				■	■	■		■	■	■										■			■		
2879				■	■	■		■	■	■						■		■	■	■	■	■		■								■	■		
2880																																			
2881					■	■	■			■	■					■		■	■	■		■		■							■				
2882																																			
2883					■				■	■						■				■		■					■		■		■	■			
2884																■																			
2885					■	■		■		■						■			■	■	■	■		■						■					
2886					■	■	■	■		■																									
2887				■	■		■	■	■	■		■	■		■	■		■		■	■	■			■		■		■	■	■				
2888					■	■	■			■					■	■		■	■						■		■			■	■	■	■		
2889	■				■	■	■		■	■			■	■	■	■					■	■	■				■		■				■		
2890					■	■			■	■					■	■			■	■		■									■				
2891					■	■			■	■						■		■	■			■					■					■		■	■
2892					■	■	■	■	■	■									■	■	■				■		■	■	■	■	■		■		
2893					■	■		■	■	■							■		■			■			■				■	■	■		■		

▲ **Sequence Number—indicates the order of the college in this book only. Do *not* use this number with admissions tests or need analysis services.**

1 No campus room and board facilities
2 Room only or board only
3 Most freshmen required to live on campus
4 City or district residency requirements
5 Accredited by regional accrediting association or a recognized candidate for accreditation
6 All female freshman class
7 All male freshman class
8 Some admission selectivity; not all hs graduates accepted
9 Requirements more stringent for nonresidents
†Accredited by a nationally recognized accrediting body other than one of the regional accrediting associations

New Jersey
(continued)

Sequence Number	School name (upper entry) / City (lower entry)	Enrollment	Costs: Resident tuition/fees + room/board	Costs: Room/board (upper entry) / Nonresident tuition/fees (lower entry)	Gen. Info.: Affiliation (upper entry) / Religious observance (lower entry)	Gen. Info.: Size of community	Gen. Info.: Type of community	Admissions: Fall term application deadline (upper entry) / Test required or desired (lower entry)	Admissions: Calendar	Financial Aid: Fall term application deadline (upper entry) / Forms to be filed (lower entry)	No. in 10 who- -have need, rec some aid	-are women	-live on campus	-are minority students	-are nonresidents	-return as sophomores	-complete assoc degree	-transfer to 4-year college
2894	Union Co C / Cranford	4325	1300	[1] / 4500	Pub	S		A=S	E [5]	10/01 / FAF	2	6	0	5	0			
2895	Upsala C Wirths / Sussex	425	4100	[1]	Luth	T [8]		8/15 / S/A	4 [5]	8/01 / FAF	9	7	0	0	0	7		7
New Mexico																		
2896	Albuquerque Tech Voc / Albuquerque	4937	500	[1] / 2900	Pub	L	U	Oth	T [5]	9/06 / FA/FF	2	5	0	5	1		9	
2897	Clovis CC / Clovis	635	500	[1] / 1500	Pub	S		A=S	S [5]	7/01 / FA/FF	4	6	0	2	1	7	3	4
2898	E NM U Roswell CC / Roswell	745	3200	2500 / 4400	Pub	S		None	E [5]	FA/FF	8	6	1	3	1	6	3	2
2899	Inst Amer Indian Art / Santa Fe	186	5100	3200	Pub	M [8]		4/15 / A/S	E [5]	5/01 / FF=FA	5	5	6	8	5	5	4	3
2900	Luna Voc-Tech Inst / Las Vegas	495	0	[1] / 1200	Pub	S		Oth	S [5]	4/01 / FAF	9	5	0	8				
2901	NM Gallup Br,U of / Gallup	610	600	[1] / 1400	Pub	S		8/15 / ACT	S [5]	5/15 / FAF	6	7	0	8	2	4	1	
2902	NM JC / Hobbs	895	3200 [3]	2800 / 3700	Pub	S		A/S	E [5]	4/01 / FF=FA	3	6	0	2	1	6	6	3
2903	NM Military Inst / Roswell	393	3600	2300 / 5000	Pub / O	M [8]		8/15 / A/S	E [5]	FA/FF	7	1	9	1	6	7	6	9
2904	NM St U Alamogordo / Alamogordo	540	600	[1] / 1800	Pub	S		None	E [5]	3/01 / FA/FF	9	6	0	3		5	2	6
2905	NM St U Carlsbad / Carlsbad	427	600	[1] / 1800	Pub	S		9/24 / Oth	E [5]	FF=FA	5	6	0	3	1	4	2	5
2906	NM St U Grants / Grants	200	600	[1] / 1700	Pub	S		A/S	E [5]	FA/FF	3	7	0	5	0	7	1	1
2907	Northern NM CC / Espanola	777	3200	2700 / 4100	Pub	S		Oth	E [5]	5/01 / FA/FF	9	7	1	8	1	4	2	
2908	San Juan C / Farmington	1011	400	[1] / 600	Pub	S		None	S [5]	5/01 / FA/FF	5	6	0	4	0	3	1	1
2909	Santa Fe CC / Santa Fe	340	500	[1] / 1400	Pub	M		A=S	E [5]	FA/FF	2	6	0	5	1			
2910	Southwst Indian Poly / Albuquerque	429	0		Pub	L	S	8/17 / None	S [5]	8/27 / FA/FF	7	6	4	9	6			
2911	Tech Training Inst / Las Cruces	60	4800	[1]	Priv	M	U	9/15 / Oth	Q †	9/01 / FF=FA	9	5	0	7	1		8	
New York																		
2912	Adirondack CC / Queensbury	1570	3300 [2]	1800 / 4700	Pub	S		8/15 / None	S [5]	6/15 / FF=FA	4	6	0	1	1	7	5	4
2913	Albany,JC of / Albany	750	10200	4200	Priv	M [8]	U	8/01 / A=S	E [5]	3/15 / FAF	7	6	2	1	1	7	7	5
2914	Amer Acad Dram Arts / New York	219	7200	[1]	Priv	V [8]	U	Oth	S [5]	FAF	6	5	0	1	8	0	4	1

Educational Programs Available — College Transfer Courses

Sequence Number	Agriculture	Bus-Commerce	Communications	Education	Engineering	Fine, Applied Arts	Foreign Lang	Health	Home Ec	Humanities	Mathematics	Computer/Info Sci	Biological Sci	Physical Sci	Social Sci
2894		■	■	■	■	■		■		■		■	■		■
2895		■	■			■	■			■		■	■	■	■
2896		■				■		■		■	■		■	■	■
2897		■	■	■	■	■	■		■	■	■		■	■	■
2898		■	■			■	■	■	■	■	■	■	■	■	■
2899			■			■			■	■					■
2900								■							
2901		■	■	■		■	■	■		■	■		■	■	■
2902	■	■	■	■	■	■	■	■		■	■	■	■	■	■
2903		■	■	■	■	■	■	■		■	■	■	■	■	■
2904		■		■	■	■	■	■	■	■	■	■	■	■	■
2905		■		■	■	■	■	■	■	■	■	■	■	■	■
2906	■	■		■	■	■	■		■	■	■	■	■	■	■
2907				■		■	■			■	■	■	■	■	■
2908		■	■	■	■	■	■	■		■	■	■	■	■	■
2909		■	■	■		■	■	■	■	■	■	■	■	■	■
2910															
2911															
2912	■	■	■	■	■	■	■	■	■	■	■	■	■	■	■
2913		■	■	■		■		■				■		■	■
2914															

Educational Programs Available — Career-oriented Programs (Agri, Business, Arts)

Sequence Number	Agri: Ag Business	Ag/Farm Mgmt	Ag Mechanics/Tech	Horticulture	Business: Accounting	Bus Mgmt & Admin	Hotel/Rest Mgmt	Office Mgmt	Marketing/Purchasing	Secretarial Studies	Arts: Architecture Tech	Applied Design	Photography/Cinema
2894					■					■			
2895					■	■							
2896					■	■			■	■			
2897					■	■		■	■				
2898						■		■		■			
2899												■	■
2900		■		■	■	■	■	■	■	■			
2901						■		■		■			
2902						■		■		■			
2903													
2904										■			
2905					■			■	■	■			
2906								■		■			
2907					■	■		■		■			
2908										■			
2909					■	■	■	■	■	■			
2910					■			■	■	■			
2911					■			■		■			
2912					■	■		■	■	■			■
2913					■	■		■	■	■			■
2914													

Educational Programs Available — Career-oriented Programs (Health, Math, SocSci, Technical/Skilled Trades)

Sequence Number	Health: Dental Assistant	Medical or Lab Tech	Nursing (RN)	Nursing (LPN)	Radiologic Technology	Math: Computer Prog	Data Processing Tech	Computer Operating	SocSci: Crim Just/Law Enforce	Parks/Rec Mgmt	Social Work	Technical/Skilled Trades: Air/Refrig/Heat Tech	Auto Body Repair	Auto Mechanics	Carpentry/Constr	Drafting/Eng Draft	Electric Eng Tech	Civil Eng Tech	Indus/Mfg Eng Tech	Mech Eng Tech	Machinework	Welding
2894		■		■	■	■		■									■	■		■		
2895									■	■												
2896		■		■		■	■		■			■	■	■	■	■		■			■	■
2897			■	■	■	■	■		■			■		■	■	■						
2898		■	■	■					■				■	■		■						■
2899																						
2900	■	■	■	■		■		■				■		■	■	■	■					■
2901		■	■					■	■	■				■	■							■
2902		■	■	■		■	■	■	■	■				■		■					■	■
2903																						
2904		■		■			■		■								■					
2905			■		■		■	■	■													■
2906							■		■								■					
2907			■	■	■	■	■	■	■		■			■	■	■	■				■	■
2908						■	■						■	■	■	■				■	■	■
2909			■			■		■	■						■	■						
2910						■	■	■								■				■		
2911						■	■	■									■					
2912			■			■	■	■	■						■	■				■		
2913			■								■											
2914																						

▲ Sequence Number—indicates the order of the college in this book only. Do *not* use this number with admissions tests or need analysis services.

1 No campus room and board facilities
2 Room only or board only
3 Most freshmen required to live on campus
4 City or district residency requirements
5 Accredited by regional accrediting association or a recognized candidate for accreditation
6 All female freshman class
7 All male freshman class
8 Some admission selectivity; not all hs graduates accepted
9 Requirements more stringent for nonresidents
†Accredited by a nationally recognized accrediting body other than one of the regional accrediting associations

New York
(continued)

Sequence Number	School name (upper entry) City (lower entry)	Enrollment	Resident tuition/fees + room/board	Room/board (upper entry) Nonresident tuition/fees (lower entry)	Affiliation (upper entry) Religious observance (lower entry)	Size of community	Type of community	Fall term application deadline (upper entry) Test required or desired (lower entry)	Calendar	Fall term application deadline (upper entry) Forms to be filed (lower entry)	-have need, rec some aid	-are women	-live on campus	-are minority students	-are nonresidents	-return as sophomores	-complete assoc degree	-transfer to 4-year college
			Costs		**Gen. Info.**			**Admissions**		**Financial Aid**	**Student Profile** (No. in 10 who-)							
2915	Amer Acad McAllister New York	137	4900	[1]	Priv	V	U	8/15 None	S †		5	3	0	5	4	6	5	
2916	Arnot Ogden Sch Nsg Elmira	155	8100	2500	Priv	M[8]		6/30 A=S	T †	9/15 FA/FF	7	9	1	1	1	9	5	
2917	Berkeley Sch NY City New York	725	9900	[1]	Priv	V[8]	U	None	Q[5]	None	9	9	0	5	1	5	6	1
2918	Berkeley Sch Wh Plns White Plains	495	12200	4200	Priv	M	S	None	Q[5]	FA/FF	8	9	3	4	2	8	8	2
2919	Bible Bapt Inst & C Hudson Falls	21	700	[1]	Bapt OS	M		9/01 A=S	S			5	0				9	5
2920	Broome CC Binghamton	3200	1300	[1] 2600	Pub	M	S	None	E[5]	4/15 FF/FA	7	6	0	1	1	7		2
2921	Bryant Stratn Bus In Rochester	480	5000	[1]	Priv	M[8]		Oth	Q †	10/01 FFS	8	8		1		9	5	1
2922	Bryant-Stratton Inst Albany	295	4700	[1]	Priv	M[8]	S	A=S	Q †	FF=FA	8	7	0	5	1	7	5	1
2923	Bryant-Stratton Inst Buffalo	894	5000	[1]	Priv	V[8]	U	9/29 None	Q	FA/FF	0	7	0	3	1	6	8	1
2924	Bryant-Stratton Inst Syracuse	560	7000[2]	2300	Priv	M[8]	U	A=S	Q †	FA/FF	9	7	2	2	0	6	8	1
2925	Cayuga Co CC Auburn	2600	1400	[1] 2900	Pub	S		A=S	S[5]	5/01 FA/FF	7	5	0	1	1	8	7	
2926	Central City Bus Ins Syracuse	457	7600[3]	2900	Priv	M	U	None	S †	6/01 FF=FA	9	9	4	9	1	7	7	1
2927	Chas Gregory Sch Nsg Perth Amboy	100	1400	[1] 2000	Priv	T[8]		8/01 SAT	S †		1				1	1		
2928	Clinton CC Plattsburgh	1097	1500	[1] 2800	Pub	S		8/31 A/S	S[5]	6/01 FF=FA	9	5	0	1	1	6	6	7
2929	Columbia-Greene CC Hudson	890	1400	[1] 2800	Pub	S		None	E[5]	5/01 FAF	8	6	0	1	1	5	3	5
2930	Corning CC Corning	1920	1800	[1] 2400	Pub	S		None	E[5]	6/30 FAF	8	5	0	1	1	6	4	5
2931	Crouse-Irvng Sch Nsg Syracuse	307	6800	2400	Priv	L[8]	U	7/15 A=S	S †	4/30 FF=FA	8	9	2	1	1	8		
2932	CUNY Bronx CC Bronx	3728	1300	[1] 2100	Pub	V	U	None	S[5]	Oth	9	7	0	7	1	6	3	4
2933	CUNY Hostos CC Bronx	4231	1500	[1] 2100	Pub	V	U	8/15 Oth	S[5]	Oth	9	7	0	9				
2934	CUNY La Guardia CC Long Island	7125	1500	[1] 2000	Pub	V	U	None	O[5]	6/30 Oth	7	6	0	8	0	6		6
2935	CUNY Manhattan CC New York	7625	1500	[1] 2100	Pub	V	U	9/01 None	E[5]	8/31 FF=FA	9	7	0	9	1	7	1	3
2936	CUNY Queensborough C New York	5453	1500	[1] 2100	Pub	V	U	None	S[5]	9/01 Oth	9	5	0	5			5	4
2937	CUNY-Kingsborough CC Brooklyn	5578	1500	[1] 2100	Pub	V	U	None	O[5]	Oth	7	6	0	4	1	7	3	2

Educational Programs Available — College Transfer Courses

Sequence Number	Agriculture	Bus-Commerce	Communications	Education	Engineering	Fine, Applied Arts	Foreign Lang	Health	Home Ec	Humanities	Mathematics	Computer/Info Sci	Biological Sci	Physical Sci	Social Sci
2915								■							
2916								■							
2917															
2918															
2919				■						■				■	■
2920		■			■			■				■		■	■
2921		■	■			■		■				■			
2922		■							■			■			
2923		■	■			■		■				■			
2924		■						■				■			
2925	■	■	■	■	■	■	■	■	■	■	■	■	■	■	■
2926		■													
2927								■					■	■	■
2928		■		■		■	■	■		■	■		■	■	■
2929		■	■			■	■	■		■	■	■	■	■	■
2930	■	■	■	■	■	■	■	■	■	■	■	■	■	■	■
2931															
2932		■		■			■	■		■	■		■		■
2933															
2934		■	■	■	■	■	■			■	■	■	■	■	■
2935		■	■	■	■	■	■	■		■	■	■	■	■	■
2936		■		■	■	■	■	■		■	■	■	■	■	■
2937		■	■	■	■	■	■	■		■	■	■	■	■	■

Educational Programs Available — Career-oriented Programs

Sequence Number	Agri: Ag Business	Agri: Ag/Farm Mgmt	Agri: Ag Mechanics/Tech	Agri: Horticulture	Business: Accounting	Business: Bus Mgmt & Admin	Business: Hotel/Rest Mgmt	Business: Office Mgmt	Business: Marketing/Purchasing	Business: Secretarial Studies	Arts: Architecture Tech	Arts: Applied Design	Arts: Photography/Cinema	Health: Dental Assistant	Health: Medical or Lab Tech	Health: Nursing (RN)	Health: Nursing (LPN)	Health: Radiologic Technology	Math: Computer Prog	Math: Data Processing Tech	Math: Computer Operating	SocSci: Crim Just/Law Enforce	SocSci: Parks/Rec Mgmt	SocSci: Social Work	Technical/Skilled Trades: Air/Refrig/Heat Tech	Auto Body Repair	Auto Mechanics	Carpentry/Constr	Drafting/Eng Draft	Electric Eng Tech	Civil Eng Tech	Indus/Mfg Eng Tech	Mech Eng Tech	Machinework	Welding
2915																																			
2916																■																			
2917					■	■			■	■																									
2918					■				■	■																									
2919																																			
2920					■	■		■	■	■			■		■	■		■		■		■								■	■		■		
2921					■	■	■		■	■									■	■															
2922					■	■			■	■									■	■															
2923					■	■			■	■		■		■					■	■															
2924					■	■	■		■	■					■				■	■	■														
2925					■	■			■	■						■			■	■		■							■	■					
2926					■	■															■														
2927																																			
2928					■	■		■		■					■	■						■								■					
2929					■	■				■			■			■				■	■	■					■								■
2930					■	■										■				■	■			■		■	■		■	■		■	■		
2931																■																			
2932					■				■	■									■	■															
2933					■	■				■		■			■	■		■		■				■											
2934					■	■		■		■		■				■			■	■															
2935					■	■		■	■	■						■			■	■				■											
2936					■	■			■	■		■			■	■				■	■								■	■		■	■		
2937					■	■			■	■						■			■	■			■												

▲ **Sequence Number—indicates the order of the college in this book only. Do *not* use this number with admissions tests or need analysis services.**

[1] No campus room and board facilities
[2] Room only or board only
[3] Most freshmen required to live on campus
[4] City or district residency requirements
[5] Accredited by regional accrediting association or a recognized candidate for accreditation
[6] All female freshman class
[7] All male freshman class
[8] Some admission selectivity; not all hs graduates accepted
[9] Requirements more stringent for nonresidents
†Accredited by a nationally recognized accrediting body other than one of the regional accrediting associations

New York
(continued)

Sequence Number	School name (upper entry) / City (lower entry)	Enrollment	Costs: Resident tuition/fees + room/board	Costs: Room/board (upper entry) / Nonresident tuition/fees (lower entry)	Gen. Info.: Affiliation (upper entry) / Religious observance (lower entry)	Gen. Info.: Size of community	Gen. Info.: Type of community	Admissions: Fall term application deadline (upper entry) / Test required or desired (lower entry)	Admissions: Calendar	Financial Aid: Fall term application deadline (upper entry) / Forms to be filed (lower entry)
2938	Dutchess CC Poughkeepsie	2845	1400	[1] 2800	Pub	S		None	E[5]	4/15 FAF
2939	Ellis Hosp Sch Nsg Schenectady	54	2500	[1] 3500	Priv	M[8]	U	9/01 A=S	O†	9/01 FF=FA
2940	Erie CC City Cam Buffalo	2383	1500	[1] 2800	Pub	L	U	8/12 A=S	E[5]	8/12 FAF
2941	Erie CC North Cam Williamsville	3553	1500	[1] 2800	Pub	T		8/12 A=S	E[5]	8/12 FAF
2942	Erie CC South Cam Orchard Park	1859	1500	[1] 2800	Pub	S		8/12 A=S	E[5]	8/12 FAF
2943	Finger Lakes,CC of Canandaigua	2012	1500	[1] 2800	Pub	S		None	E[5]	5/01 FF=FA
2944	Five Towns C Seaford	600	5600	[1]	Priv	S[8]		9/01 A=S	S[5]	9/01 FAF
2945	Fulton-Montgomery CC Johnstown	1998	1400	[1] 2800	Pub	S		None	4[5]	FAF
2946	Genesee CC Batavia	2050	1400	[1] 2700	Pub	S		9/04 Oth	E[5]	6/01 FAF
2947	Grumman Data Systems Woodbury	1000	5800	[1]	Priv	L	S	Oth	O†	FAF
2948	Herkimer Co CC Herkimer	1825	1600	[1] 3100	Pub	T		8/01 A/S	E[5]	8/01 FAF
2949	Hilbert C Hamburg	464	9200	3800	Priv	S[8]		9/01 A=S	S[5]	3/31 FA/FF
2950	Hudson Valley CC Troy	5518	1300	[1] 2900	Pub	M[8]	S	A=S	S[5]	5/31 FFS
2951	Interboro Inst New York	740	5000	[1]	Priv	V	U	Oth	T	3/15 None
2952	Jamestown Bus C Jamestown	303	4600	[1]	Priv	S[8]		9/01 None	S†	Oth
2953	Jamestown CC Jamestown	2117	1500	[1] 2800	Pub	S		8/15 None	E[5]	5/01 FAF
2954	Jefferson CC Watertown	1227	1500	[1] 2800	Pub	S		A/S	E[5]	FA/FF
2955	Katharine Gibbs Sch Mevil Hunt Sta	550	7000	[1]	Priv	M	[6]	Oth	S	
2956	Katharine Gibbs Sch New York	520	7000	[1]	Priv	V[8]	U	Oth	Q	
2957	Maria C Albany	511	4000	[1]	Cath S	M[8]	S	8/15 S/A	S[5]	FA/FF
2958	Mater Dei C Ogdensburg	455	7200	2900	Cath S	S[8]			E[5]	FF=FA
2959	Mohawk Valley CC Utica	3950	4800	3300 6200	Pub	M	S	None	E[5]	5/01 FAF
2960	Monroe CC Rochester	6967	1700	[1] 3400	Pub	L	S	3/01 A=S	E[5]	5/01 FAF

Student Profile (No. in 10 who-) and College Transfer Courses

Sequence Number	-have need, rec some aid	-are women	-live on campus	-are minority students	-are nonresidents	-return as sophomores	-complete assoc degree	-transfer to 4-year college	Agriculture	Bus-Commerce	Communications	Education	Engineering	Fine, Applied Arts	Foreign Lang	Health	Home Ec	Humanities	Mathematics	Computer/Info Sci	Biological Sci	Physical Sci	Social Sci
2938	5	6	0	2	1	5	4	4	■	■	■		■						■	■	■		■
2939	5	9	0	1	0	8	6	1															
2940	9	6	0	3				2	■	■				■	■			■	■		■	■	■
2941	8	5	0	1				3	■	■	■		■	■	■			■	■	■	■	■	■
2942	5	5	0	1				2		■	■			■	■			■	■	■	■	■	■
2943	9	6	0	1	1	6	6	3	■	■	■	■	■	■		■	■	■	■	■	■	■	■
2944	6	3	0	2	1		3	2		■				■					■	■			■
2945	7	5	0	1	1	8	6	3		■	■	■	■	■	■	■	■	■	■	■	■	■	■
2946	8	6	0	1	0	5	3	3		■	■	■	■	■	■			■	■	■	■	■	■
2947	9	3	0	1			8																
2948	8	6	0	1	0	9	5	3	■	■	■	■	■	■		■	■	■	■	■	■	■	■
2949	8	7	2	1	1	8	7	6		■								■	■	■	■		■
2950	4	5		1	1	6	6	4		■		■	■		■	■	■	■	■	■	■	■	■
2951	8	6	0	9	1	7	7	2		■						■				■			
2952	9	8	4	1	2	7	6	1		■										■			
2953	8	5	0	1	1	7	3	4	■	■			■	■	■	■	■	■	■	■	■	■	■
2954	9	6	0	1	1	7	6	4	■	■	■	■	■	■		■	■	■	■	■	■	■	■
2955		9	0		0													■					■
2956		9	0	3	1	9	8	1		■													
2957	6	8	0	1	1	8	6	2		■		■		■		■	■	■	■	■	■	■	■
2958	8	8	3	2	1	5	4	4		■		■		■	■	■		■	■		■	■	■
2959	9	5	1	1	0	5	6	5	■	■	■	■	■	■	■	■	■	■	■	■	■	■	■
2960	7	5	0	2	1	7		3		■	■		■	■	■	■		■	■	■	■	■	■

Educational Programs Available — Career-oriented Programs (Agri: Ag Business – Horticulture; Business: Accounting – Secretarial Studies; Arts: Architecture Tech – Photography/Cinema; Health: Dental Assistant – Radiologic Technology; Math: Computer Prog – Computer Operating; SocSci: Crim Just/Law Enforce – Social Work; Technical/Skilled Trades: Air/Refrig/Heat Tech – Welding)

Sequence Number	Ag Business	Ag/Farm Mgmt	Ag Mechanics/Tech	Horticulture	Accounting	Bus Mgmt & Admin	Hotel/Rest Mgmt	Office Mgmt	Marketing/Purchasing	Secretarial Studies	Architecture Tech	Applied Design	Photography/Cinema	Dental Assistant	Medical or Lab Tech	Nursing (RN)	Nursing (LPN)	Radiologic Technology	Computer Prog	Data Processing Tech	Computer Operating	Crim Just/Law Enforce	Parks/Rec Mgmt	Social Work	Air/Refrig/Heat Tech	Auto Body Repair	Auto Mechanics	Carpentry/Constr	Drafting/Eng Draft	Electric Eng Tech	Civil Eng Tech	Indus/Mfg Eng Tech	Mech Eng Tech	Machinework	Welding
2938					■	■			■	■	■				■	■						■	■		■				■	■		■			■
2939																■																			
2940						■	■			■						■		■		■		■			■						■	■			
2941						■				■					■	■				■		■								■	■	■	■		
2942						■				■	■									■							■		■			■			
2943				■	■	■	■		■	■						■			■	■	■	■		■					■	■			■		
2944					■	■		■	■	■			■						■	■	■														
2945					■	■				■					■	■				■	■	■		■			■	■		■					
2946					■		■		■	■					■	■			■			■							■	■					
2947					■					■									■	■	■								■	■					
2948					■	■	■	■	■	■	■				■				■	■	■	■		■				■	■						
2949					■	■			■	■										■	■	■													
2950					■				■						■	■		■		■		■	■	■	■	■	■	■	■	■	■	■	■	■	
2951					■	■				■																									
2952					■			■	■	■																									
2953					■	■									■	■						■			■					■			■		
2954					■	■	■	■	■	■					■	■				■	■	■		■											
2955					■	■		■		■																									
2956					■	■	■	■		■																									
2957					■	■		■		■						■					■														
2958					■	■				■												■		■											
2959					■	■			■	■		■	■		■	■				■		■		■	■				■	■	■		■		
2960					■		■		■	■						■		■		■		■	■		■		■		■	■	■		■		

▲ **Sequence Number—indicates the order of the college in this book only. Do *not* use this number with admissions tests or need analysis services.**

[1] No campus room and board facilities
[2] Room only or board only
[3] Most freshmen required to live on campus
[4] City or district residency requirements
[5] Accredited by regional accrediting association or a recognized candidate for accreditation
[6] All female freshman class
[7] All male freshman class
[8] Some admission selectivity; not all hs graduates accepted
[9] Requirements more stringent for nonresidents
†Accredited by a nationally recognized accrediting body other than one of the regional accrediting associations

New York
(continued)

Sequence Number	School name (upper entry) City (lower entry)	Enrollment	Costs: Resident tuition/fees + room/board	Costs: Room/board (upper entry) Nonresident tuition/fees (lower entry)	Gen. Info.: Affiliation (upper entry) Religious observance (lower entry)	Gen. Info.: Size of community	Gen. Info.: Type of community	Admissions: Fall term application deadline (upper entry) Test required or desired (lower entry)	Admissions: Calendar	Financial Aid: Fall term application deadline (upper entry) Forms to be filed (lower entry)	No. in 10 who- -have need, rec some aid	-are women	-live on campus	-are minority students	-are nonresidents	-return as sophomores	-complete assoc degree	-transfer to 4-year college
2961	Nassau CC Garden City	10220	1600	[1] 3200	Pub	S		8/26 None	E [5]	5/01 Oth	3	6	0	2	0	7	3	6
2962	Niagara Co CC Sanborn	2955	1400	[1]	Pub	T		Oth	E [5]	FA/FF	6	6	0	1	0	6	3	4
2963	North Country CC Saranac Lake	1453	1500	[1] 3500	Pub	T		9/01 A=S	S [5]	4/30 Oth	8	6	0	1	1	6	5	7
2964	Olean Business Inst Olean	195	4000	[1]	Priv	S [8]		8/15 None	S	6/15 FAF	8	9	1	1	3	4	8	1
2965	Onondaga CC Syracuse	3857	1400	[1] 4200	Pub	L	S	S/A	S [5]	4/15 FF/FA	8	6	0	4	1	4	6	4
2966	Orange Co CC Middletown	2423	1400	[1] 2800	Pub	S		8/01 None	E [5]	5/01 FAF	6	6	0	2	1	4		4
2967	Paul Smith's C Paul Smiths	792	10900	3700	Priv	T [8]		8/30 None	S [5]	FAF	8	3	9	1	3	8	6	5
2968	Plaza Bus Inst Jackson Heights	706	1600	[1]	Priv	V [8]	U	Oth	O †	Oth	9	8		7			8	
2969	Practical Bible Sch Bible School Pk	115	6200 [3]	2700	Bapt OS	L [8]	S	A/S	E †	8/01 FF/FA	7	3	7	1	3	8	9	5
2970	Rockland CC Suffern	3726	1700	[1] 3200	Pub	S		None	E [5]	Oth		6	0	3	1	5	1	6
2971	Samaritan Sch of Nsg Troy	43	6600	2900 7500	Priv	M [8]	U	A/S	S †	FAF	6	9	2	1	0	9	5	1
2972	Schenectady CC Schenectady	1290	1600	[1] 2900	Pub	M	U	A=S	E [5]		7	6	0	1	0	6	3	7
2973	Simmons Sch Mort Sci Syracuse	65	11400	[1]	Priv	L	U	A/S	T †	9/01 Oth	5	1	0	1	1		9	0
2974	St Elizabeth Sch Nsg Utica	97	6200	2400	Cath	M [8]		6/15 Oth	S †	8/01 FA/FF	9	8	2	1		8	7	3
2975	Suffolk Co CC Selden	6807	1400	[1] 2800	Pub	S		8/31 A/S	S [5]	FF=FA	6	6	0	1	0	6	6	3
2976	Sullivan Co CC Loch Sheldroke	1300	6000	4500 7600	Pub	T		A=S	4 [5]	4/15 Oth	7	5	6	3	1	4		4
2977	SUNY Ag-Tech Coblskl Cobleskill	2630	5200 [3]	3500 8600	Pub	T [8]		A=S	S [5]	4/01 FA/FF	7	5	8	1	1	6	5	4
2978	SUNY Ag-Tech Morisvl Morrisville	2686	5300	3600 8600	Pub	T [8]		A=S	E [5]	FAF	7	5	8	1	1	7	6	4
2979	SUNY C Environ Sci Wanakena	48	6800	4900 10100	Pub	T [8]		6/01 A=S	E [5]	3/15 FF/FA	8	1	9	0	0		8	2
2980	SUNY C Tech Alfred Alfred	3405	5600 [3]	3800 9000	Pub	T [8]		A=S	E [5]	FA/FF	8	4	8	1	1	9	8	3
2981	SUNY C Tech Canton Canton	2107	5500 [3]	3800 7800	Pub	T [8]		8/15 A=S	E [5]	FFS	8	4		1	1	7		3
2982	SUNY C Tech Delhi Delhi	2374	5300 [3]	3500 8700	Pub	T [8]		A=S	E [5]	4/01 FAF	8	4	7	1	1	5	6	3
2983	SUNY C Tech Farmndl Farmingdale	5400	5900	3900 9200	Pub	T [8]		A=S	S [5]	FAF	9	5	2	3	1	6		

Educational Programs Available — College Transfer Courses

Sequence Number	Agriculture	Bus-Commerce	Communications	Education	Engineering	Fine, Applied Arts	Foreign Lang	Health	Home Ec	Humanities	Mathematics	Computer/Info Sci	Biological Sci	Physical Sci	Social Sci
2961		■	■	■	■	■		■			■	■	■	■	■
2962			■	■		■				■	■		■	■	■
2963	■	■	■	■		■		■		■	■		■	■	■
2964															
2965	■	■	■		■	■	■	■		■	■	■	■	■	■
2966		■	■	■	■	■	■	■	■	■	■	■	■	■	■
2967	■	■	■						■		■		■		■
2968															
2969							■			■					
2970	■	■	■		■	■		■	■	■	■	■			■
2971								■							
2972		■		■	■	■	■		■	■	■	■	■	■	■
2973												■			
2974								■							
2975	■	■	■	■	■	■	■	■	■	■	■	■	■	■	■
2976	■	■	■	■	■	■	■	■		■	■	■	■	■	■
2977	■	■	■	■	■	■		■	■	■	■	■	■	■	■
2978	■	■	■		■	■		■	■	■	■	■	■	■	■
2979	■														
2980	■	■			■	■		■		■	■	■		■	■
2981		■			■					■	■		■	■	■
2982	■	■					■			■	■	■	■	■	■
2983	■	■	■	■	■	■	■	■	■	■	■	■	■	■	■

Educational Programs Available — Career-oriented Programs (Agri, Business, Arts, Health)

Sequence Number	Agri: Ag Business	Ag/Farm Mgmt	Ag Mechanics/Tech	Horticulture	Business: Accounting	Bus Mgmt & Admin	Hotel/Rest Mgmt	Office Mgmt	Marketing/Purchasing	Secretarial Studies	Arts: Architecture Tech	Applied Design	Photography/Cinema	Health: Dental Assistant	Medical or Lab Tech	Nursing (RN)	Nursing (LPN)	Radiologic Technology
2961					■		■		■	■			■		■	■		■
2962				■	■	■			■	■						■	■	
2963					■	■			■	■					■		■	■
2964					■	■				■								
2965					■	■	■	■			■		■		■	■		
2966					■	■		■	■	■					■	■		■
2967						■	■											
2968					■	■		■		■								
2969																		
2970				■	■	■	■	■	■			■			■	■		
2971																■		
2972					■	■	■	■		■								
2973																		
2974																■		
2975				■	■	■	■	■	■	■				■		■		
2976					■	■	■	■	■	■			■			■		
2977	■	■		■	■	■	■	■	■	■					■			
2978	■	■	■	■	■	■	■			■					■	■		
2979																		
2980	■			■	■	■		■	■	■	■				■	■		
2981					■	■	■			■					■	■		
2982				■	■	■	■		■	■						■	■	
2983				■		■	■			■	■	■			■	■		

Educational Programs Available — Career-oriented Programs (Math, SocSci, Technical/Skilled Trades)

Sequence Number	Math: Computer Prog	Data Processing Tech	Computer Operating	SocSci: Crim Just/Law Enforce	Parks/Rec Mgmt	Social Work	Technical/Skilled Trades: Air/Refrig/Heat Tech	Auto Body Repair	Auto Mechanics	Carpentry/Constr	Drafting/Eng Draft	Electric Eng Tech	Civil Eng Tech	Indus/Mfg Eng Tech	Mech Eng Tech	Machinework	Welding
2961		■										■	■	■			
2962		■	■	■			■					■			■		
2963				■	■												
2964																	
2965	■	■	■	■	■	■			■	■	■	■			■	■	
2966			■	■							■	■					
2967					■												
2968			■														
2969																	
2970		■		■					■			■					
2971																	
2972	■	■	■	■		■						■					
2973																	
2974																	
2975	■	■	■	■		■						■	■		■		
2976		■	■	■													
2977	■	■	■		■				■								
2978	■	■	■		■				■	■	■	■			■		
2979																	
2980	■	■				■	■	■	■	■	■	■	■		■		
2981		■					■		■	■		■	■		■		
2982					■		■		■	■	■	■	■				■
2983		■	■	■			■					■	■		■		

▲ Sequence Number—indicates the order of the college in this book only. Do *not* use this number with admissions tests or need analysis services.

1 No campus room and board facilities
2 Room only or board only
3 Most freshmen required to live on campus
4 City or district residency requirements
5 Accredited by regional accrediting association or a recognized candidate for accreditation
6 All female freshman class
7 All male freshman class
8 Some admission selectivity; not all hs graduates accepted
9 Requirements more stringent for nonresidents
†Accredited by a nationally recognized accrediting body other than one of the regional accrediting associations

New York
(continued)

Sequence Number	School name (upper entry) City (lower entry)	Enrollment	Resident tuition/fees + room/board	Room/board (upper entry) Nonresident tuition/fees (lower entry)	Affiliation (upper entry) Religious observance (lower entry)	Size of community	Type of community	Fall term application deadline (upper entry) Test required or desired (lower entry)	Calendar	Fall term application deadline (upper entry) Forms to be filed (lower entry)
2984	Taylor Bus Inst New York	1000	6300	[1]	Priv	V[8]	U	 Oth	Q †	 Oth
2985	Tech Career Inst New York	2300	6300	[1]	Priv	V	U	9/15 None	Q †	 Oth
2986	Tobe-Coburn Sch New York	200	15900	6900	Priv	V[8]	U	8/30 A=S	E †	9/15 FA/FF
2987	Tompkins-Cortland C Dryden	1437	1500	[1] 3000	Pub	T		 A/S	S[5]	 FA/FF
2988	Trocaire C Buffalo	499	4900	[1]	Cath S	L[8]	U	 S/A	S[5]	 FAF
2989	Ulster Co CC Stone Ridge	1547	1700	[1] 3400	Pub	T		 None	E[5]	6/01 FA/FF
2990	Utica Sch of Comm Utica	475	4100	[1]	Priv	M[8]		 None	O †	5/01
2991	Villa Maria C Buffalo	356	4900	[1]	Cath OS	L[8]	S	/00 Oth	S[5]	 FA/FF
2992	Westchester CC Valhalla	3627	1600	[1] 3600	Pub	S		 A=S	S[5]	 Oth
2993	Wood Sch,The New York	492	8000	[1]	Priv	V[8]	U[6]	 Oth	O †	
2994	Word Life Bible Inst Pottersville	537	5600[3]	3000	Oth OS	T		 A=S	Q	 FF/FA

North Carolina

Sequence Number	School name (upper entry) City (lower entry)	Enrollment	Resident tuition/fees + room/board	Room/board (upper entry) Nonresident tuition/fees (lower entry)	Affiliation (upper entry) Religious observance (lower entry)	Size of community	Type of community	Fall term application deadline (upper entry) Test required or desired (lower entry)	Calendar	Fall term application deadline (upper entry) Forms to be filed (lower entry)
2995	Alamance CC Haw River	1159	400	[1] 3900	Pub	S		9/01 Oth	O[5]	8/01 FF/FA
2996	Albemarle,C of Elizabeth City	852	400	[1] 4000	Pub	S		 Oth	Q[5]	3/01 FF/FA
2997	Anson CC Ansonville	204	300	[1] 3000	Pub	S		 None	Q[5]	 FF/FA
2998	Asheville-Buncombe Asheville	1383	500	[1] 4000	Pub	M		 Oth	O[5]	5/31 FFS
2999	Beaufort Co CC Washington	1194	300	[1] 3000	Pub	S		 Oth	Q[5]	8/15 FA/FF
3000	Bladen CC Dublin	377	300	[1] 3000	Pub	T		9/01 Oth	Q[5]	8/15 FF=FA
3001	Blue Ridge Tech C Flat Rock	601	500	[1] 4000	Pub	S		8/29 None	O[5]	8/29 FF=FA
3002	Brevard C Brevard	780	7100[3]	3500 8200	Meth S	T[8]		 A=S	S[5]	7/01 FA/FF
3003	Brunswick CC Supply	344	300	[1] 2800	Pub	S		9/07 None	Q[5]	 FA/FF
3004	Caldwell CC/Tch Inst Hudson	920	300	[1] 3000	Pub	S		 Oth	Q[5]	 FF/FA
3005	Cape Fear CC Wilmington	1376	400	[1] 3900	Pub	M		9/01 Oth	Q[5]	3/01 FA/FF

Student Profile — No. in 10 who-

Sequence Number	-have need, rec some aid	-are women	-live on campus	-are minority students	-are nonresidents	-return as sophomores	-complete assoc degree	-transfer to 4-year college
2984		7		8	1	6	6	
2985	9	1	0	6	2	8	5	1
2986	7	9	0	5	5	8	8	
2987	7	6		1			5	4
2988	9	9	0	1		7	5	2
2989	9	5	0	1	1	5	3	2
2990	9	7	0	2	0	3	9	4
2991	7	8	0	1	1	5	4	3
2992	6	5	0	3	1			4
2993	9	9	0	8	1		8	
2994	1	5	9	1	8			
2995	5	6	0	2	1	4	3	1
2996	3	6	0	2	1	4	5	4
2997	5	6	0	3	0	4	4	1
2998	1	5	0				7	1
2999	3	6	0	3	1	2	2	1
3000	4	5	0	3	1	5	5	5
3001	9	6	0	1	1	3	1	1
3002	7	5	9	1	5	8	7	9
3003	4	6	0	2	1	4	1	
3004	2	6	0	1	1	4	1	1
3005	8	5	0	2	1	5	6	1

Educational Programs Available — College Transfer Courses

Sequence Number	Agriculture	Bus-Commerce	Communications	Education	Engineering	Fine, Applied Arts	Foreign Lang	Health	Home Ec	Humanities	Mathematics	Computer/Info Sci	Biological Sci	Physical Sci	Social Sci
2984		■													
2985		■													
2986															
2987	■	■	■		■	■		■		■	■	■	■	■	■
2988										■	■				■
2989		■	■	■	■	■	■	■		■	■	■	■	■	■
2990		■										■			
2991		■		■		■						■			■
2992		■	■	■	■	■	■	■	■	■	■	■	■	■	■
2993		■													
2994										■					
2995		■	■	■	■	■	■	■	■		■	■			■
2996	■	■		■		■	■	■		■	■	■	■	■	■
2997		■	■	■		■	■	■	■	■	■	■	■	■	■
2998		■						■				■			■
2999		■		■		■	■	■		■	■	■	■	■	■
3000		■		■								■			■
3001	■	■			■			■				■			
3002	■	■	■	■	■	■	■	■		■	■	■	■	■	■
3003		■			■					■	■	■	■		■
3004	■	■		■	■	■	■		■	■	■	■	■	■	■
3005															

Educational Programs Available — Career-oriented Programs (Agri, Business, Arts, Health)

Sequence Number	Ag Business	Ag/Farm Mgmt	Ag Mechanics/Tech	Horticulture	Accounting	Bus Mgmt & Admin	Hotel/Rest Mgmt	Office Mgmt	Marketing/Purchasing	Secretarial Studies	Architecture Tech	Applied Design	Photography/Cinema	Dental Assistant	Medical or Lab Tech	Nursing (RN)	Nursing (LPN)	Radiologic Technology
2984					■	■		■		■								
2985																		
2986						■			■	■								
2987					■	■	■	■	■	■					■	■	■	
2988								■		■					■	■		■
2989				■	■	■			■	■						■		
2990					■	■		■		■								
2991						■	■		■				■					
2992					■	■	■	■	■	■					■	■	■	■
2993					■					■								
2994																		
2995					■	■			■	■		■		■	■	■	■	
2996						■	■	■		■						■	■	
2997					■	■		■	■	■		■	■				■	
2998					■	■	■	■	■	■				■	■	■	■	■
2999					■	■				■					■	■	■	
3000						■				■								
3001				■		■				■						■		
3002																		
3003						■		■		■							■	
3004					■	■	■			■						■	■	■
3005					■	■		■		■						■	■	

Educational Programs Available — Career-oriented Programs (Math, SocSci, Technical/Skilled Trades)

Sequence Number	Computer Prog	Data Processing Tech	Computer Operating	Crim Just/Law Enforce	Parks/Rec Mgmt	Social Work	Air/Refrig/Heat Tech	Auto Body Repair	Auto Mechanics	Carpentry/Constr	Drafting/Eng Draft	Electric Eng Tech	Civil Eng Tech	Indus/Mfg Eng Tech	Mech Eng Tech	Machinework	Welding
2984																	
2985																	
2986																	
2987		■		■		■				■		■			■		
2988																	
2989		■		■							■						
2990		■	■														
2991																	
2992		■		■		■			■		■	■	■		■	■	
2993																	
2994																	
2995	■	■		■			■		■	■	■	■				■	■
2996	■	■	■	■			■		■	■	■	■				■	
2997		■	■			■	■	■	■	■		■			■		■
2998	■		■	■			■		■	■	■		■		■	■	■
2999	■	■		■		■			■		■	■			■	■	■
3000				■					■	■		■				■	■
3001		■					■	■	■	■		■				■	■
3002																	
3003	■	■	■						■	■							■
3004		■						■	■		■					■	■
3005				■			■		■	■	■	■			■	■	■

▲ Sequence Number—indicates the order of the college in this book only. Do *not* use this number with admissions tests or need analysis services.

[1] No campus room and board facilities
[2] Room only or board only
[3] Most freshmen required to live on campus
[4] City or district residency requirements
[5] Accredited by regional accrediting association or a recognized candidate for accreditation
[6] All female freshman class
[7] All male freshman class
[8] Some admission selectivity; not all hs graduates accepted
[9] Requirements more stringent for nonresidents
†Accredited by a nationally recognized accrediting body other than one of the regional accrediting associations

North Carolina
(continued)

Sequence Number	School name (upper entry) City (lower entry)	Enrollment	Resident tuition/fees + room/board	Room/board (upper entry) Nonresident tuition/fees (lower entry)	Affiliation (upper entry) Religious observance (lower entry)	Size of community	Type of community	Fall term application deadline (upper entry) Test required or desired (lower entry)	Calendar	Fall term application deadline (upper entry) Forms to be filed (lower entry)	-have need, rec some aid	-are women	-live on campus	-are minority students	-are nonresidents	-return as sophomores	-complete assoc degree	-transfer to 4-year college
			Costs		**Gen. Info.**			**Admissions**		**Financial Aid**	**Student Profile: No. in 10 who-**							
3006	Carteret CC Morehead City	679	300	[1] 2600	Pub	S		None	Q[5]	9/01 FAF	3	6	0	1	1	5	5	1
3007	Catawba Valley CC Hickory	1267	300	[1] 3000	Pub	M	S	Oth	Q[5]	10/15 FF/FA	1	6	0	1	1	7	6	2
3008	Central Carolina Tec Sanford	1904	400	[1] 4000	Pub	S		None	Q[5]	FF=FA	1	6	0	2	1	4	3	1
3009	Central Piedmont CC Charlotte	5038	400	[1] 3400	Pub	L	U	Oth	Q[5]	FA/FF	1	6	0	2	1		2	1
3010	Cleveland CC Shelby	518	300	[1] 3000	Pub	S		None	Q[5]	FF=FA	1	5	0	2	1	2	4	1
3011	CMHA Sch of Nsg Charlotte	40	3500		Pub	V[8]	U	7/30 A=S	T[5]	7/30 FF=FA		7	1	2			9	
3012	Coastal Carolina CC Jacksonville	1500	300	[1] 2900	Pub	S		9/05 Oth	Q[5]	8/15 FA/FF	7	5	0	2	3	3	4	2
3013	Craven CC New Bern	965	400	[1] 4000	Pub	S		Oth	Q[5]	4/01 FF/FA	2	6	0	2	1	6		
3014	Davidson Co CC Lexington	990	300	[1] 3000	Pub	S		A=S	Q[5]	7/01 FF/FA	3	6	0	1	0	7	5	1
3015	Durham Tech CC Durham	1497	400	[1] 3900	Pub	M	U	8/16 Oth	O[5]	FF/FA	4	6	0	4	1	0	2	
3016	Edgecombe CC Tarboro	675	300	[1] 3000	Pub	S		9/01 Oth	Q[5]	9/01 Oth	5	7	0	5	0	6	2	1
3017	Fayetteville Tech CC Fayetteville	6000	900	[1] 3100	Pub	M	S	Oth	Q[5]	3/15 FFS	4	6	0	4	1	3	5	1
3018	Forsyth Tech CC Winston-Salem	4999	300	[1] 2900	Pub	L[8]	U	8/31 Oth	Q[5]	5/01 FF/FA	6	6	0	2	0	7	6	2
3019	Gaston C Dallas	1704	300	[1] 3000	Pub	M	S	A/S	Q[5]	FA/FF	1	6	0	1	1	5	5	3
3020	Guilford Tech CC Jamestown	3200	400	[1] 3000	Pub	L	S	Oth	Q[5]	7/01 FF/FA	2	5	0	2	1	7	2	1
3021	Halifax CC Weldon	496	300	[1] 2500	Pub	S		9/17 Oth	Q[5]	6/01 FFS	6	7	0	5	1	5	4	1
3022	Haywood Tech C Clyde	708	400	[1] 3900	Pub	T		Oth	Q[5]	FF/FA	2	5	0	1	1	6	5	1
3023	Isothermal CC Spindale	386	300	[1] 2900	Pub	M	U	Oth	Q[5]	9/01 FF/FA	2	6	0	1	1	4	1	4
3024	James Sprunt CC Kenansville	571	300	[1] 3000	Pub	T		Oth	Q[5]	7/01 FF/FA	3	6	0	4	1	6	5	1
3025	Johnston CC Smithfield	949	300	[1] 2500	Pub	T		8/15 None	Q[5]	FAF	3	6	0	2	1	2	3	1
3026	King's C Charlotte	430	10400[2]	3300	Priv	L[8]	U	None	O†	Oth	9	9	5	2	3			
3027	Lenoir CC Kinston	1113	500	[1] 4000	Pub	S		9/09 Oth	Q[5]	8/01 Oth	3	6	0	3	1	7	3	2
3028	Louisburg C Louisburg	800	8400	2800	Meth	T[8]		A=S	E[5]	FA/FF	8	4	8	1	1	6	4	9

Educational Programs Available — College Transfer Courses

Sequence Number	Agriculture	Bus-Commerce	Communications	Education	Engineering	Fine, Applied Arts	Foreign Lang	Health	Home Ec	Humanities	Mathematics	Computer/Info Sci	Biological Sci	Physical Sci	Social Sci
3006		■				■		■				■			■
3007	■	■	■	■	■	■	■			■	■	■	■	■	■
3008		■		■	■		■	■			■	■	■	■	■
3009	■	■	■	■	■	■	■	■	■	■	■	■	■	■	■
3010		■	■			■	■			■	■	■	■	■	■
3011															
3012		■	■	■		■	■			■	■		■	■	■
3013															
3014		■			■					■		■			■
3015				■											■
3016															
3017															
3018	■	■		■	■	■		■				■			■
3019		■	■	■	■	■	■	■	■	■	■	■	■	■	■
3020	■	■	■	■	■	■		■	■	■	■	■	■	■	■
3021		■	■	■	■	■	■	■	■	■	■	■			■
3022															
3023		■		■	■			■		■	■	■	■	■	■
3024				■		■		■		■	■		■	■	■
3025		■	■			■		■	■			■			■
3026															
3027	■	■		■	■	■	■	■			■	■			■
3028		■	■	■	■	■	■	■		■	■	■	■	■	■

Educational Programs Available — Career-oriented Programs (Agri, Business, Arts, Health)

Sequence Number	Ag Business	Ag/Farm Mgmt	Ag Mechanics/Tech	Horticulture	Accounting	Bus Mgmt & Admin	Hotel/Rest Mgmt	Office Mgmt	Marketing/Purchasing	Secretarial Studies	Architecture Tech	Applied Design	Photography/Cinema	Dental Assistant	Medical or Lab Tech	Nursing (RN)	Nursing (LPN)	Radiologic Technology
3006						■				■							■	■
3007				■	■				■		■					■		
3008					■	■			■	■						■	■	
3009				■	■	■	■	■	■	■	■	■		■		■	■	
3010					■	■			■	■							■	■
3011																■		
3012					■	■		■	■	■				■	■	■	■	
3013					■	■			■	■						■	■	
3014					■	■				■						■		
3015					■					■							■	
3016						■				■						■	■	■
3017				■	■	■		■	■	■				■		■	■	■
3018										■							■	■
3019					■	■		■	■	■						■		
3020					■			■	■	■	■		■	■		■	■	
3021						■				■					■	■	■	
3022				■		■				■		■				■		
3023					■	■		■	■	■							■	
3024	■				■	■				■		■				■	■	
3025				■													■	
3026					■		■	■	■	■					■			
3027	■	■	■	■	■	■		■	■	■						■	■	
3028						■				■								

Educational Programs Available — Career-oriented Programs (Math, SocSci, Technical/Skilled Trades)

Sequence Number	Computer Prog	Data Processing Tech	Computer Operating	Crim Just/Law Enforce	Parks/Rec Mgmt	Social Work	Air/Refrig/Heat Tech	Auto Body Repair	Auto Mechanics	Carpentry/Constr	Drafting/Eng Draft	Electric Eng Tech	Civil Eng Tech	Indus/Mfg Eng Tech	Mech Eng Tech	Machinework	Welding
3006				■			■		■	■		■					■
3007		■	■	■	■		■		■		■	■				■	■
3008	■	■	■	■			■		■		■					■	■
3009	■	■	■	■			■	■	■		■	■	■	■	■	■	■
3010			■	■			■	■	■	■		■				■	■
3011																	
3012	■			■			■	■	■		■	■	■			■	■
3013	■	■		■			■	■	■	■		■				■	■
3014		■		■			■	■	■		■					■	■
3015	■			■					■	■	■	■				■	
3016	■	■		■		■		■	■								
3017	■			■	■		■	■	■	■			■			■	■
3018							■	■	■	■	■	■		■	■	■	■
3019	■	■		■		■	■		■		■	■	■	■	■	■	■
3020	■		■	■			■	■	■	■	■	■	■		■	■	■
3021	■	■	■	■		■			■								■
3022			■	■				■	■	■						■	■
3023	■	■	■	■				■	■		■	■			■	■	■
3024	■			■					■	■		■					■
3025							■	■	■	■						■	■
3026			■														
3027	■	■	■	■			■		■		■				■	■	■
3028																	

▲ Sequence Number—indicates the order of the college in this book only. Do *not* use this number with admissions tests or need analysis services.

[1] No campus room and board facilities
[2] Room only or board only
[3] Most freshmen required to live on campus
[4] City or district residency requirements
[5] Accredited by regional accrediting association or a recognized candidate for accreditation
[6] All female freshman class
[7] All male freshman class
[8] Some admission selectivity; not all hs graduates accepted
[9] Requirements more stringent for nonresidents
†Accredited by a nationally recognized accrediting body other than one of the regional accrediting associations

North Carolina
(continued)

Sequence Number	School name (upper entry) / City (lower entry)	Enrollment	Resident tuition/fees + room/board	Room/board (upper entry) / Nonresident tuition/fees (lower entry)	Affiliation (upper entry) / Religious observance (lower entry)	Size of community	Type of community	Fall term application deadline (upper entry) / Test required or desired (lower entry)	Calendar	Fall term application deadline (upper entry) / Forms to be filed (lower entry)	-have need, rec some aid	-are women	-live on campus	-are minority students	-are nonresidents	-return as sophomores	-complete assoc degree	-transfer to 4-year college
3029	Martin CC Williamston	352	300	[1] 3000	Pub	T		Oth	Q [5]	8/01	3	7	0	3	1	4	3	1
3030	Mayland CC Spruce Pine	411	300	[1] 3000	Pub	S		Oth	Q [5]	FF/FA	6	6	0	1	1	7	2	1
3031	McDowell Tech CC Marion	395	400	[1] 3900	Pub	T		Oth	Q [5]	FF=FA	7	6	0	1		6	4	1
3032	Mitchell CC Statesville	1232	400	[1] 2600	Pub	S		None	Q [5]	7/01 FF/FA	6	6	0	1	1	8	7	6
3033	Montgomery CC Troy	543	400	[1] 3900	Pub	T		9/06 Oth	Q [5]	FF/FA	4	4	0	2	1	4	4	2
3034	Nash CC Rocky Mount	525	300	[1] 3000	Pub	M	S	Oth	Q [5]	FF=FA	1	6	0	2	1		3	1
3035	Pamlico Tech C Grantsboro	144	300	[1] 3000	Pub	S		Oth	Q [5]	FFS	4	8	0	2	1	1	7	1
3036	Peace C Raleigh	416	7800	3600	Pres OS	L [8]	U [6]	S/A	S [5]	FA/FF	4	9	9	1	1	8	9	9
3037	Piedmont CC Roxboro	355	400	[1] 3900	Pub	T		Oth	Q [5]	4/15 FF/FA	7	5	0	4	1	6	4	1
3038	Pitt CC Greenville	1385	500	[1] 4000	Pub	S		9/01 Oth	Q [5]	7/10 FF=FA	4	6	0	3	1	6	5	1
3039	Randolph CC Asheboro	689	300	[1] 3000	Pub	S		Oth	Q [5]	5/01 FF/FA	2	6	0	1	1	5	2	1
3040	Richmond Tech C Hamlet	599	300	[1] 3000	Pub	M		Oth	Q [5]	FA/FF	4	6	0	3	1	6	6	
3041	Roanoke-Chowan Tech Ahoskie	506	700	[1] 4200	Pub	T		Oth	O [5]	11/30 FFS	8	7	0	5	1	6	5	2
3042	Robeson CC Lumberton	873	300	[1] 2200	Pub	M		9/10 Oth	Q [5]	9/10 FF=FA	8	7	0	6	1	1	1	1
3043	Rockingham CC Wentworth	850	300	[1] 3000	Pub	T		Oth	Q [5]	5/01 FAF	3	6	0	2	1		5	
3044	Rowan-Cabarrus CC Salisbury	2000	400	[1] 3000	Pub	S		Oth	Q [5]	6/30 FFS	7	6	0	1	1		6	1
3045	Saint Mary's C Raleigh	271	11600	5300	Oth OS	L [8]	U [6]	A=S	E [5]	4/01 FA/FF	3	9	9	1	4	7	8	9
3046	Salisbury Business C Salisbury	155	2200	[1]	Priv	S [8]		A=S	Q	6/01 FF/FA		9	0	3	0		0	1
3047	Sampson CC Clinton	473	300	[1] 3000	Pub	T		Oth	Q [5]	7/15 FF=FA	9	7	0	3	1	6	3	1
3048	Sandhills CC Pinehurst	1388	300	[1] 3000	Pub	S		9/12 None	Q [5]	9/01 FF/FA	6	6	0	2	1	5	2	1
3049	Southeastern CC-NC Whiteville	939	300	[1] 2500	Pub	S		Oth	Q [5]	FA/FF	3	7	0	2	1	4	6	3
3050	Southwestern CC Sylva	583	300	[1] 2500	Pub	T		Oth	Q [5]	FA/FF	3	6	0	1	1	5	3	1
3051	Stanly CC Albemarle	560	300	[1] 2900	Pub	S		9/01 Oth	Q [5]	5/15 FA/FF	2	6	0	1		6	3	1

Column groups: Costs (Resident tuition/fees + room/board; Room/board / Nonresident tuition/fees); Gen. Info. (Affiliation / Religious observance; Size of community; Type of community); Admissions (Fall term application deadline / Test required or desired; Calendar); Financial Aid (Fall term application deadline / Forms to be filed); Student Profile (No. in 10 who-).

Educational Programs Available — College Transfer Courses (Agriculture … Social Sci); Career-oriented Programs: Agri (Ag Business … Horticulture), Business (Accounting … Secretarial Studies), Arts (Architecture Tech … Photography/Cinema), Health (Dental Assistant … Radiologic Technology), Math (Computer Prog … Computer Operating), SocSci (Crim Just/Law Enforce … Social Work), Technical/Skilled Trades (Air/Refrig/Heat Tech … Welding)

Sequence Number	Agriculture	Bus-Commerce	Communications	Education	Engineering	Fine, Applied Arts	Foreign Lang	Health	Home Ec	Humanities	Mathematics	Computer/Info Sci	Biological Sci	Physical Sci	Social Sci	Ag Business	Ag/Farm Mgmt	Ag Mechanics/Tech	Horticulture	Accounting	Bus Mgmt & Admin	Hotel/Rest Mgmt	Office Mgmt	Marketing/Purchasing	Secretarial Studies	Architecture Tech	Applied Design	Photography/Cinema	Dental Assistant	Medical or Lab Tech	Nursing (RN)	Nursing (LPN)	Radiologic Technology	Computer Prog	Data Processing Tech	Computer Operating	Crim Just/Law Enforce	Parks/Rec Mgmt	Social Work	Air/Refrig/Heat Tech	Auto Body Repair	Auto Mechanics	Carpentry/Constr	Drafting/Eng Draft	Electric Eng Tech	Civil Eng Tech	Indus/Mfg Eng Tech	Mech Eng Tech	Machinework	Welding
3029		■		■											■					■	■		■		■											■				■		■	■						■	■
3030		■		■	■	■									■					■	■				■							■		■			■				■		■						■	■
3031		■	■	■								■								■	■		■	■	■		■	■				■		■	■	■	■			■	■	■	■		■				■	■
3032		■	■	■	■	■	■	■		■	■	■	■	■	■					■	■		■	■	■		■				■			■	■		■		■	■		■		■	■			■		■
3033		■		■					■			■			■					■	■				■							■				■	■			■	■	■								
3034		■		■	■			■				■			■	■				■	■			■	■						■	■		■		■	■					■								■
3035		■			■							■								■	■		■	■	■																	■	■							■
3036		■	■	■	■	■	■	■	■	■	■	■	■	■	■					■					■										■															
3037		■		■								■			■					■	■				■						■			■					■	■			■	■						■
3038		■		■						■	■				■			■		■	■			■	■		■				■	■	■	■	■		■		■	■		■	■		■		■		■	■
3039	■	■			■	■	■	■		■	■	■	■	■	■				■	■	■				■		■	■			■				■		■				■	■			■				■	■
3040		■			■			■				■			■										■							■										■	■		■				■	■
3041		■		■				■				■			■						■				■						■			■			■			■		■	■	■						■
3042		■						■				■			■					■	■		■	■	■						■	■		■		■	■			■			■		■					
3043		■	■	■	■	■	■	■	■	■	■	■	■	■	■					■			■								■	■					■			■	■		■	■					■	■
3044		■					■													■				■					■		■	■	■	■			■			■		■	■	■	■		■	■	■	■
3045																																																		
3046																				■			■		■																									
3047	■	■		■		■		■		■	■	■	■	■	■				■	■	■				■						■			■			■													■
3048	■	■	■	■	■	■	■	■	■	■	■	■	■	■	■				■	■	■	■	■		■	■				■	■	■	■	■	■	■			■		■	■		■		■	■			
3049		■		■		■	■	■		■	■	■	■	■	■						■		■		■						■	■			■		■	■		■		■	■		■					■
3050	■	■		■	■	■			■	■	■	■	■		■					■	■			■						■	■	■	■	■			■	■		■		■	■		■					■
3051																			■	■	■			■	■						■			■		■	■				■	■							■	■

▲ **Sequence Number—indicates the order of the college in this book only. Do *not* use this number with admissions tests or need analysis services.**

[1] No campus room and board facilities
[2] Room only or board only
[3] Most freshmen required to live on campus
[4] City or district residency requirements
[5] Accredited by regional accrediting association or a recognized candidate for accreditation
[6] All female freshman class
[7] All male freshman class
[8] Some admission selectivity; not all hs graduates accepted
[9] Requirements more stringent for nonresidents
†Accredited by a nationally recognized accrediting body other than one of the regional accrediting associations

North Carolina
(continued)

Sequence Number	School name (upper entry) / City (lower entry)	Enrollment	Costs: Resident tuition/fees + room/board	Costs: Room/board (upper entry) / Nonresident tuition/fees (lower entry)	Gen. Info.: Affiliation (upper entry) / Religious observance (lower entry)	Gen. Info.: Size of community	Gen. Info.: Type of community	Admissions: Fall term application deadline (upper entry) / Test required or desired (lower entry)	Admissions: Calendar	Financial Aid: Fall term application deadline (upper entry) / Forms to be filed (lower entry)	No. in 10 who- -have need, rec some aid	-are women	-live on campus	-are minority students	-are nonresidents	-return as sophomores	-complete assoc degree	-transfer to 4-year college
3052	Surry CC / Dobson	1085	300	[1] / 3000	Pub	T		None	Q[5]	5/01 / FA/FF	5	6	0	1	1	7	6	3
3053	Tri-County CC / Murphy	804	400	[1] / 3900	Pub	T		9/15 / Oth	Q[5]	8/01 / FF/FA	5	6	0	1	1	5	4	3
3054	Vance Granville CC / Henderson	2316	300	[1] / 3000	Pub	S		9/01 / Oth	Q[5]	8/15 / FF/FA	6	6	0	5	1	6	5	9
3055	Wake Tech C / Raleigh	1821	400	[1] / 3900	Pub	L	S	8/25 / Oth	O[5]	8/01 / FAF	2	6	0	2	1	5	5	1
3056	Wayne CC / Goldsboro	1470	300	[1] / 3000	Pub	M		Oth	Q[5]	7/01 / FA/FF	3	6	0	2	1	5	4	2
3057	Western Piedmont CC / Morganton	965	300	[1] / 3000	Pub	S		Oth	Q[5]	FF=FA	5	6	0	1		6	3	2
3058	Wilkes CC / Wilkesboro	1039	300	[1] / 3000	Pub	T		Oth	Q[5]	4/01 / FF=FA	2	6	0	1	1	6	5	3
3059	Wilson Tech CC / Wilson	563	400	[1] / 3000	Pub	S		9/04 / Oth	Q[5]	8/15 / FF/FA	5	6	0	3	0	3	3	1
North Dakota																		
3060	Bismarck St C / Bismarck	1569	3500	1900 / 5900	Pub	M		8/15 / A/S	S[5]	5/01 / FF/FA	5	5	1	1	1	2	3	3
3061	Fort Berthold CC / New Town	155	1600	[1]	Pub	T		9/07 / A/S	S[5]	8/24 / FFS	5	5	0	9	0	3		3
3062	Interstate Bus C / Fargo	420	3800	[1]	Priv	M[8]	S	Oth	Q†	Oth	7	6	0	1			8	
3063	Medcenter QR RT Prog / Bismarck	9	400	[1]	Pub	M[8]		1/01 / A/S	O	None	5	7	0	1	2	9	9	
3064	ND St C of Science / Wahpeton	2200	3200	1600 / 5600	Pub	T		A/S	Q[5]	4/15 / FFS	7	3	8	1	2	9	7	1
3065	ND St U Bottineau / Bottineau	403	3600[3]	2000 / 6000	Pub	T		9/01 / A/S	Q[5]	4/01 / FF/FA	6	4	8	1	3	6	6	5
3066	ND Williston,U of / Williston	527	3100	1500 / 5500	Pub	S		A/S	E[5]	FFS	6	6	2	1	2	7	6	4
3067	ND-Lake Region,U of / Devils Lake	412	3600	2000 / 6000	Pub	T		A/S	E[5]	FF/FA	8	5	2	1	1		4	3
3068	Standing Rock CC / Fort Yates	198	2100	[1]	Pub	T		9/05 / A=S	S[5]	2/15 / FF=FA	8	5	0	9	5	6	3	4
3069	Turtle Mountain CC / Belcourt	408	1200	[1]	Priv	T		ACT	Q[5]	5/01 / FFS	9	6	0	9	0			
Ohio																		
3070	Aultman Hosp Sch Nsg / Canton	108	5500[2]	1400	Priv	L[8]	U	3/31 / A/S	S†	5/01 / FF=FA	8	9	1	1	0	8	9	0
3071	Aultman Sch Rad T / Canton	28	600	[1]	Priv	L[8]	U	1/31 / ACT	O†		0	9	0	1	0		9	
3072	Aultman/Ultrasonogra / Canton		1000	[1]	Pub	M[8]	U	1/15 / Oth	O†		0	5		0			9	

Educational Programs Available (College Transfer Courses; Career-oriented Programs: Agri, Business, Arts, Health, Math, SocSci, Technical/Skilled Trades)

Sequence Number	Agriculture	Bus-Commerce	Communications	Education	Engineering	Fine, Applied Arts	Foreign Lang	Health	Home Ec	Humanities	Mathematics	Computer/Info Sci	Biological Sci	Physical Sci	Social Sci	Ag Business	Ag/Farm Mgmt	Ag Mechanics/Tech	Horticulture	Accounting	Bus Mgmt & Admin	Hotel/Rest Mgmt	Office Mgmt	Marketing/Purchasing	Secretarial Studies	Architecture Tech	Applied Design	Photography/Cinema	Dental Assistant	Medical or Lab Tech	Nursing (RN)	Nursing (LPN)	Radiologic Technology	Computer Prog	Data Processing Tech	Computer Operating	Crim Just/Law Enforce	Parks/Rec Mgmt	Social Work	Air/Refrig/Heat Tech	Auto Body Repair	Auto Mechanics	Carpentry/Constr	Drafting/Eng Draft	Electric Eng Tech	Civil Eng Tech	Indus/Mfg Eng Tech	Mech Eng Tech	Machinework	Welding
3052	■	■		■	■							■			■	■			■	■	■			■	■						■	■				■	■					■	■	■				■	■	■
3053		■		■			■			■	■		■	■	■																	■									■	■	■		■				■	■
3054		■		■	■	■	■		■	■	■	■	■		■					■	■										■	■	■	■		■				■		■	■		■					■
3055																				■	■	■		■	■	■			■	■	■		■	■	■	■	■			■		■		■		■	■	■	■	■
3056									■				■	■	■				■	■	■			■	■				■		■	■				■	■	■		■	■	■							■	■
3057	■	■	■	■	■	■		■	■	■	■	■	■	■	■				■	■	■				■				■	■	■			■	■		■					■	■	■			■		■	■
3058		■	■	■		■	■	■	■	■	■	■	■	■	■					■	■	■			■				■		■			■	■	■	■		■		■	■	■	■						
3059		■		■	■			■				■			■					■	■				■						■	■		■	■		■			■		■	■	■	■			■	■	■
North Dakota																																																		
3060	■	■	■	■	■	■	■	■		■	■	■	■	■	■	■	■				■	■	■	■	■					■										■	■	■	■							■
3061	■	■	■	■	■	■	■			■	■	■	■	■	■			■					■		■							■							■	■	■		■							
3062																				■	■		■		■									■	■	■														
3063								■																									■																	
3064	■	■	■	■	■	■		■		■	■	■	■	■	■					■									■		■	■								■	■	■			■	■		■	■	■
3065	■	■		■		■		■		■	■	■	■	■	■	■	■		■	■			■	■	■					■						■		■												
3066	■	■	■	■	■	■	■	■	■	■	■	■	■	■	■	■	■			■	■		■	■	■						■	■			■	■						■								
3067	■	■	■	■		■			■	■	■	■	■	■	■	■	■						■	■	■										■	■	■					■								
3068	■	■								■	■	■	■		■		■								■												■													
3069		■	■	■	■	■		■	■	■	■	■	■		■					■			■		■											■							■							■
Ohio																																																		
3070								■																							■																			
3071																																	■																	
3072																																																		

▲ Sequence Number—indicates the order of the college in this book only. Do *not* use this number with admissions tests or need analysis services.

[1] No campus room and board facilities
[2] Room only or board only
[3] Most freshmen required to live on campus
[4] City or district residency requirements
[5] Accredited by regional accrediting association or a recognized candidate for accreditation
[6] All female freshman class
[7] All male freshman class
[8] Some admission selectivity; not all hs graduates accepted
[9] Requirements more stringent for nonresidents
†Accredited by a nationally recognized accrediting body other than one of the regional accrediting associations

Ohio
(continued)

Sequence Number	School name (upper entry) / City (lower entry)	Enrollment	Costs: Resident tuition/fees + room/board	Costs: Room/board (upper entry) / Nonresident tuition/fees (lower entry)	Gen. Info.: Affiliation (upper entry) / Religious observance (lower entry)	Gen. Info.: Size of community	Gen. Info.: Type of community	Admissions: Fall term application deadline (upper entry) / Test required or desired (lower entry)	Admissions: Calendar	Financial Aid: Fall term application deadline (upper entry) / Forms to be filed (lower entry)
3073	Belmont Tech C / St Clairsville	1123	1000	[1] / 1500	Pub	T		None	Q[5]	FF=FA
3074	Bliss C / Columbus	650	5800	[1]	Priv	V	U	Oth	Q †	10/03 / FFS
3075	Bowling Grn Firelnds / Huron	601	2200	[1] / 5500	Pub	T		8/01 / A/S	E[5]	4/01 / FA/FF
3076	Central Ohio Tech C / Newark	750	1800	[1] / 2500	Pub	S		9/19 / Oth	Q[5]	4/15 / FA/FF
3077	Christ Hosp Sch Nsg / Cincinnati	205	8800	2100	Priv	L[8]	S	A=S	O †	5/01 / FFS
3078	Cinci Clermont C,U / Batavia	462	2700	[1] / 6600	Pub	T		9/20 / A=S	Q[5]	3/01 / FA/FF
3079	Cinci Ray Walters,U / Cincinnati	1496	2700	[1] / 6600	Pub	L	S	A=S	Q[5]	2/01 / FF=FA
3080	Cinci Tech C / Cincinnati	4961	2100	[1] / 3400	Pub	V	U	Oth	O[5]	3/01 / FA/FF
3081	Clark St CC / Springfield	1013	1600	[1] / 3300	Pub	M	S	Oth	Q[5]	8/01 / FAF
3082	Columbus St CC / Columbus	4756	1600	[1] / 3500	Pub	V	U		Q[5]	3/31 / FA/FF
3083	Community Hos Sc Nsg / Springfield	105	3700[2]	1000	Priv	M[8]		A/S	O †	FA/FF
3084	Cuyahoga CC East Cam / Warrensvl Tnshp	1207	1200	[1] / 2800	Pub	V	S	None	Q[5]	9/01 / FF=FA
3085	Cuyahoga CC Metro / Cleveland	2236	1200	[1] / 2800	Pub	V	U	Oth	Q[5]	9/01 / FA/FF
3086	Cuyahoga CC West Cam / Parma	2872	1300	[1] / 3300	Pub	L	S	None	Q[5]	
3087	Davis C / Toledo	527	4600	[1]	Priv	L[8]	U	Oth	Q[5]	Oth
3088	Edison St CC / Piqua	728	1600	[1] / 3000	Pub	S		A/S	Q[5]	FF=FA
3089	ETI Tech C-Niles / Niles	160	4000	[1]	Priv	S[8]		Oth	T †	Oth
3090	Fairview Hos Sch Nsg / Cleveland	165	3400	[1]	Priv	V[8]	S	Oth	O †	FAF
3091	Good Samartn Sch Nsg / Cincinnati	320	7400[2]	2300	Cath	V[8]	U	A/S	E †	FA/FF
3092	Hocking Tech C / Nelsonville	5209	5100	3600 / 6700	Pub	T		Oth	Q[5]	FA/FF
3093	Jefferson Tech C / Steubenville	839	1100	[1] / 1800	Pub	S		Oth	Q[5]	FF=FA
3094	Kent St Ashtabula / Ashtabula	401	2400	[1]	Pub	S		8/31 / A/S	S[5]	8/15 / FA/FF
3095	Kent St E Liverpool / East Liverpool	429	2400	[1] / 5400	Pub	S		A/S	E[5]	8/01 / FA/FF

Student Profile — No. in 10 who-

Sequence Number	-have need, rec some aid	-are women	-live on campus	-are minority students	-are nonresidents	-return as sophomores	-complete assoc degree	-transfer to 4-year college
3073	5	6	0	1	1	5	5	1
3074	6	7	0	3	1	3	5	1
3075		6	0	1		6		
3076	5	6	0	1	0	7	4	1
3077	8	9	3	1	1	9	7	
3078	3	6	0	1	0	5	4	3
3079	9	7	0	1	1	6	6	3
3080	4	5	0	2	1	6	5	1
3081		7	0	1	0	7		
3082	3	6	0	2	1	4	6	2
3083	4	9	7	1	1	5		
3084	7	7	0	5	1	2	1	3
3085	7	6	0	6	1	9		
3086	4	6	0	1	1	2	2	2
3087	7	7	0	1	1	6	5	1
3088	9	6	0	1	0	6	5	
3089	7	7		1	1	8	7	1
3090		9	0	1	0	7		
3091	7	9	5	1	1	7	7	
3092	7	4	1	1	1	7	6	1
3093	9	6	0	1	2	5	2	2
3094	5	6	0	1	1	4	3	3
3095	6	7	0	1	1	7	6	3

Educational Programs Available — College Transfer Courses

Sequence Number	Agriculture	Bus-Commerce	Communications	Education	Engineering	Fine, Applied Arts	Foreign Lang	Health	Home Ec	Humanities	Mathematics	Computer/Info Sci	Biological Sci	Physical Sci	Social Sci
3073															
3074		■	■						■		■	■			■
3075		■	■	■	■	■	■	■		■	■	■	■	■	■
3076		■			■										
3077								■							
3078		■	■	■	■	■	■	■		■	■	■		■	■
3079		■	■	■	■	■	■	■		■	■	■	■	■	■
3080	■	■	■			■		■	■	■		■			
3081	■	■	■		■			■				■			■
3082		■	■	■		■	■	■	■		■	■			■
3083								■							
3084		■	■	■	■	■	■	■		■	■	■	■	■	■
3085	■	■	■	■	■	■	■			■	■	■	■	■	■
3086		■	■	■	■	■	■	■		■	■	■	■	■	■
3087		■	■									■			■
3088		■	■	■	■	■	■	■		■	■	■	■	■	■
3089					■							■			■
3090								■							
3091															
3092	■	■	■		■	■		■	■			■	■	■	■
3093		■			■			■		■	■	■		■	■
3094	■	■		■	■	■	■	■	■	■	■	■	■	■	■
3095		■	■	■		■		■		■	■	■			■

Educational Programs Available — Career-oriented Programs (Agri, Business, Arts, Health)

Sequence Number	Agri: Ag Business	Agri: Ag/Farm Mgmt	Agri: Ag Mechanics/Tech	Agri: Horticulture	Business: Accounting	Business: Bus Mgmt & Admin	Business: Hotel/Rest Mgmt	Business: Office Mgmt	Business: Marketing/Purchasing	Business: Secretarial Studies	Arts: Architecture Tech	Arts: Applied Design	Arts: Photography/Cinema	Health: Dental Assistant	Health: Medical or Lab Tech	Health: Nursing (RN)	Health: Nursing (LPN)	Health: Radiologic Technology
3073					■	■			■	■						■	■	
3074					■	■		■	■	■								
3075					■	■		■	■	■								
3076					■	■										■		■
3077																■		
3078					■	■	■	■		■								
3079					■	■		■	■	■					■	■		■
3080				■	■	■	■		■	■	■				■	■		
3081	■			■	■	■				■					■	■	■	
3082					■	■	■		■	■	■				■	■		
3083																■		
3084					■	■	■	■	■	■		■				■		
3085					■	■	■	■	■	■				■	■	■	■	■
3086					■	■		■	■	■						■		■
3087					■	■		■	■	■								
3088					■	■		■	■	■						■		
3089										■					■			
3090																■		
3091																■		
3092					■	■	■		■	■						■	■	
3093					■	■	■		■	■				■	■		■	■
3094					■	■		■	■	■						■		
3095					■	■		■	■	■						■		

Educational Programs Available — Career-oriented Programs (Math, SocSci, Technical/Skilled Trades)

Sequence Number	Math: Computer Prog	Math: Data Processing Tech	Math: Computer Operating	SocSci: Crim Just/Law Enforce	SocSci: Parks/Rec Mgmt	SocSci: Social Work	Air/Refrig/Heat Tech	Auto Body Repair	Auto Mechanics	Carpentry/Constr	Drafting/Eng Draft	Electric Eng Tech	Civil Eng Tech	Indus/Mfg Eng Tech	Mech Eng Tech	Machinework	Welding
3073	■	■	■				■		■		■	■	■	■			■
3074	■	■	■														
3075	■	■	■	■		■						■		■	■		
3076	■			■							■	■			■		
3077																	
3078	■		■	■		■						■					
3079	■	■	■						■								
3080	■		■						■				■	■	■		
3081	■			■		■					■	■	■		■		
3082	■	■	■	■		■	■		■	■	■		■	■	■		
3083																	
3084	■	■	■	■													
3085	■	■		■								■	■		■		
3086	■			■					■								
3087	■	■	■														
3088	■	■	■	■		■					■	■	■		■		■
3089												■					
3090																	
3091																	
3092	■	■		■	■				■		■						
3093		■	■	■							■	■		■	■		■
3094				■								■			■		
3095	■	■		■													

▲ **Sequence Number—indicates the order of the college in this book only. Do *not* use this number with admissions tests or need analysis services.**

[1] No campus room and board facilities
[2] Room only or board only
[3] Most freshmen required to live on campus
[4] City or district residency requirements
[5] Accredited by regional accrediting association or a recognized candidate for accreditation
[6] All female freshman class
[7] All male freshman class
[8] Some admission selectivity; not all hs graduates accepted
[9] Requirements more stringent for nonresidents

†Accredited by a nationally recognized accrediting body other than one of the regional accrediting associations

Ohio
(continued)

Sequence Number	School name (upper entry) City (lower entry)	Enrollment	Resident tuition/fees + room/board	Room/board (upper entry) Nonresident tuition/fees (lower entry)	Affiliation (upper entry) Religious observance (lower entry)	Size of community	Type of community	Fall term application deadline (upper entry) Test required or desired (lower entry)	Calendar	Fall term application deadline (upper entry) Forms to be filed (lower entry)	-have need, rec some aid	-are women	-live on campus	-are minority students	-are nonresidents	-return as sophomores	-complete assoc degree	-transfer to 4-year college
3096	Kent St Stark Cam Canton	1002	2400	[1] 5400	Pub	L	S	 A/S	S [5]	3/01 FA/FF	3	6	0	1		7	1	4
3097	Kent St Trumbull Warren	713	2400	[1] 5500	Pub	M		 A/S	E [5]	4/01 FA/FF	7	6	0	1	1	3	2	4
3098	Kent St Tuscarawas New Philadelphi	612	2400	[1] 5400	Pub	S		 A/S	E [5]	5/01 FA/FF	5	6	0	1	0	5	1	2
3099	Kent St U Geauga Burton	579	2400	[1] 5000	Pub	T		 A/S	E [5]	4/01 FA/FF	4	6	0	1	1	6	3	
3100	Kent St U Salem Salem	385	2400	[1] 5400	Pub	S		8/30 A/S	E [5]	 FA/FF	4	6	0	1	0	6	1	4
3101	Kettering C Kettering	357	7300	2500	Oth OS	S [8]		 A/S	E [5]	 FF/FA	3	8	3	1	1	9	8	3
3102	Lakeland CC Mentor	2011	1500	[1] 3600	Pub	L	S	9/21 ACT	Q [5]	 FAF		6	0	1	1		3	
3103	Lima Tech C Lima	1242	1600	[1] 3100	Pub	M	S	 ACT	Q [5]	3/15 FA/FF	5	7	0	1	0	5	3	1
3104	Lorain Co CC Elyria	7400	1600	[1] 4200	Pub	L	S	9/15 None	Q [5]	8/15 FF=FA	3	6	0	1	0	4	5	4
3105	Mansfield Sch Nsg Mansfield	80	4700	1100 5600	Priv	M [8]		8/01 ACT	Q †	8/01 FF=FA	4	9	4	0	0	8	5	
3106	Marion Tech C Marion	619	1900	[1] 3500	Pub	S		9/15 ACT	Q [5]	7/01 FF=FA	6	7	0	1	0	6		
3107	Mercy Sch of Nsg Toledo	118	6900 [2]	1500 7500	Cath S	L [8]	U	 A/S	Q †	5/15 FFS	5	9	2	1	1	9	7	
3108	Meridia Huron Sc Nsg Cleveland	128	3600	[1] 5600	Priv	V [8]	U	8/30 A/S	Q †	6/01 FA/FF	5	9	0	4	0		8	
3109	Metro Health Med Ctr Cleveland	135	3300	[1] 3700	Pub	V [8]	U	 A/S	O †	4/15 FF/FA		9		1	0	9		
3110	Miami U Hamilton Hamilton	746	2500	[1] 6500	Pub	M	U	8/28 A=S	E [5]	2/15 FA/FF	3	6	0	1	1	5	5	5
3111	Miami U Middletown Middletown	910	2500	[1] 6500	Pub	M	S	8/31 A=S	E [5]	3/01 FA/FF	4	6	0	1	0	6	2	4
3112	Miami-Jacobs JC Dayton	635	4300	[1]	Priv	L [8]	U	9/01 Oth	Q †	9/01 Oth	8	9	0	3	1	7	7	2
3113	Muskingum Area Tech Zanesville	1042	1800	[1] 3100	Pub	S		9/01 Oth	Q [5]	6/15 Oth	7	6	0	1	0	5	4	1
3114	Natl Educ Center Cuyahoga Falls	290	5000	[1]	Priv	M		 Oth	O [5]	 Oth		1	0	4	1	8		
3115	North Central Tech Mansfield	2274	1900	[1] 3500	Pub	M	S	9/20 Oth	Q [5]	 Oth	5	6	0	1		7	4	1
3116	Northwest Business C Lima	1050	8500 [2,3]	1900	Priv	M			O [5]	8/01	4	4	4	6	6	7	6	2
3117	Northwest Tech C Archbold	491	1800	[1] 3100	Pub	T		 Oth	Q [5]	 FA/FF	3	6	0	1	1	1	1	1
3118	Ohio St-Agr Tech Wooster	606	4100 [2]	1800 8700	Pub	S		8/15 A/S	Q [5]	5/01 FA/FF	7	3	6	1	1	6		

Educational Programs Available — College Transfer Courses

Sequence Number	Agriculture	Bus-Commerce	Communications	Education	Engineering	Fine, Applied Arts	Foreign Lang	Health	Home Ec	Humanities	Mathematics	Computer/Info Sci	Biological Sci	Physical Sci	Social Sci
3096		■	■	■		■	■	■	■	■	■	■	■	■	■
3097		■	■	■	■	■	■	■	■	■	■	■	■	■	■
3098		■	■	■		■	■	■		■	■	■	■	■	■
3099		■	■	■	■	■	■	■		■	■	■	■	■	■
3100	■	■		■		■	■	■		■	■	■	■	■	■
3101					■			■							
3102		■	■	■	■	■	■	■	■	■	■	■	■	■	■
3103		■						■	■			■			■
3104		■	■	■	■	■	■	■		■	■	■	■	■	■
3105															
3106		■			■			■				■			■
3107															
3108								■							
3109								■							
3110	■	■	■	■		■	■	■	■	■	■	■	■	■	■
3111		■	■	■	■	■	■	■		■	■	■	■	■	■
3112		■						■				■			
3113	■	■						■			■	■	■	■	■
3114															
3115		■		■	■			■	■		■	■	■		■
3116		■	■							■	■	■			■
3117	■	■		■	■			■	■	■	■	■	■	■	■
3118	■	■	■								■				■

Educational Programs Available — Career-oriented Programs

Sequence Number	Agri: Ag Business	Agri: Ag/Farm Mgmt	Agri: Ag Mechanics/Tech	Agri: Horticulture	Business: Accounting	Business: Bus Mgmt & Admin	Business: Hotel/Rest Mgmt	Business: Office Mgmt	Business: Marketing/Purchasing	Business: Secretarial Studies	Arts: Architecture Tech	Arts: Applied Design	Arts: Photography/Cinema	Health: Dental Assistant	Health: Medical or Lab Tech	Health: Nursing (RN)	Health: Nursing (LPN)	Health: Radiologic Technology	Math: Computer Prog	Math: Data Processing Tech	Math: Computer Operating	SocSci: Crim Just/Law Enforce	SocSci: Parks/Rec Mgmt	SocSci: Social Work	Technical/Skilled Trades: Air/Refrig/Heat Tech	Auto Body Repair	Auto Mechanics	Carpentry/Constr	Drafting/Eng Draft	Electric Eng Tech	Civil Eng Tech	Indus/Mfg Eng Tech	Mech Eng Tech	Machinework	Welding
3096																																			
3097					■	■		■	■	■									■			■					■			■			■		
3098					■			■		■						■			■			■								■		■	■		
3099					■														■																
3100				■	■	■		■		■								■												■			■		
3101																																			
3102					■	■		■		■					■	■			■	■		■							■	■	■		■		
3103					■	■			■	■						■		■	■	■		■		■					■			■	■		
3104					■	■		■	■	■					■	■	■	■			■	■									■	■	■		
3105																■																			
3106					■	■		■	■	■					■	■				■	■								■	■			■		
3107																■																			
3108																■																			
3109																■																			
3110					■	■										■														■		■			
3111					■	■		■		■						■			■											■			■		
3112					■	■		■	■	■									■	■	■														
3113					■	■			■	■								■				■								■			■		
3114																			■	■										■					
3115					■	■	■			■						■	■	■	■		■	■		■					■				■		
3116					■	■		■													■						■								
3117	■		■		■	■		■	■	■						■	■		■	■										■			■		
3118	■	■	■	■																															

▲ **Sequence Number—indicates the order of the college in this book only. Do *not* use this number with admissions tests or need analysis services.**

[1] No campus room and board facilities
[2] Room only or board only
[3] Most freshmen required to live on campus
[4] City or district residency requirements
[5] Accredited by regional accrediting association or a recognized candidate for accreditation
[6] All female freshman class
[7] All male freshman class
[8] Some admission selectivity; not all hs graduates accepted
[9] Requirements more stringent for nonresidents
†Accredited by a nationally recognized accrediting body other than one of the regional accrediting associations

Ohio (continued)

Sequence Number	School name (upper entry) City (lower entry)	Enrollment	Costs: Resident tuition/fees + room/board	Costs: Room/board (upper entry) Nonresident tuition/fees (lower entry)	Gen. Info.: Affiliation (upper entry) Religious observance (lower entry)	Gen. Info.: Size of community	Gen. Info.: Type of community	Admissions: Fall term application deadline (upper entry) Test required or desired (lower entry)	Admissions: Calendar	Financial Aid: Fall term application deadline (upper entry) Forms to be filed (lower entry)
3119	Ohio U Belmont St Clairsville	570	2200	[1] 5300	Pub	T		A/S	Q [5]	4/01 FA/FF
3120	Ohio U Lancaster Lancaster	926	2100	[1] 4900	Pub	S		A/S	Q [5]	FA/FF
3121	Ohio U Zanesville Zanesville	695	2200	[1] 5300	Pub	S		9/12 A/S	Q [5]	4/01 FAF
3122	Ohio Valley Sch Nsg Steubenville	91	4100 [2]	1000	Priv	S [8]		6/01 A=S	Q †	FF=FA
3123	Owens Tech C Toledo	2499	1600	[1] 2900	Pub	L	S	A/S	S [5]	3/15 FF=FA
3124	Providence Sch Nsg Sandusky	100	5600	1600	Cath	S [8]		3/01 A/S	Q †	5/01 FA/FF
3125	Providence Sch Rad T Sandusky	15	1600 [2]	800	Cath	S [8]	[6]	2/28	Q †	5/01 FF=FA
3126	Riverside Sch Rad T Columbus	18	1400	[1]	Meth	V [8]	S	4/01 Oth	Q †	Oth
3127	Sinclair CC Dayton	4182	1300	[1] 2700	Pub	L	U		Q [5]	4/15 FAF
3128	Southern Ohio C Cincinnati	563	6000	[1]	Priv	V [8]	U	Oth	Q [5]	Oth
3129	Southern St CC Hillsboro	754	1800	[1] 3300	Pub	T		A=S	Q [5]	FF=FA
3130	St Elizabeth Sch Nsg Youngstown	173	5100 [2]	1000 6100	Cath O	L [8]	U	A=S	Q †	4/01 FA/FF
3131	St Thomas Sch Nsg Akron	108	4400	[1]	Priv	L [8]	U	Oth	O †	9/10 FA/FF
3132	St Vincent Sch Nsg Toledo	160	6600 [2]	1100	Cath	L [8]	U	A=S	O †	3/01
3133	Stark Tech C Canton	1672	1800	[1] 2800	Pub	M		9/01 A/S	Q [5]	6/01 FAF
3134	Terra Tech C Fremont	717	1600	[1] 3800	Pub	S		9/01 None	Q [5]	7/30 FF=FA
3135	Washington St CC Marietta	608	1900	[1] 3800	Pub	S		None	Q [5]	9/23 FF=FA
3136	Wayne Gen & Tech C Orrville	676	2200	[1] 5000	Pub	T		A=S	E [5]	4/15 FA/FF
3137	Wright St U-Lake Celina	387	2200	[1] 4300	Pub	S		A=S	Q [5]	FAF
Oklahoma										
3138	Bacone C Muskogee	454	5200 [3]	2600	Bapt OS	S [8]		A/S	E [5]	FF/FA
3139	Carl Albert JC Poteau	663	3000	2100 4500	Pub	T		8/15 A/S	E [5]	7/15 FFS
3140	Central Okla Vo-Tech Drumright	410	1100	[1] 2100	Pub	S		Oth	S [5]	

Student Profile (No. in 10 who-)

Sequence Number	-have need, rec some aid	-are women	-live on campus	-are minority students	-are nonresidents	-return as sophomores	-complete assoc degree	-transfer to 4-year college
3119	5	6	0	1	1	3	1	7
3120	2	6	0	1	1	6	5	5
3121		7	0	1	0			
3122	7	9	3	1	2		7	3
3123	3	5	0	1	1	6	3	2
3124	5	9	5	1	0	7	7	1
3125	4	9	2	0	0	9	9	
3126	3	8	0	1	1	9	9	
3127	4	6	0	1	1		3	3
3128	9	6		4	1	6	3	1
3129	4	7	0	1	1	2		
3130	7	9		1	1	9	9	
3131	7	9	0	1		9	8	
3132	4	9	4	1	3			
3133	7	5	0	1		6	6	1
3134	4	4	0	1	1	6	4	1
3135	8	6	0	1	1	6	3	1
3136	2	5	0	1	1	8	4	6
3137	5	6	0	1	0	6	2	6
3138	9	7	3	6	1	6	3	2
3139	6	7	1	1	1	2	2	1
3140	9	6	0	1	1	1		

Educational Programs Available — College Transfer Courses

Sequence Number	Agriculture	Bus-Commerce	Communications	Education	Engineering	Fine, Applied Arts	Foreign Lang	Health	Home Ec	Humanities	Mathematics	Computer/Info Sci	Biological Sci	Physical Sci	Social Sci
3119		■	■	■	■	■	■	■	■	■	■	■	■	■	■
3120		■	■	■	■	■	■	■	■	■	■		■	■	■
3121		■	■	■		■	■	■		■	■	■	■	■	■
3122															
3123	■	■		■		■		■	■			■			■
3124															
3125															
3126															
3127		■	■	■	■	■	■	■	■	■	■	■	■	■	■
3128															
3129	■	■	■	■	■	■	■	■		■	■	■	■	■	■
3130															
3131															
3132								■							
3133		■						■			■	■			■
3134		■	■	■	■	■		■	■	■	■	■		■	■
3135		■	■	■	■			■	■			■			■
3136		■	■	■	■	■	■	■	■	■	■	■	■	■	■
3137		■	■	■	■		■			■	■	■	■	■	■
3138	■	■	■			■	■	■	■	■	■	■	■	■	■
3139	■	■	■	■	■	■	■	■	■	■	■	■	■	■	■
3140															

Educational Programs Available — Career-oriented Programs (Agri, Business, Arts, Health)

Sequence Number	Agri: Ag Business	Agri: Ag/Farm Mgmt	Agri: Ag Mechanics/Tech	Agri: Horticulture	Business: Accounting	Business: Bus Mgmt & Admin	Business: Hotel/Rest Mgmt	Business: Office Mgmt	Business: Marketing/Purchasing	Business: Secretarial Studies	Arts: Architecture Tech	Arts: Applied Design	Arts: Photography/Cinema	Health: Dental Assistant	Health: Medical or Lab Tech	Health: Nursing (RN)	Health: Nursing (LPN)	Health: Radiologic Technology
3119												■						
3120					■					■								
3121																■		
3122																■		
3123	■				■	■	■		■	■	■					■		■
3124																■		
3125																		■
3126																		■
3127					■	■		■	■	■	■	■				■		■
3128					■	■		■	■	■								
3129					■	■				■						■	■	
3130																■		
3131															■	■		■
3132																■		
3133					■	■	■		■	■					■			
3134					■	■			■	■	■							
3135					■	■			■	■					■		■	
3136								■	■	■								
3137					■	■		■										
3138				■	■			■		■						■		■
3139	■				■	■	■	■		■						■		
3140		■						■	■	■	■			■			■	

Educational Programs Available — Career-oriented Programs (Math, SocSci, Technical/Skilled Trades)

Sequence Number	Math: Computer Prog	Math: Data Processing Tech	Math: Computer Operating	SocSci: Crim Just/Law Enforce	SocSci: Parks/Rec Mgmt	SocSci: Social Work	Air/Refrig/Heat Tech	Auto Body Repair	Auto Mechanics	Carpentry/Constr	Drafting/Eng Draft	Electric Eng Tech	Civil Eng Tech	Indus/Mfg Eng Tech	Mech Eng Tech	Machinework	Welding
3119																	
3120											■	■					
3121																	
3122																	
3123	■	■		■			■	■	■		■	■	■	■	■	■	■
3124																	
3125																	
3126																	
3127		■	■	■		■	■		■		■		■	■	■	■	
3128	■	■										■					
3129	■										■	■			■		
3130																	
3131																	
3132																	
3133	■	■							■		■	■	■	■	■		
3134	■			■			■		■		■	■	■		■	■	■
3135		■				■	■		■		■	■		■			■
3136		■	■														
3137	■					■					■			■			
3138			■														
3139		■															
3140		■	■	■			■		■	■	■	■			■	■	■

▲ Sequence Number—indicates the order of the college in this book only. Do *not* use this number with admissions tests or need analysis services.

1 No campus room and board facilities
2 Room only or board only
3 Most freshmen required to live on campus
4 City or district residency requirements
5 Accredited by regional accrediting association or a recognized candidate for accreditation
6 All female freshman class
7 All male freshman class
8 Some admission selectivity; not all hs graduates accepted
9 Requirements more stringent for nonresidents
†Accredited by a nationally recognized accrediting body other than one of the regional accrediting associations

2-YEAR COLLEGES

Oklahoma
(continued)

Sequence Number	School name (upper entry) City (lower entry)	Enrollment	Costs: Resident tuition/fees + room/board	Costs: Room/board (upper entry) Nonresident tuition/fees (lower entry)	Gen. Info.: Affiliation (upper entry) Religious observance (lower entry)	Gen. Info.: Size of community	Gen. Info.: Type of community	Admissions: Fall term application deadline (upper entry) Test required or desired (lower entry)	Admissions: Calendar	Financial Aid: Fall term application deadline (upper entry) Forms to be filed (lower entry)	Student Profile (No. in 10 who-): -have need, rec some aid	-are women	-live on campus	-are minority students	-are nonresidents	-return as sophomores	-complete assoc degree	-transfer to 4-year college
3141	Connors St C Warner	1348	2700 [3]	1800 4100	Pub	T		 A/S	E [5]	 FF/FA	7	6	1	2	1	5	5	6
3142	Eastern Okla St U Wilburton	1578	2900	2000 4200	Pub	T		 A/S	E [5]	 FFS	7	6	4	2	1	5	3	6
3143	El Reno JC El Reno	429	900	1 2300	Pub	S		 A/S	E [5]	3/01 FF/FA	4	6	0	1	1	4	4	4
3144	Murray St C Tishomingo	827	3200 [3]	2300 4700	Pub	T		 ACT	E [5]	8/01 FFS	6	5	3	1	1	5	2	3
3145	Northeast Okla A&M Miami	1972	2700	1900 4200	Pub	S		9/01 A/S	E [5]	9/01 FF/FA	8	5	4	2	1	3	4	6
3146	Northern Okla C Tonkawa	1123	2500 [3]	1700 4000	Pub	T		9/01 ACT	E [5]	 FFS	9	5	2	1	1	5	5	3
3147	Okla City CC Oklahoma City	2331	900	1 2700	Pub	L	S	 A/S	O [5]	9/01 FA/FF	4	6	0	1	1	4	1	4
3148	Okla JC Tulsa	1120	8600	1	Priv	L [8]	S	 Oth	O [5]	 FFS	9	7	0	2	1	7		
3149	Okla St U Tech Oklahoma City	1133	1000	1 3300	Pub	V	U	 A/S	S [5]	6/01 FFS	1	5	0	1		3	2	3
3150	Okla St U Tech Okmulgee	2109	4300 [3]	3000 7700	Pub	S		 A/S	T [5]	4/01 FFS	6	3	5	2	1	6	4	
3151	Rogers St C Claremore	2151	3500	2400 4700	Pub	S		 ACT	E [5]	4/15 FF/FA	7	6	1	2	1	6	3	6
3152	Rose St C Midwest City	3179	800	1 2400	Pub	L	S	8/30 A/S	E [5]	6/01 FF/FA	2	6	0	2	1		2	5
3153	Saint Gregory's C Shawnee	260	6400	2700	Cath	S [8]		 ACT	E [5]	 FFS	7	5	9	2	2	7	6	8
3154	Seminole JC Seminole	728	2800	1900 4300	Pub	T		 A/S	E [5]	 FF=FA	4	6	1	1	0	6	5	4
3155	Southwest Okla St U Sayre	465	1200	1 2900	Pub	T		 ACT	E [5]	 FF/FA	9	7	0	1	1	7	3	4
3156	Spartan Sch Aeronaut Tulsa	2668	13200	1	Priv	L	U	 A/S	Q [5]	 FAF	8	1	0	3	8	7	4	1
3157	Tulsa JC Tulsa	3951	900	1 2300	Pub	L	U	 A/S	E [5]	5/01 FFS		6	0	1	1	3		5
3158	Western Okla St C Altus	1017	800	1 2300	Pub	S		 A/S	S [5]		6	5	0	2	1	3	5	8
Oregon																		
3159	Blue Mountain CC Pendleton	1024	800	1 2300	Pub	S		0/06 Oth	Q [5]		6	6	0	1	1	3	4	2
3160	Central Oregon CC Bend	1241	3700	2900 6300	Pub	S		 None	Q [5]	 FAF	6	6	1	1	2	4	1	2
3161	Chemeketa CC Salem	3437	800	1 3000	Pub	M		 Oth	Q [5]	9/04 FAF	6	6	0	1	1		6	
3162	Clackamas CC Oregon City	1895	800	1 2700	Pub	S		 Oth	Q [5]	1/15 FAF	4	4	0	1		2	1	2

Educational Programs Available — College Transfer Courses

Sequence Number	Agriculture	Bus-Commerce	Communications	Education	Engineering	Fine, Applied Arts	Foreign Lang	Health	Home Ec	Humanities	Mathematics	Computer/Info Sci	Biological Sci	Physical Sci	Social Sci
3141	■	■	■	■	■	■	■	■	■	■	■	■	■	■	■
3142	■	■	■	■	■	■		■		■	■	■	■	■	■
3143	■	■	■	■	■	■		■		■	■	■	■	■	■
3144	■	■	■	■	■	■	■	■	■	■	■	■	■	■	■
3145	■	■	■	■	■	■	■	■	■	■	■	■	■	■	■
3146	■	■	■	■	■	■	■	■	■	■	■	■	■	■	■
3147		■	■		■	■	■			■	■		■	■	■
3148		■			■			■				■			
3149	■	■	■		■	■	■	■		■	■	■	■	■	■
3150	■	■	■			■			■		■	■		■	■
3151	■	■	■	■	■	■	■	■	■	■	■	■	■	■	■
3152	■	■	■	■	■	■	■	■	■	■	■	■	■	■	■
3153		■	■	■	■	■	■	■	■	■	■	■	■	■	■
3154		■	■	■	■	■	■		■	■	■	■	■	■	■
3155		■		■				■							
3156															
3157	■	■	■	■	■	■	■	■	■	■	■	■	■	■	■
3158	■	■	■	■	■	■	■	■	■	■	■	■	■	■	■
3159	■	■	■	■	■	■	■	■		■	■		■	■	■
3160	■	■	■	■	■	■	■	■	■	■	■	■	■	■	■
3161	■	■	■	■	■	■	■	■	■	■	■	■	■	■	■
3162	■	■	■	■	■	■	■	■	■	■	■	■	■	■	■

Educational Programs Available — Career-oriented Programs

Sequence Number	Agri: Ag Business	Ag/Farm Mgmt	Ag Mechanics/Tech	Horticulture	Business: Accounting	Bus Mgmt & Admin	Hotel/Rest Mgmt	Office Mgmt	Marketing/Purchasing	Secretarial Studies	Arts: Architecture Tech	Applied Design	Photography/Cinema	Health: Dental Assistant	Medical or Lab Tech	Nursing (RN)	Nursing (LPN)	Radiologic Technology	Math: Computer Prog	Data Processing Tech	Computer Operating	SocSci: Crim Just/Law Enforce	Parks/Rec Mgmt	Social Work	Technical/Skilled Trades: Air/Refrig/Heat Tech	Auto Body Repair	Auto Mechanics	Carpentry/Constr	Drafting/Eng Draft	Electric Eng Tech	Civil Eng Tech	Indus/Mfg Eng Tech	Mech Eng Tech	Machinework	Welding
3141	■	■				■		■	■	■	■				■	■					■	■							■			■			
3142		■		■					■	■						■			■				■			■	■		■					■	■
3143	■	■			■					■					■	■			■			■								■					
3144		■				■		■		■						■												■	■	■			■		
3145		■						■	■	■						■			■						■		■	■							
3146	■				■				■	■						■			■	■		■						■	■	■			■	■	■
3147					■			■					■			■				■		■					■	■	■					■	■
3148					■	■	■	■	■	■									■	■															
3149				■		■		■			■					■			■	■		■			■			■	■		■				
3150					■	■			■	■	■										■				■	■	■	■	■	■		■		■	
3151					■	■		■		■						■			■			■													
3152					■	■		■		■				■	■			■	■	■	■	■							■	■			■		
3153																																			
3154					■	■				■					■	■			■	■		■													
3155										■					■																				
3156																																			
3157	■			■	■	■	■	■	■	■					■	■		■	■			■			■			■	■	■			■	■	
3158	■	■			■	■		■		■		■				■				■		■						■	■						■
3159	■	■	■		■			■	■	■				■			■			■		■				■	■		■	■	■				■
3160					■	■	■	■	■	■						■	■				■						■		■	■				■	■
3161					■	■		■	■	■				■		■	■		■	■	■	■					■	■	■	■	■	■		■	■
3162				■	■	■		■		■						■	■			■		■			■	■	■		■			■	■	■	■

▲ Sequence Number—indicates the order of the college in this book only. Do *not* use this number with admissions tests or need analysis services.

[1] No campus room and board facilities
[2] Room only or board only
[3] Most freshmen required to live on campus
[4] City or district residency requirements
[5] Accredited by regional accrediting association or a recognized candidate for accreditation
[6] All female freshman class
[7] All male freshman class
[8] Some admission selectivity; not all hs graduates accepted
[9] Requirements more stringent for nonresidents
†Accredited by a nationally recognized accrediting body other than one of the regional accrediting associations

Oregon
(continued)

Sequence Number	School name (upper entry) City (lower entry)	Enrollment	Costs: Resident tuition/fees + room/board	Costs: Room/board (upper entry) Nonresident tuition/fees (lower entry)	Gen. Info.: Affiliation (upper entry) Religious observance (lower entry)	Gen. Info.: Size of community	Gen. Info.: Type of community	Admissions: Fall term application deadline (upper entry) Test required or desired (lower entry)	Admissions: Calendar	Financial Aid: Fall term application deadline (upper entry) Forms to be filed (lower entry)	No. in 10 who- -have need, rec some aid	-are women	-live on campus	-are minority students	-are nonresidents	-return as sophomores	-complete assoc degree	-transfer to 4-year college
3163	Clatsop CC Astoria	461	900	[1] 3300	Pub	T		None	Q[5]	FAF	6	5	0	2	2	4	1	1
3164	Columbia Gorge CC The Dalles	133	900	[1] 1400	Pub	S		Oth	Q[5]	Oth	5	6	0	1				
3165	Lane CC Eugene	3892	800	[1] 3300	Pub	L	S	None	Q[5]	FAF		5	0	1			1	1
3166	Linn-Benton CC Albany	2384	900	[1] 3600	Pub	S		Oth	Q[5]	FAF	6	5	0	1	1	2	1	1
3167	Mount Hood CC Gresham	3215	800	[1] 3700	Pub	M	S	9/24 Oth	Q[5]	4/01 FAF	3	5	0	1	1	4	4	6
3168	Oregon Coast CC Newport	75	900	[1] 3600	Pub	S		0/01 Oth	Q[5]	Oth	2	7	0	2	0		1	1
3169	Portland CC Portland	6361	800	[1] 3600	Pub	V	U	None	Q[5]	FF=FA	2	5	0	2	1		1	2
3170	Rogue CC Grants Pass	884	900	[1] 3000	Pub	S		Oth	Q[5]	FF=FA	5	6	0	1	0	3	2	2
3171	Southwest Oregon CC Coos Bay	631	800	[1] 2300	Pub	S		Oth	Q[5]	FAF	6	6	0	1			2	1
3172	Tillamook Bay CC Tillamook	23	1000	[1] 3200	Pub	T		None	Q[5]	FA/FF	5	7	0	1	0			
3173	Treasure Valley CC Ontario	747	3500	2800 4200	Pub	S		None	Q[5]	FA/FF	7	6	2	1	4		3	4
3174	Umpqua CC Roseburg	900	300	[1] 1300	Pub	S		None	Q[5]	FAF	6	6	0	1	1	4	7	5
	Pennsylvania																	
3175	Allegheny Co CC Boyc Monroeville	1724	1300	[1] 3900	Pub	M	S	None	S[5]	5/01 Oth	4	6	0	1		6	7	4
3176	Allegheny Co CC No Pittsburgh	871	1300	[1] 3900	Pub	L	S	None	E[5]	5/01 Oth	4	5	0	1	0	6	7	4
3177	Allegheny Co CC So West Mifflin	2185	1300	[1] 3900	Pub	L	S	None	E[5]	5/01 Oth	4	6	0	1	0	6	7	5
3178	Allegheny Co CC-Alle Pittsburgh	3289	1300	[1] 3900	Pub	L	U	None	E[5]	5/01 Oth	4	6	0	2		6	7	6
3179	Beaver Co CC Monaca	1409	1300	[1] 4400	Pub	T		9/01 Oth	E[5]	FA/FF	6	5	0	1	1	7	6	2
3180	Bucks Co CC Newtown	3168	1400	[1] 4600	Pub	S		5/01 A=S	S[5]	5/01 FF/FA	3	6	0	1	1			5
3181	Butler Co CC Butler	1489	1200	[1] 3500	Pub	S		8/20 None	E[5]	5/01 Oth	7	6	0	1	1	7	6	5
3182	Central Pa Bus Sch Summerdale	641	6400[2]	2100	Priv	T[8]		/00 None	T[5]	5/01 Oth	7	9	6	1	1	7	6	1
3183	Clarion U Venango Oil City	300	2800	[1] 5000	Pub	S[8]		A=S	E[5]	5/01 Oth	7	7	0	1	1	7	8	2
3184	Delaware Co CC Media	3061	1100	[1] 3500	Pub	S		9/11 Oth	E[5]	8/01 Oth	2	6	0	1	0	5		

Educational Programs Available — College Transfer Courses

Sequence Number	Agriculture	Bus-Commerce	Communications	Education	Engineering	Fine, Applied Arts	Foreign Lang	Health	Home Ec	Humanities	Mathematics	Computer/Info Sci	Biological Sci	Physical Sci	Social Sci
3163	■	■	■	■	■	■	■	■		■	■	■	■	■	■
3164		■				■	■	■		■	■	■	■	■	■
3165	■	■	■	■	■	■	■	■	■	■	■	■	■	■	■
3166	■	■	■	■	■	■	■	■	■	■	■	■	■	■	■
3167	■	■	■	■	■	■	■	■		■	■	■	■	■	■
3168		■		■		■	■		■	■	■	■	■	■	■
3169	■	■	■	■	■	■	■	■	■	■	■	■	■	■	■
3170		■		■	■	■	■	■		■	■	■	■	■	■
3171	■	■	■	■	■	■	■	■	■	■	■	■	■	■	■
3172		■						■	■	■		■	■	■	■
3173	■	■	■	■	■	■	■	■	■	■	■	■	■	■	■
3174	■	■	■	■	■	■	■	■	■	■	■	■	■	■	■
3175		■	■	■	■	■	■	■		■	■	■			■
3176		■		■	■	■		■		■	■	■			■
3177	■	■	■	■	■	■	■	■	■	■	■	■		■	■
3178		■	■	■	■	■	■	■	■	■	■	■	■	■	■
3179		■	■	■		■	■			■	■	■			■
3180		■	■	■	■	■	■	■		■	■	■	■	■	■
3181		■		■	■		■	■		■	■		■	■	■
3182	■	■	■					■	■			■			■
3183		■	■	■		■		■		■	■	■	■	■	■
3184		■			■							■			

Educational Programs Available — Career-oriented Programs (Agri, Business, Arts, Health)

Sequence Number	Agri: Ag Business	Agri: Ag/Farm Mgmt	Agri: Ag Mechanics/Tech	Agri: Horticulture	Business: Accounting	Business: Bus Mgmt & Admin	Business: Hotel/Rest Mgmt	Business: Office Mgmt	Business: Marketing/Purchasing	Business: Secretarial Studies	Arts: Architecture Tech	Arts: Applied Design	Arts: Photography/Cinema	Health: Dental Assistant	Health: Medical or Lab Tech	Health: Nursing (RN)	Health: Nursing (LPN)	Health: Radiologic Technology
3163					■	■		■		■						■	■	
3164					■	■		■		■								
3165			■		■	■		■	■	■				■		■	■	
3166		■		■	■	■	■	■	■	■				■		■		
3167				■	■	■	■	■		■	■	■				■	■	
3168					■	■		■	■	■								
3169			■	■	■	■	■	■	■	■	■	■		■	■		■	■
3170					■	■		■		■						■	■	
3171					■	■		■	■	■						■	■	
3172		■			■	■		■		■								
3173	■	■	■		■	■		■		■		■				■	■	
3174																		
3175					■	■	■									■		■
3176					■	■	■		■	■						■	■	
3177				■	■	■	■	■	■	■	■			■	■	■	■	
3178					■	■			■	■					■	■	■	
3179					■	■				■	■	■			■	■	■	
3180					■	■	■		■	■						■	■	
3181					■	■	■		■	■						■		
3182					■	■	■	■	■	■								
3183					■			■		■						■		
3184					■	■	■	■	■	■	■					■		

Educational Programs Available — Career-oriented Programs (Math, SocSci, Technical/Skilled Trades)

Sequence Number	Math: Computer Prog	Math: Data Processing Tech	Math: Computer Operating	SocSci: Crim Just/Law Enforce	SocSci: Parks/Rec Mgmt	SocSci: Social Work	Air/Refrig/Heat Tech	Auto Body Repair	Auto Mechanics	Carpentry/Constr	Drafting/Eng Draft	Electric Eng Tech	Civil Eng Tech	Indus/Mfg Eng Tech	Mech Eng Tech	Machinework	Welding
3163		■		■					■			■				■	■
3164			■														
3165			■	■			■	■	■	■	■			■	■		■
3166	■	■	■	■			■	■	■		■		■			■	■
3167									■		■		■	■		■	■
3168																	
3169	■	■	■	■				■	■	■	■	■	■		■	■	■
3170	■		■	■		■			■	■				■		■	
3171			■	■	■	■			■		■					■	■
3172			■														
3173		■	■	■				■	■		■	■					■
3174																	
3175	■	■					■				■	■	■				■
3176	■	■	■	■			■		■	■	■	■	■	■	■	■	■
3177	■	■	■			■	■	■		■	■	■	■		■		■
3178	■	■	■	■		■					■	■					
3179	■	■		■					■		■		■				■
3180	■	■		■							■	■					
3181	■	■	■		■						■		■		■		
3182																	
3183			■														
3184	■	■	■	■			■		■	■	■			■		■	■

▲ **Sequence Number—indicates the order of the college in this book only. Do *not* use this number with admissions tests or need analysis services.**

[1] No campus room and board facilities
[2] Room only or board only
[3] Most freshmen required to live on campus
[4] City or district residency requirements
[5] Accredited by regional accrediting association or a recognized candidate for accreditation
[6] All female freshman class
[7] All male freshman class
[8] Some admission selectivity; not all hs graduates accepted
[9] Requirements more stringent for nonresidents
†Accredited by a nationally recognized accrediting body other than one of the regional accrediting associations

Pennsylvania
(continued)

Sequence Number	School name (upper entry) City (lower entry)	Enrollment	Costs: Resident tuition/fees + room/board	Costs: Room/board (upper entry) Nonresident tuition/fees (lower entry)	Gen. Info.: Affiliation (upper entry) Religious observance (lower entry)	Gen. Info.: Size of community	Gen. Info.: Type of community	Admissions: Fall term application deadline (upper entry) Test required or desired (lower entry)	Calendar	Financial Aid: Fall term application deadline (upper entry) Forms to be filed (lower entry)	-have need, rec some aid	-are women	-live on campus	-are minority students	-are nonresidents	-return as sophomores	-complete assoc degree	-transfer to 4-year college
3185	Harcum JC Bryn Mawr	569	9200 [3]	3600	Priv	S [8]		S/A	E [5]	5/01 Oth	6	9	7	2	3	8	6	4
3186	Harrisburg Area CC Harrisburg	3162	1500	[1] 4400	Pub	M	S	8/02 Oth	E [5]	6/01 Oth	4	6	0	1	1		2	2
3187	Keystone JC La Plume	763	10900	4100	Priv	T [8]		A=S	S [5]	5/01 Oth	5	6	5	2	2	0		
3188	Lackawanna JC Scranton	353	4800	[1]	Priv	M		9/10 A=S	E [5]	5/01 Oth	8	7	0	1	0	9	9	3
3189	Lancaster Sch Nsg Lancaster	260	7100	2800 9000	Priv	L [8]	U	S/A	E †	4/01 Oth	6	9	7	1	1	8	7	1
3190	Lehigh Co CC Schnecksville	1594	1300	[1] 4500	Pub	T		None	E [5]	3/31 Oth	2	6	0	1	1	4	3	3
3191	Luzerne Co CC Nanticoke	2217	1500	[1]	Pub	S		Oth	4 [5]	Oth	7	6	0	1	0		7	5
3192	Manor JC Jenkintown	374	8600	3000	Oth S	T [8]		8/31 Oth	E [5]	4/15 FA/FF	8	9	1	2	1	6	6	3
3193	Montgomery Co CC Blue Bell	2600	1500	[1] 4400	Pub	T		A=S	E [5]	3/15 Oth	3	6	0	1	1	6	4	7
3194	Mount Aloysius JC Cresson	786	9400	3000	Cath S	T [8]		A=S	E [5]	5/01 Oth	9	7	4	1	1	7	9	2
3195	Natl Educ-Vale Tech Blairsville	589	6300 [2]	1000	Priv	T		None	O †	8/01 Oth	9	1	1	1	1			
3196	Northampton Co CC Bethlehem	1802	4700	3100 8200	Pub	M	S	None	E [5]	3/31 FA/FF	3	6	1	1	1	6	2	2
3197	Northeast Christian Villanova	188	7900 [3]	3400	Oth OS	T		S/A	S [5]	9/30 FA/FF	9	5	9	4	6	6	6	8
3198	Pa C Tech Agri & Sci Williamsport	3281	4500	[1] 6800	Pub	S		Oth	E [5]	5/01 Oth	6	4	0	1	1	7	6	1
3199	Pa St U Allentown Fogelsville	452	3900	[1] 8400	Pub	T [8]		S/A	E [5]	FA/FF	5	5	0	1	1	6		
3200	Pa St U Altoona Altoona	2080	7400	3500 11900	Pub	M [8]		S/A	E [5]	FA/FF	6	5	2	1	2	6	2	
3201	Pa St U Beaver Monaca	795	7400	3500 11900	Pub	T [8]		S/A	E [5]	FA/FF	6	4	2	1	1	6	2	
3202	Pa St U Berks Reading	976	7400	3500 11900	Pub	M [8]		S/A	E [5]	FA/FF	5	4	0	1	1	6	2	
3203	Pa St U Delaware Media	1068	3900	[1] 8400	Pub	T [8]		S/A	E [5]	FA/FF	4	5	0	1	1	6	2	
3204	Pa St U DuBois DuBois	725	3900	[1] 8400	Pub	T [8]		S/A	E [5]	FA/FF	7	4	0	1	1	6	2	
3205	Pa St U Fayette Uniontown	607	3900	[1] 8400	Pub	S [8]		S/A	E [5]	FA/FF	6	5	0	1	1	6	2	
3206	Pa St U Hazleton Hazleton	1197	7400	3500 11900	Pub	S [8]		S/A	E [5]	FA/FF	6	4	3	1	2	6	2	
3207	Pa St U Ogontz Abington	1895	3900	[1] 8400	Pub	T [8]		S/A	E [5]	FA/FF	5	5	0	1	1	6	2	

Educational Programs Available — College Transfer Courses

Sequence Number	Agriculture	Bus-Commerce	Communications	Education	Engineering	Fine, Applied Arts	Foreign Lang	Health	Home Ec	Humanities	Mathematics	Computer/Info Sci	Biological Sci	Physical Sci	Social Sci
3185		■		■		■	■	■	■	■	■		■	■	■
3186		■	■	■	■	■	■	■	■	■	■	■	■	■	■
3187	■	■	■	■	■	■		■	■			■	■	■	
3188		■								■	■	■			■
3189															
3190		■	■	■	■	■	■	■		■	■	■	■	■	■
3191		■	■	■	■	■	■	■		■	■	■	■	■	■
3192	■	■		■				■	■	■	■	■	■	■	■
3193		■	■	■	■	■	■	■		■	■	■	■	■	■
3194		■		■		■	■	■		■	■	■	■	■	■
3195															
3196		■		■		■					■	■	■	■	■
3197		■	■	■	■	■	■	■	■	■	■	■	■	■	■
3198			■			■									
3199	■	■	■	■	■	■	■	■	■	■	■	■	■	■	■
3200	■	■	■	■	■	■	■	■	■	■	■	■	■	■	■
3201	■	■	■	■	■	■	■	■	■	■	■	■	■	■	■
3202	■	■	■	■	■	■	■	■	■	■	■	■	■	■	■
3203	■	■	■	■	■	■	■	■	■	■	■		■	■	■
3204	■	■	■	■	■	■	■	■	■	■	■	■	■	■	■
3205	■	■	■	■	■	■	■	■	■	■	■	■	■	■	■
3206	■	■	■	■	■	■	■	■	■	■	■	■	■	■	■
3207	■	■	■	■	■	■	■	■	■	■	■	■	■	■	■

Educational Programs Available — Career-oriented Programs: Agri, Business, Arts

Sequence Number	Ag Business	Ag/Farm Mgmt	Ag Mechanics/Tech	Horticulture	Accounting	Bus Mgmt & Admin	Hotel/Rest Mgmt	Office Mgmt	Marketing/Purchasing	Secretarial Studies	Architecture Tech	Applied Design	Photography/Cinema
3185						■	■	■					
3186					■		■	■	■		■		■
3187							■						
3188					■	■			■	■			
3189													
3190					■	■	■	■	■	■			
3191					■	■	■			■			
3192					■	■		■		■			
3193					■	■	■	■	■	■			
3194					■		■						
3195													
3196					■	■	■		■	■	■		■
3197										■			
3198				■	■	■		■	■	■	■		
3199													
3200	■												
3201	■					■							
3202	■					■	■						
3203	■					■							
3204	■					■							
3205	■												
3206	■					■							
3207	■												

Educational Programs Available — Career-oriented Programs: Health, Math, SocSci

Sequence Number	Dental Assistant	Medical or Lab Tech	Nursing (RN)	Nursing (LPN)	Radiologic Technology	Computer Prog	Data Processing Tech	Computer Operating	Crim Just/Law Enforce	Parks/Rec Mgmt	Social Work
3185	■	■						■			■
3186	■	■	■	■	■		■	■	■		■
3187											
3188									■		
3189			■								
3190			■	■		■	■	■	■		
3191	■		■				■	■	■		
3192	■	■					■				
3193		■	■				■		■		■
3194		■	■						■		
3195											
3196	■	■	■	■	■		■		■		
3197							■				■
3198			■	■	■			■			
3199											
3200											
3201											
3202											
3203											
3204		■									
3205											
3206		■									
3207											

Educational Programs Available — Career-oriented Programs: Technical/Skilled Trades

Sequence Number	Air/Refrig/Heat Tech	Auto Body Repair	Auto Mechanics	Carpentry/Constr	Drafting/Eng Draft	Electric Eng Tech	Civil Eng Tech	Indus/Mfg Eng Tech	Mech Eng Tech	Machinework	Welding
3185											
3186			■			■		■	■		
3187											
3188											
3189											
3190	■		■		■	■			■		
3191			■			■			■		
3192											
3193					■	■					
3194											
3195		■	■								
3196			■			■				■	■
3197											
3198	■	■	■	■	■	■	■	■	■	■	■
3199											
3200						■			■		
3201						■			■		
3202						■			■		
3203						■					
3204									■		
3205	■					■			■		
3206						■			■		
3207						■			■		

▲ **Sequence Number—indicates the order of the college in this book only. Do *not* use this number with admissions tests or need analysis services.**

[1] No campus room and board facilities
[2] Room only or board only
[3] Most freshmen required to live on campus
[4] City or district residency requirements
[5] Accredited by regional accrediting association or a recognized candidate for accreditation
[6] All female freshman class
[7] All male freshman class
[8] Some admission selectivity; not all hs graduates accepted
[9] Requirements more stringent for nonresidents
†Accredited by a nationally recognized accrediting body other than one of the regional accrediting associations

Pennsylvania
(continued)

Sequence Number	School name (upper entry) City (lower entry)	Enrollment	Costs: Resident tuition/fees + room/board	Costs: Room/board (upper entry) Nonresident tuition/fees (lower entry)	Gen. Info.: Affiliation (upper entry) Religious observance (lower entry)	Gen. Info.: Size of community	Gen. Info.: Type of community	Admissions: Fall term application deadline (upper entry) Test required or desired (lower entry)	Admissions: Calendar	Financial Aid: Fall term application deadline (upper entry) Forms to be filed (lower entry)	Student Profile (No. in 10 who-): -have need, rec some aid	-are women	-live on campus	-are minority students	-are nonresidents	-return as sophomores	-complete assoc degree	-transfer to 4-year college
3208	Pa St U Schuylkill Schuylkill Havn	707	7400	3500 11900	Pub	T [8]		S/A	E [5]	FA/FF	6	6	1	1	2	6	2	
3209	Pa St U Wilkes-Barre Lehman	629	3900	[1] 8400	Pub	M [8]		S/A	E [5]	FA/FF	6	3	0	1	1	6	2	
3210	Pa St U Worthington Dunmore	938	3900	[1] 8400	Pub	S [8]		S/A	E [5]	FA/FF	6	4	0	1	1	6	2	
3211	Pa St U York York	935	3900	[1] 8400	Pub	L [8]	S	S/A	E [5]	FA/FF	5	4	0	1	1	6	2	
3212	Pa St U-McKeesport McKeesport	861	7200	3300 11700	Pub	S [8]		S/A	E [5]	FA/FF	6	4	1	1	1	6	2	
3213	Pa St U-Mont Alto Mont Alto	751	7400	3500 11900	Pub	T [8]		S/A	E [5]	FA/FF	6	4	5	1	2	6	2	
3214	Pa St U-N Kensgtn New Kensington	761	3900	[1] 8400	Pub	S [8]		S/A	E [5]	FA/FF	7	4	0	1	1	6	2	
3215	Pa St U-Shenango Vly Sharon	490	3900	[1] 8400	Pub	S [8]		S/A	E [5]	FA/FF	6	6	0	1	1	6	2	
3216	Philadelphia,CC of Philadelphia	4330	1700	[1] 5000	Pub	V	U	Oth	E [5]	5/01 FF=FA		6	0	5	1		4	5
3217	Pierce JC Philadelphia	722	7800 [2]	2400	Priv	V [8]	U	8/01 Oth	E [5]	6/01 Oth	8	8	1	5	1	7	5	2
3218	Pinebrook JC Coopersburg	107	8200	3000	Oth OS	T		8/31 SAT	4 †	8/01 FF=FA	7	6	9	1	6	5	5	4
3219	Pittsbg Titusvl,U of Titusville	322	7100 [3]	3200 11000	Priv	T [8]		6/01	T [5]	3/01	7	5		1	1			
3220	Reading Area CC Reading	655	1300	[1] 4000	Pub	M		None	Q [5]	9/01 Oth	6	7	0	2		5	1	1
3221	Sawyer Sch Pittsburgh	650	9200	3200	Priv	V [8]	U	Oth	O †	Oth	7	8		2				
3222	South Hills Bus C State College	300	5600	[1]	Priv	M [8]		Oth	T †	Oth	9	8	0	1	1	9	8	1
3223	St Fran Respiratory Pittsburgh	19	4100	[1]	Cath	V [8]	U	A=S	O †	Oth	7	5		1			7	2
3224	Valley Forge Mil JC Wayne	140	15200 [3]	3400	Priv O	T [8]	[7]	A=S	E [5]	FA/FF	6	0	9	3			7	9
3225	Westmoreland Co CC Youngwood	2105	1200	[1] 3700	Pub	T		None	E [5]	5/01 Oth	6	6	0	1	0	6		2
3226	York Tech Inst York	450	5000	[1]	Priv	L [8]	S	Oth	Q †		8	4	0	1	1	9	9	
3227	Yorktowne Bus C York	272	3500	[1]	Priv	L [8]		Oth	T †	Oth	3	7	0	1		9	7	1

Educational Programs Available

Sequence Number	College Transfer Courses															Career-oriented Programs: Agri				Business						Arts			Health					Math			SocSci			Technical/Skilled Trades										
	Agriculture	Bus-Commerce	Communications	Education	Engineering	Fine, Applied Arts	Foreign Lang	Health	Home Ec	Humanities	Mathematics	Computer/Info Sci	Biological Sci	Physical Sci	Social Sci	Ag Business	Ag/Farm Mgmt	Ag Mechanics/Tech	Horticulture	Accounting	Bus Mgmt & Admin	Hotel/Rest Mgmt	Office Mgmt	Marketing/Purchasing	Secretarial Studies	Architecture Tech	Applied Design	Photography/Cinema	Dental Assistant	Medical or Lab Tech	Nursing (RN)	Nursing (LPN)	Radiologic Technology	Computer Prog	Data Processing Tech	Computer Operating	Crim Just/Law Enforce	Parks/Rec Mgmt	Social Work	Air/Refrig/Heat Tech	Auto Body Repair	Auto Mechanics	Carpentry/Constr	Drafting/Eng Draft	Electric Eng Tech	Civil Eng Tech	Indus/Mfg Eng Tech	Mech Eng Tech	Machinework	Welding
3208	■	■	■	■	■	■	■	■	■	■	■	■	■	■	■	■																	■												■					
3209	■	■	■	■	■	■	■	■	■	■	■	■	■	■	■	■					■																								■			■		
3210	■	■	■	■	■	■	■	■	■	■	■	■	■	■	■	■					■																			■					■			■		
3211	■	■	■	■	■	■	■	■	■	■	■	■	■	■	■	■					■																								■			■		
3212	■	■	■	■	■	■	■	■	■	■	■	■	■	■	■	■					■																								■			■		
3213	■	■	■	■	■	■	■	■	■	■	■	■	■	■	■	■					■																													
3214	■	■	■	■	■	■	■	■	■	■	■	■	■	■	■	■					■									■			■												■			■		
3215	■	■	■	■	■	■	■	■	■	■	■	■	■	■	■	■					■																			■					■			■		
3216		■		■	■	■	■	■	■	■	■		■	■	■					■	■	■	■	■	■	■		■	■	■	■		■	■	■	■	■							■						
3217		■										■			■					■	■	■	■	■	■									■	■	■														
3218		■	■	■		■	■			■	■	■			■						■				■																									
3219		■	■	■	■	■	■	■		■	■	■	■	■	■					■				■											■															
3220		■		■	■			■		■			■	■	■					■	■		■		■					■	■	■	■		■				■			■							■	
3221																				■		■			■					■					■															
3222		■	■					■		■	■	■			■					■	■		■	■	■									■	■	■														
3223																																																		
3224		■				■	■			■	■	■		■	■																																			
3225		■	■	■	■	■	■	■	■	■	■		■	■	■				■	■	■	■		■	■	■			■		■	■		■	■	■	■			■		■		■	■					■
3226																				■		■	■																					■	■	■		■		
3227		■										■								■	■	■	■	■	■									■	■	■														

▲ **Sequence Number—indicates the order of the college in this book only. Do *not* use this number with admissions tests or need analysis services.**

[1] No campus room and board facilities
[2] Room only or board only
[3] Most freshmen required to live on campus
[4] City or district residency requirements
[5] Accredited by regional accrediting association or a recognized candidate for accreditation
[6] All female freshman class
[7] All male freshman class
[8] Some admission selectivity; not all hs graduates accepted
[9] Requirements more stringent for nonresidents
†Accredited by a nationally recognized accrediting body other than one of the regional accrediting associations

Sequence Number	School name (upper entry) City (lower entry)	Enrollment	Costs: Resident tuition/fees + room/board	Costs: Room/board (upper entry) Nonresident tuition/fees (lower entry)	Gen. Info.: Affiliation (upper entry) Religious observance (lower entry)	Gen. Info.: Size of community	Gen. Info.: Type of community	Admissions: Fall term application deadline (upper entry) Test required or desired (lower entry)	Admissions: Calendar	Financial Aid: Fall term application deadline (upper entry) Forms to be filed (lower entry)	No. in 10 who- -have need, rec some aid	-are women	-live on campus	-are minority students	-are nonresidents	-return as sophomores	-complete assoc degree	-transfer to 4-year college
	Rhode Island																	
3228	Katharine Gibbs Sch Providence	333	6800	[1]	Priv	M[8]	S	 A/S	O †	9/15 FA/FF	6	9	0	1	2	0	9	0
3229	Rhode Island,CC of Warwick	5020	1100	[1] 1900	Pub	M	S	 None	S[5]	 FAF	6	6	0	1	1	6	3	5
	South Carolina																	
3230	Aiken Tech C Aiken	809	600	[1] 900	Pub	M	S	 Oth	Q[5]	9/01 FA/FF	3	6	0	3	1	6		1
3231	Chesterfield Tech Cheraw	570	600	[1] 900	Pub	S		 Oth	Q[5]	6/15 FAF	3	6	0	3	0			1
3232	Clinton JC Rock Hill	90	3100	1900	Meth O	S		9/22 None	E	 FA/FF	9	3	9	9	1	9	9	
3233	Denmark Tech C Denmark	536	3900	2900 6800	Pub	T		 A=S	Q[5]	6/01 FA/FF	9	5	6	9	1	6	6	1
3234	Florence Darlington Florence	1173	1000	[1] 1500	Pub	S		 Oth	Q[5]	4/01 FA/FF	4	7	0	2	0	7	3	2
3235	Greenville Tech C Greenville	3887	800	[1] 1300	Pub	L[8]	U	 A=S	Q[5]	 FF=FA	3	6	0	1	1		4	
3236	Horry Georgetwn Tech Conway	1096	1000	[1] 2000	Pub	S		 Oth	Q[5]	5/01 FA/FF	8	5	0	2	1	4	4	1
3237	Midlands Tech C Columbia	3846	900	[1] 2300	Pub	M[8]	U	9/01 A=S	Q[5]	5/01 FA/FF	3	6	0	3	1		2	1
3238	North Greenville C Tigerville	507	9300	3400	Oth OS	T		8/27 A=S	S[5]	7/01	8	3	8	3	2	4	2	7
3239	Orangeburg Calhoun Orangeburg	1506	800	[1] 1200	Pub	S		9/04 Oth	Q[5]	8/30 FFS	8	7	0	4	0	8	8	1
3240	Piedmont Tech C Greenwood	1157	800	[1] 1200	Pub	S		9/13 Oth	Q[5]	 FF/FA	7	5	0	3	0	3	2	1
3241	SC at Salkehat,U of Allendale	351	1400	[1] 3000	Pub	T[8]		 S/A	S[5]	 FF/FA	5	7	0	3	1	5	8	7
3242	SC at Sumter,U of Sumter	698	1200	[1] 3000	Pub	S[8]		8/28 A=S	E[5]	4/01 FF/FA	9	6	0	2	1			
3243	SC at Union,U of Union	368	1500	[1] 3000	Pub	S		 S/A	E[5]	8/15 FF/FA	4	6	0	1	1	5	8	8
3244	SC Beaufort,U of Beaufort	220	1400	[1] 3000	Pub	S[8]		 S/A	E[5]	8/01 FF=FA	5	5	0	2	1	7	2	5
3245	SC Lancaster Cam,U Lancaster	517	1200	[1] 3000	Pub	S[8]		 A=S	S[5]	 FF=FA	2	6	0	1	1	4	3	3
3246	Spartanburg Meth C Spartanburg	882	8700	3300	Meth OS	S[8]		 A=S	S[5]	 FF=FA	7	5	5	2	1	7	6	8
3247	Spartanburg Tech C Spartanburg	1764	700	[1] 1400	Pub	S		 A=S	Q[5]	 FAF		5						
3248	Sumter Area Tech C Sumter	866	900	[1] 1400	Pub	S		 Oth	Q[5]	7/15 FFS	5	6	0	4	0	4	7	1
3249	Tech C Lowcountry Beaufort	411	800	[1] 1100	Pub	S		 Oth	Q[5]	 FF/FA	7	7	0	5	0	3	2	1

Educational Programs Available — College Transfer Courses

Sequence Number	Agriculture	Bus-Commerce	Communications	Education	Engineering	Fine, Applied Arts	Foreign Lang	Health	Home Ec	Humanities	Mathematics	Computer/Info Sci	Biological Sci	Physical Sci	Social Sci
3228															
3229					■	■	■			■	■		■	■	■
3230		■	■	■	■					■	■	■	■	■	■
3231		■		■	■			■				■			■
3232				■		■	■		■	■	■	■	■		■
3233		■							■			■			■
3234		■		■				■				■			■
3235		■		■	■	■	■	■		■	■	■	■	■	■
3236	■	■			■						■	■			■
3237		■			■			■				■			■
3238		■	■	■		■	■	■		■	■	■	■	■	■
3239	■	■			■			■				■			■
3240		■		■	■			■	■			■			■
3241		■	■	■	■	■	■	■		■	■	■	■	■	■
3242		■	■	■	■	■	■			■	■	■	■	■	■
3243		■	■	■	■	■	■	■		■	■	■	■	■	■
3244		■	■	■	■	■	■	■		■	■	■	■	■	■
3245		■	■	■	■	■	■	■		■	■	■	■	■	■
3246		■		■	■		■	■		■	■				■
3247		■													
3248							■			■					■
3249		■										■			

Educational Programs Available — Career-oriented Programs (Agri, Business, Arts, Health)

Sequence Number	Agri: Ag Business	Ag/Farm Mgmt	Ag Mechanics/Tech	Horticulture	Business: Accounting	Bus Mgmt & Admin	Hotel/Rest Mgmt	Office Mgmt	Marketing/Purchasing	Secretarial Studies	Arts: Architecture Tech	Applied Design	Photography/Cinema	Health: Dental Assistant	Medical or Lab Tech	Nursing (RN)	Nursing (LPN)	Radiologic Technology
3228								■		■								
3229					■	■		■	■	■				■	■	■	■	■
3230					■	■				■				■			■	
3231										■						■		
3232										■								
3233					■			■		■								
3234																		
3235					■	■		■	■	■				■	■	■		■
3236			■	■	■	■	■	■		■							■	
3237					■	■		■	■	■				■	■	■	■	■
3238						■												
3239					■			■		■					■	■	■	■
3240					■	■		■	■	■						■	■	■
3241										■								
3242																		
3243																		
3244																		
3245																		
3246									■	■								
3247				■	■	■				■				■	■		■	■
3248					■	■			■	■					■	■		
3249				■	■		■		■		■					■	■	

Educational Programs Available — Career-oriented Programs (Math, SocSci, Technical/Skilled Trades)

Sequence Number	Math: Computer Prog	Data Processing Tech	Computer Operating	SocSci: Crim Just/Law Enforce	Parks/Rec Mgmt	Social Work	Technical/Skilled Trades: Air/Refrig/Heat Tech	Auto Body Repair	Auto Mechanics	Carpentry/Constr	Drafting/Eng Draft	Electric Eng Tech	Civil Eng Tech	Indus/Mfg Eng Tech	Mech Eng Tech	Machinework	Welding
3228																	
3229	■	■	■	■		■						■		■	■		
3230	■	■	■				■		■		■	■				■	■
3231	■			■			■		■		■				■	■	■
3232																	
3233	■			■			■		■	■							■
3234			■														■
3235	■			■			■	■	■	■	■	■			■	■	■
3236	■	■	■	■	■		■		■		■	■	■			■	■
3237		■		■		■	■		■		■	■	■		■	■	
3238					■												
3239			■	■			■		■		■	■				■	■
3240	■			■		■	■		■	■	■	■		■		■	■
3241				■													
3242																	
3243																	
3244																	
3245																	
3246				■													
3247	■		■				■		■			■	■	■	■	■	■
3248		■		■			■		■		■	■	■			■	■
3249		■		■			■	■	■	■		■					■

▲ **Sequence Number—indicates the order of the college in this book only. Do *not* use this number with admissions tests or need analysis services.**

[1] No campus room and board facilities
[2] Room only or board only
[3] Most freshmen required to live on campus
[4] City or district residency requirements
[5] Accredited by regional accrediting association or a recognized candidate for accreditation
[6] All female freshman class
[7] All male freshman class
[8] Some admission selectivity; not all hs graduates accepted
[9] Requirements more stringent for nonresidents
†Accredited by a nationally recognized accrediting body other than one of the regional accrediting associations

South Carolina
(continued)

Sequence Number	School name (upper entry) / City (lower entry)	Enrollment	Costs: Resident tuition/fees + room/board	Costs: Room/board (upper entry)	Costs: Nonresident tuition/fees (lower entry)	Gen. Info.: Affiliation (upper entry)	Gen. Info.: Religious observance (lower entry)	Gen. Info.: Size of community	Gen. Info.: Type of community	Admissions: Fall term application deadline (upper entry)	Admissions: Test required or desired (lower entry)	Admissions: Calendar	Financial Aid: Fall term application deadline (upper entry)	Financial Aid: Forms to be filed (lower entry)	No. in 10 who- have need, rec some aid	-are women	-live on campus	-are minority students	-are nonresidents	-return as sophomores	-complete assoc degree	-transfer to 4-year college
3250	Tri-Co Tech C / Pendleton	1821	900	[1]	1800	Pub		T			Oth	Q [5]	6/01	FA/FF	2	6	0	1	1	6	6	1
3251	Trident Tech C / Charleston	3058	1100	[1]	2000	Pub		M	U	8/19	Oth	O [5]	5/01	FA/FF		6	0	3	1	6	1	1
3252	Williamsburg Tech C / Kingstree	165	600	[1]		Pub		T			Oth	Q [5]	3/15	FFS	4	8	0	5	0	4	4	1
3253	York Tech C / Rock Hill	1530	500	[1]	1000	Pub		S		9/01	A=S	Q [5]	7/01	FFS	3	5	0	2	1		5	2
South Dakota																						
3254	Cheyenne River CC / Eagle Butte	120	2000	[1]		Pub		T		8/30	A/S	S	3/15	FF/FA		7	0	8		7		
3255	Kilian CC / Sioux Falls	142	4500	[1]		Priv		M	U		None	Q [5]	8/31	FF=FA	8	8	0	1	1	7	7	1
3256	Lake Area Voc-Tech / Watertown	749	1600	[1]		Pub		S			Oth	Q [5]	4/15	Oth	9	3	0	1	1			1
3257	McKennan Hos Sch Rad / Sioux Falls	16	500	[1]		Cath		M [8]	S	2/01	ACT	S †	9/31	FFS	5	9	0	0	1	9		
3258	Mitchell Voc-Tech / Mitchell	550	1300	[1]		Pub		S			Oth	Q [5]		FF=FA	8	3	0	1	1	3		
3259	Nettleton C / Sioux Falls	444	4400	[1]		Priv		M [8]	U		A=S	Q †		FF=FA	9	7	0	1	4	5	8	1
3260	Sacred Heart Sch Rad / Yankton	8	900	[1]		Cath		S [8]		4/15	A/S	S †		Oth	7	7	0	0	5	9	9	
3261	Sioux Vly Hos Sch RT / Sioux Falls	24	100	[1]		Pub		M [8]	U	1/31	ACT	O †		FFS	9	8		0	1	9	9	
3262	Southeast Area V-T / Sioux Falls	650	2500	[1]		Pub		M	S		A=S	O [5]	5/15	FF/FA	8	4	0	1	1			
3263	St Joseph Sch Radiol / Mitchell	5	1500	[1]		Priv		S				O †		FFS								
3264	West Dakota Voc-Tech / Rapid City	455	2000	[1]		Pub		M			Oth	Q [5]		FF=FA	8	2	0	2	1	3	8	1
Tennessee																						
3265	Aquinas JC / Nashville	280	3100	[1]		Cath	OS	L [8]	U	8/01	Oth	S [5]	9/01	FF/FA	2	6	0	1	0	3	6	4
3266	Athens St Voc-Tech / Athens	224	300	[1]		Pub		S			Oth	O [5]		FF/FA		5	0	1				
3267	Baptist Hosp Sch Nsg / Memphis	582	4600 [2]	1600		Bapt	S	V [8]	U	7/31	A/S	O †		Oth	9	9	5	1				
3268	Chattanooga Tech CC / Chattanooga	2145	800	[1]	3300	Pub		L	U		Oth	S [5]		FF/FA	9	6	0	1	1	4	3	2
3269	Cleveland St CC / Cleveland	1399	900	[1]	3300	Pub		S			A/S	E [5]		FF=FA	4	6	0	1	1	6	2	2
3270	Columbia St CC / Columbia	1328	800	[1]	3200	Pub		S			A/S	S [5]	4/30	FF=FA	7	7	0	1	1	4	3	3

Educational Programs Available — College Transfer Courses; Career-oriented Programs: Agri

Sequence Number	Agriculture	Bus-Commerce	Communications	Education	Engineering	Fine, Applied Arts	Foreign Lang	Health	Home Ec	Humanities	Mathematics	Computer/Info Sci	Biological Sci	Physical Sci	Social Sci	Ag Business	Ag/Farm Mgmt	Ag Mechanics/Tech	Horticulture
3250		■	■	■	■	■	■	■	■	■	■	■	■	■	■				
3251	■	■	■	■		■	■	■		■	■	■	■	■	■				■
3252						■	■			■	■		■	■	■				
3253																			
3254		■		■		■		■		■	■		■		■				
3255		■	■	■		■	■			■	■	■		■	■	■			
3256																■	■	■	
3257								■											
3258											■				■	■	■	■	
3259																			
3260								■											
3261																			
3262		■	■			■			■	■	■	■		■	■				■
3263																			
3264	■	■		■							■				■	■			
3265		■		■		■	■			■	■		■	■	■				
3266																			
3267																			
3268	■	■	■	■	■	■	■	■	■	■	■	■	■	■	■				
3269		■	■	■	■	■	■	■		■	■	■	■	■	■				
3270	■	■	■	■	■	■	■	■		■	■	■	■	■	■	■			

Educational Programs Available — Career-oriented Programs: Business, Arts, Health, Math, SocSci, Technical/Skilled Trades

Sequence Number	Accounting	Bus Mgmt & Admin	Hotel/Rest Mgmt	Office Mgmt	Marketing/Purchasing	Secretarial Studies	Architecture Tech	Applied Design	Photography/Cinema	Dental Assistant	Medical or Lab Tech	Nursing (RN)	Nursing (LPN)	Radiologic Technology	Computer Prog	Data Processing Tech	Computer Operating	Crim Just/Law Enforce	Parks/Rec Mgmt	Social Work	Air/Refrig/Heat Tech	Auto Body Repair	Auto Mechanics	Carpentry/Constr	Drafting/Eng Draft	Electric Eng Tech	Civil Eng Tech	Indus/Mfg Eng Tech	Mech Eng Tech	Machinework	Welding
3250	■	■				■				■	■	■	■		■	■	■	■			■		■		■			■		■	■
3251	■	■	■	■	■	■				■	■		■	■	■			■			■	■	■		■	■	■		■	■	■
3252				■		■												■					■	■	■					■	■
3253	■	■		■		■				■	■	■		■	■						■		■	■	■		■	■	■	■	■
3254	■																	■					■	■							■
3255	■	■		■	■	■									■	■	■														
3256					■	■				■	■		■		■								■	■	■					■	■
3257														■																	
3258	■			■		■	■				■				■	■	■				■		■	■	■	■					■
3259	■	■		■	■	■									■	■	■														
3260														■																	
3261														■																	
3262	■	■	■	■		■	■				■				■	■	■				■	■	■	■	■		■				■
3263														■																	
3264				■			■						■				■	■				■	■	■	■	■					■
3265												■						■													
3266						■							■									■	■		■	■				■	■
3267												■																			
3268	■	■	■	■	■	■				■		■	■	■	■	■					■	■	■		■	■	■		■	■	■
3269	■			■		■					■	■																			
3270	■	■			■						■	■		■	■			■								■		■			

▲ Sequence Number—indicates the order of the college in this book only. Do *not* use this number with admissions tests or need analysis services.

1 No campus room and board facilities
2 Room only or board only
3 Most freshmen required to live on campus
4 City or district residency requirements
5 Accredited by regional accrediting association or a recognized candidate for accreditation
6 All female freshman class
7 All male freshman class
8 Some admission selectivity; not all hs graduates accepted
9 Requirements more stringent for nonresidents
†Accredited by a nationally recognized accrediting body other than one of the regional accrediting associations

Tennessee
(continued)

Sequence Number	School name (upper entry) / City (lower entry)	Enrollment	Costs: Resident tuition/fees + room/board	Costs: Room/board (upper entry) / Nonresident tuition/fees (lower entry)	Gen. Info.: Affiliation (upper entry) / Religious observance (lower entry)	Gen. Info.: Size of community	Gen. Info.: Type of community	Admissions: Fall term application deadline (upper entry) / Test required or desired (lower entry)	Admissions: Calendar	Financial Aid: Fall term application deadline (upper entry) / Forms to be filed (lower entry)	No. in 10 who- have need, rec some aid	-are women	-live on campus	-are minority students	-are nonresidents	-return as sophomores	-complete assoc degree	-transfer to 4-year college
3271	Covington St Vo-Tec / Covington	130	300	[1]	Pub	T		Oth	O [5]	FFS	4	4	0	2	0	8		
3272	Crossville Area Sch / Crossville	200	300	[1]	Pub	S		Oth	O [5]	FFS		3	0	1	0	5		
3273	Dickson Voc-Tech Sch / Dickson	151	300	[1]	Pub	S		Oth	O [5]	FFS		7	0	1	0	0		
3274	Draughons JC / Knoxville	400	4300	[1]	Priv	V	U	None	Q †	9/28 / FF=FA	9	8	1	1	1	6	3	1
3275	Dyersburg St CC / Dyersburg	908	800	[1] / 2400	Pub	S		8/23 / ACT	E [5]	FF/FA		5	0	1	1	2	1	
3276	Edmondson JC / Chattanooga	703	2900	[1]	Priv	M [8]	U	Oth	Q †	Oth	9	8	0	2	3	3		1
3277	Elizabethton Area Sc / Elizabethton	133	300	[1]	Pub	S		Oth	Q [5]	FFS	7	5	0	1			8	1
3278	Harriman St Voc-Tech / Harriman	175	300	[1]	Pub	T		None	Q [5]	FF/FA	6	5	0	1		6		
3279	Hartsville St Vo-Tec / Hartsville	130	300	[1]	Pub	T		None	O [5]	FFS	6	3	0	1	0	8		
3280	Hiwassee C / Madisonville	421	6400	2600	Meth / O	T [8]		A/S	S [5]	FA/FF	8	5	7	2	3	6		
3281	Hohenwald St Vo-Tech / Hohenwald	69	300	[1]	Pub	T		Oth	Q [5]		4	3	0					
3282	Jacksboro St Vo-Tech / Jacksboro	180	300	[1]	Pub	T		Oth	Q [5]	FFS		4		1				
3283	Jackson Area Sch / Jackson	245	300	[1]	Pub	S		Oth	Q [5]	None		3	0	9				
3284	Jackson St CC / Jackson	1499	800	[1] / 3400	Pub	M		8/15 / A/S	S [5]	5/01 / FF/FA	2	6	0	1	0		3	2
3285	John A Gupton C / Nashville	41	2500	[1]	Priv	L	U	ACT	S [5]			5						
3286	Knoxville Business C / Knoxville	189	3900	[1]	Priv	L	U	0/05 / A/S	Q †	10/05 / FF=FA	9	9	0	3	0		6	1
3287	Knoxville C / Morristown	147	8800	3600	Pres / S	S		9/01 / A/S	E [5]	11/15 / FF/FA	9	4	9	9	8	8	8	6
3288	Knoxville St Voc-Tec / Knoxville	450	300	[1]	Pub	M	U	Oth	Q [5]	FF/FA	5	3	0	1	0		8	1
3289	Martin Methodist C / Pulaski	390	7100	2600	Meth / OS	T [8]		9/01 / A/S	E [5]	5/15 / FF/FA	8	5	5	3	1	6	5	7
3290	McKenzie St Vo-Tech / McKenzie	150	300	[1]	Pub	T		None	Q [5]	FF=FA	3	2	0	1	0			
3291	McMinnville St V-T / McMinnville	298	300	[1]	Pub	S		Oth	O [5]		4	3	0	1	0	0		
3292	Memphis Area Vo-Tec / Memphis	560	300	[1]	Pub	V	U	Oth	Q [5]		7	5	0	6			5	1
3293	Methodist Hosp Nsg / Memphis	240	2700 [2]	1100	Meth	V [8]	U		O †	6/15 / FFS	8	9	3	3	1	9		

Educational Programs Available — College Transfer Courses; Career-oriented Programs: Agri, Business

Sequence Number	Agriculture	Bus-Commerce	Communications	Education	Engineering	Fine, Applied Arts	Foreign Lang	Health	Home Ec	Humanities	Mathematics	Computer/Info Sci	Biological Sci	Physical Sci	Social Sci	Ag Business	Ag/Farm Mgmt	Ag Mechanics/Tech	Horticulture	Accounting	Bus Mgmt & Admin	Hotel/Rest Mgmt	Office Mgmt	Marketing/Purchasing	Secretarial Studies
3271																				■			■		■
3272																				■					■
3273																				■					■
3274		■	■					■	■	■	■	■			■					■	■	■	■	■	■
3275		■		■	■	■		■		■	■	■	■	■	■					■	■			■	■
3276		■	■		■	■		■	■	■	■	■			■					■	■		■	■	■
3277																				■					■
3278																							■		■
3279																							■		■
3280	■	■	■	■	■	■	■	■	■	■	■	■	■	■	■		■			■	■		■		■
3281																				■					■
3282																									■
3283																									■
3284	■	■	■	■	■	■	■	■	■	■	■	■	■	■	■	■	■				■		■	■	■
3285								■																	
3286		■								■	■	■			■					■	■				■
3287		■	■	■		■		■		■	■	■	■	■	■					■					■
3288																				■					■
3289	■	■	■	■	■	■	■	■		■	■	■	■	■	■										
3290																				■			■		■
3291																							■		■
3292																							■		■
3293								■																	

Educational Programs Available — Career-oriented Programs: Arts, Health, Math, SocSci, Technical/Skilled Trades

Sequence Number	Architecture Tech	Applied Design	Photography/Cinema	Dental Assistant	Medical or Lab Tech	Nursing (RN)	Nursing (LPN)	Radiologic Technology	Computer Prog	Data Processing Tech	Computer Operating	Crim Just/Law Enforce	Parks/Rec Mgmt	Social Work	Air/Refrig/Heat Tech	Auto Body Repair	Auto Mechanics	Carpentry/Constr	Drafting/Eng Draft	Electric Eng Tech	Civil Eng Tech	Indus/Mfg Eng Tech	Mech Eng Tech	Machinework	Welding
3271							■								■		■							■	■
3272				■			■				■				■	■	■	■	■	■				■	■
3273							■			■					■		■							■	
3274																									
3275						■			■	■	■	■								■		■			
3276									■	■	■	■													
3277							■		■						■		■			■					■
3278							■										■			■				■	■
3279									■	■	■						■		■					■	■
3280									■										■						
3281																	■	■	■	■				■	■
3282							■								■		■		■	■				■	■
3283							■									■	■		■	■				■	■
3284					■	■		■	■	■															
3285																									
3286																									
3287												■		■											
3288				■			■				■				■	■	■		■	■				■	■
3289																									
3290										■					■		■		■	■				■	■
3291							■				■				■		■		■	■				■	■
3292	■		■	■	■		■			■	■				■	■	■		■	■	■		■	■	■
3293						■																			

▲ Sequence Number—indicates the order of the college in this book only. Do *not* use this number with admissions tests or need analysis services.

[1] No campus room and board facilities
[2] Room only or board only
[3] Most freshmen required to live on campus
[4] City or district residency requirements
[5] Accredited by regional accrediting association or a recognized candidate for accreditation
[6] All female freshman class
[7] All male freshman class
[8] Some admission selectivity; not all hs graduates accepted
[9] Requirements more stringent for nonresidents
†Accredited by a nationally recognized accrediting body other than one of the regional accrediting associations

Tennessee
(continued)

Sequence Number	School name (upper entry) / City (lower entry)	Enrollment	Costs: Resident tuition/fees + room/board	Costs: Room/board (upper entry) / Nonresident tuition/fees (lower entry)	Gen. Info.: Affiliation (upper entry) / Religious observance (lower entry)	Gen. Info.: Size of community	Gen. Info.: Type of community	Admissions: Fall term application deadline (upper entry) / Test required or desired (lower entry)	Admissions: Calendar	Financial Aid: Fall term application deadline (upper entry) / Forms to be filed (lower entry)	Student Profile (No. in 10 who-): -have need, rec some aid	-are women	-live on campus	-are minority students	-are nonresidents	-return as sophomores	-complete assoc degree	-transfer to 4-year college
3294	Moore Sch of Techn Memphis	57	1100	[1]	Priv	V	U	None	T [5]	11/30 None		1	0	5				
3295	Morristown St Vo-Tec Morristown	300	300	[1]	Pub	S			O [5]		8	3	0	1	0	0		
3296	Motlow St CC Tullahoma	1370	900	[1] 3500	Pub	S		7/24 A/S	S [5]	5/01 FF/FA	6	7	0	1			6	4
3297	Nashville St Tech Nashville	1348	800	[1] 3300	Pub	V	S	A/S	E [5]	5/01 FA/FF		5	0	2	1	5	3	1
3298	Newbern Area Sch Newbern	180	300	[1]	Pub	T		Oth	O [5]	FF=FA	6	2	0	1				
3299	Northeast St Tech CC Blountville	860	900	[1] 1200	Pub	L	S	8/15 A=S	E [5]	7/01 FF=FA	3	4	0	1	1	8	7	1
3300	Oneida Area Vo-Tech Oneida	116	300	[1]	Pub	T		Oth	O [5]	FFS	7	5	0	1				
3301	Paris Area Sch Paris	230	400	[1]	Pub	S		Oth	O [5]	FF=FA	6	5	0	1				
3302	Pellissippi St Tech Knoxville	4702	900	[1] 3100	Pub	L	S	Oth	E [5]	8/01 FF/FA	3	5	0	1	1	6	4	3
3303	Pulaski Area Sch Pulaski	125	200	[1]	Pub	T		None	O [5]			2	0	1				
3304	Ripley Area Sch Ripley	75	300	[1]	Pub	T		Oth	O [5]			6	0	4				
3305	Roane St CC Harriman	2473	800	[1] 3300	Pub	S		A/S	S [5]	FF/FA	3	6	0	1	1	7	2	3
3306	Saint Joseph Sch Nsg Memphis	144	4500 [2]	1300	Cath	V [8]	U	5/01 A/S	Q [5]	7/01 FFS	9	9	1	4	1	8		
3307	Saint Joseph Sch Rad Memphis	16	1200 [2]	700	Cath	V [8]	U	4/01 ACT	O †			8	2	0	1			
3308	Savannah Area Sch Crump	143	300	[1]	Pub	T		None	O [5]		7	5	0	1	1			1
3309	Shelby St CC Memphis	2072	800	[1] 3300	Pub	V	U	Oth	E [5]	FFS		6	0	6	1			
3310	Shelbyville Voc-Tech Shelbyville	242	300	[1]	Pub	S		Oth	O [5]	FFS	3	4	0	1				
3311	St Tech Inst Memphis Memphis	2763	800	[1] 2400	Pub	V	U	Oth	E [5]	FFS	3	5	0	3	1		1	
3312	Volunteer St CC Gallatin	1945	800	[1] 3300	Pub	S		8/23 Oth	E [5]	4/15 FF=FA	3	6	0	1	1	6		
3313	Walters St CC Morristown	1991	800	[1] 3300	Pub	S		A=S	E [5]	3/31 FF/FA	2	6	0	1		6	2	2
3314	Whiteville Voc-Tech Whiteville	126	300	[1]	Pub	T		Oth	O [5]	FF/FA	7	5	0	6				

Educational Programs Available

Sequence Number	College Transfer Courses															Career-oriented Programs: Agri				Business						Arts			Health					Math			SocSci			Technical/Skilled Trades										
	Agriculture	Bus-Commerce	Communications	Education	Engineering	Fine, Applied Arts	Foreign Lang	Health	Home Ec	Humanities	Mathematics	Computer/Info Sci	Biological Sci	Physical Sci	Social Sci	Ag Business	Ag/Farm Mgmt	Ag Mechanics/Tech	Horticulture	Accounting	Bus Mgmt & Admin	Hotel/Rest Mgmt	Office Mgmt	Marketing/Purchasing	Secretarial Studies	Architecture Tech	Applied Design	Photography/Cinema	Dental Assistant	Medical or Lab Tech	Nursing (RN)	Nursing (LPN)	Radiologic Technology	Computer Prog	Data Processing Tech	Computer Operating	Crim Just/Law Enforce	Parks/Rec Mgmt	Social Work	Air/Refrig/Heat Tech	Auto Body Repair	Auto Mechanics	Carpentry/Constr	Drafting/Eng Draft	Electric Eng Tech	Civil Eng Tech	Indus/Mfg Eng Tech	Mech Eng Tech	Machinework	Welding
3294																																								■				■	■				■	■
3295																							■		■							■			■	■				■	■	■	■	■	■		■	■	■	■
3296	■	■	■	■	■	■	■	■		■	■	■	■	■	■					■	■		■	■	■						■															■		■		
3297		■	■			■		■		■	■	■	■	■	■					■	■				■	■		■						■	■	■						■			■	■	■	■		
3298																									■							■								■		■		■					■	■
3299		■																		■					■										■							■			■		■	■	■	■
3300																							■		■							■								■		■	■						■	■
3301																		■														■									■	■							■	■
3302		■	■	■	■	■	■	■	■	■	■	■	■	■	■					■	■		■	■										■	■	■								■	■	■		■		
3303																							■		■							■				■						■		■	■				■	■
3304																				■			■		■																	■								
3305		■	■	■	■	■	■	■		■	■	■	■	■	■					■	■		■		■					■	■		■		■	■	■													
3306								■																							■																			
3307																																	■																	
3308																				■			■		■	■			■			■			■	■				■	■			■	■			■	■	■
3309		■		■		■	■	■	■	■	■				■					■	■		■	■	■					■	■		■				■													
3310																				■					■				■			■								■	■	■		■	■				■	■
3311		■		■	■	■					■	■	■	■	■					■	■	■				■								■	■	■						■			■	■	■	■		
3312	■	■	■	■	■	■		■							■					■	■	■	■	■	■				■			■	■																	
3313	■	■	■	■	■	■	■	■	■	■	■	■	■	■	■	■			■	■	■	■			■					■	■		■				■						■		■		■			
3314																				■					■							■		■	■					■		■							■	■

▲ **Sequence Number—indicates the order of the college in this book only. Do *not* use this number with admissions tests or need analysis services.**

1 No campus room and board facilities
2 Room only or board only
3 Most freshmen required to live on campus
4 City or district residency requirements
5 Accredited by regional accrediting association or a recognized candidate for accreditation
6 All female freshman class
7 All male freshman class
8 Some admission selectivity; not all hs graduates accepted
9 Requirements more stringent for nonresidents
†Accredited by a nationally recognized accrediting body other than one of the regional accrediting associations

Texas

Sequence Number	School name (upper entry) City (lower entry)	Enrollment	Costs: Resident tuition/fees + room/board	Costs: Room/board (upper entry) Nonresident tuition/fees (lower entry)	Gen. Info.: Affiliation (upper entry) Religious observance (lower entry)	Gen. Info.: Size of community	Gen. Info.: Type of community	Admissions: Fall term application deadline (upper entry) Test required or desired (lower entry)	Admissions: Calendar	Financial Aid: Fall term application deadline (upper entry) Forms to be filed (lower entry)	No. in 10 who- -have need, rec some aid	-are women	-live on campus	-are minority students	-are nonresidents	-return as sophomores	-complete assoc degree	-transfer to 4-year college
3315	Alvin CC Alvin	1457	400	[1] 1500	Pub	S		9/10 Oth	E [5]	 FF=FA	3	5	0	2	1	2		
3316	Amarillo C Amarillo	1879	500	[1] 1700	Pub	M	U	8/27 Oth	E [5]	6/01 FFS	4	6	0	2	1	5		7
3317	Ambassador C Big Sandy	1150	4500 [3]	2500	Oth OS	T [8]		3/01 S/A	S †	 None		5	9	0	9	9	9	5
3318	Angelina C Lufkin	1371	3300	2800 3700	Pub	S		 A/S	S [5]	6/15	5	6	1	2	1	6	3	4
3319	Austin CC Austin	4928	700	[1] 3200	Pub	L	U	8/30 Oth	S [5]	4/01 FF=FA	1	5	0	3				
3320	Bee Co C Beeville	1390	2500	2100 5800	Pub	S			E [5]	4/01 FAF	5	6	1	6		5	5	2
3321	Blinn C Brenham	4034	2800	2200 4500	Pub	S		 A/S	S [5]	 FF/FA	3	5	4	2	1	3	2	8
3322	Brazosport C Lake Jackson	867	300	[1] 600	Pub	M	S	 Oth	E [5]		2	5	0	2	1	3		3
3323	Brookhaven C Farmers Branch	8359	300	[1] 1500	Pub	V	S	8/26 A=S	S [5]	8/15 FA/FF	2	6	0	2	1	6	2	4
3324	Cedar Valley C Lancaster	877	600	[1] 2400	Pub	S		 Oth	E [5]	6/30 FA/FF	2	5	0	5	1			
3325	Central Texas C Killeen	1612	3200	2600 3900	Pub	M	S	 A/S	E [5]	9/01 FF/FA	2	6		4	1			
3326	Chenier Business Bulmont	125	4800	[1]	Priv	M	U	 Oth	O [5]	 Oth	9	6	0	6	0		8	1
3327	Cisco JC Cisco	700	2600	2000 3000	Pub	T		 A=S	E [5]	9/13 FF/FA	8	5	5	2	1			8
3328	Clarendon C Clarendon	470	2100 [3]	1500 2300	Pub	T		8/24 A/S	S [5]	8/24 FFS	8	5	7	1	1	7	4	6
3329	Collin Co CC McKinney	2585	500	[1] 1500	Pub	M	S	 None	S [5]	 FA/FF	1	6	0	1	1		1	7
3330	Commonwlth Funeral C Houston	130	4900	[1]	Priv	V	U	9/05 None	O †	 FFS	2	4	0	4	2	0		
3331	Cooke Co C Gainesville	807	1000 [2]	600 1400	Pub	S		 A/S	S [5]	6/01 FFS	3	6	1	1	2	3	3	3
3332	Dallas Inst Funl Ser Dallas	200	4900	[1]	Priv	V	U	9/20 None	O [5]	9/09 FF/FA	6	1	0	2	5		8	
3333	Del Mar C Corpus Christi	3657	500	[1] 1500	Pub	L	U	 A=S	E [5]	6/01 FAF	9	6	0	5	1	2	1	6
3334	Eastfield C Mesquite	4844	400	[1] 1900	Pub	V	S	 Oth	E [5]	 FF=FA	7	5	0	2	1	2	3	6
3335	El Centro C Dallas	1007	300	[1] 1500	Pub	V	U	 Oth	S [5]	7/01 FAF	4	7	0	6	1		3	3
3336	El Paso CC El Paso	8097	600	[1] 1800	Pub	V	U	 None	S [5]	6/01 FF=FA	6	6	0	8	1	2		
3337	Frank Phillips C Borger	962	1900	1500 2200	Pub	S		 Oth	E [5]	 FF/FA	8	6	2	1		6		5

Educational Programs Available

College Transfer Courses

Sequence Number	Agriculture	Bus-Commerce	Communications	Education	Engineering	Fine, Applied Arts	Foreign Lang	Health	Home Ec	Humanities	Mathematics	Computer/Info Sci	Biological Sci	Physical Sci	Social Sci
3315	■	■	■	■	■	■	■	■	■	■	■	■	■	■	■
3316		■	■	■	■	■	■	■	■	■	■	■	■	■	■
3317			■			■			■	■					■
3318	■	■	■	■	■	■	■	■	■	■	■	■	■	■	■
3319		■	■	■	■	■	■	■	■	■	■	■	■	■	■
3320	■	■	■	■	■	■	■	■		■	■	■	■	■	■
3321	■	■	■	■	■	■	■	■	■	■	■	■	■	■	■
3322		■	■	■	■	■	■	■		■	■	■	■	■	■
3323		■	■	■	■	■	■	■	■	■	■	■	■	■	■
3324	■	■		■		■	■	■		■	■	■	■	■	■
3325	■	■	■	■	■	■	■	■		■	■	■	■	■	■
3326															
3327	■	■	■	■	■	■	■	■		■	■	■	■	■	■
3328	■	■	■	■	■	■	■	■	■	■	■		■	■	■
3329		■	■		■	■	■		■	■	■	■	■	■	■
3330															
3331	■	■		■	■	■	■	■		■	■	■	■	■	■
3332															
3333		■	■	■	■	■	■	■	■	■	■	■	■	■	■
3334		■	■		■	■	■	■		■	■	■	■	■	■
3335		■		■		■	■	■	■	■	■	■	■	■	■
3336	■	■	■	■	■	■	■	■	■	■	■	■	■	■	■
3337	■	■	■	■	■	■	■	■	■	■	■	■	■	■	■

Career-oriented Programs

Sequence Number	Agri: Ag Business	Agri: Ag/Farm Mgmt	Agri: Ag Mechanics/Tech	Agri: Horticulture	Business: Accounting	Business: Bus Mgmt & Admin	Business: Hotel/Rest Mgmt	Business: Office Mgmt	Business: Marketing/Purchasing	Business: Secretarial Studies	Arts: Architecture Tech	Arts: Applied Design	Arts: Photography/Cinema	Health: Dental Assistant	Health: Medical or Lab Tech	Health: Nursing (RN)	Health: Nursing (LPN)	Health: Radiologic Technology
3315					■	■		■	■	■					■	■	■	
3316					■	■		■		■				■	■		■	■
3317						■												
3318					■	■				■					■	■	■	■
3319					■	■	■	■	■	■		■			■	■	■	■
3320					■			■	■	■							■	
3321					■			■		■							■	■
3322								■		■						■	■	
3323					■	■		■	■	■								
3324					■	■		■	■	■								
3325		■	■		■	■	■	■	■	■					■		■	
3326					■	■		■		■							■	
3327										■							■	
3328	■	■				■				■							■	
3329				■	■			■		■			■			■	■	
3330																		
3331		■						■		■						■	■	
3332					■													
3333					■	■	■		■	■				■	■	■	■	■
3334					■	■		■	■	■		■						
3335					■	■		■		■					■	■	■	■
3336					■	■	■	■	■	■	■	■	■	■	■		■	■
3337	■	■	■	■	■	■		■		■							■	

Sequence Number	Math: Computer Prog	Math: Data Processing Tech	Math: Computer Operating	SocSci: Crim Just/Law Enforce	SocSci: Parks/Rec Mgmt	SocSci: Social Work	Technical/Skilled Trades: Air/Refrig/Heat Tech	Auto Body Repair	Auto Mechanics	Carpentry/Constr	Drafting/Eng Draft	Electric Eng Tech	Civil Eng Tech	Indus/Mfg Eng Tech	Mech Eng Tech	Machinework	Welding
3315	■	■		■		■	■		■		■	■					■
3316	■		■	■			■		■		■						
3317	■																
3318	■	■		■		■	■		■		■						■
3319	■			■			■		■	■	■						■
3320		■	■	■			■		■		■						■
3321	■			■													
3322		■		■			■		■	■	■	■				■	■
3323		■	■					■	■								
3324	■						■		■								
3325	■	■		■			■	■	■	■	■						■
3326		■	■														
3327	■	■		■					■	■	■	■					■
3328									■								
3329												■					
3330																	
3331	■	■	■	■				■	■		■					■	■
3332																	
3333	■			■		■	■	■	■		■	■				■	■
3334	■	■	■			■	■	■	■		■						■
3335	■	■		■													
3336	■	■	■	■	■		■		■	■	■	■		■	■	■	■
3337	■			■			■		■		■				■		■

▲ Sequence Number—indicates the order of the college in this book only. Do *not* use this number with admissions tests or need analysis services.

[1] No campus room and board facilities
[2] Room only or board only
[3] Most freshmen required to live on campus
[4] City or district residency requirements
[5] Accredited by regional accrediting association or a recognized candidate for accreditation
[6] All female freshman class
[7] All male freshman class
[8] Some admission selectivity; not all hs graduates accepted
[9] Requirements more stringent for nonresidents
†Accredited by a nationally recognized accrediting body other than one of the regional accrediting associations

Texas
(continued)

Sequence Number	School name (upper entry) City (lower entry)	Enrollment	Costs: Resident tuition/fees + room/board	Costs: Room/board (upper entry) Nonresident tuition/fees (lower entry)	Gen. Info.: Affiliation (upper entry) Religious observance (lower entry)	Gen. Info.: Size of community	Gen. Info.: Type of community	Admissions: Fall term application deadline (upper entry) Test required or desired (lower entry)	Admissions: Calendar	Financial Aid: Fall term application deadline (upper entry) Forms to be filed (lower entry)	Student Profile (No. in 10 who-): -have need, rec some aid	-are women	-live on campus	-are minority students	-are nonresidents	-return as sophomores	-complete assoc degree	-transfer to 4-year college
3338	Galveston C Galveston	562	300	[1] 600	Pub	M	U	 A=S	E[5]	8/01	4	7	0	4	1	6	5	4
3339	Grayson Co C Denison	3146	2200	1600 3400	Pub	M			E[5]	 FFS	2	6	1	1	1	7	6	4
3340	Hendrick Sch Rad Tec Abilene	10	800	[1]	Bapt	M[8]	U	3/01 Oth	O†	 None	0	7	0	1	0		9	
3341	Hill C Hillsboro	800	3100	2500 3700	Pub	T		9/01 A/S	S[5]	9/01 FF/FA	7	4	1	3	1	6	5	5
3342	Houston CC Houston	6642	800	[1] 2000	Pub	V	U	8/19 A=S	E[5]	4/15 FA/FF	1	5	0	4	1	5		
3343	Howard C Big Spring	1153	2700	2000 3000	Pub	S		9/06 Oth	E[5]	7/01 FF/FA	7	6	3	2	1	5	2	4
3344	Jacki Nell Secr Sch Austin	145	5600	[1]	Priv	L	U[6]	 Oth	O†	 Oth	8	9		6			9	
3345	Jacksonville C Jacksonville	261	4500[3]	2200	Bapt OS	S		 A=S	E[5]	 FF=FA	7	5	5	2	1	5	3	7
3346	Kilgore C Kilgore	1915	2300	2000 3100	Pub	S		8/12 A=S	E[5]	8/01 Oth	6	6	1	1	1	6	3	3
3347	Lamar U-Port Arthur Port Arthur	808	1000	[1] 4300	Pub	M	U	8/24 S/A	S[5]	8/25	3	3	0	4	1	2	4	1
3348	Laredo JC Laredo	5000	2100[2]	1500 3600	Pub	M	S	 A=S	S[5]	5/01 FA/FF	8	6		9	1	7		3
3349	Lee C Baytown	625	300	[1] 1300	Pub	M		 A/S	E[5]	7/01 FF/FA	9	4	0	2	1	2	1	6
3350	Lon Morris C Jacksonville	328	6800	3200	Meth OS	S[8]		 A/S	S[5]	8/15 FA/FF	7	4	8	3	1	6		9
3351	Mainland,C of the Texas City	3762	100	[1] 800	Pub	M	S	8/07 Oth	E[5]	 FF=FA	8	6	0	3	1	4	2	3
3352	McLennan CC Waco	2265	500	[1] 2500	Pub	M	U	 Oth	E[5]	 FF/FA	6	6	0	2	1		1	4
3353	Midland C Midland	1420	600	[1] 1200	Pub	M	U	 A/S	E[5]	6/01 FF=FA	3	6	0	2	1	4	3	4
3354	Mountain View C Dallas	1212	300	[1] 1800	Pub	V	U	 Oth	E[5]	8/20 FA/FF	9	4	0	4	1	5	2	5
3355	N Harris Co C-Tombal Tomball	1063	300	[1] 1000	Pub	M	S	 A=S	E[5]	 FF=FA		6			1			
3356	Natl Ed Center Texas Dallas	1086	7800	[1]	Priv	V	S	0/15 Oth	Q†	9/16 Oth	7	4	0	4	1	8	6	
3357	Navarro C Corsicana	1592	3000	2600 4000	Pub	S		 A=S	E[5]	 FF/FA	9	6	1	3	1	7	2	4
3358	North Harris Co C Houston	7200	300	[1] 800	Pub	V	S	 A/S	S[5]	8/01 FF/FA	3	5	0	2	1		3	3
3359	North Harris Co C Kingwood	1600	300	[1] 800	Pub	V	S	 A=S	E[5]	8/01 FF/FA	3	5	0	2	1	4	5	
3360	North Lake C Irving	1361	400	[1] 1900	Pub	L	S	8/27 A=S	E[5]	8/27 FA/FF	1	5	0	1	1		1	2

Educational Programs Available — College Transfer Courses

Sequence Number	Agriculture	Bus-Commerce	Communications	Education	Engineering	Fine, Applied Arts	Foreign Lang	Health	Home Ec	Humanities	Mathematics	Computer/Info Sci	Biological Sci	Physical Sci	Social Sci
3338		■	■	■	■	■	■	■	■	■	■	■	■	■	■
3339	■	■	■	■	■	■	■	■			■	■	■	■	■
3340															
3341	■	■	■	■	■	■	■	■	■	■	■	■	■	■	■
3342		■	■	■	■	■	■	■	■	■	■	■	■	■	■
3343	■	■	■	■	■	■	■	■	■	■	■	■	■	■	■
3344															
3345		■	■			■	■	■		■	■	■	■	■	■
3346	■	■	■	■	■	■	■	■	■	■	■	■	■	■	■
3347		■	■	■	■	■	■	■	■	■	■	■	■	■	■
3348		■	■	■	■	■	■	■	■	■	■	■	■	■	■
3349	■	■	■	■	■	■	■	■	■	■	■	■	■	■	■
3350		■	■	■	■	■	■	■		■	■	■	■	■	■
3351	■	■	■	■	■	■	■	■	■	■	■	■	■	■	■
3352	■	■	■	■	■	■	■	■	■	■	■	■	■	■	■
3353		■	■	■	■	■	■	■		■	■	■	■	■	■
3354		■	■	■		■	■			■	■	■	■	■	■
3355		■		■		■	■	■	■	■		■	■	■	■
3356															
3357	■	■	■	■	■	■	■	■	■	■	■	■	■	■	■
3358		■	■	■	■	■	■	■	■	■	■	■	■	■	■
3359		■	■	■	■	■	■	■	■	■	■		■	■	■
3360		■	■	■		■	■	■		■	■	■	■	■	■

Educational Programs Available — Career-oriented Programs

Sequence Number	Agri				Business						Arts			Health					Math			SocSci			Technical/Skilled Trades										
	Ag Business	Ag/Farm Mgmt	Ag Mechanics/Tech	Horticulture	Accounting	Bus Mgmt & Admin	Hotel/Rest Mgmt	Office Mgmt	Marketing/Purchasing	Secretarial Studies	Architecture Tech	Applied Design	Photography/Cinema	Dental Assistant	Medical or Lab Tech	Nursing (RN)	Nursing (LPN)	Radiologic Technology	Computer Prog	Data Processing Tech	Computer Operating	Crim Just/Law Enforce	Parks/Rec Mgmt	Social Work	Air/Refrig/Heat Tech	Auto Body Repair	Auto Mechanics	Carpentry/Constr	Drafting/Eng Draft	Electric Eng Tech	Civil Eng Tech	Indus/Mfg Eng Tech	Mech Eng Tech	Machinework	Welding
3338				■	■		■	■		■						■	■	■				■			■										
3339				■	■	■		■	■	■		■	■	■	■	■	■		■	■	■	■		■	■	■	■		■	■				■	■
3340																		■																	
3341	■	■			■	■		■		■							■		■	■		■			■	■	■	■	■	■				■	■
3342				■	■	■	■	■	■	■	■		■	■	■	■	■	■		■	■	■			■	■	■	■	■	■	■		■	■	■
3343				■	■	■		■		■						■	■		■	■	■	■		■		■	■		■						■
3344										■																									
3345					■					■									■	■															
3346			■		■			■	■	■		■			■	■	■		■	■		■			■		■		■	■				■	■
3347					■	■		■		■							■		■	■	■	■				■	■			■					
3348					■	■	■	■	■						■	■	■	■	■	■	■	■			■		■	■		■					■
3349				■		■		■	■	■						■	■		■	■		■			■	■	■		■	■				■	■
3350																■																			
3351					■	■		■	■	■					■	■		■	■	■	■	■			■	■	■		■	■					■
3352					■	■		■	■	■					■	■	■	■	■	■	■	■		■											
3353					■	■		■	■	■						■	■	■	■		■	■			■		■		■					■	■
3354					■	■				■																			■	■				■	■
3355					■			■		■						■				■	■	■													
3356								■	■	■									■	■	■									■					
3357	■	■	■		■					■		■			■	■	■	■	■	■		■			■				■	■					■
3358					■	■		■	■	■				■		■	■		■	■		■			■		■		■						■
3359					■	■		■	■	■							■		■	■							■		■	■					
3360					■			■		■									■	■					■			■							

▲ Sequence Number—indicates the order of the college in this book only. Do *not* use this number with admissions tests or need analysis services.

[1] No campus room and board facilities
[2] Room only or board only
[3] Most freshmen required to live on campus
[4] City or district residency requirements
[5] Accredited by regional accrediting association or a recognized candidate for accreditation
[6] All female freshman class
[7] All male freshman class
[8] Some admission selectivity; not all hs graduates accepted
[9] Requirements more stringent for nonresidents
†Accredited by a nationally recognized accrediting body other than one of the regional accrediting associations

Texas
(continued)

Sequence Number	School name (upper entry) City (lower entry)	Enrollment	Resident tuition/fees + room/board	Room/board (upper entry) Nonresident tuition/fees (lower entry)	Affiliation (upper entry) Religious observance (lower entry)	Size of community	Type of community	Fall term application deadline (upper entry) Test required or desired (lower entry)	Calendar	Fall term application deadline (upper entry) Forms to be filed (lower entry)	-have need, rec some aid	-are women	-live on campus	-are minority students	-are nonresidents	-return as sophomores	-complete assoc degree	-transfer to 4-year college
3361	Northeast Texas CC Mount Pleasant	722	600	[1] 1000	Pub	S		A=S	E[5]	6/01 FF/FA	2	7	0	1	0			
3362	Odessa C Odessa	1655	3100	2600 3300	Pub	M	U	None	E[5]	FF/FA	2	6	1	3	1	6		
3363	Palo Alto C San Antonio	1348	600	[1] 1500	Pub	V	S	9/01 Oth	S[5]	6/01	3	6	0	6	1			
3364	Panola C Carthage	846	2300	2000 2600	Pub	T		A/S	E[5]	7/15 FFS	6	6	1	2	1	4		3
3365	Paris JC Paris	1637	2900	2400 3400	Pub	S		Oth	S[5]	FFS	9	6	1	1			2	3
3366	Ranger JC Ranger	718	2800	2200 3100	Pub	T		8/21 A=S	S[5]	8/01 Oth	7	3	8	3	1	7	5	7
3367	Richland C Dallas	3552	400	[1] 1900	Pub	V	S	A=S	S[5]	FA/FF	1	5	0	1	1	2	1	5
3368	Saint Philip's C San Antonio	3782	500	[1] 1200	Pub	V	U	9/01 A=S	E[5]	6/01 Oth	3	4	0	7		7	3	4
3369	San Antonio C San Antonio	7051	500	[1] 1500	Pub	V	U	Oth	E[5]	FF=FA		6	0	5			1	1
3370	San Jacinto C Cent Pasadena	3236	300	[1] 1300	Pub	L	S		S[5]	6/01 FF=FA	3	5	0	2	1	2	1	
3371	San Jacinto C North Houston	1201	300	[1] 700	Pub	V	S	9/04 None	E[5]	Oth	1	6	0	4	1	2		
3372	San Jacinto C South Houston	1391	200	[1] 1300	Pub	V	S	None	S[5]	7/01 Oth	1	6	0	2				
3373	South Plains C Levelland	2328	2500	2000 2600	Pub	S		9/01 A/S	E[5]	6/01 FF/FA	3	5	2	3	1	6	6	4
3374	Southwest Christian Terrell	250	5900	2300	Oth O	S		7/31 Oth	S[5]	8/01 FA/FF	9	4	8	9	6	8	7	8
3375	Southwest Texas JC Uvalde	1223	2500	2000 4000	Pub	T		8/23	S[5]	9/01	4	5		5				
3376	Tarrant Co JC NE Cam Hurst	3400	300	[1] 3000	Pub	S		9/01 Oth	E[5]	9/01 Oth	1	6	0	1	1			
3377	Tarrant Co JC NW Cam Fort Worth	1157	300	[1] 3800	Pub	L	U	9/02 A=S	S[5]	6/01 FFS	1	5	0	2	1			
3378	Tarrant Co JC S Cam Fort Worth	4700	400	[1] 1400	Pub	L	U	None	E[5]	Oth	9	5	0	3	0			3
3379	Temple JC Temple	2469	3000	2400 4100	Pub	S		A=S	E[5]	FFS	3	6	1	2	1	4	1	3
3380	Texarkana C Texarkana	1625	500	[1] 900	Pub	M		A/S	S[5]	6/01 FFS	9	6	0	1	4	7	2	4
3381	Texas Southmost C Brownsville	2618	700	[1] 2500	Pub	M		Oth	Q[5]	4/01 Oth	6	6	0	9	0	5	1	2
3382	Texas St Harlingen Harlingen	2900	4600	3000	Pub	S		A=S	Q[5]	5/13 FFS								
3383	Texas St Tech Inst Amarillo	435	3400	2800 6600	Pub	M	S	9/07 Oth	O[5]	FFS	7	2	1	2	1	6	6	1

Educational Programs Available — College Transfer Courses

Sequence Number	Agriculture	Bus-Commerce	Communications	Education	Engineering	Fine, Applied Arts	Foreign Lang	Health	Home Ec	Humanities	Mathematics	Computer/Info Sci	Biological Sci	Physical Sci	Social Sci
3361	■	■	■	■		■	■	■		■	■	■	■	■	■
3362		■	■	■	■	■	■	■	■	■	■	■	■	■	■
3363	■	■		■		■		■		■	■	■	■	■	■
3364	■	■	■	■	■	■	■	■	■	■	■	■	■	■	■
3365	■	■	■	■	■	■	■	■		■	■	■	■	■	■
3366		■	■	■	■	■	■	■	■	■	■	■	■	■	■
3367	■	■	■		■	■	■			■	■	■	■	■	■
3368		■	■	■	■	■	■	■	■	■	■	■	■	■	■
3369		■	■	■	■	■	■	■	■	■	■	■	■	■	■
3370	■	■	■	■	■	■	■	■	■	■	■	■	■	■	■
3371		■	■	■	■	■	■	■	■	■	■	■	■	■	■
3372		■	■	■	■	■	■	■		■	■	■	■	■	■
3373	■	■	■	■	■	■	■	■	■	■	■	■	■	■	■
3374		■		■		■	■	■	■	■	■	■	■	■	■
3375	■	■					■					■			
3376		■	■	■	■	■	■	■		■	■	■	■	■	■
3377	■	■	■	■	■	■	■			■	■	■	■	■	■
3378		■	■	■	■	■	■	■	■	■	■	■	■	■	■
3379	■	■	■	■	■	■	■	■		■	■	■	■	■	■
3380	■	■	■	■	■	■	■	■	■	■	■	■	■	■	■
3381		■	■	■	■	■	■	■	■	■	■	■	■	■	■
3382	■	■			■	■		■			■	■			
3383		■	■			■						■			

Educational Programs Available — Career-oriented Programs (Agri, Business, Arts, Health)

Sequence Number	Ag Business	Ag/Farm Mgmt	Ag Mechanics/Tech	Horticulture	Accounting	Bus Mgmt & Admin	Hotel/Rest Mgmt	Office Mgmt	Marketing/Purchasing	Secretarial Studies	Architecture Tech	Applied Design	Photography/Cinema	Dental Assistant	Medical or Lab Tech	Nursing (RN)	Nursing (LPN)	Radiologic Technology
3361	■	■			■	■		■		■						■	■	
3362						■			■	■			■		■		■	■
3363				■		■		■		■								
3364								■		■							■	
3365		■	■					■		■						■	■	■
3366										■							■	
3367				■	■	■				■								
3368					■	■	■	■		■					■		■	■
3369					■	■		■	■	■		■		■		■		
3370				■	■	■	■	■	■	■		■	■		■	■		■
3371					■		■	■	■	■		■					■	
3372					■	■		■	■		■						■	
3373	■	■	■		■	■	■	■	■			■				■	■	■
3374										■								
3375	■			■	■	■			■				■	■			■	
3376					■				■	■				■	■			■
3377				■	■					■								
3378					■			■	■	■						■		
3379						■		■	■	■					■		■	
3380	■									■						■	■	
3381					■	■				■					■	■	■	■
3382			■		■			■		■							■	
3383																		

Educational Programs Available — Career-oriented Programs (Math, SocSci, Technical/Skilled Trades)

Sequence Number	Computer Prog	Data Processing Tech	Computer Operating	Crim Just/Law Enforce	Parks/Rec Mgmt	Social Work	Air/Refrig/Heat Tech	Auto Body Repair	Auto Mechanics	Carpentry/Constr	Drafting/Eng Draft	Electric Eng Tech	Civil Eng Tech	Indus/Mfg Eng Tech	Mech Eng Tech	Machinework	Welding
3361		■		■			■		■			■					■
3362						■	■	■	■	■	■	■				■	■
3363	■	■	■														
3364	■	■		■					■								■
3365	■	■		■			■			■	■	■				■	■
3366		■							■								■
3367	■	■								■	■	■	■		■		
3368							■	■	■		■	■				■	■
3369	■	■	■	■	■					■	■	■		■			
3370	■	■	■	■			■		■		■	■	■	■	■		■
3371	■	■	■	■			■	■	■	■	■	■					■
3372							■	■		■	■	■					
3373	■	■	■	■			■	■	■		■	■		■		■	■
3374	■	■															
3375							■		■								■
3376				■							■		■				
3377	■	■						■	■		■						
3378	■						■	■	■		■				■	■	■
3379	■	■		■					■		■						■
3380	■	■		■			■	■	■		■	■					■
3381		■	■	■		■	■	■	■	■	■					■	■
3382							■	■	■	■	■					■	■
3383	■																

▲ Sequence Number—indicates the order of the college in this book only. Do *not* use this number with admissions tests or need analysis services.

[1] No campus room and board facilities
[2] Room only or board only
[3] Most freshmen required to live on campus
[4] City or district residency requirements
[5] Accredited by regional accrediting association or a recognized candidate for accreditation
[6] All female freshman class
[7] All male freshman class
[8] Some admission selectivity; not all hs graduates accepted
[9] Requirements more stringent for nonresidents
†Accredited by a nationally recognized accrediting body other than one of the regional accrediting associations

Texas
(continued)

Sequence Number	School name (upper entry) City (lower entry)	Enrollment	Costs: Resident tuition/fees + room/board	Costs: Room/board (upper entry) Nonresident tuition/fees (lower entry)	Gen. Info.: Affiliation (upper entry) Religious observance (lower entry)	Gen. Info.: Size of community	Gen. Info.: Type of community	Admissions: Fall term application deadline (upper entry) Test required or desired (lower entry)	Admissions: Calendar	Financial Aid: Fall term application deadline (upper entry) Forms to be filed (lower entry)	No. in 10 who- -have need, rec some aid	-are women	-live on campus	-are minority students	-are nonresidents	-return as sophomores	-complete assoc degree	-transfer to 4-year college
3384	Texas St Tech Inst Sweetwater	759	4300	3400 9400	Pub	S		Oth	Q[5]	FF/FA	7	3	4	3	1		4	1
3385	Texas St Tech Inst Waco	3254	3800	3000 6800	Pub	M	S	Oth	Q[5]	5/30 FF=FA	8	2		2	1	2	3	1
3386	Trinity Valley CC Athens	1581	2400	2100 4100	Pub	S		9/01	E[5]	8/15 Oth	4	6	1	2	1	6	2	4
3387	Tyler JC Tyler	5000	2500	2000 3200	Pub	M		9/01 Oth	E[5]	4/15 FF=FA	2	5	1	2	1	5	2	4
3388	Vernon Regional JC Vernon	575	2500	1700 2800	Pub	S		A=S	E[5]	FFS	7	6	1	2	1	6	4	3
3389	Victoria C Victoria	2000	400	[1] 1300	Pub	M		Oth	E[5]	Oth		6	0	2	1	6	4	4
3390	Weatherford C Weatherford	941	3000	2500 5100	Pub	S		A=S	E[5]	FF/FA	2	5	1	1	1	2	2	4
3391	Western Texas C Snyder	597	2400[3]	1900 2600	Pub	S		A/S	E[5]	FF/FA	7	5	3	2	1	7	4	3
3392	Wharton Co JC Wharton	1674	2500	1900 3800	Pub	S		A/S	E[5]	7/15 FFS	3	6	1	3	1	4	2	3
Utah																		
3393	Dixie C St George	3100	3300	2200 5300	Pub	S		A/S	Q[5]	FF=FA	6	5	3	1	2	3	3	7
3394	Eastern Utah,C of Price	2960	3100	2100 4800	Pub	T		A/S	Q[5]	5/01 Oth	7	5	2	3	1		4	2
3395	Latter-Day Sts Bus C Salt Lake City	573	3100[2]	1300	LDS OS	L	U	A/S	Q[5]	FFS	5	7	1	1	5	5	2	1
3396	Salt Lake CC Salt Lake City	13344	1200	[1] 3100	Pub	L	S	9/20 Oth	Q[5]	7/01 FF/FA	5	5	0	1	1	6	4	4
3397	Snow C Ephraim	1798	3200	2200 5000	Pub	T		ACT	Q[5]	8/01 FA/FF	4	5	5	1	1	4	4	5
3398	Stevens Henager C Ogden	265	9500[2]	2000	Priv	M[8]	U	A=S	Q†	FF=FA	9	8	0	1	1	6	6	1
3399	Stevens Henager C Provo	277	7000[2]	1800	Priv	M			O†		9	7	0	1	1	7	8	1
3400	Utah Valley CC Orem	7886	1200	[1] 3300	Pub	M	S	None	E[5]	FFS	6	5	0	1				
Vermont																		
3401	Landmark C Putney	174	23900[3]	4400	Priv	T[8]		Oth	S[5]	8/01 FAF	1	3	9	1	9	5	1	9
3402	Sterling C-Voc Tech Craftsbury Comm	83	14800[3]	4400	Priv	T[8]		9/15 S/A	O[5]	FA/FF	5	3	9	1	9	6	9	
3403	Vermont Tech C Randolph	714	7600[3]	4100 10400	Pub	T[8]		A=S	S[5]	FF/FA	5	2	9	1	3	7	5	2
3404	Vermont,CC of Waterbury	210	2000	[1] 4000	Pub	T		None	S[5]	FF=FA	9	7	0	1	1	4	2	4

Educational Programs Available — College Transfer Courses; Career-oriented Programs (Agri, Business, Arts, Health, Math, SocSci, Technical/Skilled Trades)

Sequence Number	Agriculture	Bus-Commerce	Communications	Education	Engineering	Fine, Applied Arts	Foreign Lang	Health	Home Ec	Humanities	Mathematics	Computer/Info Sci	Biological Sci	Physical Sci	Social Sci	Ag Business	Ag/Farm Mgmt	Ag Mechanics/Tech	Horticulture	Accounting	Bus Mgmt & Admin	Hotel/Rest Mgmt	Office Mgmt	Marketing/Purchasing	Secretarial Studies	Architecture Tech	Applied Design	Photography/Cinema	Dental Assistant	Medical or Lab Tech	Nursing (RN)	Nursing (LPN)	Radiologic Technology	Computer Prog	Data Processing Tech	Computer Operating	Crim Just/Law Enforce	Parks/Rec Mgmt	Social Work	Air/Refrig/Heat Tech	Auto Body Repair	Auto Mechanics	Carpentry/Constr	Drafting/Eng Draft	Electric Eng Tech	Civil Eng Tech	Indus/Mfg Eng Tech	Mech Eng Tech	Machinework	Welding
3384											■	■											■	■	■						■	■		■	■	■				■	■	■	■						■	
3385	■		■		■			■	■			■					■	■	■					■					■											■	■	■	■	■		■	■	■	■	■
3386	■	■	■	■	■	■	■	■	■	■	■	■	■	■	■		■		■	■	■		■	■	■			■			■	■		■	■	■	■					■		■						■
3387	■	■	■	■	■	■	■	■	■	■	■	■	■	■	■		■							■	■					■	■	■	■	■	■		■	■		■				■	■	■				■
3388	■	■			■	■	■			■	■	■	■	■	■		■			■				■	■							■			■		■					■		■				■		■
3389		■	■	■	■	■	■	■	■	■	■	■	■	■	■										■							■			■		■			■				■	■					■
3390	■	■	■	■	■	■	■	■		■	■	■	■	■	■		■								■							■		■										■						■
3391	■	■	■	■		■	■	■		■	■	■	■	■	■					■	■		■									■					■					■								■
3392	■	■	■	■	■	■	■		■	■	■			■	■		■				■		■		■					■	■	■	■	■	■		■			■		■		■	■					■
Utah																																																		
3393	■	■	■	■	■	■	■	■	■	■	■	■	■	■	■								■	■	■						■	■									■	■		■						■
3394	■	■	■	■	■	■		■	■	■	■	■	■	■	■					■					■							■									■	■		■		■			■	■
3395		■	■	■		■		■	■	■	■	■	■	■	■					■	■		■	■	■									■	■	■														
3396		■	■	■	■	■	■	■	■	■	■	■	■	■	■					■	■		■	■	■					■	■	■	■	■	■	■	■			■	■	■	■	■	■			■	■	■
3397	■	■	■	■	■	■	■	■	■	■	■	■	■	■	■	■	■						■	■	■										■							■	■		■					■
3398		■						■												■	■	■	■	■	■																									
3399		■						■				■								■	■			■	■																									
3400		■	■		■	■	■	■	■	■	■	■		■	■					■		■	■	■	■							■	■			■				■	■	■	■	■	■				■	■
Vermont																																																		
3401		■								■	■	■	■		■										■																									
3402	■			■				■					■		■																																			
3403	■	■			■	■		■								■	■	■	■				■		■	■																■	■		■	■	■	■		
3404		■		■				■																																										

▲ Sequence Number—indicates the order of the college in this book only. Do *not* use this number with admissions tests or need analysis services.

1 No campus room and board facilities
2 Room only or board only
3 *Most freshmen required to live on campus*
4 City or district residency requirements
5 Accredited by regional accrediting association *or a recognized candidate for accreditation*
6 All female freshman class
7 All male freshman class
8 Some admission selectivity; not all hs graduates accepted
9 *Requirements more stringent for nonresidents*
†Accredited by a nationally recognized accrediting body other than one of the *regional accrediting associations*

Virginia

Sequence Number	School name (upper entry)	City (lower entry)	Enrollment	Resident tuition/fees + room/board	Room/board (upper entry)	Nonresident tuition/fees (lower entry)	Affiliation (upper entry) / Religious observance (lower entry)	Size of community	Type of community	Fall term application deadline (upper entry)	Test required or desired (lower entry)	Calendar	Fall term application deadline (upper entry)	Forms to be filed (lower entry)	-have need, rec some aid	-are women	-live on campus	-are minority students	-are nonresidents	-return as sophomores	-complete assoc degree	-transfer to 4-year college
				Costs			Gen. Info.			Admissions			Financial Aid		Student Profile: No. in 10 who-							
3405	Blue Ridge CC	Weyers Cave	1374	900	[1]	4300	Pub	T			None	E [5]	6/01	FAF	9	6	0	1	1	3	2	1
3406	Career Devel Inst	Arlington	225	8600	[1]		Priv	V	S		Oth	O †		FAF	9	3	0	6			9	
3407	Central Virginia CC	Lynchburg	1010	1100	[1]	4600	Pub	M	S		None	E [5]		Oth	2	5	0	1	1	3	2	2
3408	Commonwealth C	Norfolk	2500	8200	3000		Priv	L [8]	U		A=S	Q [5]	10/01		9	8	1	5		7	5	1
3409	Dabney Lancaster CC	Clifton Forge	501	900	[1]	4000	Pub	T			Oth	S [5]		FF=FA	6	6	0	1	1	6	5	2
3410	Danville CC	Danville	1079	1100	[1]	4300	Pub	M		9/30	Oth	S [5]	9/30	FAF	9	5	0	2	1	5	6	1
3411	Eastern Shore CC	Melfa	211	900	[1]	4500	Pub	T			Oth	S [5]			2	7	0	3	1	6	4	2
3412	Germanna CC	Locust Grove	645	1100	[1]	4300	Pub	T			None	E [5]		FAF	8	6	0	1	1	6	4	
3413	J S Reynolds CC	Richmond	2690	800	[1]	4000	Pub	V	U		None	E [5]	7/01	FAF		6	0	3	1			1
3414	John Tyler CC	Chester	1036	900	[1]	4500	Pub	S			None	E [5]	6/30	FF=FA	2	6	0	3	1	5	1	2
3415	Kee Business C	Newport News	250	5000	[1]		Priv	M [8]	S	9/27	Oth	O		FAF	9	9	0	4				
3416	Lord Fairfax CC	Middletown	712	900	[1]	4500	Pub	T		8/27	None	E [5]			3	6	0	1	1			
3417	Mountain Empire CC	Big Stone Gap	1057	1100	[1]	4300	Pub	T		9/05	None	E [5]	6/01	Oth	7	5	0	1	1		4	1
3418	National Business C	Roanoke	453	6800	2400		Priv	M [8]	U	9/01	Oth	Q †	9/15		9	6	1	3	1	7	7	2
3419	New River CC	Dublin	1534	900	[1]	4300	Pub	T			None	S [5]		Oth	4	6	0	1	1	2	1	1
3420	Northern Virginia CC	Annandale	9193	900	[1]	4500	Pub	V	S		None	S [5]		FAF	1	5	0	2	1	1		
3421	Patrick Henry CC	Martinsville	565	1000	[1]	4000	Pub	S			None	E [5]	7/01	FAF	6	6	0	1	0	4		
3422	Paul D Camp CC	Franklin	298	900	[1]	4500	Pub	S		0/01	None	S [5]	8/01	FA/FF	5	6	0	5	1	3	4	1
3423	Piedmont Virginia CC	Charlottesville	881	800	[1]	4000	Pub	M			Oth	S [5]		FAF	6	6	0	1	1	7		3
3424	Rappahannock CC	Glenns	351	800	[1]	4000	Pub	M		8/28	Oth	S [5]	6/01	FA/FF	4		0	2	1	5	3	1
3425	Richard Bland C	Petersburg	1205	1400	[1]	3600	Pub	S [8]		8/15	S/A	S [5]		FAF	4	6	0	2	1	7	5	9
3426	Roanoke Sch Prac Nsg	Roanoke	45	2500	1800		Priv	M [8]	U		Oth	O †		Oth		9		1				
3427	Southern Seminary C	Buena Vista	277	12900 [3]	4300		Priv	T [8]	[6]	8/15	S/A	E [5]	8/15	FF=FA	5	9	9	1	4	7	7	8

Educational Programs Available

Sequence Number	Agriculture	Bus-Commerce	Communications	Education	Engineering	Fine, Applied Arts	Foreign Lang	Health	Home Ec	Humanities	Mathematics	Computer/Info Sci	Biological Sci	Physical Sci	Social Sci	Ag Business	Ag/Farm Mgmt	Ag Mechanics/Tech	Horticulture	Accounting	Bus Mgmt & Admin	Hotel/Rest Mgmt	Office Mgmt	Marketing/Purchasing	Secretarial Studies	Architecture Tech	Applied Design	Photography/Cinema	Dental Assistant	Medical or Lab Tech	Nursing (RN)	Nursing (LPN)	Radiologic Technology	Computer Prog	Data Processing Tech	Computer Operating	Crim Just/Law Enforce	Parks/Rec Mgmt	Social Work	Air/Refrig/Heat Tech	Auto Body Repair	Auto Mechanics	Carpentry/Constr	Drafting/Eng Draft	Electric Eng Tech	Civil Eng Tech	Indus/Mfg Eng Tech	Mech Eng Tech	Machinework	Welding
	College Transfer Courses															Career-oriented Programs: Agri				Business						Arts			Health					Math			SocSci			Technical/Skilled Trades										
3405	■	■		■	■	■				■			■		■					■	■		■	■							■			■	■	■	■					■		■				■		
3406																									■									■	■	■														
3407		■		■		■	■			■	■		■	■	■					■	■			■						■			■	■	■		■					■		■					■	
3408		■						■		■		■											■						■						■	■														
3409		■		■		■	■		■	■	■	■	■	■	■						■		■								■				■	■	■							■				■		■
3410		■		■	■	■	■	■		■	■		■	■	■					■	■			■	■							■		■	■		■		■	■	■	■		■	■				■	
3411		■		■				■		■	■	■	■	■	■						■				■																			■	■					■
3412		■		■	■			■		■	■	■	■	■	■					■	■				■						■						■					■		■	■					
3413		■		■	■							■							■	■	■	■	■	■	■				■	■	■			■	■		■		■	■		■	■	■	■	■				
3414		■		■						■	■				■					■	■			■	■	■		■			■			■			■			■		■	■		■				■	■
3415																				■			■		■																									
3416		■	■	■	■	■		■	■	■	■	■			■	■			■	■	■				■	■	■								■	■		■						■		■		■		
3417	■	■		■	■	■		■		■	■	■	■	■	■					■	■		■		■						■						■			■				■	■					■
3418		■						■				■			■					■	■	■	■	■	■									■	■															
3419		■										■			■					■	■			■	■	■					■	■				■			■			■		■	■				■	■
3420	■	■	■	■	■	■	■	■	■	■	■	■	■	■	■				■	■	■	■	■	■	■	■		■		■	■		■	■	■	■	■	■		■	■	■		■		■			■	■
3421		■		■		■		■		■		■			■					■				■	■						■	■		■		■	■					■		■	■			■		■
3422		■		■	■			■		■		■			■						■				■												■					■		■	■					■
3423		■		■	■	■	■	■		■	■	■	■	■	■					■	■			■	■						■			■			■							■	■					
3424	■	■		■		■				■	■	■	■	■	■						■		■		■						■	■				■	■					■	■	■	■					
3425	■	■	■	■	■	■	■	■		■	■	■	■	■	■																																			
3426																																■																		
3427		■	■	■		■	■			■	■	■	■	■	■						■			■																										

▲ **Sequence Number—indicates the order of the college in this book only. Do *not* use this number with admissions tests or need analysis services.**

[1] No campus room and board facilities
[2] Room only or board only
[3] Most freshmen required to live on campus
[4] City or district residency requirements
[5] Accredited by regional accrediting association or a recognized candidate for accreditation
[6] All female freshman class
[7] All male freshman class
[8] Some admission selectivity; not all hs graduates accepted
[9] Requirements more stringent for nonresidents
†Accredited by a nationally recognized accrediting body other than one of the regional accrediting associations

Virginia (continued)

Sequence Number	School name (upper entry) City (lower entry)	Enrollment	Costs: Resident tuition/fees + room/board	Costs: Room/board (upper entry) Nonresident tuition/fees (lower entry)	Gen. Info.: Affiliation (upper entry) Religious observance (lower entry)	Gen. Info.: Size of community	Gen. Info.: Type of community	Admissions: Fall term application deadline (upper entry) Test required or desired (lower entry)	Admissions: Calendar	Financial Aid: Fall term application deadline (upper entry) Forms to be filed (lower entry)	No. in 10 who- -have need, rec some aid	-are women	-live on campus	-are minority students	-are nonresidents	-return as sophomores	-complete assoc degree	-transfer to 4-year college
3428	Southside Va CC Alberta	876	900	— 4300	Pub	T		None	E[5]	FAF	5	6	0	4	0	7		
3429	Southwst Virginia CC Richlands	2476	1000	— 4800	Pub	T		Oth	S[5]	FAF	6	6	0	1	1	5	4	2
3430	Thomas Nelson CC Hampton	1676	900	— 4500	Pub	L	U	None	S[5]	6/01	2	6	0	3	1	7	1	2
3431	Tidewater CC Portsmouth	4671	900	— 4500	Pub	L	U	Oth	S[5]	8/01 FAF		6	0	2	1	4	4	3
3432	Virginia C Roanoke	65	2500	—	Priv	M	U	A=S	T †		2	3	0	1	0	8	6	1
3433	Virginia Highlnds CC Abingdon	983	1100	— 4300	Pub	T		Oth	S[5]	8/15 FAF	6	5	0	1	1		7	4
3434	Virginia Western CC Roanoke	1847	700	— 4000	Pub	L	U	None	E[5]	FA/FF	6	6	0	1	1	5	3	1
3435	Wytheville CC Wytheville	828	900	— 4500	Pub	T		Oth	E[5]	6/01 FAF	5	6	0	1	1		3	1
	Washington																	
3436	Bellevue CC Bellevue	5043	1000	— 3800	Pub	M	S	None	Q[5]	5/01 FF=FA	2	6	0	1			1	2
3437	Big Bend CC Moses Lake	1062	4100	3200 6600	Pub	S		None	Q[5]	FA/FF	4	5	1	1	1	6		
3438	Centralia C Centralia	1262	900	— 3400	Pub	S		A=S	Q[5]	FAF	5	6	0	1	1	4	3	2
3439	Clark CC Vancouver	3750	900	— 3300	Pub	M		Oth	Q[5]	5/01 FAF	9	5	0	1	1		2	2
3440	Columbia Basin C Pasco	2675	1000	— 3700	Pub	S		9/01	Q[5]	FA/FF	3	6	0	1	1	7	3	3
3441	Edmonds CC Lynnwood	3510	1000	— 3800	Pub	M	S	None	Q[5]	FAF	2	6	0	1	1	6	3	1
3442	Everett CC Everett	2687	900	— 3400	Pub	M		Oth	Q[5]	FAF	3	5	0	1	1		1	
3443	Gray's Harbor C Aberdeen	1352	900	— 3400	Pub	S		9/25 Oth	Q[5]	5/15 FA/FF	9	6	0	1	1	4	3	2
3444	Green River CC Auburn	8049	900	— 3400	Pub	S		ACT	Q[5]	FA/FF	3	4	0	1	1	4	2	1
3445	Highline CC Des Moines	3000	800	— 3200	Pub	S		9/24 None	Q[5]	4/01 FAF	2	6	0	2	1	2	4	3
3446	Lake Washington Voc Kirkland	1200	900	—	Pub	S		None	O[5]	7/01 FAF	6	6	0					
3447	Lower Columbia C Longview	1814	1000	— 3700	Pub	S		Oth	Q[5]	FF=FA	3	6	0	1	1	6	3	2
3448	North Seattle CC Seattle	8292	1000	— 3700	Pub	V	U	9/23 Oth	Q[5]	8/16 FAF	4	5	0	2	1		2	2
3449	Olympic C Bremerton	2730	900	— 3400	Pub	S		9/15 None	Q[5]	8/01 FAF	5	5	0	1	1	2	3	2

Educational Programs Available

Sequence Number	Transfer: Agriculture	Transfer: Bus-Commerce	Transfer: Communications	Transfer: Education	Transfer: Engineering	Transfer: Fine, Applied Arts	Transfer: Foreign Lang	Transfer: Health	Transfer: Home Ec	Transfer: Humanities	Transfer: Mathematics	Transfer: Computer/Info Sci	Transfer: Biological Sci	Transfer: Physical Sci	Transfer: Social Sci	Agri: Ag Business	Agri: Ag/Farm Mgmt	Agri: Ag Mechanics/Tech	Agri: Horticulture	Business: Accounting	Business: Bus Mgmt & Admin	Business: Hotel/Rest Mgmt	Business: Office Mgmt	Business: Marketing/Purchasing	Business: Secretarial Studies	Arts: Architecture Tech	Arts: Applied Design	Arts: Photography/Cinema	Health: Dental Assistant	Health: Medical or Lab Tech	Health: Nursing (RN)	Health: Nursing (LPN)	Health: Radiologic Technology	Math: Computer Prog	Math: Data Processing Tech	Math: Computer Operating	SocSci: Crim Just/Law Enforce	SocSci: Parks/Rec Mgmt	SocSci: Social Work	Trades: Air/Refrig/Heat Tech	Trades: Auto Body Repair	Trades: Auto Mechanics	Trades: Carpentry/Constr	Trades: Drafting/Eng Draft	Trades: Electric Eng Tech	Trades: Civil Eng Tech	Trades: Indus/Mfg Eng Tech	Trades: Mech Eng Tech	Trades: Machinework	Trades: Welding
3428		■		■			■	■		■	■	■	■	■	■						■				■						■	■					■			■		■		■	■					
3429	■	■	■	■	■	■	■	■	■	■	■	■	■	■	■					■	■				■						■		■				■					■		■	■				■	■
3430		■		■	■	■														■	■	■		■	■		■	■		■	■						■		■	■		■			■			■	■	
3431	■	■	■	■	■	■	■	■	■	■	■	■	■	■	■				■	■	■		■		■		■	■		■			■	■		■	■	■	■	■				■	■	■		■	■	■
3432												■													■									■																
3433		■		■		■	■			■	■	■	■	■	■					■	■				■						■		■		■		■			■				■	■				■	
3434	■	■		■	■	■	■			■	■	■	■	■	■				■	■	■				■						■		■		■	■	■		■	■		■			■	■		■		
3435		■	■	■				■												■	■			■	■				■	■	■		■	■		■	■							■		■			■	
3436		■	■	■	■	■	■		■	■	■	■	■	■	■					■	■			■				■			■		■	■			■	■												
3437		■	■	■	■	■	■	■		■	■	■	■	■	■					■	■		■		■						■	■		■	■	■						■		■						■
3438	■	■	■	■	■	■	■	■	■	■	■	■	■	■	■					■	■		■	■	■							■										■		■	■	■				■
3439	■	■	■	■	■	■	■	■	■	■	■	■	■	■	■				■	■	■		■	■	■		■				■	■		■	■		■					■	■	■	■	■		■	■	■
3440	■	■	■	■	■	■	■	■	■	■	■	■	■	■	■	■	■	■			■		■	■	■	■					■	■					■				■	■	■	■	■	■			■	■
3441	■	■		■	■	■	■	■	■	■	■	■	■	■	■				■	■	■		■	■	■										■				■											
3442	■	■	■	■	■	■	■	■	■	■	■	■	■	■	■					■	■	■			■						■	■		■	■		■	■				■		■						■
3443	■	■	■	■	■	■	■	■	■	■	■	■	■	■	■						■		■		■						■	■			■							■	■						■	■
3444	■	■	■	■	■	■	■	■	■	■	■	■	■	■	■					■	■		■	■	■							■		■		■	■	■			■	■	■	■	■				■	■
3445		■	■	■	■	■	■	■	■	■	■	■	■	■	■					■	■	■	■	■	■		■		■		■			■	■		■							■			■	■		■
3446																			■	■		■		■	■				■						■					■	■	■		■	■		■		■	■
3447	■	■	■	■	■	■	■	■	■	■	■	■	■	■	■					■	■		■		■						■	■		■	■		■				■	■	■	■				■	■	■
3448	■	■		■	■	■	■	■		■	■	■	■	■	■					■			■		■							■		■	■	■				■				■	■	■		■		
3449	■	■	■	■	■	■	■	■	■	■	■	■	■	■	■					■	■		■	■	■					■	■	■		■	■	■	■					■	■	■	■	■		■	■	■

▲ Sequence Number—indicates the order of the college in this book only. Do *not* use this number with admissions tests or need analysis services.

1 No campus room and board facilities
2 Room only or board only
3 Most freshmen required to live on campus
4 City or district residency requirements
5 Accredited by regional accrediting association or a recognized candidate for accreditation
6 All female freshman class
7 All male freshman class
8 *Some admission selectivity; not all hs graduates accepted*
9 Requirements more stringent for nonresidents
†Accredited by a nationally recognized *accrediting body other than one of the* regional accrediting associations

Washington
(continued)

Sequence Number	School name (upper entry)	City (lower entry)	Enrollment	Resident tuition/fees + room/board	Room/board (upper entry)	Nonresident tuition/fees (lower entry)	Affiliation (upper entry)	Religious observance (lower entry)	Size of community	Type of community	Fall term application deadline (upper entry)	Test required or desired (lower entry)	Calendar	Fall term application deadline (upper entry)	Forms to be filed (lower entry)	-have need, rec some aid	-are women	-live on campus	-are minority students	-are nonresidents	-return as sophomores	-complete assoc degree	-transfer to 4-year college
				Costs			**Gen. Info.**				**Admissions**			**Financial Aid**		**Student Profile — No. in 10 who-**							
3450	Peninsula C	Port Angeles	865	4000	3100	6500	Pub		S			Oth	Q[5]	6/01	FAF	7	6	1	1	1		3	2
3451	Pierce C	Tacoma	5180	900	[1]	3500	Pub		L	S		Oth	Q[5]	4/01	FA/FF	2	5	0	3	1	4	4	2
3452	Renton Voc-Tech Inst	Renton	3066	900	[1]		Pub		S			Oth	O[5]		FF=FA	2	5	0	2	1	6	6	
3453	Seattle Central CC	Seattle	4459	900	[1]	3400	Pub		V	U	9/24	A=S	Q[5]	5/15	FF=FA	2	6	0	4	1	5	1	1
3454	Shoreline CC	Seattle	4035	900	[1]	3700	Pub		V	S		Oth	Q[5]		FA/FF	3	6	0	1				
3455	Skagit Valley C	Mount Vernon	2101	900	[1]	3700	Pub		S			Oth	Q[5]	6/01	FA/FF	6	6	0	1	1	7	3	
3456	South Seattle CC	Seattle	2079	900	[1]	3700	Pub		V	U		None	Q[5]		FAF	4	4	0	3	1	7	3	6
3457	Spokane CC	Spokane	4105	900	[1]	3700	Pub		M	S	9/18	A=S	Q[5]	4/01	FA/FF	3	5	0	1	1	5	6	1
3458	Spokane Falls CC	Spokane	3359	900	[1]	3700	Pub		M	S	9/18	Oth	Q[5]	4/01	FA/FF	5	5	0	1	1	5	5	4
3459	Tacoma CC	Tacoma	3121	1000	[1]	3700	Pub		M	U	9/23	Oth	Q[5]	4/01	FAF	2	6	0	2				
3460	Valley C	Kent	250	1700	[1]		Priv		L	S		A/S	O†		Oth	1	5	0	1	1		7	2
3461	Walla Walla CC	Walla Walla	1760	900	[1]	3700	Pub		S				Q[5]	9/30	FF=FA	4	5	0	1	1	5	5	3
3462	Wenatchee Valley C	Wenatchee	1475	4100	3200	6900	Pub		S		9/01	None	Q[5]	5/01	FA/FF	2	5	0	1	1	5	2	2
3463	Whatcom CC	Bellingham	720	800	[1]	3200	Pub		M			None	Q[5]		FAF	3	6	0	1	1	3	2	3
3464	Yakima Valley CC	Yakima	2801	4000	3100	6800	Pub		M			Oth	Q[5]	5/01	FA/FF	5	5	1	3	1	3	2	1
West Virginia																							
3465	Beckley C	Beckley	929	2500	[1]		Priv		S		9/06	ACT	E[5]	4/01	FA/FF	3	7	0	1		7	3	
3466	Greenbrier CC	Lewisburg	240	1100	[1]	1900	Pub		T			ACT	E[5]		FAF	6	7		1	1		4	2
3467	Kanawha Co Sch Elec	Charleston	32	1100	[1]		Pub		M[8]		5/01	Oth	Q[5]		Oth	6	1	0	1	1	9	8	5
3468	Mountain St C	Parkersburg	492	4900	[1]		Priv		S[8]			Oth	Q†			9			1			8	
3469	Natl Ed Center W Va	Cross Lanes	480	5400	[1]		Priv		S			Oth	Q†		Oth	7	1	0	2	1	8	6	
3470	Potomac St C of W Va	Keyser	998	4000	2700	6000	Pub		T		8/22	A/S	E[5]	8/15	FAF	8	4	3	1	3	2	4	5
3471	South W Va CC Logan	Logan	1541	800	[1]	2500	Pub		T			ACT	E[5]	4/15	FA/FF	3	7	0	1	0	4	5	4

Educational Programs Available

Sequence Number	College Transfer Courses															Career-oriented Programs: Agri				Business						Arts			Health					Math			SocSci			Technical/Skilled Trades										
	Agriculture	Bus-Commerce	Communications	Education	Engineering	Fine, Applied Arts	Foreign Lang	Health	Home Ec	Humanities	Mathematics	Computer/Info Sci	Biological Sci	Physical Sci	Social Sci	Ag Business	Ag/Farm Mgmt	Ag Mechanics/Tech	Horticulture	Accounting	Bus Mgmt & Admin	Hotel/Rest Mgmt	Office Mgmt	Marketing/Purchasing	Secretarial Studies	Architecture Tech	Applied Design	Photography/Cinema	Dental Assistant	Medical or Lab Tech	Nursing (RN)	Nursing (LPN)	Radiologic Technology	Computer Prog	Data Processing Tech	Computer Operating	Crim Just/Law Enforce	Parks/Rec Mgmt	Social Work	Air/Refrig/Heat Tech	Auto Body Repair	Auto Mechanics	Carpentry/Constr	Drafting/Eng Draft	Electric Eng Tech	Civil Eng Tech	Indus/Mfg Eng Tech	Mech Eng Tech	Machinework	Welding
3450	■	■	■	■	■	■	■			■	■	■	■	■	■					■	■				■						■				■	■	■					■								
3451	■	■	■	■	■	■	■	■	■	■	■	■	■	■	■					■	■		■	■	■					■				■	■	■	■	■	■											
3452																			■	■	■		■	■	■	■			■	■		■		■	■	■	■			■	■	■	■	■	■	■		■	■	■
3453		■	■	■	■	■	■	■	■	■	■	■	■	■	■					■		■			■		■		■		■			■	■								■	■					■	■
3454		■	■	■	■	■	■	■	■	■	■	■	■	■	■					■	■	■	■	■	■			■		■	■					■	■					■		■	■	■		■	■	■
3455	■	■	■	■	■	■	■	■	■	■	■	■	■	■	■							■	■	■	■						■	■				■	■	■	■		■	■		■	■	■				■
3456				■			■			■	■		■	■	■				■	■		■	■		■																■	■		■		■		■	■	
3457	■	■	■		■	■	■	■	■	■	■	■	■	■	■	■	■	■	■	■	■	■	■	■	■	■			■		■	■		■	■	■	■	■		■	■	■	■	■	■	■		■	■	■
3458		■	■	■	■	■	■	■	■	■	■	■	■	■	■					■	■		■	■	■		■	■											■											
3459	■	■	■	■	■	■	■	■		■	■	■	■	■	■					■	■		■		■						■		■			■	■		■											
3460		■			■					■	■	■		■						■			■		■																			■						
3461	■	■	■	■	■	■	■	■	■	■	■	■	■	■	■	■	■	■		■			■	■	■						■	■		■			■	■		■	■	■	■	■		■			■	■
3462	■	■	■	■	■	■	■	■	■	■	■	■	■	■	■						■		■	■	■					■	■	■								■		■	■							■
3463		■	■			■	■	■	■	■	■	■	■	■	■					■	■		■		■										■	■	■													
3464	■	■	■	■	■	■	■	■	■	■	■	■	■	■	■	■	■	■		■		■			■						■	■	■	■		■	■		■			■				■				■
West Virginia																																																		
3465	■	■		■	■	■		■		■	■			■	■					■	■				■					■																				
3466		■		■		■				■	■	■	■	■	■					■	■		■		■																									
3467																																																		
3468		■	■					■				■			■					■	■	■	■		■									■		■														
3469																																		■	■								■	■						
3470	■	■	■	■	■	■	■	■		■	■	■	■	■	■		■	■	■	■	■		■		■									■	■										■		■		
3471		■	■	■		■		■	■	■	■	■	■	■	■					■			■	■	■					■	■				■		■					■		■						■

▲ Sequence Number—indicates the order of the college in this book only. Do *not* use this number with admissions tests or need analysis services.

[1] No campus room and board facilities
[2] Room only or board only
[3] Most freshmen required to live on campus
[4] City or district residency requirements
[5] Accredited by regional accrediting association or a recognized candidate for accreditation
[6] All female freshman class
[7] All male freshman class
[8] Some admission selectivity; not all hs graduates accepted
[9] Requirements more stringent for nonresidents
†Accredited by a nationally recognized accrediting body other than one of the regional accrediting associations

West Virginia
(continued)

Sequence Number	School name (upper entry) / City (lower entry)	Enrollment	Resident tuition/fees + room/board	Room/board (upper entry) / Nonresident tuition/fees (lower entry)	Affiliation (upper entry) / Religious observance (lower entry)	Size of community	Type of community	Fall term application deadline (upper entry) / Test required or desired (lower entry)	Calendar	Fall term application deadline (upper entry) / Forms to be filed (lower entry)	-have need, rec some aid	-are women	-live on campus	-are minority students	-are nonresidents	-return as sophomores	-complete assoc degree	-transfer to 4-year college
3472	St Mary's Sch Nsg / Huntington	176	3300	[1] / 4500	Cath	M [8]		5/01 / ACT	4 †	6/01 / FAF	6	9	0	1	2	9	7	
3473	W Va Career C / Charleston	140	6000	[1]	Priv	M [8]	U	0/01 / Oth	Q †	10/01 / Oth	7	8	0	2	0	3	7	1
3474	W Va Northern CC / Wheeling	1086	900	[1] / 2700	Pub	S		A/S	E [5]	6/01 / FA/FF	4	7	0	1	2		7	3
3475	W Va U Sch Radiology / Morgantown	30	800	[1]	Priv	S [8]		ACT	S †	5/15 / FF/FA	3	8		0	5		9	
3476	W Va U-Parkersburg / Parkersburg	1662	700	[1] / 2100	Pub	M	S	ACT	E [5]	5/01	3	6	0	1	1		1	1
3477	Wood Co Sch Nsg / Parkersburg	50	900	[1] / 1000	Pub	S [8]		3/30 / A=S	O [5]	Oth	7	9	0	1			9	
Wisconsin																		
3478	Blackhawk Tech C / Janesville	2300	900	[1] / 4500	Pub	M		8/15 / Oth	E [5]	4/15 / FF/FA	6	6	0	1	1		6	1
3479	Chippewa Vly Tech C / Eau Claire	3800	1100	[1] / 8100	Pub	M		8/20 / Oth	S [5]	3/01 / FAF	7	5	0	1	0	6	4	1
3480	Fox Valley Tech C / Appleton	4256	1300	[1] / 9100	Pub	M	S	Oth	Q [5]	FFS	8	5	0	1	1	6	6	1
3481	Gateway Tech C / Kenosha	2119	1100	[1] / 8300	Pub	M	U	8/29 / Oth	S [5]	FAF	6	6	0	1	1	6	5	1
3482	Lakeshore Tech C / Cleveland	1090	1200	[1] / 7000	Pub	T		A=S	S [5]	FAF	9	5	0	1	1	3	6	1
3483	Madison Area Tech C / Madison	7252	1200	[1] / 9400	Pub	M	U	8/01 / Oth	S [5]	FAF	7	5	0	1	1			
3484	Madison Business C / Madison	271	3100	[1]	Priv	L	S	9/23 / None	T †		5	8	0	1	1	7	5	
3485	Mid-State Tech C / Wisconsin Rapid	933	1300	[1] / 8400	Pub	S		Oth	S [5]	FF/FA	7	6	0	1	1	6	4	1
3486	Milwaukee Area Tech / Milwaukee	5546	1500	[1] / 8600	Pub	V [8]	U	8/20 / Oth	S [5]	FFS	7	5	0	3	1	4		1
3487	Milwaukee Sch Nsg / Milwaukee	152	4300 [2]	1400 / 4700	Pub	V [8]	U	A/S	S †	7/30 / FF/FA		9	1	1	1	7	8	
3488	Moraine Park Tech / Fond du Lac	739	1300	[1] / 9100	Pub	S		5/01 / Oth	S [5]	5/01 / FA/FF	4	6	0	1	1	8	7	1
3489	Moraine Park Tech / West Bend	322	1300	[1] / 9100	Pub	S		5/01 / Oth	S [5]	5/01 / FA/FF	4	6	0	1	1	6	7	1
3490	Nicolet Area Tech C / Rhinelander	434	1300	[1] / 7300	Pub	T		9/04 / Oth	S [5]	FF/FA	8	7	0	1	1	6	2	2
3491	North Central Tech / Wausau	2200	3800	2400 / 11100	Pub	S		7/01 / None	E [5]	FFS	9	6		1	1	6	6	1
3492	Northeast Wis Tech / Green Bay	2144	1300	[1] / 9400	Pub	M	S	ACT	S [5]	FA/FF	4	6	0	1	0		4	1
3493	Southwest Wis Tech C / Fennimore	606	1400	[1] / 10000	Pub	T		Oth	E [5]	7/15 / FA/FF	9	6	0	1	1	6		1

Educational Programs Available — College Transfer Courses; Career-oriented Programs (Agri, Business)

Sequence Number	Agriculture	Bus-Commerce	Communications	Education	Engineering	Fine, Applied Arts	Foreign Lang	Health	Home Ec	Humanities	Mathematics	Computer/Info Sci	Biological Sci	Physical Sci	Social Sci	Ag Business	Ag/Farm Mgmt	Ag Mechanics/Tech	Horticulture	Accounting	Bus Mgmt & Admin	Hotel/Rest Mgmt	Office Mgmt	Marketing/Purchasing	Secretarial Studies
3472																									
3473																				■	■		■		■
3474		■	■	■	■	■		■	■	■	■	■	■	■	■					■	■		■		■
3475																									
3476			■	■	■	■	■	■		■	■		■	■	■					■				■	■
3477																									
3478	■	■	■		■	■		■	■		■	■			■	■	■			■				■	■
3479																■	■	■		■		■		■	■
3480																■	■	■	■	■		■	■	■	■
3481			■														■		■	■		■	■	■	■
3482																	■			■				■	■
3483	■	■	■			■	■		■	■	■		■	■	■			■		■	■	■	■	■	■
3484		■										■								■	■			■	■
3485		■							■			■			■		■			■	■	■		■	■
3486	■	■	■	■	■	■	■	■	■	■	■	■	■	■	■	■	■		■	■			■		■
3487																									
3488		■																		■	■		■	■	
3489																				■				■	■
3490		■		■		■	■		■	■	■		■	■	■					■	■	■	■	■	■
3491		■			■					■		■				■	■	■		■				■	■
3492		■						■				■	■	■	■	■				■				■	■
3493	■	■						■	■			■				■	■	■		■	■			■	■

Educational Programs Available — Career-oriented Programs (Arts, Health, Math, SocSci, Technical/Skilled Trades)

Sequence Number	Architecture Tech	Applied Design	Photography/Cinema	Dental Assistant	Medical or Lab Tech	Nursing (RN)	Nursing (LPN)	Radiologic Technology	Computer Prog	Data Processing Tech	Computer Operating	Crim Just/Law Enforce	Parks/Rec Mgmt	Social Work	Air/Refrig/Heat Tech	Auto Body Repair	Auto Mechanics	Carpentry/Constr	Drafting/Eng Draft	Electric Eng Tech	Civil Eng Tech	Indus/Mfg Eng Tech	Mech Eng Tech	Machinework	Welding
3472						■																			
3473					■					■	■														
3474					■	■		■	■	■		■													
3475								■																	
3476						■						■		■	■		■		■				■		■
3477							■																		
3478				■		■			■	■		■				■	■	■	■	■				■	■
3479					■	■	■	■	■			■			■	■	■	■	■	■	■		■	■	■
3480				■		■	■		■	■	■	■				■	■	■	■	■			■	■	■
3481				■	■	■	■		■	■	■	■		■		■	■		■	■	■	■	■	■	■
3482				■		■		■		■		■				■	■		■	■			■	■	■
3483	■	■	■	■	■	■	■	■	■	■	■	■				■	■	■	■		■		■	■	■
3484									■																
3485					■					■	■	■				■	■	■		■	■	■	■	■	■
3486					■	■	■	■	■						■	■	■	■	■	■				■	■
3487						■																			
3488						■	■		■			■			■	■	■			■	■	■	■	■	
3489						■																		■	
3490						■				■	■						■		■				■	■	■
3491	■					■		■	■			■				■	■		■				■	■	■
3492				■			■			■						■	■	■	■	■		■		■	■
3493						■	■		■	■	■					■	■						■	■	■

▲ **Sequence Number—indicates the order of the college in this book only.** ***Do not use this number with admissions tests or need analysis services.***

1 No campus room and board facilities
2 *Room only or board only*
3 Most freshmen required to live on campus
4 City or district residency requirements
5 *Accredited by regional accrediting association* or a recognized candidate for accreditation
6 All female freshman class
7 All male freshman class
8 *Some admission selectivity; not all hs graduates accepted*
9 Requirements more stringent for nonresidents
†Accredited by a nationally recognized *accrediting body other than one of the* regional accrediting associations

Wisconsin

(continued)

Sequence Number	School name (upper entry) City (lower entry)	Enrollment	Costs: Resident tuition/fees + room/board	Costs: Room/board (upper entry) Nonresident tuition/fees (lower entry)	Gen. Info.: Affiliation (upper entry) Religious observance (lower entry)	Gen. Info.: Size of community	Gen. Info.: Type of community	Admissions: Fall term application deadline (upper entry) Test required or desired (lower entry)	Admissions: Calendar	Financial Aid: Fall term application deadline (upper entry) Forms to be filed (lower entry)
3494	Stratton C Milwaukee	381	5400	[1]	Priv	V[8]	U	Oth	Q †	Oth
3495	Waukesha Co Tech C Pewaukee	1308	1200	[1] 8100	Pub	M		None	E[5]	FF=FA
3496	West Wis Tech C La Crosse	1676	4800	3600 12400	Pub	M		Oth	Q[5]	FA/FF
3497	Wis Center Barron,U Rice Lake	400	1400	[1] 4300	Pub	T[8]		8/15 ACT	E[5]	10/01 FF=FA
3498	Wis Ctr Baraboo,U Baraboo	285	1300	[1] 4200	Pub	T[8]		A/S	E[5]	FA/FF
3499	Wis Ctr Fox Vly,U of Menasha	710	1400	[1] 5500	Pub	M	U	9/01 ACT	E[5]	4/15 FF=FA
3500	Wis Ctr Manitowoc,U Manitowoc	354	1400	[1] 4100	Pub	S		A/S	E[5]	FF=FA
3501	Wis Ctr Marathon,U Wausau	878	1400	[1] 4200	Pub	M		8/01 A/S	E[5]	FA/FF
3502	Wis Ctr Marinette,U Marinette	232	1500	[1] 4400	Pub	S[8]		ACT	E[5]	FF=FA
3503	Wis Ctr Marshfld,U Marshfield	386	1400[2]	4300	Pub	S		ACT	E[5]	FF=FA
3504	Wis Ctr Richland,U Richland Center	425	4900	3300 7900	Pub	T[8]		8/04 ACT	E[5]	4/15 FF=FA
3505	Wis Ctr Rock Co,U of Janesville	469	1400	[1] 4200	Pub	M		ACT	E[5]	3/01 FF=FA
3506	Wis Ctr Sheboygan,U Sheboygan	436	1400	[1] 4200	Pub	S[8]		8/15 ACT	E[5]	3/01 FF=FA
3507	Wis Ctr Washington,U West Bend	569	1400	[1] 4300	Pub	S[8]		ACT	E[5]	FF=FA
3508	Wis Ctr Waukesha,U Waukesha	1234	1400	[1] 4200	Pub	M[8]	S	ACT	E[5]	3/01 FA/FF
3509	Wis Fond Du Lac,U Fond Du Lac	449	1400	[1] 4300	Pub	S[8]		ACT	E[5]	FA/FF
3510	Wis Indianhead Tech Ashland	203	1200	[1] 9400	Pub	T[8]		Oth	S[5]	FF/FA
3511	Wis Indianhead Tech New Richmond	339	1200	[1] 9400	Pub	T		9/15 Oth	S[5]	FF/FA
3512	Wis Indianhead Tech Rice Lake	576	1200	[1] 9400	Pub	T		8/23 Oth	S[5]	FAF
3513	Wis Indianhead Tech Superior	421	1200	[1] 9400	Pub	S		0/30 Oth	S[5]	
3514	Wisconsin Sch Electr Madison	325	5500	[1]	Priv	M	U	0/10 Oth	T †	Oth

Student Profile — No. in 10 who- and **Educational Programs Available — College Transfer Courses**

Sequence Number	-have need, rec some aid	-are women	-live on campus	-are minority students	-are nonresidents	-return as sophomores	-complete assoc degree	-transfer to 4-year college	Agriculture	Bus-Commerce	Communications	Education	Engineering	Fine, Applied Arts	Foreign Lang	Health	Home Ec	Humanities	Mathematics	Computer/Info Sci	Biological Sci	Physical Sci	Social Sci
3494	9	7	0	5						■						■				■			
3495	2	4	0	1	0	5	4			■													
3496	6	6	1	1	1	7	4	1	■	■				■			■			■			■
3497	7	5	0	1	1	6	5	7	■	■	■	■	■	■	■	■	■	■	■	■	■	■	■
3498	7	6	0	1	1	5	2	6	■	■	■	■	■	■	■	■	■	■	■	■	■	■	■
3499	3	6	0	1	1	7	2	7	■	■	■	■	■	■	■	■	■	■	■	■		■	■
3500	5	5	0	1	0	7	3	7	■	■	■	■	■	■	■	■	■	■	■	■	■	■	■
3501	7	6	2	1	1	8	5	5	■	■	■	■	■	■	■	■	■	■	■	■	■	■	■
3502	6	6	0	1	3	5			■	■	■	■	■	■		■	■	■	■	■	■	■	■
3503	5	6	0	1	0	4	1	8	■	■	■	■	■	■	■	■	■	■	■	■		■	■
3504	7	5	1	1	1	5	5	7	■	■	■	■	■	■		■	■	■	■	■	■	■	■
3505	3	6	0	1	1	7	5	4	■	■	■	■	■	■	■	■	■	■	■	■		■	■
3506	3	5	0	1	0	3				■	■	■	■	■	■	■	■	■	■	■	■	■	■
3507	4	5	0	1	1	6			■	■	■	■	■	■	■	■	■	■	■	■	■	■	■
3508	2	5	0	1	1	5		9	■	■	■	■	■	■	■	■	■	■	■	■	■	■	■
3509	4	5	0	1	0	2			■	■	■	■	■	■	■	■	■	■	■	■	■	■	■
3510	7	8	0	1	1		7	1		■						■	■						
3511	7	6	0	1	1		7	1		■						■							
3512	7	5	0	1	1		7	1		■						■				■			
3513	7	5		1	1		7	1		■						■				■			
3514		1	0	1	1	9	8																

Educational Programs Available — Career-oriented Programs (Agri, Business, Arts, Health)

Sequence Number	Ag Business	Ag/Farm Mgmt	Ag Mechanics/Tech	Horticulture	Accounting	Bus Mgmt & Admin	Hotel/Rest Mgmt	Office Mgmt	Marketing/Purchasing	Secretarial Studies	Architecture Tech	Applied Design	Photography/Cinema	Dental Assistant	Medical or Lab Tech	Nursing (RN)	Nursing (LPN)	Radiologic Technology
3494					■	■	■	■	■	■								
3495					■				■	■						■		
3496	■	■			■	■		■	■	■				■	■	■	■	■
3497																		
3498																		
3499																		
3500																		
3501																		
3502																		
3503																		
3504																		
3505																		
3506																		
3507																		
3508																		
3509																		
3510		■			■					■						■		
3511		■	■		■				■	■						■		
3512	■	■			■				■	■						■		
3513					■				■	■								
3514																		

Educational Programs Available — Career-oriented Programs (Math, SocSci, Technical/Skilled Trades)

Sequence Number	Computer Prog	Data Processing Tech	Computer Operating	Crim Just/Law Enforce	Parks/Rec Mgmt	Social Work	Air/Refrig/Heat Tech	Auto Body Repair	Auto Mechanics	Carpentry/Constr	Drafting/Eng Draft	Electric Eng Tech	Civil Eng Tech	Indus/Mfg Eng Tech	Mech Eng Tech	Machinework	Welding
3494	■	■	■														
3495		■	■	■				■	■		■	■			■	■	■
3496	■	■		■			■	■	■	■	■	■		■	■	■	■
3497																	
3498																	
3499																	
3500																	
3501																	
3502																	
3503																	
3504																	
3505																	
3506																	
3507																	
3508																	
3509																	
3510																■	
3511												■				■	
3512				■				■	■	■	■				■	■	■
3513		■							■		■					■	■
3514											■						

▲ Sequence Number—indicates the order of the college in this book only. Do *not* use this number with admissions tests or need analysis services.

[1] No campus room and board facilities
[2] Room only or board only
[3] Most freshmen required to live on campus
[4] City or district residency requirements
[5] Accredited by regional accrediting association or a recognized candidate for accreditation
[6] All female freshman class
[7] All male freshman class
[8] Some admission selectivity; not all hs graduates accepted
[9] Requirements more stringent for nonresidents
†Accredited by a nationally recognized accrediting body other than one of the regional accrediting associations

Wyoming

Sequence Number	School name (upper entry) City (lower entry)	Enrollment	Costs: Resident tuition/fees + room/board	Costs: Room/board (upper entry) Nonresident tuition/fees (lower entry)	Gen. Info.: Affiliation (upper entry) Religious observance (lower entry)	Gen. Info.: Size of community	Gen. Info.: Type of community	Admissions: Fall term application deadline (upper entry) Test required or desired (lower entry)	Admissions: Calendar	Financial Aid: Fall term application deadline (upper entry) Forms to be filed (lower entry)
3515	Casper C Casper	1913	2700	2100 3300	Pub	M		8/15 A/S	E 5	FA/FF
3516	Central Wyoming C Riverton	655	3100	2400 3600	Pub	T		Oth	E 5	3/16 FF=FA
3517	Eastern Wyoming C Torrington	485	2600	2000 3200	Pub	T		9/01 A/S	E 5	4/01 FF=FA
3518	Laramie Co CC Cheyenne	1202	3600	3000 4200	Pub	M		8/29 None	E 5	4/01 FA/FF
3519	Northwest CC Powell	1000	3000 3	2200 3400	Pub	T 8		8/15 A/S	E 5	FF/FA
3520	Sheridan C Sheridan	888	2900	2200 3400	Pub	S		A/S	E 5	4/01 FF=FA
3521	Western Wyoming CC Rock Springs	780	2700	2100 3300	Pub	S		A/S	E 5	4/01 FA/FF

Student Profile — No. in 10 who-

Sequence Number	-have need, rec some aid	-are women	-live on campus	-are minority students	-are nonresidents	-return as sophomores	-complete assoc degree	-transfer to 4-year college
3515	6	5	3	1	1	4	4	6
3516	4	6	5	2	1	4		3
3517	8	7	4	1	2	7	6	5
3518	5	6	1	1	1	3	2	2
3519	7	5	7	1	2	7	6	7
3520	7	6	3	1	1	6	3	4
3521	6	7	2	1	1		4	3

Educational Programs Available — College Transfer Courses

Sequence Number	Agriculture	Bus-Commerce	Communications	Education	Engineering	Fine, Applied Arts	Foreign Lang	Health	Home Ec	Humanities	Mathematics	Computer/Info Sci	Biological Sci	Physical Sci	Social Sci
3515	■	■	■	■	■	■	■	■	■	■	■	■	■	■	■
3516	■	■	■	■	■	■	■	■		■	■	■	■	■	■
3517	■	■	■	■		■	■	■	■	■	■	■	■	■	■
3518	■	■	■	■	■	■	■	■		■	■	■	■	■	■
3519	■	■	■	■	■	■	■	■	■	■	■	■	■	■	■
3520	■	■		■	■	■	■	■		■	■	■	■	■	■
3521		■	■	■	■	■	■	■		■	■	■	■	■	■

Educational Programs Available — Career-oriented Programs (Agri, Business, Arts, Health)

Sequence Number	Agri: Ag Business	Agri: Ag/Farm Mgmt	Agri: Ag Mechanics/Tech	Agri: Horticulture	Business: Accounting	Business: Bus Mgmt & Admin	Business: Hotel/Rest Mgmt	Business: Office Mgmt	Business: Marketing/Purchasing	Business: Secretarial Studies	Arts: Architecture Tech	Arts: Applied Design	Arts: Photography/Cinema	Health: Dental Assistant	Health: Medical or Lab Tech	Health: Nursing (RN)	Health: Nursing (LPN)	Health: Radiologic Technology
3515			■		■	■		■	■	■		■				■	■	■
3516	■				■	■		■	■	■						■		
3517	■	■	■					■		■								
3518	■	■	■							■						■		■
3519	■	■		■	■			■	■	■		■			■		■	
3520										■				■		■	■	
3521					■	■				■				■			■	■

Educational Programs Available — Career-oriented Programs (Math, SocSci, Technical/Skilled Trades)

Sequence Number	Math: Computer Prog	Math: Data Processing Tech	Math: Computer Operating	SocSci: Crim Just/Law Enforce	SocSci: Parks/Rec Mgmt	SocSci: Social Work	Air/Refrig/Heat Tech	Auto Body Repair	Auto Mechanics	Carpentry/Constr	Drafting/Eng Draft	Electric Eng Tech	Civil Eng Tech	Indus/Mfg Eng Tech	Mech Eng Tech	Machinework	Welding
3515		■	■	■					■	■	■					■	■
3516		■	■	■		■			■		■						■
3517			■	■			■										■
3518	■			■				■	■	■	■		■				■
3519		■															■
3520				■					■			■	■			■	■
3521		■	■							■	■	■				■	■

▲ Sequence Number—indicates the order of the college in this book only. Do *not* use this number with admissions tests or need analysis services.

1 No campus room and board facilities
2 Room only or board only
3 Most freshmen required to live on campus
4 City or district residency requirements
5 Accredited by regional accrediting association or a recognized candidate for accreditation
6 All female freshman class
7 All male freshman class
8 Some admission selectivity; not all hs graduates accepted
9 Requirements more stringent for nonresidents
†Accredited by a nationally recognized accrediting body other than one of the regional accrediting associations

Index of additional career-oriented programs at two-year colleges

On the two-year college **Search** pages, indicators (■) show which of 15 college transfer course areas and 35 career-oriented programs are offered by each college. On the following pages, sequence numbers are provided to identify two-year schools offering the 39 **additional career-oriented programs** shown in the outline on the next page.

These career-oriented programs are intended primarily to prepare students for employment and vary in length from less than a year to more than two years; some may result in a two-year associate degree.

Suggestions for using this index

Which colleges in a state offer a specific career-oriented program?

To identify colleges in a state that offer one of the career-oriented programs on the list on the next page, follow these steps:

1. Turn back to the two-year **Search** section and note the lowest and highest sequence numbers for schools in that state.

2. Find the career-oriented program you are considering on the following pages. Scan the numbers listed under that program to see if any are in the sequence number range for the state that interests you.

For example, assume you would like to find out which schools in Alabama offer agricultural technology programs. First note that the sequence number range for colleges in Alabama is 2001-2055.

Then turn to the listing for **1. Agriculture, Forestry, Wildlife Technologies** on page 266. There you will see that only the college assigned sequence number 2014 offers this program in Alabama. Jot down this sequence number and turn back to the **Search** pages to identify the college and check other information about it.

Is a specific career-oriented program available at the college you are considering?

Identify the sequence number for the college you're interested in by checking the **College Index** or the **Search** pages. Then, look for that sequence number among those listed for that specific career-oriented program.

Additional career-oriented programs at two-year colleges

Agriculture*

1. Agriculture, Forestry, Wildlife Technologies
2. Agronomy
3. Animal Science
4. Fish, Game, and Wildlife Management
5. Food Science and Technology
6. Forestry
7. Natural Resources Management

Business*

8. Banking and Finance
9. Real Estate and Insurance
10. Recreation and Tourism
11. Transportation and Public Utilities

Communications

12. Journalism
13. Radio/Television (related to broadcasting)
14. Advertising

Education

15. Education, general

Engineering (see Technical/Skilled Trades)

Fine/Applied Arts*

16. Community and Regional Planning
17. Interior Design
18. Art (painting, drawing, sculpting)

Health Professions*

19. Dental Hygiene
20. Dental Lab Technology
21. Medical Assistant or Medical Office Assistant
22. Occupational Therapy
23. Physical Therapy
24. Radiology
25. Surgical Technology
26. Veterinary Medicine

Home Economics

27. Clothing and Textiles
28. Family Relations, Child Development
29. Foods and Nutrition

Math/Physical Sciences*

30. Biological Sciences, general
31. Physical Sciences, general

Social Sciences*

32. Community Service, general
33. Social Sciences, general
34. Psychology
35. Sociology

Technical/Skilled Trades*

36. Aeronautical, Aviation Technology
37. Data Systems Repair
38. Engineering Technology-Electrical
39. Engineering Technology-Aeronautical

---

*Other career-oriented programs in this area are shown on pages 195-263 in the two-year college **Search** section.

1. Agriculture, Forestry Wildlife Technologies

2014 2065 2102 2104 2107 2111 2129 2135 2138 2146
2155 2162 2167 2170 2174 2175 2178 2190 2195 2197
2198 2210 2224 2269 2296 2303 2368 2369 2380 2386
2387 2390 2392 2424 2428 2438 2461 2478 2486 2492
2494 2500 2511 2514 2515 2523 2583 2634 2703 2711
2716 2718 2735 2752 2758 2761 2777 2785 2793 2830
2845 2847 2849 2851 2977 2978 3022 3065 3066 3118
3129 3142 3146 3158 3163 3173 3236 3258 3264 3268
3325 3375 3382 3447 3455 3457 3461 3462 3470 3480
3516 3519

2. Agronomy

2065 2104 2107 2126 2129 2143 2146 2167 2169 2170
2174 2175 2190 2195 2204 2207 2210 2224 2288 2303
2362 2383 2390 2392 2413 2428 2476 2486 2512 2514
2516 2523 2531 2583 2692 2735 2736 2795 2842 2847
2851 2854 2977 2978 2980 3117 3118 3159 3173 3328
3337 3361 3375 3457 3464 3511

3. Animal Science

2065 2074 2104 2107 2143 2146 2150 2155 2163 2167
2169 2170 2174 2181 2190 2195 2196 2197 2198 2204
2207 2224 2303 2342 2353 2362 2363 2385 2390 2424
2471 2472 2478 2486 2507 2509 2512 2513 2514 2516
2519 2535 2583 2633 2634 2711 2725 2735 2736 2752
2761 2773 2793 2795 2797 2804 2830 2847 2851 2977
2978 2980 3024 3029 3056 3066 3117 3118 3159 3163
3166 3173 3185 3192 3325 3337 3342 3357 3361 3375
3382 3405 3416 3457 3478 3483 3519

4. Fish, Game, or Wildlife Management

2104 2107 2129 2135 2146 2167 2170 2178 2190 2209
2303 2363 2424 2461 2479 2486 2492 2583 2617 2711
2735 2756 2758 2937 2943 2977 3022 3056 3065 3092
3145 3167 3204 3268 3325 3375 3409 3443 3450 3457
3480

5. Food Science and Technology

2077 2091 2104 2107 2113 2114 2116 2121 2129 2137
2138 2148 2151 2152 2163 2167 2170 2174 2177 2178
2190 2195 2204 2210 2239 2255 2281 2284 2293 2303
2355 2356 2357 2413 2424 2427 2461 2467 2474 2483
2516 2546 2573 2583 2601 2605 2607 2640 2667 2669
2670 2675 2676 2678 2687 2694 2698 2699 2702 2735
2736 2738 2749 2771 2778 2813 2820 2842 2844 2863
2871 2888 2912 2945 2954 2967 2975 2977 2978 2981
2983 2987 2998 3004 3020 3027 3050 3085 3117 3152
3157 3161 3166 3167 3181 3182 3235 3236 3258 3314
3336 3338 3342 3348 3361 3368 3370 3373 3375 3385
3393 3420 3438 3439 3441 3442 3448 3451 3454 3455
3456 3480 3481 3488

6. Forestry

2028 2036 2038 2056 2075 2076 2103 2104 2107 2114
2118 2129 2135 2146 2167 2170 2178 2181 2190 2195
2198 2264 2269 2284 2303 2349 2350 2427 2479 2583
2606 2607 2640 2711 2714 2727 2735 2756 2778 2832
2863 2907 2943 2945 2967 2978 2981 3022 3033 3049
3056 3065 3092 3118 3142 3160 3161 3167 3171 3173
3187 3198 3213 3236 3239 3268 3364 3409 3420 3438
3444 3457 3480

7. Natural Resources Management

2034 2102 2104 2107 2114 2118 2129 2146 2155 2167
2170 2175 2190 2197 2198 2204 2217 2230 2303 2391
2424 2438 2471 2476 2479 2486 2516 2550 2583 2605
2617 2634 2640 2684 2698 2711 2721 2735 2756 2758
2847 2851 2863 2907 2938 2943 2945 2977 2978 3065
3092 3113 3118 3143 3169 3173 3236 3248 3325 3375
3416 3455 3457 3480

8. Banking and Finance

2003 2007 2009 2013 2014 2020 2025 2026 2030 2040
2041 2042 2045 2054 2065 2068 2069 2070 2071 2072
2077 2078 2079 2080 2088 2090 2091 2093 2100 2102
2104 2105 2107 2108 2113 2114 2116 2117 2119 2125
2129 2130 2132 2133 2137 2138 2140 2142 2148 2151
2152 2153 2154 2156 2157 2158 2162 2163 2166 2167
2168 2169 2170 2172 2173 2175 2176 2177 2178 2179
2180 2182 2183 2185 2186 2187 2190 2191 2192 2193
2194 2195 2196 2197 2198 2200 2201 2202 2204 2205
2206 2210 2212 2213 2227 2239 2251 2252 2253 2254
2255 2257 2258 2259 2261 2262 2263 2264 2265 2266
2270 2271 2273 2275 2277 2279 2280 2284 2286 2290
2293 2295 2299 2309 2317 2319 2323 2334 2340 2341
2342 2357 2359 2365 2367 2369 2371 2372 2379 2380
2381 2383 2384 2388 2392 2393 2397 2404 2406 2408
2410 2413 2414 2416 2417 2420 2423 2426 2434 2439
2440 2458 2461 2464 2467 2477 2486 2488 2494 2497
2507 2508 2509 2516 2523 2524 2528 2535 2536 2538
2541 2545 2546 2550 2552 2557 2561 2569 2575 2582
2583 2595 2607 2609 2611 2613 2615 2619 2620 2622
2625 2627 2634 2638 2647 2651 2653 2657 2665 2667
2673 2675 2677 2678 2679 2681 2683 2684 2685 2686
2687 2688 2698 2702 2703 2711 2712 2716 2721 2722
2726 2735 2749 2753 2754 2769 2771 2780 2784 2789
2790 2808 2814 2817 2820 2821 2822 2825 2826 2853
2858 2859 2860 2868 2871 2872 2877 2883 2886 2887
2889 2890 2891 2892 2897 2898 2901 2905 2907 2909
2911 2912 2926 2929 2935 2940 2942 2945 2948 2949
2950 2954 2955 2959 2965 2966 2970 2975 2978 2980
2987 2989 2991 2992 2995 2996 2997 2998 3007 3008
3009 3017 3019 3020 3023 3027 3032 3034 3038 3042
3050 3054 3055 3057 3059 3066 3074 3081 3082 3084
3085 3086 3088 3092 3093 3094 3095 3097 3102 3103
3104 3106 3110 3111 3115 3117 3123 3127 3129 3134
3135 3145 3147 3152 3154 3157 3161 3165 3166 3167
3168 3169 3170 3171 3175 3176 3177 3179 3180 3182
3184 3186 3188 3191 3196 3216 3220 3225 3237 3239
3255 3256 3259 3262 3268 3269 3275 3277 3280 3284
3296 3297 3299 3302 3305 3309 3311 3312 3315 3316
3318 3319 3320 3322 3325 3332 3333 3336 3337 3338
3339 3342 3343 3346 3348 3352 3358 3359 3361 3367
3369 3370 3371 3375 3376 3379 3380 3381 3389 3396
3400 3405 3407 3409 3410 3413 3416 3429 3430 3431
3434 3435 3446 3447 3452 3458 3465 3466 3474 3476
3478 3480 3481 3482 3483 3486 3491 3493 3496 3510
3512 3521

9. Real Estate and Insurance

2009 2013 2025 2026 2034 2040 2041 2042 2054 2065
2071 2077 2078 2080 2088 2104 2107 2108 2110 2111
2113 2114 2119 2120 2121 2122 2124 2127 2136 2138
2141 2145 2147 2149 2152 2154 2155 2158 2159 2164
2165 2166 2167 2170 2171 2172 2173 2176 2180 2181
2182 2183 2185 2186 2188 2192 2193 2194 2195 2197
2198 2199 2207 2209 2211 2212 2229 2236 2247 2255
2258 2261 2272 2273 2275 2276 2277 2279 2280 2284
2290 2291 2292 2293 2295 2299 2327 2336 2339 2367
2369 2371 2375 2376 2379 2380 2386 2387 2389 2390
2391 2393 2396 2404 2406 2408 2410 2413 2414 2419
2420 2423 2424 2426 2427 2434 2439 2440 2461 2467
2470 2497 2516 2523 2538 2541 2546 2549 2557 2582
2610 2614 2619 2638 2643 2652 2654 2665 2679 2712
2726 2735 2737 2754 2760 2822 2841 2842 2845 2846
2849 2851 2858 2860 2861 2868 2872 2876 2877 2883
2885 2889 2892 2897 2909 2924 2929 2942 2944 2948
2961 2966 2970 2976 2980 2987 2990 2992 2995 3001
3003 3005 3008 3009 3017 3023 3031 3044 3048 3049
3051 3055 3057 3078 3079 3080 3082 3084 3086 3087
3088 3092 3093 3103 3104 3106 3117 3119 3127 3129
3134 3135 3136 3141 3145 3152 3157 3158 3161 3164
3165 3168 3169 3173 3176 3177 3178 3184 3186 3190
3191 3193 3196 3216 3222 3229 3236 3255 3284 3305
3315 3316 3318 3320 3321 3322 3325 3329 3331 3336

9. Real Estate and Insurance (continued)

3337 3339 3341 3342 3343 3347 3348 3351 3352 3353 3358 3359 3362 3368 3369 3370 3371 3372 3373 3376 3379 3386 3387 3389 3396 3405 3414 3416 3420 3421 3424 3429 3431 3434 3435 3436 3437 3439 3440 3444 3446 3448 3449 3451 3452 3458 3479 3481 3483 3485 3490 3491 3495

10. Recreation and Tourism

2013 2057 2077 2078 2102 2103 2104 2107 2109 2113 2117 2125 2136 2138 2143 2149 2152 2156 2158 2159 2160 2170 2177 2178 2180 2185 2186 2187 2188 2202 2206 2207 2208 2212 2215 2217 2219 2226 2227 2237 2253 2255 2258 2272 2275 2276 2282 2291 2294 2295 2323 2338 2357 2360 2371 2375 2376 2379 2383 2384 2395 2398 2402 2404 2408 2409 2413 2418 2419 2420 2435 2439 2458 2461 2463 2464 2465 2467 2468 2478 2479 2503 2510 2512 2523 2527 2557 2564 2595 2598 2615 2622 2630 2631 2633 2636 2639 2641 2645 2647 2648 2649 2651 2653 2654 2655 2660 2661 2679 2687 2690 2696 2702 2708 2711 2712 2735 2740 2760 2788 2796 2806 2814 2821 2843 2859 2861 2871 2872 2873 2874 2875 2886 2887 2892 2900 2912 2917 2918 2920 2921 2922 2923 2924 2934 2935 2937 2943 2946 2948 2954 2956 2957 2960 2966 2967 2970 2972 2975 2976 2977 2978 2984 2987 3001 3009 3026 3043 3062 3074 3082 3087 3092 3102 3104 3112 3116 3128 3145 3148 3182 3185 3187 3190 3191 3194 3196 3220 3221 3222 3227 3228 3236 3259 3276 3312 3316 3336 3342 3359 3387 3393 3396 3398 3399 3418 3420 3441 3444 3445 3468 3479 3481 3483 3494 3510

11. Transportation and Public Utilities

2026 2057 2078 2127 2141 2152 2170 2200 2219 2254 2284 2371 2375 2381 2404 2410 2413 2434 2503 2610 2630 2670 2679 2722 2741 2742 2877 2887 2961 3007 3009 3014 3074 3084 3086 3127 3135 3149 3169 3186 3225 3284 3322 3334 3336 3342 3368 3381 3396 3481 3492

12. Journalism

2013 2025 2102 2103 2104 2108 2114 2120 2121 2125 2129 2132 2133 2137 2138 2140 2141 2148 2151 2152 2155 2156 2157 2158 2164 2167 2169 2170 2173 2174 2177 2178 2180 2182 2183 2185 2187 2190 2197 2200 2202 2203 2207 2213 2219 2236 2250 2263 2281 2295 2303 2326 2372 2379 2381 2386 2413 2435 2440 2461 2467 2479 2511 2515 2522 2529 2548 2557 2563 2583 2633 2679 2692 2760 2851 2870 2876 2890 2893 2937 2948 2978 3032 3127 3139 3146 3154 3158 3159 3166 3167 3176 3177 3178 3191 3198 3268 3316 3336 3345 3353 3362 3370 3371 3372 3375 3386 3421 3431 3444 3445 3476 3519

13. Radio/Television (related to broadcasting)

2009 2020 2025 2033 2065 2078 2085 2104 2107 2113 2114 2119 2120 2121 2133 2138 2142 2148 2150 2151 2152 2158 2167 2169 2170 2173 2174 2175 2177 2178 2182 2185 2186 2187 2190 2192 2194 2195 2202 2227 2233 2238 2240 2261 2263 2275 2284 2286 2320 2367 2381 2389 2392 2393 2413 2438 2442 2446 2461 2463 2476 2486 2512 2514 2516 2523 2557 2598 2608 2609 2618 2619 2622 2623 2633 2639 2650 2651 2657 2665 2670 2676 2679 2687 2691 2692 2694 2707 2710 2714 2734 2743 2748 2756 2757 2774 2776 2784 2820 2842 2849 2851 2876 2887 2890 2909 2912 2925 2937 2946 2948 2965 2975 2987 3008 3019 3023 3027 3050 3058 3092 3121 3128 3135 3146 3147 3152 3159 3165 3167 3169 3180 3190 3191 3196 3250 3284 3315 3316 3337 3353 3357 3362 3369 3373 3380 3421 3431 3444 3458 3465 3481 3516

14. Advertising

2033 2043 2069 2102 2104 2106 2107 2111 2113 2116 2117 2122 2125 2129 2140 2141 2151 2152 2170 2177 2178 2180 2185 2187 2191 2210 2268 2275 2284 2309 2319 2363 2375 2395 2402 2408 2413 2420 2423 2426 2461 2476 2486 2510 2511 2516 2522 2528 2529 2548 2573 2579 2619 2622 2630 2633 2669 2676 2678 2679 2692 2702 2712 2713 2725 2734 2747 2754 2759 2777 2793 2814 2820 2842 2861 2870 2876 2888 2959 2965 2970 2976 2986 3009 3021 3087 3185 3186 3196 3251 3262 3268 3323 3329 3373 3387 3431 3441 3445 3454 3458 3483 3511 3519

15. Education, general

2014 2018 2026 2043 2054 2057 2061 2066 2068 2075 2078 2095 2097 2103 2104 2105 2107 2108 2109 2110 2111 2122 2125 2126 2129 2135 2138 2141 2142 2145 2146 2147 2149 2150 2152 2154 2156 2163 2165 2169 2170 2171 2174 2175 2179 2185 2187 2188 2194 2198 2202 2204 2207 2209 2210 2212 2213 2229 2232 2238 2241 2242 2243 2244 2247 2253 2255 2266 2278 2280 2281 2284 2285 2288 2290 2295 2301 2308 2314 2335 2344 2353 2356 2360 2361 2371 2374 2379 2381 2386 2388 2392 2393 2399 2404 2407 2410 2413 2423 2424 2426 2434 2439 2479 2492 2494 2508 2509 2511 2516 2518 2521 2522 2529 2540 2548 2572 2573 2574 2583 2585 2586 2591 2593 2607 2612 2613 2614 2618 2620 2629 2632 2636 2638 2639 2641 2643 2648 2650 2653 2654 2655 2656 2657 2662 2678 2679 2692 2696 2704 2711 2725 2727 2754 2755 2759 2760 2778 2796 2808 2810 2831 2833 2851 2858 2861 2876 2877 2879 2881 2887 2888 2890 2891 2901 2909 2925 2932 2934 2938 2948 2957 2958 2961 2965 2976 2977 2988 2991 2997 3003 3004 3013 3015 3016 3017 3020 3021 3030 3031 3032 3038 3041 3042 3047 3051 3055 3058 3059 3069 3075 3082 3085 3086 3102 3115 3117 3123 3127 3134 3141 3145 3147 3152 3154 3158 3161 3162 3165 3168 3169 3170 3176 3177 3178 3180 3184 3185 3187 3190 3191 3192 3193 3194 3220 3229 3232 3250 3254 3258 3280 3291 3292 3309 3315 3319 3323 3336 3339 3342 3347 3350 3352 3353 3369 3372 3375 3381 3386 3396 3404 3409 3410 3417 3419 3420 3422 3427 3428 3429 3430 3433 3434 3436 3438 3439 3441 3442 3444 3445 3446 3447 3448 3449 3451 3454 3458 3488 3518

16. Community and Regional Planning

2104 2194 2195 2399 2622 2623 3078 3149 3369 3420

17. Interior Design

2033 2041 2044 2054 2077 2078 2080 2102 2104 2106 2107 2109 2114 2120 2121 2124 2125 2133 2138 2142 2148 2149 2151 2152 2160 2168 2169 2170 2173 2174 2177 2178 2180 2185 2186 2190 2192 2194 2202 2209 2212 2255 2258 2261 2264 2265 2266 2275 2278 2281 2285 2290 2291 2293 2311 2362 2367 2375 2381 2386 2414 2434 2440 2446 2453 2456 2457 2461 2472 2486 2495 2499 2509 2525 2573 2610 2619 2622 2623 2630 2632 2639 2647 2651 2665 2669 2670 2679 2698 2703 2712 2730 2742 2773 2814 2822 2834 2844 2845 2873 2913 2920 2921 2923 2954 2960 2965 2975 2991 3006 3009 3021 3039 3057 3084 3087 3127 3146 3151 3185 3196 3335 3336 3342 3359 3368 3370 3371 3387 3393 3395 3405 3416 3420 3427 3431 3440 3445 3452 3458 3480 3481 3483 3486 3496

18. Art (painting, drawing, sculpting)

2014 2026 2054 2071 2073 2074 2076 2080 2088 2095 2103 2104 2106 2109 2111 2114 2116 2120 2125 2126 2129 2130 2134 2139 2142 2146 2147 2152 2154 2155 2156 2157 2160 2162 2169 2170 2171 2173 2174 2182 2187 2190 2194 2196 2197 2199 2203 2207 2209 2210 2213 2217 2240 2243 2264 2268 2281 2284 2288 2289 2295 2334 2364 2365 2381 2399 2413 2414 2443 2486

18. Art (painting, drawing, sculpting) (continued)

2509 2514 2520 2527 2573 2579 2583 2613 2625 2643
2650 2669 2670 2676 2678 2679 2684 2731 2739 2796
2841 2845 2870 2881 2897 2899 2913 2923 2933 2935
2937 2945 2959 2965 2989 2997 3031 3032 3043 3058
3138 3147 3151 3158 3169 3170 3175 3176 3177 3178
3185 3216 3315 3318 3328 3334 3336 3339 3342 3345
3350 3353 3358 3362 3363 3370 3371 3372 3373 3375
3386 3396 3420 3430 3431 3445 3449 3458

19. Dental Hygiene

2039 2077 2104 2108 2111 2113 2125 2129 2130 2136
2137 2178 2184 2208 2218 2228 2249 2251 2254 2256
2261 2266 2275 2281 2283 2284 2290 2292 2297 2299
2319 2323 2324 2328 2329 2381 2392 2413 2414 2424
2440 2467 2472 2525 2549 2583 2603 2607 2609 2635
2638 2649 2655 2657 2665 2669 2675 2676 2679 2686
2691 2740 2749 2780 2787 2789 2821 2842 2858 2872
2878 2881 2888 2894 2920 2933 2941 2950 2960 2965
2966 2983 2998 3009 3012 3017 3020 3056 3064 3079
3085 3102 3103 3123 3127 3152 3165 3167 3185 3186
3191 3193 3196 3198 3216 3229 3235 3237 3268 3305
3312 3316 3320 3333 3336 3339 3343 3375 3376 3387
3392 3420 3434 3435 3439 3451 3454 3464 3483 3486
3491 3520

20. Dental Lab Technology

2027 2049 2078 2116 2125 2130 2152 2163 2178 2183
2195 2266 2268 2274 2281 2284 2307 2309 2434 2486
2549 2609 2623 2649 2671 2698 2741 2742 2787 2789
2822 2842 2894 2942 3015 3082 3085 3256 3268 3292
3413 3420 3453

21. Medical Assistant or Medical Office Assistant

2003 2007 2009 2014 2015 2017 2018 2020 2025 2026
2027 2031 2034 2039 2042 2045 2049 2053 2054 2059
2070 2085 2088 2093 2100 2103 2107 2108 2111 2113
2114 2115 2116 2120 2121 2123 2125 2127 2129 2132
2133 2137 2142 2151 2152 2163 2168 2170 2173 2174
2180 2181 2182 2183 2185 2188 2192 2195 2197 2208
2212 2219 2228 2243 2251 2255 2256 2258 2264 2268
2270 2271 2272 2275 2278 2280 2284 2291 2294 2298
2304 2306 2307 2309 2314 2315 2316 2319 2320 2328
2333 2339 2341 2344 2345 2350 2355 2365 2368 2374
2381 2393 2402 2408 2413 2416 2434 2440 2445 2446
2447 2449 2450 2451 2452 2453 2454 2455 2456 2457
2458 2461 2467 2483 2486 2488 2494 2500 2503 2507
2509 2523 2527 2528 2539 2540 2547 2555 2564 2568
2569 2571 2575 2589 2595 2598 2602 2605 2608 2615
2623 2628 2629 2631 2632 2640 2648 2649 2654 2657
2658 2660 2661 2665 2667 2669 2670 2671 2674 2676
2678 2679 2681 2690 2691 2694 2695 2698 2704 2714
2716 2726 2732 2749 2754 2761 2770 2771 2787 2789
2805 2806 2807 2816 2821 2825 2837 2842 2845 2850
2853 2868 2872 2877 2885 2893 2896 2920 2921 2923
2924 2936 2941 2961 2962 2965 2980 2987 2988 3003
3006 3007 3009 3012 3016 3017 3019 3020 3026 3027
3029 3035 3038 3042 3048 3057 3058 3062 3065 3073
3080 3082 3085 3086 3087 3089 3092 3093 3104 3112
3113 3116 3123 3127 3128 3129 3133 3140 3141 3148
3157 3158 3161 3167 3171 3175 3177 3178 3182 3184
3185 3190 3191 3192 3194 3198 3216 3218 3221 3235
3237 3239 3240 3247 3248 3250 3251 3253 3256 3259
3262 3268 3274 3276 3288 3292 3297 3316 3319 3326
3333 3335 3336 3338 3342 3346 3362 3368 3369 3370
3373 3379 3382 3386 3395 3396 3398 3399 3431 3441
3445 3446 3448 3449 3452 3457 3459 3462 3463 3473
3474 3478 3481 3482 3483 3485 3486 3491 3492 3494
3495 3496 3511 3519 3521

22. Occupational Therapy

2003 2009 2014 2015 2017 2018 2020 2025 2026 2027
2034 2039 2045 2051 2053 2054 2104 2228 2281 2355

22. Occupational Therapy (continued)

2371 2375 2379 2381 2399 2426 2461 2486 2610 2632
2647 2652 2655 2669 2694 2698 2704 2706 2707 2714
2755 2756 2813 2822 2834 2864 2871 2894 2934 2941
2948 2957 2966 2970 3004 3051 3064 3080 3085 3095
3113 3127 3133 3147 3167 3175 3185 3190 3194 3198
3297 3319 3331 3342 3351 3368 3373 3444 3464 3480
3483

23. Physical Therapy

2003 2009 2014 2015 2017 2018 2020 2025 2026 2027
2033 2034 2039 2041 2045 2051 2053 2054 2078 2127
2170 2188 2194 2212 2222 2228 2236 2255 2275 2284
2290 2345 2355 2365 2381 2386 2406 2410 2461 2474
2514 2525 2546 2561 2582 2583 2609 2614 2632 2651
2652 2657 2665 2670 2676 2681 2704 2706 2714 2755
2813 2822 2858 2864 2871 2881 2894 2900 2920 2934
2946 2957 2961 2962 2965 2966 2975 3004 3009 3017
3029 3032 3034 3050 3051 3076 3085 3095 3103 3123
3127 3133 3140 3147 3151 3157 3167 3175 3182 3185
3190 3206 3213 3235 3268 3284 3305 3309 3312 3316
3318 3319 3336 3339 3342 3348 3352 3368 3376 3420
3431 3435 3444 3452 3492 3496

24. Radiology

2003 2009 2014 2015 2017 2018 2020 2025 2026 2027
2033 2034 2039 2042 2045 2051 2053 2054 2070 2078
2084 2088 2089 2095 2099 2103 2104 2108 2109 2114
2116 2119 2125 2136 2137 2151 2152 2163 2164 2170
2174 2178 2188 2190 2193 2195 2210 2219 2228 2238
2239 2240 2247 2254 2255 2258 2261 2265 2266 2273
2275 2281 2284 2286 2290 2292 2299 2304 2313 2327
2332 2345 2350 2351 2355 2365 2366 2369 2371 2375
2381 2383 2387 2388 2390 2391 2396 2399 2404 2412
2413 2423 2424 2425 2426 2433 2434 2437 2442 2447
2455 2466 2474 2480 2485 2490 2491 2495 2496 2499
2504 2523 2525 2528 2533 2537 2539 2547 2549 2550
2554 2566 2573 2590 2601 2605 2607 2613 2618 2623
2625 2627 2636 2644 2647 2648 2649 2652 2653 2655
2657 2664 2665 2669 2674 2676 2678 2679 2682 2683
2684 2691 2693 2697 2700 2716 2723 2729 2734 2740
2741 2748 2750 2777 2778 2781 2782 2783 2789 2800
2813 2818 2819 2821 2838 2839 2853 2859 2872 2877
2878 2879 2881 2887 2888 2891 2894 2897 2905 2907
2920 2933 2940 2950 2960 2961 2963 2966 2988 2992
2998 3004 3006 3010 3016 3017 3018 3038 3044 3048
3050 3054 3055 3063 3071 3076 3079 3085 3086 3093
3100 3103 3104 3113 3115 3123 3125 3126 3127 3131
3138 3152 3157 3169 3175 3186 3196 3198 3208 3214
3216 3220 3229 3235 3237 3239 3240 3247 3251 3253
3257 3260 3261 3263 3268 3270 3284 3305 3307 3309
3312 3313 3316 3318 3319 3321 3333 3335 3336 3338
3340 3342 3348 3351 3352 3353 3357 3362 3365 3368
3370 3373 3376 3381 3387 3392 3396 3400 3407 3420
3429 3431 3433 3434 3435 3436 3459 3464 3474 3475
3479 3482 3483 3486 3491 3496 3515 3518 3521

25. Surgical Technology

2003 2007 2009 2014 2015 2017 2018 2020 2025 2026
2027 2031 2034 2039 2042 2045 2049 2053 2054 2059
2070 2085 2088 2093 2100 2103 2107 2108 2111 2113
2114 2115 2116 2120 2121 2123 2125 2127 2129 2132
2133 2137 2142 2151 2152 2163 2168 2170 2173 2174
2180 2181 2182 2183 2185 2188 2192 2195 2197 2208
2212 2219 2228 2243 2251 2255 2256 2258 2264 2268
2270 2271 2272 2275 2278 2280 2284 2291 2294 2298
2304 2306 2307 2309 2314 2315 2316 2319 2320 2328
2333 2339 2341 2344 2345 2350 2355 2365 2368 2374
2381 2393 2402 2408 2413 2416 2434 2440 2445 2446
2447 2449 2450 2451 2452 2453 2454 2455 2456 2457
2458 2461 2467 2483 2486 2488 2494 2500 2503 2507
2509 2523 2527 2528 2539 2540 2547 2555 2564 2568
2569 2571 2575 2589 2595 2598 2602 2605 2608 2615

25. Surgical Technology (continued)

2623 2628 2629 2631 2632 2640 2648 2649 2654 2657
2658 2660 2661 2665 2667 2669 2670 2671 2674 2676
2678 2679 2681 2690 2691 2694 2695 2698 2704 2714
2716 2726 2732 2749 2754 2761 2770 2771 2787 2789
2805 2806 2807 2816 2821 2825 2837 2842 2845 2850
2853 2868 2872 2877 2885 2893 2896 2920 2921 2923
2924 2936 2941 2961 2962 2965 2980 2987 2988 3003
3006 3007 3009 3012 3016 3017 3019 3020 3026 3027
3029 3035 3038 3042 3048 3057 3058 3062 3065 3073
3080 3082 3085 3086 3087 3089 3092 3093 3104 3112
3113 3116 3123 3127 3128 3129 3133 3140 3141 3148
3157 3158 3161 3167 3171 3175 3177 3178 3182 3184
3185 3190 3191 3192 3194 3198 3216 3218 3221 3235
3237 3239 3240 3247 3248 3250 3251 3253 3256 3259
3262 3268 3274 3276 3288 3292 3297 3316 3319 3326
3333 3335 3336 3338 3342 3346 3362 3368 3369 3370
3373 3379 3382 3386 3395 3396 3398 3399 3431 3441
3445 3446 3448 3449 3452 3457 3459 3462 3463 3473
3474 3478 3481 3482 3483 3485 3486 3491 3492 3494
3495 3496 3511 3519 3521

26. Veterinary Medicine

2014 2020 2216 2372 2381 2386 2423 2514 2582 2583
2633 2647 2736 2804 2858 3008 3032 3078 3079 3169
3220 3318 3333 3336 3339 3388

27. Clothing and Textiles

2007 2019 2022 2033 2049 2077 2078 2101 2104 2106
2114 2120 2123 2129 2130 2138 2142 2143 2149 2151
2157 2158 2167 2170 2173 2174 2176 2178 2180 2183
2185 2187 2190 2194 2195 2197 2209 2255 2264 2266
2268 2275 2280 2281 2284 2291 2292 2298 2302 2303
2304 2315 2328 2341 2353 2354 2362 2440 2472 2476
2486 2525 2574 2632 2637 2639 2665 2669 2712 2729
2735 2738 2742 2751 2774 2841 2845 2899 2965 2986
3252 3259 3280 3309 3335 3336 3342 3349 3370 3386
3387 3393 3445 3446 3452 3453 3483 3492 3496

28. Family Relations, Child Development

2025 2040 2041 2049 2054 2060 2065 2069 2071 2077
2078 2079 2085 2104 2107 2110 2111 2113 2114 2118
2119 2120 2124 2127 2129 2132 2138 2142 2145 2146
2150 2154 2159 2164 2165 2167 2169 2170 2172 2173
2174 2175 2176 2177 2179 2180 2181 2182 2183 2185
2186 2187 2188 2194 2195 2198 2199 2209 2211 2212
2219 2227 2229 2232 2243 2253 2254 2255 2258 2261
2264 2265 2270 2272 2279 2280 2284 2286 2291 2292
2293 2295 2298 2303 2304 2307 2328 2330 2341 2360
2361 2363 2367 2371 2374 2375 2376 2379 2380 2384
2388 2389 2390 2393 2404 2410 2413 2417 2423 2424
2427 2432 2434 2438 2439 2440 2448 2449 2451 2455
2461 2467 2470 2472 2483 2496 2503 2506 2508 2511
2512 2519 2523 2527 2608 2629 2632 2634 2639 2665
2669 2675 2679 2681 2691 2694 2704 2710 2725 2726
2729 2735 2742 2747 2749 2754 2755 2760 2774 2776
2778 2788 2797 2813 2821 2834 2841 2844 2845 2849
2853 2857 2858 2859 2866 2871 2883 2898 2900 2925
2950 2965 2966 2970 2976 3007 3009 3017 3020 3023
3025 3048 3049 3050 3056 3058 3067 3082 3102 3103
3115 3117 3123 3127 3134 3135 3139 3141 3142 3145
3147 3152 3154 3158 3160 3161 3167 3169 3170 3178
3182 3185 3186 3187 3196 3198 3216 3225 3230 3249
3250 3253 3256 3264 3280 3301 3313 3315 3318 3319
3323 3329 3336 3342 3343 3347 3348 3351 3352 3369
3370 3371 3373 3381 3387 3396 3400 3413 3414 3420
3431 3440 3446 3450 3451 3452 3458 3461 3463 3464
3480 3481 3488 3490 3493 3496

29. Food and Nutrition

2005 2007 2013 2019 2025 2027 2046 2054 2066 2077
2078 2080 2094 2098 2104 2107 2108 2111 2114 2118
2120 2125 2142 2148 2151 2152 2157 2163 2166 2167

29. Food and Nutrition (continued)

2170 2173 2174 2175 2177 2180 2181 2183 2185 2188
2190 2192 2193 2194 2195 2197 2202 2204 2210 2220
2226 2227 2228 2229 2247 2253 2255 2256 2264 2265
2266 2268 2270 2272 2275 2276 2278 2279 2280 2281
2283 2284 2285 2291 2293 2294 2295 2299 2301 2304
2307 2309 2312 2335 2341 2356 2367 2371 2374 2375
2376 2380 2386 2389 2391 2393 2394 2399 2404 2413
2417 2423 2424 2434 2440 2448 2449 2452 2455 2461
2467 2474 2483 2486 2499 2525 2539 2540 2547 2569
2572 2573 2579 2593 2600 2601 2605 2606 2607 2608
2609 2632 2634 2635 2640 2644 2648 2651 2667 2669
2670 2679 2681 2685 2690 2691 2694 2697 2698 2699
2702 2703 2704 2712 2713 2714 2715 2721 2722 2724
2729 2735 2739 2740 2742 2749 2751 2753 2756 2766
2771 2774 2775 2788 2812 2820 2828 2834 2841 2842
2844 2845 2853 2858 2859 2863 2871 2876 2878 2885
2888 2890 2896 2900 2909 2910 2912 2934 2938 2940
2941 2945 2954 2959 2962 2965 2967 2970 2972 2975
2976 2977 2978 2980 2992 2995 3004 3009 3010 3017
3020 3025 3027 3058 3064 3080 3082 3085 3092 3103
3127 3150 3165 3166 3169 3170 3178 3180 3181 3186
3187 3190 3191 3198 3221 3225 3233 3258 3268 3283
3292 3295 3309 3322 3333 3335 3336 3337 3338 3342
3349 3358 3359 3362 3370 3371 3373 3378 3385 3413
3416 3420 3429 3430 3431 3439 3441 3446 3448 3449
3451 3452 3453 3454 3455 3456 3457 3464 3474 3478
3479 3480 3481 3483 3485 3488 3495 3496 3510

30. Biological Sciences, general

2104 2112 2114 2120 2129 2130 2142 2157 2171 2187
2210 2213 2216 2241 2243 2251 2268 2276 2280 2295
2379 2399 2479 2569 2583 2814 2858 2871 2937 2943
2967 3032 3061 3158 3170 3178 3318 3332 3336 3339
3345 3353 3375 3386

31. Physical Sciences, general

2104 2114 2120 2130 2133 2138 2142 2146 2148 2152
2163 2185 2187 2207 2213 2216 2241 2251 2268 2276
2280 2295 2298 2379 2399 2511 2569 2779 2814 2820
2858 2871 2893 2930 2937 2943 2960 2977 2978 3032
3141 3151 3158 3170 3177 3178 3318 3332 3336 3339
3345 3363 3375 3386 3454 3519

32. Community Service, general

2007 2008 2009 2012 2014 2022 2025 2026 2027 2030
2034 2037 2038 2039 2040 2041 2043 2048 2052 2053
2054 2055 2065 2068 2069 2071 2075 2077 2078 2079
2080 2091 2095 2105 2107 2108 2112 2113 2115 2117
2120 2121 2122 2125 2126 2130 2133 2141 2145 2147
2148 2150 2159 2162 2163 2164 2165 2166 2167 2168
2170 2176 2179 2180 2183 2185 2186 2187 2190 2192
2193 2194 2196 2197 2198 2199 2200 2201 2206 2210
2211 2219 2221 2226 2227 2229 2230 2236 2249 2253
2254 2255 2258 2259 2261 2262 2264 2265 2266 2268
2269 2270 2271 2272 2274 2275 2276 2277 2279 2280
2281 2283 2284 2285 2288 2289 2290 2291 2293 2294
2295 2296 2297 2299 2301 2302 2304 2306 2307 2309
2312 2314 2315 2316 2324 2328 2329 2330 2334 2335
2336 2339 2341 2343 2344 2345 2347 2353 2354 2357
2365 2369 2371 2375 2376 2377 2380 2381 2386 2387
2388 2389 2391 2392 2393 2396 2397 2399 2404 2410
2423 2426 2427 2434 2440 2447 2449 2452 2455 2461
2467 2478 2482 2483 2488 2495 2500 2501 2502 2506
2508 2509 2511 2515 2522 2525 2527 2536 2540 2543
2544 2547 2573 2583 2584 2605 2609 2610 2616 2618
2622 2627 2634 2635 2636 2638 2640 2643 2648 2649
2652 2655 2657 2665 2667 2670 2674 2675 2676 2677
2679 2681 2683 2685 2691 2697 2710 2714 2721 2722
2725 2726 2733 2734 2738 2742 2751 2753 2755 2756
2759 2760 2761 2762 2773 2774 2776 2778 2779 2783
2788 2790 2796 2808 2813 2814 2820 2830 2836 2845
2846 2855 2865 2866 2879 2885 2887 2888 2890 2891

32. Community Service, general (continued)

2893 2894 2897 2898 2899 2901 2902 2904 2907 2908
2912 2920 2930 2935 2938 2949 2953 2958 2959 2960
2963 2965 2970 2972 2975 2987 2989 2991 2992 2996
2997 2999 3000 3001 3004 3006 3012 3013 3015 3016
3017 3019 3020 3022 3023 3024 3027 3029 3031 3032
3034 3037 3038 3041 3043 3044 3047 3049 3050 3051
3052 3053 3054 3055 3057 3059 3061 3073 3075 3079
3082 3084 3092 3102 3104 3111 3123 3127 3133 3136
3140 3149 3152 3160 3162 3169 3170 3171 3173 3184
3191 3193 3196 3204 3225 3229 3233 3249 3251 3252
3254 3276 3280 3281 3292 3301 3316 3320 3324 3325
3326 3327 3329 3331 3335 3336 3338 3339 3342 3343
3346 3347 3352 3353 3355 3361 3362 3369 3370 3371
3372 3373 3375 3379 3381 3386 3387 3396 3400 3405
3407 3413 3416 3419 3420 3423 3428 3430 3431 3433
3434 3436 3440 3441 3446 3452 3454 3457 3458 3459
3464 3474 3480 3481 3483 3485 3488 3490 3492 3493
3512 3513 3515 3516 3517 3518

33. Social Sciences, general

2014 2044 2062 2068 2071 2073 2077 2095 2097 2104
2107 2109 2111 2114 2120 2137 2139 2146 2147 2152
2154 2156 2162 2163 2170 2171 2181 2186 2187 2190
2193 2194 2196 2200 2203 2207 2209 2210 2212 2213
2217 2231 2239 2241 2243 2250 2251 2258 2261 2266
2273 2276 2279 2281 2290 2292 2293 2295 2297 2298
2372 2379 2398 2399 2402 2424 2440 2455 2461 2467
2479 2510 2525 2555 2569 2583 2598 2608 2614 2641
2649 2651 2653 2656 2665 2679 2681 2691 2695 2726
2743 2760 2773 2784 2814 2816 2817 2822 2837 2842
2843 2844 2845 2848 2857 2858 2872 2879 2881 2885
2887 2889 2893 2895 2898 2909 2911 2913 2928 2930
2933 2937 2949 2953 2954 2972 2975 2978 2986 2989
3004 3005 3008 3009 3014 3015 3017 3019 3020 3032
3043 3048 3050 3052 3057 3059 3067 3075 3079 3082
3102 3106 3116 3127 3141 3152 3158 3162 3169 3170
3171 3176 3177 3178 3182 3183 3186 3191 3192 3194
3196 3217 3228 3237 3248 3249 3251 3255 3259 3264
3286 3325 3336 3339 3343 3353 3355 3363 3369 3371
3375 3386 3387 3396 3400 3420 3438 3439 3440 3451
3452 3455 3457 3463 3468 3492 3496 3515 3518

34. Psychology

2012 2043 2071 2085 2095 2104 2114 2120 2133 2145
2152 2153 2180 2187 2207 2210 2213 2241 2280 2295
2351 2381 2399 2402 2510 2555 2569 2583 2654 2658
2814 2871 2876 2893 2895 2897 2928 2933 3032 3061
3158 3170 3177 3178 3192 3332 3336 3339 3345 3350
3353 3363 3367 3375 3386

35. Sociology

2043 2071 2085 2095 2104 2114 2120 2126 2133 2153
2180 2187 2213 2241 2295 2381 2399 2402 2510 2569
2583 2654 2814 2871 2893 2895 2928 2933 3032 3061
3141 3158 3170 3177 3204 3206 3215 3332 3336 3339
3345 3353 3363 3375 3386

36. Aeronautical, Aviation Technology

2001 2034 2054 2067 2068 2078 2098 2104 2114 2125
2136 2151 2170 2174 2186 2192 2195 2197 2211 2218
2219 2226 2255 2261 2272 2273 2275 2284 2290 2307
2330 2335 2343 2365 2372 2387 2396 2413 2420 2461
2472 2474 2476 2477 2479 2483 2515 2519 2521 2526
2529 2613 2616 2668 2674 2677 2679 2681 2690 2691
2695 2698 2704 2726 2727 2735 2738 2743 2758 2760
2762 2769 2770 2773 2788 2801 2804 2835 2855 2868
2879 2887 2897 2898 2928 2945 2959 3020 3027 3056
3080 3082 3085 3087 3127 3147 3151 3152 3156 3158
3165 3167 3169 3173 3178 3179 3182 3190 3191 3198
3225 3235 3251 3256 3292 3342 3347 3354 3355 3363
3370 3375 3380 3385 3393 3396 3413 3420 3437 3442
3456 3457 3464 3474 3480 3481 3515

37. Data Systems Repair

2005 2012 2020 2021 2034 2035 2040 2041 2048 2052
2056 2064 2068 2069 2078 2091 2092 2093 2098 2100
2104 2109 2110 2113 2114 2117 2120 2133 2136 2137
2138 2152 2157 2158 2164 2167 2169 2170 2183 2186
2202 2212 2224 2226 2229 2230 2252 2253 2256 2258
2261 2263 2264 2265 2268 2269 2272 2276 2280 2283
2284 2285 2288 2292 2293 2294 2295 2299 2304 2307
2309 2314 2315 2341 2343 2345 2360 2365 2367 2371
2381 2382 2386 2387 2390 2393 2404 2410 2413 2414
2419 2423 2424 2461 2467 2472 2474 2476 2483 2486
2493 2494 2499 2509 2523 2525 2526 2527 2531 2536
2540 2547 2552 2553 2562 2568 2575 2579 2586 2591
2596 2600 2601 2605 2610 2613 2620 2635 2642 2647
2655 2656 2657 2666 2669 2670 2679 2681 2687 2691
2694 2695 2699 2704 2717 2718 2720 2722 2724 2725
2728 2729 2731 2738 2739 2742 2747 2749 2751 2754
2761 2766 2771 2782 2785 2787 2801 2812 2815 2817
2820 2835 2836 2837 2841 2849 2852 2855 2861 2864
2866 2868 2876 2883 2893 2894 2909 2910 2911 2922
2925 2934 2942 2943 2945 2946 2947 2960 2965 2970
2980 2995 2996 3000 3005 3007 3009 3014 3018 3025
3042 3050 3055 3075 3079 3080 3082 3089 3092 3104
3111 3114 3123 3127 3136 3140 3149 3151 3152 3161
3169 3175 3176 3177 3180 3190 3198 3225 3226 3230
3235 3237 3247 3258 3262 3264 3268 3272 3279 3288
3295 3297 3303 3311 3314 3315 3316 3322 3342 3346
3347 3348 3356 3357 3358 3363 3370 3371 3381 3382
3384 3385 3387 3396 3406 3431 3432 3440 3441 3446
3452 3455 3459 3460 3469 3481 3488 3496 3510 3511
3515

38. Engineering Technology-Electrical

2001 2026 2043 2047 2048 2054 2066 2068 2071 2088
2091 2100 2103 2104 2105 2108 2112 2119 2136 2139
2151 2154 2155 2158 2160 2166 2167 2169 2170 2174
2180 2186 2187 2190 2192 2194 2197 2202 2204 2205
2210 2241 2245 2248 2250 2251 2252 2255 2258 2263
2265 2269 2275 2284 2286 2289 2292 2313 2315 2323
2336 2341 2367 2369 2373 2376 2383 2385 2386 2393
2399 2404 2414 2417 2420 2423 2432 2434 2438 2442
2486 2494 2500 2507 2529 2536 2546 2551 2554 2568
2569 2573 2583 2595 2597 2605 2608 2612 2635 2636
2638 2642 2650 2653 2657 2658 2667 2669 2676 2678
2684 2686 2697 2698 2704 2714 2717 2731 2746 2751
2754 2757 2769 2777 2783 2789 2795 2802 2804 2820
2821 2829 2841 2863 2878 2881 2887 2888 2889 2890
2893 2904 2910 2911 2925 2932 2950 2960 2962 2965
2966 2970 2978 2980 2987 2995 2999 3000 3001 3003
3004 3005 3007 3008 3012 3013 3014 3020 3021 3022
3023 3027 3030 3032 3034 3035 3038 3039 3042 3044
3048 3049 3050 3051 3054 3055 3056 3078 3088 3089
3092 3094 3097 3111 3120 3127 3129 3137 3140 3146
3148 3149 3152 3159 3161 3162 3167 3175 3176 3177
3178 3179 3180 3193 3200 3201 3202 3203 3204 3205
3206 3207 3208 3209 3210 3211 3212 3214 3215 3229
3230 3231 3235 3236 3239 3240 3250 3256 3262 3266
3268 3270 3273 3300 3302 3311 3316 3318 3328 3329
3333 3334 3353 3354 3357 3358 3359 3367 3369 3372
3385 3387 3389 3405 3412 3414 3417 3420 3422 3424
3431 3435 3438 3439 3440 3444 3448 3449 3451 3452
3454 3465 3467 3476 3478 3481 3482 3486 3492 3516

39. Engineering Technology-Aeronautical

2001 2034 2067 2116 2124 2125 2129 2136 2146 2165
2174 2186 2195 2202 2213 2255 2275 2284 2354 2413
2526 2573 2610 2616 2656 2670 2679 2681 2983 3020
3082 3150 3152 3198 3280 3370 3375 3431 3456 3481
3514

Abbreviations for the College Index

Words that are always abbreviated

Academy — Acad
American — Amer
Campus — Cam
College — C
Community College — CC
Community Junior College — CJC
Conservatory — Consv
County — Co
Engineer — Engr
Hospital — Hosp
Institute — Inst
Junior College — JC
School — Sch
State — St
Technical — Tech
Technology, Technological — Techn
University — U

Schools

City University of New York — CUNY
Fairleigh Dickinson — Farlgh Dcksn
State University of New York — SUNY

City and state names that are always abbreviated

Cities

Cincinnati — Cinci
Los Angeles — Los Ang
New Orleans — New Orls
Philadelphia — Phila
Pittsburgh — Pittsbg
San Francisco — San Fran

States

Alaska — Alas
Arizona — Ariz
California — Cal
Colorado — Colo
Connecticut — Conn
Delaware — Del
Illinois — Ill
Indiana — Ind
Louisiana — La
Maryland — Md
Massachusetts — Mass
Michigan — Mich
Minnesota — Minn
Mississippi — Miss
New Hampshire — NH
New Jersey — NJ
New Mexico — NM
New York — NY
North Carolina — NC
North Dakota — ND
Oklahoma — Okla
Pennsylvania — Pa
South Carolina — SC
South Dakota — SD
Tennessee — Tenn
West Virginia — W Va
Wisconsin — Wis

Region

New England — New Eng

Other abbreviations

Accounting — Acct
Aeronautical — Aero
Agricultural — Agri
Agriculture — Agr
Applied Sciences — App Sci
Architecture — Arch
Baptist — Bapt
Branch — Br
Business — Bus
Business Administration — Bus Adm
Center — Ctr
Central — Cent
Design — Des
East, Eastern — E
Education — Ed
English — Eng
Finance — Fin
Foundation — Found
General — Gen
Health — Hlth
Health Sciences — H S
Industrial — Indus
International — Intern
Lutheran — Luth
Maintenance — Main
Marine, Maritime — Mar
Mechanical — Mech
Medical — Medl
Medicine — Med
Methodist — Meth
Military — Mil
Mineral — Minrl
Minor — Min
Missionary — Msnry
Mortuary Science — Mort Sci
Mount — Mt
Mountain — Mtn
National — Natl
Normal — Norm
North, Northern — N
Nursing — Nsg
Polytechnical — Poly
Presbyterian — Presb
Radiology, Radiological — Rad
Regional — Reg
Saint — Snt
Science — Sci
Seminary — Sem
South, Southern — S
Study, Studies — Stud
Teachers — Tchrs
Theology, Theological — Theol
Valley — Vly
Vocational — Voc
Vocational-Technical — Voc-Tech
West, Western — W

College Index

The **College Index** lists virtually all college-level institutions in the United States that offer two-year associate or four-year bachelor's degree programs. Colleges are listed in alphabetical order, according to the first key word in the institution's name. "University," "College," and "Community College" are **not** considered key words. Thus, "University of Montana" appears in the M section as "Montana, U of." (Note: Because of limited space, the prepositions "in," "at," and "of" used in school names are frequently omitted.) Words such as "Saint" and "Northwest" have been spelled out completely and alphabetized according to the complete spelling. As a general rule, a word is abbreviated when it is not a key word.

Before using the Index, examine the three lists in "Abbreviations for the **College Index**" on page 271. The first list contains words that are abbreviated every time they occur (for example, "College" is always "C," "Technical" always "Tech," and so on). In the second list are city, state, and region names that are always abbreviated. (For example, "Louisiana" is always abbreviated "La" and "Maryland" as "Md." Colleges with these names in their titles are consistently alphabetized and ordered according to the abbreviated spelling.) Finally, the list of other abbreviations contains all abbreviations that occur often in the **College Index.** Sometimes, words in lengthy school names have been shortened (generally by dropping vowels). Since the meaning in these cases is usually clear, they are not included in "Abbreviations for the **College Index.**"

The first line of each **College Index** entry includes the college name and the sequence number that may be used to locate information about the college in the book. The second line of each entry contains the city, state, and ZIP code.

Four-year college and university sequence numbers range between 0001 and 1737; information displays for four-year colleges (blue) begin on page 56. Two-year college sequence numbers begin at 2001 and run through 3521; information displays for two-year colleges (purple) begin on page 195.

Note: The sequence numbers indicate the order of the colleges in this book only. Do not use them with admissions tests or need analysis services.

Name	Sequence Number
A	
Abbott NW Sch Rad Techn Minneapolis, MN 55407	2700
ABC Tech Trade Sch Tucson, AZ 85713	2064
Abilene Christian U Abilene, TX 79699	0840
Abraham Baldwin Agri C Tifton, GA 31794	2303
Acad of Accountancy Minneapolis, MN 55416	2701
Acad of Aeronautics Flushing, NY 11371	1326
Acad of the New Church Bryn Athyn, PA 19009	1304
Adams St C Alamosa, CO 81102	0106
Adelphi U Garden City, NY 11530	1498
Adirondack CC Queensbury, NY 12804	2912
Adrian C Adrian, MI 49221	0591

Name	Sequence Number
Aero-Space Inst Chicago, IL 60605	0520
Agnes Scott C Decatur, GA 30030	1235
Aiken Tech C Aiken, SC 29802	3230
Aims CC Greeley, CO 80632	2211
Akron, U of Akron, OH 44325	0461
Alabama A&M U Normal, AL 35762	0844
Alabama Aviation & Tech Ozark, AL 36361	2001
Alabama Bible C Guin, AL 35563	2002
Alabama in Birmingham, U Birmingham, AL 35294	0925
Alabama in Huntsville, U Huntsville, AL 35899	0957
Alabama St U Montgomery, AL 36101	0763
Alabama, U of Tuscaloosa, AL 35487	0981

Name	Sequence Number
Alamance CC Haw River, NC 27258	2995
Alameda, C of Alameda, CA 94501	2101
Alas Anchorage, U of Anchorage, AK 99508	0020
Alas Bible C Glennallen, AK 99588	0030
Alas Fairbanks, U of Fairbanks, AK 99775	0107
Alas Juneau, U of Juneau, AK 99801	0001
Alas Pacific U Anchorage, AK 99508	0088
Albany C of Pharmacy Albany, NY 12208	1462
Albany St C Albany, GA 31705	1091
Albany Tech Inst Albany, GA 31708	2304
Albany, JC of Albany, NY 12208	2913
Albemarle, C of Elizabeth City, NC 27906	2996

Name	Sequence Number
Albert Lea Tech C Albert Lea, MN 56007	2702
Albertus Magnus C New Haven, CT 06511	1639
Albion C Albion, MI 49224	0668
Albright C Reading, PA 19612	1508
Albuquerque Tech Voc Albuquerque, NM 87106	2896
Alcorn State U Lorman, MS 39096	0826
Alderson-Broaddus C Philippi, WV 26416	1137
Alexander City CC Alexander City, AL 35010	2003
Alexandria Tech C Alexandria, MN 56308	2703
Alexandria Voc-Tech Alexandria, LA 71307	2565
Alfred U Alfred, NY 14802	1511
Alice Lloyd C Pippa Passes, KY 41844	0789
Allegany CC Cumberland, MD 21501	2607
Allegheny C Meadville, PA 16335	1512
Allegheny Co CC Pittsburgh, PA 15212	3178
Allegheny Co CC Boyce Monroeville, PA 15146	3175
Allegheny Co CC North Pittsburgh, PA 15237	3176
Allegheny Co CC South West Mifflin, PA 15122	3177
Allegheny Wesleyan C Salem, OH 44460	0462
Allen Co CC Iola, KS 66749	2508
Allen Hosp Sch Nsg Waterloo, IA 50701	2462
Allen U Columbia, SC 29204	1022
Allentown C Center Valley, PA 18034	1350
Alma C Alma, MI 48801	0663
Alpena CC Alpena, MI 49707	2659
Alvernia C Reading, PA 19607	1391
Alverno C Milwaukee, WI 53215	0586
Alvin CC Alvin, TX 77511	3315
Amarillo C Amarillo, TX 79178	3316
Ambassador Baptist C Shelby, NC 28150	1042
Ambassador C Big Sandy, TX 75755	3317
Amber U Garland, TX 75041	0942
Amer Acad Dramatic Arts New York, NY 10016	2914
Amer Acad McAllister Inst New York, NY 10019	2915
Amer Acad of Art Chicago, IL 60603	2364
Amer Baptist C Nashville, TN 37207	0740
Amer Consv of Music Chicago, IL 60602	0475
Amer Inst of Business Des Moines, IA 50321	2464
Amer Inst of Commerce Davenport, IA 52807	2463
Amer International C Springfield, MA 01109	1661
Amer Islamic C Chicago, IL 60613	0468
Amer River C Main Cam Sacramento, CA 95841	2102
Amer U Washington, DC 20016	1278
Amer U of Paris New York, NY 10003	1409
Amherst C Amherst, MA 01002	1723
Ancilla C Donaldson, IN 46513	2443
Anderson C Anderson, SC 29621	1065
Anderson U Anderson, IN 46012	0596
Andrew C Cuthbert, GA 31740	2305
Andrews U Berrien Springs, MI 49104	0457
Angelina C Lufkin, TX 75901	3318
Angelo St U San Angelo, TX 76909	0956
Anna Maria C Paxton, MA 01612	1632
Anne Arundel CC Arnold, MD 21012	2608
Anoka Tech C Anoka, MN 55303	2704
Anoka-Ramsey CC Cambridge, MN 55008	2705
Anoka-Ramsey CC Coon Rapids, MN 55433	2706
Anson Tech CC Ansonville, NC 28007	2997
Antelope Valley C Lancaster, CA 93536	2103
Antietam Bible C Hagerstown, MD 21740	1007
Antioch C Main Cam Yellow Springs, OH 45387	0569
Antioch Sch Adult Learn Yellow Springs, OH 45387	0718
Antioch U Los Ang Marina Del Rey, CA 90292	0023
Antioch U Santa Barbara Santa Barbara, CA 93101	0225
Antioch U Seattle Seattle, WA 98121	0024
Appalachian Bible C Bradley, WV 25818	1054
Appalachian St U Boone, NC 28608	1209
Aquinas C Grand Rapids, MI 49506	0604
Aquinas JC Nashville, TN 37205	3265
Aquinas JC at Milton Milton, MA 02186	2628
Aquinas JC at Newton Newton, MA 02158	2629
Arapahoe CC Littleton, CO 80160	2212
Ariz C of Bible Phoenix, AZ 85021	0006
Ariz St U Tempe, AZ 85287	0198
Ariz Western C Yuma, AZ 85364	2065
Ariz, U of Tucson, AZ 85721	0197
Ark Med Science, U of Little Rock, AR 72205	0756
Arkansas Baptist C Little Rock, AR 72202	0738
Arkansas C Batesville, AR 72503	0946
Arkansas Little Rock, U of Little Rock, AR 72204	0771
Arkansas Main Cam, U of Fayetteville, AR 72701	0927
Arkansas Monticello, U of Monticello, AR 71655	0760
Arkansas Pine Bluff, U of Pine Bluff, AR 71601	0761
Arkansas St U Beebe Beebe, AR 72012	2083
Arkansas St U Main Cam St University, AR 72467	0773
Arkansas Tech U Russellville, AR 72801	0823
Armstrong C Berkeley, CA 94704	0078
Armstrong St C Savannah, GA 31419	1094
Arnot Ogden Sch Nsg Elmira, NY 14905	2916
Art Academy of Cincinnati Cincinnati, OH 45202	0534
Art Center C of Design Pasadena, CA 91103	0156
Art Inst Boston Boston, MA 02215	1597
Art Inst Fort Lauderdale Fort Lauderdale, FL 33316	1035
Art Inst of Chicago Chicago, IL 60603	0592
Arts, U of the Philadelphia, PA 19102	1493
Asbury C Wilmore, KY 40390	0908
Asheville-Buncombe C Asheville, NC 28801	2998
Ashland C Ashland, OH 44805	0611
Ashland CC Ashland, KY 41101	2538
Asnuntuck CC Enfield, CT 06082	2231
Assoc Arts, C of St Paul, MN 55102	0304
Assumption C Worcester, MA 01615	1668
Athens Area Tech C Athens, GA 30610	2306
Athens St C Athens, AL 35611	1000
Athens St Voc-Tech Athens, TN 37303	3266

Name	Sequence Number
Atlanta Area Tech Sch Atlanta, GA 30310	2307
Atlanta C of Art Atlanta, GA 30309	1135
Atlanta Christian C East Point, GA 30344	1051
Atlanta Metro C Atlanta, GA 30310	2308
Atlantic Baptist Bible C Chester, VA 23831	1014
Atlantic CC Mays Landing, NJ 08330	2871
Atlantic Union C South Lancaster, MA 01561	1616
Atlantic Voc-Tech Coconut Creek, FL 33063	2253
Atlantic, C of the Bar Harbor, ME 04609	1642
Auburn at Montgomery, U Montgomery, AL 36117	0819
Auburn U Auburn, AL 36849	0982
Augsburg C Minneapolis, MN 55454	0398
Augusta Area Tech Sch Augusta, GA 30906	2309
Augusta C Augusta, GA 30910	1112
Augustana C Sioux Falls, SD 57197	0393
Augustana C of ILL Rock Island, IL 61201	0674
Aultman Hosp Sch Nsg Canton, OH 44710	3070
Aultman Hosp Sch R-T Canton, OH 44710	3071
Aultman/Ultrasonography Canton, OH 44710	3072
Aurora U Aurora, IL 60506	0508
Aurora, CC of Aurora, CO 80011	2213
Austin C Sherman, TX 75091	0970
Austin CC Austin, TX 78714	3319
Austin CC of Minn Austin, MN 55912	2707
Austin Peay St U Clarksville, TN 37044	0852
Averett C Danville, VA 24541	1199
Avila C Kansas City, MO 64110	0283
Ayers Tech C Anniston, AL 36201	2004
Azusa Pacific U Azusa, CA 91702	0120

B

Name	Sequence Number
Babson C Wellesley, MA 02157	1703
Bacone C Muskogee, OK 74403	3138
Bainbridge C Bainbridge, GA 31717	2310
Baker C Flint, MI 48507	0453
Baker C Muskegon, MI 49442	0455
Baker C-Mt Clemens Mount Clemens, MI 48043	0429
Baker C-Owosso Owosso, MI 48867	0435
Baker C-Pontiac Pontiac, MI 48053	2660
Baker C-Port Huron Port Huron, MI 48060	2661
Baker U Baldwin City, KS 66006	0352
Bakersfield C Bakersfield, CA 93305	2104
Baldwin-Wallace C Berea, OH 44017	0657
Ball St U Muncie, IN 47306	0632
Baltimore Hebrew C Baltimore, MD 21215	1226
Baltimore, CC of Baltimore, MD 21215	2609
Baltimore, U of Baltimore, MD 21201	1301
Baptist Bible C Springfield, MO 65803	0232
Baptist Bible C East Boston, MA 02136	1588
Baptist Bible C of Pa Clarks Summit, PA 18411	1317
Baptist Christian Shreveport, LA 71108	0863
Baptist Hosp Sch Nsg Memphis, TN 38104	3267
Baptist System Sch Nsg Little Rock, AR 72210	2084
Barat C Lake Forest, IL 60045	0552
Barber-Scotia C Concord, NC 28025	1055
Barclay C Haviland, KS 67059	0272
Bard C Annandale Hudsn, NY 12504	1518
Barnard C-Columbia U New York, NY 10027	1564
Barnes C of Nsg St Louis, MO 63110	0309
Barry U Miami, FL 33161	1204
Barstow C Barstow, CA 92311	2105
Bartlesville Wesleyan C Bartlesville, OK 74003	0809
Barton C Wilson, NC 27893	1183
Barton Co CC Great Bend, KS 67530	2509
Bassist C Portland, OR 97201	0048
Bates C Lewiston, ME 04240	1730
Baton Rouge Rad Techn Baton Rouge, LA 70806	2566
Baton Rouge Sch Nsg Baton Rouge, LA 70821	2567
Baton Rouge Voc-Tech Baton Rouge, LA 70805	2568
Bauder Fashion C Atlanta, GA 30326	2311
Bay De Noc CC Escanaba, MI 49829	2662
Bay Path C Longmeadow, MA 01106	2630
Bay Ridge Christian C Kendleton, TX 77451	0733
Bay St C Boston, MA 02116	2631
Baylor C of Dentistry Dallas, TX 75246	0992
Baylor U Waco, TX 76798	0975
Beal C Bangor, ME 04401	2598
Beaufort Co CC Washington, NC 27889	2999
Beaver C Glenside, PA 19038	1432
Beaver Co CC Monaca, PA 15061	3179
Becker C Worcester Worcester, MA 01609	2632
Becker JC Leicester Leicester, MA 01524	2633
Beckley C Beckley, WV 25802	3465
Bee Co C Beeville, TX 78102	3320
Bel-Rea Inst Animal Techn Denver, CO 80231	2214
Belhaven C Jackson, MS 39202	0874
Bellarmine C Louisville, KY 40205	0961
Belleville Area C Belleville, IL 62221	2365
Bellevue C Bellevue, NE 68005	0260
Bellevue CC Bellevue, WA 98009	3436
Bellin C of Nsg Green Bay, WI 54305	0639
Belmont Abbey C Belmont, NC 28012	1110
Belmont C Nashville, TN 37212	0913
Belmont Tech C St Clairsville, OH 43950	3073
Beloit C Beloit, WI 53511	0675
Bemidji St U Bemidji, MN 56601	0348
Bemidji Tech C Bemidji, MN 56601	2708
Ben Hill Irwin Tech Fitzgerald, GA 31750	2312
Benedict C Columbia, SC 29204	1033
Benedictine C Atchison, KS 66002	0338
Bennett C Greensboro, NC 27401	1121
Bennington C Bennington, VT 05201	1695
Bentley C Waltham, MA 02154	1699
Berea C Berea, KY 40404	0955
Bergan Mercy Sch Rad Tech Omaha, NE 68124	2839
Bergen CC Paramus, NJ 07652	2872

COLLEGE INDEX

Name	Sequence Number
Berkeley C Business Waldwick, NJ 07463	2873
Berkeley C Business Woodbridge, NJ 07095	2875
Berkeley C of Business West Paterson, NJ 07424	2874
Berkeley Sch NY City New York, NY 10017	2917
Berkeley Sch White Plains White Plains, NY 10604	2918
Berklee C of Music Boston, MA 02215	1619
Berkshire CC Pittsfield, MA 01201	2634
Berry C Rome, GA 30149	1252
Bessemer St Tech Bessemer, AL 35021	2005
Beth-El C of Nsg Colorado Sprgs, CO 80909	0077
Bethany Bible C Santa Cruz, CA 95066	0045
Bethany C Bethany, WV 26032	1234
Bethany C Lindsborg, KS 67456	0323
Bethany C of Missions Bloomington, MN 55438	0297
Bethany Lutheran C Mankato, MN 56001	2709
Bethel C McKenzie, TN 38201	0865
Bethel C Mishawaka, IN 46544	0529
Bethel C North Newton, KS 67117	0317
Bethel C St Paul, MN 55112	0360
Bethune-Cookman C Daytona Beach, FL 32115	1102
Beulah Heights Bible C Atlanta, GA 30316	1010
Bible Baptist Inst & C Hudson Falls, NY 12839	2919
Big Bend CC Moses Lake, WA 98837	3437
Billings Voc-Tech Center Billings, MT 59102	2828
Biola U La Mirada, CA 90639	0161
Birmingham-Southern C Birmingham, AL 35254	0969
Bismarck St C Bismarck, ND 58501	3060
Black Hawk C Moline, IL 61265	2367
Black Hawk C East Kewanee, IL 61443	2368
Black Hills St U Spearfish, SD 57783	0287
Blackburn C Carlinville, IL 62626	0640
Blackhawk Tech C Janesville, WI 53547	3478
Bladen CC Dublin, NC 28332	3000
Blessing Hosp C of Nsg Quincy, IL 62301	0530
Blinn C Brenham, TX 77833	3321
Bliss C Columbus, OH 43214	3074
Bloomfield C Bloomfield, NJ 07003	1321
Bloomington-Norml Sch Rad Normal, IL 61761	2366
Bloomsburg U Bloomsburg, PA 17815	1524
Blue Mountain C Blue Mountain, MS 38610	0798
Blue Mountain CC Pendleton, OR 97801	3159
Blue Ridge CC Weyers Cave, VA 24486	3405
Blue Ridge Tech C Flat Rock, NC 28731	3001
Bluefield C Bluefield, VA 24605	1067
Bluefield St C Bluefield, WV 24701	1026
Bluffton C Bluffton, OH 45817	0643
Bob Jones U Greenville, SC 29614	1103
Boca Raton, C of Boca Raton, FL 33431	1111
Boise St U Boise, ID 83725	0070
Boricua C New York, NY 10032	1308
Bossier Parish CC Bossier City, LA 71111	2569
Boston C Chestnut Hill, MA 02167	1732
Boston Consv of Music Boston, MA 02215	1635
Boston U Boston, MA 02215	1737
Bowdoin C Brunswick, ME 04011	1724
Bowie St U Bowie, MD 20715	1175
Bowling Green Firelands Huron, OH 44839	3075
Bowling Green St U Bowling Green, OH 43403	0697
Bowling Green Voc-Tech Bowling Green, KY 42102	2539
Bradford C Bradford, MA 01835	1644
Bradley U Peoria, IL 61625	0695
Brainerd CC Brainerd, MN 56401	2710
Brainerd Tech C Brainerd, MN 56401	2711
Brandeis U Waltham, MA 02254	1729
Brazosport C Lake Jackson, TX 77566	3322
Brenau Women's C Gainesville, GA 30501	1150
Brescia C Owensboro, KY 42301	0876
Brevard C Brevard, NC 28712	3002
Brevard CC Cocoa, FL 32922	2254
Brewer St JC Fayette, AL 35555	2006
Brewton-Parker C Mt Vernon, GA 30445	1031
Briar Cliff C Sioux City, IA 51104	0354
Bridgeport Engr Inst Fairfield, CT 06430	1589
Bridgeport, U of Bridgeport, CT 06601	1672
Bridgewater C Bridgewater, VA 22812	1202
Bridgewater St C Bridgewater, MA 02325	1682
Brigham Young U Hawaii Laie, HI 96762	0058
Brigham Young U Main Cam Provo, UT 84602	0194
Bristol CC Fall River, MA 02720	2635
Bronson Hosp Sch Nsg Kalamazoo, MI 49007	2663
Bronson Hosp Sch Rad Tech Kalamazoo, MI 49007	2664
Brookdale CC Lincroft, NJ 07738	2876
Brookhaven C Farmers Branch, TX 75244	3323
Brooks C Long Beach, CA 90804	2106
Brooks Inst Photography Santa Barbara, CA 93108	0081
Broome CC Binghamton, NY 13902	2920
Broward CC Fort Lauderdale, FL 33301	2255
Brown Mackie C Salina, KS 67402	2510
Brown U Providence, RI 02912	1735
Brunswick CC Supply, NC 28462	3003
Brunswick JC Brunswick, GA 31520	2313
Bryan C Dayton, TN 37321	0881
Bryan Memorial Sch Nsg Lincoln, NE 68506	2840
Bryant C Smithfield, RI 02917	1696
Bryant Stratton Bus Inst Rochester, NY 14623	2921
Bryant-Stratton Inst Albany, NY 12205	2922
Bryant-Stratton Inst Buffalo, NY 14202	2923
Bryant-Stratton Inst Syracuse, NY 13202	2924
Bryn Mawr C Bryn Mawr, PA 19010	1565
Bucknell U Lewisburg, PA 17837	1557
Bucks Co CC Newtown, PA 18940	3180
Buena Vista C Storm Lake, IA 50588	0362
Bunker Hill CC Boston, MA 02129	2636
Burdett Sch Boston, MA 02116	2637
Burge Sch of Nursing Springfield, MO 65802	2792

Name	Sequence Number
Burlington C Burlington, VT 05401	1590
Burlington Co C Pemberton, NJ 08068	2877
Butler Co CC Butler, PA 16001	3181
Butler Co CC El Dorado, KS 67042	2511
Butler U Indianapolis, IN 46208	0670
Butte C Oroville, CA 95965	2107
Butte Voc-Tech Center Butte, MT 59701	2829

C

Name	Sequence Number
Cabrillo C Aptos, CA 95003	2108
Cabrini C Radnor, PA 19087	1401
Cal Baptist C Riverside, CA 92504	0042
Cal Berkeley, U of Berkeley, CA 94720	0223
Cal C of Arts Oakland, CA 94618	0053
Cal Davis, U of Davis, CA 95616	0219
Cal Inst of Techn Pasadena, CA 91125	0212
Cal Inst of the Arts Valencia, CA 91355	0171
Cal Irvine, U of Irvine, CA 92717	0220
Cal Los Ang, U of Los Angeles, CA 90025	0221
Cal Lutheran U Thousand Oaks, CA 91360	0121
Cal Maritime Acad Vallejo, CA 94590	0029
Cal Poly-San Luis Obispo San Luis Obispo, CA 93407	0204
Cal Riverside, U of Riverside, CA 92521	0216
Cal San Diego, U of La Jolla, CA 92093	0224
Cal Santa Barbara, U of Santa Barbara, CA 93106	0222
Cal Santa Cruz, U of Santa Cruz, CA 95064	0217
Cal St Poly U Pomona Pomona, CA 91768	0185
Cal St U Bakersfield Bakersfield, CA 93311	0154
Cal St U Chico Chico, CA 95929	0187
Cal St U Dominguez Hills Carson, CA 90747	0152
Cal St U Fresno Fresno, CA 93740	0192
Cal St U Fullerton Fullerton, CA 92634	0181
Cal St U Hayward Hayward, CA 94542	0180
Cal St U Long Beach Long Beach, CA 90840	0195
Cal St U Los Ang Los Angeles, CA 90032	0126
Cal St U Northridge Northridge, CA 91330	0202
Cal St U Sacramento Sacramento, CA 95819	0196
Cal St U San Bernardino San Bernardino, CA 92407	0183
Cal St U Stanislaus Turlock, CA 95380	0155
Cal U of Pa California, PA 15419	1448
Caldwell C Caldwell, NJ 07006	1351
Caldwell CC & Tech Inst Hudson, NC 28638	3004
Calumet C of St Joseph Whiting, IN 46394	0515
Calvary Bible C Kansas City, MO 64147	0267
Calvin C Grand Rapids, MI 49546	0590
Camden Co C Blackwood, NJ 08012	2878
Cameron U Lawton, OK 73505	0888
Campbell U Buies Creek, NC 27506	1220
Campbellsville C Campbellsville, KY 42718	0808
Canada C Redwood City, CA 94061	2109
Canisius C Buffalo, NY 14208	1418
Canyons, C of the Valencia, CA 91355	2110
Cape Cod CC West Barnstable, MA 02668	2638
Cape Fear CC Wilmington, NC 28401	3005
Capital City Business C Little Rock, AR 72214	2085
Capital U Columbus, OH 43209	0615
Capitol C Laurel, MD 20708	1068
Cardinal Stritch C Milwaukee, WI 53217	0588
Career Devel Inst Arlington, VA 22204	3406
Carl Albert JC Poteau, OK 74953	3139
Carl Sandburg C Galesburg, IL 61401	2369
Carleton C Northfield, MN 55057	0415
Carlow C Pittsburgh, PA 15213	1357
Carnegie-Mellon U Pittsburgh, PA 15213	1574
Carroll C Waukesha, WI 53186	0664
Carroll C of Montana Helena, MT 59625	0087
Carson-Newman C Jefferson City, TN 37760	0914
Carteret CC Morehead City, NC 28557	3006
Carthage C Kenosha, WI 53140	0612
Carver St Tech Inst Mobile, AL 36617	2007
Case Western Reserve U Cleveland, OH 44106	0714
Casper C Casper, WY 82601	3515
Castleton St C Castleton, VT 05735	1657
Catawba C Salisbury, NC 28144	1139
Catawba Valley CC Hickory, NC 28602	3007
Catholic U of Amer Washington, DC 20064	1267
Catonsville CC Catonsville, MD 21228	2610
Cayuga Co CC Auburn, NY 13021	2925
Cazenovia C Cazenovia, NY 13035	1332
Cecil CC North East, MD 21901	2611
Cedar Crest C Allentown, PA 18104	1373
Cedar Valley C Lancaster, TX 75134	3324
Cedarville C Cedarville, OH 45314	0585
Centenary C Hackettstown, NJ 07840	1322
Centenary C of La Shreveport, LA 71134	0950
Center Creative Studies Detroit, MI 48202	0560
Center for Robotic Tech Chicago, IL 60631	0513
Central Ala CC-Childrsbrg Childersburg, AL 35044	2008
Central Ariz C Coolidge, AZ 85228	2066
Central Arkansas, U of Conway, AR 72032	0848
Central Baptist C Conway, AR 72032	0859
Central Bible C Springfield, MO 65803	0302
Central C McPherson, KS 67460	0276
Central C Pella, IA 50219	0394
Central Carolina Tech C Sanford, NC 27330	3008
Central CC Platte Columbus, NE 68601	2841
Central CC-Hastings Hastings, NE 68901	2842
Central City Bus Inst Syracuse, NY 13203	2926
Central Conn St U New Britain, CT 06050	1683
Central Florida CC Ocala, FL 32678	2256
Central Florida, U of Orlando, FL 32816	1273
Central Kentucky Voc-Tech Lexington, KY 40510	2540
Central Maine Sch Nsg Lewiston, ME 04240	2599
Central Maine Tech C Auburn, ME 04210	2600
Central Methodist C Fayette, MO 65248	0327
Central Mich U Mt Pleasant, MI 48859	0689

Name	Sequence Number
Central Missouri St U, Warrensburg, MO 64093	0295
Central Ohio Tech C, Newark, OH 43055	3076
Central Okla Area Vo-Tech, Drumright, OK 74030	3140
Central Okla, U of, Edmond, OK 73034	0845
Central Oregon CC, Bend, OR 97701	3160
Central Pa Bus Sch, Summerdale, PA 17093	3182
Central Piedmont CC, Charlotte, NC 28235	3009
Central St U, Wilberforce, OH 45384	0452
Central Texas C, Killeen, TX 76541	3325
Central Texas, U of, Killeen, TX 76540	0996
Central Virginia CC, Lynchburg, VA 24502	3407
Central Washington U, Ellensburg, WA 98926	0133
Central Wesleyan C, Central, SC 29630	1071
Central Wyoming C, Riverton, WY 82501	3516
Centralia C, Centralia, WA 98531	3438
Centre C, Danville, KY 40422	0985
Cerritos C, Norwalk, CA 90650	2111
Cerro Coso CC, Ridgecrest, CA 93555	2112
Chabot C, Hayward, CA 94545	2113
Chadron St C, Chadron, NE 69337	0242
Chaffey C, Rancho Cucamung, CA 91701	2114
Chaminade U of Honolulu, Honolulu, HI 96816	0118
Champlain C, Burlington, VT 05402	1615
Chandler Gilbert CC, Chandler, AZ 85225	2067
Chapman C, Orange, CA 92666	0124
Charity Hosp Sch Nsg, New Orleans, LA 70112	2570
Charity Hosp Surg Tech, New Orleans, LA 70140	2571
Charles Co CC, La Plata, MD 20646	2612
Charleston Southern U, Charleston, SC 29411	1187
Charleston, C of, Charleston, SC 29424	1215
Charleston, U of, Charleston, WV 25304	1140
Chas Gregory Sch Nsg, Perth Amboy, NY 08861	2927
Chatham C, Pittsburgh, PA 15232	1468
Chattahoochee Tech Inst, Marietta, GA 30060	2314
Chattahoochee Valley CC, Phenix City, AL 36867	2009
Chattanooga Tech CC, Chattanooga, TN 37406	3268
Chemeketa CC, Salem, OR 97309	3161
Chenier Business, Bulmont, TX 77706	3326
Chesapeake C, Wye Mills, MD 21679	2613
Chesterfield Tech, Cheraw, SC 29520	3231
Chestnut Hill C, Philadelphia, PA 19118	1466
Cheyenne River CC, Eagle Butte, SD 57625	3254
Cheyney U, Cheyney, PA 19319	1327
Chicago C of Commerce, Chicago, IL 60603	2370
Chicago City-Wide C, Chicago, IL 60606	2371
Chicago St U, Chicago, IL 60628	0498
Chicago, U of, Chicago, IL 60637	0715
Chipola JC, Marianna, FL 32446	2257
Chippewa Valley Tech C, Eau Claire, WI 54701	3479
Chowan C, Murfreesboro, NC 27855	1061
Christ C Irvine, Irvine, CA 92715	0093
Christ C of Okla, Tulsa, OK 74169	0856
Christ Hosp Sch Nsg, Cincinnati, OH 45219	3077
Christendom C, Front Royal, VA 22630	1142
Christian Brothers C, Memphis, TN 38104	0965
Christian Heritage C, El Cajon, CA 92021	0089
Christian Union C, Greenfield, OH 45123	0469
Christopher Newport C, Newport News, VA 23606	1158
Cinci Bible C, Cincinnati, OH 45204	0437
Cinci C of Mort Sci, Cincinnati, OH 45206	0720
Cinci Clermont C, U of, Batavia, OH 45103	3078
Cinci Ray Walters, U of, Cincinnati, OH 45236	3079
Cinci Tech C, Cincinnati, OH 45223	3080
Cinci, U of, Cincinnati, OH 45221	0630
Circleville Bible C, Circleville, OH 43113	0471
Cisco JC, Cisco, TX 76437	3327
Citadel of SC, The, Charleston, SC 29409	1173
Citrus C, Glendora, CA 91740	2115
City C of San Fran, San Francisco, CA 94112	2116
City U, Bellevue, WA 98008	0018
Clackamas CC, Oregon City, OR 97045	3162
Claflin C, Orangeburg, SC 29115	1053
Claremont McKenna C, Claremont, CA 91711	0206
Clarendon C, Clarendon, TX 79226	3328
Clarion U, Clarion, PA 16214	1442
Clarion U Venango, Oil City, PA 16301	3183
Clark Atlanta U, Atlanta, GA 30314	1109
Clark CC, Vancouver, WA 98663	3439
Clark St CC, Springfield, OH 45505	3081
Clark U, Worcester, MA 01610	1594
Clarke C, Dubuque, IA 52001	0342
Clarke C, Newton, MS 39345	2764
Clarkson C of Nursing, Omaha, NE 68131	0301
Clarkson U, Potsdam, NY 13676	1554
Clarksville Baptist C, Clarksville, TN 37043	0731
Clatsop CC, Astoria, OR 97103	3163
Clayton St C, Morrow, GA 30260	1078
Clearwater Christian C, Clearwater, FL 34619	1024
Cleary C, Ypsilanti, MI 48197	0432
Clemson U, Clemson, SC 29634	1274
Cleveland CC, Shelby, NC 28150	3010
Cleveland Inst of Art, Cleveland, OH 44106	0566
Cleveland Inst of Music, Cleveland, OH 44106	0649
Cleveland St CC, Cleveland, TN 37320	3269
Cleveland St U, Cleveland, OH 44115	0460
Clinton Area Voc Tech, Clinton, MO 64735	2793
Clinton CC, Clinton, IA 52732	2465
Clinton CC, Plattsburgh, NY 12901	2928
Clinton JC, Rock Hill, SC 29731	3232
Cloud Co CC, Concordia, KS 66901	2512
Clovis CC, Clovis, NM 88101	2897
CMHA Sch of Nsg, Charlotte, NC 28232	3011
Coahoma CC, Clarksdale, MS 38614	2765
Coastal Carolina CC, Jacksonville, NC 28540	3012
Coastline CC, Fountain Valley, CA 92708	2117

Name	Sequence Number
Cochise C Douglas, AZ 85607	2068
Coe C Cedar Rapids, IA 52402	0382
Coffeyville CC Coffeyville, KS 67337	2513
Cogswell C Cupertino, CA 95014	0080
Coker C Hartsville, SC 29550	1141
Colby C Waterville, ME 04901	1725
Colby CC Colby, KS 67701	2514
Colby-Sawyer C New London, NH 03257	1643
Colgate U Hamilton, NY 13346	1558
Collier Voc-Tech New Orleans, LA 70126	2572
Collin Co CC McKinney, TX 75070	3329
Colo at Denver, U of Denver, CO 80217	0151
Colo Boulder, U of Boulder, CO 80309	0199
Colo C Colorado Sprgs, CO 80903	0211
Colo Christian U Lakewood, CO 80226	0083
Colo Mountain C Alpine Steamboat Sprgs, CO 80477	2215
Colo Mountain C Sprg Vly Glenwood Sprgs, CO 81601	2216
Colo Mountain C Timberln Leadville, CO 80461	2217
Colo Northwestern CC Rangely, CO 81648	2218
Colo Sch of Mines Golden, CO 80401	0209
Colo St U Fort Collins, CO 80523	0203
Colo Tech C Colorado Sprgs, CO 80907	0033
Colo-Colo Springs, U of Colorado Sprgs, CO 80933	0104
Columbia Basin C Pasco, WA 99301	3440
Columbia Bible C Columbia, SC 29230	1123
Columbia C Chicago, IL 60605	0450
Columbia C Columbia, MO 65216	0326
Columbia C Columbia, SC 29203	1228
Columbia C Columbia, CA 95310	2118
Columbia C of Nsg Waukesha, WI 53186	0645
Columbia Christian C Portland, OR 97216	0086
Columbia Gorge CC The Dalles, OR 97058	3164
Columbia St CC Columbia, TN 38402	3270
Columbia U Columbia C New York, NY 10027	1568
Columbia U Engr-App Sci New York, NY 10027	1561
Columbia U Sch Gen Study New York, NY 10027	1549
Columbia U Sch of Nsg New York, NY 10032	1582
Columbia Union C Takoma Park, MD 20912	1147
Columbia-Greene CC Hudson, NY 12534	2929
Columbus C Columbus, GA 31993	1083
Columbus C of Art Columbus, OH 43215	0602
Columbus St CC Columbus, OH 43215	3082
Columbus Tech Inst Columbus, GA 31995	2315
Commonwealth C Norfolk, VA 23510	3408
Commonwealth Funeral C Houston, TX 77090	3330
Community Hosp Sch Nsg Springfield, OH 45501	3083
Compton CC Compton, CA 90221	2119
Conception Seminary Conception, MO 64433	0306
Concord C Athens, WV 24712	1092
Concordia C Ann Arbor, MI 48105	0541
Concordia C Bronxville, NY 10708	1360
Concordia C Portland, OR 97211	0049
Concordia C Seward, NE 68434	0311
Concordia C at Moorhead Moorhead, MN 56560	0389
Concordia C at Saint Paul St Paul, MN 55104	0355
Concordia C-Alabama Selma, AL 36701	2010
Concordia Lutheran C Austin, TX 78705	0815
Concordia U Mequon, WI 53092	0506
Concordia U of Ill River Forest, IL 60305	0546
Conn C New London, CT 06320	1704
Conn Main Cam, U of Storrs, CT 06269	1711
Connors St C Warner, OK 74469	3141
Contra Costa C San Pablo, CA 94806	2120
Converse C Spartanburg, SC 29301	1230
Cooke Co C Gainesville, TX 76240	3331
Cooper Union New York, NY 10003	1550
Coosa Valley Sch Nsg Sylacauga, AL 35150	2011
Coosa Valley Voc-Tech Rome, GA 30161	2316
Copiah-Lincoln CC Wesson, MS 39191	2767
Copiah-Lincoln CC Natchez, MS 39120	2766
Coppin St C Baltimore, MD 21216	1080
Corcoran Sch of Art Washington, DC 20006	1152
Cornell C Mount Vernon, IA 52314	0404
Cornell U Ithaca, NY 14853	1577
Corning CC Corning, NY 14830	2930
Cornish C Seattle, WA 98102	0040
Corpus Christi St U Corpus Christi, TX 78412	1002
Cosumnes River C Sacramento, CA 95823	2121
Cottey C Nevada, MO 64772	2794
Covenant C Lookout Mt, GA 30750	1145
Covenant Sch Rad Techn Waterloo, IA 50702	2466
Covington St Voc-Tech Covington, TN 38019	3271
Cowley Co CC Arkansas City, KS 67005	2515
Crafton Hills C Yucaipa, CA 92399	2122
Craven CC New Bern, NC 28560	3013
Creighton U Omaha, NE 68178	0408
Crichton C Memphis, TN 38175	0795
Crossville Area Sch Crossville, TN 38555	3272
Crouse-Irving Sch Nsg Syracuse, NY 13210	2931
Crowder C Neosho, MO 64850	2795
Crowley's Ridge C Paragould, AR 72450	2086
Cuesta C San Luis Obispo, CA 93403	2123
Culver-Stockton C Canton, MO 63435	0312
Cumberland C Williamsburg, KY 40769	0901
Cumberland Co C Vineland, NJ 08360	2879
Cumberland U Lebanon, TN 37087	0806
CUNY Bernard Baruch C New York, NY 10010	1438
CUNY Bronx CC Bronx, NY 10453	2932
CUNY Brooklyn C Brooklyn, NY 11210	1437
CUNY C of Staten Island Staten Island, NY 10301	1312
CUNY Hostos CC Bronx, NY 10451	2933
CUNY Hunter C New York, NY 10021	1523
CUNY La Guardia CC Long Island, NY 11101	2934
CUNY Manhattan CC New York, NY 10007	2935
CUNY Medgar Evers C Brooklyn, NY 11225	1306

Name	Sequence Number
CUNY NY City New York, NY 10001	1314
CUNY NY City Tech C Brooklyn, NY 11201	1311
CUNY Queens C Flushing, NY 11367	1522
CUNY Queensborough C New York, NY 11364	2936
CUNY York C Jamaica, NY 11451	1323
CUNY-City College New York, NY 10031	1439
CUNY-John Jay C Crim Just New York, NY 10019	1374
CUNY Kingsborough CC Brooklyn, NY 11235	2937
CUNY-Lehman C Bronx, NY 10468	1475
Curry C Milton, MA 02186	1679
Cuyahoga CC East Cam Warrensvl Tnshp, OH 44122	3084
Cuyahoga CC Metro Cam Cleveland, OH 44115	3085
Cuyahoga CC Western Cam Parma, OH 44130	3086
Cuyamaca C El Cajon, CA 92019	2124
Cypress C Cypress, CA 90630	2125

D

Name	Sequence Number
D-Q U Davis, CA 95617	2126
D'Etre U Grosse Pointe, MI 48236	0524
D'Youville C Buffalo, NY 14201	1393
Dabney Lancaster CC Clifton Forge, VA 24422	3409
Daemen C Amherst, NY 14226	1395
Dakota Co Tech C Rosemount, MN 55068	2712
Dakota St U Madison, SD 57042	0300
Dakota Wesleyan U Mitchell, SD 57301	0313
Daley C Chicago, IL 60652	2372
Dallas Baptist U Dallas, TX 75211	0875
Dallas Christian C Dallas, TX 75234	0794
Dallas Inst Funeral Serv Dallas, TX 75227	3332
Dallas, U of Irving, TX 75062	0967
Dalton C Dalton, GA 30720	2317
Dalton Vocational Sch Dalton, GA 30720	2318
Dana C Blair, NE 68008	0318
Daniel Webster C Nashua, NH 03063	1638
Danville Area CC Danville, IL 61832	2373
Danville CC Danville, VA 24541	3410
Dartmouth C Hanover, NH 03755	1726
Darton C Albany, GA 31707	2319
Davenport C Grand Rapids Grand Rapids, MI 49503	0456
Davenport C Lansing Lansing, MI 48933	0442
Davenport C-Kalamazoo Kalamazoo, MI 49007	0438
David Lipscomb U Nashville, TN 37203	0838
Davidson C Davidson, NC 28036	1290
Davidson Co CC Lexington, NC 27293	3014
Davis & Elkins C Elkins, WV 26241	1073
Davis C Toledo, OH 43623	3087
Dawson CC Glendive, MT 59330	2830
Dawson Tech Inst Chicago, IL 60609	2374
Dayton, U of Dayton, OH 45469	0631
Daytona Beach CC Daytona Beach, FL 32120	2258
DC, U of Washington, DC 20008	1036
De Anza C Cupertino, CA 95014	2127
De Paul U Chicago, IL 60604	0696
De Pauw U Greencastle, IN 46135	0679
Deaconess C Nursing St Louis, MO 63139	0307
Dean JC Franklin, MA 02038	2639
Deep Springs C Via Dyer NV, CA 89010	2128
Defiance C Defiance, OH 43512	0493
DeKalb C Decatur, GA 30034	2320
Del Mar C Corpus Christi, TX 78404	3333
Del St C Dover, DE 19901	1165
Del Tech & CC Stanton Newark, DE 19702	2251
Del Tech & CC Terry Dover, DE 19903	2252
Del Tech & CC-South Georgetown, DE 19947	2250
Del, U of Newark, DE 19716	1277
Delaware Co CC Media, PA 19063	3184
Delaware Valley C Doylestown, PA 18901	1402
Delgado CC New Orleans, LA 70119	2573
Delta C University Ctr, MI 48710	2665
Delta State U Cleveland, MS 38733	0824
Denison U Granville, OH 43023	0687
Denmark Tech C Denmark, SC 29042	3233
Denver, CC of Denver, CO 80204	2219
Denver, U of Denver, CO 80208	0190
Des Moines Area CC Ankeny Ankeny, IA 50021	2467
Des Moines Area CC Boone Boone, IA 50036	2468
Des Moines Area CC-Crl Carroll, IA 51401	2469
Des Moines Area CC-Urb Des Moines, IA 50314	2470
Desert, C of the Palm Desert, CA 92260	2129
Detroit C Bus-Warren Warren, MI 48092	0433
Detroit C of Business Dearborn, MI 48126	0451
Detroit Lakes Tech C Detroit Lakes, MN 56501	2713
Detroit, U Mercy MC Detroit, MI 48221	0659
DeVry Inst of Techn Chicago, IL 60618	0501
DeVry Inst of Techn Columbus, OH 43209	0503
DeVry Inst of Techn Irving, TX 75038	0833
DeVry Inst of Techn Kansas City, MO 64131	0289
DeVry Inst of Techn Lombard, IL 60148	0502
DeVry Inst of Techn Phoenix, AZ 85021	0062
DeVry Inst Techn City Industry, CA 91746	0063
DeVry Inst Techn Decatur, GA 30030	1097
DeVry Tech Inst Woodbridge, NJ 07095	2880
Diablo Valley C Pleasant Hill, CA 94523	2130
Dickinson C Carlisle, PA 17013	1559
Dickinson St U Dickinson, ND 58601	0243
Dickson Voc-Tech Sch Dickson, TN 37055	3273
Dillard U New Orleans, LA 70122	0910
Divine Word C Epworth, IA 52045	0269
Dixie C St George, UT 84770	3393
Doane C Crete, NE 68333	0334
Dodge City CC Dodge City, KS 67801	2516
Dominican C Orangeburg, NY 10962	1320
Dominican C of San Rafael San Rafael, CA 94901	0102
Don Bosco Tech Inst Rosemead, CA 91770	2131
Donnelly C Kansas City, KS 66102	2517
Dordt C Sioux Center, IA 51250	0350

Name	Sequence Number
Dowling C Oakdale Long Is, NY 11769	1331
Drake St Tech Huntsville, AL 35811	2012
Drake U Des Moines, IA 50311	0401
Draughons JC Knoxville, TN 37919	3274
Drew U Madison, NJ 07940	1556
Drexel U Philadelphia, PA 19104	1537
Drury C Springfield, MO 65802	0387
Dubuque, U of Dubuque, IA 52001	0345
Duke U Durham, NC 27706	1296
Dull Knife C Lame Deer, MT 59043	2831
Duluth Tech C Duluth, MN 55811	2714
Dundalk CC Baltimore, MD 21222	2614
Dunwoody Inst Minneapolis, MN 55403	2715
DuPage, C of Glen Ellyn, IL 60137	2375
Duquesne U Pittsburgh, PA 15282	1533
Durham Tech CC Durham, NC 27703	3015
Dutchess CC Poughkeepsie, NY 12601	2938
Dyersburg St CC Dyersburg, TN 38025	3275
Dyke C Cleveland, OH 44115	0465

E

Name	Sequence Number
Earlham C Richmond, IN 47374	0681
East Arkansas CC Forrest City, AR 72335	2087
East Carolina U Greenville, NC 27858	1211
East Central C Union, MO 63084	2796
East Central JC Decatur, MS 39327	2768
East Central U Ada, OK 74820	0817
East Coast Bible C Charlotte, NC 28214	1016
East Georgia C Swainsboro, GA 30401	2321
East Grand Forks Tech C East Grand Fork, MN 56721	2716
East Los Ang C Monterey Park, CA 91754	2132
East Miss CC Scooba, MS 39358	2770
East Miss CC-Golden Cam Mayhew, MS 39753	2769
East Stroudsburg U E Stroudsburg, PA 18301	1375
East Tenn St U Johnson City, TN 37614	0919
East Texas Baptist U Marshall, TX 75670	0870
East Texas St U Commerce, TX 75428	0895
East-West U Chicago, IL 60605	0434
Eastern Ariz C Thatcher, AZ 85552	2069
Eastern C St Davids, PA 19087	1404
Eastern Christian C Bel Air, MD 21014	1013
Eastern Conn St U Willimantic, CT 06226	1650
Eastern Idaho Tech C Idaho Falls, ID 83404	2360
Eastern Ill U Charleston, IL 61920	0623
Eastern Kentucky U Richmond, KY 40475	0785
Eastern Maine Tech C Bangor, ME 04401	2601
Eastern Mennonite C Harrisonburg, VA 22801	1133
Eastern Mich U Ypsilanti, MI 48197	0629
Eastern Montana C Billings, MT 59101	0016
Eastern Nazarene C Quincy, MA 02170	1601
Eastern NM U Portales, NM 88130	0056
Eastern NM U Roswell CC Roswell, NM 88202	2898
Eastern Okla St U Wilburton, OK 74578	3142
Eastern Oregon St C La Grande, OR 97850	0114
Eastern Shore CC Melfa, VA 23410	3411
Eastern Utah, C of Price, UT 84501	3394
Eastern Washington U Cheney, WA 99004	0131
Eastern Wyoming C Torrington, WY 82240	3517
Eastfield C Mesquite, TX 75150	3334
Eastman Sch of Music Rochester, NY 14604	1472
Eckerd C St Petersburg, FL 33733	1268
Edgecombe CC Tarboro, NC 27886	3016
Edgewood C Madison, WI 53711	0487
Edinboro U Edinboro, PA 16444	1444
Edison CC Fort Myers, FL 33907	2259
Edison St CC Piqua, OH 45356	3088
Edison St Ext Degree C Trenton, NJ 08625	1309
Edmonds CC Lynnwood, WA 98036	3441
Edmondson JC Chattanooga, TN 37411	3276
Edward Waters C Jacksonville, FL 32209	1227
El Camino C Torrance, CA 90506	2133
El Centro C Dallas, TX 75202	3335
El Paso CC El Paso, TX 79998	3336
El Reno JC El Reno, OK 73036	3143
Elgin CC Elgin, IL 60123	2376
Elizabeth City St U Elizabeth City, NC 27909	1084
Elizabethton Area Sch Elizabethton, TN 37644	3277
Elizabethtown C Elizabethtown, PA 17022	1552
Elizabethtown CC Elizabethtown, KY 42701	2541
Ellis Hosp Sch Nsg Schenectady, NY 12308	2939
Ellsworth CC Iowa Falls, IA 50126	2471
Elmhurst C Elmhurst, IL 60126	0597
Elmira C Elmira, NY 14901	1499
Elms C Chicopee, MA 01013	1636
Elon C Elon College, NC 27244	1192
Embry Riddle Aero U Daytona Beach, FL 32114	1188
Embry-Riddle Aero U Prescott, AZ 86301	0117
Emerson C Boston, MA 02116	1681
Emmanuel C Boston, MA 02115	1641
Emmanuel C Franklin Sprgs, GA 30639	2322
Emmaus Bible C Dubuque, IA 52001	0299
Emory & Henry C Emory, VA 24327	1143
Emory U Atlanta, GA 30322	1295
Emporia St U Emporia, KS 66801	0245
Endicott C Beverly, MA 01915	1608
Enterprise St JC Enterprise, AL 36331	2013
Erie CC City Cam Buffalo, NY 14203	2940
Erie CC North Cam Williamsville, NY 14221	2941
Erie CC South Cam Orchard Park, NY 14127	2942
Erskine C Due West, SC 29639	1148
Essex Agri & Tech Inst Hathorne, MA 01937	2640
Essex CC Baltimore Co, MD 21237	2615
Essex Co C Newark, NJ 07102	2881
ETI Tech C-Cleveland Cleveland, OH 44103	0521
ETI Tech C-Niles Niles, OH 44446	3089
Eugene Lang C New York, NY 10011	1471

Name	Sequence Number
Eureka C Eureka, IL 61530	0558
Evangel C Springfield, MO 65802	0290
Evangeline Voc-Tech St Martinville, LA 70582	2574
Evansville, U of Evansville, IN 47722	0660
Eveleth Tech C Eveleth, MN 55734	2717
Everett CC Everett, WA 98201	3442
Evergreen St C Olympia, WA 98505	0112
Evergreen Valley C San Jose, CA 95135	2134

F

Name	Sequence Number
Fairfield U Fairfield, CT 06430	1701
Fairmont St C Fairmont, WV 26554	1029
Fairview Hosp Sch Nsg Cleveland, OH 44111	3090
Faith Baptist Bible C Ankeny, IA 50021	0305
Faith Baptist Inst & C Oliver Springs, TN 37840	0732
Faribault Tech C Faribault, MN 55021	2718
Farlgh Dcksn U Ed Wm Hackensack, NJ 07601	2882
Farlgh Dcksn U Madison Madison, NJ 07940	1422
Farlgh Dcksn U Rutherford Rutherford, NJ 07070	1423
Farlgh Dcksn U Teaneck Teaneck, NJ 07666	1424
Fashion Inst of Techn New York, NY 10001	1379
Faulkner St JC Bay Minette, AL 36507	2014
Faulkner U Montgomery, AL 36193	0807
Faulkner U Birmingham Birmingham, AL 35222	2015
Faulkner U Florence Florence, AL 35630	2016
Faulkner U Huntsville Huntsville, AL 35805	2017
Faulkner U Mobile Mobile, AL 36604	2018
Fayetteville St U Fayetteville, NC 28301	1161
Fayetteville Tech CC Fayetteville, NC 28303	3017
Feather River C Quincy, CA 95971	2135
Felician C Lodi, NJ 07644	1339
Fergus Falls CC Fergus Falls, MN 56537	2719
Ferris St U Big Rapids, MI 49307	0511
Ferrum C Ferrum, VA 24088	1189
Findlay, U of Findlay, OH 45840	0601
Finger Lakes, CC of the Canandaigua, NY 14424	2943
Fisher C Boston, MA 02116	2641
Fisk U Nashville, TN 37203	0945
Fitchburg St C Fitchburg, MA 01420	1652
Five Towns C Seaford, NY 11783	2944
Fla Baptist Theol C Graceville, FL 32440	1008
Flagler C St Augustine, FL 32085	1182
Flathead Valley CC Kalispell, MT 59901	2832
Florence Darlington Florence, SC 29501	3234
Florida A&M U Tallahassee, FL 32307	1114
Florida Atlantic U Boca Raton, FL 33431	1272
Florida Baptist C Brandon, FL 33509	1005
Florida Bible C Kissimmee, FL 32758	1049
Florida C Temple Terrace, FL 33617	2260
Florida CC Jacksonville Jacksonville, FL 32205	2261
Florida Christian C Kissimmee, FL 32743	1044
Florida Inst of Techn Melbourne, FL 32901	1259
Florida International U Miami, FL 33199	1270
Florida Keys CC Key West, FL 33040	2262
Florida Memorial C Miami, FL 33054	1034
Florida Southern C Lakeland, FL 33801	1195
Florida St U Tallahassee, FL 32306	1299
Florida, U of Gainesville, FL 32611	1282
Floyd C Rome, GA 30162	2323
Fontbonne C St Louis, MO 63105	0331
Foothill C Los Altos Hills, CA 94022	2136
Fordham U Bronx, NY 10595	1538
Forsyth Sch Dental Hyg Boston, MA 02115	1645
Forsyth Tech CC Winston-Salem, NC 27103	3018
Fort Berthold CC New Town, ND 58763	3061
Fort Hays St U Hays, KS 67601	0248
Fort Lauderdale C Ft Lauderdale, FL 33301	1020
Fort Lewis C Durango, CO 81301	0059
Fort Peck CC Poplar, MT 59255	2833
Fort Scott CC Fort Scott, KS 66701	2518
Fort Valley St C Fort Valley, GA 31030	1089
Fox Valley Tech C Appleton, WI 54913	3480
Framingham St C Framingham, MA 01701	1649
Francis Marion C Florence, SC 29501	1096
Franciscan U Steubenville, OH 43952	0594
Frank Phillips C Borger, TX 79007	3337
Franklin & Marshall C Lancaster, PA 17604	1519
Franklin C of Indiana Franklin, IN 46131	0563
Franklin Inst of Boston Boston, MA 02116	2642
Franklin Pierce C Rindge, NH 03461	1618
Franklin U Columbus, OH 43215	0446
Fredd St Tech C Tuscaloosa, AL 35401	2019
Frederick CC Frederick, MD 21702	2616
Free Will Baptist C Nashville, TN 37205	0746
Freed-Hardeman U Henderson, TN 38340	0903
Fresno City C Fresno, CA 93741	2137
Fresno Pacific C Fresno, CA 93702	0095
Friends U Wichita, KS 67213	0291
Friends World C Huntington, NY 11743	1366
Front Range CC Westminster, CO 80220	2220
Frontier CC Fairfield, IL 62837	2377
Frostburg St U Frostburg, MD 21532	1176
Fullerton C Fullerton, CA 92634	2138
Fulton-Montgomery CC Johnstown, NY 12095	2945
Furman U Greenville, SC 29613	1288

G

Name	Sequence Number
Gadsden St CC Gadsden, AL 35902	2020
Gainesville C Gainesville, GA 30503	2324
Gallaudet U Washington, DC 20002	1184
Galveston C Galveston, TX 77550	3338
Gannon U Erie, PA 16541	1435
Garden City CC Garden City, KS 67846	2519
Gardner-Webb C Boiling Springs, NC 28017	1136
Garland Co CC Hot Springs, AR 71913	2088
Garrett CC McHenry, MD 21541	2617
Gaston C Dallas, NC 28034	3019

Name	Sequence Number
Gateway C Evangelism Florissant, MO 63031	0261
Gateway CC Phoenix, AZ 85034	2070
Gateway Tech C Kenosha, WI 53144	3481
Gavilan C Gilroy, CA 95020	2139
General Motors Inst Flint, MI 48504	0707
Genesee CC Batavia, NY 14020	2946
Geneva C Beaver Falls, PA 15010	1392
George Fox C Newberg, OR 97132	0096
George Mason U Fairfax, VA 22030	1218
George Washington U Washington, DC 20052	1279
Georgetown C Georgetown, KY 40324	0911
Georgetown U Washington, DC 20057	1297
Georgia Baptist C College Park, GA 30349	1116
Georgia Baptist Sch Nsg Atlanta, GA 30312	1117
Georgia C Milledgeville, GA 31061	1081
Georgia Inst of Techn Atlanta, GA 30332	1292
Georgia Military C Milledgeville, GA 31061	2325
Georgia Southern U Statesboro, GA 30460	1115
Georgia Southwestern C Americus, GA 31709	1085
Georgia St U Atlanta, GA 30303	1222
Georgia, U of Athens, GA 30602	1283
Georgian Court C Lakewood, NJ 08701	1348
Germanna CC Locust Grove, VA 22508	3412
Gettysburg C Gettysburg, PA 17325	1517
Glassboro St C Glassboro, NJ 08028	1452
Glen Oaks CC Centreville, MI 49032	2666
Glendale CC Glendale, CA 91208	2140
Glendale CC Glendale, AZ 85302	2071
Glenville St C Glenville, WV 26351	1028
Gloucester Co C Sewell, NJ 08080	2883
God's Bible Sch & C Cincinnati, OH 45210	0466
Goddard C Plainfield, VT 05667	1609
Gogebic CC Ironwood, MI 49938	2667
Golden Gate U San Francisco, CA 94105	0105
Golden West C Huntingtn Beach, CA 92647	2141
Goldey Beacom C Wilmington, DE 19808	1063
Gonzaga U Spokane, WA 99258	0162
Good Samaritan Sch Nsg Cincinnati, OH 45220	3091
Gordon C Barnesville, GA 30204	2326
Gordon C Wenham, MA 01984	1673
Goshen C Goshen, IN 46526	0549
Goucher C Towson, MD 21204	1243
Governors St U University Park, IL 60466	0719
Grace Bible C Grand Rapids, MI 49509	0522
Grace C Winona Lake, IN 46590	0535
Grace C of Bible Omaha, NE 68108	0303
Graceland C Lamoni, IA 50140	0281
Graceland U New Albany, IN 47150	0481
Graham Hosp Sch Nsg Canton, IL 61520	2378
Grambling St U Grambling, LA 71245	0783
Grand Canyon U Phoenix, AZ 85017	0116
Grand Rapids Bapt C Grand Rapids, MI 49505	0527
Grand Rapids Bible C Grand Rapids, MI 49506	2668
Grand Rapids JC Grand Rapids, MI 49503	2669
Grand Valley St U Allendale, MI 49401	0628
Grand View C Des Moines, IA 50316	0240
Granite Falls Area V-T Granite Falls, MN 56241	2720
Gratz C Melrose Park, PA 19126	1316
Gray's Harbor C Aberdeen, WA 98520	3443
Grayson Co C Denison, TX 75020	3339
Great Falls Voc-Tech C Great Falls, MT 59405	2834
Great Falls, C of Great Falls, MT 59405	0005
Great Lakes Bible C Lansing, MI 48901	0473
Greater Hartford CC Hartford, CT 06106	2232
Green Mountain C Poultney, VT 05764	1630
Green River CC Auburn, WA 98002	3444
Greenbrier CC Lewisburg, WV 24901	3466
Greenfield CC Greenfield, MA 01301	2643
Greensboro C Greensboro, NC 27401	1128
Greenville C Greenville, IL 62246	0555
Greenville Tech C Greenville, SC 29606	3235
Griffin-Spaulding Vo-Tech Griffin, GA 30223	2327
Grinnell C Grinnell, IA 50112	0414
Grossmont C El Cajon, CA 92020	2142
Grove City C Grove City, PA 16127	1479
Grumman Data Systems Woodbury, NY 11797	2947
Guilford C Greensboro, NC 27410	1264
Guilford Tech CC Jamestown, NC 27282	3020
Gulf Area Voc-Tech Sch Abbeville, LA 70510	2575
Gulf Coast CC Panama City, FL 32401	2263
Gustavus Adolphus C St Peter, MN 56082	0399
Gwynedd-Mercy C Gwynedd Valley, PA 19437	1355

H

Name	Sequence Number
Hagerstown JC Hagerstown, MD 21740	2618
Hahnemann U Philadelphia, PA 19102	1394
Halifax CC Weldon, NC 27890	3021
Hamilton C Clinton, NY 13323	1562
Hamline U St Paul, MN 55104	0402
Hammond Area Tech Inst Hammond, LA 70404	2576
Hampden-Sydney C Hampden-Sydney, VA 23943	1231
Hampshire C Amherst, MA 01002	1706
Hampton U Hampton, VA 23668	1181
Haney Voc-Tech Center Panama City, FL 32405	2264
Hannibal-La Grange C Hannibal, MO 63401	0270
Hanover C Hanover, IN 47243	0652
Harcum JC Bryn Mawr, PA 19010	3185
Hardin-Simmons U Abilene, TX 79698	0899
Harding U Searcy, AR 72143	0960
Harford CC Bel Air, MD 21014	2619
Harold Washington C Chicago, IL 60601	2379
Harriman St Voc-Tech Harriman, TN 37748	3278
Harris Voc-Tech Opelousas, LA 70570	2577
Harris-Stowe St C St Louis, MO 63103	0298
Harrisburg Area CC Harrisburg, PA 17110	3186
Hartford C for Women Hartford, CT 06105	2234

COLLEGE INDEX

Name	Location	Sequence Number
Hartford Camerata Consv	Hartford, CT 06105	2233
Hartford St Tech C	Hartford, CT 06106	2235
Hartford, U of	West Hartford, CT 06117	1680
Hartnell C	Salinas, CA 93901	2143
Hartsville St Voc-Tech	Hartsville, TN 37074	3279
Hartwick C	Oneonta, NY 13820	1436
Harvard-Radcliffe U	Cambridge, MA 02138	1731
Harvey Mudd C	Claremont, CA 91711	0207
Haskell Indian JC	Lawrence, KS 66046	2520
Hastings C	Hastings, NE 68901	0337
Haverford C	Haverford, PA 19041	1560
Hawaii at Manoa, U of	Honolulu, HI 96822	0182
Hawaii Hilo, U of	Hilo, HI 96720	2353
Hawaii Loa C	Kaneohe Oahu, HI 96744	0097
Hawaii Pacific U	Honolulu, HI 96813	0115
Hawkeye Inst of Techn	Waterloo, IA 50704	2472
Haywood Tech C	Clyde, NC 28721	3022
Hazard CC	Hazard, KY 41701	2542
Hazard St Voc-Tech Sch	Hazard, KY 41701	2543
Heald Inst of Tech	San Francisco, CA 94103	2144
Hebrew C	Brookline, MA 02146	1587
Hebrew Theological C	Skokie, IL 60077	0483
Heidelberg C	Tiffin, OH 44883	0671
Helena Voc-Tech Center	Helena, MT 59601	2835
Helene Fuld Sch Nsg	Camden, NJ 08104	2884
Hellenic C-Holy Cross Sch	Brookline, MA 02146	1627
Henderson CC	Henderson, KY 42420	2544
Henderson St U	Arkadelphia, AR 71923	0762
Hendrick Sch Rad Techn	Abilene, TX 79601	3340
Hendrix C	Conway, AR 72032	0962
Hennepin Tech-Brklyn Park	Minneapolis, MN 55441	2721
Hennepin Tech-Edn Prairie	Minneapolis, MN 55441	2722
Henry Ford CC	Dearborn, MI 48126	2670
Heritage Baptist U	Indianapolis, IN 46227	0463
Heritage C	Orlando, FL 32808	1015
Heritage C	Toppenish, WA 98948	0004
Herkimer Co CC	Herkimer, NY 13350	2948
Herzing Inst of Alabama	Birmingham, AL 35205	2021
Hesser C	Manchester, NH 03103	2861
Hesston C	Hesston, KS 67062	2521
Hibbing CC	Hibbing, MN 55746	2723
Hibbing Tech C	Hibbing, MN 55746	2724
High Point C	High Point, NC 27261	1191
Highland CC	Freeport, IL 61032	2380
Highland CC	Highland, KS 66035	2522
Highland Park CC	Highland Park, MI 48203	2671
Highline CC	Des Moines, WA 98198	3445
Hilbert C	Hamburg, NY 14075	2949
Hill C	Hillsboro, TX 76645	3341
Hillsborough CC	Tampa, FL 33631	2265
Hillsdale C	Hillsdale, MI 49242	0661
Hillsdale FW Baptist C	Moore, OK 73153	0743
Hinds CC-Jackson	Jackson, MS 39213	2771
Hinds CC-Rankin	Pearl, MS 39208	2772
Hinds CC-Raymond	Raymond, MS 39154	2773
Hinds CC-Utica Cam	Utica, MS 39175	2774
Hinds CC-Vicksburg	Vicksburg, MS 39180	2775
Hiram C	Hiram, OH 44234	0647
Hiwassee C	Madisonville, TN 37354	3280
Hobart C	Geneva, NY 14456	1520
Hobson St Tech	Thomasville, AL 36784	2022
Hocking Tech C	Nelsonville, OH 45764	3092
Hofstra U	Hempstead, NY 11550	1534
Hohenwald St Voc-Tech	Hohenwald, TN 38462	3281
Hollins C	Roanoke, VA 24020	1237
Holmes C of the Bible	Greenville, SC 29601	1039
Holmes CC	Goodman, MS 39079	2776
Holy Apostles C	Cromwell, CT 06416	1591
Holy Cross C	Notre Dame, IN 46556	2444
Holy Cross, C of the	Worcester, MA 01610	1728
Holy Family C	Philadelphia, PA 19114	1382
Holy Name Hosp Sch Nsg	Gadsden, AL 35902	2023
Holy Names C	Oakland, CA 94619	0143
Holyoke CC	Holyoke, MA 01040	2644
Honolulu CC, U Hawaii	Honolulu, HI 96817	2354
Hood C	Frederick, MD 21701	1240
Hope C	Holland, MI 49423	0658
Hopkinsville CC	Hopkinsville, KY 42241	2545
Horry Georgetown Tech	Conway, SC 29526	3236
Houghton C	Houghton, NY 14744	1488
Housatonic CC	Bridgeport, CT 06608	2236
Houston Baptist U	Houston, TX 77074	0959
Houston CC	Houston, TX 77270	3342
Houston Clear Lake, U of	Houston, TX 77058	0998
Houston Downtown C, U of	Houston, TX 77002	0766
Houston Main Cam, U of	Houston, TX 77004	0980
Howard C	Big Spring, TX 79720	3343
Howard CC	Columbia, MD 21044	2620
Howard Payne U	Brownwood, TX 76801	0768
Howard U	Washington, DC 20059	1221
Hudson Co CC	Jersey City, NJ 07306	2885
Hudson Valley CC	Troy, NY 12180	2950
Huey Long Voc Sch	Winnfield, LA 71483	2578
Human Services, C of	New York, NY 10014	1319
Humboldt St U	Arcata, CA 95521	0186
Humphreys C	Stockton, CA 95207	0010
Huntingdon C	Montgomery, AL 36194	0948
Huntington C	Huntington, IN 46750	0550
Hurley Sch Nsg	Flint, MI 48502	2672
Huron U	Huron, SD 57350	0277
Husson C	Bangor, ME 04401	1592
Huston-Tillotson C	Austin, TX 78702	0754
Hutchinson CC	Hutchinson, KS 67501	2523
Hutchinson Tech C	Hutchinson, MN 55350	2725
Hyles-Anderson C	Crown Point, IN 46307	0448

Name	Sequence Number
I	
Idaho St U Pocatello, ID 83209	0021
Idaho, C of Caldwell, ID 83605	0094
Idaho, U of Moscow, ID 83843	0069
Ill Benedictine C Lisle, IL 60532	0609
Ill C Jacksonville, IL 62650	0536
Ill Central C East Peoria, IL 61635	2381
Ill Chicago, U of Chicago, IL 60680	0704
Ill Inst of Techn Chicago, IL 60616	0680
Ill St U Normal, IL 61761	0633
Ill Tech C Chicago, IL 60605	2382
Ill Valley CC Oglesby, IL 61348	2383
Ill Wesleyan U Bloomington, IL 61702	0709
Ill-Urbana Chpgn, U of Champaign, IL 61820	0716
Immaculata C Immaculata, PA 19345	1356
Immanuel Lutheran C Eau Claire, WI 54701	0514
Imperial Valley C Imperial, CA 92251	2145
Incarnate Word C San Antonio, TX 78209	0917
Ind Inst of Techn Fort Wayne, IN 46803	0489
Ind St U Main Cam Terre Haute, IN 47809	0626
Ind U at Bloomington Bloomington, IN 47405	0637
Ind U at Kokomo Kokomo, IN 46904	0570
Ind U at South Bend South Bend, IN 46634	0571
Ind U East Richmond, IN 47374	0512
Ind U Northwest Gary, IN 46408	0572
Ind U Southeast New Albany, IN 47150	0573
Ind U-Purdue Fort Wayne Fort Wayne, IN 46805	0575
Ind U-Purdue Indianapolis Indianapolis, IN 46202	0617
Ind Voc Tech C-South Bend South Bend, IN 46619	2446
Ind Voc Tech-Lafayette Lafayette, IN 46903	2445
Ind Voc Tech-Wabash Terre Haute, IN 47803	2447
Ind Voc Tech-Whitewater Richmond, IN 47374	2448
Ind Voc-Tech C Columbus Columbus, IN 47203	2450
Ind Voc-Tech C Kokomo Kokomo, IN 46901	2456
Ind Voc-Tech C NE Ind Fort Wayne, IN 46805	2449
Ind Voc-Tech C SW Ind Evansville, IN 47710	2457
Ind Voc-Tech C-East Cent Muncie, IN 47302	2451
Ind Voc-Tech C-NW Gary, IN 46409	2452
Ind Voc-Tech C-SE Madison, IN 47250	2454
Ind Voc-Tech C-South Sellersburg, IN 47172	2453
Ind Voc-Tech Cen Ind Indianapolis, IN 46206	2455
Ind Wesleyan U Marion, IN 46953	0551
Independence CC Independence, KS 67301	2524
Indian Hills CC Centervle Centerville, IA 52544	2473
Indian Hills CC Ottumwa Ottumwa, IA 52501	2474
Indian River CC Fort Pierce, FL 34981	2266
Indiana U of Pa Indiana, PA 15705	1527
Indianapolis, U of Indianapolis, IN 47227	0603
Inst Amer Indian Arts Santa Fe, NM 87504	2899
Insurance, C of New York, NY 10007	1469
Interboro Inst New York, NY 10019	2951
International Baptist C Tempe, AZ 85282	0032
International Bible Florence, AL 35630	0791
International Business C Fort Wayne, IN 46804	2458
International Fine Arts C Miami, FL 33132	2267
International Inst Lewisville, TX 75067	0984
Interstate Business C Fargo, ND 58103	3062
Intl Acad Merch Design Tampa, FL 33609	1021
Inver Hills CC Inver Grove Hts, MN 55076	2726
Iona C New Rochelle, NY 10801	1425
Iowa Central CC Fort Dodge, IA 50501	2476
Iowa Central CC Webster City, IA 50595	2477
Iowa Central CC Eagle Gr Eagle Grove, IA 50533	2475
Iowa Lakes CC Emmetsburg Emmetsburg, IA 50536	2478
Iowa Lakes CC Estherville Estherville, IA 51334	2479
Iowa Methodist Sch Nsg Des Moines, IA 50309	2481
Iowa Methodist Sch Rad Des Moines, IA 50309	2480
Iowa St U Ames, IA 50011	0410
Iowa Wesleyan C Mount Pleasant, IA 52641	0284
Iowa Western CC Council Bluffs, IA 51502	2483
Iowa Western CC Clarinda Clarinda, IA 51632	2482
Iowa, U of Iowa City, IA 52242	0377
Isothermal CC Spindale, NC 28160	3023
Itasca CC Grand Rapids, MN 55744	2727
Itawamba CC Fulton, MS 38843	2777
Ithaca C Ithaca, NY 14850	1456
ITT Tech Inst Fort Wayne, IN 46825	0476
J	
J E M H Sch Nsg Council Bluffs, IA 51501	2484
J E M H Sch Rad Techn Council Bluffs, IA 51501	2485
J S Reynolds CC Richmond, VA 23261	3413
Jacki Nell Secretary Sch Austin, TX 78704	3344
Jacksboro St Voc-Tech Jacksboro, TN 37757	3282
Jackson Area Sch Jackson, TN 38301	3283
Jackson Business Inst Jackson, MI 49201	2673
Jackson CC Jackson, MI 49201	2674
Jackson St CC Jackson, TN 38301	3284
Jackson St U Jackson, MS 39217	0853
Jackson Tech C Jackson, MN 56143	2728
Jacksonville C Jacksonville, TX 75766	3345
Jacksonville St U Jacksonville, AL 36265	0774
Jacksonville U Jacksonville, FL 32211	1197
James Madison U Harrisonburg, VA 22807	1219
James Sprunt CC Kenansville, NC 28398	3024
Jamestown Business C Jamestown, NY 14701	2952
Jamestown C Jamestown, ND 58401	0320
Jamestown CC Jamestown, NY 14701	2953
Jarvis Christian C Hawkins, TX 75765	0802
Jefferson C Hillsboro, MO 63050	2797
Jefferson CC Louisville, KY 40202	2546
Jefferson CC Watertown, NY 13601	2954
Jefferson Davis CC Brewton, AL 36427	2024
Jefferson Parish Voc Metairie, LA 70003	2579
Jefferson Sch Nsg Pine Bluff, AR 71603	2089
Jefferson St CC Birmingham, AL 35215	2025

Name	Sequence Number
Jefferson St Voc-Tech Louisville, KY 40203	2547
Jefferson Tech C Steubenville, OH 43952	3093
Jefferson Westbank V-T Harvey, LA 70058	2580
Jersey City St C Jersey City, NJ 07305	1384
Jewish Hosp Sch Nsg St Louis, MO 63110	2798
Jewish Theol Sem of Amer New York, NY 10027	1463
Jimmy Swaggart Bible C Baton Rouge, LA 70828	0742
John A Gupton C Nashville, TN 37203	3285
John A Logan C Carterville, IL 62918	2384
John Brown U Siloam Springs, AR 72761	0877
John C Calhoun St CC Decatur, AL 35602	2026
John Carroll U University Hts, OH 44118	0673
John F Kennedy U Orinda, CA 94563	0035
John Tyler CC Chester, VA 23831	3414
John Wesley C High Point, NC 27265	1043
John Wood CC Quincy, IL 62301	2385
Johns Hopkins U Baltimore, MD 21218	1291
Johnson & Wales U Providence, RI 02903	1620
Johnson Bible C Knoxville, TN 37998	0803
Johnson C Smith U Charlotte, NC 28216	1104
Johnson Co CC Overland Park, KS 66210	2525
Johnson St C Johnson, VT 05656	1658
Johnston CC Smithfield, NC 27577	3025
Joliet JC Joliet, IL 60436	2386
Jones C Main Campus Jacksonville, FL 32211	1041
Jones Co JC Ellisville, MS 39437	2778
Jordan C Cedar Springs, MI 49319	0447
Jordan Energy Inst Cedar Springs, MI 49319	0464
Judaism, U of/Lee C Los Angeles, CA 90077	0144
Judson C Elgin, IL 60123	0561
Judson C Marion, AL 36756	0943
Juilliard Sch, The New York, NY 10023	1548
Jumonville Voc-Tech Port Allen, LA 70767	2581
Juniata C Huntingdon, PA 16652	1502

K

Name	Sequence Number
Kalamazoo C Kalamazoo, MI 49007	0677
Kalamazoo Valley CC Kalamazoo, MI 49009	2675
Kanawha Co Sch Electronic Charleston, WV 25301	3467
Kankakee CC Kankakee, IL 60901	2387
Kansas C of Tech Salina, KS 67401	2526
Kansas City Art Inst Kansas City, MO 64111	0285
Kansas City C of Bible Overland Park, KS 66204	0266
Kansas City Kans CC Kansas City, KS 66112	2527
Kansas Newman C Wichita, KS 67213	0321
Kansas St U Manhattan, KS 66506	0259
Kansas Wesleyan U Salina, KS 67401	0314
Kansas, U of Lawrence, KS 66045	0258
Kapiolani CC, U Hawaii Honolulu, HI 96816	2355
Kaskaskia C Centralia, IL 62801	2388
Katharine Gibbs Sch Boston, MA 02116	2645
Katharine Gibbs Sch Montclair, NJ 07042	2886
Katharine Gibbs Sch New York, NY 10017	2956
Katharine Gibbs Sch Norwalk, CT 06851	2237
Katharine Gibbs Sch Providence, RI 02906	3228
Katharine Gibbs Sch-NY Mevil Hunt Sta, NY 11747	2955
Kauai CC, U Hawaii Lihue, HI 96766	2356
Kean College of NJ Union, NJ 07083	1333
Kee Business C Newport News, VA 23606	3415
Keene St C Keene, NH 03431	1653
Kellogg CC Battle Creek, MI 49017	2676
Kemper Military C Boonville, MO 65254	2799
Kenai Peninsula C Soldotna, AK 99669	2056
Kendall C Evanston, IL 60201	0492
Kendall C of Art/Design Grand Rapids, MI 49503	0479
Kennebec Valley Voc-Tech Fairfield, ME 04937	2602
Kennedy-King C Chicago, IL 60621	2389
Kennesaw C Marietta, GA 30061	1079
Kent St Ashtabula Ashtabula, OH 44004	3094
Kent St E Liverpool East Liverpool, OH 43920	3095
Kent St Stark Cam Canton, OH 44720	3096
Kent St Trumbull Warren, OH 44483	3097
Kent St Tuscaraws New Philadelphi, OH 44663	3098
Kent St U Main Cam Kent, OH 44242	0638
Kent St U Salem Salem, OH 44460	3100
Kent St U Geauga Burton, OH 44021	3099
Kentucky Christian C Grayson, KY 41143	0801
Kentucky Main Cam, U of Lexington, KY 40506	0979
Kentucky St U Frankfort, KY 40601	0830
Kentucky Wesleyan C Owensboro, KY 42301	0947
Kenyon C Gambier, OH 43022	0686
Ketchikan Cam, U Alas SE Ketchikan, AK 99901	2057
Kettering C Kettering, OH 45429	3101
Keuka C Keuka Park, NY 14478	1464
Keystone JC La Plume, PA 18440	3187
Kilgore C Kilgore, TX 75662	3346
Kilian CC Sioux Falls, SD 57105	3255
King C Bristol, TN 37620	0949
King's C Briarcliff, NY 10510	1354
King's C Charlotte, NC 28204	3026
King's C Wilkes-Barre, PA 18711	1407
Kings River CC Reedley, CA 93654	2146
Kirkwood CC Cedar Rapids, IA 52406	2486
Kirtland CC Roscommon, MI 48653	2677
Kishwaukee C Malta, IL 60150	2390
Knox C Galesburg, IL 61401	0650
Knoxville Business C Knoxville, TN 37927	3286
Knoxville C Knoxville, TN 37921	0841
Knoxville C Morristown, TN 37814	3287
Knoxville St Voc-Tech Knoxville, TN 37919	3288
Kodiak C Kodiak, AK 99615	2058
Kuskokwim C Bethel, AK 99559	2059
Kutztown U Kutztown, PA 19530	1440

L

Name	Sequence Number
La C Pineville, LA 71359	0867

Name	Sequence Number
La Roche C Pittsburgh, PA 15237	1346
La Salle U Philadelphia, PA 19141	1494
La St U A&M Baton Rouge Baton Rouge, LA 70803	0938
La St U Alexandria Alexandria, LA 71302	2582
La St U Eunice Eunice, LA 70535	2583
La St U Sch Allied Hlth Shreveport, LA 71130	0995
La St U Sch Dentistry New Orleans, LA 70119	0941
La St U Shreveport Shreveport, LA 71115	0757
La Tech U Ruston, LA 71272	0779
La Verne, U of La Verne, CA 91750	0122
Lab Inst of Merchandising New York, NY 10022	1344
Labette CC Parsons, KS 67357	2528
Laboure C Boston, MA 02124	2646
Lackawanna JC Scranton, PA 18505	3188
Lafayette C Easton, PA 18042	1555
LaGrange C LaGrange, GA 30240	1127
Lake Area Voc-Tech Inst Watertown, SD 57201	3256
Lake City CC Lake City, FL 32055	2269
Lake Co Voc-Tech Center Eustis, FL 32726	2270
Lake County, C of Grayslake, IL 60030	2391
Lake Erie C Painesville, OH 44077	0559
Lake Forest C Lake Forest, IL 60045	0683
Lake Land C Mattoon, IL 61938	2392
Lake Mich C Benton Harbor, MI 49022	2678
Lake Superior St C Sault Ste Marie, MI 49783	0581
Lake Tahoe CC S Lake Tahoe, CA 95702	2147
Lake Washington Voc Sch Kirkland, WA 98033	3446
Lake-Sumter CC Leesburg, FL 32788	2271
Lakeland C Sheboygan, WI 53082	0554
Lakeland CC Mentor, OH 44060	3102
Lakeshore Tech C Cleveland, WI 53015	3482
Lakeview C of Nursing Danville, IL 61832	0516
Lakewood CC White Bear Lake, MN 55110	2729
Lamar CC Lamar, CO 81052	2221
Lamar U Beaumont, TX 77710	0847

Name	Sequence Number
Lamar U-Port Arthur Port Arthur, TX 77641	3347
Lambuth C Jackson, TN 38301	0871
Lancaster Bible C Lancaster, PA 17601	1318
Lancaster Sch of Nsg Lancaster, PA 17603	3189
Lander C Greenwood, SC 29649	1168
Landmark Baptist C Haines City, FL 33844	1118
Landmark C Putney, VT 05346	3401
Lane C Jackson, TN 38301	0753
Lane CC Eugene, OR 97405	3165
Laney C Oakland, CA 94607	2148
Langston U Langston, OK 73050	0765
Lanier Tech Inst Oakwood, GA 30566	2328
Lansing CC Lansing, MI 48901	2679
Laramie Co CC Cheyenne, WY 82007	3518
Laredo JC Laredo, TX 78040	3348
Las Positas C Livermore, CA 94550	2149
Lasell C Newton, MA 02166	1611
Lassen C Susanville, CA 96130	2150
Latter-Day Saints Bus C Salt Lake City, UT 84111	3395
Lawrence Tech U Southfield, MI 48075	0584
Lawrence U Appleton, WI 54912	0710
Lawson St CC Birmingham, AL 35221	2027
Le Cox Sch of Radiology Springfield, MO 65807	2800
Le Moyne C Syracuse, NY 13214	1495
Le Tourneau U Longview, TX 75607	0883
Lebanon Valley C Annville, PA 17003	1369
Lee C Baytown, TX 77520	3349
Lee C Cleveland, TN 37320	0835
Lees C Jackson, KY 41339	2548
Lees-McRae C Banner Elk, NC 28604	1066
Leeward CC, U Hawaii Pearl City, HI 96782	2357
Lehigh Co CC Schnecksville, PA 18078	3190
Lehigh U Bethlehem, PA 18015	1539
LeMoyne-Owen C Memphis, TN 38126	0827
Lenoir CC Kinston, NC 28501	3027

Name	Sequence Number
Lenoir-Rhyne C Hickory, NC 28603	1255
Lesley C Cambridge, MA 02138	1676
Lewis & Clark CC Godfrey, IL 62035	2393
Lewis and Clark C Portland, OR 97219	0174
Lewis C of Business Detroit, MI 48235	2680
Lewis U Romeoville, IL 60441	0608
Lewis-Clark St C Lewiston, ID 83501	0014
Lexington Baptist C Lexington, KY 40508	0787
Lexington CC Lexington, KY 40506	2549
Lexington Inst Chicago, IL 60643	2394
Liberty Christian C Pensacola, FL 32516	1012
Liberty U Lynchburg, VA 24506	1038
Life Bible C Los Angeles, CA 90086	0036
Life Bible C East Christiansburg, VA 24073	1045
Lima Tech C Lima, OH 45804	3103
Limestone C Gaffney, SC 29340	1131
Lincoln C Lincoln, IL 62656	2395
Lincoln Christian C Lincoln, IL 62656	0472
Lincoln Land CC Springfield, IL 62794	2396
Lincoln Memorial U Harrogate, TN 37752	0896
Lincoln Sch of Commerce Lincoln, NE 68501	2843
Lincoln Trail C Robinson, IL 62454	2397
Lincoln U Jefferson City, MO 65101	0249
Lincoln U Lincoln Univ, PA 19352	1324
Lincoln U San Francisco, CA 94118	0027
Lindenwood C St Charles, MO 63301	0359
Lindsey Hopkins Tech Ctr Miami, FL 33127	2268
Lindsey Wilson C Columbia, KY 42728	0770
Linfield C McMinnville, OR 97128	0165
Linfield Sch Nsg Portland, OR 97210	0142
Linn Tech C Linn, MO 65051	2801
Linn-Benton CC Albany, OR 97321	3166
Lively Voc-Tech Center Tallahassee, FL 32304	2272
Livingston U Livingston, AL 35470	0825
Livingstone C Salisbury, NC 28144	1120

Name	Sequence Number
Lubbock Christian U Lubbock, TX 79407	0811
Lock Haven U Lock Haven, PA 17745	1376
Lockyear C Evansville, IN 47706	0431
Loma Linda U Riverside, CA 92515	0067
Lon Morris C Jacksonville, TX 75766	3350
Long Beach City C Long Beach, CA 90808	2151
Long Island U Brooklyn Brooklyn, NY 11201	1408
Long Island U C W Post Brookville, NY 11548	1455
Long Island U Sthampton Southampton, NY 11968	1426
Longview CC Lee's Summit, MO 64081	2802
Longwood C Farmville, VA 23901	1179
Lorain Co CC Elyria, OH 44035	3104
Loras C Dubuque, IA 52001	0358
Lord Fairfax CC Middletown, VA 22645	3416
Los Ang City C Los Angeles, CA 90029	2152
Los Ang Harbor C Wilmington, CA 90744	2153
Los Ang Mission San Fernando, CA 91340	2154
Los Ang Pierce C Woodland Hills, CA 91371	2155
Los Ang Southwest C Los Angeles, CA 90047	2156
Los Ang Trade-Tech C Los Angeles, CA 90015	2157
Los Ang Valley C Van Nuys, CA 91401	2158
Los Medanos C Pittsburg, CA 94565	2159
Louisburg C Louisburg, NC 27549	3028
Louisville, U of Louisville, KY 40292	0937
Lourdes C Sylvania, OH 43560	0467
Lowell, U of Lowell, MA 01854	1687
Lower Columbia C Longview, WA 98632	3447
Lowthian C Minneapolis, MN 55402	2730
Loyola C Baltimore, MD 21210	1265
Loyola Marymount U Los Angeles, CA 90045	0125
Loyola U in New Orls New Orleans, LA 70118	0971
Loyola U of Chicago Chicago, IL 60611	0693
Luna Voc-Tech Inst Las Vegas, NM 87701	2900
Lurleen Wallace St JC Andalusia, AL 36420	2028
Luther C Decorah, IA 52101	0400
Lutheran C Hlth Prof Fort Wayne, IN 46807	0519
Lutheran Med Ctr Sch Nsg St Louis, MO 63118	2803
Luzerne Co CC Nanticoke, PA 18634	3191
Lycoming C Williamsport, PA 17701	1430
Lynchburg C Lynchburg, VA 24501	1208
Lyndon St C Lyndonville, VT 05851	1659

M

Name	Sequence Number
Macalester C St Paul, MN 55105	0413
MacCormac JC Chicago, IL 60604	2398
MacMurray C Jacksonville, IL 62650	0547
Macomb CC Warren, MI 48093	2681
Macon C Macon, GA 31297	2329
Macon Technical Inst Macon, GA 31206	2330
Madison Area Tech C Madison, WI 53704	3483
Madison Business C Madison, WI 53705	3484
Madisonville CC Madisonville, KY 42431	2550
Madonna C Livonia, MI 48150	0583
Magdalen C Bedford, NH 03278	1598
Magnolia Bible C Kosciusko, MS 39090	0734
Maharishi International U Fairfield, IA 52556	0322
Maine Augusta, U of Augusta, ME 04330	1586
Maine Farmington, U of Farmington, ME 04938	1651
Maine Fort Kent, U of Fort Kent, ME 04743	1595
Maine Machias, U of Machias, ME 04654	1621
Maine Maritime Acad Castine, ME 04420	1625
Maine Orono, U of Orono, ME 04469	1688
Maine Presque Isle, U of Presque Isle, ME 04769	1614
Maine U C, U of Orono, ME 04469	2603
Mainland, C of the Texas City, TX 77591	3351
Malcolm X C Chicago, IL 60612	2399
Malone C Canton, OH 44709	0653
Manatee CC Bradenton, FL 34207	2273
Manchester C N Manchester, IN 46962	0598
Manchester CC Manchester, CT 06040	2238
Manhattan C Riverdale, NY 10471	1506
Manhattan Christian C Manhattan, KS 66502	0236
Manhattan Sch of Music New York, NY 10027	1547
Manhattanville C Purchase, NY 10577	1505
Mankato St U Mankato, MN 56001	0370
Mankato Tech C North Mankato, MN 56002	2731
Manna Bible Inst Philadelphia, PA 19144	1303
Manna Christian C Fayetteville, NC 28304	1040
Mannes C of Music New York, NY 10024	1467
Manor JC Jenkintown, PA 19046	3192
Mansfield Hosp Sch Nsg Mansfield, OH 44903	3105
Mansfield U Mansfield, PA 16933	1386
Maple Woods CC Kansas City, MO 64156	2804
Maranatha Bapt Bible C Watertown, WI 53094	0436
Maria C Albany, NY 12208	2957
Marian C Indianapolis, IN 46222	0543
Marian C of Fond Du Lac Fond Du Lac, WI 54935	0505
Marian Hlth Ctr Rad Sioux City, IA 51105	2487
Marietta Bible C Marietta, OH 45750	0422
Marietta C Marietta, OH 45750	0678
Marin, C of Kentfield, CA 94904	2160
Marion Military Inst Marion, AL 36756	2029
Marion Tech C Marion, OH 43302	3106
Marist C Poughkeepsie, NY 12601	1419
Marlboro C Marlboro, VT 05344	1694
Marquette Sch Radiography Marquette, MI 49855	2682
Marquette U Milwaukee, WI 53233	0694
Mars Hill C Mars Hill, NC 28754	1186
Marshall U Huntington, WV 25755	1214
Marshalltown CC Marshalltown, IA 50158	2488
Martin CC Williamston, NC 27892	3029
Martin Luther C New Ulm, MN 56073	0263
Martin Methodist C Pulaski, TN 38478	3289
Mary Baldwin C Staunton, VA 24401	1153
Mary Hardin Baylor, U of Belton, TX 76513	0900
Mary Holmes C West Point, MS 39773	2779

COLLEGE INDEX

Name	Sequence Number
Mary Washington C Fredericksburg, VA 22401	1248
Mary, U of Bismarck, ND 58504	0349
Marygrove C Detroit, MI 48221	0587
Maryland Baptist Bible C Elkton, MD 21921	1011
Marylhurst C Marylhurst, OR 97036	0009
Marymount C Tarrytown, NY 10591	1368
Marymount C Palos Verdes Rancho Palos Ve, CA 90274	2161
Marymount Manhattan C New York, NY 10021	1362
Marymount U of Virginia Arlington, VA 22207	1205
Maryville C Maryville, TN 37801	0951
Maryville C St Louis St Louis, MO 63141	0380
Marywood C Scranton, PA 18509	1399
Mass Amherst Cam, U of Amherst, MA 01003	1713
Mass Bay CC Wellesley Hills, MA 02181	2647
Mass C of Art Boston, MA 02115	1715
Mass C of Pharmacy/Health Boston, MA 02115	1675
Mass Inst of Techn Cambridge, MA 02139	1733
Mass Maritime Acad Buzzards Bay, MA 02532	1622
Massasoit CC Brockton, MA 02402	2648
Massey Business C Atlanta, GA 30308	2331
Master's C, The Newhall, CA 91321	0092
Matanuska-Susitna C Palmer, AK 99645	2060
Mater Dei C Ogdensburg, NY 13669	2958
Mattatuck CC Waterbury, CT 06708	2239
Maui CC, U Hawaii Kahlului, HI 96732	2358
Mayland CC Spruce Pine, NC 28777	3030
Maysville CC Maysville, KY 41056	2551
Mayville St U Mayville, ND 58257	0233
McCook CC McCook, NE 69001	2844
McDowell Tech CC Marion, NC 28752	3031
McFatter Voc-Tech Davie, FL 33317	2274
McHenry Co C Crystal Lake, IL 60012	2400
McIntosh C Dover, NH 03820	2862
McKendree C Lebanon, IL 62254	0531
McKennan Hosp Sch Rad Tec Sioux Falls, SD 57101	3257
McKenzie St Voc-Tech McKenzie, TN 38201	3290
McLennan CC Waco, TX 76708	3352
McMinnville St Voc-Tech McMinnville, TN 37110	3291
McMurry U Abilene, TX 79697	0904
McNeese St U Lake Charles, LA 70609	0775
McPherson C McPherson, KS 67460	0329
Md Baltimore Co Cam, U of Baltimore, MD 21228	1275
Md College Park Cam, U of College Park, MD 20742	1286
Md Eastern Cam, U of Princess Anne, MD 21853	1100
Md Inst C of Art Baltimore, MD 21217	1154
Md U C, C of College Park, MD 20742	1025
Med/Dental, C of Atlanta, GA 30309	2333
Medaille C Buffalo, NY 14214	1328
Medcenter One Sch of Nsg Bismarck, ND 58501	0418
Medcenter QR RT Prog Bismarck, ND 58501	3063
Medical C of Georgia Augusta, GA 30912	1160
Medical Center-Sch Rad Columbus, GA 31994	2332
Medical Inst of Minn Minneapolis, MN 55404	2732
Memphis Area Voc-Tech Memphis, TN 38105	3292
Memphis C of Art Memphis, TN 38112	0816
Memphis St U Memphis, TN 38152	0923
Mendocino C Ukiah, CA 95482	2162
Menlo C Atherton, CA 94027	0055
Mennonite C of Nursing Bloomington, IL 61701	0725
Merced C Merced, CA 95348	2163
Mercer Co CC Trenton, NJ 08690	2887
Mercer U Macon Macon, GA 31207	1201
Mercy C-NY Dobbs Ferry, NY 10522	1313
Mercy Hosp Sch Nsg Des Moines, IA 50314	2489
Mercy Hosp Sch Radiology Des Moines, IA 50314	2490
Mercy Sch of Nsg Toledo, OH 43624	3107
Mercy-St Luke Sch Rad Tec Cedar Rapids, IA 52402	2491
Mercyhurst C Erie, PA 16546	1397
Meredith C Raleigh, NC 27607	1251
Meridia Huron Sch Nsg Cleveland, OH 44112	3108
Meridian CC Meridian, MS 39305	2780
Merrimack C North Andover, MA 01845	1674
Merritt C Oakland, CA 94619	2164
Mesa CC Mesa, AZ 85202	2072
Mesa St C Grand Junction, CO 81502	0017
Mesabi CC Virginia, MN 55792	2733
Messiah C Grantham, PA 17027	1415
Methodist C Fayetteville, NC 28311	1194
Methodist Center Sch Nsg Peoria, IL 61636	2401
Methodist Hosp Sch Nsg Memphis, TN 38104	3293
Metro Business Cape Gir Cape Girardeau, MO 63701	2805
Metro Business Jeff City Jefferson City, MO 65109	2806
Metro Business Rolla Rolla, MO 65401	2807
Metro Health Med Center Cleveland, OH 44109	3109
Metropolitan CC Omaha, NE 68103	2845
Metropolitan St C Denver, CO 80204	0068
Metropolitan St U St Paul, MN 55101	0417
MGW Sch of Nsg Easton, MD 21601	2621
Miami Christian C Miami, FL 33167	1124
Miami U Oxford, OH 45056	0692
Miami U Hamilton Hamilton, OH 45011	3110
Miami U Middletown Middletown, OH 45042	3111
Miami-Dade CC Miami, FL 33132	2275
Miami-Jacobs JC Dayton, OH 45401	3112
Miami, U of Coral Gables, FL 33124	1280
Mich Ann Arbor, U of Ann Arbor, MI 48109	0717
Mich Christian C Rochester Hills, MI 48307	0439
Mich Dearborn, U of Dearborn, MI 48128	0706
Mich Flint, U of Flint, MI 48502	0651
Mich St U East Lansing, MI 48824	0701
Mich Techn U Houghton, MI 49931	0691
Mid America Funeral C Jeffersonville, IN 47130	2459
Mid Mich CC Harrison, MI 48625	2683
Mid-Amer Nazarene C Olathe, KS 66061	0254
Mid-America Bible C Oklahoma City, OK 73170	0804

Name	Sequence Number
Mid-Florida Tech Orlando, FL 32809	2276
Mid-Plains CC North Platte, NE 69101	2846
Mid-South Christian C Memphis, TN 38181	0790
Mid-State Tech C Wisconsin Rapid, WI 54494	3485
Midcontinent Bible C Mayfield, KY 42066	0735
Middle Georgia C Cochran, GA 31014	2334
Middle Georgia Tech Warner Robins, GA 31056	2335
Middle Tenn St U Murfreesboro, TN 37132	0846
Middlebury C Middlebury, VT 05753	1721
Middlesex CC Bedford, MA 01730	2649
Middlesex CC Middletown, CT 06457	2240
Middlesex Co C Edison, NJ 08818	2888
Midland C Midland, TX 79705	3353
Midland Lutheran C Fremont, NE 68025	0332
Midlands Tech C Columbia, SC 29205	3237
Midstate C Peoria, IL 61602	2402
Midway C Midway, KY 40347	0813
Midwestern St U Wichita Falls, TX 76308	0828
Miles C Birmingham, AL 35208	0745
Miles CC Miles City, MT 59301	2836
Millersville U Millersville, PA 17551	1528
Milligan C Milligan, TN 37682	0878
Millikin U Decatur, IL 62522	0667
Mills C Oakland, CA 94613	0176
Millsaps C Jackson, MS 39210	0972
Milwaukee Area Tech C Milwaukee, WI 53233	3486
Milwaukee Inst of Art Milwaukee, WI 53202	0523
Milwaukee Med Sch Nsg Milwaukee, WI 53226	3487
Milwaukee Sch Engr Milwaukee, WI 53201	0656
Mineral Area C Flat River, MO 63601	2808
Minn Bible C Rochester, MN 55902	0262
Minn Duluth, U of Duluth, MN 55812	0375
Minn Morris, U of Morris, MN 56267	0412
Minn Rivlnd Tech C Austin, MN 55912	2734
Minn Tech Inst, U of Crookston, MN 56716	2735
Minn Twin Cities, U of Minneapolis, MN 55455	0378
Minn Waseca, U of Waseca, MN 56093	2736
Minneapolis C Art Design Minneapolis, MN 55404	0340
Minneapolis CC Minneapolis, MN 55403	2737
Minneapolis Tech C Minneapolis, MN 55403	2738
Minot St U Minot, ND 58701	0251
Miracosta C Oceanside, CA 92056	2165
Misericordia, C Dallas, PA 18612	1352
Miss Bapt Sch Rad Techn Jackson, MS 39201	2781
Miss C Clinton, MS 39058	0902
Miss Co CC Blytheville, AR 72316	2090
Miss Delta CC Moorhead, MS 38761	2782
Miss Gulf CC Jackson Gautier, MS 39553	2783
Miss Gulf CC Jeff Davis Gulfport, MS 39507	2784
Miss Gulf CC Perkinston Perkinston, MS 39573	2785
Miss Main Cam, U of University, MS 38677	0930
Miss Medical Center, U of Jackson, MS 39216	1003
Miss St U Miss State, MS 39762	0855
Miss U for Women Columbus, MS 39701	0834
Miss Valley St U Itta Bena, MS 38941	0832
Mission C Santa Clara, CA 95054	2166
Missoula Voc-Tech Center Missoula, MT 59801	2837
Missouri Baptist C St Louis, MO 63141	0252
Missouri Baptist Med Ct St Louis, MO 63131	2809
Missouri Columbia, U of Columbia, MO 65211	0411
Missouri Kansas City, U of Kansas City, MO 64110	0407
Missouri Rolla, U of Rolla, MO 65401	0385
Missouri Saint Louis, U of St Louis, MO 63121	0405
Missouri Southern St C Joplin, MO 64801	0286
Missouri Valley C Marshall, MO 65340	0363
Missouri Western St C St Joseph, MO 64507	0241
Mitchell C New London, CT 06320	2241
Mitchell CC Statesville, NC 28677	3032
Mitchell Voc-Tech C Mitchell, SD 57301	3258
Moberly Area CC Moberly, MO 65275	2810
Mobile C Mobile, AL 36613	0837
Modesto JC Modesto, CA 95350	2167
Mohave CC Kingman, AZ 86401	2073
Mohawk Valley CC Utica, NY 13501	2959
Mohegan CC Norwich, CT 06360	2242
Molloy C Rockville Centr, NY 11570	1388
Monmouth C Monmouth, IL 61462	0646
Monmouth C W Long Branch, NJ 07764	1414
Monroe CC Rochester, NY 14623	2960
Monroe Co CC Monroe, MI 48161	2684
Montana C Minrl Sci-Techn Butte, MT 59701	0109
Montana St U Bozeman, MT 59717	0134
Montana, U of Missoula, MT 59812	0132
Montay C Chicago, IL 60659	2403
Montcalm CC Sidney, MI 48885	2685
Montclair St C Upper Montclair, NJ 07043	1532
Monterey Inst Inter Study Monterey, CA 93940	0228
Monterey Peninsula C Monterey, CA 93940	2168
Montevallo, U of Montevallo, AL 35115	0893
Montgomery C Rockville Rockville, MD 20850	2622
Montgomery C Takoma Park Takoma Park, MD 20912	2623
Montgomery C-Germantown Germantown, MD 20874	2624
Montgomery CC Troy, NC 27371	3033
Montgomery Co CC Blue Bell, PA 19422	3193
Montreat-Anderson C Montreat, NC 28757	1060
Montserrat C of Art Beverly, MA 01915	1596
Moody Bible Inst Chicago, IL 60610	0579
Moore C of Art Philadelphia, PA 19103	1371
Moore Sch of Techn Memphis, TN 38104	3294
Moorhead St U Moorhead, MN 56560	0371
Moorhead Tech C Moorhead, MN 56560	2739
Moorpark C Moorpark, CA 93021	2169
Moraine Park Tech Inst Fond du Lac, WI 54935	3488
Moraine Park Tech Inst West Bend, WI 53095	3489
Moraine Valley CC Palos Hills, IL 60465	2404

Name	Sequence Number
Moravian C Bethlehem, PA 18018	1504
Morehead St U Morehead, KY 40351	0851
Morehouse C Atlanta, GA 30314	1253
Morgan CC Fort Morgan, CO 80701	2222
Morgan St U Baltimore, MD 21239	1180
Morningside C Sioux City, IA 51106	0346
Morris Brown C Atlanta, GA 30314	1190
Morris C Sumter, SC 29150	1023
Morris, Co C of Randolph, NJ 07869	2889
Morrison C/Reno B C Reno, NV 89503	0002
Morrison Inst of Techn Morrison, IL 61270	2405
Morristown St Area Vo-Tec Morristown, TN 37814	3295
Morton C Cicero, IL 60650	2406
Motlow State CC Tullahoma, TN 37388	3296
Mott CC Flint, MI 48503	2686
Mount Aloysius JC Cresson, PA 16630	3194
Mount Angel Seminary St Benedict, OR 97373	0079
Mount Carmel C of Nsg Columbus, OH 43222	0641
Mount Holyoke C South Hadley, MA 01075	1718
Mount Hood CC Gresham, OR 97030	3167
Mount Ida C Newton, MA 02159	1593
Mount Marty C Yankton, SD 57078	0274
Mount Mary C Milwaukee, WI 53222	0532
Mount Mercy C Cedar Rapids, IA 52402	0335
Mount Olive C Mount Olive, NC 28365	1069
Mount Saint Clare C Clinton, IA 52732	0278
Mount Saint Joseph, C of Mount St Joseph, OH 45051	0600
Mount Saint Mary C Newburgh, NY 12550	1349
Mount Saint Mary's C Emmitsburg, MD 21727	1206
Mount Saint Mary's C Los Angeles, CA 90049	0147
Mount Saint Vincent, C of Riverdale, NY 10471	1363
Mount San Antonio C Walnut, CA 91789	2170
Mount San Jacinto C San Jacinto, CA 92383	2171
Mount Senario C Ladysmith, WI 54848	0484
Mount Union C Alliance, OH 44601	0672
Mount Vernon C Washington, DC 20007	1157
Mount Vernon Christian C Mount Vernon, IL 62864	2407
Mount Vernon Nazarene C Mount Vernon, OH 43050	0482
Mount Wachusett CC Gardner, MA 01440	2650
Mountain Empire CC Big Stone Gap, VA 24219	3417
Mountain St C Parkersburg, WV 26101	3468
Mountain View C Dallas, TX 75211	3354
Muhlenberg C Allentown, PA 18104	1513
Multnomah Sch of Bible Portland, OR 97220	0084
Mundelein C Chicago, IL 60660	0556
Murray St C Tishomingo, OK 73460	3144
Murray St U Murray, KY 42071	0921
Muscatine CC Muscatine, IA 52761	2492
Museum Fine Arts, Sch of Boston, MA 02115	1602
Muskegon CC Muskegon, MI 49442	2687
Muskingum Area Tech C Zanesville, OH 43701	3113
Muskingum C New Concord, OH 43762	0616

N

Name	Sequence Number
N Harris Co C-Tomball Tomball, TX 77375	3355
Napa Valley C Napa, CA 94558	2172
Nash CC Rocky Mount, NC 27804	3034
Nashville St Tech C Nashville, TN 37209	3297
Nassau CC Garden City, NY 11530	2961
Natchez C Natchez, MS 39120	2786
Natchitoches Central Natchitoches, LA 71457	2584
National Business C Roanoke, VA 24017	3418
National C Rapid City, SD 57709	0239
National C Chiropractic Lombard, IL 60148	0726
National Career C Decatur, AL 35601	2030
National Career C Tuscaloosa, AL 35405	2031
National Ed Center Fort Lauderdale, FL 33334	1032
National Ed Center Texas Dallas, TX 75238	3356
National Ed Center W Va Cross Lanes, WV 25313	3469
National Ed Ctr Alabama Birmingham, AL 35209	2032
National Ed Ctr Kentucky Louisville, KY 40213	2552
National Ed Ctr of Iowa West Des Moines, IA 50265	2493
National Educ Center Cuyahoga Falls, OH 44221	3114
National Educ-Vale Tech Blairsville, PA 15717	3195
National U San Diego, CA 92108	0073
National-Louis U Evanston, IL 60201	0599
Natl Ed Ctr Ark Tech Little Rock, AR 72207	2091
Navajo CC Tsaile, AZ 86556	2074
Navarro C Corsicana, TX 75110	3357
Nazarene Bible C Colorado Sprgs, CO 80935	2223
Nazareth C Rochester, NY 14610	1420
NC Agrl & Tech St U Greensboro, NC 27411	1113
NC at Asheville, U of Asheville, NC 28804	1163
NC at Chapel Hill, U of Chapel Hill, NC 27599	1298
NC at Charlotte, U of Charlotte, NC 28223	1210
NC at Greensboro, U of Greensboro, NC 27412	1271
NC at Wilmington, U of Wilmington, NC 28403	1213
NC Central U Durham, NC 27707	1164
NC Sch of the Arts Winston-Salem, NC 27117	1046
NC St U Raleigh, NC 27695	1281
NC Wesleyan C Rocky Mount, NC 27801	1138
ND Main Cam, U of Grand Forks, ND 58202	0255
ND St C of Science Wahpeton, ND 58075	3064
ND St U Bottineau Bottineau, ND 58318	3065
ND St U Main Cam Fargo, ND 58105	0256
ND Williston, U of Williston, ND 58801	3066
ND-Lake Region, U of Devils Lake, ND 58301	3067
Ne C of Tech Agri Curtis, NE 69025	2847
Nebraska at Omaha, U of Omaha, NE 68182	0293
Nebraska C of Business Omaha, NE 68131	2848
Nebraska Christian C Norfolk, NE 68701	0234
Nebraska Lincoln, U of Lincoln, NE 68588	0376
Nebraska Medical Ctr, U of Omaha, NE 68105	0420
Nebraska Methodist C Nsg Omaha, NE 68114	0379
Nebraska Wesleyan U Lincoln, NE 68504	0386
Nebraska-Kearney, U of Kearney, NE 68849	0294

Name	Sequence Number
Neosho Co CC Chanute, KS 66720	2529
Nettleton C Sioux Falls, SD 57106	3259
Neumann C Aston, PA 19014	1342
Nevada Las Vegas, U of Las Vegas, NV 89154	0137
Nevada Reno, U of Reno, NV 89557	0072
New C of Cal San Francisco, CA 94102	0031
New C-U of S Florida Sarasota, FL 34243	1287
New Eng C Henniker, NH 03242	1612
New Eng Consv of Music Boston, MA 02115	1693
New Eng, U of Biddeford, ME 04005	1666
New Haven, U of West Haven, CT 06516	1664
New Orls, U of New Orleans, LA 70148	0926
New River CC Dublin, VA 24084	3419
New Rochelle, C of New Rochelle, NY 10805	1364
Newbern Area Sch Newbern, TN 38059	3298
Newberry C Newberry, SC 29108	1134
Newbury C Brookline, MA 02146	2651
Newman Hosp Sch Nsg Emporia, KS 66801	2530
NH C Manchester, NH 03104	1669
NH Tech C Berlin Berlin, NH 03570	2863
NH Tech C Claremont Claremont, NH 03743	2864
NH Tech C Laconia Laconia, NH 03246	2865
NH Tech C Manchester Manchester, NH 03102	2866
NH Tech C Nashua Nashua, NH 03061	2867
NH Tech C Stratham Stratham, NH 03885	2868
NH Tech Inst Concord, NH 03301	2869
NH, U of Durham, NH 03824	1710
Niagara Co CC Sanborn, NY 14132	2962
Niagara U Niagara, NY 14109	1403
Nicholls St U Thibodaux, LA 70310	0776
Nichols C Dudley, MA 01570	1607
Nicolet Area Tech C Rhinelander, WI 54501	3490
Niles C of Loyola Chicago, IL 60631	0494
NJ Inst Techn Newark, NJ 07102	1487
NM Gallup Branch, U of Gallup, NM 87301	2901
NM Highlands U Las Vegas, NM 87701	0057
NM Inst Mining & Techn Socorro, NM 87801	0153
NM JC Hobbs, NM 88240	2902
NM Military Inst Roswell, NM 88201	2903
NM St U Alamogordo Alamogordo, NM 88310	2904
NM St U Carlsbad Carlsbad, NM 88220	2905
NM St U Grants Branch Grants, NM 87020	2906
NM St U Main Cam Las Cruces, NM 88003	0128
NM, U of Albuquerque, NM 87131	0074
Norfolk St U Norfolk, VA 23504	1037
Normandale CC Bloomington, MN 55431	2740
North Adams St C North Adams, MA 01247	1654
North Alabama, U of Florence, AL 35632	0889
North Arkansas CC Harrison, AR 72601	2092
North Central Bible C Minneapolis, MN 55404	0271
North Central C Naperville, IL 60566	0610
North Central Mich C Petoskey, MI 49770	2688
North Central Missouri C Trenton, MO 64683	2811
North Central Tech C Mansfield, OH 44901	3115
North Central Tech Inst Wausau, WI 54401	3491
North Central Voc-Tech Beloit, KS 67420	2531
North Central Voc-Tech Farmerville, LA 71241	2585
North Country CC Saranac Lake, NY 12983	2963
North Florida JC Madison, FL 32340	2277
North Florida, U of Jacksonville, FL 32216	1245
North Georgia C Dahlonega, GA 30597	1162
North Georgia Tech Clarkesville, GA 30523	2336
North Greenville C Tigerville, SC 29688	3238
North Harris Co C East Kingwood, TX 77339	3359
North Harris Co C South Houston, TX 77073	3358
North Hennepin CC Brooklyn Park, MN 55445	2741
North Idaho C Coeur D'Alene, ID 83814	2361
North Iowa Area CC Mason City, IA 50401	2494
North Kentucky St Voc-Tch Covington, KY 41011	2553
North Lake C Irving, TX 75038	3360
North Park C Chicago, IL 60625	0567
North Seattle CC Seattle, WA 98103	3448
North Shore CC Beverly, MA 01915	2652
North Tech Ed Ctr Riviera Beach, FL 33404	2278
North Texas, U of Denton, TX 76203	0934
Northampton Co CC Bethlehem, PA 18017	3196
Northeast Alabama St JC Rainsville, AL 35986	2033
Northeast Iowa CC Calmar, IA 52132	2496
Northeast Iowa CC Calmr Calmar, IA 52132	2495
Northeast La U Monroe, LA 71209	0777
Northeast La Voc Sch Winnsboro, LA 71295	2586
Northeast Metro Tech White Bear Lake, MN 55110	2742
Northeast Miss CC Booneville, MS 38829	2787
Northeast Missouri St U Kirksville, MO 63501	0406
Northeast St Tech CC Blountville, TN 37617	3299
Northeast Texas CC Mount Pleasant, TX 75455	3361
Northeast Wis Tech Green Bay, WI 54303	3492
Northeastern CC Norfolk, NE 68701	2849
Northeastern Christian JC Villanova, PA 19085	3197
Northeastern Ill U Chicago, IL 60625	0500
Northeastern JC Sterling, CO 80751	2224
Northeastern Okla A&M C Miami, OK 74355	3145
Northeastern Okla St U Tahlequah, OK 74464	0920
Northeastern Sch Commerce Bay City, MI 48708	2689
Northeastern U Boston, MA 02115	1689
Northern Ariz U Flagstaff, AZ 86011	0127
Northern Colo, U of Greeley, CO 80639	0135
Northern Essex CC Haverhill, MA 01830	2653
Northern Ill U De Kalb, IL 60115	0635
Northern Iowa, U of Cedar Falls, IA 50614	0369
Northern Kentucky U Highland Height, KY 41076	0772
Northern Maine Voc-Tech Presque, ME 04769	2604
Northern Mich U Marquette, MI 49855	0510
Northern Montana C Havre, MT 59501	0108
Northern Nevada CC Elko, NV 89801	2857

Name	Sequence Number
Northern NM CC Espanola, NM 87532	2907
Northern Okla C Tonkawa, OK 74653	3146
Northern St U Aberdeen, SD 57401	0347
Northern Virginia CC Annandale, VA 22003	3420
Northland Baptist C Dunbar, WI 54119	0518
Northland C Ashland, WI 54806	0496
Northland CC Thief Rvr Falls, MN 56701	2743
Northland Pioneer C Holbrook, AZ 86025	2075
Northrop U Los Angeles, CA 90045	0099
Northwest Business C Lima, OH 45805	3116
Northwest C Kirkland, WA 98083	0041
Northwest C Nome, AK 99762	2061
Northwest CC Phil Campbell, AL 35581	2034
Northwest CC Powell, WY 82435	3519
Northwest Christian C Eugene, OR 97401	0011
Northwest Iowa Tech C Sheldon, IA 51201	2497
Northwest La Voc-Tech Sch Minden, LA 71058	2587
Northwest Miss CC Senatobia, MS 38668	2788
Northwest Missouri St U Maryville, MO 64468	0367
Northwest Missouri Vo-Tec Maryville, MO 64468	2812
Northwest Nazarene C Nampa, ID 83651	0044
Northwest Tech C Archbold, OH 43512	3117
Northwest Tech Inst Eden Prairie, MN 55344	2744
Northwestern Bus C Chicago, IL 60630	2408
Northwestern C Orange City, IA 51041	0353
Northwestern C St Paul, MN 55113	0292
Northwestern C of Wis Watertown, WI 53094	0517
Northwestern Conn CC Winsted, CT 06098	2243
Northwestern Mich C Traverse City, MI 49684	2690
Northwestern Okla St U Alva, OK 73717	0820
Northwestern St U of La Natchitoches, LA 71497	0767
Northwestern U Evanston, IL 60208	0713
Northwood Inst West Palm Beach, FL 33409	1075
Northwood Inst Midland Midland, MI 48640	0507
Northwood Inst of Texas Cedar Hill, TX 75104	0884
Norwalk CC Norwalk, CT 06854	2244
Norwalk St Tech C Norwalk, CT 06854	2245
Norwich U Northfield, VT 05663	1678
Notre Dame C of NH Manchester, NH 03104	1628
Notre Dame C-Ohio Cleveland, OH 44121	0533
Notre Dame of Md Baltimore, MD 21210	1232
Notre Dame, C of Belmont, CA 94002	0098
Notre Dame, U of Notre Dame, IN 46556	0712
Nova U Ft Lauderdale, FL 33314	1193
NW Bus C-SW Cam Palos Hills, IL 60465	2409
NY Inst of Techn Old Westbury, NY 11568	1334
NY Sch of Interior Design New York, NY 10022	1341
NY U New York, NY 10011	1544
Nyack C Nyack, NY 10960	1347

O

Name	Sequence Number
Oak Hills Bible C Bemidji, MN 56601	0265
Oakland CC Bloomfield Hill, MI 48303	2691
Oakland City C Oakland City, IN 47660	0441
Oakland U Rochester, MI 48309	0690
Oakton CC Des Plaines, IL 60016	2410
Oakwood C Huntsville, AL 35896	0842
Oberlin C Oberlin, OH 44074	0711
Occidental C Los Angeles, CA 90041	0214
Ocean Co C Toms River, NJ 08753	2890
Odessa C Odessa, TX 79764	3362
Oglethorpe U Atlanta, GA 30319	1233
Ohio Dominican C Columbus, OH 43209	0488
Ohio Northern U Ada, OH 45810	0676
Ohio St Lima Lima, OH 45804	0424
Ohio St Mansfield Mansfield, OH 44906	0425
Ohio St Marion Marion, OH 43302	0426
Ohio St Newark Newark, OH 43055	0427
Ohio St U Columbus Columbus, OH 43210	0702
Ohio St-Agr Tech Wooster, OH 44691	3118
Ohio U Athens Athens, OH 45701	0703
Ohio U Belmont St Clairsville, OH 43950	3119
Ohio U Chillicothe Chillicothe, OH 45601	0423
Ohio U Ironton Ironton, OH 45638	0444
Ohio U Lancaster Lancaster, OH 43130	3120
Ohio U Zanesville Zanesville, OH 43701	3121
Ohio Valley C Parkersburg, WV 26101	1057
Ohio Valley Hosp Sch Nsg Steubenville, OH 43952	3122
Ohio Wesleyan U Delaware, OH 43015	0682
Ohlone C Fremont, CA 94539	2173
Oil Belt Voc-Tech El Dorado, AR 71730	2093
Okaloosa-Walton JC Niceville, FL 32578	2279
Okla Baptist C-Inst Oklahoma City, OK 73127	0741
Okla Baptist U Shawnee, OK 74801	0897
Okla Christian U Oklahoma City, OK 73136	0836
Okla City CC Oklahoma City, OK 73159	3147
Okla City U Oklahoma City, OK 73106	0906
Okla Health Sci Ctr, U of Oklahoma City, OK 73190	1001
Okla JC Tulsa, OK 74133	3148
Okla Missionary Baptist C Marlow, OK 73055	0729
Okla Panhandle St U Goodwell, OK 73939	0759
Okla St U Stillwater, OK 74078	0936
Okla St U Tech OK City Oklahoma City, OK 73107	3149
Okla St U Tech Okmulgee Okmulgee, OK 74447	3150
Okla, U of Norman, OK 73019	0929
Old Dominion U Norfolk, VA 23529	1225
Olean Business Inst Olean, NY 14760	2964
Olive-Harvey C Chicago, IL 60628	2411
Olivet C Olivet, MI 49076	0540
Olivet Nazarene U Kankakee, IL 60901	0504
Olney Central C Olney, IL 62450	2412
Olympic C Bremerton, WA 98310	3449
Omaha C of Health Omaha, NE 68105	2850
Oneida Area Voc-Tech Oneida, TN 37841	3300
Onondaga CC Syracuse, NY 13215	2965
Opelika St Tech Opelika, AL 36801	2035

Name	Sequence Number
Oral Roberts U Tulsa, OK 74171	0912
Orange Co CC Middletown, NY 10940	2966
Orange Coast C Costa Mesa, CA 92628	2174
Orangeburg Calhoun Tech Orangeburg, SC 29115	3239
Oregon Bible C Oregon, IL 61061	0430
Oregon Coast CC Newport, OR 97365	3168
Oregon Inst of Techn Klamath Falls, OR 97601	0060
Oregon St U Corvallis, OR 97331	0129
Oregon, U of Eugene, OR 97403	0193
Orlando C Orlando, FL 32810	1027
Orlando Voc Tech Ctr Orlando, FL 32801	2280
Otero JC La Junta, CO 81050	2225
Otis Art Inst Los Angeles, CA 90057	0145
Ottawa U Ottawa, KS 66067	0324
Otterbein C Westerville, OH 43081	0614
Ouachita Baptist U Arkadelphia, AR 71923	0898
Our Lady of Lake Sch Nsg Baton Rouge, LA 70808	2588
Our Lady of the Lake U San Antonio, TX 78285	0915
Our Lady Surgical Baton Rouge, LA 70808	2589
Owens Tech C Toledo, OH 43699	3123
Owensboro CC Owensboro, KY 42303	2554
Owensboro JC of Business Owensboro, KY 42302	2555
Oxford C of Emory U Oxford, GA 30267	2337
Oxnard C Oxnard, CA 93030	2175
Ozark Christian C Joplin, MO 64801	0235
Ozarks, C of the Point Lookout, MO 65726	0383
Ozarks, U of the Clarksville, AR 72830	0862

P

Name	Sequence Number
Pa C Tech Agri & Sci Williamsport, PA 17701	3198
Pa St U Allentown Cam Fogelsville, PA 18051	3199
Pa St U Altoona Cam Altoona, PA 16601	3200
Pa St U Beaver Cam Monaca, PA 15061	3201
Pa St U Berks Cam Reading, PA 19610	3202
Pa St U Delaware Cam Media, PA 19063	3203
Pa St U DuBois Cam DuBois, PA 15801	3204
Pa St U Erie Behrend Erie, PA 16563	1387
Pa St U Fayette Cam Uniontown, PA 15401	3205
Pa St U Harrisburg Cam Middletown, PA 17057	1584
Pa St U Hazleton Cam Hazleton, PA 18201	3206
Pa St U Ogontz Cam Abington, PA 19001	3207
Pa St U Schuylkill Cam Schuylkill Havn, PA 17972	3208
Pa St U Wilkes-Barre Cam Lehman, PA 18627	3209
Pa St U Worthington Cam Dunmore, PA 18512	3210
Pa St U York Cam York, PA 17403	3211
Pa St U-McKeesport McKeesport, PA 15132	3212
Pa St U-Mont Alto Mont Alto, PA 17237	3213
Pa St U-New Kensington New Kensington, PA 15068	3214
Pa St U-Shenango Vly Sharon, PA 16146	3215
Pa St U-U Park University Park, PA 16802	1541
Pa, U of Philadelphia, PA 19104	1578
Pace U NY City New York, NY 10038	1410
Pace U Pleasantville Pleasantville, NY 10570	1411
Pace U White Plains White Plains, NY 10603	1361
Pacific Christian C Fullerton, CA 92631	0047
Pacific Lutheran U Tacoma, WA 98447	0166
Pacific NW C of Art Portland, OR 97205	0037
Pacific Oaks C Pasadena, CA 91103	0227
Pacific States U Los Angeles, CA 90006	0007
Pacific U Forest Grove, OR 97116	0159
Pacific Union C Angwin, CA 94508	0066
Pacific, U of the Stockton, CA 95211	0178
Paducah Area Voc Center Paducah, KY 42001	2556
Paducah CC Paducah, KY 42002	2557
Paine C Augusta, GA 30910	1058
Palm Beach CC Lake Worth, FL 33461	2281
Palm Beach-Atlantic C West Palm Beach, FL 33401	1106
Palm Beaches, C of West Palm Beach, FL 33407	2282
Palmer C of Chiropractic Davenport, IA 52803	0421
Palmer Chiro Sch Tech Davenport, IA 52803	2498
Palo Alto C San Antonio, TX 78224	3363
Palo Verde C Blythe, CA 92225	2176
Palomar C San Marcos, CA 92069	2177
Pamlico Tech C Grantsboro, NC 28529	3035
Pan American U Edinburg, TX 78539	0782
Panola C Carthage, TX 75633	3364
Paradise Valley CC Phoenix, AZ 85032	2076
Paris Area Sch Paris, TN 38242	3301
Paris JC Paris, TX 75460	3365
Park C Parkville, MO 64152	0315
Parkland C Champaign, IL 61821	2413
Parks C of St Louis U Cahokia, IL 62206	0593
Parsons Sch of Design New York, NY 10011	1510
Pasadena City C Pasadena, CA 91106	2178
Pasco-Hernando CC Dade City, FL 33525	2283
Passaic Co CC Paterson, NJ 07509	2891
Patrick Henry C Monroeville, AL 36461	2036
Patrick Henry CC Martinsville, VA 24115	3421
Patten C Oakland, CA 94601	0082
Patterson Tech C Montgomery, AL 36116	2037
Paul D Camp CC Franklin, VA 23851	3422
Paul Quinn C Waco, TX 76704	0744
Paul Smith's C Paul Smiths, NY 12970	2967
Peabody Inst Baltimore, MD 21202	1241
Peace C Raleigh, NC 27604	3036
Pearl River CC Poplarville, MS 39470	2789
Pellissippi St Tech Knoxville, TN 37933	3302
Pembroke St U Pembroke, NC 28372	1159
Peninsula C Port Angeles, WA 98362	3450
Penn Valley CC Kansas City, MO 64111	2813
Pensacola Christian C Pensacola, FL 32523	1099
Pensacola JC Pensacola, FL 32504	2284
Pepperdine U Malibu Malibu, CA 90263	0215
Peru St C Peru, NE 68421	0247
Petit Jean Voc Tech Morrilton, AR 72110	2094
Pfeiffer C Misenheimer, NC 28109	1132

Name	Sequence Number
Phila C of Pharm Sci, Philadelphia, PA 19104	1490
Phila C of Textiles & Sci, Philadelphia, PA 19144	1417
Phila C of the Bible, Langhorne, PA 19047	1345
Philadelphia, CC of, Philadelphia, PA 19130	3216
Philander Smith C, Little Rock, AR 72202	0793
Phillips C, Atlanta, GA 30309	2338
Phillips Co CC, Helena, AR 72342	2095
Phillips U, Enid, OK 73701	0885
Phoenix C, Phoenix, AZ 85013	2077
Pickens Area Tech Inst, Jasper, GA 30143	2339
Pickens Tech Ctr, Aurora, CO 80011	2226
Piedmont Bible C, Winston-Salem, NC 27101	1050
Piedmont C, Demorest, GA 30535	1056
Piedmont CC, Roxboro, NC 27573	3037
Piedmont Tech C, Greenwood, SC 29648	3240
Piedmont Virginia CC, Charlottesville, VA 22901	3423
Pierce C, Tacoma, WA 98498	3451
Pierce JC, Philadelphia, PA 19102	3217
Pikes Peak CC, Colorado Sprgs, CO 80906	2227
Pikeville C, Pikeville, KY 41501	0748
Pillsbury Bible C, Owatonna, MN 55060	0237
Pima CC, Tucson, AZ 85702	2078
Pine Manor C, Chestnut Hill, MA 02167	1613
Pine Tech C, Pine City, MN 55063	2745
Pinebrook JC, Coopersburg, PA 18036	3218
Pinellas Voc-Tech, Clearwater, FL 34620	2285
Pitt CC, Greenville, NC 27835	3038
Pittsbg Bradford Cam, U of, Bradford, PA 16701	1343
Pittsbg Greensburg, U of, Greensburg, PA 15601	1329
Pittsbg Johnstwn Cam, U of, Johnstown, PA 15904	1484
Pittsbg Main Cam, U of, Pittsburgh, PA 15260	1542
Pittsburg St U, Pittsburg, KS 66762	0246
Pittsburg Titusvl, U of, Titusville, PA 16354	3219
Pitzer C, Claremont, CA 91711	0150
Platt CC, St Joseph, MO 64506	2814
Platte Valley Bible C, Scottsbluff, NE 69361	0230
Plaza Business Inst, Jackson Heights, NY 11372	2968
Plymouth St C, Plymouth, NH 03264	1655
Point Loma Nazarene C, San Diego, CA 92106	0119
Point Park C, Pittsburgh, PA 15222	1406
Polk CC, Winter Haven, FL 33881	2286
Polytechnic U, Brooklyn, NY 11201	1553
Pomona C, Claremont, CA 91711	0213
Pontifical C Josephinum, Columbus, OH 43235	0477
Porterville C, Porterville, CA 93257	2179
Portland CC, Portland, OR 97219	3169
Portland Sch of Art, Portland, ME 04101	1631
Portland St U, Portland, OR 97207	0136
Portland, U of, Portland, OR 97203	0157
Potomac St C of W Va U, Keyser, WV 26726	3470
Practical Bible Sch, Bible School Pk, NY 13737	2969
Prairie St C, Chicago Heights, IL 60411	2414
Prairie View A&M U, Prairie View, TX 77446	0894
Pratt CC, Pratt, KS 67124	2532
Pratt Inst, Brooklyn, NY 11205	1434
Presbyterian C, Clinton, SC 29325	1257
Presentation C, Aberdeen, SD 57401	0273
Prestonsburg CC, Prestonsburg, KY 41653	2558
Prince George's CC, Largo, MD 20772	2625
Prince Wm Sound CC, Valdez, AK 99686	2062
Princeton U, Princeton, NJ 08544	1575
Principia C, Elsah, IL 62052	0568
Prospect Hall C, Hollywood, FL 33020	2287
Providence C, Providence, RI 02918	1698
Providence Hosp Sch Nsg, Sandusky, OH 44870	3124
Providence Hosp Sch Rad T, Sandusky, OH 44870	3125
Pueblo CC, Pueblo, CO 81004	2228
Puget Sound Christian C, Edmonds, WA 98020	0038
Puget Sound, U of, Tacoma, WA 98416	0167
Pulaski Area Sch, Pulaski, TN 38478	3303
Purdue U Calumet Cam, Hammond, IN 46323	0574
Purdue U Main Cam, West Lafayette, IN 47907	0699
Purdue U North Cent Cam, Westville, IN 46391	0499
Q	
Queens C, Charlotte, NC 28274	1198
Quincy C, Quincy, IL 62301	0654
Quincy C, Quincy, MA 02169	2654
Quinebaug Valley CC, Danielson, CT 06239	2246
Quinnipiac C, Hamden, CT 06518	1665
Quinsigamond CC, Worcester, MA 01606	2655
R	
Rabbinical C of Amer, Morristown, NJ 07960	1305
Rabbinical Sem of Amer, New York, NY 11375	1459
Radford U, Radford, VA 24142	1217
Rainy River CC, Internatl Falls, MN 56649	2746
Ramapo C of NJ, Mahwah, NJ 07430	1383
Rancho Santiago CC, Santa Ana, CA 92706	2180
Randolph CC, Asheboro, NC 27203	3039
Randolph-Macon C, Ashland, VA 23005	1262
Randolph-Macon Women's C, Lynchburg, VA 24503	1238
Ranger JC, Ranger, TX 76470	3366
Ranken Tech C, St Louis, MO 63113	2815
Rapides Hosp Sch Rad Tech, Alexandria, LA 71301	2590
Rappahannock CC, Glenns, VA 23149	3424
Raritan Valley CC, Somerville, NJ 08876	2892
Ravenswood Sch of Nsg, Chicago, IL 60640	2415
Ray C of Design, Chicago, IL 60611	0478
Reading Area CC, Reading, PA 19603	3220
Red Rocks CC, Lakewood, CO 80401	2229
Red Wing Tech C, Red Wing, MN 55066	2747
Redlands, U of, Redlands, CA 92373	0177
Redwoods, C of the, Eureka, CA 95501	2181
Reed C, Portland, OR 97202	0179
Reformed Bible C, Grand Rapids, MI 49505	0440

Name	Sequence Number
Regis C Denver, CO 80221	0163
Regis C Weston, MA 02193	1640
Reid St Tech C Evergreen, AL 36401	2038
Reinhardt C Waleska, GA 30183	2340
Rend Lake C Ina, IL 62846	2416
Rensselaer Polytech Inst Troy, NY 12180	1576
Renton Voc-Tech Inst Renton, WA 98056	3452
Research C of Nursing Kansas City, MO 64132	0343
Rhode Island C Providence, RI 02908	1686
Rhode Island Sch Design Providence, RI 02903	1702
Rhode Island, CC of Warwick, RI 02886	3229
Rhode Island, U of Kingston, RI 02881	1709
Rhodes C Memphis, TN 38112	0989
Rice U Houston, TX 77251	0986
Rich Mountain CC Mena, AR 71953	2096
Richard Bland C Petersburg, VA 23805	3425
Richland C Dallas, TX 75243	3367
Richland CC Decatur, IL 62521	2417
Richmond Tech C Hamlet, NC 28345	3040
Richmond, U of Richmond, VA 23173	1263
Ricks C Rexburg, ID 83460	2362
Rider C Lawrenceville, NJ 08648	1428
Ringling Sch Art/Design Sarasota, FL 33580	1077
Rio Grande, U of Rio Grande, OH 45674	0449
Rio Hondo C Whittier, CA 90608	2182
Rio Salado CC Phoenix, AZ 85003	2079
Ripley Area Sch Ripley, TN 38063	3304
Ripon C Ripon, WI 54971	0648
Riverside CC Riverside, CA 92506	2183
Riverside Hosp Sch R-T Columbus, OH 43214	3126
Rivier C Nashua, NH 03060	1629
Roane St CC Harriman, TN 37748	3305
Roanoke C Salem, VA 24153	1203
Roanoke Sch Prac Nsg Roanoke, VA 24033	3426
Roanoke-Chowan Tech C Ahoskie, NC 27910	3041
Robert Morris C Chicago Chicago, IL 60601	2419
Robert Morris C Coraopols Coraopolis, PA 15108	1330
Robert Morris C-Sprfld Springfield, IL 62704	2418
Roberts Wesleyan C Rochester, NY 14624	1465
Robeson CC Lumberton, NC 28359	3042
Rochester CC Rochester, MN 55904	2748
Rochester Inst of Techn Rochester, NY 14623	1536
Rochester Tech C Rochester, MN 55904	2749
Rochester, U of Rochester, NY 14627	1573
Rock Valley C Rockford, IL 61111	2420
Rockford C Rockford, IL 61108	0565
Rockhurst C Kansas City, MO 64110	0391
Rockingham CC Wentworth, NC 27375	3043
Rockland CC Suffern, NY 10901	2970
Rocky Mountain C Billings, MT 59102	0091
Rocky Mtn C Art Design Denver, CO 80224	0003
Roger Williams C Main Cam Bristol, RI 02809	1671
Rogers St C Claremore, OK 74017	3151
Rogue CC Grants Pass, OR 97527	3170
Rollins C Winter Park, FL 32789	1269
Roosevelt U Chicago, IL 60605	0605
Rosary C River Forest, IL 60305	0562
Rose St C Midwest City, OK 73110	3152
Rose-Hulman Inst of Techn Terre Haute, IN 47803	0708
Rosemont C Rosemont, PA 19010	1358
Rowan-Cabarrus CC Salisbury, NC 28144	3044
Roxbury CC Roxbury Crossng, MA 02120	2656
Rush U Chicago, IL 60612	0727
Russell Sage C Troy, NY 12180	1427
Rust C Holly Springs, MS 38635	0797
Rutgers-C of Engr New Brunswick, NJ 08903	1551
Rutgers-C of Nursing Newark, NJ 07102	1461
Rutgers-C of Pharmacy New Brunswick, NJ 08903	1546
Rutgers-Camden C of A&S Camden, NJ 08102	1480
Rutgers-Cook C New Brunswick, NJ 08903	1485
Rutgers-Douglass C New Brunswick, NJ 08903	1482
Rutgers-Livingston C New Brunswick, NJ 08903	1483
Rutgers-M Gross Sch Art New Brunswick, NJ 08903	1340
Rutgers-Newark C of A&S Newark, NJ 07102	1481
Rutgers-Rutgers C New Brunswick, NJ 08903	1571
Rutgers-U C, Camden Camden, NJ 08102	1335
Rutgers-U C, New Brunswick New Brunswick, NJ 08903	1302
Rutgers-U C, Newark Newark, NJ 07102	1315
Rutledge-Phillips C Springfield, MO 65806	2816

S

Name	Sequence Number
S D Bishop CC Mobile, AL 36690	2039
Sabine Valley Voc-Tech Many, LA 71449	2591
Sacramento City C Sacramento, CA 95822	2184
Sacred Heart Sch Rad Tech Yankton, SD 57078	3260
Sacred Heart Seminary Detroit, MI 48206	0470
Sacred Heart U Fairfield, CT 06432	1663
Saddleback C Mission Viejo, CA 92692	2185
Saginaw Valley St U University Ctr, MI 48710	0582
Saint Ambrose U Davenport, IA 52803	0357
Saint Andrew's Presb C Laurinburg, NC 28352	1149
Saint Anselm C Manchester, NH 03102	1670
Saint Anthony C Nsg Rockford, IL 61108	0723
Saint Augustine C Chicago, IL 60640	2421
Saint Augustine Tech Ctr St Augustine, FL 32084	2288
Saint Augustine's C Raleigh, NC 27611	1107
Saint Basil's C Stamford, CT 06902	1626
Saint Benedict, C of St Joseph, MN 56374	0395
Saint Bernard Parish CC Chalmette, LA 70043	2592
Saint Bonaventure U St Bonaventure, NY 14778	1412
Saint Catharine C Saint Catharine, KY 40061	2560
Saint Catherine, C of St Paul, MN 55105	0361
Saint Charles CC St Charles, MO 63301	2817
Saint Clair Co CC Port Huron, MI 48060	2692
Saint Cloud Hosp Sch Xray St Cloud, MN 56303	2750
Saint Cloud St U St Cloud, MN 56301	0372

Name	Sequence Number
Saint Cloud Tech C St Cloud, MN 56301	2754
Saint Edward's U Austin, TX 78704	0966
Saint Elizabeth Sch Nsg Lafayette, IN 47904	2460
Saint Elizabeth Sch Nsg Utica, NY 13501	2974
Saint Elizabeth Sch Nsg Youngstown, OH 44501	3130
Saint Elizabeth, C of Convent Station, NJ 07961	1413
Saint Francis C Brooklyn, NY 11201	1377
Saint Francis C Fort Wayne, IN 46808	0544
Saint Francis C Loretto, PA 15940	1416
Saint Francis C of Nsg Peoria, IL 61603	0722
Saint Francis Rad Sch Wichita, KS 67214	2533
Saint Francis Rad Techn Peoria, IL 61637	2422
Saint Francis Sch Nsg Evanston, IL 60202	2430
Saint Francis, C of Joliet, IL 60435	0642
Saint Gregory's C Shawnee, OK 74801	3153
Saint Hyacinth C & Sem Granby, MA 01033	1624
Saint John Fisher C Rochester, NY 14618	1405
Saint John Sch Rad Techn Detroit, MI 48236	2693
Saint John Vianney C Miami, FL 33165	1126
Saint John's C Santa Fe, NM 87501	0148
Saint John's of Md Annapolis, MD 21404	1242
St John's Rad Tech Springfield, MO 65802	2818
Saint John's River CC Palatka, FL 32177	2289
Saint John's Sch Nsg Springfield, MO 65804	2823
Saint John's Sch Nsg Springfield, IL 62702	0724
Saint John's Sch Res Ther Springfield, IL 62769	2431
Saint John's Sem C Camarillo, CA 93010	0075
Saint John's Seminary Brighton, MA 02135	1623
Saint John's U Collegeville, MN 56321	0397
Saint John's U Jamaica, NY 11439	1453
Saint Joseph C West Hartford, CT 06117	1690
Saint Joseph C of Nsg Joliet, IL 60435	0721
Saint Joseph Rad Techn Mason City, IA 50401	2504
Saint Joseph Sch Nsg Memphis, TN 38105	3306
Saint Joseph Sch of Rad Mitchell, SD 57301	3263
Saint Joseph Sch Rad Tech Memphis, TN 38101	3307
Saint Joseph Sem & C St Benedict, LA 70457	0814
Saint Joseph, C of Rutland, VT 05701	1600
Saint Joseph's C Brooklyn, NY 11205	1380
Saint Joseph's C Rensselaer, IN 47978	0613
St Joseph's C Windham, ME 04062	1633
Saint Joseph's U Philadelphia, PA 19131	1500
Saint Lawrence U Canton, NY 13617	1514
Saint Leo C Saint Leo, FL 33574	1144
Saint Louis C of Pharmacy St Louis, MO 63110	0319
Saint Louis CC Flo Vly St Louis, MO 63135	2820
Saint Louis CC Forest Pk St Louis, MO 63110	2821
Saint Louis CC Meramec St Louis, MO 63122	2822
Saint Louis Christian C Florissant, MO 63033	0264
Saint Louis U St Louis, MO 63103	0409
Saint Luke, C of Kansas City, MO 64111	2824
Saint Luke's Sch Nsg Sioux City, IA 51104	2505
Saint Lukes Sch Rad Kansas City, MO 64111	2819
Saint Martin's C Lacey, WA 98503	0054
Saint Mary C Leavenworth, KS 66048	0325
Saint Mary of Plains C Dodge City, KS 67801	0275
Saint Mary Plains C Nsg Topeka, KS 66604	0419
Saint Mary-of-the-Woods C St Mary-Woods, IN 47876	0564
Saint Mary, C of Omaha, NE 68124	0328
Saint Mary's C Notre Dame, IN 46556	0665
Saint Mary's C Orchard Lake, MI 48324	0474
Saint Mary's C Raleigh, NC 27603	3045
Saint Mary's C Saint Marys, KS 66536	2534
Saint Mary's C Winona, MN 55987	0356
Saint Mary's C of Md St Mary's City, MD 20686	1249
Saint Mary's of St Cath Minneapolis, MN 55454	2755
Saint Mary's Sch of Nsg Huntington, WV 25701	3472
Saint Mary's U San Antonio, TX 78228	0964
Saint Marys C of Cal Moraga, CA 94575	0172
Saint Meinrad C St Meinrad, IN 47577	0485
Saint Michael's C Colchester, VT 05439	1700
Saint Norbert C De Pere, WI 54115	0669
Saint Olaf C Northfield, MN 55057	0403
Saint Paul Bible C St Bonifacius, MN 55375	0279
Saint Paul-Tech C St Paul, MN 55102	2751
Saint Paul's C Lawrenceville, VA 23868	1059
Saint Peter's C Jersey City, NJ 07306	1396
Saint Petersburg JC St Petersburg, FL 33733	2290
Saint Petersburg Voc-Tech St Petersburg, FL 33711	2291
Saint Philip's C San Antonio, TX 78203	3368
Saint Rose, C of Albany, NY 12203	1398
Saint Scholastica, C of Duluth, MN 55811	0364
Saint Thomas Aquinas C Sparkill, NY 10976	1389
Saint Thomas Med Sch Nsg Akron, OH 44310	3131
Saint Thomas U Miami, FL 33054	1196
Saint Thomas, U of Houston, TX 77006	0916
Saint Thomas, U of St Paul, MN 55105	0392
Saint Vincent C Latrobe, PA 15650	1489
Saint Vincent Sch Nsg Toledo, OH 43608	3132
Saint Xavier C Chicago, IL 60655	0606
Salem C Winston-Salem, NC 27108	1236
Salem CC Penns Grove, NJ 08069	2893
Salem St C Salem, MA 01970	1685
Salem Teikyo Salem, WV 26426	1070
Salisbury Business C Salisbury, NC 28144	3046
Salisbury St C Salisbury, MD 21801	1177
Salt Lake CC Salt Lake City, UT 84130	3396
Salve Regina C at Newport Newport, RI 02840	1677
Sam Houston St U Huntsville, TX 77341	0918
Samaritan Hosp Sch of Nsg Troy, NY 12180	2971
Samford U Birmingham, AL 35229	0963
Sampson CC Clinton, NC 28328	3047
Samuel Merritt C Oakland, CA 94609	0101
San Antonio Art Inst San Antonio, TX 78209	0868
San Antonio C San Antonio, TX 78284	3369

Name	Sequence Number
San Bernardino Valley C San Bernardino, CA 92410	2186
San Diego City C San Diego, CA 92101	2187
San Diego Mesa C San Diego, CA 92111	2188
San Diego St U San Diego, CA 92182	0139
San Diego, U of San Diego, CA 92110	0169
San Fran Art Inst San Francisco, CA 94133	0141
San Fran Consv Music San Francisco, CA 94122	0043
San Fran Mort Sci San Francisco, CA 94115	2189
San Fran St U San Francisco, CA 94132	0191
San Fran, U of San Francisco, CA 94117	0170
San Jacinto C Central Pasadena, TX 77505	3370
San Jacinto C North Houston, TX 77015	3371
San Jacinto C South Houston, TX 77089	3372
San Joaquin Delta C Stockton, CA 95207	2190
San Jose Christian C San Jose, CA 95108	0039
San Jose City C San Jose, CA 95128	2191
San Jose St U San Jose, CA 95192	0200
San Juan C Farmington, NM 87401	2908
San Mateo, C of San Mateo, CA 94402	2192
Sandhills CC Pinehurst, NC 28374	3048
Sangamon St U Springfield, IL 62794	0728
Santa Barbara CC Santa Barbara, CA 93109	2193
Santa Clara U Santa Clara, CA 95053	0189
Santa Fe CC Gainesville, FL 32601	2292
Santa Fe CC Santa Fe, NM 87502	2909
Santa Fe, C of Santa Fe, NM 87501	0052
Santa Monica C Santa Monica, CA 90405	2194
Santa Rosa JC Santa Rosa, CA 95401	2195
Sarah Lawrence C Bronxville, NY 10708	1521
Sauk Valley CC Dixon, IL 61021	2423
Savannah Area Sch Crump, TN 38327	3308
Savannah Area Tech Savannah, GA 31499	2341
Savannah C Art Design Savannah, GA 31401	1256
Savannah St C Savannah, GA 31404	1086
Sawyer Sch Pittsburgh, PA 15222	3221
SC at Aiken, U of Aiken, SC 29801	1166
SC at Beaufort, U of Beaufort, SC 29901	3244
SC at Lancaster, U of Lancaster, SC 29720	3245
SC at Salkehatchie, U of Allendale, SC 29810	3241
SC at Spartanburg, U of Spartanburg, SC 29303	1167
SC at Sumter, U of Sumter, SC 29150	3242
SC at Union, U of Union, SC 29379	3243
SC Coastal Cam, U of Conway, SC 29526	1171
SC Main Cam, U of Columbia, SC 29208	1284
SC St C Orangeburg, SC 29117	1178
Schenectady CC Schenectady, NY 12305	2972
Schiller Intl U Dunedin, FL 34698	1076
Schoolcraft C Livonia, MI 48152	2694
Schreiner C Kerrville, TX 78028	0886
Sci & Arts of Okla, U of Chickasha, OK 73018	0857
Scott CC Bettendorf, IA 52722	2499
Scottsdale CC Scottsdale, AZ 85250	2080
Scranton, U of Scranton, PA 18510	1491
Scripps C Claremont, CA 91711	0149
SD Sch Mines & Techn Rapid City, SD 57701	0384
SD St U Brookings, SD 57006	0366
SD, U of Vermillion, SD 57069	0368
Seattle Central CC Seattle, WA 98122	3453
Seattle Pacific U Seattle, WA 98119	0123
Seattle U Seattle, WA 98122	0160
Selma U Selma, AL 36701	0736
Seminole CC Sanford, FL 32773	2293
Seminole JC Seminole, OK 74868	3154
Sequoias, C of the Visalia, CA 93277	2196
Seton Hall U South Orange, NJ 07079	1433
Seton Hill C Greensburg, PA 15601	1353
Seward Co CC Liberal, KS 67901	2535
Shasta C Redding, CA 96099	2197
Shaw U Raleigh, NC 27611	1105
Shawnee C Ullin, IL 62992	2424
Shawnee St U Portsmouth, OH 45662	0443
Shelby St CC Memphis, TN 38174	3309
Shelbyville St Voc-Tech Shelbyville, TN 37160	3310
Sheldon Jackson C Sitka, AK 99835	0012
Shelton St CC Tuscaloosa, AL 35405	2040
Shenandoah C Winchester, VA 22601	1151
Shepherd C Shepherdstown, WV 25443	1247
Sheridan C Sheridan, WY 82801	3520
Sheridan Vo-Tech Ctr Hollywood, FL 33021	2294
Shimer C Waukegan, IL 60079	0490
Shippensburg U Shippensburg, PA 17257	1443
Shoals CC Muscle Shoals, AL 35662	2041
Shoreline CC Seattle, WA 98133	3454
Shorter C Arkansas N Little Rock, AR 72114	2097
Shorter C of Georgia Rome, GA 30161	1130
Siena C Loudonville, NY 12211	1492
Siena Heights C Adrian, MI 49221	0538
Sierra C Rocklin, CA 95677	2198
Sierra Nevada C Incline Village, NV 89450	0046
Silver Lake C Manitowoc, WI 54220	0491
Simmons C Boston, MA 02115	1705
Simmons Sch Mort Sci Syracuse, NY 13207	2973
Simon's Rock of Bard C Gr Barrington, MA 01230	1691
Simpson C Indianola, IA 50125	0396
Simpson C Redding, CA 96003	0085
Sinclair CC Dayton, OH 45402	3127
Sinte Gleska C Rosebud, SD 57570	0229
Sioux Falls C Sioux Falls, SD 57105	0330
Sioux Valley Hosp Sch Rad Sioux Falls, SD 57117	3261
Siskiyous, C of the Weed, CA 96094	2199
Sitka Cam, U Alas SE Sitka, AK 99835	2063
Skagit Valley C Mount Vernon, WA 98273	3455
Skidmore C Saratoga Sprgs, NY 12866	1515
Skyline C San Bruno, CA 94066	2200
Slidell Voc-Tech Sch Slidell, LA 70459	2593

COLLEGE INDEX

Name	Sequence Number
Slippery Rock U Slippery Rock, PA 16057	1445
Smith C Northampton, MA 01063	1722
Snead St JC Boaz, AL 35957	2042
Snow C Ephraim, UT 84627	3397
Solano CC Suisun City, CA 94585	2201
Somerset CC Somerset, KY 42501	2561
Sonoma St U Rohnert Park, CA 94928	0184
South Alabama, U of Mobile, AL 36688	0928
South Central CC New Haven, CT 06511	2247
South Chicago Sch Rad Chicago, IL 60617	2425
South Florida CC Avon Park, FL 33825	2295
South Florida, U of Tampa, FL 33620	1223
South Georgia C Douglas, GA 31533	2342
South Georgia Tech Americus, GA 31709	2343
South Hills Business C State College, PA 16801	3222
South La Voc-Tech Houma, LA 70361	2594
South Mountain CC Phoenix, AZ 85040	2081
South Plains C Levelland, TX 79336	3373
South Seattle CC Seattle, WA 98106	3456
South Suburban C South Holland, IL 60473	2426
South, U of the Sewanee, TN 37375	0973
Southeast Area Voc-Tech Sioux Falls, SD 57107	3262
Southeast CC Cumberland, KY 40823	2562
Southeast CC-Lincoln Lincoln, NE 68520	2853
Southeast CC Milford Milford, NE 68405	2852
Southeast CC-Beatrice Beatrice, NE 68310	2851
Southeast Missouri St U Cape Girardeau, MO 63701	0296
Southeastern Baptist C Laurel, MS 39441	0739
Southeastern Bible C Birmingham, AL 35243	0864
Southeastern C Assemb God Lakeland, FL 33801	1098
Southeastern CC West Burlington, IA 52655	2500
Southeastern CC S Iowa Keokuk, IA 52632	2501
Southeastern CC-NC Whiteville, NC 28472	3049
Southeastern FW Bapt C Wendell, NC 27591	1048
Southeastern Ill C Harrisburg, IL 62946	2427
Southeastern La U Hammond, LA 70402	0780
Southeastern Mass U North Dartmouth, MA 02747	1708
Southeastern Okla St U Durant, OK 74701	0821
Southeastern U Washington, DC 20024	1052
Southern Arkansas U El Dorado, AR 71730	2099
Southern Arkansas U Magnolia, AR 71753	0822
Southern Arkansas U Tech Camden, AR 71701	2098
Southern C Collegedale, TN 37315	0843
Southern C Tech Inst Marietta, GA 30060	1169
Southern Cal C Costa Mesa, CA 92626	0090
Southern Cal, U of Los Angeles, CA 90089	0205
Southern Colo, U of Pueblo, CO 81001	0113
Southern Conn St U New Haven, CT 06515	1684
Southern Idaho, C of Twin Falls, ID 83303	2363
Southern Ill U Carbondale Carbondale, IL 62901	0634
Southern Ill U Edwardsvl Edwardsville, IL 62026	0625
Southern Ind, U of Evansville, IN 47712	0445
Southern JC Birmingham, AL 35203	2043
Southern JC-Huntsville Huntsville, AL 35805	2044
Southern Maine Voc-Tech South Portland, ME 04106	2605
Southern Maine, U of Portland, ME 04103	1656
Southern Methodist U Dallas, TX 75275	0977
Southern Miss, U of Hattiesburg, MS 39406	0974
Southern Nazarene U Bethany, OK 73008	0905
Southern Nevada, CC North Las Vegas, NV 89030	2858
Southern Ohio C Cincinnati, OH 45237	3128
Southern Ohio C-N KY Cam Fort Mitchell, KY 41017	2559
Southern Oregon St C Ashland, OR 97520	0061
Southern Seminary C Buena Vista, VA 24416	3427
Southern St CC Hillsboro, OH 45133	3129
Southern U New Orls New Orleans, LA 70126	0758
Southern U Shreveport Shreveport, LA 71107	2595
Southern U-Baton Rouge Baton Rouge, LA 70813	0781
Southern Union JC Wadley, AL 36276	2045
Southern Utah U Cedar City, UT 84720	0015
Southern Vermont C Bennington, VT 05201	1604
Southern Vocational C Tuskegee, AL 36083	2046
Southern W Va CC Logan Logan, WV 25601	3471
Southside Virginia CC Alberta, VA 23821	3428
Southwest Baptist U Bolivar, MO 65613	0253
Southwest C Christian Min Bethany, OK 73008	0861
Southwest Indian Polytech Albuquerque, NM 87184	2910
Southwest Miss CC Summit, MS 39666	2790
Southwest Missouri St U Springfield, MO 65804	0373
Southwest Okla St U Sayre Sayre, OK 73662	3155
Southwest St Tech C Mobile, AL 36605	2047
Southwest St U Marshall, MN 56258	0288
Southwest Tech C-Canby Canby, MN 56220	2752
Southwest Texas JC Uvalde, TX 78801	3375
Southwest Texas St U San Marcos, TX 78666	0940
Southwest Virginia CC Richlands, VA 24641	3429
Southwest Wis Tech C Fennimore, WI 53809	3493
Southwest, C of the Hobbs, NM 88240	0076
Southwestern Advent C Keene, TX 76059	0755
Southwestern Assem God C Waxahachie, TX 75165	0751
Southwestern C Chula Vista, CA 92010	2202
Southwestern C Phoenix, AZ 85032	0034
Southwestern C Winfield, KS 67156	0308
Southwestern CC Creston, IA 50801	2502
Southwestern CC Sylva, NC 28779	3050
Southwestern Christian C Terrell, TX 75160	3374
Southwestern La, U of Lafayette, LA 70504	0778
Southwestern Mich C Dowagiac, MI 49047	2695
Southwestern Okla St U Weatherford, OK 73096	0818
Southwestern Oregon CC Coos Bay, OR 97420	3171
Southwestern Tech C Pipestone, MN 56164	2753
Southwestern U Georgetown, TX 78626	0987
Spalding U Louisville, KY 40203	0880
Sparks St Tech CC Eufaula, AL 36027	2048
Spartan Sch Aeronautics Tulsa, OK 74158	3156

Name	Sequence Number
Spartanburg Methodist C Spartanburg, SC 29301	3246
Spartanburg Tech C Spartanburg, SC 29305	3247
Spelman C Atlanta, GA 30314	1254
Spencer Sch of Business Spencer, IA 51301	2503
Spokane CC Spokane, WA 99207	3457
Spokane Falls CC Spokane, WA 99207	3458
Spoon River C Canton, IL 61520	2428
Spring Arbor C Spring Arbor, MI 49283	0539
Spring Garden C Philadelphia, PA 19119	1359
Spring Hill C Mobile, AL 36608	0952
Springfield C Springfield, MA 01109	1667
Springfield C of Ill Springfield, IL 62702	2429
Springfield Tech CC Springfield, MA 01101	2657
Spurgeon Baptist C Mulberry, FL 33860	1017
St Fran Respiratory Pittsburgh, PA 15201	3223
St Joseph's/Suffolk Patchogue, NY 11772	1381
St Patrick Rad Tech Missoula, MT 59806	2838
St Tech Inst Memphis Memphis, TN 38134	3311
Standing Rock CC Fort Yates, ND 58538	3068
Stanford U Stanford, CA 94305	0218
Stanly CC Albemarle, NC 28001	3051
Staples Tech C Staples, MN 56479	2756
Stark Tech C Canton, OH 44720	3133
State CC East St Louis, IL 62201	2432
State Fair CC Sedalia, MO 65301	2825
Stephen Austin St U Nacogdoches, TX 75962	0922
Stephens C Columbia, MO 65215	0365
Sterling C Sterling, KS 67579	0280
Sterling C-Voc Tech Craftsbury Comm, VT 05827	3402
Stetson U De Land, FL 32720	1261
Stevens Henager C Ogden Ogden, UT 84401	3398
Stevens Henager C Provo Provo, UT 84606	3399
Stevens Inst of Techn Hoboken, NJ 07030	1516
Stillman C Tuscaloosa, AL 35403	0800
Stockton St C Pomona, NJ 08240	1478
Stonehill C North Easton, MA 02357	1697
Stratton C Milwaukee, WI 53202	3494
Strayer C Arlington, VA 20036	1095
Sue Bennett C London, KY 40741	2563
Suffolk Co CC Selden, NY 11784	2975
Suffolk U Boston, MA 02108	1660
Sul Ross St U Alpine, TX 79832	0831
Sullivan C Louisville, KY 40205	0812
Sullivan Co CC Loch Sheldroke, NY 12759	2976
Sullivan Voc-Tech Bogalusa, LA 70427	2596
Summit Christian C Fort Wayne, IN 46807	0525
Sumter Area Tech C Sumter, SC 29150	3248
SUNY Ag Tech Cobleskill Cobleskill, NY 12043	1579
SUNY Ag-Tech Cobleskill Cobleskill, NY 12043	2977
SUNY Agrl-Tech Morrisvl Morrisville, NY 13408	2978
SUNY at Albany Albany, NY 12222	1525
SUNY at Binghamton Binghamton, NY 13902	1570
SUNY at Brockport Brockport, NY 14420	1449
SUNY at Buffalo Buffalo, NY 14222	1446
SUNY at Buffalo Buffalo, NY 14260	1540
SUNY at Cortland Cortland, NY 13045	1441
SUNY at Fredonia Fredonia, NY 14063	1378
SUNY at Geneseo Geneseo, NY 14454	1569
SUNY at New Paltz New Paltz, NY 12561	1447
SUNY at Old Westbury Old Westbury, NY 11568	1325
SUNY at Oneonta Oneonta, NY 13820	1530
SUNY at Oswego Oswego, NY 13126	1526
SUNY at Plattsburgh Plattsburgh, NY 12901	1531
SUNY at Potsdam Potsdam, NY 13676	1476
SUNY at Purchase Purchase, NY 10577	1477
SUNY at Stony Brook Stony Brook, NY 11794	1529
SUNY C Environmental Sci Wanakena, NY 13695	2979
SUNY C Tech Alfred Alfred, NY 14802	2980
SUNY C Tech Canton Canton, NY 13617	2981
SUNY C Tech Delhi Delhi, NY 13753	2982
SUNY C Tech Farmingdale Farmingdale, NY 11735	1580
SUNY C Tech Farmingdle Farmingdale, NY 11735	2983
SUNY Empire St C Saratoga Sprgs, NY 12866	1307
SUNY Envrnmtl Sci-Forsty Syracuse, NY 13210	1486
SUNY Health Brooklyn Brooklyn, NY 11203	1585
SUNY Health Syracuse Syracuse, NY 13210	1337
SUNY Inst Tech Utica Utica, NY 13504	1583
SUNY Maritime C Ft Schylr Bronx, NY 10465	1460
Suomi C Hancock, MI 49930	2696
Surry CC Dobson, NC 27017	3052
Susquehanna U Selinsgrove, PA 17870	1509
Suwannee-Hamilton Vo-Tech Live Oak, FL 32060	2296
Swainsboro Tech Inst Swainsboro, GA 30401	2344
Swarthmore C Swarthmore, PA 19081	1567
Swedish-Amer Sch Rad Rockford, IL 61104	2433
Sweet Briar C Sweet Briar, VA 24595	1239
Syracuse U Syracuse, NY 13244	1543

T

Name	Sequence Number
Tabor C Hillsboro, KS 67063	0316
Tacoma CC Tacoma, WA 98465	3459
Taft C Taft, CA 93268	2203
Talladega C Talladega, AL 35160	0866
Tallahassee CC Tallahassee, FL 32304	2297
Tampa C Tampa, FL 33614	1030
Tampa, U of Tampa, FL 33606	1260
Tarkio C Tarkio, MO 64491	0310
Tarleton St U Stephenville, TX 76402	0850
Tarrant Co JC NE Cam Hurst, TX 76054	3376
Tarrant Co JC NW Fort Worth, TX 76179	3377
Tarrant Co JC South Fort Worth, TX 76119	3378
Taylor Business Inst New York, NY 10119	2984
Taylor U Upland, IN 46989	0607
Tech C Lowcountry Beaufort, SC 29902	3249
Tech Career Inst New York, NY 10001	2985
Tech Training Inst Las Cruces, NM 88001	2911

Name	Sequence Number
Teche Area Voc-Tech Sch New Iberia, LA 70560	2597
Teikyo Marycrest U Davenport, IA 52804	0333
Teikyo Post U Waterbury, CT 06723	1606
Teikyo Westmar U Lemars, IA 51031	0344
Temple Baptist C Cincinnati, OH 45240	0428
Temple JC Temple, TX 76501	3379
Temple U Philadelphia, PA 19122	1457
Tenn at Chattanooga, U of Chattanooga, TN 37403	0932
Tenn at Knoxville, U of Knoxville, TN 37996	0939
Tenn Martin, U of Martin, TN 38238	0891
Tenn Memphis, U of Memphis, TN 38163	0997
Tenn St U Nashville, TN 37203	0764
Tenn Tech U Cookeville, TN 38505	0924
Tenn Temple U Chattanooga, TN 37404	0805
Tenn Wesleyan C Athens, TN 37303	0810
Terra Tech C Fremont, OH 43420	3134
Texarkana C Texarkana, TX 75501	3380
Texas A&I U Kingsville, TX 78363	0887
Texas A&M Galveston Galveston, TX 77553	0860
Texas A&M U Main Cam College Station, TX 77843	0983
Texas at Arlington, U of Arlington, TX 76019	0931
Texas at Austin, U of Austin, TX 78712	0991
Texas at Dallas, U of Richardson, TX 75083	0954
Texas at El Paso, U of El Paso, TX 79968	0849
Texas at Tyler, U of Tyler, TX 75701	0999
Texas Baptist C Longview, TX 75604	0737
Texas C Tyler, TX 75702	0749
Texas Christian U Fort Worth, TX 76129	0976
Texas Health Sci Ctr, U of San Antonio, TX 78284	0786
Texas Hlth Sci Ctr, U of Dallas, TX 75235	0993
Texas Lutheran C Seguin, TX 78155	0944
Texas Medical Br, U of Galveston, TX 77550	1004
Texas Permian Basin, U of Odessa, TX 79762	0994
Texas San Antonio, U of San Antonio, TX 78285	0933
Texas Sch Allied H Sci, U Houston, TX 77225	0872
Texas Southern U Houston, TX 77004	0784
Texas Southmost C Brownsville, TX 78520	3381
Texas St Harlingen Harlingen, TX 78551	3382
Texas St Tech Inst Sweetwater, TX 79556	3384
Texas St Tech Inst Amar Amarillo, TX 79111	3383
Texas St Tech Inst Waco Waco, TX 76705	3385
Texas Tech U Lubbock, TX 79409	0935
Texas Tech U Sch Nsg Lubbock, TX 79430	0858
Texas Wesleyan U Fort Worth, TX 76105	0907
Texas Woman's U Denton, TX 76204	0892
Thames Valley St C Norwich, CT 06360	2248
Thief River Falls Tech Thief Rvr Falls, MN 56701	2757
Thiel C Greenville, PA 16125	1365
Thomas Aquinas C Santa Paula, CA 93060	0146
Thomas C Thomasville, GA 31792	1009
Thomas C Waterville, ME 04901	1605
Thomas Jefferson U Philadelphia, PA 19107	1581
Thomas More C Crestview Hills, KY 41017	0882
Thomas More Inst Merrimack, NH 03054	1599
Thomas Nelson CC Hampton, VA 23670	3430
Thomas Tech Inst Thomasville, GA 31799	2345
Three Rivers CC Poplar Bluff, MO 63901	2826
Tidewater CC Portsmouth, VA 23703	3431
Tiffin U Tiffin, OH 44883	0486
Tillamook Bay CC Tillamook, OR 97141	3172
Tobe-Coburn Sch New York, NY 10012	2986
Toccoa Falls C Toccoa Falls, GA 30598	1122
Toledo, U of Toledo, OH 43606	0636
Tomlinson C Cleveland, TN 37320	0747
Tompkins-Cortland C Dryden, NY 13053	2987
Topeka Tech C Topeka, KS 66618	2536
Tougaloo C Tougaloo, MS 39174	0799
Touro C New York, NY 10001	1454
Towson St U Towson, MD 21204	1276
Transylvania U Lexington, KY 40508	0953
Traviss Voc-Tech Center Lakeland, FL 33840	2298
Treasure Valley CC Ontario, OR 97914	3173
Trenholm St Tech Montgomery, AL 36108	2049
Trenton St C Trenton, NJ 08650	1572
Trevecca Nazarene C Nashville, TN 37210	0769
Tri-Co Tech C Pendleton, SC 29670	3250
Tri-County CC Murphy, NC 28906	3053
Tri-State U Angola, IN 46703	0595
Trident Tech C Charleston, SC 29411	3251
Trinidad St JC Trinidad, CO 81082	2230
Trinity Bible C Ellendale, ND 58436	0238
Trinity C Hartford, CT 06106	1719
Trinity C of DC Washington, DC 20017	1155
Trinity C of Florida Holiday, FL 34690	1018
Trinity C of Ill Deerfield, IL 60015	0557
Trinity C of Vermont Burlington, VT 05401	1634
Trinity Christian C Palos Heights, IL 60463	0545
Trinity U San Antonio, TX 78212	0988
Trinity Valley CC Athens, TX 75751	3386
Triton C River Grove, IL 60171	2434
Trocaire C Buffalo, NY 14220	2988
Troy St U Dothan Dothan, AL 36304	0788
Troy St U Montgomery Montgomery, AL 36103	0730
Troy St U-Troy Troy, AL 36082	0890
Truckee Meadows CC Reno, NV 89512	2859
Truett-McConnell C Cleveland, GA 30528	2346
Truman C Chicago, IL 60640	2435
Tufts U Medford, MA 02155	1736
Tulane U New Orleans, LA 70118	0978
Tulsa JC Tulsa, OK 74135	3157
Tulsa, U of Tulsa, OK 74104	0968
Tunxis CC Farmington, CT 06032	2249
Turtle Mountain CC Belcourt, ND 58316	3069
Tusculum C Greeneville, TN 37743	0879
Tuskegee U Tuskegee, AL 36088	0909

Name	Sequence Number
Twentieth Century C Mobile, AL 36602	2050
Tyler JC Tyler, TX 75711	3387

U

Name	Sequence Number
Ulster Co CC Stone Ridge, NY 12484	2989
Umpqua CC Roseburg, OR 97470	3174
Union C Barbourville, KY 40906	0873
Union C Lincoln, NE 68506	0282
Union C Schenectady, NY 12308	1563
Union Co C Cranford, NJ 07016	2894
Union Inst Cincinnati, OH 45206	0454
Union Memorial Sch Nsg Baltimore, MD 21218	2626
Union U Jackson, TN 38305	0958
United Med Ctr Sch Nsg Moline, IL 61265	2436
United Samaritan Rad Tech Danville, IL 61832	2437
Unity C Unity, ME 04988	1603
Upper Iowa U Fayette, IA 52142	0339
Upsala C E Orange East Orange, NJ 07019	1370
Upsala C Wirths Sussex, NJ 07461	2895
Upson Co Voc-Tech Thomaston, GA 30286	2347
Urbana U Urbana, OH 43078	0495
Ursinus C Collegeville, PA 19426	1507
Ursuline C Pepper Pike, OH 44124	0553
US Air Force Acad USAF Academy, CO 80840	0208
US Coast Guard Acad New London, CT 06320	1714
US International U San Diego, CA 92131	0158
US Merchant Marine Acad Kings Point, NY 11024	1458
US Military Acad West Point, NY 10996	1474
US Naval Acad Annapolis, MD 21402	1244
USNY Regents C Degree Albany, NY 12203	1310
Utah St U Logan, UT 84322	0071
Utah Valley CC Orem, UT 84058	3400
Utah, U of Salt Lake City, UT 84112	0138
Utica C Utica, NY 13323	1497
Utica Sch of Commerce Utica, NY 13501	2990

V

Name	Sequence Number
Valdosta St C Valdosta, GA 31698	1212
Valencia CC Orlando, FL 32802	2299
Valley C Kent, WA 98032	3460
Valley C Comm/Tech Kent, WA 98032	0025
Valley City St U Valley City, ND 58072	0231
Valley Forge Christian C Phoenixville, PA 19460	1336
Valley Forge Mil JC Wayne, PA 19087	3224
Valparaiso U Valparaiso, IN 46383	0655
Vance Granville CC Henderson, NC 27536	3054
Vanderbilt U Nashville, TN 37212	0990
Vandercook C Music Chicago, IL 60616	0497
Vassar C Poughkeepsie, NY 12601	1566
Vennard C University Park, IA 52595	0268
Ventura C Ventura, CA 93003	2204
Vermilion CC Ely, MN 55731	2758
Vermont Tech C Randolph, VT 05061	3403
Vermont, CC of Waterbury, VT 05676	3404
Vermont, U of Burlington, VT 05405	1712
Vernon Regional JC Vernon, TX 76384	3388
Victor Valley C Victorville, CA 92392	2205
Victoria C Victoria, TX 77901	3389
Villa Julie C Stevenson, MD 21153	1119
Villa Maria C Buffalo, NY 14225	2991
Villanova U Villanova, PA 19085	1535
Vincennes U Vincennes, IN 47591	2461
Virginia C Roanoke, VA 24017	3432
Virginia Clinch, U of Wise, VA 24293	1172
Virginia Commonwealth U Richmond, VA 23284	1216
Virginia Highlands CC Abingdon, VA 24210	3433
Virginia Intermont C Bristol, VA 24201	1072
Virginia Military Inst Lexington, VA 24450	1250
Virginia St U Petersburg, VA 23803	1101
Virginia Tech Blacksburg, VA 24061	1285
Virginia Union U Richmond, VA 23220	1108
Virginia Wesleyan C Norfolk, VA 23502	1200
Virginia Western CC Roanoke, VA 24038	3434
Virginia, U of Charlottesville, VA 22906	1300
Vista C Berkeley, CA 94704	2206
Visual Arts, Sch of New York, NY 10010	1421
Viterbo C La Crosse, WI 54601	0589
Volunteer St CC Gallatin, TN 37066	3312
Voorhees C Denmark, SC 29042	1019

W

Name	Sequence Number
W Va Career C Charleston, WV 25301	3473
W Va Inst of Techn Montgomery, WV 25136	1170
W Va Northern CC Wheeling, WV 26003	3474
W Va St C Institute, WV 25112	1088
W Va U Morgantown, WV 26506	1224
W Va U Sch of Radiology Morgantown, WV 26506	3475
W Va U-Parkersburg Parkersburg, WV 26101	3476
W Va Wesleyan C Buckhannon, WV 26201	1207
Wabash C Crawfordsville, IN 47933	0644
Wabash Valley C Mt Carmel, IL 62863	2438
Wadena Tech C Wadena, MN 56482	2759
Wadhams Hall Seminary-C Ogdensburg, NY 13669	1338
Wagner C Staten Island, NY 10301	1429
Wake Forest U Winston-Salem, NC 27109	1294
Wake Tech C Raleigh, NC 27603	3055
Waldorf C Forest City, IA 50436	2506
Walker C Jasper, AL 35501	2051
Walker St Tech Sumiton, AL 35148	2052
Walker Tech Inst Rock Spring, GA 30739	2348
Walker Voc-Tech Naples, FL 33942	2300
Walla Walla C College Place, WA 99324	0065
Walla Walla CC Walla Walla, WA 99362	3461
Wallace St CC-Dothan Dothan, AL 36303	2053
Wallace St CC-Hanceville Hanceville, AL 35077	2054
Wallace St CC-Selma Selma, AL 36701	2055
Walsh C Canton, OH 44720	0526

Name	Sequence Number
Walters St CC Morristown, TN 37813	3313
Warner Pacific C Portland, OR 97215	0050
Warner Southern C Lake Wales, FL 33853	1064
Warren Wilson C Swannanoa, NC 28778	1129
Wartburg C Waverly, IA 50677	0390
Washburn U of Topeka Topeka, KS 66621	0250
Washington & Jefferson C Washington, PA 15301	1503
Washington and Lee U Lexington, VA 24450	1289
Washington Bible C Lanham, MD 20706	1062
Washington C Chestertown, MD 21620	1156
Washington Co Voc-Tech Calais, ME 04619	2606
Washington St CC Marietta, OH 45750	3135
Washington St U Pullman, WA 99164	0140
Washington U St Louis, MO 63130	0416
Washington-Holmes Vo-Tec Chipley, FL 32428	2301
Washington, U of Seattle, WA 98195	0201
Washtenaw CC Ann Arbor, MI 48106	2697
Watterson C Louisville, KY 40218	2564
Waubonsee CC Sugar Grove, IL 60554	2439
Waukesha Co Tech C Pewaukee, WI 53072	3495
Waycross C Waycross, GA 31501	2349
Waycross Ware Tech Waycross, GA 31501	2350
Wayland Baptist U Plainview, TX 79072	0750
Wayne CC Goldsboro, NC 27533	3056
Wayne Co CC Detroit, MI 48226	2698
Wayne Gen & Tech C Orrville, OH 44667	3136
Wayne St C Wayne, NE 68787	0244
Wayne St U Detroit, MI 48202	0705
Waynesburg C Waynesburg, PA 15370	1390
Weatherford C Weatherford, TX 76086	3390
Webb Inst of Naval Arch Glen Cove, NY 11542	1545
Webber C Babson Park, FL 33827	1125
Weber St U Ogden, UT 84408	0022
Webster U St Louis, MO 63119	0351
Wellesley C Wellesley, MA 02181	1720
Wells C Aurora, NY 13026	1470
Wenatchee Valley C Wenatchee, WA 98801	3462
Wentworth Inst Techn Boston, MA 02115	1617
Wentworth Military Acad Lexington, MO 64067	2827
Wesley C Dover, DE 19901	1074
Wesley C Florence, MS 39073	0792
Wesley Center Rad Techn Wichita, KS 67214	2537
Wesleyan C Macon, GA 31297	1229
Wesleyan U Middletown, CT 06457	1717
West Chester U West Chester, PA 19383	1450
West Coast Christian C Fresno, CA 93710	0008
West Coast U Main Cam Los Angeles, CA 90020	0019
West Dakota Voc-Tech C Rapid City, SD 57701	3264
West Florida, U of Pensacola, FL 32514	1246
West Georgia C Carrollton, GA 30118	1093
West Georgia Tech Inst Lagrange, GA 30240	2351
West Hills C Coalinga, CA 93210	2207
West Liberty St C West Liberty, WV 26074	1090
West Los Ang C Culver City, CA 90230	2208
West Los Ang, U of Los Angeles, CA 90066	0226
West Shore CC Scottville, MI 49454	2699
West Suburban C Nsg Oak Park, IL 60302	0548
West Texas St U Canyon, TX 79016	0829
West Valley C Saratoga, CA 95070	2209
Westark CC Fort Smith, AR 72913	2100
Westbrook C Portland, ME 04103	1637
Westchester CC Valhalla, NY 10595	2992
Western Baptist C Salem, OR 97301	0051
Western Carolina U Cullowhee, NC 28723	1082
Western Conn St U Danbury, CT 06810	1647
Western Ill U Macomb, IL 61455	0624
Western Iowa Tech CC Sioux City, IA 51102	2507
Western Kentucky U Bowling Green, KY 42101	0854
Western Md C Westminster, MD 21157	1266
Western Mich U Kalamazoo, MI 49008	0700
Western Montana C Dillon, MT 59725	0028
Western Nebraska CC Scottsbluff, NE 69361	2854
Western Nebraska CC Sidney, NE 69162	2855
Western Nevada CC Carson City, NV 89703	2860
Western New Eng C Springfield, MA 01119	1662
Western NM U Silver City, NM 88062	0013
Western Okla St C Altus, OK 73521	3158
Western Oregon St U Monmouth, OR 97361	0111
Western Piedmont CC Morganton, NC 28655	3057
Western St C Gunnison, CO 81231	0110
Western Texas C Snyder, TX 79549	3391
Western Washington U Bellingham, WA 98225	0188
Western Wis Tech C La Crosse, WI 54602	3496
Western Wyoming CC Rock Springs, WY 82901	3521
Westfield St C Westfield, MA 01086	1648
Westminster C Fulton, MO 65251	0381
Westminster C New Wilmington, PA 16172	1496
Westminster C Salt Lake City, UT 84106	0064
Westminster Choir C Princeton, NJ 08540	1372
Westmont C Santa Barbara, CA 93108	0173
Westmoreland Co CC Youngwood, PA 15697	3225
Westside Voc Tech Ctr Winter Garden, FL 32787	2302
Wharton Co JC Wharton, TX 77488	3392
Whatcom CC Bellingham, WA 98226	3463
Wheaton C Norton, MA 02766	1707
Wheaton C Wheaton, IL 60187	0662
Wheeling Jesuit C Wheeling, WV 26003	1146
Wheelock C Boston, MA 02215	1610
White Pines C Chester, NH 03036	2870
Whiteville Voc-Tech Whiteville, TN 30875	3314
Whitman C Walla Walla, WA 99362	0168
Whittier C Whittier, CA 90608	0175
Whitworth C Spokane, WA 99251	0164
Wichita St U Wichita, KS 67208	0257
Widener U Chester, PA 19013	1431

Name	Location	Sequence Number
Wilberforce U	Wilberforce, OH 45384	0528
Wiley C	Marshall, TX 75670	0752
Wilkes C	Wilkes-Barre, PA 18766	1400
Wilkes CC	Wilkesboro, NC 28697	3058
Willamette U	Salem, OR 97301	0210
William & Mary Main Cam, C	Williamsburg, VA 23185	1293
William Carey C	Hattiesburg, MS 39401	0869
William Jewell C	Liberty, MO 64068	0388
William Paterson C	Wayne, NJ 07470	1451
William Penn C	Oskaloosa, IA 52577	0336
William Rainey Harper C	Palatine, IL 60067	2440
William Smith C	Geneva, NY 14456	1473
William Tyndale C	Farmington Hill, MI 48331	0480
William Woods C	Fulton, MO 65251	0341
Williams Baptist C	Walnut Ridge, AR 72476	0796
Williams C	Williamstown, MA 01267	1727
Williamsburg Tech C	Kingstree, SC 29556	3252
Willmar CC	Willmar, MN 56201	2760
Willmar Tech C	Willmar, MN 56201	2761
Wilmington C	New Castle, DE 19720	1047
Wilmington C	Wilmington, OH 45177	0542
Wilson C	Chambersburg, PA 17201	1367
Wilson Tech CC	Wilson, NC 27893	3059
Windward CC, U Hawaii	Kaneohe, HI 96744	2359
Wingate C	Wingate, NC 28174	1185
Winona St U	Winona, MN 55987	0374
Winona Tech C	Winona, MN 55987	2762
Winston-Salem Bible C	Winston-Salem, NC 27102	1006
Winston-Salem St U	Winston-Salem, NC 27110	1087
Winthrop C	Rock Hill, SC 29733	1174
Wis Center Baraboo, U of	Baraboo, WI 53913	3498
Wis Center Barron Co, U of	Rice Lake, WI 54868	3497
Wis Center Fond Du Lac, U	Fond Du Lac, WI 54935	3509
Wis Center Manitowoc, U of	Manitowoc, WI 54220	3500
Wis Center Marathon, U of	Wausau, WI 54401	3501
Wis Center Marinette, U of	Marinette, WI 54143	3502
Wis Center Marshfld, U of	Marshfield, WI 54449	3503
Wis Center Richland, U of	Richland Center, WI 53581	3504
Wis Center Rock Co, U of	Janesville, WI 53546	3505
Wis Center Sheboygan, U of	Sheboygan, WI 53081	3506
Wis Center Washingtn, U of	West Bend, WI 53095	3507
Wis Center Waukesha, U of	Waukesha, WI 53188	3508
Wis Ctr Fox Valley, U of	Menasha, WI 54952	3499
Wis Eau Claire, U of	Eau Claire, WI 54701	0619
Wis Green Bay, U of	Green Bay, WI 54311	0578
Wis Indianhead Tech	Ashland, WI 54806	3510
Wis Indianhead Tech Inst	New Richmond, WI 54017	3511
Wis Indianhead Tech Inst	Rice Lake, WI 54868	3512
Wis Indianhead Tech Supr	Superior, WI 54880	3513
Wis La Crosse, U of	La Crosse, WI 54601	0688
Wis Lutheran C	Milwaukee, WI 53226	0537
Wis Madison, U of	Madison, WI 53706	0698
Wis Milwaukee, U of	Milwaukee, WI 53201	0627
Wis Oshkosh, U of	Oshkosh, WI 54901	0618
Wis Parkside, U of	Kenosha, WI 53141	0580
Wis Platteville, U of	Platteville, WI 53818	0620
Wis River Falls, U of	River Falls, WI 54022	0576
Wis Sch of Electronics	Madison, WI 53704	3514
Wis Stevens Point, U of	Stevens Point, WI 54481	0622
Wis Stout, U of	Menomonie, WI 54751	0509
Wis Superior, U of	Superior, WI 54880	0577
Wis Whitewater, U of	Whitewater, WI 53190	0621
Wittenberg U	Springfield, OH 45501	0684
Wofford C	Spartanburg, SC 29303	1258
Wood Co Sch Nsg	Parkersburg, WV 26101	3477
Wood JC	Mathiston, MS 39752	2791
Wood Sch, The	New York, NY 10016	2993
Woodbury U	Burbank, CA 91510	0103
Wooster, C of	Wooster, OH 44691	0685
Wor Wic Tech CC	Salisbury, MD 21801	2627
Worcester Poly Inst	Worcester, MA 01609	1716
Worcester St C	Worcester, MA 01602	1646
Worcester Tech Inst	Worcester, MA 01605	2658
Word of Life Bible Inst	Pottersville, NY 12860	2994
World C West	Petaluma, CA 94952	0100
World Studies Prgm	Marlboro, VT 05301	1692
Worsham C of Mort Sci	Des Plaines, IL 60018	2441
Worthington CC	Worthington, MN 56187	2763
Wright C	Chicago, IL 60634	2442
Wright St U	Dayton, OH 45435	0458
Wright St U-Lake	Celina, OH 45822	3137
Wyoming, U of	Laramie, WY 82071	0130
Wytheville CC	Wytheville, VA 24382	3435

X

Name	Location	Sequence Number
Xavier U	Cincinnati, OH 45207	0666
Xavier U of La	New Orleans, LA 70125	0839

Y

Name	Location	Sequence Number
Yakima Valley CC	Yakima, WA 98907	3464
Yale U	New Haven, CT 06520	1734
Yavapai C	Prescott, AZ 86301	2082
Yellowstone Baptist C	Billings, MT 59106	0026
Yeshiva U	New York, NY 10033	1501
York C	York, NE 68467	2856
York C of Pa	York, PA 17403	1385
York Tech C	Rock Hill, SC 29730	3253
York Tech Inst	York, PA 17402	3226
Yorktowne Business C	York, PA 17404	3227
Young Harris C	Young Harris, GA 30582	2352
Youngstown St U	Youngstown, OH 44555	0459
Yuba C	Marysville, CA 95901	2210

Accredited by the American Association of Bible Colleges

Name	Sequence Number
A	
Alas Bible C Glennallen, AK 99588	0030
Amer Baptist C Nashville, TN 37207	0740
Appalachian Bible C Bradley, WV 25818	1054
Ariz C of Bible Phoenix, AZ 85021	0006
Atlanta Christian C East Point, GA 30344	1051
B	
Baptist Bible C Springfield, MO 65803	0232
Baptist Bible C East Boston, MA 02136	1588
Barclay C Haviland, KS 67059	0272
Bay Ridge Christian C Kendleton, TX 77451	0733
Bethany C of Missions Bloomington, MN 55438	0297
C	
Calvary Bible C Kansas City, MO 64147	0267
Central Baptist C Conway, AR 72032	0859
Central Bible C Springfield, MO 65803	0302
Cinci Bible C Cincinnati, OH 45204	0437
Circleville Bible C Circleville, OH 43113	0471
D	
Dallas Christian C Dallas, TX 75234	0794
E	
Emmaus Bible C Dubuque, IA 52001	0299
F	
Faith Baptist Bible C Ankeny, IA 50021	0305
Florida Christian C Kissimmee, FL 32743	1044
Free Will Baptist C Nashville, TN 37205	0746
G	
God's Bible Sch & C Cincinnati, OH 45210	0466
Grace C of Bible Omaha, NE 68108	0303
Grand Rapids Bible C Grand Rapids, MI 49506	2668
Great Lakes Bible C Lansing, MI 48901	0473
I	
International Bible Florence, AL 35630	0791
J	
John Wesley C High Point, NC 27265	1043
K	
Kansas City C of Bible Overland Park, KS 66204	0266
L	
Life Bible C Los Angeles, CA 90086	0036
M	
Magnolia Bible C Kosciusko, MS 39090	0734
Manhattan Christian C Manhattan, KS 66502	0236
Manna Bible Inst Philadelphia, PA 19144	1303
Miami Christian C Miami, FL 33167	1124
Minn Bible C Rochester, MN 55902	0262
Multnomah Sch of Bible Portland, OR 97220	0084
N	
Nazarene Bible C Colorado Sprgs, CO 80935	2223
Nebraska Christian C Norfolk, NE 68701	0234
O	
Oak Hills Bible C Bemidji, MN 56601	0265
Ozark Christian C Joplin, MO 64801	0235
P	
Piedmont Bible C Winston-Salem, NC 27101	1050
Practical Bible Sch Bible School Pk, NY 13737	2969
Puget Sound Christian C Edmonds, WA 98020	0038
R	
Reformed Bible C Grand Rapids, MI 49505	0440
S	
Saint Louis Christian C Florissant, MO 63033	0264
San Jose Christian C San Jose, CA 95108	0039
Southeastern Baptist C Laurel, MS 39441	0739
Southeastern Bible C Birmingham, AL 35243	0864
Southeastern FW Bapt C Wendell, NC 27591	1048
Southwestern C Phoenix, AZ 85032	0034
T	
Tenn Temple U Chattanooga, TN 37404	0805
Trinity Bible C Ellendale, ND 58436	0238
Trinity C of Florida Holiday, FL 34690	1018
V	
Valley Forge Christian C Phoenixville, PA 19460	1336
Vennard C University Park, IA 52595	0268
W	
Washington Bible C Lanham, MD 20706	1062
Wesley C Florence, MS 39073	0792

Accredited by the Association of Independent Colleges and Schools

Name	Sequence Number
A	
Acad of Accountancy Minneapolis, MN 55416	2701
Amer Inst of Commerce Davenport, IA 52807	2463
B	
Beal C Bangor, ME 04401	2598
Berkeley C Business Waldwick, NJ 07463	2873
Bliss C Columbus, OH 43214	3074
Brooks Inst Photography Santa Barbara, CA 93108	0081
Bryant Stratton Bus Inst Rochester, NY 14623	2921
Bryant-Stratton Inst Albany, NY 12205	2922
Bryant-Stratton Inst Syracuse, NY 13202	2924
Burdett Sch Boston, MA 02116	2637
C	
Chicago C of Commerce Chicago, IL 60603	2370
Cleary C Ypsilanti, MI 48197	0432
D	
Draughons JC Knoxville, TN 37919	3274
E	
Edmondson JC Chattanooga, TN 37411	3276
F	
Fort Lauderdale C Ft Lauderdale, FL 33301	1020
G	
Grumman Data Systems Woodbury, NY 11797	2947
I	
International Business C Fort Wayne, IN 46804	2458
Interstate Business C Fargo, ND 58103	3062
Intl Acad Merch Design Tampa, FL 33609	1021
J	
Jacki Nell Secretary Sch Austin, TX 78704	3344
Jackson Business Inst Jackson, MI 49201	2673

Name	Sequence Number
Jamestown Business C Jamestown, NY 14701	2952
Johnson & Wales U Providence, RI 02903	1620
Jones C Main Campus Jacksonville, FL 32211	1041

K

Name	Sequence Number
Katharine Gibbs Sch Boston, MA 02116	2645
Katharine Gibbs Sch Montclair, NJ 07042	2886
Katharine Gibbs Sch Norwalk, CT 06851	2237
Katharine Gibbs Sch Providence, RI 02906	3228
King's C Charlotte, NC 28204	3026
Knoxville Business C Knoxville, TN 37927	3286

L

Name	Sequence Number
Lincoln Sch of Commerce Lincoln, NE 68501	2843
Lockyear C Evansville, IN 47706	0431
Lowthian C Minneapolis, MN 55402	2730

M

Name	Sequence Number
Madison Business C Madison, WI 53705	3484
McIntosh C Dover, NH 03820	2862
Metro Business Cape Gir Cape Girardeau, MO 63701	2805
Metro Business Jeff City Jefferson City, MO 65109	2806
Metro Business Rolla Rolla, MO 65401	2807
Miami-Jacobs JC Dayton, OH 45401	3112
Morrison C/Reno B C Reno, NV 89503	0002
Mountain St C Parkersburg, WV 26101	3468

N

Name	Sequence Number
National Business C Roanoke, VA 24017	3418
National Career C Decatur, AL 35601	2030
National Career C Tuscaloosa, AL 35405	2031
National Ed Center Fort Lauderdale, FL 33334	1032
Nebraska C of Business Omaha, NE 68131	2848
Nettleton C Sioux Falls, SD 57106	3259
Northeastern Sch Commerce Bay City, MI 48708	2689
Northwestern Bus C Chicago, IL 60630	2408
NW Bus C-SW Cam Palos Hills, IL 60465	2409

O

Name	Sequence Number
Orlando C Orlando, FL 32810	1027
Owensboro JC of Business Owensboro, KY 42302	2555

P

Name	Sequence Number
Palm Beaches,C of West Palm Beach, FL 33407	2282
Plaza Business Inst Jackson Heights, NY 11372	2968
Prospect Hall C Hollywood, FL 33020	2287

R

Name	Sequence Number
Rutledge-Phillips C Springfield, MO 65806	2816

S

Name	Sequence Number
Sawyer Sch Pittsburgh, PA 15222	3221
Schiller Intl U Dunedin, FL 34698	1076
South Hills Business C State College, PA 16801	3222
Spencer Sch of Business Spencer, IA 51301	2503
Stevens Henager C Ogden Ogden, UT 84401	3398
Stevens Henager C Provo Provo, UT 84606	3399
Stratton C Milwaukee, WI 53202	3494

T

Name	Sequence Number
Tampa C Tampa, FL 33614	1030
Taylor Business Inst New York, NY 10119	2984
Tobe-Coburn Sch New York, NY 10012	2986
Twentieth Century C Mobile, AL 36602	2050

U

Name	Sequence Number
Utica Sch of Commerce Utica, NY 13501	2990

V

Name	Sequence Number
Virginia C Roanoke, VA 24017	3432

W

Name	Sequence Number
W Va Career C Charleston, WV 25301	3473
Watterson C Louisville, KY 40218	2564
Wood Sch,The New York, NY 10016	2993

Y

Name	Sequence Number
Yorktowne Business C York, PA 17404	3227

Planning for college doesn't stop when you decide which college to attend!

Planning for college also means getting ready to be **IN** college!

Have you thought about what's going to happen when you actually get to college? How will it be different from high school? How will it be different from living at home?

More independence? Sure!
More activities? Yes!
More responsibility for yourself? Immediately!
More studying? Definitely!

Coping with that first year of college won't be easy. In fact, one out of every three students in your freshman class probably won't come back as a sophomore. But you can survive and succeed with *A Guide to College Survival.*

ACT publishes this book because we believe it can make a difference in helping you accomplish your goals in college. With *A Guide to College Survival,* you'll learn what to expect in college and what works best to avoid the dreaded "freshman frenzies."

- Balancing social and academic interests
- Budgeting time for study
- Creating a good study environment
- Reading college textbooks
- Taking lecture notes
- Preparing for and taking various kinds of tests
- Setting goals and keeping a positive attitude

A small investment now in *A Guide to College Survival* will pay big dividends on campus. Meet the challenges of your freshman year with confidence! Mail the order form at right, with your payment, to **ACT Publications, P.O. Box 168, Iowa City, IA 52243.** Allow 3-4 weeks for delivery.

ACT

Order Form

Please send *A Guide to College Survival.*

____ copies × $8.00 $______
CA residents add 6% state sales tax $______
Add $2 shipping/handling per book $______
Total amount enclosed $______

Name ______________________

Address ______________________

City ____________ State ________ ZIP ________

Mail your completed order form with a check or money order payable to ACT. Address your order to **ACT Publications, P.O. Box 168, Iowa City, IA 52243.** DO NOT SEND CASH.

Acknowledgments

American College Testing (ACT) is a not-for-profit organization dedicated to the enrichment of education. The **College Planning/Search Book** is one of many services ACT offers to help students make the transition from high school to postsecondary education and careers.

This book describes college policies and programs in effect for the 1991-92 academic year. All college information was provided directly by representatives of individual colleges between March and May 1991. Sincere appreciation is extended to the college admissions officers and staff members who furnished up-to-date information about their institutions.

Every reasonable effort has been made to ensure accuracy of information. Institutions occasionally do revise policies or fees after the data for the book have been collected. Notification of errors in the data would be most appreciated. Readers are invited to make comments and suggestions about this book.

For information about ordering additional copies, write:

College Planning/Search Book
ACT Publications
P.O. Box 168
Iowa City, Iowa 52243